The Growth of the American Republic

George Washington (1732-99) by Edward Savage

The Growth of the American Republic

VOLUME ONE

SAMUEL ELIOT MORISON

HENRY STEELE COMMAGER

AND

WILLIAM E. LEUCHTENBURG

SEVENTH EDITION

New York   Oxford

OXFORD UNIVERSITY PRESS

Library of Congress Cataloging in Publication Data
Morison, Samuel Eliot, 1887–1976.
The growth of the American Republic.
Includes bibliographies and index.
1. United States — History. I. Commager,
Henry Steele, 1902–   joint author.
II. Leuchtenburg, William Edward, 1922–
joint author. III. Title.
E178.M85   1980   973   79-52432
ISBN 0-19-502595-4 (two-vol. set)
ISBN 0-19-502593-8 (v. 1)
ISBN 0-19-502594-6 (v. 2)

This leather-bound edition has been published by
Gryphon Editions, Inc. exclusively for the members of its
Classics Libraries with the permission of Oxford University
Press, Inc.

Printed in the United States of America

printing, last digit: 10 9 8 7 6

Preface

The publication of the seventh edition of *The Growth of the American Republic* marks the fiftieth anniversary of this history. It first appeared in 1930 as a single volume, beginning the story in 1763 and terminating it in 1917. Over the next three decades, the two senior authors brought out four more editions, covering a much longer span, from the first arrival of Indians on this continent to the most recent events, an enterprise which required publication in two volumes and a division of editorial responsibility. In the fifth edition, which appeared in 1962, Morison was responsible for the period up to the Civil War, and for the chapters on World War II in Vol. II; Commager for the period since 1860, except for the chapters on World War II.

With the appearance of the sixth edition in 1969, Leuchtenburg joined the two senior authors for the first time. In that edition, Leuchtenburg had the main responsibility for a substantial revision, and for writing new chapters on the Kennedy and Johnson years, but Morison and Commager also made revisions, especially on those chapters which they contributed to the previous edition.

This seventh edition is the first to appear without the direct involvement of Samuel Eliot Morison, though his significant contribution to the sixth edition has been retained. His death on 15 May 1976 evoked widespread expressions of sorrow together with a sense of fulfillment for a life so rich in achievement. In his eighty-eight years Admiral Morison had written more than fifty books, taught with distinction at Harvard for four decades, served his country in two world wars, and, an accomplished mariner, had retraced the voyages of Columbus and Magellan. Born in the nineteenth century, with intimate associations with the world of eighteenth-century Boston, he embraced in his own life much of the history of the American republic about which he wrote with such felicity.

For this seventh edition, the final chapter of the second volume of this work was revised, and new material was added to embrace the period from the fall of 1968 until nearly the end of the next decade, including such momentous events of the Carter presidency as the recognition of the People's Republic of China.

We write for young men and women of all ages, for whom economy in truth-telling is neither necessary nor appropriate. We believe that history embraces the whole of a people's activity: economic and social, literary and spiritual, as well as political and military. We have endeavored therefore to give such stress to these different aspects that our story will be that of a growing and changing civilization in an expanding United States of America.

This new edition, marking a half-century of continuous publication, is dedicated to the rising generation. May they continue to further the Growth of the American Republic!

HENRY STEELE COMMAGER
WILLIAM E. LEUCHTENBURG

Contents

Maps

Illustrations

At Massaponax Church, Virginia. General Ulysses S. Grant (left end of bench nearest tree) sits on a pew from Bethesda Church writing a dispatch, May 21, 1864.

Richmond in Ruins. Photograph by Mathew Brady.

Southern Freedmen in Richmond. Photograph by Mathew Brady.

Horace Greeley (1811–72).

Hamilton Fish (1808–93).

Thaddeus Stevens (1792–1868). Brady-Handy photograph.

Charles Sumner (1811–74). Photograph by Mathew Brady.

Andrew Johnson (1808–75) by Washington Cooper.

Samuel Eliot Morison
1887–1976

For the whole earth is the sepulchre of famous men, and their
story lives on, woven into the stuff of other men's lives.

PERICLES, The Funeral Speech

The Growth of the American Republic

Isolated America

1. THE FIRST DISCOVERY

One summer day somewhat over 25,000 and less than 40,000 years ago, a tribe of Mongolian savages stood on lofty Cape Dezhnev, the easternmost promontory of Siberia, about 30 miles south of the Arctic Circle. They or their parents had abandoned their old home in what is now the Gobi Desert, because that area was beginning to dry up. They had had a long, hard trek of at least 3000 miles, living off the country and fighting the natives all along the way for several years. Perhaps only the magic of their medicine man, his promise of a new world toward the rising sun, had kept them going. Food was scarce, the latest enemy to resent their intrusion followed hard at their heels, and their skin garments were in tatters; in fact they were a tough-looking lot, even according to Siberian standards of that very unrefined era. Looking southeastward over Bering Strait, our hard-pressed savages saw clearly, only 23 miles away, a dome-shaped island over 1700 feet high rising above the sea. They had no experience in navigation, but something had to be done quickly. So, either by fastening together whatever logs and driftwood they could procure, or (more likely) by stealing native kayaks, they ferried themselves over to Big Diomede Island, as we call it, and shook off their pursuers.

Big Diomede and its companion Little Diomede, between which runs today the U.S.-U.S.S.R. boundary, are rocky and barren, affording little in the way of food. So our harassed pioneers, unconscious that they were men of destiny, resumed their voyage to a high rocky land that they sighted 25 miles to the eastward. This was on the Seward Peninsula of Alaska, now the westernmost point of continental United States. Our Mongoloid pilgrim fathers were the forerunners of the mighty race which Christopher Columbus mistakenly named the Indians.

Alaska to them was a land of promise indeed, for it afforded the first square meals they had had for many a long day. In the rivers and the sea there were salmon, seal, and sea-otter. In the back-country there were lots of big, hairy beasts that roared in an amusing manner and rolled over dead when you struck them in a vital spot with your stone-pointed spear; animals whose meat filled the belly and whose pelt kept you warm all winter. And no rival human beings to fight for all this plenty! Our pilgrims so fell in love with this new country that they completely forgot about the old; it never occurred to them to found a Society of Gobi Desert Descendants.

Indulge your historian this little flight of imagination before he settles down to hard fact! After all, the consensus of scientists is that the American continent was discovered by man in some such way as we have described. *Homo sapiens* is a relative newcomer on our planet, and he must have come from some other continent to America, because no near relatives, such as the bigger and brighter apes, have been found here. Great animals like the dinosaur had it all their own way in the pre-glacial age, 50,000 years ago and earlier. This is not to say that all the many million Indians who inhabited North, Central, and South America in 1492 were descended from the passengers on our hypothetical fleet of Mongoloid *Mayflowers*. Biologically it was perfectly possible, but other migratory bands from Siberia must have followed the same course to safety and a square meal.

All ancestors of the American Indians came from Asia via Siberia, and America received no addition from any other source for at least 25,000 years. Africa was once joined to South America, and there was a bridge for plant and insect life between the Old World and the New; but that was long before humankind appeared on the earth. The 'lost continents' of Atlantis and Mu are myths. The Polynesians, although very skillful in canoe navigation, never reached America, because in the South Pacific the prevailing winds are easterly, and in the North Pacific there is a 2000-mile jump from the Hawaiian Islands to California. An occasional Chinese junk or Japanese fishing boat may have drifted across to the coast of Vancouver Island or Oregon; but the human survivors, if any, were undoubtedly killed and probably eaten.

During the next twenty-five to perhaps thirty-five millennia, these Asiatic immigrants migrated southward, perhaps through a corridor in the ice cap that then covered much of North America, until they had reached the southernmost part of Patagonia. Although they lived in the Western Hemisphere for a period some fifty to seventy times as long as the interval from Columbus's landfall to the present day, we know little of their history save what may be surmised from scattered artifacts and skeletons. In these silent eons, Niagara Falls was created, Crater Lake erupted into birth, and mastodons, enormous ground sloths, and camels roamed the continent. The Indians hunted mammoths with spears tipped with ivory; painted pictures and made beads; and showed their precocity by working copper and planting maize at a surprisingly early point in time.

2. THE HIGH CULTURE OF THE INDIANS

Somewhere between 500 B.C. and A.D. 500, the pace of Indian life quickened, especially among the Maya of northern Central America, the Inca of Peru, and the Chibcha of Colombia. In Guatemala arose the Maya empire, a civilization so advanced that its calendar was more accurate than the Julian calendar. It abandoned the stone-built cities of Guatemala in favor of a new location in Yucatán, where its civilization reached its height around A.D. 1100. About a hundred years later a warrior tribe from the north called the Toltec, traditionally led by a remarkable king named Quetzalcoatl, conquered most of the Maya and absorbed their culture, much as the Romans did that of the Greeks. The Toltec empire fell before the onslaught of a new warrior race from the north, the Aztec, a ruthless people who practiced human sacrifice to satisfy the blood lust of their unattractive deities. In South America, the Inca ruled over a great Andean empire; a totalitarian society, it excelled in stone architecture and imperial organization.

The only area north of Mexico where any long historical sequence can be given to Indian life is New Mexico and Arizona. Here a hunting group that had already learned the rudiments of agriculture settled down somewhere about the beginning of the Christian era, abandoned their semi-subterranean log and earth lodges, and built adobe-walled towns with apartment-house dwellings, community courts, and build-ings where religious dances and other ceremonies were practiced. These pueblos were so defensible that succeeding waves of Indian conquerors passed them by. And their inhabitants, of the Hopi, Zuñi, and other tribes, were such good farmers and weavers that they seldom lacked food or clothing. First conquered by the Spaniards in the sixteenth cen-tury, they managed to unite and throw out their masters in 1680; and although reconquered, they, more than other North American Indians, have been unmolested by Spaniards and Americans, so today they afford the best example of a well-rooted Indian culture. Using a 'tree-ring' method of dating,[1] it has been possible to establish a sequence of basket weaving and pottery for the Pueblos, in different styles, from the first centuries of the Christian era to the present.

In the 1300 years that elapsed between A.D. 217 (year of the oldest pueblo roofbeam that can be dated) and 1540, when the Spaniards burst in on them, these Indians became fairly sophisticated by Euro-pean standards. There gradually grew up what archaeologists call the Anasazi culture, from a Navajo word meaning 'the old people,' who were there before them. This culture is divided into six consecutive pe-riods. In the oldest, that of the basket-makers, the people lived in caves or built round adobe huts, wove baskets in which they stored wild seeds and little nubbin-like ears of corn, which they cultivated with a digging-stick. They kept dogs and possibly turkeys, hunted with flint-headed spears, smoked tobacco in a pipe shaped like a cigar-holder, and went completely naked, except for sandals on their feet and fur in the winter.

In their second stage, the basket-makers learned to make pottery, as the inhabitants of Mexico had done somewhat earlier; and this art spread throughout America. The second basket-maker people wove crude fabrics from plant fibers and the women began to adorn them-selves with bracelets of shell, seed, and turquoise beads. The bow and arrow, another independent invention of the Indians which had already been adopted in the Old World, replaced the spear.

The third Pueblo period, from about A.D. 1050 to 1500, curiously cor-

1. Rings of trees make definite patterns, owing to the amount of sunshine and moisture they receive in the growing season. Thus, in the Southwest, where wooden beams were used for the pueblos, the rings on them can be compared with those of a pueblo known to have been destroyed four centuries ago, and these with rings on deeper buried beams, giving us a dating sequence extending about 2100 years.

responds to the 'glorious thirteenth century' in Europe. It was the golden age of the Anasazi culture, that of the cliff-dwellings which discouraged enemies, of great masonry-walled communal dwellings built in the open, with terraced set-backs like modern skyscrapers; of big *kivas* like built-in drums where the priests danced. The close-weave basketry and decorated black-on-white pottery of this period are remarkable. But the Pueblo people used no metals, except occasionally some copper acquired by trade.

After 1300 the area occupied by the Pueblo civilization was seriously reduced, owing to drought, arroyo cutting, and invasions by wild tribes; the people were forced together into larger pueblos where there was a good supply of water, and their arts, ritual, and organization expanded. These were the ancestors of the Zuñi, Hopi, Tewa, and Kere nations of today. The Navajo and Apache of the Athabascan language stock moved in and absorbed the Anasazi culture, which the Navajo have maintained to this day. These people had no sense of political organization beyond the single town, but they have been very tenacious of their way of life; at Acoma, Walpi, Oraibi, Laguna, Zuñi, and other modern pueblos, Indians today live very much as they did before the Europeans arrived.

Of the Indian history of North America east of the Rockies even less is known because the Indians there did not stay put, as did those of the pueblos. Whence came the 'mound-builders,' as the older Indians of the Ohio and upper Mississippi valley are popularly called, we do not know. There is an intriguing theory that they were Toltec tribes, pushed out of Mexico by the Aztec, who piled into canoes somewhere near Vera Cruz, crossed the Gulf of Mexico, and paddled up the Mississippi until they felt safe. Certainly they did not arrive there until about the beginning of the Christian era. If not Toltec in origin, the mound-builders picked up agriculture and pottery from the Anasazi of the Southwest, and went on from there. They traded with other Indians, replaced the pointed sticks with which the Anasazi tilled the earth by stone and shell hoes; they carved out of stone elaborate tobacco pipes with realistic pictures of birds and fishes, and painted their bodies with red ochre. They made elaborate ornaments out of shell, bone, and copper which they obtained from the Lake Superior deposits. Mound-builders were the best metal workers north of Central America before the European discovery, and even used a musical instrument, panpipes of bone and copper. These disappeared when they disappeared, along with the tunes that a thousand years ago resounded through the oak groves of our Middle West. Above all, these people were famous for the massive earthen mounds, sometimes built in shapes of serpents and birds, in which they buried their dead. That is why they were called the 'mound-builders' in the nineteenth century.

At the time the first white men arrived in North America, the Indians of the Great Plains between the Rocky Mountains and the forested areas bordering on the Mississippi lived partly by corn culture but mostly by hunting the buffalo, on foot with bow and arrow. Although Europeans regarded all Indians except the Pueblos as nomads (a convenient excuse for denying them title to the land they occupied), only the Plains Indians really were nomadic; and even they did not become so until about A.D. 1550, when they began to break wild mustangs, offspring of European horses brought in by the Spaniards. Use of the horse gave the men mobility in pursuit of the buffalo herds, while women followed with children and baggage on *travois*, shafts attached to big dogs or old horses; or, in winter, on toboggans, another Indian invention.

The Algonquin included the Abnaki of Maine and Nova Scotia, all the Indian tribes of southern New England, the Delaware and Powhatan of the Middle States and Virginia, the Sauk and Fox, Kickapoo and Pottawatomi in the Middle West, and Blackfoot in the Plains. This complex of tribes, semi-sedentary and agricultural, we know fairly well from the observations of the English and French, with whom they made their first European contacts. They cultivated beans, pumpkins, tobacco, and maize, which on many occasions saved English colonists from starvation. The New England settler found the Indians not in the forest primeval but in the fields, tending crops. The Algonquin was an excellent fisherman with nets and a good hunter. He lived sociably and filthily in long bark-covered communal houses. He invented one of the lightest and most efficient of the world's small boats — the birch-bark canoe; and in regions where no white birch of sufficient girth was available he built dugouts, as did the other coastal Indians. He hunted deer and moose with bow and arrow for meat and skins, and trapped beaver, with which his women folk made smart jackets. The men went almost naked, even in winter, except for 'shorts' and moccasins of deerskin. They got about easily in winter on snowshoes, an Algonquian invention. These tribes produced some great and even noble characters: Powhatan, Massasoit, King Philip, Tammany, Pontiac, Tecumseh, and Keokuk. The Algonquin were susceptible to Christianity and assimilated European culture somewhat better than most Indians, although some of the chiefs we have named tried to unite their people against the English and perished in the attempt.

The Five Nations (Mohawk, Cayuga, Oneida, Onondaga, and Seneca) of the Iroquois had the reputation of being the toughest fighters in North America; and they had to be, to hold their own against the Algonquin. In 1600, when first seen by Europeans, they occupied the territory from Lake Champlain to the Genesee river, and from the Adirondack mountains to central Pennsylvania. Hard pressed when the Europeans arrived, the Iroquois survived, and even extended their dominion, partly by Hiawatha's League which prevented war among themselves, and later through alliance with the Dutch and English. Their folkways were similar to those of the Algonquin, except that they were not good fishermen. Among their famous leaders were Hendrick, Cornplanter, Red Jacket, Brant, and Logan. The Tuscarora, who in 1720 moved north and became the Sixth Nation, and the southern Cherokee were also of Iroquoian stock. The Cherokee produced one of the greatest of American Indians, Sequoya, who invented an alphabet for his people and led them in a great advance in civilization.

In the southeastern United States the Muskhogean stock, which included the Apalachee, Chickasaw, Choctaw, Creek, Natchez, and Seminole nations, was regarded by Europeans of the colonial era as the elite of North American Indians. They had an elaborate system of castes, from the 'Suns' down to the 'Stinkards,' which were not allowed to intermarry. All Muskhogean tribes were planters of maize, which they accented with the annual 'busk,' or green corn festival; and they were expert potters, weavers, and curers of deerskin for clothing. They learned very quickly from Europeans to plant orchards and keep cattle.

If further evidence is wanted that these advanced civilizations of the Indians were of purely American origin, we have only to consider the simple things of immemorial use in Europe, which even the most gifted Indians never discovered. Although they mined, smelted, and worked gold, silver and platinum, tin, lead, and copper, their use of iron was limited to chance finds of meteoric deposits. Indians invented the bark and the dugout canoes, yet only one or two primitive tribes in California learned to build a boat from plank and timber and only the Peruvian Indian learned to sail on balsa rafts. Although they made pottery that could stand a hot fire, they never discovered the potter's, or any other kind of wheel; the only beasts of burden in all the Americas (apart from the women) were the dog and the llama.

But despite all their deficiencies — notably in political organization — the American Indians were a great and noble race, which we of European or African origin are proud to claim as predecessors, and ashamed to have treated as barbarians, which they were not.

3. THE FIRST EUROPEAN IMPACT — THE NORTHMEN

Outside Peru, Mexico, Central America, and the Iroquois country, the Indians were completely decentralized; each tribe controlled but a small territory, lived in a state of permanent hostility with its near neighbors, and knew nothing of what went on elsewhere. Hence it was possible for Europeans to impinge here and there on the New World without affecting tribes a few hundred miles away, and without breaking down American isolation. One such impingement, and the only one which is positively known to have occurred, was that of the Norsemen in the eleventh century A.D.

In the ninth century A.D. Scandinavians from Norway occupied Iceland, driving out the Christian Irish colonists who had been living there in isolation for almost two centuries. These Celtic wanderers were bold and skillful navigators in their skin-covered boats, and the sea-voyage from Iceland to Greenland, or from Greenland to the Labrador, is much shorter than that from Ireland to Iceland. Hence, it is possible that Irish from Iceland were the first Europeans to reach the American continent. If so, they were absorbed or exterminated by the Indians, leaving no trace that has been uncovered.

However that may be, it is a matter of historic record that in the late tenth century a tough Norseman from Iceland named Eric the Red discovered Greenland, and founded on its west coast a colony named Brattalid that flourished for several centuries by raising cattle and exporting walrus ivory and white falcons to Norway. After one Biarni had seen land to the west c. 986, Eric's son Leif in 1001 reached a coast where he saw long sand beaches, spent a winter in northern New-foundland, and returned to Greenland.

Around 1010–15 another Icelander named Thorfinn Karlsefni, with a group of Eric the Red's kindred and neighbors, explored the coast of this 'Vinland the Good,' and attempted to found a colony where Leif had been. They spent two or three winters in northern Newfoundland, but the natives, whom they called 'Skrellings,' proved so hostile that the Norsemen gave up and returned to Greenland. Their adventures were related in two sagas first written down in the thirteenth century.

These Norsemen were not Vikings, and they used a round, one-masted trading ship, not the long Viking ship so often pictured. Ordinary farmers and traders, with weapons little better than those of the American natives, they were unable to cope with these people. Certain traces of them have been found at L'Anse aux Meadows, Newfoundland by a Norse archaeologist, Helge Ingstad, and a fifteenth-century map now at Yale shows an island west of Greenland labeled 'Vinlandia Insula.' The wild grapes which gave this short-lived colony its name were probably wild currants or cranberries. After Thorfinn's colony failed, Greenlanders occasionally made voyages to the coasts of Labrador to cut wood, and the Greenland colony seems to have lasted until the late fifteenth century, when it faded out, owing to attacks by Eskimos, and the failure of a then impoverished Norway to send them a ship. The significance of this discovery as the key to a brave New World never seems to have occurred to the Norsemen, or to anyone else. Biarni, the predecessor of Leif Ericsson, may justly be called the European discoverer of America; but he only lifted a corner of the veil, and his people let it drop. Nothing that he or Thorfinn Karlsefni observed was of any interest to a Europe just emerging from the Dark Ages. And there is no trace of Norse influence in the legends or customs of the northern Indians, or in American fauna and flora.

4. INDIAN AND EUROPEAN

Thus America enjoyed almost five centuries more of complete isolation. Nothing was done to prepare for the next European attack, because the existence of Europe and Asia was unsuspected. No Indian tribe or nation knew much about its own continent a few hundred miles away. Among them there was nothing even approaching a sentiment of racial or continental solidarity, not even a name for race or country. Almost every Indian tribe called itself something equivalent to 'We the People,' and used some insulting title for its near neighbors. Wherever Europeans appeared, for a century or more after 1492, the first thought of the Indians was 'Men from the Sky!' and the second, 'Heaven-sent allies against our enemies.' European invasions fitted perfectly into the Indian's own pattern of warfare. The white man did not have to divide and conquer, because the Indian continent was already cut up into almost microscopic divisions; he only had to conquer them piecemeal, and he found plenty of native assistance for the task.

Lack of iron and gunpowder, ships and horses, handicapped the Indians, but the earliest Europeans who came had few of these, and the Indians in time learned to use them well enough. Certain tribes, like the Cuna Cuna of Panama, have retained their lands and their cultural integrity to this day because they combined the offensive power of poisoned arrows with lack of anything valuable to Europeans. But the Indians of the Western Hemisphere were a heterogeneous group with great differences in language and in level of culture. Primarily, inability to unite was responsible for the European conquest. If, for instance, the Iroquois or a confederacy like theirs had been in possession of the localities where the first Spaniards, English, and Dutch landed, white colonization might have been postponed to the nineteenth century, when European pressures and techniques became irresistible. If the Aztec had had a little more time to consolidate his empire, Mexico might have emerged as a native state like Japan. As it was, the three authoritarian Indian empires were the first to fall. For, as a conquistador put it, when you captured *the* Inca or *the* Montezuma, it was as if a keystone fell from an arch. In Mexico, Peru, and Colombia the Spaniards simply took the place of an Indian aristocracy or theocracy, and exploited the natives for their own profit.

Yet there was no consistent pattern of conquest. Certain free but feeble peoples, such as the Arawak of the West Indies, were exterminated by being forced to labor. Others, like the Plains Indians, were humbled and degraded in the nineteenth century because their food supply was destroyed. Still others, like the Carib and a good part of the Algonquin (as in our own day many of the Polynesians), were destroyed by the religion as well as by the vices and diseases of white men who wished them well. Anthropologists have ascertained that if we wish to conserve a people of lower culture, we must respect their religion and folkways, and not attempt to clothe their bodies or dethrone their gods. Some nations managed for many years to live peaceably side by side with a European colony. But if the tribe wished to keep its virtue, it had to raid or fight; and the lower sort of white men could always be counted on to provoke hostilities, which at best ended in land cession, removal, and the same thing starting over again. Here and there a successful amalgamation took place: on the St. Lawrence the natives were folded into the French Canadians, as a pastry-cook folds butter into pie-crust dough, and the same process went on in many parts of Central America, between Europeans and Indians, or between Indians and Negroes. Yet it should be added that war was far less important in the extermination of the Indian than the ravages of new forms of disease, an unintended contribution of the white man.

Since Indian societies were diverse, and since their experience with the white man differed, the intrusion of the European had a variety of results, some of them unexpected. In New England, the Puritans, who regarded the redmen as potential Christians descended from the ten lost tribes of Israel, sought to convert and educate these 'Jewes' and to deal with them fairly. In the Pacific Northwest, where native craftsmen carved bone, horn, and wood, the metal tools the whites brought with them stimulated a marked artistic advance. In the South, the Indian, adapting himself to the white man's ways, acquired Negro slaves. In the Great Plains, the arrival of the Spaniard with his horses had the unanticipated consequence of the explosive development of the horse-and-bison culture. Yet even where the initial result of the advent of the white man was benign, the ultimate outcome of the pressure of a technologically advanced European civilization on the American Indian was almost always extinction or dispersal.[2]

2. However, the Indians are so far from being exterminated that in the United States and Canada today their numbers are approaching the estimated 1.5 million of 1500.

II

The Century of Discovery

1. THE DECADENCE OF EUROPE

At the end of the year 1492 most thinking men in western Europe felt gloomy about the future. Christian civilization appeared to be shrinking in area and dividing into hostile units. For over a century there had been no important advance in natural science, and registration in the universities dwindled as the instruction they offered became increasingly barren and lifeless. Institutions were decaying, well-meaning people were becoming cynical or desperate, and many intelligent men were endeavoring to escape the present through studying the pagan past.

Islam was now expanding at the expense of Christendom. Every effort to recover the Holy Sepulchre at Jerusalem, touchstone of Christian prestige, had been a failure. The Ottoman Turks, after snuffing out all that remained of the Byzantine Empire, had overrun most of Greece, Albania, and Serbia; presently they would be hammering at the gates of Vienna. For half a century each successive Pope had proclaimed a new crusade, but Europe regarded these appeals to duty as a mere device to raise money. One scandal of Western Christendom, the great schism, had been overcome, but only at the cost of suppressing reforms within the Church, thus rendering the greater and more permanent Protestant schism all but inevitable. And in 1492 the papacy touched bottom when Rodrigo Borgia, a corrupt ecclesiastical politician, was elected to the throne of Saint Peter as Alexander VI.

If one turned to the Holy Roman Empire, secular counterpart to the Roman Catholic Church, the picture was no brighter. The amiable but lazy Emperor Frederick III, driven from his Austrian lands by the king of Hungary, had retired to dabble in astrology and alchemy; his son Maximilian was full of promise but short in performance. In England the Wars of the Roses were over, but few expected the House of Tudor to last long. Only in the Iberian peninsula, in Portugal and Castile, were there signs of new life; but these kingdoms were too much on the periphery of Europe to alter the general picture of decay.

With an empire incurably weak and the Church low in moral prestige, Christians had little to which they might cling. The great principle of unity represented by emperor and pope was a dream that had not come true. It seemed as if the devil had adopted as his own the principle 'divide and rule.' Throughout western Europe the general feeling was one of profound disillusion, cynical pessimism, and black despair.

One may catch the prevailing mood by reading the final pages of the *Nuremberg Chronicle*. The colophon of this stately folio, dated 12 July 1493, declares that it contains 'the events most worthy of notice from the beginning of the world to the calamity of our time.' And that time was painted in the most gloomy colors, suggesting the end of the world; a few blank pages were left to record events between 1493 and the Day of Judgment. Yet, even as the chroniclers of Nuremberg were correcting their proofs from Koberger's press, a Spanish caravel named *Niña* scudded before a winter gale into Lisbon, with news of a discovery that was to give old Europe another chance.

In a few years we find the picture completely changed. Strong monarchs are stamping out privy conspiracy and rebellion; the Church, purged and chastened by the Protestant Reformation, puts her house in order; new ideas flare up throughout Italy, France, Germany, and the northern nations; faith in God revives and the human spirit is renewed. The change is complete and astounding. A new world view has begun, and people no longer sigh after an imaginary golden age in the distant past, but lay plans for a golden age in the near future.

2. COLUMBUS DISCOVERS AMERICA

Christopher Columbus discovered America by accident when looking for Japan and China. Few people cared anything about it, when found;

and the Atlantic coast of America from Hudson's Bay to the Strait of Magellan was explored by navigators who were seeking a passage to India through or around this unwanted continent. Yet Columbus was the effective discoverer of America for Europe, because he was the first to do anything with it. The 'Enterprise of the Indies,' as he called his plan of sailing west to the Orient, was his very own, suggested by no previous information, produced by no economic forces. He promoted this design for at least eight years before he could persuade any European prince to grant him the modest equipment required; and a less persistent or stout-hearted captain would have been forced to turn back before reaching land. News of his discovery was immediately spread throughout Europe by the recent invention of printing. Columbus personally led the first colony to the New World in 1493; he discovered the South American continent in 1498; and he obtained the first definite news of the Pacific Ocean. The history of the Americas stems from his four voyages.

This great seaman was born at Genoa in 1451, the son of a weaver of woolen cloth. At about the age of twenty he went to sea; and after making voyages in the Mediterranean suffered shipwreck in Portugal, and settled in Lisbon around the year 1477.

Portugal was then the most progressive and western-minded of the European kingdoms. Under the direction of Prince Henry the Navigator, the nine islands of the Azores were discovered and colonized between 1439 and 1453; Corvo, farthest west of the Azores, is only 1024 nautical miles from Newfoundland. The Portuguese, supposing that other islands lay to the westward, made many voyages in search of them; but none succeeded. Boisterous westerly winds in the North Atlantic make the westward passage, even in our day, difficult and dangerous for sailing vessels; and the vessels of that day could not sail nearer the wind than 66°; with a heavy sea they could make no progress to windward. Only a lucky break, such as John Cabot evidently had in 1497, plus the certainty of land to the westward, could make that northern route the road to discovery — unless indeed you followed the Iceland-Greenland-Labrador stepping stones. Nobody thought of that, because nobody except the Norsemen had ever known about the land to the westward, and they had written it off as unprofitable.

Portugal could use a few more Atlantic islands, but what she really wanted was a sea route to 'the Indies' (India, China, and the eastern islands), there to obtain at their source the spices, drugs, and gems which reached Europe in small quantities over caravan routes, and the gold and silver about which Marco Polo had told tall tales. The most promising route lay to the southward, along the coast of Africa; and by the time Columbus settled in Portugal, the mariners of that nation were opening up new stretches of the West African coast every year. As early as 1460 they had passed the site of Dakar, had dispelled the Arabian legends of a 'sea of pitchy darkness,' and disproved what the ancients had said on the uninhabitable nature of tropical countries. Fifteen years later they had completed the exploration of the Gulf of Guinea, and opened up a trade in gold and ivory, slaves and pepper, that made Lisbon the envy of Europe. And for this traffic, which required a round voyage of many thousand miles, the Portuguese developed a type of sailing vessel, the caravel, which was fast, seaworthy, and weatherly. Ships capable of making the voyage to America and back had existed long before Columbus was born; but the caravel, the type he chose, made the voyage far less difficult and dangerous.

Columbus proposed to open a much shorter sea route to 'the Indies' by sailing west, around the world. A poor mathematician, he had satisfied himself by a series of lucky miscalculations that Japan lay only 2400 to 2500 miles west of the Canaries. In 1484 began his long and arduous efforts to obtain backing for his enterprise. He first offered it to the king of Portugal, and then to the sovereigns of Spain, while his brother Bartholomew hawked it about the courts of northern Europe. Unfortunately for Columbus, the learned men and mathematicians had much more accurate notions of the size of the globe and the distribution of land and water than he had. Not that he needed to demonstrate that the earth was round. The earth had been known to be spherical for centuries; a spherical earth was taught in all European universities. Everyone agreed that a westward route to 'the Indies' was theoretically possible, like flying in 1900; but nobody considered it practicable with such means as were then available.

During his eight years of agitation, the eloquence and personality of Columbus gave him enthusiastic friends and backers; but his scheme was rejected by two successive royal committees. Finally the intuition of a woman, Queen Isabella, gave him his chance. After all, the man might be right about the size of the earth. Nobody really knew — it was simply one theory against another. The equipment he asked for was cheap enough; the honors he demanded were not unreasonable, if he succeeded, and the glory and gain for Spain would be incalculable. If he failed, not much would be lost. Why not try it? So Ferdinand and Isabella, the joint sovereigns of Spain, undertook to pay the bills and to make Columbus viceroy, governor, and admiral over any lands he might discover and acquire. They gave him a Latin letter of introduction to the Emperor of China, and a passport stating that he was on a legitimate voyage 'to regions of India.'

Columbus sailed from Palos on 3 August 1492, as commander of a fleet of three vessels, *Niña, Pinta,* and *Santa Maria,* each about 70 to 80 feet long. All were equipped at the royal expense, and manned by about 90 picked Spaniards. His plan was to sail due west from the Canary Islands, because according to the best available maps these lay on the same latitude as Japan; and the mythical islands named Antilia, which he hoped to sight en route, would be a good place of call for wood and water. And if these islands were missed, the fleet would be sure to hit China. Their course lay along the northern edge of the belt of northeast trade winds which blow steadily in the late summer between the Canaries and America. This most important voyage in history was also one of the easiest; during most of the outward passage the Spaniards enjoyed fair wind, soft air, a serene sky, and an ocean smooth as a river. The three vessels dropped the last of the Canaries on 9 September 1492. Mutiny flared up on 10 October but Columbus persuaded the men to go on for three days more. At 10 p.m. of 11 October, Columbus and a few others saw for a short time a dim light ahead. This may have been a brush fire kindled by natives on a high point of an island, whose sand cliffs showed up in the moonlight at 2 a.m. on the 12th. It was the Bahamian island that Columbus named, and we call, San Salvador.

Many other discoveries have been more spectacular than that of this small, low, sandy island that rides out ahead of the American continent, breasting the trade winds. But it was there that the Ocean for the first time 'loosed the chains of things' as Seneca had prophesied, gave up the secret that had baffled Europeans since they began to inquire what lay beyond the western horizon's rim. Stranger people than the gentle Arawak, more exotic plants than the green verdure of San Salvador, had been discovered, even by the Portuguese before Columbus; but the discovery of Africa was but an unfolding of a continent already glimpsed, whilst San Salvador, rising from the sea at the end of a 33-day westward sail, was a clean break with past experience. Every tree, every plant, that the Spaniards saw was strange to them, and the natives were not only strange but completely unexpected, speaking an unknown tongue and resembling no race of which even the most educated of the explorers had read in the tales of travelers from Herodotus to Marco Polo. Never again may mortal man hope to recapture the amazement, the wonder, the delight of those October days in 1492 when the New World gracefully yielded her virginity to the conquering Castilians.

With America's virginity went her isolation. Neither could ever be restored or re-established, despite the efforts of soothsayers and statesmen.

The natives of these islands, whom Columbus hopefully called Indians, welcomed the 'men from the sky' and several were impressed to act as guides to 'Cipangu' and 'Cathay.' They piloted Columbus through the Bahamas to northwestern Cuba. There he dispatched his Arabic interpreter inland to meet a cacique whom he took, from the Indians' description, to be the Emperor of China. The village of thatched huts that they found bore little resemblance to the Cambaluk where Marco Polo had hobnobbed with Kubla Khan; but on the way back to the ships the envoys met Indians inhaling cigars through the nostrils, 'to drink the smoke thereof as they are accustomed.' Unknowingly, Columbus had discovered one of the greatest gifts of the New World to the Old.

Eastward along the coast of Cuba sailed the fleet, Columbus eagerly examining every new plant as evidence that this was the southeastern promontory of China. He then crossed the Windward Passage to *La Isla Española*, 'The Spanish Island,' which we still call Hispaniola in English. There he found golden grains in river sands, rumors of a gold mine up-country, and an abundance of gold ornaments on the Indians which they readily swapped for brass rings, glass beads, and bits of cloth. The flagship ran hard and fast on a coral reef, so Columbus built a fort of her timbers, garrisoned it with her crew, and sailed for home on board *Niña,* accompanied by *Pinta.* Sailing as close to the trade wind as they could, the two caravels worked their way north to the latitude of Bermuda where they caught the winter westerlies and went roaring home, superbly handled through two severe storms. Both dropped anchor the same day, 15 March 1493, in the harbor of Palos whence they had departed.

Columbus and his men were received as heroes, and everyone

assumed that they had discovered islands 'in the Indian Sea,' if not the continent of Asia itself. The Pope conferred on Spain the sovereignty of all discoveries already made or to be made, beyond the meridian 100 leagues (318 nautical miles) west of the Cape Verde Islands. Portugal protested, and by mutual consent in a treaty the next year, the line was moved 270 leagues farther west; and this new line of demarcation gave Portugal her title to Brazil.

After six months in Spain Columbus sailed in command of a gallant fleet of seventeen vessels, discovered all the Caribbee Islands north and west of Martinique, had his first fight with the Carib Indians at St. Croix, called at Puerto Rico; and at Hispaniola, after ascertaining that his garrison had been wiped out, he landed men and began building the fortified trading station of Isabella on the north coast.

There his troubles began. The first European colony in America was nothing more than a glorified gold hunt. Columbus expected to obtain the precious metal by trade; but the Indians' demand for jingly trading truck was soon exhausted, and the Spaniards began taking gold by force. As elsewhere in America where Europeans came, the newcomers were first welcomed by the Indians as visitors, then resented as in-truders, and finally resisted with fruitless desperation. The Spaniards, who had come for gold and nothing else, resented their governor's orders to build houses, tend crops, and cut wood; the wine and food supplies from Spain gave out; and before long bands of men in armor were roving about the fertile interior of Hispaniola, living off the coun-try, and torturing the natives to obtain gold. In the summer of 1494, which Columbus spent exploring the southern coasts of Cuba and His-paniola and discovering Jamaica, the colonists got completely out of hand; and the Admiral's attempts to impose an iron discipline resulted in malcontents seizing vessels and returning to Spain to complain of him and of 'the Indies.' So Columbus, leaving his brother Bartholomew in charge, sailed for home in 1496.

Everybody in Spain had wanted to go to 'the Indies' in 1493; four years later nobody wanted to go there. America seemed a fraud and a delusion; even the gold, it was rumored, was no good. The air was pes-tilential, the food inedible, and the Columbus brothers were merciless foreign taskmasters. Ferdinand and Isabella would doubtless have dropped the whole thing had not their honor been involved. After a year's lobbying at court, Columbus could only obtain their grudging consent to send out convicts as colonists, and to let him make a new voyage in search of the Asiatic continent.

In the meantime, a second nation had stumbled on America when searching for Asia, and through the efforts of another Genoese. John Cabot, a compatriot of Columbus but a naturalized citizen of Venice, was one of a colony of foreign merchants established at Bristol in England. He had carried spices from the Levant to England, and believed that the Far East could best be reached by sailing westward in the short high latitudes. After making a contract with Henry VII of England similar to that of Columbus with the Spanish sovereigns, he sailed from Bristol in late May 1497 in the *Matthew*, a ship so small that she carried a crew of but eighteen men. On 24 June after a voyage of thirty-five days, he raised land (probably Cape Bonavista, Newfoundland), enjoyed good codfishing, saw nets ashore but no natives, sailed for home not later than 20 July, and arrived in Bristol 6 August. He proceeded to court, where King Henry gave him £10 and a pension of £20. That is practically all we know of Cabot's first voyage; and the facts of his second, made in 1498, are impossible to disentangle from later voyages of his more famous son Sebastian. In any event, the English did practically nothing to follow up Cabot's voyages for three-quarters of a century, and their only influence on American history was to give the English Crown a 'legal' title to North America against the claims of Spain and the Netherlands.

If the Spaniards had heard of Cabot's voyage by 1498, they were not interested in codfish or rocky, spruce-clad shores. Columbus on his third voyage followed a southerly course in search of a continent which, it was suspected, filled the vast unknown spaces of the globe in that direction. On 31 July 1498 he sighted the island of Trinidad, and a few days later entered the Gulf of Paria between it and the mainland, of which he took possession for Spain. He then stretched across the Caribbean to Santo Domingo, the new capital of Hispaniola that had been established in his absence, and found the island in a turmoil. Most of the Indians had been brought under subjection, but the chief justice, Francisco Roldán — first of a long line of American rebels — was heading a revolt of ex-criminals and robust individualists against the government of Columbus's brother, in the hope of obtaining a larger share of the women and the gold-diggings than regulations allowed. Columbus had so few loyal and healthy followers that he was forced to appease

Roldán with a system of land and labor allotments. To each man was granted a tract of land with the Indians who lived on it, whose labors he was entitled to exploit as he saw fit. These *encomiendas,* as they were subsequently called, marked the beginning not only of agricultural colonization, but of a system that the Spaniards applied throughout their conquests on the continent, in order to induce settlement and supply the colonists with the cheap labor that they wanted.

In the meantime Vasco da Gama had rounded the Cape of Good Hope, reached Calicut in India, and returned; a triumphant voyage that gave Portugal the sea route to the Orient which Columbus had first sought. Pedro Alvarez Cabral, on his voyage to India in 1500, called at a bay in Brazil, now named after him, and took possession of that mighty country for Portugal. Several Spaniards who had been officers under Columbus made voyages of their own to the South American continent, and on one of them sailed a Florentine merchant, Amerigo Vespucci. Amerigo's amusingly inflated and pre-dated account of the voyage that he made with Hojeda in 1499 made his name familiar to northern Europe. Thus, when a German geographer in 1507 suggested that the new continent be called *America,* after him, the name caught on. A year earlier Columbus, after an unsuccessful fourth voyage to try to find a strait through his 'Other World,' as he called America, had died in obscurity at Valladolid.

Columbus did not exaggerate when he boasted, 'Over there I have placed under their Highnesses' sovereignty more land than there is in Africa and Europe, and more than 1700 islands, not counting Hispaniola. . . . In seven years I, by the divine will, made that conquest.' And the mystical strain in him, which made him venture unafraid into the unknown, led him to predict, 'Your Highnesses will win these lands, which are an Other World, and where Christianity will have so much enjoyment, and our faith in time so great an increase.' No discoverer in the world's history had such marvelous success as Columbus, even though he never found what he first sought; no navigator save Magellan or da Gama may be compared with him for courage, persistence, and skill; no other great benefactor of the human race was so ill rewarded in his lifetime; none other is so justly revered today in the New and Other World of his Discovery.

3. CARIBBEAN COLONIES

For about twenty years after the first voyage of Columbus, Hispaniola was the only European colony in America. It was an agricultural and mining colony based on cattle and cotton raising, gold mining, and the culture of the sugar cane, which the Spaniards introduced from the Canaries. In 1512 Hispaniola was exporting annually to Spain not far short of a million dollars in gold. The enslaved Indians died off under forced labor, and were replaced, first by Indians kidnapped from other islands, who suffered the same fate, and then — beginning in 1510 — by Negro slaves, bought from the Portuguese, who procured them in Africa.

Santo Domingo became the center from which the rest of America, to a great extent, was explored and colonized. The more adventurous spirits, dissatisfied with the humdrum life of sugar planter, mine overseer, or petty official, obtained royal permission to conquer and colonize other islands, and then the mainland.

Juan Ponce de León, the first of these *adelantados* (advancers), explored in 1508 the island of Puerto Rico. It was conquered and colonized, as was Jamaica in 1509–10, and Cuba between 1511 and 1515.

Next, the Spaniards extended their explorations to the mainland. Ponce de León had heard the story of a marvelous spring on Andros in the Bahamas which restored youth and vigor to the old and impotent. This seemed to fit in with a classical myth of the waters of the terrestrial paradise; and Ponce, who at the age of 53 was pretty well used up by fighting and rapine, decided to search for it. In April 1513, after threading his way through the Bahamas and ascertaining (what Columbus might have told him) that there were neither springs nor streams in these coral islands, Ponce landed near the mouth of the St. John's river, and named the land Florida after that fair Easter season (*Pascua Florida*). Hugging the coast to avoid the Gulf stream, he rounded the Florida Keys and sailed up the Gulf coast, possibly as far as the site of Pensacola. But he returned without an ounce of gold or a drink of invigorating water; and tough Indians thwarted his attempt to found a colony on the peninsula in 1521. St. Augustine was founded by Menéndez de Aviles in 1566 in order to protect the treasure fleets from

French and English marauders. Within two years he had established a string of posts from Tampa Bay to Port Royal, South Carolina, and was prepared to enter the real-estate business; but for that, Florida had to wait until 1886 when Henry M. Flagler began the 'development' whose devastating results we witness today. Spanish missionaries ranged as far north as Chesapeake Bay, and several missions were later established on the Gulf coast, among the Creek Indians; but the few settlers who came soon withdrew, the Indians remained hostile, and Florida during three centuries of Spanish rule was little more than a military outpost of Mexico and Cuba.

The acquisition of Mexico and South America almost ruined the Spanish colonies in the Caribbean. Hispaniola in 1574 contained only 1000 Spaniards, less than Columbus brought over in 1493, and 12,000 Negro slaves. Spanish Hispaniola has never to this day recovered her pristine prosperity; it is as if the tortured Indians had put a curse on the land.

4. BALBOA AND MAGELLAN

The Pacific Ocean was discovered by Vasco Núñez de Balboa, a stowaway from Hispaniola who had made himself master of a relatively insignificant Spanish post on the Gulf of Darien. In 1513 Balboa had several hundred Indians hack the way across the treacherous isthmus of Darien for him and his 189 hidalgos; the distance was only 45 miles as the crow flies, but it took them 25 days to reach the spot where 'silent, upon a peak in Darien,' he first gazed upon the Pacific. The discoverer was soon after put to death by his rival Pedrarias, whose energy was so vast that small sailing vessels and their gear were transported across the divide in sections, and set afloat on *El Mar del Sur*, the great South Sea. Presently the city of Panama was founded, and Spain had a Pacific base.

Across that ocean — how far across nobody had yet guessed — lay the Spice Islands, whence King Manoel of Portugal was deriving far greater wealth than did his Spanish cousins from the gold-washings of Hispaniola. So the discovery of Balboa only stimulated efforts to get around, through, or past, America. For a time it seemed that the Portuguese would discover the western as well as the eastern route to the real Indies; their exploration of the Brazilian coast took them down to the River Plate by 1514. But they made the same mistake that John II did with Columbus.

A short, stocky, and dour captain named Ferdinand Magellan, who had spent seven years with the Portuguese in the Far East, believed that the Spice Islands — the modern Indonesia — could better be reached by sailing westward; but King Manoel was not interested. So Magellan turned to the king of Spain (Charles I, later the V), who gave him a fleet of five ships. They sailed from Seville in August 1519, and reached the River Plate in January. A careful search proved that this estuary was no strait, and the voyage continued south along the coast of Patagonia. While the fleet was wintering, the captains of four ships mutinied; Magellan hanged some of the leaders, and marooned the others. At the Antarctic summer solstice the voyage was renewed, and on 21 October 1520, Magellan discovered the entrance to 'that Strait which shall forever be honored with his name,' as Camoëns wrote in the *Lusiads.*

The fleet, now reduced by shipwreck and desertion to three sail, required 38 days to thread the 325-mile passage that cuts through the tail end of the Andes. Tortuous channels, many of them dead-ends that lead only to destruction; cliff-rimmed waters so deep that a ship will strike before she can anchor; icy squalls that blow right down your mast at a moment's notice; penetrating cold and dangerous fog; this Strait has everything that a seaman dreads. Yet Magellan's three ships sailed safely through on 28 November 1520.

Then came the most terrible part of the voyage. This South Sea was calm enough, once they were off shore — that is why Magellan renamed it the Pacific Ocean — but they were fourteen weeks without sight of land, excepting two small coral atolls where neither water nor food was found. The scurvy-ridden men were reduced to eating sawdust and biscuit which had become mere powder swarming with worms, even to broiling the leather chafing-gear of the yards. Relief was obtained on 6 March 1521, at Guam, in the group that Magellan named the Ladrones; and ten days later they reached Leyte Gulf in the Philippines. Sailing through Surigao Strait, the fleet anchored off a tiny island named Limasaua, off Leyte. There occurred the most dramatic event of the voyage. Magellan's Malay servant Henriquez, whom he had brought home from a previous voyage, was able to make himself understood. West had met East; Henriquez was the first man in history to sail around the world.

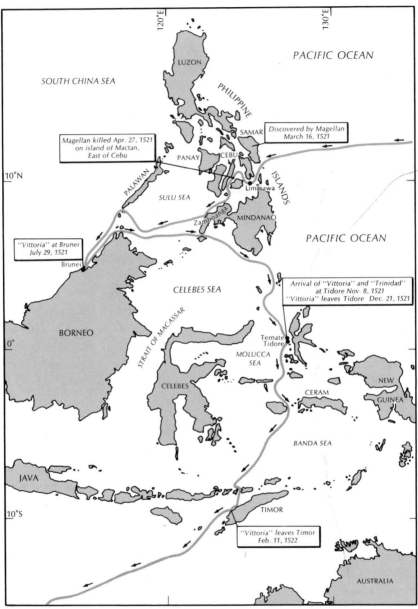

ROUTE OF MAGELLAN'S FLEET
through the Philippines and Moluccas, 1521-1522

At Cebu, the Moslem rajah pretended to embrace Christianity in order to obtain Magellan's aid against a local enemy; and in the ensuing fight at Mactan, on 27 April 1521, as he was covering the retreat of his men to the boats, Magellan lost his life.

After two ships had been abandoned, the *Vittoria,* laden with spices, set forth alone, on 21 December 1521, under Captain Juan Sebastian de El Cano. She crossed the Indian Ocean, rounded the Cape of Good Hope, and on 9 September 1522, this greatest voyage of all time ended at Seville, with only eighteen of the 239 men who set forth three years earlier. But the cargo of spices more than paid expenses. Captain de El Cano was ennobled, and Europe for the first time learned the width of the Pacific Ocean and the real relation of the New World to the Orient.

The most substantial fruit of this marvelous voyage for Spain was the Philippine Islands, as they were named after the *infante* who became King Philip II in 1556. Permanent occupation of this archipelago began with the expedition of Miguel López de Legaspi in 1564. Owing to Legaspi's tact, the friendly attitude of the natives, and (not least) the fact that they had no gold or other precious commodities,[1] the Philippines were conquered, converted, and held by a mere handful of soldiers and friars. Thus the nation which had rolled back the westernmost wave of Islam from Europe, met and checked the eastern wave of Mohammedanism in the Philippines. Manila, founded by Legaspi in 1571, became a wealthy trading post between West and East, such as Columbus had hoped to establish on his first voyage.

5. THE SPANISH EMPIRE

The entire east coast of South America had been explored, and Magellan was already on his way, before the two most splendid native civilizations in America, those of Mexico and Peru, had yielded their secrets.

In 1519 the governor of Cuba, wishing to establish a trading post on the Mexican coast, sent an expedition of eleven ships, carrying only 550 Spaniards, under 32-year-old Hernando Cortés. Arriving at a time when the caciques of Mexico were chafing under the cruel sovereignty

1. The Philippines now are one of the leading gold-producing countries of the world, but the Spaniards did not discover the gold deposits.

of the Aztecs, Cortés was welcomed by many as their fabled hero, Quetzalcoatl, and he had the wit to take advantage of it. For all that, the conquest of Mexico was one of the most amazing military and diplomatic feats in the world's history. The march up from Vera Cruz to the great interior plateau, the audacious capture of Montezuma's lake-rimmed capital (1521), and the defeat of a vast army on the plains of Teotihuacan, completed the ruin of Aztec power and firmly established Cortés as master of Mexico.

This conquest, with its spectacular yield of treasure, was only a beginning. The whole southern section of the United States from South Carolina across to California was explored by Spanish conquistadors in search of more valuable treasure, of new empires that might challenge Mexico, and of the fabled Strait of Anian which was supposed to cross North America from east to west, and might be the long-sought passage to India.

Pánfilo de Narvaez, who sailed to Florida from Spain in 1527, was the most unfortunate of the conquistadors. After losing two ships in a hurricane, he landed somewhere on the Gulf coast of Florida, fought his way up to the site of Tallahassee, retreated to the coast, and there built a fleet of boats from native wood fastened with spikes fashioned from spurs and stirrups, rigged with hair cordage and sails made from the hides of horses which his men had eaten. In these crazy craft Narvaez sailed past the mouths of the Mississippi, only to be wrecked on the coast of Texas. The survivors, Cabeza de Vaca, two other Spaniards, and a Negro, spent six years among the Indians, eventually reaching Mexico with tales of wild 'hunchback cows' that covered the plains as far as the eye could see, and of cities with emerald-studded walls, of which they had heard. These 'Seven Cities of Cibola' were more readily believed in than were the buffalo.

In 1539 the viceroy of Mexico sent Fray Marcos, accompanied by Esteban, the Negro companion of Cabeza de Vaca, up into the future New Mexico in search of the fabled 'Seven Cities.' There they discovered the disappointing foundation of this myth, the Zuñi pueblos, and so reported; but the honest tale of Fray Marcos was so blown up by popular imagination that the viceroy sent forth the most splendid expedition of all, that of Francisco Vásquez Coronado. One of Coronado's lieutenants discovered the Grand Canyon in 1540; Coronado himself marched eastward across the panhandle of Texas into eastern Kansas, only to prick another rumor; and returned, disappointed, to Mexico.

Hernando de Soto, who had obtained a grant of Florida from the king, landed at Tampa Bay and marched about the interior of the future Gulf States for many months, led on by tales of splendid cities. In 1541 he came upon the Mississippi near Memphis, crossed to the west bank, spent the winter near Fort Smith, Arkansas, returned to the Father of Waters, and there died. His men built boats, descended the Mississippi, crossed the Gulf, and reached Tampico in safety, after an absence of over four years.

Owing to their failure to find treasure or a strait, these Spanish explorations of North America had no immediate result; the tide of conquest turned toward South America. Only at the end of the sixteenth century, when the frontier of settlement and mining in Mexico had been pushed so near to the Rio Grande that conquest of the Pueblo Indians seemed desirable, did Juan de Oñate formally take possession 'of all the kingdoms and provinces of New Mexico.' The Pueblos promptly submitted, colonization began, and the next governor founded Santa Fe in 1609. Thus New Mexico, the forty-seventh state to be admitted to the Union, was settled at the same time as the first permanent English colony in North America.

By that time Spain had conquered almost the whole of South America, down to the River Plate. Francisco Pizarro had overthrown the mighty Inca empire of Peru and founded Lima by 1535. Other conquistadors swarmed southward and eastward, overrunning the whole of the continent. By mid-century the foundations had been laid for every one of the twenty republics of Central and South America, excepting the Argentine.

There has been no other conquest like this in the annals of the human race. In one generation the Spaniards acquired more new territory than Rome conquered in five centuries. Genghis Khan swept over a greater area, but left only destruction in his wake; the Spaniards organized and administered all that they conquered, brought in the arts and letters of Europe, and converted millions to their faith. Our forebears in Virginia and New England, the pathfinders of the Great West, and the French-Canadian pioneers were stout fellows indeed; but their exploits scarcely compare with those of Spanish conquistadors and friars who hacked their way in armor through solid jungle, across endless plains, and over snowy passes of the Andes to fulfill their dreams of gold and glory, and for whom reality was greater even than the dream.

The Spanish empire was much like those later established by England and France; yet there were important differences too. Since Spain carved out its empire a century earlier than England and France, Spanish America had a more medieval character. A conquistador like Cortés self-consciously modelled himself on the Amadis of Gaul of medieval chivalry. Spain had much the largest of the empires in America, a vast domain extending from California to Tierra del Fuego, but most of its settlers preferred to concentrate in cities. Spain, like France, was an absolute monarchy, while England was developing parliamentary institutions; yet the Spanish Crown proved much more willing to compromise than did the French monarchs, and Spain was more effective than France in planting European institutions in the New World. The Catholic Church, too, showed a flexibility in Spanish America which helped bridge the old order and the new. As Eric Wolf has written, 'Just as the cloak of the Virgin hid many a local Persephone or Isis along the shores of the European Mediterranean, . . . so a Hummingbird-on-the-Left became a Spanish St. James riding down upon the heathens; . . . and Our Lady Spirit, the Virgin of Guadalupe.'

The most important characteristic that distinguishes the Spanish empire results from the fact that Spain encountered an Indian population more numerous and more advanced than England and France found. Unlike the English and French, the Spanish incorporated the Indian into their society. The intermarriage of whites, Indians, and Negroes created a heterogeneous culture less marked by racial prejudice. But it was also a highly stratified social order in which social distinction rested on pigmentation, with a white elite at the top.

Hispanic America is rich in paradox. Guilty of revolting cruelty toward the Indian, Spain, however, sought persistently, and with some success, to preserve his personal liberty. A medieval society, it nonetheless welcomed the Enlightenment and the Scientific Revolution. Mexico City and Lima, the 'City of Kings,' became seats of urban civilization within fifteen years of the conquest; in each a university was founded in 1551; the first printing press in the New World came to Mexico City in 1539. Even today an air of superb magnificence rests on the churches and palaces built by these 'children of the sun' in their provincial capitals hundreds of miles from the sea.

Thus, the Spanish empire in America had more than a century's head start on the English and French; and the stupendous results of that conquest, materially as well as spiritually, were the envy of every European power. Spanish prestige reached its height in the year 1580 when Philip II succeeded to the throne of Portugal as well as that of Spain, uniting under his person two vast empires that now stretched their arms around the world, the left arm to the west coast of Mexico, the right arm to Manila. At that moment not another nation had placed a single permanent settler on the shores of the New World.

Yet the end of that monopoly was near. The autumn gales of 1580 blew up the English Channel and into Plymouth harbor Francis Drake in the *Golden Hind,* worm-eaten and weed-clogged after her three years' voyage around the world, laden with the spoil of a Peruvian treasure ship. Only eight years more, and Spain suffered her first major defeat on the ocean that she had mastered; twenty years more, and Virginia was founded.

6. ENTER FRANCE AND ENGLAND

Spanish conquest was too swift and successful for the health of Spain. American treasure ruined her manufactures, financed useless military adventures of her kings, and finally led to poverty and stagnation. Yet the immediate success, which alone was visible, stimulated three other nations, France, England, and the Netherlands, to acquire colonial possessions of their own. As early as 1521 French corsairs bagged part of the booty that Cortés was sending home; and this process of muscling into the Spanish empire continued until England and France were firmly established in North America, and the Dutch in the Far East.

John Cabot discovered the teeming cod-fisheries of the Grand Bank of Newfoundland, but French and Portuguese fishermen were first to profit by them. Norman fishermen were on the banks by 1504, and the Portuguese were so active about Newfoundland for a generation after Corte-Real's discovery, that even today the principal bays and headlands of Newfoundland have Portuguese names. These fishermen were practical men who were only concerned in catching and curing the firm-fleshed cod of northern waters that found a ready market in Europe. The important explorations in northern waters, as along the Spanish Main, were made by navigators seeking a passage to India.

Francis I of France, who liked to be in the swim, engaged a Florentine navigator to find for him the water route to China. This Giovanni Verrazzano in the summer of 1524 made the first voyage (of which we have definite record) along the Atlantic coast of the United States from Cape Fear to Maine, searching for the Strait. He entered the future New York harbor sailing past the site of the twentieth-century bridge named after him, but decided that the Hudson was not a passage; he tried Narragansett Bay and again drew a blank; he sailed among the spruce-clad islands of Maine, which meant nothing to him, and then home. By that time Francis I had been captured at the Battle of Pavia, and could no longer finance exploration. Verrazzano's brother made a map of his voyages that showed a mythical gulf of the Pacific stretching to within a few miles of Chesapeake Bay. Probably the efforts of Indians to tell about the Great Lakes was the origin of this 'Sea of Verrazzano,' the search for which lasted almost two centuries. Every Englishman who marched inland from the Atlantic coast, even Governor Spotswood as late as 1716, hoped to gaze on the Pacific from the crest of the Blue Ridge.

Jacques Cartier is the Columbus of French Canada. This hardy seaman of St.-Malo made three voyages to the Gulf of St. Lawrence (1534–41) in search of the passage to the Orient. On the second he discovered the rock of Quebec, in a region which the natives called Canada, and then proceeded upstream, past Montreal (so named by him), to the lowest rapids of the St. Lawrence, which he humorously called La Chine. He wintered near the mouth of the Saguenay, and collected from the Indians a cycle of tall tales about an inland kingdom of that name, where gold and silver were as plentiful as in Mexico or Peru. Francis I, much excited at this prospect, then equipped Cartier with a fleet so formidable that the Spanish government seriously discussed sending naval vessels to sink it. But the Spanish king wisely concluded that it would be a good thing to keep the French busy chasing northern will-o'-the-wisps. Cartier brought back nothing but a shipload of iron pyrites, or fool's gold, and quartz crystals that he believed to be diamonds. France then fell into a cycle of religious wars, and although every year Norman and Breton fishermen visited the banks and cured their fish ashore, and traded with the natives for fur, no progress was made toward establishing a French-American empire until the next century.

England approached America very gingerly; the Cabot voyages were not her only false starts. For England was a small and poor country, hemmed in by enemies. Independent and hostile Scotland sat on her northern border; the hereditary enemy France lay across one channel; and Ireland, who still refused to admit she had been conquered, across another. English monarchs of the House of Tudor were cautious, impecunious, and anxious to placate the Spanish sovereigns. Yet England was growing stronger year by year. No small share of the treasure from Mexico and Peru went to buy English woolens, and the English gradually assumed control of their foreign trade. Henry VIII's breach with the Church of Rome, whatever his motive, stimulated English nationalism and made a break with Spain inevitable sooner or later.

Under Queen Elizabeth I (1558–1603) it became a religious as well as a patriotic duty to 'singe the king of Spain's beard.' The obvious place to harry that monarch's whiskers was in the West Indies. Spanish commerce with her overseas possessions was conducted by convoys. The outward-bound fleet from Spain made the West Indies at Guadeloupe and then split, separate squadrons proceeding to Santo Domingo, Cartagena, Porto Bello on the isthmus of Panama, and Vera Cruz, the port of Mexico. Commerce with Peru and the west coast was conducted through Panama; the precious metals were transported by mule train across the isthmus to Porto Bello, where at the time of the annual fair, ingots of silver were piled up in the market place like cordwood. On the homeward passage, galleons from the Caribbean sailed through the Yucatán Channel and made rendezvous with those from Mexico at Havana, whence the Gulf Stream helped them through the Straits of Florida to the zone of westerly winds.

In the 1560's John Hawkins of Plymouth began slaving voyages from England to Africa and then to Spanish America, where his courtly manners and attractive prices ensured a good reception, although it was illegal for Spanish colonists to trade with foreigners. After Hawkins had been set upon by the Spanish fleet in Vera Cruz and roughly handled, his flag captain, Francis Drake, became the most implacable enemy of Spain. 'El Draque' as the Dons called him, raided the isthmus of Panama and the coast towns again and again, and on his memorable voyage to California and around the world (1577–80) he terrorized the coasts of Chile and Peru. Captain Thomas Cavendish bagged the grandest prize of all in 1587, a Manila galleon; his ships entered the

Thames rigged with damask sails, and each sailor wore a silk suit and a chain of pure gold round his neck.

The great age of Elizabeth and of Shakespeare, in which English genius burned brightly in almost every aspect of life, was reaching its acme.

> This happy breed of men, this little world,
> This precious stone set in the silver sea,

awakened from long lethargy to a feeling of exuberant life, such as few people had known since ancient Greece. That was an age when the scholar, the divine, and the man of action were often one and the same person — for the Elizabethans knew, what many of us have forgotten, that life is empty without religion, that the tree of knowledge is barren unless rooted in love, and that learning purchased at the expense of living is a sorry bargain. Man in those days was not ashamed to own himself an animal, nor so base as to quench the divine spark that made him something better; but above all, he exulted in the fact that he was a man. Chapman, in *The Conspiracy and Tragedy of Byron,* spoke for his age and generation when he cried out, 'Be free, all worthy spirits, and stretch yourselves!'

The age of discovery in England was closely integrated with English literature, promoted by her governing class, and a matter of great moment to the government. Sir Humphrey Gilbert, Oxonian, educational reformer, and courtier, published a *Discourse of a Discovery for a New Passage to Cataia* (i.e. China), and attempted the first English colony. His half-brother Sir Walter Raleigh, courtier, soldier, and historian, founded Virginia and sought El Dorado up the Orinoco. And the Reverend Richard Hakluyt, student of Christ Church, Oxford, compiled his great collection of *Navigations, Voyages Traffiques and Discoveries of the English Nation,* in order to fire his countrymen to worthy deeds overseas. The English empire down to the American Revolution was but a fulfillment of the plans made by Hakluyt, Gilbert, Raleigh, and a number of other promoters in the reign of Queen Bess.

What these men wanted was an overseas empire that would make England self-sufficient, and employ a great merchant marine. It should be in a climate where Englishmen might live, and where they and the natives would provide a new market for English goods. The colonies should produce tar and timber for shipbuilding, gold and silver, dye-woods, wine, spices and olives, and everything else that England was then buying from abroad. The Indians must be converted to Protestant Christianity, in order to stay the progress of the Counter-Reformation. A passage through to the real Indies was sought that would serve as an English Strait of Magellan. Yet, with all this energy, gallantry, and enthusiasm, the chronicle of English colonization in the sixteenth century is one of repeated failure. Martin Frobisher sought gold and the Northwest Passage in the 1570's, discovered Hudson's Strait, and brought back shiploads of worthless iron pyrites. Sir Humphrey Gilbert took possession of Newfoundland for the Queen in 1583, but was lost on the voyage home. Sir Walter Raleigh then took over his patent to the whole of North America above Florida, named it Virginia, and planted two successive colonies on Roanoke Island. The first gave up after a year; the second, a well-chosen group of 117 men, women, and children, had completely disappeared by the time a relief expedition arrived in 1590.

Reasons for these and other failures are not far to seek. England's efforts in overseas expansion were left to individuals, and the experience of Gilbert and Raleigh proved that 'it is a difficult thing to carry over colonies into remote countries upon private men's purses.' The English Crown was too impecunious to finance colonies; and individual enterprise preferred the gay adventure and certain profit of raiding Spanish possessions and capturing Spanish ships. These activities increased both the confidence and the sea-knowledge of the English, and so contributed in the end to imperial achievement; but as long as the war with Spain lasted (and it lasted as long as did Elizabeth I), it was impossible to obtain enough capital or men for the prosaic business of planting and maintaining a colony. The Roanoke venture failed, too, for more immediate reasons: inept planning, the lack of a good harbor, and a poorly chosen site on an exposed island. So the sixteenth century closed like the fifteenth, without a single Englishman on American soil — unless survivors of Raleigh's lost colony were still wandering through the forests of Carolina.

This should have been discouraging, but the English were past discouragement. For, underlying all their efforts, the earlier failures as well as later successes, was a powerful drive which thrust them forward. This *daimon* of the English was the burning desire to found a new England, a new society, in which all the best of the past would be conserved, but where life would have a different and better quality from anything then conceivable in Europe.

It was typical of an English discoverer that Sir Humphrey Gilbert, when last seen on the quarterdeck of the *Squirrel,* was reading a book; and from the phrase that he joyfully shouted to his men — 'We are as near Heaven by sea as by land' — that book must have been Sir Thomas More's *Utopia.*[2] The Utopian ideal for America, in the mind of every important group of English pioneers from Maine to Georgia, takes off from the *Utopia* of Sir Thomas More, first printed in 1516. The ideal commonwealth of that saintly mind is described as an island set in the Ocean Sea, somewhere in the New World. It is in the northern zone, the 'air soft, temperate, and gentle; the ground covered with green grass,' 'full of people, governed by good and wholesome laws' (but no lawyers), where everyone is honestly employed, and no one exploited or overworked. In the cities, planted not less than a day's journey apart, dwell the handicraftsmen and men of learning; but each city possesses a great rural district studded with co-operative farms. Burghers and farmers change places every two years, so that each has his share of necessary labor, and nobody becomes bored. All alike labor six hours a day, leaving ample time for recreation. Husbandry is made pleasant and easy by having oxen do the heavy work, and by inventions such as incubators for raising chickens. In the cities the streets are laid out 'very commodious and handsome,' and the houses are each of three stories, fireproof, amply windowed, and provided with a garden. Government is carried on by a series of town meetings. Free and compulsory education is continued for adults by daily lectures, which all attend except such as wish 'to bestow the time well and thriftily upon some other science, as shall please them'; for Utopians like nothing better than 'free liberty of the mind, and the garnishing of the same.' Greek literature is the favorite study of these workers' educational classes.

Utopia cultivates community life as well as individual achievement. Medicine is socialized. Whoever wishes to make a pleasure trip is provided by the government with an ox wagon, but he has to work on the farms or in the cities that he visits. The Utopians hate warfare 'as a thing very beastly,' yet both men and women submit to compulsory military training in case other and less happy people seek to invade them, or attack countries that are their friends. All their wars heretofore have been in defense of friendly countries, the Utopians knowing that if these were conquered by tyrants their turn would come next. The

2. 'The way to heaven out of all places is of like length and distance.' One of the maxims of Raphael the Portuguese, who discovered Utopia, in Book 1.

Utopians enjoy complete religious liberty; and although they cultivate virtue, they mean not 'sharp and painful virtue,' or to 'banish the pleasure of life.'

Thus, out of the welter of misery, insecurity, and corruption that were the lot of the common man in England of 1516, came this vision of a new and better society: the American dream. One constant thread of American history has been this quest for peace, liberty, and security; this effort, often frustrated, never realized but in part, yet ever hopeful, ever renewed, to make true the Utopian dream of the blessed Thomas More.

III

First Foundations

1. VIRGINIA

Two waves of colonizing activity were responsible for founding twelve of the thirteen English colonies which federated as the United States of America, and the French colonies which became the nucleus of the Canadian Commonwealth. The first wave, which began in 1606 and lasted until 1637, planted three groups of English colonies and three French colonies: Virginia and Maryland on the Chesapeake, the Puritan commonwealths of New England, and the British West Indies; French L'Acadie (Nova Scotia), Quebec, and the Antilles; and also the Dutch colony of New Netherland, which became New York. All within one generation!

The death of Elizabeth I and the accession of James I in 1603 brought peace with Spain and Scotland, and released capital and manpower for fruitful purposes. The lesson that 'private purses are cold comforts to adventurers' had been well learned. Excellent results had already been obtained in foreign trade by joint-stock corporations, which combined the capital of many under the management of a few, chosen by the stockholders. The Muscovy Company and the Levant Company, first of these overseas trading corporations, had done well in trading with Russia and the Near East; spectacular profits were in store for the East India Company. Each company received a monopoly of English trade with a specified portion of the world, and full control over whatever trading posts or colonies it might see fit to establish.

In such wise the English colonization of Virginia was effected. Two groups of capitalists were formed, one centering in Bristol and the other in London. The price of a share was £12 10s (about $62 in gold) and every stockholder could take part in the quarterly meetings (called general courts) and had a vote in choosing the board of directors, known as the treasurer and council.[1] Between these two companies, the English claim to North America was divided. Northern Virginia, renamed New England in 1620, fell to the Bristol group; Southern Virginia, which also included the future Maryland and Carolina, to the Londoners. The Northern Company's one attempt to plant came to grief because of an 'extreme unseasonable and frosty' Maine winter. But the 'Old Dominion' of Virginia was established by the London Company. That corporation was no mere money-making scheme, although the expectation of profit certainly existed; rather was it a national enterprise with hundreds of stockholders great and small.

Three ships under Captain Christopher Newport, *Susan Constant, Godspeed,* and *Discovery,* dropped down the Thames at Christmastide 1606, cheered by Michael Drayton's 'Ode to the Virginia Voyage':

> Britans, you stay too long,
> Quickly aboord bestow you,
> And with a merry gale,
> Swell your stretch'd sayle,
> With vows as strong
> As the winds that blow you.

'Virginia's Tryalls' (as an early tract on the colony was entitled) began at once. The voyage, by the Columbus route, was long and tedious and fatal to sixteen of the 120 men aboard — no women were taken. Almost everything was done wrong. The Virginia Company, having inherited the ample ambitions of the Hakluyt and Gilbert era, expected to convert Indians, locate gold mines, discover the Northwest Passage, produce 'all the commodities of Europe, Africa and Asia, and supplye the wantes of all our decayed trades.' But no gold was found, neither the James nor the Chickahominy rivers led to the Pacific, and the only commodities sent home for several years were of the forest, such as oak clapboard, cedar and walnut paneling. The company proposed to establish a new home for the unemployed who swarmed into English

1. In the reorganizations of 1609 and 1612; in the original charter, the council was appointed by the king.

towns, when ousted from the land; but these 'sturdy beggars' did not care to emigrate as landless wage-slaves to a company. So the first colony consisted largely of decayed gentlemen, released prisoners, with a few honest artisans who found nothing to do. The Company provided them with a poor sort of local government; and although Captain Newport was instructed to choose a healthy location, he selected for Jamestown a very malarial site which was eventually abandoned. As in Columbus's first colony over a century earlier, the men were upset by the strange food, drenched through flimsy housing (for the tight, warm log cabin of the American frontier was a later Swedish contribution), racked by disease, and pestered by mosquitoes and the Indians. By the spring of 1608 only 53 Englishmen were left alive; and they were saved only through the bustling activity of Captain John Smith in placating Indians and planting corn.

The Virginia Company would not hear of failure. Relief was sent in 1608, and again in 1609 — a fleet of nine ships under Sir Thomas Gates. The flagship was wrecked on the Bermudas, providing material for Shakespeare's *Tempest*, and securing for England the lovely islands that are now her oldest colony. When the survivors reached Jamestown in a vessel they constructed of Bermudian cedar, the colony was reduced to the last stage of wretchedness. 'Everie man allmost laments himself of being here,' wrote Governor Dale in 1611. He despaired of making a success with 'sutch disordered persons, so prophane, so riotous . . . besides of sutch diseased and crased bodies.' He hoped the king would send to Virginia, out of the common jails, all men condemned to die; they at least might be glad 'to make this their new Countrie.' One is not astonished at the 'murmurs' and 'treasonable Intendments' of these workers when one reads of their regime. Twice a day they were marched into the fields by beat of drum or into the forests to cut wood, and twice a day marched back to Jamestown to eat and pray. The only thing that kept the colony alive was the deep faith and gallant spirit of men who refused to admit defeat. These men believed that they had hold of something which must not be allowed to perish. 'Be not dismayed at all,' says the author of *Newes from Virginia* (1610), 'God will not let us fall':

> Let England knowe our willingnesse,
>   For that our worke is good;
> *Wee hope to plant a nation,*
>   *Where none before hath stood.*

Virginia needed more than faith and a gallant spirit to ensure permanence. She needed a profitable product, a system of landholding that gave immigrants a stake in the country; discipline to be sure, but also liberty. In ten years' time she obtained all these. Between 1615 and 1625 Virginia was transformed from an unsuccessful trading post, ruled by iron discipline and hated by most of the settlers, into a commonwealth that began to open a new and wonderful life to the common man of England.

Tobacco culture, which never entered into the founders' plans, saved Virginia. Smoking was probably brought to England by Sir John Hawkins in the 1560's. Tobacco is the Arawak Indian word for the cigars which they inhaled through the nostrils; but North American Indians used long-stemmed pipes, with stone bowls from 'the great Red Pipestone Quarry,' if they could get them. English smokers complained that the variety of tobacco that the Indians cultivated around Roanoke bit the tongue viciously, and so continued to import West Indian leaf through Spain. John Rolfe, husband to Pocahontas, is said to have been responsible for procuring seed from the West Indies around 1613, and the leaves grown from this seed on Virginian soil smoked well. Some 2500 pounds were exported to England in 1616; 20,000 in 1617; 50,000 in 1618. Here at last was something to attract capital and labor, and make large numbers of Englishmen wish to emigrate. Unfortunately there was a strong anti-nicotine movement in England led by King James, who described smoking as 'a custome lothsome to the eye, hatefull to the Nose, harmefull to the braine, dangerous to the Lungs, and in the blacke stinking fume thereof, neerest resembling the horrible Stigian smoke of the pit that is bottomelesse.' Tobacco planting was almost too successful for the good of the colony, which was still importing foodstuffs from England a decade after her foundation. Yet nothing could stop the colonists from planting or Englishmen from buying and smoking Virginia tobacco.

Private property in land also stimulated the growth of Virginia. As the indentures of the hired servants expired, they became tenant farmers on a share-cropping basis; by 1619 the tenant farms extended twenty miles along the James, and the population had passed a thousand souls. Groups of settlers organized by some man of substance were granted large tracts called 'hundreds,' which formed autonomous communities within the colony. And in 1618 the company devised 'head-rights,' which became the basis of land tenure in all the Southern English Colonies. By this system persons who emigrated at their own expense were granted 50 acres free for each member of their party, or for any subsequent immigrant whose passage money they paid. Thus private gain and individual enterprise were enlisted to build up the colony, and the labor supply kept pace with that of arable land.

English law and liberty came as well. In 1618 the company instructed the new governor to introduce English common law and the orderly processes thereof and summon a representative assembly with power to make by-laws, subject to the company's consent in England. Democracy made her American debut on 30 July 1619, when 22 'burgesses,' two from each settled district, elected by the vote of all men aged seventeen and upward, met with the governor's council in the church at Jamestown. The session lasted but six days, the few laws passed had to be validated by the company in England, and another assembly was not chosen until 1621. But the Virginia Assembly of 1619 was the earliest representative body in the New World. From that time forth, government of the people, however limited or thwarted, has been a fundamental principle of the English colonies and the United States. And the rule of law, replacing the law of governors or captains, was equally important; no other European colony had that.

As long as it lasted, the parent company in England exerted far more power in Virginia than this popular assembly. But the company itself was democratic in spirit; a movement of stockholders in 1619 unseated Sir Thomas Smyth, the experienced London merchant adventurer who had been treasurer and executive head during the most difficult years, and elected Sir Edwin Sandys, second son of the Archbishop of York, a leader of the opposition in the House of Commons, tolerant in religion and liberal in outlook. Convinced that the colony's exclusive preoccupation with tobacco was unsound and politically dangerous, Sandys induced the stockholders to adopt a five-year plan for Virginia. French vines, vintners, and olive trees, lumbermen from the Baltic, ironworkers from England, were procured or hired to start new industries, and thousands of poor Englishmen and women were assisted to emigrate. Unfortunately this required more expense than the company was able to bear, and the colony was ill-prepared to receive an influx of 4000 people in four years. Of those sent from England in the Sandys regime, more than three-fourths perished. Ships were overcrowded, housing facilities inadequate, and the loss of life from typhus, malaria, malnutrition, and overwork was appalling. Moreover, most of the artisans and specialized farmers, whose passages had been paid, dropped what they were supposed to do in order to cultivate the great cash crop. Plantations were laid out too far apart, defense was neglected, and in 1622 a surprise attack by Indians destroyed the infant ironworks at the falls of the James river, erased almost every settlement outside Jamestown, massacred more than 300 men, women, and children, and in a night wiped out the gains of three years. This gave the enemies of Sandys a handle against him, convinced the king that the bankrupt, faction-torn colony had been grossly mismanaged, produced legal proceedings against the charter, and, in 1624, a judicial dissolution of the Virginia Company of London.

Virginia now became a royal province or crown colony; but she did not lose the large measure of self-government that she had won. The assembly, the courts of justice, and other organs of local government already being evolved were retained. Governor and council, however, were now appointed by the king of England and subject to royal instructions. This change was not unpopular in the colony; Virginia never has liked economic planning. Charles I, not unaffected by the large revenue he was obtaining from the customs on Virginia tobacco, interfered with the colony less than the company had, and development continued along tobacco plantation lines.

When we think of seventeenth-century Virginia we should first banish from our minds the cavalier myth of gallants and fair ladies living a life of silken ease, which was created by politicians and romantic novelists of the nineteenth century. We must picture a series of farms and plantations lining the James, the York, and the Rappahannock rivers up to the fall line, and beginning to extend along the south bank of the Potomac. Very few houses are more than a mile or two from tidewater. The average farm, not above 300 or 400 acres, is cultivated by the owner and his family and a few white indentured servants of both sexes. The house is a story-and-a-half frame cottage, kept warm in winter by great log fires; around it is a vegetable garden and orchard; beyond, corn and tobacco fields, enclosed by zigzag Virginia fences of split rails; and beyond that, woodland, where the cattle and hogs fend for themselves. In the course of a few years, when the original tobacco fields are exhausted, the woodland will be cleared and put under tillage, while the 'old fields,' after a few diminishing crops of corn, will revert to brush and woodland. Few horses and still fewer wheeled vehicles will be seen outside Jamestown until after 1650, but almost every farmer keeps a yoke of oxen for plowing, and a boat on creek or river. If the owner prospers, he will procure more land from someone who has more head rights than he cares to take up, or by importing his poor relations as servants.

The few great plantations, established by men who came out with considerable capital, have large houses and more outbuildings, keep a store for selling English goods to their neighbors, and a wharf and warehouse for handling their tobacco. Every so often the big planter orders the London merchant who handles his tobacco crop to send him out another parcel of indented servants, for each of whom he will obtain 50 acres more land; if no ungranted land is available near the homestead he will 'seat' a second plantation elsewhere, and put his son, or a trusty servant whose time is up, in charge.

If Virginia had few cavaliers, it nonetheless was, even at the outset, a colony with a sharply defined ruling class, although it took almost a century for a stable aristocracy to develop. The original leaders of the Virginia colony were men of social position in England who brought to the New World a sophisticated interest in literature and science, men such as Christopher Dawson, the colony's secretary, who was the son of Queen Elizabeth's secretary. But they were soon succeeded by a rough, ambitious crowd with an eye for the main chance but few of the attributes of social authority. This group in turn was displaced by new arrivals from England, often younger sons well connected both in London and in Virginia. Although they too had to make room for still more recent immigrants, who insisted on a share of power, the generation which came to Virginia between 1635 and 1670, including men who bore such names as Byrd, Carter, and Mason, were the founders of the eighteenth-century aristocracy.

The First Families of Virginia worked hard to win and maintain their position, but a man like William Byrd II, an active farmer, trader, and land-grabber, also found time for cultural pursuits. Byrd entered in his diary:

> January 27, 1711 I rose at 5 o'clock and read two chapters in Hebrew and some Greek in Lucian. I said my prayers and ate boiled milk for breakfast. I danced my dance. It rained all night but held up about 8 o'clock this morning. My sick people were all better,

thank God Almighty. I settled several accounts; then I read some English which gave me great light into the nature of spirit. . . . In the afternoon my wife and I took a little walk and then danced together. Then I read some more English. At night I read some Italian and then played at piquet with my wife. . . . I said my prayers and had good health, good thoughts, and good humor, thank God Almighty.

During the first half-century, the manners and customs of Virginia were Puritan. The code of laws passed by the first Virginia Assembly 'Against Idleness, Gaming, drunkenes and excesse in apparell,' might well have been passed by a New England colony; the Virginia laws against Sabbath-breaking and contempt of the Bible or the ministry were almost as severe as in Massachusetts; several thanksgiving days were appointed before the Pilgrim Fathers had time to think of one, and days of fasting and humiliation were held to placate the Almighty after a pestilence or an Indian victory. Witchcraft was prosecuted in Virginia as in New England, although no witches were hanged except in Massachusetts. The typical library of a Virginia settler contained about the same proportion of religious literature as that of his fellow in New England; for the neo-paganism of Elizabeth's reign had by now worn off, and Englishmen like other Christians were eager to learn and do the will of God.

Yet there were important differences between Virginia and New England too. The Church of England was early established in Virginia, and Puritan congregations were outlawed in 1643; the Book of Common Prayer had to be read. Such Puritanism as there was in the Virginia church came from absence of Anglican discipline and authority rather than from an aggressive Puritan doctrine and a cohesive Puritan community. And as time flowed on, and great fortunes were built up from tobacco, the Puritan tinge faded from the Old Dominion.

Below the independent landowners in Virginia were the English indented servants. These were the main source of labor in the Chesapeake colonies throughout this pioneer period, and an important source in other colonies. Indented servants were mostly lads and lasses in their late 'teens or early twenties, members of large families in the English towns and countryside, who were looking for a better chance than the overcrowded trades of the old country. They were attracted by 'Come all Ye' ballads like 'The Maydens of London's Brave Adventures':

Then come, brave Lasses, come away, conducted by Apollo,
Although that you do go before, your sweet-hearts they will follow.

Nor were they much deterred by counter-propaganda, such as the ballad
of 'The Trapann'd Maiden,' [2] of which this stanza is a sample:

Instead of drinking Beer, I drink the water clear,
   In the Land of Virginny, O;
Which makes me pale and wan, do all that e'er I can,
   When that I am weary, weary, weary, weary, O.

The loss of beer was indeed serious, because beer, as then brewed in
England, contained vitamins which were lacking in a diet of 'hog and
hominy.'

Men and women servants alike performed any sort of labor their
master required for a period of five years, which might be extended for
ill-conduct; at the end of that time they were dismissed with a few tools
and clothes; in Maryland each servant was given 50 acres of land by the
Lord Proprietor. The more energetic freedmen would then earn money
by wage labor, and set up as farmers themselves. A hard system it was,
according to modern lights; yet it enabled thousands of Englishmen and
women, and, in the eighteenth century, tens of thousands of Scots, Irish,
Germans, and Swiss, to make a fresh start in life and take an active part
in forming the American nation.

A Dutch ship brought the first Africans to Jamestown as early as 1619.
The first Negroes were indented servants; slavery is not mentioned in
any statute until after 1660, although it may have developed before that.
Slavery carried with it a racist assumption of the inferiority of the
Negro. Slavery did not become a characteristic feature of Virginia society until nearly the end of the seventeenth century. It became so then
for three reasons: England restricted the emigration of white bond servants; the Royal African Company became more efficient in the slave
trade; and a catastrophic fall in the price of tobacco ruined the small
farmers, permitting profits only to men who had the capital to purchase
cheap and self-propagating labor.

Virginia was the most English of the English colonies, and more rural
than most parts of England. Local government was set up on the English model; Anglican parishes run by wardens and vestry, with care for
the poor and for good morals as one of their duties; counties with

2. 'Trapanned' was seventeenth-century English for 'kidnapped,' and also included
those who were persuaded to sell their services for five years by false promises.

justices appointed by the royal governor. As long as each farm or plantation had access to tidewater, which in general was true throughout the
century, each had its own 'tobacco road' by sea to London, and handled
its own imports and exports, provided the ship cleared at Jamestown.
Until Norfolk and Williamsburg were founded, at the close of the century, there was no settlement with more than a few score persons; even
Jamestown was almost deserted when the assembly was not in session. It
was so easy to import articles of necessity and luxury from England in
exchange for tobacco that local trades did not prosper. The Virginians
were intensely loyal to their mother country, and proud of being Englishmen. Yet seeds of antagonism were early sown by the exploitation of
Virginia at the hands of English merchants who, if the assembly pegged
the price of tobacco, cynically raised the price of English goods. A traveler reported of Jamaica in 1763, that most of its inhabitants 'look upon
themselves as passengers only.' That might have been true of Virginia a
century earlier, when the average big planter hoped to sell out at a profit
and return 'home' to England; but it was no longer true in 1750.

2. LORD BALTIMORE'S AND OTHER PROPRIETARY COLONIES

Maryland, a colony with the same soil, climate, economic and social
system as Virginia, owed her separate existence and her special character to the desire of a great Englishman to create a feudal domain for his
family, and a refuge for members of his faith. Sir George Calvert, first
Lord Baltimore, was a stockholder of the Virginia Company who aspired to found his own colony. He failed once, in Newfoundland; then
he emigrated to Virginia, but was ordered out, because he was a Roman
Catholic convert. He then asked for and obtained from Charles I a
liberal slice of the Old Dominion. This original Maryland grant extended from the south [3] bank of the Potomac river north to New England, but was later cut into by another royal hand-out, Pennsylvania.
Lord Baltimore died while the Maryland charter was going through in
1632, but it was confirmed to his son and heir Cecilius. This second Lord
Baltimore dispatched the first group of colonists, who settled at St.
Mary's near the mouth of the Potomac, in 1634.

Cecilius Calvert planned Maryland to be not only a source of profit,

3. This was the cause of the 'oyster war' between Virginia and Maryland that still
goes on.

but a refuge for English and Irish Roman Catholics. One required faith and fortitude to be a good Catholic in the England of that era; yet, for reasons still unexplained, comparatively few English Catholics emigrated to Maryland. Almost from the start the colony had a Protestant majority. Calvert coped with this situation in a statesmanlike manner by inducing the Maryland Assembly to pass a law of religious toleration in 1649. He had summoned an assembly, since his charter required that the laws have the consent of the freemen; but he allowed it little power, and conferred most of the lucrative offices on his relatives and Catholic friends. The local civil war that broke out in Maryland in 1654 was essentially a class war of Protestant small farmers against the Catholic magnates and lords of manors. The majority won, and the Act of Toleration was repealed; but Lord Baltimore eventually recovered his rights.

In the West Indies, English and French used the proprietary method of colonization for a time with success. The Caribbean is the American Mediterranean in a strategic as well as a climatic sense. There the Spaniards established their base for the conquest of Mexico; there, in the late sixteenth and early seventeenth centuries, English, French, and Dutch seized vantage points that destroyed Spain's American monopoly and rendered her communications insecure. The superb arc of islands has an amazing fertility; the extension of sugar culture around 1650 made even the smallest of them immensely valuable, and the slaves imported from Africa thrived beyond all expectation. Far more money and men were spent on defending and capturing these islands in the colonial era than on the continental colonies that became the United States, because they were much more profitable to their owners.

As none of the islands east of Puerto Rico were effectively occupied by the Spaniard, these Lesser Antilles attracted small-time English and French adventurers, who were unable to swing a continental venture like Maryland or Canada. Often families split between islands and continent; John Winthrop, governor of Massachusetts, had a son Samuel in Antigua, and another in Barbados, who sent him tobacco that the governor described as 'verye ill conditioned, fowle, full of stalkes and evill coloured.' The John Jefferson who represented Flowerdew Hundred in the first Virginia Assembly, later helped Sir Thomas Warner to found the English colony on St. Kitts, and also became a leading planter in Antigua. Thomas Jefferson was descended from his brother.

In the 1650's the French and English turned from bad tobacco to

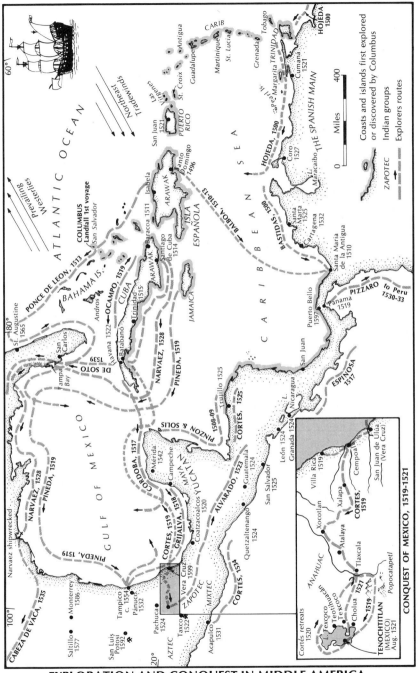

EXPLORATION AND CONQUEST IN MIDDLE AMERICA

Coasts and islands first explored
or discovered by Columbus

Indian groups

Explorers routes

0   Miles   400

CONQUEST OF MEXICO, 1519–1521

good sugar cane. Once sugar came in, white labor went out. For instance, Barbados in 1645 had a white population of 30,320 and 5680 Negro slaves. Ten years later there were only 23,000 whites but 20,000 slaves. The islands enjoyed remarkable prosperity. Twenty acres in Barbados planted with cotton and sugar cane yielded more profit than a great tobacco plantation in Virginia. Barbados, too, had its representative assembly, which yielded nothing to Massachusetts Bay and Virginia in its solicitude for the liberties of Englishmen.

Thus, within a generation of founding their first continental colonies, at Quebec and Jamestown, France and England had tropical possessions which were small in extent, but worthy competitors to the Spanish empire in sugar, dyewoods, cotton, and coffee. In the second half of the century, Spain was despoiled of Jamaica by Cromwell, while smaller islands such as St. Martin, St. Croix, St. Thomas, and Tobago were picked up by Dutch, Norwegians, and Danes. It seemed in 1700 as if the Spanish empire were on the way out — but it was an unconscionable time a-dying!

These non-Spanish colonies in the West Indies were closely integrated with the next group we have to consider, the English colonies in New England. With slave labor it was more profitable for the planters to concentrate on tropical crops of high profit, and procure elsewhere every other essential to living, such as salt meat and fish, breadstuffs and ground vegetables, lumber and livestock. These were exactly the commodities that New England produced, yet could find no vent for in England; and New England built the ships to carry these products of her farms, forests, and fisheries to the West Indies. The Chesapeake colonies, and later the Middle Colonies and the Carolinas, also shared this trade and, like New England, imported the molasses and distilled it into the fiery beverage first known as 'rumbustion' or 'kill-devil.' New England, however, would have long remained a string of poor fishing stations and hardscrabble farms, but for commerce with these superb tropical islands set in the sapphire Caribbean.

3. THE PURITAN COLONIES

New England was founded without reference to the West Indies, and largely as a result of the religious movement known as Puritanism. Puritanism both as a religion and a social force has been so pervasive and permanent an influence in the United States, extending far beyond New England and the colonial period, that we may well pause to inquire what it originally meant.

The Puritans were that party in the Church of England who wished to carry through the Protestant Reformation to its logical conclusion, and establish both a religion and a way of living based on the Bible — as interpreted by themselves. The Church of England, an English compromise between Rome and the reform, did not satisfy them. With official Anglican doctrine the Puritans had no quarrel; but they wished to do away with bishops, deans, and all clergy above the rank of parish priests, to abolish set prayers, and to reorganize the Church either by a hierarchy of councils (Presbyterianism), or on the basis of a free federation of independent parishes (Congregationalism). They were disgusted with the frivolity, extravagance, and moral corruption that pervaded both extremes of English society in the early Stuart era, with gaming and 'stage-plays,' and with the rough, semi-pagan festivals that marked rural life. In other words, they wished to establish such patterns of behavior as would make it possible for people to lead something approaching the New Testament life. They believed that men were predestined for salvation or perdition, but although good behavior could not change a man's fate, a good life might be a sign that he was among the elect. English Puritan divines frowned on idleness as a sin, eschewed mysticism and monasticism, and taught that a good businessman served God well, provided he were honest; hence Puritanism appealed largely to the middle class of tradesmen and rising capitalists whose center was London. It made a wide appeal also in certain rural regions such as East Anglia and the West Country, where 'the hungry sheep look up and are not fed' (to use Milton's phrase) by the common run of English clergyman, incapable of delivering a proper sermon. And it enlisted the devoted support of many young intellectuals in the universities, especially in Cambridge; hence the stress of the Puritans on education. Puritanism was no class revolt, or economic movement in religious clothing, as sundry irreligious writers have claimed, but a dynamic religious revival. A burning desire to know and to do the will of God seemed to pass through the land; neighbors subscribed to establish Puritan 'lectureships' in parishes where the parson was a poor preacher, and then met in their homes for the exchange of religious views and experiences.

These desires of the serious-minded were thwarted in an increasing degree by the first two Stuart kings. James I, remembering the days

when the Scots churchman Andrew Melville had called him 'God's silly
vassal,' promised to harry the Puritans out of the land if they would not
conform; and he harried one little band to such good purpose that it
founded the first New England colony. Things became worse under
Charles I. The Anglo-Catholic polity of Bishop Laud, a move toward re-
establishing the Eucharist as the central point of Christian worship,
appealed to the king, and was enforced; clergymen who refused to
follow this 'back to Rome' movement, as they regarded it, were persecuted, and Puritan lecturers were silenced.

The Pilgrim Fathers were a group of Separatists who, unlike the majority of Puritans, despaired of reforming the Church of England and
broke away to create a new institution. They were a small band of
humble folk of East Anglia, whose religious meetings were so interfered
with that they removed to Leyden in 1609 and formed an English Congregational Church. After ten years' exile in a foreign land where the
people were tolerant but the living was hard, and where war threatened,
they decided to remove to America. Sir Edwin Sandys, who recognized
the quality of these people although he did not share their faith, procured for them a grant from the Virginia Company, and a group of
English merchants consented to finance their migration. After intermina-
ble delays the *Mayflower* set sail in the worst season of the year for an
ocean crossing, and after a rough passage, anchored on 11 November
1620 in the harbor of Cape Cod, outside the Virginia jurisdiction. Accordingly, with that instinct for self-government which Englishmen even
then possessed, the Pilgrims signed a compact to be governed by the will
of the majority until permanent provision should be made for their
colony.

This Mayflower Compact of 1620 stands with the Virginia Assembly
of 1619, as one of the two foundation stones of American institutions.
Nothing like them happened anywhere else in the world for almost two
centuries.

But the Pilgrims also had to eat. Their grim, almost desperate, situation, arriving in a harbor enclosed by barren sand dunes at the beginning of a New England winter, is vividly described by their leader,
Governor William Bradford:

> If they looked behind them, there was the mighty ocean which they
> had passed and was now as a main bar and gulf to separate them
> from all the civil parts of the world . . . What could now sustain

them but the Spirit of God and His grace? May not and ought not
the children of these fathers rightly say: 'Our fathers were Englishmen which came over this great ocean, and were ready to perish
in this wilderness; but they cried unto the Lord, and He heard their
voice and looked on their adversity,' etc. 'Let them therefore praise
the Lord, because He is good: and His mercies endure forever.'

No group of settlers in America was so ill-fitted by experience and
equipment to cope with the wilderness as this little band of peasants,
town laborers, and shopkeepers; yet none came through their trials so
magnificently. For, as Bradford put it, 'they knew they were pilgrims,
and looked not much on those things, but lift up their eyes to the
heavens, their dearest country'; and, as another wrote to Sandys, 'It is
not with us as with other men, whom small things can discourage, or
small discontentments cause to wish themselves at home again.' Their
only good luck was to find deserted fields ready for tillage at the harbor
already named Plymouth by Captain John Smith, and to be joined by
Squanto, a lonely Indian who taught them how to catch fish and plant
corn. Half the company died the first winter; but when the *Mayflower*
set sail in April not one of the survivors returned in her. No ship came
with supplies for a whole year. Around mid-October 1621, after the
gathering of a fair harvest and a big shoot of waterfowl and wild turkey,
the Pilgrims held their first Thanksgiving feast, with Chief Massasoit of
the Wampanoag and 90 of his subjects, 'whom for three days we entertained and feasted.' Although the Indians contributed several deer for a
venison barbecue, this was an expensive entertainment, and the Pilgrims, with 35 new arrivals on the *Fortune* to feed, were soon again on
short allowance; for several years the colony ran neck-and-neck with
famine. But they never lost heart or considered giving up and going
home. These simple folk were exalted to the stature of statesmen and
prophets in their narrow sphere, because they ardently believed, and so
greatly dared, and firmly endured. They set forth in acts as in words the
stout-hearted idealism in action that Americans admire; that is why
Plymouth Rock has become a symbol. For, as Governor Bradford concluded his annals of the lean years,

Thus out of small beginnings greater things have been produced by
his hand that made all things of nothing, and gives being to all
things that are; and as one small candle may light a thousand; so
the light here kindled hath shone unto many, yea, in some sort, to
our whole nation.

Only small beginnings were apparent for ten years; at the end of that time the total population of the Colony of New Plymouth was only 300. In the meantime a dozen straggling fishing and trading posts had been founded along the New England coast from southern Maine to Massachusetts Bay, with or without permission from the Council for New England.

One of these developed into the important Bay Colony. A company, which planted a small settlement at Salem in 1628, was taken over by a group of leading Puritans, including Sir Richard Saltonstall, Thomas Dudley, and John Winthrop, who wished to emigrate. Obtaining from Charles I a royal charter as the Massachusetts Bay Company in 1629, when Anglo-Catholic pressure began to be severely felt, they voted to transfer charter, government, and members to New England. A fleet of seventeen sail bearing 900 to 1000 men and women, the largest colonizing expedition yet sent out from England, crossed in the summer of 1630 to Massachusetts Bay, founded Boston, and six or seven towns near by.

This transfer of the Massachusetts Bay charter had an important bearing on colonial destiny and American institutions. As long as the charter remained in England, the Salem settlement had the same relation to the company as Jamestown had to the Virginia Company. With both charter and company in America, the colony became practically independent of England. The 'freemen,' as stockholders were then called, became voters; the governor, deputy-governor, and assistants whom the freemen annually elected, and who in England had been president and directors of a colonizing company, were now the executives, upper branch of the legislative assembly, and judicial officers of a Puritan commonwealth. A representative system was devised, as it was inconvenient for the freemen to attend the 'general court' or assembly in person, and by 1644 the deputies and assistants had separated into two houses. Neither king nor parliament had any say in the Massachusetts government. The franchise was restricted to church members, which prevented non-Puritan participation in the government; but this did not matter in the long run. What mattered was that this organization made for independence, and that the annual election on a definite date of all officers — governor and upper branch as well as deputies — became so popular in the colonies as to be imitated wherever the king could be induced to grant his consent. An integral feature of the state constitutions of 1776–82, it even survives in the Federal Government, with the election of President, senators, and representatives on the same day. This corporate precedent has given the American system of government a very different complexion from the parliamentary system that was slowly developing in England. Thus, American institutions began to diverge from English institutions in 1630.

With the greater part of their English heritage the Puritan leaders had no quarrel. The new colonies were to preserve the liberties of the 'freeborn Englishmen,' foster education and learning, and preserve the distance between social classes that Englishmen of all eras seem to value. But they proposed to subordinate all that to setting up and maintaining what they deemed to be true religion. That included an insistence on sobriety of manners, purity of morals, and an economy that would neither exalt the rich nor degrade the poor. Unlike the Pilgrims of Plymouth, they were not Separatists, but remained nominally within the Church of England. Unlike the Presbyterians, they were Congregationalists, who denied the need for a superstructure of church organization and who stipulated that membership in the church would be restricted to those 'visible saints' who gave unmistakable evidence of their Christian beliefs.

Church and state in New England were dominated by the covenant idea. 'We are entered into a covenant' with God 'for this work,' preached Winthrop on the voyage over. 'We have taken out a Commission; the Lord hath given us leave to draw our own Articles,' and He 'will expect a strict performance.' Each Congregational church was formed by a new convenant, and so was each new settlement. Thus there was a social and a religious sanction, as well as a civic obligation.

It soon appeared that Massachusetts Bay was the sort of colony that English Puritans wanted; for heavy Puritan migration to it began in 1631 and continued until the outbreak of civil war in England. By that time New England had some 20,000 people. Most of this emigration, unlike that which was going on at the same time to Virginia, Maryland, and the West Indies, was against the will of the royal government; but nothing could stop it. According to a popular ballad, satirizing the Old Testament names beloved by Puritans,

> Our Company we feare not —
> There goes my cousin Hannah;
> And Reuben doe persuade to goe

His sister, faire Susanna;
With Abigail and Lydia
And Ruth noe doubt comes after,
And Sarah kinde will not stay behinde
My cousin Constance' daughter
Then for the truth's sake come along, come along!
Leave the place of superstition,
Were it not for we that brethren be,
You'd sink into perdition.

The community character of the New England migration dictated the method of land settlement. Neighborhood groups from the old country, often accompanied by an ousted parson, insisted on settling together, obtained a grant of land from the general court, established a village center, laid out lots, and so formed what was called in New England a town. Yet there was no 'typical New England town,' in part because the settlers brought with them dissimilar experiences of community life in England; some had dwelt in open-field manorial villages, others in boroughs, still others in the enclosed-farm villages of East Anglia. Furthermore, they found, especially at the outset, that the customs and institutions of England — the courts-leet, seneschals, and ale tasters — were inappropriate for life on the frontier, and towns differed in the kinds of adaptations they made.

Around each village green were situated the meeting-house (as the Puritans called a church edifice), the parsonage, and the houses of the principal settlers. Each person admitted as an inhabitant received a house lot, a planting lot for his corn, and a strip of river mead or salt meadow for winter forage. The cattle ranged the common woods for most of the year, attended by the town herdsman. In town meeting, everyone taking part, each settlement determined local affairs such as support of the school, laying out highways, regulations for cutting timber, and deciding when cattle could be turned into meadows and cornfields. Here democracy seeped into New England, unwanted by the founders of these colonies.

The Puritan leaders were disturbed, too, by the rising spirit of egalitarianism. Men like John Winthrop, a superior statesman of noble character, had no doubt that God had ordained a hierarchy of classes, so that 'in all times some must be rich some poore, some highe and eminent in power and dignitie; others meane and in subieccion.' When a Puritan synod met in 1679, it expressed its concern not only about the rise of bastardy, the attempt to set up a brothel in Boston, and the displaying of naked necks and arms, 'or, which is more abominable, naked Breasts,' but, above all, about the spirit of insubordination of inferiors toward their betters. In particular, the church leaders noted: 'Day-Labourers and Mechanicks are unreasonable in their demands.'

As the population of the towns grew, clashes frequently developed between the first generation, which insisted on respect for rank, and the second generation, determined on winning a share of meadow rights. If demands of the new generation were not met, they would threaten to secede from the town. 'If you persecute us in one city, wee must fly to another,' a Sudbury man warned. When such clashes were unresolved, a few hardy spirits would break away and repeat the process of town-building farther west.

This community form of settlement, which extended throughout New England and later affected the federal land system, had an important bearing both on defense and on education. The frontier advanced in an orderly manner, as fast as the Indians could be persuaded to retire. In order to keep them persuaded, universal military training was early adopted. Each male settler eighteen years old and upward had to provide himself with a flintlock musket 'not under three foot nine inches in length,' a pound of gunpowder, 20 bullets, and '2 fathom of match.' He took part in frequent drills on the village green, and annual regimental musters. Civilian defenders took turns at a nightly 'watch and ward' against prowling wolves and Indians; and boys from ten to sixteen years of age were instructed 'in the exercise of arms, as small guns, half pikes, bows and arrows.'

Education was a particular concern of the Puritans. Their movement was directed by university-trained divines, and embraced largely by middle-class merchants and landowning farmers, who enjoyed the benefits of education in Elizabethan England. Moreover, it was necessary for godliness that everyone learn to read the Bible. There had come to New England by 1640 about 130 university alumni; and these men insisted that their children have the same advantages as themselves, or better. Consequently, in the New England colonies, parents were required to teach their children and servants to read, or to send them to a village school for that purpose. Above these primary schools, about two dozen of the larger New England towns had secondary public grammar schools on the English model, supported by taxation, which boys en-

tered at the age of eight or nine, and where they studied Latin and
Greek, and little else, for six years. At the end of that time they were
prepared to enter Harvard College, founded by the Massachusetts government in 1636, and named after a young clergyman who bequeathed
to it his library and half his estate. There, the more ambitious New
England lads (with some from other colonies as far as Bermuda) studied the same seven arts and three philosophies as at Oxford, Cambridge,
or Dublin, using the same Latin manuals of logic and metaphysics,
Greek texts, Euclid, and 'Hebrew in Twenty-four Hours,' as in European
universities. Scholarships were founded by family contributions of corn
and wampum, the small change of the Indian trade; and for want of
currency students paid their term bills in all manner of agricultural
products. About half the graduates entered the Puritan ministry, and
became the pastors of frontier communities, where they labored a lifetime to maintain civilized standards; others became magistrates, merchants, physicians, or plain farmers.

Coeval with Harvard College was the first, and for a generation the
only, printing press in the English colonies, with a considerable output
of almanacs, catechisms, primers, and such locally delivered sermons as
London publishers rejected. Nor were the fine arts neglected. Seventeenth-century New Englanders had a natural good taste in house design and village layout; artisans like John Hull, John Coney, and
Timothy Dwight fashioned beautiful articles of silver for home and
communion table; writers such as Anne Bradstreet, Urian Oakes, and
Edward Taylor produced religious and other poetry of great charm.
Thus the classical and humanist tradition of the English went hand in
hand with conquering Puritanism into the clearings of the New England
wilderness.

Although the founders of Massachusetts Bay hoped to stretch her
borders to include all New England, except the Colony of New Plymouth whose separate existence they somewhat grudgingly respected,
there was too much individualism among the Puritans for complete
unity. Massachusetts did succeed in annexing New Hampshire for a
time, and the population of southern Maine also turned to Boston for
protection; but three other colonies, which formed two states of the
Union, sprang up before 1640. Under the lead of Master Thomas
Hooker, the first westward migration in the English colonies took place
in 1636, to the Connecticut river, where a Bible Commonwealth was

organized on the Massachusetts model. New Haven, founded by a London merchant named Theophilus Eaton and his pastor the Rev. John Davenport, maintained a separate existence from Connecticut until 1662, and spread along both shores of Long Island Sound.

Both these colonies were like-minded with the Bay Colony and Plymouth; but Rhode Island, the creation of four separate groups of Puritan heretics, was distinctly otherwise-minded. As everywhere in the Protestant world, so in Massachusetts the rulers were unable to maintain religious conformity. Anne Hutchinson of Boston, who set up as a personal prophetess, and Master Roger Williams, who differed with Bay authorities on many matters, were banished, and on Narragansett Bay formed settlements which federated as Rhode Island and Providence Plantations in 1644. A separatist, Roger Williams denied the authority of civil or ecclesiastical hierarchy over a man's conscience. A devout religious enthusiast, he opposed the use of force to compel adherence to church doctrine. 'Forced worship,' he asserted, 'stinks in God's nostrils.' Imbued with the spirit of Christian love, he treated Indians as brothers. Under Williams, Rhode Island became a haven for the persecuted, and the ideas of this seventeenth-century Puritan have inspired a host of secular twentieth-century civil libertarians, even though their views of the universe have been very different from those of this remarkable divine.

One thing these New England colonies had in common until 1680: all were virtually independent, acknowledging allegiance to whatever authority had control in England, but making their own laws, trading where they pleased, defending themselves without help from home, and working out their own institutions. Their connection with the mother country was one of sentiment and tradition rather than compulsion.

4. NEW NETHERLAND

Between New England and Virginia the indomitable Dutch, with that uncanny instinct for sources of wealth that has always characterized their commercial ventures, planted a colony that in due time became New York. In 1602 Dutch capitalists organized the Netherlands East Indies Company, a corporation in comparison with which the Virginia Company was a petty affair. Persistently but inexorably this company pushed the Portuguese out of most of their trading posts in the Far East, where they created a rich empire. The East Indies Company, seeking a shorter way to the Orient than the stormy and dangerous Cape route, made several efforts to find a northeast or a northwest passage to India. That is what Henry Hudson was looking for in 1609 when he sailed the *Half-Moon* up the noble river that shares his name with the mighty bay where he met his death. The Hudson river proved to be a passage indeed, to the heart of the Iroquois Confederacy and the richest fur-bearing country south of the St. Lawrence. Hudson's employers were not interested in the fur trade, but other Dutchmen were; and after skippers Block and May had explored the coast from Maine to the Delaware Capes, fur traders began to frequent the rivers and trade with the natives. The grim prospect of the renewal of the fierce war with Spain impelled the Pilgrim fathers to leave Holland for America, and inspired the founding of the Dutch West India Company, a corporation less concerned with colonization than with privateering.

New Netherland began as a trading-post colony in 1624, with the foundation of Fort Orange (Albany) up the Hudson. Fort Amsterdam on the tip of Manhattan Island was permanently established in 1626, Fort Nassau at the site of Gloucester, N. J., in 1623, and Fort Good Hope on the Connecticut river, near Hartford, in 1633. But, as the Dutch looked east rather than west, and even the West India Company was primarily interested in privateering, the future state of New York received very little attention from the Company, and still less from their High Mightinesses, the States General of the Netherlands. New Netherland was governed much as Virginia had been before 1619, by a governor and council appointed by the Company, without representative institutions. New Amsterdam was the center of the fur trade — it was from Dutch traders that the Pilgrim fathers learned the use of wampum — and a base for the Dutch merchant ships that entered the Virginia tobacco trade. As early as 1630 it was a typical sailormen's town, with numerous taverns, smugglers, and illicit traders, as well as a Dutch Reformed Church, and a number of substantial houses. Everywhere they went, from New York down to Curaçao and Brazil, or around the world to Ternate and Timor, the Dutch imposed their architecture, their neatness, and their good business methods.

When in 1638 the States General threw open the seaborne trade of New Netherland to all Dutch subjects, New Amsterdam became practically a free port. A half-hearted attempt to encourage settlement was made by the company in 1629 by issuing the Charter of Privileges to

Patroons. Anyone who brought out 50 families of tenants at his own expense could have an extensive tract of land, with full manorial privileges of holding court, issuing fishing and hunting licenses, and mill monopoly. The directors of the company, such as Kiliaen Van Rensselaer, promptly snapped up all the best sites, like Staten Island and the Hudson valley above Poughkeepsie; and these privileges, which were confirmed under the English regime, meant that the most valuable land in the Hudson valley was held in vast estates on a feudal basis. A certain number of Dutchmen and Walloons acquired 'bouweries' (farms) outside the wall on Manhattan, or in the pretty villages of Haerlem, Breucelen on Long Island, or Bergen across the North (as the Dutch called the Hudson) river; a few hundred New England Puritans spilled over into Westchester County and Long Island. Yet New Netherland did not prosper; it was the neglected child of a trading company whose main interests were elsewhere.

'Diedrich Knickerbocker' (Washington Irving) created a myth of New Netherland that will never die; the jolly community of tipplers and topers, of waterfront taverns, broad-beamed fraus, and well-stocked farms. The actual New Netherland was a frustrated community. The successive governors, Wouter van Twiller, William Kieft, and Peter Stuyvesant, of whom Irving drew comic pictures, were, in reality, petty autocrats and grafters who ruled New Amsterdam with a rod of iron, used torture to extract confessions, and mismanaged almost everything, especially Indian relations. Kieft, assuming that if the Dutch did not exterminate the natives, the reverse would happen, attacked in cold blood a tribe of River Indians who were disposed to be friendly because they dreaded the Iroquois; but these Indians declined to be exterminated, and put up so stout a fight that assistance had to be summoned from New England before the burghers of New Amsterdam dared venture north of the Wall Street wall. This was in 1644, a time when Virginia, New England, and the Caribbean colonies were humming with activity. But a committee of the Dutch colonists wrote home that, through 'foolish hankering after war,' their fields 'lie fallow and waste,' their 'dwellings and other buildings are burnt.' A prominent settler named Adriaen Van der Donck drew up a remonstrance to the Netherlands government in 1649, begging it to take over the colony and establish schools, churches, and other apparatus of civilized life.

Peter Stuyvesant, who had been governor of Curaçao, and had lost a leg storming a French fort at St. Martin's, attempted to pull things together by crushing political or religious dissenters and jailing his critics. Some of these shared the worthy American trait of talking back. In 1657, 30 English inhabitants of Flushing protested against Stuyvesant's decree that anyone who took in a Quaker for the night would be fined 50 florins. They were commanded by the Bible, they said, to do good to all men and they wished not to offend any of Christ's children. They would, therefore, continue to shelter Quakers 'as God shall persuade our consciences.'

Stuyvesant enlarged New Netherland at the expense of his neighbors. In 1655 he seized and annexed the colony of New Sweden that centered about Fort Christina (Wilmington) on the Delaware. But on the other side, Fort Good Hope on the Connecticut river was squeezed out by English settlers.

English governments, royal, commonwealth, and colonial, had never ceased protesting against the existence of New Netherland as an intrusion on English America; and as the Dutch and English in Europe drew apart from their traditional alliance and engaged in naval and commercial wars, a clash in the New World was inevitable. One Anglo-Dutch war was concluded in 1654 just in time to call off a Cromwellian expeditionary force against New Netherland. That gave Peter Stuyvesant another decade to retard development of Manhattan's superb advantages for trade and commerce. He ended the free-trade policy which had brought vessels to New Amsterdam. He did nothing to conciliate the varied population of the colony. The West India Company, bankrupt after its costly venture in Brazil,[4] and unable to secure even the profits of the fur trade from corrupt officials, took less and less interest in its North American colony. Thus, when a small English fleet appeared off New Amsterdam one summer's day in 1664 and ordered the Dutch to surrender, Governor Stuyvesant stomped his wooden leg in vain, and New Netherland became New York without a blow or a tear.

The population of the city had then reached only 1500, and that of the colony less than 7000; New England outnumbered New Netherland ten

---

4. An interesting result of the Portuguese recapture of Brazil was the emigration of a small number of Portuguese-speaking Jews, to whom the Dutch had extended toleration, from Brazil to New Amsterdam and Newport, R.I., where many of them became successful merchants.

to one. But the Dutch stamp was already placed indelibly on New York, and most of the Dutch families, such as the Van Rensselaers, Van Burens, and Roosevelts, kept their property and prospered under English rule.

5. TWO DECADES OF NEGLECT

That 'salutary neglect' by England, which Edmund Burke later asserted to be one of the main reasons for American prosperity, was never more evident than in the twenty years between 1640 and 1660. The civil war and other commotions which lasted from 1641 to 1653, when Oliver Cromwell became Lord Protector of the English Commonwealth, afforded all three groups of colonies a chance to grow in their own way, with a minimum of interference; and Oliver too decided to let well enough alone. They were thrown on their own resources, sought their own markets, undertook their own defense, and developed their own institutions. When interference was threatened, colonies as wide apart as Massachusetts and Barbados stood stiffly on their privileges. The Barbadian assembly declared in 1651, 'Shall we be bound to the government and lordship of a Parliament in which we have no representatives? . . . This would be a slavery far exceeding all that the English nation hath yet suffered.' Massachusetts asserted, 'Our allegiance binds us not to the laws of England any longer than while we live in England, for the laws of the Parliament of England reach no further.' In other words, dominion status was asserted by Barbados implicitly and by Massachusetts explicitly. The Long Parliament, Puritan itself, respected the Puritan colonies overseas, and interfered in New England only to the extent of protecting Rhode Island from being partitioned by her three neighbors. Parliament sent a fleet to blockade Barbados in 1651, but the commander, in return for nominal allegiance, agreed that no taxes be imposed save by act of the assembly, and that free trade with the Dutch continue. The Virginia Assembly, which proclaimed Charles II king after hearing of the execution of Charles I, capitulated without a blow to a parliamentary fleet in 1652, and in return was allowed to elect the governor and council. In Maryland, the only colony where English events touched off a civil war, Lord Baltimore triumphed in the end.

Perhaps the most significant colonial development of the period was the formation of the New England Confederacy in 1643, largely for defense against the Dutch, the French, and the Indians. A board of commissioners representing Plymouth, Massachusetts, Connecticut, and New Haven, the 'United Colonies of New-England,' formed a 'firm and perpetual league of friendship and amity, for offense and defense, mutual advice and succor upon all just occasions.' Several boundary controversies between the member colonies and one with the Dutch were settled, provision was made for the return of runaway servants, contributions were taken up for Harvard College, and an English fund for the conversion of the Indians was administered. In several respects the New England Confederacy anticipated the Confederation of 1781; and the league held together long enough to direct offensive and defensive operations during the Indian war of 1675–76.

During the brief rule of Cromwell as Lord Protector, he entertained a 'Western Design' to obtain more tropical colonies for England at the expense of Spain. An expedition under Admiral Penn (the father of William) in 1655 easily acquired the beautiful and fertile island of Jamaica for the English empire. Under the new regime, and with the aid of slave labor, Jamaica became the most valuable of England's tropical colonies.

6. NEW FRANCE

New France, too, had taken on character and substance in this period. Samuel de Champlain, who unfurled the lilies of France on the rock of Quebec in 1608, protected missionaries and defended the beaver line of his Huron allies to the Great Lakes from Iroquois assaults. But the companies that employed him, up to his death in 1635, were even less interested in settlement than was the Dutch West India Company. Not a furrow was plowed or a seed planted in Canada until 1628. Shortly after, the Company of the Hundred Associates, which then ruled New France, began establishing seigneuries, not unlike the Dutch patroonships in character, though smaller and more numerous, along both banks of the St. Lawrence. Each seigneur was supposed to bring out a certain number of habitants, or settlers. But the system caught on very slowly. There were two main interests in New France, conversion of the Indians and conversion of beaver into peltry. The French Crown, which wished Canada to be a country of peasant farms like Normandy, abolished the

Company regime in 1663, and Canada became a Crown colony under the direct government of Louis XIV. But even *Le Grand Monarque* was unable to make his transatlantic empire change character.

Thus, in a little more than half a century after the founding of Jamestown, the French, English and Dutch had a firm foothold on the shores of five American areas — the St. Lawrence, New England, the Hudson, the Delaware, Chesapeake Bay — and the West Indies. They had planted those attitudes, folkways, and institutions which were destined to endure and to spread across the North American continent. In 1660 New England, Virginia, and Maryland were already full-fledged commonwealths possessing most of the apparatus of civilized life as developed up to that time, reproducing or attempting to improve on the institutions of the homeland, yet conscious of their peculiar interests and capable of defending themselves against any foreign enemy. Utopia was still far off, but the essential nuclei of the American Republic were already formed.

The Empire Comes of Age

1. THE ACTS OF TRADE AND NAVIGATION

Although the English colonies were already conscious of themselves, England was hardly yet conscious of them. The average Englishman of the governing class still regarded overseas settlements as 'plantations' of slight worth compared with the Spanish imperial domain. Every English colony except Virginia had grown up through the unco-ordinated efforts of individuals and small groups. The home government as yet had no clear policy about colonial trade, development, or the administrative connection between colonies and mother country.

With the restoration of the monarchy in 1660 came a perceptible drift into something that may be called a colonial policy. Charles II conquered New Netherland, and filled the gap between New England and Maryland with four new English colonies. He extended the southern frontier by founding the Carolinas. Parliament laid down a definite economic policy for the empire in the Acts of Trade and Navigation. Next, James II tried to consolidate all continental settlements into two viceroyalties, Spanish style, a scheme thwarted by his expulsion from England. William and Mary, more tactfully, brought all England's American colonies under some measure of political control. And a protracted struggle began between the English on the one side and the French and Spanish on the other for the control of North America.

By 1660 the economic doctrine known as mercantilism, the pursuit of economic power in the interest of national self-sufficiency, was taken for granted by all European states. Mercantilism had been implicit in the founding of Virginia; it now became explicit in the Acts of Trade and Navigation. Everyone, even colonists, admitted that the profits of an empire should center in the mother country. Spain and Portugal had seen to that since the beginning; but England, what with haphazard colonization and civil tumults, had allowed her overseas subjects to trade with foreign countries in almost everything except tobacco, and even tobacco was often carried abroad in foreign ships. Now, through a series of Acts of Trade and Navigation (1660–72), an effort was made to make the English empire a self-sustaining unit, and to confine profits to English subjects.

These acts embodied three principles. All trade between England and her colonies must be conducted by English or English-colonial-built vessels, owned and manned by English subjects. All European imports into the colonies, with the exception of perishable fruit and wine from the Atlantic Islands, must first be 'laid on the shores of England' — i.e., unloaded, handled, and reloaded — before being sent to the colonies; but many of the duties were repaid on re-exportation. And, finally, certain colonial products 'enumerated' in the laws must be exported to England and England only. In the seventeenth century the only enumerated products were tobacco, sugar, cotton, and other tropical commodities grown only in the West Indies. Rice and molasses, furs, and naval stores (tar, pitch, turpentine, and ships' spars) were added between 1705 and 1722, but nothing more until 1764.

Opinions still differ about the effect of this system on the colonies. It certainly did not stop growth and prosperity in the century after 1660. But the cutting off of direct tobacco exports to the European continent, which had been practised in the Cromwellian period, helped to depress the price of tobacco in Virginia. As time went on, more and more colonial products were added to the enumerated list, until, on the eve of the American Revolution, the only important non-enumerated article was salt fish. As England developed a special technique in handling, grading, and marketing her colonial imports, the enumerated principle was not too severe, as proved by the fact that Americans after independence continued to use England as an entrepôt for rice and tobacco. Nor should it be forgotten that Parliament paid bounties to colonial producers of naval stores and indigo, prohibited the growing of tobacco in

England, and laid preferential duties which excluded Cuban and other Spanish-American leaf from the English market.

English colonists, like other English subjects, were excluded from trading with Asia by the East India Company's monopoly. But all the colonists, whether continental or insular, were encouraged to trade with one another. Nor was there any legal bar to trading with the French and other foreign West Indies. In fact a large part of the specie circulating in the continental colonies until the Revolution consisted of French and Spanish coins (especially the dollar or 'piece of eight') which were procured in the islands in exchange for the products of northern farms, forests, and fisheries. Scotland was a foreign country so far as the Acts of Trade were concerned until the Act of Union in 1707, and Ireland remained so until after the American Revolution, except that Irish 'servants, horses and provisions' could be exported directly to the English colonies.

A curious feature of this system, according to modern notions, was the English customs tariff on colonial products, which yielded so large a revenue to the Crown that its abolition was never even contemplated. There were export duties payable in the colonies on certain products, in order to support the colonial governments; import duties in England on almost everything that came from the English colonies, and import duties in the colonies on European goods that came through England. As colonial collectorships were regarded as sinecures, the laws were very inefficiently enforced, and the cost of the customs service generally exceeded the income until just before the American Revolution.

It was also in 1660 that England adopted a new policy respecting emigration. The Earl of Shaftesbury wrote, 'I take it for granted that the strength and glory of your Majesty and the wealth of your Kingdom depends . . . on the multitude of your subjects. . . . We must stop the drain that carries our natives from us.' Accordingly, skilled artisans were forbidden to leave England for the colonies, and as there was no serious unemployment problem in the last third of the century, English emigration to her colonies dwindled to a mere trickle. The new colonies established or conquered after 1660 drew for their population largely on the older colonies, on foreign countries, and on Africa. A leading English interest was the supplying of the colonies with Negro slaves, a traffic in which colonial ships and merchants participated to a limited extent.

It followed from these mercantilist ideas and policies that the most valuable colonies from the English point of view were those from the Chesapeake south, which produced tropical or semi-tropical raw materials that England wanted, and imported almost every luxury and necessity of life from home. And the least valuable colonies were those of New England, which were Old England's competitors rather than her complements. In the year 1698 seven-eighths of England's American trade was with the West Indies, Virginia, Maryland, and the Carolinas; the New England and Middle Colonies, with Newfoundland and Hudson's Bay, accounted for only one-eighth. As time went on, and the Northern Colonies acquired wealth through the West Indies trade, this unequal balance was redressed. By 1747 half, and by 1767, two-thirds, of England's colonial exports were to colonies north of Maryland.

2. FOUNDING OF THE CAROLINAS

After 1660 the impulse toward colonial expansion came mainly from three sources: English merchants and shipowners who wanted new areas for trade and exploitation, courtiers and politicians who planned to recoup their shattered fortunes with great colonial estates, and religious dissenters who sought a refuge for members of their faith.

Restoration of the Stuart monarchy set all doubtful English colonial claimants polishing up their old claims and seeking validation from Charles II. A major claim was one the Carolina Proprietors purchased. This group of eight promoters and politicians obtained from Charles II a proprietary patent to all North America between the parallels of 31° and 36° N (and the next year had this enlarged to embrace all the territory between Daytona, Fla., and the Virginia-North Carolina boundary), under the name Carolina. They hoped to achieve a more diversified colonial economy by encouraging such products as silk, wines, olives, and almonds. The two leading spirits among the proprietors were Sir John Colleton, a wealthy Barbadian planter who sought new homes for the surplus white population of Barbados, and Anthony Ashley Cooper, better known by his later title of Earl of Shaftesbury, Chancellor of the Exchequer. Shaftesbury, in collaboration with John Locke, wrote a charter for the colony, the 'Fundamental Constitutions of Carolina' in 120 articles; an extraordinary document which attempted to provide for this pioneer colony a revived feudalism, with five 'estates,' eight supreme courts, a chamberlain and lord high admiral, and native titles of baron, cacique, and landgrave, depending on the amount of land one bought. After several false starts, a small number of colonists from England and several hundred Barbadians founded Charleston in 1670.[1]

Ten years later the proprietors obtained a group of French Huguenots, and in 1683 a band of Scots settled Port Royal at the site of an abandoned Spanish post. The Spaniards broke it up three years later, but the Scots kept coming. Thus South Carolina was racially heterogeneous from the first. By 1700 the population of the colony was about 5000, half of them Negro slaves; the principal exports were provisions for the West Indies trade, naval stores, and peltry. These early South Carolinians were as expert fur-traders as the French Canadians, sending agents around the southern spurs of the Appalachians into the future Alabama in search of deerskins; and they followed the Spanish example in enslaving Indians. At the turn of the century the cultivation of rice and indigo began on the low coastal plain and along the rivers; and these gradually replaced the more pioneer pursuits. By 1730 South Carolina was a planting colony like Virginia, with a different staple, and a centralized instead of a dispersed social and political system. There were no county or local units of government. Every planter had a town house near the battery in Charleston where he spent the summer months, when river plantations were unhealthful. The French Huguenots, the most important element in the ruling class, imparted a high-spirited and aristocratic tone to the colony; unlike other foreigners in the English colonies they quickly adopted the English language and joined the Established Church of England.

In the meantime a wholly different form of society was developing in the northern or Albemarle section of the province, which became North Carolina. There the original settlers had been adventurers from New England or poor whites from Virginia; and as these settlements were separated from Charleston by several hundred miles of forest, the proprietors granted them a separate governor and assembly. Apart from the Swiss-German settlement of New Bern there were few foreigners before 1713, and still fewer colonists of family or means. The principal products were tobacco and naval stores; and lack of harbors suitable for seagoing vessels meant heavy transportation costs. North Carolina was poor, turbulent, and democratic, with relatively few slaves. In 1736 the white

1. The original site was 25 miles up the Ashley river; the present site, on the best harbor between Chesapeake Bay and the Gulf of Mexico, was chosen in 1680.

population was estimated to be one-third greater than that of the southern colony, but the production very much less.

On the whole, the proprietors of Carolina did a good job in planting these two colonies, but they reaped more headaches than profit from them. All except Lord Granville sold out to the Crown in 1729, when the two halves became the royal provinces of North Carolina and South Carolina.

In both colonies the first land system, apart from the few big purchases made by persons who desired one of the fancy titles, was a modification of the Virginia head-right system, the amount granted for each person varying from 20 to 80 acres at different times. Wherever the land could support a profitable staple, which was mostly in South Carolina, men of capital brought in Negro slaves from the West Indies or from Africa, and by combining their head-rights, created large plantations. In North Carolina it was unprofitable to do this; consequently the northern province became a community of small farms.

3. NEW YORK AND THE JERSEYS

The Duke of York's brief and unsuccessful reign as James II should not blind us to the fact that he was an excellent seaman and an able administrator. His brother Charles II appointed him Lord High Admiral at the age of 26; he brought the Royal Navy to a high state of efficiency and accompanied the fleet into action in the Dutch War of 1664. As head of the navy he wished to deprive the Dutch of their base at New Amsterdam, and as an impecunious member of the House of Stuart he needed a profitable colony. England had always protested against the Dutch seizing any part of the coast discovered by John Cabot, and now was in a position to make that protest good. With parliamentary approval the king conferred on his brother in 1664 the most extensive English territorial grant of the century. 'The Duke of York's Grant' included the continent between the Connecticut and Delaware rivers, together with Long Island, Nantucket, and Martha's Vineyard, and Maine east of the Kennebec. And the Duke lost no time in taking over. On 18 August a small English fleet entered the Narrows of New York harbor; Peter Stuyvesant surrendered New Netherland without firing a shot. The Duke of York, aged 30, now owned a section of America with boundless possibilities, one destined to be the wealthiest area in the world. As Lord

Proprietor, unhampered even by the Maryland proviso of obtaining consent of the freemen for his laws, he was absolute master of this domain, under the king.

The Duke's rule of New York, as he renamed the Dutch colony, was fairly enlightened. He summoned no assembly, but ordered his governor, Richard Nicolls, to treat the Dutch with 'humanity and gentleness,' and made no effort to impose on them the English language or his own religion. But he intended to make money out of the colony, and drew up his own schedule of customs duties, quit-rents, and taxes. That made trouble. There were already too many English in the colony for any proprietor to raise taxes without representation. A code of laws, 'The Duke's Laws,' similar to those of New England, was promulgated for Long Island; but the English there were discontented because they had no hand in them, and were taxed without 'consent,' so the governor had to keep the taxes low. And the cost of administering a government that extended from eastern Maine to Maryland was so great that the Duke was still in the red in 1673 when New York was recaptured by the Dutch. They restored it to England by treaty in 1674. Again there was trouble about taxation, and finally the Duke's Irish governor, Thomas Dongan, summoned a representative assembly in 1683.

Realizing that he had bitten off a little more than he could chew, the Duke began giving away slices of his grant as early as 1664. To his friends Lord John Berkeley and Sir George Carteret, both proprietors of Carolina, he ceded all land between the Hudson and Delaware rivers as the 'Province of Nova Caesaria or New Jersey.' A few hundred Dutch and English Puritans from New England were already there, and, in order to attract more, Berkeley and Carteret promulgated the 'Concessions and Agreements of the Proprietors of New Jersey,' granting freedom of conscience, liberal terms for land, and an assembly. In 1674 Berkeley sold out his half share in New Jersey to two Quakers, who took the southwestern half of the province, while Carteret kept the northeastern part. Carteret's widow in 1680 sold out East New Jersey for the modest sum of £3400 to a group of proprietors, and the two Quakers let William Penn in on West New Jersey. The net result of this was a heterogeneous settlement, a minimum of social cohesion, and a bad confusion in land titles that bedeviled New Jersey politics until the Revolution.

4. PENN'S HOLY EXPERIMENT

The founding of Pennsylvania, more so than any other American commonwealth, is the lengthened shadow of one man and of his faith in God and in human nature.

Out of the religious ferment of Puritan England came a leader named George Fox, who founded the Society of Friends, commonly known as Quakers. They believed that religious authority rested neither in the Bible nor in a priestly hierarchy but in the Inner Light of Jesus Christ in the soul of every man. They viewed the Scriptures as 'a secondary Rule, subordinate to the Spirit,' and they denied the distinction between the laity and a 'hireling clergy.' A mystical faith, Quakerism encouraged not quietistic contemplation but an 'enthusiastic' crusade to persuade their fellow men that they could enter a 'paradise of God' on earth. Since every man had some of God's spirit, all men were brothers and all were equal; they addressed one another as 'thee' and 'thou,' and observed literally the divine command 'thou shalt do no murder,' even under the name of war. To persecution they opposed passive resistance; and like the early Christians they gathered strength from oppression and victory from defeat. Over 3000 Quakers were imprisoned in England during the first two years of the Restoration; yet the sect spread like wildfire, and as far as Russia made converts eager to wear the martyr's crown. In 1652 the first Quaker missionaries appeared in the English colonies. Severe laws were passed against them in every colony but Rhode Island, and in Boston three were hanged; but finally by passive resistance they wore down the authorities and won a grudging toleration. The same thing happened in England. Fox and his courageous missionaries converted thousands of Puritans and Anglicans wearied of the austerities of the one or the indifference of the other, and who sought brotherhood and peace. They won converts especially among the poorer tenants in the countryside and among the workingmen of London and Bristol. As Puritanism had been in 1600, and as Methodism would be in 1770, so Quakerism became the dynamic form of English Protestantism from about 1650 to 1700.

Even without William Penn the Quakers would have had a small colony of their own, West New Jersey; with William Penn they obtained one of the greatest. The founder of Pennsylvania, born in 1644, was the son of Admiral Sir William Penn, conqueror of Jamaica. Although he had showed sufficient interest in unfashionable religion as a lad to be expelled from Christ Church, Oxford, young William was not converted to Quakerism until 1667, when, after a grand tour of the Continent, and residence at the gay viceregal court of Dublin, he listened to the sermon of a Friend on the text 'There is a Faith that overcometh the World.' And for the remaining 51 years of his life, William Penn was steadfast in that faith.

The Admiral, who swore and threatened when he heard this news, was reconciled before his death and left his Quaker son a considerable fortune. A share of West New Jersey far from satisfied the young man's ambition. What he wanted was a proprietary colony of his own, where he could experiment with political as well as religious liberty. The Friends no longer needed a refuge; but, like the Puritans of half a century before, they wanted a colony where they could live their ideal of the New Testament life, free from the pressure of bad example and worldly corruption. In 1677 Penn made a journey to the European continent with George Fox. In Germany he met members of several German sects, some akin to the Quakers in doctrine, who were uneasy and eager to leave. That tour enlarged his conception of a colony to that of a refuge for the persecuted of every race and sect.

Fortunately, Penn's conversion had never caused him to break with his father's friends, among whom was counted the Duke of York. A tactful reminder that the Admiral had lent the king's brother £16,000 that had never been repaid, secured for William and his heirs in 1681 a generous slice of the Duke's grant. At the grantor's insistence it was named Pennsylvania. The king implemented this grant by a charter creating the province a proprietary one on the model of Maryland.

Settlement began without delay. In 1681 Penn published in English, French, German, and Dutch *Some Account of the Province of Pennsylvania,* which (in accordance with Quaker business ethics) underestimated rather than exaggerated the natural advantages. He urged peasants and artisans to come, and get-rich-quick adventurers to stay away; gave instructions for the journey and the outfit; and promised political and religious liberty. Even more persuasive were the easiest terms for land yet offered in North America: a 50-acre head-right free; 200-acre tenant farms at a penny an acre rent; estates of 5000 acres for £100, with a city lot thrown in. In three months Penn disposed of warrants for over 300,000 acres, and in 1682 he came over himself.

Neither the banks of Delaware Bay nor the lower reaches of the rivers were a wilderness in 1682. About a thousand Swedes, Finns, and Dutch survivors of the colonies of New Sweden and New Netherland were already there. These were given free land grants, and proved useful in providing the first English colonists with food, housing, and labor. Choosing an admirable site for his capital, Penn laid out Philadelphia between the Delaware and the Schuylkill rivers in checkerboard fashion — which had a permanent and pernicious effect on American city planning — and undertook the government himself.

William Penn liked to allude to his province as the 'Holy Experiment.' It is difficult for us to put ourselves in the place of those seventeenth-century idealists, Winthrop and Calvert, Williams and Penn, who actually tried to found Cities of God in the wilderness. Yet, even though they made idealism pay dividends — at least Calvert and Penn did — there is no reason to doubt their sincerity. Penn, unlike the Puritans, believed in the essential goodness of human nature. 'When the great and wise God had made the world, of all his creatures it pleased him to choose man his deputy to rule it,' reads Penn's *Frame of Government* for Pennsylvania. 'And to fit him for so great a charge and trust, He did not only qualify him with skill and powers but with integrity to use them justly. This native goodness was equally his honor and his happiness.' Herein the note later stressed in American history by Jefferson and Emerson is first boldly struck. And since Quakers regarded it as nobody's business how a man worshipped, or if he worshipped at all, Penn made religious liberty and trust in humanity the twin cornerstones of his Holy Experiment.

Yet Penn never ceased to be cavalier when he went Quaker, or gentleman when he became democrat. His instincts and tastes were those of the English aristocracy; he appreciated a thoroughbred horse, a well-built ship, good food and drink, and handsome women. Penn brought over from England Tamerlane, sire of famous American race-horses; and had built a six-oared rowing barge, to convey him from his country seat on the Delaware to Philadelphia.

As a friend and admirer of Algernon Sidney and other radical publicists of the day, Penn believed in the traditional liberties of Englishmen, and intended that they should be respected in his province. He had been made to feel in his own person the value of civil liberties, and the aristocrat in him made him fight back when his rights were infringed, a thing that the average Quaker was too poor or pacifistic to do. Yet Penn was no nineteenth-century democrat. He believed in government for the people, by liberally educated gentlemen like himself. And the first Frame of Government that he issued for Pennsylvania in 1682 reflected this idea. He was the governor. He provided a small council, elected by taxpayers from landowners 'of best repute for wisdom, virtue and ability,' to initiate the laws; and a large elective assembly to accept or reject the bills — but if the assembly 'turn debaters, you overthrow the charter,' said he. Such a system was unpalatable to discussion-loving Englishmen. It worked fairly well in 1682–84 when Penn was in his province, for his generous nature and personal charm would have made any system work; but when he returned to England, his government almost blew up. He was a poor business man, and his too great trust in human nature led him to make unsuitable appointments of land agents who robbed him, and of deputy governors who antagonized or scandalized the people.

Penn returned to Philadelphia in 1699 and issued a Charter of Privileges, which remained the constitution of the province until 1776. It provided the usual colonial set-up of a governor and council (appointed by the proprietor but confirmed by the king), and an assembly composed of four representatives for each county, elected by a property franchise.

The three 'Lower Counties,' as the future state of Delaware was then called, were purchased by Penn from the Duke of York, much against the wishes of Lord Baltimore, who regarded that region as part of Maryland. The Lower Counties acquired an assembly of their own in 1702, but the Charter of Privileges was their charter too, and the Governor of Pennsylvania was their governor.

Pennsylvania began with the most generous grant of religious liberty and the most liberal and humane code of laws in the world. Capital punishment, which existed for a dozen different offenses in the other English colonies and for more than twenty in England, was inflicted in Pennsylvania only for murder. The grant of religious liberty was never retracted; but a crime wave at the turn of the century caused the criminal code to be stiffened to such a point that the Privy Council in England rejected half the new laws. Accordingly, by 1717, there was little difference between Pennsylvania and other colonies in the rigor of their laws. However, Quaker compassion provided Philadelphia with the best charitable institutions in the English colonies.

Pennsylvania prospered as did no other early settlement. For it was founded at a time when in England business was good but liberty in danger. The Popish Plot, the Rye-house Plot, Monmouth's Rebellion, and religious persecution on the Continent, made thousands of good people eager to seek peace, liberty, and prosperity overseas. The province attracted both labor and capital, and found a ready market in the West Indies for agricultural produce. In two years' time Philadelphia boasted 357 houses; in 1685 the population of the province was little short of 9000. Germans of the Mennonite sect, mostly linen-weavers from Krefeld, settled Germantown in 1683 under their cultivated minister, Francis Daniel Pastorius; Welsh Quakers founded Radnor and Haverford; a Free Society of Traders, organized by English Quakers, started fisheries and established brick kilns, tanneries, and glass works. Penn could state without boasting in 1684, 'I have led the greatest colony into America that ever any man did upon a private credit, and the most prosperous beginnings that were ever in it are to be found among us.'

William Penn himself fell on evil days at the turn of the century. His business affairs went from bad to worse. He had a protracted boundary controversy with Lord Baltimore — eventually settled in 1763–67 by the Mason-Dixon Line.[2] His eldest son, the second proprietor, turned out a spendthrift and a rake. The quarrels among council and governor and assembly distressed him; 'For the love of God, me, and the poor country,' he once wrote to Thomas Lloyd, leader of the opposition, 'Do not be so litigious and brutish!' But he never lost faith in the Holy Experiment, or in human nature.

Pennsylvania was a portent of America to be; the first large community in modern history where different races and religions lived under the same government on terms of equality. There was, to be sure, much quarreling and contention between the races; yet, for all that, they did

2. The Mason and Dixon Line lies along latitude 39° 43' 26.3" N between the southwestern corner of Pennsylvania and the arc of a circle of twelve miles' radius drawn from Newcastle (Delaware) as a center; and along that arc to the Delaware river. It was run by two English surveyors named Mason and Dixon, in consequence of Lord Hardwicke's decision, in 1750. But there have been interstate controversies about parts of it even in the present century.

not slaughter one another. For these reasons Pennsylvania interested liberal philosophers of eighteenth-century Europe as a successful experiment in the life of reason; Voltaire never tired of holding it up as proof that man could lead the good life without absolute monarchy, feudalism, or religious and racial uniformity.

5. TIME OF TROUBLES IN VIRGINIA AND NEW ENGLAND 1675–92

Virginia, ever loyal to the house of Stuart, suffered grievously from its restoration. In 1672 Charles II even proposed to grant the whole of Virginia to two courtiers, Lords Arlington and Culpeper. That was prevented, but Culpeper got the 'Northern Neck,' between the Potomac and the Rappahannock rivers. Sir William Berkeley was reappointed Governor of Virginia, and in a wave of loyalty the people elected a house of burgesses in 1661 which proved so pliant that Berkeley kept this 'long assembly' going for fifteen years by successive adjournments, and managed to get the whole machinery of government, central and local, in his hands.

More serious for the Old Dominion than the Stuarts was overproduction and the low price of tobacco. Virginia's population had doubled in the 1650's, from 15,000 to 30,000. Then came the Acts of Trade and the Dutch wars, curtailing the foreign market and raising the cost of transportation. In 1662 Governor Berkeley reported the price of tobacco to be so low that it would not pay the cost of freight. 'Forty thousand people are impoverished,' he wrote, 'in order to enrich little more than forty merchants in England.' In 1668 tobacco prices in Virginia reached an all-time low of a farthing a pound, one-quarter of the customs duty on it in England. The assembly for ten years made attempts to curtail production and peg prices; these were thwarted partly by Maryland's refusal to come in, partly by difficulty of enforcement, and partly because the English merchants raised prices of goods sent in exchange when they could not make their usual profit. Fifteen years after the Restoration, Virginia, the land of opportunity for poor and industrious Englishmen, had become a place of poverty and discontent. There the first serious rebellion in North American history broke out.

The immediate cause of Bacon's Rebellion was the Indian question. At this time the Indians were restive all along the rear of the English colonies. The Susquehannock, forced south to the Potomac by the Seneca, clashed with militia from Virginia and Maryland, broke up into small bands, and began harrying the frontier in the summer of 1675. Governor Berkeley, hoping to avoid a general Indian war (such as had already broken out in New England), decided on a defensive policy, building a chain of mutually supporting forts around the settled part of Virginia. That infuriated the frontier planters, who believed the Berkeley clique had put the planters' lives in jeopardy in order to profit from the Indian trade. Nathaniel Bacon, an impetuous 28-year-old gentlemen fresh from England whose plantation had been attacked, protested: 'These traders at the head of the rivers buy and sell our blood.' As spokesman for and leader of discontented planters, Bacon commanded an unauthorized military force which slaughtered the peaceful Oconeechee tribe, and then advanced on Jamestown. Bacon is said to have exclaimed, 'Damn my blood, I'll kill Governor, Council, Assembly and all!' As this improvised rebel army approached Jamestown, Berkeley decided to dissolve his 'long assembly' and issued writs for a new one, which met shortly and passed some important bills for relief, reform, and defense. What had begun as a sectional quarrel over Indian policy had developed into an assault on political privilege, although in this confused upheaval the poorer farmers had as many grievances against the Bacon faction as against the Berkeley circle.

For a time, Bacon ruled most of Virginia. But Berkeley plucked up courage, called out the loyal militia of the Eastern Shore, appealed to England for troops, and civil war began. Exactly how far Bacon intended to go is not clear, but there is some evidence that he hoped to unite Virginia, North Carolina, and Maryland as a 'free state.' He did set up a government of his own, but cavalier feeling in Virginia was still too strong to support a rebellion against royal authority. After Bacon's premature death (26 October 1676) and before the 'red-coats' arrived from England, the rebellion collapsed. Berkeley rounded up the leaders and had twenty-three of them executed for treason. 'That old fool has hanged more men in that naked country than I have done for the murder of my father,' exclaimed Charles II.

Many years elapsed before the economic structure improved by reason of increased demand for tobacco and higher prices. No longer could a yeoman farmer 'make a crop' with the aid of his family, or white indented servants earn their keep. Planters who could afford to import slaves made money, but the poor farmers grew poorer.

New England under the Restoration of 1660 not only flourished economically, since the increase of sugar production in the West Indies
created a demand for her ships and products, but also preserved its right
of self-government. Massachusetts Bay was allowed to continue for a
quarter-century more under her corporate charter, and Connecticut and
Rhode Island obtained similar charters from the Crown in 1662 and
1663, through sending the 'right people' as agents to London. The Connecticut charter included the old New Haven Colony in its boundaries,
which impelled some diehard Puritans of New Haven to found Newark,
N. J. Both charters not only granted complete self-government, as had
existed in Plymouth and Massachusetts from the beginning, but protected them against sundry courtiers who were seeking to carve up their
territory.

Nevertheless, New England too had its time of troubles. In 1675–77
broke out the most devastating war in her entire history. King Philip's
War it was called, after the Wampanoag chief who began hostilities.
The natives were reacting desperately against their diminishing power
in New England. As they were now skilled in the use of firearms, the
Indians were now able to attack frontier settlements at will, destroy
crops, cattle, and houses, and endanger the very existence of white New
England. A dozen towns were levelled, and the rate of casualties was
higher than in any subsequent war. But the Puritans had the New England Confederacy, while the Indians were not united; some 2500 converted Indians remained loyal to England; and gradually the New England militia, accompanied by loyal Indian scouts, broke up Indian con-
centrations, destroyed their food supply, and hunted down their bands
one by one. With the death of King Philip on 12 August 1676 the
rebellion collapsed, and Philip's wife and son were sold into slavery in
the West Indies. The power of the natives in southern New England was
broken forever; but the Abnaki of Maine and New Hampshire turned to
Canada for aid, and kept the English at bay in northern New England
for another seventy-five years.

Not until 1720 did New England recover the frontier thrown back by
this fierce war. The losses in men and property were heavy. And the
royal government chose this time to bring the Bay Colony to book for
her recalcitrance. Massachusetts offended Charles II by coining the pine-
tree shilling, and by purchasing from the Gorges proprietors the Province of Maine, which the king intended to buy for one of his bastards.

The province refused to obey the Navigation Acts on the ground 'that the laws of England are bounded within the four seas, and do not reach America. The subjects of his majesty here being not represented in Parliament, so we have not looked at ourselves to be impeded in our trade by them.' She declined to allow appeals to English courts, or to grant freedom of worship and the franchise to Anglicans. Consequently, in 1684, the High Court of Chancery declared the old Massachusetts Bay charter to be 'vacated, cancelled and annihilated.' The government was now in the king's hands to do as he saw fit; and the death of Charles II threw the problem into King James's lap.

James II, like most members of his family, was an enemy to representative institutions; and as a professional sailor he thought it an easy matter to throw them overboard. The colonial situation was disquieting. Even with the Massachusetts government gone, there were three separate colonies in New England and four in the middle region, each with its own assembly; all of them flouting the Acts of Trade and Navigation as much as they dared. French Canada, with which the English had lived on fairly good terms hitherto, now began to loom as a menace. It was now a united Crown colony under a great administrator, Count Frontenac, who sent explorers like Joliet, Marquette, and La Salle to the Far West and down the Mississippi, and attempted to seduce the Iroquois from their English alliance. Obviously there must be unity in English colonial administration to meet this danger.

The royal solution to these colonial problems was consolidation. Between 1685 and 1688 the New England colonies, New York, and the Jerseys were combined into one viceroyalty called the Dominion of New England. The Dominion was ruled by an appointed governor (Sir Edmund Andros) and council, but had no representative institutions. This reform, as it was intended to be, appealed to the non-Puritan minority in New England, and to some of the wealthier merchants elsewhere, but to nobody else; and the merchants soon wished they were back under the Puritan 'saints,' who accounted it no sin to smuggle. Andros and his council did not interfere with the Puritan churches, schools, and colleges; but they did question the validity of land titles, which alarmed every farmer in New England. And they taxed without a legislative grant, which no Englishman would allow. One curious result of the autocratic government was a currency shortage, brought on by the suppression of piracy; for pirates, as good spenders who 'put money in circulation,' had been treated tenderly by the former governments at Boston, Newport, and New York.

If James II had succeeded in suppressing English liberties at home, he would probably have combined the other continental colonies in a second dominion, and the English empire would have been governed like the Spanish viceroyalties of Mexico and Peru. But he was expelled from England in the 'Glorious Revolution' of 1688, which brought in William III and Mary II as joint sovereigns of the British Isles. As soon as news of this event reached the colonies, a succession of popular revolutions overthrew dominion authorities and put the several colonies back where they had been before 1685.

The only conspicuous leader in these revolts was Jacob Leisler, a New Yorker of German birth. Leisler, by flouting the patroons and other important groups in his colony, and by firing on the royal troops sent to take over the government, placed himself in a position where he could be accused of treason. He was judicially murdered in 1691. Elsewhere the Dominion of New England fell apart with scarcely a blow.

By that time King William's War with the French was going full blast, no English frontier farm was safe; and to cap the catalogue of woes in this seventeen-year period of terror and trouble, a famous witchcraft scare broke out in Massachusetts.

To the already vast literature on witchcraft the Reverend Cotton Mather, boy wonder of the New England clergy, contributed a book entitled *Memorable Providences,* describing a case of alleged witchcraft in Boston for which a poor old woman was executed, and how he had handled the accusing children to prevent a witch-hunting epidemic. The second edition of this work (1691) got into the hands of a group of young girls in a suburb of Salem. More or less as a prank, they accused a half-Indian, half-Negro family slave of being a witch. Flogged by her master into confessing, to save her skin she accused two respectable goodwives of being her confederates. The 'afflicted' children, finding themselves the objects of attention, and with the exhibitionism natural to young wenches, persisted in their charges for fear of being found out, and this started a chain reaction. A special court was set up to try the witches. The innocent people whom the girls accused, implicated others to escape the gallows, confessing broomstick rides, flying saucers, witches' sabbaths, sexual relations with the devil, and everything which, according to the book, witches were supposed to do. Honest folk who declared the whole thing nonsense were cried out upon for witches. The vicious business continued through the summer of 1692, until nineteen persons, including a Congregational minister and fourteen women, had been found guilty of witchcraft and hanged; and one man, Giles Corey, pressed to death. About 55 more had pleaded guilty and accused others, 150 of whom were in jail awaiting trial. The frenzy was only halted because the witch-finders were beginning to go after prominent people. On the tardy advice of Increase Mather and other clergymen, the assembly dissolved the special court and released all prisoners.

As a witchcraft scare, the Salem one was small compared with others at the time in Europe; and it had a few redeeming features. The condemned witches were hanged, not burned to death as elsewhere. Almost everyone concerned in the furor later confessed his error (Judge Sewall doing so in open church meeting), and twenty years later the Massachusetts courts annulled the convictions and granted indemnity to the victims. But the record reveals an appalling moral cowardice on the part of ministry and gentry, and credulity and hatred among the people at large. It was one of those times which unfortunately have occurred more frequently in the present century, when the safeguards of liberty, religion, and plain decency are ripped asunder by popular fear and passion, whipped up by some tyrant or demagogue, and the evil in human nature is given full sway.

6. COLONIAL REORGANIZATION

Colonial reorganization, begun under William and Mary, took place gradually by a series of typical English compromises. Rhode Island and Connecticut were allowed to keep their corporate charters. New York, and later the Jerseys and Carolinas, became royal provinces. Pennsylvania and Maryland were restored to their proprietors, in deference to the growing theory of vested rights among the whigs who had brought in the new regime. A part of the Dominion of New England was salvaged by creating the royal province of Massachusetts Bay, including the old Bay colony, the Plymouth colony, and Maine. In all these units, representative institutions were confirmed or granted, and, by an act of Parliament of 1696, a new system of admiralty courts was instituted to enforce the Acts of Trade and Navigation. Submission of all acts of colonial assemblies to the Privy Council for possible disallowance was insisted on, and appeals from colonial courts to the Privy Council were encouraged.

This reorganization was manifestly incomplete. After the admiralty courts, which required no jury trial, began to function, it became possible with the aid of revenue cutters to suppress the grosser forms of piracy and smuggling. A certain amount of European goods leaked into the Thirteen Colonies by way of Newfoundland and Jamaica, but direct importation from continental Europe was stopped. Acts of Parliament, such as those organizing the postal service, or granting bounties on colonial products, were enforced. The Crown could balk colonial legislation that it considered undesirable, both by the royal governor's veto which could not be overridden, and by the royal disallowance. About 2½ per cent of all acts passed by colonial assemblies were disallowed by the Privy Council. Most of those thrown out deserved it; for instance, discriminatory legislation against religious minorities, or laws discriminating against ships, products, or subjects of neighboring English colonies, and unbacked paper currency emissions. But some good colonial laws, such as those restricting the slave trade, were also thrown out.

These colonial laws were disallowed after investigation and report by the Board of Trade and Plantations. That body, appointed by the king under an act of 1696, was the nearest thing to a colonial office in the English government; but its powers were only advisory. Most colonial matters were routed through the Board, which meant a certain uniformity in administration, but the decisions were made either by the king, the lords of the admiralty, or the war department. In other words, the imperial system, as it existed from 1689 to 1776, was a mere outgrowth of the government of the realm; it would have been cumbrous and inefficient even if competently and honestly administered, as it was not.

The principal officials in the colonies who were expected to enforce English laws and regulations were the royal and proprietary governors. The former were appointed by the king during his good pleasure; the proprietary governors had to be acceptable to the Crown. All observed considerable pomp and circumstance, but fell into that most unfortunate political category: officials with responsibility but no power. All except the governors of Virginia and of certain West Indian islands were dependent on the assemblies for their salaries. Executive patronage, which might have been an important lever, was taken away from them both by the English secretary of state, who needed it for his own henchmen, and

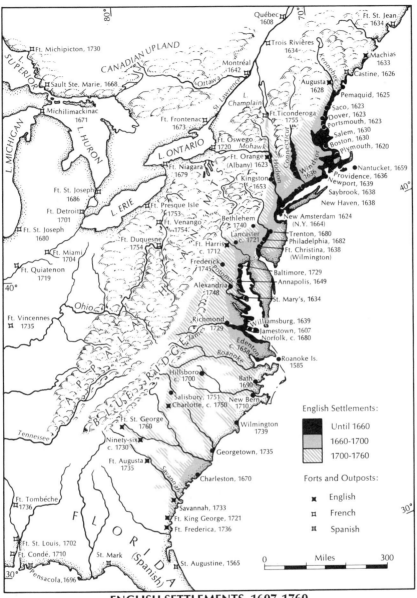

ENGLISH SETTLEMENTS, 1607-1760
English, French and Spanish Outposts

Québec 1608
Ft. St. Jean 1634
Ft. Michipicton, 1730
Trois Rivières 1634
Machias 1633
Montréal 1642
Castine, 1626
Sault Ste. Marie, 1668
Augusta 1628
Pemaquid, 1625
Michilimackinac 1671
Saco, 1623
Ft.Ticonderoga 1755
Dover, 1623
Portsmouth, 1623
Ft. Frontenac 1673
Salem, 1630
Boston, 1630
Ft. Oswego 1720
Plymouth, 1620
Ft. Orange (Albany) 1623
Ft. Niagara 1679
Nantucket, 1659
Providence, 1636
Kingston 1653
Newport, 1639
Ft. St. Joseph 1686
Saybrook, 1638
New Haven, 1638
Ft. Detroit 1701
Ft. Presque Isle 1753
Ft. St. Joseph 1680
Ft. Venango 1754
New Amsterdam 1624 (N.Y. 1664)
Bethlehem 1740
Ft. Miami 1704
Trenton, 1680
Lancaster c. 1721
Philadelphia, 1682
Ft. Duquesne 1754
Ft. Harris c. 1712
Ft. Christina, 1638 (Wilmington)
Ft. Quiatenon 1719
Frederick 1745
Baltimore, 1729
Alexandria 1748
Annapolis, 1649
St. Mary's, 1634
Ft. Vincennes 1735
Richmond 1729
Williamsburg, 1639
Jamestown, 1607
Norfolk, c. 1680
Edenton c. 1658
Roanoke
Roanoke Is. 1585
Hillsboro c. 1700
Bath 1690
Salisbury, 1751
New Bern 1710
Charlotte, c. 1750
Ft. St. George 1760
Wilmington 1739
Ninety-six c. 1730
Georgetown, 1735
Ft. Augusta 1735
Charleston, 1670
Ft. Tombéche 1736
Savannah, 1733
Ft. King George, 1721
Ft. St. Louis, 1702
Ft. Frederica, 1736
Ft. Condé, 1710
St. Mark
St. Augustine, 1565
Pensacola, 1696

English Settlements:
Until 1660
1660-1700
1700-1760

Forts and Outposts:
☒ English
⌗ French
⌗ Spanish

0 Miles 300

85

by the assemblies, which generally elected the colonial treasurer and other minor officials themselves. The royal governors on the whole were honest and able men, and no small number of them were colonists; but they had an unhappy time, for they were expected to enforce the regulations of an overseas government without the power to do so. In the proprietary as in the royal governments, the assemblies, representing local interests, demanded greater control of their local affairs than the governors' instructions permitted; the governors demanded more power for their royal and proprietary masters than the people were disposed to admit; and distance, as well as the power of the purse, tended to keep the governor's power at a low ebb.

Even in time of war, each colonial assembly had the privilege of honoring or dishonoring the requisitions made upon it by the home government for men, money, and supplies. War grants generally had a number of strings attached which prevented the governor from employing colonial troops to best advantage, and often the grants were forthcoming only after concessions had been made on some issue over which governor and assembly had long been quarreling.

7. IMPERIAL WARS

William III brought the English colonies into the orbit of world politics. As stadholder of the Netherlands he had organized a league of European states to resist the pretensions of Louis XIV to the hegemony of Europe. Having obtained the English crown, he made that league into the Grand Alliance, which brought the English and French colonies to blows. There then began the first of the international colonial wars,[3] which took up a large part of colonial effort and energy, and which ended with the complete overthrow of French power in North America.

Informal hostilities between England and Spain on the southern border had been going on for years, and a clash between English and

3. The colonial wars may be summarized as follows:

Colonial Name	European Name	Dates	Peace Treaty
I King William's	League of Augsburg	1689–97	Ryswick
II Queen Anne's	Spanish Succession	1702–13	Utrecht
III King George's	Austrian Succession	1745–48	Aachen
IV Old French and Indian	Seven Years War	1754–63	Paris

King George's War began in the Southern Colonies and Caribbean in 1739 as the 'War of Jenkins' Ear' between England and Spain.

French on the northern border was inevitable because of the conflict of the Iroquois Confederacy with Canadian ambitions. In the century after 1650, every young Canadian of spirit became an explorer or a coureur de bois, and the more adventurous of these traveling salesmen of the fur business had reached the Dakotas before Englishmen had attained the crest of the Appalachians. On the other hand, the Iroquois Confederacy, whose sphere of influence covered upstate New York, most of Pennsylvania, and the old Northwest, remained faithful to their alliance with the Dutch and the English, who could provide them with cheaper blankets and liquor than did the French. The Iroquois not only remained impervious to French missionary efforts, but occasionally indulged in raids on the canoe fur route of the St. Lawrence basin. Consequently French fur traders had to travel north of and around the Iroquois country in order to reach the upper Mississippi valley, which by 1715 had become a more valuable source of fur than the basin of the Great Lakes.

In the summer of 1682 the Sieur de La Salle, greatest of French explorers, sailed and rowed down the Mississippi, planted the white banner of St. Louis on its banks below New Orleans, and named the region Louisiana. The king declared La Salle's expedition to be 'altogether useless,' and ordered the Governor of Canada to prevent further enterprises of that nature. But La Salle, back in France, managed to 'sell' Louisiana to his sovereign on the ground that a post on the Gulf would annoy the King of Spain, with whom France was then at war. He was then allowed to recruit a few score Frenchmen, mostly convicts, to make a settlement near the mouth of the great river. Unfortunately on his next voyage La Salle missed the Passes and pitched his colony on the Gulf coast of Texas, where he was killed by his own men, who were then finished off by the Comanche Indians. La Salle's expedition was not aimed at the English, nor did they take much notice of it; and this exploration, one of the glories of French enterprise, so little affected French policy that in 1696 Louis XIV actually issued an edict ordering the Canadian coureurs de bois to take wives, settle down, and cease exploring the wilderness in search of fur! For Louis was entering his pious old age, and the Church objected that these adventurers spoiled the work of the missionaries. Governor Frontenac, hand in glove with the fur-trading interests, largely ignored his sovereign's orders.

Louis XIV, however, had no objection to Count Frontenac's using coureurs de bois and friendly Indians to raid the frontiers of New England and New York. So King William's War, as well as that of Queen Anne, took the character of a series of winter attacks on English frontier settlements. Schenectady, New York, was the first place to be destroyed, in February 1690. Other raids followed against the Maine and New Hampshire frontiers, while Canadian privateers from L'Acadie (Nova Scotia) preyed on Yankee fishermen and traders. New England's reply (1690) was to capture Port Royal on the Bay of Fundy, and to send an unsuccessful expedition against Quebec. King William's War ended in Europe with the Treaty of Ryswick (1697), which did not change a single colonial boundary but restored Port Royal to the French. In New England the war dragged along until 1699. By that time there was hardly a white settler left in the future state of Maine.

During the interval between King William's and Queen Anne's wars, Spain strengthened her position on the northern and eastern borders of Mexico; and Spain was England's enemy in the next three colonial wars. Father Kino founded the mission of San Xavier near Tucson, Arizona, in 1696, which became the center of a border province called Pimería Alta. Spaniards had by 1700 reoccupied New Mexico, whence the Pueblo Indians had driven them out in the 1680's; and Pensacola was founded by Spain in 1696.

Next year, Count Frontenac sent Le Moyne d'Iberville to take effective possession of Louisiana. Owing to the difficulty of sailing vessels up the Mississippi, he pitched his first settlement at Biloxi, and shifted it to Mobile in 1702. About the same time the Canadians founded three posts — Kaskaskia, Cahokia, and Vincennes — in the Illinois country, partly as a check to Iroquois influence, and partly as connecting links between Canada and Louisiana.

In 1700 came a shifting of European alliances. The king of Spain died without issue, Louis XIV claimed the throne for his grandson, the Grand Alliance supported a rival claimant, and the War of the Spanish Succession broke out — Queen Anne's War the colonists called it after their new sovereign. France and Spain now became allies, and the feeble little colonies of Louisiana and Florida became friends. They found a common enemy in the vigorous young English colony of South Carolina.

Owing to the lack of an Appalachian barrier to the west, the South Carolinians developed much the same sort of fur-trading frontier as had the Canadians. In this region deer and buffalo skins, which European carriers valued as a raw material for fine leather, were the important peltry. By 1700 the Carolinian traders had penetrated the entire region back of the eastern Gulf of Mexico, and were even obtaining skins from the Quapaw across the Mississippi. The Yamassee Indians, who had revolted against the Spaniards in Florida, established themselves in South Carolina, and made slaving raids on the Creek and the Cherokee, selling their captives to the English of Charleston, who in turn sold them to good advantage in the West Indies and even in New England. Le Moyne d'Iberville allied with the Choctaw, and Queen Anne's War on this southern border took on the character of a preliminary skirmish in the contest for mastery of the Mississippi — a contest that ended only with Andrew Jackson's victory before New Orleans in 1815. And, just as Massachusetts was begging the English Crown for help to conquer Canada, so the South Carolina Assembly urged on the Board of Trade in London the advantage of extending Carolina to the 'Mischisipi' river, since 'half the Canada fur trade and skins must of necessity come this way, besides a vast internal trade of furs and skins.' Throughout the last three colonial wars the flank English colonies of Massachusetts and South Carolina were more imperialist than the home government, ever urging action on the part of England; while the Middle and Chesapeake Colonies, protected by the Iroquois, hung back until they were directly menaced.

The West Indian sugar islands were so much more valuable to Europe than the continental colonies, and those waters were so rich in possible prizes, that the French and British navies usually confined their efforts to the Caribbean, where their success did not help the mainland settlements.

On the northern frontier, Queen Anne's War began with border raids by the French and Indians, of which the most famous was the one which wiped out Deerfield, Mass. New York remained neutral to the end of the war largely because the Albany merchants wished to continue their trade with Montreal. Massachusetts, after two failures, captured Port Royal, this time permanently; it became Annapolis Royal, Nova Scotia. In 1711 the English sent a fleet with 12,000 men under incompetent leaders, to co-operate with the New Englanders in an attack on Quebec, while a land force moved up the Hudson valley toward Montreal. As in the previous war, the land force stalled at Lake Champlain, and the naval-military expedition turned back after some of the ships had run aground in the Gulf of St. Lawrence.

The Treaty of Utrecht (1713), which ended this war, was a significant event in the territorial history of North America. Great Britain obtained French recognition of her sovereignty over Nova Scotia and Hudson's Bay, where the great fur-trading corporation of that name had been operating since 1670. But the value of Nova Scotia was largely nullified by allowing France to retain Cape Breton Island, where Louis XV constructed Louisbourg, the 'Gibraltar of the New World.' The negotiators at Utrecht paid no attention to the southern frontier. There the Tuscarora Indians in the coastal plain of North Carolina rose against the English in 1711. South Carolina came to the aid of her neighbor, defeated the Tuscarora tribe, and carried a large part of it off to be sold as slaves; the remnant withdrew to the Iroquois country and became the sixth nation of that confederacy. The Yamassee in South Carolina also revolted, and were driven into Spanish Florida in 1715.

Although the Treaty of Utrecht did not resolve any of the power rivalries that were constantly bringing the American colonies to blows, it became an important landmark. In the first place, England, through her naval victories and the acquisition of Gibraltar and Minorca, became the greatest sea power, a power under whose aegis the English race and speech expanded into all parts of the world. Secondly, the year 1713 marks the beginning of a generation of peace, broken only by the brief King George's War, an era in which the English colonies expanded westward, drew on new sources for their population, diversified their economic life, and began to enjoy the fruits of a century of enlightenment.

V

A Half-Century of Expansion

1. NEW LANDS, NEW PEOPLE

The Treaty of Utrecht opens the last half-century of the old British empire, a period marked by change and expansion in almost every department of colonial life. Only two new continental colonies, Nova Scotia and Georgia, were founded; but immigrants poured into the other twelve, and the frontier of settlement marched westward, creating a new section, the 'Old West,' that ran along the back-country from New Hampshire to South Carolina. The empire became integrated by war and governmental reorganization but disintegrated at the same time, owing to the growing consciousness of colonists that they were Americans as well as Englishmen. Population and trade increased manyfold, and began to strain at the bonds of the Acts of Trade and Navigation. Religion took a new turn with the Great Awakening; new schools and colleges were founded; and in the Eastern section an upper class, growing in wealth and in self-confidence, acquired the refinements and the sophistication of eighteenth-century Europeans. In 1713 nobody predicted or suspected that the English colonies would ever seek union, unless in an imperial war, much less free themselves from English rule; in 1763 union if not independence was a distinct possibility.

In 1713 the population of the twelve continental colonies was nearly 360,000. In 1760, with Georgia added, it approached 1.6 million, a fourfold increase. And the area of settlement had tripled since 1713.

Whence came this vast increase, proportionally greater than that of any subsequent half-century of our history? In part from large families, for whom there was always plenty of employment; in part from immigration. The outstanding feature of this migration was its non-English character. The two most important contributions were German and Scots-Irish. Discontented Germans came to English America because the German states had no overseas possessions, and no colonies except those of the English would take foreigners. The principal groups that came over were the so-called Palatines, ruined by French invasions of the Rhenish Palatinate; the Mennonites, the Unitas Fratrum or Moravians, the Dunkards (German Quakers); and Pietists whose relation to the Lutherans was somewhat similar to that of the Methodists to the Church of England. Many of the vanguard were assisted by the English government to come to America and to obtain land grants; thousands of others came over as 'redemptioners.' These people were given free transportation from Germany or Holland by shipowners, who recouped themselves by selling their passengers as indented servants. Most Germans entered America at Philadelphia, whence they spread out fanwise into the back-country; but small groups were also to be found all the way from Dresden, Maine, to Ebenezer, Georgia. In Pennsylvania thrifty Germans took up the best land, in the Triassic belt that runs diagonally across that state, and became the most prosperous and successful farmers in North America. They brought their own language and culture, established printing presses and newspapers, and at Bethlehem, a musical tradition that eventually flowered into the annual festival devoted to the works of Johann Sebastian Bach.

Equal in importance to the German-speaking immigrants were the English- (and sometimes Gaelic-) speaking Scots-Irish from Ulster. These were largely descendants of the Scots who had colonized Northern Ireland when the English were first settling Virginia. After 1713 the pressure of the native Catholic Irish and the restrictive legislation of the British Parliament forced them to emigrate in droves. As land was dear in the Eastern colonies, these fighting Celts drifted to the frontier. By 1763 they formed the outer belt of defense against the Indians all the way from Londonderry, New Hampshire, to the upper country of South Carolina. A considerable number of southern Irish, mostly Protestants but including Catholic families like the Kavanaghs of Maine and the Carrolls of Maryland, came at the same time; but these were mostly men of property who invested in land and remained in the older-settled regions.

A third non-English strain was the French Protestant. In 1685 the revocation of the Edict of Nantes by Louis XIV destroyed their religious liberty, and sent tens of thousands of the most solid and enterprising French subjects to enrich Germany, the Netherlands, England, and the English colonies. Comparatively few Huguenots, as they were called, came to America; but those that did were of such high quality that they soon rose to positions of prominence, and acquired an influence out of proportion to their numbers. They were particularly prominent in South Carolina (Huger, Petigru), Virginia (Maury), Massachusetts (Revere), and New York (Jay, De Lancey).

After 1713 new and speculative methods of land allotment were evolved from older systems in which the profit motive was unimportant. In the seventeenth century it was possible for any immigrant to obtain free allotments in a New England township, or free farms by the head-right system in the Middle and Southern Colonies. The Crown, or the proprietor, looked for gain from annual quit-rents rather than from sales. But by 1713 the older settlers and their descendants saw no reason why they should not profit by this new flood of immigration by buying land cheap and selling dear. In New England the colonial legislatures began the practice of laying out belts of six-mile-square townships beyond the settled frontier, which were granted to groups of veterans of earlier colonial wars. Most of the veterans promptly sold their shares to a small group of proprietors, who organized, granted home lots to a selected number of pioneers, and sold part of the remaining land. In the Middle and Southern Colonies land was sold outright in small lots by the proprietors or the assemblies, and immense free grants were made (such as Lord Fairfax's vast domain of 6 million acres in Virginia, Lord Granville's grant of the northern strip of North Carolina) to English or colonial land speculators who promised to obtain settlers. Even by 1720 so much land had been taken up by these methods that the only recourse for a poor man who had not the wherewithal to satisfy a land speculator, was to 'squat' without leave on Crown or proprietary land; and to repeat the process if he were forced to move on, selling out his improvements to a later comer who had the means to pay. His descendants generally had to wait until the Revolution to secure a good title.

Governor Spotswood's gay cavalcade of the 'Knights of the Golden Horseshoe' explored the Shenandoah valley in 1716, and opened large areas of the piedmont to settlement. About 1726 Germans and Scots-Irish who had entered America at Philadelphia began to pour into this valley at Harpers Ferry. Their motive was to acquire cheap land; for William Penn's heirs, reversing his policy, charged £10 for a hundred acres, as against £2 in Maryland, or 10s by some of the Virginia speculators. The 'Old Wagon Road' up the valley became a veritable funnel of the frontier. Some pioneers settled along it and sprinkled the Shenandoah valley with log cabins and German names; others turned south, through one of the many gaps in the Blue Ridge, into the piedmont of Virginia and the Carolinas. For a long time there was an unsettled strip of piedmont. Richmond, on its eastern edge, was founded only in 1729, but during the eighteenth century small farmers and indented servants from the tidewater pushed into that region and the great valley beyond.

In North Carolina the defeat of the Tuscarora opened up not only the coastal plain but part of the piedmont, and that colony increased sixteenfold in population between 1713 and 1760. At the latter date it contained more people than New York, where Iroquois mastery of the Mohawk valley and the feudal institutions of the Hudson river patroons retarded settlement.

The important social fact of this settlement of the Old West was the building up of a new internal tension in many of the colonies. South of New England and New York, the older-settled region was English in race and Anglican or Quaker in religion; the Old West was a mixture of German, Scots-Irish, and English in race, and either Presbyterian, Baptist, or German sectarian in religion. The eastern belt of settlement controlled the assemblies, often neglected or discriminated against the frontier, building up a West-East antagonism that broke out, later, in movements like the Paxton Boys, the Regulators, and Shays's Rebellion.

2. GEORGIA AND NOVA SCOTIA

The eighteenth century is full of contradictions and paradoxes. This happens in every age when new modes of thought and action, new forms of society and industry, are struggling to emerge from the womb of the past. On the one hand, this was an era of formalism, indifference, and decay in the established churches; on the other, it saw the birth of new religious and philosophical movements, such as Methodism in England, Jansenism in France, the 'natural religion' that stems from Newton, the idealism associated with Berkeley, and the rational philosophy that prepared the way for the French Revolution. In England the age was one of social smugness, brutality, and complacency toward poverty and other social evils; yet it was also an age of benevolence and humanitarianism, when the first effective protests were made against the slave trade, high infant mortality, and imprisonment for debt. While the colonies as a whole were exploited for the benefit of ruling classes in England, a steady flow of charitable funds reached America from England for the foundation of libraries, schools, and colleges, and for the conversion and education of Indians and Negroes.

The new colony of Georgia was the result of a combination of several charitable individuals and forces for a single well-defined object. Thomas Bray, 'the great little man,' a small but energetic Anglican clergyman, initiated several of these schemes. Sent out to Maryland in 1699 to organize the Church of England there, he was impressed with the dearth of good books, and the difficulty for colonial clergymen to keep abreast of recent literature. Accordingly he founded parochial libraries for each of the 30 Anglican parishes of Maryland, many more for the Anglican churches from Boston to Charleston, South Carolina; and a number of laymen's libraries as well. These were the first semi-public libraries in the colonies after those of the colleges; for Dr. Bray insisted that 'any inhabitant' should have the right to 'borrow any Book out of the Library.' Returning to England, Dr. Bray around 1700 founded two great missionary societies which still exist: the Society for the Propagation of the Gospel, and the Society for the Promotion of Christian Knowledge. Later he organized his particular friends as 'The Associates of Dr. Bray,' for carrying out other benevolent schemes.

One of the four Associates, a London parishioner of Dr. Bray, was a very different type of man from the busy little parson. Captain Thomas Coram, a big, tough, two-fisted shipmaster with a tender heart, made a fortune trading with the colonies after he retired from the sea, and devoted it to various charitable enterprises. Moved by compassion for abandoned infants, bastards of sailors' drabs who were left by the roadside in the hope that some passer-by might take pity on them, he founded the great Foundling Hospital of London in 1735, yet yearned to do still more for suffering humanity. Already, in 1717, Coram had planned to have Maine east of the Kennebec detached from the Province of Massachusetts Bay and erected into a colony called Georgia, with the object of providing new homes for discharged soldiers and other unemployed. But various claimants to Maine under earlier grants frustrated his scheme, and 'Georgia' moved south.

James Edward Oglethorpe, a young gentleman of rank and fortune, left Oxford to fight under Eugene of Savoy in the war of Germany against Turkey. After that war he entered Parliament, where, 'driven by strong benevolence of soul' (as Alexander Pope wrote of him), he served on a committee to inquire into the state of jails. That state was bad indeed; so horrible that a released prisoner was apt to be a broken man for life. The worst part of the system was imprisonment for debt. A debtor once committed to jail could not be released until his debt was paid, and in jail he had no means of discharging it; if released by charity after many years, he was usually incapable of supporting himself. It occurred to Oglethorpe that the way to meet this social evil was to assist poor debtors to emigrate to America under conditions that would enable them to start afresh and lead happy and useful lives. At his instance the Associates of Dr. Bray petitioned the Crown for a grant of land in Carolina, and then founded a new corporation, which obtained a propri-etary grant of the land between the Savannah and the Altamaha rivers, under the name of Georgia.

These Trustees of Georgia, men prominent in English society, politics, and business, financed the biggest publicity campaign that any English colony ever enjoyed. Inspired accounts of the healthy climate and fertile soil of Georgia were liberally paid for in the now flourishing newspaper press of London. As several of the trustees were members of Parliament, they were able to obtain grants of public money, in order to transport and settle the deserving poor. So Georgia began as a colony de luxe, the pet project of wealthy and powerful philanthropists. The royal charter created it a proprietary colony with limited tenure; after 21 years the jurisdiction should revert to the Crown, which appointed the customs officials from the first. English officials welcomed the colony as a cheap buffer for the Carolina frontier.

General Oglethorpe, appointed the first governor by the trustees, came out with the first shipload of settlers in 1733 and founded Savan-nah. During the first eight years of the colony the trustees sent over 1810 charity colonists, of whom almost half were Germans, Scots, and Swiss, and the rest English. In the same period 1021 persons arrived on their own; 92 of these were Jews. Each settler received 50 acres of land free, and the trustees forbade the importation of slaves and rum. The charity settlers were not all poor debtors or jailbirds; many were small trades-people and artisans, for the trustees wished to establish a colony in which many occupations were represented, as in New England. Unfortunately, the climate and soil of coastal Georgia did not lend themselves to these liberal views.

Friendly relations were cultivated with the near-by Creek, Choctaw, and Chickasaw Indians, who gladly joined General Oglethorpe and the Scots Highland regiment he brought out with him, in an attack on Spanish St. Augustine, Florida (June 1740). That campaign was a failure, as was a Spanish counterattack two years later. Oglethorpe then returned to England, but continued his benevolent interest in Georgia, which properly regards him as a colonial founder in a class with Penn and Shaftesbury.

Georgia did not prosper under this benevolent despotism of her trustees. The settlers found it impossible to live off 50 acres, or without slave labor; and having no quinine, rum became a necessity of life in the malarial lowlands. The contrast with South Carolina, where white colonists were growing rich through applying slave labor to rice and indigo plantations, made the 50-acre freeholders envious and discontented, and the more ambitious drifted to the older colony. The trustees gradually liberalized the conditions of land-owning, removed the slavery and liquor prohibitions, and granted an assembly in 1751; but the colony lost many people through fever and removal — the population was only 1735 whites and 349 Negroes in 1752. In that year, when the twenty years' proprietorship lapsed, the trustees were glad to turn Georgia over to the Crown, which assumed almost all expenses of government. Gradually the economy of Georgia was assimilated to the rice-plantation pattern of South Carolina, and eventually it received an up-country population by way of the intermountain trough. At the outbreak of the Revolution Georgia was still the weakest and least populous of the Thirteen Colonies; but the enterprise cannot be considered a failure in organized philanthropy, for it did assist several thousand people, whose lives would have been wasted in England, to a new life in the New World.

Captain Coram, although he had consented to serve as a trustee of Georgia, never approved of planting a charity settlement so far south; and he began agitating for a northern counterpart in Nova Scotia. He was almost at the point of having Nova Scotia made a colony of unemployed artisans in 1745, when King George's War broke out and the scheme was postponed. At the end of that war, in 1749, Halifax was founded by the British government with 1400 settlers, mostly charity colonists like those of Georgia. The Crown designed Nova Scotia, its fourteenth continental colony, as a bastion against the French, just as it viewed Georgia as a shield against the Spanish. Most of the pioneers of Nova Scotia during the next quarter-century came from New England; but the British government did so much for the people of that colony that in 1765 Nova Scotia obeyed the Stamp Act, and in 1775 remained loyal to the empire.

3. INDUSTRY AND COMMERCE

Despite the increasing controls of the imperial system — perhaps to some extent because of them — colonial industry and commerce prospered as never before, during the half-century following the Treaty of Utrecht. The key to this prosperity was a rise in prices for colonial produce in the British Isles and continental Europe. This rise kept so far ahead of production that the fourfold increase of population in the continental colonies did not dilute prosperity.

The increased European demand for colonial produce hit first the West Indies; and West Indian prosperity almost automatically affected the continental colonies. The French West Indies were an important source of supply of cheap molasses, which New England made into rum, and they provided a valuable market for fish, lumber, and farm products from the Northern colonies. The British island planters, annoyed by the competition of the French colonies, induced Parliament in 1733 to pass the Sugar or Molasses Act, charging a prohibitory duty on foreign molasses and sugar entering English colonies. By that time, rum distilleries had become so numerous in continental towns from Portsmouth to Philadelphia that the French Antilles, where molasses was cheapest and most abundant, were necessary to them as a source of supply. The act was simply ignored; shipmasters obtained false invoices at Jamaica to cover their shipments from French islands.

So brisk was the demand for flour in the West Indies that within a few years the export of grain and flour from Chesapeake Bay ports pushed tobacco for first place. Baltimore was founded in 1729, largely because Jones Falls turned mills which ground the wheat of Pennsylvania and up-country Maryland into flour. However, Philadelphia remained the principal place of export for grain and other provisions. Virginia recovered her ancient prosperity with a rise in the price of tobacco and shared in the flour trade as well. And, as in the previous century, the West Indies

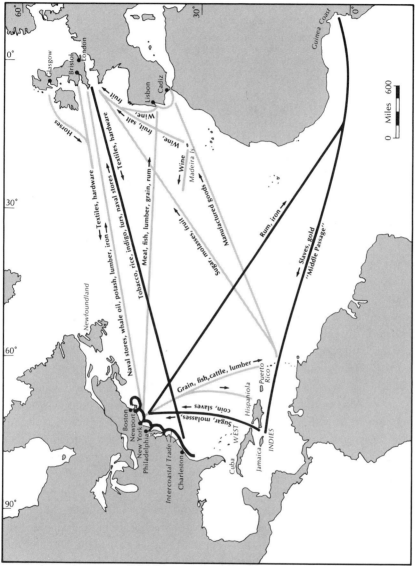

COLONIAL TRADE ROUTES

trade was vital for southern New England. The islands appeared to have an indefinite capacity to absorb salt fish, wood for boxes, barrels, and house construction, work horses, salt meat, and ground vegetables. In northern New England and North Carolina, the export to England of ship timber and naval stores, such as pitch and tar, was of great importance.

In South Carolina fortunes were built up out of rice and indigo a few years after the Treaty of Utrecht. In the year 1731, over 200 vessels cleared from Charleston, carrying 42,000 barrels (or about 21 million pounds) of rice, 14,000 barrels of pitch, tar, and turpentine, about 250,000 deer skins, and a large quantity of provisions. Parliament in 1729 allowed rice to be sent directly to all European ports south of Cape Finisterre, and by 1771 South Carolina's rice exports were threefold what they had been in 1731. Indigo, stimulated by a production bounty from the British Parliament, was introduced into South Carolina from the foreign West Indies about 1740, and quickly produced a crop of 'indigo millionaires.' Both rice and indigo required a substantial capital and a large labor force for profitable cultivation, thus accelerating the development of slavery and the African slave trade. The products of these Southern colonies found a ready market in Britain, but New England and the Middle Colonies imported more from England than they exported. To pay for these imports, the Northern colonies traded not only with the West Indies but with Newfoundland, southern Europe, and the Wine Islands.

New York was still the principal place of export for furs. The merchants of Albany had a monopoly of trade with the Six Nations, who by this time were acting as middlemen, and obtaining their peltry from an extensive watershed in the Far West. Governor Burnet founded the trading post at Oswego and attempted to break up a secondary activity of Albany merchants, supplying rum and woolens to England's rivals in Canada; but Albany had sufficient influence in London to have Governor Burnet removed to Massachusetts, and the prohibition repealed. As a result, there was a gradual infiltration of French influence among the Iroquois, which broke down what contemporaries called the 'impenetrable fence' around the Middle Colonies and lessened the usefulness of these Indians to the British empire in subsequent colonial wars.

Although the English ruling classes did not object to the colonists' indulging in crude manufacturing processes, such as milling grain, distilling molasses into rum, and making candles from spermaceti, they attempted to suppress colonial competition with any leading English industry, which by mercantilist doctrine should have a monopoly of the colonial market. Emigration of skilled artisans to the colonies with the tools of their trade was forbidden, but not strictly enforced. Three acts of Parliament were aimed at protecting English staples. The Woolens Act of 1699 forbade colonial woolen cloth to be sold outside the place or plantation where it was woven; but as most rural families carded, spun, and wove their own wool, this caused no hardship in America. On complaint of London's Worshipful Company of Hatters that the colonists were beginning to make up their own furs into the wide-brimmed beaver hats of the era, instead of importing headgear from England, a law was passed in 1732 limiting the number of hatter apprentices and banning exports of hats from one colony to another. And in 1750 the British iron interests induced Parliament to remove British duties from colonial pig and bar iron, in the hope of encouraging Americans to supplant the importations from Sweden to England. The same act forbade the establishment of new slitting mills (which slit bar iron into nail rods) or plating forges using a trip hammer, or steel tool furnaces, in order to protect the export of English ironmongery and steel. But this law had little effect. It was so flagrantly disregarded that Pennsylvania, New Jersey, and Massachusetts even granted bounties for new plants after the law was on the statute books! By 1760 there was a thriving colonial iron industry wherever a combination of surface iron ore, wood for smelting, and water power was found. So, even though the acts restraining manufactures were restrictive in motive, they were hardly so in practice; and before indulging in virtuous indignation over them, we should remember that it was formerly the policy of Congress to levy tariffs or set quotas on Philippine products, such as sugar, which competed with those of the United States.

Far more serious than all Acts of Trade and Navigation as brakes on colonial enterprise were English restrictions on the colonial use of money, and attempts of colonial assemblies to get around them. The treatment of the colonial money problem by Parliament was both selfish and irritating. No precious metals were produced in any of the English colonies, and the balance of trade with the mother country was against them; so their want of metallic currency was constant. Yet Parliament refused to allow the export of English coin to English colonies, or to allow them to mint coinage of their own [1] from the foreign bullion that they obtained through trade with the West Indies.

Colonial assemblies endeavored to meet this situation in a variety of ways. Each colony or group of colonies established a currency of account, 'lawful money' as it was called, in pounds, shillings, and pence that were worth less than sterling in England. The general standard for this 'lawful money' was the Spanish-milled dollar or 'piece of eight' weighing 17½ pennyweight, which was the commonest foreign coin that came into the continent from the Caribbean, and so eventually was chosen as standard for the United States silver dollar. The Spanish dollar was worth 4s 6d in terms of English sterling, but in South Carolina and Georgia it was valued at 4s 8d, in New England and Virginia at 6s, in New York at 8s, and in the other colonies at 7s 6d. The colonial assemblies fondly imagined that by this overvaluation of foreign coins in terms of sterling, these coins would stay in the colonies and not be re-exported; and that the colony which overvalued them most would acquire the whole stock. But the only result was a corresponding mark-up of all prices of English goods in the local £ s d of account.

Since overvaluing the Spanish dollar and undervaluing sterling did not help the colonists, they resorted to paper money. Personal promissory notes, tobacco-warehouse receipts, and bills of exchange had long been used as money in the colonies, even for very small sums. In Virginia, for instance, a man might pay his reckoning at a tavern with an order for the amount on the London merchant who handled his tobacco. From this it was a short step for the Massachusetts Assembly in 1690 to issue official promissory notes to pay for Sir William Phips's expedition against Quebec, in anticipation of loot and of tax collections. The loot did not materialize and the taxes were not sufficient to 'sink' the notes, so they stayed in circulation a couple of years. Before the close of Queen Anne's War eight or nine colonies had followed suit. This earlier colonial paper currency was generally legal tender for taxes only, and though not redeemable in silver it did not depreciate greatly, because the colonial governments bought it back from the holders fairly promptly.

These 'bills of credit' (whence we derive our phrase, a dollar 'bill') so well relieved the currency shortage in time of war that a demand grew

1. The Massachusetts 'pine-tree' coinage, begun in 1652 without authorization, ended in 1684 when the Bay Colony lost its charter.

up for issuing them in time of peace. The American farmer believed then (as some still believe) that currency inflation, raising prices of farm produce, would benefit him and ease his burden of debt. Massachusetts and South Carolina, which had borne a disproportionate share of the war burden, continued issuing bills after the Treaty of Utrecht, and in the southern colony the two houses of assembly, the council representing the creditor-mercantile, and the commons the debtor-farmer interest, became completely deadlocked on the subject. In some colonies, notably Pennsylvania, where Benjamin Franklin urged the value of the system in a growing country, issues of paper currency were promptly redeemed, and depreciated very little. They were, in effect, a lien on future prosperity, like government loans today. But in a small colony like Rhode Island, whose possibilities of future growth were limited, one issue succeeded another, until prices in terms of paper money rose about thirty-fold.

South Carolina thought up another scheme that the farmers liked even better — the so-called Land Bank. Under this system the colony, instead of issuing bills in the first instance to merchants who furnished government supplies, lent them to farmers on landed security. It was a wonderful bonus for the land-poor planter — practically a gift: for if he could not redeem the paper debt, he and his fellows could generally induce the assembly to 'stay' collection, or to let him discharge it in produce at an inflated value. In order to make the bills effective, the assemblies had to declare them legal tender for all payments. But nothing that a colonial assembly did in the way of fiat money could legally discharge debts due to English merchants; hence it was the country storekeeper or seaport merchant who suffered from this sort of legislation and sought redress in England. Royal governors were always instructed to veto paper-money laws unless they provided for prompt redemption out of taxes; and when the governor was forced by political pressure to disobey his instructions, the law was disallowed by the Privy Council.

Although few colonial assemblies showed sufficient wisdom and restraint to be entrusted with so dangerous a power as the issuance of paper money, the British government did nothing to provide a substitute. By forbidding the colonies to import English coin, or to mint the bullion they acquired from the Spanish West Indies into coin, they made some other form of currency necessary, and inflation inevitable.

4. SOCIETY AND RELIGION

While the Thirteen Colonies were expanding their trade and population and increasing their wealth and diversifying their racial content, their social and intellectual ties with England were becoming closer. Every royal governor's mansion provided a little court where the latest European fashions were displayed and London coffee-house gossip was repeated. Transatlantic travel, except during three or four winter months, was relatively safe in the small packet ships and 'constant traders' of the day. Merchants in the seaport towns made a point of visiting London every few years, and sent their sons on long voyages as supercargoes; many sons of rich Southern planters attended school in England; or, if they studied at a colonial college, took a medical course at the University of Edinburgh or read law in the Inns of Court. Even so middle-class an American as Benjamin Franklin managed to spend many years in England, and was no worse an American for that. English books and periodicals reached the colonies only a few months late. Between 1713 and 1773, thirteen colonial Americans were accorded the highest scientific honor in the English-speaking world, a fellowship in the Royal Society of London.

Commerce and land speculation were the principal ways to wealth in all the colonies, Virginia included; although some large fortunes were made in the Chesapeake colonies and South Carolina by planting combined with official position. Every year, new families rose through wealth into the class of gentry.

Professional architects were very few; Peter Harrison of Newport, Rhode Island, who catered to the slave-trading merchants of that flourishing town, appears to have been the earliest in the colonies. When Harvard College wanted a new building in 1764, Governor Bernard obligingly drew the plans. Local builders, with the aid of books of design from England, erected mansions in the balanced, well-proportioned Georgian style, and churches modeled on those of Sir Christopher Wren in London. Even the middling sort of town and farm houses reflected the 'century of enlightenment.' When young Ben Franklin, around 1720, cracked his head on a low smoke-blackened beam in the Reverend Cotton Mather's house in Boston, that sententious cleric gave him a maxim that stood him well through life — 'When you come to a low place, stoop!' Had it been a new house, there would have been one saying of 'Poor Richard' the less; for the beam would have cleared Ben's head, and also have been concealed under plaster. After 1720 paint was used freely to preserve the exterior and adorn the interior of wooden dwelling houses; square-paned sash windows replaced the leaded casements of the seventeenth century, and white paneled doors surmounted by graceful fanlights replaced the massive nail-studded oak portals that were designed to resist Indian tomahawks. Fireplaces were built much smaller, now that wood was less plentiful, and chimneys were placed at the ends instead of the center, allowing a vista from front door to garden. Gambrel roofs with dormer windows afforded good space in the attic story; the greater mansions were built in three stories, surmounted by a low roof and a classic balustrade. In the South we have the first colonnaded porches, as at Mount Vernon, a balanced layout with detached offices and kitchen (for the eighteenth century was becoming susceptible to smells), and landscaped grounds. In the back-country and new settlements from Maine to Georgia the log cabin, made either of round logs or of squared timbers well mortised together, and chinked with chips and clay, became universal.

The reconstruction of Williamsburg, Virginia, most of whose buildings were erected after 1720, affords a living picture of a colonial court town. Broad streets, well laid out; a governor's palace with formal garden; a capitol or state house with chambers for the two houses of assembly, and offices for other colonial officials; a tavern with a large room for banquets, concerts, stage plays, and dances; a Georgian church with high-backed square pews; fair brick dwelling houses with extensive gardens; and, of course, a jail. Even colonial towns of 2000 or 3000 inhabitants afforded more social amenities in the eighteenth century than do American cities today of many times their population. There would always be a market house and merchants' exchange, a tavern where the latest English gazettes were taken in and where clubs of gentlemen or tradesmen met to talk, smoke, drink, and sing; a dancing assembly for the social elite; a circulating library; and, in five or six places, a musical society. Philadelphia had a theater as early as 1724, and in 1749 an excellent English company of players began trouping through the colonies south of New England; for in the Puritan colonies only private theatricals were permitted. College commencements, horse races, and fairs gave entertainment to everyone. Williamsburg, for instance, established two annual fairs for livestock, goods, and merchandise. In 1739 the *Virginia Gazette* announced:

> And for the Entertainment and Diversion of all Gentlemen and others, that shall resort thereto, the following PRIZES are given to be contended for, at the Fair, viz.
>
> A Saddle of 40s value, to be run for, once round the Mile Course, adjacent to this City, by any Horse, Mare or Gelding, carrying Horseman's Weight, and allowing Weight for Inches.
>
> A Pair of Silver Buckles, value 20s, to be run for by Men, from the College to the Capitol. . . . A Pair of Pumps to be danc'd for by Men.
>
> A handsome Firelock to be exercis'd for; and given to the Person that performs the Manual Exercise best.
>
> A Pig, with his tail soap'd to be run after; and to be given to the Person that catches him, and lift him off the Ground fairly by the Tail.

A common interest in field sports, boxing, and horse racing (perhaps the main reason why England escaped a bloody revolution) gave all classes in Virginia a fellow-feeling. The period from 1740 to the French and Indian War was the golden age of the Old Dominion. Peace reigned over the land, high prices ruled for tobacco, immigrants poured into the back-country; and the Virginia of Thackeray and Vachel Lindsay — 'Land of the gauntlet and the glove' — came into being. Living in Virginia at that time was like riding on the sparkling crest of a great wave just before it breaks and spreads into dull, shallow pools. In that wholesome rural society with lavish hospitality and a tradition of public spirit, was bred the 'Virginia dynasty' which (with some help from elsewhere, one must admit!) would guide the destinies of the young republic yet unborn.

This period was marked by increasing missionary effort on the part of the Anglican Church, among both the English colonists and the Indians, conducted largely by ministers sent out by the Society for the Propagation of the Gospel. These efforts seldom reached the Old West, which was served mainly by Baptists, Presbyterians, or German parsons; and the Church of England's organization in the colonies always remained decentralized and haphazard because of the lack of a bishop. All English colonies belonged to the diocese of London. Bishop Sherlock proposed in 1749 that the English government provide a number of colonial bishops; but this notion provoked a violent controversy from colonists, both

Anglican and dissenters, who feared increased control, taxes, and tithes; so nothing was done.

In Rhode Island and in the second group of colonies founded after 1660, where toleration prevailed, dissenting sects enjoyed a large measure of religious liberty; but in the rest of New England, Baptists, Quakers, and Anglicans were constantly struggling against being forced to contribute to the Congregational churches. In Maryland the Catholics were severely discriminated against by the Established Church of England, now that the lords Baltimore had turned Protestant; and in Virginia the dissenters (in the English sense) were taxed for the Anglican Church, which had a monopoly of performing marriages. By mid-century, however, the dissenters in every colony had made tremendous gains, especially among the common people, through the religious revival known as the Great Awakening. This was the first important and spontaneous movement of the entire English colonial population.

The Great Awakening began in three different colonies. Theodore Frelinghuysen, a German parson of the Dutch Reformed Church, started a revival in the Raritan valley, New Jersey, in 1719. William Tennent, a Presbyterian Scot, in 1736 established the so-called Log College for revivalists at Neshaminy, Pa. In 1734 Jonathan Edwards, graduate of Yale and minister of Northampton, Mass., began his famous imprecatory sermons in order to recall the people to a sense of sin, and bring them to that sense of communion with God which evangelicals call conversion. His description of this revival, *A Faithful Narration of the Surprising Work of God in the Conversion of Many Hundred Souls in Northampton* (Boston, 1737), was promptly reprinted in London and Edinburgh, translated into German and Dutch, and became, as it still is, a classic. John Wesley read it afoot between London and Oxford. 'Surely this is the Lord's doing,' he wrote in his journal; presently he began to obtain the same effects from his own preaching, and in a little while the Methodist Church was born. George Whitefield, an eloquent young minister sent out to Georgia by the trustees, read *A Faithful Narration* in Savannah, and his amazing career as a revivalist dates from that hour.

Whitefield began the second phase of the Great Awakening by preaching at Philadelphia in 1739, and touring New England in 1740. In 73 days he rode 800 miles and preached 130 sermons. His voice could be heard by 20,000 people in the open air. He made violent gestures, danced about the pulpit, roared and ranted, greatly to the delight of the common people who were tired of gentlemanly, unemotional sermons from college-bred ministers. He introduced the second stage of revivalism with which many parts of America are still familiar — sinners becoming vocally and violently 'saved.' Whitefield preached, as he explained, with 'much Flame, Clearness and Power. . . . The People were exceedingly attentive. Tears trickled down their cheeks.' Gilbert Tennent, son of the proprietor of the Log College, and several score of lay exhorters and itinerant preachers followed Whitefield. The 'New Lights,' as their followers called themselves, proved to be the first blossom of that amazing tree that was to bear the Shakers and the Mormons, Holy Rollers and the Millerites, and a score of other sects. Not one colony or county was unaffected by the Great Awakening. Intermittently, but over the entire decade of the 1740's, it raged through New England, the Middle Colonies, and the South.

The Awakening brought more people into the Protestant churches and split them up, setting congregations against their ministers, and reviving intolerance. Connecticut, for instance, repealed its toleration act in 1743. After ignorant and emotional people had tasted the strong drink of revivalism they cared no more for traditional worship; new congregations were formed, some of which died out after a few years, while others became Baptist, Methodist, or 'New Light' Presbyterian. Calmer souls sought refuge in the Anglican churches or Quaker meetings, the least affected by the Awakening.

Jonathan Edwards stayed with the movement, although he deplored its excesses; but the backwash of reaction drove him from the pleasant Connecticut valley of his ministry. He became a missionary to the Indians in Stockbridge, and there, in the solitude of the wilderness, wrote three of his greatest works — *The Nature of True Virtue, Original Sin,* and *Freedom of the Will*. Edwards faced, as few modern men have dared or cared to face, the problem of evil and the problem of free will. The system of Calvinist theology that he and his disciple Stephen Hopkins worked out, emphasized the splendid but terrible omnipotence of Almighty God and the miserable impotence of sinful man. And certain passages in his works express more effectively the beauty of holiness and the supreme importance of man's relation to God than any other in American literature.

Although the more extreme religious enthusiasts were anti-intellectual, and even encouraged book-burning, the Great Awakening gave to the colonies three new colleges; for the 'New Lights' soon perceived that without seminaries to educate an evangelical ministry, their movement would be killed by ignorant hot-gospelers. The College of New Jersey at Princeton (1746), the first colonial school of higher learning to be founded since Yale (1701), was the Presbyterian seminary, replacing the unorganized Log College; Dartmouth (1769) was founded by Eleazar Wheelock, a disciple of Edwards and Whitefield, ostensibly for the training of Indian preachers; and the Baptists, who hitherto had been without an educated ministry, were driven by competition to build the College of Rhode Island (later Brown University), at Providence in 1764. King's College (Columbia University), founded in New York City in 1754, was Anglican; Queen's College (Rutgers University), founded at New Brunswick, N. J., in 1766, was Dutch Reformed. The Philadelphia Academy (University of Pennsylvania), founded as a secondary school in 1740, was the only colonial college whose impetus and control was wholly non-sectarian, although promoters affiliated with library companies were active in the founding of Rhode Island and King's. These men sought to encourage independent inquiry free of clerical influence.

All these colleges were very small, according to modern standards; the largest student body was 200, and the record colonial graduating class numbered 63. Several, including the older William and Mary (1693), had to maintain preparatory schools in order to render freshmen fit to follow college studies. Princeton, Yale, and Harvard offered graduate training in theology; Philadelphia and King's established medical schools in 1765 and 1767. In the two decades before the Revolution, increasing emphasis was given to modern languages and science, although science instructors were hard to find. But the great majority of undergraduates followed a prescribed course in rhetoric, philosophy, mathematics, and the ancient classics (including a good deal of political theory), which proved an excellent preparation for public life. Out of 56 signers of the Declaration of Independence, 29 were alumni of colonial or British schools of higher learning; and most of the important framers of state and federal constitutions were college-trained men.

Nevertheless, only one of the three greatest Americans of the age, Jonathan Edwards, was a college graduate. George Washington (born 1732) attained his superb poise, self-discipline, and character that met every test, partly through manly sports, and partly through contact with his gentle neighbors, the Fairfaxes of Belvoir, who employed him as a surveyor in his young manhood. They introduced him to the Stoic philosophy that breathes through Plutarch's *Lives,* Seneca's *Dialogues,* and Addison's *Cato:*

> Turn up thy eyes to Cato!
> There may'st thou see to what a godlike height
> The Roman virtues lift up mortal man,
> While good, and just, and anxious for his friends,
> He's still severely bent against himself;
> Renouncing sleep, and rest, and food, and ease,
> He strives with thirst and hunger, toil and heat . . .

Benjamin Franklin, born in 1706, three years younger than Edwards, was the very antithesis of New England's saint in character and career. Essentially worldly and practical, he found little time for theology or philosophy, and none for sports. Yet his moral maxims in *Poor Richard's Almanack* provided ethics for the unchurched, and he organized schools and libraries that others might learn. His industry enabled him to accumulate a competence early, after which the application of his inquiring mind to problems made him a leading scientist of that era. His pioneer work on electricity was of the highest significance, and led eventually, after countless experiments by others, to the dynamo, the telephone, and radio communication. Franklin suggested or initiated theories that required a century to verify and realize. His passion for improvement made him the first inventor of his time. Finding that most of the heat from open fireplaces went up the chimney, he designed the 'Pennsylvania fireplace' or Franklin stove in 1740. Worried by the fires set by lightning, he invented the lightning rod. In an age when night air was popularly supposed to breed distempers, he advised people to sleep with open windows, in order to avoid colds. And during long ocean passages under sail, of which he made many, he thought up improvements in the mariner's art, many of which have since been adopted. He was over a century ahead of naval architects in pointing out that wind resistance should be taken into account when designing the hulls and rigging of vessels, and that the same amount of canvas, if divided into a number of triangular sails, gives more speed than a few big square sails.

Franklin knew the art of living better than any other American or European of his day. He was on good terms with the world that he was eager to improve. He urged reform with a joke and a smile and never lost his temper with unprogressive people who preferred the ways of their ancestors. He loved music, played four different instruments, and invented a fifth, the glass harmonica, for which even Mozart and Beethoven composed music. The most eminent statesmen, scientists, and men of letters in England and France consorted with Franklin, and valued his conversation; yet he never ceased to be a good democrat. Unlike many clever and successful men who have risen from lowly origins, he believed in the common people; so they believed in him. He certainly knew more people, and more types of people, than anyone else in his day; for colonial Philadelphia, as we have seen, was a microcosm of the America of the future. In that future, Franklin firmly believed. Of all Americans of his day, he was the greatest optimist; yet his vision fell short of the reality.

Franklin's college was the newspaper office, which still is an effective seat of education. Colonial journalism began with the colorless *Boston News-Letter* of 1704; within twenty years James Franklin, with teen-aged Ben as printer's devil and anonymous contributor, brought out *The New-England Courant*. 'Mr. Coranto,' as this paper called itself, was a sprightly sheet that attacked Harvard College and the Mather dynasty, even when those clerical autocrats, far ahead of public opinion, were advocating inoculation for smallpox. But when Mr. Coranto attacked the Massachusetts assembly, he got in trouble; and Ben left Boston for Philadelphia. There and in London, Franklin continued his trade of printer; and he was one of the first to sense the use of almanacs to enlighten farm folk who could not afford a newspaper. In 1725 there were only five newspapers in the continental colonies; by 1765 there were twenty-five, two of them in German, and every colony but Delaware and New Jersey had at least one. All were four-page weekly journals, filled largely with foreign news clipped from London papers, but carrying a certain amount of local items, assembly debates, advertisements of runaway slaves and 'fine assortments' of English and West Indian goods for sale.

Libel laws in all the colonies were severe, and governments had to be criticized by innuendo rather than directly; yet one of the landmarks in the long struggle for the freedom of the press was the Zenger case in New York. John Peter Zenger, publisher of *The New-York Weekly Journal,* lent his columns to criticism of Governor Cosby, who haled him into court for false and scandalous libel. Andrew Hamilton, an aged Philadelphia lawyer who defended Zenger, offered the then unheard of de-

fense that the articles complained of told the truth! Chief Justice De
Lancey rejected this contention and insisted on the English common law
rule that the greater the truth the greater the libel. Hamilton countered
with a ringing appeal to the jury, declaring that the cause of English
liberty, not merely the liberty of a poor printer, was at stake, and won a
verdict of 'not guilty' in August 1735. Although the Zenger verdict failed
either to alter the common law or to provide the basis for a fully developed philosophy of freedom of expression, it encouraged editors to criti-
cize governors, and an account of the trial published by Zenger the
following year became, save perhaps for Cato's *Letters*, the best-known
source of libertarian ideas in England and America in the eighteenth
century. Gouverneur Morris called the Zenger case 'the morning star of
that liberty which subsequently revolutionized America.'

It also marked the rise of a lawyer class. In the seventeenth century
there was no legal profession in the colonies except in New York and
Maryland; practitioners were regarded with contempt, and usually deserved it. The increase of commerce brought more litigation and the
need for skilled lawyers; and in one colony after another the men of best
repute who had defended clients in the courts formed a bar, with rules
of entry and of conduct that had the force of law. Prominent lawyers
naturally were elected to the assemblies, where they were very clever in
tying up the royal governors in legal knots, and making every local
dispute a matter of the 'liberties of Englishmen.' So, when weightier
matters were at issue in the 1760's, the legal profession as well as the
press was prepared.

5. THE LAST COLONIAL WARS, 1739–63

The last colonial war began in 1739 with the 'War of Jenkins' Ear'
between England and Spain,[2] which was fought on the Georgia-Florida
border and in the Caribbean. There the principal events were raids on
Porto Bello and Cartagena by Admiral Vernon, with thousands of volunteers from the continental colonies, nine-tenths of whom succumbed to
yellow fever. One survivor was George Washington's elder brother, who
named Mount Vernon after the popular but unlucky admiral.

In 1744 the Anglo-Spanish conflict merged into the War of the Aus-

2. So called because Parliament declared war after being outraged by a smuggler
named Jenkins having his ears cropped by a Spanish coast guard.

trian Succession, and France again came to grips with England in North America, where the conflict was called King George's War. Again there was *la petite guerre* along the New York-New England border; and *la grande guerre* also, but not according to the book. The New Englanders' attack on the strong French fortress of Louisbourg, planned by Governor Shirley and led by a Maine merchant, Sir William Pepperell, was one of the maddest schemes in the history of modern warfare, a sort of large-scale 'commando'; but it worked. The Yankee yokels who pitched camp before the 'impregnable' fortress refused to obey any of the rules of eighteenth-century warfare, and the French governor was so baffled and alarmed by their odd antics that he surrendered (1745). By the Treaty of Aachen, which ended this war in 1748, the English restored Louisbourg to France in return for Madras; the disappointment of New England was assuaged by the Crown's paying the entire expenses of the expedition.

This treaty was only a truce in the final conflict for mastery in North America. In Virginia, Thomas Lee, president of the council, organized in 1747 the first Ohio Company, with the object of opening a route from the Potomac to the Ohio for Indian trade, and making a profit from Western land. Shortly after, the Loyal Company and the Greenbrier Company were organized by other prominent Virginians, such as Peter Jefferson, the father of Thomas, Dr. Thomas Walker, and Thomas Nelson; while George Fairfax and George Washington's elder brothers were taken into the Ohio Company. These rival ventures constituted a threat to communications between Canada, the Illinois country, and Louisiana, which the French could not afford to ignore.

In 1749 the governor of Canada sent Céleron de Bienville with several hundred Canadians and Indians in a fleet of batteaux and canoes to take possession of the Ohio valley. They carried over from Lake Erie to Lake Chautauqua, paddled down the Allegheny river past the site of Pittsburgh into the Ohio, down the Ohio and up the Miami, and returned to Canada by the Maumee river and Lake Erie. This expedition was followed up in 1753 by the Marquis Duquesne, who established a chain of log forts on the Allegheny and upper Ohio.

French Canada had a population of only 50,000 or 60,000 farmers and fur-traders in 1750 when the English colonies numbered 1.25 million, and the pretension of France to reserve for herself the unsettled parts of North America was one that the English could hardly be expected to admit. Governor Dinwiddie of Virginia sent young George Washington up to the Allegheny to protest, in 1753. Protest being unavailing, the governor commissioned George (aged 22) lieutenant-colonel of Virginia militia, and the next year sent him with 150 men to forestall the French at the forks of the Ohio. But the French had arrived first, and built Fort Duquesne on the site of Pittsburgh. At Great Meadows in western Pennsylvania, our young lieutenant-colonel, unmindful that one must always let the enemy make the first aggression, fired a shot on a French force under Jumonville that began the last and greatest of the colonial wars. The enemy rallied and Washington's troops had to capitulate and go home; for this was only a cold war — not declared for two years more.

Both Virginia and New England were eager to call it a hot war and get going. Virginia wished to preserve her ancient charter rights to all the territory west and northwest of her settled area; Massachusetts was still aiming to clear the French out of Canada. But the governments of George II and Louis XV hoped to localize hostilities. So in the fall of 1754 George II sent General Braddock to America with only two regiments, and the powers of commander in chief.

In the meantime eight of the Thirteen Colonies had made an attempt to agree on a plan of union for common defense. The Board of Trade instructed the royal governors in 1753 to meet representatives of the Six Nations at Albany and take measures 'to secure their wavering friendship'; for the Iroquois, impressed by the Great Meadows affair, were wondering which side to take. Leading Americans, however, wished this congress to undertake a more ambitious task. Before it met, Governor Shirley thus addressed the assembly of Massachusetts: 'For forming this general union, gentlemen, there is no time to be lost: the French seem to have advanced further toward making themselves masters of this Continent within the past five or six years than they have done ever since the first beginning of that settlement.'

The Albany Congress, which met in June 1754, spent most of its time debating colonial union. The resulting Albany Plan of Union was the work of Benjamin Franklin and Thomas Hutchinson. There was to be a president-general appointed by the Crown, and a 'grand council' appointed by the colonial assemblies, in proportion to their contributions to the common war chest — a typical bit of Ben Franklin foxiness, to ensure that taxes were really paid. The president, with the advice of the grand council, would have sole power to negotiate treaties, declare war, and make peace with the Indians; to regulate the Indian trade, to have sole jurisdiction over land purchases outside particular colonies, and to make grants of land to settlers and govern the Western territory until the Crown formed it into new colonial governments. The Union would have power to build forts, raise armies, equip fleets, and levy taxes for the same, to be paid into a general treasury with branches in each colony.

This plan showed far-sighted statesmanship, in advance of its time, but was a closer federal union than the Thirteen Colonies were willing to conclude even during the War of Independence. Whether the British authorities would have accepted it is doubtful; but they never had a chance to express their views. Not one colonial assembly ratified the Plan. Every one refused to give up any part of its exclusive taxing power, even to a representative body. So the war which then began was carried through under the old system. No British commander had authority to raise troops or money from a colony without the consent of its assembly. As in previous wars, the assemblies of provinces that were not directly menaced, and also some of those that were, like Pennsylvania, refused to make any substantial contribution to the common cause.

Although the Seven Years War (1756–63) was not formally declared for two more years, it was already being hotly waged in America, where it was called the French and Indian War. The haughty Braddock marched north and west from Virginia against Fort Duquesne. His defeat when only a few miles from the site of Pittsburgh was complete, and lost him his life. Braddock's stunning defeat brought the Indians of the Northwest over to the French side, threw back the English frontier, and exposed the western settlements of Pennsylvania, Maryland, and Virginia to a series of devastating attacks.

The other operations of the English in 1755 were inept, though not disastrous. Governor Shirley failed to take Fort Niagara, on which the whole English effort should have been concentrated; for Niagara was the French gateway to the West. William Johnson, a clever Irishman of the Mohawk valley who kept the Six Nations quiet, defeated the French on Lake George and was rewarded with a baronetcy for having gained the only English victory that year. But he was unable to capture Crown Point on Lake Champlain, and the French built Fort Ticonderoga to back up Crown Point.

This war might have been localized but for a shift in alliances in Europe; Austria came over to the side of France, and Frederick the Great tore in on the other side. Before the war was over every European power was involved and hostilities had extended to all parts of the world. There was naval warfare between England, France, and Spain in the Atlantic, the Mediterranean, the West Indies, and the Indian Ocean; battles on the Asiatic continent between Dupleix and Clive and their East Indian allies. Hostilities even reached the Philippines, where the English captured Manila after the war was over in Europe.

The years 1756–57 were disastrous for England, in America and elsewhere. The Earl of Loudoun, who became commander-in-chief in America, was justly described by Governor Shirley as 'a pen and ink man whose greatest energies were put forth in getting ready to begin.' Washington's Virginia militia with great difficulty held the line of the Shenandoah valley against the Indians. Oswego, the English fort on Lake Ontario, was captured by the French General Montcalm, who then advanced down Lake Champlain to Lake George, captured Fort William Henry, and isolated the English garrison there. Three thousand French troops reached Canada, despite efforts of the British navy. Admiral Byng lost Minorca in the Mediterranean to the French, and was court-martialed and shot for cowardice, 'pour encourager les autres,' as Voltaire quipped. In India, the British lost Calcutta. On the European continent, Frederick the Great was defeated by the French and Austrians, and the English and Hanoverian army surrendered to the French. At the end of 1757 the military experts confidently predicted that France would win, hands down; and that England and Prussia would soon be compelled to sign a peace, which would give France all North America west of the Alleghenies, and reduce Prussia to a second-rate power.

Yet the whole complexion of the war was changed in 1758 when William Pitt, the future Earl of Chatham, became Secretary of State, head of the ministry, and virtual dictator of the English empire. Pitt had a genius for organization, a knack for grand strategy, and a knowledge of men. While most Englishmen regarded the American scene as a secondary theater of war, Pitt saw that the principal object for England should be the conquest of Canada and the American West, thus carving out a new field for Anglo-American expansion. Pitt's policy was simple and direct: subsidize Frederick the Great to carry on warfare in the European theater; use the navy to command the high seas and contain

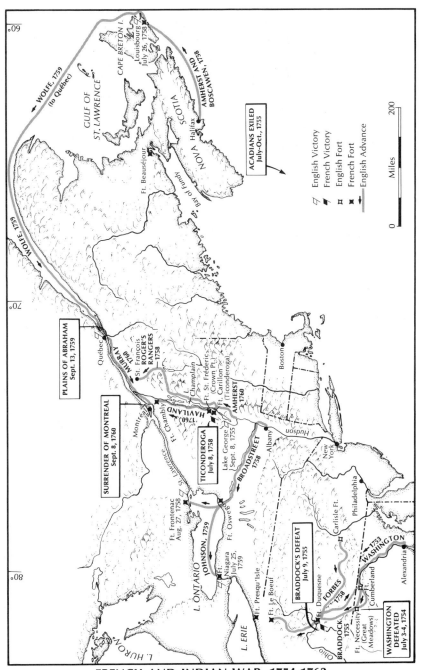

FRENCH AND INDIAN WAR, 1754-1763

the French fleet in port; and concentrate the military might of England in America, under young and energetic generals.

James Wolfe, son of a country squire, was a tall, lanky, narrow-shouldered young man with vivid red hair. Ambition, audacity, genius, and a fierce concentration on becoming master of his profession made Wolfe the most Napoleonic soldier in English history; and if his victory on the Plains of Abraham paved the way for American independence, it was lucky for America that he lost his life that day, and did not live to command British armies against the United States. Wolfe was only 31 years old in 1758, when Pitt made him first brigadier general under General Jeffrey Amherst, who was just ten years older, and whom Pitt had selected as commander in chief by passing over whole columns of senior officers. These two formed a perfect team with Admiral Boscawen in assaulting Louisbourg, which, though infinitely better fortified than in 1745 and more skillfully defended, was captured in July 1758.

That same year Colonel John Bradstreet of Massachusetts, with a force of New Englanders, captured Fort Frontenac at the site of Kingston, Ontario; and General Forbes, with George Washington as his right-hand man, marched across Pennsylvania and seized Fort Duquesne, renaming it Pittsburgh after the great war minister. Clive won the upper hand in India, and Frederick the Great broke out from his encirclement of French, Russian, and Austrian enemies.

Then came 1759, England's *annus mirabilis* — the acme of the old empire, when England reached a pinnacle of glory that she had never touched before, and, as Horace Walpole wrote, the very bells of London were worn threadbare pealing out victories. It was then that David Garrick wrote the words for that stirring old song 'Heart of Oak':

> Come, cheer up, my lads! 'tis to glory we steer,
> To add something more to this wonderful year;
> To honor we call you as freemen, not slaves,
> For who are so free as the sons of the waves?
> > Heart of oak are our ships, heart of oak are our men;
> > We always are ready, steady! boys, steady!
> > We'll fight and we'll conquer again and again.

Off the coast of France, Admiral Hawke won the battle of Quiberon Bay, which rendered the French incapable of sending reinforcements to Canada; in the West Indies, a combined naval and military expedition conquered Guadeloupe; in North America, Sir William Johnson captured Fort Niagara, key to the West.

Yet the greatest campaign that year was the one for Canada. Wolfe advanced in transports up the St. Lawrence river to Quebec. There General Amherst with a land force was supposed to co-operate with him. Amherst captured Crown Point and Ticonderoga, but never got within striking distance of Quebec. Thrice in previous wars this failure in co-ordination had meant that the great fortress-city remained French. But Wolfe's forces carried on. He had only 4000 men, with Robert Monckton (aged 33) his second in command, and George Townshend (aged 35) his third brigadier.

Wolfe, for all his youthfulness, was well prepared for his task. So earnest a student of military strategy that some of his brother officers considered him a little queer, he could size up a situation at a glance and tell instinctively what risks to take. He had learned the necessity of co-operation between army and navy. He anticipated Frederick the Great in recognizing the value of a concentrated musketry. And he was the first English or European officer to train his troops in precision and accuracy of fire. After abortive attacks on Quebec from two sides, and failing also to draw the defenders away, Wolfe worked out a ruse for placing a force on the plains above the city. And with a single concentrated volley on the Plains of Abraham, a volley withheld until his men could see the white of their enemies' eyes, Wolfe won Quebec on 13 September 1759 — as he learned just before his death on the battlefield.

After the surrender of Quebec, the issue was doubtful for a year. But with the surrender of Montreal in 1760, French power ceased on the North American continent. War continued only in the West, where the Indians could not believe that their old friends the French were beaten; but after a last flare-up, the conspiracy of Pontiac, the Western conflict flickered to a close.

In Europe the war dragged on, and Spain came in, which gave the British an opportunity to capture Havana and Manila in 1762. In the meantime the new king, George III, wearied of Mr. Pitt, who was becoming altogether too powerful for royalty, dismissed him, opened negotiations with the enemy, and purchased peace by renouncing a number of the conquests. By this Peace of Paris (1763), French Canada and the Spanish Floridas were ceded to Great Britain; while France, in order to compensate Spain for her losses, ceded Louisiana and all French claims to the west of the Mississippi to Spain. There was some talk of returning Canada to France in exchange for the sugar island of Guadeloupe; this scheme was defeated not so much by prescience for the future, as from the fear of the British planters that their market would be flooded with sugar.

Even with the return of these islands to France, and of Havana and the Philippines to Spain, this war was a mighty victory for England. The British empire bestrode the world like a colossus; India gained, all North America to the Mississippi won, and the best of the West Indies; supremacy of the seas confirmed. As the historian Seeley wrote, 'through all that remained of the eighteenth century the nation looked back upon these splendid years as upon a happiness that could never return; . . . long it continued to be the unique boast of the Englishman,

> That Chatham's language was his mother tongue
> And Wolfe's great name compatriot with his own.'

English, Scots, Irish, and colonists spilled over with expressions of loyalty; and at a meeting in Boston to celebrate the peace, James Otis declared that the true interests of Britain and her colonies were identical, and warned, 'What God in his providence has united, let no man dare attempt to pull asunder!'

Yet the war was not paid for, and the price of glory comes high. The French menace was ended forever; but a flock of new domestic problems within the empire came home to roost on post-war statesmen and to clamor for solution.

VI

1763 1770

Liberty and Empire

1. LIBERTY AND AUTHORITY

The American generation that came to maturity between the Peace of Paris and the inauguration of President Washington was confronted by more serious and original political problems than any later generation, not excepting our own. It was then that the great beacons of American principles, such as the Declaration of Independence, the Virginia Bill of Rights, and the Federal Constitution, were lighted; it was then that institutions of permanent importance in the history of America and of liberty were crystallized. The period was revolutionary and destructive for the old British empire, but creative and constructive for the United States.

This period from 1763 to 1789 has a singular unity, from which the rush of events and the din of arms can easily distract our attention. We must not let the high-strung debates that preceded the American Revolution, or the vivid events of the War for Independence, hide from us the real meaning of these years. Just as the Greek tragedies of the Periclean Age are concerned not merely with the conflicts of gods and heroes, but with the depths of human nature; just as the stories of the Old Testament explore the mysterious relation between God and man, so we may discern, behind the noisy conflict of words and arms in the American Revolution, the stirring of a political problem older than recorded history: the balancing of liberty with authority. That underlay all the tumult and the shouting. And this ancient question of liberty or

121

authority resolves itself into two: the horizontal or federal problem of distributing power between one central and many regional governments; and the vertical or democratic one of how far the masses of mankind shall be entrusted with control. These two problems are the warp and woof of American history through the Civil War; and the circumstances of our own time have simply restated these ancient problems in terms of liberty versus security and permissiveness versus discipline.

By excluding the French from continental North America, the British took over more responsibility than they could handle. At one stroke British possessions in North America more than doubled, and a race alien in language and religion was brought into the empire. Baffling questions of Indian relations, fur trade, land policy, and military and political administration were created. For the next twenty-five years, Great Britain attempted unsuccessfully to solve the great riddle of imperial organization. And the new American government found itself confronted with the same difficulties.

From 1763 to 1775 Americans asserted their rights, while Englishmen reminded them of their duties; yet thinking men on both sides of the Atlantic were grappling with the same task: how to organize this vast empire so that the interests of the whole would be furthered, the various parts nicely adjusted to each other, and a certain degree of local autonomy preserved. Americans argued, and until 4 July 1776 fought, not for independence but for a guaranteed free status within the empire. Englishmen until 1775 agreed, and until 1782 fought, not to reduce Americans to political 'slavery' but to their 'proper place' in the empire: to a political status similar to that which Puerto Rico had before it became a commonwealth in 1952.

For two centuries the English empire had been commercial, dominated largely by merchants in profitable alliance with the landed gentry, committed to the mercantilist philosophy. These people regarded the empire as valuable only in so far as all parts contributed to the wealth of Great Britain. But the immense acquisitions of the Seven Years War produced a subtle transition from commercial to territorial imperialism, from the idea of governing colonies with a view to their trade, to governing colonies with a view to their revenue and manpower. This meant, as Governor Hutchinson of Massachusetts wrote in a sentence that lost him his job, that 'there must be an abridgment of so-called English Liberties in America.' The new idea did not replace the old, but reinforced it; so that the Acts of Trade were tightened up and strengthened to an extent that began to impose real hardships on important colonial interests. In the years after 1763 British statesmen felt that their bigger empire required more ships and soldiers. These would cost money; and unless the British taxpayer supplied it all, the colonies must contribute. Revenue could be extracted from the colonies only through a stronger central administration, at the expense of colonial self-government. The Thirteen Colonies tried to escape this vicious circle by squaring it, and finally broke through with independence. Then they found much the same problem of adjustment between parts and whole confronting their new nation. Federalism — a form of government which seemed as inadmissible to eighteenth-century Englishmen as squaring the circle does to twentieth-century mathematicians — provided America with a solution.

During the half-century since 1713 the lower houses of the colonial assemblies had managed to seize control of the purse and patronage and had taken advantage of the Seven Years War to transform themselves into 'miniature parliaments.' The system worked well enough, for the British government by veto or disallowance was able to prevent things, such as abuse of paper money, that it did not like; but it was unable to get positive things done, such as full co-operation in time of war, or a financial contribution to imperial defense. The royal governors, who for the most part were able and honest gentlemen, were endowed with legal authority in America of a sort that had gone out in England with the Glorious Revolution; governors in royal and proprietary colonies had an absolute veto over legislation, the authority to prorogue and dissolve the lower houses in most colonies, and the power to dismiss judges and create courts. Yet in fact, despite this panoply of executive powers, the governors were weak, because they had short tenure, received uncertain support in England, were hampered by rigid instructions from Whitehall, and, most important, were dependent on the assemblies for their salaries.[1] The assemblies also encroached on the governors' patronage powers, essential to the wielding of political influence; in particular, they won control of the crucial post of treasurer, often political boss as well as finance minister and, in the South, speaker of the House as well. The

1. Exceptions: governors of Georgia and Nova Scotia were paid by the Crown, and the governors of Virginia and Maryland enjoyed so much income from fees that their salaries were so much 'gravy.'

Board of Trade reported in 1754, with truth, that members of the New York Assembly 'have wrested from Your Majesty's governor, the nomination of all offices of government, the custody and direction of the public military stores, the mustering and direction of troops raised for Your Majesty's service, and in short almost every other part of executive government.' South Carolina even pushed encroachment to such an extent that the Anglican churches of the colony were instructed to pray for the assembly instead of the governor!

The whole system was very chancy. A few royal governors, such as Shirley of Massachusetts and Dinwiddie of Virginia, through wisdom and personality, became so popular that it looked as if the empire would go on forever. Given patience in the colonies and also at London, there might conceivably have been a gradual broadening of colonial autonomy (as has occurred in the last century of British imperial history) until the Thirteen Colonies acquired dominion home rule; and after that they might have seceded peaceably. By 1763 there had been worked out a compromise between imperial control and colonial self-government; between the principle of authority and the principle of liberty. King and Parliament had undisputed control of foreign affairs, war and peace, and overseas trade. Parliament directed colonial trade into channels that it deemed profitable to the empire, colonies included. In almost every other respect the Americans had acquired home rule. They had acquired far more autonomy than Ireland then enjoyed, and infinitely more than the colonies of France, Spain, or any other country had before the next century.

So, apart from minor discontents, the Americans were fairly well satisfied with this compromise in 1763. But the government of George III was not. It had devised no method of exacting a uniform contribution from the colonies for defense. There were still leaks in the enforcement of the Acts of Trade and Navigation, largely owing to the fact that royal customs officials in the colonies were few in number, and so underpaid that they could only make both ends meet by accepting presents from smugglers.

Thus the situation between England and her American colonies, while it had points of friction, was not explosive. 'The Abilities of a Child might have governed this Country,' wrote Oliver Wolcott of Connecticut in 1776, 'so strong has been their Attachment to Britain.' But the Americans were a high-spirited people who claimed all the rights for which

Englishmen had fought since Magna Carta, and would settle for nothing less. They were not security-minded but liberty-minded. That is why they met attempts of the government of George III to impair these liberties first with loyal expostulation, then with indignant agitation, finally with armed resistance.

Make no mistake; the American Revolution was not fought to *obtain* freedom, but to *preserve* the freedom that the colonies already had. Independence was no conscious goal, but a last resort, reluctantly adopted, to preserve 'life, liberty, and the pursuit of happiness.'

2. THE WEST

The North American West created the most pressing and immediate problem of imperial reorganization. This Western problem may be likened to a rope of many strands, now twisted in a regular pattern, but more often tangled with each other, and with strands from other ropes, or tortured into Gordian knots which only war could sever. Of these strands we can distinguish the most important: the international and military question, the Indians, the fur trade, the dilemma of territorial administration and land policy, and the political problem, particularly with reference to the French Canadians.

The international question was whether the American West would be won by France, Spain, or Great Britain, or partitioned among them. This was only partially solved by the Seven Years War. To the south and west of the new British possessions lay the Spanish empire, rich and well organized, if sparsely populated. Spain was still a power to be reckoned with, still the largest and the most powerful empire in the New World, embracing most of South America and all Central America, together with California, Texas, and the west bank of the Mississippi. Under Charles III, an able and ambitious monarch, Spain expanded again for a brief time. Jealously she guarded Mexico; and in spite of her acquisition of a new bulwark in the shape of Louisiana, she was eager to recover the two Floridas which had gone to England, and the east bank of the Mississippi as well.

Although the Peace of 1763 presumably disposed of the French danger to the English colonies, they by no means felt safe; over the centuries France has never really renounced territory which she has been forced to relinquish. Napoleon's recovery of Louisiana in 1800 may

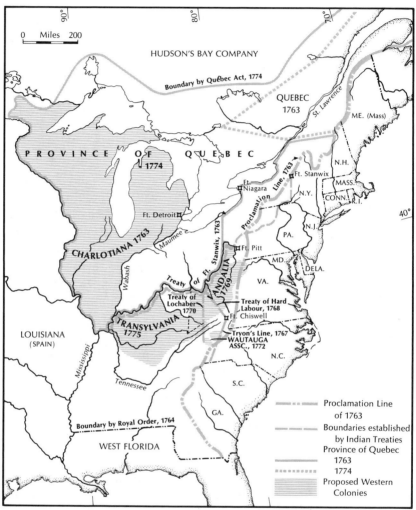

ORGANIZATION OF THE WEST AFTER 1763

Map labels:

HUDSON'S BAY COMPANY

Boundary by Québec Act, 1774

QUEBEC 1763

St. Lawrence

ME. (Mass)

P R O V I N C E   O F   Q U E B E C
1774

Ft. Stanwix

Proclamation Line 1763

Ft. Niagara

N.H.

MASS.

CONN.

R.I.

N.Y.

Ft. Detroit

Maumee

PA.

N.J.

CHARLOTIANA 1763

Wabash

Proclamation Line, 1763

Ft. Pitt

MD.

DELA.

Treaty of Ft. Stanwix, 1763

VANDALIA 1769

VA.

Treaty of Lochaber 1770

Treaty of Hard Labour, 1768

Ft. Chiswell

LOUISIANA (SPAIN)

TRANSYLVANIA 1775

Tryon's Line, 1767
WAUTAUGA ASSC., 1772

N.C.

Mississippi

Tennessee

S.C.

Boundary by Royal Order, 1764

GA.

WEST FLORIDA

40°

90° 80° 70°

0   Miles   200

Legend:
Proclamation Line of 1763
Boundaries established by Indian Treaties
Province of Quebec 1763
1774
Proposed Western Colonies

be said to have vindicated English fears in 1770. The French government continued mischievous intrigues with its former Indian allies, and
kept its finger on the pulse of colonial discontent.

While the danger from French and Spanish ambitions always loomed
on the horizon, the Indian danger was immediate. Pontiac's conspiracy
of 1763 was the most formidable Indian outbreak of the century.
Goaded to desperation by the tactics of the English traders and trappers, affronted by the refusal of the English to continue the French
practice of annual gifts, and foreseeing the future crowding by English
settlers, the Indians of the Ohio valley formed a grand confederacy
under the leadership of Pontiac, chief of the Ottawa. Every Western fort
except Detroit and Pittsburgh was captured by the savages, the frontier
was ravaged from Niagara to Virginia, and hundreds of pioneer families
were wiped out. Virginia and Maryland struck back at the foe; but
Pennsylvania, the worst sufferer, failed to provide adequate defense for
her frontiersmen. The uprising was not crushed by Americans, but by
British red-coats. If the colonies could not even co-operate for their own
defense against the Indians, could there be any doubt that stronger
imperial control was needed?

Nor was the Indian question merely one of putting down a rebellion.
How were the Indians to be treated after they had been brought to
terms? Should their hunting grounds be reserved for them in the interests of humanity and the fur trade, or, if not, by what means were they
to be secured against speculators and land-hungry frontiersmen? In
short it was imperative to work out some broad Indian policy; to provide
not only for present emergency but for future developments. Such a task
was pre-eminently one that required centralized control.

Closely connected with the Indian problem was the fur trade. Peltry
still dominated the economic life of Canada and West Florida, and was
a leading interest in New York, South Carolina, and Louisiana. This fur
trade was not merely an international rivalry, but a ruthless competition
among people of the same country, in a business which knew no ethics;
and this competition became more intense when the Peace of Paris
opened up a new field for colonial and English greed. As fast as the
peltry of one region was exhausted, the trappers and traders moved
farther west, where they competed with the Spaniards for an Indian
clientele; or by too eager salesmanship they stirred up the nearer Indians, who retaliated on the nearest white family. So here was another

ungrateful task for the harassed officials in London: regulation of a group of unprincipled traders who could not be brought to see that contented Indians trapped the most fur. Subsequently this aspect too of the Western problem was inherited by the United States government.

Even more perplexing, and also more permanent, was the problem of territorial administration and land policy. This was as old as the first English settlement in America and one that lasted into the twentieth century. Should the extensive domain acquired from France be conserved as an Indian reserve, or opened in whole or part to white settlement? If the latter, should land be regarded as a source of revenue, and assessed with quit-rents, or should quick settling be encouraged? And if so, how? By ceding it to land companies in large tracts, or in small farms to individual settlers? The British government had to do something about this question because as soon as the war was over, the Board of Trade was bombarded with petitions for big grants of land in the newly acquired West. And whose was the West to grant?

Almost every colony had claims. The rights of some, such as Virginia, were long-established and well-founded; the claims of others, such as New York, were doubtful and tenuous. Almost any policy Great Britain adopted would step on someone's corns. But everyone will now admit that the land question was essentially imperial, and that a land policy ought to be administered by a central authority.

Finally, there was the political problem. If new settlements were to be established in the West, what degree of self-government should be permitted them, and what should be their relation to the older colonies and to the mother country? Moreover, the Treaty of 1763 had given England jurisdiction over some 60,000 French Canadians, men alien in race and faith, and unaccustomed to English traditions of law and administration. Some general scheme of government had to be provided for these new additions to the empire and some method discovered to gain the friendship and support of the powerful Church, to which the habitants of Canada were unbreakably faithful.

The Western problem proved to be permanent. Before 1775 the diverse strands of defense, Indian relations, furs, land policy, and politics were English and colonial problems; after that time they entered into the web of American development, and all continued to occupy a prominent position in American politics far into the twentieth century.

3. THE COLONIES IN 1763–73

Let us now briefly survey the British continental colonies,[2] starting at the southern end. West Florida, defined in 1763 as old Spanish Florida west of the Apalachicola and a section of French Louisiana including Mobile, Biloxi, and Natchez, had very few European inhabitants. Pensacola was still a stockaded fort which Spain had used as a penal colony. Mobile, a well-built little town, was inhabited by exactly 112 Frenchmen. Governor George Johnstone, an energetic Scots naval officer, set up civil government at Pensacola, summoned an elective assembly in 1766, and advertised for English settlers; within ten years the population had risen to 3700 Europeans and 1200 Negro slaves, most of them at the Mississippi end. Governor Johnstone's ambition to make Pensacola a great port of commerce with Spanish America (to which New Orleans now belonged) was not realized. But the West Floridians traded profitably with the Creek and Choctaw nations, who ceded their lands north of a line approximately 35 miles from the sea, and with whom Johnstone cemented friendly relations.

The only settlements in East Florida, when the British took possession in 1763, were St. Augustine, and St. Mark at the mouth of the Apalachicola. That was all Spain had to show for over two centuries of her rule; and St. Augustine's population had been dependent on the bounty of the Spanish Crown. In contrast to Canada, where the French habitants loved their land more than their king, and, when promised religious liberty, readily swore allegiance to England, the people of St. Augustine, though granted toleration, chose to leave when England took over; no Spaniard could imagine living under alien heretics, compatriots of *El Draque*. The Spanish authorities provided transportation to Havana for all white inhabitants and several hundred fugitive slaves from Georgia

2. The reader is reminded that Britain now had several insular colonies — Bermuda, the Bahamas, Jamaica, Barbados, and the Leeward Islands (Antigua, St. Kitts, Montserrat, and Nevis) which had self-government through elective assemblies; together with British Guiana, Newfoundland, and the Windward Islands ceded by France in 1763 (Tobago, St. Vincent, Grenada, Dominica) which as yet had no assemblies. The Peace of Paris left France in possession of only Saint-Domingue (Haiti), Martinique, Guadeloupe, half St. Martin, and French Guiana. Dutch possession of Surinam, the Curaçao group, and the St. Eustatius group, was unchanged. Spain still held Trinidad, Puerto Rico, Cuba, and two-thirds of Hispaniola, the present Dominican Republic.

and South Carolina who had settled near the garrison town.[3] South of St. Augustine lived only Indians, mostly of the Seminole branch of the Creek nation; no white man had yet penetrated the Everglades. Speculators obtained land grants on the condition of settling a certain number of white Protestants, but hardly anybody then wished to live in Florida. One Robert Turnbull recruited 1500 settlers from Minorca, Greece, and Italy, and established them at New Smyrna, to grow indigo; and their descendants are still there, known as 'Minorcans.'[4] In addition to these, the census of 1771 showed only 288 whites and 900 Negroes in all East Florida, not enough to warrant the calling of an assembly.

To travel in the 1760's from St. Augustine to Savannah or Charleston, you would have had to go by sea or Indian trail. Georgia had passed her heroic period. No longer was General Oglethorpe drilling kilted Highlanders to pounce on the dons; evangelists like Whitefield and Wesley had gone on to richer fields. An estimated population of 10,000, including a good proportion of Negro slaves, was scattered along or near the coast, planting indigo and rice. Lord Adam Gordon, who visited Savannah in 1765, reported that the royal governor, Sir James Wright, and his council and assembly lived 'in all love and unanimity' — which nobody could have said ten years later.

South Carolina, having passed the 100,000 mark, had become very prosperous. The powerful Cherokee nation had been decisively beaten when they went on the warpath in 1759 and had been forced to cede more land, and the back-country was opened to settlement. Charleston had become a gay little city with a good number of merchants and professional men; it was the only town in America north of Mexico that had a permanent theater. The wealthiest Charlestonians sent their sons to England to be educated; but when it came to a showdown in 1775, the South Carolinian fresh from Christ Church, or the Inns of Court, became as flaming a patriot as an alumnus of Princeton or William and Mary.

North Carolina, by contrast, seemed more of a social democracy. Josiah Quincy of Boston, who traveled through the Carolinas in 1773, wrote:

3. Throughout the colonial period and later, Spain, though a slaveholding power, liberated slaves from other countries who fled to her jurisdiction.
4. They are mentioned in that remarkable novel of life in Volusia County, Marjorie K. Rawlings's *The Yearling* (1938).

The soils and climates of the Carolinas differ, but not so much as their inhabitants. . . . The number of Negroes and slaves is much less in North than in South Carolina. . . . Husbandmen and agriculture increase in number and improvement. Industry is up in the woods, at tar, pitch, and turpentine; in the fields, ploughing, planting, clearing, or fencing the land. Herds and flocks become more numerous. You see husbandmen, yeomen, and white laborers scattered through the country instead of herds of Negroes and slaves. Healthful countenances and numerous families become more common as you advance north. . . . They . . . have no metropolis, though Newbern is called the capital, as there is the seat of government.

Yet North Carolina's democratic manners concealed the fact that there was a large proportion of landless whites; more recently formed than Virginia, North Carolina had more *nouveaux riches*, with some of the planters boasting very great fortunes.

The more patrician colony of Virginia was still highly decentralized, a congeries of individual plantations. Towns there were none, except Williamsburg and the growing seaport of Norfolk. With only 200 houses and less than 1000 permanent residents, Williamsburg was a capital of distinction, with a brick state house, governor's palace, and William and Mary College, then attended by about 80 students. While the assembly was in session, Williamsburg was gay with balls, dinners, and assemblies; and the taverns did a roaring business. During the rest of the year most Virginians lived on their plantations.

The Virginia aristocracy, now fairly stable, dominated the politics of a province which sheltered no political parties. Political power was diffused among the members of the leading families by intermarriage. As Bernard Bailyn has written, 'The unpruned branches of these flourishing family trees, growing freely, met and intertwined until by the Revolution the aristocracy appeared to be one tangled cousinry.' Three families — the Robinsons, the Randolphs, the Lees — provided most of the leaders of the House of Burgesses, which was dominated by a small number of wealthy planters, many of whom also speculated in Western lands.

The gentry were delightful people — open-handed, liberal, and so hospitable that there were very few inns in the colony. Lord Adam Gordon declared that a Virginia planter's family would drive 60 miles in a six-horse coach to attend a dinner party; the trip must have taken them

10 to 12 hours! Virginians were so intensely proud of their English
nationality that any attempt to treat them as in any respect inferior to
the English landed gentry was certain to cause resentment. Andrew
Burnaby, an English clergyman who traveled through the province in
1759, observed: 'They are haughty and jealous of their liberties, impatient of restraint, and can scarcely bear the thought of being controlled
by any superior power. . . . The women are, generally speaking, handsome, though not to be compared with our fair countrywomen in England. They have but few advantages, and consequently are seldom
accomplished; this makes them reserved, and unequal to any interesting
or refined conversation. They are immoderately fond of dancing, and
indeed it is almost the only amusement they partake of.'

One important asset that the reverend gentleman missed was the good
classical education that the men obtained at William and Mary, and
their addiction to reading and study, especially in the ancient classics
and political theory. This, together with the responsibility required to
manage a plantation or serve in council or assembly, gave excellent
training in statesmanship, as is proved by the careers of some who were
young men or boys in 1763 — George Washington, the Lees, Thomas
Jefferson, John Marshall, and James Madison.

From Baltimore to Philadelphia, as travelers journeyed along a tolera-
bly good road for wheeled vehicles, they found the aspect of the country
changing. In Delaware, fifteen or twenty miles from Philadelphia, farms
became smaller, more frequent, and better cultivated. Neat farmhouses
were surrounded by gardens, fruit trees, and even hedges. An Englishman crossing the Schuylkill and entering Philadelphia felt at home; the
capital of Pennsylvania, remarked Lord Adam Gordon with evident astonishment, was 'a great and noble city,' like one of the larger towns in
England, with the difference of a Quaker primness and regularity. Some
of the neatly laid-out streets were paved, lined with sidewalks, lighted
by whale-oil lamps, and policed at night. Philadelphia, with 18,766 people according to a census of 1760, was the largest and most prosperous
town in English America. In another ten years it increased by another
10,000 and acquired some fine public buildings, including the handsome
Carpenters' Hall, where the First Continental Congress would meet in
1774, and the Old State House where independence was declared and
the Federal Constitution drafted.

Pennsylvania had always been faithful to the religious liberty ideas of her founder, and Philadelphia was then the only place in North America between Florida and Canada that had a Catholic church. But the 'brotherly love' idea had not worked very well. There were many tensions between the English Quakers, who had the highest social standing, the Germans, whom they regarded as uneducated boors, and the tough Scots-Irish who had settled the frontier and back-country, and had not been given their due weight in the assembly. In 1765, Philadelphia, Chester, and Bucks counties, with one-third of the population, elected three-quarters of the assemblymen while Philadelphia city and the other five counties, with two-thirds of the population, shared the other one-quarter of the seats. Philadelphia was run by an oligarchy of Philadelphia lawyers and merchants, kept in power by a high property qualification for voting which shut out the lower middle class and the working people.

Proceeding eastward, our traveler of 1763 would cross the Delaware by ferry to Trenton, and drive across New Jersey, probably choosing to spend a night at the pretty village of Princeton, where he could admire Nassau Hall, largest building in the English colonies. He would then cross the Hudson by ferry from Perth Amboy to New York City.

There he would find a compactly built little town, third in population in the English colonies, still bearing marks of the Dutch regime, and still the capital. The cosmopolitan little city presented vast differences in wealth. A few blocks away from the stately mansions of merchants facing the Bowling Green or the river were evil slums where day laborers, dockhands, and free Negroes lived. There were already enough Irish in New York to celebrate St. Patrick's Day, enough Jews to maintain a synagogue, enough Scots to support a Presbyterian church, and enough Germans to maintain four churches where the services were in their language. The two Anglican churches, Trinity and St. Paul's, worshipped according to the Book of Common Prayer, praying daily for 'George, our most gracious King and Governour.'

In the Province of New York, most aristocratic of the continental colonies, the landed gentry controlled politics, despite the fact that the franchise was widely held, especially in New York City and Albany. Up-river the Livingston and Van Rensselaer manors comprised almost a million acres; the Philipse family had two manors, which amounted to little less; six manors covered over half of Westchester County; four families owned 200 square miles of Long Island, and on Manhattan

Island itself, hundreds of acres were owned by the Stuyvesant, Bayard, De Lancey, and De Peyster families, to the subsequent enrichment of their descendants.

Political parties in New York derived from two rival aristocratic factions whose origins can be traced to Leisler's Rebellion: the Livingston or Presbyterian, and the De Lancey or Anglican. The Livingstons, more adaptable to the rising tide of democracy, produced several leaders of the pre-Revolutionary period such as John Morin Scott and Philip Livingston the 'singer'; and, under the later leadership of Edward Livingston and Aaron Burr, merged into the Jeffersonian Republican party.

The New England colonies owed their prosperity largely to fishing, shipbuilding, and maritime commerce. Boston with 17,000 inhabitants was the largest town, but no metropolis; there were a dozen little seaports along the coast from Bridgeport to Portland, each with some maritime specialty; and off-shore Nantucket had already gone in for deep-sea whaling in a big way. All these towns had comfortable brick and wooden houses built in the Georgian style, with excellent interior decoration and well-kept gardens. The shipowning merchants who owned them shared top status with the clergy, a few lawyers, and the physicians. New England as yet had no landed aristocracy, because land was not valuable enough to acquire as an investment, only for resale, and wild land was the only way, other than overseas trading, to make a fortune.

New Englanders were mostly members of one of the Congregational churches, which by this time were far from uniform in theology. Some were strictly Calvinist, having been stirred up during the Great Awakening; others, especially in the larger towns, had become liberal almost to the point of Unitarianism. Every village had a meetinghouse which served as town hall and church; and all, except in Boston and in Rhode Island, were supported by public taxation. In addition, there were in 1763 about a hundred Anglican and Baptist churches and Quaker meetings in New England. Every village had a free school, the towns supported grammar schools (roughly equivalent to our present high schools), and most of the people knew how to read and write. Boston supported four weekly newspapers, and Hartford one — the *Connecticut Courant* which is still published.

New England had a more democratic social and political organization than any other section, in large part because land was distributed more equally. In a town like Kent, Connecticut, almost every adult male could participate in town government. When on the eve of the Revolution, George III commented that Rhode Island was 'a strange form of government,' the tory governor of Massachusetts, Thomas Hutchinson, a descendant of Anne Hutchinson, replied: 'They approach, Sir, the nearest to a democracy of any of your colonies. Once a year all power returns to the people and all their officers are new elected. By this means the governor has no judgment of his own, and must comply with every popular prejudice.' Of his own colony he complained: 'In most of the public proceedings of the town of Boston persons of the best character and estates have little or no concern. They decline attending town meetings where they are sure to be outvoted by men of the lowest order, all being admitted and it being very rare that any scrutiny is made into the qualifications of voters.'

Yet even in New England, the electorate deferred to the leading personages who held offices almost as though they were hereditary prerogatives. New Hampshire under the Wentworths was notorious for politics by kinship. When Benning Wentworth became governor of that state in 1741, the council included four of his relatives and two remote connections; in his twenty-five-year tenure he added three more relatives and then turned over the office to his nephew who added yet others. Despite Connecticut's republican form of government, two-thirds of the top offices were held by men bearing but twenty-five surnames of 'ancient' families, precisely the same pattern as in 'aristocratic' Virginia. John Adams wrote toward the close of the century: 'Go into every village in New England, and you will find that the office of justice of the peace, and even the place of representative, which has ever depended only on the freest election of the people, have generally descended from generation to generation, in three or four families at most.'

Government by town meeting, both in seaports and the farming villages, gave everyone a chance for oratory. Town offices or a seat in the assembly afforded political training similar to that which the Virginians obtained from county government and service in the House of Burgesses. This enabled the Yankees to concert resistance against the new imperial policy; and, more important, to govern themselves during a revolution. Every seaport had a rough working class of sailors, fishermen, and shipbuilders — the caulkers who invented the political caucus — who were easily welded by agitators into mobs, as many

Crown officials and wealthy gentlemen were to learn unpleasantly; and who were always ready to help 'run in' a cargo without paying duty.

The subject of smuggling is a delicate one, because British writers on the American Revolution like to argue that the British government's effort to stop it caused the upheaval. It is true enough that the Yankees smuggled, Yorkers and Jerseymen smuggled, Philadelphians smuggled, and Southerners smuggled; but so did the English and Scots smuggle, in a big way, and very respectably. The latest English historian of smuggling, Neville Williams, calls the period 1713–75 'the heyday of illicit trade,' when smuggled tea became that nation's beverage. A good country parson such as the Reverend James Woodforde enters in his diary the periodic visits of his bootlegger, who charged half a guinea a pound for tea which, if the duty of 119 per cent had been paid, would have cost him more than double.

Apart from smuggling, the New England people were law-abiding, even on the frontier. More respect was entertained for the clergy and other educated people than for men of wealth. Professional lawyers had only recently come into existence; but several, such as James Otis and John Adams, were learned in the classics and the common law. A large part of the interior of New England was still wilderness; and much of the rest, settled in the preceding twenty years, still in the log-cabin stage of development. But in parts that had been settled for 40 years or more, you found the village green, the spired meeting-house, and the white-painted dwelling built around a huge brick chimney, which still impart charm to rural New England. The necessities of life were in great plenty and families were large, but Puritanism had preserved a certain simplicity and economy in social intercourse.

4. BRITISH POLITICS AND GEORGE III

British politics were important in the American Revolution because Parliament initiated the new colonial policy and passed the laws which precipitated the War of Independence. The English political situation in 1760–70 was not unlike that of the United States in the 'Era of Good Feelings.' Whigs had successfully eliminated tories by fastening on them the stigma of rebellion in 1745, just as the Jeffersonian Republicans eliminated the Federalists by the stigma of disloyalty in the War of 1812. The dominant party was breaking up into factions. Even King

George called himself a whig, and all the ministries with which the colonists had to deal were whig ministries.

These ministries were formed much as they were in France before de Gaulle: by making a *bloc*. The king asked someone to be premier, and the premier assembled a group of ministers who controlled enough votes in the House of Commons to pass bills which the ministry wanted and reject those it did not like. Ministries fell because some important person did not get the job he wanted for a relative or supporter, and so voted his gang against the government; or because the premier did not please the king. The American question did not cause a single ministerial crisis until 1781.

Of the different whig factions, the one which showed most sympathy for the Americans was the 'old whig,' so called because its members claimed to inherit the traditions of 1688. These included the Duke of Richmond, General Conway, the Marquess of Rockingham, his secretary Edmund Burke, Lord Camden, and Isaac Barré; names given to American towns and counties in recognition of their efforts. Usually allied with them were the 'Pittites,' William Pitt and his large personal following. These were the most liberal groups in British politics, and also the most conservative; they opposed taxation of the colonies as much because it was new as because it was unfair. Pitt's following included the Duke of Grafton, who succeeded him as Prime Minister in 1767, and Lord Shelburne, who had a broader vision of colonial problems than any English statesman of his time, especially of the Western question.

Unfortunately the old whigs, though rich in talents, were poor in leadership. Rockingham, a young man better known on the turf than in politics, was well-meaning but weak, and a halting speaker in the Commons. Pitt, a peerless leader in time of war, became inept in time of peace; and some strange malady thrust him out of the picture in 1767 almost as soon as he became premier.

Next, there were a number of factions following such political freelances as George Grenville and the Duke of Bedford, whose 'Bloomsbury gang' was notorious for being on hand when the plum-tree was shaken; and finally there was the king, and his friends.

George III, only 22 years old at his accession in 1760, had been brought up under the tutelage of his mother, a strong-minded German princess. His private life was impeccable and his simple tastes ran to farming and country sports. A strong sense of duty made him precise and

methodical, and a glutton for work. 'George, be a *king!*' was his mother's
frequent injunction, which he appears to have interpreted as 'George, be
a politician!' The young man knew what he wanted, and got it, even
though it cost him an empire. He wished to beat the whigs at their own
game, and restore the power of the Crown by creating and eventually
governing through a political party of his own. By this means he hoped
to rescue England from the baneful effects of party politics, and govern
the realm with an eye single to the public weal. His first ministry, under
his personal friend Lord Bute, was a failure. He then induced George
Grenville to construct a ministry, but inserted enough personal friends
into it so that nothing could be done against his will. Grenville fell, not
because the colonists made a row about the Stamp Act, but because he
endeavored to turn out Stuart Mackenzie, one of the king's numerous
Scottish friends; and the next ministry, Rockingham's, resigned rather
than admit some of Mackenzie's henchmen to office. Finally, after the
heterogeneous Pitt-Grafton ministry had crumbled, George III obtained
exactly the government he wanted under his subservient friend, Lord
North; and it was this ministry that drove the colonists into revolt, and
lost the war.

For the first ten years of his reign, George III was conciliatory toward
the colonists. He ordered his friends in Parliament to vote for the repeal
of the Stamp Act. When Lord Hillsborough in 1769 proposed to punish
Massachusetts by altering her charter, the king refused. But the Boston
Tea-Party, the first challenge to his personal rule, aroused his liveliest
resentment. In great measure he may be held responsible, through his
choice of ministers, for the Coercive Acts of 1774, and for the inefficient
conduct of the war. If George III, for all his private virtues and well-
meaning patriotism, is a pitiable figure in history, it is largely for the
opportunities he lost. He might have been a patriot king indeed, by
reaching out over the heads of the politicians to his colonial subjects,
who were devotedly loyal and attracted by his youth and personality.
He did his best for the empire according to his lights; but his best was
not good, and his lights were few and dim.

The British electoral system, with its rotten boroughs and family controls, was a strange mixture of medieval survival and eighteenth-century
cynicism; but there is no reason to suppose that a more uniform or
democratic system would have produced any different result, so far as
the colonies were concerned. The worst feature, from the colonial point

Christopher Columbus (1451-1506) by Sebastiano del Piombo

Cotton Mather (1663-1728) by Peter Pelham.
The first American mezzotint engraving.

PENN'S TREATY with the INDIANS, made 1681 with out an Oath, and never broken. The foundation of Religious and Civil LIBERTY, in the U.S. of AMERICA.

Jonathan Edwards (1703-58) by Joseph Badger.

Benjamin Franklin (1706-90) with His Lightning Detector by Mason Chamberlain

of view, was the lack of continuity, and the preoccupation of ministers with local politics. No sooner did a really capable man like Halifax or Shelburne come to know the colonial ropes than out he went. And a man like Burke, whose intelligent imagination enabled him to grasp how to deal with colonists, never received a responsible position. Every ministry, even North's, meant well toward the Americans and wished to keep them quiet and happy, but none adopted anything but temporary expedients.

George III's ministers were no gang of unprincipled villains, subservient to a royal tyrant. Lord Dartmouth, for instance, who sponsored the Coercive Acts, was a kind and pious gentleman, patron of Dartmouth College and protector of the poet Cowper. But almost all were incompetent. The situation called for statesmanship of the highest order; and the political system which George III manipulated to his personal advantage put statesmanship at a discount, political following at a premium. In the end it was ignorance, confusion, and unresponsiveness to crying needs and issues, rather than corruption or deliberate ill will, which convinced the Americans that their liberties were no longer safe within the British empire. And these three factors — ignorance, confusion, and irresponsiveness — have brought down more governments than we can count, and will continue to do so in the future unless replaced by knowledge, order, and sensitivity.

VII

Reform and Resistance

1. THE ORGANIZATION OF THE WEST

The immediate task that confronted the Crown at the close of hostilities was the administration and defense of new acquisitions. To this problem the ministry of George Grenville addressed itself, adopting emergency measures to meet what was thought to be a temporary situation.

The ministry decided that settlers must be excluded from the trans-Allegheny country until the Indians were pacified, and a definite land policy worked out. This decision was registered in the Royal Proclamation of 7 October 1763. By its terms all Western lands between the Appalachians, the Floridas, the Mississippi, and Quebec were reserved for the Indians. 'We do strictly forbid, on pain of our displeasure, all our loving subjects from making any purchases or settlements whatever in that region.' Thus at one stroke the Crown swept away each and every Western land claim of the Thirteen Colonies, and drew a 'Proclamation Line,' as it was called, on the map, along the crest of the Appalachians.

In the following year, 1764, an elaborate plan for the regulation of Indian affairs was advanced. As early as 1755 General Braddock had laid the foundations of an imperial Indian policy by appointing two highly capable colonists, Sir William Johnson and John Stuart, superintendents respectively of the Northern and Southern Indians. The 'Plan of 1764' recommended a well-organized Indian service under the control of these superintendents; licenses, regulations, and fixed tariffs for traders; and the repeal of all conflicting colonial laws. This was too ambitious a program for immediate fulfillment, but it looked in the right direction.

Before opening the country west of the Proclamation Line to white settlement, it was necessary to purchase territory from the Indians and establish a new boundary west of the Alleghenies. Superintendents Stuart and Johnson were already working on that. In 1763 Stuart negotiated with the Cherokee nation the Treaty of Augusta, establishing the Indian boundary line west of Georgia and the Carolinas. The Treaty of Hard Labour (a frontier post in South Carolina) of 24 October 1768, extended this boundary north to the Ohio at the confluence of that river with the Great Kanawha. This line called forth a storm of protest from Virginian land speculators and was subsequently adjusted to meet their views. In the same year, 1768, Johnson established the line north of the Ohio by the Treaty of Fort Stanwix. The Iroquois ceded for some £10,000 their rights to a large part of central New York and Pennsylvania as well as their claims to territory south of the Ohio river.

Intimately associated with Indian affairs was the pressing question of defense. 'What military establishment will be sufficient? What new forts to be erected?' inquired the secretary of state of the Board of Trade. Pontiac's rebellion made the issue acute. The Board of Trade proposed establishing a chain of garrisons from the St. Lawrence to Florida, and from Niagara to Michilimackinac. It estimated that 10,000 soldiers would be required to garrison these forts and maintain the military establishment in America. This estimate was excessive, if protection of the frontier were the only object — double the number that General Amherst, commander-in-chief in America, asked for. It is so seldom in history that a government proposes to provide more soldiers than the generals want, that one naturally inquires whether some other motive than frontier defense was not involved in this generous estimate. Obviously if the colonies could be persuaded to pay for 10,000 men, a number of deserving veterans of the Seven Years War would be taken care of without expense to the people of Great Britain. With the failure of the Stamp Act of 1765, an effort to force the colonies to pay for this military establishment, the cost of maintaining 10,000 soldiers seemed prohibitive. But for the time being adequate defense had been provided, the frontiers sufficiently garrisoned, the Indians pacified, the malpractices of Indian traders stopped, and an Indian demarcation line drawn.

Colonial fur traders and British military men wished to keep the West beyond the treaty lines an Indian reservation for the use of the fur traders. 'Let the savages enjoy their deserts in quiet . . . were they drove from their forests, the peltry trade would decrease,' wrote General Gage to the Board of Trade, and the ministry snapped up this bright thought as a reason for doing nothing further about the West. Opposed to the policy of doing nothing further about the West were the promoters of several big speculative companies, who disliked this negative policy. Of these the largest and most important was the Walpole or Vandalia Company, promoted by Benjamin Franklin, George Croghan, and Thomas Wharton of Philadelphia. The Vandalia was organized on the basis of 72 shares, some of which were issued free to important English politicians like the Walpoles, Lord Camden, and George Grenville. Their original modest object of acquiring a million and a quarter acres in the Ohio valley, on Franklin's advice was swollen to 10 million acres, for which they proposed to pay the Crown £10,000. They did, to be sure, promise to assume the cost of administration, and of satisfying the Indians, who of course were not consulted. The Vandalia Company put forth pleasing propaganda about the great national benefits it would confer; one might think it to be a charitable scheme, like Georgia. It let in leading English politicians on the ground floor to enlist their active interest, and bribed freely when it thought bribery would do good. It even succeeded in getting rid of Lord Hillsborough, the Colonial Secretary, who opposed the scheme because he was afraid it would depopulate Ireland, where he owned vast estates. Some of the other schemes then pressing for Crown grants were 'Charlotiana,' embracing most of Illinois and Wisconsin, promoted by Franklin and Sir William Johnson, General Phineas Lyman's 'Military Adventurers' who asked for Kentucky and half of Tennessee, and Major Thomas Mant's scheme for settling veterans on a tract covering somewhat more than the present state of Michigan. Later, Richard Henderson of North Carolina promoted 'Transylvania' in Tennessee.

Lord Shelburne, though not financially interested, favored making the Vandalia and other Western grants because he foresaw that expansion of the North American population would be irresistible. But he was overruled. The Board of Trade and Plantations reported against big land companies on the ground that they would make trouble with the Indians, and that 'the proposition of forming inland colonies in America' was new and contrary to British interests. Let the restless Americans fill up Nova Scotia and the Floridas, where they will export directly to

England, and buy British goods! This policy became official in a Royal Proclamation of 1774. It doubtless contributed toward making the big land speculators favor an independent America, which might look more kindly on their schemes, and did.

2. TWO ATTEMPTS TO TAX THE COLONIES

The national debt of Great Britain on the conclusion of the Seven Years War had mounted to some £130 million, double what it had been in 1754, and acquisitions in two hemispheres greatly increased administrative expenses. The annual cost of maintaining the civil and military establishments in America alone had risen from some £70,000 in 1748 to well over £350,000 in 1764. In the light of this situation, George Grenville, Chancellor of the Exchequer, felt that it was both necessary and just to extract some revenue from the colonies. Parliament greeted this proposition with enthusiastic approval, and even the level-headed Franklin anticipated no trouble from America. Early in 1764 Grenville introduced into the House of Commons a series of resolutions for securing a revenue from America, and upon these the Revenue Act and the Stamp Act were based.

The exact extent of colonial contributions to the upkeep of the empire is not easy to determine. English landowners, paying an income tax of 20 per cent, felt that the colonists could well afford to shoulder some of their burden. But the Americans insisted that they were already carrying their full share, and contributing, directly and indirectly, to the maintenance of the imperial government up to the limit of their capacities. The colonies had incurred a debt of over £2.5 million for the prosecution of the war, and, notwithstanding the generosity of Parliament in assuming a part of that debt, a large portion of it remained. Massachusetts, for example, with a population of approximately 300,000, was raising £37,500 annually for the payment of her war debt. Propertied members of that colony asserted, with some justice, that they were taxed as heavily as propertied Englishmen; but few inhabitants of other colonies could make the same claim. If little direct revenue was derived from the American customs or the royal lands, it must be remembered that the mercantilist system was designed to control, not to tax, trade. Indirect contributions in the form of English port duties and the monopoly of colonial trade were considerable; William Pitt estimated that colonial commerce brought an annual profit of not less than £2 million to British merchants. Whatever the right of these new revenue measures may have been, events proved their inexpediency quickly enough.

The Revenue Act of 1764 — often known as the Sugar Act — was the first of these measures. The preamble stated frankly its purposes: 'That a revenue be raised in your . . . Majesty's dominions in America for defraying the expenses of defending, protecting and securing the same.' It was also designed to plug leaks in the Acts of Trade and Navigation. The law reduced the duty on foreign molasses from the uncollectable 6d per gallon of 1733 to 3d, but levied additional duties on foreign sugar and on English or European luxuries such as wine, silk, and linen, when imported into the American colonies. It 'enumerated' more colonial products such as hides and skins, which could be exported only to England; and it withdrew some earlier exemptions that the colonies had enjoyed, such as free importation of madeira wine. That favorite beverage of well-to-do Americans now became subject to a customs duty of £7 per double hogshead, as against 10s on port wine imported through England — an obvious attempt to change the drinking habits of the colonial aristocrats to profit the British exchequer.

Colonial leaders promptly seized on the declared revenue-raising purpose of this act as a constitutional point. As the New York Assembly observed in a respectful petition to Parliament on 18 October, 'Exemption from burthen of ungranted, involuntary taxes, must be the grand principle of every free state,' without which 'there can be no liberty, no happiness, no security.' If Parliament got away with taxing their trade, it might proceed to tax their lands, or anything. This seemed prophetic when Parliament on 22 March 1765 passed the famous Stamp Act.

In the meantime, a movement had begun to boycott the products taxed by the Revenue Act. This seems to have started at New Haven, as the *New York Gazette* smugly announced on 22 November 1764:

> The young Gentlemen of Yale College have unanimously agreed not to make use of any foreign spirituous Liquors. . . . The Gentlemen of the College cannot be too much commended for setting so laudable an Example. This will not only greatly diminish the Expences of Education, but prove, as may be presumed, very favourable to the Health and Improvement of the Students. At the same Time all Gentlemen of Taste, who visit the College, will think themselves better entertained with a good Glass of Beer or Cider, offered them upon such Principles, than they could be, with the best Punch or Madeira.

New England rum, however, did not come under the boycott!

Parliament's Stamp Act of 1765 was the first direct, internal tax ever to be laid on the colonies by Parliament; indeed, the first tax of any sort other than customs duties. It provided for revenue stamps costing (in specie) from a halfpenny to upward of twenty shillings sterling, to be affixed to all newspapers, broadsides, pamphlets, licenses, commercial bills, notes and bonds, advertisements, almanacs, leases, legal documents, and a number of similar papers. All the revenue was to be expended in the colonies, under the direction of Parliament, solely for the purpose of 'defending, protecting and securing the colonies.' Offenses against the law were to be tried in admiralty courts with no jury. As a sugar-coating to the pill only Americans were to be appointed as agents, and a number of unsuspecting colonials such as Richard Henry Lee and Jared Ingersoll applied for such positions. The measure, if extended to the West Indies, was calculated to secure an annual revenue of over £60,000; the costs of collection, it was hoped, would be relatively small, and the burden of the tax so evenly distributed as to arouse little opposition.

The Stamp bill appeared very reasonable to Parliament. The debate in the House of Commons, which Edmund Burke described as 'languid,' was enlivened only by a memorable passage at arms between Charles Townshend and the fiery young Irishman Isaac Barré, in which the latter endeared himself to Americans by referring to them as 'Sons of Liberty.' Despite the Colonel's eloquence, the bill passed the Commons by a vote of 204 to 49.

The reaction to the Stamp Act everywhere in the Thirteen Colonies was violent, for it was the peculiar misfortune of the Act to offend the most powerful and articulate groups in the colonies: merchants and business men, lawyers, journalists, and clergymen. Soon the merchants of New York, Philadelphia, and Boston, whose every bill of lading would be taxed, and who faced the prospect of a ruinous drain of hard money, organized for resistance and formed non-importation associations. Lawyers, bankers, land-dealers, and newspaper men were aroused; even the clergy joined the din. Business came to a temporary standstill; trade with the mother country fell off £300,000 in the summer of 1765. Respectable men organized as 'Sons of Liberty,' coerced stamp distributors into resigning, burned the stamped paper, and incited people to attack unpopular local characters.

On the very day (1 November 1765) that the Stamp Act came into operation, a howling New York mob, led by a shipmaster named Issac Sears, forced Lieutenant-Governor Colden to take refuge on board a British warship. The mob then attacked the fort at the Battery, broke into the governor's coach house, destroyed his carriages, and forced the officer in charge of stamped paper to burn the lot. A part of the rabble then marched up Broadway to a country estate on the Hudson (between the present Chambers and Warren Streets), leased by an officer of the garrison who had threatened 'to cram the Stamp Act down the people's throats.' They gutted his house, destroyed furniture, books, and china, drank up his liquor, uprooted the garden, and departed in the early morning carrying the regimental colors as a trophy.

In Charleston, Henry Laurens, wrongly suspected by the local mob of hiding stamped paper in his house, was pulled out of bed at midnight while the house was searched by his friends, whom he recognized under black-face and sailor disguise. In Boston the stamp distributor was hanged in effigy and his shop pulled down, after which the mob turned its attention to the royal customs collectors and Chief Justice Hutchinson, gutting their houses, burning their furniture, and tossing their books and papers into the street. The voters, in town meeting the next day, expressed their 'utter detestation' of this 'horrid scene,' but nobody compensated the victims.

The law was completely nullified by violence. Courts reopened, vessels cleared and entered, and business resumed without the use of stamps. It was an amazing exhibition of what a closely knit revolutionary organization could do, anticipating the Jacobins in the French Revolution, and the Communist, African, and other uprisings of our own times. *Absit omen!*

All this on the assumption that the law was unconstitutional and void. Virginia led the way in expressing that view. On 30 May, Patrick Henry made his famous 'Caesar had his Brutus, Charles I his Cromwell' speech, after which the assembly passed a set of resolves declaring that it had 'the only and sole exclusive right and power to lay taxes . . . upon the inhabitants of this Colony,' who were 'not bound to yield obedience to any law' of Parliament attempting to tax them. These Virginia resolutions were an 'alarum bell to the disaffected' in Boston (said Governor Bernard), and pointed the way to common colonial action.

A few days after Henry had stirred up Virginia, Massachusetts invited all continental colonies to appoint delegates to a congress to consider the Stamp Act menace. This congress, which met at New York in October 1765, was the first intercolonial meeting summoned by American initiative. Delegates from nine colonies were present, among them James Otis of Massachusetts, Philip Livingston of New York, Daniel Dulany of Maryland, John Dickinson of Pennsylvania, and Christopher Gadsden of South Carolina. Gadsden sounded the keynote: 'We should stand upon the broad common ground of natural rights. . . . There ought to be no New England man, no New Yorkers, known on the continent, but all of us Americans.' After the debate the congress adopted a set of resolutions more moderate than those of Virginia, but asserting once more that 'no taxes ever have been, or can be constitutionally imposed on them, but by their respective legislatures,' and that the Stamp Act had a 'manifest tendency to subvert the rights and liberties of the colonists.'

The constitutional issue, thus drawn, centered on the question of 'no taxation without representation.' In the American colonies there had developed the custom that an assemblyman must reside in the district which he represented. From the colonial point of view, Americans were not represented in Parliament, since they had no right to vote for members of the House of Commons. And they knew very well that it would do them no good to elect members to a Parliament where they would be in a hopeless minority, at least for many years. The orthodox English principle was that of 'virtual representation' — representation of classes and interests rather than of localities. English parliamentarians insisted that the American colonies were represented in the same way as the cities of Liverpool, Sheffield, or Birmingham, which elected no members of their own. William Pitt denounced this theory as 'the most contemptible' idea 'that ever entered into the head of man.'

In August 1765, even before the Stamp Act Congress met, the Grenville ministry fell. An 'old whig' ministry led by the Marquess of Rockingham now came into power. Parliament, after a hot debate, but encouraged by the king, repealed the Stamp Act in mid-March 1766. The law was repealed simply because it could not be enforced against united opposition, and because English merchants and manufacturers suffered from a boycott of British goods promoted by the Sons of Liberty. Parliament did not thereby renounce the right to tax the colonies, as proved by the fact that on almost the same day as the repeal, it passed the Declaratory Act affirming Parliament's right, as the sovereign legislature of the British empire 'to bind the colonies . . . in all cases whatsoever.'

News of the Stamp Act repeal, which began to trickle into the colonies in May 1766, aroused an ecstasy of loyalty; the more so because William Pitt, the Winston Churchill of that era, had moved it. In New York City the king's birthday and the repeal were celebrated at the same time; every window was illuminated with candles, two oxen were barbecued, and free beer and grog were provided for the happy crowd. The assembly voted an equestrian statue of George III to be erected at the Battery, and a statue of William Pitt too. Tablets or busts of 'the Great Commoner' were set up at Williamsburg; and even in country villages.

The Americans had won a political victory. United opposition (and not for 50 years would they be so united again) forced the repeal. Their fundamental loyalty is proved by their taking no notice of the fact that the Revenue Act of 1764 was not repealed, and no notice of the Declaratory Act, almost word-for-word a copy of the Irish Declaratory Act of 1719 which held Ireland in bondage. In reality the British government had taken three steps forward — Proclamation of 1763, Revenue Act, Declaratory Act; and only one back, repeal of the Stamp Act.

VIII

Crisis, Calm, and Crisis Again

1. THE TOWNSHEND ACTS

During the general jubilation that followed the repeal of the Stamp Act, no serious effort was made by the British government to find out what, if anything, could be done to raise defense funds through colonial assemblies. No royal commission was sent to America to study and report. Instead, a fresh attempt was made by Parliament to tax the colonists, and a plan of imperial reorganization was placed in effect without consulting them.

Since the Thirteen Colonies had gained enormously in strength and security from the conquest of Canada and the West, was it not fair that they should either pay some part of the cost, or propose some constructive alternative? And did not Parliament twice back down before colonial opposition, in 1766 and 1770, only to find the colonists preferring new claims and discovering new rights? Perhaps, say those who ask these awkward questions, if the British government had been unyielding in 1765 it could have prevented trouble in 1775. Or, putting it another way, if English politicians had not encouraged colonial rebels, would not these rebels soon have acquiesced in parliamentary regulation? To which one can only reply, as 'Junius' did, that logic is not much use in politics, 'the fate of nations must not be tried by forms,' and the principles of police administration cannot be extended to imperial administration. Or, one may point to the complete failure of a 'hard-boiled' British policy toward Ireland over a period of centuries, and of the doctrinaire approach by France to her colonial problems subsequent to World War II. England maintained her empire and transformed it into a league of free commonwealths under Elizabeth II, by following a policy diametrically opposed to that of George III; one strikingly similar to what Jefferson and John Adams demanded in 1774 as the price of colonial loyalty.

The Rockingham ministry repealed the Stamp Act; but for reasons of internal politics and royal displeasure, that ministry fell in 1766. King George then turned to Pitt as one who commanded the confidence of Parliament yet was not unfavorable to the king's idea of one big party. The 'Great Commoner,' now Earl of Chatham, formed a ministry of talents, including three known friends to the American colonies, Shelburne, Conway, and Camden, and others, like Charles Townshend, who were not so friendly.

At a critical juncture in 1767, when Chatham was laid low by a mysterious malady, a young and amiable peer with no sense of leadership, the Duke of Grafton, became Prime Minister, and the government drifted. It was under these distressing circumstances, 'while the western horizon was still in a blaze with Pitt's descending glory, on the opposite quarter of the heavens arose another luminary, and, for his hour, became lord of the ascendant.' That was Charles Townshend, brilliant, ambitious, and unprincipled, who, taunted by George Grenville in the Commons that he dared not try to tax America, retorted, 'I will, I will!' and did. With breathtaking audacity he proposed to reduce the British land tax from 20 per cent to 15 per cent, and meet the resulting deficit of some £400,000, in part, by obtaining revenue from the colonies. This was to be done by collecting import duties in the colonies on English paint, lead, and paper; and on tea. These duties were expected to yield not less than £40,000 annually; and as the colonies had always paid some customs duties, how could they object to these? For more efficient collection the customs service was reorganized, and a Board of Commissioners of the Customs was established at Boston: an important administrative reform. New vice-admiralty courts were created, and writs of assistance, whose legality had been challenged by James Otis in a famous speech of 1761, were authorized. Most important of all, the moneys thus raised in the colonies, instead of going to support the garrisons, were to be used to create a colonial civil list and thus render the royal governors and judges independent of colonial assemblies.

The Townshend Acts took Americans by surprise. Their trade was in the usual depression that is apt to set in four or five years after the end of a great war. It was hard for them to find the sterling money to pay these new taxes, and the regulations of the Commissioners of the Customs required so many bonds and documents that for a time it was difficult to do business at all. But colonial leaders were hard put to find a legal argument against the Townshend duties. They wished to deny Parliament's power to tax them, yet to acknowledge Parliament's power to regulate their commerce. They were not prepared to break loose from the protective system of the Acts of Trade and Navigation, nor could they deny that many of the new regulations were designed to stop lawbreaking.

The colonial leader who came closest to resolving this dilemma was John Dickinson of Pennsylvania, who styled himself 'the Pennsylvania Farmer.' Actually, he was a conservative Philadelphia lawyer, born in Maryland and educated in England. Although a delegate to the Stamp Act Congress, and the member who drafted its resolutions, Dickinson was neither agitator nor politician. A public-spirited citizen, devoid of personal ambition or vanity, he abhorred violence and hoped to settle all pending disputes with England by persuasion.

The twelve 'Farmer's Letters,' which began coming out in colonial newspapers at the end of 1767, were exactly what Americans wanted; and the loyal, respectful tone of them appealed to many in England. Here are some of the key passages:

> The Parliament unquestionably possesses a legal authority to regulate the trade of Great Britain and all her colonies. . . . We are but parts of a whole; and therefore there must exist a power somewhere to preside, and preserve the connexion in due order. This power is lodged in the Parliament; and we are as much dependent on Great Britain as a perfectly free people can be on another. . . .
>
> The cause of Liberty is a cause of too much dignity to be sullied by turbulence and tumult. It ought to be maintained in a manner suitable to her nature. Those who engage in it should breathe a sedate, yet fervent spirit, animating them to actions of prudence, justice, modesty, bravery, humanity, and magnanimity. . . .
>
> Let us behave like dutiful children, who have received unmerited blows from a beloved parent. Let us complain to our parent; but let our complaints speak at the same time the language of affliction and veneration.

The most interesting of these extracts, for the future, was the first; for it shows that Dickinson was moving, somewhat fumblingly, toward the principle of federalism. Unfortunately, no responsible Englishman of that day seemed able to grasp this federal principle. Even Benjamin Franklin, who had spent several years in England as agent for Massachusetts and Pennsylvania, did not comprehend it. After reading Dickinson he wrote, 'I know not what the Boston people mean by the "subordination" they acknowledge in their assembly to Parliament, while they deny its powers to make laws for them, nor what bounds the Farmer sets to the power he acknowledges in Parliament to "regulate the trade of the colonies," it being difficult to draw lines between duties for regulation and those for revenue.'

Samuel Adams of Boston, boss of the town meeting and leader in the assembly, had already reached the point in his thinking that Parliament had no right to legislate for the colonies on any subject. But he was too clever a politician to let that out now. An austere, implacable member of Boston's middle class, this 'Matchiavel of Chaos,' alone of the forerunners of American independence, was a typical revolutionary. A master of propaganda, he realized that the general run of people prefer drama and ritual to a well thought-out exposition. The New England people enjoyed no ritual in their religion, and permitted no public theater, but Adams provided them with both in highly agreeable forms. There was dancing around the Liberty Tree, a big elm near Boston Common selected for that purpose; unpopular characters were hanged in effigy from its branches, those whom the radicals wished to become popular were serenaded, and the British ministers and their apologists were damned over bowls of rum punch. He employed classic symbols of liberty such as the Phrygian liberty cap, a Liberty Song with new words by John Dickinson set to the rousing tune 'Heart of Oak,' which anyone could roar even if he couldn't sing; and on every appropriate occasion he organized a demonstration with consummate artistry. These devices were copied by Sons of Liberty throughout the continent as far away as Charleston, where Christopher Gadsden selected a live oak as liberty tree. John Adams, after a Sons of Liberty dinner attended by delegates from Philadelphia, observed that these things 'tinge the minds of the people; they impregnate them with the sentiments of liberty; they render the people fond of their leaders in the cause, and averse and bitter against all opponents.' And, he added, that in spite of drinking 45 toasts, he 'did not see one person intoxicated, or near it.' We don't have to believe that.

Well educated in the ancient classics, Samuel Adams thought in terms of Roman virtue, and his favorite motto, chosen from the unlikely source of Ovid's *Remedia Amoris,* was *principiis obsta,* 'Take a stand at the start,' lest by one appeasement after another you end in complete subjection. He was no orator — he had a quavering voice and a shaky hand — so he let other Sons of Liberty like Joseph Warren and the firebrand Otis make the speeches, while he wrote provocative articles for the newspapers and pulled political strings.

In February 1768, after the full impact of the Townshend Acts began to be appreciated, Adams and Otis drafted (and the Massachusetts assembly adopted) a circular letter to the lower houses of all continental colonies, to call their attention to the new laws. The assembly, stated this letter, has 'preferred a humble, dutiful and loyal petition to our most gracious sovereign . . . to obtain redress.' The language of this circular letter was as moderate and loyal as that of Dickinson, but the Grafton ministry decided to make it the occasion for a showdown. Lord Hillsborough, the new secretary for the colonies, ordered the Massachusetts assembly to rescind the letter, and Governor Bernard to dismiss them if they refused. The assembly did refuse, by a vote of 92 to 17. And it was supported at Williamsburg by a set of Virginia resolves introduced by the burgess from Fairfax County, Colonel George Washington, and signed, among others, by the new burgess from Albemarle County, Thomas Jefferson. Adams and the Sons of Liberty everywhere seized on this incident as a golden opening for propaganda, and made heroes of the patriotic '92,' who refused to rescind.

In Boston the chief contributor to the Sons of Liberty war chest for printing, banners, and free rum at liberty tree rallies, was a 31-year-old merchant named John Hancock. The new Commissioners of the Customs therefore determined to put him out of business. He was 'framed' by a prosecution of his sloop *Liberty,* falsely charged with smuggling madeira wine. The Boston mob rescued him and his vessel, and gave the royal customs officials a very rough time. They then retired to the castle in Boston harbor, and Governor Bernard asked for and got protection. Two regiments of the Halifax garrison were sent to Boston.

Although the Grafton ministry failed to intimidate Boston, it dealt successfully with New York, where two regiments of the British army had been stationed since 1766. Parliament's Quartering (or Mutiny) Act required local authorities, wherever the king's troops were stationed, to provide quarters or barracks, and to furnish the men free, various house-keeping items and five pints of beer or a gill of rum *per diem*. The New York Assembly boggled at paying for the beverages, but voted the other required supplies for 1100 men. Lord Hillsborough announced that this was not enough and ordered the assembly to be suspended like that of Massachusetts. In the next election, in the fall of 1769, New York voters surprisingly returned a majority of the conservative De Lancey faction, and the new assembly voted everything that the British troops wanted. Sons of Liberty, led by Isaac Sears and Alexander McDougall, de-nounced this as a 'contemptible betrayal,' and Governor Colden threw McDougall into prison for sedition. McDougall became a hero and held receptions in jail.

In January 1770, New York City became the scene of a serious riot. British troops cut down a liberty pole erected by the radicals and piled the pieces in front of the Sons of Liberty headquarters. A fight followed on Gordon Hill, the mob using clubs and staves against the soldiers' cutlasses and bayonets, and one citizen was killed. This affair is New York's claim for having been the scene of the 'first bloodshed' of the Revolution.

In general, however, the agitation that followed the Townshend Acts was less violent than that against the Stamp Act. Merchants again re-sorted to non-importation agreements. Importations fell off by one-half in Boston and Philadelphia, and by 83 per cent in New York. Princeton students gave up imported cloth for homespun, ladies found substitutes for tea, newspapers used colonial-made paper, and houses went un-painted, all to protest the new duties. New colonial industries sprang up, and an agreement among planters to purchase no more slaves cost the Liverpool slave traders dear. Yet, owing to the opening of new markets for English goods in Europe and the Far East, these non-importation agreements of 1768–69 were not very effective in British trading circles.

The presence of British red-coats in Boston was a standing invitation to disorder. Antagonism between citizens and soldiery flared up in the so-called 'Boston Massacre' of 5 March 1770. A snowballing of the red-coats degenerated into a mob attack, someone gave the order to fire, and four Bostonians, including a Negro named Crispus Attucks, lay dead in the snow. Although the provocation came from the civilians, radicals such as Samuel Adams and Joseph Warren seized upon the 'massacre' for purposes of propaganda. Captain Preston and the British soldiers were courageously defended by young John Adams and Josiah Quincy, and acquitted of the charge of murder; but the royal governor was forced to remove the garrison from the town to the castle, and the strategic advantage lay with the radicals.

On the very day of the 'Boston Massacre,' the new British ministry headed by Lord North, concluding that colonial duties on English manufactures were preposterous, repealed all the Townshend duties except the one on tea. A tax of three pence per pound was kept on this article primarily as an assertion of parliamentary authority. 'A peppercorn in acknowledgment of the right is of more value than millions without it,' George Grenville had said; and easy-going Lord North acquiesced in this glib fallacy.

Except for that teasing little duty on tea, all outward grievances of the colonists had been removed by the summer of 1770. The radicals found themselves without an issue. Sam Adams did his best to keep up the agitation, with annual exhibits of bloody relics of the 'Boston Massacre,' but the people showed what they thought of him by defeating him for registrar of deeds in his home county. After that blow, his cousin John Adams confided to his diary, 'I shall certainly become more retired and cautious; I shall certainly mind my own farm and my own office.' New York quieted down; soldiers of the garrison could now promenade their girls on the Battery without being insulted. 'Virginia,' wrote Thomas Jefferson, 'seemed to fall into a state of insensibility.' A general prosperity reigned, imports into New England alone jumped from £330,000 to £1.2 million. Short harvests in Europe created a demand for American corn and wheat, and for the first time in history, specie was sent from England in payment. It really looked as if colonial agitation were at an end.

But Sam Adams was simply waiting for some unwise move by the North ministry to revive it.

2. BACK-COUNTRY TURMOIL

Parts of the 'back-country' were full of turmoil during the years of agitation against the Stamp and Townshend Acts; but this turmoil had nothing to do with the America versus England controversy. It was caused by discontent with local governing classes. In Pennsylvania, in 1764, a band of frontier hoodlums known as the 'Paxton Boys,' furious at their lack of protection during Pontiac's rebellion by the Quaker-dominated assembly, took a cowardly revenge by massacring some peaceful survivors of the Conestoga tribe in Lancaster County, whose ancestors had made the celebrated (though fictitious) 'treaty that was never broken' with William Penn. The 'Paxton Boys' then threatened to wipe out the so-called Moravian Indians, an Algonquian tribe which had been converted by German Moravian missionaries and settled on a reservation near Bethlehem. These Indians fled to Philadelphia where the government quartered them in barracks, protected by British regulars. The 'Boys,' 1500 strong, heavily armed, and uttering 'hideous outcries in imitation of the war whoop,' marched on the capital in February 1764, bent on killing every redskin refugee. Philadelphia was in a panic, and it took Ben Franklin to talk the ruffians into returning home, by promising more frontier protection and legislative bounties for Indians' scalps. The Pennsylvania back-country then quieted down, but bided its time to obtain more weight in the assembly.

This situation became most explosive in the Carolinas, where back-country society differed in origin, religion, and even race, from that of the seaboard. Almost half the total population of South Carolina, and 79 per cent of the white population, lived in the back-country of that province in 1776. Yet the provincial government was completely centralized at Charleston, with neither counties nor courts in the interior, much less schools or police; and a man had to own 500 acres and twenty slaves to qualify for membership in the assembly. The Western settlers were at the mercy of border ruffians, horse thieves, and Indian raiders; a band of Creeks murdered fourteen people in the frontier settlement at Long Canes on Christmas Eve 1763, and were only driven off because Patrick Calhoun, the father of John C. Calhoun, took command of the survivors. The people formed associations known as 'Regulators' to refuse payment of taxes until they got effective government. In 1769 the assembly set up six new circuit courts, and revised the fee table. But most of the Westerners' grievances in this province were still unredressed when the War of Independence broke.

In North Carolina the separation between coastal region and interior was even sharper. Here the Western grievances were not lack of government, but bad government — unequal taxation, extortion by centrally appointed judges and corrupt sheriffs, greedy lawyers, uncertainty of land titles, scarcity of hard money to pay taxes, refusal of the assembly to provide paper money or to allow taxes to be paid in produce, consequent tax levies 'by distress' and sheriffs taking over poor men's farms.[1] A particular complaint was a province law which allowed only Anglican clergymen to perform marriage ceremonies, when there were no such clergy in the back-country! It was reported that the Regulators were about to march on New Bern and wreck the royal governor's palace. March they did; but being untrained and partly unarmed, they were easily defeated by half their number of loyal militia, 16 May 1771, at the so-called Battle of the Alamance. Casualties were only nine men killed on each side, since the Regulators ran away after the first volley. But fifteen of them were captured and tried for treason, and six were hanged. Governor Tryon and his army then made a triumphal progress through Regulator country and exacted an oath of allegiance from every male inhabitant.

That was the end of the 'War of the Regulation,' the most serious internal rebellion in the English colonies since Nat Bacon's. It was put down largely by whigs who later became patriots; but Martin Howard, the hanging judge, became a prominent loyalist. The next assembly passed some remedial legislation such as fixing maximum fees, and establishing tobacco warehouses whose receipts could be tendered for taxes. But the North Carolina back-country was still so full of discontent in 1776 that many former rebels emigrated to Tennessee to avoid taking part in the war, and others became tories.

Back-country brawls from New Hampshire to South Carolina seem never to have interested the British government, which thereby missed a golden opportunity to win support from frontiersmen against the silk-stockinged Sons of Liberty and their 'wharf-rat' mobsters. But the British government was involved in another Western problem. How far were land speculators to be allowed to encroach on and monopolize Indian country? Would George III countenance Western expansion, or turn the Royal Proclamation of 1763 into a permanent policy?

Events in Virginia precipitated a decision on that particular Western

1. Note similarity of these grievances to those of Shays's rebels in Massachusetts in 1786. And it is significant that Herman Husband, leader of the North Carolina Regulators, turns up 25 years later as a Whiskey rebel in Pennsylvania.

problem. Although the land speculators had received no encouragement in London, they sent Daniel Boone and other pioneers across the Appalachians to 'spy out' land. Lord Dunmore, governor of Virginia since 1772, followed the line of least resistance, and sought to gain popularity by supporting the Western landowners and pioneers in a border conflict which they provoked with the Shawnee. As a result of a battle in which the Shawnee were defeated, the Delaware, Shawnee, and Mingo tribes renounced all their hunting rights south of the Ohio. Yet, a little more than a year later, Lord Dunmore was driven from Virginia by the very men he had led against the Indians!

Dunmore did not even have the consolation of pleasing his king; for while he was marching through the wilderness with his jovial band, the British government sought to put a stop to all such doings. It ordered royal governors to grant no land, and permit no new settlements, except after prior survey, allotment, and sale by auction. Although not put into effect outside Canada, this order of 1774 called forth Thomas Jefferson's bold *Summary View of the Rights of British America*, denying the Crown's right to dispose of any Western land and furnished one more grievance for the Declaration of Independence. Yet the United States public land system was based on exactly the same British concept.

3. THE ISSUE JOINED

Samuel Adams's genius, unlike that of his young cousin John, was for agitation and destruction. Yet he was no mere rabble-rouser, greedy for power. He believed (and the Lees of Virginia, the New York Sons of Liberty, and Gadsden of South Carolina agreed) that 'every day' in the calm period of 1770–73 'strengthens our opponents and weakens us.' And Adams was right. Prosperity dulled watchfulness for freedom, and the efficiency of the Commissioners of the Customs brought in such ample customs revenue even after the Townshend duties were repealed, that the British government put one royal governor and judge after another on the Crown payroll. The radicals fumed against this in vain — the average colonist thought it fine to be relieved of paying his governors and judges! Adams felt that if this system were allowed to go on, colonial liberties would be completely suppressed; Americans would wake up some day and find that they were helpless under royal officials.

But he needed a spectacular, emotional issue to bring home this danger before it was too late.

In the tea affair, he found it.

The powerful East India Company, being in financial straits, appealed to the British government for aid and was granted a monopoly on all tea exported to the colonies. The Company decided to sell tea through its own agents, thus eliminating the independent merchants, and disposing of the tea at less than the usual price either in America or in England. It was this monopoly aspect that aroused the colonial merchants and threw them again into alliance with the radicals. 'America,' wrote one of them, 'would be prostrate before a monster that may be able to destroy every branch of our commerce, drain us of all our property, and wantonly leave us to perish by the thousands.' These fears were groundless, but none the less powerful. Burke, in his speech on conciliation, gauged well the American temper. 'In other countries, the people . . . judge of an ill principle in government only by an actual grievance; here they anticipate the evil. . . . They augur misgovernment at a distance, and snuff the approach of tyranny in every tainted breeze.'

Colonial reaction to the tea monopoly took various forms. In Charleston the tea was landed, but not offered for sale; at Philadelphia and New York the consignments were rejected and returned to England. But in Boston the ingenious brain of Sam Adams brought about a dramatic showdown. Here, on the night of 16 December 1773, Sons of Liberty disguised as Mohawks boarded the three tea ships and dumped the offending leaves into the water. The radicals had called the ministerial bluff. They had refused even the peppercorn in acknowledgment of right.

The Boston Tea-Party accomplished just what Sam Adams wanted; it goaded the North ministry into a crack-down on the mutterings over home rule. The destruction of property — and tea at that — aroused John Bull more than mobbing officials and beating up red-coats. 'The dye is now cast,' wrote George III to Lord North. 'The Colonies must either submit or triumph.'

The House of Commons, now obedient to the king and Lord North, retaliated by passing in May and June 1774 a series of Coercive Acts. These closed the port of Boston to commerce until the tea was paid for, radically changed the provincial government in Massachusetts, and provided for the transportation of certain offenders to England for trial. These laws threatened the very life of Boston. To exclude her from the sea, the element that made her great, was a punishment comparable to the destruction of Carthage.

These 'Intolerable Acts,' as the colonists called them, were quickly followed by the enactment by Parliament of the Quebec Act of 1774. This statute, the outcome of a carefully thought-out scheme to give a permanent government to Quebec, was received by the colonists as yet another punitive measure. They viewed the provisions of the act, which extended the boundaries of Quebec to embrace the vast country west of the Appalachians and north of the Ohio, as a deliberate attempt to discourage expansion by the colonists beyond the mountains and to ignore their land claims. Perhaps most important, the colonists were disturbed by the reinstatement of the privileges of the Catholic Church, including the legalization of tithes. Young Alexander Hamilton, who warned that 'priestly tyranny' might 'find as propitious a soil in Canada as it ever has in Spain and Portugal,' asked: 'Does not your blood run cold to think that an English Parliament should pass an act for the establishment of arbitrary power and Popery in such a country?' Furthermore, Congregationalists and Presbyterians feared that the law would serve as a precedent for the establishment of an Anglican episcopate in the American colonies. The Quebec Act, aimed at conciliating the French habitants, had the unanticipated consequence of pushing American ministers toward a break with the Crown.

Instead of isolating Massachusetts, as they had been planned to do, the Coercive Acts rallied the other colonies to Massachusetts. For they demonstrated a parliamentary power far more dangerous to colonial liberty than mere taxing. On 27 May 1774 members of the Virginia Assembly, meeting in the Raleigh Tavern at Williamsburg, called for a congress of all continental American colonies. On 5 September the delegates of twelve colonies assembled in Carpenters' Hall, Philadelphia, 'to consult upon the present unhappy state of the Colonies.' This was the famous First Continental Congress.

'Clouds, indeed, and darkness,' said Edmund Burke, 'rest upon the future.'

IX

The Revolution Precipitated

1. GATHERING CLOUDS

The First Continental Congress which assembled in Philadelphia on 5 September 1774, had been summoned by a popular demand; not for independence, but for liberty, as Americans understood that word. They expected Congress to take steps to ward off parliamentary wrath, vigorously to assert colonial rights, and happily to restore imperial relations to their former agreeable status. This Continental Congress was an extra-legal body chosen by provincial congresses, or popular conventions, and instructed by them. This meant that the patriot party was in control of the situation, and that extreme conservatives who would have nothing to do with resistance to the laws were not represented. Otherwise, the membership of the Congress was a fair cross-section of American opinion. Here were extremists like the Adamses of Massachusetts, Stephen Hopkins of Rhode Island, Thomas Mifflin of Pennsylvania, Richard Henry Lee and Patrick Henry of Virginia, and Christopher Gadsden of South Carolina; moderates like Peyton Randolph (chosen president of the Congress) and George Washington of Virginia, John Dickinson of Pennsylvania, and the Rutledges of South Carolina; conservatives like James Duane and John Jay of New York and Joseph Galloway of Pennsylvania. The varied interests of the colonies were well represented. Every colony except Georgia sent at least one delegate, and the total number was fifty-five — large enough for diversity of opinion, small enough for genuine debate and effective action.

Able as this Congress was, it faced a distressing dilemma. It must give an appearance of firmness to persuade or frighten the British government into concessions, but at the same time avoid any show of radicalism or 'spirit of independency' that might alarm conservative Americans and encourage the spirit of lawlessness and leveling that was already abroad in the country.

Lawlessness, as the conservatives called it, got in the first lick. Congress was discussing a statesmanlike plan of union presented by Joseph Galloway, the essence of which provided for an American legislature, to have joint control with Parliament over all American affairs. No act of Parliament would apply to the colonies unless accepted by their legislature, which would have jurisdiction over Indian affairs, Western land grants, and raising men and money in time of war. While Galloway's plan (similar to the Albany plan of 1754) was being debated, Paul Revere came galloping from Boston to Philadelphia with the radical Suffolk Resolves in his saddlebags. These resolutions, drafted by Joseph Warren and adopted by a convention of the towns around Boston, declared the Coercive Acts to be unconstitutional and void, urged Massachusetts to arm and act as a free state until these 'attempts of a wicked administration to enslave America' were repealed, and urged Congress to adopt economic sanctions against Great Britain. All this brought Congress up short, and made debating of a plan of union seem like discussing insurance while your house was on fire. The members knew that their constituents wished to 'do something' about beleaguered Boston, for whose benefit an astonishing contribution of money and provisions was collected in all the other colonies.

So Congress, by a majority of one colony, shelved the Galloway plan and endorsed the Suffolk Resolves, which Galloway considered 'a declaration of war against Great Britain.' Congress then proceeded to adopt a series of retaliatory measures against the Coercive Acts. Mindful of the success of commercial boycott in 1765, it adopted new and stringent non-importation, non-exportation, and non-consumption agreements. John Adams was skeptical of the value of these 'economic sanctions,' which to this day have been a favorite resource of American statesmen (Jefferson's embargo, Madison's non-intercourse, Confederacy holding back cotton, restrictions on trade with Red China and Castro's Cuba). But Lee of Virginia was certain that this 'Association' would wring immediate concessions from Parliament, although in practice the system, by denying the colonists needed supplies, hurt the Americans more than the British.

Having agreed upon this counteroffensive, Congress passed a Declaration of Rights and Grievances addressed to the people of Great Britain and the colonies; and, as a sop to the moderates, a petition to the king. These papers, taken together, led the Earl of Chatham to declare in the House of Lords: 'For genuine sagacity, for singular moderation, for solid wisdom, manly spirit, sublime sentiment and simplicity of language . . . the Congress of Philadelphia shines unrivalled.' The Declaration of Rights summed up anew the traditional arguments of American protest and anticipated in many particulars the grievances of the Declaration of Independence. It did, however, concede parliamentary regulation of commerce, for Chatham had given due warning that otherwise Americans could expect no sympathy from him.

This concession did not please the radicals. Independently of one another, James Wilson, a close-reasoning Scot of Pennsylvania, Thomas Jefferson, and John Adams had reached the conclusion that Parliament had no rightful jurisdiction over the colonies. 'All the different members of the British Empire,' said Wilson, 'are distinct States, independent of each other, but connected together under the same sovereign in right of the same Crown.' Wilson's *Considerations on the Authority of Parliament,* Jefferson's *Summary View,* and Adams's *Novanglus* papers published this startling theory between August 1774 and February 1775. Historically they found no ground for Parliament's authority, although they admitted that the colonies had weakly accepted it; logically there was no need for it, since the colonial legislatures were competent. The colonists should honor and obey the king, follow his lead in war, observe the treaties he concluded with other princes; but otherwise govern themselves. Thus a federal solution for the problem of liberty versus authority, which John Dickinson found to be implicit in the old empire, was now made explicit by these three hard-thinking Americans in 1774-75. They demanded for the Thirteen Colonies the same dominion status which Canada, Australia, New Zealand, India, Pakistan, the West Indies, and other former colonies now enjoy in the British Empire, and which is now the official basis of the British Commonwealth of Nations. But these doctrines had no remote chance of acceptance. Very few Englishmen could understand how a community could be in the empire, unless parliamentary authority over it were sovereign and complete.

The most important work of the Congress was an agreement called 'The Association.' This provided for committees of inspection in every town or county, in order to supervise the non-importation, non-exportation, and non-consumption agreements. The Association was charged to publish the names of merchants who violated these sanctions, to confiscate their importations, and to 'encourage frugality, economy, and industry.' The Puritan streak common to most great revolutions appears in an exhortation to 'discourage every species of extravagance and dissipation, especially all horse-racing, and all kinds of gaming, cock-fighting, exhibitions of shews, plays, and other expensive diversions and entertainments,' including elaborate funerals, a favorite colonial diversion. Congress also started a dry war by voting to give up imported tea and wines. Rum, however, was still a patriotic beverage.

Thus the Congress called to protest against parliamentary usurpation ended by creating extra-legal machinery for supervising American daily life. The Association caused many moderate men to draw back in alarm. 'If we must be enslaved,' wrote the loyalist Samuel Seabury, 'let it be by a king at least, and not by a parcel of upstart, lawless committeemen.'

Having done all this, Congress rose on 22 October 1774, resolving to meet again the following May if colonial grievances had not then been redressed.

Even now the Crown might have effected an alliance with the large body of conservative opinion in the colonies, and by timely concession have averted hostilities. For not willingly would the propertied men in the colonies ally themselves with mob leaders and snooping committees. But the king had no intention of making concessions; and what the king said determined what the North ministry did. In September 1774, George III wrote, 'the Colonies must either submit or triumph'; and in November: 'the New England Governments are now in a State of Rebellion, blows must decide whether they are subject to this Country or independent.'

Chatham on 20 January 1775, supported by Camden, made a motion to repeal the Coercive Acts and withdraw the troops — 'I tell you the Acts must be repealed. . . . My Lords, there is no time to be lost; every moment is big with dangers. Nay, while I am now speaking the decisive blow may be struck, and millions are involved in the consequence.' But Chatham's motion was heavily defeated. Three days later, a similar motion to repeal, for which Burke delivered the first of his famous speeches on conciliation with America, was presented in the House of Commons and lost, 82 to 197. Next, Chatham got introduced in the lower house a bill conceding every practical point demanded by Congress; it was roundly defeated. Lord North then pushed through Parliament a resolution providing that if any colony would raise the cost of its own government, plus a proper quota (determined in England) for defense, Parliament would forbear to tax that colony, and would pay the customs duties collected within its borders into the colony treasury. The king liked this because he fondly thought it would 'put an end to Congresses.' But from the American point of view this North Conciliatory Resolve of 27 February 1775 conceded nothing on taxation and failed to meet the latest issue of closing a port and altering a government. And news of it arrived in America at a moment fatal to any reconciliation — just as the news of Lexington and Concord was being shouted through the length and breadth of the land.

2. HOSTILITIES BEGIN

The decisive blow that Chatham predicted was struck on 19 April 1775. General Thomas Gage, an amiable gentleman with an American wife, was not only governor of Massachusetts but in command of the garrison at Boston. Dr. Joseph Warren, one of the leading radicals of that town, wrote to Arthur Lee in London on 20 February 1775:

> It is not yet too late to accommodate the dispute amicably. But I am of the opinion that if once General Gage should lead his troops into the country with the design to enforce the late Acts of Parliament, Great Britain may take her leave, at least of the New England colonies, and, if I mistake not, of all America. If there is any wisdom in the nation, God grant it may be speedily called forth! Every day, every hour widens the breach. A Richmond, a Chatham, a Shelburne, a Camden, with their noble associates, may yet repair it; it is a work which none but the greatest of men can conduct.

Unfortunately, these noble lords and their associates were in opposition, without a dog's chance of ousting North's well-nourished majority; and General Gage's duty was to enforce the Coercive Acts. Since the previous autumn Massachusetts, as suggested by the Suffolk Resolves, had become a free state, governed by a popularly elected provincial congress, and a committee of safety which organized armed resistance.

Gage had no authority outside Boston. On 18 April 1775, when news that the revolutionary committee was collecting powder and military stores at Concord came to his ears, he sent a strong detail of his garrison to confiscate these munitions. But the signal was given: Paul Revere and Will Dawes aroused the whole countryside. When Major Pitcairn, after a night of marching, led his column of light infantry into the village of Lexington, he saw through the mists of the early morning a grim band of minute-men lined up across the common. There was a moment of hesitation, cries and orders from both sides, and in the midst of the confusion somebody fired. Then firing broke out along both lines and the Americans dispersed, leaving eight of their number dead on the green. The first blood of the War for American Independence had been shed. Who first fired, American or Englishman, is one of the unsolved riddles of history; but the patriots managed to circulate their own view of it as a brutal and wanton attack on peaceful villagers.

The British continued their march to Concord, where the 'embattled farmers' at the bridge 'fired the shot heard round the world.' Their purpose partially accomplished, the British regiments began their return march. All along the road, behind stone walls, hillocks, and houses, the minute-men arriving from 'every Middlesex village and farm' made targets of the bright red coats. When the weary column finally stumbled into Boston it had lost 247 in killed and wounded. And inside of a week Boston was a beleaguered city.

On 10 May 1775, while the country was still resounding with the alarms and 'atrocities' of Lexington and Concord, the Second Continental Congress assembled in Philadelphia. The prophetic words of Patrick Henry were still ringing in the ears of the delegates: 'It is vain, sir, to extenuate the matter. Gentlemen may cry "peace, peace" but there is no peace. The war is actually begun! The next gale that sweeps from the north will bring to our ears the clash of resounding arms! Our brethren are already in the field! Why stand we here idle?' Why, indeed? Congress was in no conciliatory mood. War had already begun. Would it be accompanied by independence? Even as delegates were asking these questions, Ethan Allen and his Green Mountain Boys were crashing through the defenses of Fort Ticonderoga and raising the standard of revolt in the North. Control of events was rapidly drifting out of the hands of law-abiding men, and Congress was forced to register, in one form or another, the accomplished facts.

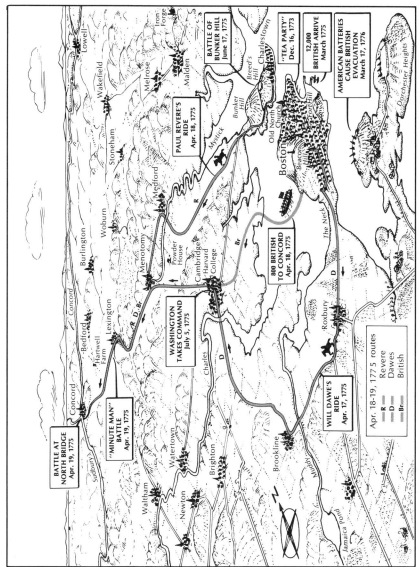

THE BOSTON REGION
at the Opening of the War of Independence, 1773-1776

Map labels:
Lowell, Iron Forge, BATTLE OF BUNKER HILL June 17, 1775, Charlestown, "TEA PARTY" Dec. 16, 1773, 12,000 BRITISH ARRIVE March 1775, AMERICAN BATTERIES CAUSE BRITISH EVACUATION March 17, 1776, Dorchester Heights, Wakefield, Malden, Melrose, Breed's Hill, Bunker Hill, Old North Church, Fort Hill, Stoneham, PAUL REVERE'S RIDE Apr. 18, 1775, Mystick, Boston, Beacon Hill, Medford, Woburn, Burlington, Menotomy, Powder House, Harvard College, Cambridge, Br, 800 BRITISH TO CONCORD Apr. 18, 1775, The Neck, R, D, Roxbury, Concord, Bedford, Lexington, R D Br, WASHINGTON TAKES COMMAND July 5, 1775, Charles, D, WILL DAWE'S RIDE Apr. 17, 1775, Hartwell Farm, BATTLE AT NORTH BRIDGE Apr. 19, 1775, "MINUTE MAN" BATTLE Apr. 19, 1775, Concord, Sudbury, Waltham, Watertown, Brighton, Newton, Brookline, Muddy, Jamaica Pond

Apr. 18-19, 1775 routes
R — Revere
D — Dawes
Br — British

167

This second Congress was as distinguished a group as ever assembled in America, and they have achieved historical immortality as the 'signers.' John Hancock, the wealthy Boston merchant, was chosen president after the death of Peyton Randolph. Young Thomas Jefferson was there, fresh from composing his *Summary View;* and the venerable Dr. Franklin, so discouraged by his vain search for conciliation in London as to have become an exponent of independence. Yet the radicals did not push through their program of accepting war and declaring independence without a severe struggle. John Dickinson again raised his voice in favor of conciliation, and persuaded his reluctant colleagues to adopt another petition to the king.

The real temper of Congress was revealed by a stirring Declaration of the Causes and Necessity of Taking up Arms, the joint product of Dickinson and Jefferson.

> Our cause is just. Our union is perfect. Our internal resources are great, and, if necessary, foreign assistance is undoubtedly attainable. . . . The arms we have been compelled by our enemies to assume, we will . . . employ for the preservation of our liberties, being with one mind resolved to die free men rather than live slaves.

And then came the ominous if oblique threat,

> We mean not to dissolve that union which has so long and so happily subsisted between us. Necessity has not yet driven us into that desperate measure, or induced us to excite any other nation to war against them. We have not raised armies with ambitious designs of separating from Great Britain, and establishing independent States. . . .

The inference was unmistakable.

Even as this resolve was being debated Congress took the militia besieging Boston into its service, and appointed Colonel George Washington commander-in-chief of the armed forces of the United Colonies. On 23 June Washington rode off from Philadelphia to take charge of the army. En route he was met by breathless couriers with the stirring story of Bunker Hill. On 17 June 1775 the British garrison in Boston made a frontal assault on a hill in near-by Charlestown, which the patriot militia had fortified. They won the hill, but it cost them 1054 killed and wounded out of 2200 troops engaged. And, as the first real stand-up battle between New England troops and British red-coats, it was a strategic victory for the Americans.

Shortly after, Congress authorized a project which the British could only consider as wantonly aggressive: an overland expedition to Quebec under Benedict Arnold, to bring Canada into the Union as the fourteenth colony. In October 1775 Congress began organizing a navy, on 10 November it created the Marine Corps, and in December it sent the Continental fleet of eight converted merchantmen, under Commodore Esek Hopkins, to raid Nassau in the Bahamas.

3. INDEPENDENCE

Nevertheless, over a year elapsed after Bunker Hill, a year in which not one gesture of conciliation was made by the British government, before Congress could make up its mind to declare independence. The very idea was repugnant to many members of Congress and to a large part of the American people. The loyalties of Americans were torn between the old and tried, and the new and uncertain. They were members of the greatest empire since Rome. Although the word *revolution* aroused no terrors, owing to the bloodless affair of 1688, the word *republic* did; complete independence of England meant one, or more, American republics. In the past, republics had been turbulent and of short duration; they required Roman virtue to maintain, and did we have it? John Adams feared that we did not — there was 'so much Venality and Corruption, so much Avarice and Ambition, such a Rage for Profit and Commerce among all Ranks and Degrees of Men even in America,' he wrote early in 1776, that he doubted whether we had 'public Virtue enough to Support a Republic.' Could we succeed where Rome failed? No European colony had ever thrown off dependence or even wished to. Would we not fight among ourselves and perhaps drift into becoming a satellite to France or Spain?

Independence meant sailing forth on an unchartered sea. America was not like Ireland, Poland, or other nations which had a romantic past that appealed to popular emotion. All the mystic chords of memory which (as Abraham Lincoln said) make a people a nation, responded in 1775 to English names and events — Magna Carta, Sir Francis Drake, Queen Elizabeth, the Glorious Revolution, the Bill of Rights, Marlborough, Wolfe. These were English memories and British glories in which the colonies had shared. Must one break with all that?

The two Continental Congresses had been summoned to get the Coercive Acts repealed, restore imperial relations as before 1763, and thus avert both war and independence. On 8 July 1775, after the news of Bunker Hill had reached Philadelphia, Congress adopted, at Dickinson's urgent request, the 'Olive Branch Petition' to George III, assuring his majesty in most loyal and respectful terms that they 'ardently desire the former harmony' between Britain and the colonies to be restored, and that 'a happy and permanent reconciliation' be effected. This petition was signed by John Hancock and almost every subsequent signer of the Declaration of Independence. As late as the autumn of 1775, the legislatures of North Carolina, Pennsylvania, New Jersey, New York, and Maryland went on record against independence, and in January 1776 the king's health was toasted nightly in the officers' mess presided over by General Washington. The flag first raised by Lieutenant John Paul Jones in the ship *Alfred* of the new Continental navy on 3 December 1775 carried thirteen stripes to mark the colonial union, but still displayed the British union jack in the canton.[1]

Yet the colonies could not forever remain half in, half out of the empire, professing allegiance while refusing obedience. The popular theory that they were not fighting the king or the mother country, but a 'ministerial' army, the 'unprincipled hirelings of a venal ministry,' made little sense. Many, however, still believed in it, hoping for a political crisis in England that would place the friends of America in power.

No compromise came from England. King George, naturally regarding as insincere an olive branch petition from a body that was carrying on armed rebellion, refused to receive it, and instead issued a proclamation declaring the colonies to be in a state of rebellion (23 August 1775). And on 22 December 1775, all trade and intercourse with the Thirteen Colonies was interdicted by Parliament.

In January 1776, before news of that vital step toward severance reached America, Thomas Paine's pamphlet *Common Sense* was published. The impact of this book on the American Revolution was comparable to that of *Uncle Tom's Cabin* on the Civil War. Paine presented in popular form the natural rights philosophy that was to be embodied in the Declaration of Independence. 'Society in every state is a blessing, but Government, even in its best state, is but a necessary evil; in its worst, an intolerable one. Government, like dress, is the badge of lost

1. This 'Grand Union Flag' as it was called was not replaced by the Stars and Stripes until June 1777.

innocence; the palaces of kings are built upon the ruins of the bowers of Paradise.' With ruthless disregard for tradition and sentiment Paine attacked the monarchy and the British Constitution. Monarchy itself, he argued, is an absurd form of government; one honest man worth 'all the crowned ruffians that ever lived'; and George III, 'the Royal Brute of Great Britain,' the worst of monarchs. Such words were sweet music to democratic ears. How absurd, too, that a continent should be governed by an island! This unnatural connection merely subjected the colonies to exploitation, and involved them in every European war. Separation would not only avert these evils, but bring positive benefits — such as a world market for American trade. Anticipating the policy of isolation, Paine announced it to be 'the true interest of America to steer clear of European contentions, which she can never do while, by her dependence on Great Britain, she is made the make-weight in the scale of British politics.'

Thus with persuasive simplicity Paine presented the alternatives: continued submission to a tyrannical king, an outworn government, and a vicious economic system; or liberty and happiness as a self-sufficient republic. And he closed with the eloquent peroration:

> O! ye that love mankind! Ye that dare oppose not only the tyranny but the tyrant, stand forth! Every spot of the old world is overrun with oppression. Freedom hath been hunted round the Globe. Asia and Africa have long expelled her. Europe regards her as a stranger and England hath given her warning to depart. O! receive the fugitive and prepare in time an asylum for mankind.

This amazing pamphlet within a month had been read by or to almost every white American. It rallied the undecided and the wavering, and proved a trumpet call to the radicals. 'Every Post and every Day rolls in upon us Independence like a Torrent,' observed John Adams exultantly.

In each colony a keen struggle was going on between conservatives and radicals for control of its delegation in Congress. As yet only a few delegations were definitely instructed for independence; it was the task of the radicals to force all into line. The alternative that faced the conservatives in such colonies as New York, Pennsylvania, Maryland, and South Carolina was not pleasant. If they tried to stem the popular tide, they would see themselves denounced as tories and hurled out of office, and old institutions exposed to the mercies of the radicals. They could maintain their accustomed position and influence, and save their property, only by acquiescing in a policy of war and separation. In Pennsylvania the struggle was particularly bitter, coinciding as it did with the ancient feud of Scots-Irish frontiersmen and city artisans against the Quaker oligarchy and the wealthier Germans. The success of the radicals here was achieved only by overthrowing the old government, establishing a new one with full representation of their frontier counties, and drawing up a new constitution. This new revolutionary government promptly instructed the Pennsylvania delegates for independence. The effect on the Congress sitting in Philadelphia was overpowering.

Events now moved rapidly toward independence. In January 1776 came the burning of Norfolk by the patriots to prevent its falling into the power of Governor Dunmore, and Virginia loyalists had to seek the protection of the British fleet. Next month, the embattled farmers of North Carolina repulsed royal troops and native loyalists at Moore's Creek Bridge. In March the legislature of that colony instructed its delegates to declare independence and form foreign alliances. Congress then threw the ports of America open to the commerce of the world, and sent an agent to France to obtain assistance. In early May news arrived that George III was sending over 12,000 German mercenaries to dragoon his American subjects. On 10 May, Congress advised the colonies to establish independent state governments. Virginia and others proceeded to do so. On 7 June Richard Henry Lee rose in Congress and moved 'That these United Colonies are, and of right ought to be, Free and Independent States.' After a terrific debate in which sturdy John Adams pled the cause of independence, Lee's motion was carried on 2 July. In the meantime Congress had appointed a committee consisting of Thomas Jefferson, John Adams, Benjamin Franklin, Roger Sherman, and Robert Livingston to prepare a formal declaration 'setting forth the causes which impelled us to this mighty resolution.' This Declaration of Independence, written by Thomas Jefferson, was adopted 4 July 1776.

4. THE GREAT DECLARATION

The Declaration of Independence announced not only the birth of a new nation; it expressed a theory which has been a dynamic force throughout the world. Out of a 'decent respect to the opinions of mankind,' Jefferson summed up, not only the reasons which impelled Americans to independence, but the political and social principles upon which the Revolution itself rested. The particular 'abuses and usurpations' charged against the king are not advanced as the basis for revolution, but merely as proof that George III's objective was 'the establishment of an absolute tyranny over these states.' The Declaration rests, therefore, not upon particular grievances but upon a broad basis which commanded general support not only in America but in Europe as well. Some of the grievances, examined in the candid light of history, seem distorted, others inconsequential. One of the strongest, an indictment of British support of the African slave trade, was struck out at the insistence of Southern and New England delegates. But Jefferson was not writing history; he was trying to influence its course.

The indictment is drawn against George III, despite the fact that for twelve years the dispute between the colonies and Britain had centered on the question of parliamentary authority. The only reference to Parliament is in the clause, 'He has combined with others to subject us to a jurisdiction foreign to our constitution and unacknowledged by our laws, giving his assent to their acts of pretended legislation.' Thus the odium of parliamentary misdeeds is transferred to the hapless George III. The reason for this shift was simply that Congress had accepted the position of Adams, Jefferson, and Wilson, according to which Parliament was merely the legislature of Great Britain, each colonial legislature being its equal, having exclusive power under the king over that particular colony. Another reason for fixing all the blame on poor George was to undermine the traditional American loyalty to the British Crown. Government, according to the theory which almost everyone then believed, was the result of a compact between ruler and people, a compact formed to protect 'life, liberty, and the pursuit of happiness.' And, to quote the Declaration, 'Whenever any form of government becomes destructive to these ends, it is the right of the people to alter or abolish it, and to institute new government, laying its foundation on such principles and organizing its powers in such form, as to them shall seem most likely to effect their safety and happiness.' It had to be proved that the king had broken the compact, which released his subjects from their allegiance. To the troublesome charge that a popular assumption of power would lead to anarchy, Jefferson replied, 'all experience hath shown that mankind are more disposed to suffer while evils are sufferable, than to right them by abolishing the forms to which they are accustomed.' The revolutionary leaders in every state but Pennsylvania cast their new state governments in accustomed forms.

Whatever the origin of government may have been in prehistoric times, in America it often arose just as Jefferson described. As in the Mayflower Compact of 1620, so in countless frontier settlements from the Watauga to the Willamette, men came together spontaneously and organized their own governments. Jefferson's philosophy seemed to them merely the common sense of the matter.

5. THE LOYALISTS

The Declaration of Independence divided those who hoped to solve the problem of imperial order by evolution from those who preferred to solve it by revolution. By calling into existence a new nation it made loyalty to King George treason; and in most colonies patriot committees went about forcing everyone, on pain of imprisonment and confiscation of property, to take an oath of allegiance to the United States. Thus it strengthened the hands of the patriots or whigs, and gave to the loyalists or tories the unpleasant alternative of submission or flight.

There were loyalists in every colony and in every walk of life. In New York, New Jersey, and Georgia they probably comprised a majority of the population, and in Pennsylvania and the Carolinas, regions where British arms were most successful, they were very strong. The loyalists were weakest in Virginia, Maryland, Connecticut, and Massachusetts: the oldest settled colonies with the proudest traditions. Although it is impossible to ascertain their number, the fact that some 80,000 loyalists left the country during the war or after, and that everyone admitted these to be a minority of the party, gives some index of their strength. The greater part of the loyalists took the required oaths and paid taxes, while praying for the defeat of the American cause, simply because they had no place to go. As late as 1830 there were old ladies in New York and Portsmouth, N. H., who quietly celebrated the king's birthday, but drew curtains and closed shutters on the Fourth of July!

The American Revolution was a civil rather than a class war, with tories and whigs finding supporters in all classes. Outside Virginia and Maryland, most of the greatest landowners were loyal, although many remained passive during the war to save their property. Yet the loyalists also won the allegiance of many back-country farmers in New York and the Carolinas, just as peasants in France rallied to the King. Royal officials went tory as a matter of course; so, too, most of the Anglican clergy, whose church prescribed loyalty to one's lawful sovereign as a Christian duty. The merchants in the North, except in Boston and the smaller New England seaports, were pretty evenly divided; and many lawyers remained faithful to the Crown. In general the older, conservative, established, well-to-do people were inclined to oppose revolution, but there were countless exceptions. Jonathan Trumbull, an arch-conservative, was nonetheless the only colonial governor to repudiate his oath of allegiance to the king and throw in his lot with the rebels.

Many families such as the Randolphs of Virginia, Morrises of New York, and Otises of Massachusetts were divided. Gouverneur Morris's mother was a tory; so too was Benjamin Franklin's natural son, William, the royalist governor of New Jersey. A Connecticut tory complained: 'Nabour was against Nabour, Father against Son and the son against the Father, and he that would not thrust his one blaid through his brothers heart was cald an Infimous fillon.'

Although most of the prominent leaders of the Revolution were gentlemen, it is easy to understand that they could not carry their entire class into a revolution which involved not merely separation from the mother country but the stability of society. The question of home rule in the empire could not be divorced from the question of who would rule in America. The country was much less united in 1776 than in 1765, or even 1774. When the conservatives realized that liberty could be won only by opening the floodgates to democracy, many drew back in alarm; others, like John Jay and John Dickinson, held their noses and carried on with the majority. Even some of the radical patriots had their bad moments. John Adams, riding home from the Continental Congress, was accosted by a horse-jockey, who exclaimed, so he tells us:

> 'We can never be grateful enough to you. There are no courts of justice now in this province, and I hope there never will be another.' Is this the object for which I have been contending? said I to myself. . . . Are these the sentiments of such people, and how many of them are there in the country? . . . If the power of the country should get into such hands, and there is a great danger that it will, to what purpose have we sacrificed our time, health and everything else?

To what purpose indeed! This question forced itself upon the consideration of every thoughtful man, and when independence was achieved, it became one of the burning questions of American society.

The loyalist minority helped the war. Those who fled to England whipped up British public opinion by their stories of persecution (unfortunately for the most part true); and they were forever telling anyone who would listen that 'if Lord George would only dispatch a few regiments to my section of the country, Sir, the countryside would rise as one man, Sir, and flock to the king's colors.' This policy was occasionally tried, but loyal rustics learned early in the war that if they rallied to a British force, it presently marched away and left them at the mercy of patriot committees. There were never enough loyalists anywhere to control the country; even in the South, where some back-country communities were almost completely loyalist, they were badly roughed up as soon as Cornwallis had passed by. There were enough, however, to do some very effective fighting for the king. Somewhat late in the war, the British discovered that Americans were the best people to fight Americans. Several tory regiments were then organized. New York furnished more soldiers to George III than to George Washington. Loyalist forces quartered in New York City frequently harried the shores of Long Island by marauding expeditions, and did other dirty work with which the regulars would not soil their hands. It was Butler's Tory Rangers and St. Leger's Loyal Greens who with Mohawk Indians perpetrated the Wyoming massacre of civilians in northern Pennsylvania. But the British waited too long to make use of the loyalists, and relied on them too much.

Tory 'partisans' in the war, often allied with Indians, committed atrocities on civilians of the other side; and the patriots retaliated where they could. But for the most part the loyalists were good men, and their principles were respectable. The attitude of those Americans who fought to hold the empire together in 1776 was no different from that of Southern Unionists like General Thomas and Admiral Farragut in 1861; and the difference between success and failure, more than that of right and wrong, explains the different 'verdict of history' toward these two great civil wars.

The War of Independence (1)

1. FACTORS AND CONDITIONS

If Americans had really been so united and determined as the ringing phrases of the Declaration of Independence suggest, they could have achieved independence within a year. For they already controlled 99 per cent of the country; the English people were half-hearted in the war; and the difficulties of conquering a determined people 3000 miles overseas were enormous. But there was so much loyalist feeling and sheer apathy that Congress found it very difficult to keep an army together and to feed those who fought. On the other hand, the Americans had so many sympathizers in Great Britain that German mercenaries had to be hired by George III. In other words, the War of Independence was a civil war, one in which, like the civil war of 1936–39 in Spain, assistance from outside was very important. American loyalists were incapable of carrying on the struggle a week without British assistance, and but for French aid the American patriots would have had to give up complete independence in 1778, or take a bad beating.

Indeed the surprising thing about the War of Independence when you compare it with other wars of liberation is not that the Americans won, but that they did not win more easily. All they had to do to win independence was to hold what they had. The British, on the contrary, had to reconquer a vast territory in order to win. It was the military problem of 1861, on a vaster scale, and with the dice loaded in favor of the 'rebels.' For the British government, in order to get troops in action against the 'rebels' of 1775–83, had to send them by bulky, slow-moving sailing vessels which never took less than four weeks (and often ten) to cross the Atlantic against the prevailing winds. Many soldiers succumbed en route to typhus, and the rest had to be conditioned after they landed, weak and groggy, in a strange land with a perplexing climate. Moreover, those who 'came three thousand miles and died, to keep the Past upon its throne,' had to be armed, clothed, and even partly fed from England, which meant more shipping, more delays, more losses from American privateers and hazards of the sea, and such expense as had never been known in English history.

The direction of the war came under the Colonial Secretary of the North ministry, Lord George Germain, who is represented in the savage political cartoons of the day as wearing a white feather. He had been dismissed from the army after the Battle of Minden for something that looked like cowardice, yet had risen in politics through a combination of personal effrontery, family influence, and royal favor. His field commanders objected that he issued fussy orders but would not accept responsibility. 'For God's sake, my Lord, if you wish me to do anything, leave me to myself,' protested Sir Henry Clinton. 'If not, tie me down to a certain point and take the risk of my want of success.' Yet Germain's real shortcoming was that he never grasped the revolutionary character of the uprising.

The Revolutionary War was fought under the peculiar condition of want of enthusiasm on each side. There were many instances of British officers who resigned their commissions rather than fight their overseas brethren. On the other side, the Americans were hampered by the small number who were willing to fight or to make any sacrifice for independence. Washington himself wrote, when trying to get the New England troops to re-enlist in the fall of 1775, 'Such a dearth of public spirit, and want of virtue, such stock-jobbing, and fertility in all the low arts to obtain advantages of one kind or another . . . I never saw before and pray God I may never witness to again. . . . Could I have foreseen what I have, and am likely to experience, no consideration upon Earth should have induced me to accept this command.' He was to experience less virtue and more politics as the war went on; but his own steadfast patriotism never wavered for a moment, and he endured a degree of neglect, disobedience, and even disloyalty, which would have induced almost any other general in history to resign his sword and give up the cause.

Washington was more than a general: he was the embodiment of all that was noblest and best in the American people. With no illusions about his own grandeur, no thought of the future except an intense longing to return to his beloved Mount Vernon, he assumed every responsibility thrust upon him, and fulfilled it. He not only had to lead an army, but to write constant letters to Congress, state leaders, and state governments, begging them for the wherewithal to create and maintain an army. He had to compose quarrels among his officers, many of them volunteers from Europe, and placate cold, hungry, unshod troops. After France sent aid, he had quasi-diplomatic functions to fulfill. Although asking and receiving no salary, he bought clothing for his men from his own pocket, and sent aid to the destitute families of his companions in battle. Thus Washington brought something more to the cause than his military ability and statesmanship; he contributed the priceless gifts of generosity and character.

Washington organized his army in line regiments, each one coming from a specific state; and the states were supposed to keep these filled. But Americans were not then — nor are they now — a military people. They were eager for a fight, but not for sustained warfare. The sort of fighting they enjoyed was militia warfare: turning out under a popular local leader like John Stark or Francis Marion to repel an invasion or do a little bushwacking, then go home to plant the corn or get in the hay. Steady service in an army so ill-fed, paid, and clothed as Washington's, was distasteful; and the average American, though he wished his side to win, saw no need of continuous fighting. When New England was cleared of the enemy, it was difficult to get Yankees to go to the aid of the Middle States or the South; after the first enthusiasm of 1775 it was equally difficult to get Southerners to serve in the North; and the people of the Middle States, where most of the fighting occurred, hung back even there. The states and local communities to which states often passed on their responsibilities were compelled to offer bounties to raise troops, and the value of the bounties had to be increased steadily as the war continued. The total enlistments in the war, regulars and militia, i.e. the total number of men who counted as veterans and as ancestors for members of patriotic societies, were several hundred thousand. But

Washington's army reached its first peak of strength with 18,000 in the summer of 1776. It fell to 5000 by the end of that year, rose to a little over 20,000 in mid-1778, and then declined. No provision was made for the families of men in service, and no pensions were paid to the dependents of those who fell; so enlistments were largely restricted to the very young, the adventurous, the floating population, and the super-patriotic. But with all these allowances the fact remains that a disgracefully small number of Americans were willing to do any sustained fighting for their country's cause.

Many in Congress, having inherited the traditional English aversion to standing armies, believed the war could be fought by militia alone; but the wiser saw that a regular army was absolutely necessary if only as a stiffener to the rest, and that it took time to train soldiers. The militia were the same sort of men as the regular 'Continentals'; it was training and proper leadership that they lacked. In the Southern campaign of 1781 General Greene used to beg the militia to fire just two volleys before they ran away, and they often did not get off even two.

These volleys were fired from smooth-bore, muzzle-loading muskets by soldiers drawn up in three lines — hence the term 'line regiments' for the infantry. The front line knelt, the second and third stood, the third firing over the shoulders of the second. The rifle was used mainly by frontier units like General Daniel Morgan's brigade, and the best tactical use of riflemen was to post them on the flanks as sharpshooters. They could not be used in line because the rifle took too long to load, and the opposing forces fired at such short range (30 to 50 yards) that before a rifleman could reload he would become victim of a British bayonet charge. And you could not fix a bayonet to a rifle. At the beginning of the war, Americans made no use of cold steel, but Washington insisted that bayonets be procured and that bayonet practice be introduced in the regular drill. Stony Point on the Hudson was captured in 1779 by a brilliant night assault of Anthony Wayne's light infantry corps, with muskets unloaded and bayonets fixed.

This light infantry was an elite corps, like the marines today, composed of young, agile lads who had proved themselves good fighters. Every ambitious officer wished to command a light infantry unit; Lafayette and Alexander Hamilton were among those who did. The 'legions' of which we hear in the Southern campaigns were cavalry units; horses were used mainly for quick transportation, the troopers fighting on foot.

Field artillery, firing twelve-pound cannon balls or, more often, grape-shot, was posted on the flanks and was not effective beyond 400 yards.

Although the spokesmen of Irish-Americans, German-Americans, and other racial minorities like to claim that the American army was largely composed of themselves, there is no evidence of racial groups favoring either side. Members of every non-English race then in America can be found on American army rolls; but so can they also be found on British army rolls and lists of loyalists. Nor was there any age limit. The Bay State sent such young boys as part of her quota in 1780 that in Washington's army they were called 'the Massachusetts miscarriages.'

Negroes served in every line regiment of the Continental army and in John Paul Jones's ships. Virginia slaves in the armed forces were liberated at the end of the war. Yet the large numbers of slaves who escaped to British lines to gain their freedom gave a note of doubt to the claim of the Patriots that they were fighting for liberty. The American General Thomas Sumter even set a pay scale for his troops in slaves plundered from the tories; a colonel would get 3½ slaves a year, a private an adult slave for each month of his enlistment. After the war the British refused to repatriate refugee slaves, and it is possible that as many Negroes departed America as did white tories.

2. SUPPLY AND FINANCE

The weakness of the American government contributed to slackness in the fight. The Continental Congress had no legal authority. Like NATO and SEATO it was dependent on the member states. It passed resolutions, not laws; it issued requisitions, not orders, for men, money, and supplies. Although Congress had the good sense to give Washington supreme control of military operations at the end of 1776, and to resist all intrigues to relieve him, it did not support him adequately — indeed it could not, dependent as it was on the good will of the states and the people for the wherewithal to carry on the war.

In providing arms and munitions, Congress, aided by supplies from France, captures by privateers, and local enterprise, did rather well, but in raising troops and in coping with feeding and clothing the army it did very ill. According to Louis C. Hatch, the principal authority on army administration, 'The army starved, not because the country could not furnish food, but because the people were unwilling to endure taxation, and because Congress themselves did not understand the importance of administrative centralization. Some of the hardships that the army endured were, indeed, unavoidable; but the greater part of them were caused by incompetent, or negligent officials, bad management, and an excess of paper money.'

The war was financed by national bills of credit (the famous Continental currency), state bills of credit, requisitions on the states in money and in kind (which were met by state loans or taxes), domestic loans and foreign loans. Of these the most important was the Continental currency, the first of which was issued shortly after the Battle of Bunker Hill. It was expected that each state would make these bills of credit legal tender, and make provision for 'sinking' (redeeming) its share of them, according to congressional apportionment; but while the states were ready enough to legalize the bills for all payments, they failed to provide for their redemption at the times fixed, and instead issued bills of credit of their own. Consequently both Continental and state bills depreciated rapidly from 1778 on, and acted as a forced loan on the people, each holder losing part of his equity as prices rose and money declined. In all, Continental bills to the face value of about $241.5 million and state bills to the face value of $210 million were issued. Congress recognized in 1780 that Continental currency was worth only one-fortieth of its specie value, and began receiving it for state requisitions at that rate, and issuing 'new tenor' bills at 5 per cent interest, redeemable in specie; but they too depreciated. The old Continental currency within a year ceased to pass, and became a byword and a jest — 'not worth a continental' was a rustic phrase for complete worthlessness well into the nineteenth century.

Requisitions of money on the states began with a sum of $5 million in 1777. These were no better honored than the parliamentary requisitions on the colonies during the French and Indian War. Three specie requisitions to the amount of over $10 million in the desperate year 1780 yielded only $1.5 million. Congress then resorted to requisitions in kind: so much beef, pork, flour, and rum; so many blankets, coats, and stockings. About $5 million worth of goods were obtained in this way. Domestic loans were floated from 1776, at first at 4 per cent and then at 6 per cent; but with the lack of liquid capital in the states, or of banks to make it available, only some $67 million in paper (about $10 million specie) was subscribed by 1780, when the loan offices were closed.

The government adroitly managed to secure significant sums from Europe. The French secret subsidies amounted to $1.6 million. Loans from France, which began in 1777, yielded $6.4 million in specie value; and, while most of this was spent on supplies in Europe, enough came to America to pay the interest on the domestic debt until 1782. Spain made a token loan of $150,000 in 1781–82; and John Adams borrowed $1.3 million from private bankers in the Netherlands during the peace negotiations.

American Revolutionary finance used to be held up to ridicule as an example of everything vicious in public finance; but since the inflation of two world wars and ever since, we have become more understanding of the old patriots. Considering the popular prejudice against taxation (with or without representation) and Congress's lack of real authority, it is surprising that the war did not collapse in the winter of 1780–81 for want of financial support. There was great improvement after February 1781, when Congress appointed Robert Morris, a wealthy Philadelphia merchant, superintendent of finance. Morris stopped waste and corruption in spending, introduced proper administrative methods, placed government finances on a specie basis, organized the first American bank of deposit and issue (the Bank of North America), fed the army by contract, and procured decent uniforms; so that during the last year of the war, after Yorktown, the army was much better paid, clothed, and fed than ever before. But he did not and could not improve revenue; and it was mainly the increased financial help from France at this time, the slackening of fighting, and the specie circulated by the French and British armies that enabled Morris to do as well as he did. Practically the whole country was on a specie basis by 1782, and European bankers were so favorably impressed by the results of Morris's efforts, that the new loan in Holland was obtained at the low interest of 5 per cent. But a financial collapse was just around the corner when the war ended.

3. MILITARY OPERATIONS, 1775–77

Even before the Declaration of Independence there were military operations which had an important effect on the outcome of the war. The North Carolina loyalists, led by Donald McDonald, kinsman of Bonnie Prince Charlie's girl guide Flora, tried to cut their way through to the coast, and with a great skirling of pipes and flashing of claymores attacked patriot militia at Moore's Creek Bridge near Wilmington, N.C., on 27 February 1776. But they were badly defeated, which made it impossible for the British to erect a military base in that region. That was the object of a new expeditionary force from Ireland commanded by Lord Cornwallis, with a detachment of British regulars from Boston under Sir Henry Clinton. They were forced to try Charleston, S.C., instead. Charleston is a remarkably hard nut to crack, as Spaniards, British, and Yankees have discovered to their cost. Washington detached Charles Lee to take charge; but before he arrived, the local patriots had erected Fort Moultrie, which drove off the attacking ships when they endeavored to force a passage (28 June 1776). Clinton and Cornwallis, baffled, retired to join Sir William Howe in his attack on New York. So the British acquired no Southern base in 1776, and the large number of Carolina loyalists had to fend for themselves.

About the time of the Moore's Creek fight, Washington, who had been besieging Boston for eight months with an army composed of New England militia and Southern riflemen, decided to finish up. Seizing and fortifying Dorchester Heights, which the British had neglected after their dearly bought capture of Bunker Hill, Washington placed his artillery in a position to blast the enemy out of Boston. General Billy Howe decided it was time to leave, and, happily for modern Boston, chose St. Patrick's Day 1776 to evacuate his army.

After Ethan Allen had taken Ticonderoga and Crown Point on Lake Champlain early in 1775, Benedict Arnold, an enterprising Connecticut militia officer, led a march on Canada in two divisions. The French Canadians were expected to revolt on the appearance of an American force, and bring in Canada as the fourteenth member of the half-formed American confederation. But as a result of the outbursts of anti-Catholic bigotry in the Northern Colonies provoked by the Quebec Act of 1774, few French habitants cared to change masters. Seldom has religious intolerance been so promptly chastised by the 'frowns of Providence.'

Richard Montgomery, with a little over a thousand men, taking the classic route of the Hudson and Lake Champlain, captured Montreal on 12 November 1775. About six hundred of Benedict Arnold's equal force got through the wilderness of Maine to Quebec, after incredible hardships. They poled, pushed, and dragged their way in flat-bottomed boats up the Kennebec river, across a twelve-mile carry, through a complicated chain of ponds and small streams, across a snow-covered mountain

pass, and — those who had boats left — down the rapids of the Chaudière river, while the rest, cold and starving, stumbled north along deer
trails. Rendezvous was made with Montgomery near Quebec. As many
of the troops' terms of enlistments expired on New Year's Day 1776,
Montgomery and Arnold delivered a premature assault on Quebec, the
strongest fortress in America, in a blinding snowstorm on the last night of
1775. Montgomery was killed, Arnold wounded; and although Congress
sent reinforcements, the expeditionary force was compelled to retreat
in the spring, and Canada remained British. The Arnold-Montgomery
campaign had an important bearing on the war. It alarmed the British
government for the safety of Canada, and induced it to divide the largest
force of regulars yet dispatched across the Atlantic and to send almost
half to Quebec. The attempt of this section under Burgoyne to push
through to New York in 1777 would result in the most decisive American victory of the entire war.

Before that took place, the Americans had lost in succession New York
and Philadelphia. Washington, rightly foretelling that New York would
be the next British objective, marched thither from Boston in April 1776,
with as much of his army as could be induced to stay under the colors.
Had it not been for the presence of Washington's force in New York
City that colony would certainly have stayed loyalist: as it was, the
Provincial Congress did not vote for independence until 9 July 1776, and
patriot committees had great difficulty in keeping the tories quiet by
strong-arm methods. If the British expeditionary force had arrived in
April or May, there would have been a different story. But Howe, after
retreating from Boston on 17 March, had to wait at Halifax, N.S., until 7
June for reinforcements to arrive from England; and his transports and
convoying fleet did not sail through the Narrows of New York harbor
until 2 July 1776.

The Howe brothers, liberal in politics and friendly to America,
brought an olive branch as well as a sword. All they had to offer (so Ben
Franklin drew from them at a conference on Staten Island) was royal
clemency to the rebels if they would stop fighting, but no guarantee of
future liberty within the empire. Franklin, as instructed, refused to
negotiate save on the basis of independence. It would have been well for
both countries if the British had accepted this condition then, instead of
six years later; but national honor forbade them to relinquish the Thirteen Colonies without a fight. And with 30,000 men and a navy to

oppose Washington's land force of 18,000, it seemed as if the fight would soon be over.

Washington, on his side, felt that he could not honorably abandon New York City without a struggle. Commanded both by Brooklyn Heights and by ships already in the harbor, the metropolis was difficult to defend. Washington promptly fortified the Heights, and prepared to defend them; but Howe quickly shifted his army to the Americans' rear. In the ensuing Battle of Long Island (27 August 1776) Washington's plan was faulty, his generals did not execute their assignments, all the breaks went against him, and British numbers were overwhelming. Brooklyn Heights became untenable, and Washington on 29 August executed a masterly retreat in small boats to the Manhattan shore. Providentially the wind held north, so the British warships could not come up the East River, and Sir William Howe apparently never knew what was going on. He lost his greatest chance to end the war by a single stroke: for if Washington's army had then been captured, it would have been impossible for the Congress to have raised another. Indeed the War of Independence was remarkably punctuated by 'ifs.'

Howe now occupied New York City, forcing Washington to retire to Harlem Heights; and during the remainder of the war that city remained a British base and a tory refuge.

Arnold, in the meantime, was stubbornly contesting every mile of the American retreat from Canada. His greatest feat was to construct a fresh-water navy on Lake Champlain which, despite a bad beating in the Battle of Valcour Bay (11 October 1776), held up Sir Guy Carleton. It was then so late in the fall that he retired to Montreal and gave up for that year an attempt to form a junction with Howe. Thus Benedict Arnold a second time helped the cause that he later betrayed.

Washington, his army weakened in morale as in men by the militia contingents' going home, abandoned his position to the north of Manhattan Island and retreated into New Jersey. This strategy was to save his army to save the cause. By the end of 1776 his army was hardly five thousand strong. The rest had simply dwindled away: deserted, gone absent without leave, or left when terms of enlistment were up. These were 'the times that tried men's souls,' wrote Tom Paine. And how few souls survived the ordeal!

Howe, in that dreary autumn, lost several chances to capture Washington's army; for Howe waged war in the dilatory manner of European

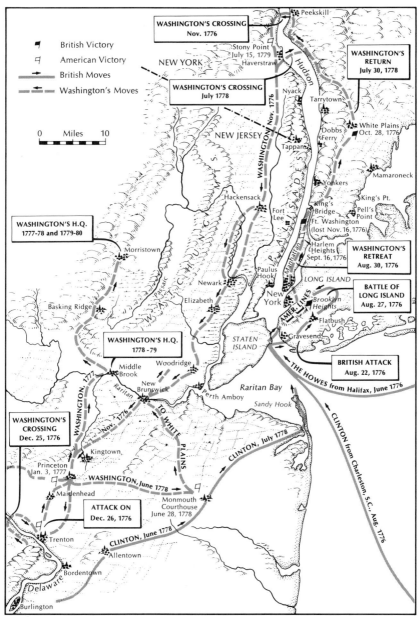

Legend:

- ⚑ British Victory
- ⚐ American Victory
- → British Moves
- → Washington's Moves

0 — Miles — 10

Map Labels
Peekskill
WASHINGTON'S CROSSING Nov. 1776
Stony Point July 15, 1779
Haverstraw
WASHINGTON'S RETURN July 30, 1778
NEW YORK
WASHINGTON'S CROSSING July 1778
Nyack
Tarrytown
NEW JERSEY
Dobbs Ferry
White Plains Oct. 28, 1776
Tappan
Mamaroneck
Yonkers
King's Pt.
WASHINGTON'S H.Q. 1777-78 and 1779-80
Hackensack
King's Bridge
Pell's Point
Morristown
Fort Lee
Ft. Washington (lost Nov. 16, 1776)
Harlem Heights Sept. 16, 1776
WASHINGTON'S RETREAT Aug. 30, 1776
Paulus Hook
Newark
LONG ISLAND
BATTLE OF LONG ISLAND Aug. 27, 1776
Basking Ridge
Elizabeth
New York
Brooklyn Heights
Flatbush
WASHINGTON'S H.Q. 1778-79
Middle Brook
Woodridge
STATEN ISLAND
Gravesend
BRITISH ATTACK Aug. 22, 1776
New Brunswick
Perth Amboy
Raritan Bay
THE HOWES from Halifax, June 1776
WASHINGTON'S CROSSING Dec. 25, 1776
Kingtown
Sandy Hook
CLINTON, July 1778
Princeton Jan. 3, 1777
CLINTON from Charleston, S.C., Aug. 1776
Maidenhead
WASHINGTON, June 1778
Monmouth Courthouse June 28, 1778
ATTACK ON Dec. 26, 1776
Trenton
CLINTON, June 1778
Allentown
Bordentown
Delaware
Burlington

THE LONG ISLAND and NEW JERSEY CAMPAIGNS, 1776-1778

campaigns. There seemed to be no hurry. Every month the Americans grew weaker; Jersey loyalists were hospitable; gentlemen did not fight in winter. So Washington reached the far bank of the Delaware before Howe's outposts reached the near bank. By then, Congress had given what amounted to an independent command to General Charles Lee. He was an English soldier of fortune, one of those showy, loud-mouthed military men who are apt to impress simpler folk. Lee insolently refused to co-operate with Washington, and when he finally did, he carelessly permitted himself to be captured. It was well for the American cause that he was, for his army was now placed under Washington; unfortunately, according to an amiable military practice of that era, he was later exchanged for a British general.

Congress now invested Washington with power to appoint and replace all officers except the generals, who had to be apportioned among the states for political reasons. And Congress recruited vigorously. But in March 1777, when the roads began to thaw, Washington had only 4000 men.

General Burgoyne now sold a plan of campaign for 1777 to Lord George Germain. His idea was to cut off New England from the rest of the states, and capture Philadelphia. Burgoyne would bring 7000 men south by the line of Lake Champlain and the Hudson to Albany. Sir John Johnson, son of old Sir William of the Mohawks, promised to bring thousands of Mohawk valley tories and Iroquois braves to help. Howe, after detaching a force to meet Burgoyne up-river, would himself capture Philadelphia, and perhaps proceed farther south. The weakness of the plan lay partly in the difficulty of obtaining coordination at such a distance. Howe did not learn that he was expected to help Burgoyne until 16 August, when the bulk of his force was embarked in transports in Chesapeake Bay. But the fatal British mistake was to ignore the conditions of warfare in America. The several transfers between Lake Champlain, Lake George, and the Hudson meant an enormous apparatus of baggage and portable boats, many delays, and plenty of warning to the enemy. Lexington and Concord had showed on a small scale what would happen to a British force advancing into a hostile country. And European tactics were helpless against a countryside in arms: for the countryside in Europe never rose; warfare over there was a professional game.

In the summer of 1777, General Howe advanced on Philadelphia. All

Washington could do against greatly superior forces was to retard Howe's advance, at the Brandywine Creek (9 September 1777). Howe occupied Philadelphia on 26 September, and Washington's gallant attack on the British forces at Germantown (3–4 October) was a complete failure. The British settled down to a comfortable winter at the former seat of Congress, while Washington went into desolate winter quarters at Valley Forge, only a few miles away.

In the meantime the greatest American victory of the war had been won, on the line of the Hudson. The British army in Canada, some seven thousand strong with a thousand Canadian militia and Indians, jumped off from the St. Lawrence on 1 June, and began a southward advance in good season and with bright prospects. On 6 July, Burgoyne took Fort Ticonderoga. By 29 July he had reached Fort Edward on the upper Hudson, and was forced to wait for more supplies from Canada. 'Gentleman Jack' Burgoyne would make no concession to wilderness conditions; he must have his service of plate, his champagne, and thirty wagons for his personal baggage. Burgoyne's ideas of American geography were not as hazy as those of Bernard Shaw, who in his delightful play, *The Devil's Disciple*, places New Hampshire south of Boston; but he did imagine that it would be an easy matter for a raiding force to march in two weeks across Vermont to Bellows Falls, down the Connecticut river to Brattleborough, and back 'by the great road to Albany.' For this exploit he chose 375 dismounted German dragoons, the slowest marchers in his army, and about 300 tories, Canadians, and Indians. They did not even reach the Vermont line. John Stark and his Green Mountain Boys marched out from Bennington to meet them; and after that battle, on 16 August, very few of the Germans returned. Much the same fate met Colonel Barry St. Leger, who commanded a raid from Oswego to Fort Stanwix. He and Sir John Johnson's forces were no match for the Mohawk valley militia under General Herkimer, when reinforced by a column under Benedict Arnold; St. Leger retreated to Canada on 22 August.

In militia fighting, nothing succeeds like success. The Battle of Bennington brought a general turnout of the fighting population of northern New England, and Burgoyne's delay at Fort Edward enabled Washington to dispatch regulars from the lower Hudson. When in early September Burgoyne finally got his unwieldy force in motion, he marched into a hornets' nest of Yankee militia, flushed with the success of their fellows,

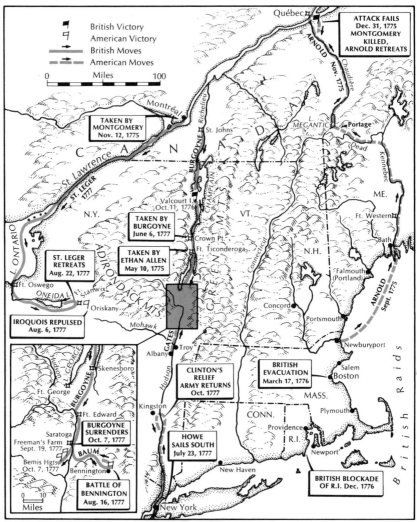

British Victory
American Victory
British Moves
American Moves
0   Miles   100

ATTACK FAILS
Dec. 31, 1775
MONTGOMERY
KILLED,
ARNOLD RETREATS

Québec

ARNOLD Nov. 1775

Chaudière

Montréal

TAKEN BY
MONTGOMERY
Nov. 12, 1775

St. Johns

Richelieu

C   A   N   A   D   A

L. MEGANTIC   Portage

Dead.

St. Lawrence

ST. LEGER
1777

N.Y.

Kennebec

ME.

Valcourt I.
Oct. 11, 1776

CHAMPLAIN

VT.

Ft. Western

TAKEN BY
BURGOYNE
June 6, 1777

Crown Pt.

Bath

L. ONTARIO

Ft. Ticonderoga

N.H.

TAKEN BY
ETHAN ALLEN
May 10, 1775

ST. LEGER
RETREATS
Aug. 22, 1777

ADIRONDACK MTS.

Connecticut

GREEN MTS.

Falmouth
(Portland)

Ft. Oswego

ONEIDA L.

Stanwix

ARNOLD Sept. 1775

Oriskany

Concord

Portsmouth

IROQUOIS REPULSED
Aug. 6, 1777

Mohawk

GATES

Albany

Troy

Newburyport

British Raids

L. GEORGE

Skenesboro

Hudson

CLINTON'S
RELIEF
ARMY RETURNS
Oct. 1777

BRITISH
EVACUATION
March 17, 1776

Salem

Boston

Ft. George

BURGOYNE

MASS.

Ft. Edward

Kingston

CONN.

Plymouth

BURGOYNE
SURRENDERS
Oct. 7, 1777

Saratoga
Freeman's Farm
Sept. 19, 1777

HOWE
SAILS SOUTH
July 23, 1777

Providence

R.I.

Bemis Hgts.
Oct. 7, 1777

BAUM

Bennington

Newport

New Haven

0   10
Miles

BATTLE OF
BENNINGTON
Aug. 16, 1777

New York

BRITISH BLOCKADE
OF R.I. Dec. 1776

British Raids

THE NORTHERN CAMPAIGN OF 1775-1777

190

stiffened by regulars, and commanded by a general of the regular army. The American Northern army, which now outnumbered Burgoyne's two to one, was commanded by Horatio Gates, a timid general who fortunately had the ardent Arnold as his second in command. As the early frosts were turning the foliage of the upper Hudson to colors bright as the British soldiers' coats, the fighting began. At the battle of Freeman's Farm (19 September) Arnold's audacious leadership and tactical skill won the day. Only a quick retreat could have saved Burgoyne then; but he had little notion of what stout fellows were mustering behind the screen of woods; and Sir Henry Clinton appeared to be coming up the Hudson to his rescue. On 7 October Burgoyne lost another fight at Freeman's farm,[1] and retreated to Saratoga. The autumn rains began, the Germans and Indians deserted in shoals, Americans were now in front, rear, and flank in overwhelming numbers. So on 17 October 1777, at Saratoga, Burgoyne surrendered his entire army, still over five thousand strong, to General Gates.

This was the decisive blow of the war, for it brought England's hereditary enemy to the American side.

1. Also called Battle of Stillwater, or Bemis Heights.

XI

The War of Independence (2)

1. ENTER FRANCE

France had been waiting for her *revanche* since 1763, and America provided the occasion. As early as November 1775, Congress had appointed a committee on foreign relations, and the next spring it sent Silas Deane to France to procure clothing, munitions, and supplies. These he obtained from the government of Louis XVI through the medium of a bogus company, organized by Beaumarchais the playwright, who wrote *The Barber of Seville* and *The Marriage of Figaro*. After independence had been declared, Franklin and Arthur Lee were sent to join Deane, with instructions to obtain secret or open assistance, and to offer a treaty of amity and commerce. John Adams then, and always, was against an 'entangling alliance,' but the American military situation became so desperate toward the close of 1776 that Congress authorized Franklin to conclude an offensive-defensive alliance if necessary to get France into the war.

Here indeed was a spectacle to delight the gods — smooth Ben, sleek Silas, and suspicious Arthur trying to sell revolution to the most absolute monarch in Europe, and a highly sophisticated court. Actually the sale was not difficult. The French intellectual world, though not yet republican in sentiment, hated feudalism and privilege. Voltaire admired the society of Pennsylvania, where men had showed it possible to live the good life on the basis of religious liberty, and thus had paved the way for a warm reception to Franklin. Condorcet was so charmed with what he read of simple, rustic Connecticut that he signed one of his tracts *Un Bourgeois de New-Haven;* Rousseau imagined the Indians to be genuine children of nature. The Declaration of Independence was greeted ecstatically; Washington seemed a new Cincinnatus; and ardent young men, of whom the Marquis de Lafayette was easily the first, hastened to place themselves under his command.[1]

If intellectual France was ready to fling up her cap for independence, the rulers had practical reasons for helping the United States. A shrewd statesman, the Comte de Vergennes, directed the foreign affairs of a rather stupid young monarch, Louis XVI. England must be humbled and the balance of power redressed in favor of France, whose lowered prestige had lately been signalized by a partition of Poland without her consent or participation. 'Providence has marked this era,' Vergennes wrote to the Spanish government in 1778, 'for the humiliation of a proud and greedy power . . . glory and inestimable advantages will result for the two crowns.' And the French manufacturers were eager for a new market in America, closed to them by the British Acts of Trade. 'Always keep in mind,' wrote Vergennes to his minister of finance after the war was over, 'that in separating the United States from Great Britain it was above all their commerce which we wanted.' And so, for practical reasons of state, the French government from the first gave the United States unneutral aid in the shape of munitions and supplies, and welcomed Yankee privateers to French seaports. But Vergennes shrank from the expense of direct intervention and open war with England.

This 'short of war' policy lasted until after the news of Burgoyne's surrender at Saratoga. It then changed because Vergennes feared lest this disaster induce the English government to make such liberal concessions as would reunite the empire. He was not far wrong. Lord North was eager to recognize American independence as soon as he heard of the defeat at Saratoga; but the king refused. He declared he would rather lose his crown than submit to the old whigs and abandon the war. Nevertheless, the King was ready to concede everything short of independence in order to keep the American states nominally under his

1. Other foreign officers who greatly helped the American cause were Baron von Steuben, who introduced a modified Prussian drill and discipline in the Continental army; Thaddeus Kosciuszko of Poland, an admirable artillery officer; Count Casimir Pulaski of Poland, mortally wounded at Savannah; the Baron de Kalb, who died of his wounds at the Battle of Camden; and the Chevalier du Portail, an accomplished officer of engineers.

sovereignty. A bill introduced by North appointed a peace commission with authority to make the following amazingly broad offer: parliamentary taxation of the colonies to be renounced; no military forces to be kept in the colonies without their consent; the Coercive Acts of 1774 and all other Acts of Parliament to which Congress objected — even the Acts of Trade — to be repealed, if America would but acknowledge the sovereignty of the king; these concessions to be guaranteed by treaty. This was more than Congress had wanted in 1775, all that Adams, Wilson, and Jefferson suggested in their pamphlets, all that Canada enjoyed in the 1920's. If the peace commission under the Earl of Carlisle had reached America before news of the French alliance, its terms might well have been accepted; for the British still held New York, Newport, and Philadelphia; and Washington was at Valley Forge. But, as usual, the British offer came too late.

On 6 February 1778, eleven days before the conciliatory bill passed Parliament, Franklin signed treaties of commerce and of alliance with Vergennes. Each nation promised to make common cause with the other until American independence was recognized. It was a generous treaty, in which America obtained everything and promised nothing except to defend French possessions in the West Indies. Vergennes had been brought to this point by Franklin's playing on his fears that otherwise a British peace offer would be accepted. Great Britain promptly declared war on France, and the War of Independence became world-wide. Spain entered as an ally of France in 1779, and proved very useful to the American cause by opening New Orleans as a base for privateers and by capturing the British posts in West Florida. The Netherlands, which had been reaping a fortune as the principal neutral sea power, was forced into the war by England in 1780; and Catherine II of Russia formed a League of Armed Neutrality which considerably cramped the operations of the British navy against neutral traders. United, the enemies of England would have been irresistible; but of them only France and America acted in concert, and then not until 1780.

So, by 1780, the shot at Concord bridge literally had been heard around the world. There were naval operations on the Atlantic Ocean, the Mediterranean, the Caribbean, the North Sea, the English Channel, even the Indian Ocean. And in far off Hindustan, Warren Hastings was fighting the local allies of France to create a new empire for England in Asia.

2. MILITARY OPERATIONS 1778–81

The year 1778 was one of incompetence and failure on all sides, re-deemed only by the indomitable patriotism of Washington. While Washington's troops suffered in frigid Valley Forge, Sir William Howe's men reveled in Philadelphia. But Howe was recalled in the spring of 1778, and his successor, Sir Henry Clinton, was ordered to evacuate the city and to concentrate on New York in preparation for a new campaign. On 28 June, Washington attacked Clinton's retiring army at Monmouth Court House, New Jersey: a confused battle in which an American disaster was barely averted by Washington's sending Charles Lee off the field, and saving the day himself. Clinton's army reached New York safely; and all that Washington could do was to encamp at White Plains, fortify West Point, and look on.

The only successful American campaign of 1778 was that of George Rogers Clark, acting for the state of Virginia. He shot the rapids of the Ohio, and, undismayed by a total eclipse which frightened his men, led his little force across the wilderness to take the British post of Kaskaskia in Illinois, first in a series of bloodless victories. When the British struck back and threatened to recapture each of the posts he had taken, the intrepid Clark in February 1779 marched his men 180 miles in the dead of winter through icy floods, sometimes shoulder-high, until sick, sodden and weary they arrived at Vincennes to surprise the disbelieving British. Clark is often credited with saving the West for his country; but if the peace negotiators in 1782 were aware of his exploits, they did not allude to them in a single one of their numerous notes and dispatches.

The war had now reached the nasty stage common to many wars, when one side or the other, unable to reach a military decision, resorts to desultory and haphazard operations that have no useful military result but arouse bitterness and hatred. The British raided Egg Harbor, N.J., and New Bedford, Mass., burned Portsmouth, Va., and Fairfield and Norwalk, Conn., and plundered New Haven.

The first break in this dismal strategy came at the other end of the Atlantic seaboard. An amphibious operation commanded by Brigadier Archibald Campbell captured Savannah from its weak Continental gar-rison on 29 December 1778. With the help of the British garrison of East Florida, under General Augustine Prevost, Campbell then overran the settled part of Georgia, reinstated the royal governor, summoned an assembly, and virtually restored that state to the British empire. From Savannah (which he looted), Prevost marched overland against Charleston, burning plantations and kidnapping slaves en route. Charleston was successfully defended by its small Continental garrison under General Benjamin Lincoln, and in Prevost's absence Savannah was attacked by a formidable expedition under the commander of the French fleet, Admiral the Comte d'Estaing. In the assault (9 October 1779) Count Pulaski was killed at the head of his legion. D'Estaing, twice wounded, re-embarked his landing force and sailed for France. A year and a half had elapsed since the French alliance, and so far it had produced little but disappointment.

The recovery of Georgia and the repulse of D'Estaing gave the British a bold strategic idea: a big amphibious expedition to capture Charleston, and with the aid of local tories to set up loyal governments in the Carolinas, to roll up all American fighting forces into Virginia, then to secure that pivotal state, and Chesapeake Bay. There was nothing wrong with the plan, but three unexpected factors wrecked it. The Carolina tories were neither numerous enough nor tough enough to play their part, the British army treated the people so savagely as to drive even loyal men into rebellion, and the French navy intervened at a crucial moment.

This Southern campaign opened brilliantly for Britain when a massive amphibious operation compelled the surrender on 12 May 1780 of Charleston and 5500 men, the worst disaster of the war for American arms. Washington now detached all Southern line regiments from his army which was watching New York and sent them on the long march south, to stiffen local militia and form a new army. Congress, against Washington's advice, appointed to this command Horatio Gates and placed him over the able and courageous Baron de Kalb. Cornwallis beat Gates badly at Camden, S.C., on 16 August; Gates (like the famous Duke of Plaza Toro) leading the rout on his fast thoroughbred. And De Kalb was mortally wounded.

Lord Cornwallis was an excellent soldier and leader, and by this time, using cavalry leaders like Banastre Tarleton and Patrick Ferguson to bolster the local loyalists, he had South Carolina pretty well in hand. But Ferguson went a bit too far when he threatened the 'hill-billies' of the Watauga country to pay them a visit and hang their leaders. They swarmed around his tory force at its position on Kings Mountain near the border, and completely wiped it out on 7 October 1780. In retro-spect, Kings Mountain marks the turn of the tide in South Carolina. The back-countrymen, mostly loyalist when Clinton landed, or joining his 'band wagon' after the fall of Charleston, had been alienated by his harsh measures. Kings Mountain proved that the British were not invin-cible, and thousands of small farmers enlisted under partisan leaders like Francis Marion, 'the swamp fox,' Andrew Pickens, and Thomas Sumter.

Congress now shelved galloper Gates for good, and let Washington choose a general for the Southern army, Nathanael Greene. This gifted son of a Rhode Island farmer, generally conceded to be the ablest gen-eral officer after Washington on the American side, found the defeated army in a terrible state, morally and materially. 'Nothing can be more wretched and distressing than the condition of the troops,' he wrote to Washington, 'starving with cold and hunger, without tents and camp equipage. Those of the Virginia line are literally naked, and a great part totally unfit for any kind of duty, and must remain so until clothing can be had from the northward.' Only about a thousand men were effective. Somehow, Greene instilled a new spirit in them, obtained food and clothes (not uniforms, nobody ever saw a Continental uniform on any-one under a colonel in the Carolina campaign) from the countryside; and in a brilliant, shifty campaign inflicted so many losses on Cornwallis at Cowpens (17 January 1781) and Guilford Courthouse (15 March) that the British army had to retire to the coast. Greene then lashed back into South Carolina, and at Eutaw Springs (8 September) and in several minor engagements recovered control over the interior of that state.

Cornwallis, reinforced and refreshed after contacting his ocean supply line at Wilmington, N.C., marched north into Virginia. There Benedict Arnold, now a British general, and Lafayette, an American major-general, were chasing each other — and Governor Jefferson. On 1 August 1781 Cornwallis occupied Yorktown and began turning that little town into a military base, to help the Royal Navy to control Chesapeake Bay, Maryland, and Virginia.

3. THE NAVIES, AND YORKTOWN

Sea power was decisive in the War of Independence, as Washington appreciated from the first; but it was not until 1780 that the allies were able to challenge British sea supremacy. An American navy was improvised by Washington from some Marblehead fishing schooners during the siege of Boston, and the New England states began to fit out privateers with letters of marque and reprisal, authorizing them to capture British merchantmen wherever found. At least 2000 American privateers were commissioned during the war. Some were armed merchantmen who only took prizes as a side line. Yet in helping themselves the privateersmen served the cause, for they intercepted military supplies, forced up insurance rates, and obtained consumer goods for the army and the people. There were also several state navies, which were used mostly for harbor defense but occasionally cruised offshore. The Continental forces engaged almost exclusively in commerce-destroying, for naval warfare had to pay for itself. Congress in December 1775 authorized an ambitious building program of thirteen frigates — ships mounting twenty to thirty nine- and twelve-pounders each [2] — but fewer than half of them ever got to sea.

The most successful ships were those fitted out or operated in European waters with the co-operation of French and Spanish authorities. *Revenge* of fourteen guns, under Captain Gustavus Conyngham, captured 60 prizes in two years. Captain John Paul Jones, after two successful prize-taking cruises in the Gulf of Maine, was sent across the Atlantic in command of sloop-of-war *Ranger*. Using Brest as a base, he raided English shipping in the narrow seas, and spiked the guns at Whitehaven near his old home in Scotland. Subsequently Franklin got him a small fleet in France, of which the flagship was an old French Indiaman, which Jones renamed *Bonhomme Richard*. She won a desperate battle with H.M. frigate *Serapis* off Flamborough Head on 23 September 1779. Paul Jones's exploits pinned down British forces which might otherwise have been used in America, and he became the hero of countless ballads, chapbooks, and fireside tales. Yet the Royal Navy continued to command American waters, and enabled the British army to be moved from place to place by sea at will, while Washington's army had to walk if it wanted to get anywhere.

Fortunately for America, the French navy had been reorganized since 1763, and was at a high point of morale and efficiency; whilst the British navy under Lord Sandwich, a corrupt and inefficient First Lord of the

2. The three largest classes of warships of that era were the '74' or ship of the line, with three gun decks, the frigate with two, and the sloop-of-war with one. All had three masts, square rigged. The U.S. Navy also had a number of two-masted brigs and schooners, and single-masted sloops.

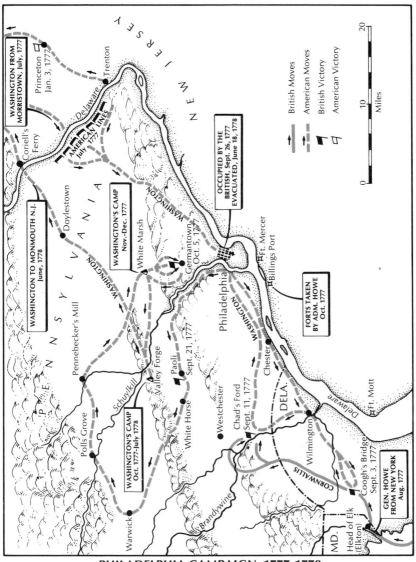

Map labels:

WASHINGTON FROM MORRISTOWN, July, 1777

Princeton Jan. 3, 1777

Trenton

N E W   J E R S E Y

Delaware

AMERICAN LINES July, 1777

Coriell's Ferry

WASHINGTON

OCCUPIED BY THE BRITISH. Sept. 26, 1777 EVACUATED, June 18, 1778

WASHINGTON TO MONMOUTH N.J. June, 1778

Doylestown

WASHINGTON'S CAMP Nov.-Dec. 1777

White Marsh

P E N N S Y L V A N I A

WASHINGTON

Pennebecker's Mill

Germantown Oct. 5, 1777

Philadelphia

Ft. Mercer

Billings Port

FORTS TAKEN BY ADM. HOWE Oct. 1777

Schuylkill

Valley Forge

Paoli Sept. 21, 1777

WASHINGTON

Chester

Polls Grove

White Horse

Westchester

Chad's Ford Sept. 11, 1777

WASHINGTON'S CAMP Oct. 1777-July 1778

DELA.

Wilmington

Ft. Mott

Delaware

CORNWALLIS

Coogh's Bridge Sept. 3, 1777

GEN. HOWE FROM NEW YORK Aug. 1777

Warwick

Brandywine

MD.

Head of Elk (Elkton)

Legend:

British Moves
American Moves
British Victory
American Victory

20

10

Miles

0

PHILADELPHIA CAMPAIGN, 1777-1778

199

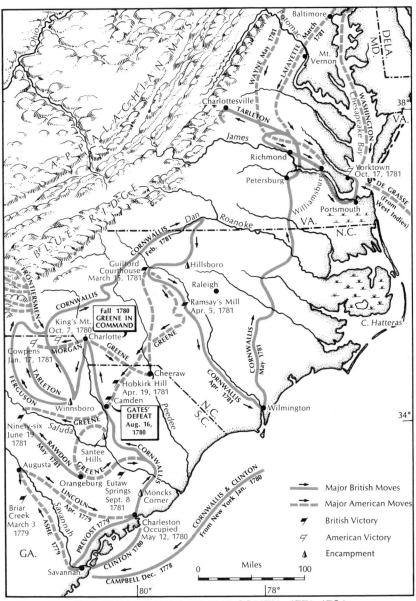

THE SEAT OF WAR IN THE SOUTH, 1779-1781

Admiralty, was full of dry rot and mismanagement. Persuaded by La-fayette to make a real effort to bring the war to an end, Louis XVI sent over a splendid expeditionary force of 6000 men under General Ro-chambeau, which occupied Newport in the summer of 1780. For a year it did nothing except enrich the Rhode Island farmers and fascinate their daughters. Rochambeau's army was no use without a French high-seas fleet. Fortunately, in May 1781, a powerful fleet under the com-mand of a first-rate seaman, Admiral Grasse, arrived at Cape Haitien with orders to clean up in the West Indies and then repair to that part of the coast of the United States where he could do the most good.

The military-naval campaign of Yorktown was one of the most bril-liantly conceived and smoothly executed operations in the history of warfare, considering that it involved co-ordinated movements between two French fleets, an American and a French army, all widely separated, and with no faster means of transport or communication than sailing ships and horses.

Although Washington preferred to dislodge the British from New York, he wisely recognized that the French navy must have the casting vote, and in July 1781, Grasse decided to strike Cornwallis's army at the Chesapeake. On 5 August he sailed with his grand fleet and 4000 men of the Haiti garrison under General the Marquis de Saint-Simon. Precisely one month later, as the forces of Washington and Rochambeau were marching southward to join him, Grasse inflicted a bad beating on a portion of the British fleet in the Battle of the Capes of the Chesapeake.

The French were now masters of Chesapeake Bay and able to boat Washington's and Rochambeau's armies to positions about Yorktown. The siege began on 30 September, under the direction of French engi-neers. The combined allied armies under Washington, Rochambeau, and Saint-Simon, together with Virginia militia, totaled 15,000 men; Corn-wallis had about half that number, but his position was well fortified. Two of his redoubts were carried by American and French assaulting parties, and an attempt to escape across the York river was unsuccessful. Casualties had been surprisingly light, less than those of the naval battle, but Cornwallis knew he was beaten. On 17 October 1781 he surrendered his entire force. As the British passed through the allied lines to stack arms, the military bands played 'The World Turned Upside Down.'

Lafayette joyfully wrote the news to Paris, concluding, 'The play is over; the fifth act has just come to an end.'

It was not quite so simple as that. Grasse's fleet sailed for the West Indies (where it was badly beaten by the British on 12 April 1782); Rochambeau's army was lifted to the West Indies, and Washington at the close of 1781 found himself back at White Plains watching Clinton, with no French allies at hand. During the summer of 1782 British warships and privateers based on New York were sweeping the waters off our coast. General Washington, who with slight success had been urging the states to reinforce his army, reminding them that the war was not over and that the enemy still held New York and other strategic points, felt this to be the most critical moment of the war. On 18 July he wrote to James McHenry, 'At present, we are inveloped in darkness. . . . Providence has done much for us in this contest, but we must do something for ourselves.' He did not realize that the British will for victory, feeble at best, had completely evaporated.

The only fighting on American soil in 1782 was in the West. That year the British won the ascendancy throughout the Northwest, owing largely to their better treatment of the Indians. Colonel William Crawford, Washington's old associate in land speculation, was ambushed and killed by a force of tories and Indians at the site of Sandusky, Ohio, on 4 June 1782. This brought into the war many more Indians, who began raiding deep into Pennsylvania, western Virginia, and Kentucky. Bryan's Station, a fort near Lexington, Ky., was besieged in August by tories and Indians, who on the 19th routed a relieving force of frontier militia at the Lower Blue Licks. George Rogers Clark then collected 1100 mounted riflemen and on 10 November 1782 routed the Shawnee and burned their villages near Chillicothe, Ohio. That was the last land battle of the War of American Independence.

4. THE PEACE OF PARIS

If the soldiers had spoken all their parts, the sailors still had something to say; and the diplomats were just warming up behind the scenes.

Before Cornwallis's surrender, it rather looked as if the United States could only obtain peace and independence on the basis of a *uti possidetis* truce — 'keep what you have' — which would have meant that Great Britain would retain the principal seaports from New York to Savannah, and Spain (France's ally but not ours) would hold both banks of the Mississippi and the shores of the Gulf of Mexico. No progress had been made toward peace when news of the happy victory at Yorktown reached Europe. George III, hearing the news, declared he would never sanction 'getting a peace at the expense of a separation from America.' When Lord North, who had frequently threatened to resign since Burgoyne's surrender, finally threw in the sponge, George III went so far as to draft a message of abdication. But he thought better of it, and in March 1782 called Rockingham — the same minister who had repealed the Stamp Act — to form a ministry, together with Shelburne, Charles James Fox, and others who were traditional friends of America. Shelburne at once sent Richard Oswald to Paris to sound out Dr. Franklin. He proved remarkably complaisant when Franklin suggested not only independence and peace, but the cession of Canada to the United States to prevent future quarrels. It was lucky for British Canada that the negotiations were not pushed through at once, for at that time Shelburne was willing to concede almost anything to get home the 30,000 troops who were doing nothing in America at enormous expense. But there were endless complications and delays.

Franklin, however, was not to be the sole negotiator, only one of a commission of five appointed by Congress four months earlier. They had complete discretion as to peace terms, provided France consented. These instructions, practically dictated by the French minister at Phila-delphia, were intended to place the United States completely under the guidance of Vergennes in the forthcoming negotiations. Franklin seems to have been willing to play that role; but fortunately John Jay, a mem-ber of the peace commission who arrived in time to take part in the negotiations, was by nature suspicious. As a member of Congress he had witnessed intrigues of the French minister at Philadelphia to detach the West from the United States, in favor of Spain. Thus when Oswald presented credentials that were rather unhappily phrased, and it looked as if the United States must negotiate as 'dependent states,' Jay insisted that he return to London and get a new commission. Oswald did not return to Paris with credentials satisfactory to Jay until 28 September, almost a year after Yorktown.

His new credentials enabled Richard Oswald 'to treat with the Com-missioners appointed by the Colonies under the title of Thirteen United States.' This change was taken by the Americans to mean a recognition of independence, and formal negotiations began at Paris toward the end of September. John Adams arrived from The Hague in October and took the same point of view as Jay; Franklin, too, was converted to this separate negotiation with England. Jay, however, is the one who deserves the greatest credit, for he smoked out a plan of Vergennes to buy Spain's consent to peace with the American West; and, in spite of the instructions from Congress to be guided in all things by France, he insisted on direct negotiation. The preliminary treaty was signed 30 November 1782, with the proviso that it was not to take effect until France concluded peace with Great Britain. There was not even an Anglo-American armistice until 20 January 1783, the day that England and France ceased hostilities; and the definitive peace was not concluded until 3 September 1783.

This Peace of Paris certainly gives the lie to the epigram that 'America never lost a war, or won a peace conference.' Considering that the British still held New York, Charleston, Savannah, Detroit, and several other posts in the Northwest, that Washington's army was almost incapable of further effort, and that the British navy had recovered command of the sea, it is surprising what wide boundaries and favorable terms the United States obtained. Almost every article except the one acknowledging the independence of the United States was subject to double construction, and occasioned long diplomatic controversy. The northeast boundary was laid down in a very sketchy manner, and not settled until 1842. The northern boundary along the line of the St. Lawrence and the Great Lakes was fairly definite, until it reached the Grand Portage on Lake Superior, where it was left hanging in the air. Franklin wanted all Canada; the Quebec fur interests, on the contrary, expected that the Ohio river boundary of 1774 would be retained. Shelburne, always a friend to westward expansion, probably accepted the compromise in the hope that it would leave both countries free to expand along parallel lines.

As for the other articles, the Americans retained fishing privileges in the territorial waters of British North America, which they had enjoyed as British subjects. That was Yankee John Adams's contribution to the treaty. Article IV provided that 'creditors on either side shall meet with no lawful impediment' to the recovery of pre-war debts. As unpaid bills for goods furnished to America before the war amounting to several million pounds were still in the strong-boxes of English merchants, this proved a strong plea for ratification; but this article the United States found itself powerless to enforce for many years. The problem of the loyalists caused the greatest difficulty. Shelburne dared not face Parliament without some provision that would take those unfortunate exiles off the books of the treasury, by giving them restitution or compensation. Franklin, contrary to his usual benevolence, cherished most ferocious sentiments against the loyalists (perhaps because his son had gone tory), and had even circulated false atrocity stories to prejudice European opinion against them. He refused to go beyond an innocuous agreement that Congress should 'earnestly recommend' to the several states to restore tory property, and a positive stipulation that no future confiscations should be made. Both parties knew that the earnest recommendations would amount to nothing, but Shelburne accepted them to save the ministry's face before Parliament.

In the other treaties signed the same day between England and France and Spain, a clause of great interest to the United States provided for the retrocession of West and East Florida to Spain, as compensation for England's keeping Gibraltar. Thus North America was divided between Spain, the British empire, and the United States, Spain retaining the lion's share: everything west of the Mississippi and south of the thirty-first parallel of latitude. But the expansion of the United States in another generation wiped out the Florida and the Mississippi boundaries, and by 1846 flung back the Spanish-American frontier to the Rio Grande. France got nothing out of the war but a few West Indian islands, a bankrupt treasury, and the prospect of a new market and an ally in America: a prospect which failed to materialize.

The comment of George III, in a letter to Shelburne, was characteristic:

> I cannot conclude without mentioning how sensibly I feel the dismemberment of America from this Empire, and that I should be miserable indeed if I did not feel that no blame on that Account can be laid at my door, and did I not also know that knavery seems to be so much the striking feature of its Inhabitants that it may not in the end be an evil that they become Aliens to this Kingdom.

A very different reception was accorded to the new republic by the enlightened and generous souls of Europe. In England itself, Washington remained a hero to the liberals; and many old whigs, though smarting with the sting of defeat, consoled themselves with the thought that the king's personal rule had been discredited. On the European continent the feeling about America may be gathered from a vivid account by Henrich Steffens, a Norwegian who later made a brilliant career in

Germany. He described his boyhood impressions at Elsinore in Denmark:

> I was well enough instructed on the significance of the North American War to be vitally interested in a people that fought so boldly for freedom. Among the great men of that time Washington and Franklin stood forth, and the verse of Juvenal with which the latter was greeted:
>
> *Eripuit coelo fulmen sceptrumque tyrannis,*[3]
>
> made a great impression on me. The hero aroused my wonder, but more enviable appeared to me the career of Franklin, who from a simple bourgeois family (the son of a printer) rose to be a famous writer and distinguished scientist, as well as representative of his struggling people, admired by the most intelligent men of his time. There were very few lively young fellows in the countries then at peace who did not follow North American affairs . . .
>
> When we ponder the significance of this war by which the gleaming spark that later burst forth into the mighty flame of Revolution was first thrown into France, it is interesting to remember how near that spark came to our quiet family circle in a far-off, peaceful land. I still remember vividly the day when the conclusion of peace, the victory of struggling liberty, was celebrated at Elsinore and in the harbor. It was a fair day, the harbor was full of merchant ships of all nations, men-of-war too. All the vessels were dressed, their mastheads adorned with long pennants; the most splendid flags were hoisted on the main flagstaffs, and there were others on the jackstaffs and strung between the masts. There was just wind enough to make flags and pennants fly free. This unusual decoration, the joyful people who swarmed over the decks, and the gun salutes from warships and from every merchantman that possessed a pair of cannon made the day festive for us all. Father had invited home a few guests, and, contrary to the prevailing custom, we boys were bidden to table; father explained the significance of this festival, our glasses too were filled with punch, and as toasts were drunk to the success of the new republic, a Danish and a North American flag were hoisted in our garden. The victory of the North Americans and the liberty of other peoples were discussed in lively fashion; and a certain anticipation of the great events to be derived from this victory was in the minds of those rejoicing. It was the friendly morning light of a bloody day in history.[4]

Alas! The friendly morning light soon grew dim and countless bloody days lay ahead.

3. 'He snatched the thunderbolt from Heaven, and the sceptre from tyrants.'
4. Translated from Henrich Steffens, *Was Ich Erlebte* (Breslau, 1840), i. 78–80.

XII

From Colony to Commonwealth

1. THE PROCESS OF FORMING NEW GOVERNMENTS

At the same time that the Americans were winning independence from Great Britain they were transforming colonies into commonwealths, creating new political institutions, and readjusting their society and business to new conditions. The Revolution furnished Americans an opportunity to give legal form to their political ideals as expressed in the Declaration of Independence; and to remedy some of their grievances through state constitutions and through legislation. As James Madison wrote, 'Nothing has excited more admiration in the world than the manner in which free governments have been established in America; for it was the first instance, from the creation of the world . . . that free inhabitants have been seen deliberating on a form of government, and selecting such of their citizens as possessed their confidence, to determine upon and give effect to it.' Americans are so accustomed to living under written constitutions that they take them for granted; yet the institution of a written constitution came out of America.

As early as 10 May 1776 Congress passed a resolution advising the colonies to form new governments 'such as shall best conduce to the happiness and safety of their constituents.' Some, such as New Hampshire and South Carolina, had already done so, and Massachusetts, to meet the Coercive Acts, had established a provisional government in the fall of 1774. Within a year after the Declaration of Independence every state except Massachusetts, Connecticut, and Rhode Island had drawn up a new constitution.[1] Massachusetts labored under her provisional government until 1780, while the two others retained their colonial charters, with a slight change in the preamble, until well into the nineteenth century.

The Pennsylvania constitution thanked God for 'permitting the people of this State, by common consent, and without violence, deliberately to form for themselves such just rules as they shall think best for governing their future society.' Yet a method of giving effect to this 'compact' theory was not easily found. The states adopted new constitutions in a variety of ways. The South Carolina, Virginia, and New Jersey constitutions of 1776 were framed by legislative bodies without any specific authorization, and promulgated by them without popular consent. In New Hampshire, Georgia, Delaware, New York, and Vermont, the legislative bodies or provincial congresses which framed the constitutions did so by express authority, but failed to submit the finished product to popular approval. In Maryland, Pennsylvania, and North Carolina the constitutions framed by authorized legislatures were in some manner ratified by the people. Only Massachusetts (1780) and New Hampshire (1784) had constitutional conventions specifically elected for that purpose, and a popular referendum on the result. This has become the standard method of constitution making.

Massachusetts illustrates the most deliberate and effective transition from colony to commonwealth. The process took five years and the delay was fortunate, for in Massachusetts the sort of people who made John Adams wince by shouting 'no courts, no taxation,' were numerous. The hired men, tinkers, and village drunkards who had enjoyed tarring and feathering tories, ransacking the premises of suspected profiteers, and turning out with the militia for a few days or weeks, were a force to be reckoned with, and sundry rural townships had a village demagogue advocating a crack-brained scheme of government. Yet there was a

---

1. The dates of the adoptions of the state constitutions are as follows:

New Hampshire (1)	6 Jan.	1776	North Carolina	18 Dec.	1776
South Carolina (1)	26 Mar.	1776	Georgia	5 Feb.	1777
Virginia	29 June	1776	New York	20 April	1777
New Jersey	2 July	1776	Vermont	8 July	1777 *
Delaware	22 Aug.	1776	South Carolina (2)	19 Mar.	1778
Pennsylvania	28 Sept.	1776	Massachusetts	15 June	1780
Maryland	11 Nov.	1776	New Hampshire (2)	13 June	1784

* Vermont was not accepted as a state until 1791.

shrewd common sense in the New England population, which sustained the leaders in establishing a sound state constitution.

The first step was for the colonial assembly to resolve itself into a provincial congress. On 5 May 1775 this congress deposed Governor Gage and ordered the election of a new assembly, as though the royal charter were in force and the governor absent. That made such an awkward government that the assembly drafted a state constitution and submitted it to the people. It was a poor sort of constitution and the voters showed good sense in rejecting it by a five-sixths majority. The chastened assembly then put into effect a new method, which at least two rural towns, Middleborough and Concord, had suggested. It asked the people to decide in their town meetings whether or not they wanted a constitutional convention. They so voted. The convention, its delegates elected by manhood suffrage, duly met and chose a committee to draft a constitution; and on that committee John Adams did all the work. His draft, adopted 2 March 1780 by the convention, was then submitted to the people. Citizens were invited to discuss the constitution in town meeting, to point out objections and suggest improvements, to vote on it article by article, and to empower the convention to ratify and declare it in force if two-thirds of the men aged 21 and upward were in favor. This complicated procedure was followed. The town meetings that spring had a beautiful time discussing the constitution clause by clause, and drafting criticisms that in the main were sensible. When the convention tabulated the returns, it found a two-thirds majority for every article, and declared the entire constitution ratified and in force on 15 June 1780.

It would be difficult to devise a more deliberate method of securing a government by popular consent. At every step the rights of the people were safeguarded, and their views consulted. By the constitutional convention, the written constitution, and popular ratification, Americans had discovered a way to legalize revolution.

2. THE NEW STATE CONSTITUTIONS

Most of the new constitutions showed the impact of democratic ideas, but none made any drastic break with the past, and all but two were designed to prevent a momentary popular will from overriding settled practices and vested interests. They were built by Americans on the solid foundation of colonial experience, with the timber of English practice, using Montesquieu as consulting architect. A few men, who saw eye-to-eye on the fundamentals of popular government, did the main work of drafting. That of New York, one of the best, was written by three young graduates of King's College: John Jay, Robert Livingston, and Gouverneur Morris, of whom the first two were just over 30 and the third, 24 years old.

Naturally the first object of the framers was to secure those 'inalienable rights,' the violation of which by George III had caused them to repudiate the British connection. Consequently, each constitution began with a 'Declaration' or 'Bill' of Rights. That of Virginia, framed by George Mason of Gunston Hall, served as a model for other states. It enumerated the fundamental liberties for which Englishmen had been struggling since Magna Carta — moderate bail and humane punishments, militia instead of a standing army, speedy trials by law of the land with judgments by one's peers, and freedom of conscience — together with others, based on recent experience, which Englishmen had not yet secured — freedom of the press, of elections, of the right of a majority to reform or alter the government, prohibition of general warrants. Other states enlarged the list by drawing upon their own experience, or upon English constitutional documents such as the Bill of Rights of 1689 — freedom of speech, of assemblage, of petition, of bearing arms, the right to a writ of habeas corpus, inviolability of domicile, equal operation of the laws. State governments were generally forbidden to pass *ex post facto* laws, to define treason in such a way as to 'get' undesirables, to take property without compensation, to imprison without warrant, to apply martial law in time of peace, or to force people to testify against themselves.

In other respects, too, the Americans had long English memories. The English people in the seventeenth century had tasted absolutism under Charles I, the Long Parliament, Cromwell, and James II. Unhappy experience of these authoritarian regimes impressed the English mind with the need for separation between those who make laws (the legislative), those who execute the laws (king, governor, or executive council), and those who interpret the laws (the judiciary); and with the need for checks even within these departments. By 1700 the English had obtained a government in which the legislative and executive functions

were separated,[2] and the judges had obtained tenure during good behavior. George III upset this balance by acquiring an undue influence
over Parliament, which was all the more reason for the Americans hark-
ing back to what they conceived to be the 'true principles' of the British
Constitution, brilliantly expounded by their Bible of political wisdom,
Montesquieu's *Spirit of Laws*.

Accordingly, all state constitutions paid allegiance to the theory of
separation of powers and attempted to carry it out in fact. But this
principle was less well observed in the first round of constitution-making
in 1776. The Virginia framers, impressed by Locke's dictum, 'The legislative is the supreme power of the commonwealth,' allowed the legislature to elect governor, council, and all judges except justices of the
peace. The Pennsylvania constitution was consciously drafted by radicals to give the popular will immediate effect. No one could be a member of the Pennsylvania legislature more than four years in every seven,
or of the executive council (out of which a president was chosen) more
than three years in seven. This rotation was prescribed (the constitution
explained) in order to preclude 'the danger of establishing an inconvenient aristocracy.' The classical education of leading men, who knew
what Julius Caesar did to the Roman Republic, was reflected by a weakening of the executive power in every state except New York, Massachusetts, and New Hampshire. Only two states granted their governor
veto power, and that could be overridden. The judiciary in most states
was appointed by the legislature, and in three states for a limited term;
but every state endeavored to make the judiciary independent by protecting the judges from arbitrary removal or pressure through reduction
of salaries.

Although the people were everywhere recognized as sovereign, every
constitution but that of Vermont placed control of the government in the
hands of persons possessing more or less property. It was accepted that
the body politic consisted of those who had a 'stake in society.' Even the
democratic Franklin declared that 'as to those who have no landed
property . . . the allowing them to vote for legislators is an impropriety.' There were property qualifications for voting, and proportionately

2. Their subsequent blending, in the modern parliamentary system, took place after
the American Revolution, and so was outside the experience of Americans at that
time.

higher ones for office-holding — £1000 in New Jersey and Maryland for a state senator, twice that in South Carolina. In most states, too, there were religious qualifications for office-holding, or test oaths of office that were designed to keep out former loyalists and Roman Catholics.

Few early constitutions provided any special method of amendment; yet when necessity arose, amendment could be effected by a new convention. Despite the haste with which many were drafted, five of these constitutions lasted over half a century, and that of Massachusetts is still in effect, although amended out of all resemblance to John Adams's constitution of 1780. Mistakes were made; but these amateur constitution-makers fully proved themselves worthy of their trust, and their states ripe for self-government.

3. POLITICAL REFORM

In most of the states a struggle between democratic and conservative elements started during the war, but did not break out in the open until after it was over. In states such as New York, Massachusetts, South Carolina, Maryland, and Virginia, where the conservative classes had taken the lead before 1775, they were in a position to direct the course of events and stem the democratic tide. In Pennsylvania and Georgia, where the initial decision in favor of independence had been a radical victory, the democratic elements had things much their own way.

The constitutional history of three typical states, Pennsylvania, Virginia, and South Carolina, illustrates the clash of classes and the essential continuity of this period with the pre-war years.

In the Quaker commonwealth the struggle between east and west culminated early in 1776 in a reapportionment of representation, a smashing victory for the western counties. Triumph tasted sweet, and the radicals wanted more. The constitution that they produced was democratic; the principal authors were George Bryan, an intense, idealistic Irishman, Thomas Young, a former Boston Son of Liberty, and Benjamin Franklin. It did away with governor and upper chamber, and provided for a council of censors to examine the operation of the government every seven years. There were no qualifications for voting or for office-holding, except the payment of a state tax and the touching proviso that membership in the House should consist of 'persons most noted for wisdom and virtue.' Vermont copied this constitution almost verbatim, and in that frontier democratic community it worked well enough. But in Pennsylvania, where there were deep class, racial, and religious divisions, it established the nearest thing to a 'dictatorship of the proletariat' that we have had in America. 'You would execrate this state if you were in it,' wrote a Pennsylvanian to Jefferson. 'The supporters of this government are a set of workmen without any weight. of character.' During the war, the Pennsylvania Assembly expended more energy in plundering tories, cracking down on profiteers, and persecuting conscientious objectors, than in supporting the Revolution. James Wilson made himself so unpopular by opposing the state constitution that his house was attacked by a radical mob in 1779. The legislature annulled the charter of Philadelphia College, the most liberal in the United States, because the provost and trustees were anti-constitutionalists, and handed over the college property to the newly chartered University of Pennsylvania, but gave that university very little support. Eventually the people of Pennsylvania turned against this constitution, and in 1790 obtained the election of a convention which drafted a new one with a bicameral legislature.

In Virginia the gentry who led the patriot party wanted a conservative constitution and got it. George Mason, Patrick Henry, and 25-year-old James Madison were on the drafting committee; Jefferson and John Adams exerted their influence from Philadelphia. Colonial property qualifications for voting and office-holding remained unchanged, and the eastern counties retained their control of the legislature through the device of giving each county exactly two members. As the western counties were large, populous, and growing fast, this disproportion became greater every year. In 1790 the five valley counties with an average white population of 12,089 had two representatives each, and five tidewater counties with an average white population of 1471 had two representatives each. And the Presbyterians were disappointed in not obtaining separation of church and state. Yet the Virginia constitution was distinguished for its noble Declaration of Rights, which served as a model for other states, and even for France. Although the Virginia gentry were unyielding in matters threatening their political supremacy, they went further in reform legislation than the governing class of any other state, not excepting Pennsylvania. Their constitution, brief and flexible, allowed this; and within a few years, under the driving leadership of Jefferson, Madison, and Mason, quit-rents, primogeniture, and entails were abolished, church and state separated, the legal code revised, and the slave trade abolished.

The South Carolina constitution of 1778 continued those class and sectional inequalities that made trouble in the colonial period. Suffrage was limited to men with a 50-acre freehold, and property qualifications for office-holding were almost prohibitory. A state senator had to hold an estate worth £2000, while the governor, lieutenant governor, and councillors had to own property to the value of £10,000. The coastal region continued to be grossly over-represented. The Anglican Church was disestablished, but only Protestants were guaranteed civil rights. This conservative triumph left that state under the control of low-country planters, who made it the stronghold of Southern conservatism until it blew up in 1865.

4. SOCIAL PROGRESS

Although democracy had little or nothing to do with starting hostilities, the war released it as a major force in American life. Tory estates were confiscated, land reforms were adopted and relics of feudalism such as titles of nobility, quit-rents, and tithes were swept away. Progress was made in achieving complete religious freedom and separation of church and state, and a concerted attack was made on slavery and the slave trade. The democratic philosophy of the Revolution percolated through politics into the structure of American society.

During the Revolution the Crown lands, extensive domains of proprietors such as the Penns and Calverts, and the princely estates of loyalists such as Lord Fairfax of Virginia, Roger Morris of New York, Henry Harford of Maryland, and the Wentworths of New Hampshire were confiscated. This was done not to equalize landholding but to punish the recalcitrant and to raise money. Confiscated lands were not given away but sold to the highest bidder. In cities like New York and Annapolis, speculators acquired most of the valuable property. Rural estates, however, were frequently subdivided so that in areas like Dutchess County, New York, manor tenants were able to become freeholders. The abolition of entail and primogeniture, chiefly of symbolic importance, indicated a determination to wipe out the remnants of feudalism and create a more egalitarian society.

An important leader in the fight for separation of church and state was the Reverend John Witherspoon, who came to America after fighting the established church in Scotland, became president of the college at Princeton, and signed the Declaration of Independence. He was forever preaching that mere toleration was not enough, since toleration implied superiority and condescension; the only proper principle for a republic was complete liberty to worship how one chose, or not at all; and every church should be supported by its own members or invested funds without help from the taxing power of the state.

In Maryland, where the Anglican Church was unpopular both with the Catholics of the coast and the Presbyterians of the interior, it was separated from the state in 1776. In North Carolina the feeble establishment completely disappeared, and the constitution of 1776 stated simply that 'there shall be no establishment of any one religious church or denomination in this State in preference to any other.' There was a struggle in South Carolina, where the Church was firmly entrenched in the affections of the ruling class; but the constitution of 1778 provided that all Protestant churches should enjoy equal civil and religious liberties. In the Middle Colonies, where religious liberty already existed, the principle was embodied in the new constitutions as a matter of course.

In Virginia the struggle by Madison, Jefferson, and Richard Henry Lee for religious liberty was long and arduous. Dissenters were still forced to pay tithes, and none but the Episcopal clergy could perform the marriage ceremony. It took ten years of what Jefferson called the severest contest in which he was ever engaged to do away with these privileges. In January 1786, after a state-wide campaign of education, the legislature passed the Statute of Religious Liberty which Jefferson had introduced seven years earlier, and which he accounted one of his three great contributions to his country, the others being the Declaration of Independence and the establishment of the University of Virginia. The statute roundly declares that 'No man shall be compelled to frequent or support any religious worship, place or ministry whatsoever.' It even warns later assemblies that any attempt on their part to tamper with this law 'will be an infringement of natural right.' None, to this day, has ventured to do so; the statute is still in force.

Only in New England did this principle fail of recognition. Here the Congregational clergy had been early and eloquent on the winning side; the Reverend Thomas Allen of Pittsfield even led his parishioners into action at Bennington. It was argued that the town church, like the town meeting and the town school, had made New England great, and should be equally respected. Rhode Island had always enjoyed religious liberty, Vermont adopted it at once; but the other three states set up a sort of quasi-establishment, according to which everyone had to pay a religious tax to the Congregational church of the parish within which he lived, unless he belonged to a recognized dissenting church. In that case the dissenting pastor received the tax. The Episcopalians in Connecticut and the Baptists elsewhere attacked this system intermittently, but it lasted in New Hampshire until 1817, in Connecticut until 1818, and in Massachusetts until 1833. The Congregational churches, therefore, were left in exactly the same position after the war as before: they had no central organization to be troubled by political changes. The same applied to the Quakers.

The Methodists, or Wesleyans, on the contrary, seized this opportunity to form a separate church. As a religious society within the Church of England, they did not prosper during the war, when (as Francis Asbury said) the minds of men were 'full of sin and politics.' Asbury, who had been John Wesley's superintendent before the war, organized the Methodist Episcopal Church of America at a Baltimore Conference in 1784, with himself as first bishop and premier circuit rider — his horseback mileage averaged 5000 annually for the next five years.

The Anglican communion, although decimated by loyalism and the withdrawal of English support, had sufficient strength and spirit to organize itself as the Protestant Episcopal Church of America at a series of conventions between 1784 and 1789. A constitution giving far more power to the laity than in England was adopted, references to English royalty were deleted from the Book of Common Prayer, and apostolic succession was secured through the election of several bishops over state-wide dioceses, who were consecrated in England or Scotland. In 1785, when Bishop Seabury (the former tory pamphleteer) returned to his new diocese in lawn sleeves, the Massachusetts legislature laid a stamp tax; this caused the *Boston Gazette* to exclaim, 'Two wonders of the world — a Stamp Act in Boston and a Bishop in Connecticut!'

No religious body was so well prepared for independence as the Presbyterians. They had numbers, wealth, Scotch respect for learning, Irish joy in battle, and President Witherspoon. At a series of synods between 1785 and 1788 a form of government and discipline, a confession of faith, a directory of worship, and two catechisms were adopted for the Presbyterian Church in the United States. The several German and

Dutch sects also broke loose from their old-world organizations, and formed new ones.

There was a lively struggle between English, French, and Irish Roman Catholics for control of that Church in the United States, which in 1785 counted only 24 priests and as many thousand souls, most of it in Maryland and Philadelphia. The London vicar apostolic made no effort to exercise jurisdiction after 1776; but in France there was an active movement, led by that Bishop of Autun who is better known in history as M. de Talleyrand, to place American Catholics under a French vicar apostolic and provide a seminary at Bordeaux for training American priests. This did not please the faithful in America, who rallied and persuaded Pope Pius VI to appoint the Reverend John Carroll of Maryland his apostolic prefect in 1784. That office did not carry enough authority to keep the French and Irish Catholics in order; and in 1786 a chapter of the Maryland clergy petitioned the Holy See to grant them episcopal government. The Pope did so, and John Carroll was duly elected, confirmed, and consecrated Bishop of Baltimore, a diocese that covered the entire United States until 1804.

The inconsistency of demanding life, liberty, and happiness for themselves while denying those 'natural rights' to Negroes was apparent to Americans even before unfriendly English criticism called it to their attention.[3] On the eve of the Revolution, a pamphleteer wrote: 'Blush ye

3. It is impossible to ascertain the exact number of slaves in the American colonies in 1776. The table below gives the approximate number in 1776 and the actual number according to the census of 1790.

	1776	1790
New Hampshire	700	157
Rhode Island	4,000	958
Connecticut	6,000	2,648
Massachusetts	5,249 *	0
New York	20,000	21,193
New Jersey	10,000	11,423
Pennsylvania	6,000	3,707
Delaware	?	8,837
Maryland	70,000	103,036
Virginia	200,000	292,627
North Carolina	70,000	100,783
South Carolina	100,000	107,094
Georgia	10,000	29,264
Kentucky	?	12,440
Southwest Territory	?	3,417
	501,949	699,374

* Including free Negroes.

pretended votaries for freedom! ye trifling patriots! who are making a vain parade of being advocates for the liberties of mankind, who are thus making a mockery of your profession by trampling on the sacred natural rights and privileges of Africans; for while you are fasting, praying, nonimporting, nonexporting, remonstrating, resolving, and pleading for a restoration of your charter rights, you at the same time are continuing this lawless, cruel, inhuman, and abominable practice of enslaving your fellow creatures.'

The first point of attack was the African slave trade. Time and again the American colonies had protested against this traffic, maintained chiefly for the benefit of the Royal African Company, but their protests had been in vain and their prohibitory laws had been disallowed by the Privy Council. Even the pious Lord Dartmouth denounced the colonies for their attempts 'to check or discourage a traffic so beneficial to the nation.' One of the first acts of the Continental Congress was to conclude a non-importation agreement interdicting the slave trade. Soon the states took separate action. Delaware prohibited it in 1776, Virginia in 1778, Pennsylvania in 1780, and Maryland in 1783. Even in South Carolina the trade was temporarily outlawed, while North Carolina placed a heavy tax on all slaves imported into that state. Within ten years after independence every state except Georgia had banned or severely restrained the traffic, and Georgia followed tardily in 1798 with an absolute prohibition. But a good many ships from New York and New England continued to bring slaves illegally from Africa and sell them in the West Indies and the lower South.

The struggle for Negro emancipation was more difficult, and marked by a sectional division. It was relatively easy for the Northern states, where slavery was unprofitable. As early as 1774 Rhode Island provided that all slaves thereafter brought into that commonwealth were to be free, because 'those who are desirous of enjoying all the advantages of liberty themselves should be willing to extend personal liberty to others.' The constitution of Vermont abolished slavery outright. In Massachusetts, Quork Walker sued his master for freedom in 1781 on the ground that the state constitution declared: 'All men are born free and equal.' He won, and slavery ended in that state. The New Hampshire courts, under a similar clause, freed only the *post nati*. Pennsylvania, stronghold of anti-slavery Quakers, provided for gradual emancipation in 1780; Connecticut and Rhode Island followed four years later. New York and

New Jersey made similar provisions in 1799 and 1804. So the Revolution put slavery well on the way to extinction, north of the Mason-Dixon Line.

In the South slaves were so numerous that to free them would have shaken the economic and social system. The dilemma of liberal Southerners is presented in a letter written by Patrick Henry:

> I take this Oppertunity to acknowledge the receit of Anthony Benezets Book against the Slave Trade. I thank you for it. . . . Would any one believe that I am Master of Slaves of my own purchase! I am draw along by the general Inconvenience of living without them; I will not, I cannot justify it. However culpable my Conduct, I will so far pay my devoir to Virtue, as to own the excellence and rectitude of her Precepts and to lament my want of conformity to them. I believe a time will come when an oppertunity will be offered to abolish this lamentable Evil.

'I tremble for my country,' Jefferson wrote, 'when I reflect that God is just; that his justice cannot sleep forever.' Yet proposals for gradual emancipation were defeated in Virginia and every Southern state. Several states, however, encouraged voluntary manumission by the masters, and thousands of Negroes obtained their freedom by this means. Practically every Southern gentleman looked upon slavery as an evil, but a necessary one; in time it became so necessary that it ceased to appear evil.

An unintended consequence of the Revolution was to diffuse political power. Rarely has a revolution been led by men so conservative. James Otis responded to a call for reform of the Massachusetts government in 1776 by sneering: 'When the pot boils, the scum will rise.' A year earlier John Adams had warned: 'Such a levelling spirit prevails . . . that I fear we shall be obliged to call in a military force to do that which our civil government was originally designed for.' Yet revolutionary leaders found that when they employed the rhetoric of popular rights in their quarrel with Britain, they encouraged mechanics and tenant farmers to use the same arguments to press for greater liberties in this country.

The Revolutionary era saw a modest growth in political democracy. There was new insistence that representatives heed instructions given them by their constituents. The people, a Philadelphia group explained, 'should be consulted in the most particular manner that can be imagined.' To emphasize the right of the electorate to supervise legislators,

New Hampshire and Massachusetts erected public galleries in their assemblies. In Williamsburg in 1774, the electors ended the patrician practice of being treated to strong drink by the candidates, and announced
that, as befitted free men, they would entertain the candidate instead. In
1775, New Hampshire and Georgia abolished the freehold qualification
for voting.

The American Revolution was no social upheaval, but it did have
social consequences. It encouraged the tendency to question the claims
of those in authority. 'The distinction of classes,' observed Washington in
1788, 'begins to disappear.' Still, the main significance of the American
Revolution was unquestionably political. Although there had been small-
scale revolts earlier in Geneva and Corsica, it was the American rebellion that touched off the explosion that shook the world. A war of
liberation, it set an example of how to achieve both decolonization and
constitutional republican government, and the force of it is not yet
spent. In a Fourth of July address in 1787 Benjamin Rush declared:
'There is nothing more common than to confound the terms American
Revolution with those of the late American War. The American War is
over, but this is far from being the case with the American Revolution.
On the contrary but the first act of the great drama is closed.'

5. ARTS, LETTERS, AND EDUCATION

The American Revolution also stimulated intellectual and humanitarian
movements. Especially in the South, where before the war there had
been but one college, new opportunities for higher education were
created. Governor Jefferson, as chairman of the board of regents, partly
secularized the College of William and Mary in 1779 by turning the
chairs of divinity and Hebrew into professorships of law and modern
languages, and by allowing students considerable latitude of choice in
their studies. It was also during the war that William and Mary students
founded the Phi Beta Kappa Society, and initiated a young Harvard
graduate who established chapters at his alma mater and at Yale. The
Presbyterians founded at least four new colleges in the 1780's: Hampden-
Sidney, Virginia (1782); Liberty Hall, which became the nucleus of
Washington and Lee University; Dickinson College (1783) at Carlisle,
Pa.; and Transylvania Seminary (1785), the first institution of secondary
education beyond the mountains, which a decade later became a univer-

sity. The Lutherans and Dutch Reformed Church, with the aid of a contribution from Benjamin Franklin, established the German-speaking Franklin College at Lancaster, Pa., in 1787; and the Protestant Episcopal Church between 1782 and 1785 founded Washington College at Chesterton, Maryland, St. John's at Annapolis, and the 'Citadel' at Charleston. Bishop Carroll opened Georgetown, the first Roman Catholic college in 1789. Within the same period the legislatures of Georgia, Maryland, and North Carolina took the initiative in providing state universities.

All the older colleges were injured by the war, but most of them picked up rapidly thereafter, Yale graduating a record-breaking class of 70 in 1785.[4] King's College was closed during the British occupation of New York, but reopened as Columbia College in 1784 under a distinguished president, William Samuel Johnson. Higher education in Philadelphia suffered, as we have seen, from political tinkering, yet the distinguished Benjamin Rush made the Pennsylvania Medical School the best in the country, and Quaker influence made Philadelphia easily the leading American city in humanitarian enterprises. A college of physicians, a free medical dispensary for the poor, an abolition society, and a society for the relief of prisoners were founded there under the Confederation.

In other branches of arts, letters, and learning this era of war and upheaval was prolific. The versatile Judge Francis Hopkinson, signer of the Declaration of Independence, also excelled as poet, painter, pamphleteer, musician, organist of Christ Church, Philadelphia, and designer of the American flag — even though Betsy Ross put together the first one. Hopkinson's *Battle of the Kegs* (1778) was a roaring satire on an incident of the Revolution; his oratorio *The Temple of Minerva* was performed in 1781 'in Presence of His Excellency General Washington and his Lady.' David Rittenhouse, a Philadelphia mathematician and astronomer, was the first man of science in America at this time; but everywhere ingenious people were seeking out the secrets of nature. In Massachusetts, for instance, the Rev. Manasseh Cutler during the war prepared the first systematic account of New England flora, measured (very inaccurately) the height of Mt. Washington, observed eclipses,

4. The numbers of other graduating classes that year, so far as is recorded, are: Harvard, 32; Princeton, 10; Dartmouth, 20; Brown, none (15 in 1786); Columbia, none (9 in 1786); Pennsylvania, 4.

and in 1787 promoted the Ohio Company; the Rev. John Prince invented a new air pump in 1783; and the Rev. Joseph Willard recorded all manner of phenomena. In the Philosophical Library that this group formed at Salem, largely from an Irish scientist's library brought in by a local privateer, young Nathaniel Bowditch, the future navigator, first fed his appetite for mathematical science. Philadelphia even before the war had her learned academy, the American Philosophical Society, of which Franklin was the founder and Rittenhouse the president; in 1780 Boston and Salem virtuosi founded the American Academy of Arts and Sciences.

A 25-year-old schoolmaster named Noah Webster declared in 1783, 'America must be as independent in *literature* as she is in *politics*, as famous for *arts* as for *arms*.' And he did more than his share to make her so. His famous blue-backed speller, the first edition of which appeared in 1783, became one of the best sellers of all time: over 15 million copies sold in the author's lifetime; 60 million in a century. It was followed in 1785 by his *American Selection*, the first school reader, including rules for elocution, a brief American history, and a geography of the United States. Joel Barlow, Webster's classmate at Yale, wrote his epic *Vision of Columbus* in the intervals of preaching, fighting, and teaching, and had it sumptuously printed at Hartford in 1787; by that time he and other 'Hartford Wits' were contributing squibs on democracy and the agrarian rebel Dan Shays to *The Anarchiad*. When poor Dan fled to New York he once more unwittingly contributed to American literature, for Royall Tyler, sent thither to demand Shays's extradition, saw Sheridan's *School for Scandal* and was inspired to write *The Contrast*. This delightful comedy was professionally produced in 1787.[5] John Trumbull, son of the governor of Connecticut but educated at Harvard, served in the war, studied painting at London under the expatriated Pennsylvanian Benjamin West, and there in 1786 completed his two famous paintings, *The Battle at Bunker's Hill near Boston*, and *The Death of General Montgomery*. St. John de Crèvecoeur's *Letters of an American Farmer* were published in 1782; and four years later appeared the first collection edition of the poems of Philip Freneau. The concluding stanzas of one of them, 'On the Emigration to America and Peopling the Western Country,' well express the spirit of this age:

5. *The Prince of Parthia* by Thomas Godfrey of Philadelphia, there produced in 1767, was the first play by an Anglo-American to be put on professionally; *The Contrast* was the second.

O come the time, and haste the day,
When man shall man no longer crush,
When Reason shall enforce her sway,
Nor these fair regions raise our blush,
Where still the *African* complains,
And mourns his yet unbroken chains.

Far brighter scenes a future age,
The muse predicts, these States will hail,
Whose genius may the world engage,
Whose deeds may over death prevail,
And happier systems bring to view,
Than all the eastern sages knew.

6. WESTERN STATE-MAKING

While the thirteen seaboard colonies were being metamorphosed into states and adjusting themselves to the conditions of independence, new commonwealths were being created in Vermont and in the trans-Appalachian country. Here, under primitive conditions, the processes of commonwealth-building and state-making were going on simultaneously throughout the revolutionary period, and here the democratic theories of that era were given a rude but effective application. Nothing more eloquently bespeaks the vital energy of Americans of this generation than their hewing new empires out of the wilderness.

Ethan Allen was the first leader of the Vermonters. Patriot and speculator, adventurer and capitalist, he was typical of those frontier leaders who directed the expansive forces of that era. Defying a pre-war decision of the British Privy Council allotting the Green Mountain country to New York, defying also Congress and Governor Clinton and General Washington, who regarded this decision as valid, the Allens and their party created and defended the independent commonwealth of Vermont. Although the Allen brothers used the language of patriotism, they were primarily interested in land. They controlled a land company which claimed title to over 300,000 acres in central Vermont, and Ethan himself declared that 'Congress shall not have the parcelling of his Lands to their avaricious Minions.' To forestall so sad an event they carried on intrigues with the Governor of Canada, looking to a guarantee of independence in return for neutrality during the war, or even to a return to the British empire after the war. Like true Vermonters they acted with such silent shrewdness that only recently have the archives revealed their doings. In 1789 Levi Allen went to London to obtain a commercial treaty, and offered 'to raise a regiment of Green Mountain boys for His Majesty's service.' George III was not interested. The people of Vermont, who knew naught of these intrigues, were active supporters of the American cause, but Congress was estopped from recognizing their claims to statehood in fear of antagonizing New York. In 1790 New York finally relinquished her claims, a convention at Bennington ratified the Federal Constitution, and on 18 February 1791 Congress admitted Vermont as the fourteenth state.

The creation of new commonwealths west of the Appalachians was attended with even greater difficulties than in Vermont. Lured by the finest hunting and some of the richest land yet spied out in America, the pioneers poured into the 'dark and bloody ground' of Kentucky and Tennessee. As early as 1769 settlers from western Virginia, defying the royal proclamation, established a small community on the upper waters of the Watauga river. In the following years James Robertson and John Sevier led a body of 80 men from North Carolina to the Watauga settlements; and by 1775 there were several thousand settlers scattered along the banks of the Watauga, Holston, and other tributaries of the Tennessee river. North Carolina organized this region as a county in 1776. The people took care of themselves throughout the war, and, as we have seen, 'took care' of Major Ferguson at the Battle of Kings Mountain. But in 1784, when the Cherokee went on the warpath, frontier leaders called a convention at Jonesboro, organized the state of Franklin, elected John Sevier governor, and adopted a constitution. Taxes were payable in beaver skins, well-cured bacon, clean tallow, rye whisky, or peach and apple brandy. After a few years Franklin became part of the state of Tennessee, which was admitted to the Union in 1796.

Central Kentucky, the blue-grass country, began to be settled shortly after the Watauga. This region was the scene of a colossal land speculation that assumed the full panoply of sovereignty — the Transylvania Company, of which the leading spirit was Judge Richard Henderson of North Carolina. On 17 March 1775 this company purchased from the Cherokee for a few thousand pounds all lands lying between the Kentucky, the Ohio, and the Cumberland rivers, although they had no authority from king or colony, and the Cherokee had no right to make the sale. A few bold pioneers, encouraged by the defeat of the Shawnee in Lord Dunmore's War, had already found their way into the blue-grass and founded Harrodsborough. Henderson and the celebrated scout Daniel Boone now conducted a few dozen more men to a place on the Kentucky river that they named Boonesborough; and there on 23 May 1775, under a great elm in the clover-carpeted meadow, Henderson called a meeting of delegates from all settlements in the Transylvania domain. The convention drafted articles of government, passed laws, organized Transylvania Colony, and petitioned the Continental Congress for recognition. It did not get it. Virginia was not ready to surrender title and jurisdiction over 17 million acres of her Western territory, Henderson alienated settlers by attempting to collect quit-rents, and the upshot was that most of the settlers sought protection from Virginia, which organized the region as Kentucky County in 1776. The Transylvania Company obtained 200,000 acres by way of compensation, for it had done much to open up Kentucky; it was Henderson who employed Daniel Boone to hew out what later was known as the Wilderness Road.[6] After fourteen years' agitation Virginia relinquished her jurisdiction over this region, and on 1 June 1792 Kentucky was admitted to the Union as the fifteenth state.

Despite their isolation from the main theaters of conflict, the Kentucky and Tennessee settlements suffered severely during the war. They were exposed to merciless Indian warfare, and the ravages of desperadoes and cattle-thieves who always flock to the frontier. At the end of the war these communities attracted a flood of emigration from the older states. Settlers from North Carolina and Virginia pressed through the Cumberland Gap into the fertile river bottoms of Kentucky, the hardwood forests between the Cumberland and the Tennessee, or the rolling blue-grass prairies; while another stream of settlers from Maryland and Pennsylvania followed the Potomac or the Juniata to their headwaters, then crossed the Alleghenies to Wheeling or Pittsburgh, and sailed down the Ohio into the promised land. The trans-Appalachian

6. The Wilderness Road, which remained a mere trail until about 1796, began at the Holston and Watauga settlements, swung north at Knoxville, passed through the Cumberland Gap where it joined the Indian 'Warrior's Path' that led to the junction of the Scioto and Ohio rivers, branched off by a buffalo trace northwesterly across the Rockcastle, crossed the Kentucky river at Boonesborough, and continued to Lexington. Just before the crossing of the Rockcastle the Wilderness Road forked, and the west branch, which led to Crab Orchard, Danville, and Louisville, soon became the most heavily traveled.

population, only a few thousand on the outbreak of the war, numbered well over 120,000 by 1790.[7] In the year ending November 1788, some 967 boats containing 18,370 men, women, and children floated down the Ohio, while almost equal numbers were spilling over the mountain barriers to the South.

The most striking features of this migration were its spontaneity and the intense individualism of its members. No government provided the pioneer's means of transport, or protected him at his destination. No church or benevolent society provided him with priest or minister, school or poor relief. But — and this exception is as American as the rule — he generally had to secure a land title from speculators. Both ideal and practice were individual liberty, restrained only by spontaneous organizations to secure defense, and to protect property from the lawless fellows. The earlier settlements were in stockades, or 'stations' as they were called. Perhaps 20 or 30 families lived within a wooden palisade, with blockhouses at the corners, encircled by a swath cleared from the surrounding forest as a precaution against surprise. Thus, ten centuries before in England, countless 'stokes' had looked out on unbroken fen and forest. But the American stockades were fortuitous and temporary. Some vague instinctive fear, perhaps, that village life would mean serfdom to him as to his Saxon ancestor broke up the stations before it was safe to do so, and each pioneer made haste to satisfy his ambition for a wilderness farm with clearing and log cabin in the center. And the instinct for self-government and the yearning for improvement were only submerged, never lost by privation and danger. It was typical of West as well as East when the Watauga leaders of 1784 declared: 'If we should be so happy as to have a separate government, vast numbers from different quarters with a little encouragement from the public, would fill up our frontier, which would strengthen us, improve agriculture, perfect manufactures, encourage literature and everything laudable.'

7. The census of 1790 gave the population of Kentucky as 73,677, that of Tennessee as 35,691. The Tennessee census was very incomplete, with five districts missing. It is estimated that there were between 4000 and 5000 inhabitants north of the Ohio.

XIII

The Confederation

1. ARTICLES OF CONFEDERATION

The Articles of Confederation and Perpetual Union, drafted by John Dickinson but altered by Congress, were adopted by that body on 15 November 1777. All states but one had ratified by early 1779. Maryland held out for two years more, until the states which had Western land claims ceded them to the United States. These cessions were delayed by the machinations of speculative land companies, but after Virginia made a tentative cession to the United States of her claims, Maryland ratified the Articles of Confederation on 1 March 1781, and the same day Congress proclaimed that they were in effect.

The change of government did little more than legalize what Congress had been doing since 1775. The Congress of the Confederation was organized in the same way and had the same powers as the Continental Congress. Each state was represented by not less than two or more than seven members, as it might choose, but no member could serve for more than three years in any six. Each state had one vote; in the event of disagreement within a state delegation, the majority gave the state's vote. The new provisions were these: (1) assent of nine out of thirteen states was required for decisions in important matters such as making war or concluding treaties, borrowing money, raising armed forces, and appointing a commander-in-chief. (2) Congress acquired the power to appoint executive departments, and shortly created five — foreign affairs with Robert R. Livingston as secretary; finance with Robert Morris as superintendent; war with General Lincoln as secretary; a board of admiralty of which Robert Morris was the only effective member, and a post office department. (3) The Articles also provided for a Committee of the States, consisting of one delegate from each state, to sit between sessions of Congress and exercise all powers except those that required the consent of nine out of the thirteen.

The Articles of Confederation sought to preserve the independence and sovereignty of the states. The Federal Government received only those powers which the colonies had recognized as belonging to king and parliament. Thus, Congress was given all powers connected with war and peace, except the important one of taxation to support a war. It could conclude no commercial treaty limiting the states' rights to collect customs duties. It had power to establish post offices and charge postage (the only taxing power it possessed), to set standards of weights and measures, and to coin money. These were sovereign powers which the king had exercised without question. The one exception to this principle was that Congress had power of 'regulating the trade and managing all affairs with the Indians, not members of any of the states'; a recognition that Indian affairs must be under central control. In view of the land cessions by the states to Congress, a strange oversight was the failure to give the new government power over federal territories; but as somebody had to see to that, Congress went ahead and did, and the greatest permanent success of the Confederation was in working out a new territorial policy.

The essence of federalism is the distribution of national and local powers between governments, and in the Articles of Confederation this distribution was not well done. But the Articles did outline a federal system, and marked an improvement over the constitution of any previous confederation in modern history.

The main defects in the Articles — failure to give Congress control over taxation and trade, want of a federal executive or judiciary, and lack of any sanction for federal powers — resulted from the unwillingness of the states to grant to a federal legislature what they had refused to Parliament, or to surrender the substance of sovereignty for the shadow of union. Even when the inadequacies of the Articles became glaringly apparent, unanimous consent for amendments was impossible to obtain. Rhode Island defeated a proposal in 1781 to provide Congress with a 5 per cent customs duty; and when Rhode Island was later induced to part with this 'most precious jewel of sovereignty,' the proposal was rejected by the New York Assembly.

Requisition worked as ill as under the colonial system. As provided for in the Articles, payments should have been apportioned according to the value of real estate in each state, but as Congress never had the money to make any real estate assessment, requisitions were made by guesswork. Naturally some states claimed they were unfairly treated and refused to pay, and several adopted the practice of using their requisition money to pay federal debts due to their own citizens, leaving little or nothing for the Federal Government. Members of Congress had no salary, and were forbidden to hold any public salaried position. It is a tribute to the strong public spirit of that decade that men of high caliber consented to serve, and that not one was ever accused, or suspected, of trying to line his pockets with 'kick-backs' from contracts.

Thus, it was not so much *powers* that the Confederation wanted as *power*. Requisitions might have served in lieu of taxes had Congress possessed authority to enforce them. As James Madison observed in a paper written in 1787:

> A sanction is essential to the idea of law, as coercion is to that of government. The federal system being destitute of both, wants the great vital principles of a political constitution. Under form of such a constitution, it is in fact nothing more than a treaty of amity of commerce and of alliance, between independent and Sovereign States.

Noah Webster pointed out the same defect and indicated the remedy that was eventually adopted:

> The general concerns of the continent may be reduced to a few heads; but in all the affairs that respect the whole, Congress must have the same power to enact laws and compel obedience throughout the continent, as the legislatures of the States have in their respective jurisdictions.

All this was apparent only to a few far-sighted statesmen. It took time and experience to convince the average man of the folly of particularism. Furthermore, the Confederation was launched under difficult circumstances, the darkest period of the war, which was followed within a few years by economic depression.

2. A NEW COLONIAL SYSTEM

Now the old Western question came home to roost. All those pesky problems of land, Indians, fur trade, settlement, and government of dependencies, which had troubled British ministers for half a century, were now up to Congress to settle. In these Western matters it did remarkably well during the troubled 1780's, formulating policies and inaugurating practices which made a permanent mark on American history.

A good precedent had been created by the Continental Congress's passage of a resolution on federal lands, on October 1780:

> The unappropriated lands that may be ceded or relinquished to the United States . . . shall be disposed of for the common benefit of the United States, and be settled and formed into distinct republican States, which shall become members of the Federal Union, and have the same rights of sovereignty, freedom and independence as the other States.

By virtue of successive state cessions, Congress by 1786 was in possession of all land south of Canada, north of the Ohio, west of the Alleghenies, and east of the Mississippi. This common possession of millions of acres of land was the most tangible evidence of nationality that existed during these troubled years. Yet possession itself was fraught with difficulties. Ancient problems of land, Indians, and administrative policy pressed for a solution.

Congress feebly attempted to regulate the fur trade. It obtained land cessions from the Iroquois and the Northwest Indians, who in alliance with Britain had waged a terrible and relentless war against the backwoods settlements; but most of these treaties it was unable to enforce. New forts were built on the Ohio, and in 1787 a detachment of the United States Army moved down the right bank, burning the cabins of frontiersmen who had staked out claims there by 'tomahawk right.' But Congress was not strong enough to prevent repeated Indian forays into Kentucky and Virginia. In the transmontane region south of the Ohio, where *de facto* state governments had been set up by pioneers, and no land claims had been made over to the Confederation, the period 1785–88 was one of bitter warfare.

Thomas Jefferson, chairman of a committee of Congress, reported the

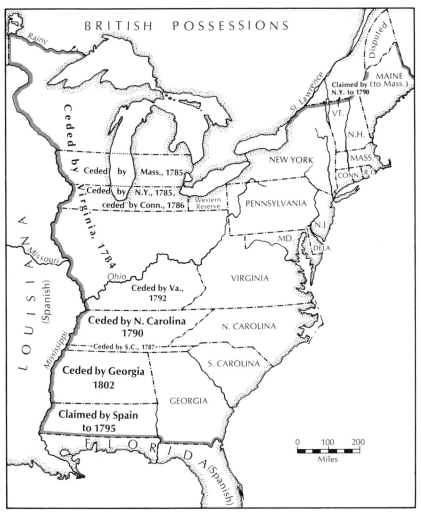

BRITISH POSSESSIONS

Rainy

Disputed

St. Lawrence

MAINE
Claimed by (to Mass.)
N.Y. to 1790

VT.

N.H.

Ceded by Virginia, 1784

NEW YORK

MASS.

CONN. R.I.

Ceded by Mass., 1785

Ceded by N.Y., 1785,
ceded by Conn., 1786

Western
Reserve

PENNSYLVANIA

N.J.

MD.

DELA.

L O U I S I A N A
(Spanish)

Missouri

Ohio

Ceded by Va.,
1792

VIRGINIA

Mississippi

Ceded by N. Carolina
1790

N. CAROLINA

Ceded by S.C., 1787

Ceded by Georgia
1802

S. CAROLINA

GEORGIA

Claimed by Spain
to 1795

F L O R I D A (Spanish)

0	100	200

Miles

CESSIONS OF STATE CLAIMS, 1783-1802

Land Ordinance of 1785. This Ordinance provided for a rectangular survey of public lands and a division into townships six miles square, each to consist of 36 sections of 640 acres each. Land offices were to be established at convenient points in the West and lands sold in orderly progress at a price of not less than one dollar an acre. Four sections of every township were to be set aside for the United States government, and one section reserved for the maintenance of public schools. This land system was modeled on that of New England, with some features derived from the projected imperial land survey of 1774. It looked forward to using the national domain as a source of revenue rather than granting it free, or on easy terms, to settlers. And as no less than one section could be sold, and $640 was too much for a pioneer farmer to pay, private land companies did most of the land-office business for many years. Although there were numerous changes in detail during the next 50 years, the Ordinance of 1785 remained the basis of American public land policy until the Homestead Act of 1862.

The activities of private land companies finally forced Congress to make provision for the political administration of its Western territory. The most important of these land companies were promoted in New England largely by officers of the Revolutionary army. In the summer of 1787 General Rufus Putnam and the Reverend Manasseh Cutler appeared before Congress requesting the sale of millions of acres of land north of the Ohio river on highly favorable terms. The prospect of money for the impoverished federal treasury attracted Congress, and the purchase was agreed upon at a bargain price. The Ohio Company of Associates obtained 1.5 million acres of land along the banks of the Ohio and Muskingum rivers at an average price of less than nine cents an acre, reserving one section in each township for education and one for religious purposes.

With this immediate prospect of settlement in the Ohio country, Congress, then sitting in New York,[1] had to make some provision for government. On 13 July 1787 a session of eighteen members representing only eight states, passed the Northwest Ordinance, the most momentous act in the Confederation's history. This enactment, largely the work of Nathan Dane and Rufus King, bridged the gap between wilderness and

1. Congress, chased out of Philadelphia by mutinous soldiers, moved to Princeton, N.J., then to Annapolis in 1783, to Trenton the next year, and in 1785 to New York, where it remained until its dissolution in 1789.

statehood by providing a system of limited self-government, the essence of which has been repeated for all continental and most insular possessions of the United States. The Northwest Territory was first organized as a single district and ruled by a governor and judges appointed by Congress. When this territory should contain 5000 free male inhabitants of voting age it could elect a territorial legislature, with the status of a subordinate colonial assembly, and send a non-voting delegate to Congress. No more than five nor less than three states were to be formed out of the Northwest Territory, and whenever any part had 60,000 free inhabitants it could be admitted to the Union 'on an equal footing with the original States in all respects whatever.' Six 'articles of compact between the original States and the people and States in the said Territory' guaranteed the customary civil rights and liberties, and declared 'Religion, morality, and knowledge, being necessary to good government and the happiness of mankind, schools and the means of education shall forever be encouraged.' Further, 'There shall be neither slavery nor involuntary servitude in the said territory. . . .'

Thus a new colonial policy was inaugurated, based upon the principle of equality. The time-honored doctrine that colonies existed for the benefit of the mother country and were politically subordinate and socially inferior was repudiated. In its stead was established the principle that colonies were but the extensions of the nation, entitled, not as a privilege but by right, to equality. The Ordinance of 1787 is one of the great creative contributions of America, for it showed how to get rid of friction in the relations of colony to metropolis. The enlightened provisions of the Land Ordinance of 1785 and the Northwest Ordinance of 1787 laid permanent foundations for the American territorial system and colonial policy, and enabled the United States to expand westward to the Pacific, and from thirteen states with relatively little trouble.

3. LIQUIDATING THE TREATY OF PARIS

The Treaty of Paris satisfied neither England nor the United States, and its terms provoked future quarrels. Boundary disputes, arising from loose wording and the ignorance of geography on the part of the negotiators, were postponed to a later generation. But there were immediate controversies over matters in which it was claimed that one or the other party failed to fulfill its obligations, such as debts, Negroes, loyalists, and the presence of British garrisons on United States soil. Congress on 14 January 1783 made the required 'earnest recommendation' to the states to restore confiscated loyalist estates, and a few complied to some extent. Pennsylvania, for instance, paid the Penn family $650,000 in compensation for their proprietary rights, but most of the states failed to act. The treaty requirement that loyalists should be free to reside for a year in any part of the United States, in order to endeavor to recover their property, was not always respected; tory raiders or partisan troops who returned to the districts they had ravaged were fortunate to get off with a term in jail. The treaty requirement, 'that there shall be no future confiscations made,' nor fresh prosecutions commenced against loyalists, was generally obeyed. New York passed a Trespass Act, encouraging owners of property formerly within the British lines to recover damages against loyalist occupants through actions of trespass. But Alexander Hamilton successfully defended the first loyalist so prosecuted, in the case of *Rutgers v. Waddington,* and obtained a judgment from the Mayor's Court of New York, nullifying the statute on the ground of its conflict with the treaty. South Carolina authorized fresh confiscations in 1783, but rescinded them in 1786. Other states passed laws having reference to the disposition of property already confiscated during the war, taking the ground that the treaty had no retroactive effect, a construction vigorously maintained by the British government in respect of a different article, which forbade British commanders to deport Negro slaves.

American tories were less harshly treated than royalists in the French Revolution, or than bourgeois, Jew, Catholic, and other dissidents in more recent upheavals. And the 80,000 tories who departed from the United States during the war, or left it voluntarily afterwards, were but a minority of the loyalist party. None was forcibly expelled after 1776. Even in New York most of the tories remained, and many of the exiles drifted back — men such as Cadwallader Colden, who became mayor of the city, and commanded a regiment in the War of 1812; and Henry Cruger, elected to the New York senate while still a member of Parliament.

A second obligation placed on the Thirteen States by the peace treaty was to open their courts freely to British subjects seeking to recover their pre-war debts. This article was violated both in letter and in spirit. Virginia, where the debts were heaviest, and the attitude toward financial obligations, aristocratic and feudal, led the way in passing laws hampering the recovery of British debts. George Mason wrote to Patrick Henry: 'If we are now to pay the debts due to the British merchants, what have we been fighting for all this while?' John Jay induced Congress to send a circular letter to the states, adverting strongly on their breach of public faith, and requesting the repeal of these acts. Most of them had complied by 1789, when the Constitution superseded all state laws contrary to treaty obligations and opened the new federal judiciary to British litigants. Thereafter, the recovery of British debts was a matter of judicial process, and no impediment was imposed. Delays, however, were prolonged, and the matter was not finally resolved until 1802.

The treaty of peace required all British garrisons on American soil to be withdrawn 'with all convenient speed.' New York was completely evacuated by December 1783, but seven military and fur-trading posts [2] on the American side of the new Canadian boundary remained. The British claimed they were retaining the posts because the United States had not complied with the peace treaty. In fact, they were motivated by desire to control the fur trade and control the Indians of the Northwest. Within a decade of the Quebec Act of 1774, Scots-Canadian fur merchants had so developed the fur trade that peltry to the annual value of £200,000 passed through Montreal on its way to London. Then, in the peace treaty, this immense imperial asset, the land between the Lakes and the Ohio river, was ceded to the new republic. As soon as the bad news reached Canada, remonstrances from Canadian fur merchants began to pour in upon the governor general. American possession of the Northwest army posts, they complained, would divert the fur trade to New York and Philadelphia, and alienate the loyal Western Indians who had been guaranteed the Ohio boundary in 1768. The Canadians requested a delay to reorganize the trade before evacuating the posts. In answer to these petitions the Home Office gave orders to retain the Northwest posts until further notice.

Not only was this act a deliberate breach of treaty obligations but there were even more serious implications, of which the actors may have

2. From east to west these posts were Dutchman's Point and Pointe-au-Fer at the head of Lake Champlain, guarding the military and trading route between Montreal and Albany; Oswegatchie on the St. Lawrence river, near Ogdensburg, N.Y.; Oswego, N.Y., on Lake Ontario, guarding the portage route to the Mohawk; Niagara, on the American side of the falls; Detroit; and Michilimackinac, on an island in the strait between Lakes Huron and Michigan.

been unconscious. Detroit and Michilimackinac were sally-ports of empire, looking toward New Orleans. Twice the Thirteen Colonies had
fought to keep French Canada from their back doors. Must the Thirteen
States fight again to keep British Canada within her legal boundaries?
Would the United States ever be secure until British power, like French
power, was expelled from the North American continent? No answer to
that question was found until 1815.

4. FOREIGN AFFAIRS DURING THE CONFEDERATION

America emerged from the War of Independence entangled by an alliance with France — the only treaty of alliance the United States ratified
before 1949. Isolation could not be even approximate until that alliance
ended; and until the two gates that closed westward advance — Britain's
in the Ohio country, and Spain's along the Mississippi — swung open on
their hinges at Montreal and New Orleans. Not until then could America
pretend 'to dictate the terms of the connexion between the old and the
new world,' as Hamilton predicted in *The Federalist*. Until then the
United States had to balance France against Britain in the old world,
and Spain against Britain in the new.

The war also ended America's favored economic position within the
British empire. Lord Sheffield argued that England could now absorb
the commerce of America without the expense of governing her, and
without concessions to the American interests.

> Our great national object is to raise as many sailors and as much
> shipping as possible. Parliament should endeavor to divert the
> whole Anglo-American trade to British bottoms. America cannot re-
> taliate. It will not be an easy matter to bring the American States to
> act as a nation. They are not to be feared as such by us. . . . We
> might as reasonably dread the effects of a combination among the
> German as among the American States.

And he concluded with the tempting suggestion that the Union was
breaking up; that New England, if made to feel the rod of British
maritime power, might return to her old allegiance.

Sheffield's policy prevailed over that of the free traders. By a series of
Orders in Council of 1783 American vessels were excluded absolutely
from Canada and the West Indies. In British ports they were placed on
the same footing as the ships of any European country, in carrying the

produce of other European countries. American tobacco, timber, and other raw materials, provided they came directly from America, were admitted to British ports in American or British bottoms, practically on a colonial footing. This privilege was a great concession: no European country enjoyed as much from Great Britain. It was not, however, secured by a commercial treaty, but revocable at pleasure. And, for all its apparent liberality, the Order in Council of 1783 was carefully designed for 'strangling in the birth' American shipping, as the loyalist author of it boasted. It might well have done so, if the American states had not formed an effective combination somewhat more promptly than those of Germany.

The immediate success of this policy established Sheffield's reputation and discredited the free traders; although it was the free-trade element in it — the free admission of American materials — that made it successful. By 1789 the Board of Trade could boast that British exports to the United States had recovered pre-war dimensions; and that their excess over imports from America was even greater than in 1772. Anglo-American trade was so largely triangular that the exclusion of American vessels from the West Indies, and from all but a direct trade in American products with England, threw the traffic into British bottoms. The Confederation of 1781–89 had no jurisdiction over commerce, and all efforts of the states to retaliate separately were completely futile. If Massachusetts closed her ports to British ships, British goods came overland from New Hampshire and Rhode Island; Connecticut and New Jersey similarly poached trade from New York City.

Four European powers concluded commercial treaties with the American Confederation. France opened up her West Indian ports to American shipping and to most American products, and admitted American-built vessels to French registry. Havana and Santiago de Cuba were opened by the Spanish about the same time; and the Dutch were completely hospitable. Yet American relations with Spain were no more satisfactory than those with Great Britain. Alarmed by the expansive tendencies of the United States, and the danger of republican institutions to the Spanish empire, Spain sought to acquire a satellite state between the Appalachians and the Mississippi. To accomplish this, Spain retained posts on United States territory, choked the southern outlet of the West, corrupted some of its leading citizens, and allied with near-by Indian nations.

In 1784 the Creek, Choctaw, and Chickasaw, who inhabited United States territory south of the Tennessee river and west of Georgia, concluded treaties placing themselves under Spanish protection. A loyalist refugee from Georgia organized a trading company, which, with Spanish approval, established trading posts in Florida and sent its factors, with ammunition and other Indian truck, up the rivers toward the Tennessee frontier. Creek and Cherokee, now well furnished with weapons, began to harry American settlements on the Cumberland and upper Tennessee rivers, and in Georgia. The frontiersmen were not slow to retaliate. During 1787–88 the border from Nashville to southern Georgia was the scene of hideous barbarities.

Natchez, on the left bank of the Mississippi and within the boundary of the United States as recognized by Great Britain, had been captured in 1779 by the Spaniards, who now refused to give up to the United States. Natchez and New Orleans gave Spain control of the lower Mississippi — a powerful means of pressure on the West. The people of Kentucky, Tennessee, western Virginia, and even western Pennsylvania, discovered that the long river journey south was their only practical way to market. Their cheap and bulky products could not stand the cost of being sweated over the Appalachian passes. The Mississippi led to natural markets in lower Louisiana, where the Creole planters preferred to concentrate on sugar cane and purchase their livestock, horses, corn, and bacon from up-river. New Orleans was the natural port of transshipment for the New York and European markets. Permission to navigate the lower Mississippi, and to enjoy a 'right of deposit' or free transshipment at New Orleans, was for the American West a question of life and growth, or strangulation.

Although formally denied to the United States as a right, both navigation and deposit were frequently accorded as a privilege, by the dispensing power of the Spanish Governor Miró, in favor of such Westerners as would promise to serve Spanish policy. That policy was to detach their communities from the United States. General James Wilkinson of Kentucky, who accepted not only favors but bribes to make his state a 'bastion of Mexico,' was the most notorious of these conspirators. When John Jay, secretary of the Confederation for foreign affairs, proposed in 1786 to waive the right of deposit temporarily in return for privileges to American shipping in Spanish ports, Spain's Western following increased. A surprising number of backwoods politicians accepted Spanish gold and intrigued for secession because they had lost hope of obtaining their outlet from the United States. What made matters worse was that many leading Easterners, disliking frontiersmen as political bedfellows, wished the West well out of the Union.

The rough-necked pioneer was an undependable ally for the polished don. The backwoodsman had a fundamental contempt for the Spaniard, and to the southward his ambition knew no limit but Panama and the Pacific. As the Germans in the dark Teutoburger forest yearned for the sunny, fertile plains of Italy, so the backwoodsman of Tennessee, as he tilled his patch of corn in the shade of girdled trees, while kinsmen watched with loaded rifles, dreamed of the day when he would go whooping down the great river of the West to loot the Spaniard of his undeveloped land. And his dream, like the other, came true.

5. THE DAY OF THE DEBTOR

The radical weakness of the Confederation, as we have seen, was its complete dependence — like the old German Diet and the United Nations — upon the good will of member states. Government starved upon the meager rations delivered by state legislatures. Only half a million dollars on an average was annually paid into the federal treasury by the states between 1781 and 1786: a sum hardly sufficient to meet the running expenses of government, let alone war costs and the interest on foreign loans.[3] Robert Morris, the able finance minister of the Confederation, was fortunate to prevent repudiation and, by the grace of loans from Dutch bankers, to stave off bankruptcy. But so hopeless had the financial situation become by 1783 that Morris resigned in despair, confessing 'it can no longer be a doubt . . . that our public credit is gone.' Overdue interest on the debt accumulated, Continental securities fell below 15 cents to the dollar, and demobilized army officers had to sell at a heavy discount the scrip they had received in lieu of pay.

At the close of the war most of the states stopped issuing paper money and tried to pay off war debts and collect long over-due taxes, at a time when the loss of markets injured their capacity to pay and districts were

3. In 1783 the foreign debt of the United States stood at $7,885,085. By 1789 the principal of foreign debts had increased to $10,098,706, and the arrears of interest to $1,760,277. Approximately $350,000 of interest had been remitted by the French government.

burdened by an increase in debt to merchant-bankers and storekeepers. There were war damages to repair, especially in the South; discharged soldiers took up new land on credit; and after seven years of war, people purchased more European luxuries than they could afford. A currency famine made matters worse. Debtors began to press state legislatures for relief in the form of 'tender acts' making land or produce at fixed prices a legal discharge, 'stay laws' postponing the collection of debts, and laws providing cheap money. It was this radical movement within the states, threatening the property interests, which, according to James Madison, 'contributed more to that uneasiness which produced the Constitution, and prepared the public mind for a general reform' than any political inadequacies of the Articles of Confederation. Seven states issued paper money in 1786, when the depression was at its worst. This virtual confiscation seemed intolerable to many when the necessity of war was removed. 'They are determined,' wrote General Knox to Washington, 'to annihilate all debts, public and private, and have agrarian laws, which are easily effected by the means of unfunded paper money.' North Carolina purchased tobacco from the farmers at double its sale value. In Charleston young radicals formed the Hint Club, which made a practice of sending sections of rope to planters who would not receive state paper for their rice. Rhode Island, where the debtors put through their whole program, furnished an example of what gentlemen might expect elsewhere. The state lent large sums of paper money to landowners, and forced it on others by heavy penalties. If a creditor refused to accept state paper to the face value of his due, the debtor could discharge his obligation by depositing the currency with the nearest judge. Of course the merchants shut up shop and fled the state to escape purchasers, as did hundreds of harassed creditors, pursued by implacable debtors seeking to make the legal proffer of paper money!

In Massachusetts, where desperate farmers lacked the political power to obtain relief, civil war broke out. Farm produce was a glut on the market, owing to the stoppage of West Indian trade, and taxes were heavier than elsewhere. The commercial interests, having obtained control of the state senate, put the state finances on a specie basis, which meant a rapid deflation, and shifted the weight of taxation onto land and polls — the latter accounting for no less than 40 per cent of the entire taxes. Courts were clogged with suits for debt, the cost of justice was exorbitant, and lawyers were more grasping than usual. All through the summer of 1786 popular conventions and town meetings demanded reform in the state administration, the removal of the capital from Boston, and an issue of fiat money as in Rhode Island. One petition from a hill town read:

> We beg leave to informe your Honours that unless something takes place more favourable to the people, in a little time att least, one half of our inhabitants in our oppinion will become banckerupt . . . Sutes att law are very numerous and the atturneys in our op- pinion very extravigent and oppressive in their demands. And when we compute the taxes laid upon us the five preceding years: the state and county, town and class taxes, the amount is equil to what our farms will rent for. Sirs, in this situation what have we to live on — no money to be had; our estates dayly posted and sold. . . . Suerly you honours are not strangers to the distresses of the people but doe know that many of our good inhabitants are now confined in gole for det and for taxes; many have fled, others wishing to flee to the State of New York or some other State. . . . Honoured Sirs, are not these imprisonments and fleeing away of our good inhabi- tants very injurious to the credit or honour of the Commonwealth?

No relief was to be had from the legislature, since the state senate wished deflation to take its natural course. Even Samuel Adams, grown cautious with age, denounced the unhappy farmers as 'wicked and un- principled men.' The process of distraining upon cattle and land for the debts and accumulated taxes went rigorously on. Some yeomen faced debtors' prison, many others were sold into servitude for a term to pay off their debt. That many resorted to violence is not so surprising as the sense of law and order that prevented the majority of sufferers from following them.

In the autumn of 1786 mobs of farmers, under the unwilling lead of a former army captain, Daniel Shays, began forcibly to prevent the county courts from sitting. The object of the leaders appears to have been to prevent further judgments for debt, pending the next state election. They met with stout resistance from the state government. The mobs were ordered to disperse, the leaders declared outlaws, and a price placed upon their heads.

Shays and his comrades then resolved to become rebels indeed. For a few days there was danger that the state government might be besieged in Boston by an infuriated yeomanry, as had happened to the last royal government in 1775. But the rebels lacked firearms, and their attempt to capture the federal arsenal at Springfield was repulsed with grape-shot. Loyal militia, financed by forced contributions of merchants, was set in motion from the eastern counties, and college boys formed a cavalry regiment to terrify the country folk. The rebel bands, armed for the most part with staves and pitchforks, were scattered into the barren hills of central Massachusetts, where they were hunted like game in the heavy snow. Many fled to the western wilderness; cold and hunger forced the remnant to surrender.

Fortunately the state government acted with wisdom and mercy. Fourteen leaders were captured and sentenced to death, but all were either pardoned or let off with short prison terms. The newly elected legislature, in which a majority sympathized with the rebels, granted some of their demands, such as allowing soldiers' notes to be tendered for taxes. And the return of prosperity in 1787 caused the eruption to simmer down, leaving no bitter slag as in North Carolina after the War of the Regulation.

Nevertheless, Shays's Rebellion had a great influence on public opinion. News of it delighted the English tories, as proof that Americans were incapable of self-government. Jefferson, from his snug retreat in the Paris legation, remarked, 'A little rebellion now and then is a good thing . . . the tree of liberty must be refreshed from time to time with the blood of patriots and tyrants.' But most American leaders were alarmed. 'But for God's sake tell me what is the cause of all these commotions?' Washington implored. 'I am mortified beyond expression that in the moment of our acknowledged independence we should by our conduct verify the predictions of our transatlantic foe, and render ourselves ridiculous and contemptible in the eyes of all Europe.' When Massachusetts appealed to the Confederation for help, Congress was unable to do a thing. That was the final argument to sway many Americans in favor of a stronger federal government.

Thus, the net effect of Shays's Rebellion was to arouse an emotional surge — without which nothing great can be accomplished in America — toward a new Federal Constitution.

XIV

The Federal Convention
and Constitution

1. CHARACTER AND AIMS OF THE CONVENTION

While it would be too much to say that the Confederation was falling apart in 1786, there was enough evidence of growing disunion to alarm thinking men. George Washington, Robert Morris, John Adams, Roger Sherman, the Rutledges, and others of the generation who had won independence, had come to the conclusion that the Union of the States could not endure without a major operation on the government. All attempts to give it a limited taxing power by amendment had failed, owing to the selfishness of one state or another. In foreign affairs, an offer by John Adams to the British government to negotiate a new treaty which would settle disputes left over in 1783, was met by the sarcastic comment that, since the Confederation was unable to enforce existing treaties, His Majesty's government could only negotiate with each of the Thirteen States. Individual states could not cope with a depression caused largely by the dislocation of foreign trade. The credit of the Confederation was at a low ebb, and on top of all this came Shays's Rebellion, during which Massachusetts called on the Confederation in vain for help, since Congress had neither armed forces nor money.

In addition, several interstate brawls caused grave disquiet. One, however, proved indirectly useful to the cause of a stronger union. The New York Assembly in 1787 increased customs duties on foreign merchandise and assessed heavy entrance and clearance fees on all vessels coming from or bound to New Jersey and Connecticut. New Jersey retaliated by taxing the lighthouse on Sandy Hook £30 a month! Virginia and Maryland, long at loggerheads because Maryland's charter gave her jurisdiction over the Potomac up to the Virginia shore, managed to make a peaceable settlement. Pennsylvania and Delaware were also concerned because some of their commerce had to pass through Virginia's territorial waters. Virginia's assembly, at this juncture in a nationalist mood, invited all the states to send delegates to a convention at Annapolis, 'to take into consideration the trade of the United States.'

This Annapolis Convention, which met in September 1786, was attended by delegates from only five states. Two of its youngest members, Alexander Hamilton and James Madison, took the lead in persuading their colleagues that nothing could be accomplished by so slim a body, and to adopt a report which Hamilton drafted. This report pointed up the critical situation of the Confederation and proposed that all thirteen states choose delegates to a convention, 'to devise such further provisions as shall appear to them necessary to render the constitution of the federal government adequate to the exigencies of the Union.'

That was the genesis of the Federal Convention. On 21 February 1787, Congress invited the states to send delegates to a convention at Philadelphia in May, 'for the sole and express purpose of revising the Articles of Confederation,' to 'render the federal constitution adequate to the exigencies of government, and the preservation of the Union.'

Twelve states (Rhode Island having sulkily declined the invitation) were represented in the Federal Convention by 55 delegates. Of these, thirty-one, including all who took leading parts in the debates, were college-educated. Two (Johnson and Baldwin) were college presidents; three (Wythe, Wilson, and Houston) were or had been professors, and a dozen or more had taught school. Four of the delegates had read law at the Inns of Court in London; nine, including James Wilson, the most useful member after Madison, were foreign-born. Twenty-eight had served in Congress, and most of the others in state legislatures. The surprising thing about the delegates, however, was their youthfulness. Five members, including Charles Pinckney, were under thirty years old; Alexander Hamilton was thirty-two or thirty-three; and the next oldest group, James Madison, Gouverneur Morris, and Edmund Randolph, were within a year of thirty-five. James Wilson, Luther Martin, Oliver Ellsworth, and William Paterson were between forty-one and forty-five. General Washington who, much against his desire, was 'drafted' for the Convention, was now fifty-five, the same age as John Dickinson and George Wythe. Only four members had reached or passed the age of sixty: William Samuel Johnson (president of Columbia College), George Mason, Roger Sherman, and Benjamin Franklin who, at eighty-one, was the oldest member by fifteen years. Practically every American who had useful ideas on political science was there. Notable exceptions were Pelatiah Webster whose pamphlet *Dissertation on the Political Union* (1783) had done much to educate the public; John Jay, who was busy with the foreign relations of the Confederation; and John Adams and Thomas Jefferson who were absent on foreign missions.

The states chose men well qualified for the work. Samuel Adams, George Clinton, Patrick Henry, Christopher Gadsden, and others whose political talents had proved to be on the destructive side, were not elected. The four men of this stamp who were chosen — Luther Martin, Abraham Yates, John Lansing, and Elbridge Gerry — 'bolted' the Convention and became Antifederalists.

It is always a temptation to read present interest into past events. Richard Hildreth, when writing about the Federal Convention in 1849, features the slavery issue. George Ticknor Curtis and George Bancroft, writing in 1854 and 1882, stressed state rights against nationalism. Charles A. Beard's *Economic Interpretation of the Constitution* (1913) sounded the note of economic determinism; and several writers of that school, with even less reverence for fact than Beard showed, have pictured the Convention as preoccupied with the protection of property and the exploitation of the common people. Another school of thought, building upon Jefferson's qualification of the framers as 'demi-gods' (a phrase that he lived to regret), regards them as inspired to draft a document of almost divine sanction.

A careful reading of Madison's and Yates's notes on the debates — an exercise in which popular writers on the Convention seldom indulge — reveals that slavery interested the members only as an aspect of sectional balance, that there was substantial agreement on the extent to which the states should yield powers to the Federal Government, and that they were chiefly interested in political technique — that is, in the organization of the government and the distribution of powers. Members were indeed conscious of sectional interests — they had to be; but the determining consideration throughout the debates was to erect a government that would be neither too strong nor too shocking to popular prejudices for adoption, and yet be sufficiently strong and well-contrived to work. There was no disagreement over some of the most important clauses of the Constitution such as federal control of defense and of interstate and foreign commerce.

The temper of the Convention, in marked contrast to that of the French Constituent Assembly of 1789, was realistic and objective, rather than idealistic and theoretical. 'Experience must be our only guide. Reason may mislead us,' was the keynote struck by Dickinson. Most of the members were public creditors, who stood to lose personally by a dissolution of the Union, and to gain by a restoration of public credit; but it would be unjust to attribute their views to property alone, as it is absurd to pronounce them superior to forces that move the best of men. All the members hoped to remedy the proved defects of the Articles of Confederation. A few saw that something more was at stake. As Madison said from the floor, 'They were now to decide the fate of republican government.' No fair-minded person can read their debates without wonder that a country of just 4 million people could produce so many men of vision.

2. THE CONVENTION AT WORK

The Convention had been authorized merely to draft amendments to the Articles of Confederation. But events at the beginning gave nationalists like Madison and Wilson, who wished to scrap the Articles, a start over those who thought that tinkering would suffice. The nationalists, or large-state party as they came to be called, having quietly organized their forces before the convention opened at a series of private meetings in Philadelphia, decided to bring in a plan for a new national government.

The Convention opened on 25 May 1787, in the Old State House where independence had been declared. On the 29th Randolph presented the result of the preliminary conferences — the Virginia or large-state plan. This plan, foreshadowing the stronger government that was subsequently adopted, became the first basis of discussion. It provided a 'National Executive,' a 'National Judiciary,' and a 'National Legislature' of two branches, with members of both House and Senate apportioned according to population, empowered 'to legislate in all cases to which the separate States are incompetent.' As to the basic question of how the states could be persuaded to abide by these Articles of Union, the Virginia plan offered three solutions: an oath of office, a negative on all state laws contravening the Constitution, and power to call forth the forces of the Union to coerce recalcitrant states. All this was not essentially different from the methods that prevailed under the British connection. A negative on state laws was no better than the practice of disallowance by the Privy Council, and the power to coerce a state was little improvement on the Coercive Acts of 1774. The Virginia plan did not get at the root of the problem of maintaining a federal state. This is all the more remarkable, since both Madison and Wilson had shown a real grasp of the federal idea. It would seem that the terror inspired by Shays's Rebellion, or over-enthusiasm for strong government, had deflected them from the course that they later followed to a brilliant conclusion.

After two weeks of discussion of the Virginia plan, William Paterson presented a counter-project, the New Jersey or small-state plan, containing almost every feature of the Articles of Confederation that made for weakness and uncertainty. A single legislative body in which each state was equally represented, and whose acts were to be enforced by armed coercion of the states, was the central feature of this plan. Yet it did contain one clause of far-reaching importance, which in a modified form became the key clause of the Federal Constitution. 'All Acts of the United States in Congress made in pursuance of the powers hereby and by the articles of confederation vested in them, and all Treaties made and ratified under the authority of the United States shall be the supreme law of the respective States . . . and the Judiciary of the several States shall be bound thereby in their decisions, anything in the respective laws of the individual states to the contrary notwithstanding.' Here we see the germ of the doctrine that the Constitution is supreme law, that acts contrary to it are void, and that the courts are the proper agents to enforce it.

To this New Jersey plan the smaller states rallied. Some of their delegates preferred the Virginia plan, but thought it too 'high-mounted' for popular acceptance; others were influenced by the fact that their states enjoyed equality with the larger ones in the Congress of the

Confederation, and did not propose to give up that privilege. This division between large and small states, which threatened time and again to wreck the work of the Convention, rested upon prejudice rather than logic. There was no natural antagonism between the interests of large and small states as such — between Pennsylvania and New Jersey, or Virginia and Maryland. The real divisions of interest in the country were sectional and economic in character; divisions between North and South or East and West, between the commercial and the agrarian interests, the creditor and the debtor.

By using their superior voting power, the large states were able to shelve the New Jersey plan on 19 June and make that of Virginia again the order of the day. But the small states' delegates were unappeased. July brought hot weather, bad temper, and deadlock. Dr. Franklin was moved to suggest that the sessions be opened henceforth with prayer; his motion was lost; not because the members disbelieved in prayer, but because the Convention had no money to pay a chaplain! Fortunately the large states met the small ones halfway. After all, it was not the best possible constitution that must be drafted, but the best that the people would be likely to accept. The same practical consideration ruled out Hamilton's plan for a centralized unitary constitution that would have made the states mere counties — a plan that revealed how completely Hamilton failed to grasp the value of federalism.

The deadlock was finally broken by the appointment of a grand committee of one member from each state to deal with the vexatious problem of representation. This committee brought in a report distinctly favorable to the small states — known as the Connecticut or Great Compromise. By the terms of this compromise (adopted 16 July) every state was conceded an equal vote in the Senate irrespective of its size, but representation in the House was to be on the basis of the 'federal ratio' — an enumeration of the free population plus three-fifths of the slaves. At the same time it was also provided that all money bills should originate in the popularly elected House of Representatives.

The alignment of large against small states then dissolved; but almost every question raised new parties and was decided only by a new compromise. State delegations were not even united within themselves. Certain members wished no branch of the Federal Government to be popularly elected, whilst others, like Wilson, thought that the 'federal pyramid' must be given as broad a basis as possible in order that it might be 'raised to a considerable altitude.' In the end the qualifications for voting for the House of Representatives had to be left to each state to decide for itself. Gouverneur Morris struggled to exclude the growing West from statehood, arguing that 'The busy haunts of men, not the remote wilderness, was the proper school of political talents. If the Western people get the power into their hands they will ruin the Atlantic interests.' Fortunately, others like Wilson and Mason had a vision of future expansion, and eventually Congress was given full discretion in the matter. There was no serious difference of opinion on such national economic questions as paper money, tender laws, and laws impairing the obligation of contracts. These were forbidden to the states with little or no debate. But there was a distinct balancing of sectional economic interests. Charles Pinckney remarked in debate that there were five distinct commercial interests. (1) The fisheries and West Indian trade, which belonged to the New England states. (2) Foreign trade, the interest of New York. (3) Wheat and flour, staples of two Middle states (New Jersey and Pennsylvania). (4) Tobacco, the staple of Maryland and Virginia, and partly of North Carolina. (5) Rice and indigo, the leading exports of South Carolina and Georgia.

Madison, in reply to the South Carolinian's contention that a two-thirds majority must be required for all commercial subjects to avoid sectional discrimination, made one of the most prophetic speeches in the Convention. He observed that the larger the political unit the less likelihood of class or sectional injustice; he pointed out that Rhode Island was the place where one class and interest had been riding roughshod over the others. 'All civilized Societies,' he said, were 'divided into different sects, factions, and interests, as they happened to consist of rich and poor, debtors and creditors, the landed, the manufacturing, the commercial interests, the inhabitants of this district, or that district. . . . The only remedy is to enlarge the sphere, and thereby divide the community into so great a number of interests and parties, that . . . a majority will not be likely . . . to have a common interest separate from that of the whole or of the minority.'

Nevertheless, the Southern delegates long contended for a two-thirds majority of both houses for laws such as a navigation act, or regulating interstate or foreign commerce. They were persuaded to abandon this demand by the Northern states' agreeing to prohibit export taxes (which would obviously have fallen largely on the South) and to cease meddling with the slave trade for twenty years. The only two-thirds requirements embodied in the Constitution were for overriding a presidential veto, for proposing constitutional amendments, and for senatorial consent to treaties; this last being the result of a feeling that John Jay, in a treaty he had negotiated with Spain, and sacrificed the interests of the West to those of the East.

For sixteen weeks the Convention held sessions every weekday, except when it adjourned for committees to catch up; it was almost continuously at work. Then, the draft Constitution was entrusted to a committee on style, where the brilliant Gouverneur Morris polished up the language. Finally, on 17 September 1787, the finished Constitution was engrossed and signed 'By unanimous consent of the States present.' As Washington arose from his armchair inscribed with a gilded half-sun the venerable Franklin observed:

> I have often and often in the course of this session, and the vicissitudes of my hopes and fears as to its issue, looked at that . . . without being able to tell whether it was rising or setting; but now at length I have the happiness to know that it is a rising and not a setting sun.

The Federal Convention was over. The members 'adjourned to the City Tavern, dined together, and took a cordial leave of each other.'

Yet the crucial part of the struggle for a more perfect union had not begun. For the document upon which the Federal Convention had expended so much thought and labor required the consent of popularly elected conventions in at least nine states to become a constitution.

3. THE NATURE OF THE FEDERAL CONSTITUTION

The essence of the Constitution, and a secret of its success, was the complete and compulsive operation of the central government upon the individual citizen, within the scope of its limited powers. It was carefully discussed whether the new government, like the old, should depend upon the sanction of state governments, and, in the last resort, upon the coercion of sovereign states by force of arms; or whether the Federal Government should create its own sanctions, enforce them by its own courts and officials, and, in the last resort, by the coercion of individuals. The latter system, which Oliver Ellsworth called the coercion of law, was finally adopted.

> Congress shall have power . . . to make all laws which shall be necessary and proper for carrying into execution the . . . powers vested by this constitution in the Government of the United States. (Art. I, Sec. viii § 18.)
>
> This Constitution, and the laws of the United States, which shall be made in pursuance thereof, and all treaties made, or which shall be made, under the authority of the United States, shall be the Supreme Law of the land; and the judges in every State shall be bound thereby, anything in the Constitution or laws of any State to the contrary notwithstanding. (Art. VI, § 2.)

Further, state legislators and executive and judicial officers are 'bound by oath or affirmation to support this Constitution' (Art. VI). Thus, the police power of every state is required to enforce the laws of the Union as well. State authorities, in these national aspects, are under the oversight of the federal courts, which have jurisdiction over 'all cases . . . arising under this Constitution, the laws of the United States, and treaties made . . . under their authority.' As a last resort, Congress has power 'to provide for calling forth the militia' under the President's command 'to execute the laws of the Union.'

These are the central clauses of the Constitution. They went far to solve the more perplexing problems of the period following the Revolution. They provide the Federal Government with means for a peaceful enforcement of its laws in normal times, and for coercion of organized law-breaking in abnormal times. That a great civil war occurred in spite of these provisions is true; but it is no less certain that without them the Federal Government would have been successfully defied by several states before the Constitution had been in effect a generation.

Yet the Constitution is not a unitary one, for although the government it creates is supreme within its sphere, that sphere is defined and limited. As the Tenth Amendment made clear in 1791, 'the powers not delegated to the United States by the Constitution, nor prohibited by it to the States, are reserved to the States respectively or to the people.' And the supremacy of federal laws is limited to such as 'shall be made in pursuance of the Constitution.' The states are co-equally supreme within their sphere; in no legal sense are they subordinate corporations. Both governments rest on the same broad bottom of popular sovereignty. And although the scope of federal power has been widely extended by amendment, by implication, by judicial interpretation, and by the necessities of national crises, so has that of the states. Even in the twentieth century, the American citizen comes more frequently in contact with his state government than with the national government. To the states belong, not by virtue of the Federal Constitution but of their own sovereign power, the control of municipal and local government, the chartering of corporations, the statutory development and judicial administration of civil and criminal law, the supervision of religious bodies, the control of education insofar as it is not limited by the Fourteenth Amendment, and the general 'police power' over the health, safety, and welfare of the people. And the Federal Constitution cannot be amended without the consent of three-fourths of the states.

Article IV of the Constitution, copied almost word for word from the Articles of Confederation, has an international flavor. Each state shall give 'full faith and credit' to the public acts, records, and judicial proceedings of its sister states, shall extend to their citizens every privilege of their own, shall extradite criminals and return fugitive slaves. The United States guarantees to every state its territorial integrity, a republican form of government, and protection against invasion or domestic violence — another reflection of Shays's Rebellion. The Supreme Court is open to suits by states and has appellate jurisdiction over disputes between citizens of different states. As the Supreme Court later held, 'For all national purposes embraced by the Federal Constitution, the States and the citizens thereof are one, united under the same sovereign authority, and governed by the same laws. In all other respects the States are necessarily foreign to and independent of each other.'

In conferring powers on the new government, the Convention included all those of the Confederation, such as the conduct of war, foreign and Indian relations, posts, coinage, fixing the standards of weights and measures, and administering the Western territories. To these were added a limited taxing power, the judiciary, a general supervision over state militia, copyright, patent, naturalization, and bankruptcy laws, and the regulation of foreign and interstate commerce. The power to pass all necessary and proper laws for executing these defined powers rendered the Federal Government sufficiently elastic to meet the needs of later generations, and of a greatly expanded body politic. Between the powers expressly or implicitly granted to the Federal Government, and those reserved to the states, is a sphere of possible governmental action in which the lines between federal power, state power, and concurrent power have as yet been merely pricked out by decisions of the Supreme Court.

Madison thus concludes his analysis of the nature of the new Constitution:

> The proposed Constitution . . . is, in strictness, neither a national nor a federal Constitution, but a composition of both. In its foundation it is federal, not national; in the sources from which the ordinary powers of the government are drawn, it is partly federal and partly national; in the operation of these powers, it is national, not federal; in the extent of them, again, it is federal not national; and finally, in the authoritative mode of introducing amendments, it is neither wholly federal nor wholly national.

Without perhaps realizing it, the framers of the Constitution had applied the principle that they always believed to be implicit in the Constitution of the British empire and that they had boldly maintained in face of the counter-theory of parliamentary sovereignty and centralization. By showing that federalism and nationalism were not mutually exclusive, they made the most successful reconciliation in modern history between liberty and empire.

4. A FEW LEADING FEATURES

The two-year term of the House of Representatives struck a compromise between the current American practice of annual elections and the four-year presidential term; the six-year term of senators, expiring biennially by thirds, was meant to be a brake on hasty action. Compared with other second chambers, the Senate has a very small membership: 22 in 1789, gradually increasing to 100 in 1960. Until 1913, when the Seventeenth Amendment was ratified, senators were chosen by state legislatures. The Senate was intended both to defend the interests of the small states — that was the talking point for it outside the Convention — and to protect property against numbers, as Madison freely admitted.

It is not, however, correct to say that the sentiment of the Convention was 'undemocratic.' Members did not propose to set up an unlimited democracy as did the Pennsylvania constitution; but they insisted on giving democracy its share in what they intended to be a 'mixt' government, with the democratic, aristocratic, and authoritative elements properly balanced. That was the recipe of all leading political writers since Polybius for the successful constitution of a state, whether republican or monarchical in form. There was no question, of course, that the United States should be a republic. Alexander Hamilton might think monarchy the best form of government, but he realized that it was wholly unsuited to America. Washington, it was believed, had refused to assume a crown during the war, and who could be king if not Washington?

Apart from setting up the Senate, as Madison said, 'to protect the minority of the opulent against the majority,' the delegates did not insert any safeguards to property in the Constitution. Certain confiscatory practices of the states during the immediately preceding years, such as breaking contracts and issuing paper money, were forbidden to them, but not to the Federal Government — as the Civil War period and our own have learned. The Constitution gave Congress power to pay the national debt but did not require it to do so, as Elbridge Gerry and other members of the Convention demanded it should. And in one respect the Constitution was more democratic than that of any state except Pennsylvania. No property qualifications were imposed for any federal office, although several Southern delegates argued that not only officials but voters should be men of property. George Mason, whose professed democratic principles did not go very deep, wished congressmen to have the same landed requirements as those imposed on members of the House of Commons in the reign of Queen Anne. Charles Pinckney wanted a property qualification of at least $100,000 for the President, and $50,000 for federal judges, congressmen, and senators. But John Dickinson, reverting to his original character of the Pennsylvania farmer, 'doubted the policy of interweaving into a Republican constitution a veneration for wealth.' Franklin, consistently democratic, expressed his dislike of everything that tended 'to debase the spirit of the common people,' or to discourage the emigration of such people to America. So these movements to make the Federal Government hightoned were emphatically defeated.

The curious method adopted of indirectly choosing a President of the United States was the result of several compromises, especially between the large and small states. It was assumed that Washington would be the first President, and the number of presidential terms was not limited; but the Convention, not anticipating the rise of a two-party system, expected each state to vote for a 'favorite son,' so that seldom would one candidate obtain a majority of electoral votes. That is why it provided for a final election by the House of Representatives where the voting would be by states, a majority of states being necessary to elect. Thus, the large states would nominate popular leaders, but the small states would have a preponderant share in electing them. Madison thought this would happen 'nineteen times out of twenty'; but the two-party system has allowed it to occur but twice, in 1801 and 1825. Political parties have made the nominations since 1792, and the presidential electors merely register the will of the state pluralities. That they should do so is now an unwritten convention, although defied in the election of 1960. In this one department where the Federal Convention had no experience to go by, it created a clumsy system which had to be supplemented by the Twelfth Amendment, and has recently been threatened with another overhaul.

If the method of electing the President was clumsy, his powers were clean-cut. This was the boldest feature of the new Constitution, for most of the states had a mere figurehead of a governor, chosen by the legislature. The example of Massachusetts, where a strong and popularly elected chief magistrate had put down rebellion, encouraged the Convention to clothe the President with ample powers. He is not only the responsible head of the executive and administrative branches but also supreme war chief and, by virtue of his suspensive veto over acts of Congress, a part of the legislative branch as well. He is not hampered by a council, although the Senate has a check on his appointing and treaty-making powers. He is responsible only to the people. It has often been said that the President of the United States is a republican monarch and a monarchical premier rolled into one; but the comparison is inexact. He is more independent of the legislative power than either; but Congress is also independent of him. He cannot dissolve Congress and can adjourn it only in case of disagreement between House and Senate, which has never occurred. The state authorities issue writs of election for the House of Representatives every two years, and the Constitution requires Congress to assemble every year, whether the President wants it or not. The President's four-year term, originally fixed by the Congress of the Confederation to begin on 4 March in order to give time for votes to be counted and congressmen to assemble in that day of slow transportation, was altered by the Twentieth Amendment of 1933 to begin on 20 January. The Twenty-second Amendment, adopted in 1951, limits the number of presidential terms to two. President Eisenhower, whose party pushed this through as a posthumous slap at Franklin D. Roosevelt, once remarked that 'this may have been a mistake.'

The Federal Constitution is a very brief document, as constitutions go; the framers had the good sense not to try to anticipate every need or provide for every eventuality. They left it to Congress, the President, and the courts to supplement and implement much that was left optional or inchoate in the Constitution itself.

In no department is this preference of 'may' over 'must' more evident than in Article III on the judiciary, which required an organic act of Congress to become operative. The framework and jurisdiction of the federal courts and the judges' tenures are covered in two sections of some 400 words. Owing to this brevity, the power of the Supreme Court to declare acts of Congress unconstitutional has been challenged whenever an unpopular decision has been handed down. Where, if anywhere, did the federal courts obtain the power of judicial review? In the first place, from the Constitution, Article III, sec. 2, which declares that the judicial power shall extend to all cases arising under the Constitution and the laws and treaties of the United States; and secondly, from Article VI, sec. 2, which declares that the Constitution, and laws 'made in pursuance thereof,' and treaties, 'shall be the Supreme Law of the land.'

As former English colonists, members of the Convention were familiar with judicial review by the Privy Council of acts of colonial assemblies that were deemed 'contrary to the laws of England,' although it should be noted that the relationship of the Privy Council to an assembly was not the same as that of the Supreme Court to a co-ordinate branch of the national government. State courts had already [1] declared acts of state legislatures void, as contrary to the state constitution or to 'natural right.'

Certain important members wished to vest in the Supreme Court the power to invalidate acts of Congress. Madison himself said, in the Convention, 'A law violating a constitution established by the people themselves, would be considered by the Judges as null and void.' Hamilton discussed the question of judicial review in No. 78 of *The Federalist* — one of the best expositions of the theory that we have. Oliver Ellsworth in the Connecticut ratifying convention declared the Supreme Court to be 'a constitutional check' if Congress 'should at any time overleap their limits.' So it is not surprising that as early as 1796, in the case of Hylton *v.* United States, Justices Paterson and Wilson, both members of the

---

1. For instance, Bayard *v.* Singleton in North Carolina, and Trevett *v.* Weeden in Rhode Island.

Federal Convention, exercised the right to pass upon the constitution-ality of an act of Congress. The weight of evidence supports the view that the power of judicial review, already familiar to the framers of the Constitution, was conferred on the judiciary with intention that it should be exercised.

5. THE RATIFICATION CONTEST

The Convention, anticipating that the influence of many state politicians would be antifederalist, provided for the ratification of the Constitution by a popularly elected convention in each state. Suspecting that Rhode Island, if not other states, would prove recalcitrant, it declared that the Constitution would go into effect as soon as nine states ratified. The convention method had the further advantage that judges, ministers, and others ineligible to state legislatures, could be chosen to such a body. The nine-state provision was, of course, mildly revolutionary. But the Congress of the Confederation, still sitting in New York to carry on federal government until relieved, formally submitted the new Constitution to the states and politely faded out before the first presidential inauguration.

In the contest for ratification the Federalists (as the supporters of the new government called themselves) had the assets of youth, intelli-gence, something positive to offer, and the support of Washington and Franklin. Everyone knew that the General favored the Constitution, and the Philosopher promptly made it clear that he did too. That was unexpected, since Franklin believed in unicameral constitutions like that of Pennsylvania. But on the last day of the Convention he made his famous harmony speech, saying, 'The older I grow, the more apt I am to doubt my own judgment.' Not only was he astonished that a con-stitution the result of so many compromises could be as good as this one; but, he predicted, 'It will astonish our enemies, who are waiting with confidence to hear that our councils are confounded. . . . Thus I consent, Sir, to this Constitution *because I expect no better, and because I am not sure that it is not the best.*' He hoped that every member who disliked the Constitution would join him in keeping his objections to himself.

Many delegates did not follow his example; only 39 of the 55 signed the Constitution. Some of the non-signers, such as Martin, Yates, and

Lansing, opposed it *in toto*. Mason, Randolph, and Gerry abstained largely because of wounded vanity, since some of their pet projects were not adopted. All delegates who opposed, except Randolph, who changed his mind, took leading parts against the Constitution.

The Federalist-Antifederalist lineup was not by class, section, or economic interest. Some of the wealthiest men in the country were in opposition. George Mason, who looked down his nose at Washington as an upstart surveyor, and James Winthrop, scion of New England's most aristocratic family, wrote pamphlets against the Constitution. Delegates to the Virginia ratifying convention from the old tidewater region were mostly Antifederalist; those from the recently settled valley, Federalist. And so it went, all over the country. Among the Antifederalists were Patrick Henry and the Lees of Virginia, George Clinton of New York, and (for a time) Samuel Adams and John Hancock of Massachusetts. The warmest advocates of the Constitution were eager young men such as the thirty-two-year-old Rufus King. In contrast, the ages of Antifederalist leaders varied from Luther Martin's forty to Sam Adams's sixty-five.

Opponents of the Constitution appealed to the popular sentiment, announced by Tom Paine, 'That government is best which governs least.' They viewed with alarm the fact that two popular principles, annual elections and rotation in office, were not embodied in the Constitution. Old radicals such as General James Warren and his gifted wife Mercy, who believed that the states were the true guardians of 'Republican Virtue,' predicted that the new Constitution would encourage speculation and vice, and that America would soon go the way of imperial Rome.

The Federalists, however, were convinced that the natural rights philosophy, taken straight, would go to the nation's head and make it totter or fall; believed that the slogans of 1776 were outmoded; that America needed integration, not state rights; that the immediate peril was not tyranny but disorder or dissolution; that certain political processes such as war, foreign affairs, and commerce, were national by nature; that the right to tax was essential to any government; and that powers wrested from king and parliament should not be divided among thirteen states, if the American government were to have any influence in the world.

Supporters of the Constitution promptly opened a campaign of education through pamphlets and newspaper articles. Most famous and effective was the series of essays that came out in a New York newspaper, written by Madison, Hamilton, and Jay over the common signature 'Publius,' later republished as a book under the title *The Federalist*. This collection forms a remarkable treatise on federal government. Numerous editions have been published in many languages, and *The Federalist* has been a mine of arguments as to the nature of the Constitution and what the founding fathers thought of it. Important as these essays were, the knowledge that Washington and Franklin were in favor of the new Constitution probably did more to affect public opinion than all the pamphlets and oratory.

Even so, the struggle for ratification was tough. There is little doubt that the Antifederalists would have won a Gallup poll. Only in a few small states was there no contest, since their leaders knew that with an equal vote in the Senate and two extra votes for presidential electors they had got more than their fair share. The Delaware Convention ratified unanimously in December 1787. Pennsylvania, second state in population, was also the second to ratify, since the Federalist policy there was to rush things through before the Antifederalists could organize.

Next came Massachusetts, where the situation was critical, since Shays's Rebellion had only lately been suppressed. Shortly after the ratifying convention met on 9 January 1788, a straw vote polled 192 members against the Constitution and only 144 in favor. John Hancock, elected president of the convention, refused to take his seat, pleading 'indisposition' until three leading Federalists made a deal promising to support him for Vice President if the Constitution were ratified — a promise that they never fulfilled. Samuel Adams, so far Antifederalist, was reached through a backfire kindled by the Federalists among his old cronies, the ship caulkers of Boston. After some leading merchants had promised to build new ships as soon as the Constitution was ratified, the shipwrights and other artisans passed strong Federalist resolutions, and Sam listened to *vox pop*.

The most important piece of strategy by the Bay State Federalists was to propose a bill of rights to supplement the Constitution. This had not been provided by the Federal Convention, partly because the Constitution was one of limited and specific powers for which it was felt no bill of rights was necessary; but mostly because when the members got around to the subject, they were worn out and wanted to go home. Lack of a bill of rights, however, was a strong Antifederalist talking point. In Massachusetts the Federalists agreed to support one to be recommended to the states as a set of amendments, and John Hancock presented this outline bill of rights. That settled it; the Massachusetts convention ratified, 6 February 1788, by the close vote of 187 to 168.

The Maryland convention, also proposing bill-of-rights amendments, ratified on 28 April by an emphatic vote; partly, it seems, because the members became weary of listening to Luther Martin's three-hour Antifederalist speeches. South Carolina came in next. Charles Pinckney made strong arguments in favor of union, which he lived long enough to regret; and on 23 May his state ratified the Constitution by a strong majority. New Hampshire had the honor of being the ninth state, whose ratification put the Constitution into force.

But four states, with about 40 per cent of the total population, were still outside, including Virginia without whom no union could be a success. Here took place the most ably and bitterly contested struggle over ratification. Nowhere were the opposing forces so well led. On the Antifederalist side were George Mason, Richard Henry Lee, and Patrick Henry, who liked nothing about the new Constitution. It 'squints toward monarchy.' The President will 'make one push for the American throne.' The time-honored system of requisitions would be abolished. 'Never will I give up that darling word requisitions!' These withering blasts of oratory were patiently met with unanswerable logic by Madison and Edmund Pendleton, and the objections disposed of, point by point. Thirty-two-year-old John Marshall, in 1788, made an excellent defense of the federal judiciary which he was later to adorn. The Virginia convention ratified unconditionally on 23 June by a vote of 89 to 79. At the same time it adopted a list of amendments similar to those proposed by Massachusetts, which the new Congress and the states were asked to ratify.

Virginia made the tenth state, but New York was still out; and in New York, as Washington remarked, there was 'more wickedness than ignorance' in Antifederalism. The party led by Governor Clinton opposed the Constitution, as did most of the big landowners, who feared heavier land taxes if the state lost her right to levy customs duties. John Jay and Alexander Hamilton led the Federalist forces in the state convention with great skill; but it was only through their threat that if New York as a state failed to ratify, New York City would secede and join the Union as a separate state, that the convention finally voted to ratify by the narrow margin of three, out of 57 voting.

Only Rhode Island and North Carolina remained outside. The former, still controlled by the debtor element, called no convention until 1790, when it tardily came into the Union. The North Carolina convention, dominated by Willie Jones, refused to take a vote at its first session, but met again in November 1788 and decided to join.

The Congress of the Confederation, still sitting in New York, declared the new Constitution duly ratified, arranged for the first presidential and congressional elections, and appointed the date 4 March 1789 for the first presidential term to begin. Owing to the difficulty of communications, this had to be postponed for several weeks.[2] The old Congress also decided on New York as the first capital of the new government, and the city undertook to clean and refurbish Federal Hall on Wall Street, where Congress had sat since 1785.

On 10 July 1788 the New York *Public Advertiser,* under the heading 'Ship News — Extra,' noted the entrance of the good ship *Federal Constitution,* Perpetual Union master, from Elysium. Her cargo included thirteen large parcels of Union, Peace, and Friendship; on her passenger list were Messrs. Flourishing Commerce, Public Faith, and National Energy. Below is noted the clearance of *Old Confederacy,* Imbecility master, with a cargo of paper money, legal-tender acts, local prejudices, and seeds of discord; and the total loss with all hands of the sloop *Anarchy,* wrecked on the Rock of Union.

2. The presidential electors met and cast their votes on 4 Feb. 1789, but the House of Representatives did not have a quorum in New York until 1 April, or count the electoral ballots until the 6th. Washington did not learn officially that he had been chosen until the 14th. He started by carriage for New York on the 16th and, owing to the celebrations en route, did not arrive until 23 April. He was then given a week to get ready for his inauguration.

XV

The United States in 1790

Twenty-five years had now elapsed since the Stamp Act, and fourteen years since the Thirteen Colonies declared 'to a candid world' that they were 'and of right ought to be, free and independent States.' It is time to take stock, and see what sort of country we had when Washington had been President for less than a year.[1]

Much had been said in the debates over the Constitution about the enhanced prestige that it would give to the United States. Official opinion in Europe was not impressed. Not that Europeans perceived danger in American republicanism. With Washington's army disbanded and the navy dismantled, the United States was hardly a feather in the balance of power. Merchants and traders, however, were not indifferent to the new nation. As a source of raw materials for Europe, the United States was not yet in a class with the West Indies; but, for a country of vast empty spaces, it was an important market. Even with the Mississippi as its western boundary, the United States equaled the area of the British Isles, France, Germany, Spain, and Italy. Less than half this territory had yet come under the effective jurisdiction of the United States or of any state; and the population of a little less than four million, including 700,000 Negro slaves, was dispersed over an expanse

1. We have taken the year 1790, rather than 1789, as the central point of this description, because it was the year of the first federal census, which supplies the first statistics, incomplete to be sure and not very accurate, for the United States.

of coastal plain and upland slightly more extensive than France. But if the trans-Appalachian country were ever settled, it would surely break off from the Thirteen States. So at least believed the few Europeans who gave the matter a thought.

Furthermore, America was attempting simultaneously three political experiments, which the accumulated wisdom of Europe deemed likely to fail: independence, republicanism, and federal union. While the British and the Spanish empires touched the states on their north, west, and south, it looked as if independence could only be maintained with more of that European aid by which it had been won, perhaps even by becoming a satellite state. Since the Renaissance, the uniform tendency in Europe had been toward centralized monarchy; federal republics had maintained themselves only in small areas, such as the Netherlands and Switzerland. Most European observers believed that the history of the American Union would be short and stormy.

Indeed the larger part of the American people then lived under isolated conditions. Amerians had not yet conquered the forest. Volney wrote that during his journey in 1796 through the length and breadth of the United States, he scarcely traveled for more than three miles together on open and cleared land. Only in southern New England, and the eastern portion of the Middle States, did the cultivated area exceed the woodland.

Yet Americans dwelt in a land of such plenty that exertion had no attraction for the unambitious. The ocean and its shores yielded plenty of fish; the tidal rivers teemed with salmon, sturgeon, herring, and shad in due season, and the upland streams with trout; every kind of game was plentiful, from quail and raccoon to wild turkey and moose; and flights of wild pigeon darkened the air. Cattle and swine throve on the woodland herbage and mast; Indian corn ripened quickly in the hot summer nights; even sugar could be obtained from the maple, or honey from wild bees. The American of the interior, glutted with nature's bounty and remote from a market, had no immediate incentive to produce much beyond his own actual needs; yet the knowledge that easier life could be had often pressed him westward to more fertile lands, or to a higher scale of living. Hence the note of personal independence that was, and in the main still is, dominant in American life. Although the ordinary American recognized the claims of social rank, he was no longer so willing to defer to the gentry, and social attitudes in the new nation contrasted markedly with those in Europe. 'The means of subsistence being so easy in the country,' wrote an English observer in 1796, 'and their dependence on each other consequently so trifling, that spirit of servility to those above them so prevalent in European manners, is wholly unknown to them; and they pass their lives without any regard to the smiles or the frowns of men in power.'

However independent of those above him the average American might be, he depended on those about him for help in harvest, in raising his houseframe, and in illness. In a new country you turn to your neighbors for many things that, in a more advanced community, are performed by the government or by specialists. Hence the dual nature of the American: individualism and community spirit, indifference and kindliness. Isolation in American foreign policy was a projection of family isolation, and the Marshall Plan was a world-wide extension of neighborly help.

In 1790 there were only six cities (Philadelphia, New York, Boston, Charleston, Baltimore, and Salem) in the United States with a population of 8000 or more; and their combined numbers included only 3 per cent of the total. No city boasted as many as 50,000 inhabitants. Their aspect resembled that of provincial towns in Great Britain, for no distinctly American architectural style would be invented for another century: brick houses in the Georgian style, often detached and surrounded with gardens and shrubbery; inns with capacious yards and stables; shops and stores with overhanging signs; churches and meeting-houses with graceful spires after Sir Christopher Wren; market houses or city halls of the same style, often placed in the middle of a broad street or square, with arcades to serve as stalls or merchants' exchange; unpainted wooden houses where the poorer people lived, but hardly one without a yard or vegetable garden. Wealth was not a conspicuous feature of the American city in 1790. Nor was there anything to match the poverty of a European city; and even the slave population of the Carolina rice-fields was less wretched than the contemporary Russian peasant.

Agriculture was the main occupation of nine-tenths of the people. Except along the Hudson, practically every farmer was a freeholder. Save among the Pennsylvania Germans and the more enlightened gentry of the South, methods of agriculture were wasteful and primitive, with little sign of the improved culture and implements that were then transforming rural England. Wheat bread was largely an upper-class luxury. Indian corn was the principal food crop, with rye a poor second. Brown 'rye and Injun' bread, corn-pone or hoe-cake, potatoes, and hasty-pudding or hominy, with salt pork or codfish, washed down by rum, cider, or whisky, formed the farmer's staple diet from Maine to Georgia, but most of them were able to supplement it by fishing and shooting game. Nobody had heard of vitamins, but they were supplied nonetheless from apple orchards and wild berries. In the large part of the Old West which had been settled within the preceding fifty years, houses were commonly log cabins of one or two rooms and a cockloft; the fields were full of stumps, and acres of dead trees strangled by girdling made a depressing sight for travelers.

Bad roads were one of the penalties that Americans paid for their dispersed settlement and aversion from taxation. In 1790 the difficulties of communication were so great that a detour of several hundred miles by river and ocean was often preferable to an overland journey of 50 miles. It was almost as difficult to assemble the first Congress of the United States as to convene church councils in the Middle Ages. There was a main post-road from Wiscasset in Maine to Savannah in Georgia, over which passengers and mails were shaken and jolted in light, open stage-wagons. It took 29 days for the news of the Declaration of Independence to reach Charleston from Philadelphia. Fords and ferries had not yet been supplanted by bridges; the wooden pile structure across the Charles river at Boston was considered an immense feat of engineering. Washington managed to visit almost every state in the Union in his own coach without serious mishap; but he had to choose a season when the roads were passable, and to undergo discomfort and even danger. Most of the roads were merely wide tracks through the forest, full of rocks and stumps and enormous holes. Many that are marked on the early maps were mere bridle-paths or Indian trails, that would admit no wheeled vehicle.

Now that America has become famous for sanitation, it is a shock to find, at this era and down to the Civil War, that the country impressed European visitors as uncommonly dirty. From persons accustomed to contemporary London or Paris, this meant really dirty! Even in the larger towns streets were seldom paved and never cleaned; offal was deposited in the street or thrown off docks, and, without wire screens, houses were defenseless against swarms of flies and other winged pests.

As no one had yet heard of disease germs, there were intermittent outbreaks of typhoid and yellow fever in the seaports as far north as New Hampshire; one at Philadelphia in 1793 caused 4000 deaths — almost 10 per cent of the total population. Frontiersmen were racked every summer by malarial fevers and agues, transmitted by mosquitoes. Flower gardens were rare; and the pioneer, regarding trees as enemies, neither spared them nor planted them for shade. Country farmhouses in the older-settled region were almost invariably of wood, usually unpainted, resembling dingy boxes surrounded by unseemly household litter. Yet stoutly and honestly built as they were, the colonial houses that have survived long enough to acquire white paint, green blinds, lawns, shrubs, and century-old shade trees, are seen to have both distinction and beauty.

The United States of 1790 was not, by any modern standard, a nation. Materials of a nation were present, but cohesive force was wanting. The English origin of the bulk of the people made for cultural homogeneity; the Maine fisherman could understand the Georgian planter much more readily than a Kentishman could understand a Yorkshireman, or an Alsatian a Breton. Political institutions, though decentralized, were fairly constant in form through the length and breadth of the land. But there was no tradition of union behind the War of Independence, and it was difficult to discover a common interest upon which union could be built. Most citizens of the United States in 1790, if asked their country or nation, would not have answered American, but Carolinian, Virginian, Pennsylvanian, Jerseyman, New Yorker, or New Englander. A political nexus had been found, but unless a national tradition were soon established, the states would develop rivalries similar to those of the republics of Latin America. It would require the highest statesmanship to keep these new commonwealths united. The Federal Constitution made it possible; but few observers in 1790 thought it probable.

2. NEW ENGLAND

In New England, climate, soil, and religion had produced in a century and a half a strongly individualized type, the Yankee, perhaps the most persistent ingredient of the American mixture.

The Yankee was the American Scot; and New England was an eighteenth-century Scotland without the lairds. A severe climate, a grudging soil that had to be cleared of boulders as well as trees, and a stern puritan faith, dictated the four gospels of education, thrift, ingenuity, and righteousness. By necessity rather than choice, the New Englanders had acquired an aptitude for maritime enterprise and trading. They hailed with joy the new and wider opportunities for seafaring opened by freedom from the Acts of Trade. Seamen of Salem had already ventured to the East Indies with success when Boston, in 1790, celebrated the return of her ship *Columbia*, laden with tea, silk, and porcelain, from a voyage around the world. On her next voyage the *Columbia* sailed up a great river that Vancouver had passed by, gave it her name, and to its banks her flag.

The five New England States were divided politically into townships, about 30 square miles on an average, each containing from less than a hundred to several thousand people. Each was a unit for purposes of local government, conducting its own affairs by town meeting and selectmen, supporting common schools by local taxes, and electing annually to the state legislature a representative, whose votes and doings were keenly scrutinized by his constituents. The nucleus of every township was the meeting-house, part town hall, part place of worship, bordering the village green. Outlying farms, by 1790, in most places outnumbered those with a village house-plot. Most of the common fields had been divided in severalty and enclosed by uncemented stone walls. Families were large, but estates were seldom divided below a hundred acres; a Yankee farmer hoped to make a scholar or minister out of one son, to provide for a second with a tract of wilderness, and let the rest earn their living by working for hire, going to sea, or learning a trade. Until about 1830 the American merchant marine was manned largely by New England lads who were seeking the wherewithal to purchase land and set up housekeeping.

Puritanism had considerably softened during the eighteenth century. The puritan Sabbath was still observed; but there were plenty of frolics at barn-raisings and corn-huskings, and heavy drinking on public occasions such as ship-launchings, ordinations, college commencements, and Thanksgiving Day — the puritan substitute for Christmas, which in course of time became an additional day of merry-making. On the whole, living was plain in New England. Even in the family of President Adams, the children were urged to eat a double portion of hasty-pudding, in order to spare the meat that was to follow. Idleness was the cardinal sin. If a Yankee had nothing else to do, he whittled barrel-bungs from a pine stick, or carved a model of his latest ship; and he usually had much else to do. New England housewives spun, wove, and tailored their woolen garments and made cloth for sale. Small fulling mills and paper mills were established at the numerous waterfalls, and distilleries in the seaports turned West Indian molasses into that pleasant if fiery beverage, New England rum. Wooden-ware was made by snowbound farmers for export to the West Indies, nails were cut and headed from wrought iron rods at fireside forges, and in some towns shoes were made for export. Connecticut, in particular, had attained a nice balance between farming, seafaring, and handicraft, which made the people of that state renowned for steady habits and mechanical ingenuity. Before the century was out, Eli Whitney of New Haven devised the cotton gin and local gunsmiths employed at the federal arsenal, Springfield, Mass., established the first approximation to the modern assembly line, enabling a small labor force to turn out 442 muskets a month. New England was ripe for transition from handicraft to the factory system; but the success of her seafarers, and the facility of emigration, postponed industrial revolution for another generation.

The South American patriot Francisco de Miranda, who traveled through New England in the summer of 1784, found much that was kindly, pleasant, and in good taste. At New Haven he is taken over Yale College by President Stiles, converses with a classically educated miller who had been a cavalry captain in the war, and views the famous 'blue laws' in the town archives. Proceeding to Wethersfield, he attends Sunday meeting, and admires the manner in which the psalms and responses are sung by the congregation, trained by a music master. At Windsor he enjoys a lively literary conversation with John Trumbull, the painter, as well as with the innkeeper, who is discovered reading Rollin's *Ancient History*, and stoutly maintains Ben Franklin to be a better man than Aristides. Thence to Middletown, and a boat excursion on the river with General Parsons and other jolly fellows, drinking copiously of punch 'in pure republican style.' Newport he thinks justly called the paradise of New England, containing, besides hospitable natives, many ladies and gentlemen from Charleston, S.C., who were using it as a summer resort. The leading lights of Providence, on the other hand, are provincial and vulgar, Commodore Esek Hopkins, formerly of the United States Navy, even insisting that there was no such place as the City of Mexico.

Miranda enters Boston armed with letters of introduction to the 'best people,' whose ladies he finds vain, luxurious, and too much given to the use of cosmetics; he predicts bankruptcy for Boston within twenty years. Sam Adams, however, is still faithful to republican simplicity. After carefully inspecting Harvard College, Miranda reports it better suited to turn out Protestant clergymen than intelligent and liberal citizens. He visits the studio of the self-taught painter Edward Savage, and predicts that with a European education his talent will take him far. (Savage did visit Europe, and his portrait of Washington is said by contemporaries to be the best likeness of the great man.) From Boston, Miranda takes the post road to Portsmouth, N.H., and is much impressed by evidences of thrift and prosperity along the north shore of Massachusetts. 'Liberty inspires such intelligence and industry in these towns . . . that the people out of their slender resources maintain their large families, pay heavy taxes, and live with comfort and taste, a thousand times happier than the proprietors of the rich mines and fertile lands of Mexico, Peru, Buenos Aires, Caracas, and the whole Spanish-American continent.'

For Portsmouth itself we have a flattering description from Count Francisco dal Verme; a 25-year-old aristocrat from Milan who toured the United States in 1783–84. After attending 'meeting' on an August Sunday with Colonel Langdon, he wrote in his diary that he couldn't begin to describe 'either the beauty or the number' of the ladies in the congregation, 'nor the elegance of their clothes, made in the fashion of the latest taste in France.' They almost made him forget to listen to the sermon! Next day, he went for a sail, attended a horse race and a dancing school of 30 couples, dined with General Whipple, and 'with difficulty took leave of my good host.' Another Milanese gentleman, Count Luigi Castiglione, was similarly impressed in 1787. He pushed on by horseback through Maine to Camden, beyond which horses were useless; so he chartered a schooner to sail up the Penobscot and visited the Abnaki Indian reservation at Oldtown, the object of this long detour. He admired their basketry, moccasins, and snowshoes, and sketched these and other Indian possessions.

The New Englanders were very well satisfied with themselves in 1790 and had reason to be; they had struck root in a region where nature was not lavish, produced a homogeneous and happy society, won liberty, and, by their own enterprise, got out of the depression. Disorderly when royal governors attempted to thwart their will, the Yankees had sloughed off cruder phases of democracy; for another generation the leadership of their clergy, well-to-do merchants, and conservative lawyers would not be successfully challenged. Outside New England, where they were familiar as sailors or peddlers, the Yankees were regarded much as Scotsmen then were by the English: often envied, sometimes respected, but generally disliked.

3. THE MIDDLE STATES

New York State, heterogeneous in 1790, never was destined to attain homogeneity. The Dutch 'Knickerbocker' families shared a social ascendancy with the descendants of English and Huguenot merchants. There were many villages where Dutch was still spoken, and Albany was still thoroughly Dutch, ruled by mynheers who lived in substantial brick houses with stepped gables. But the Netherlands element comprised only one-sixth of the 300,000 inhabitants of New York State. For the rest, there were Germans in the Mohawk valley and Ulster county, a few families of Sephardic Jews in New York City, an appreciable element of Scots and Irish, and a strong majority of English blood, mostly the fast-increasing Yankee element.

New York was only the fifth state in population in 1790: a fourfold increase in 30 years made it first in 1820. Settlement of the interior explains the difference. In 1790 the inhabited area of New York followed the Hudson river from New York City to Albany, whence one branch of settlement continued up the Mohawk toward Lake Erie, and a thin line of clearings pushed up by Lake George and Lake Champlain, which Burgoyne had found a wilderness. There were also a few islands of settlement such as Cooperstown, where James Fenimore Cooper was cradled in the midst of the former hunting grounds of the Six Nations. Socially, New York was still the most aristocratic of the states, in spite of the extensive confiscation and subdividing of loyalists' estates; for most of the patroons managed to retain their vast properties. One out of every seven New York families held slaves in 1790, and nine years elapsed before gradual emancipation began. The qualifications for voting and for office were high.

New York City owed its prosperity, and its 33,000 inhabitants, to a unique position at the mouth of the Hudson river, the greatest tidal inlet between the St. Lawrence and the River Plate. It was the natural gateway to the Iroquois country, which now began to be settled by white people. In 1825 the Erie Canal, following the lowest watershed between the Atlantic states and the Lakes, made New York City the principal gateway to the West and the financial center of the Union. The merchants did not need to be so venturesome as those of New England and Baltimore, and they spent more on good living than on churches and schools. They too had a family college — Columbia (late King's); but while Boston was forming learned institutions, and Philadelphia supporting a literary journal and a Philosophical Society, New York was founding the Columbian Order, better known as Tammany Hall. In the midst of this wealthy, gay, and somewhat cynical society, Alexander Hamilton reached manhood and Washington Irving was born.

New Jersey, a farming state of less than 200,000 people, has been compared with a barrel tapped at both ends by New York and Philadelphia. Travelers along the road between these two cities admired the Jersey apple orchards, the well-cultivated farms, and, at the pleasant village of Princeton, the College of New Jersey whose Nassau Hall, 180 feet long and four stories high, was reputed to be the largest building in the Thirteen States. At the falls of the Passaic river, near Newark, an incorporated company had just founded Paterson, the first factory village in America. South of this main road lay a region of pine barrens and malarial marshes.

Pennsylvania, second largest state in the Union, with a population of 435,000, had acquired a certain uniformity in diversity. Her racial heterogeneity, democratic polity, and social structure, ranging from wealthy merchants to crude frontiersmen, made Pennsylvania a microcosm of the America to be. Philadelphia was the principal port of immigration between 1725 and 1825; and the boat-shaped Conestoga wagons of the Pennsylvania Dutch needed but slight improvement to become the 'prairie schooner' of westward advance. Pennsylvania was still in the throes of democratic experiment. Her radical state government, with a unicameral legislature and a plural executive, had become notoriously factious and incompetent. In 1791 a new constitution with a bicameral legislature was adopted, but manhood suffrage was retained; and this laid a firm foundation for subsequent democratization of Pennsylvania.

Philadelphia, at the junction of the Delaware and Schuylkill rivers, and with a population of 45,000 in 1790, was easily the first city in the United States for commerce, architecture, and culture. During the next ten years it was the seat of the Federal Government and of a more brilliant 'republican court' than the city of Washington could show for a century to come. Owing largely to Quaker influence, Philadelphia was well provided with charitable institutions, and amateur scientists. Strangely enough, here as elsewhere in the United States, the good start in a really American literature made by such men as Noah Webster, Joel Barlow, Joseph Hopkinson, and Philip Freneau during the creative period 1782–89, came to a halt. When Tom Moore visited 'Delaware's green banks' in 1804, Joseph Dennie, Jared Ingersoll, and Brockden Brown, whom he hailed as the 'sacred few' who would save 'Columbia' from Boeotian aridity, were producing pallid imitations of *The Spectator*, dreary tragedies of medieval Europe, novels of mystery and horror. Hugh Brackenridge of Pittsburgh alone expressed the rich color and wilderness flavor of youthful Pennsylvania.

A few miles from Philadelphia one reached the garden spot of eighteenth-century America, a belt of rich limestone soil that crossed the Susquehanna river and extended into Maryland and the Valley of Virginia. The fortunate inhabitants of this region were reaping huge profits in 1790 by reason of European crop failures, and were to prosper still more through the wars that flowed from the French Revolution. 'The whole country is well cultivated,' wrote a Dutch financier who passed through this region in 1794, 'and what forests the farmers keep are stocked with trees of the right kind — chestnut, locust, walnut, maple, white oak. It is a succession of hills, not too high, and the aspect of the country is very beautiful.' Lancaster, with 4000 inhabitants, was the largest inland town in the United States. Here, and in the limestone belt, most of the farmers and townspeople were German. They were by far the best husbandmen in America, using a proper rotation, with clover and root crops. Their houses, heated by stoves, were commonly built of stone; their fences of stout posts and rails; but what most impressed strangers were the great barns, with huge gable-end doors, through which a loaded wagon could drive onto a wide threshing-floor, flanked by spacious hay-lofts, cattle and sheep pens, and horse stables. The Germans were divided into a number of sects, some of which, like the Amish Mennonites, have retained their quaint costumes and puritanism into the twentieth century. They supported six weekly newspapers in their own language and were as keen household manufacturers as the Yankees; but Chastellux found them lacking in public spirit, compared with the English-speaking Americans, 'content . . . with being only the spectators of their own wealth,' and with the standards of a German peasant.

Lancaster was the parting point for two streams of westward emigration. One wagon road took a southwesterly direction, crossed the Potomac at Harpers Ferry, and entered the Shenandoah valley of Virginia, between the Blue Ridge and the Unakas. The Pittsburgh wagon road struck out northwesterly, crossed the Susquehanna by ford or ferry at Harrisburg (the future capital of Pennsylvania), and followed the beautiful wooded valley of the Juniata to its headwaters. This region was inhabited mainly by Ulstermen, although in the easternmost section they were rapidly being bought out by the more thrifty and land-hungry Germans. To the north and west of the upper Susquehanna, Pennsylvania was still a mountainous virgin forest. After a long, painful pull up the rocky, rutty wagon road, to an elevation of some 2500 feet, you attained the Allegheny front, an escarpment from which, by a rolling, densely wooded plateau, you descended westward to where the Allegheny and Monongahela rivers come together to form the Ohio. At this point you reached Pittsburgh, a thriving village in the midst of virgin coal and iron deposits, the most important of three inner gateways to the Far West. Already fleets of covered wagons were bringing in settlers destined for Kentucky and goods to be distributed down the mighty valley of the Ohio and Mississippi.

4. THE SOUTH

Twenty-five miles south of Philadelphia the post-road crossed the Mason-Dixon Line, an internal boundary that bulks large in American history. Originally drawn to divide Pennsylvania from Delaware and Maryland, in 1790 it was already recognized as the boundary between the farming, or commercial, and the plantation states. From 1804 to 1865 it divided the free and the slave states; and even yet it is the boundary of sentiment between North and South.

Little Delaware, apart from flour mills around Wilmington, was a farming community, steadfastly conservative in politics. In Maryland, with 320,000 souls, one-third slaves, we reach the first state where slavery underlay the economic system. The old English Catholic families still retained some of the better plantations on both shores of Chesapeake Bay; but it was the Irish Carrolls who provided a 'signer,' a

United States Senator, and the first Roman Catholic bishop in the United States. Maryland produced the best wheat flour in America, and a dark variety of tobacco chiefly appreciated by the French. The lowland planters were famous for hospitality, and for the various and delicious methods devised by their black cooks for preparing the oysters, soft-shell crabs, terrapin, shad, canvas-back ducks, and other delicacies afforded by Chesapeake Bay. Annapolis, the pleasant and hospitable state capital, had just been made the seat of St. John's College.

Baltimore, a mere village before the War of Independence, approached Boston in population. A deep harbor in Chesapeake Bay, water-driven flour mills, and proximity to wheat-growing regions made it the metropolis for an important section of Pennsylvania. Baltimore was already famous for belles, two of whom married kings, but did not quite make queens. Her swift schooners, the Baltimore clippers, made excellent privateers. The Maryland piedmont resembled the limestone belt of Pennsylvania: a rich rolling grain country tilled by English and German farmers, with the aid of a few slaves. This region, in combination with Baltimore, neutralized the tidewater aristocracy and gradually drew Maryland into the social and economic orbit of the Northern states.

From Baltimore a road that long remained the despair of travelers traversed Maryland to Georgetown, just below the Great Falls of the Potomac. Here, at the head of navigation, the city of Washington was being planned. Crossing the river, one entered the Old Dominion, with a population of 748,000, of which 40 per cent were slaves.[2]

The tidewater section of Virginia, east of the fall line which passes through Georgetown, Richmond, and Petersburg, by 1790 had seen its best days. The state capital had been transferred to Richmond, at the falls of the James; only William and Mary College kept Williamsburg alive. Norfolk had not yet recovered from the fire of 1776. The 'old fields,' the exhausted tobacco lands, were now reverting to forest, and the wisest planters were emigrating to Kentucky.

One of the best plantations of the Virginia tidewater was Mount Vernon, where General Washington had hoped to spend the remainder of his days as a modern farmer, improving American husbandry by experiment and example. He studied the best works on the subject, corresponded with English experts such as Arthur Young, imported im-

2. Not including the 74,000 in Kentucky (17 per cent slaves).

proved implements, and applied new methods. Tobacco culture had long since been given up at Mount Vernon, and now wheat, flax, and root crops were being substituted for corn, a five-year rotation of crops adopted, and flocks of sheep raised on turnips or clover.

Washington's relation to Mount Vernon was like that of an industrial manager to his plant. He inherited an estate of 2500 acres and added about 5500 more, until his estate stretched ten miles along the Potomac. The 3500 acres under cultivation around 1790 were divided by tracts of woodland into separate farms, each with its own force of slaves and an overseer, who must report weekly how he had employed every hand. Brood-mares and blooded stallions occupied the best pastures. Royal Gift, a fifteen-hand jackass presented by the King of Spain, had a special paddock and groom, as befitted the ancestor of the American army mule. The General's cattle were undersized and of low breed; his hogs ran at large through the woodlands, affording illicit sport for a pack of French boar-hounds, an unwelcome gift from Lafayette. Mount Vernon was an industrial as well as an agricultural unit. There were slave blacksmiths, carpenters, and even bricklayers; a cider press and still-house, where excellent rye and Bourbon whisky were made, and sold in barrels made by slave coopers from home-grown oak. Herring and shad fisheries in the Potomac provided food for the slaves; a grist-mill turned Washington's improved strain of wheat into the finest grade of flour, which went to market in his own schooner. There was a weaving-shed, where a dozen different textiles were produced from local wool and flax and West Indian cotton.

For recreation the General hunted the fox with his own and his neighbors' packs of hounds; shot wild fowl, attended Masonic lodge at Alexandria, and with Martha danced at assemblies in the same pleasant town. A constant stream of relations and friends flowed through the mansion house, few distinguished travelers came South unprovided with a letter to the great man, and no gentleman could be turned away from his door. The guests, in fact, ate up most of the increase not consumed by the slaves, whose children Washington was too humane to sell away from their parents.

This was the life that Washington loved, and in which he hoped to spend his declining years. Even on his campaigns, and in the Presidency, he would write sixteen-page letters of instruction to his overseers. 'The more I am acquainted with agricultural affairs, the better I am pleased with them,' he wrote to Arthur Young in 1788. 'How much more delightful . . . is the task of making improvements in the earth than all the vain glory which can be acquired from ravaging it by the most uninterrupted career of conquests.'

The Virginia piedmont between the fall line and the Blue Ridge, for the most part a fruitful, rolling country, had become the seat of all that was healthy and vigorous in the plantation system; and Richmond flourished as the principal outlet of the James river valley. Most of the Virginia statesmen of the revolutionary and early federal eras were either born in this region or grew to manhood in its wilder margins. The old colonial families, excepting a few like the Randolphs, were being supplanted by others, often allied to them on the distaff side, like the Jeffersons, Madisons, Monroes, Taylors, Tylers, and Marshalls. If the proper object of society be to produce and maintain a public-spirited and intelligent aristocracy, Virginia had achieved it. If it be to maintain a high general level of comfort and intelligence, she had not. Below the 'first families,' but continually pushing into their level by marriage, was a class of lesser planters, uneducated, provincial, and often rude. Below them was an unstable and uneasy class of yeomen, outnumbering the planters in the piedmont. Descended largely from indentured servants and deported convicts, these 'peasants,' as the gentry called them, were illiterate, ferocious, and quarrelsome. Self-contained plantations, with slave artisans and mechanics, left small demand for skilled white labor, and made small farms unprofitable. Hence the Virginia yeoman had but the alternative of migrating westward, or of becoming a 'poor white' despised even by the slaves.

In the lowlands the slaves outnumbered the whites; in the piedmont they comprised about one-third of the total population. Few denied that slavery was a moral evil and a menace to the country. Almost every educated Virginian hoped to make good the opening words of his Bill of Rights 'that all men are by nature free and independent.' But a state whose population was 40 per cent Negro quailed before such a social revolution. Jefferson counted on the young abolitionists that Chancellor Wythe was making in William and Mary College. But in a few years' time the cotton gin gave chattel slavery a new lease on life; and, shortly after Jefferson died, a young professor at William and Mary began to preach the doctrine that Negro slavery was justified by history and ordained by God.

As one rode westward across the Virginia piedmont, with the crestline of the Blue Ridge looming in the distance, the forest became more dense, the large plantations less numerous, the farms of independent yeomen more frequent, and the cultivation of tobacco gave place to corn and grazing. Between the Blue Ridge and the higher folds of the Appalachians lies the Shenandoah valley, largely peopled by Scots and Germans, and feeling itself a province apart from lowland and piedmont. Here in Rockingham county, Abraham Lincoln, grandfather of the President, lived until 1784. Still less did the trans-Appalachian part of Virginia, a densely wooded plateau sloping to the upper Ohio, resemble the Virginia of the planters. In 1790 it was a more primitive frontier than Kentucky. This is the section that in 1863 became the state of West Virginia.

South from Petersburg, Virginia, a two days' journey through a sandy plain covered with pine forest, took one to Halifax, one of several pretty seaports on the rivers of North Carolina. This 'Tar-Heel State,' so called from her production of naval stores, was still marked by the geographical and demographical divisions that made trouble in the 1770's. The coastal plain, a hundred miles or more wide, consisted of pine barrens with soil too sandy for wheat or tobacco, and extensive marshes like the Dismal Swamp. The river mouths were closed against vessels drawing above ten feet by the barrier beaches that enclosed Pamlico and Albemarle Sounds, and the region was sparsely settled. President Washington, traveling through in 1791, found it 'the most barren country he ever beheld,' without 'a single house of an elegant appearance.'

The piedmont of North Carolina was a thriving region of upland farms, supporting a large population of Germans, Ulstermen, English, and Highland Scots. There was little communication between coast and piedmont through the pine barrens, and less sympathy. Petersburg, Va., and Charleston, S.C., were nearer or more convenient markets for the upland farmers than the tiny ports of their own state. Local particularism was so strong that the legislature abandoned Governor Tryon's 'palace' at New Bern and became peripatetic. Only by creating a new state capital, at Raleigh on the falls of the Neuse river, could it manage to settle down.

Although there were large tobacco plantations in North Carolina, the state on the whole was a white farmer-democracy. Honest mediocrity typified North Carolina statesmanship from the eighteenth century to the twentieth, when an industrial revolution brought material progress, enthusiasm for learning, and accomplishment in the arts. South Carolina boasted a patrician society, centered in Charleston, which in 1790, with a population of 16,000, was the fourth city in America and metropolis of the lower South. The Reverend Jedidiah Morse in his *American Geography* (1789) wrote, 'In no part of America are the social blessings enjoyed more rationally and liberally than in Charleston. Unaffected hospitality, affability, ease in manners and address, and a disposition to make their guests welcome, easy and pleased with themselves, are characteristics of the respectable people of Charleston.' One can well imagine that stiff New England Calvinist succumbing to the graceful attentions of a Charleston family, while he sipped their madeira wine on a spacious verandah overlooking a tropical garden.

The South Carolina planters went to their country houses in the coastal plain in November, when the first frosts removed the danger of fever in that subtropical climate; and took their families back to Charleston for the gay season from January to March. Early spring, a most anxious period in rice culture, was passed in the plantation mansion — shaded by a classic portico, and surrounded by groves of live oaks, hung with Spanish moss. The hot months would be spent at a summer house in the pine hills, or at Newport, Rhode Island. Popular education was little attended to, but the College of Charleston was established in 1785, and the more opulent families continued to send their sons to Old England or New England for higher education.

Rice, the economic basis of the lower country, required intensive cultivation, along such parts of the tidal rivers as permitted artificial flooding with fresh water. These regions were so unhealthy for white people that Negro labor, immune to malaria, was a necessity; and in no part of the United States were slaves so numerous. Out of 1600 heads of families in the rural part of the Charleston district, in 1790, 1300 held slaves to the number of 43,000. South Carolina not only blocked abolition of the African slave trade in the Federal Constitution, but reopened traffic by state law in 1803.

Indigo culture had been abandoned with the loss of the parliamentary bounty; but the South Carolina planters, in 1790, were experimenting with long-staple sea-island cotton; and the next year Robert Owen spun into yarn the first two bags that were sent to England. The short-staple upland cotton, which could be grown inland, was so difficult to separate from its seed as to be unmarketable until after the cotton gin was invented in 1793. One effect of this was to extend the plantation system into the more populous back-country. In 1790 the upland people won their first victory by transferring the state capital to Columbia; but the piedmont was still under-represented in the legislature, and poor men were denied office by high property qualifications. John C. Calhoun, destined to weld the South and divide the Union, was a boy of eight in the upper country, in 1790.

Across the Savannah river from South Carolina, Georgia retained few traces of General Oglethorpe's pious experiment. It had developed, like South Carolina, into a slave-holding rice coast, a belt of infertile pine barrens, and a rolling, wooded piedmont of hunter folk and frontier farmers. These Georgia 'crackers' were vigorous and lawless, hard drinkers and rough fighters. Desperately eager to despoil the Creek Indians of their fertile cornfields across the Oconee river, the up-country Georgians gave constant trouble to the Federal Government.

5. 'AMERICA THE HOPE OF THE WORLD'

Such, in their broader outlines, were the Thirteen States, and the people thereof, seven years after the war. Of such a people, so circumstanced, the friends of liberty in Europe had high expectations. The French statesman Turgot wrote in 1778:

> This people is the hope of the human race. It may become the model. It ought to show the world by facts, that men can be free and yet peaceful, and may dispense with the chains in which tyrants and knaves of every colour have presumed to bind them, under pretext of the public good. The Americans should be an example of political, religious, commercial and industrial liberty. The asylum they offer to the oppressed of every nation, the avenue of escape they open, will compel governments to be just and enlightened; and the rest of the world in due time will see through the empty illusions in which policy is conceived. But to obtain these ends for us, America must secure them to herself; and must not become, as so many of your ministerial writers have predicted, a mass of divided powers, contending for territory and trade, cementing the slavery of peoples by their own blood.

Yet there was one dominant force in United States history that neither Turgot nor anyone foresaw in 1785: expansion. With a prize such as the West at their back doors, the people of the United States would have been more than human had they been content with a 'state of nature' between the Atlantic and the Appalachians. For a century to come, the subduing of the temperate regions of North America to the purposes of civilized life was to be the main business of the United States. In 1790 the boundaries of the republic included 800,000, in 1860 3 million square miles. In 1790 the population was 4 million; in 1960 179 million. This folk movement, comparable in modern history only with the barbaric invasions of the Roman Empire, gives the history of the United States a different quality from that of Europe; different even from that of Canada and Australia, by reason of the absence of exterior control. The advancing frontier, with growing industrialism, set the rhythm of American society, colored its politics, and rendered more difficult the problem of union. Yet, as Turgot warned us, only union could secure the gain and fulfill the promise of the American Revolution.

XVI

Washington's First Administration

1. PROSPECTS AND PROBLEMS

With a new constitution the Americans challenged their own future. It remained to be seen whether a federal and republican government was workable on such a scale, whether local interests would not choke national sentiment, whether the political fabric had the strength to withstand war, or the elasticity for social and territorial growth.

The prospect seemed fair enough, outwardly, on that bright morning of 30 April 1789, when Washington, a picture of splendid manhood, stepped out onto the balcony overlooking Wall Street, New York, and took the oath: 'I do solemnly swear that I will faithfully execute the office of President of the United States and will, to the best of my ability, preserve, protect, and defend the Constitution of the United States.' His progress from Mount Vernon to New York had been a triumphal procession. His reception in the federal capital was tremendous — ships and batteries firing salutes, militia parades, civilians' cheers, triumphal arch, houses decorated. Not a single untoward note — no unrepentant tory raised a cheer for the king, no Antifederalist spat in the gutter as the President passed, no students paraded with signs saying 'George, go home!'

Yet Washington faced formidable problems. The Federal Government had to create its own machinery. Every revolutionary government of Europe, even the Communist ones, has taken over a corps of functionaries, an administrative system, and a treasury; but the American Confederation left nothing but a dozen clerks, an empty treasury, and a burden of debt. There were no taxes or other monies coming in, and no machinery for collecting taxes existed. The new Congress quickly imposed a customs tariff; but months elapsed before an administration could be created to collect it, in a loose-jointed country 2000 miles long. Until a federal judiciary could be established, there was no means of enforcing any law. The country itself was just beginning to experience the return of prosperity; but free capital was exceedingly scarce, and Washington, reputed the wealthiest of Americans, had to borrow £600 from a friend in order to meet the expense of his removal to New York. England and Spain, as we have seen, controlled spheres of influence on United States territory. A secession movement in the West threatened to split the Union along the crest of the Appalachians. The American army consisted of 672 officers and men; the navy had ceased to exist.

Still, there were saving elements in the situation. Economic conditions were vastly improved since the panic year 1786; and by 1790 easy money had returned. Virginia and the Carolinas had recovered their pre-war volume of exports in tobacco, naval stores, and rice. Poor crops in France gave a better market for the grain of the Middle States. New England was again doing business in the West Indies, because Jamaicans and Barbadians, hampered by British regulations, were helping Yankee shipmasters to smuggle in provisions. Northern shipowners, with specie borrowed from English merchant-bankers, were driving a roaring trade in Calcutta and Canton, where the number of American entries in 1789 was second only to those flying the British flag. All this had been effected by good fortune, enterprise, and individual energy, before the new government came into operation; but the Federalists were quick to claim credit for the tide on which their ship was launched.

The Federal Government could count on a good press and a favorably expectant public opinion. Not that there was much enthusiasm for the Constitution, even among its advocates. Washington, indeed, considered it a hopeful experiment, and Madison was pleased with what was chiefly his handiwork; but Hamilton, in his more cheerful moments, regarded it as a makeshift; and, in bad humor, as a 'frail and worthless fabric.' John Adams believed it would not outlast himself! Every Federalist, however, was determined to do his best to make the Constitution work. The Antifederalist attitude was ambiguous. Patrick Henry declared, when he recognized his defeat in the Virginia ratifying convention: 'I will be a peaceable citizen. My head, my hand, and my heart, shall be at liberty to retrieve the loss of liberty, and remove the defects of that system in a constitutional way.' Nevertheless, he and George Clinton continued to scream for a second federal convention, and the newspapers that had attacked the Constitution were soon sniping at Washington's administration. The important thing was the absence of any organization committed to overthrowing the Constitution: no 'Confederation in Exile' at Quebec or London, no royalist gang plotting to restore George III. Thus, the new government was launched on a sea of consent, even better than on a river of gold.

It is unlikely that the Constitution would have so soon acquired American loyalty if Washington had not consented to serve. The qualities that made him the first farmer and the first soldier in America also made him the first statesman. As landed proprietor no less than as commander-in-chief, he had shown executive ability, the power of planning for a distant end, and a capacity for taking infinite pains. In describing himself as one who inherited 'inferior endowments from nature,' Washington was too modest; but we shall underestimate the difficulties of his task if we forget that his superiority lay in character, not in talents. He had the power of inspiring respect and trust, but not the gift of popularity; directness but not adroitness; fortitude rather than flexibility; the power to think things through, not quick perception; a natural presence and dignity, but none of that brisk assertiveness which has often given inferior men political influence. The mask of dignity and reserve that concealed his inner life came from humility and stoical self-control. A warm heart was revealed in numerous kindly acts to his dependents and subordinates. And beneath his cool surface there glowed a fire that under provocation would burst forth in immoderate laughter, astounding oaths, or Olympian anger.

2. ORGANIZING AN ADMINISTRATION

Leadership in policy was expected to be one of the functions of the President. It was impossible to write this into the Constitution. Any attempt to define the presidency as either of the Roosevelts administered it would have been considered plain tyranny in 1788. The presidency was purposely left vague in its relation to Congress, with such executive departments as Congress might establish. Hence the personality of the first President would go far to determine the scope of his office.

It was here that Washington's character and prestige counted heavily. The heads of departments had to be appointed by the President with the consent of the Senate. But Congress, according to colonial usage, might have made them responsible to itself, and removable by the Senate. Instead, it made the secretaries of state and of war responsible to the President alone, and subject to his direction within their legal competence. Moreover, when the first question of dismissal from office came up, the Senate admitted that the President could remove officials without its consent. The effect of this precedent was to make the entire administrative force and diplomatic service responsible to the chief magistrate.

For Secretary of State, Washington chose Thomas Jefferson, who had been a superb minister to France. Robert Morris suggested Alexander Hamilton for the treasury, which fell in perfectly with Washington's inclinations. Henry Knox, Washington's chief of artillery and Secretary of War under the Confederation, continued as such; and Governor Edmund Randolph of Virginia was appointed Attorney-General.

The making of minor appointments turned out to be, as Washington feared, the 'most difficult and delicate part' of his duty. He deemed it necessary to reward war service, to conciliate factions, and to avoid any suspicion of personal or sectional partiality. Washington scrutinized applications conscientiously, asking the advice of senators and representatives from the applicant's state, and sought out able men where none applied. The federal civil service began with principles of efficiency and honesty that were in sharp contrast to the jobbery and corruption in contemporary European governments and in several of the state governments.

A Vice-President had been created by the Federal Constitution in order to provide an acting chief magistrate in the event of the death or disability of the President, without the need of a special election. In order to give him something to do, he was made President of the Senate, with a casting vote in case of tie. John Adams, the first Vice-President, regarded his office as 'the most insignificant . . . that ever invention of man contrived, or his imagination conceived.' Adams suffered all his life from the notion that he was not properly appreciated. A sound political scientist and a useful drafter of state constitutions, his one fault was vanity. As minister to the Dutch Republic he observed that every official was heavily titled and got the notion that without titles no republic could be respected. After all, the governors of several states were entitled 'His Excellency' by their constitutions (that of Massachusetts still is); so shouldn't the President of the United States have something more noble? Adams got through the Senate a vote in favor of the President's being called 'His Highness the President of the United States of America and the Protector of the Rights of the Same.' The House, fortunately, failed to consent, and Washington, probably to his great relief, remained simply 'Mr. President.'

Although the first Senate of only 22 members was friendly to the administration, their chamber early developed that *esprit de corps* which has been the bane of willful presidents. 'Senatorial courtesy,' the practice of rejecting any nomination not approved by the senators from the nominee's own state, soon began. In the matter of treaties, however, the Senate's sense of its own dignity defeated its ambition. The Constitution grants the President power, 'by and with the advice and consent of the Senate, to make treaties, provided two-thirds of the senators present concur.' On one memorable occasion Washington appeared before the Senate, like the Secretary of Foreign Affairs in the House of Commons, to explain an Indian treaty and see it through. Hampered in freedom of debate by the august presence, the senators voted to refer the papers in question to a select committee. The President 'started up in a violent fret.' 'This defeats every purpose of my coming here,' he said. After that he dispensed with advice until a treaty was ready for ratification. This practice has generally been followed by his successors.

'Impressed with a conviction that the due administration of justice is the firmest pillar of good government,' wrote Washington in 1789, 'I have considered the first arrangement of the judicial department as essential to the happiness of our country and the stability of its political system.' The Constitution left this branch of government even more inchoate than the others. The scope of federal judicial power was defined, the mode of appointing judges was determined, and their tenure fixed during good behavior. But it remained for Congress to create and organize the inferior federal courts, to determine their procedure, and to provide a bridge between state and federal jurisdiction. All this was done by the Judiciary Act of 24 September 1789, the essential part of which is still in force. It provided for a Supreme Court consisting of a chief justice and five associate justices, for thirteen district courts, each consisting of a single federal judge, and three circuit courts, each consisting of two Supreme Court justices and the federal judge of the district where the court sat. One section of the law set the procedure for judicial review, and resolved the problem of getting cases that involve jurisdictional disputes out of state courts and into federal courts, in order that the Constitution, laws, and treaties of the United States might indeed be 'the supreme law of the land.' A final judgment in the highest court of a state where the constitutionality of a treaty or statute of the United States is questioned, 'may be re-examined and reversed or affirmed in the Supreme Court of the United States upon a writ of error.' Without this section, every state judiciary could put its own construction on the Constitution, laws, and treaties of the Union.

On 2 February 1790 the Supreme Court opened its first session, at New York. The judges assumed gowns of black and scarlet, but honored Jefferson's appeal to 'discard the monstrous wig which makes the English judges look like rats peeping through bunches of oakum.' Under Chief Justice John Jay the federal judiciary assumed its place as the keystone to the federal arch. As early as 1791, in a case involving British debts, one of the circuit courts declared invalid a law of Connecticut which infringed Article VI of the treaty of peace. There were other cases of that nature during Washington's first administration. Later, when party and sectional interests perceived the implications of it, judicial review was vehemently attacked behind the cover of state rights and democracy; but in the early years of the republic it went almost unchallenged.

Washington was unwilling to come to any vital decision without taking the advice of people in whom he had confidence. Hence arose the American cabinet. In 1793 we find some 46 meetings of the three secretaries and the Attorney-General at the President's house. These officials were already known collectively as the President's cabinet; but not until 1907 was the cabinet officially recognized as such by law.

3. ALEXANDER HAMILTON

The clause requiring the President to recommend measures to Congress reflected a desire that the executive should take the lead in legislation.

But Washington had not the temperament to do this alone. He wanted some young and energetic man to give the impulse, and attend to his relations with the legislature. Fortunately the right man, Alexander Hamilton, was in the right office, the treasury. For the primary problems of Washington's first administration were fiscal.

If the character of Washington fortified the new government, the genius of Hamilton enabled it to function successfully. As Henry Adams wrote, he 'had at once the breadth of mind to grapple with the machine of government as a whole,' the practical knowledge to find ways and means, and 'the good fortune to enjoy power when government was still plastic and capable of receiving a new impulse.'

Alexander Hamilton was 34 years old in 1789 when Washington appointed him Secretary of the Treasury.[1] No American equaled him in administrative genius; few surpassed him in maturity of judgment. As an undergraduate at King's (Columbia) College he had brilliantly defended the rights of the colonists. At 22 he had earned a place on Washington's staff. In his twenty-seventh year he indicated the fatal defects of the Confederation, wrote a remarkable treatise on public finance, and commanded a storming party at Yorktown. Admitted to the New York bar at the conclusion of peace, he quickly rose to eminence in the law. With Madison he dominated the convention at Annapolis; in the Federal Convention he played a spectacular though hardly a useful part. His contributions to *The Federalist* helped to obtain the ratification of a constitution in which he did not strongly believe. One of the greatest of Americans, he was the least American of his contemporaries: a statesman rather of the type of the younger Pitt, whose innate love of order and system was strengthened by the lack of those qualities among his fellow citizens. Intellectually disciplined himself, Hamilton was eager to play political schoolmaster. He produced bold plans and definite policies where others had cautious notions and vague principles. When Congress was thinking of what the people would say, Hamilton told them and the people what they ought to do. He had untiring energy, loved hard work, and accepted responsibility gladly.

The treasury department was the creation of Congress, not of the Constitution; and the organic act of 1789, still in force, gave it so many duties that it remained the most powerful federal department for many

1. Recent research has established that Hamilton was born in Nevis, B.W.I., in 1755, not in 1757.

years. The secretary had the duty 'to digest and prepare plans for the improvement and management of the revenue and for the support of the public credit,' as well as estimate of the same, 'to receive, keep, and disburse the monies of the United States,' to collect customs duties and excise taxes, to run the lighthouse service, set up aids to navigation, and start a land survey of the United States. Until 1792, when the post office department was established by Congress, the treasury ran that too. Other duties, such as providing medical care for seamen, were added by Congress from time to time. By the turn of the century, the treasury included over half the total federal civil service. Jealous Jeffersonians compared it with the 'swarms of officers' sent by George III 'to harass our people and eat up their substance.' [2]

Hamilton's financial policy was determined not only by his conception of current problems, but by his political philosophy. The key to that may be found in his speeches in the Federal Convention: 'Our prevailing passions are ambition and interest; and it will ever be the duty of a wise government to avail itself of those passions in order to make them subservient to the public good.' The Constitution, he believed, could only be made an instrument for good and a guarantee of order by 'increasing the number of ligaments between the government and interests of individuals.' The old families, merchant-shipowners, public creditors, and financiers — in other words the Federalists who had procured the Constitution — must be welded into a loyal governing class, by a straightforward policy favoring their interests. His conscious purpose was to use that class to strengthen the Federal Government. As Thomas Cromwell fortified the Tudor monarchy by distributing confiscated land, and as Bonaparte promoted his own fortune by the Concordat, so Hamilton would clothe the Constitution with the sword of sovereignty and the armor of loyalty, by giving the people who then controlled the country's wealth a distinct interest in its permanence. The rest, he assumed, would go along, as they always had.

In September 1789, ten days after he took office, the House of Representatives called upon Hamilton to prepare and report a plan for the 'adequate support of public credit.' The report was laid before the

2. The treasury department, according to L. D. White's *The Federalists* (1948), had, in 1801, 78 employees in the central offices, 1615 in the field services. The post office department was run by the postmaster general and seven clerks, and the local postmasters numbered about 850.

House at its next session, on 14 January 1790. Based on the tried expedients of English finance, it was worthy of an experienced minister of a long-established government.

Hamilton first laid down principles of public economy, and then adduced arguments in support of them. America must have credit for industrial development, commercial activity, and the operations of government. Her future credit would depend on how she met her present obligations. The United States debt, foreign and domestic,

> was the price of liberty. The faith of America has been repeatedly
> pledged for it. . . . Among ourselves, the most enlightened friends
> of good government are those whose expectations [of prompt pay-
> ment] are the highest. To justify and preserve their confidence; to
> promote the increasing respectability of the American name; to
> answer the calls of justice; to restore landed property to its due
> value; to furnish new resources, both to agriculture and commerce;
> to cement more closely the Union of the States; to add to their se-
> curity against foreign attack; to establish public order on the basis
> of an upright and liberal policy; these are the great and invaluable
> ends to be secured by a proper and adequate provision, at the pres-
> ent period, for the support of public credit.

Precise recommendations of ways and means followed. The foreign debt and floating domestic debt, with arrears of interest, should be funded at par, and due provision should be made by import duties and excise taxes to provide interest and amortization. The war debts of the states should be assumed by the Federal Government in order to bind their creditors to the national interest. A sinking fund should be created in order to stabilize the price of government securities and prepare for repayment of the principal. In a subsequent report of 13 December 1790, he urged the creation of a Bank of the United States, on the model of the Bank of England, but with the right to establish branches in different parts of the country.

This daring policy could not have been carried out by Hamilton alone. Every proposal was matured by the cool judgment of the President; and in House and Senate he found eager co-operation. Congress had already passed a customs tariff, with tonnage duties discriminating in favor of American shipping — both essential parts of Hamilton's system — and his other projects were altered and in some respects improved in the process of legislation. The foreign and domestic debt was funded at par, largely through loans from the same Dutch bankers who had tided us over the last years of the war. Most of the debts of the states were assumed by Congress, after a bitter struggle not unmixed with intrigue. The Bank of the United States was chartered, and its capital subscribed in four hours after the books were open. By August 1791, United States 6 per cents were selling above par in London and Amsterdam; and a wave of development and speculation had begun. 'Our public credit,' wrote Washington, 'stands on that ground, which three years ago it would have been considered as a species of madness to have foretold.'

At the end of that year Hamilton presented to Congress his Report on Manufactures. Alone of his state papers, this report fell flat; later it became an arsenal of protectionist arguments on both sides of the Atlantic. Hamilton believed that the government should intervene to strengthen the economy by fostering industry. He was addressing a country preponderantly rural, where manufactures were still in the household or handicraft stage, where only a few experimental factories existed, and not a single steam engine. Free trade, in view of the dearness of labor and the scarcity of capital, would mean very few American manufactures.

Hamilton wished the government to give protection to infant industries, in order to increase the national wealth, induce artisans to emigrate, cause machinery to be invented, and employ woman and child labor. Hamilton's aim here, as with his funding system, was 'to increase the number of ligaments between the government and the interest of individuals.' He perceived that merchants and public creditors were too narrow a basis for a national governing class. He believed that manufactures might prosper in the South as well as in the North; the report was a distinct bid for Southern support over the heads of Jefferson and Madison. The South, however, regarded protection as another tax for Northern interests. 'What! Are they going to tax our cloth too?' was the reply of Virginia farmers to a federal agent collecting data on domestic manufactures. Hamilton's argument would have been sound, nevertheless, had not Eli Whitney's invention of the cotton gin, the following year, made the culture of upland cotton a far more profitable employment for slave labor than manufactures.

All Hamilton's other plans were adopted. He turned dead paper into marketable securities and provided for their redemption by taxes that the nation was well able to bear. He set standards of honesty and punctuality that were invaluable for a people of crude financial conceptions. His youthful country, so lately on the verge of bankruptcy, acquired a credit such as few nations in Europe enjoyed. Yet Hamilton failed to achieve his ultimate end of consolidating the Union. Although he created an interested government party, his measures encountered a dangerous opposition. Instead of attaching new interests to the Federal Government, he endowed with fresh privileges those who were already attached to it.

4. THE SECTIONAL TEST

To understand wherein Hamilton failed, we have only to glance at the effect of his measures on two commonwealths: Massachusetts and Virginia. The interests of Massachusetts, second state of the Union in population, were primarily maritime: fishermen who benefited by new bounties on dried codfish; foreign traders who benefited by the low tariff; and shipyards which were favored by discriminating tonnage duties. Good business men themselves, the merchants knew the value of sound credit and honest finance. They had invested heavily in government paper that gained enormously in value by the funding system. Since Massachusetts had the largest war debt of any state, she profited most from the assumption of state debts by the Federal Government. Maritime prosperity, percolating from the market towns to the interior, raised the price of country produce and healed the wounds of Shays's Rebellion. Boston, once the home of radical mobs, was now carried by the new Federalist party. The 'Essex junto' of Massachusetts — Cabots, Higginsons, Lowells, and Jacksons, who had been to sea in their youth and viewed politics as from a quarter-deck — hailed Hamilton as their master and kept his flag flying in the Bay State long after his death. Allied with them were the solid men of Connecticut, New York City, and seaports to the southward. But Hamilton's policy did not touch the great mass of the American people, either in imagination or in pocket. It would have been otherwise had the public debt remained in the hands of its original possessors; but farmers, discharged soldiers, petty shopkeepers, and the like who held government securities representing service rendered, goods supplied, or money advanced during the war, had been forced to part with them at a ruinous discount during the hard times that followed. By 1789 the bulk of the public debt was in the hands of the 'right people' at Philadelphia, New York, Charleston, and

Boston; and the nation was taxed to pay at par, for securities purchased at a tremendous discount.

By the same economic test, a system that appeared sound and statesmanlike in Massachusetts seemed unwarranted and unconstitutional in Virginia. Although she was well provided with a long sea frontage where small, fast vessels were built, not many of the ships were owned locally. The Virginia planter knew little of business and less of finance. A gentleman inherited his debts with his plantation, why then should debt trouble the United States? Why not pay it off at market value, as a gentleman compounds with his creditors? Some Virginians had sold their government I.O.U.'s as low as 15; why should they be taxed to pay other states' debts at 100? To men such as these, in love with 'republican virtue' of the pristine Roman model and ignorant of not only public finance but of the simplest principles of accounting, Hamilton's system looked like jobbery and corruption, as in England; might not it lead to monarchy as in England? [3]

Patrick Henry now drafted a remonstrance against the federal assumption of state debts which the Virginia Assembly adopted. Therein, on 23 December 1790, were expressed the misgivings of plain folk throughout the country, as well as those of the Virginia gentry:

> In an agricultural country like this, . . . to erect, and concentrate, and perpetuate a large monied interest, is a measure which your memorialists apprehend must in the course of human events produce one or other of two evils, the prostration of agriculture at the feet of commerce, or a change in the present form of federal government, fatal to the existence of American liberty. . . . Your memorialists can find no clause in the Constitution authorizing Congress to assume the debts of the States!

A vision of civil war flashed across Hamilton's brain as he read this remonstrance. 'This is the first symptom,' he wrote, 'of a spirit which must either be killed, or will kill the Constitution of the United States.'

Virginia could hardly form an opposition party without aid from some of her citizens who were highly placed in the Federal Government. Washington, national in his outlook, and convinced that Hamilton's policy was honest and right, signed every bill based on his recommendations. Richard Henry Lee, in 1788 elected to the Senate as an Antifeder-

3. Note some statistics of federal interest payments to citizens of different states in 1795. To Georgians, $6800; to Virginians, $62,300; to Bay Staters, $309,500; to New Yorkers, $365,000.

alist, became a convert to Hamilton's views. Thomas Jefferson, Secretary of State, and James Madison, leader of the House, wavered — but found the Virginia candle stronger than the Hamiltonian star.

5. ENTER JEFFERSON

When Thomas Jefferson returned to Virginia in November 1789, on leave of absence from his diplomatic post at Paris, he was surprised to learn of his nomination to the department of state. Only Washington's urgent request persuaded him to accept. Ambition to found a political party was remote from Jefferson's mind. 'If I could not go to heaven but with a party, I would not go there at all,' he wrote. Yet his name and reputation are indissolubly bound up with the party that he was destined to lead.

Jefferson was twelve years older than Hamilton, much more experienced, and well known in Europe, where Hamilton was unknown. While the French National Assembly was in session at Versailles, the leaders met at his dinner table, and were surprised at his prudent advice; for Jefferson, a moderate democrat in a country with a democratic social basis, was not even a republican in France. Science, literature, and the fine arts attracted Jefferson as much as they had Franklin; and he was easily the first American architect of his generation. Monticello, his Virginia mansion, designed by him and superbly located on a hill-top facing the Blue Ridge, has remained to this day one of the most admirable country estates in America. The best group of collegiate buildings in the country, at nearby Charlottesville, was designed by him. Jefferson wrote upon Neo-Platonism, the pronunciation of Greek, the Anglo-Saxon language, the future of steam engines, American archaeology, and controversial theology. But there was one subject of which he was ignorant, and that was Hamilton's specialty, finance.

Fundamentally, Hamilton wished to concentrate power; Jefferson, to diffuse power. Hamilton feared anarchy and cherished order; Jefferson feared tyranny and cherished liberty. Hamilton believed republican government could only succeed if directed by a governing class; Jefferson, that republicanism was hardly worth trying without a democratic base. Hamilton took the gloomy Hobbesian view of human nature; Jefferson, a more hopeful view: the people, he believed, were the safest and most virtuous, though not always the wisest depository of power;

education would perfect their wisdom. Hamilton would diversify the American economy, encouraging shipping and creating manufactures by legislation; Jefferson would have America remain a nation of farmers. All those differences in temper, theory, and policy were bracketed by two opposed conceptions of what America was and might be. Jefferson shared the idealistic conception of the new world to which Price and Turgot had paid homage — an agrarian republic of mild laws and equal opportunity, asylum to the oppressed and beacon-light of freedom, renouncing wealth and commerce to preserve simplicity and equality. To Hamilton this was sentimental and mischievous nonsense. Having assimilated the traditions of the New York gentry into which he had married, Hamilton believed that the only choice for America lay between a stratified society on the English model and a squalid 'mobocracy.' Jefferson, who knew Europe, where every man was 'either hammer or anvil,' wished America to be as unlike it as possible; Hamilton, who had never left America, wished to make his country a new Europe.

Their appearance was as much of a contrast as their habits of mind. Hamilton's neat, lithe, dapper figure, and air of brisk energy, went with his tight, compact, disciplined brain. He could not have composed a classic state paper such as the Declaration of Independence; yet Jefferson's mind in comparison was somewhat untidy, constantly gathering new facts and making fresh syntheses. 'His whole figure has a loose, shackling air,' wrote Senator Maclay in 1790. 'I looked for gravity, but a laxity of manner seemed shed about him.' His discourse 'was loose and rambling and yet he scattered information wherever he went, and some even brilliant sentiments sparkled from him.' His sandy complexion, hazel eyes, and much-worn clothes played up this impression of careless ease; whilst Hamilton glowed with vigor and intensity. Women found him irresistible, but they did not care much for Jefferson.

Jefferson assumed his duties as Secretary of State in March 1790, when Hamilton's financial policy was almost a year old and government circles were ringing with his praises. Jefferson approved the payment of the domestic and foreign debt at par, and he secured adoption of Hamilton's program for the assumption of the state debts by making a deal by which the federal capital was transferred from New York to Philadelphia for ten years, pending removal to the new city of Washington on the Potomac. Jefferson persuaded two Virginia congressmen to vote for assumption, and Hamilton rounded up Yankee votes for the Potomac. But from the date of Hamilton's report recommending a national bank (13 December 1790), Jefferson's attitude toward him and his policy began to change. When the President called for opinions on the constitutionality of the bank bill from his cabinet, Jefferson, in a rather labored report that foreshadows the 'strict construction' school of interpretation, declared that it was unconstitutional. He contended that the congressional power 'to make all laws necessary and proper for carrying into execution' its delegated powers did not include laws merely convenient for such purposes. A national bank was not strictly necessary — the existing state bank at Philadelphia could be used for government funds. Madison agreed — a lapse from his once strong nationalism which, in the opinion of many at that time and since, reflected his hope to be senator from Virginia. Hamilton replied with a nationalistic, 'loose-construction' interpretation of the Constitution:

> Every power vested in a government is in its nature sovereign, and includes by force of the term, a right to employ all the means requisite . . . to the attainment of the ends of such power. . . . If the end be clearly comprehended within any of the specified powers, and if the measure have an obvious relation to that end, and is not forbidden by any particular provision of the Constitution, it may safely be deemed to come within the compass of the national authority.

Congress, he pointed out, had already acted upon that theory in providing lighthouses, necessary and proper to the regulation of commerce. A bank has a similar relation to the specified powers of collecting taxes, paying salaries, and servicing the debt. This opinion satisfied Washington, and he signed the bank bill; it only needed the clarifying process of Chief Justice Marshall's brain to become the great opinion of 1819, which read the doctrine of implied powers into the Constitution.

Jefferson was neither silenced nor convinced. The Federal Constitution, from his point of view and Madison's, was being perverted into a consolidated, national government. To what end? Before many months elapsed, the two Virginians thought they knew. Hamilton was simply juggling money out of the pockets of the poor into those of the rich, building up through financial favors a corrupt control of Congress; and 'the ultimate object of all this was to prepare the way for a change from the present republican form of government to that of monarchy, of which the English constitution is to be the model.' That belief remained a fixed tenet of Jefferson for the rest of his life.

Virginian suspicions were deepened by the brisk speculation in lands, bank stock, and government funds that began in 1790. No sooner did Hamilton's financial reports come out, than Northern speculators began to comb the countryside for depreciated paper. Several friends and subordinates of Hamilton's weie implicated in big transactions of a shady character. William Duer, his first assistant secretary, and Henry Knox, Secretary of War, floated the Scioto Company, a colossal speculation in Ohio land. Duer and Macomb, an associate of Hamilton's father-in-law, formed a blind pool to speculate in government bonds, an operation which landed Duer in jail and produced a financial flurry in New York. Hamilton sincerely deprecated all this, and his own hands were clean — but the speculators were very close to him.

Jefferson's opposition, then, was based on agrarian theory, reinforced by financial ignorance, sharpened by misapprehension of Hamilton's aims and by the frenzied finance of Hamilton's friends. He did not, however, create an opposition; he joined and organized the elements of opposition.

6. THE BIRTH OF PARTIES

Political parties were in bad odor at the end of the eighteenth century. No provision for party government had been made in the Constitution, although parties or factions existed in all states as in all the colonies. Ought Jefferson to resign from the cabinet, leaving Hamilton in undisputed control? Was it proper for him openly to support opposition to a policy that Washington had accepted? The President, believing that every month and year the government endured was so much gained for stability, endeavored to keep the smouldering fire from bursting forth. To Jefferson he preached charity and to Hamilton forbearance. Both were entreated to remain in office, and both consented. But Jefferson, believing Hamilton's policy to be dangerous, used every means short of open opposition to check it; while Hamilton spared no effort to thwart Jefferson, when his management of foreign affairs appeared to be mischievous. The conduct of neither man, in view of the unprecedented circumstances and the uncertain position of the cabinet, can be called dishonorable.

The first national parties developed out of contests in Congress over Hamilton's financial program, as rival national leaders sought to win a public following for their policies. Supporters of Hamilton's government faction became known as 'Federalists.' (They should not be confused with the Federalists who had supported the Constitution in the ratification struggle; divisions over Hamilton's policies did not coincide with those over ratification.) Federalism flourished in sight of salt water; in the older seaboard communities, social cleavages were more marked and the distinction between officer and crew more honored. Before Jefferson had even reached New York, Madison had raised an opposition to Hamilton's system, and for the next seven years Madison would lead the 'Republican' interest. Disagreement over the Hamiltonian program broke on sectional lines. On the proposal to establish the Bank, southern members of the House voted 19–6 against, northern members 33–1 for. In February 1791, Jefferson wrote: 'There is a vast mass of discontent gathered in the South, and how and when it will break God knows.' Yet if Madison and Jefferson hoped to build an effective opposition, they needed backing outside their section.

A very important step toward forming an opposition party was an understanding between Virginian malcontents and those of New York. The politics of New York were still divided into two factions, of which the one that interested Jefferson was led by Governor George Clinton (the son of an Irish immigrant), the Livingston clan, and Attorney-General Aaron Burr. Opposed were the 'aristocratic' party of De Lanceys, Van Rensselaers, and General Schuyler, whose daughter Alexander Hamilton had married. George Clinton had been the war governor but, having bet on the wrong horse in opposing the Federal Constitution, he obtained neither the vice-presidency, to which he felt he was entitled, nor any federal patronage in New York. Clinton wanted Virginia's support, and the Virginians needed his. On a 'botanizing excursion' that led Jefferson and Madison up the Hudson in the summer of 1791, they undoubtedly found occasion to study *Clintonia borealis* and other hardy perennials in Ulster County and the neighborhood of Albany. They also arranged to bring Madison's classmate Philip Freneau, the poet-journalist, from New York to Philadelphia to publish an opposition newspaper, the *National Gazette*, and 'unmask' the monarchical schemes of Hamilton. In 1792 Republican leaders took a significant stride toward party organization in agreeing on Clinton as their Vice-Presidential choice, and Virginia, North Carolina, and New York gave their second electoral votes to him for Vice-President, as against John Adams. From this 'botanizing excursion,' then, we may date our first political alliance, a combination that set the pattern of the Jeffersonian Republican party and of all its successors. For more than 175 years the South and the New York democracy have been the two constant components of the Democratic party.

Outside New York, the most important group of Northern Republicans was in Pennsylvania. Here were the genuine radicals and the professional politicians of the party. Pennsylvania politics had long been a matter of class and race. The mechanics were asserting themselves. Philadelphia carpenters struck for a twelve-hour day in 1791. Journeyman shoemakers organized in 1792 the first American labor union, which by strikes and boycotts managed to force up their wages almost 100 per cent in the prosperous years of neutral trade. The New York and Pennsylvania democracy became a firm ally to the Virginia aristocracy. But the Boston shipcaulkers and shoemakers, stout fellows who had done the mobbing for Sam Adams and Jim Otis in the 1770's, were won over by a younger Otis to the party that fostered trade and shipping.

President Washington, dismayed by the growing opposition to his administration, proposed to retire in 1793. Hamilton and Jefferson both urged him to accept another four-year term; the one for obvious reasons, the other because he trusted Washington to suppress 'monarchical tendencies' and believed that the opposition needed further nursing to become an effective party. The President was unanimously re-elected. He began his new term in March 1793, in the shadow of a European war which was soon destined to precipitate all floating elements of political dissension into two national parties.

Samuel Adams (1722-1803) by John Singleton Copley

Thomas Paine (1737-1809) by A. Millière after George Romney

Congress Voting Independence, July 1776, by Robert Edge Pine and Edward Savage

Surrender of Lord Cornwallis at Yorktown, October 19, 1781, by John Trumbull

Conference of the American Commissioners for the Treaty of Peace with Great Britain, 1783, by Benjamin West. (Left to right: John Jay, John Adams, Benjamin Franklin, Henry Laurens, David Hartley)

James Wilson (1742-98)

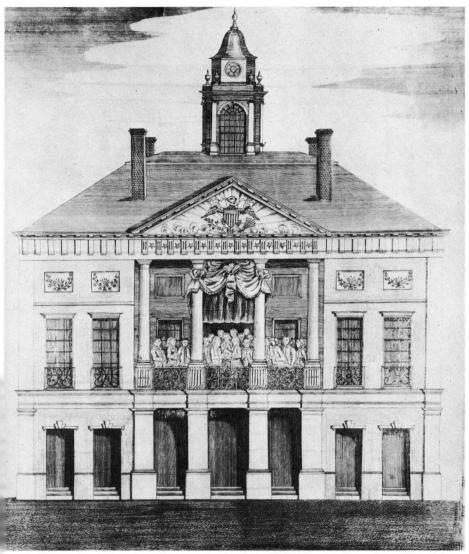

The Inauguration of George Washington as the First President of the United States at Federal Hall, New York, April 30, 1789. Engraving by Amos Doolittle (The only known contemporary representation)

Alexander Hamilton (1755-1804) by John Trumbull

XVII

Washington's Second
and Stormy Administration

1. THE FRENCH REVOLUTION AND AMERICAN POLITICS

Events of the French Revolution, beginning with the capture of the
Bastille on 14 July 1789, were followed in America with the keenest
interest, and with complete sympathy — up to a point. Few perceived
the difficulties ahead. Lafayette, Tom Paine, and the Declaration of
Rights seemed to make that revolution a continuation of ours. News
from Paris, arriving in huge stale batches by infrequent vessels, was
spread at large in the newspapers and discussed eagerly in mansions,
taverns, and the log cabins of the frontier. In December 1792 arrived
news of the previous summer — the storming of the Tuileries, the
declaration of the French Republic, and war between France and
Austria. Hard on its heels came the decree of 19 November, the 'war of
all peoples against all kings.' Enthusiasm then became hysterical. In
puritanic Boston, there was a civic feast in French style. A procession of
'citizens eight deep' escorted a roasted ox labeled 'a Peace Offering to
Liberty and Equality,' together with 1600 loaves of bread and two hogs-
heads of punch, to a spot rechristened Liberty Square.

A series of westerly gales prevented any vessel arriving from Europe
for three months. Then, in April 1793, came news that brought war to
the edge of the three-mile limit, and made the French Revolution an
issue in American politics. France had declared war on Great Britain

and Spain; the king had been guillotined; the Girondin party was in power; and Citizen Genet was coming over as minister plenipotentiary of the French Republic.

America was still, formally, an ally of France. In the treaty of 1778 the United States had guaranteed French possession of her West Indian islands. As the British navy was certain to attack them, it was difficult to see how America could honorably refuse to defend them, if France demanded it. But how to defend them without a navy?

On 18 April 1793 the cabinet met at Philadelphia. Washington, though dismayed at the turn of events, still wished the French well, but thought of his own country first. Hamilton loathed the French Revolution. It was disconcerting, just when there seemed some hope of America's settling down, to have America's favorite nation blow up and invite everyone else to follow suit! He wished to declare the treaty of 1778 in suspense now that the king was dead, declare American neutrality, and reject the French minister. Jefferson, as we might expect, considered the French Revolution 'the most sacred cause that ever man was engaged in,' but was equally anxious to keep America out of the war. To an immediate declaration of neutrality he was opposed, partly on constitutional grounds, but mainly because he regarded American neutrality, without some equivalent, as a free gift to England that she would receive only with contempt. To Washington such bargaining seemed unworthy of a self-respecting nation. Neutrality must be declared on its merits, not as part of a bargain. Accordingly, on 22 April 1793, the President issued his neutrality proclamation. It declared the disposition of the United States' to pursue a conduct friendly and impartial toward the belligerent powers,' and warned citizens that 'aiding or abetting hostilities,' or unneutral acts committed within the country, would render them liable to prosecution in the federal courts.

In the meantime Citizen Genet, quaintest of the many curious diplomatists sent by European governments to the United States, had landed at Charleston. Genet's instructions called upon him to use the United States as a base for privateering; and before presenting his credentials to Jefferson he undertook to fit out privateers against British commerce. He was instructed to recruit forces for the conquest of Florida and Louisiana, 'and perhaps add to the American constellation the fair star of Canada.' Several land speculators like George Rogers Clark, who had some dubious claims to Western land still held by Spain, showed great enthusiasm for war with that country. To them Genet distributed military commissions, forming the nucleus of an *Armée du Mississippi* and an *Armée des Florides*. In other words, France expected the same sort of aid from her sister republic that she herself had given, aid which was as certain to embroil the giver with Britain. But Hamilton refused to provide Genet with funds, in the shape of advance installments of the debt to France. So, for want of pay and subsistence, the volunteers had to return empty-handed to their log cabins. Jefferson welcomed the arrival of Genet as a sort of refresher for the opposition party, yet he enforced Washington's neutrality policy with loyal and even-handed justice. He insisted on a strict construction of French treaty privileges and lectured the minister on the law of nations.

When Genet found he could do nothing with the government, he conceived the brilliant notion of turning it out. His official notes became inconceivably truculent. In Charleston he had presided at the birth of a local Jacobin club, whose legitimacy was recognized by the parent organization at Paris; and his progress through the states was marked by similar progeny of ill portent. After a few weeks of him, Jefferson concluded that Genet was likely to become the Jonah of the Jeffersonian party: 'He will sink the Republican interest, if they do not abandon him.' In August 1793 the cabinet unanimously voted to request his recall. Robespierre gladly consented, and in return asked for the recall of Gouverneur Morris, whose intrigues at Paris had been almost as mischievous as Genet's in Philadelphia. Early in 1794 a new French minister arrived in the United States, with an order for his predecessor's arrest. Instead of returning to feed the guillotine, Genet married the daughter of Governor Clinton, and settled down to the life of a country gentleman on the Hudson.

That year, 1794, witnessed a marked acceleration in the trend toward the emergence of two national parties, a development which almost everyone viewed with dismay. Each party thought the other seditious, and even treasonable, because in a well-ordered, harmonious society there could be no place for a party system. The nation was alarmed at party feeling so intense that congressmen would not live in the same boarding house with a member of the opposite party, and a Republican had to take care not to stop at a Federal tavern. Party spirit, recalled a New Hampshire leader, 'embittered the sweets of social life, & hazarded the rights of the nation.' Not for a generation would the country recognize that parties were a medium for the expression of the popular will on national issues, that they encouraged voters to make use of the franchise, and that they enabled groups out of power to channelize their grievances.

Party divisions sharpened in Congress before they did in the states. In the 1792 election, party organization was still so rudimentary that only New York and Pennsylvania offered slates of candidates. But in Congress, party discipline was much more marked. In January 1793 the Federalist Fisher Ames wrote: 'Virginia moves in a solid column, and the discipline of the party is as severe as the Prussian. Dissenters are not spared. Madison is become a desperate party leader.' At the end of 1793, Jefferson retired, pleased to be rid of the 'hated occupations of politics,' and Madison, 'the great man of the party,' now took full responsibility for leading Republican opposition. In 1794, John Taylor of Virginia observed: 'The existence of two parties in Congress, is apparent. The fact is disclosed almost upon every important question. Whether the subject be foreign or domestic — relative to war or peace — navigation or commerce — the magnetism of opposite views draws them wide as the poles asunder.'

By 1794, party warfare, which had originated over the domestic problem of Hamiltonian finance, was coming increasingly to center on foreign affairs. European issues reached America without shadings, all black and white. Thus the French Revolution seemed to some a clear-cut contest between monarchy and republicanism, oppression and liberty, autocracy and democracy; to others, simply a new breaking-out of the eternal strife between anarchy and order, atheism and religion, poverty and property. The former joined the Republican party; the latter, the Federalist. In reverse order to expectation, democratic New England and the Eastern seaports, rivals to Liverpool and Bristol, became the headquarters of pro-British Federalists; whilst the landed interest, particularly in slave-holding communities, became gallomaniacs. For in New England the clergy had been worrying over the younger generation: students who preferred reading Voltaire and Gibbon to studying Jonathan Edwards and Rollin. Tom Paine's *Age of Reason* appeared in 1794. That scurrilous arraignment of the Bible sent liberal Christians hotfoot to the standard of reaction, eager for anything to exclude 'French infidelity.' Paine himself, by a nasty attack on Washington the next year, completely identified Jeffersonianism with Jacobinism in the mind of the average New Englander and Middle-State Presbyterian.

To the merchant shipowners of New England, New York, Philadelphia, Baltimore, and Charleston, British capital was an indispensable instrument of credit; and commerce with Britain the first condition of American prosperity. Their overseas trade was largely financed by London merchant-bankers; and after the French armies had sucked Amsterdam dry, public loans could be obtained nowhere else. Like Hamilton, they did not care to risk a quarrel with the power that could give or withhold. British spoliations on neutral trade might annoy American shipowners; but they soon discovered that British sea-power gave compensation, while French sea-power did not. Although the Acts of Trade and Navigation were technically in force in the West Indies, they were not strictly enforced after 1792. During the entire period of the French war, as in 1914–17 and 1939–41, American shipowners could make immense profits by submitting to British sea-power when they could not evade it; whilst French attacks on neutral commerce, like those of the German submarines, tended to destroy the only traffic that the British navy permitted.

Thus it came about that great Virginia planters of English race and tradition — men like John Randolph of Roanoke who would wear no boots unless made in London and read no Bible printed outside Oxford, men whose throats would have been the first cut and whose lands the first divided if Jacobinism had really infected America — screamed for the Rights of Man and railed at Britain. Thus it came about that Boston Unitarians, like William Ellery Channing, whose creed was more subversive of traditional Christianity than the crude outbursts of the Paris commune, rang the tocsin against French impiety and anarchy.

Around these two poles American opinion crystallized in 1793–95. You were either for the Republicans and France, or for the Federalists and Britain — there could be no compromise. Emotion for a principle, and for the kind of country you wanted America to be, joined interest and policy. It was not Britain and France corrupting American opinion, but American merchants and farmers stretching out to Europe for support. As a French observer wrote, 'Each party will use foreign influence as it needs, to dominate.'

2. NEUTRAL RIGHTS, THE WEST, AND JAY'S TREATY

The follies of Genet, and his disgrace, cooled American ardor for France. Yet no sooner had he been disposed of than fresh, dry timber was thrown on the hot embers of Anglo-American relations. By March 1794 the frontier and commercial controversies had become roaring furnaces.

Lord Grenville informed the American minister in London, near the end of 1793, that the British government proposed to hold the North-west posts indefinitely, abandoning all pretense that they would be evacuated when the United States gave full satisfaction for the debts. Washington's patience, Jefferson's forbearance, and Hamilton's long, uphill pull toward good understanding had apparently come to naught. What was left but war?

The other burning issue of Atlantic commerce was flaring a like signal. When England is at war, and her navy is measuring the extent of neutral rights, neutral commerce with her enemy is apt to thin out. The weaker naval powers had long endeavored to build up a positive law and neutral rights, with the doctrines of effective blockade, limited contraband, and 'free ships make free goods': doctrines which publicists long labored to write into law, only to see them go smash in 1914. The United States had subscribed to these principles in her treaties with Holland, France, and Prussia. As a neutral in the war of the French Revolution, she hoped to benefit by them. But a British order in council of unprecedented severity was issued on 6 November 1793. Among other things, it directed the detention and adjudication of all ships laden with French colonial produce, whether French or neutral property, and all vessels carrying provisions to the French colonies.

The Caribbean was swarming with Yankee schooners and brigs when the order reached naval officers on that station. It was executed in a manner that reflected the navy's sharp hunger for prize-money, and the low salaries of admiralty judges in the West Indies. If a Maine schooner laden with lumber and salt fish ventured into the harbor of St. George's, Bermuda, she would be boarded by a gang of ruffians, stripped of her rudder and sails, her seamen consigned to a calaboose or impressed into the Royal Navy, and the vessel libeled in His Majesty's court of vice-admiralty. The burden of proof that the cargo was not somehow tainted by French association was placed upon the Yankee skipper. Condemnation was certain.

News of these captures brought consternation to the American trading community, which was the backbone of Hamilton's party. Hamilton himself was exasperated. Congress began war preparations, and clapped an embargo on the seaports. In the midst of the crisis, news leaked into the American papers of a truculent speech by Governor Lord Dorchester of Canada to an Indian delegation, encouraging them to look for the king's aid shortly in driving the 'long knives' across the Ohio for good and all.

In Congress the Republican party was not eager for war, but favored Jefferson's and Madison's favorite plan of commercial retaliation, which would surely have led to war, as it did when Jefferson, Madison, and Franklin D. Roosevelt tried it. Matters were prevented from going further by a timely gesture from the British government — revocation of the order in council under color of which the commerce spoliations had been perpetrated. This information was communicated to Congress on 4 April 1794; and on the 16th, Washington nominated Chief Justice Jay as envoy extraordinary to Great Britain. 'My objects are, to prevent a war,' Washington wrote the Secretary of State, 'if justice can be obtained by fair and strong representations . . . of the injuries which this country has sustained from Great Britain in various ways,' injuries which 'leave very unfavorable impressions of their friendship, and little to expect from their justice.' Jay left immediately for London. Through the influence of the new French minister with the Republicans, the embargo was allowed to lapse. An immense fleet of provision ships then sailed from the Chesapeake and, while its French escort was fighting Admiral Lord Howe's fleet on 1 June, slipped safely into Brest, relieving the famine that accompanied the reign of terror.

A main object of Jay's mission was to obtain British evacuation of the Northwest posts. Lieutenant-Governor Simcoe of Upper Canada in 1793 encouraged the Indians of the Northwest to hold out against the United States, and established a new garrison on American soil at the rapids of the Maumee river, about a hundred miles southwest of Detroit.

The United States Army, reorganized after St. Clair's defeat and recruited to 2000 men, was now placed under the command of Major General Anthony Wayne. In the fall of 1793 he established winter quarters at the site of Greenville, Ohio. 'Mad Anthony,' as Wayne had been called after his gallant storming of Stony Point in 1779, had a cool head. An admirable disciplinarian, he trained his troops in the technique of forest warfare, and the Indians gave them plenty of practice. Several hundred Kentucky mounted riflemen, a hard-bitten lot, joined him in the spring of 1794. The lieutenant-governor of Upper Canada bent all his energy to mobilizing the Indians, despite cautious counsels from the home government. Wampum belts, 'speeches,' even Yankee scalps obtained in early skirmishes, were sent out by forest trails, in order to induce all the braves to join. Provisions, blankets, muskets, powder and ball, and vermilion warpaint were dispensed from Canadian government depots and arsenals to the enemies of a country with which His Britannic Majesty was at peace.

When the oak leaves were fully out and nature's ambush was complete, the Indians attacked Wayne's fort. After beating them off, Wayne took the offensive. Advancing cautiously through the primeval hardwood, protected by a screen of picked scouts, he debouched into the Erie plain and found himself in the granary of the Indians. The margins of the Maumee and the Auglaize were one continuous village, with log cabins, fruit trees, and fields of rustling corn extending to the forest edge. In the midst of these savage gardens Wayne built Fort Defiance, a stockade with block-house bastions. There he offered peace once more, and once more it was rejected. The Indians retreated to the vicinity of the new British fort and took cover behind a natural stockade of fallen trees. There were 1500 to 2000 of them: Miamis under Little Turtle who had ambushed St. Clair in 1791, Black Wolf with his Shawnee, the 'three fires' of the Ottawa, Chippewa, and Pottawatomi under Blue Jacket, Sauk, and Fox from Lake Superior, a few Iroquois diehards, and 70 white Canadian rangers under an old loyalist captain. On 20 August 1794 Wayne marched forth to meet them. A squadron of dragoons charged on the Indians' left flank. Both the American captains were picked off, but a lieutenant took command, and the troopers, jumping their game little horses over the fallen timber as in a steeplechase, burst in on the redskins and gave them cold steel. On their front the infantry and riflemen poured in a volley of hot stuff, and charged with fixed bayonets before the Indians had time to reload. In forty minutes it was all over.

This 'Battle of the Fallen Timbers' scattered the distant tribesmen and enabled Wayne to destroy the Indian villages and lay waste their cornfields. Fort Wayne was built at the forks of the Maumee, and the legion returned to Greenville, to await envoys of peace.

On 16 June 1795 there were enough sachems and warriors assembled for Wayne to open the peace conference. Imagine a broad clearing in the forest; the great bark-roofed council house, open at the sides and with a council fire in the middle; on one side of the fire a semicircle of war-chiefs, warriors, and sachems, splendid in their gaudy match-coats, quills, and feathers; on the other General Wayne and his lean officers; a ring of lounging soldiers beyond; and a background of hickory, oak, and buckeye trees in the green of early summer. The calumet of peace is passed around, and Wayne opens the conference in the name of the 'Fifteen Fires of America.'

> I take you all by the hand as brothers, assembled for the good work of peace. . . . The Great Spirit has favored us with a clear sky and refreshing breeze. . . .
> The heavens are bright, the roads are open; we will rest in peace and love; and wait the arrival of our brothers. In the interim, we will have a little drink, and wash the dust out of our throats. We will, on this happy occasion, be merry, without however passing the bounds of temperance and sobriety.

A little drink it had to be, for Greenville was 70 miles from the nearest frontier distillery, and fresh delegations of thirsty redskins came pouring in until warriors and sachems, representing all the tribes between the Great Lakes, the Mississippi, and the Ohio, were assembled to the number of 1130. The tedious conferences went on through interpreters.

On 20 July the articles were read, and the assembled warriors gave the 'Yo-ha!' of assent. Three days passed in eating and drinking while the treaty was engrossed; and on 3 August 1795 the General signed his name, and the chieftains their marks, to the Treaty of Greenville. By this treaty the Indians ceded the southeastern corner of the Northwest territory, together with sixteen enclaves such as Vincennes, Detroit, and the site of Chicago, in return for annuities to the value of some $10,000. So ended almost twenty years of fighting — the last phase of the War of Independence. Peace came to the border from the Genesee country of New York to the Mississippi. Pioneers began to swarm up the valleys of the Scioto and the Muskingum, and in ten years' time their insatiable greed for land made the Treaty of Greenville a mere scrap of paper.

This Battle of the Fallen Timbers occurred when John Jay was negotiating in London. Jay's treaty, signed in London on 19 November 1794, obtained the prime objects of the mission — a promise to evacuate the Northwest posts by 1796, and a limited right of American vessels to trade with the British West Indies. It preserved the peace, secured America's territorial integrity, and established a basis for Western expansion. Other pending questions were referred to mixed commissions, in accordance with which a beginning was made of settling the Maine-New Brunswick boundary. Some £600,000 was eventually paid by the United States in satisfaction of pre-war debts, and £1,317,000 by Great Britain for illegal captures of American ships.

Yet, when the terms of this treaty were printed in Philadelphia (March 1795) a howl of rage went up from all parts of the United States, especially from the West, that Jay had sold them down-river. It is difficult now to understand why, unless the treaty provided an emotional outlet for varied discontents. Jay had refused even to discuss the proposed Indian satellite state. He resisted a British demand to rectify the frontier in the Northwest so as to give Canada a corridor to the site of St. Paul; this would eventually have made latitude 45° N instead of 49° N the international boundary in the West. He declined to make any concessions on the navigation of the Mississippi. He procured the desired evacuation of the posts. A good part of the opposition to the treaty was simply the French 'party line' being repeated by Republican newspapers, for it prevented a war on which the French government was counting. A bare two-thirds majority for the treaty was obtained in the Senate, but the House of Representatives threatened to nullify it by withholding supply for the mixed commissions.

The fight over appropriations for the Jay Treaty in the House marked the crystallization of the party system. The Federalist administration appealed to the more substantial classes to bring pressure on their representatives, and petitions from merchants in support of the treaty had a telling effect. Washington's popularity also served the Federalists well. A member of the Virginia legislature cried: 'Gracious heaven, is this the return which you are about to make to a man who has dedicated the whole life to your service?' Madison conceded: 'The name of the President is everywhere used with the most wonderful success by the treaty partisans.' By the narrow vote of 51–48, the House agreed to carry out the treaty, and Michilimackinac, the last frontier post, was evacuated on 2 October 1796, thirteen years after the treaty of peace.

Jay's treaty also came as a clearing breeze to Spanish-American relations, which were badly befogged in 1795. The governor of Spanish Louisiana continued angling in Western waters with golden bait. He had established a new fort on American territory, at Chickasaw Bluffs (Memphis), and he persuaded the Creek and Cherokee to denounce their treaties with the United States. Spain had made her peace with France before Jay's treaty came out, and was preparing to enter the French system of alliances. Recognizing that Western intrigues had failed, Spain deemed it prudent to meet the United States halfway, rather than risk losing all Louisiana to American filibusters. In the Treaty of San Lorenzo (27 October 1795), known as Pinckney's Treaty after the American minister, His Catholic Majesty granted the right to navigate the lower Mississippi, as well as the 'right of deposit' at New Orleans so ardently desired by the West; and recognized the thirty-first parallel to the Chattahoochee as the southern boundary of the United States.

In 1798, after exhausting all its rich resources in procrastination, the Spanish government evacuated the posts it held north of lat. 31°. Thus, fifteen years in all elapsed before the United States obtained control of her own territories from European powers. That she did so then was due to Washington's foreign policy as much as to 'Mad Anthony's' troopers.

3. THE WHISKEY REBELLION

In the very week that Wayne crushed the Indians, President Washington was calling out 15,000 militia to put down pale-faced rebels in western Pennsylvania. This Whiskey Rebellion, as it was humorously named, tested the ability of the Federal Government to enforce federal law. Hamilton's Excise Act of 1791 appeared as unjust and tyrannical to the Westerners as had the Stamp Act to the Colonists. Beyond the mountains distillation was the only practical method to dispose of surplus corn, unless you had gold to grease the palms of Spanish officials down-river. Whiskey also did duty as currency — one-gallon jugs of 'moonshine' passing for a quarter in every store on the western slope of the Alleghenies. Modifications of the excise law obtained some measure of compliance in the Southern mountains. Western Pennsylvania, however, was largely peopled by Scots-Irish. They may not have read Robbie Burns's ballad, but they agreed with it:

> The deil's awa, the deil's awa,
> The deil's awa wi' th' Exciseman,
> He's danc'd awa, he's danc'd awa,
> He's danc'd awa wi' th' Exciseman.

Covenants were formed never to pay the hated tax; there were masked night-riders, and whippings and other methods of terrorism, familiar even yet in parts of the United States. In 1794, when a federal marshal appeared at Pittsburgh with a bundle of writs against delinquent distillers, he and the nearest exciseman were roughly handled. Led by two backwoods firebrands named Bradford and Husband (the latter a survivor of the North Carolina 'Regulators'), the people held mass meetings, appointed a committee of public safety, and called out the militia of the four western counties to protect the spirituous liberties of the people. But for the moderating influence of Albert Gallatin, an embryo statesman of the frontier, there would probably have been a declaration of independence. The governor of Pennsylvania, an old Antifederalist, minimized the affair and long refused to lend the aid of state forces.

It was the essence of the Federal Constitution that the Federal Government should have a compulsive operation on individuals. Coercion by law was preferred to coercion by arms; but to deal with forcible obstruction of judicial process, Congress was given power 'to provide for calling forth the militia to execute the laws of the Union.' By law, Congress had authorized the President to call out state militia in such contingency. It remained to be seen whether he would dare exercise the authority and whether the militia would obey. Washington, on Hamilton's urgent plea, decided to make a test case of the Pennsylvania defiance of federal law.

Everything worked smoothly. The militia of four states, including Pennsylvania, turned out upon the President's proclamation. They were given a good, stiff hike across the Alleghenies in the glorious Indian summer. The more violent leaders of the rebels fled, and the covenanters promptly caved in. Two ringleaders, who were apprehended and convicted of treason, were pardoned by the President. Henceforth, persons and interests who had a grievance against the law, had to carry their state, and evolve the doctrine of state rights as a shelter against federal authority.

4. PUBLIC LAND ACT OF 1796

Now that Jay's treaty and Wayne's victory had caused the gates of the frontier to swing open, it was time to decide how land ceded by the Indians should be disposed of. An American colonial policy had been determined once and for all by the Northwest Ordinance of 1787, but the land policy blocked out in the Ordinance of 1785 was not binding on the Federal Government. Owing to the attitude of the Northwest Indians, there had been little settlement north of the Ohio before 1796; but now that a good part of that territory was released, it was time to decide matters of land disposal.

Every feature of American society that men of Hamilton's stamp disliked — political democracy, rude plenty, an undiversified economic system — depended on an ample supply of cheap land for settlers. Albert Gallatin, in the debate on the Land Bill of 1796, said that

> if the cause of the happiness of this country was examined into, it would be found to arise as much from the great plenty of land in proportion to the inhabitants . . . as from the wisdom of their political institutions.

Forty-three years later Lord Durham in his report on Canada asserted 'that the amazing prosperity of the United States is less owing to their form of government, than to the unlimited supply of fertile land, which maintains succeeding generations in an undiminishing affluence of fertile soil.'

Yet the converse is also true; independence and self-government were necessary conditions of opening the public domain to the people. The public land system of Canada was a fair example of what the American pioneer would have had imposed upon him if the War of Independence had turned out differently. In order to foster loyalty on the basis of privilege, Lord Dorchester produced a bureaucratic travesty of the New England township system, with extensive crown and clergy reserves, and enormous free grants to loyalists and officials. During the administration of one Canadian governor, almost a million and a half acres were granted to 60 individuals; yet would-be settlers found it almost impossible to obtain land at a reasonable price.

Some such device for keeping the poor from the land would have been adopted in the United States if men like Hamilton, Jay, and Morris had determined the public land policy. Many influential Easterners, like Senator Bingham of Pennsylvania and General Knox, owned vast tracts in Maine, which they wished to dispose of before throwing open the West. Hamilton's ideas on the subject were determined by fiscal considerations and his desire to populate more thickly the Eastern states, before a general migration to the West. With labor running off to the backwoods, how could you build up manufactures? Washington, however, owned Western land and was Western-minded. In 1784 he proposed that the public domain be sold at a sufficient price to deter speculators, but to accommodate the more solid sort of settler.

If any member of Congress now wished ill to the West he did not dare avow it. William Smith of South Carolina, who reported the land bill, said that the committee had two objects in view: 'to raise revenue, and to sell land in such lots as would be most convenient for settlers.' Madison, who thought the main thing was 'to fill the treasury as soon as possible,' was for throwing the whole public domain on the market at once, in township lots, to pay off the national debt. Gallatin pointed out that this wholesale disposal would place the public domain in the hands of speculators. He proposed to encourage a gradual alienation to actual settlers, at a fixed price, in lots of 100 to 600 acres.

A few members believed the vital question to be not how fast the West could be settled, but the sort of West we would have when it was settled. American colonial experience had proven that land tenure and distribution deeply affected the nature of society. In the debates of 1796 Robert Goodloe Harper, from the South Carolina piedmont, insisted that the first object of a national land policy should be 'to secure order and good government' in the newly settled regions. William Findlay, a Pennsylvania democrat of Irish birth, pointed out that dispersion had caused much unhappiness on the frontier, whilst compact settlement enabled pioneers to obtain good schools and social intercourse. He did not think it practicable to reproduce the New England system absolutely, 'but he would have it approached to,' as in the Ordinance of 1785.

These arguments prevailed. In the Public Land Act of 1796 the township, six miles square, surveyed in compact 'ranges' or columns, starting on the western boundary of Pennsylvania, became the standard unit of public land, divided into thirty-six sections of one square mile (640 acres) each, no land to be surveyed prior to extinguishing the Indian title of occupancy, or placed on sale until surveyed. This system made for simplicity, cheapness, and a clear title, and set the pattern of the American West. Ranges, townships, and sections marched across the continent with the pioneer, imposing their rigid rectangles on forest, plain, and mountain.

The question of whether to sell the land in large plots or small was determined by a compromise, which one member called a wholesale-and-retail method. The Act of 1796 required alternate townships to be sold in blocks of eight sections each, intervening townships in single sections of 640 acres each. Government land offices were established at Philadelphia for the sale of the large lots, which were expected to appeal to moneyed men, and at Pittsburgh and Cincinnati for the convenience of actual settlers who wanted no more than one section. Both large and small lots were sold at public auction for the minimum price of two dollars an acre and one year's credit. Salt springs were reserved in order to prevent the monopolizing of that frontier necessity. The smallest unit, 640 acres, turned out to be too large and the minimum price too high for the ordinary pioneer, who at that time could buy good land from the states in Maine, New York, and the Western Reserve, for as little as 50 cents an acre. Only 50,000 acres of the national domain had been sold by 1800. Congress then lowered the unit of sale in certain areas to 320 acres (in 1804 to 160 acres), and gave four years' credit. As thus amended the 1796 law was copied for every new acquisition from the Indians in the Northwest Territory until 1820.[1] By that time eighteen federal land offices were open for sales to settlers. When Ohio, the first 'public land state,' was admitted in 1803, the Federal Government adopted the precedent of retaining title to all ungranted land within the state boundaries, excepting a donation of one section in each township to a state fund for education.

Thus, the Act of 1796, drafted by ordinary members of an average Congress, set the rhythm of American development for a century to come.

1. In 1803 it was extended to the remainder of the Mississippi Territory that was not covered by state grants; and two years later the system of survey was extended to the Louisiana purchase, although the complicated French and Spanish grants prevented the sale of government land west of the Mississippi until twelve years more had elapsed.

Until 1825 the Northwest frontier advanced not so much by settlers as by Daniel Boone, by pioneers of the Kentucky type, together with adventurous youths from New England and New York. The pioneers, inured to hardship and danger, seldom acquired a land title, and remained in one spot only long enough to kill off the game, or exhaust their clearings by crude cropping with rude implements. After large plantations and slave labor became established in Kentucky, the hardened pioneer moved southwest or northwest as a stage in his journey to Texas and the Pacific. 'No people are so adapted to encounter the fatigues and privations of the wilderness; none form such efficient pioneers of civilization,' said an English observer. They acted as a shock battalion for the permanent settlers who followed and provided the trained scouts and sharpshooters for Indian wars. Their wild, free life gave America much of its old-time gusto and savor; and if they left a taint of lawlessness and violence, they also carried forward the robust tradition of individual prowess which has created America's favorite 'image' of herself.

5. PATER PATRIAE

Organization of a government, establishment of national credit, fostering of maritime commerce, recovery of territory withheld under the Confederation, the crushing of red rebels and white, the establishment of a land policy which set the rhythm of American society, and the preservation of peace: these were the notable achievements of the two administrations of President Washington. By refusing to run for a third term he established the two-term tradition in national politics, and on 17 September 1796, he summed up his political experience in a farewell address to his countrymen.

For a paper addressed to a people in a particular stage of their development, its permanent value is surprisingly great. An eloquent plea for union is followed by a pointed exposition of disruptive tendencies: the politician's device of misrepresenting 'the opinions and aims of other districts' in order to acquire influence within his own; the forming of combinations to override or control the constituted authorities; the 'baneful effects of the spirit of party,' a spirit 'having its root in the strongest passions of the human mind.' As to foreign policy:

Observe good faith and justice towards all nations; cultivate peace and harmony with all. . . . In the execution of such a plan nothing is more essential than that permanent, inveterate antipathies against particular nations and passionate attachments for others should be excluded; and that in place of them just and amicable feelings towards all should be cultivated. The Nation which indulges towards another an habitual hatred or an habitual fondness is in some degree a slave.

Washington's famous doctrine of isolation is contained in the following sentences:

Europe has a set of primary interests, which to us have none, or a very remote relation. — Hence she must be engaged in frequent controversies, the causes of which are essentially foreign to our concerns. Hence therefore it must be unwise in us to implicate ourselves, by artificial ties in the ordinary vicissitudes of her politics, or the ordinary combinations and collisions of her friendships or enmities. Our detached and distant situation invites us to pursue a different course. . . . 'Tis our true policy to steer clear of permanent alliances, with any portion of the foreign world. . . . Taking care always to keep ourselves, by suitable establishments, on a respectable defensive posture, we may safely trust to temporary alliances for extraordinary emergencies.

The Farewell Address fell on deaf ears in a Europe ringing with the exploits of a new hero, Bonaparte. But there it was written, for whosoever cared to read, that a new power considered herself outside the European system.

Washington's valedictory, which Hamilton had played an important part in drafting, served as a Federalist campaign document in 1796. For all his abhorrence of parties, Washington was a shrewd political strategist, and the passages in the Address on foreign affairs were aimed at the Republicans' desire to base foreign policy on the French alliance. To succeed Washington, the Federalists informally settled on Vice-President John Adams. Early in 1796, Adams wrote to his wife: 'I am, as you say, quite a favorite. I am to dine again today. I am heir apparent you know, and a succession is soon to take place.' Hamilton sowed the seeds for later trouble by maneuvering to win the presidency for Thomas Pinckney of South Carolina, generally understood to be the Federalist choice for Vice-President.

The national leaders of the Republican party, centered in Congress, nominated Thomas Jefferson as their standard bearer, without consulting him. Jefferson reported: 'My name . . . was again brought forward, without concert or expectation on my part; (on my salvation I declare it.)' Most of the Republicans' second choice votes went to Aaron Burr, but party lines were still so slack that ballots for the second place were widely scattered; Virginia, for example, gave Burr one vote, George Clinton 3, and Sam Adams 15. Republicans, many of whom wore the tricolored cockade, sought to rally pro-French sentiment in a campaign in which the French ministry actively intervened. The result was a narrow Federalist victory, with the Federalists strong in the Northeast and the Republicans in the South. Adams obtained the Presidency with 71 votes in the electoral college. Jefferson's 68 votes made him Vice-President by the curious method of choice that prevailed prior to the adoption of Amendment XII. After the election, Federalists rejoiced that the 'French party is fallen.' How wrong they were!

'I now compare myself,' wrote Washington on 2 March 1797, 'to the wearied traveler who seeks a resting place, and is bending his body to lean thereon. But to be suffered to do *this* in peace is too much to be endured by *some*.' During his last year in office the President was assailed with a virulence such as few of his successors have suffered. Jefferson, in a private letter which found its way into print, referred to a certain 'Samson in the field and Solomon in the Council' whose head had been 'shorn by the harlot England' — obviously the President! The Philadelphia *Aurora,* on the morrow of Washington's retirement, proclaimed that 'this day ought to be a Jubilee in the United States . . . for the man who is the source of all the misfortunes of our country, is this day reduced to a level with his fellow citizens.'

A generation passed before Washington's services in time of peace were adequately appreciated in his own country; and as his personality has faded into legend, it becomes clothed in army uniform. Washington's unique place in history rests not only on his leadership in war and his influence in organizing the Federal Government; not merely on his integrity, good judgment, and magnanimity, but also on his courageous stand for peace when his countrymen were clamoring to embark on another unnecessary war with England. This quiet, plain-speaking gentleman of Virginia glimpsed a truth hidden from his more talented contemporaries: that the means by which a nation advances are as important as the ends which it pursues.

XVIII

John Adams's Administration

1. FRENCH POLICY AND FEDERALIST APPREHENSIONS

Washington left the country one final legacy: an example of the peaceful transfer of power in a new nation. After the inauguration of John Adams on 4 March 1797, a South Carolinian wrote: 'The change of the Executive here has been wrought with a facility and a calm which has astonished even those of us who always augured well of the government and the general good sense of our citizens. The machine has worked without a creak. On the 4th of March John Adams was quietly sworn into office, George Washington attending as a private citizen. A few days after he went quietly home to Mt. Vernon; his successor as quietly took his place.' This peaceful transition contrasted especially favorably with the turbulent changes in contemporary France.

John Adams found his situation more difficult than Washington had in 1794. Jay's treaty had embroiled the United States with a more powerful and aggressive France than the country that sent Genet to America. All political leaders friendly to the United States had been guillotined or were now in exile. France was under a five-headed executive known as the Directory, which with some justice, regarded Jay's treaty as evidence of an Anglo-American entente; for by accepting the British view of neutral rights, the United States had to order French privateers out of her harbors and to permit the British to capture provision ships destined for France. James Monroe, who had been received as American minister under an earlier regime with enthusiastic speeches and fraternal embraces, lost his balance and his usefulness under these new circumstances, and was recalled by Washington in 1796.

Party feeling in the United States was so bitter that several followers of Jefferson urged the French minister at Philadelphia to advise his government to retaliate against American shipping — largely owned by Federalists. The Directory, which needed no such urging, loosed its corsairs against the American merchant fleet. The ensuing French spoliations on commerce made those of Britain in 1793–94 seem mild by comparison. Red-bonneted ruffians who ruled the French West Indies made an open traffic of letters of marque. Even American provision ships sent to the French islands by French consuls were taken and condemned. In June 1797 the Secretary of State reported that over 300 American vessels had been captured under color of French authority.

The Directory refused to receive Charles Cotesworth Pinckney, Monroe's successor at Paris, and its official language toward the United States became insolent and provocative. President Adams declared that he would submit to no further indignities, but hoped to maintain Washington's policy of neutrality. Following the Jay precedent, he made another effort to obtain justice through diplomacy. In order to assure the Republicans that he was not seeking a quarrel, Adams appointed Elbridge Gerry, *persona grata* to them and to France; and in order to keep Gerry out of mischief, John Marshall and Pinckney were joined with him in the mission. The first year of Adams's administration passed before news arrived from the three ambassadors.

In the meantime, party cleavage deepened. When Jefferson arrived in Philadelphia to take the oath of office as Vice-President in March 1797, he noted that party animosity was so intense that 'men who have been intimate all their lives, cross the streets to avoid meeting, and turn their heads another way, lest they should be obliged to touch their hats.'

Jefferson, who had played a relatively passive role in party contests since 1794, now took over the reins of party leadership from Madison and Gallatin. Fearing that Adams intended war with France, he used his influence in Congress to frustrate the President. By the summer of 1797, William Vans Murray, about to go to Europe as minister to the Netherlands, was complaining that the Vice-President dazzled country congressmen at 'his philosophizing dinners, in which the almost treasonable theories of universal benevolence and philanthropy . . . are . . . connected, as they are unfolded over a generous glass, with the grand and enlightened views of France, with touches upon the brilliance of her *victories*, and her gorgeous strength, and the country gentleman who went well enough inclined to give a vote for plain measures of defence and preparation, gets his head turned, and comes away a philosopher, and would not for worlds interrupt such grand designs, or longer feel sentiments that evince low prejudice and narrow views.'

While the Republicans refused to believe that the French government had changed its character since 1792, the Federalists regarded France with the same fear and loathing that countless Americans have viewed the Soviet Union and Red China. Hamilton, in reviewing 'the disgusting spectacle of the French Revolution,' bewailed free love and the worship of reason, which he insisted were still officially supported in Paris. The Reverend Jedidiah Morse, the geographer, spread the word that the French Revolution was simply a conspiracy, engineered by an obscure sect called the 'Illuminati' against government, religion, and morality; and that Jefferson was their head agent to subvert American society.[1]

European events gave support to those who asserted that France was a world menace. The Directory, in its endeavors to conquer territory, erected satellite republics on its borders by exporting the Jacobinism that it proscribed at home. The civilized world was fast dividing into two camps — those who had made terms with France, and those who had not; and at the end of 1797 Britain and the United States were the only countries which had not. 'If England will persevere,' wrote Senator George Cabot, 'she will save Europe and save us; but if she yields, all will be lost.' 'She is now the only barrier between us and the deathly embraces of our dear Allies — between universal irreligion, immorality and plunder, and what order, probity, virtue and religion is left.' Surely, the alternative was to fight on England's side, or fight alone later?

So reasoned the Federalists. We now know that their fears were exaggerated, for the rulers in Paris were too well informed to try in America their favorite formula of revolution pushed home by invasion. Yet the French designs on Canada, Louisiana, and Florida were more definite and dangerous than even the Federalists suspected. Reviving a policy that brought on the Seven Years War, the Directory sought to surround

1. Similar arguments, based on John Robison's *Proofs of a Conspiracy against all the Religions and Governments of Europe, carried on in the Secret Meetings of Freemasons, Illuminati, etc.* (1797) were used against liberal and anti-militarist organizations after World War I, against Franklin D. Roosevelt, and are now being propagated by the John Birch Society.

the United States with French territory and push back her boundaries to the Appalachians. The habitants of Quebec were being plied with propaganda for a Canadian republic under French protection. Pressure was brought to bear on the Spanish court to cede the Floridas and Louisiana to France. Victor Collot, who went on a secret mission for the Directory to the Western country, stated the arguments neatly: 'France must acquire Louisiana and the Floridas by negotiation, and Canada by force, as the only means to contain the United States within peaceful bounds, to break their exclusive relations with England, to preserve our colonies exclusively to ourselves, . . . and, finally, to recover in both hemispheres that preponderance to which nature entitles us.' In 1796 relations were renewed with Genet's unpaid warriors, a fresh corps of agents was sent into the Western country, and Milfort, the half-breed 'tastenagy' or war chief of the Creek nation, was commissioned brigadier-general in the armies of the French Republic.

The American peace commission arrived in Paris at an unpropitious moment in October 1797, just after the Directors had pulled off a coup d'état against the French peace party, and concluded a successful treaty with Austria. The Directors, at least one of whom had a pecuniary interest in privateering, felt they could with impunity continue clandestine war against the United States. A comic, if one-sided, bit of bargaining ensued. Talleyrand, the Directory's minister of foreign affairs, sent some hangers-on (referred to in the dispatches as X, Y, and Z) to play on the fears of the American envoys and sound their pockets. A bribe for the minister and a loan as compensation for President Adams's 'insulting' message were prerequisites to negotiation. Pressed for an alternative, Monsieur Y hinted at the power of the French party in America, and recalled the fate of other recalcitrant nations. The American envoys, understanding that bribery was necessary in dealing with the Directory, were prepared to come down handsomely for some definite concession; but a loan of $10 million on doubtful security, together with a present of $250,000 to Talleyrand, all in advance, seemed excessive. 'Our case is different from that of the minor nations of Europe,' John Marshall informed Monsieur Y. 'They were unable to maintain their independence, and did not expect to do so. America is a great, and, so far as concerns her self-defense, a powerful nation.' After several months of this sort of thing, Marshall and Pinckney took their leave. Gerry, fondly believing his presence necessary to avert war, remained in Paris.

The envoys' dispatches, rendering a detailed account of their Paris contacts, were submitted by President Adams to Congress and published in April 1798. The public was deeply moved by this first-hand view of French diplomacy. On the Republicans the effect was stupefying. 'Trimmers dropt off from the party like windfalls from an apple tree in September,' wrote Fisher Ames. Jefferson 'thought it his duty to be silent.' Loyal addresses poured in on President and Congress, indignation meetings were held, reams of patriotic poetry were produced, and 'Millions for Defence, but not One Cent for Tribute' became the toast of the day.

2. THE QUASI-WAR WITH FRANCE

Alexander Hamilton, underestimating his old acquaintance Talleyrand, expected the French government to be so angered by the publication of the dispatches as to declare war. On Hamilton's advice, the Federalists adopted a policy of armed neutrality, counting on a declaration of war by France to unite all honest men to their standard. Congress created a navy department, a vast improvement over treating the navy as the army's Cinderella. The United States Navy had been reborn in 1794, with Barbary pirates as midwives. By February there were 126 American sailors enslaved at Algiers, and more being brought in weekly. In response, Congress authorized the building of six ships and a modest establishment of 54 officers and 2000 ratings. But limited appropriations slowed construction of the ships, and Washington had had to buy peace with Algiers in 1796 at a cost of almost a million dollars, including the ransoming of prisoners.

Under the new navy secretary, Benjamin Stoddert, and the senior naval officer, Commodore John Barry, the United States Navy became an efficient fighting force. Congress also revived the Marine Corps. Frigates *United States, Constitution,* and *Constellation* were fitted for sea; three other frigates laid down in 1795, *President, Congress,* and *Chesapeake,* were completed; five more frigates were built by groups of merchants and sold to the government; many smaller vessels were purchased and converted, and an ambitious program of naval construction was undertaken. Land for navy yards was purchased. Privateers were fitted out, and both they and the navy were authorized to capture French armed vessels wherever found; but they were not allowed to take unarmed merchant ships, since war had not actually been declared. By the end of 1798 there were fourteen American men-of-war at sea, and some 200 merchant vessels had taken out letters of marque and reprisal. The French picaroons were fairly swept out of West Indian waters, and on 9 February 1799 the *Constellation*, Commodore Truxtun, captured off Nevis the crack French frigate *L'Insurgente*.

The navy did not attempt to come to grips with France in the Mediterranean, but several American privateers fought successful actions with French armed lateeners. In January 1799 frigate *Essex*, Captain Preble, sailed around the Cape of Good Hope to the Indian Ocean, where she recaptured many American ships from the French, drove off privateers, and escorted home a fleet of merchantmen. After the State Department had recognized the Negro general Toussaint l'Ouverture in Haiti, hoping to restore order in that unhappy land, frigate *General Greene* gave the Haitian leader gunfire support in capturing Jacmel, and U. S. Marines were landed at Puerto Plata.

In the congressional elections of 1798–99 the Federalists won a strong majority, destined to be their last. They scored especially impressive gains in North Carolina and in Virginia, where John Marshall won election to Congress from the city of Richmond. Jefferson and his party appeared to be utterly discredited by their pro-French leanings, but time was preparing their revenge. A rift appeared in the Federalist party between the President and Hamilton, and into this rift Talleyrand insinuated a wedge.

Differences in objective and temperament caused the trouble. President Adams's object was to teach the Directory good manners and force it to respect the American flag. He would have accepted war if declared by France, but hoped to avoid it. The bulk of his party agreed. Hamilton and the New England Federalists, on the contrary, regarded the French imbroglio not as an affair to be wound up, but as an occasion to be improved. It was to be a starting-point for spirited measures that would strengthen the Federal Government, discipline the American people, discredit the Republicans and all they stood for. For this reason, no less than to meet an expected French invasion, the regular army was increased, the cadres for a provisional army created, and Washington was appointed Lieutenant-General, with Hamilton his second in command. Adams growled over these excessive military preparations, but complied.

The only thing wanting, it seemed, was an open and declared war, which France was not so obliging as to offer. Talleyrand, although annoyed at the exposure of his venality to the amused laughter of all Europe, saw the real point: war with America would mean a new ally for England. Jefferson advised him, and he advised the Directory, to keep cool and not fall into the trap. No use trying to turn America Jacobin, he said. 'In no country is anarchy so much feared as in the United States.' Talleyrand had a much better scheme to draw the United States out of the British orbit and into the French. That was to force Spain to cede Louisiana and the Floridas to France, and to revolutionize Canada. Even Federalists would then have to follow French foreign policy. In the meantime, Talleyrand talked peace and friendship to America. As evidence of sincerity, privateers' letters of marque were annulled, and French agents in the West Indies were ordered to respect American ships. An official explanation of the X Y Z episode was issued, in a tone of injured dignity. The American ministers, it appeared, had been imposed upon by charlatans. The Directory had intended to treat with them, but they shut themselves up in their hotel and went off in a huff before they could be received! For just such a cue the discomfited opposition in America had been waiting. Every Republican paper took up the cry that the X Y Z affair was a Federalist hoax.

These evidences of an accommodating spirit took the war Federalists aback — but only for a moment. 'I hope we shall remember,' declared Secretary of State Pickering in January 1799, 'that the tyger crouches before he leaps upon his prey.' It was decided to treat the French overtures as insincere, to continue war preparations, and to declare war on France as soon as Congress convened.

3. THE FEDERALIST 'REIGN OF TERROR'

While organizing defense and drumming up war enthusiasm, the Federalists did not neglect their enemies at home. The Naturalization, Alien, and Sedition Acts of 1798 were aimed at domestic disaffection as much as at foreign danger. These laws provoked the first organized state rights movement under the Constitution and helped promote the election of Jefferson to the presidency. They afford a striking instance of 'feedback' against political intolerance, but it must be admitted that there was plenty of provocation.

Gouverneur Morris had remarked in the Federal Convention that he wanted none of 'those philosophical gentlemen, those citizens of the world as they call themselves, in our public councils.' The French Revolution, however, sent a good many of them to America; and one who came earlier, Albert Gallatin of Geneva, was leading the congressional minority in 1798. Dr. Joseph Priestley, accused of trying 'to decompose both Church and State' with his chemical formulas, had found refuge in Pennsylvania after being mobbed as pro-French in England. Thomas Cooper, who followed him, founded a Republican newspaper. The French minister, Adet, who interfered in the election of 1796, was also a chemist by profession; the French botanist Michaux did espionage for his government. Victor du Pont, son of the economist, was among the French consuls who had to leave the United States hastily in 1798. At the height of excitement that year, the Directory requested passports for a delegation from the Institute of France, under Victor's father, Du Pont de Nemours, to visit the United States 'with the view of improving and extending the sciences.' John Adams replied, 'We have too many French philosophers already, and I really begin to think, or rather to suspect, that learned academies . . . have disorganized the world, and are incompatible with social order.' As these were the persons whom super-patriots wished to expel in 1798, it is interesting to note that Gallatin became one of our greatest statesmen, Priestley a notable figure in the history of science, Cooper a college president; whilst the Du Ponts settled in Delaware and have since engaged in the highly respectable manufacture of plastics and explosives.

Immigrants who were neither philosophers nor gentlemen gave even more trouble to the Federal Government. Noisy Jacobins began to come over. French agents were stirring up sedition in the West. Equally unwelcome from the Federalist point of view were Irish refugees from the rebellion of '98, who lost no time in becoming citizens and joining the anti-British party. Congress responded with the Naturalization Act of 1798, which increased the required period of residence for citizenship from five to fourteen years, and the Alien Act, which gave the President power to expel foreigners by executive decree. Adams never availed himself of the privilege; but two shiploads of Frenchmen left the country in anticipation that he would.

For the Sedition Act of 1798 there was a legitimate need. There being no common law of the United States, the federal courts required statutory authority before taking cognizance of conspiracies against the government or libels on high officials. One section of the act, however, declared a misdemeanor punishable by fine or imprisonment, any speech or writing against President or Congress 'with the intent to defame' or to bring them 'into contempt or disrepute.' And it was this section only that was enforced. Federalists never recognized the value of party opposition; from their quarterdeck point of view the Republicans were little better than mutineers. In the Sedition Act prosecutions, every defendant was a Republican, every judge and almost every juror a Federalist. About twenty-five persons were arrested and ten convicted, most of them Republican editors who were conveniently got out of the way by heavy fines or jail sentences. Some of the prosecutions were downright silly. A wandering 'apostle of sedition,' who persuaded the local 'Jacobins' of Dedham, Mass., to erect a liberty pole with a provocative inscription in front of Fisher Ames's house, got four years in jail. A tavern loiterer at Newark, N.J., was jailed for expressing the wish that the wadding of the cannon shot fired in the President's honor might lodge in Adams's backside!

Akin to the sedition prosecutions was the severe action taken against John Fries, a Pennsylvania German auctioneer who headed an 'insurrection' against the direct tax. This real estate tax, laid to pay for the new army and navy, was the most unpopular feature of the Federalist defense program. 'Captain' Fries, armed with sword and pistol and wearing a French tricolor cockade, led a company of about fifty countrymen who chased all the federal tax collectors out of Bucks County and liberated prisoners from the Bethlehem jail. Although this was a far less serious affair than the Whiskey Rebellion of 1794, President Adams sent in regulars, who apprehended Fries. The auctioneer was tried for treason in Philadelphia and sentenced to death, but pardoned by the President.

All this was labeled by the Jeffersonians, 'The Federalist Reign of Terror.' Looked at in the perspective of history, it was nothing of the sort; the phrase itself was mere humbug. Nobody was drowned, hanged, or tortured, nobody went before a firing squad. A few scurrilous journalists were silenced, a few received terms in jail; but the rest went right on attacking the government, defending the French, and sneering at the United States Navy. Nobody was prevented from voting against the Federalists in the next elections, state or national.

Two startling protests to the Alien and Sedition Acts came from state legislatures: the Virginia Resolves drafted by Madison, and those of Kentucky drafted by Jefferson. Both declared the objectionable laws unconstitutional. As to the Alien Act, undoubtedly the power of expelling aliens belongs to the Federal Government, not to the states. The Sedition Act stands in a different light, for the Constitution (Amendment I) forbids Congress to pass any law abridging the freedom of speech, or of the press. Federalist lawyers, like many American lawyers today, attempted to extract all meaning from this clause by adopting Blackstone's definition that freedom of the press means merely freedom from censorship prior to publication or by asserting that it was not meant to apply in time of war. Amendment I, however, was written by men who intended to protect critics of the government from punishment.

The theory of the Virginia and Kentucky Resolves was more important than their arguments, for they develop the 'compact' or 'state rights' theory of the Constitution that Jefferson had adumbrated in his opinion on the bank bill in 1792. Kentucky declared that whenever Congress palpably transcends its powers, as in the Sedition Act, each state 'has an equal right to judge for itself, as well of infractions as of the mode and measure of redress.' She called upon her 'co-states' to 'concur . . . in declaring these acts' void, and to unite 'in requesting their repeal.' Virginia hinted at 'interposing' state authority between the persecuted citizen and his government. Exactly what Madison meant by 'interposition' is uncertain; he later explained that he meant nothing more than strong protest.

In any federal government there must be conflicts between powers of the nation and powers of the states; and a minority party, or interest, will then try to escape the consequences of its position by raising the banner of state rights. Almost every man in public life between 1798 and 1860 spurned the 'doctrine' of state rights when his section was in the ascendancy and embraced it when his constituents deemed themselves oppressed. The Civil War was supposed to have killed the Resolutions of 1798–99; but they have been defiantly quoted in the 1960's to prevent the implementation of the Supreme Court's decision against racial segregation in the schools.

4. ADAMS TAKES THE HELM

President Adams became increasingly alarmed by the acts and the ambitions of Hamilton and the 'High' Federalists. Up to the spring of 1799, Hamilton had been the power behind Adams's administration, owing to deference to his views by members of Congress and three members of the President's cabinet. He did not propose to accept the status of quasi-war with France. Hints dropped here and there in letters suggest that a grandiose plan was forming in his brain. He would lead the new American army overland against New Orleans, the British navy co-operating by blockading the mouth of the Mississippi. Louisiana and the Floridas having fallen, Hamilton would march into Mexico while the South American patriot Miranda, helped by the British, would liberate the Spanish Main. Hamilton would return laurel-crowned, at the head of his victorious legion, to become the First Citizen of America, as Bonaparte was already the First Citizen of France. And the Jeffersonian party, with all it stood for, would be completely discredited.

But the Hamiltonians reckoned without the President. John Adams was one of the first political philosophers in America, and a very human one, too. In no sense a democrat, he regarded Jefferson's belief in the common man's innate virtue as sentimental nonsense; but he was equally hostile to anything resembling plutocracy or militarism. Yet he had allowed himself to be guided by Hamilton's friends in the cabinet. In March 1799 he suddenly awoke to the dangers into which the ship of state was drifting; and without telling a single person (except the prudent Abigail) about his intentions, he threw a bombshell into the Senate in the shape of the nomination of a minister plenipotentiary to France. That stalled the war program completely. Hamilton and the High Federalists were furious, but they dared not reject the nomination and thus give color to the charge that they were seeking war when the President saw the possibility of peace.

Adams compromised to the extent of appointing a commission of three instead of a single envoy; but Secretary Pickering managed to hold up their sailing, so that the ministers did not reach Paris until the year 1800. This was a bad mistake in timing; the Directory was eager to make peace with America in 1798–99, but now Bonaparte had kicked them out, made himself First Consul, and had no desire to appease the United

States. For seven months the negotiations dragged, while Napoleon crossed the Alps to thrash the Austrians again, at Marengo. He refused to admit liability for the French spoliations, unless the United States recognized the treaties of 1778, which Congress had denounced at the height of anti-Gallic feeling. No alliance, no money! The Americans, fearing to bring home a renewed entangling alliance, signed a mere commercial convention, each party reserving its rights as to treaties and spoliations. It was high time to come to terms with France, for even England was on the point of making peace.

On the very next day, 1 October 1800, France secretly obtained the retrocession of Louisiana from Spain. If Napoleon had not tossed it to Jefferson three years later, we would probably all be saying that Hamilton was right after all.

5. THE ELECTION OF 1800–1801

If the French had been so accommodating as to land even a corporal's guard on American soil, or a 'seditious alien' had been caught in a real plot, the presidential election of 1800 might have gone very differently; but as time went on, and no enemy appeared, and the new direct tax was assessed, the patriotic fervor of 1798 faded. In the meantime there were fresh difficulties with England over impressment, the sedition prosecutions were having their effect, and Republican editors were throwing out a wide net for political martyrs.

Presidential candidates for the election of 1800–1801 were selected by party caucuses in Congress. The Republicans, as in 1796, decided to support Jefferson and Burr. The Federalists reluctantly renominated John Adams, together with Charles Cotesworth Pinckney of the X Y Z mission. No sooner had they made this decision than the Hamiltonian faction, vowing vengeance on Adams for stopping the war, planned to bring in Pinckney as President by persuading one or two electors to throw away votes that would normally have gone to Adams. Hamilton wrote of Adams: 'I will never more be responsible for him by my direct support, even though the consequence should be the election of *Jefferson*. If we must have an *enemy* at the head of the government, let it be one we can oppose, and for whom we are not responsible, who will not involve our party in the disgrace of his foolish and bad measures.'

By 1800, voters were being urged to choose a straight party ticket; it was becoming a source of pride to be known not for your independence but as a good party man. The campaign of 1800 was very dirty. Jefferson was accused of being an atheist and a fellow-traveler of the French Jacobins; Adams of being an autocrat and a slavish admirer of the British monarchy. The real issues which now stand out, of peace against war, economy against heavy taxation for defense, free speech against sedition prosecutions, were also stressed; but whether they swayed votes as much as the trumped-up issues is doubtful. John Adams was later told that he lost Pennsylvania because of a whispering campaign among the Germans, to the effect that he had imported two mistresses, one French and one German, and had sent the German girl packing!

Passionate intensity marked the campaigns of this era. The Federalists really believed, from 1793 to 1815, that the Republicans aimed to destroy property and religion, and to make the United States a satellite to republican or imperial France. The Republicans really believed that the Federalists aimed to subject the country to a Northern plutocracy and, eventually, to some little king, a satellite to George III. That is why Jefferson thought he was rescuing his country from peril, and why the Federalists in opposition played with the idea of a 'saving remnant,' an independent New England.

A majority of Republican presidential electors was chosen in 1800; but since not one dared throw away his second vote, Jefferson and Burr tied for first place with 73 votes each, as against 65 for Adams and 64 for Pinckney. The tie vote was an unwelcome tribute to the degree of party regularity that had been achieved by 1800.

In 1801 the House of Representatives, voting by states, had to choose between Jefferson and Burr, a majority of one state being necessary for election. The Federalists saw an opportunity to thwart their enemies by supporting Burr, thus electing a cynical, pliant, and corrupt politician over a 'dangerous radical.' Party division was so close that during thirty-five ballots, and until 17 February 1801, the House was deadlocked. There was talk of preventing an election and of civil war. Not until two weeks before the inauguration did several Federalists cast blank ballots, which lead to Jefferson's being elected by two states to four.[2] The Twelfth Amendment to the Constitution (1804) removed the possibility of a tie between two candidates on the same ticket. In the congressional

2. The best account of the balloting is Edward Stanwood, *History of the Presidency 1788–1897* (1898), p. 72.

elections of 1800, the Republicans obtained emphatic majorities in House and Senate. Thus, in 1801 the Federalists went out of power in every branch of government except the judiciary. The exception proved very important.

'I have this morning witnessed one of the most interesting scenes, a free people can ever witness,' wrote one observer on 4 March 1801. 'The changes of administration, which in every government and in every age have most generally been epochs of confusion, villainy and bloodshed, in this our happy country take place without any species of distraction, or disorder.' For the first time in modern history, an incumbent political party had accepted an electoral defeat and turned over the government to its opponents. The young republic had survived one of the most crucial tests that can face a new nation.

So passed into minority the party which contained more talent and virtue, with less political common sense, than any of its successors. The character of Washington, the genius of Hamilton, and the disciplined, intelligent patriotism of their colleagues and lieutenants saved the American union from disintegration before its colors were set; but the events of 1798–1800 proved that the Federalists had nothing more to contribute, outside the judiciary. Their chosen basis, an oligarchy of wealth and talent, had helped to tide over a crisis, but was neither broad nor deep enough for a permanent polity. Their patience and vision were adequate. Their old-world precepts of vigor, energy, and suppression had become fixed ideas, setting them in antagonism to deep-rooted popular prejudices; and the expanding forces of American life enveloped and overwhelmed them.

XIX

Jefferson's Administrations

1. THE 'REVOLUTION OF 1800'

Thomas Jefferson, ruminating years later on the events of a crowded lifetime, thought that his election to the Presidency marked as real a revolution as that of 1776. He had saved the country from monarchy and militarism, and brought it back to republican simplicity. But there never had been any danger of monarchy; it was John Adams who saved the country from militarism; and a little simplicity more or less cannot be deemed revolutionary. Fisher Ames predicted that, with a 'Jacobin' President, America would be in for a real reign of terror. Yet the four years that followed were one of the most tranquil of Republican olympiads, marked not by radical reforms or popular tumults, but by the peaceful acquisition of territory as large again as the United States. The election of 1800–1801 brought a change of men more than of measures, and a transfer of federal power from the Hudson to the Potomac, rather than a weakening of the central government in favor of the states. For the next quarter of a century, a Virginian would rule in the White House; Jefferson, Madison, and Monroe each served eight years, and each was succeeded by his Secretary of State.

Yet if it marked no revolution, the election of Jefferson in 1800 did harbinger the beginning of an era of greater democracy. Although in the Federalist period the right to vote was widely held, many had not chosen to exercise it, and politics were controlled by the gentry, with some exceptions such as Pennsylvania. In the Jeffersonian era, an astonishing expansion of the electorate took place. No revolutionary, Jefferson none-theless throughout his life symbolized the striving for liberty and equality. In the last letter of his life, he wrote: 'All eyes are opened, or opening, to the rights of man. The general spread of the light of science has already laid open to every view the palpable truth, that the mass of mankind has not been born with saddles on their backs, nor a favored few booted and spurred, ready to ride them legitimately, by the grace of God.'

Jefferson was no social democrat, but a slaveholding country gentleman with a classical education, exquisite taste, a lively curiosity, and a belief in the perfectibility of man. His kind belonged to the eighteenth rather than the nineteenth century. Christian but no churchman, he had the serenity of one to whom now and then the Spirit has not disdained to speak. The hold that he enjoyed on the hearts of plain people was attained without speech-making, military service, or catering to vulgar prejudice. The secret of Jefferson's power lay in the fact that he appealed to and expressed America's better self: her idealism, simplicity, youthful mind, and hopeful outlook, rather than the material and imperial ambitions which Hamilton represented. Jefferson's political object was to prove that Americans were ripe for 'a government founded not on the fears and follies of man, but on his reason, on the predominance of his social over his dissocial passions.' 'We are acting for all mankind,' he wrote to Priestley. 'Circumstances denied to others, but indulged to us, have imposed on us the duty of proving what is the degree of freedom and self-government in which a society may venture to leave its individual members.'

It is easy to be cynical about Jefferson. In order to win support, he was forced to give men offices; and Hamilton's financial schemes were mere pleached alleys compared with the golden vista opened by the acquisition of Louisiana. But in one respect he was admirably consistent. Unlike petty tyrants of our day, who attain power by preaching liberty and then turn savagely on their opponents, Jefferson never avenged himself for the Sedition Act and the insults to which he had been subjected by Federalists. To Levi Lincoln he wrote, 'I shall take no other revenge, than by a steady pursuit of economy and peace . . . to sink Federalism into an abyss from which there will be no resurrection.' And with one possible exception — his attitude toward the federal judiciary — he kept his word.

Jefferson was sensitive but not sentimental. He loved birds and flowers, lacked a sense of humor, and hated the sight of blood. Unlike most Virginians he did not engage in field sports. He despised Rousseau's romanticism; and, if he thought mankind perfectible, it was because Americans had advanced so rapidly in his own time. The dead hand of the past had been lifted from their government; why not from their religion and society? But this fastidious gentleman was a finished politician. His inaugural address of 4 March 1801 was eighteenth-century idealism rubbed through the sieve of practical politics. Instead of denouncing the Federalists as monarchists, he invited them to rejoin the true republican church: 'We are all republicans — we are all federalists. If there be any among us who wish to dissolve this Union, or to change its republican form, let them stand undisturbed as monuments of the safety with which error of opinion may be tolerated where reason is left free to combat it.' This government, 'the world's best hope,' must not be abandoned 'on the theoretic and visionary fear' that it is not strong enough. 'Sometimes it is said that Man cannot be trusted with the government of himself. Can he, then, be trusted with the government of others?'

'Separated by nature and a wide ocean from the exterminating havoc of one quarter of the globe,' 'possessing a chosen country, with room enough for our descendants to the hundredth and thousandth generation' practicing the social virtues, the only thing 'necessary to close the circle of our felicities' is 'a wise and frugal government, which shall restrain men from injuring one another, shall leave them otherwise free to regulate their own pursuits of industry and improvement, and shall not take from the mouth of labor the bread it has earned.'

Ironically enough, the net result of his administrations was to bring Hamilton's dream of a warlike and industrial nation nearer fulfillment. But that came about because of world forces beyond Jefferson's, or anyone's, control.

The new President was fortunate in the circumstances surrounding his first administration. His party had a majority in both houses of Congress, and no rival leader was hankering for the succession. The peace of Amiens (1801) brought a breathing space in the European war, which left him free to concentrate on domestic problems. There was no mess to clear up; John Adams turned over the administration and the treasury in superb order. And the Federal Government had been transferred from aristocratic Philadelphia to an appropriate setting for Republican simplicity, the new capital city of Washington.

Congress had decided in 1790 to fix the federal District of Columbia on the Potomac. President Washington chose the exact site, in a sparsely populated region a few miles upstream from Mount Vernon, just below the Great Falls. Maryland and Virginia [1] ceded their jurisdiction, local landowners were indemnified by federal commissioners, and the capital city of Washington was planned on a generous scale by a French engineer, Major L'Enfant.[2] Ten years had elapsed, but Washington was little more than a cleared space with scattered buildings, between wilderness and river. One wing of the Capitol, a graceful Palladian structure on a noble site, was ready for occupancy, and the other wing nearly completed; but the rotunda was open to the heavens. Near by were a few brick houses, wooden cabins of workmen and Negroes, and a few poor stores. Pennsylvania Avenue, a broad clearing studded with stumps and alder bushes, led northwestward from the Capitol through a morass to the simple and dignified executive mansion, or White House, designed by James Hoban of Dublin. Around that, on higher ground, were a few hundred houses, mostly of wood, the nucleus of the future residential city. Two miles further west was Georgetown, a comfortable little college town that afforded the officials an agreeable change from each other's and their landladies' society. The red clay soil of Washington became fine dust in dry weather and liquid cement in rain; swarms of mosquitoes spread malaria among the newcomers and inoculated the remainder with a parasitic attitude toward life. Several fine groves of tulip-trees were the only features of natural beauty within the city site. Jefferson's one recorded wish for despotic power was to save these trees from the inhabitants, who proceeded to fell them for firewood, regardless of property rights. Except for scornful Federalists, and a complaining diplomatic corps, everyone made light of the difficulties and looked forward to some magic transmutation of their backwoods capital into a seat of commerce and the muses;

1. In 1846 that part of the District on the right bank of the Potomac, including the town of Alexandria, was retroceded to Virginia.
2. Jefferson suggested the spacing of the Capitol and the White House. William Thornton, an American born in the Virgin Islands, and B. H. Latrobe, English-born, designed the Capitol. The two interior wings, still standing (although their proportions have been marred by the extensions of 1959–60), were their work.

> Though nought but woods and Jefferson they see,
> Where streets should run and sages ought to be,

as Tom Moore wrote after his visit in 1804. Eventually the 'City of Magnificent Distances' (as the Portuguese minister called it) grew up to its plan; but until after the Civil War it was slovenly compared with Baltimore, Charleston, or the Northern cities.

Washington, then, was a fit setting for an experiment in frugal government. Members of Congress, forced to leave their wives at home and live in crowded boarding houses, finished the public business in annual sessions of three to five months' duration. Written presidential messages were substituted for the annual 'speech from the throne,' and the answers from both houses were omitted. As a widower, Jefferson was free to establish a new code of republican etiquette. The White House lay open every morning to all comers. Anthony Merry, in full uniform as British minister plenipotentiary, was received by the President in morning undress of faded threadbare coat, red waistcoat, corduroy breeches, and slippers. White House dinners were well cooked by a French chef, and Jefferson's wine bill for one year was $2800. But the rule of first come first served, which he adopted to do away with precedence, was not understood by the diplomatic corps or relished by the secretaries' wives; and Washington has since become the most precedence-ridden capital in the western world.

Jefferson's inaugural pledges to pay the public debt, and to preserve 'the general government in its whole constitutional vigor,' created joy in the Federalist camp. Hamilton, who had prophesied that his rival would pursue a temporizing rather than a violent system, viewed the inaugural message 'as virtually a candid retraction of past misapprehensions, and a pledge to the community that the new President will not lend himself to dangerous innovations, but in essential points will tread in the steps of his predecessors.' That, in the main, was what Jefferson did. He took over Washington's administrative machine 'in the full tide of successful experiment,' but fed a slightly different material into it. Madison became his Secretary of State. For Secretary of the Treasury he chose Albert Gallatin, an offshoot of aristocratic Geneva who had arrived young in the land of promise, made his living in the backwoods of Pennsylvania, and risen by character and ability to opposition leadership in the House. He and Jefferson regarded the national debt as a mortgage to be paid off without delay. Gallatin would even have retained the excise on distilled liquors, which his former constituents in Pennsylvania had resisted; but Jefferson insisted on removing this detested relic of Federalism, and so made his name immortal in the mountains. This rendered the government even more dependent than formerly on customs revenues, so that the stoppage of foreign trade seriously embarrassed federal finances on the eve of the War of 1812.

Gallatin, who had been an unsparing critic of Hamiltonian financial methods, now gave him the compliment of continuing his procedures with little change. An act passed late in the Adams administration required the Secretary of the Treasury to prepare and submit an annual report. This led to an improvement in accounting. In Washington's administration, it had been customary for Congress to appropriate lump sums to the different departments, to spend at their discretion. The opposition naturally disliked this, and recommended detailed and specific appropriations. But not much advance in this direction was made under Jefferson and Madison; and it was not until after the War of 1812 that congressmen discovered that the useful frontier practice of 'log-rolling,' when applied to appropriations, served admirably to finance unnecessary projects and direct federal money into their constituencies.

Jefferson's remark 'We are all republicans — we are all federalists' caused no little dismay in his own camp. Gallatin's father-in-law asked if enemies were to be kept 'in office to trample upon us.' William B. Giles of Virginia reminded the President that 'a pretty general purgation of office' was expected. 'It can never be unpopular to turn a vicious man out and put a virtuous one in his room.' No one seriously pretended that the federal civil service was inefficient or corrupt; but it was almost completely Federalist, since Washington and Adams had never knowingly appointed a member of the opposition. Offices were already regarded as proper rewards for party service; and Jefferson's followers were eager to feed at the public crib. Yet, as he complained, functionaries seldom die, and never resign. The only thing to do, then, was to create vacancies by the presidential prerogative of removal. It soon became clear that, in respect of the Federalists, Jefferson 'intended to entice the flock with one hand and belabor the shepherds with the other.' There was no 'general purgation,' such as Giles wanted, but performance did not square with the bland professions of the inaugural discourse. Jefferson signified the coming of party government when he replaced the whole Adams cabinet with prominent Republicans. He and Madison were assiduous, too, in 'taking care' of Republicans defeated at the polls by giving them federal posts. In his appointments to higher federal offices, Jefferson made a modest departure in the direction of naming men of merit irrespective of social class, although most of them were from the 'top drawer' socially.

Other features of the Federalist establishment were retained, such as the discriminating tonnage duties, the fishing bounties, and the mixed commissions set up under Jay's treaty, but Jefferson carried into practice the Republican dislike of a standing army and a large navy. The army was reduced by a 'chaste reformation,' as Jefferson called it, from about 3500 to 2500 men; and Congress in 1802 established the Military Academy at West Point. During the election and before, the Republican press had viciously attacked the navy as a sink of waste and corruption, an English imitation, and the like. Jefferson, who knew nothing about ships, shared these feelings to some extent. An act of the last Federalist Congress allowed the President to reduce the respectable navy that had been built up to fight France to thirteen frigates; and Jefferson not only did that, selling the rest of the navy for merchantmen, but stopped all new construction, discharged all naval constructors, and had a majority of the frigates that were retained hauled out to save the expense of pay and rations. Naturally, they went to pieces; wooden ships could not be 'put up in mothballs' like modern steel warships.

Yet, strangely enough, the most brilliant achievements of Jefferson's first administration were in war and diplomacy!

2. A SMALL WAR AND A BIG PURCHASE

By the time Jefferson became President, almost $2 million, one-fifth of the annual revenue, had been paid for gifts, ransom, and tribute to the Moslem states of Morocco, Algiers, Tunis, and Tripoli, in order to permit American merchant ships to sail in the Mediterranean. Jefferson, after reducing the navy, looked around for profitable employment of warships remaining afloat. He found it against the Bashaw of Tripoli, who, feeling he was not getting enough cut on the tribute money, declared war on the United States in May 1801. This naval war dribbled along in a desultory fashion until 1804, when Commodore Edward Preble appeared off Tripoli in command of a respectable task force, U.S.S. *Consti-*

tution flagship, which delivered a series of bombardments. Before his arrival, frigate *Philadelphia* had grounded on a reef off Tripoli, from which the enemy floated her free. The Bashaw imprisoned Captain Bainbridge and his crew and would have equipped the frigate for his own navy, had not Lieutenant Stephen Decatur, in a captured lateen-rigged schooner named *Intrepid*, entered the harbor at night, boarded and captured *Philadelphia*, and, after setting fire to her, made a safe getaway.

Decatur performed other dashing feats in this war, but the most extraordinary exploit was that of a former army officer named William Eaton, the American consul at Tunis.

Disgusted by the evil-smelling pirate princes, Eaton believed that the American tactics of blockade and bombardment would never get results; so he persuaded the American naval commander on the Mediterranean station to espouse the cause of a pretender to the Tripolitan 'throne,' then in exile in Egypt. At Alexandria, General Eaton collected a force composed of an American midshipman and a marine lieutenant, fourteen bluejackets and marines, forty Greeks, a squadron of Arab cavalry under a native chief, a hundred nondescripts, and a fleet of camels. Under his command (and paid out of his pocket) this motley expeditionary force marched over 500 miles across the Libyan desert. Despite hardships, Arab mutinies, and the pretender's treachery, they managed to reach Derna. The indomitable Eaton then led an attack on that town, in which three American man-of-war brigs co-operated, and captured it. His exploit led to a favorable treaty with Tripoli, negotiated by the captured Captain Bainbridge. But Eaton and the rival Bashaw were repudiated. Embittered at the Jefferson administration, Eaton was 'taken up' by the Federalists as a 'martyr,' a fairly common political maneuver in our history.

While Tripoli was being taught a lesson, the boundary of the United States advanced from the Mississippi to the Rocky Mountains. The whole of that vast territory, Louisiana, had been under Spanish sovereignty since the peace of 1763. Less than 1 per cent of the area was settled. The creoles, numbering with their slaves about 40,000 in 1800, were concentrated on both banks of the lower Mississippi. There were a few garrisons and trading posts on the west bank of the river between New Orleans and St. Louis, and a few more on the Red river; the rest was in possession of the Indians. Sugar cane and cotton had recently been introduced from the West Indies. The retrocession of this great province from Spain to France, in October 1800, completed a policy aimed at replacing Canada by a new French colonial empire in North America and checking the expansion of the United States.

As France did not take immediate possession of Louisiana, the treaty of retrocession was kept secret for over a year. In May 1801 Jefferson got wind of it, and another event revealed its implications. Bonaparte dispatched an expeditionary force to Hispaniola, with orders to suppress the Negro insurrection there, and then to take possession of New Orleans and Louisiana. The prospect of a veteran French army at America's back door was not pleasant. On 18 April 1802 Jefferson wrote the American minister at Paris: 'The day that France takes possession of New Orleans . . . we must marry ourselves to the British fleet and nation.'

Astounding as this letter may appear, it was a logical development of Jefferson's policy for the preceding twelve years. The President's earlier experience convinced him that as long as a foreign country controlled the mouth of the Mississippi, the United States was in danger of being drawn into every European war. Isolation was not a fact but a goal; and to attain it Jefferson was ready to adopt Washington's formula of 'temporary alliances for extraordinary emergencies.'

Up to this point Jefferson's Louisiana diplomacy had been secret: but another event almost forced his hand. Late in 1802 the Spanish governor at New Orleans withdrew the 'right of deposit' from American traders. This privilege had been guaranteed only for three years by Pinckney's treaty of 1795; but the inhabitants of the Ohio valley, who were annually trans-shipping a million dollars' worth of produce at New Orleans, believed they had secured it for ever. An explosion of indignation followed in the West. Jefferson remained imperturbable; Congress passed an appropriation of $2 million for 'expenses in relation to the intercourse between the United States and foreign nations.' And in March 1803 the President commissioned James Monroe as envoy extraordinary to France, with interesting instructions to himself and to the resident minister, Robert Livingston.

First they were to offer anything up to $10 million for New Orleans and the Floridas, which would give the United States the whole east bank of the Mississippi, and the Gulf coast to the eastward. If France refused, three-quarters of the sum should be offered for the Island of

New Orleans alone; or space on the east bank should be purchased for an American port. Failing here, they must press for a perpetual guarantee of the rights of navigation and deposit. That was Jefferson's ultimatum. If this were refused, Monroe and Livingston were ordered to 'open a confidential communication with ministers of the British Government,' with a view to 'a candid understanding, and a closer connection with Great Britain.' A mutual promise not to make a separate peace with France could not 'be deemed unreasonable.' More than even Hamilton had dared suggest!

Livingston began the negotiation before Monroe sailed, and for a time made little progress. But on 11 April 1803, when Livingston approached the minister of foreign affairs to repeat his usual offer for New Orleans, Talleyrand suddenly asked, 'What will you give for the whole of Louisiana?' And on 30 April the treaty of cession was signed. Twelve million dollars were paid for the province of Louisiana, 'as acquired from Spain' in 1800. The United States guaranteed the inhabitants the rights of American citizens and eventual admission to the Union.

We owe this amazing opportunity to two factors — the Negroes of Haiti and the British navy. Napoleon had poured 35,000 troops into Hispaniola, the Vietnam of 1800, and lost almost all; the blacks under Toussaint l'Ouverture killed those who invaded the interior, and yellow fever finished off the rest. Without Hispaniola, Louisiana lost most of its value to France. Secondly, Napoleon had decided to renew war with England, whose navy would certainly blockade and probably capture New Orleans. So Napoleon deemed it best to sell the whole of Louisiana to fatten up his war chest.

This greatest bargain in American history, the Louisiana purchase, put a severe strain on the Constitution, which said nothing about acquiring foreign territory, much less promising it statehood. Jefferson at first wanted an amendment to the Constitution, but decided to take a broad view of it when Livingston warned him that Napoleon might change his mind. The Senate promptly consented, not without sarcastic grumblings by the Federalists, and on 20 December 1803 the French prefect at New Orleans formally transferred Louisiana to the United States.

Even before the purchase, Jefferson had ordered his secretary, Captain Meriwether Lewis, and Lieutenant William Clark, officers of the regular army, to conduct an exploring expedition. Their first object was to find 'water communication across this continent' in United States territory.

Alexander Mackenzie in 1793 had already done this in Canadian territory by poling up the Peace river from Lake Athabaska, crossing the continental divide in British Columbia, and reaching the Pacific at Dean Channel. Other objects of the Lewis and Clark expedition were to secure American title to the Oregon country, and impress upon the Sioux and other Indians that their 'Great White Father' lived in Washington, not Windsor. Both young men were amateur scientists and accustomed to handling Indians.

The expedition started from St. Louis on 14 May 1804 with 32 soldiers and ten civilians, embarked in a 55-foot keelboat and two periaguas. These, propelled by sails and oars, took them up the Missouri as far as the South Fork, in what is now Montana. In September, at the mouth of the Teton river, they outfaced and managed to get by a party of touchy Sioux. The winter of 1804–5 they spent among the Mandan in North Dakota. A fleet of dugout canoes, built above the Great Falls in June 1805, took them to the foothills of the Rocky Mountains in what is now Idaho, where their interpreter, the Snake Indian girl Sacajawea, made friendly contact with the Shoshone Indians. These furnished horses for the men and squaws to carry the baggage. Crossing the Lemhi pass, the expedition moved north down the Bitterroot valley, and in the Nez Percé country reached the Clearwater, a turbulent but navigable branch of the Snake river, flowing westward. There they made more dugouts, entered the Columbia river, and after many difficulties with rocks and rapids, reached tidewater on 7 November. 'Great joy in Camp,' wrote Clark in his diary, 'we are in view of . . . this great Pacific Ocean which we have been so long anxious to see.' And they built Fort Clatsop within sound of the great Pacific surges, there to spend another winter.

Lewis and Clark learned that New England trading vessels had visited the Columbia, through the coastal Indians' use of such elegant phrases as 'heave the lead' and 'sun-of-a-pitch.' So they hoped to sail home; but as months passed and no ship called, the explorers decided to return overland. Lewis took the shorter route from the site of Missoula, Montana, to the Great Falls, while Clark followed their outward trail to the three forks of the Missouri (which they had named Jefferson, Madison, and Gallatin), made a short-cut overland to the Yellowstone, and floated down that river, past the picturesque mesa that he named Pompey's Tower, to its junction with the Missouri at the site of Fort Union. There Lewis met Clark again, and the expedition reached St. Louis 23

September 1806 with the loss of only one man and without having had a single fight with the Indians.

Jefferson, delighted with their reports, their conduct, and the specimens that they brought to Washington, appointed Meriwether Lewis governor of Louisiana Territory. They had found no water route through the Rockies, since there was none; but the land and river route they discovered served later pioneers, and their handling of Indian relations was beyond praise.

'Never was there an administration more brilliant than that of Mr. Jefferson up to this period,' said John Randolph in later years. 'We were indeed in the "full tide of successful experiment." Taxes repealed; the public debt amply provided for, both principal and interest; sinecures abolished; Louisiana acquired; public confidence unbounded.'

3. CRUMBLING FEDERALISM

Jefferson yearned to convert New England from her perverse Federalist ways. He appreciated the danger of attempting to govern a loose-knit federal union by a sectional party, and hoped by his moderation to persuade the Yankees that their commercial and shipping interests were safe in Republican hands. Gains in the congressional elections of 1802 showed that he was succeeding; but the Federalist leaders grew bitter and desperate as their power waned.

To the clergy and party leaders of New England, Jefferson's victory was the triumph of democracy, which they believed would lead to terror, atheism, and autocracy. 'The principles of democracy are everywhere what they have been in France,' wrote Fisher Ames. New England was yet pure; but the barriers to her virtue were falling. 'And must we with folded hands wait the result?' wrote Senator Pickering of Massachusetts. 'The principles of our Revolution point to the remedy — a separation.'

Thus Virginians like John Taylor had reasoned in 1798, when Virginia was hag-ridden by Hamilton. Jefferson then had calmed them with a promise of victory. No such hope could console the Federalists. Their majority was dwindling, and they knew it. Ohio, admitted to the Union in 1803, looked to Virginia for guidance, although largely settled by Yankees. New states to be formed from Louisiana would follow the same light; and their political weight would be increased by the federal ratio of representation. The annexation of Louisiana, upsetting the balance of power within the Union, absolved New England from allegiance to the Union; at least so the Federalists reasoned. Before 1803 was out the 'Essex Junto' of Massachusetts and the 'River Gods' of Connecticut began to plan a Northern Confederacy, in Pickering's words, 'exempt from the corrupt and corrupting influence and oppression of the aristocratic democrats of the South': a confederacy with New England as a nucleus.

Knowledge of this conspiracy was confined to the inner circle of New England federalism and the British minister at Washington, who gave it his blessing. Hamilton would have none of it. Intrigue was repulsive to his character, and reasoning such as Pickering's, to his intellect. The conspirators then turned to Aaron Burr.

Burr had carried New York for Jefferson in 1800, and without that state Jefferson would not have been elected. Yet Jefferson, once safe in office, ignored the Vice-President in distributing patronage and dropped him from the presidential ticket in 1804. Burr then decided to contest the governorship of New York with the regular Republican candidate. We know very little for certain of what went on; it seems highly probable that, in return for Federalist aid to elect him governor, Burr agreed, if successful, to swing New York into a Northern Confederacy and become its president. But most Federalist leaders opposed the scheme. Burr was defeated, and the Federalist conspiracy then dissolved. How remote was its chance of success the presidential election of 1804 proved. Jefferson carried every state but Connecticut and Delaware, with 162 electoral votes to 14 for Pinckney.

At the age of forty-eight, Burr was a ruined politician. He had broken with the Republicans and failed the Federalists. Hamilton was responsible. It was not the first time that Hamilton had crossed his path; it must be the last. On 18 June 1804, six weeks after the New York election, Burr wrote to his rival, demanding 'a prompt and unqualified acknowledgment or denial' of a slur upon his character reported in the press. Hamilton refused to retract, and answered, 'I trust on more reflection you will see the matter in the same light with me. If not, I can only regret the circumstances, and must abide the consequences.'

According to the 'code of honor' observed by the gentry of the South and of New York, such language was an invitation to a challenge; and the challenge came quickly. Hamilton had no business to accept. He did not need to prove his courage; he had a wife and a large family dependent on him. Moreover, he believed it murder to kill an adversary in a duel. Yet the infirmity of a noble mind forced him to accept the challenge.

Poor Hamilton had become enmeshed in a double net of theory and ambition. He might differ from the New England Federalists as to the cure for democracy, but he judged the future by their gloomy formula. A crisis was impending. The year 1804 in America corresponded to 1791 in France. Jefferson would disappear like Mirabeau and Lafayette, dissolution and anarchy would follow; then America would demand a savior. Hamilton intended to be ready at the call — but no one under suspicion of cowardice could save his country. So Hamilton went to his doom, resolved to prove his courage and yet not to kill: to reserve and throw away his first fire, in the hope that Burr would miss and honor be satisfied. Aaron Burr did not intend to miss.

At six o'clock on a bright summer morning, 11 July 1804, Hamilton and his second were ferried across the Hudson to a grove of trees under the Palisades, where the Vice-President and his friends were engaged in clearing the dueling ground. The distance agreed upon was ten paces. When the signal *present* was given, Burr raised his arm slowly, took deliberate aim, and fired. Hamilton received the bullet just below his chest, and as he fell a convulsive movement of the fingers discharged his pistol without aim. Death relieved him after 30 hours of intense suffering.

So perished one of the greatest men of the age, for his little faith in the government he had helped to form and in the people he had served so well.

4. THE ASSAULT ON THE JUDICIARY

Aaron Burr fled to Washington, where the President received him amiably and conferred upon his friends the three best offices in Louisiana Territory. It was not that Jefferson wished to reward the slayer of Hamilton, but that he wanted something of Burr. For as Vice-President he must preside over the United States Senate, sitting as a court of impeachment to try Justice Chase of the Supreme Court.

This trial was part of a Republican attempt to rid the federal judiciary of partisan Federalists. Under Chief Justice Jay the federal courts had exercised their constitutional powers without much opposition. They had, however, made two false steps. In Chisholm *v.* Georgia (1793), a case involving confiscations contrary to the peace treaty, the Supreme Court ordered that state to appear before the bar as defendant and entered judgment against it by default. State susceptibilities, thus aroused, produced the Eleventh Amendment to the Constitution, forbidding suits against states by citizens of other states or nations. It was ratified in 1798. That same year certain federal judges, excited by the supposed Jacobin menace, enforced the Sedition Act with unholy zeal and delivered political harangues to grand juries. In February 1801, when Congress increased the number of federal courts, President Adams filled the new places with members of his party and conferred the chief justiceship on John Marshall, a kinsman whom Jefferson hated bitterly and wished to humiliate.

The feud was intensified when Chief Justice Marshall, at the first session of the Supreme Court subsequent to Jefferson's inauguration, defied him in the case of Marbury v. Madison. Marbury was a justice of the peace for the District of Columbia, a 'midnight appointment' by President Adams in the last hours of his administration. Madison, the new Secretary of State, refused to deliver his commission to Marbury, who applied to the Supreme Court for a writ of mandamus, under section 13 of the Judiciary Act of 1789. Chief Justice Marshall, delivering the opinion of the Court (February 1803), first considered the point whether Madison had a right to withhold the commission of a properly appointed official and decided against the Secretary of State. 'Is it to be contended that the heads of departments are not amenable to the laws of their country?' But Marbury's hopes were dashed by the rest of the opinion, on the point whether the Supreme Court was competent to grant him a remedy. The Federal Constitution, in defining the original jurisdiction of the Supreme Court, did not include the issue of writs to executive officers. The real question, then, was whether the Court should follow section 13 of the Judiciary Act, or the Constitution.

Marshall's opinion on this point contains statements that have vitally influenced the development of constitutional law in the United States:

> It is a proposition too plain to be contested, that the Constitution controls any legislative act repugnant to it.
>
> A legislative act contrary to the Constitution is not law.
>
> It is emphatically the province and duty of the judicial department to say what the law is.
>
> A law repugnant to the Constitution is void . . . *courts*, as well as other departments, are bound by that instrument.

It followed that section 13 of the Judiciary Act was unconstitutional and the Court could not take jurisdiction. A nicer sense of propriety might have suggested to Marshall that if the Court had no jurisdiction it should not announce how it would have decided the case if it had. But Marshall was bent on rebuking Jefferson and Madison for what he considered an arbitrary act.

Jefferson now incited some of his henchmen in the House to move against certain federal judges. A district judge who had become intemperate to the point of insanity was impeached and removed. The next victim was to be Justice Samuel Chase of the Supreme Court, a signer of the Declaration of Independence, who on the bench had made himself peculiarly obnoxious to the Republicans, predicting that under Jefferson 'our republican constitution will sink into a mobocracy, the worst of all possible governments.' By a straight partisan vote, the House of Representatives impeached him on several counts of malfeasance and misfeasance in office. Strange to relate, after all that had been said about the danger of following British precedents, the Senate was fitted up in imitation of the House of Lords at the impeachment of Warren Hastings. Vice-President Burr presided; John Randolph of Roanoke prosecuted for the House, and Luther Martin and Robert Goodloe Harper defended Chase. There was no evidence to substantiate the serious charges against him, although his manners on the bench had been rough; and when it came to a vote on 1 March 1805, enough Republican Senators joined the federalists to acquit the Justice of 'crimes and misdemeanors.'

Had Chase been found guilty on the evidence presented, there is good reason to believe that the entire Supreme Court would have been purged. As it was, this trial proved to be the high-water mark of Jefferson's radicalism. Under Chief Justice Marshall conservatism rallied, and from the Supreme Court there developed a subtle offensive of ideas — the supremacy of the nation and the sanctity of property. 'The Federalists,' wrote Jefferson bitterly, 'defeated at the polls, have retired into the Judiciary, and from that barricade they hope to batter down all the bulwarks of Republicanism.' To a large measure they succeeded.

5. SECOND TERM BEGINS SOMBERLY

Thomas Jefferson, returned to the presidency by an overwhelming majority, started his second term on 4 March 1805, expecting to pursue the 'wise and frugal' policy of 1801 to its logical conclusion. Instead, his party began to break up into its constituent sections: land-hungry Westerners, New England underdogs, Virginian Republicans who cared only for principle, and Middle-state democrats who cared little for principle but much for place. Peace in Europe had been the condition of Jefferson's earlier success, but there was to be no peace in Europe for ten years. Before the end of 1805 Napoleon was supreme on land, and Britain at sea. Each side sought to starve or strangle the other by continental or maritime blockade. It was a more difficult situation for the American government than in the wars of 1792 to 1801.

Jefferson first tried fishing for Florida in the troubled waters of European diplomacy. He believed that both Floridas should have been thrown in with Louisiana, and he wanted especially West Florida, which included Mobile Bay, the only good naval harbor in the Gulf, and the lower courses of the rivers that drained Mississippi Territory and the Creek Nation.

Informed by the American minister at Paris that Napoleon might be persuaded to extort West Florida for the United States from Spain if it were made worth his while, Jefferson in December 1805 sent a secret message to Congress, hinting at his need for $2 million for 'diplomatic intercourse.' This message was the signal for a schism in the Republican party. John Randolph, brilliant in intellect, erratic in conduct, but steadfast in the faith of ideal republicanism that had carried Jefferson into office, had for some time been chafing under the yoke of party discipline. He now announced that he would stand for no shifting of responsibility; if the President wanted money, he must ask for it without evasion. Invited to a conference with the Secretary of State, Randolph was told by Madison that 'France wants money, and we must give it to her or have a Spanish and a French war' — a phrase that Randolph promptly published, and that the Federalists never allowed the country to forget. In the end Congress voted the $2 million, but that proved to be useless in a shifting Europe. Jefferson lost the support of John Taylor, high priest of Virginia Republicanism, and the Federalists were convinced that Jefferson had sold out to Bonaparte.

The concluding episode of this crucial year in Jefferson's fortunes was the Burr conspiracy. Before leaving Washington at the expiration of his term as Vice-President, Burr approached the British minister with an offer to detach Louisiana from the Union for half a million dollars, provided the Royal Navy would co-operate. Mr. Merry thought well of it and urged his government to pay, but Downing Street was not interested in promoting American secession.

Burr then proceeded to the headwaters of the Ohio and, with a few friends, sailed down-river in a luxury flat-boat, stopping here and there to propose a different scheme at every place. The Westerners, duelers themselves, were charmed by the polished gentleman from New York. Harman Blennerhasset, a romantic Irish exile, was fascinated with a plan to conquer Mexico, make Burr emperor and himself a grand potentate. In Tennessee Burr met and won the friendship of Andrew Jackson, who proposed to get him elected to the Senate if he would settle there. General Wilkinson, still in Spanish pay while governor of Louisiana Territory and ranking general of the United States Army, had already discussed with Burr a project to 'liberate' Mexico from Spain and make Louisiana an independent republic. At New Orleans Burr got in touch with certain creoles who disliked being sold by Napoleon and with an association of American filibusters who were eager to invade Mexico. The Catholic bishop of New Orleans and the mother superior of the Ursuline convent gave him their support and blessing. Returning overland, Burr found Westerners everywhere eager for war with Spain. In Washington again, Burr obtained $2500 from the Spanish minister, ostensibly for the purpose of capturing the United States naval vessels then in the Potomac and embarking a filibustering expedition to 'liberate' Louisiana!

In the summer of 1806 the former Vice-President established headquarters at Lexington, Ky., and began active recruiting for his expedition. What was his real object? Ostensibly it was to take up and colonize an enormous land claim he had purchased in western Louisiana. Those supposedly 'in the know' expected him to move into Texas and 'liberate' Mexico. Evidence is strong that Burr did have his eye on Mexico, but that, first, he would promote a secession of Louisiana Territory and become its president.

At this juncture General Wilkinson, deciding that Burr was worth more to betray than to befriend, sent a lurid letter to President Jefferson denouncing 'a deep, dark, wicked, and wide-spread conspiracy' to dismember the Union. Similar warnings reached Washington from loyal Westerners. In the late autumn of 1806 the President issued a proclamation ordering the arrest of Burr. He was apprehended and brought to

Richmond for trial, on a charge of treason against the United States. Fortunately for the prisoner, Chief Justice Marshall, who presided at his trial, took care that the constitutional definition of treason, 'levying war against the United States or adhering to their enemies,' and the constitutional safeguard of 'two witnesses to the same overt act,' should be strictly observed. Hence it followed that merely recruiting with treasonable intent was not treason. Burr was acquitted and sought exile in France, regretting no doubt that he had not killed Jefferson instead of Hamilton. Wilkinson, a traitor to every cause he embraced, retained his command and the confidence of the President.

This was the most formidable secession conspiracy prior to 1860, one which very probably would have succeeded if Burr had reached New Orleans. Hundreds of respectable characters, as well as adventurers, were behind Burr, although most of them had no clear idea of his intentions. Now visiting England and France, he interested important people in various schemes — to revolutionize Mexico, to win Canada back for France, to mobilize unemployed American sailors to overthrow Jefferson, to mediate peace between England and France and turn them both against the United States. But he never won official support. In 1812 he managed to obtain a passport and return to New York, where he built up a good law practice; and in 1833, at the age of 77, he married an attractive widow, who used to boast that she was the only woman in the world who had been embraced both by George Washington and Napoleon Bonaparte.

6. FOREIGN COMPLICATIONS AND THE EMBARGO

The acquittal of Justice Chase and of Aaron Burr marked a turning point in Jefferson's fortunes and popularity. His second term was compared by John Randolph to Pharaoh's dream of the seven lean kine that ate up the seven fat kine. Many old Virginia Republicans felt that Jefferson had deserted his own principles with the acquisition of Louisiana; as he certainly did when, in his second inaugural address, he recommended spending federal money on roads and other internal improvements. As John Randolph put it, Jefferson spelled Federalism backwards for four years, and now began spelling it forwards again, by adopting policies which he had formerly condemned. The President began to rely for support in Congress on Republicans from the Northern states, who for the most part were a rather sad lot, interested mainly in patronage. Randolph called one of them, Barnabas Bidwell of Massachusetts (who later fled to Canada to escape the consequence of stealing public money), 'the president's clerk of the water-closet.'

Jefferson increased the powers of the Federal Government largely in order to cope with the situation in Europe, where Napoleon and Britain sought to starve or strangle each other by continental or maritime blockade. Washington and Adams had had to deal with but one belligerent at a time; Jefferson was confronted with both at once. A clever diplomat might conceivably have played off one country against the other, with an armed force as stake in the game. But neither Jefferson nor Madison could grasp the realities of Napoleonic Europe, and the President began a further reduction of the United States Navy even before concluding peace with Tripoli. Instead of building frigates, which naval officers wanted, he ordered the construction of gunboats, which were less expensive but proved to be of slight value in naval warfare.[3]

As soon as the Royal Navy considered the renewal of war with France inevitable, it resumed the practice of impressing British subjects from American vessels on the high seas; and men were plucked off American ships even outside New York harbor. Britain never claimed the right to take native-born Americans, but to impress her own subjects from foreign vessels wherever found. British seamen were constantly deserting to the American merchant marine and navy. The U.S.S. *Constitution* in 1807 had 149 avowed British subjects, and only 241 who claimed American citizenship, in her crew of 419. And neither country then admitted the right of expatriation.

When a short-handed man-of-war visited an American merchantman, the boarding officer was apt to impress any likely looking lad who had the slightest trace of an Irish or English accent. Mistakes were inevitable, and difficult to rectify. There were enough instances of brutality and injustice to create indignation, quite apart from the question of law.

At the same time, old controversies over neutral rights were revived. Jefferson's instructions, to persuade England to renounce impressment and respect neutral trade, were unrealistic, as the American envoys James Monroe and William Pinkney soon realized. They followed Jay's

3. For instance, Matthew Lyon, hero of the first fistfight in Congress, jailed under the Sedition Act and returned to Congress in time to cast the vote of his state for Jefferson, was given a contract for five gunboats at Eddyville, Ky., on the Ohio river.

precedent of disregarding instructions and signed (31 December 1806)
the best terms they could obtain, a treaty very similar to Jay's — which
Monroe had vehemently denounced. But this treaty had so little reference to what Jefferson had in mind that he did not even submit it to the
Senate. There followed a British order in council (7 January 1807)
further narrowing the scope of neutral commerce, and an impressment
outrage which brought the two countries to the verge of war.

A British squadron, stationed within the Capes of the Chesapeake to
watch French frigates up the Bay, lost many men by desertion, and had
reason to believe that Jenkin Ratford, the ringleader, had enlisted in the
United States frigate *Chesapeake.* That was true; and she had other
British-born tars in her crew. On 22 June the *Chesapeake,* flying the
broad pennant of Commodore Barron, got under way from Hampton
Roads. H.M.S. *Leopard* detached herself from the British squadron and
followed. When both vessels were about ten miles outside the Capes, the
Leopard luffed up about half a cable's length to windward and signaled
'Dispatches.' Barron supposed that she wished him to carry mail to
Europe, a common courtesy between the two navies in those days. He
backed his main topsail and invited the British captain to send a boat on
board. The dispatches proved to be an order from Admiral Berkeley to
search for and remove deserters. Barron, ignorant of Ratford's presence,
replied that the only deserters from the Royal Navy in his crew were
three Americans who had escaped after impressment, and that he would
permit no search. Within ten minutes *Leopard* fired a full broadside into
the American, and poured in two more before Barron could reply; for
the *Chesapeake's* decks were littered with stores, and few of her guns
were mounted. After three men had been killed, Barron struck his flag.
His crew were then mustered by the *Leopard's* officers, and three Americans and Ratford were impressed.

News of this insult to the flag brought the first united expression of
American feeling since 1798. Even the Federalists, who had hitherto
defended every move of British sea power, were confounded. If Jefferson had summoned Congress to a special session, he could have had war
at the drop of a hat, and it would have been a far more popular war
than the one declared in 1812. But Jefferson's serenity was undisturbed.
He instructed Monroe to demand apology and reparation in London,
and ordered British warships out of American territorial waters. When
Congress met, in late October, the President obtained an appropriation

of $850,000 for building 188 more gunboats, and ordered three of the largest ships of the small sea-going navy to be hauled out.

7. JEFFERSON'S EMBARGO

No suggestion of war, or of preparation for war, came from the President. For Jefferson imagined he had England by the throat, and could strangle her by a mere turn of the wrist. For years he had been wanting an opportunity to try commercial exclusion as a substitute for war. Jefferson reasoned that since the United States was the world's largest neutral carrier and the chief market for British manufactures, Britain could be brought to terms. The President urged: 'Let us see whether having taught so many other useful lessons to Europe, we may not add that of showing them that there are peaceable means of repressing injustice, by making it to the interest of the aggressor to do what is just.' Jefferson now sent a brief message to Congress and in one day, 22 December 1807, it passed the famous Embargo Act. American or other vessels were forbidden to sail foreign, all exports from the United States whether by sea or land were prohibited, and certain specified articles of British manufacture were refused entrance.[4] The embargo went into effect immediately; and for fourteen months every American ship that was not already abroad, or could not escape, lay in port or went coasting.

The embargo struck a staggering blow to foreign trade, the most important source of America's economic growth in these years. After the outbreak of war in Europe in 1793, ships of every belligerent save England had vanished from the seas, leaving the enormous colonial trade of Europe to neutrals, and especially the United States. To avoid being intercepted, ships with tropical products — sugar, coffee, tea, pepper, cocoa — sailed to the United States, and their cargoes were then re-shipped. From 1790 to 1807 domestic exports had doubled; re-exports in that same period grew from $300,000 to more than $59 million. The war also proved a boon for grain and cotton growers when Europe's sources of these staples were cut off. During this period of flourishing commerce, the population of Philadelphia more than doubled, Boston nearly

---

4. The last measure was not, strictly speaking, a part of the embargo of December 1807, but the Non-importation Act of 16 April 1806, which did not go into effect until the embargo was adopted.

doubled, and Baltimore and New York almost tripled. Much of the increase came from shipping and shipbuilding, and their effect on dependent industries such as ropewalks, sailmaking, lumbering, provisioning, marine insurance companies, and even banks. The young nation's economic growth in this period was largely based on its ability to take advantage of neutrality in a world at war. The embargo snuffed out this profitable trade and threw thousands of sailors and shipwrights out of jobs. To the Yankees it seemed as outrageous for Congress to decree 'Thou shalt not sail!' as it would have to the South, had Congress said 'Thou shalt not plant!'

It is true that between British orders and French decrees, American vessels could visit no part of the world without rendering themselves liable to capture by one belligerent or the other. But the American merchant marine throve on such treatment; shipowners wanted no protection other than that which the British navy afforded them. European restrictions merely increased the profit with the risk; and there were plenty of lines of trade open to neutral shipowners who were willing to put up with British inspection and license, which was far less rigorous than a similar system during the two world wars. At Smyrna, for instance, American ships enjoyed the privileges of the Levant Company and the protection of the British consul. In 1810 a Salem ship that forced the Dardanelles was saved from Turkish confiscation by the British ambassador. Hence the embargo was detested by the very interest it was supposed to protect. Smuggling of British goods and American products went on over the Canadian and Florida boundaries, but unemployed seamen and shipwrights emigrated in such large numbers to the British provinces that a sarcastic loyalist called the embargo 'an act for the better encouragement of the British Colonies in America.' The greater shipowners who had a fleet abroad survived the embargo well enough; but many small ones were ruined, and some of the lesser seaports such as Newburyport and New Haven never recovered their earlier prosperity. Jefferson even tried to hold up the coasting trade by executive orders, but Justice William Johnson, whom he had appointed to the Supreme Bench to counteract Marshall, stopped that by writ of mandamus. The embargo also hurt the South, where cotton prices were almost halved, but New England spoke out most loudly against the policy, because it was the stronghold of the Federalists, who viewed the embargo as a sectional and partisan conspiracy. One Federalist wrote: 'The sky is lowering. What it will produce no one can tell. That the Administration is bent on checking the spirit of Commerce, and gradually undermining it I have no doubt. That it is favorably disposed towards the French Government I more than suspect.'

To succeed as a weapon of diplomacy, commercial retaliation requires an unusual combination of circumstances — which very seldom occur, and did not occur in 1807–9. The embargo caused a shortage of provisions in the French West Indies and of colonial produce in France; but Napoleon confiscated every American vessel that arrived at a French port, on the ground that he was helping Jefferson to enforce the measure! In the English manufacturing districts the embargo caused some distress, but the usual exports soon found their way into the United States through Canada, and British shipowners loved a measure that removed American competition.

Jefferson's mistake was the Federalists' opportunity. Their strength had been dwindling, even in New England, where in 1807 every state government except Connecticut's went Republican. The Federalists had been unable to overcome the stigma of monarchism and militarism the Republicans had fastened on them, and they were handicapped by a late start in developing effective party organization. 'We must court popular favor,' wrote Fisher Ames in 1801. 'We must study popular opinion and accommodate measures to what it is.' But in 1807 he was moaning: 'I fear Federalism will not only die, but all remembrance of it be lost.' Now, unexpectedly, Jefferson had handed them an issue on which they might make a popular appeal. Senator Pickering, the conspirator of 1804, rallied New England opinion by a public letter, roundly asserting that the embargo was dictated by Napoleon and adopted by Jefferson in the hope of destroying the shipping interest and impoverishing New England.

The Federalists approached the 1808 election with high hopes. A New Englander recorded in his diary: 'Electioneering opened. Pamphlets flying like wild geese in a storm.' Northern republicans were restive under a measure that turned their constituents Federalist; and in New York City the embargo produced a schism in the Republican party. When Madison was nominated for the presidential succession by a congressional caucus, the New York legislature placed George Clinton in nomination as an anti-embargo Republican. In Virginia John Randolph's sect of 'pure Republicans' nominated Monroe, who had been disaffected since the rejection of his treaty. If a union could have been effected between these factions and the Federalists, Madison might have been defeated. But the Federalist candidate, C. C. Pinckney, carried little but New England, save Vermont, and Delaware, and Madison was elected President by a comfortable majority, 122–47.

Jefferson intended to maintain the embargo until the British orders or the French decrees were repealed. In January 1809 Congress passed the 'Force Act,' permitting federal officials without warrant to seize goods under suspicion of foreign destination and protecting them from legal liability for their actions. Watchmen patrolled Atlantic wharves, and revenue officers seized sails and unshipped rudders. George III and Lord North had been tender in comparison. The people of New England, now in their second winter of privation and distress, began to look to their state governments for protection; and by this time all state governments of New England were Federalist again. The legislatures hurled back in the teeth of Jefferson and Madison the doctrines of the Kentucky and Virginia resolves of 1798. Connecticut resolved that 'whenever our national legislature is led to overleap the prescribed bounds of their constitutional powers,' it becomes the duty of the state legislatures 'to interpose their protecting shield between the right and liberty of the people, and the assumed power of the General Government.' A proposal to summon a New England convention for nullification of the embargo was being discussed in February 1809.

By that time the embargo had been in force fourteen months. The Northern Republicans revolted; and Jefferson was shaken by a volley of protests from New England town meetings, some of them threatening secession. A bill for the repeal of the embargo was rushed through Congress and, on 1 March 1809, approved by Jefferson. Three days later his term ended and he retired to Monticello.

The embargo was intended to be the crowning glory of Jefferson's second administration, as Louisiana had been of his first, but it proved a dismal failure. It neither influenced the policy of Britain or of Napoleon nor protected the merchant marine. It wasted the fruit of Jefferson's first administration: the creation of a broad, country-wide party in every state of the Union. It convinced many good people that the 'Virginia dynasty' was bound to that of Bonaparte, that the Republican party was a greater enemy than British sea power to American shipping. Whatever President Madison might do or neglect to do, he would never have such united support as Jefferson had enjoyed in 1807.

Yet despite the failure of the embargo, Jefferson was one of the greatest of Presidents, and the most tolerant of revolutionists. Few men have combined in like degree a lofty idealism with the ability to administer a government. He deliberately preferred the slow process of reason to the short way of force. By his forbearance, even more than by his acts, Jefferson kept alive the flame of liberty that Napoleon had almost quenched in Europe.

XX

The Second War
with Great Britain

1. DIPLOMACY AND DRIFT

Owing to James Madison's labors on the Federal Constitution he must
be accounted a great statesman, but he was a very poor politician; and a
poor politician usually makes a bad President, although a good 'pol' does
not necessarily make a good chief magistrate. Slight in stature and un-
impressive in personality, eager to please but wearing a puzzled look on
his face as though people were too much for him, 'Jemmy' Madison had
few intimate friends, and among the people at large he inspired little
affection and no enthusiasm. He had a talent for writing logical diplomatic notes; but logic was not much use in dealing with Europeans
locked in a deadly struggle. He was negative in dealing with Congress,
allowing Jefferson's system of personal influence with members to fall
apart. And Madison was stubborn to the point of stupidity.

Yet, within six weeks of his inauguration on 4 March 1809, Madison
was being greeted as a great peacemaker. Congress, when repealing
Jefferson's embargo, substituted a non-intercourse act aimed at both
Britain and France, with the promise of resuming commercial relations
with whichever nation first repealed its decrees injuring American commerce. Madison, eager to reach an understanding with England, arranged a treaty with David Erskine, the British minister in Washington,
by virtue of which His Majesty's government would rescind their orders

357

against American shipping, and the United States would resume normal trading relations with Britain but maintain non-intercourse against France. And touchy subjects such as impressment and the *Chesapeake* affair were postponed.

If this draft treaty had been accepted by George Canning, the British minister of foreign affairs, there would have been no second war with England. But Canning brutally repudiated both Erskine and the treaty, and Anglo-American relations returned to their then normal state of mutual recrimination.

The Congress that assembled in December 1809 had no idea what to do, and received no lead from Madison. On 16 April 1810 it voted to reduce both the army and the navy, weak though they already were. And on 1 May Congress reversed the principle of the earlier Non-Intercourse Act by passing Macon's Bill No. 2. This law restored intercourse with both Britain and France, but promised to the first power which recognized neutral rights, to stop trading with her enemy. American ships promptly resumed making juicy profits under British license, and merchant tonnage reached figures that were not again attained for another twenty years.

Madison took advantage of this interlude in commercial warfare to take a bite out of West Florida. The Republican administrations claimed to have bought that province with Louisiana, and now, when the Spanish empire appeared to be breaking up, was the time to act. Accordingly, the inhabitants of that portion of West Florida bordering on the Mississippi 'self-determined' for the United States, in 1810, seized Baton Rouge, and were incorporated by presidential proclamation into the Territory of Orleans, which two years later became the state of Louisiana. In May 1812 a second bite was taken, when the district between the Pearl and Perdido rivers was annexed by Act of Congress to Mississippi Territory.

The Emperor Napoleon found time between his campaigns, and divorcing Josephine and marrying Marie Louise, to cast his eye over Macon's Act, and observe an opportunity to incorporate the United States into his Continental system. That system was strikingly similar to Hitler's scheme of bringing England to her knees without winning control of the sea. It meant getting the European continent under his control, in order to impoverish England, the country which he, like Hitler, considered 'a nation of shopkeepers.' America could help this strategy by adding a sea-power component; as she actually did in 1812, too late to help Napoleon.

For five years Napoleon had treated American shipping harshly and arbitrarily. In the summer of 1810 our merchantmen at Naples were seized by imperial command, and ordered sold. But on the same day Napoleon's minister of foreign affairs informed the American minister to France that 'His Majesty loves the Americans,' and as proof of his solicitude had declared that his decrees against neutral shipping after 1 November would be revoked; 'it being understood that the English are to revoke their orders in council.'

John Quincy Adams, minister to Russia, warned Madison that this note was 'a trap to catch us into a war with England.' But the President, searching desperately for an effective policy, fell into the trap. By proclamation on 2 November 1810 he announced that France had rescinded her anti-neutral system, hence non-intercourse would be revived against Britain, if within three months she did not repeal the orders in council. Almost every mail, for the next two years, brought news of fresh seizures and scuttlings of American vessels by French port authorities, warships, and privateers. But Madison, having taken his stand, obstinately insisted that 'the national faith was pledged to France.' On 2 March 1811 he forbade intercourse with Great Britain, under authority of Macon's Act. This practically brought the United States within Napoleon's Continental system. This time, economic sanctions really worked against England — but too late to preserve the peace. The winter of 1811–12 was the bitterest that the English people experienced between the Great Plague of 1665 and the German blitz of 1940–41. Napoleon had now closed all western Europe except Portugal to British goods. American non-intercourse shut off the only important market still open except Russia, which Napoleon was about to try to force into his cordon. A crop failure raised the price of wheat to $4.50 a bushel, warehouses were crammed with goods for which there was no market, factories were closing, workmen rioting. Deputations from the manufacturing cities besought Parliament to repeal the orders in council, to recover their American market.

During these critical months several accidents postponed repeal, which, had it taken place in time, would have maintained peace with America. On 16 May 1811 there was an off-the-record fight between U.S. frigate *President* and H.M. corvette *Little Belt,* the result of which seemed to prove that the United States Navy was not to be feared. The American legation at London was vacant, except for a silly young chargé d'affaires, when the conciliatory Lord Castlereagh entered the foreign office. Spencer Perceval, the prime minister, was assassinated just after he had made up his mind to repeal the orders in council, and the business of finding a successor brought another and fatal delay. Finally on 16 June 1812, Castlereagh announced that the orders in council would be suspended immediately. If there had been a transatlantic cable, this would not have been too late. But Congress, having no word of the concession, declared war against Great Britain on 18 June 1812.

2. WAR FEVER RISES

Congress so acted in response to a message from President Madison recommending war with Britain on four grounds — impressment of seamen, repeated violations of American territorial waters by the Royal Navy, declaring an enemy coast blockaded when it was not blockaded in fact, and the orders in council against neutral trade. Yet six senators and a large majority of the congressmen from the New England states, and a majority in both houses from New York, New Jersey, and Maryland, voted against the declaration of war; whilst representatives of the inland and Western states from Vermont to Tennessee, and of the states from Virginia south, were almost solidly for war. New England, where three-quarters of American shipping was owned, and which supplied more than that proportion of American seamen, wanted no war and agitated against it to the brink of treason; whilst back-country congressmen who had never smelled salt water (unless in the Potomac), and whose constituents would as soon have thought of flying to the moon as enlisting in the United States Navy, screamed for 'Free Trade and Sailors' Rights.'

The explanation? Republican party leaders believed that they had tried to prevent war by diplomacy and economic sanction and, since both had failed, they had no choice left but capitulation or war. As Jefferson observed: 'Every hope from time, patience, and love of peace is exhausted and war or abject submission are the only alternatives left to us.' If they did not choose war, they feared they would jeopardize both the confidence of the nation in the strength of republican institutions and the future of the Republican party. If the government gave in, wrote a Baltimore leader, 'we may as well give up our Republican Government & have a Despot to rule over us.' A generation with a keen memory of the recent revolution thought that submission to the orders in council would mean acceptance of colonial status and loss of national honor.

The South and West felt that it also had economic grievances which justified war with Britain. Westerners and Southerners had no stake in the carrying trade, in which New Englanders made profits despite British restrictions, but they had a growing interest in overseas markets. Worried over the declining prices of staple exports like cotton, tobacco, and hemp, they blamed their troubles, unjustifiably, on the British. A South Carolinian protested: 'Inquire into the state of the cotton market; where is the crop of 1810? A curse to him who meddled with it. Where is that of 1811? Rotting at home in the hands of the grower, waiting the repeal of the Orders in Council.'

Some of the newer Republican leaders were much more ardent for war than was President Madison. The elections of 1810–11 had sent to Congress a remarkably able group of newcomers, who quickly assumed positions of leadership. There were thirty-four-year-old Henry Clay and Richard M. Johnson from Kentucky; equally young Felix Grundy and aged but very bellicose John Sevier from Tennessee; Peter B. Porter, also in his thirties, from Buffalo, N.Y.; and twenty-nine-year-old John C. Calhoun from the backcountry of South Carolina. These men, dubbed 'war hawks' by John Randolph, combined with other new members to brush aside old Nathaniel Macon and elect Henry Clay speaker of the house; and Clay named his friends chairmen of the important committees. Clay found lodgings at a Washington boardinghouse which was soon known as 'the strongest war mess in Congress.' The war hawks wished to scuttle diplomacy and economic sanctions, and declare war against Great Britain, using arguments that reminded old hands of the Hamiltonian reasons for war with France in 1798. They passed a bill to raise a regular army of 25,000, but did nothing for the navy; for it was still Republican doctrine that navies were evil. Richard M. Johnson, in a burst of oratory, appealed to the examples of Tyre, Sidon, Athens, and Carthage to prove that navies had always been 'engines of power, employed in projects of ambition and war.' Some of the war hawks wished also to declare war on France, but Madison used his influence to stop that. Stubbornly, against cumulative evidence of Napoleon's bad faith and outrages to American shipping, the President insisted that France had repealed her anti-neutral decrees.

The war hawks were disgusted with the wordy diplomacy of Madison and Secretary of State Monroe; they felt that national honor demanded a fight. Furthermore, war with Great Britain, if successful, would conquer Canada, end the Indian menace on the Western frontier, and throw open more forest land for settlement by United States pioneers. John Randolph of Roanoke, leader of the old-fashioned 'pure' Republicans who wished to keep the peace, poured his scorn on this 'cant of patriotism,' this 'agrarian cupidity,' this chanting 'like the whippoorwill, but one monotonous tone — Canada! Canada! Canada! Not a syllable about Halifax, which unquestionably should be our great objective in a war for maritime security.'

As Andrew Jackson, commander of the militia in western Tennessee, summed up the reasons for war: 'We are going to fight for the reestablishment of our national character, misunderstood and vilified at home and abroad; for the protection of our maritime citizens, impressed on board British ships of war and compelled to fight the battles of our enemies against ourselves; to vindicate our right to a free trade, and open a market for the productions of our soil, now perishing on our hands because the *mistress of the ocean* has forbid us to carry them to any foreign nation; in fine, to seek some indemnity for past injuries, some security against future aggressions, by the conquest of all the British dominions upon the continent of north america.'

Western concern over the Indian menace was a major cause of war, although areas in which the alarm was most intense — Mississippi, Indiana, Illinois, and Michigan — were still territories with no vote in Congress. The 1795 Treaty of Greenville ended a period in which the Northwest Indians had usually been the aggressors, and put them on the defensive. Jefferson professed benevolent principles toward them, but looked forward to moving all Indians across the Mississippi in order to encourage western migration and keep the United States agricultural. The harshness of such a policy could be mitigated only by protecting the red men from the whites during the process, and that was not done. Although the redskins faithfully fulfilled their treaty stipulations, white pioneers in the Northwest committed the most wanton and cruel murders of Indians, for which it was almost impossible to obtain a conviction from a pioneer jury. From time to time a few hungry and desperate chiefs were rounded up by government officials and plied with oratory and whiskey until they signed a treaty alienating forever the hunting grounds of their tribe, perhaps of other nations as well. Jefferson encouraged this process; and William Henry Harrison, superintendent of the Northwest Indians and governor of Indiana Territory,[1] pushed it so successfully that during the fourteen years following the 1795 Greenville treaty the Indians of that region parted with some 48 million acres. In 1809 this process came to a halt, owing in part to renewed efforts by British authorities in Canada to stiffen Indian resistance. Their efforts, as much as land hunger and far more than indignation over sailors' rights, contributed to war fever west of the Appalachians.

After the British evacuated the Northwest posts in 1796, they established two new ones on Canadian soil, St. Joseph's near Michilimackinac and Amherstburg near Detroit. These were used peacefully, to promote Canadian fur trade, until 1808, when new Canadian officials took office who believed that war with the United States was likely if not inevitable. In view of the weakness of Canada, and Britain's inability to give her much help while fighting Napoleon, these officials felt that the only way to prevent a conquest of Canada by the United States was to get the Indians of the Northwest on their side. Matthew Elliott, an Irish-born American loyalist and old fur trader, who had a Shawnee wife and spoke her language, was now British superintendent of the Northwest Indians, with headquarters at Amherstburg. He was directed to steer an uneasy course — to remind the Indians of the 'artful and clandestine manner' in which the Americans had obtained their lands, but dissuade them from actual warfare; to play them along until their help was needed to keep Canada under the Great White Father at London.

At this juncture appeared two really noble savages, the twin brothers Tecumseh and Tenskwatawa, sons of a Shawnee chief. The former, a lithe, handsome, and stately warrior, had been one of those who defeated St. Clair in 1791; Tenskwatawa, better known as The Prophet, was a half-blind medicine man who won ascendancy over his people by such simple means as foretelling an eclipse of the sun. The two, around 1808, bravely undertook the task of saving their people. They sought to reform their habits, stop the alienation of their land, keep them apart from the whites, and to weld all tribes on United States soil into a confederacy. It was a movement of regeneration and defense, a menace indeed to the expansion of the West but in no sense to its existence.

1. Indiana Territory, created in 1800, included all the old Northwest Territory except Ohio, which became a state in 1803. Michigan Territory was detached in 1805, and Illinois Territory (including Wisconsin), in 1809.

The Indians had so decreased in the last decade that scarcely 4000 warriors could be counted on in the region bounded by the Great Lakes, the Mississippi, and the Ohio. Opposed to them were at least 100,000 white men of fighting age in the Ohio valley.

For a time the partnership of warrior and priest was irresistible. The Prophet kindled a religious revival among the tribes of the Northwest, and actually induced them to give up intoxicating liquor. All intercourse with white men, except for trade, ceased; rum and whiskey were refused with disdain. In 1808 the two leaders, forced from their old settlement by the palefaces, established headquarters at a great clearing in Indiana, where Tippecanoe creek empties into the Wabash river. The entire frontier was alarmed. Indian prohibitionists were something new to backwoods experience.

There was, indeed, cause for alarm, although a similar reform in pioneer habits and a change in Madison's Indian policy would have removed it. The Prophet's moral influence extended as far south as Florida, and northwest to Saskatchewan, and naturally he was unfriendly to the United States. Governor Harrison met the situation with an act that Tecumseh could only regard as a challenge. Rounding up a few score survivors of tribes whom he frankly described as 'the most depraved wretches on earth,' the governor obtained from them several enormous tracts, to the amount of some three million acres, cutting up both banks of the Wabash into the heart of Tecumseh's country. This deprived Tecumseh of his remaining hunting grounds and brought the white border within fifty miles of the Tippecanoe.

With justice Tecumseh declared this treaty null and void. He called on Elliott at Amherstburg in November 1810, and declared that he was ready for war; but Canada was not. More Western nations joined his confederacy, and in July 1811, assuring Governor Harrison that his object was defensive, he journeyed south to obtain the allegiance of the Creek nation. Tecumseh was making good progress in that direction when Harrison decided to force the issue. With the tacit approval of the war department, he collected about 1100 soldiers, marched up the Wabash valley, and encamped hard by Tecumseh's village. The Prophet had been strictly enjoined by his brother to avoid hostilities; but instead of retiring he allowed himself to be maneuvered into battle by a few reckless young braves, who raised the war-whoop and pierced the first line of American tents. The engagement then became general; the Americans were almost surrounded, but after two hours' fighting Harrison drove the Indians into a swamp and destroyed their village. The Governor brought his army safely back to Vincennes and was hailed throughout the West as their savior. This Battle of Tippecanoe (7 November 1811) helped to elect him President in 1840.

Throughout the West it was believed that Britain had backed Tecumseh's confederacy. In fact, Tecumseh's league was the result of two Indian leaders trying to counteract an American policy which threatened to wipe out their people; as eventually it did. After Tippecanoe, however, the new governor general, Sir George Prevost, decided that war with the United States was inevitable, and his agents welcomed Tecumseh and 1800 warriors at Amherstburg in June 1812.

Thus many, if not most Westerners, were keen for war with England in order to annex Upper Canada and wipe out the assumed source of Indian troubles.

3. THE WAR OF 1812: AGGRESSIVE PHASE

Everyone knew, well before the declaration of 18 June 1812, that this war for 'Free Trade and Sailors' Rights' would be fought largely on land, preferably in Canada. That made strategic sense, just as England's attacking Napoleon in Spain made sense; Canada was the only part of the British empire that Americans could get at dry-shod. But Canada was a very long, strung-out country, and a good deal depended on where she was attacked.

The population of British North America was less than half a million; that of the United States, by the census of 1810, 7.25 million. In the States in 1811, the enrolled militia totaled about 700,000; and the regular army, by the time the war broke out, had been recruited to about 7000 officers and men. There were fewer than 5000 British regulars in North America when war broke out, and little chance that Britain, deeply engaged in the Peninsular Campaign, could spare reinforcements. Upper Canada had been largely settled from the United States, and the French Canadians in Quebec were not expected to do much to help Britain. The former American loyalists who had peopled the Maritime Provinces were ready to fight again for King George, but the war never swung their way. Canada, however, could count on Tecumseh's braves.

Moreover, the war was far from popular in the United States. New

England's attitude was largely dictated by the prejudices and predilec-
tions of the Federalist party, stronger here than anywhere else except
Maryland and Delaware. Every Federalist vote in Congress was cast
against the declaration of war, which was greeted in New England by
mournful tolling of church bells and half-masting of American flags.
Federalists approved neither the Westerners' land-hunger for Canada,
nor the Southerners' lust for the fertile acres of the Creek nation. Jefferson's embargo had convinced them of the administration's insincerity in
claiming to protect commerce; and Madison's acquiescence in Napoleon's deceptive diplomacy suggested that the Emperor had nudged us
into war. And the fact that, as soon as the orders in council were rejected, the British government through its admiral on the American
station, offered an unconditional armistice which Madison contemptu-
ously refused, convinced the doubters in the party that the administration was bent on glory and conquest.

Federalists were incensed when Congress adjourned 6 July 1812
without making any provision to increase the navy, whose total strength
until the spring of 1813 was six frigates, three sloops-of-war, and seven
smaller vessels, not counting the fleet of gunboats, which proved to be
completely useless. To refuse to increase one's naval force in a war with
the world's greatest sea power for 'Free Trade and Sailors' Rights'
seemed gross hypocrisy to the Federalists. And the President, instead
of trying to rally them to the flag, drove them to fury by publishing,
three months before his war message, the letters of a British spy in an
attempt to incriminate Federalists as British agents. A man named John
Henry, sent by the governor of Canada to report on New England, had
not been rewarded as he thought he should, and approached Secretary
of State Monroe with the offer of his reports. These contained nothing
more than accounts of dinner-table conversations in Boston castigating
'the Little Man in the Palace,' as they called Madison. From the secret-
service fund, Madison paid $50,000 (almost the cost of a sloop-of-war)
for the Henry letters, hoping that they would whip up war fever. But
they backfired. At the time they came out, the Massachusetts state government was Republican, as a result of the first 'gerrymander' signed by
Governor Gerry; but in the spring elections the Bay State went Federalist again. The lower house issued a manifesto urging the country to
'organize a peace party' and 'let there be no volunteers.' The new governor, as well as his colleagues in Rhode Island and Connecticut, refused

to call state militia into national service, and Federalist merchants would neither subscribe to war bonds nor fit out privateers.

Opponents of the war sometimes met with violence. At Baltimore the plant of a Federalist newspaper which came out for peace was demolished by a mob. The friends of Alexander C. Hanson, the editor, although refusing to be intimidated, consented to be lodged for safety in the city jail; they were dragged out by a waterfront mob led by a Frenchman, and beaten to a pulp. Hanson and General Henry Lee were badly injured, and General James M. Lingan, another Revolutionary veteran, was killed. Federalists throughout the country shuddered over this episode, recalling as it did the cowardly massacres of prisoners in the French Revolution; and it turned Maryland Federalist for the duration.

Robert Smith, Monroe's predecessor as Secretary of State, issued a public address against the war; Chief Justice Marshall wrote to him that as an American he was mortified by his country's base submission to Napoleon and that the only party division henceforth should be between the friends of peace and the advocates of war. That was indeed the division in the presidential election of 1812. The Federalists supported De Witt Clinton, who had been placed in nomination by an anti-war faction of the New York Republicans, and carried every state north of the Potomac except two. But Madison was re-elected.

The administration's military strategy was also very stupid. The settled portions of Canada (excluding the Maritimes) may be compared to a tree, of which the St. Lawrence river is the trunk, the Great Lakes and their tributaries the branches, and the sea lanes to England the roots. The Britain of William Pitt had conquered Canada in 1759–60 by grasping the roots and grappling the trunk. Madison had no proper navy to attempt the former; but he might well have tried to hew the trunk by a sharp stroke at Montreal or Quebec. Instead, he attempted several feeble and unsystematic loppings at the branches.

Three weeks before war was declared, Governor William Hull of Michigan Territory, a sixty-year-old veteran of the War of Independence, was given a brigadier's commission and ordered to march to Detroit from Dayton, Ohio, cutting his own road through the wilderness; then to invade Upper Canada. By the time Hull crossed into Canada on 12 July, a small military encounter in the far Northwest had made his situation precarious. The commander of the British post at St.

Joseph's on the Sault forced the American garrison at Michilimackinac to surrender (17 July). General Hull then fell back on Detroit, and ordered the American commander at Fort Dearborn (Chicago) to come to his assistance; but the Indians captured a part of that small force and massacred the rest. General Isaac Brock, the British commander in Upper Canada, having transported to Detroit the few troops he could spare from the Niagara front, paraded them in red coats in sight of General Hull and summoned him to surrender. A broad hint in Brock's note, that the Indians would be beyond his control the moment the fighting began, completely unnerved the elderly general. Dreading massacre, deserted by some of his militia, and cut off from his base, Hull surrendered his army on 16 August 1812.

So ended the first invasion of Canada. The effective military frontier of the United States was thrown back to the Wabash and the Ohio.

Major General Samuel Hopkins, another veteran of Hull's vintage, was now ordered to lead 4000 Kentucky militiamen, assembled at Vincennes, on a punitive expedition against the Indian tribes who had massacred the Fort Dearborn garrison. Henry Clay had boasted he could conquer Canada with Kentucky militia alone; and declared that his problem was to quench, rather than to fan, the ardor of his native state. In this instance, ardor cooled so quickly that after five days the Kentucky militia became mutinous and unmanageable. When Hopkins asked for 500 volunteers to press forward, not one man offered himself, and Hopkins retreated.

One week after Hull's surrender, General Brock was back at Niagara, eager to attack his enemy on the New York side of the Niagara river. Governor Prevost restrained him, letting the Americans take the initiative on 13 October 1812. Captain John E. Wool led a small detachment of regulars across the river, to a successful attack on Queenston heights, in which General Brock was killed. Wool should have been supported by the New York militia under General Stephen Van Rensselaer; but the militia refused to budge. They had turned out to defend their homes, not to invade Canada. In vain the Patroon exhorted them. They calmly watched their countrymen on the other bank being enveloped, shot down, and forced to surrender.

Command of the American troops on the Niagara front was now given to a curious character named Alexander Smyth, known as 'Apocalypse Smyth' because he wrote an 'explanation' of the Book of Revelation. He owed his brigadier's commission to his reputation in Virginia for oratory, a gift which he proceeded to employ in speeches to his command. On a sleety November evening Smyth tumbled his army into boats to cross the Niagara, consoling them for spending the night embarked with this message: 'Hearts of War! Tomorrow will be memorable in the annals of the United States!' But on the morrow, not liking the looks of the Canadians on the further bank, Smyth called off the campaign. The soldiers joyfully discharged their muskets in every direction, showing a preference for the general's tent as a target. Brigadier Peter B. Porter, a prominent war hawk who commanded a militia regiment, publicly questioned Smyth's courage, and the two fought a pistol duel at twelve paces, but managed not to hurt each other. Smyth followed Hull and Van Rensselaer into retirement, but got himself elected to Congress, where he continued to bray for many years.

There still remained a considerable force at Plattsburg on Lake Champlain, under the immediate command of Major General Henry Dearborn, a 62-year-old veteran of Bunker Hill who had gone to seed as Jefferson's Secretary of War. Dearborn was supposed to strike the Canadian trunk at Montreal. On 19 November he marched his troops twenty miles north of Plattsburg. The militia then refused to go further, and Dearborn marched them back to Plattsburg.

On the ocean there is a different story to tell. The United States Navy was vastly outnumbered, but the Royal Navy was so deeply engaged in war with France that at first it could spare few vessels. The pride of the United States Navy were frigates *Constitution, United States,* and *President,* which threw a heavier broadside than the British frigates, and were so heavily timbered and planked as to deserve the name 'Old Ironsides'; yet with such fine, clean lines and great spread of canvas that they could outsail almost anything afloat. The crews were volunteers, and the officers, young and tried by experience against France and Tripoli, were burning to avenge the *Chesapeake.* On the other hand, the compatriots of Nelson, conquerors at Cape St. Vincent, Trafalgar, and the Nile, were the spoiled children of victory, confident of beating any vessel not more than twice their size. Hence, when U.S.S. *Constitution* (Captain Isaac Hull, a nephew of the General) knocked H.M.S. *Guerrière* helpless in two hours and a half on 19 August 1812, and on 29 December, under Captain William Bainbridge, reduced H.M. frigate *Java* to a useless hulk; when sloop-of-war *Wasp* mastered H.M.S. *Frolic*

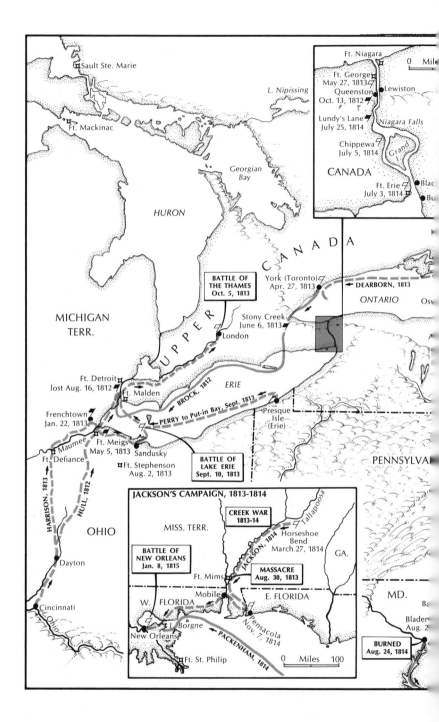

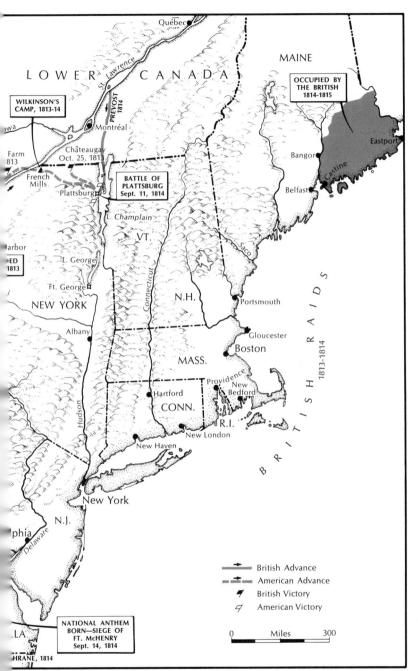

Québec

MAINE

LOWER CANADA

OCCUPIED BY
THE BRITISH
1814-1815

WILKINSON'S
CAMP, 1813-14

St. Lawrence

PREVOST
1814

Montréal

Eastport

Farm
813

Châteaugay
Oct. 25, 181

Bangor

Castine

French
Mills.

Plattsburg

BATTLE OF
PLATTSBURG
Sept. 11, 1814

Belfast

L. Champlain

VT.

arbor

Saco

L. George

ED
1813

Ft. George

Connecticut

N.H.

Portsmouth

NEW YORK

Albany

Gloucester

Boston

MASS.

Providence

New
Bedford

Hartford

CONN.

R.I.

Hudson

New London

New Haven

B R I T I S H   R A I D S

1813-1814

New York

N.J.

phia

Delaware

British Advance

American Advance

British Victory

American Victory

NATIONAL ANTHEM
BORN—SIEGE OF
FT. McHENRY
Sept. 14, 1814

LA.

HRANE, 1814

0   Miles   300

WAR OF 1812

in 43 minutes on 17 October, and U.S.S. *Hornet* (Captain James Lawrence) in a hot fight off the Demerara river, on 24 February 1813, sank
H.M.S. *Peacock* in fifteen minutes; and when frigate *United States*
(Captain Stephen Decatur) entered New London harbor with H.M.
frigate *Macedonian* as prize on 4 December 1812, there were amazement and indignation in England, and rejoicing in the United States.

The moral value of these victories to the American people, following
disaster on the Canadian border, was beyond all calculation. They even
converted some Jeffersonian Republicans from their anti-navy doctrine.
Congress accordingly made generous appropriations to increase the
navy by four ships-of-the-line and six heavy frigates. 'Frigates and
seventy-fours,' sighed Thomas Jefferson, 'are a sacrifice we must make,
heavy as it is, to the prejudices of a part of our citizens.' None of this
new construction got to sea during the war.

Unfortunately, the military value of these naval victories was slight.
Most of the American men-of-war that put into harbor during the winter
of 1812–13 never got out again. The British blockaded Delaware and
Chesapeake Bays from the fall of 1812, extended the blockade in the
spring of 1813 to New York and the seaports south of Norfolk, in November to Long Island Sound, and to New England in the spring of
1814. This blockade stifled the operations of *Constellation,* which had
enjoyed all the luck in the war with France, but was blockaded throughout this war in Norfolk, along with frigate *Adams* in the Potomac. *Constitution* entered Boston for repairs after sinking *Java,* and never got out
until December 1814, when she again distinguished herself by capturing
both H.M.S. *Cyane* and *Levant* off the African coast on 20 February
1815 — almost two months after peace had been signed.

Thus, the situation at sea for the United States in 1813–14 was much
as it had been during the War of Independence in 1779–80, but with no
help from France; the British were able to move troops by water at will.
And their base at Halifax was almost as effective as their loyalist base
had been at New York during the Revolution.

Throughout the year 1813 the Royal Navy was too busy in Europe to
lay anything better than hit-and-run raids on the Atlantic seaboard.
Randolph of Roanoke, in one of his imprecatory orations against the
war, declared, 'Go, march to Canada! Leave the broad bosom of the
Chesapeake and her hundred tributary rivers . . . unprotected.' Which
is exactly what happened. From Bermuda a powerful raiding force

under Admiral John Borlase Warren, with Rear Admiral Sir George Cockburn second in command, was sent to spread terror and destruction in Chesapeake Bay. Cockburn, a tough and ruthless old salt, within one week (April–May 1813) raided Havre de Grace, destroyed a cannon foundry up the Susquehanna and a munitions store on the Elk, and razed two villages on the Sassafras river; all without the loss of a man on either side. Hampton, where a stout militia defense inflicted casualties on the landing force, was captured, pillaged, and burned. During the rest of the year, Warren and Cockburn cruised up and down Chesapeake Bay and off the Delaware Capes, landing frequently to burn buildings and steal hogs and chickens.

In the meantime, naval history was being made on the Great Lakes. Hull's surrender at Detroit convinced President Madison that command of the Lakes was essential. The Americans surmounted great difficulties through the energy and resourcefulness of Captain Isaac Chauncey, with headquarters at Sackett Harbor on Lake Ontario, and Captain Oliver H. Perry, with headquarters at Presque Isle (Erie), Pennsylvania. Here the Americans had a logistic advantage, since Pittsburgh, not far from Erie, was already a manufacturing town. Captain Perry constructed a fleet of stout little vessels during the winter of 1812–13. That same winter, General William Henry Harrison, victor of Tippecanoe, advanced from the Ohio river toward Detroit, in three divisions. The British General Procter did not wait for them to unite, but beat two separately at Frenchtown on the Raisin river (22 January 1813) and Fort Meigs at the rapids of the Maumee (5 May) — fierce wilderness fights in which the American wounded were massacred by Indian auxiliaries. Harrison then decided to await a naval decision on Lake Erie. There Perry sought out the British squadron. He found it on 10 September, at Put-in-Bay among the islands at the western end of the lake. A strange naval battle ensued, between hastily built vessels, manned largely by militiamen, Negroes, frontier scouts, and Canadian canal men. The issue of this exceedingly bloody fight was long in doubt, but Perry refused to admit defeat. Transferring his flag to another ship in the midst of the action, he turned the tide in the American favor. Perry's laconic report, 'We have met the enemy, and they are ours,' was literally true. It was the only surrender of a complete squadron in British naval history.

The only prudent course for General Procter was to abandon Detroit and fall back on the Niagara front. But Tecumseh persuaded his ally to make a stand at an Indian village near the center of the Ontario peninsula. Thither General Harrison pursued him, after reoccupying Detroit. The Battle of the Thames or Moravian Town (5 October 1813) was a victory for the Kentucky mounted rifles. Tecumseh died on that field, his Indian confederacy broke up, Procter fled, and the American military frontier in the Northwest was re-established. This victory helped to advance the political ambitions of the 'Hero of Tippecanoe,' and Colonel Johnson's claim that he personally had slain Tecumseh made him Vice-President of the United States.

Perry's fresh-water naval squadron had obtained valuable cannon from a raid on York (Toronto), the tiny capital of Upper Canada, on 27 April 1813. A large powder magazine exploded when the Americans were advancing into the village, killing General Zebulon M. Pike and about 300 men. As a result of this incident, or of general indiscipline, the American troops got out of hand after the British had surrendered the town, and burned the two brick parliament houses, the governor's residence, and other buildings. As the British now had a considerable naval force on Lake Ontario, the Americans had to evacuate York; but Chauncey's fleet co-operated with Colonel Winfield Scott in a successful attack on Fort George.

On 10 December 1813, after another attempted American invasion of Canada had been repulsed, the British drove the American garrison out of Fort George. The American commander, a New York militia brigadier named George McClure, burned Newark and as much as he could of Queenston on retiring, turning the inhabitants out of their houses on a cold winter's night. For this act the innocent inhabitants on the American side paid dear. On 18 December Fort Niagara was taken by surprise, the Indians were let loose on the surrounding country, and the villages of Black Rock and Buffalo were destroyed.

In the meantime, an unsuccessful attempt to carry out sound strategy, a pincer attack on Montreal, was under way. General James Wilkinson (Aaron Burr's former partner) with 8000 men floated down the St. Lawrence from Sackett Harbor; and General Wade Hampton, with half that number, marched north from Plattsburg on Lake Champlain. Each allowed himself to be turned back by a mere skirmish — Hampton at Chateaugay (25 October), and Wilkinson at Chrysler's Farm (11 November 1813), seventy miles from Montreal. Thus the second year of war closed with Canada cleared of American troops, and the Canadians in possession of Fort Niagara and ready to assume the offensive. For the most part, the American performance in the initial stage of the war had been disappointing and, too often, inglorious. The war department was never able to build up the regular army to half its authorized strength, and the President got only 10,000 one-year volunteers, when 50,000 were authorized. Even Henry Clay's Kentucky furnished only 400 recruits to the army in 1812. The loyal minority in New England more than made up for the discouraging stand of the state governments; those five states provided the regular army with nineteen regiments, the Middle States with fifteen, the Southern States with only ten.[2] The war was unpopular throughout the country, after Hull's surrender had shown that it would be no walk-over. One reason, no doubt, was the uninspiring leadership of President Madison and his ministers. Albert Gallatin, the ablest, did not have the confidence of the business community, and resigned in 1813. The secretaries of war and navy were political hacks with no sense of administration. The navy enjoyed competent sea-going command; but the general officers of the army, with the exception of Jacob Brown and Andrew Jackson (who only came into the picture in 1813), were the worst military leaders of any war in which the United States has been engaged. Jackson had been eager for service at the start, and it was typical of the way this war was run that Madison refused him a federal commission because he had supported Monroe for the presidency in 1808.

4. THE WAR OF 1812: DEFENSIVE PHASE

After Napoleon's abdication on 6 April 1814, Britain was able to provide Canada with an adequate army to carry the war into the United States and to extend and intensify the naval blockade of the Atlantic coast. The war office planned to invade the United States from three points successively: Niagara, Lake Champlain, and New Orleans; and simultaneously to raid the Chesapeake.

On the Niagara front America took the initiative before British reinforcements arrived. The army had learned much from two years of

2. Winfield Scott of Virginia, who lived to be commanding general of the army in 1861, recorded that one reason he did not go with his state was his memory of the fine New England troops he had led on the Niagara front in 1813.

adversity. Incompetent officers had been weeded out, and promising young men promoted; more reliance was placed on regulars, less on militia. On 3 July 1814 General Jacob Brown boated his army of about 5000 men across the Niagara river and forced Fort Erie to capitulate. On the 5th, his subordinate, Winfield Scott, after giving his brigade a Fourth of July dinner that they had been too busy to eat the day before, was about to hold a holiday parade on a near-by plain, when three regiments of British regulars appeared to break up the celebration. The parade became the Battle of Chippewa. It was a European-style stand-up fight in open country. Both lines advanced in close order, stopping alternately to load and fire; and when they were about 60 paces from each other, it was the British who broke. On 25 July, hard by Niagara Falls, occurred the Battle of Lundy's Lane, the most stubbornly contested fight of the war. Both American generals were badly wounded, and the casualties were very heavy for a battle in that era: on the American side, 853 out of less than 2000 engaged; on the British side, 878 out of a somewhat larger force. These actions prevented an invasion of the United States from the Niagara front and gave the United States Army a new pride and character.

By mid-August General Sir George Prevost commanded some 10,000 British veterans encamped near Montreal, ready to invade the United States by the classic route of Lake Champlain and the Hudson. It was the strongest, best disciplined, and best equipped army that had ever been sent to North America. Prospects were very black for the United States, particularly since the war department had lately transferred most of the regulars from Plattsburg to Niagara. Early in September, Sir George moved down the western shore of Lake Champlain, synchronizing his movements with that of a fresh-water flotilla, and forcing the Americans back to a strong position behind the river that empties into Plattsburg Bay. There they were protected by a line of forts, and by an American lake squadron under Captain Thomas Macdonough, anchored inside the entrance to the bay.

Prevost's army reached Plattsburg on 6 September 1814. Facing them were only 1500 American regulars, and a few thousand militia. Before attacking, Prevost wished to secure control of the lake. Early in the morning of 11 September off Cumberland Head there began a murderous engagement between the two fleets composed of small vessels, without bulwarks to protect their crews, which anchored gunwale to gunwale at pistol range and attempted to pound each other to pieces. After the British flagship had silenced the starboard battery of the American flagship *Saratoga* and killed one-fifth of her crew, Captain Macdonough 'wound ship' — turned *Saratoga* completely around while at anchor — brought his fresh port battery to bear, and forced the British flagship and three other vessels to surrender. Their commander lost his life, and Prevost was so discouraged by the loss of this supporting fleet that he retreated to Canada. This naval Battle of Plattsburg — 'Macdonough's Victory' it was then called — proved to be decisive. But it was not the last battle of the war.

In June 1814 a British expeditionary force was mounted at Bordeaux in occupied France to make a diversion in the Chesapeake. The campaign that followed reflected little credit to the one side, and considerable disgrace on the other. General Robert Ross, British commander of the land forces, was instructed by Admiral Cochrane 'to destroy and lay waste such towns and districts upon the coast' as he might find assailable. A fleet of Jeffersonian gunboats, retreating up the Patuxent river, led Ross's army from Chesapeake Bay to the back door of Washington. For five days the British army marched along the banks of the Patuxent, approaching the capital of the United States without seeing an enemy or firing a shot. In the meantime, Washington was in a feverish state of preparation. About 7000 militia, all that turned out of 95,000 summoned, were placed under an unusually incompetent general and hurried to a strong position behind the village of Bladensburg, athwart the road over which the invaders must advance. President Madison and some of the cabinet came out to see the fight. After the militia had suffered only 66 casualties they broke and ran, and Ross, delayed a few hours by the bravery of marines and naval gunners, pressed on to Washington that evening (24 August 1814). Some officers arrived in time to eat a dinner at the White House that had been prepared for the President and Mrs. Madison.

Most of the public buildings of the capital were deliberately burned, partly in retaliation for the American burning of York and Newark, partly to impress the administration with the uselessness of further resistance. General Ross personally superintended the piling up of furniture in the White House before it was given to the flames, and Admiral Sir George Cockburn gave orders to burn the department buildings. The troops, under good discipline, were not allowed to indulge in looting or destruction of private property, which displeased Cockburn's superior officer, Admiral Cochrane. He wrote to him, 'I am sorry you left a house standing in Washington — depend upon it, it is mistaken mercy.'

This was a dismal period for Madison's fugitive administration. Only discouraging news had arrived from the peace commission at Ghent. Sir George Prevost was expected to march south again; and a new British expeditionary force was on its way to New Orleans. New England was disaffected, the last national war loan had failed, and all banks south of New England had suspended specie payments. John Jacob Astor, who had received many favors from the government, now combined with Stephen Girard and David Parish, Philadelphia bankers, to buy the unsubscribed part of the federal loan at 80, paying in such depreciated bank notes that they really got the bonds for half that amount.

Fortunately, the destruction of Washington only illustrated the strategic truth that hit-and-run raids accomplish nothing except to amuse the aggressors and infuriate the victims. On the night of 25–26 August 1814 the British army withdrew to its transports, and proceeded to the next objective, Baltimore. Here the inhabitants were prepared, and Maryland militia showed a very different spirit from that of the Virginia countrymen. A British naval bombardment of Fort McHenry accomplished nothing for the British, but gave us a stirring national anthem. Francis Scott Key, a prisoner on board one of the bombarding vessels, gained his inspiration for 'The Star Spangled Banner' from seeing the flag still flying over Fort McHenry 'by the dawn's early light.' General Ross fell at the head of a landing party (12 September), and that ended the Chesapeake campaign.

Before the third British expeditionary force reached New Orleans, the West had produced a great military leader, General Andrew Jackson. He had emigrated to Tennessee as a young man, represented that state in the United States Senate, and as commander of its militia had been winning laurels in warfare against the 'Red Sticks,' the Upper Creeks.

That Indian nation endeavored to remain neutral, but some of Tecumseh's warriors stirred it up. The result was a series of raids on the frontier, and the capture of Fort Mims above Mobile, together with some 250 white scalps. This news found Andrew Jackson in bed at Nashville, recovering from a pistol wound received in a street brawl with Thomas H. Benton, the future senator from Missouri. Within a month Jackson at the head of 2500 militia and a band of Choctaw and

Lower Creek auxiliaries was in the Upper Creek country. Five engagements, fought between November 1813 and January 1814, accomplished little, and the Tennessee militia showed the same disposition to panic and flee as their Northern brethren on the Canadian border. But after Jackson had executed a few militiamen to encourage the others, the spring campaign of 1814 went very well. At the Tohopeka or Horseshoe Bend of the Tallapoosa river (27 March 1814), the military power of the Creek nation was broken; 557 warriors were left dead on the battlefield, while Jackson lost only 26 of his own men and 23 Indian allies. This campaign not only had immediate strategic value by depriving the British of a powerful ally; the subsequent treaty with the Upper Creek nation opened an immense territory — about two-thirds of Alabama, the heart of the future cotton kingdom — to white settlement and Negro slavery.

In early August, a small British force landed at Pensacola in Spanish Florida. Its leader, an impetuous Irishman named Edward Nicholls, proceeded to organize and drill Creek refugees with a view to renewing the war in that quarter. Jackson invaded Florida on his own authority and crushed this diversion by capturing Pensacola on 7 November 1814.

In the meantime the most formidable British expedition of the war approached the Cochrane-Ross force, which had captured Washington and had been repulsed before Baltimore, retired for refit and rendezvous in a bay at the western end of Jamaica, the nearest staging point on British territory to New Orleans. There, the assault and landing force of 3000 men, now under command of Major General Sir Edward Pakenham, was reinforced by fresh troops from England and a fleet under Admiral Cochrane, consisting of six ships-of-the-line, fourteen frigates, dozens of smaller ships, and eleven transports capable of carrying 7450 troops. Their objective was to occupy New Orleans and as much of the Gulf coast as possible, to be used as bargaining pawns in the peace. The British government had no intention of annexing Louisiana, but that state was to be encouraged to secede and either annex herself to the Spanish empire or become a British satellite.

To meet this threat Jackson had about 5000 men, three-quarters of them militia; and for naval support, two 15-gun sloops-of-war at New Orleans and seven gunboats on Lake Borgne. The boating of an amphibious force in that era took days instead of hours, so that it was not until 23 December that the British assault force could be floated up the bayou that almost connects Lake Borgne with the Mississippi. Jackson, who had blundered in supposing that the British objective was Mobile rather than New Orleans, quickly saw his mistake. This lank, long-haired general in his 'well-worn leather cap, a short Spanish cloak of old blue cloth, and great unpolished boots whose vast tops swayed uneasily around his bony knees,' was master of the situation the moment his enemy came in sight.

At dawn 8 January began the main Battle of New Orleans. On the south bank of the river Brigadier General John Adair's Kentucky militia 'ingloriously fled' (as Jackson himself stated), before a British brigade which included a regiment of West Indian Negroes. 'This unfortunate rout' (again quoting Jackson) [3] gave the enemy a chance to attack the main American army, on the north bank, from the rear. But General Pakenham threw it away. Instead, he chose, at 6:00 a.m., to direct a foolhardy frontal assault of some 5300 men in close column formation against Jackson's 3500 on the parapet, so well protected that the British, without ladders or fascines, could not get at them. The result was more of a massacre than a battle. General Pakenham and over 2000 of all ranks were killed, wounded, or missing. The second and third generals in line of command were fatally wounded. Exactly thirteen Americans were killed and 58 wounded before the attacking columns melted. For ten days the two armies maintained their respective positions. Then General Lambert, the only surviving British general officer, withdrew the army to its transports, as London had been ordering him to do even before the battle; but communications being what they were, General Lambert never got the word until too late.

This Battle of New Orleans had no military value, since peace had already been signed at Ghent on Christmas Eve; but it made a future President of the United States, and in folklore wiped out all previous American defeats, ending the 'Second War of Independence' in a blaze of glory.

5. DISAFFECTION AND PEACE

One of the many anomalies in this curious war is the bitter opposition by the New England states, despite the fact that war built up their econ-

---

3. Jackson's aspersions on the Kentuckians were unjust, as they were ill-armed and outnumbered two to one; his report was bitterly resented in Kentucky, which never voted for him or his party in a presidential election until 1828.

omy. Since the British blockade was not extended to the New England coast until May 1814, that section of the country traded freely with the Maritime Provinces, or overland from Vermont to Quebec. And all legitimate trade passed through New England seaports, whence it was distributed to the Middle States and the South by ox wagons and sleds. Permanently important for New England was the war's stimulus to manufacturing. By 1810, after two winters of Jefferson's embargo, there were 87 cotton mills with 80,000 spindles in the region, but by 1815 half a million spindles were in operation. While John Lowell, leader of the extreme Federalist Essex Junto, was advocating a New England Confederation as the only cure for Yankee ills, his brother Francis C. Lowell was picking up information in England about power looms. After his return to the United States in 1814, Lowell invented a new power loom with which, at Waltham, Massachusetts, he equipped the first complete American cotton factory, where every process of manufacture from the raw material to the finished cloth was performed under one roof. Owing to the Peninsular War, the famous Merino flocks of Spain were broken up and sold in 1810–11, when some 20,000 sheep were imported into the United States, to the great improvement of the woolen industry.

While the War of 1812 was enriching New England, Federalists cried that their section was being ruined. Blind to new economic forces, they became as emotional over the Republicans and 'the Little Man in the Palace' as Southern leaders were in 1860 about the 'Black Republican' party and Abraham Lincoln. Yankees were assured that they were the earth's chosen people, that the Federal Constitution was weighted against them, and that the admission of Louisiana to the Union absolved them from any obligation to remain in it.

For some years there had been talk of holding a New England convention to make a concerted protest against Republican policy. Events of the summer of 1814 conspired to bring it about. Massachusetts was thrown upon her own resources for defense. The British occupied Maine east of the Penobscot, and the Royal Navy raided various parts of the coast, which received no protection from the Federal Government. That this situation existed was largely the fault of Federalist governors in refusing to place state militia under the war department; but New England was past reasoning on such matters. On 5 October 1814 Massachusetts summoned a New England Convention at Hartford, for the express purpose of conferring upon 'their public grievances and concerns,' upon 'defence against the enemy . . . and also to take measures, if they shall think proper, for producing a convention of delegates from all the United States, in order to revise the Constitution thereof.'

This language showed a compromise between the moderate and the extreme Federalists. The former, led by Harrison Gray Otis, were not disunionists, but wished to take advantage of the situation to obtain concessions for their section. Alarmed by the rising tide of secession sentiment, they hoped the Convention would act as a safety valve to let it off; their desire to concert defensive measures against the enemy was sincere. But the violent wing of the Federalist party, led by Timothy Pickering and John Lowell, had other objects in view. It was their belief that the British invasion of New Orleans would succeed, and that Aaron Burr's secession plot for Louisiana and the West would then bear fruit. They wished the Hartford Convention to draft a new federal constitution, with clauses to protect New England interests, and present it as a pistol to the original Thirteen States only, not to the democratic West. If these accepted, well and good; if not, New England would make a separate peace and go it alone. In answering echo, the London *Times* declared on 26 December, 'New England allied with Old England would form a dignified and manly union well deserving the name of Peace.'

The Hartford Convention, representing mainly Massachusetts, Rhode Island, and Connecticut, with scattered delegates from New Hampshire and Vermont, met in secret session at Hartford on 15 December 1814. Fortunately the moderates gained control and issued a calm report on 5 January 1815. An element of their caution was the strength of the Republican party in New England; the Federalists controlled all five states, but only by small majorities outside Connecticut, and there would probably have been civil war had the extremists persuaded the states to adopt ordinances of secession. Madison's administration and the war were severely arraigned by the Convention; 'but to attempt upon every abuse of power to change the Constitution, would be to perpetuate the evils of revolution.' Secession was squarely faced, and ruled out as inexpedient and unnecessary, since the causes of New England's calamities were not deep and permanent but the result of bad administration and of partisanship in the European war. The New England states were invited to nullify a conscription bill then before Congress, if it should pass. A suggestion was thrown out that the administration might permit them to assume their own defense, applying to that purpose the federal taxes collected within their borders. A few constitutional amendments were proposed. But there was no threat of a separate peace.

Secession agitation in New England now calmed down. Presently the good news from Ghent and New Orleans put Madison's administration on a high horse, and made New England the scapegoat for government mismanagement of the war. A stigma of unpatriotism, from which it never recovered, was attached to the Federalist party, and rightly so, since the leaders could not or would not see that the war had become defensive. Yet no stigma was attached to the doctrine of state rights; and within a few years it was revived by states like Virginia, which with one voice had denounced the Hartford Convention as treasonable.

Peace negotiations began almost as soon as the war did, and time was wasted over an attempted mediation by the Russian emperor. When Lord Castlereagh finally offered to treat directly with the United States, Madison replied favorably (January 1814), and Ghent in Belgium was selected as the place of negotiation. By June, when the American commissioners arrived, the British government felt in no hurry. It expected news of decisive victories on the Canadian border, which would place it in a position to dictate, rather than negotiate.

To the astonishment and distress of the American peace commissioners (John Quincy Adams, Albert Gallatin, Henry Clay, Jonathan Russell, and James A. Bayard), their opposite numbers were instructed not to admit impressment or neutral rights even as subjects of discussion. The United States must abandon her claims to the Newfoundland fisheries; the northeastern boundary must be revised to provide a direct British road between St. John, N. B., and Quebec; and the northwestern boundary must also be rectified, to give Canada access to the upper Mississippi. When the British commissioners revived that old project of an Indian satellite state north of the Ohio river, John Quincy Adams started packing. Henry Clay, untrained in diplomacy but an expert poker player, was confident that the British would recede, as they did; and on 16 September they dropped the Indian project.

The next obstacle was a British proposal to settle the boundary on the basis of *uti possidetis* — each side to keep what it held when the war ended. That would mean cession of eastern Maine and of any territory that Generals Prevost and Pakenham might conquer. The Americans refused to entertain any other basis than *status quo ante bellum*, the 1796 boundary. This deadlock was broken in mid-October by news of the British repulses at Baltimore and on Lake Champlain, which the

London *Times* described as a 'lamentable event to the civilized world.' But to the American peace commission the news from Plattsburg had 'the effect of a reprieve from execution.'

Since Napoleon had been disposed of, at least temporarily, the British premier on 4 November invited the Duke of Wellington to become commander-in-chief in America, with full powers 'to make peace, or to continue the war . . . with renewed vigor.' The Iron Duke's reply showed his sound grasp of strategy and of the American terrain. 'That which appears to me to be wanting in America is not a general, or general officers and troops, but a naval superiority on the Lakes,' he wrote. 'The question is, whether we can acquire this. . . . If we can't, I shall do you but little good in America, and I shall go there only to prove the truth of Prevost's defence; and to sign a peace which might as well be signed now. . . . I think you have no right from the state of the war to demand any concession of territory from America.' Thus, Macdonough's victory at Plattsburg was the decisive action.

By this time, the British public was sick of war, and the ministry was eager to wind it up and conclude peace all around. A third crisis occurred at Ghent over the navigation of the Mississippi, the Newfoundland fisheries, and whether Indian nations should be included in the peace or be left to their fate, as Henry Clay insisted they should. Gallatin's tact, patience, and good humor finally effected a compromise. Nothing was said in the treaty about the fisheries or the Mississippi. The United States agreed to restore Tecumseh's Indians to the lands they possessed before 1811 — an empty concession, as most of the Shawnee were dead, and most of their land had been lost before that date.

In the end, nothing much was said about anything in the Treaty of Ghent, signed on Christmas Eve 1814. Both sides agreed to disagree on everything important except the conclusion of hostilities, and restoring prewar boundaries. Madison's announced reasons for declaring war — impressment and neutral rights — were not even mentioned. But the treaty did bear good fruit in the shape of four boundary commissions to settle the line between Canada and the United States. Claims arising from the War of Independence, commercial regulations, and the Oregon question were postponed to future negotiations. And, before the next maritime war broke out, impressment had been given up as a means of recruiting for the Royal Navy.

So ended an unnecessary war, which might have been prevented by a little more imagination on the one side, and a broader vision on the other. Casualties at least were relatively light — 1877 American soldiers and sailors killed in action. Moreover, the war had a good effect on relations between the two governments. The fighters and the diplomats learned to respect one another. The United States was never again denied the treatment due an independent nation, and Americans began to grasp a basic fact of North American sovereignty, that Canada was in the British empire for as long as she wanted, not as long as we wanted. At the same time, Jackson's incursion into Florida indicated that the Spanish empire in North America was ready to fall apart.

The conduct of this conflict offered many lessons in how to fight a war and how not to organize and lead armies. Practically none was heeded. The myth of 'citizen soldiery' (the militia) being a sufficient defense, and of self-taught generals being superior to West Pointers, persisted for a century. But the almost perfect record of the navy wrought a change of public opinion toward that fighting force, leaving only 'pure Republicans' like John Randolph and Nathaniel Macon regarding the navy as a natural enemy to liberty. Most of the wartime fleet was maintained after peace, and within three months of the Treaty of Ghent it found profitable employment.

The Dey of Algeria had taken advantage of hostilities to capture American merchant ships. On 2 March 1815 Congress declared war on Algeria, and in May Commodore Decatur with frigate *Constellation*, the new *Guerrière*, and the refitted prize *Macedonian* sailed from New York for the Mediterranean. Outside the Strait of Gibraltar they encountered and captured the pirates' 44-gun flagship. The squadron then sailed to Algiers, where the Dey was presented with a treaty at gun-point. He signed it, although this time he had to pay. Similar 'stick-up' negotiations were held at Tunis and Tripoli. From that time on, the United States has maintained a naval squadron in the Mediterranean.

6. A TRIUMPH FOR REPUBLICANISM

For the United States, it had been for the most part an inglorious war. Part of the nation's capital lay in ashes, and the President had had to flee into the Virginia hills. Two days before the treaty of peace, Daniel Webster, noting that the administration could not recruit troops, collect taxes, or borrow money, wrote: 'The Govt. *cannot last*, under this war & in the hands of these men, another twelve month.'

Yet, paradoxically, the country came out of the war with an exhilarating sense of the triumph of republican institutions. It had dared a second time to wage war with the mightiest power on earth, and it had come out whole. A Republican leader in Pennsylvania explained: 'We have not got a stipulation about impressments & orders in council nor about indemnity — But victory perches on our banner & the talisman of invincibility no longer pertains to the tyrants of the Ocean — But the triumph over the Aristocrats & Monarchists is equally glorious with that over the enemy — It is the triumph of virtue over vice of republican men & republican principles over the advocates & doctrines of Tyranny.' Although the country had suffered humiliating setbacks, these were quickly forgotten in the recollection of thrilling victories. After returning from Ghent, Henry Clay reviewed the valiant deeds of Jackson, Hull, Lawrence, and Perry, and asked: 'Did the battle of Thermopylae preserve Greece but once?'

One ironic consequence of this divisive war was to intensify American nationalism. As Albert Gallatin observed: 'The War has renewed and reinstated the national feelings which the Revolution had given and which were daily lessened. The people . . . are more American; they feel and act more like a nation; and I hope that the permanency of the Union is thereby better secured.' With national honor vindicated, with a new conviction of national power, the young republic now turned away from the Atlantic and looked toward the vast continent to the west which, as Henry Adams wrote, lay before the American people 'like an uncovered ore-bed.'

XXI

Good Feelings and Bad

1. A NATIONALIST ERA

The year 1815 is a turning-point in American as in European history; and a point of divergence between the two. Hitherto the development of the United States had been vitally affected by Old World brawls; European wars and crises projected into America in spite of independence. With the Peace of Vienna, Europe turned to problems that had little interest for America; and with the Peace of Ghent, America attempted to turn her back on Europe — although she had to keep looking at the Old World over one shoulder, as the Monroe Doctrine indicates. Most of the difficulties under which the republic had labored since the War of Independence now dropped out of sight. With national union achieved, a balance between liberty and order secured, a trifling national debt, and a virgin continent awaiting the plow, there opened a serene prospect of peace, prosperity, and social progress. No one suspected that expansion would also bring its problems, that the 'self-evident truths' of the Declaration of Independence would be challenged anew, and that within half a century Americans would be slaughtering one another.

The nationalism kindled by the war shaped the direction of American politics in the next decade. When Madison submitted the peace treaty to the Senate in February 1815 he startled the country by also calling for adequate military and naval forces, direct internal taxation, a protective tariff, and a new national bank. The Federalists were astonished by the Republican volte-face, since the Republicans had long deplored peacetime armies and internal taxes and had let the first national bank expire in 1811. In his final annual message in December 1816, Madison not only called for steps toward a 'comprehensive system of roads and canals' but recommended the creation of a national university in Washington. A Federalist governor wrote: 'The Administration have fought themselves completely on to federal ground.'

The Republicans encountered little partisan opposition to their program, not only because the Federalists had long espoused such nationalist doctrine, but even more because the party had been all but destroyed by its role in the war. The Federalists, who lacked an appreciation of the importance of the presidential contest in party warfare, ran electoral slates in only three states in 1816. The Republican further weakened the Federalist forces by adopting a policy of proscription which denied their rivals any public office under their control. For a time the Federalists retained power in some of the states, but even there they were eventually displaced by the Republicans. James Monroe, once the turbulent crown prince but now the accepted heir of the Virginia dynasty, succeeded to the presidency in 1817 almost unopposed, and in 1821 obtained every electoral vote but one. Contemporaries called this period the 'era of good feelings,' but it was, in fact, an interval of stagnant politics in which it became increasingly hard for the Republicans to maintain party discipline and party zeal, and in which voting in presidential elections declined precipitously. In 1820, only 724 votes were cast in the entire state of Rhode Island.

American politics did not long continue in this placid pattern. New forces were transforming the sections; and while readjustment was taking place, everyone acquiesced in nationalism of a sort. Manufacturing was becoming the dominant interest in New England and Pennsylvania; democracy had invaded society and politics in New York. Virginia, declining as an agricultural state, had as yet found no other main interest. King Cotton's domain was advancing from South Carolina and Georgia into the new Gulf states. The Northwest, rapidly expanding in population and influence, acquired new aspirations. A series of sharp and bitter sectional conflicts brought out underlying antagonism, and by 1830 the sections had again become articulate, defining the stand they were to take until the Civil War. It became the major problem of politics to form combinations and alliances between sections whose interests were complementary, in the hope of achieving their common wants through the

Federal Government; and the first end of statesmen was to reconcile rival interests and sections through national party organizations.

With new interests came a change in the attitude of different sections toward the Constitution, completely reversing their earlier attitudes. Daniel Webster of Massachusetts, who in 1814 had warned Congress that his state would not obey conscription, in 1830 was intoning hymns to the Union; whilst John C. Calhoun of South Carolina, leader of the war-hawks in 1812 and of nationalist legislation after the war, began in 1828 to write textbooks of state rights. Of all American publicists and statesmen whose careers bridged the War of 1812, only five were consistent, and three were Virginians: Chief Justice Marshall refused to unlearn the nationalism he had been taught by Washington, John Taylor went on writing, and John Randolph went on talking, as if nothing had happened since 1798. Clay and Adams never changed their nationalist ideas of 1812.

2. THE 'AMERICAN SYSTEM'

Both Henry Clay and John C. Calhoun, the nationalist leaders in Congress at this period, feared the growing particularism of the sections. Like Hamilton, they could imagine no stronger binding force than self-interest; and their policy was but a broader version of his reports on public credit and manufactures. Their formula, which Clay christened the 'American System,' was protection and internal improvements: a protective tariff for the manufacturers, a home market and better transportation for the farmers. 'We are greatly and rapidly — I was about to say fearfully — growing,' said Calhoun in 1817. 'This is our pride and our danger; our weakness and our strength. . . . Let us, then, bind the Republic together with a perfect system of roads and canals.' Protection 'would make the parts adhere more closely. . . . It would form a new and most powerful cement.'

It was a propitious moment to raise the customs tariff. National pride had been wounded by dependence on smuggled British goods. After 1815, infant industries sustained a setback when British manufactures flooded the American market. As a consequence, the 1810–20 decade was the only one in our history in which urbanization declined. War industries were crying for protection, from which almost every section of the country expected to benefit. In New England few cotton mills managed to survive the fall in prices without adopting improved spinning machinery and the power loom. The few experimental mills in the Carolinas were staggering. Pittsburgh, already a flourishing smelter for iron deposits of the northern Appalachians, was eager to push its iron pigs and bars into the coastal region, in place of British and Swedish metal. In Kentucky a new industry of weaving local hemp into cotton bagging was menaced by the Scotch bagging industry. The shepherds of Vermont and Ohio demanded protection against English wool; the granaries of central New York, shut out of England by the corn laws, were attracted by the home market argument. Even Jefferson, outgrowing his old prejudice against factories, wrote 'We must now place the manufacturer by the side of the agriculturist.' Congressmen from states that a generation later preferred secession to protection eagerly voted for the tariff of 1816; maritime New England voted against it. Daniel Webster had said that he was 'not in haste to see Sheffields and Birminghams in America.' Yet New England and Pennsylvania were destined to pocket the earliest benefits of protection.

'Internal improvements' — public works at federal expense — were the complement to protection. Immediately after the War of 1812 there was a rush of emigrants to the West, eager to exploit the lands conquered from Tecumseh and from the Creek nation. Between 1810 and 1820 the population of the states and territories west of the Appalachians more than doubled. Four new states, Indiana (1816), Mississippi (1817), Illinois (1818), and Alabama (1819), were admitted from this region, as well as Louisiana in 1812.

Owing to the difficulty of ascending the Mississippi and Ohio rivers, Western supplies of manufactured goods came by wagon road from Atlantic seaports. After the war the increasing use of steamboats on the Western rivers threatened the Eastern cities with loss of this Western trade. In 1817 a steamboat managed to reach Cincinnati from New Orleans, and two years later 60 light-draught stern-wheelers were plying between New Orleans and Louisville. Their freight charges to the upper Ohio were less than half the cost of wagon transport from Philadelphia or Baltimore. For local and selfish reasons the Eastern cities would not combine to further the Western desire for federal roads and canals. New England and the Carolinas feared isolation. Virginia lent state assistance to two companies which hoped to pierce the Appalachians with canals. Pennsylvania went in for building roads and later canals, and New York in 1817 began the construction of the Erie canal, which was destined to make New York City outstrip all her rival seaports.

Clay and Calhoun induced Congress to push through a national road from Cumberland on the upper Potomac to Wheeling on the Ohio.[1] Connected with Baltimore by a state road, this 'national pike' became the most important route for emigrants to the Northwest until 1840. In 1817 Congress proposed to earmark certain federal revenues for bolder projects of the same sort. President Madison so far had accepted every item in the nationalist program; but here he drew the line, and vetoed this internal improvement bill. President Monroe had similar constitutional scruples; and by the time J. Q. Adams reached the White House, with even more ambitious plans for the expenditure of federal money, Congress proved disappointingly stubborn. The Appalachians were destined to be crossed and tunneled by private enterprise under state authority.

3. NATIONALISM AND THE JUDICIARY

To provide the financial ligaments for the American system, Congress in 1816 chartered a Second Bank of the United States. In introducing the bill, John C. Calhoun declared that to discuss its constitutionality would be a useless consumption of time. The B.U.S., as contemporaries abbreviated the title, began operations in 1817 as a bank of deposit, discount, and issue, having the government as principal client and holder of one-fifth of the capital stock, differing from the Bank of England mainly in the power to establish branches in the principal towns and cities. This feature, necessary for the fiscal operations of a federal government, hampered lesser banks which were operating under state charters. The Maryland legislature levied a heavy tax on the notes issued by the Baltimore branch of this 'foreign corporation.' The B.U.S. refused to pay. Maryland was sustained by the state court of appeals, whence, in accordance with the Judiciary Act of 1789, the case was appealed to the Supreme Court of the United States. This case of McCulloch v. Mary-

---

1. This National or Cumberland road was later pushed across Ohio and Indiana to Vandalia, Illinois, by successive appropriations between 1822 and 1838; but the Federal Government relinquished each section, upon its completion, to the state within which it lay.

land became a milestone in American nationalism, and gave Chief Justice Marshall an opportunity to pronounce one of the greatest of his constitutional opinions.

There were three great issues at stake. Are the states separately, or the people of the United States collectively, sovereign? Was the Act of Congress chartering the B.U.S. constitutional? If constitutional, had a state the reserved right to tax its operation? On the first point, the counsel for Maryland followed Jefferson's Kentucky Resolutions of 1798. 'The powers of the general government are delegated by the States, who alone are truly sovereign; and must be exercised in subordination to the States, who alone possess supreme dominion.' Marshall met this argument with an historical survey of the origin of the Constitution, and concluded: 'The government of the Union, then, is emphatically and truly a government of the people. In form and substance it emanates from them. Its powers are granted by them, and are to be exercised directly on them, and for their benefit.' Here is the classic definition of national sovereignty, cutting the whole ground of the state-rights theory from underneath.

On the second point, the defendant followed the Virginia remonstrance of 1790 and Jefferson's opinion on the bill chartering the first Bank of the United States. The power to charter corporations is not expressly granted to Congress by the Constitution. It cannot be inferred from the 'necessary and proper' clause. A national bank is not necessary, as the want of one since 1811 proved. All powers not granted to the Federal Government are reserved to the states, by the Tenth Amendment to the Constitution.

Marshall found little more to say on this point than Hamilton had written in his Bank opinion of 1791; but that little contained the classic expression of the doctrine of implied powers:

> The government of the Union, though limited in its powers, is supreme within its sphere of action. . . . We admit, as all must admit, that the powers of the government are limited, and that its limits are not to be transcended. But we think the sound construction of the Constitution must allow to the national legislature that discretion, with respect to the means by which the powers it confers are to be carried into execution, which will enable that body to perform the high duties assigned to it, in the manner most beneficial to the people. Let the end be legitimate, let it be within the scope of the Constitution, and all means which are appropriate, which are

plainly adapted to that end, which are not prohibited, but consist with the letter and spirit of the Constitution, are constitutional.

Finally, may a state, by virtue of its reserved power of taxation, levy a tax upon the operations of the B.U.S.? Marshall disposed of this point by a bold analogy to a state tax on the United States mails:

> The States have no power by taxation or otherwise, to retard, impede, burden, or in any manner control, the operations of the constitutional laws enacted by Congress to carry into execution the powers vested in the general government.

'A deadly blow has been struck at the sovereignty of the states,' declared a Baltimore newspaper in printing the opinion of the Court in McCulloch v. Maryland. Pennsylvania proposed a constitutional amendment prohibiting Congress from erecting a 'moneyed institution' outside the District of Columbia; and in this amendment, Ohio, Indiana, and Illinois concurred. The legislature of South Carolina, on the contrary, declared that 'Congress is constitutionally vested with the right to incorporate a bank,' and 'they apprehend no danger from the exercise of the powers which the people of the United States have confided to Congress.' South Carolina would not speak this language much longer; Pennsylvania would shortly speak no other.

The Supreme Court was not to be deterred, however, by local opposition, or influenced by public opinion. So long as Marshall was Chief Justice, it went straight ahead along the lines which he had marked out as early as 1803,[2] giving judicial sanction to the doctrine of centralization of powers at the expense of the states, and erecting judicial barriers against democratic attacks upon property rights. To the first category belong Martin v. Hunter's Lessee (1816), Cohens v. Virginia, Gibbons v. Ogden, Martin v. Mott, and Worcester v. Georgia (1832), to mention only a few of the most important. In the first named the Court upheld the constitutionality of the Judiciary Act of 1789 that gave it the power to review and reverse decisions of the state courts where they conflicted with rights guaranteed under the Constitution. In Cohens v. Virginia (1821) Marshall not only vigorously reasserted this principle, but partially nullified the purpose of the Eleventh Amendment by accepting appellate jurisdiction over a suit against a state provided the

2. So completely did Marshall dominate the Court, despite numerous changes in its personnel, that in 34 years' service he dissented only eight times. Of the 1106 opinions handed down by the Court during this period, Marshall wrote 519.

state had originally instituted the suit. In connection with this case
Marshall set forth in forceful terms the doctrine of nationalism:

> That the United States form, for many, and for most important
> purposes, a single nation, has not yet been denied. In war, we are
> one people. In making peace, we are one people. In all commercial
> relations, we are one and the same people. In many other respects,
> the American people are one; and the government which is alone
> capable of controlling and managing their interests, in all these
> respects, is the government of the Union. It is their government, and
> in that character they have no other. America has chosen to be, in
> many respects, and to many purposes, a nation; and for all these
> purposes her government is complete; to all these objects, it is com-
> petent. The people have declared, that in the exercise of all powers
> given for these objects, it is supreme. It can, then, in effecting these
> objects, legitimately control all individuals or governments within
> the American territory.

In Martin v. Mott (1827) the Court denied to a state the right, which
New England had asserted during the previous war, to withhold militia
from the national service when demanded by the President.

In Gibbons v. Ogden (1824), perhaps the most far-reaching of his
decisions, Marshall not only smashed a state-chartered monopoly
of steamboat traffic, but mapped out the course that Congress would
follow for a century in regulating interstate commerce. The case
involved an interpretation of the commerce clause of the Constitution.
The Chief Justice, in vigorous and prophetic words, defined commerce
as 'intercourse' of all kinds, and the power of Congress as complete
within its field. 'If the sovereignty of Congress, though limited to specified objects, is plenary as to those objects, the power over commerce
with foreign nations and among the several states is vested in Congress
as absolutely as it would be in a single government. . . . The power
therefore is not to be confined by state lines, but acts upon its subject
matter wherever it is to be found.'

To the second category of Marshall's decisions, those throwing the
protective veil of the Constitution over property interests, belong
Fletcher v. Peck (1810), Dartmouth College v. Woodward, and Craig v.
Missouri. In the first of these, the so-called Yazoo land fraud case, Marshall prohibited the state of Georgia from rescinding a grossly corrupt
sale of Western lands on the principle that such action impaired the
obligation of a contract. The Dartmouth College case of 1819 involved

the New Hampshire legislature's abolishing the pre-revolutionary charter of that college and placing it under state control. Daniel Webster
defended his alma mater with characteristic eloquence. Marshall's decision that a charter to a corporation was a contract within the meaning of
the Constitution, and so beyond the control of a state, was of far-
reaching importance, both for good and ill. On the one hand, it protected
privately endowed colleges, schools, and the like from political interference, and encouraged endowments for education and charity. On the
other, in conjunction with the Yazoo decision, it gave corporations an
immunity from legislative interference that was only gradually destroyed through judicial recognition of the police power of the states. In
Craig v. Missouri (1830), the Court was confronted with an attempt on
the part of a state to evade the constitutional prohibition against the
emission of paper money. Marshall's decision declaring the Missouri law
null and void and upholding the principle of sound money against the
soft-money panaceas of the frontier states aroused deep resentment
against the Court.

Marshall's opinions, and those of the Associate Justice, Joseph Story
(Martin v. Hunter's Lessee and Martin v. Mott), proved the most en-
during feature of this new nationalism. Story's monumental *Commentaries on the Constitution* (1833) inculcated nationalism in the rising
generation, as his lectures at the Harvard Law School revitalized the
teaching of law. Yet if Marshall and Story worked with the spirit of the
times in fostering nationalism, they worked against it in opposing
democracy and majority rule.

4. WESTERN PANIC AND MISSOURI COMPROMISE

The West, which deeply resented the McCulloch opinion, found other
occasions for grievances with the B.U.S. The new settlers, tempted by
rising prices of cotton, cattle, and grain, purchased land far beyond their
capacity to pay; for the Public Land Act of 1800 extended long credit.
Much of the best land was engrossed by speculators. When cotton rose
to 34 cents a pound in 1818, planters paid up to $150 an acre for
uncleared land in the black belt of Alabama. All this led to a wide
dispersal of settlers, instead of the orderly progression along a definite
frontier that the Act of 1796 had planned. Until vacant spaces were
settled, the scattered frontier farmers found themselves without schools,

means of communication, or markets, yet deeply in debt to the Federal Government or to 'wild-cat' Western banks. These in turn were indebted to the B.U.S. and to Eastern capitalists, who at the same time were erecting new manufacturing and other corporations far in advance of the country's needs. Credits piled up in a gigantic top, which could be kept whirling for some time by the lash of speculation, but was certain in the end to topple by its own weight.

The Bank of the United States, which might have put a brake on inflation, was second to none in this mad scramble, until late in 1818. Then the directors took steps to curtail credit. Branches were ordered to accept no bills but their own, to present all state bank notes for payment at once, and to renew neither personal notes nor mortgages. This hastened the inevitable panic, and in 1819 it broke. Many state banks collapsed, and enormous amounts of Western real estate were foreclosed by the B.U.S. At this juncture came the decision, in McCulloch v. Maryland, forbidding the states to tax the 'Monster.' It became the Western bogy. 'All the flourishing cities of the West are mortgaged to this money power,' declared Senator Benton. 'They may be devoured by it at any moment. They are in the jaws of the Monster. A lump of butter in the mouth of a dog — one gulp, one swallow, and all is gone!' Ohio, ignoring the Supreme Court's decision, laid a tax of $50,000 each on two local branches of the B.U.S. Ohio congressmen were shouting for 'internal improvements' at federal expense, but their state legislature declared the Kentucky and Virginia resolves of 1798 to be 'the settled construction of the Constitution.'

Would the panic and the McCulloch case, then, turn the West against nationalism, and some new Wilkinson or Burr arise to plot secession? Or would West and South shake hands, conquer the Federal Government by votes, and turn it against the money power?

When the panic came in 1819, payments due to the government for public land were in arrears many millions, most of which never were and never could be paid. It was clearly time for an alteration in the land laws. By the Public Land Act of 1820 credit was stopped, and the upset price was lowered to $1.25 an acre and the minimum unit of sale to 80 acres. This made it easier for a poor man to acquire land; but the West was not satisfied. Hard times lasted until 1824, affording an ideal culture-bed for the movement afterwards known as Jacksonian Democracy. Some of the same remedies for sectional indebtedness were tried as in 1786.

Kentucky, for instance, incorporated a bank without stockholders, with state officials as directors, and no other capital than an appropriation of $7000 for printing notes, which were to be lent on mortage security to all citizens who applied, 'for the purpose of paying his, her, or their just debts.' By this subterfuge the constitutional prohibition against the emission of paper money by states was evaded; but the courts refused to enforce acceptance of the bank notes.

While debt, deflation, and hard times were producing these preliminary symptoms of a vertical cleavage between East and West, another Western question, that of slavery extension, threatened to cut the Union horizontally into North and South. Ever since the Federal Convention of 1787 there had been a tacit political balance between these two great sections, along the old Mason-Dixon Line and the Ohio river which divided the slaveholding states and territories from those in which slavery was abolished, or in process of extinction. In 1789 North and South were approximately equal in numbers; but in 1820 the Northern or free states had a population of 5,152,000 with 105 members in the House of Representatives, while the Southern or slave states had 4,485,000 people with 81 congressmen. An even balance had been maintained in the Senate by the admission of free and slave states alternately; after the admission of Alabama in 1819 there were eleven of each.

In the territory of the Louisiana purchase, Congress had done nothing to disturb slavery as it existed by French and Spanish law. Consequently, in the westward rush after the War of 1812, several thousand slaveowners with their human property emigrated to the Territory of Upper Louisiana, establishing wheat and cotton plantations in the rich bottom lands of the lower Missouri river, or on the west bank of the Mississippi near the old fur-trading town of St. Louis. When the people of this region demanded admission to the Union as the state of Missouri, slavery was permitted by their proposed state constitution.

In February 1819 a bill admitting Missouri as a state came before the House. To the surprise and indignation of Southern members, James Tallmadge of New York offered an amendment prohibiting the further introduction of slaves into Missouri, and requiring that all children subsequently born therein of slave parents should be free at the age of 25. Thus amended, the bill passed the House, but was put down in the Senate.

Congress adjourned in March, and the question of slavery or freedom in Missouri went to the people. In state legislatures, in the newspapers, and in popular mass meetings it was discussed and agitated — not as a moral question but as one of sectional power and prestige; yet no less bitterly for that. Northerners had long been dissatisfied with the 'federal ratio' which gave the slave states twenty seats in Congress and twenty electoral votes, based on the enumeration of human chattels. They regarded the admission of Missouri, which lay almost wholly north of the then dividing line between freedom and slavery, as an aggressive move toward increasing the voting power of the South; and many threatened secession if slavery were not defeated. Southerners did not yet defend the rightfulness of slavery, but asserted their right to enjoy human property in the trans-Mississippi West, and threatened secession if that were denied. Surviving Federalist politicians and Middle-State Republicans saw an opportunity to create a solid North; to 'snatch the sceptre from Virginia for ever,' as H. G. Otis said. 'Federalism,' wrote the aged Jefferson, 'devised this decoy to draw off the weak and wicked from the Republican ranks. . . . The East is replaced in the saddle of government, and the Middle States are to be the cattle yoked to their car. . . . My hope and confidence however is . . . that they will retrace their steps back to those honester brethren of the South and West.' Jefferson's confidence was rewarded. When Congress again took up the question, in January 1820, enough Northern Republicans were detached from the anti-slavery bloc by fear of a Federalist renaissance, to get a compromise measure through. Missouri was admitted as a slaveholding state, but slavery was prohibited in United States territory north of lat. 36° 30'. As part of the compromise, Maine, which had detached herself from Massachusetts, was admitted as a free state, making twelve of each. This was the famous Missouri Compromise, which put the question of slavery extension at rest for almost a generation. The South obtained its immediate object, with the prospect of Arkansas and Florida entering as slave states in the near future; the North secured the greater expanse of unsettled territory and maintained the principle of 1787, that Congress could keep slavery out of the Territories if it would.

Angry passions quickly subsided, the sectional alignment dissolved, and politics resumed their delusive tranquillity. But a veil had been lifted for a moment, revealing a bloody prospect ahead. 'This momentous question, like a fire bell in the night, awakened and filled me with terror,' wrote Jefferson. 'I considered it at once as the knell of the Union.'

And J. Q. Adams recorded in his diary: 'I take it for granted that the present question is a mere preamble — a title-page to a great, tragic volume.'

5. ANGLO-AMERICAN ADJUSTMENTS

Almost a century of diplomacy was required to clear up all controversies between Britain and America left by the Treaty of Ghent. That diplomacy did settle them is perhaps the greatest triumph of that much abused profession during the nineteenth century. Neither the treaty, nor the situation in 1815, nor the mutual disposition of the British and American peoples, gave much ground for hope of a lasting peace. J. Q. Adams wrote before the year was out that the treaty was 'a truce rather than a peace' because nothing was settled. 'All the points of collision which had subsisted . . . before the war were left open.' Canada with a long and vague boundary, rival peltry and fishing interests, and a freshwater naval force, promised so many points of friction between the two countries that Alexander Baring wished his government would give up Canada at once. It 'was fit for nothing but to breed quarrels.'

A good beginning at adjustment was made by an Anglo-American commercial treaty in 1815, which ended British duties discriminating against United States ships, and vice-versa. But the postwar attitude in Britain toward America was defiant, even truculent. English governing classes no longer regarded 'the States' as a joke, but as a menace to British institutions. That uneasy feeling was largely responsible for sneering strictures upon American life, character, and letters with which English literature abounded during the generation following 1815, an attitude which prevented the common ties of blood and language from having their natural effect.

The three statesmen who did most to preserve peace were Presidents Madison and Monroe, and Lord Castlereagh, who had done his best to prevent war in 1812. Castlereagh was the first British statesman since Shelburne to regard friendship with America as a permanent British interest. His policy was to treat the United States in every respect as an equal, 'to smooth all asperities between the two nations, and to unite them in sentiments of good will as well as of substantial interest, with each other.' Madison and Monroe met him halfway, but not John Quincy Adams. He, too, hoped to preserve the peace, but he had a suspicious nature. Harsh and irascible in personal intercourse, Adams made a poor diplomat; as Monroe's Secretary of State his notes needed pruning and softening by the now kindly and mellow President. But Adams's perception was abnormally keen, and alone of contemporaries in either hemisphere he foresaw his country's future place in the world, and the independence of colonies everywhere.

The Treaty of Ghent provided that the contracting parties 'use their best endeavors' to abolish the African slave trade. Congress had outlawed the traffic in 1808, and in 1820 declared it to be piracy, punishable by death. But the United States refused to enter any international agreement for joint suppression, because, owing to recent memories of impressment and the like, Adams refused to allow American ships to be searched for slaves by British men-of-war. A squadron of the United States Navy was maintained off the African coast, to watch for slavers flying the American flag; but plenty of 'black ivory' got by under the flag of freedom, into Cuba or the Southern States.

Disarmament on the Great Lakes was the first fruit of Anglo-American diplomacy after the war, and the most lasting. Peace found each side feverishly building ships against the other on Lake Ontario. The Canadians, apprehensive of further American aggression, frustrated in their hope of an Indian satellite state to give them complete control of the Lakes, looked for large outlays by the British treasury to complete this building program.

The Americans, on the contrary, hoped to avoid a fresh-water building contest. An Act of Congress of 27 February 1815 authorized President Madison to sell or lay up all the Lake fleet not necessary for enforcement of the revenue laws; and this he did. The army at the same time was reduced to 10,000 men, and in 1820 to 6000. During the summer occurred several incidents on the Lakes, and from London a rumor that the Admiralty had determined to carry on its building program in Canada. President Madison then made the momentous proposal of naval disarmament on the Lakes. J. Q. Adams, United States minister at London, won over Castlereagh to the policy, and on 28–29 April 1817 an agreement was effected by an exchange of notes at Washington.

The Rush-Bagot agreement, as it is called, after the American and British ministers, provides that the naval force maintained on the Lakes shall be limited, on each side, to a single-gun vessel of 100 tons on Lake Champlain, another on Lake Ontario, and two of the same sort on the other Great Lakes. The agreement might be denounced at six months' notice; but in spite of strong pressure at periods of Anglo-American tension, it is still in force, although modified in detail by subsequent agreement in order to meet changed needs of revenue control and newer methods of naval warfare.[3]

In weighing the causes of American-Canadian amity, we must not forget that the Rush-Bagot agreement, important as it was in removing causes of irritation, was maintained only by the United States abandoning designs on Canada, and by Canada renouncing her dream of a satellite Indian state. Mutual respect and good will have kept the American-Canadian boundary undefended and unfortified, despite three subsequent periods of severe border friction.

With frigates rotting on the ways, it was a much easier matter to adjust this 4000-mile boundary, of which a scant 200 miles, the easternmost section, had as yet been determined beyond dispute. Several joint commissions for that purpose were provided in the Treaty of Ghent. The first promptly ran the boundary between Eastport, Maine, and Campobello, N.B. The second was unable to discover the whereabouts of the famous 'highlands between the St. Lawrence and the Atlantic Ocean,' mentioned by the Treaty of 1783. This question was then referred to the arbitrament of the King of the Netherlands who, pleading similar inability, recommended a compromise which the United States refused to accept; and the matter went over to the Webster-Ashburton negotiation of 1842. The third joint commission drew boundary from lat. 45° N up the St. Lawrence and through the Lakes, just short of the Sault Ste. Marie between Huron and Superior; Webster and Ashburton continued it as far as the Lake of the Woods in 1842.

At that point the international frontier had been left hanging in midair by the Treaty of 1783. No line could be drawn from 'the most northwestern point' of said Lake 'on a due west course to the river Mississippi,' because that river happened to rise to the eastward and

3. In 1838 both sides began to replace sailing revenue cutters by steamers; U.S.S. *Michigan*, an iron paddle-wheel gunboat, completed in 1844, remained in commission until 1926. In 1939, when the U.S. Navy had five ships on the Lakes, only one armed and the newest 34 years old, it was agreed by exchange of notes with the Canadian foreign minister that both navies could build vessels on the Lakes for oceanic service and maintain a few ships armed with 4-inch guns for training naval reserves. This was extended in 1946 to allow any warship to be sent to the Lakes for training purposes.

southward. This and the Oregon question were dealt with in the Convention of 1818, which extended the Canadian-American boundary along lat. 49° N to the 'Stony Mountains.'

West of the Rockies, between Spanish California and Russian Alaska, was the region vaguely known as Oregon. Britain had challenged Spain's exclusive claim to this territory at Nootka Sound in 1790, but a Boston seaman's discovery of the Columbia river mouth in 1792 gave the United States a claim, which the Lewis and Clark expedition strengthened. No settlement had yet been made, but the Hudson's Bay Company and J. J. Astor's American Fur Company had established trading posts there before the war. The British company controlled the region during the War of 1812, but American rights were recognized by the Treaty of Ghent. No agreement could be reached in the negotiation of 1818 as to the partition of Oregon, so the region was left open for ten years to the vessels, citizens, and subjects of the two powers. Before the decade elapsed, the claims of Russia and Spain had been eliminated, and in 1827 the joint occupation was extended for another ten years.

The Newfoundland fisheries question, on which the Ghent negotiators failed to agree, was also dealt with in 1818. Certain privileges within the three-mile limit on parts of the Newfoundland and Labrador coasts were restored to American fishermen. Unfortunately, this treaty was not carefully drawn, and efforts of the Newfoundland government to police the Yankee fishermen produced an almost continuous diplomatic controversy until 1910, when the Hague Tribunal gave an arbitral decision which, it is devoutly hoped, has put the question to sleep permanently.

6. JACKSON IN FLORIDA

On the southeastern border, between the southern tier of states and Florida, Anglo-American amity was gravely endangered. East Florida was a Spanish province, but Spanish authority was little exercised beyond the three fortified posts of Pensacola, St. Marks, and St. Augustine. There a situation developed like that of 1811 in the Northwest. There was meddling with the Indians on the American side of the boundary, not by Spaniards but by individual British traders. An elderly Scot named Arbuthnot, who owned a trading schooner appropriately named *Chance,* cultivated the Seminole, a branch of the Creek nation. He gained their friendship, became their informal protector, and suggested the dangerous notion that Andrew Jackson's treaty of 1814 with the Upper Creeks was voided by the Treaty of Ghent. A young adventurer named Ambrister had come to Florida in search of fun and fortune. After a short time in Arbuthnot's employ, he left it to join a group of Seminoles on the Suwanee river, under a chief whom the whites called Billy Bow-legs. Splendid fellows Ambrister found them — best soldiers in the world if properly led and equipped. If only those damned clerks at the Colonial Office in London would not interfere! One of his particular pals was the Seminole chief Hillis Hago, who sported a scarlet jacket with the insignia of a British brigadier.

In 1817 the Seminoles on the American side of the border defied settlers to enter upon the Creek lands which had been ceded three years before, and scalped some of those who did. General Andrew Jackson was ordered by President Monroe to raise a force of Tennessee militia, chastise the offenders, and pursue them into Spanish Florida if necessary. While Jackson was destroying Seminole villages, an army detachment on the way to join him, with women and children, was ambushed by other Seminoles under Himollemico, and destroyed. Jackson burst into Florida like an avenging demon. Himollemico and Hillis Hago fled to St. Marks. In the bay was a gun-boat with the Union Jack at her peak — help at last from the Great White Father! Eagerly the two chiefs rowed out to greet their allies. With mock honors they were received, and promptly clapped into irons. It was an American gun-boat and the Union Jack was a ruse. Next day (7 April 1818) Jackson entered St. Marks against the protest of the Spanish governor, hauled down the Spanish flag, hanged the two chiefs without trial, and arrested Arbuthnot. Reserving him for later attention, Jackson pushed eastward through the gloomy forest festooned with Spanish moss, to surprise Billy Bowlegs at the Suwanee river. The Indians escaped to the Everglades. Jackson, furious and baffled, learned the cause of their escape when Ambrister blundered into his camp. On one of his men was found a letter from Arbuthnot, warning Billy of Jackson's approach, and offering him ten kegs of gunpowder.

A court-martial was quickly constituted at St. Marks; Arbuthnot was placed on trial for espionage and inciting the Indians against the United States, Ambrister for actively leading them in war. Arbuthnot put up a stout defense, Ambrister threw himself on the mercy of the court. Both were found guilty and sentenced to death. The verdict was reconsidered in the case of Ambrister, whose youthful recklessness appealed to the court; but General Jackson sternly set it aside. How could he spare these 'unprincipled villains' as he deemed them, 'wretches who by false promises delude and excite an Indian tribe to all the horrid deeds of savage war'? Within a few hours Ambrister went before a firing squad, and Arbuthnot, protesting with the dignity of 70 years that his country would avenge him, was hanged from the topsail yard of the *Chance.*

The Seminoles were beaten, but Jackson was not through. After another quick march through the jungle he took Pensacola, ejected the Spanish governor, and garrisoned the fortress with Americans. Then Jackson returned, to be acclaimed once more a hero by the West. In Washington, Henry Clay reminded the Senate that 'it was in the provinces that were laid the seeds of the ambitious projects that overturned the liberties of Rome.' In Monroe's cabinet, Adams alone insisted that Jackson's every act was justified by the incompetence of Spanish authority to police its own territory; and Adams had his way.

When the news reached London in the autumn of 1818, the press rang with denunciation of America, and the 'ruffian' who had murdered two 'peaceful British traders.' Public opinion demanded instant disavowal, apology, reparation. War would have been declared 'if the ministry had but held up a finger,' wrote the American minister, Richard Rush; but Lord Castlereagh's firmness preserved the peace. Unmoved by public clamor, the Foreign Secretary examined the documents in the case, and decided that Arbuthnot and Ambrister had been engaged in 'unauthorized practices of such a description as to have deprived them of any claim on their own government for interference.'

Castlereagh, after serving the cause of Anglo-American friendship better than any English statesman of the nineteenth century, took his life in August 1822. George Canning, his successor, a man of different mettle, disliked the rising republic and wished to put her down. Five new American nations had come into existence. Let them be linked up with Britain and Canada, and the United States stew in her vaunted isolation!

XXII

Monroe and J. Q. Adams

1. REVOLUTION IN LATIN AMERICA

There were only two completely independent nations in the New World in 1815, the United States and Haiti. The next seven years saw an eruption of new republics in South America, a revolution comparable only to what has happened in Africa since 1957. An unstable situation, rich in possibilities of trouble, had been created. Anything might happen — armed intervention by the European Holy Alliance, a new balance of power, an Anglo-American entente, or a Pan-American alliance. Out of a confusion of voices came one clear note: the Monroe Doctrine, to which the policy of the United States respecting Latin America has ever since been tuned. It was invoked as recently as 1960, when Russia began to infiltrate Cuba.

In January 1817 José de San Martín, a revolutionary leader from La Plata (the Argentine), began his famous march across the Andes with 3500 men, and at Chacabuco on the Pacific slope defeated a Spanish royalist army. Chile was then liberated and organized as a republic under Bernardo O'Higgins, son of an Irish soldier in the Spanish service. In the meantime, Simon Bolívar had spread revolution up the Orinoco valley, and framed a constitution for the Republic of Venezuela.

Recognition of their independence at Washington was both sought for and expected by the three new republics. Henry Clay, in an oration describing the 'glorious spectacle of eighteen millions of people struggling to burst their chains and be free,' gave the lead to North American opinion. On President Monroe his eloquence had slight effect. J. Q. Adams, Secretary of State, 'wished well' to the new republics, but saw 'no prospect that they would establish free or liberal institutions of government. . . . Arbitrary power, military and ecclesiastical, was stamped upon their habits, and upon all their institutions. Civil dissension was infused into all their seminal principles.' Monroe's administration desired the independence of the Latin Americans as an additional bulwark for American isolation, but not with sufficient ardor to risk war. Monroe and Adams had no wish to obtain exclusive commercial privileges, or to organize and dominate a league of western republics against monarchical Europe. So long as Europe did not intervene, they were content to let Spain fight it out with her former colonies; but they would certainly oppose any general European attempt to interfere. And in 1818 Monroe instructed the American minister in London to propose a simultaneous Anglo-American recognition of the new republics.

The British government declined, torn between the desire to uphold the monarchical principle in South America and the wish to preserve newly won markets. British exports to South America by 1822 surpassed British exports to the United States; Englishmen obtained mining concessions in Mexico, Brazil, Colombia, and La Plata; and London floated several loans for the revolutionary governments. Hence England endeavored to reconcile Spain with her colonies on the basis of autonomy under the Crown and free trade; but she was strongly opposed to restoration of the exclusive Spanish colonial system, which would shut out English goods. The Spanish government took the attitude of all or nothing; and England vetoed a Franco-Russian proposal of armed intervention to re-establish Spanish absolutism in America. There matters stood in 1822.

Monroe's administration was prevented from recognizing the independence of the new republics by the Florida question. General Jackson's invasion of the province in 1818 convinced Madrid that Florida had better be sold before it was seized. Accordingly, Spain sold all her lands east of the Mississippi, together with her claim to the Oregon country, in return for $5 million (22 February 1819). In addition, the boundary between the United States and Mexico was defined. Reluctance of the Senate to relinquish the American claim to Texas, and a change of government at Madrid, delayed ratification of the Florida treaty for two years, during which Monroe dared not offend Spain by recognizing her revolted provinces.

Before the Florida treaty was ratified (22 February 1821), events in Spanish America had begun to move rapidly. The Argentine and Chile, having established their independence, went to the aid of Peru. Bolívar, at the same time, was rolling up the Spanish armies westward from the Orinoco, consolidating the liberated territory in the Great Colombian Republic. His subordinate, General Sucre, entered Quito in triumph in May 1821. A year later when Bolívar and San Martín met at Guayaquil, only one Spanish army was left in the field, and that surrendered in 1824. Dom Pedro of the House of Braganza proclaimed the independence of Brazil from Portugal in September 1822. A mutiny in the Spanish garrison at Vera Cruz forced the viceroy to accept a provisional treaty for the independence of Mexico, including Central America. Thus, by the autumn of 1822, continental America from the Great Lakes to Cape Horn was independent. European nations maintained sovereignty only in Belize, Bolivia, and the Guianas.

President Monroe, in a message to Congress of 8 March 1822, declared that the new governments of La Plata, Chile, Peru, Colombia, and Mexico were 'in the full enjoyment of their independence,' of which there was 'not the most remote prospect of their being deprived.' Formal recognition was then extended, and diplomatic relations established with the five states. 'So, Mr. Adams, you are going to make honest men of them?' asked the British minister when he heard the news. 'Yes, sir!' said Adams. 'We proposed to your government to join us some time ago, but they would not, and now we shall see whether you will be content to *follow* us!' And follow us George Canning did, for all his wrigglings — in one of which he touched a switch that released the Monroe Doctrine on an astonished world.

2. CANNING PROPOSES, MONROE DISPOSES

France successfully invaded Spain in 1823, with the avowed object of delivering Ferdinand VII from a constitution that had been forced upon him by the liberals. It was common talk that a Franco-Spanish expeditionary force to South America would follow this military promenade, with the blessing of the Holy Alliance. What possibilities did that not open up! The work of Wolfe and Chatham undone, France once more firmly seated in America, exclusively sharing Spain's colonial monopoly, deriving new wealth from the valley of Mexico, the mines of Peru, and the plains of the Argentine. 'If the Pyrenees had fallen, England would maintain the Atlantic,' wrote Canning. But by what means short of war?

The obvious policy for Canning was to follow Adams, recognize the independence of Latin America, and face Europe with an accomplished fact. But neither George IV nor the tory party was ready to admit rebel republican colonists to the family of nations. Recognition of O'Higgins might encourage O'Connell! On the other hand, if England did not do something, Canning feared that Monroe and Adams would obtain exclusive commercial advantages, and a Pan-American republican alliance.

A brilliant plan had flashed into Canning's brain, an escape from his dilemma. A joint Anglo-American protest against intervention would not only thwart the Holy Alliance and maintain England's new markets, but would break up republican solidarity in the New World. England, along with the United States, could pose as the protector of Latin America and, at the same time, throw America's weight into the British scale of power. So, on 16 August 1823, the British foreign minister put a question to Richard Rush, American minister at London. What would he say to joining England in warning France to keep hands off South America? Mr. Rush was astonished by Canning's flattering overture. In contrast to his predecessors, Rush had been made to feel that he was a person of consequence in London society; but the favor of the great and the flavor of their port had not dulled the keenness of his scent for entangling alliances. When Canning, three days later, insisted that the situation was urgent, Rush offered in the name of his government to join a British protest against intervention, provided Britain would instantly recognize the new republics. That called Canning's bluff. The tories were not yet ready to recognize republican rebels.

President Monroe sent copies of Rush's dispatches to his political mentors, ex-presidents Jefferson and Madison. The covering letter intimated that Canning's overture might be accepted. Jefferson, eighty years old, was in placid retirement at 'Monticello.' Horace and Tacitus, he wrote to Monroe, were so much more interesting than the newspapers that he was out of touch with public affairs. But this question of co-operation with Great Britain was 'the most momentous which has ever been offered to my contemplation since that of Independence. . . . America, North and South, has a set of interests distinct from those of Europe, and peculiarly her own. She should, therefore, have a system of her own, distinct from that of Europe. . . . One nation, most of all, could disturb us in this pursuit; she now offers to lead, aid and accompany us in it. . . . With her then, we should most sedulously cherish a cordial friendship; and nothing would tend more to knit our affections than to be fighting once more, side by side, in the same cause.' Here indeed was support for Canning. Jefferson, who once had regarded the touch of England as the touch of death, was once more, as in 1803, willing to accept an Anglo-American alliance! Madison, from 'Montpelier,' gave similar advice, and proposed to add an Anglo-American declaration in favor of Greek independence!

J. Q. Adams was more suspicious of Canning's astounding offer. He knew that there was slight danger of armed intervention in Latin America, and that the British navy had the power to prevent it in any case. What could be Canning's game? The clue, he thought, was a proposed pledge, in Canning's note of 20 August, against either power's acquiring a part of Spanish America. That pledge might be inconvenient if Cuba voted herself into the United States. Furthermore, it is clear that Canning was unwilling to deny Spain the right to reconquer its former colonies. Adams was right — there was a 'catch' in Canning's offer.

So, at the first subsequent cabinet meeting in Washington (7 November 1823), Adams declared, 'It would be more candid, as well as more dignified, to avow our principles explicitly to Russia and France, than to come in as a cockboat in the wake of the British man-of-war.' For Adams, moreover, the question was the larger one of future relations between the Old World and the New. While the Holy Alliance seemed to threaten South America, Russia was pushing her trading posts from Alaska southward even to San Francisco Bay. In September 1821 Emperor Alexander I issued a ukase extending Alaska to latitude 51° N, well within the Oregon country and declaring *mare clausum* the waters thence to Bering Strait. Adams believed that colonial establishments were immoral and destined to fall. With North America divided among Canada, the United States, and Mexico, and with Central and South America independent, the New World might now be considered closed to further colonization by European powers. On 17 July 1823 Adams told the Russian minister just that. Three months later, Adams received two notes from the Czar which included a characteristic homily on the Holy Alliance and disdainful references to 'expiring republicanism.'

As Adams saw it, his government had been approached or challenged on four different points, all of which could be answered at once: (1) the proposal of Anglo-American co-operation, (2) rumored European intervention in Latin America, (3) Russian extension of colonial establishments, (4) the Czar's denunciation of principles upon which every independent state in America was now based. 'I remarked,' Adams wrote of the cabinet meeting of 7 November, 'that the communications lately received from the Russian Minister . . . afforded, as I thought, a very suitable and convenient opportunity for us to take our stand against the Holy Alliance, and at the same time to decline the overture of Great Britain.'

Monroe and the cabinet appeared to agree, but Adams found it difficult to keep them straight. Calhoun, Secretary of War, wished to follow Canning, even at the cost of perpetually renouncing Cuba and Texas. Monroe vacillated between the extremes of doing nothing, for fear of the Holy Alliance, and of carrying the war into Turkey to aid Greece, whose struggle for independence had been followed in the United States with an even greater interest than was shown for South America. Daniel Webster declared that he preferred the Greeks to 'the inhabitants of the Andes, and the dwellers on the borders of the Vermilion sea.' The martyrs of Chios and the exploits of Ypsilanti were commemorated in the names of frontier hamlets. Classic colonnades were added to modest farmhouses, and Greek grammar was forced on wretched schoolboys who knew little Latin.

All this struck a reminiscent chord in Monroe's kindly heart. He had never forgotten the supreme moment of his early diplomatic career: his reception as American minister by the French Convention, the sonorous speeches against tyranny, and the fraternal accolade. Time had mellowed James Monroe without changing the quality of his mind. Another great war of revolution against tyranny, so he wrote Jefferson, was about to begin; could not America take a bolder stand for liberty than in 1793? In the first draft of his epoch-making message, Monroe proposed to reprove the French invasion of Spain, to acknowledge the independence of Greece, and to ask Congress for a diplomatic mission to Athens! President Monroe would fulfill the dreams of 'Jacobin' Monroe.

Against this meddling in European affairs Adams argued for the better part of two days, and in the end had his way. The passages on foreign relations in Monroe's annual message of 2 December 1823, although written by the President in more concise and dignified language than Adams would have used, expressed exactly the concepts of his

Secretary of State. We may summarize the original Monroe Doctrine in the President's own words:

Positive principles: (*a*) 'The American continents, by the free and independent condition which they have assumed and maintain, are henceforth not to be considered as subjects for future colonization by any European powers.' (*b*) 'The political system of the allied powers is essentially different . . . from that of America. . . . We should consider any attempt on their part to extend their system to any portion of this hemisphere as dangerous to our peace and safety.'

Negative principles: (*a*) 'With the existing colonies or dependencies of any European power we have not interfered and shall not interfere.' (*b*) 'In the wars of the European powers in matters relating to themselves we have never taken any part, nor does it comport with our policy so to do.'

Therein is the whole of President Monroe's doctrine, whatever later developments may be included under the name of the Monroe Doctrine.

Monroe's message was well received; but as no one outside the cabinet knew the dramatic circumstances of its birth, few appreciated its significance. James K. Polk was the first President to appeal to Monroe's principles by name; and it was not until after the Civil War that these principles became a doctrine, deriving their sanction no less from faith than from experience and, like religious doctrines, assuming at times a Protean shape. Critics of Monroe have pointed out that his message was a mere declaration; that European intervention had already been thwarted by the threat of the British navy; that in view of the exclusive power of Congress to declare war, a mere presidential announcement could not guarantee Latin-American independence. True, but irrelevant. What Adams accomplished was to raise a standard of American foreign policy for all the world to see, and to plant it so firmly in the national consciousness that no later President would dare to pull it down.

3. THE SECOND PRESIDENT ADAMS

In December 1823 America was much more interested in the coming presidential election than in Latin America. The Republican party was breaking into factions, and it was anyone's guess how they would divide or blend to make new parties.

The large number of candidates in 1824 signified the collapse of the old party system. With no outstanding member of the Virginia dynasty available, the burden of finding a nominee proved too much for the congressional caucus at a time when party discipline was weak. William H. Crawford, Secretary of the Treasury, was heir apparent of the Virginia dynasty, but he had suffered a paralytic stroke, and, as a spokesman for the retrenchment and simplicity of the Old Republicans, he did not command a national following. A congressional caucus dutifully nominated him, but only one-quarter of the Republicans attended. Two other members of Monroe's cabinet also aspired to the succession. John Quincy Adams was the most highly qualified, by faithful and efficient public service for thirty years. Henry Clay made a wide appeal as a Westerner and advocate of the American system; and his charming personality and oratorical gifts made 'Gallant Harry of the West' the second choice of everyone who did not place him first. But Clay had a Western rival, General Andrew Jackson, now Senator from Tennessee. John C. Calhoun, Secretary of War, was the favorite son of the lower South, but after Jackson's strength became evident he consented to be nominated for the vice-presidency, hoping to be in line for the top position.

All the candidates were Republicans. No Federalist dared raise his head, and no state-rights partisan yet ventured to come forth. Jackson carried Pennsylvania, the Carolinas, and most of the West, with a total of 99 electoral votes. Adams carried New England, most of New York,[1] and a few districts elsewhere, making 84. Crawford was a poor third, and Clay last. Since no candidate had a majority of the electoral vote, the choice between the top three went to the House — the only instance of that sort since the passage of the Twelfth Amendment.

Thus, when Congress convened in January 1825, the corridors of the Capitol and the bar-rooms and boarding houses of Washington became scenes of personal conferences, indirect offers, sly acceptances, and noncommittal refusals, as backers of Jackson and Adams tried to work up a majority for their respective candidates. Jackson would presumably hold the eleven states which had declared for him in November, but two more were needed for a majority. Adams had only seven states secured, and needed six more. Clay, no longer a candidate himself, controlled the

1. There was no uniformity at this time in methods of choosing presidential electors. In eleven states the voters chose them on a general ticket, as nowadays. In seven states they were chosen by the votes in districts; in eleven by state legislatures.

votes of three states. He opposed the elevation to the presidency of a military leader like Jackson, because he doubted 'that killing two thousand five hundred Englishmen at New Orleans' qualified a man for the chief magistracy. After it was half understood, half promised, that if Adams were elected he would appoint Clay Secretary of State, Clay threw all three for Adams. James Buchanan of Pennsylvania had already tried to make a similar deal between Clay and Jackson, but failed. The lone congressmen who represented Missouri and Illinois, states which had voted for Jackson, were 'conciliated' (Jackson men said 'bought') by Adams. New Yorkers and doubtful Marylanders who still called themselves Federalists were assured that Adams, if elected, would not take revenge on that dying party for what it had done to him and his father. And so it was that on 9 February 1825 the House on its first ballot elected John Quincy Adams President of the United States, by a majority of one state.

It was a barren victory, although perfectly legal. The cry of robbery at once went up from the Jackson forces, and active electioneering for 1828 began.

John Quincy Adams was a lonely, friendless figure, unable to express his burning love of country in any way that would touch the popular imagination. Short, thick-set, with a massive bald head and rheumy eyes, his port was stern and his manners unconciliatory. A lonely walk before dawn, or an early morning swim across the Potomac in summer, fitted him for the day's toil, which he concluded by writing in his diary. The uncomfortable labor of compiling a massive report on weights and measures during a hot summer in Washington, when he might have been playing with his children on the coast of Massachusetts, was a relaxation to Adams. 'I am a man of reserved, cold, austere and forbidding manners,' he once wrote. 'My political adversaries say a gloomy misanthrope; and my personal enemies an unsocial savage. With a knowledge of the actual defects in my character, I have not the pliability to reform it.'

Even in his own New England he was respected rather than loved, and other sections resented his election by the House over their favorite sons. His election was, said Senator Benton, with a wild plunge into what he believed to be Greek, a violation of the *demos krateo* principle. When Adams defiantly gave Clay the state department, the cry 'corrupt bargain' was raised. Jackson wrote: 'So you see the *Judas* of the West has closed the contract and will receive the thirty pieces of silver.' Randolph of Roanoke called it 'the combination, unheard of till then, of the puritan with the black-leg.' A duel followed between Randolph and Clay; fortunately both were bad shots.

Although Adams in the personal canvass of the House showed a finagling talent second to none, once in office the old New England conscience took over. He would do nothing in the way of appointments to obtain or to retain editorial support; in his anxiety to be upright he was often disagreeable. And he made the grave political error of trimming his sails to the nationalism of 1815 after the wind had changed. A sentence in his first annual message was the keynote of his domestic policy: 'The great object of the institution of civil government is the improvement of those who are parties to the social compact.' He would transcend the nationalism of Hamilton and use the ample revenues of the Federal Government to increase the navy, build national roads and canals, send out scientific expeditions, and establish institutions of learning and research. But Adams presented his ideas at a time of anti-national reaction, especially in the South which feared that a strong national government might meddle with slavery, and he offered them in a maladroit way. He antagonized old Republicans by stating that he hoped no 'speculative scruple' about constitutional limitations would trouble them, and he told Congress not to give the world the impression 'that we are palsied by the will of our constituents.'

Many sound recommendations by Adams were rudely rejected by Congress, only to be adopted years later. For instance, he wanted a national astronomical observatory, which (thinking to give it constitutional grounds) he described as a 'lighthouse of the sky.' That phrase was kicked about in Congress as if said by a half-wit. He recommended the establishment of a naval academy, and a small grant for starting one was placed in the naval appropriation bill for 1827. That touched off an outburst of the old Jeffersonian prejudice. Representative Lemuel Sawyer of North Carolina predicted that the glamor of a naval education would 'produce degeneracy and corruption of the public morality and change our simple Republican habits.' Senator William Smith of South Carolina, after pointing out that neither Julius Caesar nor Lord Nelson had attended a naval academy, predicted that American bluejackets 'would look with contempt upon trifling or effeminate leaders,' such as he assumed a naval school would produce. So the appropriation was struck out, and not until the eve of the Mexican War did Congress create the United States Naval Academy at Annapolis.

Foreign affairs were the special aptitude of Mr. Adams. But here, at every turn, he met Mr. Canning, who was deeply irritated by the 'no future colonization' clause of Monroe's message and by one of Adams's last successes as Monroe's Secretary of State — persuading the Imperial Russian government to sign a treaty in 1824, fixing lat. 54° 40′ as the southern boundary of Alaska. For Canning's American policy was to reintroduce into America the balance of power system, which Adams supposed we had got rid of with the Louisiana purchase.

President Adams's policy toward Latin America was transparently honest, and very cautious. He wished to obtain commercial treaties on the basis of most favored nation and 'free ships make free goods'; to encourage the new nations to observe republican principles and live at peace among themselves; and to discourage them from provoking Spain by attacking the *sempre fidel isla* of Cuba.[2] With Brazil, Peru, Chile, and the Argentine he was fairly successful; but Canning thwarted him by slipping into Mexico and Colombia, as a counterweight to the United States in a new balance of power.

Mexico, largest and most conservative of the new republics, having many points of possible friction with the United States and a pressing need for capital and markets that England could best supply, was the most promising ground for British influence. Joel R. Poinsett, the first United States minister to Mexico, found his British colleague serenely installed in the confidence of President Victoria, with whom he had concluded an Anglo-Mexican commercial treaty. Poinsett, an accomplished gentleman from South Carolina, appeared to have the ideal qualifications for his post: experience in public affairs, and a knowledge of the Spanish language and character, acquired by extensive travels in Europe and Latin America. But he had a superfluity of zeal, that fatal quality in diplomatists, and he was Freemason. In order to counteract Britain and the monarchists, Poinsett stood in with the *federalistas*. This party was eager to establish York rite Masonic lodges, in opposition to the Scottish rite, organized by their political enemies. Poinsett obtained charters from New York for his friends' lodges, which had a surprising and embarrassing success. All Mexico became divided into *Escoceses* and *Yorkinos;* civil war broke out between them, and Poinsett's name be-

---

2. The policy of Adams and his successors of 'hands off Cuba' was due (1) to fear that if the status quo were upset, Spain might cede Cuba to a more powerful nation such as England or France and (2) to the slave states' fear that an independent Cuba would mean the abolition of slavery there.

came the rallying point for one party and the target for the other. In the end England profited, and Poinsett was recalled under a cloud. But the cloud had a scarlet lining: *Poinsettia pulcherrima,* which the minister introduced to northern horticulture.

At the Panama Congress of 1826 Canning scored again. Bolívar the Liberator summoned this meeting of American nations, primarily to promote Latin-American solidarity and to work out some common policy toward Spain. Disliking North Americans, Bolívar proposed to leave them out, but to invite England in the hope that she might become leader of a Latin-American league. Mexico and Colombia, however, invited the United States, and President Adams accepted as a 'token of respect to the Southern republics.' By this time, midway in Adams's term, anything he proposed was sure to be defeated in Congress. His appeal for funds to pay the United States delegation was flouted, his motives were twisted, and the money was appropriated too late for the delegation to arrive in time to participate.

Only four republics took part in the Panama Conference, which accomplished nothing; but the British representative was there, and by clever propaganda managed to make the United States appear as a false friend to South America. This dangerous rivalry, which might have made Central America the Balkans of the New World, was fortunately ended by the death of Canning in 1827. The instability of the Latin-American states led his successors to drop the balance of power policy in the New World.

4. THE SECOND PARTY SYSTEM

As a consequence of the renewal of the contest for the Presidency in 1824, political leaders created a new party system. Unlike the first party system, it did not originate in Congress. Nor was it the result of a popular groundswell. The new two-party system was the deliberate creation of politicians who built cross-sectional alliances in order to capture the Presidency. Established not at one time but over a period of some sixteen years, it appeared first in the Northeast, then in the Old South, and finally in the new states.

The second party system did not continue the political alignments of the Jeffersonian era. Republicans and Federalists could be found in both the new parties: the 'friends of the Administration' who subsequently became the National Republicans and then the Whigs, and the 'Jackson men,' who would later call themselves Democrats. If Daniel Webster won former Federalists to the Adams-Clay 'Coalition,' Martin Van Buren commissioned Alexander Hamilton's son to write campaign tracts for the Jackson-Calhoun alliance. In New England, Federalists joined Adams's party; in the South, Jackson's; in the Middle States, they divided. Into the Democratic party streamed such former Federalists as Roger Taney of Maryland and James Buchanan of Pennsylvania; in 1828 as many former Federalists may have supported Jackson, who had been an early opponent of proscription, as backed Adams, whom many old Federalists viewed as an apostate.

Changes in voting procedures and the expansion of the suffrage helped shape the second party system. In 1800, only two states chose electors by popular vote; by 1832, voters cast ballots for electors in every state but South Carolina. By 1824, almost every adult white male could vote in presidential elections, save in Rhode Island, Virginia, and Louisiana. In this same period, the printed ballot replaced *viva voce* voting, and an increasing number of offices were made elective rather than appointive.

Since parties had to mobilize not a few legislators but a mass electorate, these changes revolutionized political warfare. Politicians devised institutions and techniques to win large followings for their candidates, and by so doing greatly swelled the electorate. In 1824, voting increased 130 per cent over the previous national election; in 1828, it jumped another 133 per cent. This growth resulted less from the abolition of suffrage restrictions than from the stimulus of the renewal of party competition. The transportation revolution made it possible to organize politics on a national basis, with wide-ranging campaign tours and 'monster' rallies, and the proliferation of newspapers enhanced the role of the partisan editor who fanned the flames of party feeling. As the new party system spread, the gentry yielded to professional politicians who viewed party management as a vocation.

In 1828 national leaders of the Jackson forces built a coalition in Congress, subsidized a chain of newspapers, and co-ordinated activities in the states to mobilize support for the Hero. Although the new party contained elements of a South-West alliance, sponsored by Jacksonians like Calhoun and Thomas Hart Benton, the most important aspect of what was to be the Democratic party was the renewal of the New York–

Virginia understanding between what Van Buren called the 'planters of the South and plain Republicans of the North.' The Jackson forces in 1828 tended to be more suspicious of centralized government and more favorably disposed toward unhampered capitalism than were their rivals. The South, now in full tide of reaction against nationalism, was assured that Jackson would defend state rights. In the West, loyalty to Henry Clay was impaired by Adams's professed intention to administer the public lands on business principles rather than squander them on shiftless squatters.

For the first time, a majority of states held conventions which endorsed a national candidate, but politicians in 1828 seemed less interested in democratizing politics than in manipulating the electorate. Jacksonian leaders told Dutch voters in the Middle States that the Adams forces used such expressions as 'the Black Dutch' and 'the Stupid Dutch,' unlike Jackson who 'revered' the Dutch; they informed Bostonians that Jackson was an Irishman; and they warned Westerners that Adams chatted in Latin with nuns and priests. Nor were publicists who supported Adams any more restrained. A 'coffin handbill' depicted the shooting of six militiamen by Jackson for insubordination; and the General's frontier brawls and alleged premarital relations with Mrs. Jackson were described in detail.

Jackson polled 56 per cent of the popular vote; no candidate would do so well for the rest of the nineteenth century. Party strength in the new system was very unevenly distributed; Jackson swept every state in the South and West, Adams all but two in the North. By adding Pennsylvania and most of New York, Jackson won 178 electoral votes to 83 for Adams.

John Quincy Adams never understood why he was spurned by the country he loved with silent passion, and rejected by the people he had served so faithfully. In the four sad months between the election and the end of his term, there kept running through his head the refrain of an old song he had first heard at the court of Versailles:

O Richard, O mon Roi,
L'univers t'abandonne.

Yet the noblest portion of his long career lay ahead.

XXIII

Andrew Jackson

1. JACKSONIAN DEMOCRACY

We are now in an age of great political figures. Adams, Clay, Webster, Van Buren, and Calhoun were statesmen of whom any age or country could be proud; but the man who towered above them in popularity and gave his name to an era was Major General Andrew Jackson. 'Old Hickory' as he was nicknamed in the press, 'The Gineral' as his intimates called him, 'reigned,' as his enemies said, for eight years. He practically appointed his successor, Martin Van Buren; and, after one term of Whig opposition, Jacksonian Democracy returned to the saddle in the person of James K. Polk, 'Young Hickory,' who was followed by Zachary Taylor, who died in office, and a colorless Vice-President. Then came two Democratic Presidents who had been spoon-fed by Andrew Jackson — Franklin Pierce and James Buchanan. Thus Andrew Jackson and the brand of democracy associated with him dominated the political scene for a third of a century, from 1828 to the Civil War.

Jacksonian Democracy was a national movement in that it opposed disunion and knew no geographical limits; Jackson men in Maine and Louisiana uttered the same clichés in their oratory. But it was antinational in rejecting Henry Clay's 'American System.' That is, the Democracy wanted roads, canals, and (in a few years) railroads to be chartered and aided by the states, but no Federal Government messing into the operations or sharing the expected profits. Jacksonians spoke for the men on the make who resented government grants of special privileges to rival entrepreneurs and who preferred laissez-faire to the positive state. 'The world is governed too much,' one Jacksonian allegedly said. Opponents of artificial distinctions and advocates of greater popular participation in politics, the Jackson men identified themselves with the movement toward more equality. Yet they believed in equality only for white men; they were far less charitable toward the Indian and the Negro than their 'aristocratic' foes. Jacksonian Democracy was not 'leveling' in the European sense, having no desire to pull down men of wealth to a common plane; but it wanted a fair chance for every man to level up. In the states, Jackson Democrats sometimes, but not invariably, favored free public education and a somewhat cautious humanitarianism, but dissociated themselves from most of the 'isms' of the period, such as abolitionism and feminism. In general, they shared that contempt for intellect which is one of the unlovely traits of democracy everywhere. There was no contact between political democrats like Jackson and the democratic philosophers such as Emerson. Of the greater literary figures of this era, only Nathaniel Hawthorne and, in a half-hearted way, James Fenimore Cooper were Democrats, and President Jackson could not have cared less. His attitude toward literature may be gauged by a letter he wrote late in life to President Polk, urging that his old crony Amos Kendall be appointed to the Madrid legation, a post then held by an eminent American author. 'There can be no delicacy in recalling Erwin,' he wrote; 'he is only fit to write a book and scarcely that.' He could not even remember Washington Irving's correct name! The jackass as symbol of the Democratic party was first used by the Whigs as a satire on the supposed ignorance of Old Hickory; and the party not only joyfully accepted this emblem, but has retained it to this day.

2. OLD HICKORY

Andrew Jackson was one of nature's gentlemen. And although we think of him as peculiarly American (he had never left the United States except to invade Florida), it is significant that his close friend Martin Van Buren, when minister to Great Britain, found Jackson's likeness in the Duke of Wellington. 'Old Hickory,' quick to anger and slow to forgive, rough-hewn out of live oak, accustomed as a military man to command and to be obeyed, had a fine sense of honor, a chivalrous attitude toward 'the fair' (as he generally referred to ladies), and excellent manners, provided he kept his temper. Born on the Carolina frontier in 1767 to immigrant parents from Northern Ireland, he had grown up a frontier lawyer in Tennessee, where he became owner of extensive lands, slaves, and blooded horses. But he had none of the touchiness about slavery that was common among the Southern politicians of that era; and there is little doubt that, had he lived long enough, he would have supported Lincoln against Jefferson Davis. He had sufficient knowledge of the Bible and Shakespeare to write good forcible English and to express himself well. Jackson was no champion of the poor, or even the 'common man.' But they loved him because he proved that a man born in a log cabin could get rich and become President of the United States; and, perhaps most of all, because his victory at New Orleans transformed the War of 1812 from a rout to a glorious vindication of American valor.

Washington had never held such crowds as assembled there on 4 March 1829 to see the people's champion installed. It was their day, without pomp or pageantry, scarcely even a uniform to be seen. General Jackson, a tall, lean figure dressed in black, with the hawk-like frontier face under a splendid crest of thick white hair, walked from Gadsby's Hotel up Pennsylvania Avenue, unescorted save by a few friends, to the Capitol. There, at the top of a great stone stairway to the east portico, he took the presidential oath and read his inaugural address. With difficulty he pushed through the shouting masses, all eager to shake his hand, to where his horse was waiting; then rode to the White House at the head of an informal procession of carriages, farm wagons, people of all ages, colors, and conditions. Since it would have seemed unbecoming for democracy's chieftain to make distinctions of persons, the White House was invaded by a throng of men, women, and boys who stood on chairs in their muddy boots, fought for the refreshments, and trod glass and porcelain underfoot. 'I never saw such a mixture,' said one observer. "The reign of King "Mob" seemed triumphant.' The crowd was finally drawn off like flies to honey, by tubs of punch being placed on the lawn. Washington society thought of the French Revolution, and shuddered.

Loyal, pugnacious, and honest, Jackson was also credulous, intolerant, and unlearned, with slight conception of the complex forces that were moulding themselves into the Democratic party under the shadow of his personality. His policy was summed up in a sentence, 'The Federal Constitution must be obeyed, state rights preserved, our national debt must be paid, direct taxes and loans avoided, and the Federal Union preserved. These are the objects I have in view, and regardless of all consequences, will carry into effect.'

Jackson's frontier simplicity made him over-trusting of friends and too suspicious of opponents. Yet Jackson's simplicity was his strength. His intuitive decisions were generally right; his mistakes were fewer and less costly than those of more experienced and better educated Presidents.

Jackson felt that his first task was to 'cleanse the Augean stables,' for even frontier-educated boys in those days knew about the labors of Hercules. He believed the election charges of corruption in the civil service; and his partisans, hungry for the spoils of victory, took care that he did not forget. Jackson's views of office-holding were of the eighteenth century, modified by the democratic principle of rotation. In his first annual message, he observed: 'The duties of all public offices are . . . so plain and simple. . . . No one man has any more intrinsic right to official station than another.'

Long before Jackson's day, the Republicans had followed the principle of rotation in office. In a democratic nation it served a number of commendable purposes: denying the claims of officeholders to consider their posts private property; replacing superannuated officials; preventing holdovers from frustrating the policies of a new administration and affording the citizenry a greater direct participation in government. In his eight years in office, Jackson removed only a small number of all federal officeholders, and his own appointees were mostly college graduates at a time when comparatively few Americans attended college.

Yet there is no doubt that Jackson, by stepping up the tempo of removals from office, seriously impaired the politically neutral career system which had developed in the first forty years of the republic and lowered the tone and efficiency of the civil service. Many able public servants were discarded for no other principle than to reward 'deserving Democrats,' of whom pro-Jackson newspaper editors and their friends were accounted the most deserving. Aged and respectable Jeffersonians were replaced by young, often disreputable, and sometimes corrupt Jackson men, of whom the most notorious was Samuel Swartwout, a fellow conspirator with Burr, who got the juicy plum of the Port of New York collectorship. He managed to steal over a million dollars before he was caught. Jackson fastened the spoils system on the Federal Government, from which, despite civil service reform, it has never been wholly eradicated.

3. EATON MALARIA

A woman made the first and the most lasting trouble for Jackson. She was Mrs. John H. Eaton, wife of the Secretary of War. Born Peggy O'Neale, daughter of the principal tavern keeper at the Georgetown end of Washington, she was a luscious brunette with a perfect figure, and a come-hither in her blue eyes that drove the young men of Washington wild, and some of the old ones too. Married at an early age to a purser in the navy, she became, during his long absences at sea, the mistress of John H. Eaton, bachelor senator from Tennessee and her father's star boarder. At least so 'all Washington' said, except Jackson. The Senator even bought the tavern when Papa O'Neale went broke, in order to continue this pleasant arrangement, and persuaded the navy department to give the purser plenty of sea duty. About the time of the presidential election, the complaisant cuckold, caught short some $14,000 in his accounts, died or committed suicide, nobody quite knew which; and shortly after the news arrived, on New Year's Day 1829, his bonny widow, still only thirty-two years old, married Eaton. All Eaton's friends except the President-elect tried to stop it, but Jackson practically commanded him to marry her in order (as he thought) to stop the gossip and make her an honest woman. If only Mrs. Jackson had lived, she might have taught the General better sense in such matters. Scandal made him the more determined to champion Mrs. Eaton, and to insist that official society should receive her.

Mrs. Vice-President Calhoun and the other secretaries' wives were determined to give the 'hussy' no countenance. They refused to call, and at official receptions or White House dinners failed to speak. Neither would the ladies of the diplomatic corps, nor the wives of senators and congressmen. Van Buren, however, was a widower, and Charles Vaughan, the British minister, a bachelor. They could afford to show the lady marked attention, which was not difficult, for she had both wit and beauty. But the dinners they gave in her honor were declined by other ladies, and at balls she was so snubbed that she soon gave up attempting social recognition. The President refused to surrender. He scoffed at the rumors about Peggy; after all, both Eaton and the purser had been Masons, and neither could have had 'criminal intercourse with another mason's wife, without being one of the most abandoned of men.' Jackson actually held a cabinet meeting about Mrs. Eaton, where he pronounced her 'as chaste as a virgin'; but the female rebellion continued. Even Mrs. Donelson, niece of the President and mistress of the White House, would not call on the persecuted lady; and when Jackson gave her the alternative of doing so or leaving the White House, she left. This 'Eaton malaria,' as Van Buren and the gossips called it, was not only making a breach between the administration and respectable society, but making a fool of the President.

Still, there was some use to be made of the affair by Van Buren, who coveted the presidential succession. This sly fox from New York was burrowing into the heart of the old hero. It was 'little Van' who bound up the wounds of the disappointed office-seekers, who arranged the diplomatic appointments, and directed the negotiations which brought prestige to the administration. His plump figure could be seen every fair day bobbing up and down on horseback, beside the lean, easy-seated President, on his daily constitutionals. Many a time they must have discussed the Eaton affair. Jackson, unable to account for the solid female phalanx against Mrs. Eaton, was sure there must be politics behind it. And we may be sure that Van Buren, oh! so gently and discreetly, would have eliminated one plotter after another until Jackson burst out, 'By the e-tar-nal! it's that proud aristocrat Calhoun' (for did not Mrs. Calhoun start the snubbing game, and were not all the recusant ministers Calhoun's friends?). And how Van Buren would protest that it could never, never be that high-souled pattern of chivalry! And how, if Jackson seemed too easily convinced, he would remind him of an ugly rumor that in Monroe's cabinet, at the time of the Arbuthnot and Ambrister affair, it was Calhoun who said General Jackson should be arrested and tried for insubordination! Calhoun, it will be remembered, was in his second term as Vice-President, and heir apparent.

Were all this merely a question of whether Martin or John should succeed Andrew, it would not be worth our attention. But the 'Eaton malaria,' as treated by Dr. Van Buren, was a symptom of the sectional and economic ills that presently isolated Calhoun and his adherents in a state-rights ward.

The two great issues of Jackson's presidency were nullification and the Bank of the United States. Neither issue figured in the campaign of 1828, neither had been anticipated, and Jackson did not ask for them. They were presented to him in a form that one of his wishy-washy successors might have evaded; but that he, a brave and conscientious old soldier, chose to face. And it was the manner in which he did face these issues that gave Jackson his high place in history. But for them, he might have gone down as one of several military men who made undistinguished chief magistrates.

The first issue with which Jackson had to deal was South Carolina. That state had evolved politically between 1820 and 1830 (as earlier, Massachusetts had) from the most ardent nationalism to a condition of economic flux in which everything bad was blamed on the measures of the Federal Government. The protective tariff of 1816 was largely the work of two South Carolinians, Lowndes and Calhoun, who expected their state to share the benefits. Like New England, their native state had water-power, and unlike New England she had cotton; then why not manufactures? And was it wise for her planters to depend exclusively upon the English market? But the next few years proved these expectations hollow. Competent managers were rare in the South, and Yankee mill superintendents were unable to handle slave labor, which could be employed with more immediate profit in growing cotton. All the benefits of protection appeared to be going to Northern manufacturers, while Southern planters bore the burden of higher prices. As tariff schedules rose by successive acts of Congress, and the country as a whole grew richer, South Carolina remained stationary in population, and declined in wealth. Her more enterprising planters emigrated to the black belts of Alabama and Mississippi, where their bumper crops enriched Mobile and New Orleans instead of swelling the exports of Charleston. As the cotton growing area increased, the price declined to a point below the cost of production on worn-out land. Cotton which had sold for 31 cents a pound in 1818 fetched only 8 cents in 1831.

Actually, the protective tariff only aggravated a distress for which the wasteful, land-destroying system of cotton culture was fundamentally responsible; but the South Carolina planters could hardly be expected to reason with cool logic in such a state of affairs. By 1825 there had been created among them just that atmosphere of pride, poverty, and resentment which in the twentieth century has favored the growth of Arab and African nationalism. In South Carolina this took the form of a local state-rights party, propogating the doctrine that the protective tariff and 'internal improvements' were wicked devices for taxing the South for the benefit of the North. The New England Federalists had taken the same line not long before at Hartford that had ended in talk. Charleston, however, was ten degrees of latitude south of Boston, and the South Carolina aristocracy was beginning to squirm over race relations. In particular, rice planters in the low country, where Negroes outnumbered whites five to one, had a pathological fear of Northern abolitionists, whom they held responsible for slave insurrections, and they joined the cotton growers in wanting to curb the power of the national government. Calhoun admitted in 1830 that 'the real cause of the present unhappy state of things' was 'the peculiar domestic institution of the Southern States.'

Protected interests are seldom content with what they have. Northern manufacturers were not satisfied with the tariff of 1824. In 1828 Congress passed the 'tariff of abominations,' which averaged about 50 per cent of the value of imports, compared with 33½ per cent in 1824 and 50 per cent in 1816. It was a politicians' tariff, concerned mainly with the manufacture of a President. The pro-Jackson congressmen wished to present their candidate to the South as a free-trader, and to the North as a protectionist; they therefore introduced a bill with higher duties on raw materials than on manufactures, hoping that New England votes would help defeat it, and the onus fall on Adams. As Webster said, 'Its enemies spiced it with whatever they thought would render it distasteful; its friends took it, drugged as it was.'

At a great anti-tariff meeting in Columbia, S.C., President Cooper of South Carolina College asked, 'Is it worth our while to continue this Union of States, where the North demands to be our masters and we are required to be their tributaries?' More and more South Carolinians answered this question with a thumping 'No!'

Calhoun, in the vice-presidential office, was not indifferent to this local turmoil. He had always been alive to the danger of disunion in a country so rapidly expanding. Like Hamilton, Adams, and Clay, he had sought to prevent disintegration by the cement of national legislation.

Now he believed that he had made a grave mistake. Protection, instead of a binding force, had proved an instrument of class and sectional plunder. And as Calhoun saw his beloved Carolina rushing past him down the road that led to secession, he revised his principles and produced a new and dynamic version of state rights. The measure of federal power must now be determined by the vital interest of any individual state, not by a transient majority in Congress.

Nullification was the name of this device by which Calhoun proposed to protect the peculiar interests of his state. Set forth in a document called the South Carolina Exposition, it was approved in 1828 by the legislature of that state. Nullification was based on two postulates: the common enough assertion that the Federal Constitution was a compact between states, and the theory of indivisible, indestructible sovereignty. The Constitution was established not by the American people, but by thirteen sovereign states. Sovereign in 1787, they must still be sovereign in 1828. As sovereigns, they have severally the right to judge when their agent, the Federal Government, exceeds its powers. A state convention, the immediate organ of state sovereignty, may then determine whether a given Act of Congress be constitutional or otherwise; and, in the latter event, take measures to prevent its enforcement within the state limits. Calhoun, however, recognized one constitutional authority superior to the interpretation of a single state, an interpretative federal amendment adopted by three-fourths of the states.

Nullification was not wholly original. The Kentucky and Virginia resolves of 1798 postulated the same state sovereignty; but nullification by a single state, disobeying the laws of the Union while claiming the privileges of the Union, was a very different matter. As the aged Madison declared, 'for this preposterous and anarchical pretension there is not a shadow of countenance in the Constitution.'

Calhoun's dialectic is as tedious as his noble-Roman pose; but we must concede his intelligence and his sincerity. His political principles changed, but never his object. Confronted, like Jefferson and Adams in 1775, with an accepted constitutional theory that he believed supported tyranny, he sought a new one to preserve liberty. Like them, he would preserve it within the existing body politic if possible, outside it if necessary.

Calhoun's authorship of the 'Exposition of 1828' was secret. He advised his state to hold nullification in reserve, hoping that President

Jackson would insist upon a reduction of the tariff. But Jackson was indifferent to the tariff; and Van Buren's wing of the party was interested in maintaining protection. Months stretched into years, and the 'tariff of abominations' remained on the statute books. It became clear to Southerners in the House that they could obtain no reduction without Western votes; and Western votes against nationalism could only be purchased by conceding something that the West wanted more eagerly than protection.

5. THE WEST AND DANIEL WEBSTER

The West expected Jackson to reform certain features of the national land system. The poorer public lands, unsaleable at the minimum price of $1.25 per acre, made large blocks of untaxable wilderness between the settled areas. To remedy this, Senator Benton proposed the device of 'graduation': a progressive reduction in the price of public land unsold after being offered for a given period, like the bargain basement in a modern department store. Frontiersmen who squatted on the public domain before it was placed on sale disliked having their illegal holdings sold to others. They preferred to legalize their position by a preemption act, giving them an option to purchase at the minimum price the quarter-section where they had squatted, whenever it was offered for sale by the government. The first pre-emption act was passed in 1830. It was the prelude to a new public land policy.

Older communities, both North and South, were opposed to any measure likely to encourage westward migration, which, it was assumed, would force up the wages of factory labor. To catch Western votes for protection, Henry Clay proposed a clever scheme of 'distribution.' The proceeds from land sales would be distributed among the states, for use on public works and education, giving a special bonus to those states wherein the lands lay.

It was all a game of balance between North, South, and West, each section offering to compromise a secondary interest, in order to get votes for a primary interest. The South would permit the West to plunder the public domain, in return for a reduction of the tariff. The North offered a tempting bait of distribution, in order to maintain protection. On the outcome of this sectional balance depended the alignment of parties in the future, even of the Civil War itself. Was it to be North and West against South, or South and West against North?

On 29 December 1829 Senator Foot of Connecticut proposed that Congress inquire into the expediency of putting a brake on the sale of public land. Senator Benton of Missouri denounced Foot's Resolution as a bare-faced attempt of Eastern capitalists to keep laborers from settling 'the blooming regions of the West.' He summoned the gallant South to the rescue of the Western Dulcinea; and Senator Hayne of South Carolina was the first to play Don Quixote. One after another the giants of the upper chamber rushed into the fray, and there took place one of those classic debates that America used to love — speeches hours long, each consuming a whole day's session, yet delivered from mere scraps of notes held in the palm of the hand, and every word reported in the newspapers; one of those contests of eloquence that seemed to typify the manliness and shrewdness of the nation.

The forensic duel occupied the Senate for two weeks, but was not confined to public land; it ranged over the tariff and nullification, slavery, the question of what section had done the most fighting in the Revolution, the character and objects of the Hartford Convention, and most of all, the meaning of the Constitution. The climax came on 26 January 1830, when Daniel Webster of Massachusetts replied for the second time to Hayne. Webster was the most commanding figure in the Senate, a swarthy Olympian with a craggy face, and eyes that seemed to glow like dull coals under a precipice of brows. It has been said that no man was ever so great as Daniel Webster looked. His magnificent presence and deep, melodious voice gave distinction to the most common platitudes; but his orations were seldom commonplace. He carried to perfection the dramatic, rotund style of oratory that America learned from the elder Pitt. Slumberous he was at times, even ponderous; but the South Carolinian's attack on the patriotism of New England, no less than his bold challenge to the Union in its own upper chamber, called forth all Webster's immense reserve of vitality and intellectual power. His reply is the greatest recorded American oration, thrilling to read even today in cold print, when the issues with which it deals are long since settled by the men who followed in 1861 the standard that Webster raised in 1830.

Imagine, then, the small semicircular Senate chamber in the Capitol [1]; gallery and every bit of floor space behind the desks of the forty-eight senators packed with visitors; Vice-President Calhoun in the chair, his handsome, mobile face gazing into that of the orator and reflecting every point; Daniel Webster, in blue-tailed coat with brass buttons and buff waistcoat, getting under way slowly and deliberately like a man of war, then clapping on sail until he moved with the seemingly effortless speed of a clipper ship. Hour after hour the speech flowed on, always in good taste and temper, relieving the high tone and tension with a happy allusion or turn of phrase that provoked laughter, thrilling his audience with rich imagery, crushing his opponents with a barrage of facts, passing from defense of his state to criticism of the 'South Carolina doctrine,' and concluding with an immortal peroration on the Union:

It is to that Union we owe our safety at home, and our consideration and dignity abroad. It is to that Union that we are chiefly indebted for whatever makes us most proud of our country. That Union we reached only by the discipline of our virtues in the severe school of adversity. It had its origin in the necessities of disordered finance, prostrate commerce, and ruined credit. Under its benign influences, these great interests immediately awoke as from the dead, and sprang forth with newness of life. Every year of its duration has teemed with fresh proofs of its utility and its blessings; and although our territory has stretched out wider and wider, and our population spread farther and farther, they have not outrun its protection or its benefits. It has been to us all a copious fountain of national, social, and personal happiness.

I have not allowed myself, Sir, to look beyond the Union, to see what might lie hidden in the dark recess behind. I have not coolly weighed the chances of preserving liberty when the bonds that unite us together shall be broken asunder. I have not accustomed myself to hang over the precipice of disunion, to see whether, with my short sight, I can fathom the depth of the abyss below; nor could I regard him as a safe counsellor in the affairs of this government, whose thoughts should be mainly bent on considering, not how the Union may be best preserved, but how tolerable might be the condition of the people when it should be broken up and destroyed. While the Union lasts we have high, exciting, gratifying prospects spread out before us, for us and our children. Beyond that

1. Later the Supreme Court Chamber, and after the Supreme Court obtained its own building, used by congressional committees for public hearings.

I seek not to penetrate the veil. God grant that in my day at least that curtain may not rise! God grant that on my vision never may be opened what lies behind! When my eyes shall be turned to behold for the last time the sun in heaven, may I not see him shining on the broken and dishonored fragments of a once glorious Union; on States dissevered, discordant, belligerent; on a land rent with civil feuds, or drenched, it may be, in fraternal blood! Let their last feeble and lingering glance rather behold the gorgeous ensign of the republic, now known and honored throughout the earth, still full high advanced, its arms and trophies streaming in their original lustre, not a stripe erased or polluted, not a single star obscured, bearing for its motto, no such miserable interrogatory as 'What is all this worth?' nor those other words of delusion and folly, 'Liberty first and Union afterwards'; but everywhere, spread all over in characters of living light, blazing on all its ample folds, as they float over the sea and over the land, and in every wind under the whole heavens, that other sentiment, dear to every true American heart, — Liberty *and* Union, now and forever, one and inseparable!

That peroration, declaimed from thousands of school platforms by lads of the coming generation, established in the hearts of the Northern and Western people a new, semi-religious conception of the Union. One of its earliest readers was a dreamy, gangling youth on the Indiana frontier, named Abraham Lincoln.

Time only could reveal the full import of Webster's reply to Hayne; but it went home instantly to the old patriot in the White House. Jackson counted himself a state-rights man, but he never doubted the sovereignty of the nation. State rights for him was merely a formula to prevent jobbery, corruption, and consolidation. It could never justify disobedience to the laws of the Union. Yet Calhoun and the nullification party foolishly counted upon his sympathy; and at a Jefferson's birthday dinner on 13 April 1830, they proposed to trap him into supporting their cause. The formal toasts and speeches were so worded as to prove a connection between nullification and Jeffersonian orthodoxy. Jackson sat through them outwardly impassive, inwardly fuming. When his turn came for a volunteer toast, the old soldier arose to his full height, fixing his glaring eyes on Calhoun, and flung out a challenge:

Our Federal Union — it must be preserved!

Calhoun took up the challenge with another:

The Union — next to our liberty, the most dear!

Thus each side gave notice to the other that it proposed to fight.

6. NULLIFICATION AND CALHOUN

The issue was now joined between President and Vice-President; events moved fast to separate them. An authoritative letter reached the President asserting that Calhoun, who had always posed as Jackson's defender in the Arbuthnot and Ambrister affair, had been the one cabinet member to demand his arrest and trial. Jackson enclosed it in a note to the Vice-President, inquiring if the charge were true. Calhoun replied evasively, and Jackson endorsed the letter, 'This is full evidence of the duplicity and insincerity of the man.' That form of personal disloyalty was the unforgivable sin to a man of Jackson's mettle.

To complete Van Buren's triumph and Calhoun's isolation, it now remained to cure the 'Eaton malaria' which still hung over the administration like an unwholesome fog. In the summer of 1831 the entire cabinet was persuaded to resign, thereby ridding the administration of the Calhoun influence. Van Buren, whose apparent sacrifice assured him of the presidential succession, was nominated minister to Great Britain. Eaton was consoled with the legation at Madrid — where Peggy made fresh conquests. Van Buren's place in the cabinet was given to Edward Livingston, whose penal code for Louisiana has been universally admired. Lewis Cass, a war veteran from Michigan, replaced Eaton, and Roger B. Taney of Maryland became Attorney-General. Jackson's administration was now one of the North and West, and ready for the nullifiers to do their worst.

For two years after the famous dinner, Calhoun and the nullifiers were held in check by the unionists of their own state; in 1832 Henry Clay forced their hands. With the aid of Western votes, attracted by his distribution scheme, Clay pushed a new tariff bill through Congress on 14 July 1832. Some of the 'abominations' of the 1828 tariff were removed, but high duties on iron and textiles were maintained; and the new act had an air of permanence which acted upon South Carolina as a challenge.

In the state election that autumn the state-rights party, the 'pinks of chivalry and fire-and-brimstone eaters,' as their opponents called them, won. The new legislature promptly summoned a state convention, which on 24 November 1832 declared in the name of the sovereign people of South Carolina that the tariff act was 'unauthorized by the

Constitution of the United States . . . null, void, and no law, nor binding upon this State, its officers or citizens.' This nullification ordinance forbade federal officials to collect customs duties within the state after 1 February 1833, and threatened instant secession from the Union if the Federal Government attempted to use force.

President Jackson took prompt precautions to maintain the law of the land. Forts Moultrie and Sumter were reinforced, revenue cutters were ordered to collect the duties if the customs officials were resisted, and close touch was maintained with the South Carolina unionists. On 10 December the President issued a ringing proclamation to the people of South Carolina. Their nullification ordinance, he said, was founded upon the strange proposition that a state might retain its place in the Union, and yet be bound only by those laws that it chose to regard as constitutional.

> I consider, then, the power to annul a law of the United States, assumed by one State, incompatible with the existence of the Union, contradicted expressly by the letter of the Constitution, unauthorized by its spirit, inconsistent with every principle on which it was founded, and destructive of the great object for which it was formed.

In the same proclamation the President faced the 'right of secession' and attacked Calhoun's deduction of that right from the compact method of forming the Constitution:

> The Constitution of the United States, then, forms a *government*, not a league; and whether it be formed by compact between the States, or in any other manner, its character is the same. It is a government in which all the people are represented, which operates directly on the people individually, not upon the States. . . . But each State having parted with so many powers as to constitute, jointly with the other States, a single nation, cannot, from that period, possess any right to secede, because such secession does not break a league but destroys the unity of a nation. . . . In our system . . . authority is expressly given to pass all laws necessary to carry its powers into effect, and, under this grant, provision has been made for punishing acts which obstruct the due administration of the laws.

This was the doctrine of Madison and Hamilton, Marshall and Webster, upon which Abraham Lincoln acted in 1861.

South Carolina could not be cowed by proclamation. Her legislature hurled defiance at 'King Jackson' (as his enemies began to call him) and raised a volunteer force to defend the state from 'invasion.' President Jackson, encouraged by loyal addresses that poured in from both parties and all sections, prepared to thow an army into South Carolina at the first show of resistance to the customs officers. But could he afford to? It was no question of suppressing a mere local insurrection, as Washington had done in 1794, but the very delicate and dangerous matter of coercing a state. Virginia regarded nullification as a caricature of her Resolves of 1798, Georgia 'abhorred the doctrine,' and Alabama denounced it as 'unsound in theory and dangerous in practice'; but the majority in all the Southern states probably believed in the constitutional right of secession, and Georgia had made the dangerous proposal of a Southern Convention.

Extremists aside, everyone wished to avoid bloodshed. Jackson understood the need to mix conciliation with firmness, and what the nullifiers really wanted was to reduce the tariff. Within three weeks of the President's proclamation, the House committee of ways and means proposed to lower the duties. Charleston then resolved (21 January 1833) to suspend the nullification ordinance until the new tariff bill became law, and not to molest the federal customs officials. In Congress compulsion and concession went hand in hand. On 2 March 1833 Jackson signed two bills — the Force Act, authorizing him to use the army and navy to collect duties if judicial process were obstructed, and Clay's compromise tariff, providing a gradual scaling down of all schedules until they should reach 20 per cent *ad valorem* in ten years' time. The South Carolina convention then reassembled, repealed the nullification ordinance, but saved its face by nullifying the Force Act, for which there was no longer any need.

Each party marched from the field with colors flying, claiming victory. Both seemed to have derived new strength from the contest. Nationalists were heartened by Jackson's proclamation and the Force Act, but South Carolina had proved that a single determined state could force her will on Congress, and change the commercial policy of a country which she still denied to be a nation. Jackson saw that beyond nullification lay secession. The 'next pretext,' he predicted, 'will be the Negro, or slavery question.'

7. THE U.S. BANK AND BIDDLE

In the midst of these alarums and excursions came the presidential election of 1832, memorable in the history of political organization. Jackson men from all parts of the Union, now organized as the Democratic party, sent delegates to a national party convention at Baltimore which renominated Old Hickory for the presidency and Martin Van Buren for the vice-presidency. The opposition, organized as the National Republican party (for which the name Whig, of happy memory, was shortly substituted), nominated Henry Clay.

The Democrats and Whigs were the two major parties of the future, but in 1832 there was a third party in the field, the Anti-Masons. Nineteenth-century Americans were so in love with politics that no sooner did a few earnest men capture a bit of what they took to be eternal truth than they proceeded to organize it politically. If some local success proved the scent good, it brought politicians hot-foot to the hunt to join in the kill, or lead the field in pursuit of bigger game. This Anti-Masonic party arose in 1826, out of the disappearance of a New York bricklayer named Morgan, who had divulged the secrets of his lodge. A corpse was found floating in the Niagara river. It could not be proved to be Morgan's; but, as a politician said, it was 'good enough Morgan until after election.' Both the event and the Masons' efforts to hush it up revived an old American prejudice (long since dead) against secret orders, which in a mobile, swiftly changing society appeared especially threatening to democratic institutions.[2] Furthermore, the Masons seemed to stand for all the forces of special privilege that might thwart the aspirations of ordinary men. Several young politicians, such as William H. Seward, Thurlow Weed, and Thaddeus Stevens, threw themselves into the Anti-Masonic movement, which became strong enough to elect a state governor or two. In 1831 it held a national convention and nominated William Wirt of Maryland who next year robbed Henry Clay, a Mason, of thousands of votes. In a few years the Anti-Masons faded out; but the sort of people who were quick to believe that democracy was being subverted by foreign con-

2. One aspect of this feeling was the suppression of all fraternities in American colleges except Phi Beta Kappa, which became an 'honor' organization to save its life. Not until after the Civil War did college fraternities revive.

spirators were later to be found in another one-idea party, the anti-Catholic Know-Nothings.

This presidential election decided the case of Andrew Jackson *v.* the Bank of the United States. That was the big issue in 1832, and like the nullification issue it was forced upon him. Since 1819 the Bank had been well managed, to the profit alike of the government whose funds it handled, the business community which it served, and the stockholders; but it was still unpopular in the South and Southwest. Jackson shared this dislike, together with a conviction that the money power was the greatest enemy to democracy. As the Bank's charter would expire in 1836, if not sooner renewed by Congress, Jackson's opinion was of some importance.

In the Eastern states the B.U.S. had established itself as a necessary part of the business mechanism; and the Pennsylvania Democrats and Carolina state-rights people had no complaint to make of it — the figures of stock distribution show why.[3] Calhoun had no constitutional qualms on the subject, although by any consistent standard of strict construction the chartering of a national monopoly was a more palpable invasion of state rights than a mere raising of tariff schedules to a protective level.

As the election of 1832 approached, Nicholas Biddle, president of the B.U.S., believing that Jackson would not dare risk making an issue of the Bank in an election year, precipitated a 'war' by asking for recharter immediately, four years before expiration. People warned him that such a maneuver would arouse Jackson's pugnacity, and begged him to wait until after the election. But Henry Clay wished to make the B.U.S. an issue in the campaign and encouraged Biddle to go ahead. Biddle's action demonstrated to the President that he had been right in believing that the Bank was meddling in politics, and that, as a consequence, the 'Monster of Chestnut Street' constituted a menace to democracy. When Congress voted a recharter bill on 3 July 1832, Jackson vetoed it. The bill, he declared, was not only an unconstitutional invasion of state rights; it proposed to continue a monopoly, the profits of which must

3. In January 1832 the Bank stock was distributed as follows (in round numbers): New York, 31,000; Pennsylvania, 51,000; Maryland, 34,000; South Carolina, 40,000; New England, 15,000; the West, 3,000; Europe, 84,000. Catterall, *Second B. U. S.,* p. 508. The recharter bill of 1832 was reported from a committee of which George McDuffie, Calhoun's lieutenant in the nullification movement, was chairman, and was voted for by most of Calhoun's partisans in both Houses.

come 'out of the earnings of the American people,' in favor of foreign stockholders and 'a few hundred of our own citizens, chiefly of the richest class.' Biddle called Jackson's message 'a manifesto of anarchy such as Marat or Robespierre might have issued to the mobs.'

After a fiercely fought campaign, in which the Bank was the outstanding issue, Jackson won an emphatic electoral victory with 219 votes to Clay's 49; Anti-Masonic Wirt received Vermont's seven votes, and sulky South Carolina gave its eleven to John Floyd of Virginia. Clay won four states in the Northeast, his own Kentucky, and most of Maryland, but 'Harry of the West' failed to carry any state in the New West or the Deep South, all of which backed Jackson. Yet the Bank issue hurt the Hero. Jackson is the only President in American history who won re-election to a second term with a smaller percentage of popular votes.

The election persuaded Jackson that he had to go farther than the veto and deprive the Bank of federal money. Secretary McLane got himself promoted from the treasury to the state department in order to duck the issue; his successor, Duane, was dismissed by Jackson for refusing to obey, but a third Secretary, Roger B. Taney, did; and after 1 October 1833 no more government money was deposited in the expiring 'Monster.' Federal deposits were not actually removed, but out-payments exhausted the government's account and certain state banks — called 'pet banks' by Jackson's enemies — got all the receipts. (Taney was rewarded by being appointed Chief Justice.)

Biddle refused to admit defeat. 'This worthy President thinks that because he has scalped Indians and imprisoned judges, he is to have his own way with the Bank. He is mistaken.' By constricting bank loans, Biddle helped to precipitate a panic. Yet once again his actions succeeded only in demonstrating that his enemies were correct in believing he wielded too much power.

This financial war came in the midst of a period of unparalleled speculation. The currency was already chaotic, when an Act of 1834 made matters worse by establishing the coinage ratio of 16 to 1 between silver and gold, which drove silver from the country. Yet the only embarrassment to the treasury was a surplus! This had been created by increased sales of public land, and, negatively, by the final payment of the national debt in January 1835. Henry Clay, fearing lest the administration devise some way to spend the surplus, managed to get through Congress a 'distribution' scheme in 1836. About $28 million was presented by the treasury to the state governments. Some states used the money for public works, others used it as a fund for education, one even made a *per capita* distribution; but mostly the money fed speculation. With the support of hard money men like 'Old Bullion' Benton, Jackson then administered a severe astringent, in the 'specie circular,' of 1836, ordering the treasury to receive no 'folding money' for public lands. Land speculation had reached such proportions that it added to the language the phrase 'doing a land-office business.' Shortly after, the panic of 1837 burst upon the country; and the surplus disappeared almost overnight. Short-time treasury notes tided over the crisis, but the four years of the Van Buren administration were spent in seeking a substitute for the B.U.S.; and none was found comparable with it for service and efficiency until the Federal Reserve system was established in 1913.

Although democracy won the battle with the Bank, it lost the war. Jackson, who was right in thinking no private institution should have so much uncontrolled power as this 'hydra-headed monster' held, failed to appreciate the economic functions the Bank performed and the kind of vacuum its departure would create. Out of the war the poor farmer, mechanic, and frontiersman gained nothing. Many of the bankers of New York City almost split their sides laughing over the discomfiture of Biddle, whom they cordially disliked. Wall Street picked up the pieces of the shattered institution on Chestnut Street, Philadelphia; and a new 'money power' in New York soon had more money and power than Nicholas Biddle ever dreamed of.

8. INDIAN REMOVAL

Presidents of a liberal persuasion have often in our history disregarded the interests of men of a different race, as Jackson demonstrated by carrying out a policy suggested by Jefferson: the removal of all Indian tribes to the Far West. Between 1829 and 1837, 94 Indian treaties were concluded, several million acres relinquished, and many thousand redskins more or less unwillingly transferred across the Mississippi. Tribesmen with well-developed farms, especially influential half-breeds, were given the option of staying where they were and becoming American citizens. Those who preferred to leave exchanged their property for

new lands in the West, and were promised payment for travel expenses
and the value of improvements on their relinquished property. The
'assent' of the Indians was often nominal; federal commissioners bribed
important chiefs and if necessary got them drunk enough to sign anything. 'Persuasion' often took the form of urging the Indians to sell improvements for cash with which to pay off debts to white traders.
Mixed bands of Shawnee, Delaware, Wyandot, and others were thus
'persuaded' to accept new reservations west of Missouri. Their numbers
were drastically reduced by disease on the journey. Theft by federal
officials of what was due to the Indians, and funeral rites for those who
died en route, exhausted their resources long before this 'trial of tears,'
as it was aptly called by later writers sympathetic to the Indians, came
to an end. Many groups were unable to make the trip in one season
and suffered intensely at improvised winter quarters. A cholera epidemic broke out in 1832; measles took hundreds of lives. Further trials
awaited the survivors, especially those who hoped to till the soil; the cost
of equipment reduced them to penury or debt long before they could
raise a crop or draw upon tribal annuities.

Most of the Indian tribes were too feeble to resist the process, but at
three points there was trouble. Chief Black Hawk of the Sauk and Fox
tried to retain his ancient tribal seat at the mouth of Rock river, Illinois.
Squatters encroached on his village, enclosed the Indians' cornfields,
and even plowed up the graves of their ancestors. So in 1831 Black
Hawk withdrew into Missouri Territory. There famine followed, and
hostile Sioux threatened. Hoping to find a vacant prairie in which to
plant a corn crop, Black Hawk returned the following spring with
about a thousand of the tribe. Misinterpreting this move as a hostile
expedition, the Illinois militia turned out — Abraham Lincoln commanding a company — and pursued the starving Indians up the Rock
river into the Wisconsin wilderness. It was a disgraceful frontier frolic,
stained by a wanton massacre of Indians, including women and children, when attempting to recross the Mississippi. The only redeeming
feature was the chivalrous consideration of Black Hawk by Lieutenant
Jefferson Davis of the regular army, when the captured chief was
placed in his charge. Forty years later, Davis referred to Black Hawk's
rear-guard action at Wisconsin Heights as the most gallant fight he had
ever witnessed.

In the South the Creek, Chickasaw, and Choctaw nations were fairly amenable. After some opposition and much prodding, they removed to the Indian Territory (Oklahoma), where the descendants of their survivors still live. Two nations, the Cherokee and Seminole, were refractory.

The Cherokee, after ceding their hunting grounds in the late eighteenth century, fell back on their mountainous lands in northwestern Georgia, guaranteed to them by a treaty of 1791 with the United States. It had always been a grievance against the Indians that they would not settle down to civilized ways. The Cherokee, unfortunately for themselves, took the palefaces at their word. They built neat houses and good roads, preserved the peace, received Christian missionaries, published books in an alphabet invented by their tribesman Sequoya, and adopted a national constitution. They had given as good evidence of worth and made more progress in civility than the Georgia crackers who coveted their land. In plain derogation of the Indians' treaty rights, though with some color of legalism derived from an agreement with the United States in 1802, the state of Georgia claimed the Cherokee as her subjects and tenants-at-will. An unfortunate discovery of gold in the Cherokee country in 1828 brought in a rough class of whites. By violating the treaty, Georgia raised as clear a challenge to federal supremacy as had South Carolina; but President Jackson let Georgia have her way. Regulars sent in by President Adams to protect the Indians were withdrawn; and when Chief Justice Marshall decided, on a test case brought by a missionary (Worcester v. Georgia), that the laws of Georgia had no force in Cherokee territory, Jackson is said to have remarked, 'John Marshall has made his decision. Now let him enforce it.' A portion of the Cherokee were then bribed to exchange the lands of the whole for a section of the Indian Territory, and $5 million. The rest held out for a few years; but in 1838 they too were driven westward from the lands of their ancestors. The Cherokee lost one-quarter of their number in the removal. Ralph Waldo Emerson protested in vain: 'Such a dereliction of all faith and virtue, such a denial of justice, and such deafness to screams for mercy were never heard of in time of peace and in the dealing of a nation with its own allies and wards, since the earth was made.'

A similar controversy with the Seminole of Florida had an even more tragic outcome. A tricky treaty of removal, negotiated in 1832 with a few chiefs, was repudiated by the greater portion of the tribe, led by its brave chieftain Osceola. Secure in the fastnesses of the Everglades, Osceola baffled the United States Army for years, and was only captured by treachery when bearing a flag of truce. His people kept up the fight until 1842, costing the United States some $20 million and 1500 lives. A few thousand remained in the Everglades, where their descendants, the Miccosukee, are waging a losing battle against 'progress,' represented by the bulldozer.

By the end of Van Buren's administration all but a few tribes of Eastern Indians had been removed beyond a 'permanent' barrier that ran from Lake Superior through Wisconsin and Iowa Territories, and thence along the western boundaries of Missouri and Arkansas to the Red river. A chain of military posts, garrisoned by the regular army, was established to keep whites and reds apart. Jackson declared in 1835 that the nation was pledged to keep this barrier permanent. All but the southern limb of it was torn up within twenty years.

9. FOREIGN AFFAIRS

Foreign affairs gave full scope to Jackson's liking for bold action. He scored a brilliant success by undoing the damage wrought by Adams's stiff relations with the British. As a result of this new approach, Van Buren was able to induce the British government to remove all restrictions from American produce and ships in the West Indies, except a moderate duty to maintain imperial preference. By concluding agreements with the king of Siam and the sultan of Muscat, the Jackson administration negotiated the first treaties between the United States and an Asiatic nation. But Jackson's policy toward Latin America was maladroit, and his dealings with France almost embroiled the nation in war.

The French controversy arose from a claim for spoliations under the Berlin and Milan Decrees, for which the government of Louis Philippe, in a treaty of 1831, agreed to pay $5 million, in return for the United States reducing her duties on French wine. Congress did so; but the French chambers adjourned without voting the money, and a draft of $1 million for the first installment due, drawn by the Secretary of the Treasury, 'bounced.' Jackson then alarmed American business and offended France by ordering the navy to prepare for active service and recommending Congress to authorize reprisals on French property (1

December 1834). Finally the French legislature voted the money, on the condition that it should not be paid until the United States offered 'satisfactory explanation' of the President's words. Jackson refused to apologize. The two countries were on the brink of war in 1835, when the British government mediated. Jackson then disclaimed any intention to insult France, though he would not apologize 'for the statement of truth and the performance of duty.' Wounded honor was satisfied, and the treaty was duly carried out.

10. PRESIDENT JACKSON

Jackson's aggressiveness in foreign affairs and his success in slaying the Monster Bank helped to expand the importance of the presidential office. He claimed that the President represented the people directly just as Congress did. He vetoed more bills than his predecessors had in forty years. He was the first President to insist on his right to disallow bills not for constitutional reasons but simply because he disapproved of them, and he was the first to use the pocket veto. He refused to permit the Senate to encroach on his powers, and he strengthened the unity of the executive branch by ending the ambiguous status of the Secretary of Treasury, who had previously been regarded as, in part, an agent of Congress. Jackson made clear that, as he bluntly told one Secretary, he was 'merely an executive agent, a subordinate' of the President. Jackson also enhanced the political prestige of the presidency by leading a national party with a mass appeal. Although after he left office no President until Lincoln, save Polk, proved a strong executive, Jackson left an indelible mark on the office.

Yet President Jackson had so many limitations that it is doubtful whether he should be included in the ranks of the really great Presidents. His approach to problems was too personal and instinctive; his choice of men, at times, lamentably mistaken; and, unlike the Roosevelts, who have been compared with him, he had little perception of underlying popular movements, or of the ferment that was going on in the United States. His modern counterpart, for pugnacity, chivalry, and capacity for quick but correct decisions, is Harry Truman. But one cannot help but love old Andrew Jackson. His simplicity and forthrightness, his refusal to equivocate or compromise, his gentleness where women were concerned, are admirable. And he dealt swiftly and severely with the one disruptive movement whose significance he did perceive.

Of all the Presidents, only Lincoln and the second Roosevelt have made as great an appeal to the popular imagination as Jackson. In his person he proved that the average American of sound character and common sense could win, and was fit to administer, the most powerful elective office in the world. But he left a mass of unsolved problems to his successor; and for all his hold on the people's loyalty, he did not permanently impress his party either with his strong feeling for the Union or his sincere democracy.

XXIV

The Northern States

1. AMERICA FEELING HER OATS

Statesmen and parties had done much to shape the material and moral forces pulsing through the United States in these years. Without violence they had transferred power to a new class and sectional combination. They had weathered the storm of nullification, and had evolved from the political anarchy of the 1820's two national parties, both pledged to preserve the Union. Yet, in spite of their efforts, social and economic forces were pulling North and South apart. Both were progressing, but divergently. To be sure, both North and South were affected by common experiences: nationalism, capitalism, evangelicalism, and the westward movement. But Northern society was being transformed by the industrial revolution, by cheap transportation, and by educational, humanitarian, and migratory movements that touched the border slave states very little, and the Lower South not at all. Southern society was readjusting itself to the cotton plantation, tilled by slaves. By 1850 two distinct civilizations had evolved.

In superficial appearance the Northern states had not changed much since 1790. Harriet Martineau in 1836, like Volney in 1797, was never out of sight of the woods, save in the prairies of Illinois; but there was a good deal less forest. The most striking new feature in the Northern landscape was not the occasional railway or canal, but the factory village—new and bright, built near waterfalls or rapids, containing from two to ten mills plainly built of wood, brick, or stone, as many pretentious mansions of the owners or superintendents, and hundreds of operatives' houses, exactly alike. New York City, as Dickens saw it in 1842, was low, flat, and straggling, enclosed by a hedge of masts; a city with little plumbing, lighted by gas and scavenged by pigs. Georgian architecture had given place to the neo-classic. Public buildings were being constructed of gray granite, and the wealthier farmers and country lawyers masked their wooden houses with classic colonnades and pediments. In the Middle West the white-painted farmhouse was beginning to prevail; but in the new settlements log cabins and untidy clearings dominated the landscape. American scenery now began to be appreciated for its 'romantic' contrasts of mountain with valley, sandy beach or rocky coast with island-studded sea, and its 'stupendous' gorges and cataracts. Barrack-like hotels with long covered verandas were being put up at places like Saratoga Springs, Niagara Falls, Newport, and Nahant, in order to accommodate sightseers, to provide for the brief vacations of professional and business men and the longer ones of their wives. Gimcrack Italian villas and Gothic cottages multiplied near the larger cities in the 1840's, proclaiming that wealth was being acquired faster than good taste.

It was America's awkward age. The rather attractive child who had left his parent's roof, the marvelous boy who had proclaimed great truths (or perhaps delusions) 'to a candid world,' was now a gawky hobbledehoy. The resources of a new country, exploited by the inhabitants under laws of their own making and breaking, had brought a degree of comfort and security to the common man that he had not known since the days of good Queen Bess. It was not surprising that Americans were full of bounce and bluster, contemptuous of Old World monarchies. The American had many unpleasant habits and no manners. Deference was not to be had of the white American at any price; but those who addressed him as an equal discovered a natural civility and spontaneous kindness that took the place of manners. Intercourse between man and man (provided both were white, and not too recent immigrants) was easy and pleasant. Harriet Martineau noted that in America 'the English insolence of class to class, of individuals toward each other, is not even conceived of, except in the one highly disgraceful instance of people of colour.' It was not so much the freedom, simplicity, and good humor of the people that endeared them to Miss Martineau, as the 'sweet temper . . . diffused like sunshine over the land,' and due to the 'practice of forbearance requisite in a republic.' Forbearance the Americans carried to excess in their uncritical attitude toward their own books, customs, institutions, and abuses. Almost every foreign observer of the period remarked the patience of Americans under the afflictions of contemporary travel, denounced their acceptance of majority opinion, and deplored their fear of expressing unpopular notions. Americans were becoming less independent and more gregarious, an interest in the opinion of others being a condition of social intercourse on a democratic basis. Yet so complex was the American character that the excess of one quality was balanced by its reverse. Intolerance appeared in the persecution of unpopular groups such as free Negroes, immigrants, abolitionists, and Catholics; and in hot resentment of unfavorable criticism.

Nor was distinction wanting in a country that produced in one generation Clay, Calhoun, Webster, Poe, Hawthorne, and Irving; and in the next, Emerson, Longfellow, Whitman, Lee, and Lincoln. There was merely a lack of those differences in dress, manner, and mode of living by which Europeans were accustomed to recognize the distinguished person. Clerks dressed almost as well as their employers; factory girls copied the latest Paris fashions. Scarcity of 'help,' although this was being altered by the arrival of large numbers of Irish immigrants, made it difficult for the wealthiest Northern merchant to keep up a large establishment. Young married couples in the cities often lived in hotels or boarding houses. Arthur Hugh Clough, after trying to live at Harvard like an Oxford don, wisely concluded that to enjoy America one must live roughly and simply.

It was a busy age. Eighteenth-century travelers railed at the Americans for their indolence; nineteenth-century tourists criticized their activity. 'Lazy dogs' apparently begat 'dollar-chasers.' Each Northern community was an anthill, intensely active within, and constantly exchanging with the other hills. Every man worked, or at least made a semblance of it. Nothing struck English visitors more forcibly than the total want of public parks and pleasure resorts, of games and sports, or of simple pleasures like country walking. The Northern American had not learned how to employ leisure; his pleasure came from doing things.

Yet the Northern and Western states were a land where dreams of youth came true; where the majority were doing what they wished to do, without class or official restraint. 'We were hardly conscious of the existence of a government,' wrote a Scandinavian immigrant in New York. The fun of building, inventing, creating, in an atmosphere where one man's success did not mean another's failure, gave American life that peculiar gusto that Walt Whitman caught in his poetry. Europeans often mistook this joyous activity for avidity: the incidental results for the object. Half the population was engaged in realizing the ambition of frustrated peasant ancestors for a farm of their very own, clear of rent. The other half, having achieved the farm, had tired of it; and, like the boy who loses interest in his home-made radio, had turned to some other occupation or had taken up pioneering again.

2. TRANSPORTATION AND THE WESTWARD MOVEMENT

The westward movement developed new momentum in the age of Jackson. New Englanders, who a generation before had settled the interior of New York and Ohio, were pressing forward into the smaller prairies of Indiana and Illinois, where the tough sod taxed their strength but repaid it in the end with bountiful crops of grain; where shoulder-high prairie-grass afforded rich pasturage for cattle, and groves of buckeye, oak, walnut, and hickory furnished wood and timber. A favorite objective for Yankee settlement was southern Michigan, a rolling country of 'oak openings,' where stately trees stood well-spaced as in a gentleman's park. As a popular song of the period put it:

> Come all ye Yankee farmers who wish to change your lot,
> Who've spunk enough to travel beyond your native spot,
> And leave behind the village where Pa and Ma do stay,
> Come follow me and settle in Michigania, —
> *Yea, yea, yea, in Michigania!*

Others were hewing farms from the forests of southern Wisconsin and venturing across the Mississippi into land vacated by Black Hawk's redskins — to Minnesota and

> Ioway, Ioway, that's where the tall corn grows!

Yankees direct from New England, German immigrants, and the old pioneer stock from Pennsylvania and Kentucky were swelling the stream.

Improved transportation was the first condition of this quickening life. Canals, roads, and railways took people west, and connected them with a market when they got there. By bringing the Great Lakes within reach of a metropolitan market, the Erie Canal, completed in 1825, opened up the hitherto neglected northern regions of Ohio, Indiana, and Illinois. At the same time it made New York City the principal gateway to the farther West.

As soon as it became evident that little help could be expected from the Federal Government for internal improvements, other states followed New York in constructing canals, or lending their credit to canal corporations. Ohio linked the Great Lakes with the Mississippi valley by canal in 1833–34. Cleveland rose from a frontier village to a great lake port by 1850; Cincinnati, at the other end of the state canal system, sent pickled pork down the Ohio and Mississippi by flatboat and steamboat, shipped flour by canal boat to New York, and in 1850 had a population of 115,000 — more than that of New York City in 1815. Three hundred lake vessels arrived at Chicago in 1833, although its permanent population then was only 350. Three years later the first cargo of grain from Chicago arrived at Buffalo for trans-shipment by the Erie Canal. An English traveler pronounced Chicago in 1846 to be a city of 'magnificent intentions,' and predicted that after being burned down once or twice it might amount to something. In 1856 the city was connected by railway with New York, and by 1860 it was almost as large as Cincinnati and was threatening St. Louis.

The Erie Canal forced Boston, Philadelphia, and Baltimore into rival activity. Philadelphia was shocked to find that her cheapest route to Pittsburgh was by way of New York City, Albany, Buffalo, and wagon road from Lake Erie. The state of Pennsylvania then put through the great portage canal system to Pittsburgh, surmounting the Alleghenies at an elevation of 2300 feet by a series of inclined planes, up which canal boats or railway cars were hauled by stationary steam engines. Pennsylvania had almost a thousand miles of canals in operation by 1840; twenty years later the railways rendered most of them unprofitable. Baltimore's plan for cheap transit to the West was the Baltimore and Ohio Railroad. The first spadeful was turned in 1828 by the last surviving signer of the Declaration of Independence, Charles Carroll; and the line reached the Ohio river by 1853.

American railroads were not created to connect important cities, but

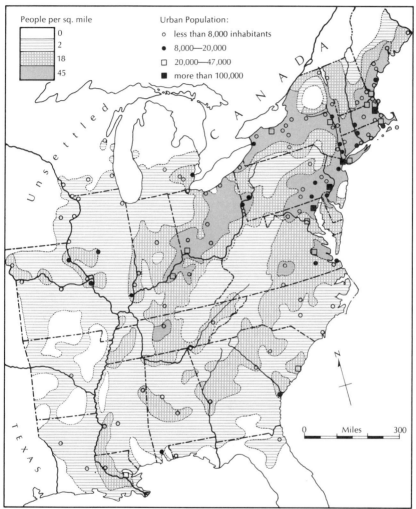

People per sq. mile

- 0
- 2
- 18
- 45

Urban Population:

- ○ less than 8,000 inhabitants
- ● 8,000—20,000
- ☐ 20,000—47,000
- ■ more than 100,000

SETTLED REGION OF THE UNITED STATES IN 1840

449

to increase the distributing radius of individual cities, around which they were disposed like sticks on a fan, each system having its own gauge, lest rivals use the line. Railways were regarded merely as an improved sort of road, and one of their chief competitors down to 1850 was the plank road built by turnpike companies as a cheap substitute for macadam. Although in the 1840's railway mileage tripled while very few canals were constructed, most bulk freight still went by water. In the early '50's the completion of the Hudson River Railway from New York to Albany (where it was connected with the New York Central for Buffalo) and of the Pennsylvania Railroad from Philadelphia to Pittsburgh, caused such an astounding transfer of freight from canals to railroads, particularly in the winter season, as to prove the superiority of rail for the long haul, and to suggest that the steam locomotive was the proper instrument for penetrating the continent.

The first locomotives used in the United States were purchased from the Stephenson works in England, and even rails were largely imported from England until the Civil War. But Americans were already experimenting in railroad equipment. The swivel or bogie truck was soon invented, as were the open one-class coach and sleeping car. In safety appliances, however, the American railroads were very backward. Collisions were frequent, and the wood-burning locomotives belched forth showers of sparks that ignited the forests, as well as the passengers' clothing.

3. THE PACKET SHIP AND IMMIGRATION

America was the first country to make practical use of the steamboat, but lagged behind England in applying steam to ocean navigation. Wooden paddle-wheel steamboats were ideal for lakes, rivers, or protected tidal waters like Long Island Sound and Chesapeake Bay, but not for rough waters. American shipbuilders concentrated on sailing vessels, which largely captured the freight and passenger traffic between Liverpool and New York. 'The reason will be evident to any one who will walk through the docks at Liverpool,' wrote an Englishman, W. N. Blane, in 1824. 'He will see the American ships, long, sharp built, beautifully painted and rigged, and remarkable for their fine appearance and white canvas. He will see the English vessels, short, round and dirty, resembling great black tubs.' The ships he admired were the

flash packets of the American marine, the famous Swallow Tail and
Black Ball liners that were driven by their dandy captains, bucko
mates, and Liverpool Irish crews across the Atlantic Ocean, winter and
summer, blow high blow low, in little more than half the average time
taken by British vessels. It was a proud seaman in those days who
earned the right to sing:

> I served my time in the Black Ball Line,
> *To me way-aye-aye-hurrah!*
> In the Black Ball Line I served my time,
> *Hurrah for the Black Ball Line!*

As late as 1846 a British emigrants' guide advised passengers to choose
an American sailing packet, rather than the new Cunard steamships, although the average westward passage by sail was six weeks.

Another favorite chanty of the square-rigger days hints at the connection between packet-ships, railroads, and immigration:

> In eighteen hundred and forty-three
> I sailed away across the sea,
> I sailed away to Amerikee
> To work upon the railway,
> O! poor Paddy works upon the railway.

Canal and railway construction created a demand for cheap labor, and
made it easier for people to reach the West. Another consequence of
the transportation revolution was the development of a safe and inex-
pensive ocean crossing. Shippers encouraged the emigrant trade in
order to have a return freight on their westward voyage.

Americans liked to believe that migrants were attracted to their
country by admiration for the unique political institutions of the United
States, but, in truth, most came for economic reasons. Cycles of prosperity in America drew them; periods of depression discouraged their
coming. They responded both to the 'pull' of the burgeoning American
economy and the 'push' of the population explosion and hard times in
Europe. After the terrible Great Famine due to the potato blights of
1845–49, the Irish peasant came to view migration as a release instead
of a banishment. In the 1846–55 decade more than a million Germans
fled to the United States to escape economic hardship.

In the century after 1815 some 30 million people migrated from
Europe to America. The country was staggered by the wave of nearly

600,000 immigrants in the 1830's, four times as many as in the previous decade, but in the 1850's a startling 2,314,000 newcomers would step ashore. The number of immigrants who came to the United States between 1815 and 1860 was greater than the total population of the country in 1790.

This enormous folk migration was carried out almost wholly by individuals or families on their own initiative with virtually no direction or assistance from governments on either side of the ocean. When European governments attempted to mitigate the hardships of the passage by requiring a minimum of space and rations, and decent treatment on the emigrant ships, they had little success. Seldom was a westward passage of the Atlantic made in less than a month. Until 1855 neither Federal nor state governments made any effort to protect the immigrant on his arrival. Many arrived penniless, having exhausted their savings on the journey; others often fell a prey to waterfront sharpers. But as soon as they recovered their shore legs the immigrants were well able to defend themselves. As early as 1835 we hear of Irishmen driving the Whigs from the polls in New York, with showers of 'Irish confetti.' Despite suffering and homesickness, most of the immigrants prospered and sent for their friends.

Almost all of the 5 million immigrants in these years came from northwestern Europe, two million from Ireland, over a million and a half from Germany, three-quarters of a million from England, Scotland, and Wales. All but a small fraction of the newcomers arrived in seaports in the Northeast and settled in the northern half of the country. Although mostly country folk, the Irish congregated in cities where thousands of them were recruited for construction work and domestic service. The impoverished Irishman lacked the cash to acquire land, had no experience of farming other than potatoes, and distrusted the land after his bitter experience in Ireland. He was too gregarious for life on the isolated American farm, and needed a community large enough to support a Catholic Church.

Peasant also were a majority of the Germans, but not in like degree; among them were thousands of artisans, a few thousand political refugees from the revolutions of 1830 and 1848 such as Carl Schurz, and a sprinkling of intellectuals such as Johann Stallo, whose writings introduced the latest German philosophy to America. German colonies were formed in such cities as New York, Baltimore, Cincinnati, and St.

Louis; Milwaukee was a German town by 1850. But the greater number bought Western land as soon as they could earn the wherewithal, especially in Wisconsin and Missouri.

Sloop *Restaurationen,* which sailed from Stavenger in 1825 with 53 pilgrims from the northern kingdoms, was the Scandinavian *Mayflower.* Her passengers, bound for western New York, were precursors of many thousands who settled among the forests and lakes of Wisconsin and Minnesota, similar to those of their native land.

This wave of immigration enhanced the wealth and progress of the country, yet encountered as bitter opposition as did Asiatics half a century later. In part, the antagonism was religious, since most of the Irish and many of the Germans were Roman Catholics. In part it was political, for most immigrants to the cities became Jackson Democrats, largely because the politicians of that party were the first to cultivate them, to see that they got jobs, and to help them in time of trouble. In part it was due to the widespread belief among native Americans that the immigrants were paupers. The greater part of the immigrants only wanted an opportunity to work, but their need for jobs was so desperate that by cutting wages they displaced some laborers, especially free Negroes. Yet the main consequence of immigration was an acceleration of economic growth that benefitted native Americans as well as the newcomers.

4. CITY, FACTORY, AND WORKSHOP

New methods and instruments of transportation, by extending the domestic market, helped the people in the North and West, hastened the industrialization of the East, threatened the self-sufficing farm, and brought farmers' boys into urban communities. Between 1820 and 1850 the combined population of New York, Philadelphia, Baltimore, and Boston increased from 343,000 to 1,162,000.[1] During the 1840's, while

1. TABLE SHOWING POPULATIONS OF PRINCIPAL CITIES:

	1790	1800	1810	1820	1830	1840	1850
Boston	18,038	24,937	33,250	43,298	61,392	93,383	136,881
New York	33,131	60,489	96,373	123,706	202,589	312,710	515,547
Philadelphia	42,520	69,403	91,874	112,772	161,410	220,423	340,045
Baltimore	13,503	26,114	35,583	62,738	80,825	102,313	169,054
Charleston	16,359	20,473	24,711	24,780	30,289	29,261	42,985
New Orleans			17,242	27,176	46,310	102,193	116,375

the population of the United States increased 36 per cent, that of the towns and cities of 8000 or more increased 90 per cent. Measured by numbers, the urban movement was stronger than westward migration, and its effect on the American character equally important.

In the generation after 1815, cotton was the greatest factor in the American economy. The South grew cotton, the Northeast converted it into cloth and supplied manufactured goods to the South, which obtained a large part of its food from the Midwest. From 1820 to 1831, the number of cotton spindles increased from 191,000 to a million and a quarter. By 1840 there were 1200 cotton factories in the United States, operating two and a quarter million spindles, two-thirds of them in New England. Ring or frame spinning had been invented, power looms were being manufactured in large numbers, and even exported.

Francis C. Lowell, inventor of the first American power loom, was a man of social vision. At New Lanark in Scotland he learned that it was possible to have factories without a degraded labor force. Farmers' daughters were attracted to the new factory city of Lowell by relatively high wages, and the scruples of their pious parents were overcome by the provision of strictly chaperoned boarding houses. For a generation the Lowell factory girls, with their neat dresses, correct deportment, and literary weekly, were a wonder. Never, unfortunately, were they typical. Yet it is also true that because of wide opportunities in a new country, no permanent proletariat was created. After three or four years, factory girls left the mills to marry, and child laborers elsewhere usually managed to find some other occupation by the time they reached their majority.

Woolen manufacturers developed more slowly and, although protected by even higher tariff schedules than those of cotton, had less success in capturing the domestic market. Power looms and spinning-jennies were generally adopted in the 1820's, and in 1840 Samuel Crompton invented a power loom for fancy woolens, just in time to produce the loud checked cassimeres favored by the beaux of the '40's. Lawrence, a woolen counterpart to Lowell, was established on the Merrimack, the same river, in 1845. By 1850 the Northern states boasted over 1500 woolen mills, most of them small, individually owned establishments with a few sets of machinery, employing country people of the neighborhood, and producing blankets, flannels, or satinet.

As a result of this factory development, spinning and weaving in the home had almost disappeared from settled communities by the Civil War, and factory-made goods had reached all but the remoter parts of the West. The picturesque linsey, fur, and buckskin of the pioneer, and the homespun of his wife, were replaced by factory cottons and woolens, made up in the clothing shops of the Eastern cities.

Of the many American industries that were still in the domestic stage at this period, the most important was shoemaking, for which no machine process of any importance was invented until 1850. In New England it was a winter occupation of farmers and fishermen, who, when the harvest was gathered, or the vessel hauled out for the winter, formed a 'crew' to make boots and shoes in a neighborhood workshop, from stock put out by some local merchant. Every man was master of his own time, and had something to fall back on when demand slackened; there was no clatter of machinery to drown discussion. A boy was often hired to read to the workers. It was said that 'every Lynn shoemaker was fit to be an United States Senator'; and Henry Wilson 'the cordwainer of Natick' became Vice-President. The shoemakers of New York and Philadelphia, more hard-pressed than their Yankee brethren by the capitalist and the immigrant, were pioneers in the first political labor movement in America.

In England the industrial revolution turned mainly on coal and iron; not so in the United States, where the iron industry developed very slowly. Suitable coal for coking was not found east of the Appalachians, but wood for making charcoal was abundant. Pennsylvania ironmasters were more adept at obtaining tariff protection against English iron than in improving their own methods of production. Even Pittsburgh used charcoal for smelting prior to 1840, rather than the bituminous coal which was plentiful in the neighborhood. And Pittsburgh, although it commanded the iron market of the Mississippi valley, could not sell its products in the industrialized Eastern states until it obtained through railroad connection with Philadelphia.

Eastern Pennsylvania was the principal coal- and iron-producing region until 1860. Here anthracite coal and iron were found in abundance, and a rather inferior method of smelting the one by the other was adopted about 1836. The production of pig-iron increased from 54,000 tons in 1810 to 564,000 tons in 1850; but by that time Great Britain's production was almost 3 million tons, and the United States was importing thence iron, steel, and the manufactures thereof to almost twice the value of its own product. Very little steel was produced in America before 1870, and the engineering trades were undeveloped. Typical iron manufactures of this period were nails, iron piping, and cast-iron air-tight stoves, which caused travelers as early as 1830 to complain of overheated American houses.

Textiles and iron do not exhaust the list of factory industries in the United States at this time, nor had mass production become a necessary condition of American industrial success. 'Their washing machines, refrigerators, rocking-chairs, all articles made of India rubber, are admirable,' wrote a visiting Englishwoman in 1846. Charles Goodyear discovered in 1844 by chance how to vulcanize rubber, an invention which within a century helped to put all America on wheels. Connecticut, in particular, was famous for small, water-driven workshops where specialized articles were produced by native ingenuity. Connecticut tinware and wooden clocks were carried by Yankee peddlers far and wide. One of the most popular exhibits at London's Crystal Palace in 1851 was the array of reapers, ranges, sewing machines, and other 'Yankee notions.' In Attleboro, Massachusetts, already a manufacturing center of cheap jewelry, President Jackson inspected a workshop during his journey through New England in 1833. The manager produced a card of lapel buttons with a palmetto tree design, which had been ordered by the South Carolina nullifiers, and humorously suggested that Jackson, having spoiled that line, should take them off his hands! The President was greatly amused to find 'that treason in South Carolina had its commercial value in Massachusetts.'

5. SCIENCE AND TECHNOLOGY

Comparatively little scientific advance was made in the United States during this era because the stress was on practice rather than theory. Benjamin Franklin started the trend; his American Philosophical Society was dedicated to 'useful knowledge,' and his loyalist contemporary Benjamin Thompson founded the Rumford professorship at Harvard in 1816 'on the Application of Science to the Useful Arts.' Alexis de Tocqueville, in his *Democracy in America* (1835), observed that in a democratic society short cuts to wealth, labor-saving gadgets, and inventions catering to the comfort of life, 'seem the most magnificent effort of human intelligence.'

The one American 'pure' scientist of this era was Joseph Henry. Son of a Scots day-laborer in Albany, he began to experiment with electricity in 1826 when, at the age of 29, he was appointed professor of natural philosophy in the local academy where he had been educated. After inventing the electromagnet, he devised means to increase the intensity of attraction produced by the same source of current; and by reversing the current he produced a rudimentary motor which he regarded as 'a philosophical toy.' His studies of induced currents, begun independently of his English contemporary Michael Faraday who first announced the discovery, led Henry to discover step-up and step-down transformers, to formulate theories of intensity (voltage) and quantity (amperage) of currents, and to make some of the earliest observations of oscillating energy discharged by electricity in a spiral coil. Outside that field he worked on solar radiation and capillary action of liquids.

In 1832 Henry was called to the College of New Jersey at Princeton, which he left in 1846 to become the first director of the Smithsonian Institution at Washington. This earliest American foundation for scientific research was established by a bequest of over £100,000 — greater than the then endowment of any American university — from a British chemist named James Smithson, for founding at Washington, 'an Establishment for the increase and diffusion of knowledge among men.' Calhoun and other strict constructionists opposed acceptance of the gift; but, largely owing to the efforts of John Quincy Adams, it was accepted in 1838, the fund invested, and the Institution organized. Congress, it appears, expected the Institution to comprise a library, art museum, and collection of scientific curiosities that would amuse congressmen and their friends. It was Henry who saw to it that the Smithsonian became an indispensable agency for the financing and wide distribution of original research in the natural and anthropological sciences.

Joseph Henry was one of three men who helped Samuel F. B. Morse to invent the electric telegraph in 1837. Morse's friends in Congress got him an appropriation of $30,000 in 1845 to establish between Baltimore and Washington the first telegraph line, which was built by Ezra Cornell of Ithaca, N. Y., who later founded Cornell University. It was typical of mid-century piety that the first message sent over this line in dots and dashes on 24 May 1844 between Morse in the Supreme Court chamber in the Capitol, and Alfred Vail in Baltimore, was 'What hath God wrought!' (Numbers xxiii:23).

The branches of science that made good progress in the generation after 1830 were natural history, chemistry, and geology. John Audubon had to visit England in order to obtain subscriptions for his classic *Birds of America* (1827), but he was acclaimed a hero on his return. In 1818 Benjamin Silliman of Yale founded and edited the first American scientific periodical, *The American Journal of Science and Arts;* in 1830 he published *Elements of Experimental Chemistry,* one of the first American scientific textbooks; in 1835 he delivered a series of lectures at Boston on geology which, pious Congregationalist though he was, made the first important dent on the Biblical account of creation. A year or two later his friend the Reverend Edward Hitchcock, a science professor of Amherst College who had already directed the geological survey of Massachusetts, discovered dinosaur tracks in the red sandstone of the Connecticut valley: a new proof of the antiquity of life on this planet.

In 1848 Louis Agassiz left his native Switzerland to lecture before the Lowell Institute of Boston. From his first public appearance, it was evident that America had found a leader in natural science who was at once an original investigator, a great teacher, and one who could appeal to the popular imagination. Promptly secured for the chair of zoology and geology in the new scientific school at Harvard, he began gathering material for a museum of comparative zoology, organized geological and biological exploring expeditions, corresponded with amateur naturalists in all parts of the country, wrote his *Contributions to the Natural History of the United States,* and trained teachers of science. Although his Harvard colleague Jeffries Wyman did more profound work in comparative anatomy, no American, native or adopted, was Agassiz's equal in stimulating both popular and scholarly interest in that segment of natural science which stretched from biology to paleontology.

6. POPULAR EDUCATION

The most tangible social gain during this period of ferment was in popular education. Since the Revolution, education had been left largely to private initiative and benevolence. Secondary academies and colleges had been founded, and of these the South now had more than the North. But almost all these institutions charged fees. Elementary education was the most neglected branch. Most of the Northern states

John Adams (1735-1826) by Mather Brown

Thomas Jefferson (1743-1826) by Rembrandt Peale

John Marshall (1755-1835) by Chester Harding

James Madison (1751-1836) by Gilbert Stuart

WASHINGTON.

The Burning of Washington by the British, August 24, 1814

Published by J. Roland & S. Lennon, Strand

Andrew Jackson (1767-1845) by Thomas Sully

had some sort of public primary school system, but only in New England was it free and open to all. In some instances a child had to know his letters before he was admitted to one of these schools, and in others only parents pleading poverty were exempted from fees. In addition the Quakers and other philanthropic bodies maintained charity schools for the poor. Consequently a stigma was attached to free schools. In New York City, around 1820, nearly half the children went uneducated because their parents were too poor to pay fees and too proud to accept charity.

Opposition to free public education came from people of property, who thought it intolerable that they should be taxed to support schools to which they would not dream of sending their children. To this argument the poor replied with votes, and reformers with the tempting argument that education was insurance against radicalism. New York City in 1832, and Philadelphia in 1836, established elementary public schools free from the taint of charity; but the growth of public schools did not keep pace with the increase of population by birth and immigration. There were half a million white adult illiterates in the country in 1840; almost a million in 1850.

In the newer states, school funds came from the proceeds of public land granted by the Federal Government in accordance with the policy of 1785, but most of these funds were mismanaged, and all proved inadequate. Pioneers of the Kentucky breed had a positive prejudice against book-learning. As a typical couple of this sort remarked to a Yankee pioneer in Illinois, they 'didn't think folks was any better off for reading, an' books cost a heap and took a power of time. 'Twant so bad for men to read, for there was a heap of time when they couldn't work out and could jest set by the fire; and if a man had books and keered to read he mought; but women had no business to hurtle away their time, 'case they could allus find something to do, and there'd been a heap of trouble in old Kaintuck with some rich men's gals that had learned to write.' Indiana was leavened by New Harmony; Robert Dale Owen helped to convert the Hoosier population to free schools. He established free traveling libraries, boxes of good books which made the rounds of the villages until read to pieces.

In the New England states the first problem was to make efficient the old colonial system. Free elementary schools, maintained by the townships and taught by birch-wielding pedagogues or college students during their vacations, were much in need of improvement. Horace Mann, a gifted politician who preferred the uphill work of reform to popular applause, sought efficient methods in Europe, and found them in Germany. He had Victor Cousin's report on Prussian education translated, and its principles were adapted to American needs when Horace Mann became chairman of the Massachusetts Board of Education (1837). Mann insisted that control of the schools should rest not with professional schoolmen but with popularly elected legislatures and school committees composed of laymen. At Lexington, Mass., in 1839, the first American teachers' college was established. After a struggle with the older teachers, who insisted that mental discipline would be lost if studies were made interesting, the elementary school ceased to be a place of terror. New England also set the pace in free public high schools; but until after the Civil War the majority of American pupils following a secondary course attended an endowed academy.

Outside New England, public schools were generally supported by the interest on a fund set up out of the proceeds of public lands or earmarked taxes, administered by a specially appointed state board. In Pennsylvania a terrific fight took place over free schools which were opposed by not only the well-to-do but the Germans, who feared the loss of their language and culture. The Pennsylvania public school law of 1834, although optional in the school districts, was bitterly attacked; and the eloquence of Thaddeus Stevens is credited with preventing its repeal the following year. By 1837, 742 out of 987 school districts had accepted it, and about 42 per cent of the children in the Keystone State went to free schools.

Ohio was fairly well provided with free public elementary schools by 1830, and six years later the state sent Calvin E. Stowe, professor of Biblical literature in Lane Theological Seminary at Cincinnati (better known as husband of the author of *Uncle Tom's Cabin*) to Europe to investigate public school systems. His *Report on Elementary Instruction in Europe* (1837) had an influence not inferior to the reports of Horace Mann. Among other things, it resulted in dividing public education in Ohio into elementary, grammar, and high school grades. By 1850 the modern system of grades one through twelve had been adopted in places where the number of pupils allowed it. Indiana established a free public school system by a narrow majority in 1848, but several years elapsed before it was properly enforced, because of the opposition of the Southern element in the population. A similar influence prevented the Illinois legislature from passing a state-wide public school law until 1855. Michigan, owing to the objections of the Germans, did not have a real public school system until about 1847. By 1860, the Midwest had a larger proportion of its children in public schools than any other region.

It was long before the free Negroes of the North had any benefit from free public education. Philadelphia opened the first school for colored children in 1822 with an apology to the public for doing something for 'this friendless and degraded portion of society.' In northern New England where Negroes were few, they were admitted to the public schools without question; but in urban centers both reformers and the Negroes themselves favored separate schools, to avoid the stigma of charity and give the children more congenial companionship. The move against segregation began with the anti-slavery agitation of the 1830's. Massachusetts in 1855 was the first state to enforce integration of all colors, races, and religions in her public schools. Other Northern states, where there was a considerable colored population, followed suit very slowly; segregation was not legally ended in New York City schools until 1900.

American schools of the nineteenth century reflected Protestant thinking. They aimed to cultivate qualities of character, such as thrift and industry, appropriate to the Puritan tradition and the cult of the self-made man, and William H. McGuffey's moralistic readers reflected the values of evangelical ministers. Yet the distinctions between public and parochial institutions were often obscured, because local schools were so flexible. Robert Cross has pointed out: 'In about the same years that a teacher in the Eliot School in Boston escaped real censure from his school board, even though he had very severely beaten an Irish Catholic student who wished to use a Douai rather than a King James Bible, Lowell, Massachusetts, was maintaining "Irish" public schools, to which only Catholic children came, in which only Catholics were employed as teachers, and where Catholic priests were allowed to conduct religious services.'

Increasingly the community expected the school to take over the roles of church and family. As the school committee of Springfield, Massachusetts, explained: 'The school-master is for the time being during school hours in loco parentis; sustaining a relation to his pupils parallel to that of a father to his children.' Even more pointed was the report of the school committee in Taunton, Massachusetts: 'New and fascinating temptations to vice have been set before our young men. Religion and virtue have not for many years had more to contend with, in their influence upon the young, than now. Hundreds of children here are idlers in the streets. Where is the remedy? The *Church* can do very little with this class. The *Home*, it is sad to say, is not often for them a place of wholesome control and is sometimes the reverse of a good school of morals. If the District School do not help save them, then their fate is sealed.'

7. HIGHER EDUCATION

This period saw an amazing multiplication of small denominational colleges; and a somewhat less surprising mortality among them. In sixteen Eastern and Midwestern states (both North and South) 516 colleges and 'universities' were founded before the Civil War; but only 104 of these were still in existence in 1929. Yale alone begat sixteen Congregationalist colleges before 1861, and Princeton 25 Presbyterian ones. The proliferation resulted from local pride, Protestant denominational rivalries, and distrust of the claims of older institutions. Community boosters preferred to launch a university rather than build an adequate grammar school. Too often, students arrived at college ill-prepared, and found there an uninspired curriculum and indifferent instruction.

It was the heyday of the small, rural college with six to a dozen professors and 100 to 300 students. Six o'clock chapel, prescribed classical-mathematical course, with chemistry and physics the most popular subjects next to Greek, and a smattering of French and German; 'philosophical apparatus,' mineralogical cabinet, and a collection of stuffed birds; freshman metaphysics, Saturday recitations on Paley's *Evidences of Christianity* followed by dismal puritan sabbath, relieved by periodic religious revivals and tremendous drinking bouts; literary and debating societies encouraged, and Greek-letter fraternities discouraged by the faculty; well-selected libraries of ancient and modern classics (Voltaire locked up); botanizing and fossil-hunting excursions over the country-side, ingenious hazing and amusing pranks, but no organized sports until the 1850's. So long as a college education meant the traditional liberal arts and three philosophies not much equipment was necessary, and a school in the country, where living was cheap, could attract more students than an urban college, and almost as good teachers. During a good part of this period, Amherst, Dartmouth, and Union colleges had as many or more students than Harvard, Yale, and Princeton. The average statesman and professional man of the Northern states completed his formal education at a small college. These were not universities as we understand them today; but for an integrated education, that cultivates manliness and makes gentlemen as well as scholars, one that disciplines the social affections and trains young men to faith in God, consideration for their fellow men, and respect for learning, America has never since had the equal of her little hill-top colleges.[2]

In the same period the movement for public and secular state universities, which had begun just before the Revolution, received a new impetus, in part from the founding of the University of Virginia. The earliest of the Western state universities was founded at Detroit in 1817, as the 'Catholepistemiead or University of Michigania' with a Presbyterian minister from Princeton as president and incumbent of seven professorial chairs, and the pioneer Catholic missionary Father Gabriel Richard as vice-president and occupant of the other six chairs. Such co-operation would have been inconceivable except on the frontier, and it was not long possible there. Despite the high-sounding title, this foundation remained a mere secondary school until 1837, when it was rechartered by the state of Michigan, removed to Ann Arbor, and endowed with proceeds from the educational land reserves. As in other Western states, so much of this land was lost by squatters' claims and legislative chicanery that tuition fees had to be charged in the early days, and state appropriations were sought later. The University was governed by a board of regents, nominated by the governor of Michigan, with full powers to dictate courses, prescribe textbooks, hire and fire professors; powers which they delighted to exercise. Henry P. Tappan, the first president who endeavored to emulate the standards of a European university, was dismissed by the regents, largely on the ground that he served wine at dinner. The University of Wisconsin, second of the state universities to become famous, was founded at

2. Oberlin in Ohio became the first co-educated college in 1833, but had very few imitators. Wesleyan College in Georgia was the first college to give degrees to women. Mary Lyon established Mount Holyoke Female Seminary in Massachusetts in 1836, but it was some years before it offered a course of college grade.

Madison in 1848, on a wilderness site crossed by Black Hawk's warriors only sixteen years before.

Harvard was the first of the older universities after the War of 1812 to feel the new spirit of progress; and the source of her inspiration was Germany. Between the years 1815 and 1820 four young Harvard graduates — George Ticknor, Edward Everett, Joseph G. Cogswell, and George Bancroft — traveled in Europe and studied at the Universities of Göttingen and Berlin. German universities were then in the first flower of their renaissance, leading Europe in almost every branch of learning. The young Americans admired the boundless erudition, critical acumen, and unwearied diligence of German scholars, marveled at the wealth of the university libraries, and envied the *Lernfreiheit* or academic freedom which permitted even theological professors to challenge the bases of the state church. They returned with an ambition to transform their little brick colleges into magnificently equipped universities, dedicated to the service of science, scholarship, and truth. All four upon their return received posts at Harvard. Everett gave prestige, by his graceful delivery and easily worn mantle of scholarship, to the lecture method of instruction; Bancroft (whom we shall meet in Polk's cabinet) applied German thoroughness to early American history; Cogswell, who secured in Germany a valuable collection of Americana, is memorable in library history; and Ticknor remained professor of belles lettres long enough to establish a worthy school of Romance and Germanic languages, and to secure the principle that undergraduates might elect them as a substitute for traditional subjects. But Ticknor's standards were too high even for the oldest American university at that period, and he was unable to obtain provision for postgraduate study. With his successor, the gentle Longfellow, came reaction; but the general level of scholarship was raised, and under these great teachers (who were first of all scholars), receptive students like Emerson, Thoreau, and J. R. Lowell, Francis Parkman and F. J. Child were encouraged to hitch their wagons to the stars. And it was in part the influence of American scholars who had caught the flame in Germany, in part the liberal tendency of Unitarianism, that made Harvard, as early as the 1830's, a steadfast defender of the scholar's freedom from political and religious pressure.

These educational reformers of 1820–40 were animated by the republican and aristocratic ideal of Jefferson. In his famous educational bill for Virginia Jefferson wrote:

it becomes expedient for promoting the publick happiness that those persons, whom nature hath endowed with genius and virtue, should be rendered by liberal education worthy to receive, and able to guard the sacred deposit of the rights and liberties of their fellow citizens, and that they should be called to that charge without regard to wealth, birth or other accidental condition or circumstance. . . .

Jefferson and the Harvard reformers proposed to train an intellectual aristocracy — one selected for 'genius and virtue,' not anyone who had the ambition — to serve the Republic. And they proposed to do this in colleges and universities free from sectarian or political control, in order to give the scholar's mind free play. Jacksonian Democracy, on the contrary, affirmed that all men were born equal, envied intellectual preeminence, and preached the doctrine of equal educational privileges for all. The American public cared nothing for academic freedom or for scholarship as such, and suspected that a liberal education made men enemies of democracy. It wanted a cheap education, directed toward the acquisition of information or skills that would be directly useful in the student's future occupation. Harvard, for instance, was criticized by the Massachusetts legislature because it did not help young men to become 'better farmers, mechanics, or merchants,' and paid professors fixed salaries, instead of so much for each student who attended their instruction. They had been reading that classic in democratic educational theory, *Thoughts on the Present Collegiate System in the United States* (1842) by President Francis Wayland of Brown University, who in one of his official reports was to proclaim the dangerously attractive principle that 'every student might study what he chose, all that he chose, and nothing but what he chose.' Jefferson's idea was a liberal education for those who could profit by it, and the training of a few selected scholars; Wayland and democracy demanded vocational training for everybody.

There was a crying need for engineering and technical schools in a country so fast developing industry and transportation. The earliest effort to meet it, outside the Military Academy at West Point, was at Norwich University in 1820; the second was the founding of the Rensselaer Polytechnic Institute in 1824. Rensselaer offered a comprehensive course of practical science, with equipment that included the first laboratories designed for students' use in the United States. Its first class in civil engineering graduated in 1835. Between 1835 and the Civil War, only three or four American universities established engineering departments.

While many of the colleges of mid-century had high standards in the subjects they professed to teach — few college students of today would or could read the large assignments of ancient classics required of their forebears — the university law and medical schools of the period were not even respectable. Yet the invention of the last century that has done the most to alleviate suffering, the application of anesthesia to surgery, was discovered independently by three graduates of American medical schools around 1842; and sulphuric ether was first used in a surgical operation at Boston in 1846. And, just as Jefferson wished to live as the founder of a university, so Dr. O. W. Holmes, author of *The Autocrat of the Breakfast Table,* considered his best title to fame the discovery in 1843 that puerperal fever could be prevented by the use of antiseptics.

Adults were not neglected in this educational awakening. In all the cities and larger towns mechanics' institutes provided vocational courses and night schools. Free public libraries were very generally established. In towns, and even villages, the lyceums offered popular lectures, scientific demonstrations, debates, and entertainments. The Lowell Institute for public lectures on literary and scientific subjects was brilliantly inaugurated in Boston by Silliman in 1839, and led to similar foundations in other cities. Popular reading was aided by mechanical improvements in printing, which made possible the penny press, one-sixth the former price of the average daily paper. The New York *Tribune,* Baltimore *Sun,* and Philadelphia *Ledger* began as penny newspapers in the 1840's. They were by no means rowdy sheets but journals of information, including pirated English novels in serial form; and the *Tribune,* under Horace Greeley's editorship, became a liberal power of the first magnitude.

By 1850, then, in the Northern and Western states there had been formulated, and to some extent established, the basic principles of American education today: (1) that free public primary and secondary schools should be available for all children; (2) that teachers should be given professional training; (3) that all children should attend school up to a certain age, but not necessarily the free public school, religious and other bodies having complete liberty to establish their own educational systems at their own cost; (4) that a liberal higher education, and professional training schools for law, medicine, divinity, and engineering be provided, largely for paying students. Although Huxley's test of a national system, 'a great educational ladder with one end in the gutter and the other in the university,' was well on its way toward being satisfied, the research function of modern universities was hardly yet thought of.

XXV

The Southern States

1. THE COTTON KINGDOM

South of the border states of Delaware, Maryland, Virginia, and Kentucky, cotton ruled from 1815 to 1861; and the principal bulwark of his throne was slavery. Almost 60 per cent of the slaves in the United States in 1850 were employed in growing cotton. Like rice, sugar, and tobacco, it was a plantation crop, requiring continuous attention of a sort that the most ignorant hands were able to perform under supervision. In 1820 the cotton crop of 160 million pounds was already the most valuable Southern interest. As more and more people in the Western world switched from linen and wool to cotton, its production doubled by 1830, and more than doubled again in the next decade. New Orleans, which in 1816 received 37,000 bales of cotton, counted almost a million in 1840. By 1850 the crop had passed a thousand million pounds; and the crop of 1860 was almost 2300 million pounds in weight, and in value two-thirds the total exports of the United States.

This growth was brought about by a rapid extension of the cotton-growing area. Like typical pioneer farmers, exploiters rather than conservers of the soil, the cotton planters advanced from South Carolina and Georgia across the 'black belts' and Indian cessions of Alabama and Mississippi, occupied the great valley up to Memphis, pushed up the Red river of Louisiana to the Indian Territory, and passed the boundary of Mexico into Texas, eating the fat of the land and leaving devastation behind. On the march King Cotton acquired new subjects:

moneyed immigrants from the North, and ambitious dirt farmers who purchased a slave or two on credit and with luck became magnates. The white population of Arkansas jumped from 13,000 in 1820 to 324,000 in 1860; the number of slaves rose from 1600 to 111,000. In every region fit for cotton, the richest lands were sooner or later absorbed by planters. Hunter folk moved westward, and poor whites settled on pine barrens, abandoned fields, and gullied hillsides. Some of the best minds of the South endeavored to arrest this process by scientific methods of agriculture; but as long as good land remained plentiful and cheap, whether within the United States or adjacent under the feeble sovereignty of Mexico, the cotton growers preferred their own ways.

Cotton plantations differed greatly both in size and character. Absenteeism was frequent in the Lower South, although hardly the rule outside the bottom lands between Vicksburg and New Orleans. Many a show plantation of the older South, where visitors were received with lavish hospitality and were impressed by the happy life of the slaves, was supported by latifundia in the new South. One of the better sort in Mississippi, described by Olmsted, covered several square miles. The mansion house, which the owner had not seen for two years, was four miles distant from the nearest white neighbor. The cleared portion, about 1400 acres, was tilled by a plough-gang of 30 men and a larger hoe-gang, mainly women, who were encouraged by a black driver with whip in hand. Enough corn and pork were usually raised to feed the cattle and the 135 slaves, who included three mechanics, two seamstresses, four teamsters and cattle-tenders, a midwife, and a nurse who had charge of a day nursery. The overseer also maintained a pack of hounds to hunt runaways. He kept the field hands working from sun to sun, but gave them most of Saturday as well as Sunday off, except in the picking season. They cut their fuel in the master's woods and were allowed to make boards for sale in their free time. Everywhere in the South slave families were allotted land to raise vegetables and poultry to eke out their rations of corn and pork.

A 'middle-class plantation,' which did not produce enough surplus to enable the owner to travel or reside elsewhere, would have 100 to 400 acres under cultivation and 10 to 40 slaves. A planter of this class might be a younger son, a self-made pioneer, an ex-overseer, or a professional man using his plantation to enhance his dignity in the community. In few instances did he enjoy comforts or amenities superior to those of the poorest farmers in the North: a bare house without conveniences, a diet largely of 'hog and hominy,' no literature but a weekly paper, no diversion but hunting and an occasional visit to the county seat. That sort of planter belonged to the governing class and had things much his own way in Alabama, Mississippi, and Arkansas. Like most Americans of the time, he distrusted other parts of the country than his own, and held the rest of the world in hearty contempt. A large part of the cotton crop was made by small farmers with one to half a dozen slaves. Mark Twain describes 'one of these little one-horse cotton plantations' in *Huckleberry Finn:*

> A rail fence round a two-acre yard; a stile, made out of logs sawed off and up-ended, in steps, like barrels of a different length, to climb over the fence with, and for the women to stand on when they are going to jump on to a horse; some sickly grass-patches in the big yard, but mostly it was bare and smooth, like an old hat with the nap rubbed off; big double log house for the white folks —hewed logs, with the chinks stopped up with mud or mortar, and these mud-stripes had been white-washed some time or another; round-log kitchen, with a big, broad, open but roofed passage joining it to the house; log smoke-house back of the kitchen; three little log nigger-cabins in a row t'other side the smokehouse; one little hut all by itself away down against the back fence, and some outbuildings down a piece the other side, ash-hopper, and big kettle to bile soap in, by the little hut; bench by the kitchen door, with a bucket of water and a gourd; hound asleep there, in the sun; more hounds asleep, roundabout; about three shade-trees away off in a corner; some currant bushes and gooseberry bushes in one place by the fence; outside the fence a garden and a watermelon patch; then the cotton fields begin; and after the fields, the woods.

Below these yeomen farmers came a class called 'pore white trash,' 'crackers,' 'peckerwoods,' and other opprobrious nicknames. Constituting less than 10 per cent of the white population, they appear to have been frontiersmen stranded on worn-out land by the westward surge of the cotton kingdom. These sallow, undernourished illiterates, whose only pride was their color, envied successful white men and hated the Negro. Twentieth-century biologists, notably Charles W. Stiles, discovered that the principal causes of the poor whites' indolence and shiftlessness were improper diet and hookworm, which they contracted by constantly going barefoot. Very different were the mountain men, the 'hillbillies' who lived in the secluded valleys and on the steep slopes of the Appalachians and the Ozarks. These proud, upstanding, independent people were expert hunters and fishermen. Almost isolated from the rest of the South, they were encountered only when they drove ox teams to market to sell moonshine whiskey made in illicit stills, and pork cured from acorn-fed pigs.

2. THE SLAVE

For more than a century writers have carried on a strenuous debate over the profitability of slavery, and the argument is as vigorous today as ever. Some historians contend that as a result of the high cost of slaves even planters opulent in nominal wealth found it difficult to keep out of debt, and the poorer ones depended on the money-lender for maintenance between crops. Thus, it is said, the system was uneconomical even for large planters in the long run; and for small farmers the first cost of labor became prohibitive. Furthermore, it has been argued that slavery retarded industrialization because the purchase of slaves absorbed an inordinate amount of capital; because slavery limited the development of a home market with widespread purchasing power; and because, by keeping the bondsmen in ignorance, the South denied itself the benefits of an educated, skilled working class. Other historians question whether the slow pace of industrialization was the consequence of slavery or of the fact that the South was an agricultural society in which capital could be more profitably employed in planting. Moreover, some historians who concede that slavery was not viable as an economic system argue that it was often very profitable as a business enterprise. There is no reason to suppose that slavery would have died out if it had not been ended by war, since even the most hopelessly inefficient master acquired status from owning slaves, even if the slave did not earn his keep.

What did the Negro himself think of this system? Here we have inferences that are poles apart. On the one hand (as stated by Jefferson Davis in his reply to Lincoln's Emancipation Proclamation), these 'several millions of human beings of an inferior race' were 'peaceful and contented laborers in their sphere.' The pampered domestic servant, the happy, carefree, banjo-playing 'darkey,' a theme of countless post-Civil

War novels, were all that many upper-class travelers saw of the South's 'peculiar institution,' as her statesmen liked to call it. On the other hand, Negro slavery in the South has been called the most oppressive and exploitative system of labor in history.

It is often forgotten that the slave trade was begun by Negroes in Africa before Europeans reached the 'Dark Continent,' that every black bought by a slave trader was sold by one of his own race, and that victims of the system who were shipped to North America were better off than those who remained in bondage in Africa; [1] better off, in fact, than many poor workers and peasants in Europe. John Randolph's slave valet who accompanied his master to Ireland in 1827, 'looked with horror upon the mud hovels and miserable food' of the Irish peasantry. But these 'white slaves,' as the scornful Virginian called them, could emigrate to America as free men, their sons could become congressmen and bishops, and their grandsons governors and even Presidents; whilst the children of Negroes in America were born into bondage.

There were social gradations among Negro slaves even before they reached America. Between a Virginian slave major-domo, whose ancestors had been American for two centuries, and a Gullah Negro of the Carolina sea-islands who might have been smuggled over from Africa within a year, there was an immense gap. Domestic slaves, naturally the favored class, were assimilated to American civilization. Many a colored butler or maid occupied a status similar to those confidential slaves that we meet in Greek and Roman literature. Field hands constituted the majority of slaves and were the most profitable. A third and intermediate class were those who learned a trade such as carpenter, blacksmith or barber, and often were hired out by their masters. In 1820 slaves made up 20 per cent of the population of Southern cities; by 1860, a half million slaves labored in factories or in other non-agricultural pursuits like railroad construction.

The distinctive aspect of slave society in the United States was the resistance offered to the bondsman who sought to escape the system. The master who contemplated freeing his slaves faced unusually great impediments. To a far less extent than in countries like Brazil, some

---

1. Compare Saint-Exupéry's account in *Wind, Sand and Stars* (1939) of an old and useless slave being turned out in the desert by his Moslem master to die of starvation — this around 1928.

slave artisans were allowed to purchase their freedom out of earnings; but state laws made that increasingly difficult, since every law-abiding and successful free Negro was a living argument against keeping the rest of his race enslaved. In the decade of the 1840's, when the number of slaves in the United States increased 29 per cent, that of free Negroes increased only 12½ per cent. The Romans usually freed their talented slaves, and in any case their progeny went free. But America offered no legal exit to the talented or intellectual slave; it subjected a writer like Frederick Douglass to the caprice of a white owner who might be his inferior in every respect. And one drop of African blood made a man or woman 'colored.' Thirteen per cent of all Negroes in the United States in 1860 were mulattoes. The beautiful octoroons of New Orleans, equal in their profession to the most talented courtesans of old France, were bought and sold like field hands — but at far higher prices.

While the average white European or North American disliked the Negro as such, there was no physical repulsion from color in the South. White children were suckled by black mammies and played with their children. In a stage coach or railroad car, as a squeamish English visitor observed, 'A lady makes no objection to ride next a fat Negro woman, even when the thermometer is at ninety degrees; provided always that her fellow travellers understand she is her property.' In every part of the South the small slaveholder worked side by side with his men in the field, and treated them like his own children, as indeed they sometimes were.

Marriage between the races was everywhere forbidden by law, but the antebellum South was curiously tolerant of irregular unions between white men and colored women. Vice-President Richard M. Johnson lived openly with a mulatto girl whom he had inherited from his father, but Washington society drew the line when he attempted to make debutantes of their two daughters.

Flogging with the rawhide or blacksnake whip was the usual method of punishing slaves. Imprisonment lost the master their time, and short rations affected their health. Although state laws forbade cruelty, a master or overseer was not often brought to book for it. A slave had rather less chance for redress at that period than a seaman against his Yankee skipper, or an enlisted man in the army against his officer. Severity pushed too far was apt to turn the slaves into runaways. Consequently, little time elapsed between detection and punishment, not softened by reflection. Instances of sadistic cruelty to slaves are so numerous in the records that they cannot be dismissed as mere abolitionist propaganda. No doubt these were extreme cases; no doubt the majority of masters were kind; but should not a system be judged by the extremes that it tolerates? May we not judge Hitler's regime by the gas chambers, or Communism by the purges, forced-labor camps, and firing squads?

The feature of slavery that most outraged humane feelings was the separation of families by private sale or auction. It was often asserted in defense that Negroes had a very slight family attachment; that Whittier's 'Farewell of a Virginia Slave Mother' with its haunting refrain, was mere abolitionist cant:

> Gone, gone, — sold and gone
> To the rice-swamps dank and lone,
> From Virginia's hill and waters:
> Woe is me, my stolen daughters!

Yet when a young Northerner asked John Randolph of Roanoke to name the greatest orator he had ever heard, the old Virginian snapped out: 'A slave, Sir. She was a mother, and her rostrum was the auction-block.'

3. SLAVE INSURRECTIONS

The years 1822–32 are a watershed in the history of Southern white people's ideas about slavery. Hitherto, the planter class apologized for slavery as something forced on them by circumstances, which they could do nothing about; many frankly called it a curse. Beginning around 1822 there was gradual tightening of the 'black codes' in the slave states, and a defiant adoption of the theory that slavery was not only the one possible means of keeping Negroes subordinate, but a positive good in itself, sanctioned by history and the Bible.

The starting point for this change of sentiment was the report that Denmark Vesey, a free mulatto, with the help of Gullah Jack, an aged African witch doctor, had hatched a plot in Charleston in 1822 involving thousands of Negroes bent on slaughter and rape. In retrospect it appears that the plot was at most a vague notion in the minds of a few men given to loose talk, and it is possible that no conspiracy existed. But in a city in which Negroes outnumbered whites, and in which, as urban blacks, they were more advanced, less servile, and free from constant surveillance, rumors of insurrection bred panic.

Betrayed by one of the conspirators, loyal to a kind master, the 'revolt' was suppressed before it really started, and 37 Negro conspirators, including Vesey, were executed. A system of control, then adopted in the Lower South, gradually spread to Virginia and the border states. Negroes were forbidden to assemble or circulate after curfew, and night patrols policed the roads. Whites were forbidden to teach slaves to read or write in every Southern state except Maryland, Kentucky, and Tennessee.

On the assumption that the great majority of slaves were happy and contented, Vesey's and subsequent insurrections were generally blamed on outside agitators — as, after the two world wars, domestic discontents were blamed on Communist agitation. In accordance with this theory, free colored sailors on Northern or European ships calling at Charleston or Savannah were by law hailed ashore and confined to the local calaboose until the ship sailed. In one case Justice William Johnson of the Supreme Court, a native of Charleston, ruled that this was unconstitutional, but gave no relief to the imprisoned Negro plaintiff; and South Carolina successfully defied his dictum. A distinguished lawyer of Massachusetts, a former member of Congress, who was sent to Charleston in 1844 to try to get the law relaxed (it being inconvenient for a shipmaster to have his colored cook impounded while in port) was accused by the South Carolina legislature of attempting to incite a slave insurrection, threatened with violence, and hustled back on board ship.

A more serious insurrection took place in tidewater Virginia in 1831. A pious slave named Nat Turner enlisted a number of others who in August killed 57 whites before they were rounded up by militia with the help of regular troops from Fortress Monroe and sailors from the navy. Between 40 and 100 Negroes were killed, and Turner was hanged.

Although the new patrol and control system prevented any slave insurrections comparable to Vesey's or Turner's during the next 30 years, a number of spontaneous and unsuccessful strikes for freedom took place. In 1845, for instance, about 75 slaves from southeastern Maryland counties attempted, without firearms, to fight their way through to Pennsylvania and freedom. They were rounded up about twenty miles north of Washington, and shot, hanged, or sold 'down the river.' Cumulative evidence proves that, however docile the majority of the slaves may have been, unrest and incipient rebellion were so widespread as to keep the master class in a constant state of apprehension.

4. SOUTHERN SOCIETY

Slavery and cotton preserved in the South a rural, almost feudal, society.[2] The eighteenth-century social contempt for trade persisted. Agriculture, the army, the church, and the law were the only proper careers for a planter's son. Northern and European merchant-bankers and ship-owners handled the cotton crop, and kept most of the profits. Shopkeepers in the market towns were often Yankees, Germans, or Jews. There were few factories; for capital was tied up in slaves, who were more valuable growing than spinning cotton. Of the 15 largest cities in America in 1860, only one (New Orleans) was in the South. European immigrants, overwhelmingly from Northern countries, shunned a region where manual labor was regarded as unfit for a free man, and where the warm climate made adjustment difficult. Railway development was slow, for the relatively sparse population of the uplands was largely self-sustaining, and cotton afforded freight traffic during but a brief season of the year. The main roads in Kentucky, Virginia, and the Carolinas were improved, and provided with decent inns; but west and south of these states one followed the usual pioneer sloughs and trails. Frontier

2. The following statistics roughly indicate the social classes in the South as a whole (including the District of Columbia) and in the cotton states (South Carolina, Georgia, Florida, Alabama, Mississippi, Louisiana, Arkansas, and Texas) in 1850:

	All Slave States	Cotton States
Number of slaveholding families	347,525	154,391
Number of families owning 1 to 9 slaves	255,258	104,956
Number of families owning 10 to 49 slaves	84,328	43,299
Number of families owning 50 or more slaves	7,939	6,144
White population	6,242,418	2,137,284
Free Negro population	238,187	34,485
Slave population	3,204,077	1,808,768

Century of Population Growth, p. 136; J. D. B. De Bow, Statistical View of the U.S. (1854), pp. 45, 63, 82, 95, 99. Slaveholding families are counted more than once if they owned slaves in different counties.

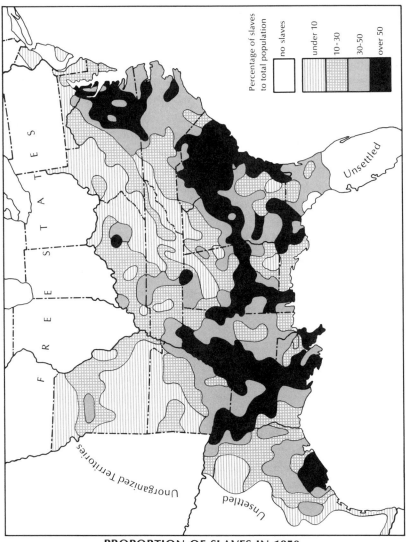

PROPORTION OF SLAVES IN 1850

477

conditions still prevailed through the greater part of the Lower South in 1850, combined with a turbulence and ignorance that seldom lingered in the Northern frontier beyond the first generation.

Theology, which had been neglected in the South when the section was liberal and anti-slavery, was much cultivated after it became conservative and pro-slavery. The influence of the evangelical sects among the planters increased in proportion as their ministers 'discovered' pro-slavery arguments in the Bible. The Catholic and Episcopalian churches remained neutral on the slavery question, and stationary in numbers. Thomas Jefferson, dying, saluted the rising sun of Unitarianism as destined to enlighten the South; but it sent only a few feeble rays beyond the Mason-Dixon Line. Horace Holley, the gifted young Unitarian who had made of Transylvania University in Lexington, Ky., a southern Harvard, was driven from his post and the university almost completely ruined by an alliance between Presbyterian bigotry and Jacksonian Democracy. Thomas Cooper, a victim of the 1798 Sedition Act, who had moved south, was promised by Jefferson the first chair of chemistry at the University of Virginia; but Cooper was a Unitarian, and the Virginians raised such an outcry that he resigned. Later, in spite of his services to the state-rights cause, Cooper was 'tried' for atheism, and ejected, at the age of 75, from the presidency of the University of South Carolina.

Presbyterians and Episcopalians appealed to the upper classes. Methodists and Baptists were more successful among middle classes, poor whites, and colored folk. For a time these churches were a bond of union between North and South; but when the Northern Methodists unreasonably insisted that a Southern bishop emancipate slaves which he had inherited and could not conscientiously get rid of, the Southern members seceded and formed the Methodist Church South (1844). The Baptists followed, and doubled their membership in fifteen years. While these Southern evangelicals condoned slavery, they banned card-playing and dancing; by 1860 the bastard puritanism of the age was more prevalent in Alabama and Mississippi than in Massachusetts and Connecticut.

The finest product of the plantation regime was the Southern gentleman. Numbering but few, the gentry ruled the older Southern states by virtue of personality even more than property, and governed them honorably and efficiently, although not with enlightenment. Discriminatingly hospitable, invariably gracious to women, endowed with a high sense of personal honor and civic virtue, they yet lacked the instinct for compromise that, time and again, has preserved the English aristocracy from annihilation.

Of this ruling class, only a small fraction belonged to the eighteenth-century aristocracy of Maryland, Virginia, and the Carolinas. The type of colonial gentleman that Washington was, appeared undiminished in his Lee kinsmen; but the old Huguenot families of Charleston were declining, and the creoles of Louisiana were easy-going and unambitious. Apart from these three persistent types, the mass of the greater planters in 1850 were self-made men like Jefferson Davis, whose parents had lived in log cabins. If not well educated themselves, their sons and daughters were. The South, despite poverty in elementary education, had good secondary schools, especially of the military type, and more students in college than the North.

Life on a resident plantation of the better sort was neither sordid as the abolitionists asserted, nor splendid as the novelists have depicted it. The mansion house, seated on rising ground, was generally a well-proportioned wooden building of neo-classic style, with a columned portico or veranda that gave dignity to the elevation and afforded shade to the ground floor and front chambers. The rooms, seldom more than fifteen in number, were high-ceiled and simply furnished. There were plenty of flowers, and masses of native flowering shrubs and creepers such as the Cherokee rose, which abounded in the Southland. Simplicity rather than ostentation was the dominant note in the planter's life. His recreations were largely field sports, but he enjoyed little leisure. On a Virginia plantation visited by Olmsted, not ten consecutive minutes elapsed even during dinner, when the proprietor was not interrupted by a servant. The owner's wife had to guard against pilferers, serve out supplies, bind up wounds, and nurse the sick.

Such a life was a continuous exercise of tact, self-control, and firmness; yet the condition of unlimited power was a constant temptation to passion. The sort of bluster considered gentlemanly in the eighteenth century remained so in the South at a time when smoother and more reticent manners had become the mark of good breeding in England and the North. The Southern gentleman had the same conflicting character as the old-regime Russian or Hungarian landlord. He would tolerate an amount of shirking and evasion that would drive any Northern employer frantic; but to cross his will, question his authority, or impugn his honor courted serious trouble. The descendants of 'cavaliers' were so afraid of being thought afraid that they were apt to see insult where none was intended and to reply in a manner that forced a fight. Governor John Lyde Wilson of South Carolina published a textbook on dueling, *The Code of Honor* (1838), but most disputes between white men were settled by other and less honorable forms of conflict. Alexander H. Stephens, future Vice-President of the Confederacy, was unable to take part in the political campaign of 1848 because he had been disabled by stabs received in an 'affray.' Items in the press such as the following were not unusual: 'The Hon. Edward P. Pitts, late state senator from Accomac Co., Va., was attacked by John C. Wise Esq. at a public vendue on December 27 last and horsewhipped by him. Mr. Wise was inflamed by a remark made by Pitts at a political meeting during a recent campaign, at which the Hon. James W. Custis knocked Mr. Wise off the stand, while speaking, for some disrespectful remark.'

5. EDUCATION AND SCIENCE

Save in New Orleans, free popular education made little progress prior to the 1850's, when Calvin H. Wiley in North Carolina and William L. Yancey in Alabama inaugurated reforms which were rudely interrupted by the Civil War. The poor white grew up largely illiterate, but the ruling classes were well served by tutors, academies, and colleges. The University of Virginia (1825), the last flowering of Jeffersonian liberalism, was the partial realization of a comprehensive scheme for public education, for which Jefferson had been striving since 1779. The essence of Jefferson's experiment was a division of the curriculum into eight vertical 'schools,' corresponding to modern faculties, or departments; and allowing every student to elect one or more, each school granting its own degree. Jefferson insisted that the university be non-sectarian, and attempted to import distinguished European scholars to set standards equal to those of the German universities. But his generous ambition was thwarted by a series of developments: the miserably inadequate support ($15,000 a year) granted by the state, so that each 'school' in practice became a one-man department; the jealousy of older colleges and the hostility of evangelicals to a 'godless university'; the inadequate preparation of Southern students and their frolicsome man-

ners—horsewhipping unpopular professors and fighting bowie-knife
duels among themselves. Nevertheless, by 1850 the University of Virginia had reached Northern standards. The South as a whole remained
faithful to the eighteenth-century type of liberal arts college. Professor
Frederick A. P. Barnard (the future president of Columbia University),
investigating the situation at the University of Alabama in 1854, found
no demand for a university of the Virginia type. The people did not
want intellectual discipline for their sons; their idea of a university was
a place to study whatever you liked, without any particular preparation. In this respect the average Southerner and Northerner saw eye to
eye.

Science in the South was still treated as a gentlemanly hobby. And
since science did not tread on the toes of slavery (as reform and letters
did) it was profitably pursued. Several Charleston gentlemen, in particular, contributed to the advancement of science: Edmund Ravenel
the pioneer conchologist, his cousin Henry W. Ravenel the mycologist,
the Reverend John Bachman, who collaborated with Audubon in *Quadrupeds of North America*. Louis LeConte, a Georgia planter, was
imbued at Columbia College with a passionate enthusiasm for science,
and maintained a botanical garden at his plantation. He was rewarded
by two sons, John and Joseph, who became eminent in biology, medicine, and geology even before the Civil War. Several Southern states
began geological surveys (but not all finished them), and Edmund
Ruffin's work on soil chemistry, first published in Virginia in 1832, did
much to bring back to fruitfulness the worn-out tobacco lands of the
tidewater.

6. THE LITERATURE OF CHIVALRY

The 'Southern chivalry' tradition was created in the generation of 1820
to 1850. In *Ivanhoe* and the flood of imitative literature that followed,
the cotton lord and his lady found a romantic mirror of their life and
ideals. A generalizing French traveler, Michel Chevalier, assumed that
all Northerners were descended from Cromwell's Roundheads, and all
Southern whites from King Charles's Cavaliers; this explained their
differences and proved infinitely comforting to the South. William A.
Caruthers's novel *The Cavaliers of Virginia* (1834) set the tradition.
Every owner of two Negroes, however dubious his origin or squalid his

existence, became a 'cavalier,' entitled to despise the low-bred shop-keepers, artisans, and clerks of the North. The rage to establish *May-flower* or 'Knickerbocker' ancestry in the North, 50 years later, was a compensation of the same sort for descendants of colonial families who were being crowded by newcomers.

To comprehend the psychology of the Southern planter we must remember that his social system was on the defensive against most of the western world. Mayor Otis of Boston, when appealed to from Virginia to suppress abolition agitation in 1831, remarked that nothing in the way of censorship could protect the South: 'The force of opinion in favor of emancipation throughout the world must blow upon them like a perpetual trade-wind, and keep them in a constant state of agitation and discomfort.' Sentiment for the abolition of slavery was world-wide. Under the leadership of Wilberforce and Clarkson in England, Parliament in 1833 passed an act emancipating all slaves in the British West Indies, allowing compensation to the owners. The Second Republic did the same in the French West Indies in 1848; Denmark and all other colonial powers in the West Indies, with the important exception of Spain, had already done so.

The white Southerner's proud assertiveness was the sign not of confidence but of fear. It was fear, not insensibility, that made him indifferent or hostile to the new tenderness that was dissolving the harsher social relations in England and the Northern states. Just as New England in 1800 refused every quickening current from France or Virginia, for fear it might bear the seeds of Jacobinism, so the South, a generation later, rejected a literature and philosophy which might conceal abolitionist sentiment. At a time when Bryant, Longfellow, and Whittier were redeeming Northern materialism with cheerful song, Southern silence was broken only by the gloomy and romantic notes of Edgar Allan Poe. It was a Pennsylvanian, Stephen C. Foster, who attuned the beauty and pathos of the old South to the human heart in 'Uncle Ned,' 'Old Black Joe,' and 'My Old Kentucky Home.'

The most distinguished and prolific man of letters of the antebellum South was William Gilmore Simms of Charleston. Bryant encouraged him, and Harper's of New York published the ten romances that he wrote between 1834 and 1842, including the famous *Guy Rivers* and *The Yemassee*, the latter an excellent historical novel; but Charleston society could not forget that Simms was not to the manner born, and failed to support the literary quarterly he founded. In the North, letters had become a recognized road to fame and fortune; historians like Bancroft, Prescott, and Irving, novelists like Cooper and Hawthorne, even the poets, won consideration and applause; a philosopher at large like Emerson and a poet-journalist like Bryant achieved warm and satisfactory contact with the educated public in the North and West. But a Southerner, as Simms's biographer wrote, had to think in certain grooves or else his writings would be ignored, or at best, smiled at as harmless eccentricities. Simms himself wrote in 1855, 'All that I have [done] has been poured to waste in Charleston.'

These 'certain grooves' in which Southern men of letters were compelled to write were glorification of the 'Southern way of life' and defense of slavery. The literary output of the South, from 1830 to the Civil War, was permeated by pro-slavery apologetics. Newspapers and periodicals, religious and secular, were filled with articles on slavery, and almost every public question was brought to that touchstone. Sermons, lectures, speeches, and discussions in literary societies revolved about the theme. It has been claimed that the South was driven to defend slavery as a reaction against the intemperate criticism of it by the abolitionists which began in 1831. On the contrary, the 'positive good' theory was an outgrowth of the 1820's, antedating the Garrisonian propaganda. Thomas Cooper published his first pro-slavery pamphlet in 1826. Governor Stephen D. Miller struck the keynote of the next 30 years in a message to the South Carolina legislature of 1829: 'Slavery is not a national evil; on the contrary, it is a national benefit.' The growth of this feeling, clashing with Northern agitation for abolition, resulted in the suppression of criticism of slavery in the South. Northern mails were seized upon and censored. Ministers, teachers, professional men, and politicians who would not bow down to mumbo-jumbo were eliminated. Laws were even passed against criticism outside the South of Southern institutions, and a price was placed on the heads of prominent abolitionists.

A positive pro-slavery theory of society, corresponding to the political doctrine of state rights, was provided by Thomas R. Dew, a bright young Virginian who returned from study in Germany to a chair at William and Mary College. In a pamphlet of 1832, he argued that slavery had been the condition of classical culture, that the Hebrew prophets and St. Paul admitted its moral validity, that civilization required the many to work and the few to think. George Fitzhugh, in a tract entitled *Cannibals All,* argued that the Negro was something less than man, and in his *Sociology for the South* provided a new set of principles to replace the 'glittering generalities' of a century of enlightenment.

John C. Calhoun gave pro-slavery doctrine the sanction of his name and character, and so cunningly combined it with American prepossessions that slavery appeared no longer the antithesis, but the condition, of democracy. Calhoun began with the axiom that no wealthy or civilized society could exist unless one portion of the community lived off the labor of others. White wage-earners, class-conscious in England and enfranchised in the Northern states, were threatening property and civilization. Chartism in England and trade-unionism in the United States proved that social stability could not be maintained where labor was free. It was too late to re-establish serfdom in Europe and the North. But to the South a beneficent providence had brought a race marked by God with mental and physical inferiority, created to be hewers of wood and drawers of water for His chosen people. In return, kind masters provided for all reasonable wants of their slaves, and saved them from the fear of misery and destitution that haunted the white proletariat. The masters themselves, relieved from manual labor and sordid competition, would reach that intellectual and spiritual eminence of which the founders of the Republic had dreamed. 'Many in the South once believed that slavery was a moral and political evil. That folly and delusion are gone. We see it now in its true light, and regard it as the most safe and stable basis for free institutions in the world.'

Such was the nonsense that became orthodox in the South by 1850. Yet it is doubtful how wide or deep this new folly really went. It was never accepted by the great Virginians who fought so valiantly for the Confederacy.[3] There was no place in the system for poor whites, from one of whom, Hinton R. Helper, came the first prophecy of disaster: *The Impending Crisis* (1857) which was suppressed throughout the South. Even the planting class did not accept the logical deduction that

3. Robert E. Lee emancipated the few slaves he inherited from his mother, and owned no others. Stonewall Jackson purchased two slaves at their own request, and allowed them to earn their freedom. J. E. Johnston and A. P. Hill never owned a slave, and disliked slavery. J. E. B. Stuart owned but two slaves, and disposed of them for good reasons, long before the war. M. F. Maury, who called slavery a 'curse.' owned but one, a family servant.

the slave trade should be reopened. John C. Calhoun, more humane than his doctrine, refused privately to condone the domestic slave trade, although he might publicly threaten that the South would secede rather than allow it to be forbidden in Washington. Many non-slaveholding whites continued to dislike slavery, but they agreed with the planters that it would never do to emancipate the slave, since the South must be kept a 'white man's country.' The white South valued the slave system less for its economic returns than because continued enslavement of the Negroes was the only possible way to maintain white supremacy. 'In the very coil of Negro complications,' as Carlyle wrote, the whites knew no way out.

It was not inevitable in 1850 that Southern society would turn to secession; but the prospect of any other result was unlikely. The Southern ruling class might have been brought to face facts. They might have tried to diversify their economic life, and to have anticipated a gradual extinction of slavery. English ruling classes have done as much, again and again; but English ruling classes were never isolated or in a position to seek a way out by secession. By 1850 the Cotton Kingdom, closing in on itself, had excluded every means of saving reform, and had resolved to make Negro slavery, in an ever-increasing radius, a permanent basis of American society.

XXVI

Ferment in the North

1. REFORMERS AND REVIVALISTS

'The ancient manners were giving way. There grew a certain tenderness on the people, not before remarked,' wrote Emerson of this period. 'It seemed a war between intellect and affection; a crack in Nature, which split every church in Christendom. . . . The key to the period appeared to be that the mind had become aware of itself. . . . The young men were born with knives in their brain.'

One of these young men was Thomas H. Gallaudet, son of a Philadelphia merchant, who studied the education of deaf-mutes under Abbé Sicard in Paris and, before he was 30, established the first American school for the deaf at Hartford, Connecticut. Samuel Gridley Howe of Boston fought for Greek independence in his early twenties, and returned with Michael Anagnos, one of his comrades in arms, to found the Perkins Institute for the Blind, a searchlight for those deprived of sight. Elihu Burritt, the 'learned blacksmith' of New Britain, Conn., in his early thirties threw himself heart and soul into the peace movement, and organized a series of international peace congresses which unfortunately were ineffective; but his efforts in a less ambitious field, the exchange of what he called 'friendly addresses' between people and municipalities in the British Isles and America, helped to prevent war over boundary and other questions. Neal Dow, a prominent Maine business man with Quaker antecedents, started a brisk campaign against Demon Rum, which had tangible results in the drinking habits of the people, and by 1857 had persuaded thirteen states to pass laws prohibiting alcohol.

Young women, too, were 'born with knives in their brain.' It was the age of the Women's Rights movement which included a number of devoted and successful women reformers, such as Elizabeth C. Stanton and Lucretia Mott, who in 1848 launched at Seneca Falls, N.Y., a movement for women's suffrage. This, carried forward by the eloquence of Lucy Stone and the energy of Susan B. Anthony, finally bore fruit in Amendment XIX to the Constitution (1920). One of their converts, Amelia Bloomer the dress reformer, should not be blamed for the baggy gym pants associated with her name; her 'bloomers' were well-cut slacks, and thousands of women adopted them for housework, although only the bravest could face the jeers and insults to which they were subjected in public.

Most remarkable of these pioneer women was Dorothea Lynde Dix, a New England gentlewoman who, after teaching for several years in a fashionable girls' school, at the age of 33 began a life-long crusade in favor of the insane. These unfortunates were then largely treated as criminals, 'chained, naked, beaten with rods and lashed into obedience,' as she described their plight in her *Memorial to the Legislature of Massachusetts* (1843). She began, so far as America was concerned, the movement for intelligent and humane treatment of the mentally afflicted. This amazing woman — beautiful, naturally timid and diffident — visited all parts of the United States investigating conditions and lobbying for the insane. She persuaded Congress to establish St. Elizabeth's Hospital. She was the only New England reformer to penetrate the South, where chivalry gave her a hearing; and, at her urging, public hospitals were established for the insane in nine Southern states between 1845 and 1852. Off then she went to Europe, where the treatment of the insane was almost equally appalling. There Dorothea enlisted the support of the Duke of Argyll and Queen Victoria, and in Rome told Pope Pius IX that the local insane asylum was 'a scandal and disgrace'; and the Pope listened to her and did something about it.

The great breeding ground of mid-century 'isms' was not New England itself, but an area peopled by Yankees in the rolling hills of central New York and along the Erie Canal. These folk were so susceptible to religious revivals and Pentecostal beliefs that their region was called 'The Burned-over District.' Anti-Masonry began there, and the temperance movement was strong. Joseph Smith sojourned at Palmyra, N. Y., and there published *The Book of Mormon* in 1830 and converted Brigham Young. William Miller, a veteran of the War of 1812, worked out at Hampton, N. Y., the theory that the Second Coming of Christ would take place on 22 October 1843. He founded the Millerite or Adventist sect which persuaded thousands to sell all their goods and, clothed in suitable robes, to await the Second Coming on roofs, hilltops, and haystacks, which they felt would shorten their ascent to Heaven. Mother Ann Lee (at New Lebanon, N. Y.) and Jemima Wilkinson (at Jerusalem, N. Y.) attempted to sublimate the sexual urges of mankind by founding Shaker and 'Universal Friend' communities on the basis of celibacy. John H. Noyes, on the contrary, sought perfection and catharsis in sexual indulgence at his Oneida Community, which ended as an arts-and-crafts organization. It seemed appropriate that spirits from the other world seeking means to communicate with this, should have chosen Rochester, metropolis of the Burned-over District. There the Fox sisters' spirit-rappings and table-turnings had the whole country agog in 1848. Out of their performances issued the cult of spiritualism which within ten years had 67 newspapers and periodicals devoted to culling messages from 'angel spheres.' And it was from central New York that a vast swarm of Yankee 'isms' descended on the West like flights of sparrows.

This attitude of 'restless, prying, conscientious criticism,' as Emerson called it, led to a wide variety of reforms. Throughout the Northern states, as well as Maryland and Kentucky, imprisonment for debt was abolished and the rigors of prison life were softened. Flogging as a punishment for white people was outlawed in most of the states, and abolished in the navy in 1850, owing partly to the influence of Herman Melville's *White Jacket*. Public and private charitable institutions multiplied.

This exuberant generation believed a man could take action not only to change society but to save his soul. Charles Grandison Finney, probably the greatest American evangelist, carried out most of his work in the final decade of the Second Great Awakening that began in 1795 and ended about 1835. Finney, who had felt God come to him 'in waves of liquid love,' struck one of the last blows at orthodox Calvinism and helped substitute a liberal Calvinism which found a place for man's effort to achieve his own salvation. As William McLoughlin has observed: 'The difference between Edwards and Finney is essentially the difference between the medieval and modern temper. One saw God as the center of the universe, the other saw man.' By 1855 the evangelical Methodists and Baptists accounted for nearly 70 per cent of all Protestant communicants. Both sects rebelled against such Calvinist ideas as man's depravity, predestination, and unconditional election; Wesley's followers, especially, responded to the promise of atonement and perfectibility. Although evangelical Protestantism eventually tended to be conservative in political outlook and divided in its attitude toward slavery, in the years of the Second Great Awakening it gave powerful support to the thrust for social reform.

2. LABOR AND THE UTOPIANS

Playing in and out of the material forces of this period, like summer lightning in heavy clouds, were thunderbolts of radicalism: portents of that clear flame of emancipation that split the American firmament.

Almost every event in the early labor history of America followed similar occurrences in the British Isles, perhaps because the industrial revolution came to the Northern states a generation later than to England. But when we reflect that thousands of skilled artisans were emigrating to the United States, that religious bodies like the Friends kept up a constant intercommunication, and that reformers like Robert Owen were flitting to and fro, it is difficult to believe that there was no conscious influence. Conversely, English radicals and reformers were heartened and inspired by American example; the six points of the People's Charter of 1838 might have been selected from the established points of American democracy.

The first labor movement in America, as in England, was initiated by urban handicraftsmen rather than factory operatives; but it took a different direction. Merchant-capitalists, in order to exploit new Western markets that the canals were opening up, organized trades such as tailoring on a larger scale, with long credits, division of labor, and wholesale marketing, that drove small shops out of business. The old-time master workman, who employed a few journeymen and apprentices, was degraded to a foreman or boss under an entrepreneur. Minute specialization broke down the apprentice system. With the introduction of gas in the cities, the old working hours of sun to sun were lengthened in the winter, making a twelve-hour day the year round. The ranks of labor were so constantly diluted by immigrants and women [1] that the artisans were alarmed over their declining status. This was an old story in England; but the American workman had the vote. Manhood suffrage was established in every Northern state except Rhode Island by 1825. Three years later a group of Philadelphia artisans organized a 'Workingmen's party,' and parties with the same name sprang up in other Eastern cities. They were not proletarian, but largely middle-class mechanics and small shopkeepers who wanted local and practical reforms like free schools, freedom from imprisonment for small debts, and laws giving workers such as carpenters liens on buildings to prevent their being cheated by rascally or bankrupt contractors.

There have always been two great obstacles to political labor parties in the United States: social democracy and federal government. Abundant opportunities for social betterment prevented the worker from becoming class-conscious. And the federal form of government made it both impossible and useless for the workers to gain control of Congress, which then claimed no power to enact social legislation. The most that a labor party could do was to wage a vigorous state campaign, and acquire enough strength to give it bargaining power with the Democratic party, whose hostility to banks made a point of contact. The Workingmen's parties, with their moderate programs of social betterment, were making progress in the cities of Pennsylvania and New York, when they fell into the hands of malpractitioners.

Robert Owen, the earliest foreign radical who imagined that because America had achieved political liberty she would be receptive to every form of libertarianism, came to reform, and remained to scold. In 1825 he purchased a German Rappite settlement at New Harmony, Indiana, and experimented in a form of communism. His son Robert Dale Owen took it over, and in two years' time New Harmony had become new discord. Young Owen now joined forces with Frances Wright (Madame d'Arusmont), a vigorous Scotswoman who had founded a community in Tennessee for the purpose of emancipating slaves. When that, too, came to an untimely end, 'Fanny' Wright be-

---

1. Although women were not generally employed in shops or in offices until after the Civil War, they were to be found in over a hundred different occupations in 1835, and had even attained trades such as printing, from which the unions later excluded them.

came a lecture-platform apostle of woman's rights, free inquiry in religion, free marital union, birth control, and a system which she called 'National, Rational, Republican Education, Free for All at the Expense of All, Conducted under the Guardianship of the State,' apart from the contaminating influence of parents.

These 'Free Enquirers' had already attracted much unfavorable attention from the Northern press in 1829, when the artisans of New York City, after a hard winter of unemployment, organized a Workingmen's party. Grateful for intellectual leadership, they eagerly accepted the aid of George Henry Evans, a young editor recently arrived from England, who was also an ardent admirer of Owen and Fanny Wright, both of whom promptly joined the workingmen in the hope of capturing their support for 'National, Rational Education.' To the consternation of conservatives, the 'Workies' polled 30 per cent of the total New York City vote in the autumn election. A press campaign then began, hortatory toward the workingmen but denunciatory toward Fanny Wright, the 'bold blasphemer and voluptuous preacher of licentiousness.' The printers' union repudiated this 'band of choice spirits of foreign origin,' and led a secession from the party, which promptly broke up. Such was American labor's first and typical experience with intellectuals. Small groups of the party then joined the Democrats, who rewarded them by obtaining a mechanics' lien law and the abolition of imprisonment for debt in New York State; and these reforms led the way to similar laws in other states.

In 1833, when a period of prosperity and increasing costs began, the American labor movement abandoned politics in favor of trade organization, the closed shop, and the strike. Unionization was pursued so rapidly and widely as to include even seamstresses. Trades' unions — federations of all the organized trades in a single community — were formed in twelve Northern cities; and in 1837 delegates from these cities organized a National Trades' Union. Strikes became frequent, and on several occasions included not only the organized workers but the unskilled laborers of an entire city. Wages were generally improved, and conditions bettered. The ten-hour day was established in several cities for municipal employees, and in the navy yards in 1836 by order of President Jackson. Harriet Martineau, visiting the Northern states at that time, took note of the well-dressed, well-fed, and even well-read 'dandy mechanics.'

Then came the panic of 1837, bringing unemployment and misery to the landless artisans. Wages fell 30 to 50 per cent, union funds were depleted, federations collapsed, and the 'dandy mechanics' were glad to sell their 'gay watch guards and glossy hats' for a bit of bread. A promising labor movement collapsed; the 300,000 trade unionists of 1837 (about half the urban skilled workers in the United States) could no longer pay their dues. Hard times followed, with long hours and lean wages, of which the workers were often mulcted by payment in kind; years of sporadic, desperate strikes. The Lowell factory girls, speeded up by improved machinery, petitioned the Massachusetts legislature in vain to reduce their twelve-hour day to ten. Immigrants took their places, and by 1850 these show workers of America, with their white gowns and literary journal, were no longer found in the cotton mills.

All this convinced the American artisan, as the panic of 1825 had taught his English brother, that mere combination was futile at a moment of widespread trade depression. He also began to question the value of his vote. Jacksonian Democracy had smashed the monster Bank, but it could not supply bread and butter. As they were searching for the root of the trouble, laborers were approached by eager, earnest idealists, each with his peculiar vision of a new world in which men and women might lead free and happy lives, neither exploiting nor being exploited. So instead of trying to assimilate and humanize this new industrial order, both workers and thinkers dissipated their energy in efforts to escape it.

Almost every known panacea was applied, with meager or negative results. Robert Owen in 1845 summoned a 'World Convention to Emancipate the Human Race from Ignorance, Poverty, Division, Sin, Misery.' Josiah Warren, the first American anarchist, devised a system of 'time stores' and 'labor notes,' inspired by Owenite 'labor bazaars.' During the depression many unions went in for producers' co-operation, others began consumers' co-operation about 1840; and from the mistakes and failures of these early efforts the later co-operative movement profited. The typical experiment of this period was some sort of association, or community. Emerson wrote to Carlyle that anyone you met in the street might produce a new community project from his waistcoat pocket. Brook Farm, the transcendentalist community described in Hawthorne's *The Blithedale Romance*, became one of forty Fourierite 'phalanxes' in the Northern states. Etienne Cabet's *Voyage en Icarie* inspired several others, and there were many 'small, sour and fierce schemes,' one of which, the Mormon Church, stuck it out through countless discouragements, emigrated to Utah, and achieved astounding success. With that exception, the associations of the 1840's solved nothing; but they gave friendship and creative joy to thousands of generous and sanguine souls, before acquisitive society sucked them back into its vortex.

Horace Greeley kept the columns of the New York *Tribune* hospitable to all these movements; but his best advice to the worker was: 'Go West, young man, go West!' Here was a point of contact with national politics. Public land at $200 the quarter-section was not for those who needed it most, but for those who had the price, or for squatters who defied all comers to dislodge them. George Henry Evans and Horace Greeley insisted that every man had the same natural right to a bit of land, as to air and sunlight. 'Equality, inalienability, indivisibility' were Evans's three points: a free homestead from the public domain to every settler; limitation of individual holdings; no alienation of the homestead, voluntary or otherwise. 'Vote yourself a farm' was his slogan.

The first free homestead bill was introduced in Congress in 1846 by Andrew Johnson, the future President. Northern Whigs and Southern Democrats combined to defeat it. But many Western states passed laws exempting a man's homestead from confiscation to pay the owner's debts, a good protection in times of agricultural depression.

For all the paucity of results, the labor movement received much public sympathy and met with little violence. If American judges found criminal conspiracy in trade union activities, their sentences were in the form of fines that were easily paid by labor sympathizers. And Chief Justice Lemuel Shaw of Massachusetts, in the memorable case of Commonwealth *v.* Hunt (1842), declared that a trade union was a lawful organization, the members of which were not collectively responsible for illegal acts committed by individuals; and that a strike for the closed shop was legal.

Yet the American of 1840 did not conceive of government as an instrument for social purposes. He permitted industrialism to cut deeper even than in England. Farmers could not see why factory operatives should work shorter hours than themselves; and perhaps feared that their own 'hired men' would demand the ten-hour day. The only factory acts passed by the states before the Civil War related to the hours of child labor, and were inspired largely by a desire to give all children an opportunity for education. The first state provision for factory inspection did not come until 1867.

3. TRANSCENDENTALISM AND LITERATURE

Just as the Virginia galaxy of political theorists was flickering to a close, the same revolutionary spirit that inspired them lighted a new constellation in a higher latitude. The year 1836, when Ralph Waldo Emerson published his essay on *Nature*, may be taken as the focus of a period in American thought corresponding to 1776 in American politics.

Transcendentalism is the name generally given to this manifestation of the revolutionary spirit in the Northern states between 1820 and 1860. It embraced so wide a spectrum of ideas that the term almost defies definition; the transcendentalists themselves took pride in their eclecticism. Optimistic about human nature, these romantic 'enthusiasts' deplored religious and literary formalism and believed that by relying on intuition Man and Society could be renovated. The new spirit appeared in some men as intense individualism, in others as a passionate sympathy for the poor and oppressed. It gave to Hawthorne his deep perception of the beauty and the tragedy of life, to Walt Whitman his robust joy in living. Transcendentalism touched the labor movement on its revolutionary side, the anti-slavery movement on its positive side; it inspired the majority of American men of letters who flourished between 1820 and 1860; and almost every aspect of it may be found in Emerson, who perfectly embodied the essential spirit, a belief in the soul's inherent power to grasp the truth. Historically speaking, transcendentalism was a movement to liberate America spiritually, as independence and democracy had liberated her politically; an attempt to make Americans worthy of their independence, and elevate them to a new stature among the mortals.

It may have been a mere accident that this outburst of intellectual activity occurred largely within a 50-mile radius of Boston, during a single generation. Transcendentalism has been called the inevitable flowering of the puritan spirit; but puritanism does not necessarily bear blossoms, and the fruit thereof is often gnarled and bitter. In New England, however, the soil had been mellowed by two centuries of cultivation and prepared by Unitarianism. The puritan ministers in and about Boston had by 1800 almost converted their congregations to a more liberal faith than Calvinism, when Boston Federalism checked the flow of sap, fearful lest it feed flowers of Jacobin red. There was just time for a gorgeous show of blossom and a harvest of wine-red fruit, between this late frost and the early autumn blight of the Civil War.

Unitarianism and her sister Universalism took a great weight off the soul of New England. The Unitarians not only denied that God was a member of a trinitarian Godhead but had an optimistic faith in man's capacity for good and rejected the Calvinist view that men predestined for damnation cannot achieve salvation. Longfellow's *Psalm of Life* which seems so trite nowadays,

> Life is real! life is earnest!
> And the grave is not its goal;
> Dust thou art, to dust returnest,
> Was not spoken of the soul.

came as a message of hope to thousands of young people reared in the fear of everlasting damnation. Yet something was lacking in mere Unitarianism. A faith in the essential goodness of human nature might be a theological counterpart to democracy; but it failed to supply the note of mysticism that democrats no less than aristocrats seek in religion.

The historical function of Unitarianism in America was to liberate the minds of the well-to-do, and to provide a church for rationalists. That church has been prolific in men of letters and reformers. But its direct influence did not go wide of the New England settlements, or deep even within them. Holmes's 'One-Hoss Shay' was a symbol of the sudden crumbling of Calvinism; but Calvinism collapsed only in eastern Massachusetts. Congregationalists, Presbyterians, Methodists, and Baptists howled down the Unitarians as atheists, and maintained their hold on the masses. The immigrants, with some notable exceptions among the Germans, remained loyal to Catholicism or to other old-country faiths. Harvard fell into Unitarian hands as early as 1806; but Yale clung to the five points of Calvinism, and some of the little Western offshoots of Yale became centers of conservative theology. Most of the reform movements were inspired by the evangelical sects rather than by liberal religion. But the influence of liberalism went far beyond those who embraced it as a faith.

The Reverend Theodore Parker began as a Unitarian, but, as James

Russell Lowell aptly wrote in his *Fable for Critics*, 'from their orthodox kind of dissent he dissented.' Parker became a fiery preacher for prison reform, the rights of factory workers, and the slave; Lincoln remembered and treasured his definition of democracy as 'the government of all, by all, for all.' His scholarship in law, philosophy, and German literature was impeccable. When he died in Florence in 1860, Parker was mourned by Emerson as 'my brave brother,' whose 'place cannot be supplied.'

Emerson in 1832, at the age of 29, laid down his pastoral office in a Unitarian church because it no longer interested him. In his next four years of reading and travel, he found God again in nature; and settled down as 'lay preacher to the world' in the placid village of Concord, which harbored during one generation Emerson, Hawthorne, Thoreau, and the Alcotts.

If Jefferson was the prophet of democracy, and Jackson its hero, Emerson was its high priest. Like Jefferson, he believed ardently in the perfectability of mankind; but the philosopher Emerson knew what Jefferson never learned, that free institutions would not liberate men not themselves free. His task was to induce Americans to cleanse their minds of hatred and prejudice, to make them think out the consequences of democracy instead of merely repeating its catchwords, and to seek the same eminence in spirit that they had reached in material things. He founded no cult and gathered no disciples, because what he said did not come from any wish to bring men to himself, but to themselves.

Henry Thoreau, whose *A Week on the Concord and Merrimac Rivers* came out in 1849, was the best classical scholar of the Concord group and the most independent of classic modes of thought. Concord for him was a microcosm of the world. His genius was little appreciated in his own country until the twentieth century. Thoreau's *Walden* (1854) has had a world-wide influence on English writers, such as W. H. Hudson, who called it 'the one golden book in any century of best books.' In the twentieth century, translations began to appear in South America and in France (where the sensitive Marcel Proust hailed Thoreau as a precursor) and in Germany, Holland, Scandinavia, and Russia. Tolstoy in 1901 sent a 'Message to the American People,' inquiring why they paid so little attention to the voices of Garrison, Emerson, Thoreau, and Theodore Parker. Thoreau has had an even greater impact on the Orient. The Chinese sage Lin Yutang called him 'the most Chinese of all American authors in his entire view of life,' and Pandit Nehru has sponsored translations of *Walden* into all the principal languages of India. When bumbling county commissioners in 1959 tried to turn the shores of Walden Pond into a beach resort, a blast of protests from all over the world halted the desecration.

At the same time, Hawthorne of Salem, later a sojourner in Concord, wrote tragedies of New England that penetrate to the core of all human life.

In these three men, Emerson, Thoreau, and Hawthorne, in Herman Melville, who was half Yankee, and in the timeless Emily Dickinson of the next generation, the New England that had slowly matured since the seventeenth century justified herself.

In the meantime, the Dennie and Brockden Brown literary group at Philadelphia had died, and the 'Knickerbocker School' was declining in New York. Bryant's collected poems, mostly written more than a decade earlier, appeared in 1832, and his last spurt of poetical activity ended in 1844; during the rest of his long life Bryant became a leading figure in American journalism. Washington Irving's *Sketch Book* appeared as early as 1818; seven years later he turned to Spain for inspiration and to history for expression; returning to New York a literary hero, he visited the West for material; but his *Astoria* and *Adventures of Captain Bonneville* lack the fresh, authentic flavor of Francis Parkman's *Oregon Trail* (1849). For the rest of his life, Irving at "Sunnyside" on the Hudson and at Madrid, well played the roles of diplomat, host, and sage. James Fenimore Cooper's 'Leather-Stocking' and 'Sea Tales' started in the 1820's, after which he embarked on a crusade to put everybody right both in England and America, and succeeded in making himself the most unpopular person in the English-speaking world.

The Knickerbocker Magazine, founded at New York in 1833, remained the leading literary periodical in America until *The Atlantic Monthly* appeared in 1857. The former published the poetry and prose of budding and established writers belonging to all parts of the country; and, more than any other magazine of the age, acquainted the American people with the wealth and variety of their own literature. 'Old Knick,' as devoted readers called the magazine, did not take himself solemnly as did the *North American Review*, and the reformers thought him regrettably frivolous; he went in for a little of everything except politics — poetry, science, short stories, humor, musical and dramatic criticism, Western travel — so long as it was American; and in a single number could boast contributions from Irving, Cooper, Bryant, Fitz-Green Halleck, Longfellow, John Greenleaf Whittier, and Lewis Cass.

The New England intellectuals had more to say than their New York contemporaries, but they too conveyed it in traditional forms. 'We all lean on England,' wrote Emerson. Not until 1851 did a distinctive American literature, original both in form and content, emerge with *Moby-Dick.* Four years later, with Emerson's blessing, *Leaves of Grass* began to sprout. Walt Whitman, half Yankee, half New York Dutch, had grown up outside the ambit of New England respectability, in direct and intimate contact with the crude realities of American life. In the 'barbaric yawp' that so deeply influenced twentieth-century poetry, Walt Whitman sang of the common American and his life in seaport, farm, and frontier.

Walt Whitman was the poet of democracy, but Henry Wadsworth Longfellow was democracy's favorite poet. The American people, when they read poetry, wished to be lifted out of themselves by verses that rhymed or at least scanned, into a world of romance and beauty. Hawthorne and Whittier and Longfellow craved beauty themselves, and found it for others: Hawthorne by his *Marble Faun* and *Wonder Book* of classical myths, Whittier and Longfellow by poetic legends from early American history, Longfellow especially by popularizing Old World stories, and translating Dante. The music of his verse was tuned to catch the ear of a busy and unlearned people. Longfellow, 'poet of the mellow twilight of the past,' as Whitman called him, 'poet of all sympathetic gentleness — and universal poet of women and young people,' had more influence on his generation than any American man of letters save Emerson. And, until Lincoln's prose poem, 'The Gettysburg Address,' was delivered, no poem had a greater effect in creating that love of the Union which made young men fight to preserve it than the peroration to Longfellow's 'Building of the Ship' (1849):

> Thou, too, sail on, O Ship of State!
> Sail on, O Union, strong and great!
> Humanity with all its fears,
> With all the hopes of future years,
> Is hanging breathless on thy fate!

4. ANTI-SLAVERY AND ABOLITION

Of all humanitarian and reform movements, the one that shook the Union to its foundation sought the abolition of slavery. An earlier anti-slavery movement, offshoot of the American Revolution, won its last victory in 1807 when Congress passed an act against the slave trade. The Quakers kept up a mild and ineffectual protest, while the cotton gin was creating a new vested interest in slavery; and in 1820, as we have seen, an effort to stay the westward advance of slavery was defeated by the admission of Missouri.

The older generation of Virginia statesmen, foreseeing the tragedy of 1861, endeavored in vain to arouse their people. Few Virginians or indeed Americans would contemplate emancipation, unless at the same time they could get rid of the colored population. Free Negroes were felt to be a menace throughout the United States. Most of the Northern states had severe laws against their immigration; most of the Southern states allowed benevolent masters to free their slaves only on condition of removing them. Yet the cotton states gagged at emancipation, even when sweetened by compensation and deportation.

The American Colonization Society proved that this last method was practical, at least on a small scale. Founded in 1817, supported by men such as President Monroe, Henry Clay, and Chief Justice Marshall, and financed by voluntary contributions, this society aimed to do for the American Negro what the Republic of Israel did for the Jews — to give him back a part of his homeland. For they observed that the greatest obstacle to Negro emancipation was not the owners, but the problem of the free Negro, who encountered bitter antagonism from the meaner sort of whites in his efforts to adapt himself to American society. They believed in the Negro's potentialities, but felt that he could only realize them through a government of his own in his ancestral continent.

Obviously the A.C.S. could not hope to repatriate all slaves in the United States, who numbered about a million and a half in 1820, nor even all the 230,000 free Negroes. But many planters were eager to emancipate their slaves, provided they could be removed to Africa instead of becoming victims of improvidence and persecution in America. The A.C.S. helped them to do so by chartering ships for the transatlantic passage, and assisting the colonists to get started in Africa. It was no hare-brained scheme. England's free Negro colony in Sierra Leone had taken care of two or three thousand former slaves, at least half from America. A free Negro of Massachusetts, Paul Cuffee, who commanded his own trading schooner, brought to Sierra Leone at his own expense a trial shipload of thirty-eight American freedmen in 1815. To further this enterprise, the A.C.S. purchased from native tribes several tracts along the Grain Coast of West Africa; and several thousand had been settled by 1847, when they organized the Republic of Liberia, with a capital named Monrovia after President Monroe, and a constitution modeled on that of the United States. The first president of Liberia was Joseph J. Roberts, son of Virginia free Negroes and a statesman in his own right. He defended his little nation against encroachment and obtained recognition of Liberian sovereignty by the principal powers of Europe.

The only obstacle to making Liberia and the adjacent Ivory Coast a Negro Israel was lack of funds. The A.C.S., having scraped the barrel of private benevolence, appealed to Congress for federal aid in 1827. Its plea was endorsed by the legislatures of at least ten states, including Kentucky, Tennessee, Delaware, and Maryland, border slave states where the colonization scheme was most popular. But South Carolina, Georgia, and Missouri passed strong resolutions against the movement, Georgia calling it 'wild, fanatical and destructive and ruinous to the prosperity, importance, and political strength, of the southern States.' They considered 'not only the retention, but the increase of the slave population to be all-important' for their welfare. And at the same time the abolitionists denounced colonization as a subtle attempt to increase the value of the remaining slaves in America. The A.C.S., though discouraged, continued its work to the Civil War and was rewarded by Liberia's successfully maintaining her independence. She is now the oldest and best governed of the African republics.

When Jackson became President in 1829, moral suasion against slavery appeared to have spent its force. Apathy could hardly have been more complete, when on 1 January 1831, the first number of *The Liberator* appeared in Boston, printed on borrowed paper with borrowed type, published by William Lloyd Garrison. On the first page he announced:

> I shall strenuously contend for the immediate enfranchisement of
> our slave population. . . . On this subject I do not wish to think,

or speak, or write, with moderation. . . . I am in earnest — I will
not equivocate — I will not excuse — I will not retreat a single
inch — AND I WILL BE HEARD.

Therein spoke the Old Testament, not the New. Garrison had less in
common with Emerson than with Stonewall Jackson. He was all contra-
diction: a fighting pacifist, an aggressive non-resistant who spurned politics as a means but employed language that made impossible the peaceful attainment of his ends. Garrison's policy was to hold up the most
repulsive aspects and exceptional incidents of Negro slavery to the
public gaze; to castigate the slaveholders and all who defended them as
man-stealers, torturers, traffickers in human flesh. He recognized no
rights of the masters, acknowledged no racial animosities, tolerated no
delay.

Blackguarding the slaveholders would have made few converts in the
South at any time, but least of all at that time. The Nat Turner slave
insurrection occurred in August 1831. Prominent Southerners at once
asserted that Garrison was responsible (although only four copies of
The Liberator had reached the South), and demanded that the Northern
states, if they valued the Union, should suppress this incendiary agitation.

Many efforts short of press censorship were made in the North to satisfy the South on this point. Garrison wrote that he 'found contempt
more bitter, opposition more stubborn, and apathy more frozen' in New
England than among slave-owners themselves. Advocates of Negro
emancipation were attacked everywhere in the free states. Whether in
city or country, in New England, New York, or the Middle West, devoted men and women addressing an abolition meeting were assailed
by barrages of rotten eggs and their voices drowned by tin horns,
drums, and sleigh bells. A philanthropist who built a school for Negro
children in a Maine village found it one day in the middle of a swamp,
hauled there by the ox-teams of indignant farmers. Elijah Lovejoy, who
persisted in printing an abolitionist paper, had his press twice thrown
into the river, and in 1837 was murdered by a mob at Alton, Ill. When
Philadelphia abolitionists held a protest meeting in Pennsylvania Hall,
which they and their reformer friends had just built, a mob burned
it down. All that summer there were outbursts of mob violence against
Negroes in the City of Brotherly Love; in 1842 a particularly bad one,
when houses of colored residents were burned.

Philadelphia was far from unique in this respect. On 21 October 1835

William Lloyd Garrison was paraded around Boston with a rope around his neck, by what was called a 'broadcloth mob'; and on the same day delegates who met at Utica to organize an anti-slavery society were dispersed by a mob of 'very respectable gentlemen' led by a congressman and a judge. Yet the abolition movement grew, and made converts at every mobbing: of Gerrit Smith, for instance, at the Utica affair; of Wendell Phillips in Boston; of Cassius M. Clay, a cousin of Henry Clay, in Kentucky. In 1836 there were more than 500 anti-slavery societies in the Northern states, and by 1840 their membership was over 150,000. Whittier's pen was already consecrated to the movement; presently James Russell Lowell would lend his gift of satire.

Garrison, mild in manner and soft of voice, yet driven by a fierce passion for righteousness to write words that cut and burned, personified this new and dreadful force to the entire South, but Theodore D. Weld of New York was the most effective abolition leader. Himself a great bear of a man, Weld could subdue a mob or whip an assailant, and often had to. He took up with another Yankee reformer, the Reverend Sylvester Graham, who was waging a one-man war against white bread (hence the name graham bread) for which he was mobbed by the bakers of Boston. Abolitionists were charged with knowing nothing of slavery firsthand; but Weld really studied it, traveling to the Gulf of Mexico in 1831–32 and observing social conditions very closely. On that trip he recruited James G. Birney, an upstanding young blood of Kentucky who owned a big plantation in Alabama; and Birney became the first anti-slavery candidate for President of the United States, polling little more than 2 per cent in 1840.

Weld and two wealthy merchants of New York City, Arthur and Lewis Tappan, organized the American Anti-Slavery Society in 1833. Weld then tried teaching at Lane Seminary, Cincinnati, so close to the slave area and so dependent on Southern trade that the trustees ordered discussion of slavery by the students to cease. He and his student converts — many of them Southerners — then seceded to Oberlin, which became the first college in the United States to admit both Negroes and women.

Owing perhaps to their Quaker connection, the abolitionists preceded other reformers in permitting women to address their meetings and serve on committees. Lucretia Mott of Philadelphia, and the Grimké sisters, gentlewomen of South Carolina who freed their slaves and came north to obtain freedom of speech, were counted among the leaders; Angelina Grimké married Theodore Weld, and it was perhaps her influence which kept hatred of the slaveholder out of Weld's agitation for freedom and which made him favor a gradual, compensated emancipation. Frederick Douglass, an escaped slave of remarkable intellect, was the first of several fugitives who wrote or dictated their memoirs. There was a close connection also with British abolitionists like Wilberforce and Daniel O'Connell. This constant intercourse and mutual aid led to a sort of English-speaking union between humane and liberty-loving persons in both countries.

The abolitionists took special pride in the 'Under Ground Railroad' which carried Negroes to liberty. Slaves who had the courage to strike out for freedom would take cover in the woods or swamps near their master's plantation until the hue and cry died down, then follow the North Star to Mason and Dixon's line, or the Ohio river. Once across, the 'U.G.' took them in charge. They were transferred from one abolitionist household to another, hidden by day in attics, haystacks, or corn shocks; piloted by night through the woods, or concealed in farm wagons; sometimes driven in a Friend's carriage, disguised in women's clothes and a deep Quaker bonnet. Others were smuggled north by sea, and made their way into Canada through the New England states. The total number of people thus rescued from slavery was not large, and their proportion to the total slave population was infinitesimal: about .03 per cent in 1850. Moreover, many of the slaves who did escape did so largely through their own devices; the runaways often fled to other parts of the South where they found refuge in swamps or in cities, among Indians, or as deckhands on ships. Yet if measured by the stimulus it gave the abolitionist cause and the rage it aroused in the breasts of Southern slaveholders, the 'Under Ground' was a brilliant success.

Conducting the 'U.G.' was dangerous business. Pursuit was often hot and ruthless, and the pursuers had the law on their side even where opinion was against them. It afforded the young men in the movement something positive to do for the slave; they became the commandos of this cold war. And it gave the Negroes a chance to show their mettle. Most famous of all 'conductors' on the 'U.G.' was Harriet Tubman, an illiterate field hand from the Eastern Shore of Maryland, who not only escaped herself but repeatedly returned southward and guided more than 300 slaves from bondage to freedom, taking some as far as Canada.

Fugitive slaves, moreover, gave the abolitionists a handle to work both on public opinion and on the Federal Government. One fugitive, telling his own story at a public meeting, made more converts than bushels of tracts.

By a federal statute of 1793, a master, or his agent, who caught a runaway in a free state could repatriate him forcibly after swearing to his identity before a magistrate. A professional slave-catcher whom the right Negro eluded was apt to conclude that 'any nigger' would answer. Kidnapping became so frequent that Pennsylvania (1826) and other Northern states passed 'personal liberty laws' to protect their free colored citizens. The abolitionists cleverly turned the local resentment against kidnapping, and the Northern dislike of domineering Southerners, into opposition to the return of genuine fugitives. Gradually the personal liberty acts were strengthened to a degree that made a runaway's identity almost impossible to establish. The Supreme Court invalidated a Pennsylavania law of that description in Prigg v. Pennsylvania (1842). But if the states had no right to obstruct, by the same token they had no obligation to assist the federal authorities; and without such assistance the slave-catchers began to receive the attention of mobs more often than abolitionists. A runaway from Virginia was forcibly rescued from his captors in Boston in 1843, and his freedom purchased by a popular collection. The abolitionists for the first time voiced a popular sentiment, when Whittier declared:

> No slave-hunt in our borders — no pirate on our strand!
> No fetters in the Bay State — no slave upon our land!

The most famous case involving slavery, until eclipsed by Dred Scott's, was that of the *Amistad,* in 1839. She was a Spanish slaver carrying 53 newly imported slaves who were being sailed from Havana to another Cuban port. Under the leadership of an upstanding young Negro named Cinqué, the 'cargo' mutinied and killed captain and crew; but, ignorant of navigation, the mutineers had to rely on the white owners who were on board to sail the ship. The owners stealthily steered north until the *Amistad* was picked up off Long Island by U.S.S. *Washington* and taken into New Haven; the Negroes were placed in charge of the federal marshal, and housed in the local jail. Then, what a legal hassle! Spain demanded that they be given up to be tried for piracy, and President Van Buren tried to do so. Southern senators insisted that, if not surrendered to Spain, the Negroes be tried for murder and piracy by a federal court. Lewis Tappan and Roger Sherman Baldwin, a Connecticut abolitionist, undertook to free them by legal process. A decision of the lower federal court that the Negroes be surrended was appealed to the Supreme Court. John Quincy Adams, persuaded to act as their attorney, argued for their liberty on the ground that the African slave trade was illegal by Spanish law and by the natural right of mankind to freedom. The Court, with a majority of Southerners, was so impressed by the old man's eloquence that it ordered Cinqué and the other Negroes set free, and they were returned to their native Africa.

The ironic epilogue is that Cinqué, once back home, set himself up as a slave trader.

At the right wing of the abolitionists were those who spurned the name and called themselves anti-slavery men. They opposed the extension of slavery into more territories of the United States, and favored severe laws against the African slave trade, but did not propose to interfere with slavery in the slave states. The anti-slavery wing included many evangelists such as Charles G. Finney, who warned 'Brother Weld,' his proselyte, in 1836, that extremist sentiment would 'roll a wave of blood over the land'; and Francis Wayland, president of Brown University, who told the militant abolitionists that their agitation had 'rendered any open and calm discussion of this subject in the slaveholding states utterly impossible.' Wayland also asserted that abolition 'would be a great calamity were it to terminate by violence, or without previous moral and social preparation.' Emerson took a similar position. But almost all these moderate anti-slavery men were eventually forced by Southern intransigence into more radical views.

The South, in general, made three tactical errors in combating abolition. It assumed that every anti-slavery person was a firebrand, an inciter of Negro insurrection. Southern legislatures passed laws making it increasingly difficult for masters to liberate slaves, and for free Negroes to make a living. And by frantic attempts to suppress all discussion of the subject, and to buttress, protect, and expand slavery, the spokesmen of the South ended in persuading the North that every man's liberty was at stake. Birney, one of the first to see this aspect of the problem, wrote from Kentucky to Gerrit Smith in 1835, 'It has now become absolutely necessary that slavery should cease in order that freedom may be preserved in any portion of the land.' William Jay, son of the Chief Justice, pointed out the next year, 'we commenced the present struggle to obtain the freedom of the slave; we are compelled to continue it to preserve our own.'

The most notorious, and least successful, attempt to suppress discussion of slavery was the 'gag resolution' passed by Congress in 1836 to prevent debate on petitions to prohibit the domestic slave trade in the District of Columbia. Washington was then a shipping point for slaves from Virginia and Maryland to the cotton states. Even from the windows of the Capitol one could watch coffles of Negroes marching by to the music of clanking chains. Why, inquired Henry Clay, should Northern members 'be outraged by a scene so inexcusable and detestable'? The slave states felt that Washington was a strategic outpost, a prestige point, to be held at all costs. Calhoun, now senator from South Carolina, declared that any intermeddling with slavery in the federal district would be 'a foul slander on nearly one-half the states of the Union'; and all such petitions were rejected. Other abolitionist petitions, not always so limited in their scope, came pouring in on the House, which at the insistence of the Southern members passed the 'gag resolution,' a rule to the effect that all petitions relating 'in any way' to slavery, 'whether within or without the legislative competence of Congress,' be laid on the table.

John Quincy Adams, now a member of the House, was not an abolitionist; but the gag rule awakened in him ancestral memories of royal tyranny. It was a thing to be resisted in its prime, like taxation without representation. Session after session he fought for the right of petition, using his deep knowledge of parliamentary practice and rich resource in harsh and bitter eloquence. Every attempt short of personal violence was made to silence, to censure, or to expel Adams; but the tough old puritan persisted. The Northern states finally forced their representatives to support him, and in 1844 the gag rule was repealed. It made no difference to the slaves. But on the day when the news reached South Carolina, the leading Whig newspaper of Columbia discontinued printing installments from Washington's Farewell Address, and substituted an appeal for secession.

How then, shall we estimate the abolitionists? Their sincerity and courage are no longer denied by friend or enemy; of their wisdom no enemy was ever convinced, and many friends are now doubtful. It must be admitted that they fanned the passions which led to civil war; but it is fatuous to argue, as Southern apologists have done, that if they had kept silent, emancipation would have come peaceably. Abolition was an irresistible power in a world then awakening to new concepts of humanity. It could no more be kept down in Boston and Indianapolis than in London and Paris. People such as Weld, Garrison, and the Grimkés, Charles Sumner and Wendell Phillips, were 'members of a family of minds that had appeared in all the Western countries, in Italy, in Germany, in France, to defend the religion of liberty, poets militant, intellectual men who were glad to fight and die for their beliefs, figures that were appearing in flesh and blood on battlefields and barricades in Europe. Brothers of Mazzini, heirs of William Tell, men of the world themselves and men of culture, they roused the indifferent minds of the thinking masses and made the American anti-slavery movement a part of the great world-struggle of darkness and light.' [2]

The trouble with the abolitionists, as we can see now, was this — they spent all their compassion on the slave and left none for the Southern white man who was equally involved in the system and could see no way to get rid of it. The cost of their agitation in hatred and bloodshed was immense; but in view of the Southern resistance to any amelioration of slavery, and Southern insistence on acquiring more slave territory and more buttresses to the system, it is doubtful whether emancipation could have come about in any other way than the worst way, civil war.

More than a century has elapsed since Lincoln's Emancipation Proclamation and Amendment XIII to the Constitution destroyed chattel slavery on United States soil. We now know that the slavery question was but one aspect of a race and class problem that is still far from solution. The grapes of wrath have not yet yielded all their bitter vintage.

2. Van Wyck Brooks, The Flowering of New England, pp. 393-4.

XXVII

Democrats and Whigs

1. THE EXPANSION OF THE SECOND PARTY SYSTEM

The controversies that revolved around Andrew Jackson stimulated the formation of a new American party system. In the second year of Jackson's presidency the National Republicans joined with dissenting Democrats to create the new Whig party. The name was chosen because it suggested that, as the Whigs of the 1770's had stood up against King George, so the Whigs of the 1830's were fighting for liberty against 'King Andrew I.' The new party appealed to a disparate set of elements united only by their opposition to Jackson: Bank Democrats and others hurt by the war with B.U.S.; old-fashioned state-righters offended by Jackson's stand on nullification; New England and Middle State Yankees who thought that all Democrats smelled bad; owners of factory stock who wanted more protection; and Westerners attracted by Henry Clay's economic policies.

The Whigs wished to use the national government in order to further capitalistic enterprise. They favored internal improvements, rechartering the Bank, and a protective tariff. Somewhat paradoxically, although partisans of strong national government, they believed in weak Presidents, in part as a consequence of their struggle with 'King Andrew.' Yet many who gravitated to the Whigs did so for non-ideological reasons. As the Democrats attracted Catholic immigrants, especially from Ireland, the Whigs drew British Protestant immigrants. While freethinkers flocked to the Democrats, the Whigs made a home for those

Protestant clerics who wished to use the State to wipe out 'moral' blemishes like the liquor traffic.

If the Democrats had the 'best principles,' wrote Emerson, the Whigs had the 'best men,' with Clay of Kentucky, Webster and Everett of Massachusetts, John Bell and Hugh L. White of Tennessee, Reverdy Johnson of Maryland, Hugh S. Legaré and James L. Petigru of South Carolina, and a dozen other statesmen of intelligence and integrity. Indeed, the Whigs suffered from a plethora of prima donnas always jostling one another for the big spot. Henry Clay, intelligent, upright, magnetic, and with a quarter-century's experience of Congress, ran for the White House more often than any major party candidate in history, but never successfully. Lincoln called Clay 'my beau ideal of a statesman, the man for whom I fought all my humble life.' Dennis Hanks, Lincoln's illiterate cousin, explained that Lincoln became a Whig because he 'always Loved Hen Clays Speaches I think was the Cause Mostly.' The insouciant 'Prince Hal' gambled for high stakes, fought a duel, enjoyed good whiskey, and attracted women. Presented by Whig orators as 'the mill-boy of the Slashes,' Clay was in fact a prosperous Kentucky planter, identified with conservative interests. 'I would rather be right than President,' he said in a speech in 1850, and he had to be content with being right.

In 1836 the Whigs by-passed Clay in favor of the strategy of running three candidates, each strong in his own section: Webster in New England, General William Henry Harrison in the West, and Hugh White in the South. They expected that these three 'favorite sons' would carry enough states to deny any one candidate a majority in the electoral college and thus throw the election into the House, where the Whigs might prevail.

To counter the Whig strategy Jackson placed Democratic party fortunes in the hands of his personal choice, the affable Martin Van Buren. Never before had a professional politician reached so high. He did have a law practice, but from the age of 25 he had lived largely by politics, and he was now 55. His home, at Old Kinderhook near Albany, in its abbreviated form 'O.K.' gave a new word to the language.[1] 'Little

1. O.K., meaning Old Kinderhook (the home of Van Buren), was the secret name for Democratic clubs in New York in the campaign of 1840. The Whigs, unable to penetrate the meaning, invented this conversation between Amos Kendall and Jackson. ' "Those papers, Amos, are all correct. I have marked them O.K. (oll korrect)." ' The Gen. never was good at spelling.'

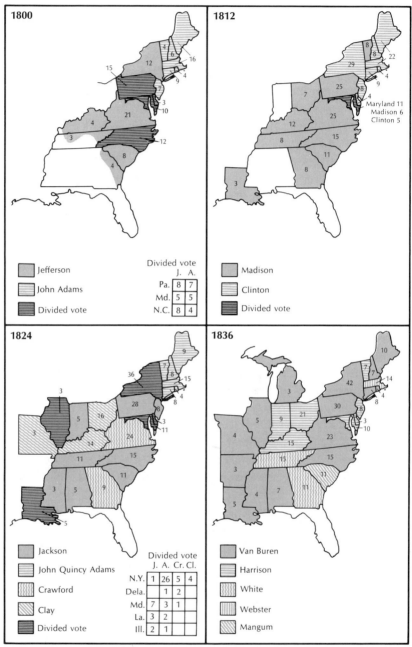

1800

Jefferson
John Adams
Divided vote

Divided vote
J. A.
Pa. | 8 | 7
Md. | 5 | 5
N.C. | 8 | 4

1812

Madison
Clinton
Divided vote

Maryland 11
Madison 6
Clinton 5

1824

Jackson
John Quincy Adams
Crawford
Clay
Divided vote

Divided vote
J. A. Cr. Cl.
N.Y. | 1 | 26 | 5 | 4
Dela. | | 1 | 2
Md. | 7 | 3 | 1
La. | 3 | 2
Ill. | 2 | 1

1836

Van Buren
Harrison
White
Webster
Mangum

PRESIDENTIAL ELECTIONS, 1800, 1812, 1824, 1836

Van' earned the nickname 'The Red Fox' from his slyness, and 'The Little Magician' from his ability to turn everything into gold. He profited by the death of De Witt Clinton to be elected governor of New York in 1828, just in time to sew up the state patronage before Jackson made him Secretary of State. He benefited from the 'Eaton malaria' to supplant Calhoun as Democratic heir apparent. Calhoun joined forces with Clay in the Senate to defeat Van Buren's nomination as minister to Great Britain; but he enjoyed several months' experience in that important post before the news reached London, and returned in time to be nominated and elected Vice-President for Jackson's second term. His perfect 'bedside manner' had already won him the complete confidence of the President, who described him as 'a true man with no guile'; and his ready wit, pleasant smile, and glad hand made him so popular that there was no opposition to his nomination in 1836.

The two-party system now took hold in areas of the South, which in recent years had been a one-party (Democratic) reserve, and in the New West, which had been conducting politics on a 'no party' basis. Since Van Buren lacked Jackson's regional appeal to the South, that section split. Yet Van Buren did well enough. With less than 51 per cent of the popular vote, he captured 170 electoral votes to 124 for his three rivals. Harrison polled 73 electoral votes, but the regional strategy broke down, for White carried only Tennessee and Georgia and Webster won only the Bay State. Van Buren thereby became the first President born under the Stars and Stripes, the first of Dutch stock, the first from New York, and the first to step from the governor's mansion at Albany into the White House at Washington. For Democratic vice-presidential candidate, Jackson dictated the nomination of Richard M. Johnson, congressman from Kentucky, who had acted as errand boy for him during the Peggy Eaton affair. Johnson was one of the original war hawks of 1812, and unlike most politicians of that kidney, had actually fought in the war; in the Battle of the Thames he claimed to have killed Tecumseh. Accordingly, as the principal Whig candidate of 1836 was campaigning on having won the Battle of Tippecanoe, Johnson's friends countered with a slogan which touched an all-time low for electioneering imbecility:

> Rumpsey dumpsey, rumpsey dumpsey
> Colonel Johnson killed Tecumseh!

Since this hero failed to obtain a majority in the electoral college, he was chosen Vice-President by the Senate, according to Amendment XII of the Constitution — the only time that has been done.

National politics long muffled the growing divergence between North and South. Churches might split, social differences might deepen, and extremists revile one another; but, so long as the Whig and Democratic parties remained national in scope, the Union was safe. The political system not only postponed disunion but survived it.

Constitutional developments in the states were quickly reflected in the national party organization. State constitutional changes between 1830 and 1850 tended toward government of, for, and by the people. Religious tests and property qualifications for office were generally swept away, and manhood suffrage adopted. The newer state constitutions, beginning with that of Mississippi in 1832, transferred many offices from the appointive to the elective class. These constitutional changes were effected by the democratic method initiated by Massachusetts in 1780: a popularly elected constitutional convention, with a popular referendum on the result.

Political partisanship began at the municipal level; a good Democrat would no more think of voting for a Whig governor or a Whig mayor than for a Whig congressman or President. Federal, state, and local politics were so closely articulated that the misconduct of a state treasurer might turn a presidential election; and the attitude of a President on the tariff or the public lands might embarrass his party's candidate for a municipal office. Every state had its captains of hundreds and captains of thousands, working for the party every day in the year and looking for reward to the spoils of victory. Both parties used the device of the nominating convention, which may have increased popular control, but also made possible greater party discipline.

In 1835 Tocqueville wrote that 'the political activity which pervades the United States must be seen in order to be understood. No sooner do you set foot upon American ground, than you are stunned by a kind of tumult . . . almost the only pleasure which an American knows is to take a part in the government, and to discuss its measures.' Annual or biennial state and local elections kept interest from flagging in the course of a presidential term and were regarded as portents of the next general election. Innumerable local rallies, often held on the same day with a county fair, barbecue, or anniversary, gave the leaders an occasion for inspiring the faithful, 'spellbinding' the doubtful, and confounding the enemy. Steamboats and railroads carried political orators long distances and enabled them to speak in other parts of the country than their own. In 1840, for instance, Senator Rives of Virginia addressed a great outdoor gathering at Auburn in New York for three hours and a half, after which Mr. Legaré of South Carolina carried on for two hours and a half more. The endurance of mid-century audiences was amazing.

2. THE PANIC OF 1837

The 'Little Magician' in the White House might turn dross into precious metal, but he reaped the whirlwind that Jackson's blasts had helped to sow. The panic of 1837 was blamed on the Democrats, as panics always are on the party in power. Speculation was the basic cause: but it was the failure of three English banking houses in 1837 that brought on the crisis, much as the Austrian Credit Anstalt failure worsened the financial crisis of 1931. The twelve-year boom in Western land, manufacturing, transportation, banking and all other business enterprises resulted in over-extension of credit, to which Jackson unwittingly contributed by withdrawing government deposits from the conservative B.U.S. in favor of 'pet banks' which used them as a base for further speculation. The same thing, in a smaller way, was happening in Europe; and American enterprises were then largely dependent on European capital. Thus, when continental Europe put pressure on English banks, they in turn demanded the payment of short-term loans to American enterprises. In pursuance of Jackson's specie circular, millions in hard money were withdrawn from deposit banks to pay for purchases of government land in the West; at the same time, the price of cotton fell from 20 to 10 cents and the wheat crop of 1836 failed, so that wheat had to be imported from Canada and even England. Demands for gold from English creditors reached the banks at the very time they were depleted to pay for Western lands.

Van Buren was no sooner in the White House than mercantile houses and banks began to fail, and there were riots in New York over the high cost of flour. In May 1837, after almost every bank in the country had suspended specie payments, the President, who so far had adopted the attitude that there was nothing really wrong, summoned Congress to an extra session. The government alone lost $9 million through the collapse of 'pet banks' in which its funds had been deposited. In the meantime, there was widespread suffering; less undoubtedly than in Herbert Hoover's administration, because the great majority of Americans were then farmers, and many industrial workers could return to parental farms. On the other hand, there was no government assistance of any kind, other than the town or county poorhouse for the desperate; cold and hungry people in the cities had to depend on private charity for fuel and food.

The special session of Congress which met in September accomplished nothing except to authorize a large issue of temporary treasury notes, which started the national debt once more. It has kept on growing, with fluctuations, ever since. As a permanent fiscal measure Van Buren proposed an 'independent treasury,' a depository for government funds located in several cities. It was devised in order to divorce government from private banking interests so that no one group or class would enjoy an advantage over another. But that was too much for state banking interests to swallow, and an alliance of conservative Democrats with the Whigs prevented it from becoming law until 1840. The Independent Treasury Act was repealed by the Whigs next year, re-enacted under President Polk, and remained the basis of the federal fiscal system until the Civil War.

In August 1839 most of the state banks that had not failed resumed specie payments, but a severe depression set in which lasted about four years. At that time about $200 million in American securities were owned in England. So much of this was lost, including $35 million worth of repudiated Pennsylvania state bonds, that when President Tyler tried to float a loan in 1842 to replenish the treasury, the English financiers turned him down flat. 'Not a dollar!' said Baron Rothschild to the President's agent. Thus, the presidential election of 1840 was held in the midst of a depression, which has always meant woe for the party in power.

3. THE NEW SUPREME COURT

Van Buren's administration inherited a virtually new Supreme Court. A number of deaths, including that of Chief Justice Marshall, disposed of all but two of the judges appointed by John Adams and the Virginia dynasty. Jackson was able to designate a new Chief Justice and four associate justices. Van Buren named three more in 1837, and this new blood dominated the Court until the Civil War.

No appointment to the supreme bench in a hundred years occasioned so much anger, disgust, and apprehension as Jackson's choice of Roger B. Taney to succeed the sainted Marshall. Taney was a gentleman (even that was denied) of an old Maryland Catholic and Federalist family, a lawyer and politician without judicial training, a Jackson partisan who had defended the right of his chief to hold views on the Constitution different from those of Marshall. His name had twice been rejected by the Senate: once as Secretary of the Treasury and once as associate justice of the court over which he was destined to preside brilliantly for 28 years. It was only the election of new Democratic senators in 1836 that made possible Taney's confirmation as Chief Justice. By that time Taney had broken completely with his Federalist background; Jackson's war with the B.U.S. taught him the arrogance and potential danger of organized finance, and his first service to the country was to provide an important limitation on Chief Justice Marshall's definition of the contract clause in the Dartmouth College case.

An old corporation which operated a toll bridge leading out of Boston sought to invalidate a recent state law which had provided a rival and parallel free bridge. Justice Story, following what would probably have been the opinion of his former chief, believed the state's action to be confiscatory and a breach of contract; the new Chief Justice, speaking for the majority, upheld Massachusetts, on the ground that no corporate charter could confer implied powers against the public. 'While the rights of private property are sacredly guarded,' he declared, 'we must not forget that the community also have rights, and that the happiness and well-being of every citizen depend on their faithful preservation' (Charles River Bridge v. Warren Bridge, 1837). Herein appears, perhaps for the first time, the modern doctrine of the social responsibilities of private property. Although denounced by conservatives as opening the floodgates to confiscation and destruction, the Charles River Bridge decision helped capital to find profitable investment by financing improved transportation, and made railroads possible without the necessity of buying up every competing stagecoach, canal, or turnpike company.

A second field in which Taney limited the consequences of earlier decisions related to interstate commerce. Marshall, in Gibbons *v.* Ogden and Brown *v.* Maryland, implied that federal power to regulate commerce was not only full but exclusive, even when not exercised by Congress, voiding state regulations even if they filled a need that the Federal Government had not yet recognized. Taney posted a different thesis in the license cases (1847):

> The controlling and supreme power over commerce with foreign nations and the several states is undoubtedly conferred upon Congress. Yet, in my judgment, the state may nevertheless, for the safety or convenience of trade, or for the protection of the health of its citizens, make regulations of commerce for its own ports and harbors, and for its own territory; and such regulations are valid unless they come in conflict with a law of Congress.

In many other respects, the Court under Taney reflected the reaction in favor of state rights. In the Passaic Bridge case (1857), for instance, the Supreme Court declined to rule as to whether a railroad bridge erected under the authority of New Jersey was or was not a nuisance and a hindrance to interstate commerce on the Passaic river. 'These questions have all been ruled by the legislature of New Jersey, having (as we believe) the sole jurisdiction in the matter.' But, in general, the new Court had the same views as to the relation between state and nation as its predecessor. On one occasion, very unfortunately chosen (the Dred Scott case), the Court found an act of Congress to be unconstitutional, as Marshall had done. Yet, despite this decision (which we shall consider in due course), Roger B. Taney, for luminous perception and sound grasp of those social and economic realities upon which judicial statesmanship rests, must be considered one of the three or four really great Chief Justices of the United States.

4. TIPPECANOE AND TYLER TOO

The reason the 1840 campaign became the jolliest — and most idiotic — presidential contest in our history is that the Whigs fought the Democrats by their own methods. They adopted no platform, nominated a military hero, ignored real issues, and appealed to the emotions rather than to the brains of the voters. Expectations of profit and patronage were employed to 'get out the vote,' and the people were given a big show. It is amusing to find Democratic politicians, even Jackson himself, complaining of Whig 'demagoguery.'

Clay, the logical Whig candidate, did not get the nomination, for he had made many enemies; whilst old General Harrison, the 'Hero of Tippecanoe,' had proved to be a good vote-getter in 1836 and could be 'built up' still further. Harrison was not politically inexperienced, having served as congressman and senator from Indiana, but unlike Clay he was not associated with any particular measures. As American minister to Colombia (appointed by Adams and recalled by Jackson) he had incurred the enmity of Bolívar by lecturing the Liberator on the duties of a republican president. But that did not hurt him with the North American public.

Harrison's nomination set the pattern that Jackson's had begun — a nationally known figure, uncommitted on controversial issues. The Whig convention even appointed a committee to supervise the General's correspondence lest he write something incautious and be quoted! The pattern was slightly changed after 1840 by nominating some inconsequential 'Mr. Throttlebottom' to the vice-presidency. That change was made because of the Whig party's experience with a very positive and rambunctious vice-president, John Tyler, whose views were as old-fashioned as those of the late John Randolph. Yet he had just turned 50 years of age, whilst Harrison was already pushing 70.

As the Whig nominating convention met in December 1839 and adjourned without building a platform, the party had plenty of time to organize without being hampered by principle, for which it substituted mass enthusiasm. 'Tippecanoe and Tyler too' was the slogan. The Whigs had so far abandoned patrician values that Van Buren was pictured with cologne-scented whiskers, drinking champagne out of a crystal goblet at a table loaded with costly viands and massive plate. An unlucky sneer in a Democratic newspaper, to the effect that Harrison would be content with a $2000 pension, a log cabin, and plenty of hard cider, gave opportunity for effective contrast. It became the log-cabin, hard-cider campaign. There were log-cabin badges and log-cabin songs, a *Log Cabin* newspaper and log-cabin clubs, big log cabins where the thirsty were regaled with hard cider that the jealous Democrats alleged to be spiked with whiskey, little log cabins borne on floats in procession, with latch-string out, cider barrel marked 'O.K.' by the door, coon-

skin nailed up beside, and real smoke coming out of the chimney, while
lusty voices bawled:

> Let Van from his coolers of silver drink wine,
> And lounge on his cushioned settee.
> Our man on his buckeye bench can recline,
> Content with hard cider is he . . .

Huge balls, supposed to represent the gathering majority, were rolled
by men and boys from village to village and state to state, singing as
they rolled:

> What has caused this great commotion, motion, motion,
>   Our country through?
> — It is the ball a-rolling on, for
> (*Chorus*) TIPPECANOE AND TYLER TOO: —
>   Tippecanoe and Tyler too.
>   And with them we'll beat little Van, Van, Van,
>   Oh! Van is a used-up man.

In vain the Democrats worked a counterline of campaign lies, to the
effect that Harrison was an abolitionist and a 'Hartford Convention
Federalist.' In vain did 'Old Rumpsey-Dumpsey' Johnson try to take the
curse off dandy Van by clowning in a red jacket he claimed to have
stripped off Tecumseh's dead body. In vain James Buchanan in his
nasal Pennsylvania twang stuffily 'endeavored, without giving personal
offense, to carry the war into Africa.'

Tippecanoe and Tyler rolled up 234 electoral votes, a four-to-one
majority, but the popular vote was much closer, Harrison winning less
than 53 per cent in an election in which almost four-fifths of the eligible electorate went to the polls. By 1840, American politics had
reached a remarkable equilibrium in which every state boasted a competitive two-party system. For the next twelve years, and for the only
time in our history, both parties were national organizations with strong
followings everywhere. This unusual situation could persist only at the
expense of ignoring divisive sectional feelings.

John Quincy Adams, who had supported Tip and Ty somewhat
wryly, remarked in his diary, 'Harrison comes in upon a hurricane; God
grant he may not go out upon a wreck!' Worse than that, he went out
in a hearse. The stress of seeing applicants for offices morning, noon,
and night brought on pneumonia; and on 4 April 1841, after one month

in office, the Hero of Tippecanoe died. John Tyler succeeded to his office, and by his actions established the precedent that a Vice-President in such a situation inherits all the powers, as well as the title, of President.

It was soon demonstrated that desire 'for office was the only binding force in the Whig party. Henry Clay expected to be 'mayor of the palace,' as well as leader of the Senate; but the new President was an obstinate man of commonplace mind and narrow views. Clay, like Hamilton, wished to integrate the Federal Government by catering to substantial interests; and his immediate ambition was to charter a new Bank of the United States. Tyler believed it his mission to assert Virginian state-rights 'principles of 1798,' and to strip the Federal Government of its 'usurped' power; but he lacked both the personal magnetism and the saving common sense of Jefferson.

Tyler signed the 'log cabin' bill which made permanent in public land policy the pre-emption principle of the Act of 1830. Any American not already an owner of 320 acres or more could now buy 160 acres in the public domain, and pay later at the rate of $1.25 an acre. This Pre-emption Act of 1841 was probably the most important agrarian measure ever passed by Congress. It was a clean-cut frontier victory.

In some respects, President Tyler fulfilled Whig expectations. He took over Harrison's cabinet intact; carried through the political purge of the civil service that Harrison had begun; and accepted an upward revision of the tariff as a necessary measure for the revenue. But he vetoed all bills for internal improvements and harbor works, and refused to accept any fiscal device that bore the remotest resemblance to the B.U.S. of detestable memory. Clay's bill for a new bank was returned with the President's veto, as was a second bill especially drafted to meet his constitutional scruples.

From that date (9 September 1841) there was open warfare between Tyler and Clay. Four days later the cabinet resigned — except Webster who wished to appear independent of Clay — and the President was read out of the Whig party.

Here was Calhoun's chance to count in the sectional balance of power. For three years (1841–43), while Tyler attempted to form a party with a corporal's guard of faithful Whigs, Calhoun played a waiting game, repressing a secession movement among his hot-headed followers in South Carolina, intriguing to obtain the Democratic nomination for the Presidency in 1844. Webster left the cabinet in 1843; and in March 1844 Calhoun became Tyler's Secretary of State.

The new combination was extraordinary. Tyler had gone over to the Democrats, and Calhoun had returned to the fold. Calhoun's purpose was to 'reform' the Democratic party on the basis of state rights, a formula which was a mere cover for the main purpose of his devoted followers, to perpetuate slavery where it was and extend it into regions where it did not exist. Calhoun tipped the internal balance of the Democratic party very definitely southward; the loss of Tyler inclined the internal balance of the Whig party slightly, but no less definitely, northward. The important question of which side the West would take would be decided when the Democrats nominated James K. Polk for the Presidency in 1844, on a platform of westward expansion. It was even more significant that in the same platform the Democrats neglected to reaffirm their faith, as had been their wont, in the principles of the Declaration of Independence.

5. ANGLO-AMERICAN RELATIONS

Both Van Buren and Tyler faced a troublesome situation on the northern border. In the autumn of 1837, rebellion broke out in Upper and Lower Canada. The long constitutional controversy that preceded this outbreak bore so marked a resemblance to the history of the Thirteen Colonies that most Americans hailed the Canadian rebellion as a new American Revolution. Northern New York and Vermont, adjoining the centers of disturbance, harbored numerous refugees from Canadian justice; and among their permanent population were thousands of active, energetic young men who were ready for any sort of row. A network of secret societies called Hunters' Lodges, pledged to expel British sovereignty from North America, was formed along the border.

President Van Buren issued a neutrality proclamation on 5 January 1838, but on the long, unfortified boundary his resources were few and feeble, while the state governments were weak in will, and not much stronger in means. Hence, for a period of over a year, the Ontario rebel William L. Mackenzie and his followers were able to recruit money, supplies, and men in the United States and return to loot and burn in Canada. A force of regulars under General Scott was stationed at Buffalo, just after Mackenzie had recruited 200 or 300 'liberators' among the bargees, lake sailors, and others who were suffering from unemployment. The rebel headquarters on Navy Island were supplied from the New York shore by a small American steamer called the *Caroline*. On the night of 29 December 1837, as she lay at her wharf in the United States, a picked band of loyal Canadians performed the hazardous feat of rowing across the Niagara river just above the head of the falls, cutting out the *Caroline,* and setting her on fire. It was a violation — or counterviolation — of neutrality analogous to that of Jackson in Florida; but New York was not a Spanish province, and peppery Palmerston instead of calm Castlereagh was in Downing Street.

In 1840, before the United States could obtain an admission from Palmerston that the attack on the *Caroline* had been deliberate and official, a Canadian named McLeod boasted in a New York barroom that he had killed an American in the affray, and was promptly arrested and indicted for murder. Palmerston then admitted that the ship had been destroyed under orders as a necessary means of defense against American 'pirates,' and demanded the immediate release of McLeod. His execution, so he wrote to the British minister at Washington, 'would produce war, war immediate and frightful in its character, because it would be a war of retaliation and vengeance.' By that time John Tyler was President, and Daniel Webster Secretary of State. They were as eager as Van Buren had been to preserve the peace, but were equally hampered by the limitations of federal government. Governor Seward of New York insisted that the justice of his state should take its course, and Webster could do no more than provide counsel for the prisoner. In the trial, fortunately, McLeod sober found an alibi for McLeod drunk, and was acquitted.

Lord Durham, who had been sent to Canada to report on conditions there, saw the real significance of the rebellion and the border incidents. No matter how firmly the rebellion might be suppressed, protracted discontent in Canada must lead to Anglo-American war, or to the liberal elements in Canada seeking annexation to the United States. At his suggestion, the British government granted responsible government to Quebec and Ontario in 1841, and to Nova Scotia and New Brunswick several years later. Canada owes this, in some measure at least, to the disturbing presence of her neighbor. Later, the federation movement was inspired by similar considerations.

Tyler, who did especially well in foreign relations, not only finished the work that Van Buren had begun of pacifying the New York–Ontario border, but he and his Secretary of State, Webster, settled the Northeastern boundary question. That controversy was already 60 years old. The British claim had no foundation in law. It had been the intention of the negotiators in 1782–83 to give the United States the territory of the old Province of Sagadahoc (eastern Maine), and the United States claimed no more. The northern part of that region was then, as much of it still is, a wilderness; hence the provincial boundaries had never been marked, and the negotiators of 1782 merely copied the terms of former grants and governors' commissions in agreeing that the international boundary should follow the 'Highlands which divide those rivers that empty themselves into the St. Lawrence from those which fall into the Atlantic Ocean.'

East of Lake Champlain, if this treaty were followed literally, the boundary would run inconveniently close to the St. Lawrence river and obstruct the natural land route between Quebec and the Maritime Provinces. Accordingly, a British case for flattening out the Maine salient was built up, largely on the quibble that the Bay of Fundy was not the Atlantic Ocean. If that interpretation were admitted, the entire valley of the St. John, which flowed into the Bay of Fundy, must be included in Canada. The War of 1812 emphasized this strategic consideration; and in course of time this interpretation became, in the minds of most British subjects, a prescriptive right, the denial of which by Americans was accounted low and grasping. Legal briefs were accumulated, more surveys were made, and Maine lumberjacks had some gorgeous fights with their rivals from New Brunswick. In 1838 British 'trespassers' along the Aroostook (a tributary to the St. John) seized a 'trespassing' official of Maine; both state and provincial governors called out their militia, and the resulting 'Aroostook War' remained bloodless only because President Van Buren was willing to arrange a *modus vivendi* until the diplomats could try their skill again.

So matters stood early in 1842, when Aberdeen sent Lord Ashburton to negotiate at Washington with Daniel Webster. Both men, and Tyler too, were ardent for peace. To that end Webster stepped down from the Olympian atmosphere in which he was wont to move, conducted the negotiations informally, discarded the treaty of 1783 as inexecutable, and compromised. The negotiation, conducted wholly in private and largely by conversation, resulted in the Webster-Ashburton treaty of 9 August 1842, which established the present boundary. Great Britain obtained about five-twelfths of the disputed territory — better than the Dutch proposal of 1831, and sufficient for a connecting link between Quebec and New Brunswick. The United States with the other seven-twelfths obtained a rectification of frontier on Lake Champlain, sufficient to include a fort that had inadvertently been built on Canadian territory. The international lake and river boundary, which a joint commission under the Treaty of Ghent had completed only to the Sault Ste. Marie, was continued thence to the Lake of the Woods.

It was one thing for Webster and Ashburton to sign a treaty, quite another to get it ratified by the Senate and accepted by Parliament. This contest was won by what Webster called the 'battle of the maps.' Professor Jared Sparks had discovered in Paris, and placed in Webster's hands, an early French map with a red line sustaining the British claim. Both he and Webster assumed that this was the map referred to by Franklin in a letter to Vergennes, as a map 'marked with a Strong Red Line [representing] the Limits of the thirteen United States, as settled in the Preliminaries between the British and American plenipotentiarys.' One look at it brought the delegates of Maine to Webster's heel, and in the Senate it helped to obtain the necessary two-thirds majority. On the other side, the director of the British Museum had discovered, and the Foreign Office impounded, a map formerly belonging to George III, which showed the 'Boundary as described by Mr. Oswald' (the British peace commissioner of 1782), along the line of the American claim! Aberdeen happily produced this map in Parliament when Palmerston attacked the treaty as the 'Ashburton capitulation.' The actual 'red-line map,' or a contemporary copy of it, was found years later in the Spanish archives. It indicates that the United States was entitled to about 5000 square miles more than she obtained.

XXVIII

Western Empire

1. THE GREAT PLAINS

Since 1806, when Lewis and Clark returned from their journey to the Oregon country, the United States government had not taken much interest in the Far West. Major Long's expedition of 1819 reported the Great Plains 'almost wholly unfit for cultivation,' and laid down on the map of that region, which now supports a thriving population of several millions, the legend 'Great American Desert.'

The Great Plains of the United States cover an area equal to that of European Russia. Their smooth or gently rolling surface, rising gradually or by step-like escarpments from an elevation of 2000 to 6000 feet, was covered with a carpet of grass, rank and thick in the eastern portions, but giving way to tufts of short buffalo grass and sagebrush in the parched high plains. An occasional rocky dome, butte, or mesa established a welcome landmark. The Platte and Missouri rivers, with their short tributaries, cut deep gashes in the soil and watered a thin line of willow, cottonwood, and wild plum trees. A short summer of blistering heat, with fierce thunderstorms and frequent cyclones, followed hard on a long winter of bitter northwest winds and heavy snow. Over this area roamed the Kansa, Pawnee, Sioux, Cheyenne, Blackfoot, Crow, and Arapaho tribes. Countless herds of buffalo grazed on the plains and supplied the redskins with every necessity of life: with meat for immediate use, or, dried and pounded into pemmican, for winter subsistence; with skins for clothing, shields, harness, vessels, and the cover of the tepees or tents; with sinews for thread, cordage, and bow-strings; with bone for arrowheads and implements; with peltry to sell the traders; even with fuel. These Indians had long since domesticated the wild mustang, off-spring of those set free by the Spanish conquista-dores, and showed marvelous skill in shooting buffalo with bow and arrow while riding bareback.

The plains Indians seldom practiced agriculture, and knew little or nothing of pottery, basketry, or weaving; but they were the finest phys-ical specimens of the race, and in warfare, once they had learned the use of the rifle, were more formidable than the Eastern tribes that had yielded so slowly to the white man. Politically they were even less de-veloped; tribe warred with tribe, and knew no common head or coun-cil. A highly developed sign language was the only means of intertribal communication. The effective unit was the band or village of a few hundred souls, which might be seen in the course of its wanderings en-camped by some watercourse with tepees erected; or pouring over the plain, squaws and children leading the dogs and pack-horses with their trailing travois, superbly dressed braves loping gaily ahead on their wiry steeds. They lived only for the day, recognized no rights of prop-erty, robbed or killed any party of whites who could not defend them-selves, inflicted cruelty without a qualm, and endured torture without flinching.

The only white men who penetrated this region before 1830 were ex-plorers, fur traders, and trappers. As soon as Lewis and Clark brought news of the untouched store of fur-bearing animals in the core of the continent, commercial companies were organized to hunt them. The plains Indians were able to supply plenty of buffalo skins, but disliked trapping; hence the trading companies organized bands of *engagés*, trappers who spent most of their time in the Rocky Mountains or Black Hills, and returned yearly to a company post on the upper Platte or Missouri in order to turn in their furs and enjoy a week's riotous living on the proceeds. Peltry was also obtained from free-lance trappers who managed by prowess or diplomacy to obtain a certain immunity from the Indians. Supplies and trading goods were sent up-river from St. Louis, the leading market for the fur trade. Every river, valley, moun-tain, and water-hole of the Far West was known to the trappers before 1830, and without their guidance and knowledge transcontinental emi-gration would have been impossible. It was they who discovered the

South Pass of the Rockies in Wyoming, a wide valley of rolling hills that takes one to the transcontinental divide by easy gradients. A party of trappers led by Jedediah Smith and William Sublette took the first covered wagons from the Missouri to the Rockies in 1830. Six years later Captain Bonneville, whose adventures provided literary material for Washington Irving, led the first loaded wagons through the South Pass and down the Snake valley to the Columbia river.

2. 'WHERE ROLLS THE OREGON' [1]

The Oregon Country, which included not only the present state of Oregon, but Washington, Idaho, part of Montana, and British Columbia, was something else again. Here climate, timber, and salmon-teeming rivers invited settlement. But how to get at it? And would the pioneer who braved the transcontinental journey or the 200-day voyage around Cape Horn find himself on United States soil when he got there?

Every diplomatic negotiation between the United States and Great Britain since 1815 had agreed to disagree on the Oregon question. The only thing they could settle upon was a temporary condominium, or joint occupation, north of lat. 42° N, where Spanish California stopped, and south of lat. 54° 40', where Russian Alaska ended. When John Jacob Astor's trading post of Astoria at the mouth of the Columbia river was sold to a Canadian fur trading company, which in 1821 amalgamated with the Hudson's Bay Company, the only American foothold in Oregon was relinquished. Three years later, the Hudson's Bay Company constructed on the north bank of the lower Columbia Fort Vancouver, which Dr. John McLoughlin, the Company factor, a shrewd, stalwart, and humane British subject, built up to be an efficient imperial outpost. With hundreds of French Canadians and half-breeds in company employ, and a fleet of small vessels, he sent out 'brigades' of trappers and traders as far as Idaho, Alaska, and California. He had some 3000 acres of land under cultivation, and treated the Indians of the region with justice and firmness. His help and hospitality to early

1. The name, derived from Jonathan Carver's *Travels*, was popularized by Bryant's 'Thanatopsis' in 1817:
> The continuous woods,
> Where rolls the Oregon and hears no sound
> Save his own dashings.

American immigrants to the Oregon Country are memorable, and eventually he became a citizen of the United States; but the flag flown at Fort Vancouver was the company's own British banner, not the Stars and Stripes.

In the meantime the West coast from San Diego to Queen Charlotte Island was being visited by Boston fur traders and 'hide droghers.' Many of these vessels also traded with Hawaii, where the American Board of Foreign Missions had established a native Congregational church in 1820 under a great missionary, the Reverend Hiram Bingham. California belonged to Mexico and to the Roman Catholic Church, but Bingham kept urging his Boston backers to do something about the free-for-all Oregon Country. His appeal reached an eccentric Yankee named Hall J. Kelley, who in 1831 founded 'The American Society for Encouraging the Settlement of the Oregon Territory.' This organization issued prospectuses praising the mild climate, and pointing out openings for Pacific trade and opportunities for converting the Indians. Kelley stirred up Nathaniel J. Wyeth, a 28-year-old man of action whose zest for oceanic trade had been whetted by successfully exporting ice from Fresh Pond, Cambridge, to the West Indies and South America.

3. THE OREGON TRAIL

Wyeth made two attempts to begin American colonization of Oregon, which ruined him but really started the far westward movement. In 1832 he sent a brig around Cape Horn, while he with 24 men and boys, guided by the fur-trapper guide William Sublette, marched overland from St. Louis, arriving at Fort Vancouver in October 1832, after a trek lasting 190 days. The brig was lost at sea; Wyeth returned to Boston, and organized a second expedition in 1834 with two ornithologists (Thomas Nuttall and John K. Townsend), the Reverend Jason Lee, and four other missionaries in his company. These last had been selected by the Methodists of New England to convert the Flathead Indians. This party cut the time between St. Louis and Fort Vancouver to 160 days, and the ship also arrived, but too late for the salmon fishing on which Wyeth had counted to meet expenses. Wyeth a second time returned empty-handed to Boston, and went back into the ice business.

Yet, from the long view, his project did more than any other to win Oregon for the United States. The ornithologists, by their writings, helped to make that country known. Jason Lee and his fellow missionaries settled in the Willamette valley, near the present Salem, Oregon, and combined with former employees of the Hudson's Bay Company to raise wheat and cattle. Jason Lee visited the East in 1838 to obtain assistance — his 'great reinforcement' of 50 people came by sea — and the same year his backers began the publication at Boston of a periodical called *The Oregonian and Indians' Advocate,* which gave a luscious and, on the whole, truthful description of the Oregon Country.

It would, in fact, have been difficult to exaggerate. Here the majestic Columbia river, teeming with salmon, broke through the Cascade range, whose snow-capped peaks (Hood, St. Helens, Adams, Rainier) soared like serene white souls above virgin fir forests. Here were the fertile valleys of the Clackamas, the Willamette, and the Umatilla, ripe for grain fields and orchards, and a mild moist climate, more like Old England's than New England's. And the continent was rimmed by an iron-bound coast, with an occasional sand beach, on which the long Pacific surges eternally tumbled and roared. Fort Vancouver offered a market for all the grain and livestock the settlers could raise.

When you had completed the difficult journey to Oregon, it was not clear what flag you were under when you got there. Presidents Jackson, Van Buren, and Tyler paid little or no attention to Oregon. Nothing was done to extend American law to this region, or to settle the question of sovereignty. Nevertheless, Lee and his neighbors, following the same instinct for self-government that had produced the Mayflower Compact and the State of Franklin, called a meeting at Champoeg in the Willamette valley and set up a provisional government for Oregon Territory, on 5 July 1843. The laws of Iowa were adopted, and arrangements were made to settle land titles, that fruitful subject of frontier disputes. By 1844, with new settlers from New England and several hundred from the Mississippi valley, there were about 2500 white people, in addition to the Fort Vancouver employees, in the Oregon Country. By 1850 the population was 13,000, almost half of it born in the slave states. Nevertheless, the territorial legislature set up under the Champoeg compact declared in 1844 that slavery was illegal in the Territory. At the same time it forbade free Negroes to enter the country, and ordered all then there to leave within three years. The Southerners in this migration wanted no more slavery; but neither did they want Negro neighbors.

In the meantime, the American Board of Foreign Missions had sent religious and medical missionaries to the eastern part of the Oregon Country, especially the future state of Idaho. In response to a Macedonian cry from four Flatheads who had visited St. Louis, the board sent the young and energetic Dr. Marcus Whitman, accompanied by a beautiful young bride with the improbable name of Narcissa, to the Far West. Their honeymoon was spent on the Oregon trail, in company with fur traders, in the spring of 1836. Narcissa Whitman, first white woman to pass the Rockies, had plenty of awed attention from the mountain men, whose aches and fractures were attended to by the doctor. One article after another was discarded, the wagon that the Doctor insisted on bringing over the South Pass was cut down to a two-wheeled cart; and, to make room for the other two wheels, the Doctor discarded Narcissa's bridal trunk. Her emotion over that loss, 'Farewell, little trunk,' is more poignant than Manon Lescaut's 'Adieu, ma petite table.' They left St. Louis on 31 March and arrived at Fort Walla Walla on 1 September 1836.

This Whitman party and those that immediately followed established missions to the Cayuse Indians at Waiilatpu 25 miles east of Walla Walla, to the Nez Percé at Lapwai on the Clearwater river, near its junction with the Snake in northern Idaho, and to the Flathead at Tshimakain, not far from the site of the present city of Spokane. For almost ten years these missions flourished, and part of the New Testament was printed in Nez Percé. But the Cayuse became estranged when rough characters of the heavy migration of 1845–47 harassed them and started a measles epidemic. A half-breed accused Dr. Whitman of administering poison in the guise of medicine, and in November 1847 Marcus, Narcissa, and most of the mission group were massacred. This provoked the first of Oregon's Indian conflicts, the Cayuse War. The settlements of the Columbia had so prospered that they were able to put 250 armed men in the field to punish the guilty Indians.

Nor did the Catholic Church neglect this Far Western mission field; by 1847 there were fourteen Jesuits in the Northwest. Father Pierre-Jean de Smet from the Catholic University of St. Louis, 'Blackrobe' to the Indians, founded the Sacré Cœur Mission in the Cœur d'Alene country as early as 1841.

In 1842 'Oregon fever' struck the frontier folk of Iowa, Missouri, Illinois, and Kentucky. By temperament and tradition these were backwoodsmen who had no use for treeless prairies or arid high plains; they wanted wood, water, and game, which the Oregon Country had in abundance, and to be rid of the fevers and agues that afflicted them in the low-lying lands bordering the Mississippi. Independence, Mo., was their jumping-off place. 'Prairie schooners,' as the canvas-covered Conestoga wagons were nicknamed, converged there in May, when the grass of the plains was fresh and green. Parties were organized, a captain appointed, an experienced trapper or fur-trader engaged as pilot; and amid a great blowing of bugles and cracking of long whips, the caravan, perhaps a hundred wagons strong with thousands of cattle on the hoof, moved off up the west bank of the Missouri. At Fort Leavenworth, one of the bastions of the Indian frontier, the emigrants for the last time enjoyed the protection of their flag.

For a long time there was neither road nor trail. Near Council Bluffs, where the Missouri is joined by the Platte, the route to Oregon turned west to follow the Platte over the Great Plains.[2] Until a road had been beaten into the sod, it was easy to lose the way. Numerous tributaries of the Platte, swollen and turbid in the spring of the year, had to be forded or swum, to the great damage of stores and baggage. Francis Parkman in 1846 found ancient tables and chests of drawers which perhaps had served some family in a dozen homes between England and the Mississippi, left cracking in the sun where this latest wave of migration had grounded them. Every night the caravan made a hollow square of wagons round its fire of cottonwood or buffalo chips. The horses and mules were kept inside, for protection, and the howling of prairie wolves was drowned by a chorus of hymns and old ballads. At dawn the horsekind were let out to graze for an hour or two, the oxen were rounded up and hitched to the wagons, bugles blew, and another start was made toward 'the sunset regions.'

Until the forks of the Platte were reached, near the present northeastern corner of Colorado, the herbage was luxuriant, and the grades easy. Following the north fork, the trail became hilly and then mountainous, as one turned north to avoid the Laramie spur of the Rockies. Beyond the South Pass came the worst part of the journey — a long,

2. Later, the Oregon trail cut straight across the prairie from Independence to the southernmost bend of the Platte, near the site of Kearney, Nebraska.

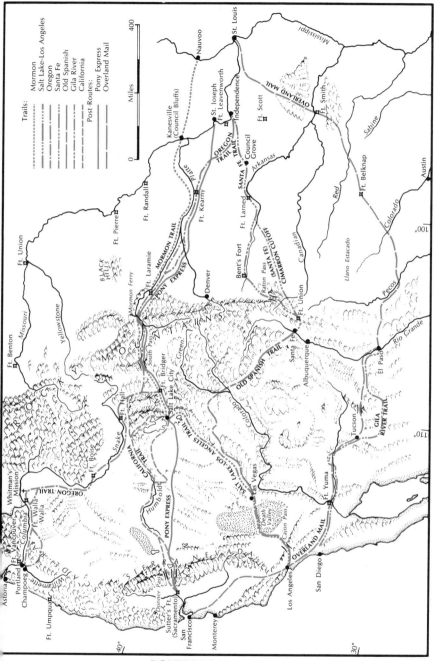

ROUTES TO THE WEST

531

hard pull across the arid Wyoming basin, where the grass was scanty, and alkali deposits made the water almost undrinkable. Between the Gros Ventre and Teton ranges of the Rockies the Oregon-bound emigrant found westward-flowing waters, and took heart; but there were still 800 miles to go to the lower Columbia, following the meanderings of the Snake river. As there was no good road in early days through the heavily forested country along the Columbia, wagons were often rafted down the stream; and with fair luck a party that left Independence in May might celebrate Thanksgiving Day in the Willamette valley. But it was a lucky caravan indeed that arrived with the same number of souls that started; and some of the weaker parties disappeared — whether by starvation after losing the trail, or at the hands of Indians, no one ever knew.

This heavy immigration of 1843–45, 4000 to 5000 strong, strained the provisional territorial organization, and convinced Congress that something must be done to provide this remote colony with government, law, and land titles. First, however, the Federal Government wished to reach a settlement with Great Britain.

In 1843, agitation for annexing the whole of Oregon up to Alaska began in the Western states, and Democratic politicians scented a good issue to win the Western vote in the next presidential election. A bill for organizing Oregon as a United States Territory passed the Senate in February 1843, but the House, fortunately ignorant of Palmerston's threat that the passage 'would be a declaration of war,' let it drop. Secretary Calhoun opened negotiations on the subject in 1844 with the British minister at Washington and repeated a proposal, thrice made by J. Q. Adams, to divide the territory along latitude 49°. But Aberdeen, like Castlereagh and Canning, refused to abandon the north bank of the Columbia.

If the question were to be decided by extent of actual occupation the British claim was just; and it would be difficult to discover any other basis of division. North of the Columbia, about Fort Vancouver and along Puget Sound, were living over 700 British subjects, and only half a dozen American citizens. The United States, however, could well afford to wait. A decline in the Columbia river fur trade was making Fort Vancouver unprofitable, and the menacing attitude of the latest American immigrants threatened its security. At Dr. McLoughlin's suggestion the company abandoned Fort Vancouver to the Americans in 1845, and erected a new post at Victoria on Vancouver Island.

By this time James K. Polk, an expansionist, had become President of the United States. In his annual message of December 1845, Polk shouted defiance at Britain; and in December, asserted that the American title to the whole of Oregon, up to lat. 54° 40', was 'clear and unquestionable,' and asked Congress for authority to terminate the joint occupation agreement of 1818. To a timid Congressman Polk remarked that 'the only way to treat John Bull was to look him straight in the eye; that he considered a bold and firm course on our part the pacific one.' He had his eye not only on the rich valleys of Oregon but on the splendid harbors of Puget Sound, which would help to exploit the immense Pacific area.

Polk, however, never intended to risk a war to acquire the whole of Oregon. His ambition was to annex California, which probably meant war with Mexico; he did not care to be responsible for fighting England and Mexico at the same time. Thus, when Lord Aberdeen formally proposed to extend the international boundary along latitude 49° N to Puget Sound, thence to the ocean through Juan de Fuca Strait, leaving Vancouver Island to Canada, President Polk decided to accept. He submitted the British offer to his cabinet on 6 June 1846, and to the Senate immediately after. It was during the Senate debate that some Western expansionist coined the slogan '54–40 or fight!' All but a few diehards supported the President, and on 15 June the Oregon treaty, describing the boundary according to Aberdeen's offer, was ratified. It took five months for the news to reach the settlements on the Willamette. Thus was completed the final section of the 3000-mile frontier between Canada and the United States.

4. THE MORMONS

Before the Oregon question was finally adjusted came the hegira of the Church of Jesus Christ of the Latter-day Saints, commonly called the Mormons, to the Great Salt Lake.

Joseph Smith was the offspring of a family of New England frontier drifters, who had made at least ten moves in nineteen years, ending at Palmyra, N. Y., in the midst of the 'burned-over district.' At the age of fifteen he began to see visions and dig for buried treasure. An angel of the Lord, so he claimed, showed him the hiding-place of a package of inscribed gold plates, together with a pair of magic spectacles which enabled him to read the characters. The resulting Book of Mormon

(first printed in 1830), a tedious anthology of personal experiences, religious notions, and wildly inaccurate history, gave the story of certain
Lost Tribes of Israel (the Indians), whom the Saints were commanded
to redeem from paganism. Joseph Smith then organized the Church of
the Latter-day Saints, a co-operative theocracy in which all power
emanated from Smith the Prophet, who stood at the head of a complicated hierarchy. Smith was an upstanding, jovial, lusty sort of man,
who 'ruled gaudily, enjoying power, publicity and worship.'

Smith set up the first Mormon community at Kirtland, Ohio, in 1830,
but persecutions drove the Mormons to Missouri and then to a spot on
the east bank of the Mississippi which the Prophet named Nauvoo. At
first the Mormons were welcomed in Illinois, courted by both political
parties, and given a charter that made Nauvoo practically an autonomous theocracy. The settlement grew rapidly — even faster than Chicago; by 1844, with 15,000 citizens, Nauvoo was the largest and most
prosperous city in Illinois. It was at Nauvoo that Joseph Smith received
the 'revelation' sanctioning polygamy, which he and the inner circle of
'elders' were already practicing. Although supported by Isaiah iv. 1,
'And in that day seven women shall take hold of one man,' this revelation split the church. The monogamous 'schismatics' started a paper at
Nauvoo; Smith caused the press to be broken up after the first issue; he
and his brother were then arrested by the authorities for destruction of
property and lodged in the county jail, whence, on June 27, 1844, they
were pulled out by a mob and lynched. Brigham Young, who succeeded to the mantle of the Prophet, and to five of his 27 widows, directed retaliation; and for two years terror reigned in western Illinois.
The Mormons were a virile, fighting people, but the time had come for
them to make another move, before they were hopelessly outnumbered.

Although polygamy was the feature of Mormonism that attracted
popular attention, it was little more than a recruiting device appropriate for a wandering tribe and was finally abandoned in 1890. The genius of the Mormons lay in a disciplined community life, integrated by
a peculiar faith and directed by able men of action.

The Saints had been making an astonishing gain in numbers. Missionaries had been raking in converts from the Northern states since
1831; and by 1840, when Brigham Young visited Liverpool, England
had become one of their principal harvest fields. For in England thou-

sands of poor laborers were allured by the prospect of a decent living and the promise of heavenly 'thrones, kingdoms, principalities and powers.' Almost 4000 English converts reached Nauvoo between 1840 and 1846, and 40 or 50 churches of Latter-day Saints in the old country contributed modest tithes to the Prophet's bulging treasury.

Under their new Moses the Mormons abandoned their homes in Nauvoo, and in 1846, several thousand strong, began their westward journey. After wintering near the Council Bluffs, Brigham Young pushed ahead with a pioneer band along a new trail on the north bank of the Platte; and in July 1847 reached the promised land, the basin of the Great Salt Lake. Many flinched from the long journey, but by the end of 1848, 5000 people had arrived in the future state of Utah, which Young named Deseret.

This new Canaan was a dry and inhospitable land. Young chose it in the hope that his Saints would no longer be molested by Gentiles, and also because it was Mexican territory; but the Mexican War would change that. Arid wastes, where salt and alkali deposits glistened among sagebrush thickets, sloped down from the Rocky Mountains to the Great Salt Lake, desolate and repulsive as another Dead Sea. But in the mountains lay natural reservoirs of rain and snow, the means of quickening life.

For such unfamiliar conditions the experience of English-speaking pioneers was inadequate, but the Mormons had resourceful leaders and a genius for disciplined community life. Brigham Young caused irrigation canals and ditches to be dug, and appointed committees to control water for the public benefit, discarding the common-law doctrine of riparian rights. He set up a system of small farms, intensively cultivated and carefully fertilized. He forbade speculation in land, but respected private property and accumulated a large fortune for himself. He kept the Indians quiet by a judicious mixture of firmness and justice. He repressed heresy and schism with a heavy hand. He organized foreign and domestic missions and financed both transatlantic and transcontinental immigration. By means of a complicated hierarchy he controlled both civil and spiritual affairs with Yankee shrewdness, rough humor, and substantial justice; and held himself responsible only to God.

For ten years there was intermittent want and starvation in Deseret, and the gold rush of 1849 to California caused unrest. Brigham Young announced in the Tabernacle at Salt Lake City, 'If you Elders of Israel want to go to the gold mines, go and be damned!' The wiser Saints found it more profitable to sell corn and potatoes to passing Argonauts. Yearly the community grew in numbers, strength, and wealth, a polygamous theocracy within a monogamous and democratic nation. Congress organized Deseret as Utah Territory in 1850, but since President Fillmore appointed Brigham Young the territorial governor, government in the hands of the Prophet continued. Federal judges were driven from Utah when they refused to do his will; Colonel Albert Sidney Johnston and 1500 regulars could obtain only a nominal submission in 1858; and in the Civil War Utah was practically neutral. The Latter-day Saints brought comfort, happiness, and self-respect to thousands of humble folk; and Brigham Young must be included among the world's most successful commonwealth builders.

XXIX

From the Sabine to Mexico City

1. THE SPANISH BORDERLANDS

While one column of pioneers deployed into the prairies of Illinois and Iowa, and another wound over the Oregon trail, a third crossed into Mexican territory and took possession of the coastal plain of Texas. Expansion in that direction was no simple matter of endurance or driving back Indians. There the English-speaking pioneer came into contact with a proud and ancient civilization, no longer upheld by a dying empire, but by the young Republic of Mexico. Who could tell whether Mexico might not develop the same expansive force as the United States, and Spain recover in the New World the moral dominion she had lost in the Old?

There was little sign of it in 1820. Upper California, New Mexico, and Texas, frontier provinces of the old viceroyalty, spread out fanwise toward the United States. Explored as early as the sixteenth century by the Spaniards, they had been thinly colonized after a long interval, and in the Roman rather than the English sense. Missions had been planted among the Indians as centers of civilization and exploitation; *presidios* or frontier garrisons established to protect the fathers in their work; and such few colonists as could be persuaded to venture so far were generously endowed by the Spanish government with lands and Indian serfs. A constant drain on the mother country, the frontier provinces had been maintained simply as a protection to Mexico against Indians to the north and 'Yanquis' to the east. In 1600, all North America had been a Spanish bastion, with feeble forts and missions studding the coast as far north as Virginia. The American conquest of Texas and California was a large chapter in the volume that began with the settlement of Jamestown in 1607 and ended with the Spanish-American War of 1898.

Spain left her stamp on the architecture, the place-names, and the customs of these frontier provinces; but her hold on them was slight, as their connection with Mexico was tenuous. Weak, distracted, lacking expansive energy, the new Mexican government did not know how to use the frontier provinces, and was too proud to dispose of them. Garrisons were withdrawn, missions secularized, and the Indians allowed to relapse into paganism. Upper California, a province the size of Asia Minor, contained little more than 6000 white men, mainly Mexican, in 1846. By 1840, hundreds of Americans had 'left their consciences at Cape Horn' to live and trade in this delightful country, and in 1840 overland emigrants began to trickle in from a branch of the Oregon trail through the passes of the Sierra Nevada.

Fifteen hundred miles from Vera Cruz, and 1000 from Mexico City, lay Santa Fe, capital and chief town of New Mexico. It was the gateway to a country of marvels and enchantments, shimmering plains that grew strange cacti, mesas striped with ochre and vermilion, aboriginal cliff-dwellings, Indian pueblos, and the stupendous canyon of the Colorado river. Annually an armed caravan of American traders assembled at Independence, Mo., and followed the Santa Fe trail with pack-mule and wagon through the country of the Osage and Comanche, to this lonely emporium of New Mexico, returning with silver and peltry.

But it was in Texas that the first compact wedge of English-speaking people was thrust across Mexico's borders. Texas, 750 miles long from the Sabine river to El Paso, and of equal depth from the tip of the 'panhandle' to the mouth of the Rio Grande del Norte, is larger than France and almost as varied in climate and natural resources. The pioneers found moist Gulf plains studded with canebrakes, and cold arid plateaus; dense forests of pine and hardwood; prairies of a deep, black, waxy loam, perfect for cotton growing, and others of lighter soil adapted for grain; sagebrush and yucca deserts; and the Llano Estacado or high plains, where roamed immense herds of buffalo and mustang.

Texas never formed part of Louisiana, and the United States's claim, renounced in the Florida Treaty of 1819, was based on nothing better than the fact that Napoleon was prepared to seize it before he decided to sell Louisiana to the United States. However, no sooner had President Monroe renounced Texas, and agreed upon the Sabine and the Red rivers as the American southwestern boundary, than he and J. Q. Adams were accused of selling out American territory. President Adams, sensitive to this charge, and President Jackson, who believed it to be true, pressed Mexico to sell the whole or a part of Texas. The mere offer was considered insulting; its repetition aroused suspicion.

Yet, with strange inconsistency, Mexico encouraged emigration from the United States to Texas. The most important grant, for the future, was made in 1821 to Moses Austin, a Connecticut Yankee of the type described by Washington Irving as disproving the adage 'a rolling stone gathers no moss.' Successively dry-goods merchant in Philadelphia and Richmond, owner of the Chiswell lead mines in Virginia, pioneer lead miner in Missouri, banker in St. Louis caught by the panic of 1819, Moses Austin died six months after obtaining his Texas grant, but the Mexican Congress confirmed it to his son Stephen in 1823. This gave Stephen F. Austin the privilege of *empresario*. He could settle 300 American families in one of the most fertile regions of Texas, and, later, the number was increased. Each family received free 177 acres of rich tillage, together with 13,000 acres of prairie pasture, Austin taking a bonus of 65,000 acres.

The Austin colony was a great success. By 1834 it comprised 20,000 white colonists and 2000 slaves, outnumbering the native Mexicans in Texas four to one. Austin, a grave and gentle young man, chose recruits for his colony with care, and ruled it with autocratic power until 1829. In social structure it resembled an English proprietary colony like Maryland; and Texas was more law-abiding and better governed than any nineteenth-century American frontier.

Although anti-slavery by preference, Austin found himself in the same dilemma as every colonist with capital: the choice between pioneer poverty and using some form of forced labor. There were no Indian peons in that part of Mexico, and the soil offered such opportunities for cotton and sugar culture that Southern planters would not come unless permitted to bring their slaves, and could not prosper without them. The Mexican Congress, the state legislature at Saltillo, and various Mexican dictators passed laws or decrees declaring the abolition of slavery throughout the Republic. But Austin was always able to obtain some 'explanation' of these decrees which allowed the Americans to hold their slaves in fact, if not by law.

Insecurity of slave property was but one of many factors pulling toward the separation of Texas from Mexico. Austin and the older American *empresarios* tried to be good Mexicans; but it was difficult to respect a government in constant turmoil. The American colonist admired the horsemanship of his Mexican neighbor, adopted his saddle and trappings — and sometimes appropriated his horse — but his attitude toward the 'natives' was condescending, and toward their government, impatient. And this irritation became mutual. There was trouble about the tariff, representation, and immigration; conflicts with Mexican garrisons whose proud officers resented the crude wit and boisterous individualism of the settlers. For in the 1830's, quiet law-abiding pioneers of Austin's type began to be outnumbered by swashbucklers like Sam Houston, former governor of Tennessee, Indian trader on the Texas frontier, and adopted Cherokee; David G. Burnet of Louisiana, who had twice followed Miranda to Caracas and later resided among the Comanches; the Bowie brothers of Louisiana, slave-smugglers who designed the long and deadly knife that bears their name; Davy Crockett, a publicity-mad professional backwoodsman from Tennessee; and many others of restless ambition and pungent personality, who had left their country for their country's good.

2. THE LONE STAR REPUBLIC

The break came in 1835, when President Santa Anna of Mexico proclaimed a unified constitution for Mexico that made a clean sweep of state rights. The American settlers of Texas set up a provisional government and expelled the Mexican garrison from San Antonio. Over the Rio Grande came Santa Anna with 3000 men. In the Alamo, the fortified mission at San Antonio, a garrison of less than 200 Texans refused to retreat or to surrender. For ten days, the defenders turned back assaults on the adobe walls. At dawn on 6 March 1836 Santa Anna assaulted the Alamo again, captured it after every Texan, including Crockett, Jim Bowie, and Colonel William Travis, had been killed or wounded, and put the wounded to death.

Already a convention elected by the American settlers had proclaimed the independent Republic of Texas, and adopted a flag with a single star. Santa Anna quickly advanced eastward with his wiry Mexican troops, the settlers fleeing before him, and for a few weeks it looked as if the Lone Star Republic would be snuffed out. Generalissimo Sam Houston managed to keep a force together, acquired volunteers from across the border, and awaited the Mexicans in an ilex grove by the ferry of the San Jacinto river, not far from the site of the city that bears his name. On 21 April, shouting 'Remember the Alamo!' the Texans and their allies burst on Santa Anna's army, scattered it, and took the general prisoner. Mexico made no serious effort toward reconquest; the Battle of San Jacinto was decisive. The Texans ratified their new constitution, legalized Negro slavery, elected Sam Houston President, and sent an envoy to Washington to demand annexation to the United States, or recognition as an independent republic.

Enthusiasm over the defense of the Alamo, and liberal land offers by the Republic, drew hundreds of American adventurers into the Texan army. President Jackson made no attempt to prevent this unneutral aid, but on the questions of recognition and annexation his attitude was diplomatically correct. Only on his last full day of office (3 March 1837), after Congress had approved, did Jackson recognize the Lone Star Republic.

Texas would have preferred annexation to the United States, but that was a year of agitation in Congress over the domestic slave trade and the 'gag resolution.' On 23 May 1836 Calhoun remarked in the Senate, that 'there were powerful reasons why Texas should be part of this Union. The Southern States, owning a slave population, were deeply interested in preventing that country from having the power to annoy them.' The same year a Quaker abolitionist named Benjamin Lundy brought out a pamphlet called *The War in Texas,* which attempted to prove that the Texas revolution was a conspiracy to open new slave markets and gain slave territory for cotton. Lundy spoke with an appearance of authority, for he had been to Texas, and with the bitterness of frustration, for he had hoped to found there a colony of free Negroes. His pamphlet, which described the Texans as a gang of horse-thieves, land-jobbers, and desperadoes, appealed to that widespread Northern sentiment opposed to the political dominance of the South and the extension of the slave territory. Almost in a moment the whole country realized that the annexation of Texas would affect the balance of power between North and South. On 1 November 1837 the Vermont legislature 'solemnly protested' against the admission 'of any state whose constitution tolerates domestic slavery.' That naturally aroused a contrary feeling in the South. Calhoun as solemnly announced that any attempt to exclude a state on account of its 'peculiar institution' would be a virtual dissolution of the Union.

The slave states were already beginning to realize that they had received the thin end of the Missouri Compromise of 1820, which prohibited slavery in federal territory north of 36° 30'. Arkansas and Michigan had just been admitted to the Union, making thirteen free and thirteen slave states. Florida was the only slave territory left; but three free territories, Wisconsin, Iowa, and Minnesota would be demanding admission in a few years, and more might well follow if the Indian barrier to the Great Plains were broken. The Alabama legislature, on Christmas Day 1837, resolved: 'It needs but a glance at the map to satisfy the most superficial observer that an overbalance is produced by the extreme northeast, which as regards territory would be happily corrected and counterbalanced by the annexation of Texas.' The Lone Star Republic, greater in area than nine free states of the Northeast, might be carved into several slave states to balance New England.

A resolution for the annexation of Texas was promptly introduced in Congress. President Van Buren, engaged at the time in delicate negotiations with Mexico, and anxious to keep slavery out of politics, used his influence against the resolution, which was finally smothered by a speech of J. Q. Adams that took three weeks to deliver (July 1838). The politicians were content to let so explosive a question rest. In the meantime, thousands of petty planters, ruined by the panic of 1837, were glad to leave their debts at home and start life anew across the Sabine.

The Lone Star Republic now belonged to the family of nations, but for how long? To be sure Britain and France had recognized her. But white population was barely 50,000; her currency had been inflated to the vanishing point and she had a debt of $7 million. In 1843 the British minister negotiated a truce between Texas and Mexico, but at any turn of the political wheel in Mexico City the truce might be denounced and hostilities renewed. Political conditions in Texas were chaotic. A Texas President who bore the conquering name of Mirabeau Buonaparte Lamar aimed to annex New Mexico, California, and the northern tier of Mexican states to the new republic, and directed an expedition against Santa Fe, which the Mexicans easily defeated. Sam Houston, who succeeded Lamar after that imperialist incursion, felt that Texas needed security, not enlargement. He favored a four-square annexation to the United States; but if the United States refused to take Texas, her best bet, thought Houston, would be a dual mediation by Britain and France to obtain Mexican recognition of her independence, and a dual guarantee to maintain it.

Such a project was certain to appeal to European statesmen. Here was a ready-made wedge between the United States and Latin America, an independent source of supply for cotton, sugar, and tobacco, a possible center of British or French influence. How Canning would have hastened to 'slip in between'! Lord Aberdeen in the foreign office toyed with the idea; Louis Philippe, king of the French, still smarting from his bout with President Jackson, was ready to go along. There was little doubt of Texas acceptance, if the offer were made in time; but it required the consent of Mexico, and no Mexican cabinet dared recognize Texan independence. More sense of reality and less of prestige at Mexico City in 1844 might have changed the entire course of American expansion.

Amid the cross-currents of notes, suggestions, and conversations between London, Paris, Washington, Austin, and Mexico City, another fact stands out clearly: the fear of Southern statesmen that Texas might abolish slavery. Calhoun believed that Aberdeen had agreed to guarantee a Texan loan if the Lone Star Republic would do just that; would even lend money to compensate Texan slave-holders, as England had done for those of the West Indies. The prospect of Texas becoming a second Canada, a refuge for fugitive slaves, alarmed the South to the point of panic. Abel P. Upshur, President Tyler's Secretary of State, at once began to negotiate a treaty of annexation with the Texan minister at Washington, and informed him that the abolition project was inadmissible.

At this juncture there occurred a fatal accident on a United States warship which influenced political history. Congress authorized the construction of U.S.S. *Princeton,* a frigate of revolutionary design. On a gala trip of *Princeton* down the Potomac on 28 February 1844, with President Tyler, cabinet ministers, diplomats, senators, and numerous ladies on board, one of its 12-inch wrought iron guns, 'Peacemaker,' burst. Secretary Upshur, the Navy Secretary, and a New York state senator were killed; Senator Thomas H. Benton and nineteen others were severely wounded.

The explosion virtually threw into President Tyler's arms the fair Julia Gardiner, daughter of the slaughtered state senator; shortly she became the second Mrs. Tyler and mistress of the White House. And the loss of the two secretaries gave the President an opportunity to reconstruct his cabinet, without a single Northerner or even a Whig, although it was that party which had elected him. John C. Calhoun was now brought back as Secretary of State.

Calhoun was appointed for two main purposes — to put Texas into the Union, and to get Tyler the Democratic (not the Whig) nomination for the presidency in 1844. Like several later Vice-Presidents who have succeeded through death, 'Tyler too' dearly wanted to be elected President 'in his own right.' Calhoun, who supposedly had retired from politics, accepted because he hoped to be able to link the Texas question with Oregon, and so forge an alliance of South and West under the Democratic aegis, and become President after Tyler.

Lord Aberdeen, as soon as the gossip about his intention to liberate Texas slaves bounced back to London, sent a dignified but imprudent denial of it to Secretary Calhoun. 'Great Britain desires, and is constantly exerting herself to procure, the general abolition of slavery throughout the world. But the means which she has adopted, and will continue to adopt, for this humane and virtuous purpose, are open and undisguised.' Calhoun replied by reading the British government a lesson on the beauties of Negro slavery. Adducing some questionable statistics, he offered to convince the noble lord that the Negro race would be reduced to wretchedness and vice by his misdirected charity. And he observed that the 'threatened danger' to the 'safety and prosperity of the Union' justified American annexation of Texas. In other words, the mere prospect of abolition in a neighboring republic was sufficient reason to absorb it.

Annexation, urged on such grounds as Calhoun's, repelled more votes from one section than it attracted from another. A second annexation treaty, which Calhoun negotiated with some difficulty (since Sam Houston was playing coy and beginning to think that a Greater Texas would be a better theater for his talents than a seat in the U.S. Senate), failed to obtain the necessary two-thirds vote. Indeed, about two-thirds of the Senate voted against it.

But President Tyler had another card up his sleeve. After the presidential election of 1844 had 'pronounced' in favor of 're-annexation,' [1] he recommended that Texas be admitted to the Union by joint resolution of both houses, which did not require a two-thirds vote. The deed was done on 28 February 1845; and President Tyler on his last day of office had the satisfaction of sending a courier to inform President Houston that only the consent of the Lone Star Republic was necessary to make Texas the twenty-eighth State of the Union. That was given promptly.

This almost indecent haste to annex Texas, in marked contrast to the administration's indifference to Oregon, was occasioned by one thing only: fear on the part of influential Southern editors and politicians that the Republic of Texas would abolish slavery. Arguments were also used that 'perfidious Albion' intended to build up Texas to rival the United States in cotton production, that she was also angling for Cuba, and that there was grave danger of the Gulf of Mexico and the Caribbean becoming an Anglo-Abolitionist lake. These were only a smoke screen for the main issue in the annexation of Texas: slavery.

3. PRESIDENT POLK AND HIS MANEUVERS

While Tyler and Calhoun were rushing Texas into the Union, wiser politicians were trying to keep it out of politics. Martin Van Buren, retired to 'O.K.' (renamed 'Lindenwald') since his defeat in 1840, expected the Democratic nomination in 1844. Two years earlier, he called on Henry Clay, who had an equally firm expectation for the Whig presidential nomination. Both men agreed to issue a letter opposing the immediate annexation of Texas, and each did. Van Buren expressed his opinion that to rush the affair would mean war with Mexico. Henry Clay declared that he would welcome Texas to the Union if it could be done 'without dishonor, without war, with the common consent of the Union, and upon just and fair terms.' These praiseworthy efforts to preserve the peace were fatal to their authors; they lost Van Buren the nomination and Clay the election.

1. The implication here was that Monroe and Adams had given Texas away.

When the Democratic nominating convention met at Baltimore in May 1844, Van Buren had a majority of the delegates. But the Southern expansionist delegates, led by Robert J. Walker of Mississippi, put over the two-thirds rule,[2] which Little Van was not strong enough to surmount. The expansionists trotted out the first 'dark horse' in presidential history. His name, new to most of the country, was James K. Polk. By holding firmly to 'Old Hickory's' coat-tails, Polk had become speaker of the House and governor of Tennessee. With Jackson pulling wires for him from 'The Hermitage,' he won the presidential nomination on the ninth ballot. Senator Silas Wright, outraged at Van Buren's being passed over, declined the vice-presidential nomination over the new electric telegraph; and a colorless Pennsylvanian, George M. Dallas, was given the second place. To please the Northern Democrats, 're-occupation of Oregon' was given equal honors on the platform with 're-annexation of Texas,' but Oregon was a minor factor in the campaign.

Henry Clay, now 67 years old, received the Whig nomination by acclamation. He had lately made a triumphal progress through the South, speaking to 'vast concourses' of people, and felt confident of the election. But Clay's open letter offended the annexationists and lost him votes in the South. Enough anti-slavery Whigs in New York voted for Birney, the Liberty party (abolitionist) candidate, to give Polk a slight edge, and New York's electoral vote was pivotal.

Save for the unusual four-way race in 1824, the victory of Polk in 1844 marked the first time that a President had been elected with less than 50 per cent of the vote. Hence, Polk's triumph was hardly a mandate for expansion. Yet it permitted the Democrats to claim that a firm conviction of America's 'manifest destiny' to extend west to the Pacific and south at least to the Rio Grande lay behind the defeat of the popular Clay. 'Reoccupation of Oregon, re-annexation of Texas,' gave an emotional accolade to the plain fact that America was again on the move. Anyone who objected had better get out of the way! The prospect of acquiring Oregon and Texas appealed to plain people who were recovering confidence after the hard times of 1837–43. Polk wanted both and California to boot; he got all three.

2. First adopted in 1836, but not used in 1840; after this it continued in Democratic national conventions until 1936. It was an admirable device for preventing strong men from obtaining the nomination, and giving it to indecisive or weak characters — but that did not happen in 1844.

James Knox Polk, though not yet 50 years of age, looked 20 years older by reason of bad health. He was a stiff, angular person, with sharp gray eyes in a sad, lean face, and grizzled hair overlapping a black coat-collar. He had majored in mathematics and the classics at the University of North Carolina to train his mind, and the event proved that he succeeded. His working day in the White House was nearer eighteen than eight hours, and in four years he was absent only six weeks from Washington. His will controlled a cabinet of experienced and distinguished men.[3] Determined and tenacious, seldom smiling and never relaxing, Polk recalls that other presidential scholar and diarist, J. Q. Adams, rather than Jackson, with whom his political supporters were apt to compare him. Their domestic policies were as wide apart as the poles, but Polk adopted the same foreign policy as Adams, and he had a way of getting things done. He aspired to reduce the tariff, re-establish Van Buren's independent treasury, settle the Oregon question, and acquire California. Within four years his ambition was fulfilled.

California — the very word used to connote mystery and romance. It was the name given to a mythical kingdom 'near the terrestrial paradise,' in a novel of chivalry written in the lifetime of Columbus, the *Esplandian* of Garcia Ordoñez de Montalvo. President Polk did not read Spanish novels, but he wanted California, a golden land with every sort of climate and soil, forests of giant pines and sequoias, broad valleys suited for wheat, and narrow vales where the vine flourishes, extensive grazing grounds, mountains abounding in superb scenery and mineral wealth, and magnificent harbors at San Francisco and San Diego. Although Oregon had been well advertised for years, almost nothing was known in the United States about California until after Fremont's exploration of 1843.

John C. Frémont, a 28-year-old second lieutenant in the topographical corps of the United States Army, wooed and won sixteen-year-old Jessie, daughter of Senator Thomas Hart Benton of Missouri. Papa Benton, equally devoted to hard money, western expansion, and daugh-

3. James Buchanan of Pennsylvania, Secretary of State; William L. Marcy of New York, who had helped Polk to win that state despite the disappointment of Van Buren, Secretary of War; Senator Robert J. Walker of Mississippi, Secretary of the Treasury; George Bancroft the historian, Secretary of the Navy. It was Bancroft who persuaded Congress to establish the Naval Academy at Annapolis.

ter Jessie, conceived the idea of sending sonny-boy on an exploring expedition, with competent guides like 'Kit' Carson to take care of him. That was not difficult for an important senator to arrange. Frémont on his first trip discovered nothing new, but on his second he struck political pay dirt. Turning south from Oregon into the future Nevada and then into the Sacramento valley, he passed through central and southern California and returned via Santa Fe. His report on this journey (largely written by Jessie), published in the fall of 1844, gave Washington its first knowledge of the feeble Mexican hold on California and the limitless riches and possibilities of that romantic land. Incidentally, it made Fremont a presidential candidate, and, later, one of the most inefficient generals on either side of the Civil War.

President Polk knew little about California except that it had three good harbors — San Francisco, Monterey, and San Diego; but he wished desperately to acquire it for the United States because he feared that England or France would grab it if he got into war with England over Oregon or with Mexico over Texas. No question of slavery was involved, only empire. There was, indeed, some reason for the President's apprehension. England and France were rapidly acquiring Pacific empires. New Zealand had been annexed in 1840 by the British, who did not want it, in order to keep it from the French, who did want it. In 1842 the French navy took the Marquesas, where Commodore Porter had hoisted the American flag in 1813, and bombarded Queen Pomaré out of Papeete. In 1843 King Kamehameha III of Hawaii proposed to place the 'Sandwich Islands' and his royal person under the protection of Queen Victoria. The British consul at Monterey repeatedly urged his government to acquire California; the British minister to Mexico suggested canceling Mexico's debt to Britain in exchange for California; and the British Admiralty wanted San Francisco Bay. Polk did not know this, but suspected the worst. He would have preferred to buy California from Mexico, but similar propositions respecting Texas had been turned down.

4. WAR WITH MEXICO

Shortly after Polk entered office, Mexico protested against the annexation of Texas, and broke diplomatic relations. From her point of view, Texas was still a rebellious province. In July 1845 Polk ordered a detachment of the regular army under General Zachary Taylor to take up a position on the Nueces river, the southwestern border of Texas, to protect the new state against a possible Mexican attack. If Polk had been content with Texas and had not reached out for something besides, there is no reason to suppose that Mexico would have initiated hostilities, although she might long have delayed acknowledging the annexation of Texas to the United States.

On 24 June 1845 the Secretary of the Navy sent secret orders to Commodore Sloat, commander of the Pacific station, to seize San Francisco if he should 'ascertain with certainty' that Mexico had declared war on the United States. In October the Secretary of War wrote to the American consul at Monterey, 'Whilst the President will make no effort and use no influence to induce California to become one of the free and independent States of the Union, yet if the people should desire to unite their destiny with ours, they would be received as brethren, whenever this can be done without affording Mexico just cause of complaint.' The situation in California was edgy — the number of North American immigrants and Mexicans was about equal, and each group hated the other.

While Polk was priming revolt in California, he proposed to see what could be got out of Mexico in exchange for claims. Like most nations at most times, the United States had claims on Mexico for repudiated bonds, revoked concessions, and damage done to American property during the civil war that broke out every few years. Hitherto the United States had been forbearing, in comparison with the French government, which sent a squadron to bombard San Juan de Ulúa in 1839. A mixed commission had awarded the United States about $1.5 million in 1841, and claims to about $3 million more had since accumulated. In 1843 the two countries ratified a convention by virtue of which Mexico was to pay the whole with accrued interest in twenty quarterly installments. After three installments Mexico suspended payment — as several states of the Union had done on their bonds — but did not repudiate the debt. Torn by civil dissension and virtually bankrupt, Mexico could not pay at that time, as President Polk knew and admitted.

On 10 November 1845 the President commissioned John Slidell minister plenipotentiary to Mexico, with instructions to offer that the United States assume the unpaid claims of its citizens against Mexico, in return for Mexican recognition of the Rio Grande as the southern boundary of Texas and of the United States. In addition, $5 million would be paid for the cession of New Mexico, and 'money would be no object' if California could also be bought. A practical man, Polk hoped to put through a business deal; but the Mexican government did not have a business mentality. Mexico refused to receive Slidell. At this juncture another revolution broke out in Mexico City, and by New Year's Day 1846 the government was in the hands of a faction which was spoiling for a fight with the United States. On 13 January 1846, the day after he had received word of Mexico's refusal to receive Slidell, Polk ordered General Taylor to take his army across the Nueces river, and to occupy the left bank of the Rio Grande del Norte. Thereby the President attempted to force the solution of a boundary controversy, and his view of the controversy was wrong. The Rio Grande had never been the southern boundary of Texas. The territory between it and the Nueces was a barren tract belonging to the Mexican state of Tamaulipas. Texas laid claim to the Rio Grande in her declaration of independence; but her authority as state or republic had never been exercised beyond the Nueces.

General Taylor, in obedience to orders, on 23 March 1846 took up a position on the left bank of the Rio Grande, with his guns bearing upon the Mexican town of Matamoros. The Mexican general in command of that district ordered him back to the Nueces (11 April). Taylor replied by blockading the Rio Grande in order to cut off food supplies from Matamoros (23 April). In spite of furious threats by the Mexican press, the Mexican government had made no military disposition threatening Texas, and had kept its forces out of the disputed territory between the two rivers.

On 25 April President Polk began to prepare a message to Congress urging war on the sole grounds of Slidell's rejection as minister and the unpaid claims — which amounted to only $3.2 million when adjudicated by a United States commission in 1851. On that very day Mexican cavalry had crossed the Rio Grande, engaged in a skirmish with United States dragoons, killed a few troopers, and captured the rest. This news reached Washington at 6:00 p.m. Saturday, 9 May. At a cabinet meeting that evening it was agreed that a war message, with documents proving the 'wrongs and injuries' the United States had suffered from Mexico, should be laid before Congress on Monday. And at noon on 11 May 1846, Congress got the message. 'The cup of forbearance has been exhausted,' declared the President. 'After reiterated menaces, Mexico has passed the boundary of the United States, has invaded our territory and shed American blood upon the American soil.' Two days later Congress declared that 'by act of the Republic of Mexico, a state of war exists between that Government and the United States.'

The record is clear: Polk baited Mexico into war over the Texas boundary question, in order to get California, after he had decided that Mexico would not sell California. One of the best exposés of the falseness of his claim that the Rio Grande flowed through United States soil was made by a freshman congressman from Illinois named Abraham Lincoln.

In the Mississippi valley the war was highly popular. Mexico evoked visions of gold and glory among the men of the frontier. Thousands of Western volunteers came forward, eager to 'revel in the halls of the Montezumas.' In the older states there was little enthusiasm and much opposition. The Mississippi valley and Texas together furnished 49,000 volunteers; the original Thirteen States only 13,000. The Whig party opposed the war, although with more wisdom than the Federalists of 1812 they voted for war credits and supplies in the hope that the Democrats would be hanged if given plenty of rope. Anti-slavery men and abolitionists regarded the war as part of an expansionist conspiracy of slave-owners:

> They just want this Californy
> So's to lug new slave-states in
> To abuse ye, an' to scorn ye,
> An' to plunder ye like sin.

Thus James Russell Lowell castigated the Mexican War in his *Biglow Papers*. And although few agreed with him that it was time to part from the slave states, the Whig legislature of Massachusetts declared that the Mexican War was a war of conquest, a war to strengthen the 'slave power,' a war against the free states, unconstitutional, insupportable by honest men, to be concluded without delay, and to be followed by 'all constitutional efforts for the abolition of slavery within the United States.'

That was nothing but talk, which not even the Whig party took seriously. Henry Thoreau, however, made his own protest against the war by refusing to pay his state poll tax. After he had spent a night in the

Concord lock-up, his aunt paid the tax and he went back to his cabin on Walden Pond. It sounds petty and futile, as one tells it. Yet, the ripples from that Concord pebble, like the shot of 19 April 1775, went around the world; Thoreau's *Essay on Civil Disobedience*, which he wrote to justify his action, became the best-known work of American literature to the peoples of Asia and Africa struggling to be free, and has earned the honor of having its sale prohibited in Communist countries.

5. GLORY AND CONQUEST

California, the main objective, lay beyond the principal seat of war, and became the scene of confusing conflicts. Frémont learned of the impending war with Mexico in May 1846, when encamped near Lower Klamath Lake. He moved his exploring expedition into the lower Sacramento valley, where his presence encouraged the settlers who wished to shake off Mexican rule. Hostilities began even before news arrived of the declaration of war; a few dozen American squatters in the Sacramento valley took possession of Sonoma with its commandant, proclaimed the 'Republic of California,' and waved a white flag with a bear and star painted on it (14 June 1846). Three weeks later Commodore Sloat, having heard of the outbreak of hostilities, raised the Stars and Stripes at Monterey and declared California a part of the United States. The Spanish-speaking Californians, not relishing these proceedings, rose in arms, re-occupied Los Angeles for a time, and had a brush with Colonel Stephen W. Kearny, who had led 500 troopers overland from Independence, mopping up Santa Fe on the way. But by the end of 1846 California was completely in the hands of the United States.

In the main theater of war, General Zachary Taylor began what he intended to be a march on Mexico City by pushing across the Rio Grande before war was even declared, and winning two minor engagements; but refused to move farther from his base until properly reinforced and supplied. Polk, who had never seen northern Mexico, thought that Taylor ought to live off the country. Finally men and munitions were sent. Taylor's army then advanced and captured the town of Monterrey (Nuevo Leon), after a tough three days' battle (21–23 September 1846).

President Polk was not too pleased with this brilliant victory. 'Old Rough and Ready' Taylor, an outspoken, blaspheming veteran of the Jackson breed, was becoming dangerously popular, and the Whigs began to talk of nominating him for the presidency in 1848. As a way out, Polk conceived the brilliant stroke of appointing Thomas H. Benton, the 64-year-old Senator from Missouri, Lieutenant General in command of the United States Army. Unfortunately for Mexico, Congress refused to create this new grade. The President then turned to Major General Winfield Scott of the regular army, a Whig indeed, but a dandy swashbuckler whose airs and foibles were unlikely to win golden opinions from democracy. Scott's plan to end the war by marching on Mexico City from Vera Cruz was now adopted.

Getting the army to Vera Cruz was the job of the United States Navy, which ruled the Gulf of Mexico virtually unopposed, having recently been strengthened by steam frigates and gunboats. Under command of Commodore David Conner, the Gulf Squadron floated Scott's army from Tampico and Brazos Santiago to a roadstead southeast of Vera Cruz and landed it, 12,000 strong, without loss, on a beach three miles from the city, on 9 March 1847. This was the biggest and most successful amphibious operation of the century. Cannon were then sited to fire on Vera Cruz and San Juan de Ulúa, both of which, after a few days' bombardment, surrendered on the 27th and were occupied by the United States for the remainder of the war. From Vera Cruz, Scott's army started for Mexico City on 8 April along the route that Cortés had followed three centuries earlier.

It was a brilliant campaign. General Scott, with little more than half the 20,000 troops he wanted, hampered by insubordinate volunteer officers who had been appointed for political reasons, thwarted by the jealousy and incompetence of the administration, often forced to live off the country and to fight with captured ammunition, managed to accomplish his ends. In two weeks' time he reached the fortified pass of Cerro Gordo. Captain Robert E. Lee found a way to outflank the Mexicans, a brilliant operation in which Captain George B. McClellan and Lieutenant Ulysses S. Grant took part. On 7 August General Scott cut connection with the coast. Three days later his army reached the divide 10,000 feet above sea level, with the wonderful Valley of Mexico stretching before, and the towers of Mexico City rising through the mist. More good staff work carried out by the engineers, and stiff battles at Contreras (7 August) and Churubusco (20 August), and the army was ready to push on into the city. At Churubusco the American forces lost 177 killed or missing and 879 wounded, or about one in seven; and most of these casualties were inflicted by the artillery of the San Patricio battalion, a Mexican outfit made up of Irish and other deserters from the United States Army. But 3000 Mexican prisoners (including eight generals!) were captured, and the victory was overwhelming.

In the meantime Polk had provided Mexico with a leader. General Santa Anna, in exile at Havana when the war broke out, was able to persuade Polk that, once in possession of the Mexican government, he would sign the sort of treaty that the President wanted. So he was allowed to slip through the United States blockading squadron into Vera Cruz to enter Mexico City in triumph in September 1846, to assume dictatorship and take command of the army facing Zachary Taylor in the north of Mexico. General Taylor beat him badly at Buena Vista (22–23 February 1847) — a splendid picture-book battle on a sun-soaked plain; a fight that advanced in politics both General Taylor and his son-in-law, Colonel Jefferson Davis, who distinguished himself and his regiment (uniformed in red shirts, white pants, and slouch hats) by breaking up a Mexican cavalry charge. Santa Anna raised more troops and turned south to oppose Scott's advance.

On that front, General Scott did not push on to the capital after his Churubusco victory, but accorded Santa Anna on armistice to start peace negotiations. Polk had attached to the American army as peace commissioner Nicholas Trist, chief clerk of the department of state. His instructions were to obtain the Rio Grande boundary for Texas, plus New Mexico, Upper California, and a right of transit across the Isthmus of Tehuantepec, one of the proposed interoceanic canal routes. The Mexican politicians, unable to face reality, made such an uproar on hearing these terms that Santa Anna decided to try another joust with Scott. The American army, refreshed by a fortnight among the orchards and orange groves of the Valley of Mexico, marched forward to a bloodbath at Molino del Rey (8 September), and five days later stormed its last obstacle, the fortified hill of Chapultepec, heroically defended by the boy cadets of the Mexican military school. On pushed Scott's troops, taking cover under the arches of the aqueducts, Lieutenants U. S. Grant and Raphael Semmes mounting howitzers on belfries and roofs. At dawn 17 September a white flag came out from Mexico City.

The Mexicans crowded windows and rooftops as a vanguard of battered, mud-stained doughboys [4] and hard-boiled marines, led by Brigadier General John A. Quitman, who had lost a boot in the latest fight, swung along to the main plaza. There the conquerors gazed with wonder on the great baroque cathedral and the lofty pink-walled palace — the Halls of the Montezumas at last. Presently a clatter of hoofs was heard on the stone-paved streets; and as the weary veterans snapped into 'Atten-*shun!* Present-*arms!*' General Scott, splendidly uniformed and superbly mounted, escorted by a squadron of dragoons with gleaming swords, came dashing into the plaza.

Santa Anna promptly abdicated, for the third but not the last time; and two months elapsed before Scott and Trist could find a Mexican government willing to negotiate peace. In the meantime the Gulf Squadron under Commodore Matthew C. Perry and the Pacific Squadron under Commodore Robert F. Stockton had established a tight blockade of both coasts of Mexico, preventing munitions and supplies, previously ordered from Europe, from reaching the Mexican army, and opening East Coast ports to neutral commerce.

Trist, recalled by Polk, remained, and negotiated the Treaty of Guadalupe Hidalgo (2 February 1848) in accordance with his original instructions. Mexico ceded Texas with the Rio Grande boundary, New Mexico, and Upper California (including San Diego) to the United States. The region embraced what would become the states of California, Utah, and Nevada, large sections of New Mexico and Arizona, and parts of Colorado and Wyoming. The victor assumed unpaid claims, and paid $15 million to boot — three-fifths of the amount Slidell had been instructed to offer for the same territory in 1846.

Democratic expansionists, intoxicated with success, chimed in with the new *vox populi* and advised the President to repudiate both Trist and the treaty. Polk coldly put the secretary in his place, and sent the treaty to the Senate, which ratified it after the usual bitter debate. One Whig senator described the treaty as 'negotiated by an unauthorized agent, with an unacknowledged government, submitted by an accidental President to a dissatisfied Senate.' With characteristic meanness, the

4. This term for infantrymen began in the Mexican War and lasted until World War II, when it was replaced by 'GI.' Army casualties in the Mexican War were 1721 killed in battle or died of wounds, 11,550 deaths from 'other causes,' mainly disease.

President then did his best to humiliate General Scott who had won the war and Mr. Trist who had made the peace. He relieved the former by a Democratic major general, and dismissed the resourceful chief clerk from the state department.

The United States had rounded out her continental area substantially to the present limits. It remained only to complete the present southwestern boundary of the United States by the 'Gadsden purchase' from Mexico (1853) of the Gila river valley, in southern Arizona. But it also remained to be seen whether these immense and valuable acquisitions would be settled peacefully, or become a bone of contention between pro- and anti-slavery interests, leading to civil war.

XXX

The Compromise of 1850

1. THE WILMOT PROVISO

John C. Calhoun was right, for once. He foresaw that the acquisition of new territory would bring the question of slavery expansion into the open. The man who opened the door was an obscure Democratic congressman from Pennsylvania named David Wilmot. On 8 August 1846, about twelve weeks after the war began, the President asked Congress for a secret appropriation of $2 million as a down payment to bribe Santa Anna into ceding California. Wilmot, in a short speech, remarked that although he understood this was not a war of conquest, it was all right with him to buy California; but he did not think it compatible with democratic principles to extend slavery into free territory. He therefore proposed as an amendment to the $2 million bill that on any territory so acquired 'neither slavery nor involuntary servitude shall ever exist.' The phrase was copied from the Northwest Ordinance of 1787, which had so dedicated the territory north of the Ohio. This was the famous 'Wilmot proviso.'

The question of slavery extension was no mere abstract principle. To be sure many believed it was; they thought the geography of the West erected a barrier against the spread of slavery. 'What do you want? — what do you want? — you who reside in the free States?' Clay would ask shortly. 'You have got what is worth more than a thousand Wilmot provisos. You have nature on your side.' Nor was the question immediately practical; even when they had a legal right to do so, few

557

slaveholders would go West in the next decade. The 1860 census numbered only two slaves in Kansas. Yet, in truth, there was no climatic or natural bar to slavery extension, or to the Negro race — after all, a Negro was one of the two men who accompanied Admiral Peary to the North Pole in 1909. If slavery could flourish in Texas, why not in New Mexico, Arizona, and points west? In the warm climate and rich soil of southern California, Negro slaves, if introduced, would undoubtedly have thrived and multiplied, just as the Chinese and Mexicans did who later filled the demands of ranchers and fruit growers for cheap labor.

The Wilmot proviso provoked bitter sectional animosity. To many Northerners it seemed monstrous for the 'land of the free' to introduce slavery, even in principle, where it had never previously existed.[1] Every Northern state legislature except one passed resolutions approving the anti-slavery proviso. The beneficiaries would not be slaves but Northern whites. As Wilmot bluntly put it: 'I would preserve for free white labor a fair country, a rich inheritance, where the sons of toil, of my own race and color, can live without the disgrace which association with negro slavery brings upon free labor.' While Northern anti-slavery men were pressing for adoption of the proviso, the Illinois constitution of 1848 excluded free Negroes, and Iowa in 1851 stipulated severe penalties for any Negro who dared enter that state. To Southerners the proviso seemed an insult to their 'peculiar institution.' The South had watched anxiously as population gains gave the North control of the House; soon the admission of new free states would upset the balance in the Senate. Eventually, the North might have enough seats in Congress and enough state legislatures to put through a constitutional amendment to interdict slavery in the South. Now Wilmot was proposing to seal off the South so that it could never hope to add even one more slave state to the Union, unless Texas split up.

President Polk proposed that lat. 36° 30′ (the old Missouri Compromise line of 1820) divide freedom and slavery in the new territories as in the old; but there were too many extremists for this common-sense compromise to be accepted. Southern Whigs who voted for the proviso in the interest of peace were denounced as traitors to the South; Northern Democrats who voted the other way, for the same reason, were branded 'dough-faces' or 'Northern men with Southern principles.' The

1. In earlier territorial acquisitions — Louisiana, Florida, and Texas — slavery had been established under the French, Spanish, and Lone Star flags.

Wilmot proviso did not pass, nor did any measure to organize the newly acquired territory. American settlers in the Far West lacked law and government, because Congress could not decide whether or not they could have slaves. Oregon in 1848 was finally organized as a territorial government without slavery, but Polk's presidential term ended on 4 March 1849 before anything had been done about California, New Mexico, or Utah.

Hitherto, it had been widely accepted that Congress could legislate slavery in or out of a territory, since the Constitution gave it the power to 'make all needful rules and regulations respecting territory or other property belonging to the United States.' Congress had recognized slavery in some territories, such as Mississippi, and banned it from others, such as Indiana and Minnesota. From the Wilmot proviso debates emerged new and conflicting theories: (1) Congress has the right and duty to prohibit slavery wherever its jurisdiction extends: freedom must be national, slavery sectional. In a little while the Free-Soil and Republican parties will be founded to enforce this doctrine. (2) Neither Congress nor any territorial government has power to prohibit slavery in the territories. In a little while the South will insist that the Government must act positively to protect the slaveholder who takes his 'property' into a territory: freedom is sectional, slavery national. (3) Not Congress but the people of the territory shall decide whether or not they will have slavery, as soon as they obtain a territorial legislature. This doctrine of 'popular sovereignty,' first put forth by Caleb Smith of Indiana, would be given prominence by Lewis Cass of Michigan and vigorously advanced by Stephen Douglas of Illinois.

It was difficult to sustain the extreme Southern view, traversing as it did a constitutional practice of sixty years; but the mind of Calhoun was equal to the task. The territories, he argued, belonged to the states united, not to the United States. Congress was merely the attorney of a partnership, and every partner had an equal right to protection for his property in the territories. Slaves were common-law property; Lord Mansfield's contrary dictum in the Sommersett case (1772) did not affect America. Consequently the Mexican laws against slavery ceased to have effect in California and New Mexico when they were annexed to the United States. If Congress had, in 1820, prohibited slavery in territories north of lat. 36° 30', that act was unconstitutional and void. Slavery followed the American flag, wherever firmly planted. Calhoun's new doctrine, embodied in resolutions by the Virginia legislature in 1847, became the 'platform of the South'; and in the Dred Scott case of 1857 it was read into the Federal Constitution. Only one more step, feared many Northerners, and slave-owning would come to be regarded as a natural right, which not even a state legislature could impair.

It is idle to debate whether Wilmot or Calhoun, North or South was the aggressor in this matter. All depends on the moral standpoint. If slavery was a positive good or a practical necessity, any attempt to restrict or to pinch it out by degrees would justify Southern indignation, if not secession. If slavery was an evil and a curse, any attempt to establish it in virgin territory, even nominally, would be an affront to the public opinion of the Christian world. Motives on both sides were fundamentally defensive. Even when Calhoun wrote of forcing the slavery issue in the North, his motive was to protect the domestic institutions of the slave states. Even when Seward and Chase asserted that every inch of the new territory must be free soil, their object was to defend Northern farmers, wage-earners, and lovers of liberty against further wars and encroachments of the 'slave power,' and against more competition to free labor by slave labor. To yield on the issue of the territories, it was feared, would merely encourage extremists on the other side to new aggressions. It is just such matters of prestige and strategic advantage that bring on great wars.

The state of the American Union in 1848 may be compared with that of Europe in 1913 and 1938; possibly with the world in the late 1960's. Political and diplomatic moves become frequent and startling. Integrating forces will win apparent victories, but in reality grow feebler. The tension increases, until some event that in ordinary times would have no great consequence precipitates a bloody conflict.

2. ELECTION OF '48; GOLD RUSH OF '49

At a time of mounting crisis, both parties in 1848 turned to men with military backgrounds, since generals have a useful talent for blurring issues and winning votes. The Democrats named Senator Lewis Cass of Michigan, an ardent expansionist, veteran of 1812, and Jackson's Secretary of War. The Whigs nominated General Zachary Taylor, hero of the Mexican war. A third party, the Free-Soil, was formed in the North by

a coalition of three hitherto separate and hostile elements — the abolitionist Liberty party, the 'conscience' or anti-slavery Whigs of New
England, and 'locofoco' or 'barnburner' faction of the New York Demo-
crats, whom Polk had ignored in distributing patronage. The Free-
Soilers also embraced a number of Northern (especially Western)
Democrats who had been angered when a tariff bill carried by the vote
of two Texas senators and when Polk, with Southern support, vetoed a
rivers and harbors bill which would have benefited the Great Lakes.
'Free soil, free speech, free labor, and free men' was the slogan. Martin
Van Buren, convinced that only slavery restriction could save the
Union, accepted the Free Soil presidential nomination, with the 'Con-
science' Whig, Charles Francis Adams, as his running mate. Among the
former Democrats who rallied to the Free-Soil standard was David
Wilmot.

Although the Free-Soil party carried not one state, it rolled up an
impressive 10 per cent of the popular vote, and by taking Democratic
votes from Cass in states like New York and Pennsylvania, made possible Taylor's victory. Since little was known of Taylor's views, the Whigs
had been able to offer him to voters in different sections according to
which posture would draw the most support. In the South, they pointed
out that 'Old Rough and Ready' was a Louisianan who held more than
a hundred slaves on a Mississippi plantation; Louisiana, Florida, and
Georgia gave the Whigs their ballots. Northern voters heard that Taylor was friendly to the Wilmot proviso. The strategy worked; Taylor,
with only 47 per cent of the popular vote, received 163 electoral votes
to Cass's 107. But the Whigs bought victory at too high a cost; for once
in office they would inevitably alienate a large section of their followers. The Southern Whigs were especially vulnerable for they were tied
to a leader said to be committed to an extreme Northern position. The
Whig party was living on borrowed time.

Nathaniel Hawthorne in 1849 lost his post in the Salem custom
house, and proceeded to write *The Scarlet Letter*. Walt Whitman the
same year was fired from the *Brooklyn Eagle* for supporting Van
Buren, and proceeded to write *Leaves of Grass*. These were among the
results of Zachary Taylor's election, and of the clean sweep that followed in the civil service. General Taylor was a simple, honest soldier,
who detested the sophistries of politicians and regarded the slavery
question as an artificial abstraction. He was ready to sign any bill Con-

gress might pass for organizing new territories; but before Congress could resolve the deadlock, California proposed to skip the territorial stage altogether, and to become a free state of the Union.

On 24 January 1848, shortly before peace was signed with Mexico, a workman in the Sacramento valley discovered gold in Sutter's millrace. The news spread rapidly, and by the end of the year everyone in America, Australia, and western Europe had heard of fortunes made from the stream beds of the Sierra Nevada, merely by separating the golden grains from the sand in a common washbowl. Farmers mortgaged their farms, pioneers deserted their clearings, workmen put down tools, clerks left their desks and even ministers their pulpits, for the California gold washings. Young men organized companies with elaborate equipment and by-laws, and were 'grub-staked' by local capitalists as the Elizabethan seadogs had been financed by merchant adventurers. The people of Cutler, in eastern Maine where living was hard, built and rigged their own ship, provisioned her with salt fish and hardtack, and sailed to San Francisco. Any and every route was taken by the 'forty-niners'; round the Horn in the slowest and craziest sailing vessels, across the continent by the Oregon or California trails, or, if pressed for time, by the Isthmus of Panama. It seemed as if all the world were chanting, to the tune of 'Oh! Susanna' —

> Oh! California,
> That's the land for me;
> I'm off for Sacramento
> With my washbowl on my knee

By the end of 1849 thousands of Argonauts from every part of Europe, North America, and the antipodes, were jumping each other's claims, drinking, gambling, and fighting in ramshackle mining villages such as Red Dog, Grub Gulch, and Poker Flat. San Francisco arose in a few months from a village to a city of 20,000 or 25,000, where eggs laid on the other side of Cape Horn sold for $10 a dozen, and a drink of whiskey cost a pinch of gold dust; where Englishmen and Frenchmen, Yankees and Hoosiers, Georgia 'crackers' and Missouri 'pukes' rubbed shoulders with Indians, Mexicans, Sydney 'ducks,' and the 'heathen Chinee.' Fortunes were made in the gold-diggings, to be lost in a night at a 'Frisco faro palace; even more were made by speculation in goods and land. It was a state of nature that would have made Rousseau a tory. Owing to neglect by Congress the government was still military in theory, though impotent in fact; *alcaldes* and *ayuntamientos* appointed by the military governor administered any sort of law they pleased — it might be the code of Mexico or of Napoleon, or of Judge Lynch.

So California went ahead and made herself a state, with the blessing of President Taylor. His military governor issued writs of election for a convention which met at Monterey in September 1849 and drafted a state constitution prohibiting slavery. This constitution was ratified by a popular vote of over 12,000 ayes to 800 noes. Without waiting for congressional sanction, the people chose a governor and legislature which began to function in 1850. Only formal admission to the Union was wanting; and on that issue the Union almost split.

Up to this time the most extreme Southerners had admitted the right of a state to prohibit slavery — for slavery was emphatically a state matter. But if California were admitted to the Union with its 'Wilmot proviso' constitution, the slave power would have lost over half the American conquests from Mexico. During 1849 the temper of the South had been steadily rising. The governor and legislature of South Carolina only hesitated from secession because they hoped to unite the entire South on that program. Calhoun wrote 'I trust we shall persist in our resistance [to the admission of California] until the restoration of all our rights, or disunion, one or the other, is the consequence. We have borne the wrongs and insults of the North long enough.' California's demand for admission, when Congress convened in December 1849, at once started a movement for a Southern Convention. Like the Hartford Convention of 1814, this was intended by extremists to form a stepping-stone toward a new confederacy.

The South felt insecure. Since 1801 the section had obtained from the Union all she really wanted, and the South had disproportionate strength in the national government. But it was hard to keep such facts in mind. From every side — England and New England, Jamaica and Mexico, Ohio and the Northwest, and now California, abolition seemed to be pointing daggers at her heart. Hence fear, the worst of political counselors, came to supersede thought. But it was not wholly fear that moved the South. What Benét called 'the purple dream,' the vision of a great slaveholding republic stretching from the Potomac into the tropic seas, monopolizing the production of cotton and so dictating to the world, was beginning to lift up the hearts of the younger and more radical Southern leaders, like Robert Barnwell Rhett and William L. Yancey. Slavery must expand to live; to contract its area, or even to admit that it might be contracted, would mean that the abolitionists had the South on the run.

3. THE UNION PRESERVED

Zachary Taylor, the fourth distinguished soldier to be elected President of the United States, was the first to have had no political experience whatsoever; he had been in the army for over 40 years, and during that time had never once cast his vote in a presidential election. He proved to be straightforward, sincere, and, although a large slaveholder, devoid of pro-slavery sentiment. He saw no reason why the South should be bribed to admit California as a free state if California wanted freedom.

The House of Representatives that met in December 1849 was so factional that 63 ballots were taken before it could elect a speaker, and the opinions on slavery of candidates even for the post of door-keeper had to be made the subject of careful inquiry. President Taylor recommended the immediate admission of California with her free constitution and the organization of New Mexico and Utah territories without reference to slavery. To protesting senators from Georgia, the old soldier declared his determination to crush secession wherever and whenever it might appear, if he had to lead the army personally.

In the Senate, leaders of the new generation such as Jefferson Davis, Stephen A. Douglas, William Seward, and Salmon P. Chase, sat with giants of other days such as Webster, Clay, and Calhoun. It was Henry Clay who divined the high strategy of the moment. Union sentiment was not ripe to meet the issue of secession. Concessions must be made to stop the movement now; time might be trusted to deal with it later. On 27 January 1850 he brought forward the compromise resolutions that kept the peace for ten years. The gist of them was (1) immediate admission of free California to the Union; (2) the organization of territorial governments in New Mexico and Utah, without mention of slavery; (3) a new and stringent fugitive slave law; (4) abolition of the domestic slave trade in the District of Columbia; (5) assumption of the Texan national debt by the Federal Government.

These resolutions brought on one of those superb Senate debates that did so much to mold public opinion. Clay defended them in a speech that lasted the better part of two days. Haggard in aspect and faltering in voice he rose to speak, but his passionate, unwavering devotion to the Union seemed to bring back all the charm and fire of 'Young Harry of the West,' and to lift him and his audience to high issues. He appealed to the North for concession and to the South for peace. He asked the North to accept the substance of the Wilmot proviso without the principle and honestly to fulfill her obligation to return fugitive slaves. He reminded the South of the great benefits she derived from the Union and warned her against the delusion that secession was constitutional, or could be peaceful, or would be acquiesced in by the Middle West. For Clay was old enough to remember the excitement in Kentucky when Spain and France had attempted to stop her river outlet. 'My life upon it,' he offered, 'that the vast population which has already concentrated . . . on the headwaters and the tributaries of the Mississippi, will never give their consent that the mouth of that river shall be held subject to the power of any foreign State.'

Calhoun, grim and emaciated, his voice stifled by the catarrh that shortly led to his death, sat silent, glaring defiance from his hawk-like eyes, while his ultimatum was voiced for him by Senator Mason of Virginia (4 March 1850). 'I have, Senators, believed from the first that the agitation of the subject of slavery would, if not prevented by some timely and effective measure, end in disunion.' 'The cords that bind the States together' are snapping one by one. Three great evangelical churches are now divided. The Federal Union can be saved only by satisfying the South that she can remain within it in safety, that it is not 'being permanently and hopelessly converted into the means of oppressing instead of protecting' her. Senator Clay cannot save the Union with his compromises. The North must 'do justice by conceding to the South an equal right in the acquired territory' — which, he explained, meant admitting slavery to California and New Mexico — returning fugitive slaves, restoring to the South through constitutional amendment the equilibrium of power she once possessed in the Federal Government.[2] And the North must 'cease the agitation of the slave question.' Note well this imperative as to free speech, even in the North.

2. There seems no doubt that Calhoun's proposed amendment would have taken the form of a dual executive, one President elected by the North and one by the South, each armed with a veto.

Three days later Webster rose for his last great speech. His voice had lost its deep resonance, his massive frame had shrunk, and his face was lined with suffering and sorrow. But in his heart glowed the ancient love of country, and the spell of his personality fell on Senate and galleries with his opening words: 'I speak to-day for the preservation of the Union. "Hear me for my cause." ' He attacked both the abolitionists and the Wilmot Proviso. 'I would not take pains to reaffirm an ordinance of nature, nor to re-enact the will of God,' he said. Viewing the situation eye to eye with Clay, Webster merely restated in richer language the points made by his old-time rival; but the North could never have been induced to swallow a new fugitive slave law, had not Webster held the spoon. Just as his reply to Hayne in 1830 stimulated the growth of Union sentiment, so the Seventh of March speech of 1850 permitted that sentiment to ripen, until it became irresistible.

Senator Seward of New York, in opposing the compromise from the opposite angle, spoke for the 'conscience' Whigs. He admitted that Congress had the constitutional power to establish slavery in the territories. 'But there is a higher law than the Constitution which regulates our authority over the domain': the law of God, whence alone the laws of man can derive their sanction. The fugitive slave bill would endanger the Union far more than any anti-slavery measure. 'All measures which fortify slavery or extend it, tend to the consummation of violence; all that check its extension, and abate its strength, tend to its peaceful extirpation.'

Yet for all the skill of Clay, the omnibus measure stalemated. Southern firebrands denounced it, and in the North abolitionists portrayed Webster as a lackey of the slavehounds. Senators exchanged blows; an official bloodied the face of a congressman; a Mississippi senator confronted Senator Benton with a cocked and loaded revolver. With the older generation stymied, the young men took over. One of the youngest in the Senate was Stephen A. Douglas of Illinois, a sturdy five-footer, chock-full of brains, bounce, and swagger. In August, with the struggle now in its eighth month, the 'little giant' put together a winning combination, with the support of fellow Democrats, who proved sturdier than the Whigs.

In early September 1850 the essential bills passed: the admission of California; a more stringent fugitive slave law; the organization of New Mexico and Utah as territories free to legislate on slavery and to enter the Union with or without slavery when sufficiently populous; curbing of the slave trade in Washington; adjustment of the Texas boundary; assumption of the Texas debt. The Compromise of 1850 did not repeal the Missouri Compromise; the 1820 enactment dealt with the Louisiana purchase land only, the 1850 law exclusively with the territory acquired from Mexico. The act had some disappointing consequences. The Fugitive Slave Law failed to bring sectional peace; the free state of California added a surprising element to the argument over sectional balance when it sent pro-slavery men to the Senate; and the slave trade continued to flourish in the District. But it was a satisfactory compromise in that it gave both North and South something each badly wanted, and the New Mexico-Utah bills avoided both the Wilmot proviso 'stigma' and the forcible introduction of slaves to regions which had none. Once more the Union was preserved by the same spirit of compromise that created it; but for the last time.

Another year elapsed before it was certain that the secession movement in the cotton states could be stopped. In the state elections Whigs and Democrats disappeared. The contest was between a Union party led by the Georgian triumvirate, Alexander H. Stephens, Robert Toombs, and Howell Cobb; and a 'Southern rights' or immediate secession party, led by Robert Barnwell Rhett, John A. Quitman, and William L. Yancey. The Unionists met the secessionists on their own ground, denying the existence of a constitutional right of secession. In every cotton state the Unionists won, although in South Carolina and Mississippi the contest was very close.

In the North, Democrats accepted the compromise, Free-Soilers and abolitionists denounced it in the most frenzied terms; the Whigs, in spite of Webster's eloquence, were divided in sentiment between acquiescence and repudiation. It was the Fugitive Slave Act which stuck in Northern throats. If only the South could have realized that the one hope for slavery was to let the North forget about it, instead of perpetually rubbing it in by hunting runaways through Northern streets and countryside! Even Emerson, the serene philosopher who had advised the abolitionists to love their white neighbors more and their colored brethren less, wrote in his journal, 'This filthy enactment was made in the nineteenth century, by people who could read and write. I will not obey it, by God!'

'Old Rough and Ready,' now 65 years old, succumbed to a combination of official scandals, Washington heat, and doctors. The scandal he knew nothing about until it broke, for like other military Presidents he trusted too many rascals. Governor G. W. Crawford of Georgia, Taylor's Secretary of War, had taken over, on a fifty-fifty basis, the settlement of an old pre-revolutionary claim which originally amounted to less than $45,000. With the help of his friends he got a bill appropriating that amount through Congress. Then, by a smart triple play with the Attorney General and Secretary of the Treasury, Crawford got an additional payment of $191,353 for 73 years' interest, the half of which made him a nice little fortune. As ventilated by Congress, this Galphin claim affair, as it was called, smelled worse than anything of the sort prior to the Credit Mobilier scandals in the administration of U. S. Grant, the next soldier President.

On 4 July 1850, already depressed by the Galphin revelations, Taylor was subjected to two hours' oratory by Senator Foote in the broiling sun, and then tried to cool off by consuming an excessive quantity of cucumbers, washed down with copious draughts of iced milk. Washington, with its open sewers and flies, was always unhealthy in the summer, and the President came down with acute gastroenteritis, then called cholera morbus. He would probably have recovered if left alone, but no President ever had that chance. The physicians of the capital, assisted by a quack from Baltimore, rallied around his bedside, drugged him with ipecac, calomel, opium, and quinine (at 40 grains a whack), and bled and blistered him too, until he gave up the ghost on the 9th. The death of Taylor, denounced in the South as a Southern man of Northern principles, helped make possible the adoption of the Compromise, for his successor, Vice-President Millard Fillmore, shared the outlook of Webster and Clay. Fillmore signed all the compromise acts before Congress adjourned on 30 September 1850, after a record session of 302 days.

One more giant of other days had already passed. Calhoun died on 31 March 1850. His coffin made a triumphal progress through the Southern states to Charleston, where friends and followers pledged devotion to his principles by the marble tombstone over his grave in St.

Philip's churchyard. Would he have led the secession party in the next decade, or would he have moderated the more rabid state-righters? We can never know. But no strong man was now left to control the new generation of angry young men in South Carolina.

Andrew Jackson had died peacefully in his 'Hermitage.' John Quincy Adams, stricken at his seat in the House, had been carried out of the Capitol to die. 'Old Bullion' Benton was defeated for re-election to the Senate in 1851; his Andrew Jackson nationalism had grown old-fashioned in Missouri. Clay and Webster, the one denounced as traitor by Southern hotspurs, the other compared with Lucifer by New England reformers, had only two years to live; but that was time enough to teach them grave doubts whether their compromise could long be maintained and whether their party could survive their departure.

With their death the second generation of independent Americans may be said to have gone. The galaxy of 1812 that had seemed to bind the heavens together, like the great constellation of Orion, was extinguished.

XXXI

Young America

1. CALM BEFORE STORM

Passage of the Compromise of 1850 caused the slavery question to sub-side for a short time, while other matters occupied the nation. Jenny Lind, the Rochester spirit-rappings, and the newly popular game of baseball supplanted the Compromise as topics of conversation. Neal Dow won a famous victory with the Maine prohibitory law, and Timothy S. Arthur's *Ten Nights in a Bar-Room* spread the gospel of temperance. Not that slavery was forgotten. *Uncle Tom's Cabin*, published in 1852, served to keep it in the back of people's minds; but everyone save Northern abolitionists and Southern 'fire-eaters' wished to let it remain there.

The country enjoyed the fruits of its flourishing economy. In the 1850's steam engine and machinery output shot up 66 per cent, cotton textile production 77 per cent, coal mined 182 per cent, hosiery goods 608 per cent. Immigration reached a new high level, and by 1860 New York City's population would exceed one million. Craft unions were negotiating agreements with their employers; the National Typographic Union (1852), the United Hatters (1856), and the Iron Moulders' Union of North America (1859) were the first permanent federations. An English traveler in 1850 noted that 'all classes of the people may be said to be well dressed and the cast off clothes of one class are never worn by another.' Yacht racing and intercollegiate rowing were introduced, together with vulgar luxury. In New York, Newport, and Saratoga, according to the season, could be found 'a set of exquisites — daintily arrayed men who spend half their income on their persons, and shrink from the touch of a woollen glove . . . delicate and lovely women, who wear the finest furs and roll in the most stylish equipages.'

The promise that America would fulfill her destiny through quality rather than quantity was never brighter than in the 1850's. Consider the great books of that decade in American literature. In 1850–51: Hawthorne's *Scarlet Letter* and *House of the Seven Gables*, Melville's *White Jacket* and *Moby-Dick*, Emerson's *Representative Men* and *English Traits*. In 1852, Melville's *Pierre*; in 1854–56, Thoreau's *Walden*, Whitman's *Leaves of Grass*, and Melville's *Piazza Tales*. In 1857 the *Atlantic Monthly* was founded, with James Russell Lowell, satirist of slavery and the Mexican War, as editor, and Longfellow, Whittier, and Dr. Holmes (whose *Autocrat* appeared in 1858) as contributors. This was Longfellow's most productive decade, with *The Golden Legend* (1851), *Hiawatha* (1855), and *The Courtship of Myles Standish* (1858). Whittier published his *Songs of Labor* in 1850 and his 'Maud Muller' and 'Barefoot Boy' in 1856. And Parkman's *Conspiracy of Pontiac* (1851) opened a great historical series that required 40 years to complete.

But all these were Northern writers. In the South, Poe was dead; John P. Kennedy had obtained his political reward as President Fillmore's Secretary of the Navy; William Gilmore Simms, still writing historical novels, was so neglected by his native Charleston as to be left out of a semi-official list of literature suitable for young Southerners. Materially, the Cotton Kingdom was consolidating and becoming more conscious of its strength. Kentucky backwoodsmen, who in the 1830's had taken up land in the black belts, were now gentleman planters, mingling on equal terms with the first families of Virginia in the White Sulphur, the Hot, the Warm, and the Sweet Springs. Their elder sons, after leading volunteers in the Mexican War, had become lawyers or planters in turn; their younger sons were patronizing the newer colleges of the Lower South, or attending the University of Virginia, with hounds and hunters and black servants. Dread of abolition, with its implication of Negro equality, bound yeomen and poor whites more closely to their slaveholding neighbors. There seemed to be no limit to cotton production. The annual crop rose from 1000 million to 2300 million pounds, but never lacked purchasers. De Bow's progressive *Review* was preaching the use of guano, conservation of soil, diversification of crops, local manufactures; and, ominously, a revival of the African slave trade.

The Southern railway network, encouraged by financial aid from states, counties, and towns, greatly extended. Georgia built a railroad across the southern end of the Appalachians, which helped to make Atlanta and Chattanooga great cities; Charleston planned a railway to the Ohio river to siphon off Western trade from New York, with a connecting steamship line to Europe; and by 1860 there was through rail connection between New York and New Orleans. Several other promising efforts were made toward bringing this section into line with dynamic and expanding America, but there was too little time to make them effective. Southern liberals and industrialists of the 1850's for the most part were lonely individuals, looked down upon by aristocratic planters, neglected by politicians, scolded by journalists, and unable to make any dent on the hardening shell of the 'slavocracy.'

The presidential election of 1852 proved that an overwhelming majority of Americans were disposed to regard the Compromise of 1850 as final and that economic questions were predominant once again. Since both parties endorsed the Compromise, party lines were drawn not on slavery but on such old economic issues as the tariff and internal improvements. The Democratic party nominated Franklin Pierce of New Hampshire, whose only apparent qualifications were a winning smile and a fair military record in the Mexican War. No more were needed. The New York 'barnburners,' starved for four lean years with the Free-Soilers, returned to their Democratic allegiance; and thousands of Southern Whigs, disgusted by the anti-slavery tendencies of Northern Whigs, went over to their opponents. General Winfield Scott, the Whig presidential candidate, made himself rather ridiculous in the campaign; and, although he was a Virginian by birth, that asset was canceled by a nationalist career which recalled Jackson, Harrison, and Taylor. Although Pierce won less than 51 per cent of the popular vote, he handed the Whigs a drubbing in the electoral column, where Scott carried only four states. The Whigs would never recover from this defeat.

2. MORE 'MANIFEST DESTINY'

Republicanism and democracy appeared to be sweeping the western world. After the revolution of 1848, France adopted a constitution which was a centralized edition of that of the United States. Within the Democratic party, a 'Young America' movement sprang up, devoted at first to creating ideals of service and duty, then to enlisting Young America's aid for democrats beyond the seas, and finally to electing Stephen A. Douglas to the presidency. Walt Whitman spoke for Young America in his poem on the flag:

O hasten flag of man — O with sure and steady step, passing highest flag
    of kings,
Walk supreme to the heavens mighty symbol — run up above them all
Flag of stars! thick-sprinkled bunting!

When the new European republics were crushed, Walt sounded the note of robust optimism that has heartened thousands of imprisoned and exiled patriots:

Liberty, let others despair of you — I never despair of you!

There had been wild talk in 1848 of annexing Ireland and Sicily to the United States, as certain revolutionists in those countries requested; and when the news came that Hungary had fallen and had been forcibly incorporated with Austria, the legislatures of New York, Ohio, and Indiana called for action. In Congress many senators from Western states voted for a resolution to suspend diplomatic relations with Austria; but the cautious Whigs and Southern Democrats voted it down. Louis Kossuth, brought to New York as guest of the nation in 1851, was given an overwhelming ovation, and a Harvard professor who exposed Hungarian humbug was forced to resign. 'Europe is antiquated, decrepit, tottering on the verge of dissolution,' declared Senator Douglas. 'It is a vast graveyard.'

American diplomacy was particularly truculent when directed by Southern gentlemen who wanted new slave territory, as compensation for the 'loss' of California. Cuba, during these eventful years, was in its usual state of unrest. Certain Southern statesmen professed to fear lest the island fall to England, or become a black republic like Haiti. Others had an eye on the large and redundant slave population there. Polk, still in the market for new territory after the vast acquisitions from Mexico, proposed to buy Cuba in 1848 for $100 million, but Spain rejected his offer with contempt. Then came filibustering expeditions, frowned upon by Taylor, tolerated by Fillmore and Pierce; and consequent interference by the Spanish authorities with Yankee traders. One such instance, the case of the *Black Warrior* (1854), seemed a good opportunity to provoke Spain into war. The Secretary of War, Jefferson Davis, urged President Pierce to take that line; but the Secretary of State, William L. Marcy, kept his head; and Spain disappointed the annexationists by apologizing.

There was a comic anticlimax when the American ministers to Spain, France, and Great Britian held a meeting at Ostend and drafted a serious recommendation to Marcy (18 October 1854) on how to settle the Cuban question. 'In the progress of human events the time has arrived,' they pompously argued, 'when the vital interests of Spain are as seriously involved in the sale as those of the United States in the purchase of the island' of Cuba. With the purchase money, Spain might 'become a centre of attraction for the travelling world,' and 'her vineyards would bring forth a vastly increased quantity of choice wines.' Should she be so unreasonable as to refuse, then, 'by every law, human and divine, we shall be justified in wresting it from Spain if we possess the power.' The New York *Herald* made a 'scoop' of this secret document and published it as the 'Ostend Manifesto.' Its only effect was to lower American prestige in Europe and that of Pierce at home. The Cubans' consent to being annexed was never asked; and it is interesting to reflect whether, if it had been, a José Martí or a Fidel Castro would have arisen to demand *Cuba Libre* from the United States.

3. JAPAN OPENED

Not only trouble but much good flowed from the territorial acquisitions of the Mexican War. The difficulty of communicating with California and Oregon by overland trail led to the project of an interoceanic canal, the perfection of the sailing ship, plans for transcontinental railways, and diplomatic relations with the Far East.

American diplomacy now crossed the Pacific. In 1844 Caleb Cushing, as the first United States minister to China, negotiated a treaty by which American ships obtained access to certain Chinese seaports, and American merchants acquired extraterritorial privileges.

Japan had been closed for two centuries to all foreign intercourse, save a strictly regulated trade with the Dutch and Chinese at Nagasaki. Her government was feudal, her economy medieval — no factories, no steamships or steam engines, only small junks allowed to be built in order to keep the Japanese at home. Foreign sailors wrecked on the shores of Japan were not allowed to leave, and Japanese sailors wrecked on foreign coasts were not permitted to return. Commodore James Biddle USN tried to open relations at Tokyo Bay in 1845, but was surrounded by small guard boats and forced to leave.

Largely to protect castaways from the growing American whaling fleet, President Fillmore decided to make another try. He entrusted the mission to Commodore Matthew C. Perry, brother of the hero of Lake Erie and commander of the Gulf Squadron in the Mexican War. The Commodore, who had had diplomatic experience dealing with Turkey, Naples, and several African kings, studied every available book on Japan. On 8 July 1853 his armed squadron, including steam frigates *Mississippi* and *Susquehanna,* anchored in the mouth of Tokyo Bay. Perry's orders forbade him to use force, except as a last resort; but the Kanagawa Shogun who then ruled Japan was so deeply impressed by the Commodore's show of force that, contrary to all precedent, he consented to receive the President's letter to the Emperor. Perry tactfully sailed to Macao, in order to give the elder statesmen time to make up their minds; and by the time he returned (February 1854), with an even more impressive squadron, they had decided to yield. Conferences were held at the little village of Yokohama, where gifts were exchanged: lacquers and bronzes, porcelain and brocades, for a set of telegraph instruments, a quarter-size steam locomotive complete with track and cars, Audubon's *Birds* and *Quadrupeds of America,* an assortment of farming implements and firearms, a barrel of whiskey, and several cases of champagne. Thus old Japan first tasted the blessings of Western civilization! Progressive Japanese leaders, who wished to put an end to isolation, persuaded the Shogun to sign the Treaty of Kanagawa (31 March 1854), allowing the United States to establish a consulate, assuring good treatment to castaways, and permitting American vessels to visit certain Japanese ports for supplies and repairs.

Such was the famous 'opening' of Japan, and it was Perry's proud boast that without firing a shot he had effected what European nations had failed to do by using force. His published *Narrative* of the Expedition (1856) included a description of Japanese manners and customs, and a prediction that Japan, not China, would become the most powerful nation in East Asia. President Buchanan sent Townsend Harris, a New York merchant, to Japan as the first American consul. Harris's fine character and genuine appreciation of the Japanese cemented friendship between the two countries, and Japan's first foreign mission visited Washington in 1860.

In the 1850's the Ryukyu and Bonin Islands were virtually independent of Japan. With the local king's unwilling permission, Perry used Naha, Okinawa, as a temporary base. Both for the navy, which was rapidly being converted from sail to steam, and for the merchant marine, Commodore Perry was eager to obtain a coaling station. He bought land for one at Chichi Jima from a group of New Englanders and Hawaiians who had settled there many years earlier, and instructed them to set up a local government under American protection. But the navy department and Congress refused to implement his actions, and a few years later Japan formally annexed both island groups. Ninety years later, Okinawa and Iwo Jima, near Chichi Jima, were occupied by the United States after heavy fighting.

Cushing's Chinese treaty and Perry's Japan Expedition were far more significant than their immediate results. They mark the beginning of an active role for the United States in East Asia.

4. ISTHMIAN DIPLOMACY

In the matter of communications between the older United States and her new Pacific territories, the simplest solution appeared to be an interocean canal. Three routes were seriously considered: across the Isthmus of Tehuantepec, the Isthmus of Panama, and via Lake Nicaragua. Over the first route, which was not practical for a canal, President Pierce obtained by the Gadsden treaty of 1853 the privilege to build a road and the right of transit, even in time of war. This concession, never used, was formally abrogated in 1937. Over the Isthmus of Panama, President Polk in 1846 obtained right of transit by treaty with Colombia, in return for guaranteeing to that republic her sovereignty over the Isthmus, and undertaking to defend its neutrality. A Panama railway, built by American capital, was completed in 1855. But the Nicaragua route brought on a sharp controversy with Great Britain.

When the Monroe Doctrine was first announced, the British had two bases in Central America: the old logwood establishment of Belize or British Honduras, and a shadowy protectorate over the Mosquito Indians of Nicaragua. Owing to the weakness of the local republics, the enterprise of British agents, and indifference at Washington, British influence increased in Central America between 1825 and 1845. The Belize government took possession of the Bay Islands off the coast of Honduras in 1838, and the British government stationed a 'resident' in 'Mosquitia,' which thus became an Indian satellite state with a flag incorporating the Union Jack. Lord Palmerston, who returned to the foreign office in 1846, believed it high time to check 'manifest destiny' in that part of the world, and in 1848 formally declared the sovereignty of 'Mosquitia' over San Juan or Greytown, the eastern terminus of the proposed Nicaragua ship canal. Both the Indians and the old picaroons who inhabited the Bay Islands hated Spanish Americans and wanted British protection.

All this created a very ticklish situation, from which the United States and United Kingdom emerged by negotiating the Clayton-Bulwer treaty (15 April 1850). It was agreed that neither government would ever fortify, or obtain exclusive control over, the proposed Isthmian canal. Both guaranteed its neutrality and invited other nations to join. Later generations of Americans regarded the Clayton-Bulwer treaty as a sellout; but at the time it was a fair compromise between the concessions that Britain had obtained in Central America when the American government was indifferent, and the new interest that the United States had acquired by becoming a Pacific power.

As American capitalists showed no enthusiasm for building a ship canal, the Clayton-Bulwer treaty might have caused no embarrassment for many years, but for ambiguous clauses. The United States government supposed that they meant British withdrawal from the Bay Islands, Greytown, and the Mosquito coast; although it did not object to the ancient custom of crowning some local chief with an old admiral's chapeau as King of Mosquitia, if that gratified him and amused the authorities of Belize. The British government insisted that the treaty merely forbade future acquisitions, and held onto what it had. This dispute became dangerous in 1854, when President Pierce and the Democrats were looking for an issue to distract the country from the slavery question. The game of 'twisting the lion's tail' then began, the object being to produce a roar that would be grateful in the ears of native and

Irish-American voters. But the game terminated in 1859–60 when Britain ceded the Bay Islands to Honduras and the Mosquito coast to Nicaragua.

In the meantime, a curious episode occurred in Nicaragua. Cornelius Vanderbilt, 'commodore' of the Hudson river steamboat fleet, organized a company to compete with the Panama railway. It ran steamers up the San Juan river and across Lake Nicaragua, whence freight was forwarded to the Pacific by muleback. Wanting political stability in that region, this company financed William Walker, a professional filibuster, known to his friends as 'the gray-eyed man of destiny,' to overthrow the existing government of Nicaragua. Walker, who had tried, and failed, to filibuster Lower California into a new slave state, in 1856 succeeded in making himself President of Nicaragua. He planned (with the approval if not the actual support of Pierce's Secretary of War, Jefferson Davis) to introduce Negro slavery and to push a scheme to conquer the rest of Central America. But he had the bad judgment to quarrel with Vanderbilt and seize his ships. The 'commodore' then supported a Central American coalition that invaded Nicaragua, and Walker surrendered in 1857. Twice more this prince of filibusters tried; on his second attempt, in 1860, he was seized and executed by a Honduran firing squad.

5. CANADIAN RECIPROCITY

Midway in the Isthmian negotiations there was established a landmark in North American commerce and diplomacy, the Canadian Reciprocity Treaty of 1854. The onward march of free trade in Britain harassed Canada's feelings and played fast and loose with her interests. Preference for colonial grain and flour had given Canada the business of milling American wheat for the British market. Sir Robert Peel's repeal of the British corn laws abolished this preference and prostrated the industry. At the request of the Canadian legislature the British government attempted to negotiate at Washington a reciprocity treaty for Canada, and Parliament passed an enabling act.

Canada could offer in return free navigation of the St. Lawrence and access to the fishing grounds off Labrador and the Gulf of St. Lawrence where the sportive mackerel was wont to elude Yankee fishermen. But it was a difficult matter to effect that exchange. The foreign office and the state department had no trouble in concluding a reciprocity treaty, but such a treaty required concurrent acts of Parliament, of Congress, and of four Canadian legislatures; and the Maritime Provinces were loath to admit Yankees to their offshore fisheries. Secretary of State Marcy greased the way at Halifax, Fredericton, and St. John by a judicious expenditure of secret service funds; and Lord Elgin, a hard-headed but genial Scot, is said to have floated the treaty through the United States Senate on 'oceans of champagne.' If true, both served their respective countries well. The treaty (5 June 1854) opened the United States market to Canadian farm produce, timber, and fish, and Canada to American rice, turpentine, and tobacco; the bait for Southern support is obvious. Yankee fishermen got new privileges in Canadian territorial waters, and the American merchant marine obtained the right to navigate the Great Lakes, the St. Lawrence, and their connecting canals. Thus Britain maintained her political dominion over Canada by sanctioning a partial economic union with the United States.

6. THE CLIPPER SHIP

While the diplomats were wrangling over future canals to the Pacific, the shipwrights of New York and New England were engaged in cutting down the time of ocean passage around Cape Horn. In one month of 1850, 33 sailing vessels from New York and Boston entered San Francisco bay after an average passage of 159 days. Then there came booming through the Golden Gate the clipper ship *Sea Witch* of New York, 97 days out. At once the cry went up for clipper ships at any price.

This new type of sailing vessel, characterized by great length in proportion to breadth of beam, an enormous sail area, and long concave bows ending in a gracefully curved cutwater, had been devised for the China-New York tea trade. The voyage of the *Sea Witch* showed its possibilities. Her record was broken by the *Surprise* of Boston within a year, and in 1851 the *Flying Cloud* of Boston made San Francisco in 89 days from New York, a record never surpassed and only twice equaled, once by herself. As California then afforded no return cargo except gold dust (the export of wheat began only in 1855), the Yankee clippers sailed in ballast to the Chinese treaty ports, where they came into competition with the British merchant marine; and the result was more impressive than the victory of the yacht *America*. Crack East-Indiamen humbly waited for cargo weeks on end, while one American clipper after another sailed off with a cargo of tea at double the ordinary freights. When the *Oriental* of New York appeared at London, 97 days from Hong Kong, crowds thronged the dock to admire her beautiful hull, lofty rig, and patent fittings; the admiralty took off her lines in dry dock, and *The Times* challenged British shipbuilders to set their 'long practised skill, steady industry and dogged determination' against the 'youth, ingenuity and ardour' of the United States.

In 1852 Donald McKay of Boston launched the *Sovereign of the Seas*, the largest merchant vessel yet built and the boldest in design: stately as a cathedral, beautiful as a terraced cloud. A young American naval officer, Lieutenant Matthew Fontaine Maury of Virginia, had been charting trade winds and ocean currents by the study of ships' logs. It was he who discovered that the strong and steady westerly gales were to be found in the 'roaring forties' south latitude. Following his sailing directions, the *Sovereign of the Seas* on her homeward passage made a day's run of 411 nautical miles, surpassed only seven times in the history of sailing vessels, only twice by the product of another shipyard than McKay's.

By this time the British Navigation Acts had been repealed, and gold had been discovered in Australia. For that destination the *Sovereign* was chartered in Liverpool, and made so successful a voyage that four clippers were ordered of Donald McKay for the Australian Black Ball Line. Three of them, *James Baines, Lightning*, and *Champion of the Seas*, were the world's fastest sailing ships. The *Baines*, with her skysail studding-sails and main moonsail, established the record transatlantic sailing passage — 12¼ days Boston to Liverpool — and then another from Liverpool to Melbourne — 63 days — that still holds good. The *Lightning* on her maiden voyage made a day's run of 436 nautical miles. From noon to noon, 11–12 December 1854, *Champion of the Seas*, whose design combined the imposing majesty of a man-of-war with the airy grace of a yacht, fulfilled the bold challenge of her name by hanging up the greatest day's run of all time by a sailing vessel, 464 nautical miles, an average of almost 20 knots.

Nightingale and *Witch of the Wave, Northern Light* and *Southern Cross, Young America* and *Great Republic, Golden Age* and *Herald of the Morning, Red Jacket* and *Westward Ho!, Dreadnought* and *Glory of the Seas* —

> I cannot tell their wonder nor make known
>
> .   .   .   .
>
> These splendid ships, each with her grace, her glory,
> Her memory of old song or comrade's story,
> Still in my mind the image of life's need,
> Beauty in hardest action, beauty indeed [1]

No sailing vessel ever approached them in power, majesty, or speed. Yankee ingenuity, with its latent artistic genius, had at last found perfect and harmonious expression. Yet the clipper fulfilled a very limited purpose: speed to the goldfields at any price or risk. When that was no longer an object, no more were built; and when the panic of 1857 brought a world-wide depression in shipping, it was the clipper-ship owners who suffered first and most. British builders, leaving glory to their rivals, were quietly evolving a more useful type of medium clipper and perfecting the iron screw steamer.

The American iron industry and engineering trades were so backward, and the extent of inland and protected waters in the United States so great, that American steamship builders clung too long to the wooden side-wheeler, unsuitable for ocean work. The Pacific Mail did well in its own sphere, and for a few years the Collins Line, heavily subsidized by Congress, challenged the Cunard; but its vessels had an unfortunate way of foundering. By 1857 the British empire had an ocean-going steam tonnage of almost half a million tons, as compared with 90,000 under the American flag. England had won back her maritime supremacy in fair competition, by the skill of her engineers and her shipbuilders. Civil war turned the Yankee mind to other objects; the two world wars revived an ancient challenge.

1. John Masefield, 'Ships'; quoted by kind permission of the late Poet Laureate and Messrs. Macmillan.

1854   1859

The Irrepressible Conflict

1. PRAIRIE SETTLEMENT AND PACIFIC RAILWAYS

In the 1850's economic change had an enormous impact on political events. Increasingly the lines of force in the American economy moved on an East-West axis rather than on a West-South axis. To be sure the Mississippi trade flourished; the Illinois Central Railroad forged a link between the South and the Northwest; and cotton still played a significant role in North-South trade. But cotton was no longer king. The Northeast, which now did not raise enough food for its own needs, provided the most important market for the Western farmer. And the Northwest, no longer so dependent on the South, turned its gaze away from the slave-tilled plantations and toward the empire of rolling prairie and Great Plains.

Down to 1850 American agricultural settlement had been largely confined to the forests and to small prairies. The pioneers depended on wood and running water, and the wide treeless tracts of Illinois and Iowa were devoid of shelter and remote from markets. Their earliest settlers had to live in sod cabins, and contend with wolves, prairie fires, and locusts. Many emigrants preferred to take the long journey to Oregon, where they could renew the backwoods life that they loved. As late as 1849 one could look northward from a knoll near Peoria, Ill., over an undulating plain, unbroken by a house or tree as far as the eye could reach.

But in the 1850's the prairie farmer became the typical American pioneer. In part the change was due to new agricultural machinery, which helped to cope with the labor shortage; for, owing to the amazing fertility of the prairies, grain crops were often too abundant to harvest with scythe, cradle, and sickle, even when all the neighbors within 30 miles pitched in. The important principle of the modern reaper, a moving knife against a fixed finger, was the basis of reaping machines invented independently by Obed Hussey at Cincinnati and Cyrus H. McCormick in Virginia, and patented respectively in 1833 and 1834. By 1851 McCormick, the better business man and organizer, was building a thousand reapers a year at his Chicago plant. Marsh's harvester, which gathered the wheat into sheaves, Appleby's self-knotting binder, and the steel-toothed cultivator followed later. An improved form of plow with a steel mold-board made it easier to break up the tough prairie sod. Steel wire solved the fencing problem. Yet the greatest impetus to prairie farming came from the rising price of wheat (from $0.93 a bushel in 1851 to $2.50 in 1855 at the New York market) and from the transportation revolution. The value of merchandise shipped to the West over the Erie Canal soared from $10 million in 1836 to $94 million in 1853. Railways linked the East with the farms and burgeoning cities of the Northwest. In 1850 railroads had hardly penetrated the Middle West; by 1860 their network covered it. The railway mileage in the old Northwest increased from 660 in 1847 to 7653 in 1861, that of the United States as a whole from 9,021 to 30,265. The prairie farmer, hitherto dependent on long wagon hauls over execrable roads, could at last market his grain and livestock to advantage. As the Illinois prairie filled up, the state moved away from its Southern ties. One Illinois politician ruined his political future in an attempt to preserve the old alliance, and another Illinois politician led a new North-and-West political party which caused the South to seek safety for slavery in secession.

A struggle over the route of the first transcontinental railway promoted the same result. Of the many schemes projected since 1845, the four most important were (1) the Northern, from the upper Mississippi to the upper Missouri and by Lewis and Clark's trail to the Columbia river; (2) the Central, from St. Louis up the Kansas and Arkansas rivers, across the Rockies to the Great Salt Lake and by the California trail to San Francisco; (3) the Thirty-fifth Parallel route from Memphis, up the Arkansas and Canadian rivers, across the Rockies near

Santa Fe, and through the Apache and Mojave country to Los Angeles; (4) the Southern, from New Orleans up the Red river and across Texas and by the Gila valley to Yuma and San Diego.[1] Either of the first two would follow existing trails and bind the Far West to the old Northwest; but the unorganized Indian country was an obstacle. The Southern route was the shortest, with the best contours, and led through states and territories already organized.

Congress, in March 1853, authorized surveys of these four routes under the direction of the war department, whose secretary was Jefferson Davis of Mississippi. He saw that the Southern route might well be the means of the South's recovering all she had lost by the Compromise of 1850; and, although a state-rights man, he advocated its construction by the Federal Government under the war power. As soon as the survey showed that a Southern railway would have to pass through Mexican territory south of the Gila river, Davis induced President Pierce and Congress to buy the land for $10 million. The Gadsden treaty of 30 December 1853 effected this purchase.

The stage was now set for Congress to sanction the Southern route.

2. THE KANSAS-NEBRASKA BILL

Stephen A. Douglas, the senior senator from Illinois, was the best orator in the Northwest and the idol of Northern Democrats. As an Illinoisan, he was sensitive to the demands of prairie folk for the organization of the trans-Missouri country to open it to settlement. He wished to erase the 'barbarian wall' of Indian tribes impeding migration to the plains and 'to authorize and encourage a continuous line of settlements to the Pacific Ocean.' A heavy speculator in Western lands, including the city site which he expected to be the eastern terminus of the railroad, he favored a Central route for the transcontinental railway. In order to contest Davis's southern route, law and government must be extended over, and settlers invited into, the region through which the Central route must pass. Ambitious politicians, Douglas and his fellow Democrats in the Washington boardinghouse known as the 'F Street Mess,' sought a promising political issue for

1. These, in order, were followed in part by (1) the Northern Pacific; (2) the Missouri Pacific, Denver & Rio Grande, and Southern Pacific; (3) the Rock Island and the Santa Fe; and (4) the Texas Pacific and Southern Pacific.

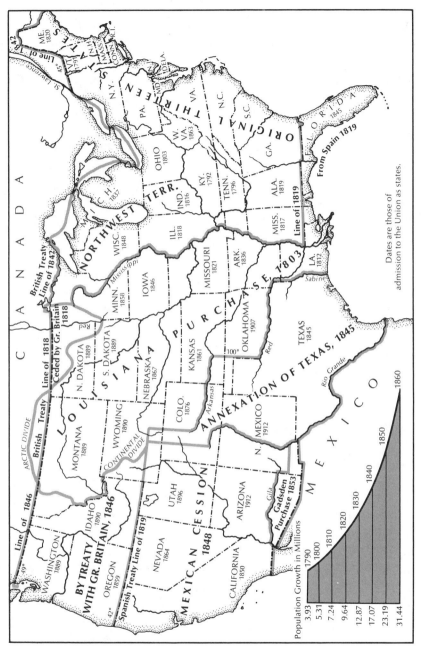

Dates are those of admission to the Union as states.

TERRITORIAL GROWTH OF THE UNITED STATES

Population Growth in Millions

Year	Millions
1790	3.93
1800	5.31
1810	7.24
1820	9.64
1830	12.87
1840	17.07
1850	23.19
1860	31.44

1856. For these reasons, and probably for others known only to himself, the 'Little Giant' reported a bill to organize the Great Plains as the Territory of Nebraska, in January 1854. Earlier bills of this nature had been defeated by Southern senators. So Douglas baited this one for Southern votes by incorporating the principle of popular sovereignty. At the insistence of Southern leaders, he made clear that his bill would render the Missouri Compromise 'inoperative and void.' Furthermore, the bill, as amended, divided the region into two distinct territories: Kansas and Nebraska.

Douglas miscalculated grievously. He thought reopening the slavery question a minor matter; personally opposed to slavery, he believed the Plains would be inhospitable to it. But Northerners were incensed at a proposal to permit the slave power to extend its domain into a virgin land which more than 30 years before the Missouri Compromise had closed to the slaveholder 'forever.' People could hardly have been more startled by a proposition to repeal habeas corpus and trial by jury than they were by the Kansas-Nebraska bill. Anti-slavery men raged at the Northern apostate; as Douglas himself said, he could have traveled from Boston to Chicago by light of his burning effigies. The North, in Lincoln's picturesque phrase, was determined to give her pioneers 'a clean bed, with no snakes in it.' Nor did Douglas realize how passionate the South had become over maintaining prestige.

For three months the bitter, angry debate dragged on. President Pierce tried to whip his party into line, and all but a few Northern Democrats obeyed. Old Sam Houston of Texas reminded the Senate in vain that by solemn treaties it had confirmed most of Kansas and Nebraska to the Indians 'as long as grass shall grow and water run.' No one else thought of the aborigines. Federal agents were already bullying them into renouncing their 'perpetual' titles. The once powerful Delaware or Leni-Lenape accepted a small reservation with an annual bounty. Others, like the Shawnee and Miami, who had once terrorized the Kentucky frontier and beaten a Federal army, were removed to the Indian Territory, which fortunately lay between the rival railway routes.

Democratic discipline triumphed. On 25 May 1854 the Kansas-Nebraska bill passed the Senate by a comfortable majority, and received President Pierce's signature. 'It is at once the worst and best Bill on which Congress ever acted,' declared Senator Charles Sumner. The worst, inasmuch as it is a present victory for slavery. The best, for 'it

Fairview Inn by Thomas Ruckle. A view of the National Road

View of the Upper Village of Lockport, New York, 1836. After a drawing by W. Wilson.

View of St. Louis from Lucas Place, 1855-60

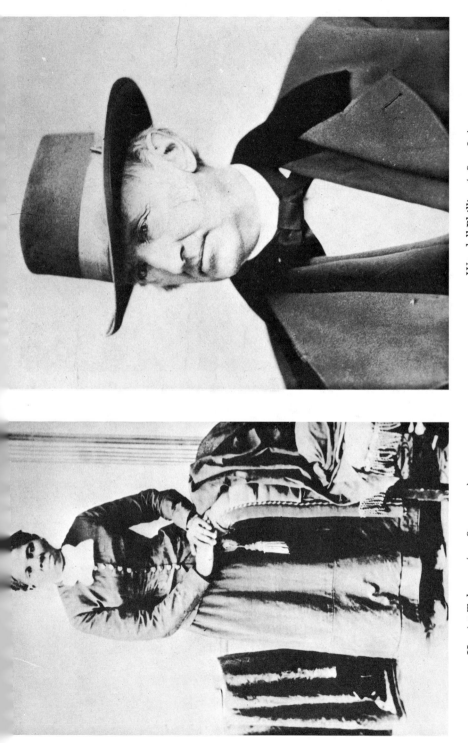

Wendell Phillips (1811-84)

Harriet Tubman (c. 1823-1913)

Herman Melville (1819-91) by Joseph Oriel Eaton

Nathaniel Hawthorne (1804-64)

The Verdict of the People by George Caleb Bingham

An Emigrant Train Fording Medicine Bow Creek, Rocky Mountains, by Samuel Colman

Laramie's Fort by A. J. Miller

The Last of the Buffalo by Albert Bierstadt

San Francisco, 1853. From Charles A. Dana,
The United States Illustrated, New York, 1853.

James K. Polk (1795-1849) by G.P.A. Healy

annuls all past compromises with slavery, and makes all future compromises impossible. Thus it puts freedom and slavery face to face, and bids them grapple. Who can doubt the result?'

'If the Nebraska bill should be passed, the Fugitive Slave Law is a dead letter throughout New England' wrote a Southerner in Boston. 'As easily could a law prohibiting the eating of codfish and pumpkin pies be enforced.' It did pass; and the very next day (26 May) a Boston mob led by a Unitarian minister tried to rescue a fugitive slave from the courthouse where he was detained for examination. They did not succeed. Anthony Burns, the slave, was identified by his master and escorted to the wharf by a battalion of United States artillery, four platoons of marines, and the sheriff's posse, through streets lined with silent spectators and covered with crepe, with every church-bell tolling a funeral dirge. It cost the United States some $40,000 to return that slave to his master; and he was the last to be returned from Massachusetts.

3. THE BREAK-UP OF PARTIES

The first palpable result of the Kansas-Nebraska Act was the creation of a new anti-slavery party. A convention held under the oaks at Jackson, Mich., on 6 July 1854, resolved to oppose the extension of slavery, and 'be known as "Republicans" until the contest be terminated.' Many places, especially Ripon, Wisconsin, claim the birthplace of the G.O.P., but Jackson at least made the happy suggestion of adopting Jefferson's old label. The new party, however, was slow in gathering momentum outside the Northwest. Seward sulked in his Whig tent; the 'Anti-Nebraska Democrats' were loath to cut all connection with their party; the Free-Soilers could not see why a new party was needed. With the old parties breaking up, many people hearkened to a new gospel of ignorance.

Know-Nothingism was a No Popery party. Nativists feared that the Catholic Church threatened republican institutions. Everyone knew that the Pope had his eye on America, for who would dwell in decaying Rome when he could live in the Mississippi Valley? Anti-Catholics had long derived a vicarious pleasure from projecting on priests and nuns their own licentious fantasies; they thrived on volumes like Maria Monk's *Awful Disclosures of the Hotel Dieu Nunnery of Montreal*

(1836), called the 'Uncle Tom's Cabin of Know-Nothingism.' Nativists were alarmed too by the rising flood of immigrants. In 1845, the immigrant tide passed the 100,000 a year mark for the first time; only two years later it had reached 200,000 and by 1854 had more than quadrupled. It was charged that the newcomers corrupted the nation's morals; one observer complained, 'They bring the grog shops like the frogs of Egypt upon us.' Even more important, nativists believed that the immigrants were sapping republican institutions. Between 1850 and 1855 in Boston, native-born voters increased 15 per cent, foreign born 195 per cent. The declining Whigs attributed Pierce's victory in 1852 to the immigrant vote.

Accordingly native-born Protestants formed a secret 'Order of the Star-Spangled Banner,' with elaborate ritual and rigid discipline. Members, when questioned by outsiders, answered 'I know nothing.' Candidates nominated secretly developed surprising strength at the polls, and many politicians joined up, thinking that this was the wave of the future. In the state elections of 1854 the Know-Nothings almost won New York and did win Massachusetts, electing a new legislature that passed some good reform laws but also conducted a clownish investigation of Catholic schools and convents. The new party sent some 75 congressmen to Washington; especially strong in New England and the border states, it also found a considerable following in the South. At Baltimore where the white working class was still largely native-born, the Know-Nothings organized 'plug-uglies,' gangs who attended the polls armed with carpenters' awls, to 'plug' voters who did not give the password. In some Baltimore wards, loaded swivel-guns were stationed at the polls to intimidate the Democrats, and bands of 'native American' hoodlums drove through the streets on election day, firing pistols and insulting women. St. Louis, in August 1854, was the scene of a series of pitched battles between Native Americans and Irish Catholics — the Germans staying carefully aloof. The police and militia were helpless, many lives were lost, and order was restored only after the mayor, Edward Bates (later Lincoln's Attorney General) had organized a force of 700 armed citizens to combat the rival mobs.

In the summer of 1855 the American party, as the Know-Nothings now called themselves, held a national convention of which the Southern members obtained control, passed pro-slavery resolutions, and nominated for the presidency old Millard Fillmore. The Northerners then lost interest; and except in Maryland, which voted for Fillmore in 1856, the movement collapsed. By 1856 it was no longer able to offer the nation an escape from the slavery question. 'Anything more low, obscene, feculent,' wrote Rufus Choate, 'the manifold heavings of history have not cast up.' Mr. Choate did not live to see the Ku Klux Klan, the American Nazi Party, the Minute Men, and similar manifestations of later eras.

4. BLEEDING KANSAS, 'BLACK' REPUBLICANISM

'Bleeding Kansas' soon diverted attention from the 'Popish peril.' Most of the settlers who came to Kansas went there to build a new life and live in peace, not to agitate the slavery question. When blood was shed, it was often not over the freedman but in a dispute about land titles, for there was no legal way a settler could register and protect his land claim until the Federal Government opened its first land office in 1856. The Kansas struggle also involved quarrels over government patronage and grants and contracts. Yet the new territory also witnessed a savage conflict over slavery which helped to plunge the nation into civil war.

In the elections for the territorial legislature in March 1855, several thousand 'border ruffians' crossed over from Missouri to stuff ballot boxes. The legislature elected by such fraudulent means then put through a drastic slave code. The free-state men responded by setting up their own rump government, and by 1856 Kansas had two governments, both illegal. Since popular sovereignty was to settle the question of slavery in Kansas, sectional rivals dispatched settlers into the state. The New England Emigrant Aid Company sent some 1240 migrants into Kansas. After Missourians had sacked their first settlement at Lawrence, the Company started arming its forces with a new breech-loading weapon, the Sharps rifle, or 'Beecher's Bible,' so called after the abolitionist preacher who advised its use. Parties of Northern 'Jayhawkers' battled with 'Kickapoo Rangers,' 'Doniphan Tigers,' and other organizations from Missouri and points south. 'We had at least seven thousand men in the Territory on the day of the election, and one-third of them will remain there,' wrote Senator Atchison of Missouri. 'The pro-slavery ticket prevailed everywhere. . . . Now let the Southern men come on with their slaves. Ten thousand families can take possession of and hold every acre of timber in the Territory of Kansas, and this secures the prairie. . . . We are playing for a mighty stake; if we win, we carry slavery to the Pacific Ocean.'

Few Southerners, however, cared to risk valuable property in such a region, and free-state settlers came in with the spirit of crusaders. The whole North thrilled to the marching song which John Greenleaf Whittier wrote for them:

> 'We cross the prairie as of old
> The pilgrims crossed the sea
> To make the West, as they the East,
> The homestead of the free.'

One of the newcomers, a fanatic named John Brown, was responsible for the murder of five men, four of whom were hacked to death, at the 'Pottawatomi massacre.' Such were the workings of popular sovereignty. The Kansas conflict was one of those contests preliminary to major wars, as were the Balkan Wars of 1912–13 to World War I, and the Spanish Civil War to World War II.

Could nothing be done to prevent a head-on collision? The abolitionists were no help. Garrison, who had long since denounced the Constitution as 'a covenant with death and an agreement with hell,' publicly burned a copy of it. Nor were Southern extremists. George Fitzhugh demonstrated conclusively that 'Southrons' were descended from the civilized peoples of France and the Mediterranean while Yankees were the offspring of German peasants, and welcomed a separation. One of the few constructive proposals came from the Sage of Concord. Before the Anti-Slavery Society of New York on 6 February 1855, Emerson proposed that slavery be extinguished by granting full compensation to the owners. Unlike the abolitionists, and Northern radicals generally, Emerson understood that the slave-owner was caught in a trap, from which emancipation on the British model seemed to be the only peaceful escape. The Federal Government and the states could give the proceeds of public lands; 'the churches will melt their plate,' wealthy benefactors will give their thousands and school children their pennies; 'every man in the land would give a week's work to dig away this accursed mountain of sorrow once and forever out of the world.' [2]

Nobody seconded the motion, and even Emerson did not say what the fate of the freed Negro was to be. The South was determined on no

2. Emerson Mss., Harvard College Library. The speech was well reported in the New York *Herald*, 7 Feb. 1855.

condition to give up slavery, and the North was unwilling to pay the masters to do it. Emerson's estimate of the cost, $200 million, was cheap enough in comparison with the Civil War.

On 19 May 1856 Senator Sumner of Massachusetts delivered a speech on 'The Crime against Kansas,' which contained some unpalatable truth, much that was neither truthful nor in good taste, and some disgraceful personal invective against Senator Andrew Butler of South Carolina. Three days later, a kinsman of Butler, Preston Brooks, attacked Sumner as he sat at his desk in the Senate chamber and beat him senseless with a stout cane, while Stephen Douglas and Robert Toombs looked on. He was following the code of a Southern gentleman in dealing with an enemy unworthy of a duel. 'Towards the last he bellowed like a calf,' Brooks reported. 'I wore my cane out completely but saved the Head which is gold.' Returning to South Carolina, the assailant was feted from place to place and presented by admirers with suitably inscribed canes. From Louisiana, Braxton Bragg wrote, 'You can reach the sensibilities of such dogs only through their heads and a big stick.'

A few days after this affair, the new Republican party held its first national nominating convention at Philadelphia. The Republicans embraced diverse elements: anti-slavery radicals like Charles Sumner; former Whigs, many of a conservative stripe such as Bates of Missouri; Free-Soil Democrats like Chase and Lyman Trumbull; and dissatisfied Know-Nothings. Glamorous John C. Frémont, the 'Pathfinder,' stampeded the convention and obtained the first Republican presidential nomination. The platform proclaimed it 'both the right and the duty of Congress to prohibit in the territories those twin relics of barbarism, polygamy and slavery.'

The Democratic convention in Cincinnati marked the first time it had met west of the Appalachians, another sign of the rising importance of the Western city. Flabby James Buchanan, for twenty-five years disappointed at not getting the Democratic presidential nomination, now wrested it from pleasant Mr. Pierce, who has the sad distinction of being the only man elected President of the United States to be denied a second term by his own party. The professional Democrats felt that Pierce had become too much involved in the Kansas-Nebraska business, on which Buchanan, as minister to Great Britain, was able to avoid commitment.

The 'Black Republicans,' as their enemies called them, conducted a lively campaign. 'Free soil, free speech, and Frémont,' was their slogan.

PRESIDENTIAL ELECTIONS, 1840, 1844, 1856

Slavery in the territories was the only real issue. Buchanan won with only 45 per cent of the popular vote. He swept the South and every border state but one, and took five Northern states as well. Frémont polled only 33 per cent, not much more than Fillmore did, although the Pathfinder had the backing of the Know-Nothings' Northern wing as well as his own party. The ominous aspect to Frémont's 1.3 million votes was that all but 1200 came from non-slaveholding states.

No previous candidate had so nearly united North and West against the South. Party divisions were approaching dangerously close to the Mason-Dixon Line; and the Lower South, even in this campaign, made it perfectly clear that it would secede if a purely Northern party elected its presidential candidate.

5. DRED SCOTT

On 6 March 1857, two days after Buchanan's inauguration, the Supreme Court published its decision on the famous case of Dred Scott v. Sandford. Dred Scott was a slave who had been taken by his master to Illinois, thence to the unorganized territory north of lat. 36° 30', where slavery had been forbidden by the Missouri Compromise, and finally back to Missouri, where he sued for freedom on the ground of having twice been resident of free soil.

Chief Justice Taney and the four Southerners among the associate justices hoped through this case to settle the question of slavery by extending it legally to all territories of the United States. President-elect Buchanan put Justice Catron up to it, in order to restore harmony to the Democratic party. Catron informed him what to expect, so that Buchanan slipped a clause into his inaugural address declaring that the Supreme Court was about to determine 'at what point of time' the people of a territory could decide for or against slavery, pledging his support to their decision, and begging 'all good citizens' to do likewise.

Poor, foolish Buchanan! He had hoped for a peaceful term of office, but the Dred Scott case unleashed the worst passions of pro- and anti-slavery when his administration was less than a week old. The nine justices filed nine separate opinions. Taney, speaking for the Court, declared against Scott's claim for freedom on three grounds: (1) as a Negro he could not be a citizen of the United States, and therefore had no right to sue in a Federal court; (2) as a resident of Missouri the laws of Illinois had no longer any effect on his status; (3) as a resident of the territory north of lat. 36° 30′ he had not been emancipated because Congress had no right to deprive citizens of their property without 'due process of law.' The Missouri Compromise, it followed, was unconstitutional and void (as Calhoun and other Southerners had long claimed), and slavery followed the flag.

On all these points the Chief Justice's opinion was either vulnerable or mistaken. As Justice Curtis asserted in his vigorous dissenting opinion, Negroes had always been considered citizens in most of the Northern states, and thus had the right to sue in the Federal courts. Under the generally accepted rule of interstate comity, Missouri had in seven earlier cases recognized the claim to freedom of a slave who had resided in free territory. And Congressional authority over slavery in the territories had been acknowledged by every branch of the government for 70 years. As for 'due process of law,'[3] that term in the Constitution referred to the method of enforcing the law, not to its substance.

Only once before, in Marbury v. Madison (1803), had the Supreme Court declared an Act of Congress unconstitutional. In that case the law directly concerned the Federal judiciary; but the Missouri Compromise was a general law, resting on the precedent of the Ordinance of 1787, on the statute books for 34 years. By its ruling the Court had sanctioned Calhoun's doctrine that slavery was national, freedom sectional, a doctrine which departed violently from the principle of international law that slavery existed only in local law. Oregon and Nebraska, as well as Kansas, were opened to the slaveholder. Squatter sovereignty thenceforth was no sovereignty; slavery was theoretically legal in every territory of the United States.

Buchanan reeled from disaster to disaster. The conclusion of the Crimean War, which deprived the farmer of a prime market in Europe, came at a time when the North was feeling the effects of the collapse of the Western land boom and paying the price for a weak banking structure and an overbuilt railway system; by October, the Panic of 1857 had hit with full force. Congressmen returned to Washington at the

3. The phrase is from Amendment V of the Constitution and is a translation of *per legem terrae* in Magna Carta. Lincoln observed in his Springfield speech of 17 June 1858 that the Chief Justice's construction of 'due process' would invalidate every state emancipatory act, since a similar clause was in the Bill of Rights of every Northern state constitution.

end of 1857 to cope with the Kansas question in an atmosphere of anxiety over the economy and in the midst of a religious revival which intensified sectional sensitiveness about slavery.

Events in Kansas pointed toward civil war. A convention chosen by a minority of the voters had adopted the 'Lecompton constitution,' an out-and-out pro-slavery charter, subsequently ratified in a bogus referendum. The free-state faction then drafted its own constitution and got it ratified in an extra-legal referendum. Each group appealed to Washington for statehood. Despite the travesty of the fraudulent elections, Buchanan insisted on pushing the Lecompton constitution through Congress. He asserted, on the authority of the Dred Scott opinion, that Kansas was 'as much a slave state as Georgia,' and warned that refusal to admit Kansas as a slave state would be 'keenly felt' by the South. At this, Stephen Douglas decided he had had enough. Embarrassed by the way popular sovereignty had worked out, he broke with Buchanan and the Southern Democrats and fought the Lecompton proposal. In the end the Democrats were compelled to submit the constitution to a new referendum, and in August 1858 in an honest election the voters of Kansas rejected it overwhelmingly. But by then both sections had found new cause for grievance, and the Democratic party, badly split between the Buchanan and Douglas factions, was rapidly losing its function as a unifier of the nation.

6. THE LINCOLN-DOUGLAS DEBATES

Before the Kansas struggle Abraham Lincoln had been distinguished from hundreds of Northwestern lawyer-politicians only by a high reputation for integrity and a habit of prolonged, abstracted contemplation. Slavery he had long regarded as an evil thing; but the abolitionist agitation seemed to him mischievous and unrealistic.

About the time of the Kansas-Nebraska Act an unseen force began to work on Lincoln's soul and to prepare him for the most arduous and distressing responsibility that has ever fallen to an American. He began to preach a new testament of anti-slavery, without malice or hatred toward slave-owners.

> I surely will not blame them for not doing what I should not know how to do myself. If all earthly power were given me, I should not know what to do as to the existing institution. . . . When they remind us of their constitutional rights, I acknowledge

them, not grudgingly, but fully and fairly; and I would give them
any legislation for the reclaiming of their fugitives which should not
in its stringency, be more likely to carry a free man into slavery than
our ordinary criminal laws are to hang an innocent one. . . . But
all this, to my judgment, furnishes no more excuse for permitting
slavery to go into our own free territory, than it would for reviving
the African slave trade by law.

Slavery is founded on the selfishness of man's nature — opposition to it in his love of justice. These principles are in eternal
antagonism; and when brought into collision so fiercely as slavery
extension brings them, shocks and throes and convulsions must
ceaselessly follow.

These quotations are from Lincoln's Peoria speech of 16 October
1854. It made him known throughout the Northwest. Four years later
he became a rival candidate to Stephen A. Douglas for election to the
Senate from Illinois. The first paragraph of his opening speech in the
campaign (16 June 1858) gave the ripe conclusion to his meditations
during the last four years and struck the keynote of American history
for the seven years to come.

We are now far into the fifth year since a policy was initiated
with the avowed object and confident promise of putting an end to
slavery agitation.

Under the operation of that policy, that agitation has not only not
ceased, but has constantly augmented. In my opinion it will not
cease until a crisis shall have been reached and passed.

'A house divided against itself cannot stand.' [4]

I believe this government cannot endure permanently half slave
and half free.

I do not expect the Union to be dissolved — I do not expect the
house to fall — but I do expect it will cease to be divided. It will
become all one thing, or all the other.

Either the opponents of slavery will arrest the further spread of it,
and place it where the public mind shall rest in the belief that it is
in the course of ultimate extinction; or its advocates will push it forward till it shall become alike lawful in all the States, old as well as
new, North as well as South.

William H. Seward echoed the same sentiment in his speech of 25
October 1858. 'It is an irrepressible conflict between opposing and en-
during forces, and it means that the United States must and will,

4. Matthew xii:25.

sooner or later, become either entirely a slave-holding nation, or entirely a free labor nation.'

Lincoln and Douglas engaged in a series of seven joint debates, covering every section of the state, through the summer and autumn of 1858. Imagine some parched little prairie town of central Illinois, set in fields of rustling corn; a dusty courthouse square surrounded by low wooden houses and stores blistering in the August sunshine, decked with flags and party emblems; shirt-sleeved farmers and their families in wagons and buggies and on foot, brass bands blaring out 'Hail! Columbia' and 'Oh! Susanna,' wooden platform with railing, perspiring semicircle of local dignitaries in black frock coats and immense beaver hats. The Douglas special train (provided by George B. McClellan, superintendent of the Illinois Central) pulls into the 'deepo' and fires a salute from the twelve-pounder cannon bolted to a flatcar at the rear. Senator Douglas, escorted by the local Democratic club in columns of fours, drives up in an open carriage and aggressively mounts the platform. His short, stocky figure is clothed in the best that Washington tailors can produce. Every feature of his face bespeaks confidence and mastery; every gesture of his body, vigor and combativeness. Abe Lincoln, who had previously arrived by an ordinary passenger train, approaches on foot, his furrowed face and long neck conspicuous above the crowd. Wearing a rusty frock coat the sleeves of which stop several inches short of his wrists, and well-worn trousers that show a similar reluctance to approach a pair of enormous feet, he shambles onto the platform. His face, as he turns to the crowd, has an air of settled melancholy.

In their debates, Douglas accused Lincoln of advocating doctrines which would lead to fratricide, while Lincoln sought to show the inconsistency of the Dred Scott decision and Douglas's doctrine of popular sovereignty. At Freeport, Lincoln asked Douglas whether the people of a territory could, in any lawful way, exclude slavery from their limits. Apparently, Douglas must either accept the Dred Scott decision and admit popular sovereignty to be a farce, or separate from his party by repudiating a dictum of the Supreme Court. But this clever statesman had already found a way out of the dilemma: the principle of 'unfriendly legislation.' 'Slavery cannot exist a day or an hour anywhere, unless it is supported by local police regulations,' said Douglas. If a territorial legislature failed to pass a black code, it would effectually keep slavery out, for no slaveholder would take valuable property into a territory unless he were sure of protection. No doubt Douglas was right. Congress could invalidate a positive enactment of the territorial legislature, but not force it to pass a law against its will. It is probable that this 'Freeport doctrine,' as it was called, won Douglas his reelection to the Senate. But by saying to the slaveholders that popular sovereignty gave them no protection, Douglas, who had already antagonized them by his role in the Lecompton affair, made himself 'unavailable' for the Democratic nomination in 1860.

If Lincoln had the more principled argument, Douglas had a more sensible position, at least for the moment. Kansas was safe for freedom; and if theoretically slavery were legal in all the territories, there was slight chance of any except New Mexico and Arizona, not even a territory until 1863, becoming slaveholding states. Yet the long-run practicality of Douglas's stand hinged on the extreme unlikelihood that the South would rest content with the Dred Scott principle, any more than she had rested content with the compromises of 1787, 1820, and 1850. As early as 1848 four Southern states had endorsed the 'Alabama platform' which called for positive action by Congress to protect slavery in the territories, and the majority platform of the national Democratic convention at Charleston in 1860 would demand that Congress enact a 'black code' and impose it on the Western settlers.

Abolition was blowing on the South like a perpetual trade wind, as Harrison Gray Otis predicted in 1833. She was fated to insist on extending slavery further and further afield until the world cried out, 'Away with this foul thing!'

Lincoln furnished an even deeper justification for Republican policy in his Quincy speech of 13 October 1858. This controversy over strategic positions, he pointed out, was an effort to dominate the fundamental moral issue:

> The difference between the men who think slavery a wrong and those who do not think it wrong. The Republican party think it wrong — we think it is a moral, a social, and a political wrong. We think it is a wrong not confining itself merely to the persons of the States where it exists, but that it is a wrong which in its tendency, to say the least, affects the existence of the whole nation. Because we think it wrong, we propose a course of policy that shall deal with it as a wrong. We deal with it as with any other wrong, in so far as we can prevent its growing any larger, and so deal with it

that in the run of time there may be some promise of an end to it. . . .

I will add this, that if there be any man who does not believe that slavery is wrong in the three aspects which I have mentioned, or in any one of them, the man is misplaced and ought to leave us. While, on the other hand, if there be any man in the Republican party who is impatient . . . of the constitutional guarantees thrown around it, and would act in disregard of these, he too is misplaced, standing with us.

In his reply Douglas took the ground that the right and wrong of slavery was nobody's business outside the slave states, and he added that for his part he did not care whether slavery was voted up or down. 'If each state will only agree to mind its own business, and let its neighbors alone . . . this republic can exist forever divided into free and slave states, as our fathers made it and the people of each state have decided.'

Lincoln, in rejoinder, thanked his opponent for the admission that slavery in America must exist forever.

7. RE-OPEN THE AFRICAN SLAVE TRADE?

Lincoln and Seward believed that the next Southern demand would be to foist slavery on the free states, as it had already been forced into the free territories. No responsible Southerner wished to thrust slavery back into New York and New England, although most vocal Southerners were becoming insistent that these states silence the abolitionists. The real desires of the more radical slavery protagonists in the late 1850's were to acquire new territory to the southward and to re-open the African slave trade.

President Buchanan, in his message of 7 January 1858, gently chided William Walker for his filibustering activities in Nicaragua, on the ground that he was hampering 'the destiny of our race to spread themselves over the continent of North America, and this at no distant day, should events be permitted to take their natural course.' At the end of that year he asked Congress for money to buy Cuba, and Senator John Slidell introduced an appropriation for that purpose; but the Republicans were on the alert and did not allow it to be brought to a vote.

Re-opening the African slave trade was the rising demand in the South. Prime field hands were becoming so highly priced — more than

$2000 for a prime field hand — that only wealthy planters could afford to buy them. Slave smuggling was on the increase. Not only pica-roons of the West Indies but respectable merchantmen of Baltimore and New York were engaged in buying 'black ivory' cheap on the west coast of Africa and unloading their cargo on coasts where customs supervision was slack. The governor of South Carolina in a public message (1856) argued at length for the repeal of the federal act of 1807 that outlawed the slave trade. The governor of Florida opposed repeal, from no 'sickly sentimentality,' so he said, but because it would alienate Virginia from the cotton states. Re-opening the slave trade was one of the principal subjects discussed by Southern business men in their annual conventions; the Vicksburg commercial convention of 1859 adopted a resolution that all laws, state or federal, prohibiting the African slave trade, ought to be repealed.' A senator from Florida proposed, as an entering wedge, that Negroes captured on slavers by the United States Navy be 'apprenticed' to kind planters, instead of being sent to Liberia. De Bow's progressive *Review* came out for repeal in 1859.

By many, if not most, Southern gentlemen, these proposals were re-garded with distaste. Yet it is difficult to see how the gentry could long have resisted the logic of William L. Yancey of Alabama: 'If it is right to buy slaves in Virginia and carry them to New Orleans, why is it not right to buy them in Cuba, Brazil, or Africa, and carry them there?' If slavery was a boon to the Negro race, as almost every Southern news-paper now declared, why not indeed extend its blessings to those in darkest Africa? And, without surplus slave population to take advan-tage of the Kansas-Nebraska Act and the Dred Scott decision, these would be barren victories.

The facile assumption of certain historians that slavery in 1860 was already on the decline in the South, and would have disappeared with-in twenty years if the South had been left alone, is rendered highly im-probable by these changes in Southern opinion during the 1850's. Eco-nomics had very little to do with these opinions; slavery never profited so few people as at the period when it had the hottest advocates. Slavery was valued fundamentally as a social necessity for keeping the South 'a white man's country.' Many high-minded Southerners like Robert E. Lee still deplored slavery; but even they saw no alternative and sug-gested none. Suppose Lincoln had not been elected, or that the

Southern states had not seceded. The South, in the natural course of events, would have demanded new and more stringent guarantees to her 'peculiar institution,' including the re-opening of the African slave trade (which, if conceded by an abject North, might have brought on war with England), and the absolute suppression of abolitionist agitation. Supposing the impossible, that the North had conceded everything, and left the South entirely free to deal with her race problem, what possible break in Southern white mentality on the subject of the Negro would have done away with slavery, even in our own day?

8. NORTHERN AGGRESSION AND JOHN BROWN

In 1859 came two startling portents of the 'irrepressible conflict.' The Anthony Burns fugitive slave case was followed by a new crop of state 'personal liberty laws.' These penalized citizens for helping federal officials to perform this unwelcome duty. A certain Booth of Wisconsin, convicted in a federal court of having rescued a runaway slave from his captors, was released by the state supreme court on the ground that the Fugitive Slave Act of 1850 was unconstitutional and void. After the Supreme Court of the United States had reversed this decision, in Ableman v. Booth (1859), the Wisconsin legislature, quoting the Kentucky resolutions of 1798 which Southern men considered canonical, declared 'that this assumption of jurisdiction by the federal judiciary . . . is an act of undelegated power, void, and of no force.' The Federal Government vindicated its power by rearresting and imprisoning Booth; but the deeper significance lies in the fact that Calhoun's nullification had been enunciated in a new quarter. Janus-like, each section turned to nationalism or state rights, as best suited its purpose. Had it been the South instead of the North that was growing and gaining power, Garrison's principle of 'no union with slaveholders' might well have become the nucleus of a strong secession movement in the Northern states.

If the Booth case aroused bitterness, the next episode of the year brought the deeper anger that comes of fear. John Brown, 'of Pottawatomi,' formed a vague project to establish an abolitionist republic in the Appalachian mountains and wage guerrilla war on slavery with fugitive Negroes and a few determined whites. To this wild scheme he rallied support from many of the leading abolitionists of New England who thought his fanaticism holy. On the night of 16 October 1859, leading an army of thirteen white men and five Negroes, Brown seized the federal armory at Harpers Ferry, killed the town's mayor, and took prisoner some of the leading townspeople. Daybreak brought the neighboring militia swarming about him, while the telegraph spread consternation through Virginia. Was this it, the irrepressible conflict?

Governor Wise called out the entire state militia and implored the Federal Government for aid. John Brown retreated to the engine-house of the armory, knocked portholes through the brick wall, and defended himself. Lewis Washington, one of his prisoners, has left us a graphic description of the scene: 'Brown was the coolest and firmest man I ever saw in defying danger and death. With one son dead by his side, and another shot through, he felt the pulse of his dying son with one hand and held his rifle with the other, and commanded his men with the utmost composure, encouraging them to be firm and to sell their lives as dearly as they could.' In the evening, when Colonel Robert E. Lee arrived with a company of marines, only four of Brown's men were alive and unwounded. The next day the marines forced an entrance and captured the slender remnant.

Eight days after his capture the trial of John Brown began in the court house of Charles Town, Virginia. From the pallet where he lay wounded the bearded old fighter rejected his counsel's plea of insanity. There could be no doubt of the result. On 31 October the jury brought in a verdict of murder, criminal conspiracy, and treason against the Commonwealth of Virginia. John Brown, content (as he wrote to his children) 'to die for God's eternal truth on the scaffold as in any other way,' was hanged on 2 December 1859.

Southerners thought of Haiti and shuddered, although not a single slave had voluntarily joined their would-be liberator. Keenly they watched for indications of Northern opinion. That Christian burial was with difficulty obtained for John Brown's body they did not know. That every Democratic or Republican newspaper condemned his acts they did not heed, so much as the admiration for a brave man that Northern opinion could not conceal. And the babble of shocked repudiation by politicians and public men was dimmed by one bell-like note from Emerson: 'That new saint, than whom nothing purer or more brave was ever led by love of men into conflict and death . . . will make the gallows glorious like the cross.'

Lincoln, Secession, and Civil War

1. THE DEMOCRATIC SPLIT

An unfortunate vote of the Democratic national convention of 1856 had decided on Charleston, the headquarters of secession sentiment, as the seat of the next national nominating convention, which assembled on 23 April 1860. Southern Democrats believed that they had been duped by Douglas, whose favorite principle now appeared as a stalking horse for abolition. They had 'bought' popular sovereignty in 1854, expecting to get Kansas; but Kansas slipped off the other way. Its territorial legislature was now in the hands of anti-slavery men, encouraged by Douglas's Freeport doctrine to flout the Dred Scott decision. Nothing less than active protection for slavery in every territory would satisfy the Southerners.

The split came on the platform. Northerners on the platform committee were willing to go along with the Southerners in supporting the Dred Scott decision, condemning personal liberty laws in the Northern states, and proposing the annexation of Cuba. But the Southerners insisted on the principle already announced by Jefferson Davis, that Congress must adopt a black code for all territories of the United States to override 'popular sovereignty.' The Democratic party must take distinctly the position 'that slavery was right,' said Yancey of Alabama. 'Gentlemen of the South,' replied Senator Pugh of Ohio, 'you mistake us — you mistake us — we will not do it.'

The minority report of the Northern delegates was adopted by the convention on 30 April as the Democratic platform. Thereupon the Alabama delegation, and a majority of the delegates from South Carolina, Georgia, Florida, Louisiana, and Arkansas, withdrew from the convention. This symbolic secession, in retrospect, seems even more rash and foolish than the actual secession, which developed from it as inevitably as vinegar from cider. For the best possible way for the South to protect the 'peculiar institution' was to elect a Democrat president; and this horizontal geographical split in the party made it impossible to elect any Democrat.

After the Southern rights men seceded from the Charleston convention, balloting started for President. Although Douglas led, neither he nor anyone could obtain the now traditional two-thirds majority. So, on 2 May, the convention adjourned, to meet again in the calmer atmosphere of Baltimore on 18 June.

At Baltimore a second split occurred on the question of re-admitting the seceding delegates. It was decided in the negative, and another secession took place. The convention then nominated for the Presidency Stephen A. Douglas, who thus became the official Democratic nominee. The seceders nominated Vice-President John C. Breckinridge of Kentucky for President, and this action was endorsed by the original seceders from Charleston on 26 June.

In the meantime, old Whigs, Know-Nothings, and moderate men of both North and South had held a convention of what they called the Constitutional Union party, and on 10 May nominated Senator John Bell of Tennessee for President and Edward Everett of Massachusetts for Vice-President. They avowed no political principle other than the Constitution, the Union, and the enforcement of the laws. This praiseworthy attempt to found a middle-of-the-road party, pledged to solve the slavery extension issue by reason rather than violence, came at least four years too late.

2. THE ELECTION OF 1860

The Republicans had already been heard from, at the first national convention held at Chicago, in a huge 'wigwam' constructed for the occasion, holding 1000 delegates and 9000 spectators. The Republicans had won the congressional elections of 1858, and had good reason to hope for victory in 1860, although the leaders of the Lower South let it be clearly understood that they would not submit to the rule of a 'Black Republican' president. The Republicans were no longer a party of one idea, but a party of the North. On the slavery question the platform adopted at Chicago on 18 May 1860 was as clear as in 1856, though less truculent: no more slavery in the territories, no interference with slavery in the states. So there was no place in the party for the abolitionists, who denounced new Republicanism as old Whiggery writ large. John Brown was condemned in the same breath with the 'border ruffians' of Missouri, and secession was called plain treason. The Chicago platform also promised the settlers a free quarter-section of public land and revived Henry Clay's old 'American system' of internal improvements and protective tariff, representing Northern desires that had been balked by Southern interests. Low tariffs and the panic of 1857 had brought distress to the iron-masters of Pennsylvania and to the wool growers of Ohio, both unable as yet to meet British competition on equal terms.

Abraham Lincoln received the presidential nomination on the third ballot; not for his transcendent merits, which no one yet suspected, but as a matter of political strategy. His humble birth, homely wit, and skill in debate would attract the same sort of Northerners who had once voted for Andrew Jackson; and no one else could carry the doubtful states of Indiana and Illinois. Seward, the most distinguished and experienced candidate, had too long and vulnerable a record.

As Minnesota and Oregon had been admitted to the Union in 1858–59, there were now eighteen free and fifteen slave states. It was the most exciting campaign since 1840, and followed the Tippecanoe pattern. In torchlight parades, a Republican organization called the 'Wide Awakes' excelled, as their uniforms included a glazed cap and cape to protect them from spilling oil. When Democrats, emulating the log cabin sneer of 1840, called Abe Lincoln a mere rail-splitter, the Wide Awakes took it up; even their tin lamps were fitted to rail-like sticks. The Bell-and-Everett processions featured the ringing of a great bell as the alarm-bell of the Union. 'Little Giants' were recruited for Douglas. There were ballads, jokes, and songs, one of the most popular tunes a minstrel show 'walk-around' called 'Dixie's Land,' used first by the Republicans in 1860, but by the Confederacy from 1861 on.

Lincoln triumphed in the four-way race by capturing every free state, save New Jersey, whose vote was divided. But in ten Southern states he did not receive one vote. Breckinridge carried every cotton state, together with North Carolina, Delaware, and Maryland. Douglas, although a good second to Lincoln in the total popular vote, won only Missouri and three electoral votes in New Jersey. Virginia, Kentucky, and Tennessee went for Bell, although his popular vote was the least. Lincoln would have won even if the opposition to him had been united, because he rolled up a large majority in the electoral college.[1]

Lincoln ran well ahead of Douglas in the East, and scored a narrower victory over the 'Little Giant' in the West. Many German-Americans remained in the Democratic party; Catholics distrusted the radicalism of Republican leaders like Carl Schurz, older Lutherans supported slavery, and in general Germans were suspicious of the nativist and temperance strains in the Republican party. But in 1860 the personality of Lincoln and the free homestead issue swept large numbers of Germans into the Republican fold; they were probably decisive in swinging Illinois to Lincoln. Before 1854 the native American artisan had been anti-Negro. Since then he had been aroused by the sneers of Southern statesmen at wage-earners, and by deadly quotations from Southern literature on the evils of a free society. He had been deeply impressed by the favorite question of Republican orators: could the free laboring man ever get two dollars a day when a slave cost his master but ten cents a day to keep? In some obscure way Northern labor had come to look upon slavery as an ally of the capitalists who did their best to exploit him. He wished to break up what Charles Sumner called an alliance between 'the lords of the lash and the lords of the loom.'

To John Bell was attributed the wisest thing said in the entire campaign: that the only way for the South to preserve slavery was to accept the result of the election and stay in the Union. But, as the New Orleans *Bee* editorialized on 14 December 1860, the South could stay in the Union only after 'a change of heart, radical and thorough' of

[1] *Candidates*	*Popular vote*	*Per Cent*	*Electoral vote*
Lincoln	1,866,432	39.9	180
Douglas	1,375,197	29.4	12
Breckinridge	845,763	18.1	72
Bell	589,586	12.6	39

These figures include no popular vote in South Carolina, where Breckinridge electors were chosen by the legislature. In the other states that seceded the popular vote was Breckinridge 736,592; Bell, 345,919; Douglas, 72,084.

'Northern opinion in relation to slavery.' That was asking the impossible.

3. SECESSION

It was a foregone conclusion that South Carolina would secede if Lincoln were elected. Since Calhoun's death, if not earlier, the radical leaders like Robert Barnwell Rhett had been waiting for an occasion that would unite the South in a new confederacy. As soon as the result of the election was certain, the South Carolina legislature summoned a state convention. On 20 December 1860 it met at Charleston and unanimously declared 'that the Union now subsisting between South Carolina and other states under the name of "The United States of America" is hereby dissolved.'

In the other cotton states Union sentiment was strong. Men like Jefferson Davis, who had traveled in the North and maintained a sense of proportion, wished to give Lincoln's administration a fair trial. Outside South Carolina secession was insisted upon by small planters, provincial lawyer-politicians, journalists, and clergymen, but they met stout opposition. After Mississippi, Alabama, and Florida seceded, the key struggle took place in Georgia, trapped between states which had pulled out of the Union. Alexander H. Stephens declared: 'This government of our fathers, with all its defects, comes nearer the objects of all good government than any other on the face of the earth.' But Senator Robert Toombs cried: 'Throw the bloody spear into this den of incendiaries!' On 19 January 1861 Georgia voted secession by a 2 to 1 plurality at its convention, but only after a motion to defer action had been narrowly defeated. 'Georgia was launched upon a dark, uncertain and dangerous sea,' Herschel V. Johnson later reflected. 'Peals of cannon announced the fact, in token of exultation. The secessionists were jubilant. I never felt so sad before. The clustering glories of the past thronged my memory, but they were darkened by the gathering gloom of the lowering future.'

By 1 February 1861, these five states had been joined by two more: Louisiana, where the vote for secessionist delegates had totalled only 20,448 to 17,296 Unionists, and Texas, over the opposition of old Sam Houston, Jacksonian nationalist to the last, subsequently deposed as governor for refusing to swear fealty to the Confederacy. On 4 Feb-

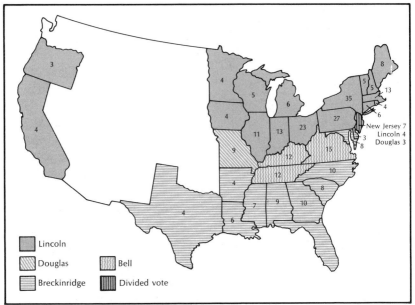

PRESIDENTIAL ELECTION, 1860

Lincoln

Douglas   Bell

Breckinridge   Divided vote

New Jersey 7
Lincoln 4
Douglas 3

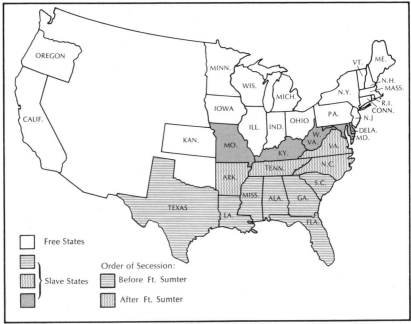

Free States

Slave States

Order of Secession:

Before Ft. Sumter

After Ft. Sumter

SECESSION, 1860-1861

ruary, delegates from the seven seceded states met at Montgomery, Alabama, and on the 8th formed the Confederate States of America. The next day this Congress elected Jefferson Davis provisional President and A. H. Stephens Vice-President of the Southern Confederacy, and proceeded to draft a constitution.

4. SECESSION, CAUSES, AND RIGHTS

The causes of secession, as they appeared to its protagonists, were plainly expressed by the state conventions. 'The people of the Northern states,' declared Mississippi, 'have assumed a revolutionary position towards the Southern states.' 'They have enticed our slaves from us,' and obstructed their rendition under the fugitive slave law. They claim the right 'to exclude slavery from the territories,' and from any state henceforth admitted to the Union. They have 'insulted and outraged our citizens when travelling among them . . . by taking their servants and liberating the same.' They have 'encouraged a hostile invasion of a Southern state to excite insurrection, murder and rapine.' To which South Carolina added, 'They have denounced as sinful the institution of slavery; they have permitted the open establishment among them' of abolition societies, and 'have united in the election of a man to the high office of President of the United States whose opinions and purposes are hostile to slavery.'

On their own showing, then, the states of the Lower South seceded as the result of a long series of dissatisfactions respecting the Northern attitude toward slavery. There was no mention in their manifestoes or in their leaders' writings and speeches of any other cause. Protection figured as a 'cause' in the Confederate propaganda abroad and in Southern apologetics since; but there was no contemporary mention of it because most of the Southern congressmen, including the entire South Carolina delegation, had voted for the tariff of 1857, and because the Congress of the Confederacy re-enacted it. The Morrill Tariff of 20 February 1861, the first strongly protective tariff since 1832, could not have been passed if the members of the seceding states had not withdrawn from Congress. Nor was any allusion made to state rights apart from slavery; on the contrary, the Northern states were reproached for sheltering themselves under state rights against the fugitive slave laws and the Dred Scott decision. A letter of Jefferson Davis to a Northern friend, written on 20 January 1861, is a fair example of what was in the Southern mind at the moment of secession: 'Many States, like Iowa, have denied our rights, disregarded their obligations, and have sacrificed their true representatives. To us it became a necessity to transfer our domestic institutions from hostile to friendly hands, and we have acted accordingly. There seems to be but little prospect that we will be permitted to do so peacefully.' All these 'rights,' 'obligations,' and 'institutions' had reference to slavery and nothing but slavery.

A strong minority regarded Southern independence as an end in itself. Their minds were filled with the vision of a great republic ruled by themselves and their own kind, affording perfect security to their social organism. Lincoln, we must remember, appeared to the South not as we know him, but as a malignant sort of baboon, with abolitionist serpents as attendants.[2]

The Southern people should have listened to Stephens when he predicted that even for the purpose of protecting slavery, secession was a colossal act of folly. 'The people are run mad,' he wrote. 'They are wild with passion and frenzy.' And so they were. Southerners and Democrats combined would have possessed a majority in both houses of Congress. Lincoln could have done nothing without their consent. At worst Republicans might eventually gain strength to outlaw slavery in the territories, but secession would immediately lose the cotton states all rights of any sort in the territories. Northern states were not enforcing the fugitive slave law, but secession would make that law a dead letter. Abolitionists were disagreeable fellow-countrymen; but their propaganda could not be stopped by international boundaries. And as Lincoln asked, 'Can enemies make treaties better than friends can make laws?' The Republicans proposed no interference with slavery in the Southern states, and those in Congress early in 1861 actually proposed a constitutional amendment to that effect. Even had they wished, they could not have freed the slaves in unwilling states except as an act of war. To free them by constitutional amendment would have been impossible even today, if the slave states had stayed united.[3]

2. This picture of Lincoln would have been amusing had it not been so pathetically wrong. Lincoln was hated by out-and-out abolitionists. Wendell Phillips referred to him as 'the slavehound of Illinois.'
3. There were fifteen slave states in 1860, enough to prevent the ratification of a constitutional amendment a century later.

The doctrine of constitutional secession, as distinct from a mere right of revolution, seems to have been first enunciated by John Taylor of Caroline, and first elaborated by the New England Federalists in 1814. There had been little difference between the two sections in this respect before 1850; every section denounced as contrary to state sovereignty national measures which were against its interests, and with complete lack of humor denounced as treasonable similar declarations by other sections. The humiliation of defeat and reconstruction would give the Southern people a sentimental devotion to the principle of state rights, without affecting their practice; whilst in Northern eyes the principle seemed befouled with treason. These attitudes were reversed in 1933, when state rights were brandished by Republicans against the New Deal. Again in the 1950's state rights were invoked and the Confederate flag waved, in attempted nullification of a decision of the Supreme Court against Negro segregation.

State rights is a relative term. Everyone then believed, and believes today, that the states have certain rights which the Federal Government has no lawful power to touch. State *sovereignty* is another matter. Admitting that the rights reserved to the states in the Federal Constitution are sovereign in their ordinary nature, they are hardly so in the condition under which they are enjoyed, since the Constitution, as interpreted by the Supreme Court, is the law of the land, and three-quarters of the states, comprising perhaps but a minority of the population, may deprive the other quarter of all their privileges by constitutional amendment. Secessionists made much of the reservation under which certain states ratified the Constitution, as if that could have had any effect on the others; and of the Kentucky and Virginia resolves of 1798, as if they were official glosses on the Constitution. The nationalists, on the other hand, could point to the fact that every presidential administration except Tyler's, and the Supreme Court under Jay, Marshall, and Taney, had acted on the assumption that a sovereign American people existed. No stronger assertions of nationalism were ever made than by three Southern Presidents: Washington, Jackson, and Polk. After all, effectiveness is the only test of sovereignty. And if the American people had not cared enough about nationalism in 1861 to maintain it by force, the sovereignty of the states would have been an accomplished fact.

5. CONFUSION AND ATTEMPTED COMPROMISE

During the awkward four months' interval between Lincoln's election in November 1860 and his inauguration on 4 March, a period in which Southern states seceded and the Confederacy was formed, the timid Buchanan was President. His cabinet included three secessionists, and only one strong nationalist, Jeremiah Black, after Cass resigned in disgust (12 December). Buchanan had the same power to defend federal property and collect federal taxes within states that obstructed federal law as President Jackson possessed in 1832, but the President did nothing. 'Vacillating and obstinate by turns, yet lacking firmness when the occasion demanded firmness, he floundered about in a sea of perplexity, throwing away chance after chance.' [4] In his annual message of 8 December, Buchanan had an opportunity to sound the Jacksonian trumpet note to recall loyal citizens to their duty. Instead, he querulously chided the abolitionists as responsible for the fact that 'many a matron throughout the South retires at night in dread of what may befall herself and her children before the morning.' And he did a notable shilly-shally on secession, which Seward not unfairly paraphrased thus: 'It is the duty of the President to execute the laws, unless somebody opposes him; and that no state has a right to go out of the Union, unless it wants to.'

Yet Buchanan confronted a situation which appeared to spell defeat no matter what course he pursued. A Jacksonian stance might only have precipitated war sooner, and he did put off hostilities long enough to permit attempts at compromise to emerge. He opposed any overt act which might drive the Upper South and the border states from the Union, and he hoped by a policy of conciliation to encourage the seceding states to return. But he found little support for his policies in any section. Washington was a Southern city. Congress, cabinet, and all the federal departments were riddled with secessionists. Secretary of the Treasury Howell Cobb resigned on 10 December to organize secession in Georgia. To onlookers like young Henry Adams, the Federal Government seemed to be dissolving; soon there would be nothing left to secede from. Public opinion gave the President no lead. The Northern people had grown so accustomed to Southern threats of secession that

4. J. F. Rhodes, *United States*, III, 150.

when the talk became a reality they could hardly credit the fact, and few had any notion what to do about it. Oliver Wendell Holmes wrote an appeal to 'Caroline, Caroline, child of the sun,' admonishing her:

> 'When heart aches and your feet have grown sore
> Remember the pathway that leads to our door.'

Horace Greeley of the New York *Tribune* struck the key-note of Northern sentiment in January with the phrase, 'Wayward sisters, depart in peace!'

'Why not?' we are entitled to ask, in an era that has seen more than fifty new nations created. 'Why not have let the cotton states form their own republic?' The answer was given in Lincoln's inaugural address: 'Physically speaking, we cannot separate.' With the best will in the world, a readjustment and redistribution of federal power would have been difficult,[5] and good will was notably wanting. Peace could not have been maintained for a year between the United States and the Southern Confederacy. Fugitive slaves, adjustment of the national debt, and of each government's share in the territories would have raised problems only solvable by force; once the right of secession had been admitted, other states would have seceded. A war between the sections was inescapable.

When South Carolina seceded, Major Robert Anderson, who commanded the small U.S. Army detachment at Charleston, shifted his command from the indefensible Fort Moultrie on the mainland, to the incomplete Fort Sumter, on an island commanding the harbor entrance. An 'embassy' from South Carolina to Washington almost bullied Buchanan into ordering Major Anderson out, or home; but at the turn of the year Attorney General Jeremiah H. Black managed to put a little ginger into the President, and he refused. Buchanan also reconstructed his cabinet, with Black as Secretary of State, and made a half-hearted attempt to reinforce Fort Sumter with 200 men and arms and ammunition in an unarmed passenger steamer which retired after gunfire from a fort flying the palmetto flag had straddled her.

Buchanan did not retaliate, because he continued to hope that one of

5. The matter of breaking up the federal postal service, for instance, was so difficult that the Confederacy permitted United States mails to run their usual course through the South until 30 June 1861, six weeks after the Civil War had begun, and almost six months after South Carolina had 'resumed her separate and equal place among nations.'

the compromise movements might succeed. None did, but they served the purpose of showing even the most reluctant Northerners that there was no middle ground between separation and coercion. The first of these was proposed on 18 December 1860 by Senator John J. Crittenden of Kentucky, a grand old statesman in the Henry Clay tradition. As amended in the Senate, the 'Crittenden Compromise' amounted to this: (1) The old 36° 30′ line between free and slave territories to be extended to the California boundary, any acquisition of new territory to the south to be slave territory; (2) Congress never to interfere with slavery in states where it existed, or in the District of Columbia; (3) Compensation to owners for fugitive slaves not recovered. These were to be submitted to the people as constitutional amendments. Lincoln, the President-elect, was willing to support the last two, if the Southern senators would issue an appeal to their states against secession, which they refused to do. Respecting the first proposition he had already written to a Republican congressman, 'Prevent, as far as possible, any of our friends from demoralizing themselves and our cause by entertaining propositions for compromise of any sort on "slavery extension." There is no possible compromise upon it but which puts us under again and leaves us all our work to do over again. . . . On that point hold firm, as with a chain of steel.'

Crittenden's measures, laid before Congress two days before South Carolina seceded, were discussed in committee for two months in the hope that they might at least keep the border states in the Union. The Republicans were willing to go so far as to admit New Mexico as a slave state if the people there chose slavery, but refused to entertain further slavery extension into newly acquired territory. Even so, the Crittenden propositions fell so far short of the Breckinridge platform that they could not possibly have stopped the secession landslide.

A second sincere but futile effort to arrest the landslide was the so-called Peace Convention of 133 delegates from twenty states and Kansas Territory. This was summoned by the Virginia legislature in the hope that it might propose a revision of the Federal Constitution that would attract the seceding states. It met and debated secretly at Willard's Hotel, Washington, under the presidency of John Tyler, between 8 and 27 February 1861. The Convention included no small number of distinguished men, such as William C. Rives of Virginia, David Dudley Field and James S. Wadsworth of New York, William Pitt Fessenden of Maine, Salmon P. Chase of Ohio, and James B. Clay of Kentucky. This

Convention had been in session only eight days when Jefferson Davis, assuming the presidency of the Southern Confederacy at Montgomery, announced that no propositions for a reconstruction of the Union would be entertained by him or the Confederate Congress. That blast limited the Convention's efforts to finding some soothing formula that might restrain Virginia and the border slave states, all of which were represented there. This was found to be impossible. A series of seven constitutional amendments, similar to Senator Crittenden's, were passed by narrow majorities, the Virginia members voting against most of them. The only ones acceptable to the Virginia delegation were (1) congressional compensation for fugitive slaves, (2) no annexation of territory without concurrence of a majority of both Northern and Southern senators, and (3) a 'never-never' amendment to the effect that neither by law nor constitutional amendment could Congress ever interfere with slavery in the states or the District of Columbia.

Senator Crittenden himself, on 4 March, the day of Lincoln's inauguration, recommended that the Peace Convention propositions be submitted to the states as constitutional amendments, but this was rejected by a vote of four to one, both senators from Virginia voting against it; and Tyler himself as soon as he returned to Richmond repudiated the recommendations of the Convention and went all out for secession. The 'never-never' amendment, however, was passed by the House of Representatives on 27 February by a vote of 133 to 65, most of the Republicans voting for it. This non-interference principle had been a leading plank in their presidential platform, and they were eager to prove their sincerity in the matter.

Thus, all formal compromises failed either to bring back the 'wayward sisters' or to keep Virginia in. The repeal by several Northern states of personal liberty laws, and the breaking up of an abolition meeting in Boston to commemorate John Brown, seemed insufficient evidence of a change of heart. Nothing further had been done toward compromise by 4 March 1861, when Abraham Lincoln was inaugurated President of the no longer United States.

6. LINCOLN INAUGURATED

Washington appeared carefree and slovenly as usual that day. Actually, the people were nervously expectant of trouble. It was rumored that secessionists from Virginia or 'plug-uglies' from Baltimore would raid the capital and prevent the inauguration. General Scott took every possible precaution, but the soldiers at his disposal were too few even to light up the black-coated sombreness of the crowd. The inaugural procession, as it moved up Pennsylvania Avenue under the harsh glare of a March sun, while a blustering wind blew clouds of dust roof-high, might have been a funeral procession. The Capitol, with its great uncompleted dome supporting an unkempt fringe of derricks, suggested ruination. President Buchanan, urbane and white-haired, and bowed old Chief Justice Taney seemed symbols of a golden age of the Republic that was over. President Lincoln, uncouth and ill at ease, inspired no confidence until his high-pitched, determined voice was heard delivering the solemn phrases of the inaugural address.

After a brief review of the constitutional issues involved in secession, Lincoln renewed the pledge of his party to respect slavery in the states, and to enforce any fugitive slave law that had proper safeguards for the colored people of the free states.

> In your hands [he addressed the South] and not in mine, is the momentous issue of the civil war. The Government will not assail you. [But] I hold that, in contemplation of universal law and the Constitution, the Union of these States is perpetual. . . . No state, upon its own mere action, can lawfully get out of the Union. . . . I shall take care, as the Constitution itself expressly enjoins upon me, that the laws of the Union be faithfully executed in all the States. . . . The power confided to me will be used to hold, occupy, and possess the property and places belonging to the Government, and to collect the duties and imposts.

7. FORT SUMTER AND SEWARD

Buchanan had flinched from defending those coigns of vantage, the federal forts in the Southern states; and we shall judge him less harshly when we reflect that it took Lincoln a month to meet the issue bravely. By the time he was inaugurated, all the forts and navy yards in the seceded states, except Fort Pickens at Pensacola, Fort Sumter at Charleston, and two minor posts off the Florida coast, had fallen unresisting to the Confederate authorities. So, too, had a string of post offices and custom houses and the mint at New Orleans. From the extreme Southern point of view, the jurisdiction of such places passed with secession to the states, and their retention by the Federal Government was equivalent to an act of war. Confederate commissioners came to Washington to treat for their surrender, a few days after Lincoln's inauguration. Although Seward refused to receive the gentlemen, he assured them indirectly that no supplies or provisions would be sent to the forts without due notice, and led them to expect a speedy evacuation.

William H. Seward, as Lincoln's chief rival for the nomination, and as the most experienced statesman in the Republican party, had been given the department of state, where he was playing a deep and dangerous game. Lincoln he regarded as an inexperienced small-town lawyer; and in truth Lincoln's public appearances during the crisis of the winter had been for the most part undignified, and some of his utterances, flippant. Of course Lincoln was always flippant when thinking most deeply, but Seward did not yet know that; nor did he know the Confederate leaders. Judging them in the light of New York politics, he suspected their sincerity. In his opinion, secession was a mere blind for obtaining concessions to Southern rights. If a collision could be avoided, the leaders would sneak back into the Union. If they did not, Seward would rally the Southern people to their old flag by a foreign war.

Major Anderson, commanding Fort Sumter, notified the war department that his supplies were giving out, and that new Confederate batteries commanded his position. Fort Sumter had no strategic value in case of civil war. Why, then, risk war by holding it? The Confederacy made it clear that any attempt to reinforce or even to supply Sumter would be regarded as a hostile act, which would probably pull Virginia into the Confederacy. In the middle of March, not only General Scott but five of the seven members of Lincoln's cabinet opposed supplying Fort Sumter. If, however, the forts were tamely yielded, would not the principle of union be fatally compromised? Could a recognition of the Confederacy thereafter be avoided?

Lincoln delayed decision, not from fear, but because he was watching Virginia. Jefferson Davis, too, was watching Virginia. The Old Dominion was a stake worth playing for. Although the state had long since fallen from her position of primacy, her sons were the ablest officers in the United States Army, and her soil was almost certain to be the theater of any war between the sections. The 'panhandle' of western Virginia thrust a salient between Pennsylvania and Ohio to within 100 miles of Lake Erie. If Virginia seceded, she must carry North Carolina with her; and Maryland, Kentucky, Tennessee, and Missouri would probably follow.

Virginia showed her union sentiment in 1860 by voting for Bell rather than Breckinridge; but unionism in Virginia meant a voluntary association of sovereign states. Delegates to a Virginia state convention were elected by the people in January 1861, and met at Richmond on 13 February. A majority of the delegates were union men, but the secessionist minority was united, aggressive, and clever; it kept the convention in session week after week, until many unionist delegates left for their homes in the western part of the state. Delegations of unionist members visited Washington and besought Lincoln to let Fort Sumter go. Twice the President offered to do so if the Virginia unionists 'would break up their convention without any row or nonsense'; but they were not strong enough to promise that. Finally Lincoln came to see that to yield Fort Sumter would not bring the 'wayward sisters' back; and Virginia would join them the moment he raised his hand to strike. If Virginia would not accept the Union as it was, she must abide the consequences.

Toward the end of March Lincoln, determined to face the issue squarely, ordered a relief expedition to be prepared for Fort Sumter. Seward then showed his hand. On April Fools' Day 1861, he presented Lincoln with a paper entitled 'Thoughts for the President's Consideration.' The most startling proposal in this extraordinary document was that the United States should at once pick a quarrel with France and Spain, possibly with England and Russia as well, as a means of reuniting North and South for glory and conquest! And Lincoln was invited to appoint Seward his prime minister to execute this mad policy! Lincoln calmly replied that he saw no reason to abandon the policy outlined in his inaugural address. As for promoting war on Europe, 'I remark that if this must be done, *I* must do it.' But Seward was too intent on his scheme to catch the President's meaning. On 6 April, when the President ordered the Sumter expedition to sail, Seward by deception obtained Lincoln's signature diverting the capital ship of the expedition to Fort Pickens.

It mattered nothing. When Lincoln's informal warning that an attempt would be made 'to supply Fort Sumter with provisions only' arrived at Montgomery, it found Jefferson Davis in a similar state of confusion and perplexity. Southern spirits were evaporating for want of a fight; in Charleston there were murmurs of dissatisfaction with the Confederacy; Rhett's *Mercury* was attacking Davis's administration almost as severely as Lincoln's. Only a collision could 'fire the Southern heart' and bring in Virginia. According to one account, Robert Toombs, Confederate secretary of state, begged for delay. To attack Fort Sumter, he predicted, would be to 'strike a hornet's nest which extends from mountain to ocean, and legions now quiet will swarm out and sting us to death.' Finally, Davis ordered Confederate General P. G. T. Beauregard, commanding the Charleston district, to fire on Sumter only if absolutely necessary to prevent its reinforcement. On the night of 11–12 April Beauregard sent four staff officers to Fort Sumter demanding surrender. Major Anderson, a Kentuckian who loathed the idea of civil war, had no desire for the sort of fame that would come from being the occasion of it. Nothing as yet had been seen or heard of the relief expedition. So, at a quarter past three in the morning, he offered to surrender as soon as he might do so with honor — in two day's time, when the garrison's food would be exhausted. The Confederate staff officers peremptorily refused this reasonable stipulation, and on their own responsibility gave orders to open fire. For, as one of them admitted in later life, they feared that Davis would clasp hands with Seward, and the chance of war would slip away forever.

On 12 April 1861, at 4:30 a.m., the first gun of the Civil War was fired against Fort Sumter. The relief expedition appeared, but for lack of its capital ship was unable to pass the batteries. All day Major Anderson replied as best he could to a concentric fire from four or five Confederate forts and batteries, while the beauty and fashion of Charleston flocked to the waterfront as to a gala. At nine o'clock the next morning, 13 April, the barracks caught fire; in the early afternoon the flagstaff was shot away, and a few hours later, although his situation was by no means desperate, Major Anderson accepted terms of surrender. On the afternoon of Sunday, 14 April, the garrison marched out with drums beating and colors flying.

Walt Whitman caught the spirit of that occasion in his

Beat! beat! drums! — blow! bugles! blow!
Through the windows — through doors — burst like a ruthless force,
Into the solemn church, and scatter the congregation,

Into the school where the scholar is studying;
Leave not the bridegroom quiet — no happiness must he have now with
    his bride,
Nor the peaceful farmer any peace, ploughing his field or gathering his
    grain.
So fierce you whirr and pound you drums — so shrill you bugles blow.

8. SECESSION COMPLETED

On 15 April President Lincoln issued a call for 75,000 volunteers in order to put down combinations 'too powerful to be suppressed by the
ordinary course of judicial proceedings,' and 'to cause the laws to be
duly executed.' Already the Virginian secessionists were organizing attacks on the Norfolk navy yard and the arsenal at Harpers Ferry, and
threatening to purge the state convention. That body was in a state of
high-strung emotion bordering on hysteria, when Lincoln's call precipitated matters. On 17 April it voted, 88 to 55, to submit an ordinance of
secession to the people. Without awaiting that verdict, the governor
placed his state under Confederate orders.

The western part of Virginia refused to leave the Union; [6] but three
more states followed the main part of the state into the Southern Confederacy. Arkansas seceded on 6 May; Tennessee on 7 May concluded
an alliance with the Confederacy, which a month later the people approved; North Carolina, having previously voted down secession, was
in the impossible position of a Union enclave until 20 May, when she
ratified the Confederate constitution. The attitude of Maryland was
crucial, for her secession would isolate the Federal Government at
Washington. The first Northern troops on their way to the capital were
mobbed as they passed through Baltimore (19 April), and Lincoln
wisely permitted the rest to be marched around the city until he could
spare enough troops to occupy it and enforce martial law. The Maryland
legislature protested against 'coercion' of the Southern Confederacy,
but refused to summon a state convention; and danger of disunion
in that quarter passed. The government of Kentucky, where opinion was evenly divided, refused to obey the call for volunteers, and endeavored in vain to enforce neutrality, but by the end of the year threw
in its lot with the Union. Missouri was practically under a dual regime

6. West Virginia was admitted as a state in 1863, but gave comparatively little aid
to the Union cause.

throughout the war; Delaware never wavered in her loyalty. In California there was a fierce struggle between Southern sympathizers and the Unionists, which the latter won; but California was too remote to give the Union cause other than pecuniary aid, in which she was generous. The Indians of the Indian Territory, many of them slaveholders, mostly threw in their lot with the South.

The motives for this second group of secessions, beginning with Virginia's, were obviously different from those of the Lower South. The Upper South had been willing to give the Lincoln administration a try. Before Lincoln's call for troops, a number of these states had, in different ways, voted their sentiments against secession. But the Upper South was drawn to the Lower by ties of blood and a determination to keep that region a 'white men's country.' This emotion was rationalized by the theory of state sovereignty, which was strong and genuine in eastern Virginia and Maryland, and in western and central Tennessee. According to this theory any state had a right to secede; hence Lincoln's call for coercion was illegal. And it forced the issue: everyone had to choose between defending the Confederacy or helping to put it down.

Yet the issue was not as simple as it might seem. Throughout the Civil War, lines were never strictly drawn between the states that seceded and those that did not. The majority of men went with their neighbors, as most people always do. But there were thousands who did not. The Confederate army contained men from every Northern state, who preferred the Southern type of civilization to their own; and some of fashionable society in Baltimore, Philadelphia, and New York was pro-Southern to the end. The United States Army and Navy contained loyal men from every seceded state, Americans who knew that the break-up of the Union would be the worst blow to the cause of self-government and republicanism since the day that Bonaparte assumed the purple. Robert J. Walker, the most efficient Union agent in Europe, was a former senator from Mississippi; Caleb Huse, the most efficient Confederate agent in Europe, was from Massachusetts. Franklin Pierce sent his one-time mentor Jefferson Davis warm greetings, and his organ of the New Hampshire Democracy attacked the Lincoln administration with a virulence hardly matched by the Charleston *Mercury*. Admiral Farragut was born in Tennessee; General George Thomas was born in Virginia, and so too the Commander in Chief of the Union forces, General Winfield Scott. Samuel P. Lee commanded the Union naval forces on the James river while his uncle, General Robert E. Lee, was resisting Grant in the Wilderness. Two sons of Commodore Porter, USN, fought under Stonewall Jackson; Senator Crittenden of the attempted compromise had two sons, Major General T. L. Crittenden, USA, and Major General G. B. Crittenden, CSA. Three brothers of Mrs. Lincoln died for the South, and the President's kinsmen on his mother's side were Southern sympathizers, whilst near kinsmen of Mrs. Davis were in the Union army. In a house on West 20th Street, New York, a little boy named Theodore Roosevelt prayed for the Union armies at the knee of his Georgia mother, whose brothers were in the Confederate navy. At the same moment, in the Presbyterian parsonage of Augusta, Georgia, another little boy named Thomas Woodrow Wilson knelt in the family circle while his Ohio-born father invoked the God of Battles for the Southern cause.

Robert E. Lee abhorred the methods of the abolitionists, but agreed with them that slavery was wrong and emancipated his few inherited slaves. He did not believe in a constitutional right of secession, and severely criticized the action of the cotton states. On 23 January 1861 Lee wrote to his son, 'I can contemplate no greater calamity for the country than a dissolution of the Union. . . . Still, a Union that can only be maintained by swords and bayonets, and in which strife and civil war are to take the place of brotherly love and kindness, has no charm for me.' To a cousin and brother officer of the United States Army, who determined to remain faithful to the flag, Lee wrote expressing sympathy and respect for his 'notions of allegiance.' But, 'I have been unable to make up my mind to raise my hand against my native state, my relatives, my children and my home.' With deep regret Colonel Lee resigned his commission in the United States Army; only a sense of duty induced him to accept a commission in the cause of which he was to be the main prop. What anguish that decision cost him we can never know. What it cost the United States we know too well.

To a third Virginian, Senator James Murray Mason, we are indebted for the most accurate definition of the great struggle that was about to begin: 'I look upon it then, Sir, as a war of sentiment and opinion by one form of society against another form of society.'

XXXIV

Conditions and Considerations

1. CONDITIONS OF VICTORY

From a distance of a century men wonder at the rash and hopeless gallantry of the Southern war for independence. A loose agrarian confederacy of 5 or 6 million whites and 3.5 million slaves challenged a federal union of 19 or 20 million freemen with overwhelming financial and industrial advantages.[1] Yet, futile as the effort proved and tragic as the consequences, the Southern cause was not predestined to defeat.

The Confederacy, in order to win, needed merely to defend her own territory long enough to weary the Northerners of war. The United States, in order to win, had to conquer an empire almost as large as the whole of western Europe and crush a people. A negotiated peace, or any less emphatic result than unconditional surrender of the Southern armies and total collapse of the Confederate government, would have meant some sort of special privilege to the Southern states within the Union, if not independence without the Union: in either event a Southern victory.

1. By the census of 1860 the white population of the eleven seceded states was 5,449,467; the white population of the nineteen free states, 18,936,579. Both figures leave out of account the white population (2,589,533) of the four border slave states (Delaware, Maryland, Kentucky, and Missouri), which did not secede, but which probably contributed as many men to the Confederacy as to the Union. Subtracting the loyal regions of Virginia and Tennessee would reduce the Confederacy's white population to about 5 million. By the census of 1860 there were 3,521,111 slaves in the Confederate states, and 429,401 in the four border states, and from those the Union recruited about 100,000 troops.

For with the one crucial exception of slavery the moral scales seemed to be weighted in favor of the South. From their point of view, Southerners were fighting for everything that men hold dear: liberty and self-government, hearth and home, the survival of their customs. They could abandon the struggle only by sacrificing the very bases of their society; and defeat for them involved the most bitter humiliation. The Northern people, on the contrary, could have stopped the war at any moment, at the mere cost of recognizing what to many seemed an accomplished fact. They were fighting for the sentiment of Union, which, translated into action, seemed to tender souls scarcely different from conquest. Negro emancipation, itself an ideal, came more as an incident than as an object of the war. It was not the abolitionist 'Battle-Hymn of the Republic' that sent the blood leaping through Northern veins in those years of trial, but the simple sentiment of:

> The Union forever, hurrah! boys, hurrah!
>   Down with the traitor, up with the star,
> While we rally round the flag, boys, rally once again,
>   Shouting the battle-cry of Freedom.

When we look to material rather than moral factors, the position of the South was less favorable. In the secession winter, a Virginia editor had warned: 'Dependent upon Europe and the North for almost every yard of cloth, and every coat and boot and hat that we wear, for our axes, scythes, tubs, and buckets, in short, for everything except our bread and meat, it must occur to the South that if our relations with the North are ever severed, . . . we should, in all the South, not be able to clothe ourselves; we could not fill our firesides, plough our fields, nor mow our meadows.' Although, the editor exaggerated, the situation was bad enough. New York state alone turned out manufactures worth four times more than the output of all the seceded states, and the North manufactured 97 per cent of the nation's firearms. The Union commanded an immense superiority in men, money, railroads, industrial potential, navy and merchant marine.

But the South too had certain advantages. As Southerners were more inclined than Northerners to make a profession of arms, the senior officers — those with the longest experience — were Southern: Albert Sidney Johnston, Joseph E. Johnston, Robert E. Lee, to name only the most prominent. The South would be fighting on home soil, with all the advantages of familiarity with the terrain, and of interior lines of communication. Third, the South was fighting on the defensive; it takes far larger armies and more formidable equipment to mount an offensive than to sustain a defense, and it was the North which would have to maintain long lines of communication deep into hostile territory. Fourth, the South had an immense coastline, with innumerable inlets and harbors, and might expect to defy a Northern blockade and import military necessities she was unable to supply. Finally, Southerners were convinced that 'Cotton was King.' As Senator Hammond of South Carolina wrote on 19 April 1860, 'Cotton, rice, tobacco and naval stores command the world; and we have the sense to know it, and are sufficiently Teutonic to carry it out successfully. The North without us would be a motherless calf, bleating about, and die of mange and starvation.' The Confederacy believed that Great Britain and France would be forced to intervene to stop the war or to aid the South in order to keep cotton supplies flowing across the Atlantic.

In these circumstances there was good reason to expect that the South would win. The Thirteen Colonies, the Netherlands, and in recent memory the South American and the Italian states had achieved their independence against greater odds. Even devoted English partisans of the American Union like John Bright hardly dared hope for its complete restoration; and among the statesmen, the military experts, the journalists, the men of letters, and the leaders of public opinion in western Europe, those who before the end of 1863 doubted the permanency of separation were few and inconspicuous. For there was one imponderable and unique factor of which almost everyone in Europe was ignorant: the steadfast devotion to the Union which alone made it possible for the superior material resources of the United States to prevail.

2. THE CONFEDERATE STATES OF AMERICA

The opposing governments were nearly identical in pattern. The Constitution of the Confederate States differed from that of the 'fathers,' said Jefferson Davis, only in so far as it was 'explanatory of their well-known intent.' In making explicit those guarantees of slave property and state rights that the South found implicit in the older document, she did not improve it as a framework of government, still less as an instrument of war. Bounties, protective tariffs, and 'internal improvements' were forbidden. Federal officials and even judges could be impeached by the legislatures of the state in which their functions were exercised. No 'law denying or impairing the right of property in negro slaves' could be passed by the Confederate Congress, and in all new territory acquired 'the institution of negro slavery, as it now exists in the Confederate States, shall be recognized and protected.' In two respects only was the Confederate Constitution an improvement over its model. Congress, unless by a two-thirds majority, could appropriate money only upon the President's transmitting the request and estimate by some head of an executive department; and these heads of departments, who constituted an informal cabinet in the new government as in the old, might be granted a seat in Congress and the privilege of discussion. The President, further, had the right to veto items of appropriation bills. Actually these provisions remained inoperative during the short lifetime of the Confederacy.

The executive branch, which should have been strong and efficient, proved to be distressingly weak. President Davis and his Congress worked less in harmony than had any President and Congress of the United States since Tyler. Nor were the other departments more successful. As under the Articles of Confederation, the pull of the individual states and of the army operated to discourage first-rate statesmen from service in the Confederate Congress in Richmond, which was consistently less effective than the Federal Congress in Washington. Finally, although the Confederate Constitution provided for a Supreme Court, this constitutional provision was never implemented, and the Confederacy fought the war without an effective judicial system.

To outsiders, the Southern Confederacy seemed animated by a single will and purpose; actually it was weakened by faction and shaken by its inherent vice of localism. Davis and most of the Southern leaders had been talking state rights but thinking Southern nationalism; yet many important men, especially in North Carolina and Georgia, loved state rights more than Southern unity and feared a centralizing tyranny at Richmond no less than they had at Washington. No Union general ever had to write, as Lee did of the Lower South when contemplating an advance: 'If these states will give up their troops, I think it can be done.' State rights stood always at Davis's elbow. The Confederacy suffered too from the absence of a two-party system, which could restrain petty personal politics and link leaders in state and nation. The composition and character of the Southern people too was unfavorable for united and disinterested effort. The gentry, more accustomed to direct slaves than to govern themselves, and as full of fixed notions on politics as on slavery, could not co-operate effectively with their President, and were only happy in active army life. The white democracy, unsophisticated and provincial, never even remotely realized what the Confederacy had to face, and the government did nothing to enlighten it. Slaves proved to be a material asset for war production. If Davis or the Congress could have made up their minds to arm them before Lincoln decided to free them, they might well have been the decisive military factor.

3. THE TWO PRESIDENTS

During the war both Davis and Lincoln were regarded by their enemies as fiends incarnate; and by many of their own people were accused of everything from incompetence and corruption to tyranny and treason. At the outset few doubted that Davis was the abler, since he appeared the more dignified figure of the two. Lieutenant of dragoons, colonel of volunteers, congressman, senator, and Secretary of War, Davis brought experience such as Lincoln had never had, and talents that he never claimed, to the Southern presidency. Courage, sincerity, patience, and integrity were his; only tact, perception, humility, and inner harmony were wanting to make him a very great man. Davis was torn between a desire to command and a taste for intellectual solitude, between nationalist instinct and state-rights faith. Isolated from the Southern democracy out of which he had sprung, he moved as to the manner born among the whispering aristocracy of Richmond; yet he had a perverse knack of infuriating the gentlemen who tried to work under him.

His pronounced military tastes and slight military experience led Davis to attempt to direct military operations as well as civil administration. Only a Bonaparte could successfully have played the dual role in the Confederacy; and even Bonaparte had a general staff and a centralized government. Davis had neither the time to exercise control nor the talent to choose effective instruments, and he allowed private sentiment to dictate military decisions. His stubborn hostility to the able

General Joseph E. Johnston and his misguided devotion to the incompetent General Braxton Bragg are cases in point. Instead of cooperating with the state governors, he first antagonized them, then quarreled with them. Worst of all he never won the affections of the plain people as Lincoln did; it is suggestive that to this day the South celebrates not Davis's birthday, but Lee's. Davis was ill-cast as the leader of a revolution. In the last years of the war his health and nerves gave way, and his state papers show an increasing querulousness which contrasts sharply with the dignity and magnanimity of all that Lincoln wrote.

Davis selected his cabinet for work, not for politics. It contained several men of distinction, but only three of the ruling planter class: Robert Toombs and Pope Walker, both of whom soon resigned, and Judah P. Benjamin. The others inspired little confidence and exerted less influence. Secretary of the Treasury Christopher Memminger was a Charlestonian of German extraction; Secretary of the Navy Stephen R. Mallory was West Indian by birth, of mixed Yankee and Irish blood; Postmaster General John H. Reagan was a Unionist from Texas. Easily the ablest member of the group and closest to Davis was Benjamin, a Louisiana planter and lawyer whose perpetual smile and imperturbable suavity masked a brilliant mind and sound judgment. An unstable amalgam, the Davis cabinet in four years had five attorneys-general and six secretaries of war.

Since the Union had a thriving party system, Lincoln could put together a cabinet which carried more political weight than that of Davis. The President's choices were determined by the need to represent every element in the Republican party and every loyal section of the Union. Seward's appointment brought the administration confidence, and eventually strength; but not until he had almost wrecked it by his aggressive foreign policy. Simon Cameron, the Secretary of War, a Pennsylvania manufacturer who proved criminally careless if not corrupt, was replaced by Edwin M. Stanton, efficient but as difficult to work with as a porcupine. Salmon P. Chase, an apostle of righteousness, received the treasury as a party chieftain and a rival for the Republican nomination in 1860; he never developed more than a moderate talent for administration and finance. Gideon Welles, formerly a bureau chief in the navy department, latterly a newspaper editor in a small Connecticut town, and a recent convert from the Democratic party, was appointed

Secretary of the Navy and proved surprisingly effective. His Biblical name and patriarchal beard made Welles the laughing stock of the administration; he took appropriate revenge by writing a pungent and voluminous diary. Edward Bates and Montgomery Blair, the Attorney General and Postmaster General, were good second-rate characters who represented the loyal slave states in the cabinet.

At the beginning of Lincoln's administration the members of the cabinet distrusted one another, and only Blair had much respect for the President. Seward assumed the role of premier — as he liked to be called and considered. After the firing on Sumter, several months elapsed before the President was really master in his own house. The change of scene, the hurly-burly of war preparations, seemed for a time to cut his contact with that unconscious, unseen force that lifted him from the common herd. Yet his feeling for the democratic medium in which he had to work, for its limitations, imperfections, and possibilities, was akin to that of a great artist for the medium of sculpture or painting. He could capture the imagination of the common soldier and citizen, and at the same time make the outstanding quality of an ill-balanced character like Stanton an instrument of his great purpose. This rail-splitter, this prairie politician with his droll stories and his few, poor, crude social devices, had innate tact and a delicacy that carried conviction of his superiority to all but the most obtuse, and a humanity that opened the hearts of all men to him in the end.

If Lincoln was slow to direct the conduct of the war, he never faltered in his conception of the purpose of the war. From Sumter to Appomattox, it was for him a war to preserve the Union. The power that lay in that word came less from an instinct of nationality than from the passionate desire of a youthful people to prove its worth by the only test that all the world recognized. The Union, which for Washington was a justification for the American Revolution, and for Hamilton a panoply of social order, had become, in the hands of Jackson, Clay, and Webster, a symbol of popular government. Lincoln drove home this conception in his every utterance, and gave it classical expression in the Gettysburg Address. He made the average American feel that his dignity as a citizen of a free republic was bound up with the fate of the Union, whose destruction would be a victory for the enemies of freedom in every country.

Lincoln could not bring everyone to this conception. Many members of the Democratic party in the North still looked upon the states as the symbol of democracy. Many believed civil war too great a price to pay for Union. The abolitionists would support him only on the condition of his serving their immediate purpose. Nor did Lincoln completely dominate his own group. Many Republicans regarded the war as a mere assertion of Northern superiority; for in 1861 they were essentially a Northern, not a Union party. Because Lincoln, ignoring all appeals to hatred, sectionalism, and humanitarianism, raised the Union standard at the beginning and kept it flying, the Union was preserved. Prominent Democrats such as Stephen Douglas promptly rallied the best elements of their party to the colors; and in a few months the entire Ohio valley, half slaveholding in fact, and largely pro-slavery in sentiment, was secure. His enemies sneered, 'Lincoln would like to have God on his side, but he must have Kentucky.' His friends doubted whether even God could preserve the Union without Kentucky. Nor did Lincoln ever forget that those whom he liked to call 'our late friends, now adversaries' must, if his object were attained, become fellow citizens once more. He could never bring himself to contemplate the South with feelings other than sorrow and compassion.

4. THE TWO ARMIES

In the matter of military preparations the Confederacy had a start of several months on the United States, and secured many of the ablest officers of the United States Army then in active service — Lee, both Johnstons, Beauregard, J. E. B. Stuart, and A. P. Hill; as well as Thomas 'Stonewall' Jackson and D. H. Hill, who were teaching in Southern military colleges. While most Southern officers went with their states, Virginia-born Winfield Scott and George Thomas and David G. Farragut of Tennessee remained loyal to the nation. The Union army found its proper leaders only through the costly method of trial and error. Most of the West Pointers who rose to prominence in the Union army were civilians at the beginning of the war; fortunately for the Union they were promptly recalled to the colors as generals of volunteers. In the regular army of the United States — only 16,000 strong — many brilliant young officers like Philip Sheridan were confined to small units until late in the war.

The 40 United States naval vessels in commission were scattered over the seven seas. Until mid-April no attempt was made to enlarge or even to concentrate these slender forces, for fear of offending the Virginia unionists. In the meantime the Confederate States had seized the United States arsenals and navy yards within their limits, had obtained munitions from the North and from Europe, and had organized state armies; by the end of April 1861 President Davis had called for and quickly obtained 100,000 volunteers for twelve months.

Winfield Scott, general-in-chief of the United States Army, infirm in body but robust in mind, advised the President that at least 300,000 men, a general of Wolfe's capacity, and two or three years' time would be required to conquer even the Upper South. No one else dared place the estimate so high; and Seward believed with the man in the street that one vigorous thrust would overthrow the Confederacy within 90 days. The President, in his proclamation of 15 April 1861, called for only 75,000 volunteers for three months. Militia regiments fell over one another in their alacrity to aid the government; New York alone voted to supply 30,000 men for three years. Within two weeks 35,000 troops were in Washington or on their way thither, and 20,000 more were waiting for transportation. Undoubtedly the government should have taken advantage of this patriotic outburst to create a really national army for the duration of the war. Instead, Lincoln on 3 May called for 40 more volunteer regiments of 1050 men each and 40,000 three-year enlistments in the regular army and navy, leaving the recruiting, organization, and equipment of all volunteer regiments to the states. That Lincoln, inexperienced and bewildered, should have lost this golden opportunity is not surprising, since the war department preferred the traditional American method of raising an army by state quotas, as in 1776, 1812, and 1846.

As a basis for the new army, every Northern state had some sort of volunteer militia force which was mobilized for an annual 'muster' and 'Cornwallis' (sham battle) — usually not much better than a frolic. The company officers were elected by the men, the regimental and general officers appointed by the state governor. A few militia regiments, like the Seventh New York, were well-officered and drilled. There were also a number of semi-social military companies, such as the Fire Zouaves and Sarsfield Guards, which performed fancy evolutions in showy uniforms. Many of these volunteered en masse, and proceeded on the road to glory without undue delay. Two Brooklyn companies were provided with pieces of rope, tied to their musket barrels, with which to bring back 'traitors' from the South. (Similarly the Southern volunteers armed themselves with huge bowie knives to terrorize their presumably pallid enemies.) But for the most part, the volunteer regiments that made up the bulk of the United States Army during the war were regiments created on the spot. A patriotic citizen would receive a colonel's commission from his state governor, and raise and even equip a regiment by his own efforts and by those who expected to be officers under him. When the regiment was reasonably complete and partially equipped, it was forwarded to a training camp and placed under federal control. The Federal Government in practice had to respect state appointments until they were found wanting in action; and its own were scarcely better. Prominent politicians like Nathaniel P. Banks and Benjamin F. Butler of Massachusetts, without the slightest military experience, received major generals' commissions from the President, and outranked seasoned officers of the regular army. There was something to be said for this system as a means of giving an unmilitary country a stake in the war, and utilizing community pride and competition. But something better was wanted before a year had elapsed.

By much the same system was the first Confederate army raised. The Southern respect for rank and caste gave prompt recognition to natural leaders. Indeed the earlier Southern armies were embarrassed by a plethora of officer material. J. E. B. Stuart remarked of one Virginia unit, 'They are pretty good officers now, and after a while they will make excellent soldiers too. They only need reducing to the ranks!' The Southern troops had the advantage of being accustomed to the use of arms — for every slaveholder had to keep weapons by him in case of insurrection, and the non-slaveholders were good marksmen. Both classes were lovers of horseflesh, and it was a poor white indeed who did not own a horse or a mule. Northern troops, unless from the West, had outgrown the hunting and horseback-riding frontier, and the Northern gentry had not yet adopted field sports or fox-hunting for recreation. Discipline, to which the more primitive individualistic Southerners were averse, soon outweighed these differences. The two armies became as nearly equal in fighting capacity, man for man, as any two in history; and they took an unprecedented amount of punishment. If the Confederates won more battles, it was due to their better leadership, which gave them a tactical superiority on the field of battle, against the strategical superiority of their enemies on the field of operations. As the North had the greater immigrant population, it had a far larger proportion of foreign-born soldiers, especially German, Irish, and Scandinavian.[2]

Throughout the war the Union army was the better equipped in shoes and clothing, and more abundantly supplied with munitions; yet the red tape of war department bureaus, and the prejudice of elderly officers, prevented the adoption of the breech-loading rifle until almost the end of the war. Both in artillery and small arms, it was largely a war of the muzzle-loader, and to a great extent of the smooth-bore. The head of the Ordnance Bureau in Washington was an old fogey, Colonel James Ripley, popularly known as Ripley Van Winkle. He not only failed to provide the Union armies with breech-loading rifles but neglected to launch an aggressive program of purchases abroad. Thanks to the energetic efforts of certain state governors and congressmen, and of General Frémont, the North did manage to buy a substantial supply of modern rifles and other military equipment in Britain, Belgium, Germany, and Austria.

The Confederacy, too, hurried agents to Britain and the Continent to buy arms, but they were for the most part unable to bid against the more affluent Union agents. Yet the Confederates managed to procure some 50,000 rifles in England. When the blockade stopped these shipments from Europe the Confederate ordnance service, under a resourceful Pennsylvanian, Josiah Gorgas, performed near-miracles to keep the army supplied. Though the Union at all times had greater fire power than the Confederacy, the South never lost a major battle for want of ammunition. Richmond was one of the principal coal- and iron-producing centers in the United States, and her Tredegar Iron Works were well equipped for the manufacture of heavy castings and ordnance. It was there that the iron armor of the *Virginia* (*ex-Merrimack*) was rolled and her rifled guns were cast, and that the first practical submarine was built. But these were the only works in the Confederacy so equipped until 1863, when a newly established plant at Selma, Alabama, began to turn out cannon. Much enterprise was also shown by

2. And many foreign-born officers like the Germans Franz Sigel and Carl Schurz, the Irish generals Corcoran and Meagher, the French Philippe de Trobriand, and the Norwegian colonels Hans Christian Heg and Hans Mattson.

the Confederate government in setting up woolen mills to weave cloth for uniforms, but the Southern armies were never properly supplied with shoes. Deficiencies in clothing, equipment, artillery, and small arms were constantly made good from the supplies abandoned by Union armies in their frequent retreats.

5. NUMBERS AND LOSSES

The problem of numbers and losses in the Civil War is almost insoluble, partly because we lack reliable statistics, especially for the Confederacy, and partly because the statistics we have are confusing. In both armies service varied from three months to three years, or the duration of the war; obviously a soldier in for three years counts for more than one serving for three months or for six. And how should one count deserters or the sick, the wounded, and other ineffectives who were in the army but not part of the fighting force?

One statistician, by reducing Union enlistments to a three-years' service standard, arrives at a total of 2,320,272 Union soldiers. Another statistician estimates the total Union soldiers at 2,898,304, of whom 230,000 failed to serve; reducing this figure to a three-year standard he arrives at a total of only 1,556,678 men in the Union ranks. To these totals must be added some 40,000 or 50,000 sailors. Most historians guess that around 900,000 is right for the Confederate armies. Perhaps the closest approximation to the truth is to be read in the census of 1890 which discovered 1,034,073 Union veterans and 432,000 Confederate veterans still surviving. As life expectancy (and medical services) favored Northerners, these figures suggest roughly a two to one ratio for the war.

The numbers actually on the army rolls at any one time give a truer comparative index:

	Union	Confederate
July 1861	186,751	112,040
Jan. 1862	575,917	351,418
Mar. 1862	637,126	401,395
Jan. 1863	918,121	446,622
Jan. 1864	860,737	481,180
Jan. 1865	959,460	445,203

Even these figures, however, are far from conclusive on the matter of relative numbers. For it must be remembered that the Union had to maintain long lines of communication in large areas of the South; that it was an occupying army with substantial numbers engaged in noncombatant work; that it took more men to put together a railroad track than to tear one up, to occupy exterior lines than interior, to fight offensive battles than defensive. If we look to the numbers actually engaged in major battles we find — somewhat to our surprise — that the Confederacy was not seriously outnumbered before 1864 and in many important battles outnumbered the Federals. After Gettysburg and Vicksburg the situation changed, and in the Wilderness and along the lines of Petersburg Lee was overwhelmingly outnumbered, as was J. E. Johnston on his retreat through Georgia and the Carolinas.

The statistics of losses are even more bewildering, for while the Federal Government kept reasonably accurate statistics, the Confederacy did not, and many records that it did compile were subsequently lost in the confusion of defeat and dispersion. In the Union army 67,058 were killed on the field of battle, and 43,012 died from wounds; 224,586 died from disease and 25,566 more from accidents and miscellaneous causes — a total of 360,222. Estimates of Confederate losses vary widely. Deaths from battle were probably around 80,000 or 90,000. If deaths from disease ran proportionately as high as in the Union ranks — and there is no reason to suppose that they were any lower — they must have reached 160,000 to 180,000.

Sickness took an appalling toll from both armies. The average soldier, whether in blue or in gray, was sick enough two or three times a year to be sent to a hospital, which was often more dangerous than the battlefield: deaths from disease were more than twice as high as deaths from battle — but we should remember that in the Mexican War the ratio was ten to one! Poor sanitation, impure water, wretched cooking, exposure, lack of cleanliness, and sheer carelessness exposed soldiers on both sides to dysentery, typhoid, malaria, and consumption — the chief killers. Medical services were inadequate and inefficient, hospitals often primitive, nursing at first almost nonexistent though it gradually improved. Care for the wounded was haphazard and callous: after Shiloh and Second Bull Run the wounded were allowed to lie for two or three days on the battlefields without relief. Behind the lines overworked doctors worked desperately in hastily improvised field hospitals. Antisepsis was unknown and anesthetics were not always available; abdominal wounds and major amputations meant probable death. Out of a total of 580 amputations in Richmond in two months of 1862 there were 245 deaths; no wonder a Confederate officer wrote that in every regiment 'there were not less than a dozen doctors from whom our men had as much to fear as from their Northern enemies.' Katherine Wormeley, later a distinguished literary figure, describes conditions on one of the hospital transports to which the wounded were brought during the Peninsular campaign:

> We went on board; and such a scene as we entered and lived in for two days I trust never to see again. Men in every condition of horror, shattered, and shrieking, were being brought in on stretchers borne by contrabands who dumped them anywhere, banged the stretchers against pillars and posts, and walked over the men without compassion. There was no one to direct what ward or what bed they were to go into. Men shattered in the thigh, and even cases of amputation, were shovelled into top berths without thought or mercy. The men had mostly been without food for three days, but there was nothing on board either boat for them, and if there had been the cooks were only engaged to cook for the ship, and not for the hospital.

It was thought not quite respectable for women to nurse soldiers, and the armies relied at first on male nurses and orderlies, mostly untrained. The heroic Dorothea Dix was appointed Superintendent of Nurses at the beginning of the war, and over 3000 intrepid women volunteered to work under her, but the army did not welcome their services. Clara Barton, 'Angel of the Battlefield,' nursed the wounded. Much of the medical care on both sides was voluntary; the United States Sanitary Commission not only inspected camps and hospitals but provided a good deal of nursing and relief both at the front and behind the lines; it combined the work which the Red Cross and the United Service Organization carried out in the Second World War. There was no comparable organization in the South, but many of the Confederate sick and wounded could be nursed in near-by homes. Confederate medical skill was no worse than that of the Union, but lack of drugs, anesthetics, and surgical instruments imposed pitiful difficulties and losses.

XXXV

The War, 1861-1862

1. TERRAIN, TACTICS, AND STRATEGY

Civil War battles were fought in rough, forested country with occasional clearings — Antietam, Gettysburg, Fredericksburg, Shiloh, and Vicksburg were the only big battles in open country. The defending infantry is drawn up in a double line, the men firing erect or from a kneeling posture. The attacking force moves forward by brigade units of 2000 to 2500 men, covering a front of 800 to 1000 yards, in double rank; captains in the front rank, the other officers and non-coms in the rear to discourage straggling. It is preceded by a line of skirmishers. Normally the attack moves forward in cadenced step and is halted at intervals to fire and reload — a slow business with old-fashioned muzzle-loading rifles — the enemy returning fire until one or the other gives ground. Occasionally the boys in blue, more often the boys in gray, advance on the double-quick, the former shouting a deep-chested 'Hurrah!', the latter giving vent to their famous 'rebel yell,' a shrill staccato hunting cry. An attack of this sort generally ends in a bayonet encounter; but both sides, ill-trained in bayonet work, prefer to club their muskets. There was slight attempt at concealment, and so little entrenchment until 1863 that the moments of actual combat were more deadly to officers and men than the battles of World War I; but as soon as contact was broken the men were comparatively safe. A regular feature of the Civil War was the fraternizing of picket guards, and even whole units of men, during the intervals between fighting.

Union strategy, aggressive by the nature of the cause, took a form dictated by the geography of the Confederate States. The Appalachians and the Mississippi river divided the Confederacy into three parts, nearly equal in area: the eastern, the western, and the trans-Mississippi theaters of war. The most spectacular campaign came in that part of the eastern theater bounded by North Carolina, the Appalachians, the Susquehanna river, and Chesapeake Bay. Here were the two capitals, Washington and Richmond, and between them a rough wooded country, crossed by numerous streams and rivers. Although destruction of the enemy's army, not occupation of the enemy's capital, is considered the proper object in warfare, in a civil war, especially, possession of the enemy capital is of immense moral value. The Union expended more effort in trying to capture Richmond than on all its other operations combined, while the Confederacy in turn allowed its military strategy to be determined by the supposed necessity of defending its capital. In the retaliating threats to Washington, the Shenandoah-Cumberland valley, pointing like a long cannon at the heart of the Union, became the scene of dashing raids and military exploits. Military operations beyond the Mississippi had little effect on the result. But the western theater of war between the Mississippi and the Appalachians was as important as the eastern. Lee might perform miracles in Virginia, and even carry the war into the enemy's country; but when Grant and the gunboats had secured the Mississippi, and Sherman was ready to swing round the southern spurs of the Appalachians into Georgia, the Confederacy was doomed. Control of the sea was a priceless asset to the Union. The navy maintained communications with Europe, cut off those of the South, captured important coastal cities, and on the Western rivers and — as Lincoln put it, 'wherever the ground was a little damp,' — co-operated with the army like the other blade to a pair of shears.

A threefold task lay before the armed forces of the Union: constriction, scission, and defeat of the Southern armies. Both the nature and the magnitude of the task were imperfectly apprehended in 1861, except by Winfield Scott, whose 'anaconda policy' of constriction was dismissed as the ravings of an old fogey, but eventually adopted, in principle, by Grant.

2. THE WAR IN 1861

The Union plan of campaign for 1861, if a series of unco-ordinated moves can be called a campaign, was to blockade the Southern coast and occupy strategic points along its edge; to mobilize and train the volunteer army in regions convenient for invading the Southern states; and to capture Richmond, which, it was assumed, would cause the Confederacy to collapse. Kentucky had to be carefully nursed out of neutrality, and Missouri, which threatened the Union right flank, saved from fanatical Southern sympathizers. Hence the first forward movements were from Cincinnati, St. Louis, and Washington.

By July some 25,000 three-month volunteers were at Washington, spoiling for a fight, and the Northern press and people clamored for action. Against General Scott's advice, President and cabinet yielded to the cry of 'On to Richmond.' General Irvin McDowell, with a 'grand army' of 30,000, crossed the Potomac in order to seek out Beauregard's army of some 22,000 near Manassas Junction, Virginia. A throng of newspaper correspondents, sight-seers on horse and foot, and congressmen in carriages came out to see the sport.

On 21 July McDowell attacked Beauregard on a plateau behind the small stream called Bull Run. The troops on both sides were so ill-trained, the officers so unused to handling large numbers, the opposing flags so similar, and the uniforms so varied that a scene of extraordinary confusion took place. For hours it was anyone's battle, but the timely arrival of 9000 Confederate reinforcements from the valley and the stand of General Thomas Jackson (who thereby earned the sobriquet Stonewall) won the day. Union retreat turned to rout. All next day, soldiers came straggling into Washington without order or formation, dropping down to sleep in the very streets; rumors flying about that Beauregard was in hot pursuit, that the Capitol would be abandoned; treason openly preached everywhere. But Lincoln did not flinch, and Beauregard did not pursue. 'The Confederate army was more disorganized by victory than that of the United States by defeat,' wrote General Johnston. There was no more talk of a 90-days war. From the dregs of humiliation the Union was nerved to make preparations for a long war; while the South, believing her proved superiority would dis-

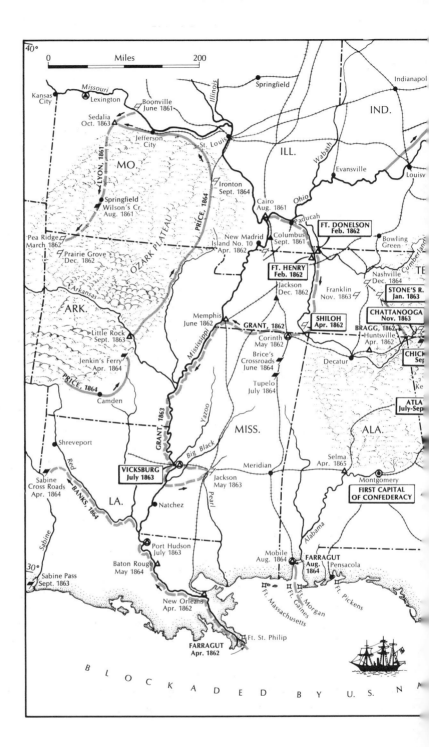

640

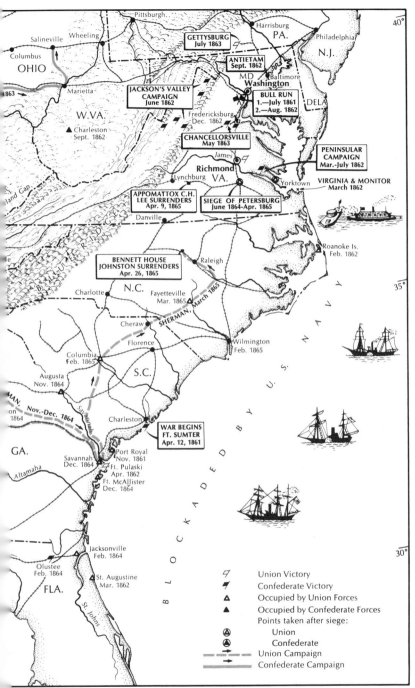

Pittsburgh

Salineville · Wheeling · Harrisburg · **PA.** · Philadelphia

Columbus · **N.J.**

OHIO · 1863

Marietta · **GETTYSBURG July 1863**

ANTIETAM Sept. 1862 · MD · Baltimore · DELA

JACKSON'S VALLEY CAMPAIGN June 1862 · **Washington**

W.VA. · **BULL RUN 1.—July 1861 2.—Aug. 1862**

▲ Charleston Sept. 1862 · Fredericksburg Dec. 1862

CHANCELLORSVILLE May 1863 · **PENINSULAR CAMPAIGN Mar.-July 1862**

James · **Richmond** · **VA.** · Lynchburg · Yorktown · **VIRGINIA & MONITOR March 1862**

...land Gap · **APPOMATTOX C.H. LEE SURRENDERS Apr. 9, 1865** · **SIEGE OF PETERSBURG June 1864-Apr. 1865**

Danville

Roanoke Is. Feb. 1862

BENNETT HOUSE JOHNSTON SURRENDERS Apr. 26, 1865 · Raleigh

Charlotte · **N.C.** · Fayetteville Mar. 1865 **SHERMAN, March 1865**

Cheraw · **SHERMAN**

Florence · Wilmington Feb. 1865

Columbia, Feb. 1865 · **S.C.**

Augusta Nov. 1864

...MAN Nov.-Dec. 1864 · ...on 1864 · Charleston · **WAR BEGINS FT. SUMTER Apr. 12, 1861**

GA. · Savannah Dec. 1864 · Port Royal Nov. 1861 · Ft. Pulaski Apr. 1862 · Ft. McAllister Dec. 1864

Altamaha

Jacksonville Feb. 1864

Olustee Feb. 1864 · St. Augustine Mar. 1862

FLA. · St. Johns

U.S. NAVY · BLOCKADED BY

40° · 35° · 30°

⚡ Union Victory
⚡ Confederate Victory
△ Occupied by Union Forces
▲ Occupied by Confederate Forces
Points taken after siege:
◉ Union
◉ Confederate
Union Campaign
Confederate Campaign

THE CIVIL WAR, 1861-1865

641

solve the Northern 'hordes' and procure foreign recognition, indulged in an orgy of self-applause.

At this point, on 24 July 1861, President Lincoln summoned General McClellan to Washington and gave him command of the army in that department. George B. McClellan was only 34 years old, a graduate of West Point on the eve of the Mexican War, in which he had performed distinguished service. His subsequent business experience accustomed him to deal with large affairs in a big way and gave him the confidence of men of property; his personal magnetism and some easy successes in western Virginia in June 1861, made him a popular hero. The Northern states provided him with plenty of three-year volunteers, Congress was generous with money and equipment, and the President gave him the fullest support. No untried general in modern times has had such abundant means as McClellan enjoyed during the nine months that followed Bull Run; and few used them to so little profit when the time came to fight.

McClellan proved an ideal organizer. His precise, methodical mind, his appetite for detail and love of work, and his attractive personality and genuine interest in his men were exactly the qualities needed to form an army from a mob. But his defects in conduct and character impaired his usefulness and weakened his support when the time came for action. His position required not only technical military ability, which he possessed, but some perception of the democratic medium in which he must work; and that perception, which was given to Grant and Lincoln, McClellan wholly lacked. Impatient democracy demanded quick results, but McClellan neither gave them nor did he clearly explain to the people why quick results could not be expected. His love of display, the French princes on his staff, too frequent mention of 'my army,' a curt way with politicians, and his contempt for Lincoln combined with frequent public statements as to what the politicians should do, seemed out of place in a republican soldier. He was the type of man who is not content merely to do well the task at hand, but must be forever dreaming of the future in terms of self: victorious McClellan, dictator McClellan, President McClellan. Yet no Union general was so beloved by the untrained volunteers whom his talent turned into a superb instrument of war, the Army of the Potomac.

Weeks stretched into months, and the newspapers had nothing to report but drills and reviews. 'All quiet along the Potomac' appeared so often in the headlines as to become a jest. The Confederate General Joseph E. Johnston extended his lines along the south bank of the Potomac and closed the river to traffic in October. McClellan estimated the enemy's number at 150,000. Actually, at that time, the Confederate army in northern Virginia was less than 50,000 strong and wretchedly equipped. Johnston, dogmatic in temper and choleric in disposition, had much the harder task of the two. President Davis found him recruits with difficulty, since every Southern state set up a big home guard, and neither then nor later did the Confederacy learn to concentrate its resources.

Lincoln refused to let the politicians worry him into ordering an advance. When General Scott got in McClellan's way, the President on 1 November appointed McClellan general-in-chief of all the armies of the republic. And Lincoln ordered the war department to take over all matters of recruiting, equipment, and organization from the states. Yet McClellan persistently snubbed the President, and on one occasion affronted him in a way that no other ruler would have pardoned. 'Never mind,' said Lincoln, 'I will hold McClellan's horse if he will only bring us success.' November passed with no preparations made for an offensive. December came, and McClellan began to play with plans for an oblique instead of a direct advance on Richmond. 'If something is not done soon, the bottom will be out of the whole affair,' said the President. 'If General McClellan does not want to use the army I would like to *borrow* it.'

It was not just a misconception of the enemy's strength that was holding McClellan back. A mere victory, he believed, would be indecisive; but one dramatic coup such as the capture of Richmond, if accompanied by satisfactory assurances as to slave property, would win back the South. 'I shall carry the thing *en grande,* and crush the rebels in one campaign,' he wrote to his young and adoring wife.

McClellan was not alone in this delusion that rebellion could be stamped out as suddenly as it arose. He differed from others only in his estimate of the preparation necessary for a fatal blow. Yet, if McClellan's strategy of delay was correct, his 'one big victory' concept was mistaken. The Union needed to postpone offensive movements until its superior resources were organized for an offensive war of attrition and constriction; the Confederacy needed to force an issue promptly. On the Confederate side, Lee certainly, and J. E. Johnston probably, had the right instinct of aggression; but they were overruled by President Davis's policy of defense and delay.

3. THE UNION NAVY, THE BLOCKADE, AND THE INLAND WATERS

In naval strategy, the policy of constriction was so obvious that it was consciously applied from the first. President Davis invited applications for letters of marque on 17 April 1861; two days later President Lincoln proclaimed a blockade of the Southern ports, thus precipitating awkward questions of constitutional and international law. The following day brought a naval counterpart to Bull Run. The navy yard at Norfolk, which the United States government had neglected to reinforce for fear of offending Virginia, was captured without a blow by the troops of that state, together with enormous stores of ordnance, munitions, and the hull of the frigate *Merrimack* — promptly rebuilt and christened *Virginia*.

The navy department then awoke, and Gideon Welles proved to be one of Lincoln's lucky finds. Painstaking and methodical as an administrator, respectful of navy traditions, he and his capable assistant secretary, Gustavus V. Fox, gave the navy much more efficient direction than the army received. But the problem of blockading 3550 miles of coastline from Washington to Matamoros, Mexico, with the vessels and seamen available, seemed at first insoluble. The 60 sailing vessels proved as obsolete as medieval galleys. Congress had begun to build a new steam navy in 1850; but as yet only 24 steamers had been placed in commission, only twelve of these were in the home squadron, and only two actually available to guard the Atlantic coast in April 1861! Although American inventors had for some years been planning ironclads, whose value had been proved in Europe, Congress had refused to appropriate money for that purpose. There was no naval reserve. Without waiting for Congress to assemble, the Administration undertook a large construction program, and side-wheelers, screw steamers, clipper ships, tugboats, and even ferryboats were purchased in wholesale quantities, at retail prices. Time and legislation were required to build ironclads, to establish promotion by merit, and to retire aged officers. Before the end of the war the navy totaled almost 700 ships of all kinds, manned by over 50,000 seamen. And in David Glasgow Farragut, with 50 years of service, who chose to stay with the Union notwithstanding his Southern birth, the nation found a naval hero in the tradition of John Paul Jones and Isaac Hull.

It was a paper blockade for two or three months after 19 April and not wholly effective for more than two years; but by the end of July 1861 four blockading squadrons were stationed off the seven or eight enemy ports that were commercially important. About 800 vessels entered and cleared from the ports of the Confederacy during the first year of the blockade; but the last year of peace had seen more than 6000. It was impossible to close the Confederate ports completely. Small vessels clearing from a Carolinian port could sneak along an inside passage until they reached an outlet to a clear horizon, and then make a dash for the high seas. It was about 600 miles from Mobile to Havana, and even less distance from the South Atlantic ports to protected waters in the Bahamas, where Nassau quickly acquired an importance it had not known since the days of the buccaneers and a prosperity it did not recover until it became a winter playground for the rich.

During the summer of 1861 the navy department began to establish bases on the Southern coast. Cape Hatteras and Hilton Head on the sea islands off Port Royal, S.C., were captured between August and November 1861. This last was the only important Union victory of that year. And in February–March 1862, General Ambrose Burnside, at the head of a joint naval-military expedition, seized Roanoke Island, New Bern, and Beaufort, N.C., giving the Union control of Albemarle and Pamlico Sounds. But Wilmington, N.C., remained a major leak in the blockade until nearly the end of the war. For want of military cooperation these successes were not followed up by raids into the interior; but they pinned down thousands of Southern troops.

The achievement of the hastily improvised Union navy on inland waters was no less important than that of the warships in the Atlantic. The Mississippi with its tributaries — the Tennessee, Cumberland, Arkansas, and Red rivers — penetrated into the heart of the Confederacy, and whoever commanded these inland waters controlled lines of communication that were cheap, accessible, and indestructible: a cavalry troop could tear up railroad tracks, but could not block a river. At the outbreak of the war most of the Mississippi and Ohio river steamboats were in federal hands, and many of these were converted to transports for Grant's campaigns against Forts Henry and Donelson and for later campaigns in the deep South. Within a short time Western energy and ingenuity created an effective fleet suited to the special needs of Western warfare. James B. Eads, an engineering genius from St. Louis, proposed to Lincoln the construction of a fleet of armored gunboats, won his approval, and launched the first of the formidable boats within 45 days. Another engineering genius, Charles Ellet, was authorized to carry out his favorite idea of ironclad rams, and in three months built a fleet of them which, in the same summer of 1862, destroyed the entire Confederate river defense fleet guarding Memphis and captured that city. Captain Andrew H. Foote, commander of naval operations on the Mississippi, built some 40 mortar-boats. These ugly little rafts carrying mortar-guns capable of hurling a 230-pound shell over two miles did terrible damage to the river towns that stood high on the bluffs above the Mississippi. In a memorable letter rejoicing in victories at Gettysburg and Vicksburg, President Lincoln paid tribute to the contributions of 'Uncle Sam's web-feet.'

4. THE ATTITUDE OF EUROPE

The British and French had an avid interest in the Civil War. They divided, on the whole, along class lines. The plain people of Europe for the most part were convinced that Union victory would vindicate democracy while destruction of the Union would be a mortal wound to democracy. To the ruling classes of Europe, however, the United States had long been obnoxious for the encouragement its success afforded to radicals and democratic reformers. 'An involuntary instinct, all-powerful and unconquerable,' wrote the Comte de Montalembert, 'at once arrayed on the side of the pro-slavery people all the open or secret partisans of the fanaticism and absolutism of Europe.' Many Englishmen even outside that category favored the South for, as Henry Adams wrote, 'the English mind took naturally to rebellion — when foreign.' Most liberals supported the North, but some, like the historian Lord Acton, could see no difference between the Southern struggle for independence and the nationalist movements in Europe with which they had sympathized. Humanitarians, who would have welcomed a war against slavery, were put off for nearly two years by the repeated declarations of Lincoln and Seward that slavery was not the issue. The commercial classes noted the return of the United States to a high protective policy, which the Confederate Constitution forbade, while shipping interests hoped for the ruin of their most formidable competitor and approved a new cotton kingdom for which they might do the carrying trade.

The Times, Punch, the leading quarterlies, and the great landed families went out of their way to show their hostility to American democracy and their sympathy for the South, but there were influential newspapers and ardent voices on the other side as well. The great reformer John Bright was a host in himself, and his friendship with Lincoln and with Senator Sumner had far-reaching consequences on both sides of the water; it was to Bright that Lincoln sent a draft of those resolutions of support which he hoped British workingmen would adopt — and which they did. The efforts of statesmen like Bright and Cobden, intellectuals like John Stuart Mill, and American emissaries like Henry Ward Beecher and Archbishop Hughes, as well as the march of events, rallied British opinion eventually to the support of the Union.

Southern expectations of victory were based upon four delusions: that 'cavaliers' were invincible; that the Ohio valley would not fight; that all border states would secede; and that Britain and France would break the blockade to get cotton. The theory that inspired the Association of 1774 and Jefferson's embargo, the old delusion that American staples ran the wheels of industry in Europe, had gathered strength with the growing export of cotton to Britain and France. By the decade of the 1850's over 80 per cent of British cotton came from America. The prospect of a cotton famine, therefore, whether by the blockade or by a Confederate embargo policy, caused consternation in the textile centers of Manchester, Liverpool, and Lyons. No wonder Senator Hammond of South Carolina could boast that 'you dare not make war upon our cotton. No power on earth dares make war upon it. Cotton is King.'

Yet, as it turned out, this was a short-sighted view. By April 1861 there was a 50 per cent oversupply of cotton in the English market. Furthermore Britain was able to get cotton from Egypt and India and, later in the war, from the United States as well; altogether from 1860 to 1865 Britain managed to import over 5 million bales of cotton from America. So instead of demanding intervention to get more cotton, the big textile interests of England and France welcomed the opportunity to work off surplus stocks and to free themselves from dependence on the American supply. It was the workingmen of Lancashire and Yorkshire who suffered most from the cotton blockade; by the winter of 1862 some 330,000 operatives were out of work. The South had assumed that these would join with the manufacturers in demanding that Britain break the blockade, but they rallied instead to the support of the Union. That winter the workingmen of Manchester assured President Lincoln that 'our interests are identified with yours. We are truly one people. . . . If you have any ill-wishers here, be assured they are chiefly those who oppose liberty at home, and that they will be powerless to stir up quarrels between us.' Understandably Lincoln called this resolution 'an instance of sublime Christian heroism.'

As luck would have it, too, the Civil War years saw poor wheat and corn harvests in Europe and exceptionally good harvests in the United States. If Britain's looms depended on Southern cotton, her dinner tables depended on American grain; British imports of American wheat rose from 17 million bushels in 1860 to 62 million in 1862, with imports of other grains and of meats rising correspondingly. With some justice it could be argued that not cotton but wheat was king.

In thinking about the blockade, the South also ignored the traditional British doctrine of naval warfare. As Lord John Russell wrote, the American blockade satisfied principles that the Royal Navy had always observed; and in view of England's dependence on sea power, it would be highly imprudent for her to insist on different principles which might hamper her in the future.

International complications arose first from the fact that the United States officially regarded the war as a domestic insurrection, yet tacitly accorded belligerent status to the Confederacy by declaring a public blockade. Lincoln might simply have declared rebel ports closed to foreign commerce, as any government would do in similar circumstances today. But the world was not then prepared to respect a blockade unless the word were pronounced and the fact proclaimed; nor would neutral vessels on any other terms submit to visit and search.

Lord Palmerston's government issued a proclamation on 13 May 1861 which declared 'strict and impartial neutrality' in the contest between 'the Government of the United States of America and certain states styling themselves the Confederate States of America.' This proclamation was greatly to the advantage of the Union, as was another order forbidding port authorities of the empire to admit prize ships. But the very promptitude and explicitness of the neutrality proclamation and its unprecedented mention of a rebel government by its chosen name seemed unfriendly to the North and raised false hopes of recognition in the South. In fact the British position was, and remained throughout the war, technically correct. There was no recognition of the South; Southern emissaries were never officially received; delivery of ships built or under construction in British shipyards was stopped — on protest from the American minister; and in the end the Confederate envoys withdrew from England and British consuls retired from the South.

Yet at the beginning, and mid-way in the war, there were episodes that threatened a serious break. The first was the *Trent* affair. The British mail steamer *Trent* was conveying to Southampton two Confederate diplomatic agents, J. M. Mason and John Slidell, when on 8 November 1861 she was boarded from the U.S.S. *San Jacinto*, Captain Charles Wilkes commanding, and the two Confederates seized and jailed. When the news of this affair reached England, the British, having conveniently forgotten their own conduct during the Napoleonic wars — clamored for a showdown, the government sent reinforcements to Canada, and Lord John Russell drafted a demand for apology and reparation in terms so offensive as to be unacceptable. Fortunately Prince Albert, then in his last illness, toned down Russell's dispatch, and Queen Victoria, more friendly to America than some of her ministers, made it clear that she wanted peace. And by a notable dispensation of Providence the Atlantic cable had ceased to function. Seward from the first saw that Mason and Slidell must be surrendered; but Lincoln feared the political effect of yielding to Britain. Not until Charles Sumner, armed with letters from Bright and Cobden, had argued before the cabinet during a long Christmas Day session, could the President be persuaded to yield. Seward's note to the British minister was designed more to placate the American public than the British public, and contained no apology; but Mason and Slidell were released and forwarded to their uncomfortable posts. Many Americans felt that Britain had been less than generous in its reaction to the *Trent* case.

Yet in the end the *Trent* episode cleared the air. Seward now appeared in the new role of conciliator — and found that he liked it; an

Anglo-American war had been faced and found intolerable to both governments; and the British cabinet was stiffened in its policy of neutrality.

5. PLANS AND PERSONALITIES

For half a year after Bull Run, the armies in Virginia marked time. Day by day McClellan's inaction increased the political difficulties that were gathering about Lincoln. The united spirit formed by the guns that fired on Fort Sumter was evaporating. Lincoln was challenged in his own party by conservatives and by the radicals led by 'Ben' Wade, 'Zach' Chandler, and 'Thad' Stevens. A diverse group which differed on many issues, the Radicals were united in their hatred of the insolent slave power. By their zeal they helped transform the war from a struggle to put down an insurrection to a crusade for human rights, but their politics were often maladroit and even nasty. The policy they wished to force upon the President was immediate emancipation and arming of the slaves — a policy which, if adopted in 1861, would have alienated the Northern Democrats and driven the border slave states into secession. General Frémont's pretense to free the slaves in Missouri by proclamation, an act which Lincoln sternly rebuked, received their hearty approbation, whilst McClellan, even more conservative than Lincoln on the slavery question, was the particular object of their jealousy and suspicion.

To the Radical standard surged the uncompromising, eager to win yet certain to lose the war if the government yielded to their misguided ardor. Radicals dominated the Joint Committee on the Conduct of the War created by Congress on 20 December 1861. Throughout the war their inquisitorial activities, *ex parte* investigations, and missions to the front, hampered the executive, undermined army discipline, and discouraged the more competent generals. Yet the Radicals differed in one crucial respect from Jefferson Davis's gadflies. While Davis's opponents often valued particularist interests more highly than winning the war, the Radicals who tormented Lincoln were urging him on to greater effort. They energetically supported the war and indeed wished to enlarge its aims.

Owing to the efforts of another House committee, corruption on a gigantic scale was uncovered in the war department, and the scandal smirched Secretary Cameron. Lincoln sent him on a foreign mission and appointed a 'War Democrat,' Edwin M. Stanton, Secretary of War. Gloomy, ill-mannered, and vituperative, Stanton was another cross for Lincoln to bear. Ignorant of military matters and contemptuous of military science, intolerant of delay and harsh to subordinates, he was hated by almost every officer with whom he came in contact; and with several he dealt injustly. Yet for all that, Stanton's determination, thoroughness, and system proved him a fit instrument for Lincoln's purpose. He stood for discipline against the President's desire to pardon all deserters. He browbeat politicians and got things done. As Lincoln remarked at a dark period for the Union cause, 'Folks come up here and tell me that there are a great many men in the country who have all Stanton's excellent qualities without his defects. All I have to say is, I haven't met 'em! I don't know 'em! I wish I did!'

When Stanton took office (15 January 1862), McClellan had already prepared, and the President had approved, the general outlines of a plan of operations for 1862. In brief, it was to capture and hold the line of the Mississippi; to occupy Kentucky and Tennessee and cut the Memphis and Charleston railway; and to catch Richmond between two nippers, one operating from Albemarle Sound, and the other from Washington. The blockade, of course, was to be pressed home by the occupation of more bases on the Southern coast.

Lincoln was so pathetically eager to have something to show for all these elaborate preparations that he issued 'War Order No. 1,' designating Washington's Birthday as the date for a general forward movement of all the sea and land forces. Needless to say, 22 February passed without any forward move from McClellan, at whom the order was aimed. But already the first substantial victory for the Union had come in an unsuspected quarter, from an unknown general.

6. GRANT AND FARRAGUT

Ulysses S. Grant, an officer who disliked war and loathed army routine, had fallen on evil days since the proud moment before Mexico City. After promotion to a captaincy he resigned from the army in order to avoid a court-martial for drunkenness. Unable to extract a living from 'Hardscrabble Farm' near St. Louis, he attempted to sell real estate, and failed again. His father bestowed a clerkship in the family leather store at Galena, Illinois. Brothers condescended, fellow townsmen sneered. Only his wife had faith; and the meanest horses were obedient to his voice and hands.

Fort Sumter fell two weeks before Grant's thirty-ninth birthday. After many rebuffs he obtained a colonelcy of volunteers. His regiment, the 21st Illinois, was promptly ordered into Missouri to dislodge a Confederate regiment under a Colonel Harris. Approaching the reported position, so Grant relates, fear gripped his heart; but he had not the moral courage to halt and consider what to do. Suddenly there opened a view of the enemy's encampment — abandoned! 'It occurred to me at once that Harris had been as much afraid of me as I had been of him. This was a new view of the question I had never taken before; but it was one I never forgot afterwards.'

In August 1861 Grant received a brigadier's commission. In the late autumn he was assigned to General Henry Halleck's department and stationed at Cairo, Ill., at the junction of the Ohio with the Mississippi. Less than 50 miles up the Ohio from Cairo the Tennessee and Cumberland rivers opened parallel routes into Tennessee, Alabama, and Mississippi. Grant observed that Fort Henry and Fort Donelson, the two Confederate earthworks which closed these rivers, were the twin keys to the Confederate West. Their capture would open navigable waterways into the enemy's center and drive in his flanks. Grant was furnished with the necessary transports and gunboats and on 7 February 1862 Fort Henry was reduced by the gunboat flotilla before Grant's army arrived.

Fifteen miles across country, on the high left bank of the Cumberland, was the strong, entrenched camp called Fort Donelson. There Albert Sidney Johnston, the Confederate commander, had stationed half his army of 30,000, and thither the Fort Henry garrison retired. Grant disposed his troops in a semicircle about Fort Donelson on the land side, while the gunboats steamed down the Tennessee and up the Cumberland. On 13 February they attacked the fort at a range of 400 yards, but were driven back disabled. It seemed that a siege would be necessary. Two days later the Union right flank occupying dense woods on either side of the road to Nashville was surprised by a sortie. Grant arrived in the thick of the battle to find his right in disorder and his center in danger. Deducing from the three days' rations in a captured Confederate's haversack that the enemy was trying to cut his way out, and perceiving a certain confusion in his movements, Grant made exactly the right tactical disposition to drive the Confederates back into their entrenchments. It was a fierce, blind battle in the forest, but the result justified Grant in asking and the Confederate generals in agreeing to 'unconditional surrender' [1] of army and fortress.

The results of this Battle of Fort Donelson (15 February 1862) were unexpected, even to Grant. Nashville, with its valuable powder and armament works, was no longer tenable by the enemy, and A. S. Johnston retreated to the Memphis-Chattanooga railway. Grant had practically restored Tennessee to the Union; and, if his victory were followed up, the whole area would be open from Chattanooga to the Mississippi. Equally important was the moral gain to the then dispirited North. The prairie boys of the new Northwest had tried their mettle with the rangy foresters of the old Southwest; and the legend of Southern invincibility collapsed.

'Unconditional Surrender' Grant still had an old army reputation to live down. His jealous and pedantic superior, General Halleck, instead of allowing him to pursue A. S. Johnston, held up his advance and withdrew his troops to attack the northernmost Confederate strongholds on the Mississippi. In consequence Johnston found time to concentrate at Corinth with Beauregard and that notable man of God, Bishop and General Leonidas Polk.

They caught Grant napping, on 6 April. His army, encamped in an ill-chosen position at Pittsburg Landing, with its rear to the swollen Tennessee river and its front unprotected by entrenchments, had the Battle of Shiloh forced upon it. For twelve hours there was confused fighting between detached portions of the Union lines and the dashing Confederates. If the Union army was not routed it was due less to Grant's steadfast coolness than to the fiery valor of divisional commanders like William Tecumseh Sherman and to the pluck of individual soldiers. By the end of the day the Confederates had captured the key position at Shiloh church, the Union lines were dangerously near the river, and thousands of stragglers were cowering under the bluffs at Pittsburg Landing. But Albert Sidney Johnston, leading a charge, was mortally wounded, leaving the Confederates leaderless. All night a torrential rain drenched both armies, and the Union gunboats dropped shells on

1. Actually it was the astonishing Ben Butler, at Hatteras Inlet in August 1861, who first used this term, which has become a controversial one since World War II.

the Confederates. When the battle re-opened at dawn on 7 April Grant had been strengthened by Lew Wallace's division and the van of General Don Carlos Buell's Army of the Ohio. After ten more hours of desperate fighting Beauregard withdrew the Confederate army to Corinth. Grant's army was too exhausted to pursue.

Shiloh was a Union victory at a dreadful price. Out of 63,000 Union troops engaged, the loss was 13,000; the Confederates lost 11,000 out of 40,000. A storm of controversy arose, and pressure was put upon the President to remove Grant. Lincoln replied: 'I can't spare this man; he fights.' But General Halleck thought he could spare Grant, and did so by taking command of his army in person, and in consequence, little more was accomplished by the army during 1862 in this western theater of the war. But the river gunboats continued their advance down the Mississippi, and on 1 July 1862 joined Farragut's fleet above Vicksburg.

Captain Farragut had to force his way up the Mississippi from the Gulf without a single ironclad, but his wooden walls housed stout hearts. Below New Orleans, the river was protected by Forts Jackson and St. Philip, by sunken hulls supporting a log boom, by a fleet of rams and armed steamers, and by a current of three- to four-knot strength. In the small hours of 24 April Farragut's column of eight steam sloops-of-war and fifteen wooden gunboats, with chain cables secured as a coat of mail abreast the engines, crashed through the boom and ran the gantlet of armored rams, fire-rafts, river defense fleet, and the two forts. In the gay creole city of New Orleans, largest and wealthiest of the Confederacy, there had been no business since the blockade closed down and little laughter since the news of Shiloh. When Farragut's fleet anchored off the levee on 25 April, New Orleans was already abandoned by the Confederacy, and the following day United States forces took possession.

After landing the army Farragut proceeded up-river, receiving the surrender of Baton Rouge and Natchez, and running past Vicksburg to join the up-river gunboat fleet. But as Halleck could not be induced to provide troops for a joint attack on Vicksburg, that 'Gibraltar of the Mississippi' held out for a year longer, enabling Richmond to maintain communication with Arkansas, Missouri, and Texas.

The Confederacy was tightly pinched along its waistline; but the blood could still circulate. Thanks to the fumbling of Halleck the Union offensive in the West had failed in its great purpose, yet thanks chiefly to Grant it accomplished much of value. That was more than could be said of the grand campaigns of this year in the eastern theater of war.

7. THE PENINSULAR CAMPAIGN BEGINS

'In ten days I shall be in Richmond,' declared General McClellan on 13 February 1862. It was one of those rash boasts that made men doubt either his judgment or his sincerity. He was planning to outflank J. E. Johnston — then stationed at Manassas — by the Rappahannock, and race him for Richmond. A glance at the map on the next page will show the extreme unlikelihood of his success; and Johnston countered by moving to Fredericksburg. McClellan promptly emulated the famous King of France by marching a portion of his army to the deserted Confederate headquarters at Manassas, and back again to Washington. For Lincoln this was the last straw.

Throughout the winter Lincoln had stood between McClellan and a rising tide of popular impatience, radical suspicion, and denunciation by the committee on the conduct of the war. His patience was now exhausted, his confidence impaired. Yet when McClellan proposed a wide flanking movement by the York peninsula Lincoln reluctantly acquiesced. The President then (11 March) stripped McClellan of his superior command, leaving him only the Army of the Potomac, gave Stanton supreme control of military operations, and created a new department in western Virginia for Frémont with more troops than the 'Pathfinder' knew how to handle. Then, just as the campaign was beginning, he allowed Stanton to stop recruiting and to dismantle the new federal recruiting machinery. McClellan was forced to do his best with the means in hand; inadequate though this army was for his ambitious plans, it was greatly superior to anything the Confederacy could organize. Indeed the Army of the Potomac, well armed, trained, and equipped, and 110,000 strong, was the most formidable military force yet seen on American soil.

McClellan's peninsular plan had one obvious advantage, that it enabled the Union army to be supplied and reinforced by sea. Fortress Monroe, at the tip of the York peninsula, was in federal possession. The navy could protect the army's right flank as it advanced up the peninsula. On its left flank the James, with deep water up to the suburbs of

For details of the Gettysburg Campaign and the Seven Days' Battles, see individual maps.

Union Victory
Confederate Victory
△ Occupied by Union Forces
▲ Occupied by Confederate Forces
Union Campaign
Confederate Campaign

0   Miles   100

PENNSYLVANIA

Harrisburg

Chambersburg   York   Philadelphia

Gettysburg
1863

MARYLAND

NEW
JERSEY

Sharpsburg
(Antietam)
1862
Harpers
Ferry
Winchester 1862
1862
Cedar Cr.   Kernstown
1864   1862
Strasburg

W. VA.

Baltimore

Potomac

Front
Royal
1862
Manassas
Junc.
1862

Washington
Alexandria
Bull Run
(Manassas)
1st 1861
2nd 1862

DELA.

Chancellorsville
1863

Cross Keys
1862
Cedar Mt.
1862
The
Wilderness
1864
Fredericksburg
1862

McDowell
1862
Port
Republic
1862
Spotsylvania
1864

Chesapeake Bay

S. Anna

James

7 Days'
Battles
1862
Cold
Harbor 1864
West
Point

APPOMATTOX C.H.
LEE SURRENDERS
Apr. 9, 1865

Richmond

Seven
Pines
1862
Williamsburg
1862

Lynchburg

GRANT Apr.
1865
VIRGINIA
Five Forks
1865
Siege of
Petersburg
1865
Siege of
Yorktown
1862

VIRGINIA & MONITOR
1862

Norfolk

Danville

Roanoke

BENNETT HOUSE
JOHNSTON SURRENDERS
Apr. 26, 1865

Albemarle S.

Greensboro

Plymouth 1864

Roanoke I.
1862

Raleigh

Goldsboro

NORTH
CAROLINA

Bentonville
1865

Pamlico S.

Cape
Hatteras

Fayetteville
1865

SHERMAN March 1865

New Bern
1862

Beaufort

Ft. Macon 1862

THE EASTERN THEATER OF WAR, 1862-1865

656

Richmond, was a better line of approach; but C.S.S. *Virginia* (ex U.S.S. *Merrimack*) closed it to the Union navy during the first few weeks of the campaign. The *Virginia* — a more powerful edition of the armored gunboats already being used on the Mississippi — met her equal in the *Monitor* in Hampton Roads on 9 March 1862. A new principle of naval armament, the revolving turret, thereupon obtained the sanction of success. But so long as the *Virginia* was afloat she protected the mouth of the James.

McClellan intended to take Richmond and crush the rebellion that summer. His sense of injury at the hands of the administration, his suspicion that they did not really wish him to win, only made him the more ardent of success. Splendid visions were in his brain. Himself, on prancing charger, entering Richmond in triumph, Davis and Stephens playing the role of suppliants. Magnanimous terms to the gallant enemy: civil rights restored, slave property guaranteed. Discomfited administration not daring to refuse ratification. Grand review at Washington. Modest savior of his country resigns sword to Congress and returns to wife and baby at Cincinnati. Nominated by acclamation for President in 1864. Yet he did not employ the only methods that had the slightest chance of realizing these dreams: mobility and dash. His strategy throughout the campaign was determined by a policy of caution which allowed the hastily constructed Confederate field-works that crossed the peninsula from Yorktown to hold up his advance for the entire month of April. When on 5 May McClellan prepared to assault the Confederate lines he found that they had been quietly evacuated! A hasty Union pursuit was checked at Williamsburg and the Confederates withdrew in good order to the defense of Richmond.

8. LEE AND JACKSON

The Confederate government had been shaken out of its lethargy by Grant's capture of Fort Donelson. Its military organization had been improved by Davis's appointment of Lee as his military adviser (13 March 1862). Yet it was difficult to see how Richmond could be saved. McClellan with over 100,000 men would soon be advancing up the York peninsula, and J. E. Johnston had less than 60,000 to oppose him. McDowell's corps of 40,000 was before Fredericksburg (21 April) with only 11,000 Confederates between him and McClellan's right flank. The repulse of Stonewall Jackson near Kernstown had apparently corked up the Shenandoah valley. Frémont with 15,000 was approaching the upper valley through the Appalachian passes, where only 3000 Confederates faced him. Upon Lee's advice President Davis on 16 April adopted the strategy of delaying McClellan before Yorktown until Jackson could confuse the Union forces in the Shenandoah valley, threaten Harpers Ferry, and thus frighten the Union government into recalling McDowell's corps from its advanced position. On the same day the Confederate Congress adopted conscription. Of doubtful constitutionality, this courageous act drove a wedge between Davis and his state-rights critics, who feared that their precious theory was being done to death in the house of its friends. But conscription retained in the ranks the men who saved Richmond.

On 14 May McClellan, at last free from the Yorktown lines and within three days' march of Richmond, wired 'for every man the War Department can send, by water.' Lee, instead of recalling the scattered legions of the Confederacy to her capital, had the glorious audacity to use Jackson to neutralize three Union units and to break up McClellan's plans by threatening Washington.

Jackson returned to the upper valley, got around behind Banks, crushed his outposts (Front Royal, 22 May), almost cut his communications with Washington, administered a stinging defeat at Winchester, and sent him whirling north to the safe side of the Potomac (25 May). Washington was panic-stricken by Jackson's rapid advance, although shielded by double his numbers. Stanton telegraphed the governors of the loyal states, 'Enemy in great force advancing on Washington'; and Lincoln did exactly what Lee intended him to do: on 25 May he recalled McDowell's corps, on the point of marching to join McClellan.

Jackson, after a feint at Harpers Ferry, doubled on his tracks, passed between his enemies' converging columns, and on two successive days, 8 and 9 June, whipped Frémont at Cross Keys, and one of Banks's divisions at Port Republic. He was then ready to transfer his army to the Richmond front, while large Union forces remained immobile in the valley to protect Washington from another attack of nerves. In a few days McClellan would be on the defensive.

After this Battle of Fair Oaks (or Seven Pines), McClellan, true to his instinctive strategy of caution and constriction, dug himself into a stronger position and waited for fair weather to advance on Richmond under cover of superior artillery. 'We are engaged in a species of warfare at which we can never win,' Johnston wrote to Lee. 'It is plain that General McClellan will adhere to the system adopted by him last summer, and depend for success upon artillery and engineering.'

On 1 June Robert E. Lee succeeded Johnston, who had been wounded, and named his force the Army of Northern Virginia. He saw that McClellan must win Richmond if he were permitted to choose his own 'species of warfare' and that the closing cordon must be broken. Lee seized the offensive and threw McClellan upon the defensive. On 11 June he ordered Jackson to attack McClellan's right flank, while he launched an assault on the front.

9. THE SEVEN DAYS' BATTLES

On 26 June Lee took the initiative, and the great Seven Days' battles [2] began. Lee planned to crumple up McClellan's right, north of the Chickahominy, with A. P. Hill's and Jackson's divisions, to cut his communications, harass his army front and rear, and force him either to retreat down the peninsula or to surrender. Superb strategy, but too ambitious for his army to execute. Neither his staff nor his commanders were yet equal to the task of moving an exact combination of several columns in a thickly wooded country. And the Jackson of the Seven Days was not the Jackson of the Valley.

After beating off the first attack on his extreme right at Mechanicsville, McClellan withdrew Fitz John Porter's corps, which occupied that wing of his army, to a much stronger position near Gaines's Mill. There the Union troops threw up hasty field entrenchments that mark a stage in modern tactics; if spades were not yet trumps, they would be shortly. Against them, on the 27th, Lee developed his plan. The massed commands of Jackson, both Hills, and Longstreet, 57,000 strong, were hurled in line after line against the Union defenders (34,000), and at nightfall broke through. Only darkness saved Porter.

Toward midnight McClellan made the great decision: to move his army by the left to the newly prepared base on the James river, where the United States Navy was ready to take them out, if necessary. This

2. Mechanicsville (26 June), Gaines's Mill or first Battle of Cold Harbor (27th), Savage Station (29th), Frayser's Farm or Glendale (30th), Malvern Hill (1 July).

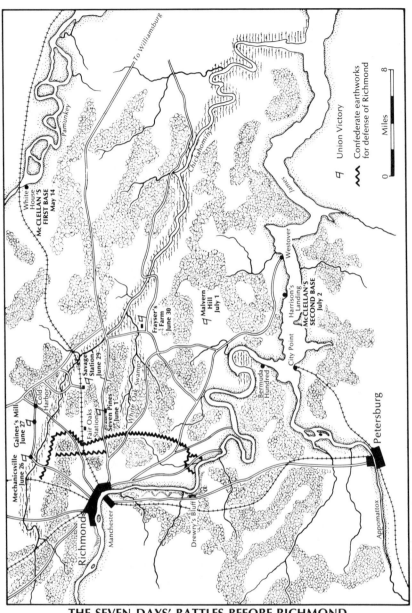

THE SEVEN DAYS' BATTLES BEFORE RICHMOND
June 26—July 2, 1862

meant giving up his cherished plan to capture Richmond. In something like despair he hurled at Stanton an unforgivable charge: 'If I save this army now I tell you plainly that I owe no thanks to you or to any other person in Washington.' On the night of 27–28 June, McClellan withdrew his right across the Chickahominy and began to move by the left southward, to the James. Lee was completely baffled. His cavalry was sent sweeping eastward, to cut communications that were no longer there. During 30 precious hours the Confederate leader lost contact and knowledge of an army of 90,000 men, whose rear-guard was only a few hundred yards from his pickets, and whose van was within a few miles of his capital. Only at sunrise on the 29th did Lee discover that he had concentrated on empty camps and deserted entrenchments. Promptly he drafted another brilliant plan of concentration, but again his staff and his divisional commanders were unequal to the task. McClellan's maneuver was conducted with the precision of a grand review. 'Throughout this campaign we attacked just when and where the enemy wished us to attack,' wrote D. H. Hill. The Army of the Potomac, 90,000 strong, with its trains of artillery, 5000 wagons, and 2500 beeves, marched by two narrow country roads crossing the highways that led from Richmond, defending itself flank and rear in fierce bayonet encounters against Lee's pursuing army. On Malvern Hill (1 July), in a position carefully chosen by its commander, the Union army stood at bay, while Lee hurled his divisions without order or unity over cannon-swept wheatfields, in a last desperate attempt to trap the host he had hoped to destroy. By the close of the second day of July, while Lee was withdrawing his decimated legions toward Richmond, the Army of the Potomac, with trains intact and morale unimpaired, was secure at Harrison's Landing on the James under Union gunboats.

It was magnificent, but it was a retreat. McClellan, outnumbered in effective force at the beginning of the Seven Days, had inflicted a superior loss on his adversaries.[3] His army was still full of fight and ready to resume the advance on Richmond if properly reinforced. The summer was still young. McClellan entreated Lincoln to give him an opportunity to attack Richmond via Petersburg. But General Halleck (who had replaced Stanton in control of operations) pronounced this plan,

3. Union effectives engaged, 91,169; Union loss (killed, wounded, and missing), 15,849. Confederate effectives engaged, 95,481; Confederate loss, 20,614. T. L. Livermore, *Numbers and Losses*, p. 86.

by which Grant subsequently brought the war to an end, to be impracticable; and Lincoln feared that the administration could no longer carry McClellan. The country could see nothing except that Richmond was still in rebel hands after a costly campaign. Accordingly, on 3 August, Halleck ordered the Army of the Potomac back to the river that gave it birth; and all the gains of the Peninsular campaign were thrown away. Not for over two years did another Union army approach so near Richmond.

So ended the first grand campaign of the war. Lee by audacious strategy, Jackson by brilliant execution of Lee's orders, had taken full advantage of the enemy's mistakes, and saved Richmond. But Richmond alone was hardly worth the loss of some 25,000 men; only the capture or destruction of the Army of the Potomac could have won Southern independence. McClellan too had been wanting. His strategy had been sound but his tactics faulty, and he had lost an opportunity to end the war promptly. If the war had ended that summer, slavery would not have been abolished by violence, and the South would have had some voice in whatever means of gradual emancipation might subsequently have been adopted. In a little while, President Lincoln would feel that he had more need of the moral forces represented by abolition than of the border slave states: that God, after all, had a higher fighting value than Kentucky.

10. WEIGHING IMPONDERABLES

The eight weeks that followed the Seven Days were pure sunshine for the Confederacy. Thousands of replacements for Lee's army came pouring into Richmond. On 28 July C.S.S. *Alabama* left Liverpool for a cruise that proved costly for the American merchant marine and eventually even more so for the British taxpayer.

'There is an all but unanimous belief that you *cannot* subject the South to the Union,' Richard Cobden wrote Senator Sumner on 11 July, when news of the Seven Days' battles reached England. The same day W. S. Lindsay, M.P., the largest shipowner and most active Southern partisan in Great Britain, introduced a motion for Franco-British mediation in the Civil War. On 16 July Napoleon III listened graciously to John Slidell's offer of 100,000 bales of cotton if France would denounce the blockade. The Emperor telegraphed to his foreign minister: 'Ask the English government if it does not think the moment has arrived to recognize the South.' Palmerston was still against recognition; but the cotton shortage was becoming acute, and Lee's army was preparing to take the offensive. Writing from London, Henry Adams concluded that only victory, or a prompt and definite stand on the slavery question, could prevent European interference.

For Lincoln the slavery question was somewhat more complicated. He always remembered what it seemed all the world had forgotten, that he was President of the United States — not of the Northern States. His policy was explained in a famous letter to Horace Greeley, editor of the New York *Tribune*, of 22 August 1862:

> As to the policy I 'seem to be pursuing,' as you say, I have not meant to leave any one in doubt. I would save the Union. I would save it the shortest way under the Constitution. The sooner the national authority can be restored, the nearer the Union will be 'the Union as it was.' If there be those who would not save the Union unless they could at the same time save slavery, I do not agree with them. If there be those who would not save the Union unless they could at the same time destroy slavery, I do not agree with them. My paramount object in this struggle is to save the Union, and is not either to save or to destroy slavery. If I could save the Union without freeing any slave, I would do it; and if I could save it by freeing all the slaves I would do it; and if I could save it by freeing some and leaving others alone, I would also do that. What I do about slavery, and the colored race, I do because I believe it helps to save the Union; and what I forbear, I forbear because I do not believe it would help to save the Union.

From the first advance into Southern territory, slaves of rebel owners had flocked into the Union lines, embarrassing both government and commanders, until the irrepressible Benjamin F. Butler declared them 'contraband of war.' The 'contrabands' were organized in labor battalions, and school teachers were provided to look after their welfare. When Union forces captured the sea islands between Charleston and Savannah in November 1861, the cotton planters fled, and their plantations and some 10,000 slaves came under the jurisdiction of the Treasury, which conducted an 'experiment in reconstruction.' Betrayed by their enemies and sometimes by their friends, the Negroes nonetheless demonstrated that they could participate in a free society in which they owned property and earned wages.

After the war some of the returning planters found themselves borrowing money from their former slaves. Unfortunately the border states blocked proposals for compensated emancipation on which the President had set his heart. Delaware lost a chance to lead in defeating by a single vote a bill for gradual emancipation of her 1800 slaves, with compensation to their owners from the Federal Government. In April and June 1862 Congress finally carried out a party pledge by abolishing slavery in the District of Columbia and the territories.

Increasingly the question intruded: of what avail to restore the Union if slavery, the original cause of disruption, remained? James Russell Lowell expressed this admirably in his 'Biglow Paper' that appeared in the *Atlantic Monthly* of June 1862. Hosea is conversing with the shade of his 'gret-gret-gret-gran'ther';

> 'Hosee,' sez he, 'I think you're goin' to fail:
> The rettlesnake ain't dangerous in the tail;
> This 'ere rebellion's nothin' but the rettle, —
> You'll stomp on thet an' think you've won the bettle;
> It's Slavery thet's the fangs an' thinkin' head,
> An' ef you want selvation, cresh it dead, —
>
> .   .   .
>
> 'God's truth! ' sez I, —'an' ef I held the club,
> An' knowed jes' where to strike — but there's the rub!'

"The moment came,' said Lincoln, 'when I felt that slavery must die that the nation might live.' In the cabinet meeting on 22 July he proposed to declare that on the next New Year's Day all slaves in rebel territory would be free. Seward pointed out that such a proclamation at such a time would be interpreted as 'our last shriek on the retreat' from Richmond. Emancipation was then put aside to be a crown to the first victory.

Victory seemed possible that summer, if one merely counted the battalions; but Union morale had been gravely impaired by McClellan's failure to take Richmond. There was a panic in Wall Street; the gold dollar reached a 17 per cent premium over paper in mid-July, when Congress authorized a new issue of $150 million in paper money. When Lincoln called upon the states for 300,000 volunteers, fewer than 90,000 enlisted, and they were organized in new nine-month regiments instead of being used, like the Confederate conscripts, as permanent replacements.

Yet, if the situation had changed for the worse, Lincoln had attained new stature. Resolute in purpose and sure of vision he had always been; yet often vacillating and uncertain in performance. From those anxious vigils at the White House during the Seven Days the perplexed, over-advised, and humble Lincoln emerged humble only before God, but the master of men. He seemed to have captured all the greater qualities of the great Americans who preceded him, without their defects: the poise of Washington without his aloofness, the astuteness of Jefferson without his indirection, the conscience of J. Q. Adams without his harshness, the forthrightness of Jackson without his ignorance, the magnetism of Clay without his vanity, the lucidity of Webster without his ponderousness; and fused them with a magnanimity peculiarly his own.

11. THE SECOND BULL RUN

From the Peninsular campaign Lincoln had learned the folly of divided command and civilian direction; but the instruments of victory he had not yet found. On 11 July he relegated Stanton to his proper place as war minister and summoned Halleck from the West to become general-in-chief in control of operations. 'Old Brains' Halleck, as the army called him, wrote excellent treatises on military science, but seemed helpless before actual problems.

McClellan was still at Harrison's Landing, begging for reinforcements to attack Richmond by way of Petersburg; but Halleck withdrew his army by driblets to reinforce the war department's favorite plan of an overland march on Richmond, covering Washington. To lead this advance, Halleck summoned General John Pope, who after winning some trifling successes on the Mississippi had the self-confidence of a Napoleon. Now was Lee's opportunity to break the wall of steel that was closing about the Confederacy, to carry the war into the free states, and to win peace and recognition on Northern soil. Again with Jackson's close co-operation in a bold maneuver, he got on Pope's flank, drew the Army of the Potomac into the spot he wanted, and attacked it front and rear in the second Battle of Bull Run, or Manassas (29 August–1 September 1862). Pope himself was hopelessly outmaneuvered and bewildered; and Fitz John Porter, with 10,000 men, failed to get into the battle at all. The result was a shattering defeat. By combining bold strategy and perfect tactics, Lee and Jackson had undone the Union gains of an entire year in the Virginia theater of war.

As the news from the front became more and more alarming, Lincoln, without consulting Halleck or his cabinet, placed McClellan in 'command of the fortifications of Washington, and of all the troops for the defence of the capital.' The General at once rode out to meet Pope's retreating army and received enthusiastic acclaim from his troops.

Lincoln now faced a cabinet meeting. Stanton and Chase were vehement in their opposition to McClellan, and all their colleagues with the exception of Seward and Blair concurred. Lincoln admitted most of their allegations — but pointed out that no one else had the confidence of officers and men, or the ability to cope with so desperate a situation. As Gideon Welles wrote:

> In stating what he had done, the President was deliberate, but firm and decisive. His language and manner were kind and affectionate, especially toward two of the members who were greatly disturbed; but every person present felt that he was truly the chief, and every one knew his decision, though mildly expressed, was as fixed and unalterable as if given out with the imperious command and determined will of Andrew Jackson.

When, three days later (5 September), news came that Lee was crossing the Potomac above Washington into Maryland, Lincoln orally gave McClellan 'command of the forces in the field.'

Of many crises for the Union this was the most acute. With Virginia clear of invaders Lee was about to break through into the heart of the Union. In the West a Confederate offensive was undoing the work of Grant and Buell: Kirby Smith had taken Lexington and was threatening Cincinnati; Braxton Bragg was racing Buell for Louisville. If he won, Kentucky would be secured for the Confederacy, and a Southern invasion of Ohio might follow. In England the sentiment for intervention came to a head.

Lee expected to win Maryland for the Confederacy; but his prime objective was the railway bridge over the Susquehanna at Harrisburg, Pa. Possession of that bridge and of the line of approach would come perilously near cutting the Union in two. It would leave Washington connected with the West only by the roundabout Atlantic Ocean, Hudson river, and Great Lakes route. The victorious Southern army would be in a central position to attack Washington, Baltimore, or Philadelphia. President Davis, on Northern soil, would propose peace on the basis of Southern independence; and if Lincoln's government refused they would have to reckon with the people in the November election and face the likelihood of foreign intervention. On 7 September the French minister at Washington informed Seward that in his opinion it was time to recognize the independence of the Confederacy. Napoleon III was only waiting for English approval, which might well have come after another Confederate victory.

12. ANTIETAM

As they splashed through the fords of the Potomac in those early September days, the regimental bands of Lee's army played the stirring air in which an ardent citizen of Maryland implored his state to 'clothe her beauteous limbs with steel' and 'be the battle-queen of yore.'

> Come, for thy dalliance does thee wrong,
> Maryland! My Maryland!
> Come, for thy shield is bright and strong,
> Maryland! My Maryland!

But she did not come. Southern influence in Maryland extended little beyond tidewater. The prudent farmers of the western counties were more impressed by the ragged uniforms of Lee's barefooted veterans than by his invitation to thow off their 'foreign yoke.' It was the harvest season in that rich section of Maryland. Orchards heavily fruited, well-stocked piggeries, and ripe 'roastin' ears' refreshed the foot-weary boys in gray and tempted many to remain. Lee lost more men by desertion than he gained by recruiting.

Lee counted on McClellan taking weeks to reorganize and thought he could safely divide his army, sending Jackson to capture Harpers Ferry while he moved into Pennsylvania. But he miscalculated. While his army scattered over the Maryland countryside, McClellan marched on him with 70,000 men. For on 13 September a soldier brought him Lee's Order No. 191 setting forth in detail the whole plan of the campaign. It was one of those strokes of chance that changes the course of history.

South Mountain, as the Blue Ridge is called where it crosses Maryland, separated the hostile armies. Sending his van to force the passes, McClellan sat his horse as in review by the roadside, pointing to where clouds of smoke showed that the Battle of South Mountain had begun. Men and officers as they passed cheered themselves hoarse, falling out of ranks to touch his charger. That day (14 September) South Mountain was carried. 'I thought I knew McClellan, but this movement of his puzzles me,' exclaimed his West Point classmate, Stonewall Jackson. Lee knew what it meant and hastened south from Hagerstown just in time to prevent the Union army from interposing between his great lieutenant and himself. Jackson crossed the Potomac and joined Lee on the 16th; but the reunited Army of Northern Virginia, outnumbered more than two to one, was caught in a cramped position between Antietam Creek and the Potomac, where Lee had no room to perform those brilliant maneuvers that were his delight and the enemy's confusion. He had no alternative but to fight or to retreat, and he chose to fight.

The Battle of the Antietam or Sharpsburg (17 September) was a series of desperate unco-ordinated attacks and equally desperate but skillful counter-attacks that exhausted Lee's army but did not drive it from position. Although fresh reserves were available, McClellan failed to use them and refused to renew the battle the next day, as Grant or Sherman would certainly have done. Relieved of further pressure, Lee recrossed the Potomac into Virginia on the night of 18 September. The crisis was ended.

Antietam was nearly decisive; it might have been really so if McClellan had not missed the opportunity for a knockout. Two years and a half more elapsed before the war ended, but the Confederacy was never so near independence or Lee's army so near a ruinous defeat as on that bloody day in the Maryland hills. McClellan by restoring morale to the army, by assuming responsibility, and through the lucky break of the lost order, had frustrated Lee's campaign and parried the most serious thrust at his country's heart. Antietam averted all danger of foreign recognition of the Confederacy; and by giving Lincoln the opportunity he sought to issue the Emancipation Proclamation, it brought the liberal opinion of the world to his side.

13. FOREVER FREE

It was on 22 September 1862, five days after Antietam, that Lincoln opened a momentous cabinet meeting by reading Artemus Ward's 'High-handed Outrage in Uticy.' The President had not summoned his cabinet for their advice, so he told them. He had made a covenant with God to free the slaves as soon as the rebels were driven out of Maryland; God had decided on the field of Antietam; his mind was fixed, his decision made. Blair and Bates, from border slave states, thought the moment inopportune; the President reminded them that for months he had urged their states to take the initiative in emancipation. He must now make the forward movement. In the Preliminary Emancipation Proclamation the President, by virtue of his power as commander-in-chief of the army and navy, declared that upon the first day of January 1863 all slaves within any state or district then in rebellion against the United States 'shall be then, thenceforward, and forever free.'

This proclamation, potentially more revolutionary in human relationships than any event in American history since 1776, lifted the Civil War to the dignity of a crusade. Though it did not actually free any slaves — for it did not apply to loyal border states — it did make clear that slavery would not survive Union victory. Yet it was slow to influence public opinion at home or abroad. The South, indignant at what she considered an invitation to the slaves to cut their masters' throats, was nerved to greater effort. The Northern armies received from it no new impetus. The Democratic party, presenting it to the Northern people as proof that abolitionists were responsible for the duration of the war, made signal gains in the autumn elections. Julia Ward Howe saw in it the glory of the coming of the Lord; but in England and Europe the proclamation was greeted by conservatives with contempt, as a flat political maneuver, though by liberals with joy. The liberal *Morning Star* called it 'indisputably the great fact of the war — the turning point in the history of the American commonwealth . . . a gigantic stride in the paths of Christian and civilized progress.'

Antietam did not alter the opinion held by almost every member of Palmerston's ministry that the Union could never conquer the South; but it did convince every member of the cabinet except Gladstone that the moment was inopportune for intervention. Joint mediation between North and South, which Lord John Russell began to advocate after the second Bull Run, died in the hands of his colleagues by the end of October. A more concrete proposal from Napoleon III, that England, France, and Russia join in proposing an armistice and lifting the blockade for six months, was definitely rejected by the British cabinet on 11 November. So passed the second great crisis in foreign relations.

14. FREDERICKSBURG

Lee's Army of Northern Virginia retreated up the Shenandoah valley in a demoralized condition. 'The absent are scattered broadcast over the land,' Lee wrote the Confederate Secretary of War on 23 September, 'unless something is done the army will melt away.' And the invasion of Kentucky had proved as disappointing as that of Maryland; the spirit of Henry Clay was too strong. 'Unless a change occurs soon, we must abandon the garden spot of Kentucky to its cupidity,' wrote Braxton Bragg on 25 September. On 8 October Buell fought a western Antietam, at Perryville; and although Bragg claimed the victory, he retreated to central Tennessee.

Public opinion in the North was not so much grateful to McClellan for what he had done as indignant because he had let Lee escape. On 6 October Lincoln ordered McClellan to 'cross the Potomac and give battle to the enemy, or drive him South.' Instead of moving at once, McClellan began to clamor for supplies and clothing and to bandy words with the President. The prospect of another winter of bickering and procrastination was more than Lincoln could bear; and the fall elections had begun. Toward the end of October Lincoln decided that if McClellan permitted Lee to get between him and Richmond, McClellan must go. Lee did just that; and on 7 November the President relieved McClellan of command of the Army of the Potomac and appointed Burnside in his place.

Distinguished chiefly for his flowing side-whiskers, Burnside proved monumentally incompetent. Learning nothing from experience, he reverted to the old plan of a 'covering advance' on Richmond, from a base behind the Rappahannock opposite Fredericksburg. Lee hastened across northern Virginia and, before Burnside had crossed, posted a mighty army of 75,000 men and over 300 guns on the south bank of the Rappahannock, on the wooded heights above Fredericksburg. There, on 13 December, they met an attack by Burnside's army of 113,000 that presented the most inspiring spectacle and the most useless slaughter of the Civil War. Burnside ordered a frontal attack on Lee's center, strongly entrenched on Marye's Heights: an 'insane attempt,' as one of the Union generals called it. Six times the Union infantry — long double lines of blue, bright national and regimental colors, bayonets gleaming in the sun — pressed across an open plain completely covered

by the Confederate artillery and entrenched riflemen. Six times the survivors were hurled back, leaving the dead and wounded lying in heaps.
The slaughter was appalling and one-sided: Burnside lost 12,700 men,
Lee 5400. 'It is well that war is so terrible,' said Lee as he watched the
battle, 'or we should grow too fond of it.'

15. POLITICAL INTRIGUE

The South hoped that this battle would end the war; but the Fredericksburg position was not one from which Lee could pursue the
enemy with profit. Yet to many loyal men in the North it must have
seemed, as it did to an English war correspondent, that the 13th day of
December would be a memorable date in the decline and fall of the
American republic. Elections in October and November to the new
House of Representatives had increased the Democratic delegation
from 44 to 75 members. New York elected a Democratic governor by
10,000 majority; Pennsylvania, Republican by 60,000 in 1860, went
Democratic by 4000 in 1862. Ohio, Indiana, and Illinois — Lincoln's
own state — together returned 33 Democrats and only 11 Republicans
to the new House; and among the Democrats were several of the 'copperheads,' as Northern opponents of the war were called. Only in New
England and the trans-Mississippi West did the Emancipation Proclamation seem to strike a responsive note; those regions and (strangely
enough) the border slave states saved the Republican majority.

Instead of being drawn more closely to the President by emancipation and misfortune, the radicals were still his bitter enemies. A few
days after Fredericksburg, the Republican members of Congress held a
caucus, and on Senator Sumner's proposal appointed a committee of
several radicals to call on the President and demand a change of men
and measures. Seward must go, for Seward was the friend of McClellan; and the jealous Chase, angling for the presidency in 1864, had convinced his friends in Congress that Seward was the cause of all the
nation's woes. That night the President confided his distress to his
friend, Senator Browning, 'We are now on the brink of destruction. It
appears to me the Almighty is against us, and I can hardly see a ray of
hope.'

Apparently, Lincoln had to make a choice: yield to the radicals by
sacrificing the indispensable Seward, or defy the Republican party
by expelling Chase. He must, in derogation of established constitutional

practice, allow Congress to choose his cabinet, or separate himself wholly from Congress. Either horn of the dilemma would entail disaster. When Browning told him that the game was to surround him with a radical cabinet, 'The President said with a good deal of emphasis that he was master, and that they should not do that.'

Seward promptly offered his resignation, and in the hope of cementing radical support, Chase followed suit. Lincoln, his eye lighting up, almost snatched the paper from his clerk's hesitating hand. Laughing, he exclaimed with a graphic frontier metaphor, 'Now I can ride! I have got a pumpkin in each end of my bag.' He wrote identical letters to both secretaries, refusing to accept their resignations; and both resumed their duties. Lincoln was master indeed.

To crown this eventful year there only remained for Lincoln to issue the definite Emancipation Proclamation, which faint-hearted Union men had urged him to postpone indefinitely. In anticipation, on New Year's Eve, pro-Union meetings were held in several English cities, and stout resolves were passed that heartened the President and his people. 'The erasure of that foul blot upon civilization and Christianity — chattel slavery — during your presidency will cause the name of Abraham Lincoln to be honored and revered by posterity,' declared a meeting of 6000 working men at Manchester, the city which suffered most from the Union blockade. To which Lincoln replied on 19 January 1863:

> I know and deeply deplore the sufferings which the working men at Manchester, and in all Europe are called to endure in this crisis. . . . Under the circumstances, I cannot but regard your decisive utterances upon the question as an instance of sublime Christian heroism which has not been surpassed in any age or in any country. It is indeed an energetic and reinspiring assurance of the inherent power of truth and of the ultimate and universal triumph of justice, humanity and freedom. I do not doubt that the sentiments you have expressed will be sustained by your great nation; and, on the other hand, I have no hesitation in assuring you that they will excite admiration, esteem and the most reciprocal feeling of friendship among the American people. I hail this interchange of sentiment, therefore, as an augury that whatever else may happen, whatever misfortune may befall your country or my own, the peace and friendship which now exist between the two nations will be, as it shall be my desire to make them, perpetual.

XXXVI

Behind the Lines

1. LIBERTY IN WARTIME

Lincoln wielded a greater power throughout the war than any later chief magistrate, excepting Franklin D. Roosevelt; a wider authority than any English-speaking ruler between Cromwell and Churchill. If Lincoln was the ideal tyrant of whom Plato dreamed, he was none the less a dictator from the standpoint of American constitutional law and practice. President Davis was open to the same charge; and in the Confederacy, as in the United States, there were many citizens who preferred to risk defeat at the hands of the enemy rather than submit to arbitrary government by their own President.

The war power of the President as commander-in-chief of the army and navy is, in practice, limited only by public opinion and the courts. At the very beginning of the war, Lincoln of his own authority called for enlistments not yet sanctioned by Congress, proclaimed the blockade, and suspended the writ of habeas corpus in parts of Maryland. The first assumption of power was shortly legalized by Congress, the second by the Supreme Court; but Chief Justice Taney protested in vain against executive suspension of the famous writ (*ex parte* Merryman). At the same time military officers, acting under orders from the state or the war department, began to arrest persons suspected of disloyalty or espionage, and to confine them without trial in military prisons for indefinite terms. Lincoln thought it unwise to indulge a meticulous reverence for the Constitution when the Union was crumbling. As he put it in his message of 4 July 1861, 'Are all the laws but one to go unexecuted, and the government itself go to pieces, lest that one be violated?' And, again, in justifying, or extenuating, acts that violated traditional concepts of due process of law: 'Must I shoot a simple-minded soldier boy who deserts, while I must not touch a hair of the wily agitator who induces him to desert?' Lincoln himself counseled moderation, but the power he wielded was grossly abused by subordinates.

Simultaneously with the Emancipation Proclamation, the President announced that all persons resisting the draft, discouraging enlistment, or 'guilty of any disloyal practice affording aid and comfort to rebels' would be subject to martial law, tried by court-martial, and denied the writ of habeas corpus. Under this proclamation, over 13,000 persons were arrested and confined by military authority, for offenses ranging from the theft of government property to treason. Earlier in 1862 — only a few days after he had scathingly denounced Lincoln's tyranny — President Davis obtained from his Congress the power to suspend the writ of habeas corpus, and promptly did so in Richmond and other places, where arbitrary and unjust proceedings occurred.

Undoubtedly the provocation was great, especially in the North, where opposition to the war was open, organized, and active. Many Northerners sincerely believed that only the obstinacy of Lincoln, or the ambition of Davis, prevented peace. The copperheads worked ceaselessly to discourage recruiting and to hamstring the government. In the Confederacy, anti-Davis sentiment evolved easily into anti-war sentiment. On both sides the opponents of war organized secret societies. In the North the 'Knights of the Golden Circle' harassed loyal households by midnight raids and barn-burnings; in the South the 'Heroes of America' gave aid and comfort to the enemy.

Neither the Union nor the Confederate government made any systematic effort to suppress these organizations: perhaps because they were too formidable. In Ohio, Indiana, and Illinois, where treason flourished side by side with the most stalwart loyalty, General Burnside attempted repression in 1863 with slight success. In a general order he declared, 'The habit of declaring sympathy for the enemy will not be allowed in this department.' For violation of this order, in a campaign speech, the prominent copperhead Clement Vallandigham was arrested, tried by a military commission, and sentenced to confinement for the duration of the war. Lincoln humorously altered the sentence to banishment, and Vallandigham was escorted within the military lines of the Confederacy. He received *in absentia* the Democratic nomination for governor of Ohio and conducted a campaign for peace and reunion from Canadian soil. In 1866 the Supreme Court took cognizance of a similar case (*ex parte* Milligan), and declared in unmistakable terms that neither the Constitution nor any custom of war could sanction the military trial of a civilian in districts where the civil courts were open.

This decision, coming after the war, helped nobody. Owing to unchecked acts of over-zealous military officers, personal liberty was subject to a more arbitrary if spasmodic control during the Civil War than during the two world wars. Yet on the whole pacifists, conscientious objectors, and critics of the government fared better under the Lincoln regime than under that of Wilson. There was no single act in the two world wars so outrageous as the trial of the conspirators in the assassination of Lincoln; but the Espionage Act of 1917, administered by a department of justice with a corps of paid spies and volunteer informers and enforced by judges and juries often maddened with war propaganda, was more unjust in its operation than the courts-martial of 1861–65; and the so-called 'relocation' of West-coast Japanese in World War II was less justifiable than anything that happened under Lincoln. Throughout the Civil War active disloyalty was effectively dealt with wherever it raised its head; but there was no general censorship of the press, and discussion of war aims and peace terms went unhindered. Hardly a Northern community lacked a few 'unterrified Democrats' who maintained with impunity that Jeff Davis was a better man than Abe Lincoln, secession was legitimate, and the Union forever dissolved. Sentences of courts-martial were comparatively mild, and offenders were pardoned promptly with the coming of peace.

In the field of civil and political liberties, the Confederate record was better than that of the Union. No Southern newspapers were suspended, or even censored, although they were often guilty of divulging important military information to Northern commanders and their attacks on the government sometimes passed the bounds of decency. Davis suspended the writ of habeas corpus on three occasions, but only with congressional authority and approval, despite the fact that the writ was widely abused to prevent military authorities from apprehending deserters and draft dodgers. On the other hand, the habits of command, bred in a slave society, expressed themselves in aggravated form. Military commanders like General Braxton Bragg established martial law and ruled their areas with an iron hand. Hordes of provost marshals infested the land, demanding passports and credentials from all who attracted their attention and suspicion. Loyalty oaths were exacted indiscriminately — even from aliens — and neutrals and Unionists were almost as badly treated as loyalists during the Revolution. These policies and practices, however, proved futile either to put down Unionism or arrest defeatism in the Confederacy.

2. NORTHERN INDUSTRY AND WESTWARD EXPANSION

It was an article of faith among subjects of King Cotton that Northern industry, cut off from its Southern markets and its supply of fiber, would collapse. On the contrary, Northern industry grew fat and saucy during the war. Union sea power maintained the routes to foreign markets; the waste of war stimulated production. In Philadelphia alone 180 new factories were built during the years 1862–64. The government, generous in its contracts and lavish in expenditure, helped to create a new aristocracy of profiteers, who became masters of capital after the war.[1] The North, prepared to endure the deprivation of war, was startled to find it was enjoying a war-boom, an experience which would be a common phenomenon in the twentieth century. After the middle of 1862 enough cotton was obtained from the occupied parts of the South, and even brought from Liverpool, to re-open many cotton mills. Indeed the only essential Northern industry that suffered from the war was the carrying trade. Only 257 American merchantmen were destroyed by Confederate cruisers, but many more took foreign registry to escape capture; and with the diversion of the better ships into government service, the foreign-flag share in American trade greatly increased.

In many ways the drain of men into the army and navy was compensated. Immigration for the five war years amounted to almost 800,000. Labor-saving devices, invented before the war, were now

---

1. The foundations of the Armour (meat packing), Havemeyer (sugar), Weyerhaeuser (lumber), Huntington (merchandise and railroads), Remington (guns), Rockefeller (oil), Carnegie (iron and steel), Borden (milk), and Marshall Field (merchandise) fortunes were laid during the war.

generally applied. The Howe sewing machine proved a boon to the clothing manufacturer and a curse to the poor seamstress, whose wage dropped to eight cents an hour in 1864. The Gordon McKay machine for sewing uppers to shoe-soles speeded up that process one hundred-fold and revolutionized the industry. Petroleum, discovered in Pennsylvania in 1859, was so rapidly extracted that production increased from 84,000 to 128 million gallons in three years; and refining methods were so rapidly improved that kerosene in cheap glass lamps had begun to replace candles and whale oil by 1865. New industries sprang up to meet the army's insatiable demand for food: Gail Borden supplied condensed milk, the packing houses of Armour and Morris provided meat, and the Van Camp Company experimented with canned vegetables to frustrate the threat of scurvy.

Like causes speeded up the revolution in American agriculture. The mechanical reaper, hitherto confined to the better prairie farms, came into general use, giving every harvest hand fivefold his former capacity with scythe and cradle. The annual pork pack almost doubled, the annual wool clip more than tripled between 1860 and 1865. Westward migration and the opening up of new prairie wheatfields were greatly stimulated by the passage of the Homestead Act in 1862, which supplemented the Pre-emption Act of 1841 by offering a settler title to 160 acres of public land after five years' residence and use, for a nominal fee. Some 15,000 homesteads were thus pre-empted during the war. Every autumn brought bumper crops of wheat and corn, while Europe suffered a succession of poor harvests. England imported fiftyfold the amount of wheat and flour in 1862 that she had in 1859. Although the lack of cotton threw many English factory operatives out of work, it was evident that any attempt to break the blockade, and consequently fight the United States, would bring the British Isles face to face with starvation. 'Old King Cotton's dead and buried, brave young Corn is King,' went the refrain of a popular song.

Apart from this extension of prairie farming, the development of the West continued. Colorado, the goal of the 'Pikes Peak or Bust' gold rush in 1859, was organized as a territory in 1861; and with the reorganization of Dakota and Nevada territories the same year, no part of the United States, on paper at least, was any longer outside the dominion of law. Kansas became a state as soon as Congress lost its Southern delegation in 1861; and Nevada was admitted prematurely in

1864, because the Republicans thought they needed its electoral vote. At least 300,000 emigrants crossed the plains to California, Oregon, and the new territories during the war — some to farm, others to seek gold, and many to escape the draft.

In general, the normal growth and activity of a civilized community continued in the North. The cities increased in wealth and population. Enrollment in the universities hardly decreased beyond the loss of Southern students, although in some of the Western colleges the undergraduates enlisted in a body for short tours of service. Fifteen new institutions of higher learning, including Cornell University, Swarthmore College, and the Massachusetts Institute of Technology, were founded in wartime, and numerous bequests and new buildings were obtained by the older colleges. The Harvard-Yale boat-races, interrupted in 1861, were resumed in 1864 while Grant was besieging Petersburg, and not a single member of either crew enlisted.

The Union was more conspicuous for organized service than for individual sacrifice. In addition to the work of the United States Sanitary Commission, there was also a United States Christian Commission which deluged the army with Bibles, tracts, and patriotic song-books. If the boys in blue and the boys in gray obtained less aid and attention than the combatants of the two world wars, they expected less; and their standard of comfort was lower. Compared with any earlier conflict the amount and variety of volunteer-organized non-combatant service was unprecedented. At the same time, contributions to private charities increased, and states undertook new construction of public institutions. One commentator observed: 'No war in history was embellished by such matchless exhibitions of benevolence.'

3. CONSCRIPTION

Lincoln had appealed to the states to raise 'three hundred thousand more' on 2 July 1862. The New York abolitionist James Gibbons responded with a song, 'We are coming, Father Abraham, three hundred thousand more' but that was almost the only response; for the states, even by drafting from their own militia, produced but 88,000 men, organized in new regiments and enlisted for nine months. Replacements for veteran regiments could not be obtained. Yet Congress flinched from a national conscription. During the winter of 1862–63 it became evident that unless these scruples were surmounted, the game was up; and Congress on 3 March 1863 passed the first United States Conscription Act.

It was a most imperfect law, a travesty of a conscription act. All men between the ages of 20 and 45 were declared liable to military service and had to be registered. As men were needed, the number was divided among the loyal states in proportion to their total population and subdivided among districts, giving credit for previous enlistments. In the first draft (1863) these credits wiped out the liability of most of the Western states, which had been most forward in volunteering. Between each subsequent call and the actual draft, every state and district had 50 days' grace to furnish its revised quota by volunteering, after which the balance was obtained by drafting names on the registered lists. No attempt was made to levy first on the younger men or bachelors, and instead of exempting specified classes such as ministers and supporters of families, money payment was made the basis of exemption. You could commute service in a particular draft upon payment of $300; or evade service during the entire war by procuring a substitute to enlist for three years — no matter if the substitute died the next month, or deserted the next day.[2]

Worst of all, the draft did not bring in soldiers: fewer than 170,000 men were added to the army by the Conscription Act! The system was inequitable to the poor, and in the working-class quarters of New York the first drawing of names in 1863 was the signal for terrible riots. Apparently the Irish-Americans of New York, always hostile to the Negro, were disaffected by the Emancipation Proclamation and inflamed by the importation of black 'contrabands' to break a stevedores' strike. On 13 July, while the names were being drawn, the provost marshal was driven from his office by a mob. Men, women, and boys paraded the

2. The system was so complicated that certain exceptions to these broad statements must be noted. (*a*) The basis of the quota was changed from total population to population registered for service, after the first draft. (*b*) Naval enlistments were not credited in the first draft. (*c*) In the first draft the married men over 35 were not to be drafted until all others had been called out; but there was no such distinction in later drafts. (*d*) From all the drafts exemption was granted to sole supporters of aged parents and eldest brothers in large families of young children, but not to supporters of families as such. Physical disability was the principal cause for exemption. (*e*) The commutation privilege was abolished for all but religious conscientious objectors by Act of 24 February 1864, but such objectors had to serve in some non-combatant branch.

streets during the better part of four days and nights, sacking shops, gutting saloons, burning mansions, lynching or torturing Negroes who fell into their clutches. The police did their best, but it was not until troops were poured into the city that order was restored, after the loss of hundreds of lives. This was equivalent to a Confederate victory, for Meade's army was so weakened by detachments for guard duty in Northern cities, that he was unable to take the offensive against Lee after Gettysburg.

In fact, although there were three more drafts after the first, a very small proportion of the Union army was furnished by direct conscription. In the fall of 1863, of 88,000 men drafted in New York, only 9000 went into the army; more than 52,000 paid fees, the rest hired substitutes. Every fresh draft began an ignoble competition between districts to reduce their quotas by fictitious credits and to fill the residue by bounty-bought volunteers. As recruits were credited to the district where they enlisted, and not to that of their residence, several wealthy communities escaped the draft altogether by purchasing cannon-fodder in the poorer country districts. These were left with only fathers of families and physical rejects to fill subsequent drafts — which, therefore, were not filled at all. Professional bounty-brokers so covered the country with their network that it was difficult for anyone to get into service without passing through their clutches, and as the state bounties or individual substitution fees were paid cash down, the brokers often induced the recruits they furnished to desert at the first opportunity and re-enlist elsewhere. 'Bounty jumpers' enlisted and deserted, ten, twenty, and even thirty times, before being apprehended.[3] Brokers had their crimps in Canada, offering fabulous bounties that were never paid, kidnapping civilians, and tempting soldiers of the British garrison to desert — there were almost 50,000 Canadian enlistments in the Union army. State agents scoured occupied portions of the South for Negroes and obtained shiploads of men from the poorhouses of Belgium and Germany, all of whom were credited to their state quotas. Federal officials were bribed to admit cripples, idiots, and criminals as recruits. One can easily imagine the effect on the morale of a veteran regiment which received replacements of this nature.

3. The United States Provost-General estimated desertions from the Union army at about one to every seven enlistments, desertions from the Confederate army, one to every nine. Ella Lonn, *Desertions in the Civil War* (1928), says one to ten for both armies. The difference is one of methods of computation rather than of fact.

The success of the Union conscription, however, is not to be measured by the very small number of actual draftees obtained, or the large proportion of deserters, but by the number of volunteers obtained under pressure. Unquestionably the average quality of both armies deteriorated as the war dragged on; but the men who followed Grant through the Wilderness and Sherman to Atlanta compare well with any soldiers of modern times for courage, discipline, and tenacity.

4. PAYING FOR THE WAR

The United States was as unprepared financially as militarily to fight a four-year war. No previous wars had provided experience on which the government might draw, except as examples to avoid. Nor did the government have fiscal machinery adequate to deal with the vast and complex financial operations required by a war of such magnitude and duration. There was no centralized banking system, and few large accumulations of capital; Americans had never paid income taxes, nor were they accustomed to many internal taxes familiar to Europeans. How finance a war which by 1864 cost over $3 million a day?

Secretary Chase, who had no experience in public finance, resorted to three obvious methods: taxes, loans, and paper money. Congress doubled the customs duties, laid a direct tax of $20 million, and imposed excise taxes on a bewildering variety of goods and services. Most important, for the future, was the decision to levy an income tax with rates varying from 3 to 10 per cent. The merchant prince A. T. Stewart paid $400,000 on an income of $4 million, yet the income tax brought in only a meager $55 million during the entire war. And all taxes — customs, excise, and income — raised less than $675 million in four years, less than the cost of one year of fighting.

Clearly the government had to do better if it was to remain solvent. When Chase took over the treasury department he found less than $2 million in the coffers and no prospect of additional income until Congress got around to new taxes. Inevitably he had recourse to borrowing. His first loan, of $150 million, cost the taxpayer the tidy sum of 7.3 per cent interest. Once inaugurated, this method of financing the war had an irresistible appeal: the government found it much the easiest way to solve its most pressing fiscal problems; the taxpayer rejoiced in the opportunity to foist the cost of the war onto the next generation; the business and banking community discovered in government loans a source of immense returns. Altogether the government borrowed some $2.6 billion at home and abroad, enough to pay for three-fourths of the total cost of the war. During World Wars I and II the government sold bonds directly to the people at low rates of interest; Secretaries Chase and Fessenden (who succeeded Chase when he went to the Supreme Court) relied on banks to take up most of their bonds on terms that brought them rich rewards. Even at that Chase had difficulty in disposing of his bonds until the Philadelphia banker Jay Cooke — who played a role analogous to that of Robert Morris in the Revolution — undertook to sell them directly to the public.

Casting about for some method of easy financing, Congress, in February 1862, authorized the treasury to issue $150 million of legal tender — the familiar 'greenbacks' that were to bedevil American politics for the next twenty years. Before the war was over the treasury had issued some $450 million of greenbacks. Chase thought they were unconstitutional, and a good many lawyers agreed with him. Because they were not redeemable in gold, and the government itself refused to accept them in payment of customs duties, greenbacks speedily depreciated. In mid-summer 1864 they fell to 39 on the gold dollar; and though they rose to 74 after Appomattox it was not until the treasury 'resumed' specie payments in 1879 that they finally reached par. This resort to paper money is estimated to have cost the taxpayer an additional $600 million; its indirect costs in inflation were of course greater.

The banking side of Chase's financial policy was more constructive. At the beginning of the war there were some 1500 banks with charters issued by 29 states, operating under a most bewildering variety of rights, privileges, and restrictions. No fewer than 7000 different kinds of bank notes circulated throughout the country, and alongside these another 5000 varieties of fraudulent notes. Chase wanted to bring some sort of order out of this chaos, to provide a national currency, and to assure a regular market for government bonds. To this end he recommended a national banking system. Under the National Bank Acts of 1863 and 1864 member banks were required to invest one-third of their capital in government bonds (on which they were paid a handsome interest); they could then issue notes up to 90 per cent of the value of these bonds (on which they could earn handsome profits). The scheme was useful to the government, profitable to the banks, and convenient to the public. Competition from state banks ended in 1865 when Congress taxed their notes out of existence, and by October 1865 over 1500 banks had joined the new national banking system.

5. THE SOUTH IN WARTIME

Compared with the Union, the Confederacy was more nearly a nation in arms. During four years war was its only business. Fighting for independence and the supremacy of the white race, the Southerners gave their government more, and asked of it less, than did the Northern people. Yet the Southern cause met hostility and indifference too. In the mountainous regions of North Carolina and Tennessee no Confederate conscription officer dared show his face. Much more costly were the inveterate provincialism and widespread ignorance, the stiff-necked insistence on the rights of states and of social position, and withal a certain shrewd instinct on the part of the poor whites that it was 'a rich man's war and a poor man's fight.'

The history of conscription illustrates these attitudes. The Confederate system was, in theory, a mass levy of Southern manhood between the ages of 18 and 35. Yet, instead of prompting solidarity, it fomented class antagonism. Originally adopted (April 1862) in order to obtain replacements, and retain in the ranks all men whose terms of enlistment were expiring, conscription was generally regarded as a mere temporary expedient of doubtful constitutionality. There was no answer to Senator Foote's question, 'If agents of the Confederate Government had the right to go into any state and take therefrom the men belonging to that state, how were state rights and state sovereignty to be maintained?' The Chief Justice of North Carolina even discharged two deserters who killed a man when resisting capture, on the ground that a state had nothing to do with enforcing Confederate conscription! Although the law granted exemptions to ministers, conscientious objectors, railway employees, postmen, apothecaries, teachers, and the like, South Carolina of her own authority extended the privilege and asserted the right of nullification in 1862 as roundly as in 1832. In Georgia, Governor Joseph E. Brown openly defied conscription, withholding Georgia soldiers for the defense of the state. A week before the fall of Atlanta, as Sherman poised for his march to the sea, Brown recalled 10,000 men he had 'loaned' to General Hood and sent them home for 30 days to harvest the crops. Congress was persuaded to add millers, blacksmiths, editors, printers, and plantation overseers, at the rate of one to every twenty slaves, to the exempted classes; whereupon there arose a great clamor from the democracy, especially against the 'twenty-Negro' provision and the privilege of substitution. So much fraud and skulking developed that Congress swung in the other direction until the Confederate war department had to supply labor for essential industries by details from the army. Substitution was stopped toward the close of 1863, when the price of a substitute had reached 6000 paper dollars. Early in 1864 the Confederate Congress extended the age of military service to seventeen and fifty.

No Southern city was disgraced by draft riots like those of New York; but fraud and evasion were widespread, and many of the remoter districts of the South were terrorized by armed bands of deserters and draft-dodgers who waged a successful guerrilla warfare against the troops sent to apprehend them. President Lincoln on 10 March 1863 proclaimed amnesty to all absentees without leave who would return within the month. In June of that same year when the percentage of absentees in the Confederate army was approaching 30 per cent, President Davis extended a similar invitation. So few came in that the offer of twenty days' grace was repeated shortly after Gettysburg, Davis declaring the South to be invincible if every man liable to service would do his duty.

That was the trouble everywhere: even when the South had the resources it was rarely able to organize and exploit them. Occasionally, it would find a genius like General Josiah Gorgas, the Pennsylvania-born Chief of Ordnance, who performed amazing feats in turning out arms and ammunition. More often the government temporized. And as Union armies penetrated ever more deeply into the South, the resource base of the Confederacy shrank dangerously. Union advances imperilled food supplies and cut the Confederacy off from cities like New Orleans, the new nation's financial center.

Railways were the weakest links in the Confederate economic chain. At the outbreak of the war the Confederacy boasted some 9000 miles of rails, compared to 22,000 miles in the North. It turned out only 4 per cent of the country's locomotives and had inadequate repair facilities. Through traffic hardly existed; at numerous 'bottle-necks' — Petersburg, Lynchburg, Knoxville, and elsewhere — freight had to be carted from one station to another. Between Danville, Va., and Greensboro, N.C., a

40-mile gap interrupted a main line into the interior. The government was slow to assert control over the railroads, or to give control to the army. Robert Barnwell Rhett opposed a national program of railroad construction, because a railroad was 'a military convenience, not a military necessity.' Not until February 1865 did the Confederate Congress appropriate any really substantial sum for railroad construction and equipment. The few rolling mills and foundries were too busy with government work to replace locomotives, freight cars, or even track. Many lines could be kept going only by using the rolling-stock and tearing up the rails of branch lines; junctions became congested with supplies; breakdowns were frequent. It took seven and a half days to move Longstreet's corps from Virginia to northern Georgia in 1863, and at the close of the war railroads were averaging six miles an hour. Without an engineering tradition, the Confederacy was unable either to organize the transportation resources that it had or to rebuild them when shattered. That is why there were bread riots in Richmond when the barns of the valley of Virginia were bursting with wheat; why government clerks had to pay fifteen dollars a bushel for corn that was bringing the farmer only a dollar in southwestern Georgia.

The Confederacy also mismanaged finances, though with more excuse. The people were even less used to heavy taxation than those in the North and less able to bear it. Cotton, the most valuable single asset of the Confederacy, was frittered away. Deluded by faith in its indispensability, the Confederacy deliberately withheld the staple from English and French markets, and restricted cultivation; Southern plantations, which had produced 4 million bales in 1861, raised only 300,000 in 1864. In addition, the Confederate Congress required owners to destroy all cotton that might fall into enemy hands; thus, over 2 million bales were sacrificed. Belatedly the government changed its policy and bought cotton for export or for security against foreign loans which it hoped to negotiate. A few thousand bales of cotton evaded the blockade and perhaps half a million bales were smuggled across the Rio Grande, but the cotton loan program was a failure. By 1863 England was getting her cotton from Egypt, India, Mexico, and New York. Only in France did the Confederacy have any success with the cotton-loan policy: the so-called Erlanger loan brought a mere $2.6 million on security of $45 million worth of cotton. At that the Confederacy did better than the French bondholders, who lost all they paid in.

The first Secretary of the Treasury, Christopher Memminger of Charleston, was bewildered and incompetent; when, in 1864, he was succeeded by the energetic George Trenholm the situation was beyond repair. The basic difficulties were the shortage of specie and of taxable assets; but mismanagement and the unwillingness of the Southern people to pay taxes contributed to the debacle. The Confederacy raised only about one per cent of its revenue from taxation. Confederate tax receipts did not exceed $27 million, while expenditures ran to a couple of billion dollars. The gap between income and outgo was bridged by bonds and by treasury notes payable in gold on the acknowledgment of independence by the United States. Altogether the Confederacy floated bonds and other loans to the value of some $700 million, and a total of $1.5 billion in treasury notes. Inevitably these depreciated: by January 1864 Confederate paper was worth five cents on the dollar, and even before Lee's surrender it had become practically worthless. By October 1864 the Confederacy had derived nearly 60 per cent of its income from paper money, compared to 13 per cent for the Union from that source. As a consequence both of the resort to paper money and the shortage of certain staples, prices rose to fantastic levels: by 1864 flour was $500 a barrel. Inflation tempted Southerners to hoard food, to speculate in essential supplies, and to trade with the Union armies for United States dollars — which throughout the war were at a premium in the Confederacy. The government in vain tried to fix maximum prices, and blockade runners often imported luxuries for profiteers rather than necessities for the army. In desperation the Confederate government resorted to wholesale impressment of supplies of all kinds, including slaves; this program, in effect confiscation, bitterly antagonized the farmers on whom it bore unfairly.

After noting these many instances of selfishness, indifference, incompetence, and defeatism on both sides, we must remember that, after all, both the Union and Confederate governments were sustained by popular suffrage in 1862 and 1864, and that no earlier war in modern history drew out so much sacrifice, energy, and heroism. Vice-President Stephens divined the situation at the beginning of 1863 when he wrote, 'The great majority of the masses both North and South are true to the cause of their side. . . . A large majority on both sides are tired of the war; want peace. . . . But as we do not want peace without independence, so they do not want peace without union.' The average American then, as in both world wars, loathed army life and only acquiesced because of patriotism and social compulsion. Union soldiers sang 'When This Cruel War Is Over,' while their enemies in gray sang the equally sentimental 'Lorena,' and both rejected the 'fighting' ballads printed by patriots behind the lines. Yet both fought gallantly to the end.

6. 'THE SABLE ARM'

The slaves were, as Lincoln later said, 'somehow the cause of the war,' but at the beginning they were denied any part in it, as were free Negroes. It is not surprising that until the last days of the war Confederate authorities rejected all proposals to use slaves as soldiers, opening the door to freedom; but it is strange that for almost two years Washington followed much the same policy. Congress was so sensitive to the feelings of the border states, and so indifferent to those of the Negroes, that it refused to enlist even free blacks in the Union ranks. And when slaves found their way to the Union armies in Virginia or Tennessee federal officers frequently returned them to their former owners. That was going farther than either common sense or public opinion required, and it was the ingenious General Benjamin F. Butler who worked out a new formula: fugitive slaves, he said, were 'contraband of war.' From that it was only a short step to using them for work around the camp — cooking, building fences, caring for horses, and so forth. Butler, too, took the next logical step. Commanding in New Orleans in the summer of 1862, he found his ranks depleted and informed the Secretary of War, 'I shall call on Africa to intervene, and I do not think I shall call in vain.' Within a few weeks the First Regiment Louisiana Native Guards was mustered into the federal service. Soon there were Negro regiments in all theaters of the war. The First South Carolina, recruited from fugitive slaves who had escaped to the sea islands, was commanded by the preacher-soldier Thomas Wentworth Higginson, whose *Army Life in a Black Regiment* is one of the classics of Civil War literature.

After the Emancipation Proclamation it was thought logical to let any and all Negroes into the ranks. For a time the government was guilty of a petty attempt to pay the Negro soldiers less than white, but eventually they fought as equals. Altogether about 180,000 Negro soldiers enlisted in the Union armies, and in addition almost 30,000 served in the Navy. Most of these were recruited from among the free Negroes of the North, and to a generation that loved dramatics there was something very stirring in the spectacle of the 54th Massachusetts Infantry swinging down the flag-decked streets of Boston — William Lloyd Garrison in the reviewing stand — to the very wharf whence less than ten years earlier the fugitive Anthony Burns had been returned to slavery. Some 50,000 of the Negro soldiers, refugees from slavery, fought under special handicaps. As Higginson tells us:

> They had more to fight for than the whites. Besides the flag and the Union they had home and wife and child. They fought with ropes around their necks, and when orders were issued that the officers of colored troops should be put to death on capture, they took a grim satisfaction. It helped their *esprit de corps* immensely. Though they had begun with a slight feeling of inferiority to white troops, this compliment substituted a peculiar sense of self-respect. And when the new colored regiments began to arrive from the North my men still pointed out this difference — that in the case of ultimate defeat, the Northern troops, black or white, would go home, while the First South Carolina must fight it out or be re-enslaved.[4]

Colored soldiers fought in every theater of the war — at Battery Wagner guarding the harbor of Charleston, where Robert Gould Shaw fell at the head of his regiment; at Port Hudson below Vicksburg; in the bayous of Louisiana; up the St. Mary's in Florida; along the Missouri borderlands; in the Wilderness and on the iron lines of Petersburg; and at Nashville where they helped shatter Hood's command. In part because they were more susceptible to such diseases as dysentery and tuberculosis, their losses — 66,000 deaths — were proportionately higher than those suffered by white troops.

4. *Army Life in a Black Regiment*, p. 251.

XXXVII

From Vicksburg to Appomattox

1. THE DIPLOMATIC FRONT

Military operations became simpler as the war progressed. In 1863 both sides concentrated upon the objectives they had failed to attain the year before: the Union on strengthening the blockade and pressing out such obstacles to military constriction as Vicksburg, Chattanooga, and Lee's army; the Confederacy on defense and breaking through into Kentucky, Pennsylvania, and the high seas. The year was a brilliant one for the Confederate navy. Two improvised 'cotton-clads' recaptured Galveston; the guns of Fort Sumter repelled three separate attacks on Charleston; the British-built *Alabama* and *Florida* were at large, destroying United States shipping; and orders were placed in England and France for some powerful armored rams, which might well have broken the Union blockade.

The interventionist forces in Europe, encouraged by Fredericksburg, began to make trouble again in 1863. Of these forces, Napoleon III was the most dangerous because the least calculable. Napoleon's American policy was determined by his Mexican adventure, which began in 1861 and became a purely French enterprise the next year; in June 1863, a French army took Mexico City, and the next year the unfortunate Maximilian of Austria accepted the imperial crown of Mexico from France. Thus the Civil War gave Napoleon III an opportunity to perform the feat of which Talleyrand, Canning, and Aberdeen had dreamed: to bring the New World into the balance of power, to re-establish European influence in North America. Slidell, the Southern agent in Paris, offered Confederate support to the Emperor in Mexico; a practical demonstration that American disunion was playing the European game. In January 1863, Napoleon III proposed a peace conference between North and South, with the object of establishing the Confederacy. Seward flatly refused the offer. Spain in a small way was pursuing the same policy. At the invitation of the conservative faction in Santo Domingo she was endeavoring to convert that unstable republic into a Spanish colony. France in Mexico, Spain in Santo Domingo, meant a counter-stroke of monarchial Europe against republican America, an after-clap of the Holy Alliance. 'A little audacity,' wrote a Spanish historian, 'and France was assured of her possessions, England of Canada . . . ourselves of the treasure of our Antilles, and the future of the Spanish race. Mexico and the Southern States . . . were the two advanced redoubts which Europe in its own interest should have thrown up against the American colossus.' [1]

Impressive was the rally of liberal sentiment to the Union in England, France, and Spain, as the meaning of the Emancipation Proclamation sank in. A Confederate agent reported of France, 'With the exception of the Emperor and his nearest personal adherents, all the intelligence, the science, the social respectability, is leagued . . . against us.' In England, the Emancipation Proclamation brought about such an upheaval of evangelical, radical, and working-class opinion in favor of the Union that no ministry dared to give aid and comfort to the slave power. Bright, John Stuart Mill, and Goldwin Smith were now believed when they asserted that the cause of the Union was the cause of liberty. There were many enthusiastic pro-Union meetings. Karl Marx organized a gathering of 3000 representatives of the London trades unions on 26 March 1863, which was addressed by Bright, and resolved 'that the success of free institutions in America was a political question of deep consequence in England, and that they would not tolerate any interference unfavorable to the North.' Henry Adams, who reported the meeting for his father, wrote, 'I never quite appreciated the moral influence of American democracy, nor the cause that the privileged classes in Europe have to fear us, until I saw directly how it works.'

Yet the Confederate partisans did not give up hope. Just one week before the trades union meeting the Confederacy launched its first for-

1. Navarro y Rodrigo, *O'Donnell y su Tiempo* (1869), p. 195.

eign loan, precursor of a new diplomatic offensive. Bonds to the amount of £3 million, redeemable in cotton at a rate of exchange that promised fabulous profits, were issued at 90 and promptly rose to 95. Slidell deemed this success 'a financial recognition of our independence'; Mason wrote, 'Cotton is King at last.'

The *Alabama* and *Florida* were active; another English-built commerce-destroyer, the *Alexandria,* was almost ready for sea; and the Lairds were building two armored rams to break the Union blockade. On 4 April Lord Russell ordered the detention of the *Alexandria.* At once King Cotton began to tremble on his new financial throne. The bonds fell to 87, and only by using the subscription money to sustain the market were Mason and Slidell able temporarily to arrest a landslide.

2. THE VICKSBURG CAMPAIGN

In the end recognition of the Confederacy would be determined by military events. During the winter of 1862–63 all eyes were fastened on the struggle for the Mississippi.

Although both sides of the Mississippi below Memphis were Confederate territory, there was nothing on the river to oppose the passage of a hostile fleet and army until it reached Vicksburg. At that point the line of bluffs that borders the valley touches the river itself and follows close beside its eastern bank for over 100 miles to Port Hudson, Louisiana. At both points the Confederates had strongly fortified the bluffs, and between them troops and supplies reached the heart of the Confederacy from Arkansas, Louisiana, and Texas.

Vicksburg was a hard nut to crack. Strongly fortified and held by General John C. Pemberton, its front was impregnable to assault from the river, its rear was 200 miles from Grant's base at Memphis, and its right was protected by the densely wooded and water-logged valley of the Yazoo, intersected with countless backwaters and bayous. Yet even after spending cold, wet months in fruitless attempts to outflank Pemberton in the slimy jungle of the lower Yazoo, Grant was not discouraged, as McClellan would have been. In order to advance he must cut loose from his base of supplies, march his army below Vicksburg along the west bank of the Mississippi, cross over to the dry ground, and attack the fortress from the rear.

'I don't know what to make of Grant, he's such a quiet little fellow,'

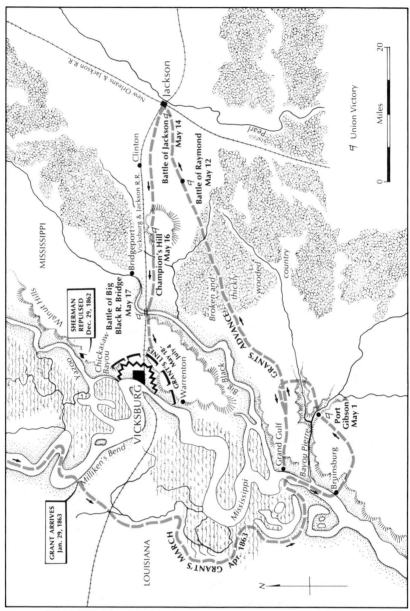

GRANT'S CAMPAIGN BEFORE VICKSBURG, Jan.-July 1863

said Lincoln, whose experience had been mainly with generals who let their presence be known to the eye and ear. 'The only way I know he's around is by the way he makes things *git!*' Grant's Army of the Tennessee worked in perfect concert with the fresh-water navy. 'Grant and Sherman are on board almost every day. Dine and tea with me often; we agree in everything,' wrote Flag Officer Porter.

Grant's plan was as audacious as any campaign by Lee; and he met difficulties that Lee never encountered. To disrupt Confederate communications he sent Colonel Grierson on a daring 600-mile raid through the very heart of Mississippi, destroying bridges and tearing up railroads all the way from the Tennessee border to Baton Rouge. Meantime the main Army of the Tennessee marched along the west bank of the Mississippi to a point south of Grand Gulf, where there was an easy crossing. The fleet had to run the gantlet of Vicksburg on the night of 16–17 April 1863. With lights doused and engines stopped, it floated downstream until discovered by a Confederate sentry. Then, what a torrent of shot and shell from the fortress, and what a cracking-on of steam in the fleet, when, lighted by flashing guns and burning cotton-bales, the gunboats, turtle-backed rams, and river steamboats with tall flaring funnels, dashed by the batteries! 'Their heavy shot walked right through us,' wrote Porter; but all save one transport got by safely.

Boldly, without waiting for support, Grant struck out for the rear of Vicksburg with 20,000 men, subsisting on the country. Pemberton came out to meet him, and Joe Johnston was moving south from Chattanooga with another army. Grant captured an important railway junction, then turned on Pemberton in quick pursuit. By a series of masterly combinations and rapid marches, fighting as he progressed, in less than three weeks he won five pitched battles against a superior force and penned the enemy army in Vicksburg.

On 22 May the siege of Vicksburg began. Civilians were living in bomb-proofs, and the Confederate defenders, reduced to eating snakes and rats, were on the point of mutiny when Pemberton, on 3 July, sent out a flag of truce, asking for a parley. The next day he surrendered his army and the 'Confederate Gibraltar.' Port Hudson capitulated on the 9th. Within a week a steamboat arrived at New Orleans from St. Louis, having passed the entire course of the Mississippi undisturbed by hostile shot or challenge.

Well might Lincoln write, in one of his happiest letters, 'The signs look better. The Father of Waters again goes unvexed to the sea. Thanks to the great Northwest for it. Nor yet wholly to them. Three hundred miles up they met New England, Empire, Keystone, and Jersey, hewing their way right and left. The sunny South, too, in more colors than one, also lent a hand. On the spot, their part of the history was jotted down in black and white. The job was a great national one, and let none be banned who bore an honorable part in it. . . . Nor must Uncle Sam's web-feet be forgotten. At all the watery margins they have been present. Not only on the deep sea, the broad bay, and the rapid river, but also up the narrow, muddy bayou, and wherever the ground was a little damp, they have been and made their tracks. Thanks to all: for the great republic — for the principle it lives by and keeps alive — for man's vast future — thanks to all.'

3. CHANCELLORSVILLE

In the eastern theater of war 'Fighting Joe' Hooker, brave, vain, and unreliable, relieved Burnside, who was commanding the Army of the Potomac, after the Fredericksburg disaster. One hundred and thirty thousand strong, it was indeed 'the finest army on the planet.' Hooker did much to restore its morale, but his first move in the direction of Richmond, on 27 April 1863, brought on Chancellorsville, one of the bloodiest battles of the war. Again, as at the second Manassas, Lee divided his army in the face of superior numbers and sent Jackson by a wood road through the Wilderness round the Union right, whose commander refused to change front in spite of ample warnings from his picket line (2 May). Earlier in the war so complete a surprise as Jackson then sprung would have meant disaster. Only individual valor saved it now, for Hooker, who had been struck by a falling brick and had lost control of the situation, seemed to forget the very rudiments of generalship, while Lee, with half his manpower, chose time and place of attack, always outnumbering him at the point of contact. Three days of this and Hooker, dazed and bewildered, retired across the Rappahannock (5 May). A well-earned Southern victory was too dearly won by the loss of Stonewall Jackson, mortally wounded by his own men when reconnoitering between the lines. Lee had lost 'his right arm.'

Lee's army was soon ready for another spring at the enemy's throat, and on enemy soil. Such a victory might knock out Northern morale, already staggering from Chancellorsville and trembling in prospect of the first draft; French and perhaps British recognition would follow. It was a bold game for the highest stake, but President Davis was not a bold player. He could not make up his mind to weaken the other Confederate forces to push this invasion home. So Lee moved northward into Pennsylvania with only 73,000 men, while 190,000 Confederate field troops were scattered between the Mississippi and the Rappahannock.

4. THE GETTYSBURG CAMPAIGN

On 3 June General Lee began to move toward the Shenandoah valley, having selected that well-screened highway to Pennsylvania. Hooker was eager to launch a counter-strike at the Confederate capital, but Lincoln rightly advised him that 'Lee's army, and not Richmond, is your objective.' Lee sent J. E. B. Stuart on a cavalry raid with orders not sufficiently precise to restrain that reckless horseman. 'Jeb' and his men enjoyed themselves as usual and cut out a wagon train within four miles of Washington; but Hooker, by crossing the Potomac on the 25th, separated them from Lee, depriving the Confederate army of its 'eyes' during the most critical days of the campaign.

By 27 June Lee's entire army was in Pennsylvania. To an anxious nation the Confederates seemed to threaten Philadelphia and Washington. Hooker, on the 28th, having concentrated the Army of the Potomac about the town of Frederick, resigned the command and Lincoln turned it over to one of his corps commanders, General George Gordon Meade, safe and sane, certain to do nothing foolish if unlikely to perform any brilliant feat of arms. Lee hoped that the mere presence of his army in Pennsylvania would strengthen the copperheads, and would force Lincoln to receive Vice-President Stephens, then proceeding toward Washington under flag of truce to open peace negotiations on the basis of independence. Yet the North showed no sign of flinching. Grave anxiety was felt, but no panic; and Lincoln did not recall a single unit from the West.

Chance placed the great battle where neither Lee nor Meade wanted it; because neither knew exactly where the other was. On 30 June a part of A. P. Hill's corps which was covering Lee's concentration, strayed into Gettysburg in search of new shoes. Boots and saddles were there — on Buford's cavalry division, masking the Army of the Potomac. Gettysburg commanded some important roads; and each army was so eager for action that this chance contact drew both into the quiet little market town as to a magnet. There, on 1 July, the great three-day battle began, each unit joining in the fray as it arrived.

The first day (1 July) went ill for the Union. Hill and Ewell drove the First Corps through the town. In the nick of time, Winfield Scott Hancock, the greatest fighting general in the Army of the Potomac, rallied the fugitives on Cemetery Ridge. The position so fortunately chosen proved to be admirable for defense: a limestone outcrop shaped like a fish-hook, with the convex side turned west and north, toward the Confederates. Along it the Union army was placed as rapidly as it arrived from the south and east, while the Confederates took up an encircling position, their right on the partially wooded Seminary Ridge, parallel to Cemetery Ridge. Lee decided to attack the following day.

Lee's great opportunity came on the evening of 2 July when Jubal Early broke the Union defenses on Cemetery Ridge and Ewell stormed up the slope of Culp's Hill on the Union right — the barb of the hook. But reinforcements failed to appear. Early was hurled back within an hour, and the next morning a withering fire drove back Ewell's veterans. Longstreet had already driven in Sickles's corps which had occupied the peach orchard in advance of Cemetery Ridge, but failed to take Little Round Top — the eye of the hook — which would have enabled his artillery to enfilade the entire Union position. Now Jeb Stuart reached the battlefield, and Lee, with his army at full strength, prepared to assault the Union lines in the morning. Longstreet, who thought the situation desperate, procrastinated all forenoon while Meade strengthened Cemetery Ridge. At one o'clock there came a deafening artillery fire from the Confederate lines, answered by even heavier bombardment directed by the Union artillerist General Henry Hunt, and for an hour the batteries blasted at each other. Then silence. Lee, against Longstreet's protest, ordered a direct attack on the strongest part of the Union center with Pickett's, Pettigrew's, and Trimble's divisions, 15,000 strong. The time had come. Pickett rode up to Longstreet and asked, 'General, shall I advance?' Longstreet, unwilling to give the word, bowed his head. 'Sir, I shall lead my division forward,' said Pickett.

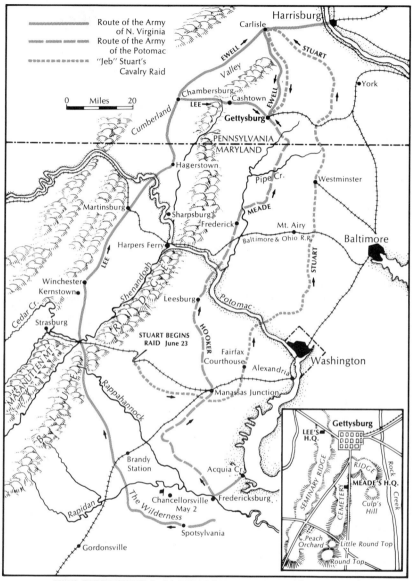

THE GETTYSBURG CAMPAIGN, June 27—July 4, 1863

From Cemetery Ridge the Union troops saw three gray lines of battle issue from the wooded ridge three-quarters of a mile away and march with bayonets glittering and the colors of 47 regiments fluttering in the breeze into the valley below. When less than half-way across the Union artillery opened up on them; a little nearer they came under a raking fire from the batteries on Round Top. The flank divisions melted away; but the Northern troops, peering through the smoke, could see Pickett's men still coming on, merged in one crowding, rushing line. Lost for a moment in a swale, they emerged so near that the expression on their faces could be seen. 'The line springs,' wrote Frank Haskell of Meade's Second Corps. 'The crest of the solid ground with a great roar heaves forward its maddened load, men, arms, smoke, fire, a fighting mass. It rolls to the wall — flash meets flash, the wall is crossed, a moment ensues of thrusts, yells, blows, shots, and undistinguishable conflict, followed by a shout universal, and the last and bloodiest fight of the battle of Gettysburg is ended and won.' Two of Pickett's brigadiers and fifteen of his regimental commanders were killed. General Armistead, with cap raised on point of sword, leaped the stone wall into the Union lines, a hundred men followed him, and for a brief moment the battle cross of the Confederacy floated on the crest of Cemetery Ridge. Then the Union lines closed in relentlessly and all Armistead's men were shot down or captured.

All next day, 4 July, Lee remained defiantly in position. That evening his army, with baggage and prisoners, retired to a position west of Sharpsburg. There the flooded Potomac stopped his retreat and gave Meade an opportunity that Lincoln begged him to seize. 'Act upon your own judgment and make your generals execute your orders,' telegraphed Halleck. 'Call no council of war. . . . Do not let the enemy escape.' Meade called a council of war, the Potomac fell, and the enemy got away.

Lee was too candid to congratulate himself for having escaped. He had seen the flower of his army wither under the Union fire. He knew that all hope for peace that summer was gone, and he must have felt that slight hope for Southern independence remained. Yet after the battle, as before, his soldiers gathered only confidence and resolution from the placid countenance of their beloved 'Marse Robert.' With justice Lee might have blamed Longstreet, whose failure to obey orders probably led to the disaster, but no word of censure escaped him. To President Davis he wrote, 'No blame can be attached to the army for its failure to accomplish what was projected by me, nor should it be censured for the unreasonable expectations of the public. I am alone to blame.' On 8 August he submitted his resignation as commander of the Army of Northern Virginia. 'To ask me to substitute you by some one more fit to command,' President Davis answered, 'is to demand an impossibility.'

Lincoln was deeply mortified by the escape of Lee's army. 'Our army held the war in the hollow of their hand, and they would not close it,' he said. 'Still, I am very grateful to Meade for the great service he did at Gettysburg.' 'General Meade has my confidence, as a brave and skilful officer and a true man.' Unpopular with his men, placed in command of an army thrice whipped within a twelve-month, on the eve of encounter with an enemy hitherto invincible, he fairly won the greatest battle of the war. And from the Wilderness to Appomattox he was the right arm of Grant.

Four months later, when a national cemetery was dedicated on the battlefield of Gettysburg, Lincoln delivered his immortal address:

Fourscore and seven years ago our fathers brought forth on this continent a new nation, conceived in liberty, and dedicated to the proposition that all men are created equal.

Now we are engaged in a great civil war, testing whether that nation, or any nation so conceived and so dedicated, can long endure. We are met on a great battle-field of that war. We have come to dedicate a portion of that field as a final resting-place for those who here gave their lives that the nation might live. It is altogether fitting and proper that we should do this.

But, in a larger sense, we cannot dedicate — we cannot consecrate — we cannot hallow — this ground. The brave men, living and dead, who struggled here, have consecrated it far above our poor power to add or detract. The world will little note nor long remember what we say here, but it can never forget what they did here. It is for us, the living, rather, to be dedicated here to the unfinished work which they who fought here have thus far so nobly advanced. It is rather for us to be here dedicated to the great task remaining before us — that from these honored dead we take increased devotion to that cause for which they gave the last full measure of devotion; that we here highly resolve that these dead shall not have died in vain; that this nation, under God, shall have a new birth of freedom; and that government of the people, by the people, for the people, shall not perish from the earth.

On the diplomatic front Gettysburg and Vicksburg bore fruit. A House of Commons motion to recognize the Confederacy was already withdrawn, but the Laird armored rams, from which the Confederacy hoped much, were being rushed to completion. Lord John Russell was most anxious to prevent another *Alabama* from swelling the tide of American resentment; but the destination of the vessels was so cleverly covered by a fictitious sale that he could find no evidence to warrant detention. Fortunately he decided to stretch a point and keep the peace. On 3 September he gave orders to prevent the departure of the rams, and a month later both were impounded.[2]

John Bigelow, the American consul-general at Paris, obtained evidence in the same month that four steam corvettes and two armored rams were being constructed for the Confederacy at Nantes and Bordeaux. Napoleon III had practically invited Slidell to place the contracts, although he was careful to insist that their destination should be concealed. Now that the secret was out, he ordered the vessels to be sold to foreign governments; but only the utmost vigilance by the American authorities prevented their falling into Confederate hands. The ram *Stonewall* eventually did, but too late to help the Southern cause.

5. FROM CHICKAMAUGA TO ATLANTA AND THE SEA

The advance of the Army of the Cumberland under General William S. Rosecrans toward Chattanooga, in July 1863, began a campaign that ended only with Sherman's march to the sea and a division of the Confederacy. Chattanooga, after Richmond and Vicksburg, was the most vital point in the Confederacy: a junction on the important Richmond-Knoxville-Memphis railway for lines running southwest and southeast. The Tennessee river there breaks through the parallel ridges of the southern Appalachians. So long as the Confederates held Chattanooga, the Union armies could not hope to penetrate far into the Lower South, however firmly they might press its periphery. Once in possession of Chattanooga, the Union armies might swing round the Great Smoky mountains and attack Atlanta, Savannah, Charleston, or even Rich-

2. Charles Francis Adams's famous note to Russell on the rams, 'It would be superfluous in me to point out to your lordship that this is war,' was written two days after Russell had decided to detain them.

mond, from the rear. Rosecrans out-maneuvered the Confederates, and, without fighting a battle marched into Chattanooga on 9 September 1863.

At first the Chattanooga campaign was conducted by third-rate generals: our old friend Burnside; General Rosecrans, who had most of McClellan's faults without his ability; and on the Confederate side Braxton Bragg, a dyspeptic martinet. From the first battle of the campaign, at Chickamauga (19 September), there emerged a great commander, the loyal Virginian George H. Thomas. After Bragg had swept the Union right and center into Chattanooga, General Thomas, for six hours, held the left against repeated assaults by the whole Confederate army; and when nightfall found him stripped of ammunition, he retired unmolested to a safe position. 'The *élan* of the Southern soldier was never seen after Chickamauga,' wrote D. H. Hill. 'That brilliant dash which had distinguished him was gone forever.' It broke against the lines of Thomas, 'the rock of Chickamauga.' Owing to his Virginian birth and the want of support in Congress, Thomas never had a command equal to his ability; but many military students today believe that, if given the opportunity, he could have proved himself peer to Lee.

Next, Rosecrans allowed his army to be penned up and besieged in Chattanooga. He was approaching a state of imbecility when Lincoln sent Grant to the rescue as supreme commander in the West. Grant placed Thomas in command of the Army of the Cumberland and ordered him to hold Chattanooga at all hazards. 'I will hold the town till we starve,' was Thomas's reply.

Grant then resumed the offensive. On 24 November he began the great Battle of Chattanooga. Simultaneous attacks delivered by Hooker, Sherman, and Thomas drove the enemy from the steep wooded ridges across the river. The capture of Missionary Ridge was perhaps the most gallant action of the war. Thomas's men, after driving the Confederates from the rifle-pits at the foot, were ordered to halt. Refusing to obey, they kept straight on up the steep rocky slope, overrunning a second and a third line of defense, rushed the Confederate guns on the crest, and turned them on the enemy; then, with Phil Sheridan leading, pursued the fleeing gray-coats down the eastern slope.

This Battle of Chattanooga placed the combined armies of the Tennessee and the Cumberland (Sherman and Thomas) in a position to advance into Georgia in the early spring. The center of gravity had

now shifted to the West. One portion of the Confederacy had been severed along the Mississippi, and a deep salient, resting on the Appalachians and the great river, had been thrust into the rest. It remained to
prolong that salient to the sea, somewhere between Charleston and
Savannah; and then to close in on Lee and the Army of Northern Virginia.

When early in 1864 Grant became general-in-chief, Sherman was left
in command of 100,000 men in Chattanooga to continue that campaign.
Sherman's objective was Joe Johnston's (late Bragg's) army, 65,000
strong, which lay between him and Atlanta, Georgia. On 7 May 1864
he opened the campaign, with an army stripped to the barest essentials
in baggage and equipment. Johnston divined the needs of the situation
when he adopted Fabian strategy. Hope for the Confederacy lay in
fighting only at a decided advantage and wearying the Northern
people of the war. Sherman restrained his natural eagerness and aggressiveness to beat Johnston 'at his own game of patience.' On 17 July
Sherman moved across the Chattahoochee river, eight miles from Atlanta, and began to besiege the capital of Georgia. With a line of communications 140 miles longer than at Chattanooga, his situation was
perilous; and the appointment of the fighting John B. Hood in Johnston's place meant that the Confederates would speedily take the offensive. Hood, however, merely wasted lives by his thrusts at Sherman. On
2 September he evacuated Atlanta, and Sherman occupied that key city.
This campaign was a military, and, even more, a political triumph, for
it did much to confound defeatism in the North and win support for
Lincoln.

President Davis assured the people of Georgia that Sherman must
sooner or later retreat from Atlanta. 'And when that day comes the
fate that befell the army of the French Empire in its retreat from Mos-
cow will be re-enacted.' Hood proposed to help by striking high into
Tennessee at the long, thin line of Union communications. The imperturbable Sherman, sending Thomas back to Nashville to cope with him,
cut loose from Atlanta in the opposite direction, toward the sea (17
October 1864), marching 62,000 men without supplies into the 'garden
spot of the Confederacy.'

The march to the sea was one of deliberate and disciplined destruction. Sherman's army cut a swath 60 miles through central Georgia,
destroying stores of provisions, standing crops and cattle, cotton-gins

and mills, railways and bridges, in fact everything that could be useful to the Confederacy and much that was not. The looting of houses, although forbidden by orders, could not altogether be prevented, and many a Georgia family was stripped of its possessions; but outrages on persons were surprisingly few. It was the sort of campaign that soldiers love — maximum of looting and destruction, minimum of discipline and fighting: splendid weather, few impedimenta; broiled turkey for breakfast and fried chicken for supper.

> Hurrah! Hurrah! we bring the jubilee!
> Hurrah! Hurrah! the flag that makes you free!
> So we sang the chorus from Atlanta to the sea,
> While we were marching through Georgia.

For a month the North lost sight of Sherman. He emerged at Savannah on 10 December 1864 and was able to offer Lincoln the city as a Christmas present.

In the meantime Hood, with 40,000 veterans, was moving into central Tennessee, hoping to catch Thomas and Schofield and whip them separately. At the end of November he caught up with Schofield at Franklin and sacrificed 6000 men in a series of gallant but futile attacks. Schofield slipped away to Nashville, where the 'Rock of Chickamauga' was in command. Disregarding frantic telegrams from Stanton and Grant, Thomas bided his time. Finally on 27 December, he inflicted on Hood at Nashville the most smashing defeat of the war.[3] Grant made prompt amends to Thomas for his impatience; but this great Virginian, who had forsaken home and kindred for loyalty to the Union, was neglected in the distribution of post-war honors.

6. THE WILDERNESS

While Sherman and Thomas were carrying on this brilliant and successful scission of the Confederacy, General Grant was having rough going

3. After the battle of Nashville a delegation called on President Lincoln to warn him that Hood's army was still potentially dangerous and to admonish him that Thomas should concentrate on the pursuit and destruction of that army. Lincoln replied with the story of Farmer Slocum and his yellow dog. Slocum's dog Rover, he said, was the terror of the neighborhood, and one day some boys tied firecrackers to him, fore and aft, lit them, and exploded Rover over the countryside. Sadly Farmer Slocum contemplated the remains. 'Rover was a good dog' he said, 'there wasn't any better dog than Rover. But I reckon that Rover's usefulness, *as a dog*, is about over.' That, said Lincoln, was the position of Hood's army.

with Lee, whose prowess very nearly conquered the Northern will to victory in the summer of 1864.

On 9 March 1864 Grant was appointed lieutenant general and general-in-chief of the armies of the United States. Summoned to Washington, where he had never been, to confer with Lincoln, whom he had never seen, this slightly seedy and very ordinary-looking individual, perpetually smoking or chewing a cigar, caused some misgivings among those who were used to the glittering generals of the Army of the Potomac. Keener observers were impressed with Grant's rough dignity, simplicity, and calm confidence. He was the first of all the commanders in the East who never doubted the greatness of his President; and Lincoln knew that he had a general at last 'who would take the responsibility and act.'

Grant assumed personal direction of the Virginia campaign against Lee. 'He habitually wears an expression as if he had determined to drive his head through a brick wall, and was about to do it,' wrote one of his officers. 'I determined,' wrote Grant himself, 'to hammer continuously against the armed force of the enemy and his resources, until by mere attrition, if in no other way, there should be nothing left to him but submission.' On 4 May 1864 Grant launched his offensive, marching his army of 102,000 men through the same tangled Wilderness from which Jackson had fallen upon Hooker at Chancellorsville. When halfway through, Lee repeated Jackson's maneuver. Grant accepted battle and changed his front, but his enormous army corps maneuvered with great difficulty in that dense undergrowth, and in two days' fierce fighting he lost 17,700 men. This first Battle of the Wilderness (5–7 May) was a draw. Grant now knew that he had to deal with a general of different mettle from Johnston or Bragg; and Lee learned that the Army of the Potomac had obtained a leader worthy of it.

Grant then tried to outflank the enemy; but clouds of dust from his marching columns warned Lee of his intention and by the time his van reached the crossroads at Spottsylvania Court House, Lee was there to check him. Both armies threw up field entrenchments, and the five-day battle that followed (Spottsylvania, 8–12 May) was the first of modern trench warfare. Grant lost 31,000 more men and a cry went up for his removal. He declared, 'I . . . propose to fight it out on this line if it takes all summer' and Lincoln stood by him. Again he moved by his left in the hope of outflanking Lee's right and again the Army of

Northern Virginia was there to welcome him, and in a position so well chosen and entrenched that Grant needed all his adroitness to withdraw in safety and continue his flanking march (26 May). Lee swung with him to McClellan's old battlefield of Gaines's Mill. Both armies entrenched. The lines were six or eight miles long. On 1–3 June came the Battle of Cold Harbor, costliest and most futile Union assault in the entire war — an assault upon the entire line of Lee's trenches. Before going over the top the Union soldiers pinned papers on their backs, giving their names and addresses to identify their corpses. Eight or nine thousand men fell in a few hours, but hardly a dent was made on the Confederate lines.

During ten more days the armies faced one another. War had now acquired many of the horrors that we associate with World War I. The wounded, unattended between the lines, died of thirst, starvation, and loss of blood. Corpses rotted on the ground. Sharpshooters kept up their deadly work. Officers and men fought mechanically without hope. The war had begun so long ago that one could hardly remember anything else, or even what it was about.

In one month Grant had advanced from the Rapidan to the Chickahominy, the exact spot where McClellan had stood two years before, and he had lost from 55,000 to 60,000 men as against Lee's 25,000 to 30,000; but he could count on a continuous flow of reinforcements, and Lee could not. On 12 June Grant began a change of base to the James. With immense skill he ferried his vast army across that broad river, unmolested by Lee. But an opportunity to push into undefended Petersburg and thus outflank Richmond was lost. Lee slipped in by the interior lines, entrenched in time, and three general assaults cost the Union 8000 more men (15–18 June). Grant's army sat down to besiege Petersburg and remained there for nine months. A war of position had arrived.

Grant never had enough men or artillery to carry the Petersburg lines by assault. One attempt to do so, by mining under the Confederate lines and breaking them by explosions of dynamite — the Battle of the Crater — ended in costly defeat. He was right in holding Lee in position while Sherman reduced the effective area of the Confederacy, for Lee unable to maneuver was not dangerous.

Such, in brief, was the most desperately fought campaign of the war. Lee, with an army that despised digging as unsoldierly and hated fighting from entrenchments, had developed the technique of trench warfare to a point that Europe reached only in 1916. He had saved his army and saved Richmond. Grant, after making mistakes and suffering losses that would have broken any of his predecessors, was still indomitable. But how long would the country suffer such stupendous losses with no apparent result? The country could not then appreciate what we now know, that Grant had brought the end near and had forced the Confederate government to concentrate its best efforts on supporting Lee, thereby denying Joseph Johnston the necessary reinforcements to stop Sherman's march to the sea.

Jubal A. Early, having qualified for the role of Stonewall Jackson's successor by driving the Union forces from the Shenandoah valley, now had an opportunity to repeat the drama of 1862, but muffed it. On 2 July 1864 his 15,000 veterans were at Winchester, marching north by the classic route; at noon on 11 July he was only five miles from the capital. Almost at the same moment two Union divisions, which Grant had hurriedly detached from the Army of the Potomac, disembarked at Washington. Early had lost his chance! Union defenders drove Early back and on 13 July the Confederates fled back to the valley.

On 18 July the President called for half a million more volunteers, any deficiency to be filled by draft on 6 September, but as usual, the country was not up to Lincoln's stature. The appalling toll of casualties seemed to have brought the war no nearer conclusion. It looked as if Grant could never beat Lee, or Sherman take Atlanta. Paper dollars fell to their lowest point on the day that Early appeared before Washington. And the cost of living had soared far beyond the rise of wages or salaries. Unable to look beyond their own troubles to the far greater ills of their enemy, the Northern people began to ask whether a further prosecution of the war would profit anyone but the profiteers. This undercurrent of doubt and despair induced some strange developments in the presidential campaign that was already under way.

7. THE PRESIDENTIAL ELECTION

Alone of democratic governments before World War II, the United States faced a general election in wartime. For, as Lincoln said, 'We cannot have free government without elections; and if the rebellion could force us to forego or postpone a national election, it might fairly claim to have already conquered and ruined us.' In June 1864 Lincoln was renominated for the presidency by acclamation by a National Union convention representing both Republicans and War Democrats; the 'Union' of the two was dramatized by the nomination of Andrew Johnson of Tennessee — a life-long Democrat — to the vice-presidency.

Yet within a few weeks, and before the Democrats had held their own convention, there developed a movement against Lincoln within his own party. Sherman was stalled in front of Atlanta; things were going badly in Virginia; Chase resigned from the cabinet and struck an alliance with political adventurers and marplots like General Butler, Roscoe Conkling, and Horace Greeley. These men had come to the conclusion that Lincoln could not win and that it was necessary to name another ticket. 'Mr. Lincoln is already beaten' wrote Greeley. 'He cannot be elected. We must have another ticket to save us from overthrow.' He suggested Grant, Sherman, or Butler for President and Farragut for Vice-President!

In July a breach developed between the President and the radicals over the manner and method of reconstructing the Union after the war. When on 8 July Lincoln pocket-vetoed a bill embodying the radical views of reconstruction, Senator Wade and Representative Henry Davis issued a public manifesto accusing the President of a 'studied outrage on the legislative authority of the people' from the basest motives of personal ambition. Greeley published this Wade-Davis Manifesto in the *Tribune* on 5 August; and two weeks later he and the radicals began to circulate among the politicians a call for a new Republican convention to reconsider the Lincoln candidacy.

It was an alarming situation. Some of Lincoln's staunchest supporters thought the election already lost. The executive committee of the Republican party implored him to make a peace move. Lincoln sent them away satisfied that he cared nothing for himself, but that so palpable a confession of weakness as an overture to Jefferson Davis, at that juncture, would be equivalent to surrender. What Lincoln really thought of the situation is clear from the paper he wrote and sealed on 23 August:

> It seems exceedingly probable that this administration will not be re-elected. Then it will be my duty to so co-operate with the Presi-

dent-elect as to save the Union between the election and the inauguration, as he will have secured his election on such ground that he cannot possibly save it afterward.

If Jefferson Davis had been adroit he could have completed the distraction of Union councils by proposing an armistice or a peace conference on any terms; for once the fighting had stopped, it would have been impossible to get it started again. Had he been a supremely wise man he would have accepted the President's condition of peace: restoration of the Union without slavery. But President Davis still believed his cause invincible. 'Say to Mr. Lincoln from me, that I shall at any time be pleased to receive proposals for peace on the basis of our Independence. It will be useless to approach me with any other.' That cleared the air.

In the face of this plain and honest statement from the Confederate President, the Democratic national convention on 29 August adopted a resolution drafted by the Ohio copperhead Vallandigham:

> After four years of failure to restore the Union by the experiment of war . . . justice, humanity, liberty, and the public welfare demand that immediate efforts be made for a cessation of hostilities . . . to the end that at the earliest practicable moment, peace may be restored on the basis of the Federal Union of the States.

General McClellan received and accepted the Democratic nomination for President. He repudiated the peace plank in the platform, but was willing to ride into the White House on a wave of opposition to war.

Jefferson Davis by his frankness, the Democrats by their defeatism, and Sherman by capturing Atlanta knocked the bottom out of the Wade-Davis-Greeley scheme. Nothing more was heard of the call for a new Republican convention. On 6 September the new draft went quietly into effect, the New England radicals held a ringing Lincoln rally in Faneuil Hall, and, marvelous to relate, Ben Wade announced he would take the stump for the President! Lincoln's election, so doubtful in August, was conceded on every side in October. After Sheridan had beaten Early at Cedar Creek (19 October) and devastated the Shenandoah valley, the Northern people, on 8 November, chose 212 Lincoln electors and only 21 for McClellan. But Lincoln's popular majority was only 400,000 in 4,000,000 votes.

'The election,' said Lincoln two days later, 'has demonstrated that a people's government can sustain a national election in the midst of a great civil war.'

8. THE COLLAPSE OF THE CONFEDERACY

The re-election of Lincoln, the failure to obtain foreign recognition, the increasing pinch of the blockade, Sherman's march to the sea, and Grant's implacable hammering at the thin lines around Petersburg, took the heart out of the South. 'Two-thirds of our men are absent . . . most of them absent without leave' admitted President Davis that September. Yet he was by no means ready to concede defeat, or even that the situation was desperate, and he still hoped to change the fortunes of the battlefield and to wring peace and independence from a weary North.

On 3 February 1865 there took place a conference on board a steamer in Hampton Roads, between the President of the United States and the Vice-President of the Confederacy, who had been his friend and mentor in Congress sixteen years before. Stephens had credentials to negotiate peace as the envoy of an independent republic. Lincoln patiently repeated his refusal to negotiate on that basis. Senator Hunter, who accompanied Stephens, alleged as precedent the negotiations during the English Civil War. Lincoln replied, 'I do not profess to be posted in history. On all such matters I will turn you over to Seward. All I distinctly recollect about the case of Charles I is that he lost his head.' But 'the war will cease on the part of the Government, whenever it shall have ceased on the part of those who began it.' Offered a lifeboat, Stephens clutched at a straw, the very straw that Seward set afloat on April Fool's Day 1861 — Union and Confederacy might ally to expel Maximilian from Mexico.

It was as Lincoln had predicted — 'Davis cannot voluntarily re-accept the Union; we cannot voluntarily yield it.' Lee might with honor surrender his army to irresistible force; Davis could not with honor surrender his nation. The inherent dignity of his refusal was marred by his frantic boast at a public meeting in Richmond that he would compel the Yankees in less than twelve months to petition him for peace on his own terms.

But by February 1865 the Confederacy was sinking fast. Even slavery was jettisoned — in principle. President Davis sent an envoy to Europe, in January 1865, to offer abolition in exchange for recognition, and on 25 March the Richmond Congress authorized arming the slaves. Sherman, as he marched northward, was proving his sulphurous synonym for war. 'Columbia! — pretty much all burned; and burned *good.*' Yet the doughty Sherman passed some anxious hours, when he learned that Lee and his grim veterans were on the loose again.

For nine months the armies of Grant and Lee had faced one another across long lines of entrenchment running through the outskirts of Petersburg. At the beginning of the siege their forces were not disparate; but by the middle of March 1865 Grant had 115,000 effectives to Lee's 54,000. If Lee did not move out of his trenches Grant would soon envelop him; but if Petersburg were abandoned, Richmond must fall. Lee first tried an assault on the Union left — a costly failure. Sheridan, having marched across Virginia from the valley, thrust back Lee's right at the Battle of Five Forks (1 April); and on the next day Grant penetrated the center of the Confederate defenses. Lee's only hope was to retreat westward and unite with Johnston, who now commanded the remnants of his former army in North Carolina.

On the night of 2–3 April Lee's army slipped out of the Petersburg lines; and the next evening the Union forces entered Richmond. Without pause Grant pursued. Sheridan blocked the Confederates' escape southward. Rations failed Lee through some mistake at Richmond; his 30,000 men had to live on a thinly populated country in springtime. On 9 April Sheridan closed the only avenue of escape westward. Whether Lee could have cut his way through to the mountains and continued guerilla warfare indefinitely may well be doubted; but as he wrote himself, it is certain that he had only to ride along the lines and all would be over. 'But it is our duty to live, for what will become of the women and children of the South, if we are not here to support and protect them?'

Lee ordered a white flag to be displayed and requested an interview with his opponent. The scene that followed, in a house of the little village of Appomattox Court House, has become a part of American folklore. Lee, in the new full-dress uniform with jewel-studded sword that he had saved in the flight, Grant in his favorite private's blouse, unbuttoned, and without a sword, 'his feelings sad and depressed at the downfall of a foe who had fought so long and valiantly.'

Formal greetings. Small talk of other days, in the old army. . . .

Grant writes the terms of surrender in his own hand. . . . Officers and men paroled . . . arms and matériel surrendered . . . not to include the officers 'side-arms, and —

'Let all the men who claim to own a horse or mule take the animals home with them to work their little farms.'

'This will do much toward conciliating our people.'

The conference is over. Lee pauses a moment in the doorway, looking out over a field blossoming with the stars and stripes. Thrice, and slowly, he strikes a fist into the palm of his gantleted hand. He mounts his horse Traveller and is gone.

A sound of cheering spreads along the Union lines.

Grant orders it to cease:

'The war is over; the rebels are our countrymen again.'

General Joshua Chamberlain who received the surrender on behalf of Grant recalled the moving scene:

Before us in proud humiliation stood the embodiment of manhood: men whom neither toils and sufferings, nor the fact of death, nor disaster, nor hopelessness could bend from their resolve; standing before us now, thin, worn, and famished, but erect, and with eyes looking level into ours, waking memories that bound us together as no other bond; — was not such manhood to be welcomed back into a Union so tested and assured?

When the head of each division column comes opposite our group, our bugle sounds the signal and instantly our whole line from right to left, regiment by regiment in succession, gives the soldier's salutation, from the 'order arms' to the old 'carry' — the marching salute. Gordon at the head of the column, riding with heavy spirit and downcast face, catches the sound of shifting arms, looks up, and taking the meaning, wheels superbly, making with himself and his horse one uplifted figure, with profound salutation as he drops the point of his sword to the boot toe; then facing to his own command, gives word for his successive brigades to pass us with the same position of the manual — honor answering honor. On our part not a sound of trumpet more, nor roll of drum; not a cheer, nor word nor whisper of vain-glorying, nor motion of man standing again at the order, but an awed stillness rather, and breath-holding, as if it were the passing of the dead! . . . How could we help falling on our knees, all of us together, and praying God to pity and forgive us all! [4]

4. Joshua Chamberlain, *The Passing of the Armies*, 258ff.

But let the last word be by a poet:

> Bury the bygone South.
> Bury the minstrel with the honey-mouth,
> Bury the broadsword virtues of the clan,
> Bury the unmachined, the planters' pride,
> The courtesy and the bitter arrogance,
> The pistol-hearted horsemen who could ride
> Like jolly centaurs under the hot stars.
> Bury the whip, bury the branding-bars,
> Bury the unjust thing
> That some tamed into mercy, being wise,
> But could not starve the tiger from its eyes
> Or make it feed where beasts of mercy feed.
> Bury the fiddle-music and the dance,
> The sick magnolias of the false romance
> And all the chivalry that went to seed
> Before its ripening.[5]

9. WHY DID THE SOUTH LOSE?

Was the defeat of the Confederacy inevitable?[6] We have seen that at the time of the attack on Fort Sumter Southerners generally expected to win the war, and that many disinterested observers abroad shared this expectation. Why was the South defeated? Was defeat the result of external factors over which the Confederacy had no control? Was it, after all, the sheer superiority of the North in population, wealth, and industrial might? Was it the blockade? Was it those big battalions which the god of war proverbially favors? Or did defeat result in any significant part from internal causes: the breakdown of the transportation system; the collapse of finances; the ineffectiveness of the political and administrative machinery; the failure of bold leadership; state rights and localism; the loss of nerve? In short, did Southern nationalism fail because of defeat on the battlefield or was the Confederacy defeated on the battlefield because Southern nationalism had failed?

It is impossible to give a conclusive answer to these questions. But recall what we observed at the very beginning: that the Confederacy

---

5. Stephen Vincent Benét, *John Brown's Body* (N.Y., 1929), book viii, pp. 374–5. By kind permission of Mrs. Stephen Vincent Benét.
6. In one sense we may say that whatever happened in history was inevitable; otherwise it would not have happened. But this is to beg the whole question.

did not need to win battles or campaigns in order to win the war; she needed only to go on fighting until the North grew weary of war and allowed the 'erring sisters' to go their way. And notwithstanding the great Union victories of mid-summer 1863, there was still danger of just such war-weariness as late as mid-summer of 1864 when Grant was hurling himself in vain against Lee's lines, when Sherman was bogged down before Atlanta, when greenbacks fell to 39 cents on the gold dollar, and when Lincoln expected to be defeated in the fall elections. There were still enough white men of fighting age in the Confederacy to provide its armies with half a million men (174,223 surrendered in April and May 1865), and enrollment of the Negroes might have brought in thousands more. Neither the Tredegar iron works outside Richmond nor the great munitions-producing center at Selma, Alabama, were captured until April 1865. As for material factors, an agricultural region should not have lacked for food, and in fact did not; the transportation system could have been improved; and financial collapse may have been a consequence, not a cause, of military setbacks and of defeatism. Senator Hill of Georgia who wrote to President Davis on 25 March 1865, 'we shall conquer all enemies yet,' admitted nine years later, all physical advantages are insufficient to account for our failure. The truth is, we failed because too many of our people were not determined to win.'

Certainly we cannot divorce the defeat of the Confederacy from internal factors. The Confederacy never really developed that sentiment of nationalism so essential to effective warfare in modern times. While military leadership compares favorably with that of the Union, its political leadership does not. Davis lacked the statesman-like qualities of Lincoln, and his cabinet and administrative officers were decidedly inferior to those of the Union. Nor could Southern state governors play the role so effectively performed by men like Andrews of Massachusetts, Curtin of Pennsylvania, Morton of Indiana, or Kirkwood of Iowa. Equally serious was the failure of the South to develop political parties. This meant that opposition to President Davis did not find expression through normal political channels, but in bitter personal attacks, state-rights nihilism, and outright subversion. And, perhaps because the ablest Southerners thought their proper place was in the army, the Confederacy failed to develop effective political or governmental machinery. Indeed the very notion of administrative efficiency conjured

up to many Southerners the specter of centralization: thus a writer in
De Bow's *Review* argued defiantly that 'the very moment any administration mistakes the Southern Confederacy for a *government proper,*
and attempts to exercise all the powers of government, that moment will
be its last, or at least the beginning of its downfall.'

In the last analysis, however, the Confederacy may have been condemned to defeat by its very *raison d'être.* Southern states seceded in
order to vindicate, and enjoy, state rights, and to preserve a way of
life based on Negro slavery. But how could one establish a nation and
win a war on the principle of state rights, a principle by its very nature
decentralizing and disintegrating? And how command the sympathy
and support of Britain and France, so essential to breaking the blockade and to eventual victory, as long as enlightened European opinion
looked on slavery as archaic and immoral? May it not be said that the
Confederacy was defeated not by inferiority in arms, man power, or resources, and certainly not by any lack of ability or of courage, but by
the two insurmountable handicaps of state rights and slavery? A strong
government might have crushed state rights; a bold government might
have liquidated slavery. But if Southerners were prepared to accept
such policies as the price of victory; secession, the Confederacy, and the
war all became meaningless.

10. THE LAST DAYS OF LINCOLN

. . . With malice toward none; with charity for all; with firmness
in the right, as God gives us to see the right, let us strive on to finish
the work we are in; to bind up the nation's wounds; to care for him
who shall have borne the battle, and for his widow, and his orphan
— to do all which may achieve and cherish a just and lasting peace
among ourselves, and with all nations.

Thus closed the second inaugural address of President Lincoln on 4
March 1865. The struggle over reconstruction was already on. Ben
Wade with his truculent vigor and fierce hatred of the slaveholders, the
Democrats eager for revenge on the President, Charles Sumner with his
passionate conviction that right and justice required the South to pass
under the Caudine forks, were certain to oppose the terms with which
Lincoln proposed to bind up the nation's wounds. But Congress would

Dred Scott (1795-1858). Contemporary painting

John Brown (1800-1859)

Stephen A. Douglas (1813-61). Photograph by Mathew Brady

Jefferson Davis (1808-89)

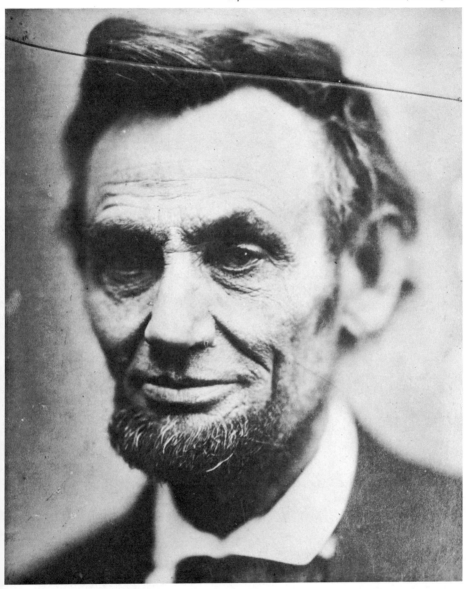

Abraham Lincoln (1809-65). His last photograph, April 1865.

Ulysses S. Grant (1822-85)

Robert E. Lee (1807-70)

The Confederate *Nashville* and the Union *Harvey Birch* in the English Channel

Camp Northumberland, 96th Pennsylvania Infantry. Photograph by Mathew Brady

At Massaponax Church, Virginia. General Ulysses S. Grant
(left end of bench nearest tree) sits on a pew from
Bethesda Church writing a dispatch, May 21, 1864.

Berlin. Photograph by Mathew Brady.

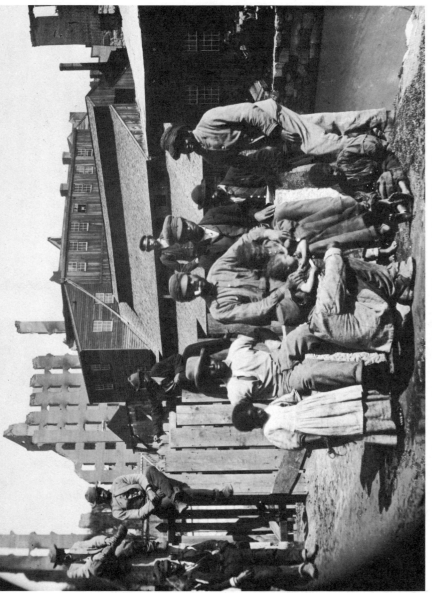

Southern Freedmen in Richmond. Photograph by Mathew Brady

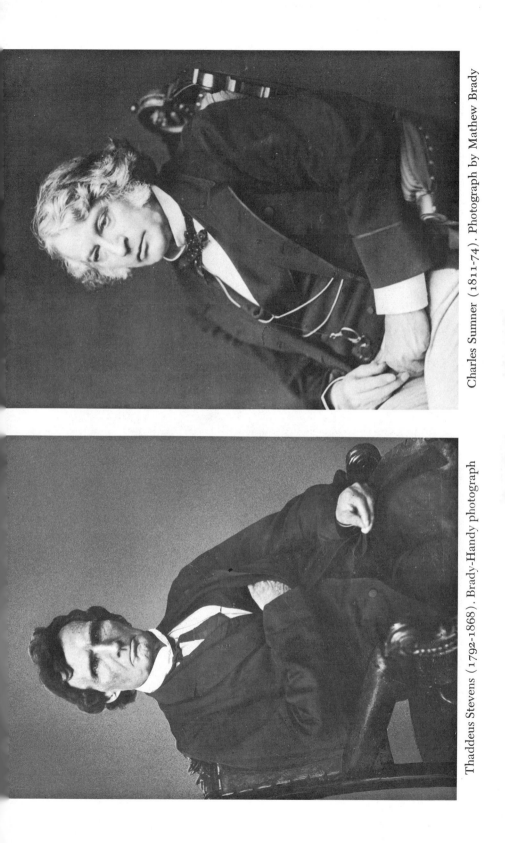

Charles Sumner (1811-74). Photograph by Mathew Brady

Thaddeus Stevens (1792-1868). Brady-Handy photograph

Andrew Johnson (1808-75) by Washington Cooper

not meet until December. It might be confronted with the established fact of a restored nation, if the South were wise, and nothing happened to Lincoln.

On 11 April, two days after Lee's surrender, Lincoln delivered his last public address. After a brief allusion to Appomattox and the hope of a speedy peace, he unfolded his reconstruction policy — the most magnanimous terms toward a helpless opponent ever offered by a victor. For Lincoln did not consider himself a conqueror. He was, and had been since 1861, President of the United States. The rebellion must be forgotten, and every Southern state re-admitted to her full privilege in the Union as soon as 10 per cent of the whites had taken the oath of allegiance, and organized a state government.

On Thursday night, 13 April, Washington was illuminated on account of Lee's surrender, and crowds paraded the streets. A general light-heartedness was in the air; everyone knew that the war was practically over. When a marine band serenaded Lincoln, he asked them to play 'Dixie' because 'we have fairly captured it.' On Good Friday, the 14th, the President held his last cabinet meeting. It was decided to lift the blockade. He urged his ministers to turn their thoughts to peace. There must be no more bloodshed, no persecution. General Grant, who attended the meeting, was asked for late news from Sherman, but had none. Lincoln remarked that it would soon come and be favorable,[7] for last night he had had a familiar dream. In a strange indescribable ship he seemed to be moving with great rapidity toward a dark and undefined shore. He had had this same dream before Sumter, Bull Run, Antietam, Murfreesboro, Vicksburg, and Wilmington. Matter-of-fact Grant remarked that Murfreesboro was no victory — 'a few such fights would have ruined us.' Lincoln looked at him curiously and said, however that might be, his dream preceded that battle.

Secretary Welles, who records this incident, may be our guide to the fearful events of that night. He had gone to bed early and was just falling sleep when someone shouted from the street that the President had been shot and the Secretary of State and his son assassinated. He dressed and crossed Lafayette Square to Seward's house on 15th Street. The lower hall was full of excited people. Welles went upstairs to the

---

7. Johnston surrendered his army to Sherman 26 April. Jefferson Davis was captured 10 May. The last Confederate force surrendered 26 May.

room where Seward was lying on a bed soaked with blood, his lower jaw sagging as if in death. In the next room lay the son, unconscious from the injuries he had received in defending his father.

Leaving the quartermaster general in charge of the house, Welles, who by this time had been joined by Stanton, hurried down to 10th Street in a carriage. The dying President had been carried across that street from Ford's Theatre to a poor lodging-house, where he was laid on a bed in a narrow back room. He never recovered consciousness. 'The giant sufferer,' writes Welles, 'lay extended diagonally across the bed, which was not long enough for him. . . . His slow, full respiration lifted the clothes with each breath that he took. His features were calm and striking.' The room and the house were uncomfortably crowded. It was a dark and gloomy night, and rain fell at dawn. Crowds remained in the street, looking in vain for hope from the watchers who came out for a breath of air. About once an hour Mrs. Lincoln would repair to the bedside of her dying husband and with lamentation and tears remain until overcome by emotion.'

A little before half-past seven the great heart ceased to beat.

Welles continues, 'I went after breakfast to the Executive Mansion. There was a cheerless cold rain and everything seemed gloomy. On the Avenue in front of the White House were several hundred colored people, mostly women and children, weeping and wailing their loss. This crowd did not appear to diminish through the whole of that cold, wet day; they seemed not to know what was to be their fate since their great benefactor was dead, and their hopeless grief affected me more than almost anything else, though strong and brave men wept when I met them.'

XXXVIII

The Aftermath of the War

1. THE HERITAGE OF WAR

Bow down, dear land, for thou has found release!
 Thy God, in these distempered days,
 Hath taught thee the sure wisdom of His ways
And through thine enemies hath wrought thy peace!
 Bow down in prayer and praise!
No poorest in thy borders but may now
Lift to the juster skies a man's enfranchised brow;
O Beautiful! My Country! Ours once more!

Thus James Russell Lowell, at the Harvard commemoration service of 1865, saluted, as he believed, a reunited nation purged by war of all grossness that had accompanied its rise to power. But the fierce passions of warfare had burned good with evil; and in the scorched soil the new growth showed tares as well as wheat. 'The Civil War marks an era in the history of the American mind,' wrote Henry James fourteen years after Appomattox. From the war, the American had gained a sense 'of the world being a more complicated place than it had hitherto seemed, the future more treacherous, success more difficult.'

The war had been fought for the preservation of the Union, yet this was not the sole object of the war. The nation whose endurance was to be tested was, as Lincoln said in his Gettysburg Address, 'a nation conceived in liberty and dedicated to the proposition that all men are created equal.' After 1862 the abolition of slavery came to be a second acknowledged objective of the war. And to many people, in Europe as in America, the maintenance of a 'government of the people, by the people, for the people' came to be a third. Union, freedom, and democracy, these things were legitimate objectives of the war, and it is proper to inquire to what extent they were achieved, and at what cost.

Union had been preserved, but it could not be said that the old Union had been restored. The long dispute over the nature of the Union had been settled, at last, in favor of the nationalist contention, but it had required force to bring that about. Nor had sectionalism disappeared. The natural influences of geography and climate which had gone to create Northern and Southern sectionalism remained, and in the generation after the war a third powerful section came into existence — the trans-Mississippi West, whose regional consciousness, like that of the South, was accentuated by its exploitation by the Northeast. Until well into the next century American political life was to be conditioned by this division of North, South, and West.

Slavery, to be sure, was gone and no more would politicians proclaim the sophistry that black servitude was necessary for white freedom. But emancipation, too, had been brought about by violence. Perhaps this was the only way it could have been brought about, but even the most ardent champions of freedom were forced to admit that the method was painful for white and black alike. Emancipation ended slavery, and that was momentous. But slavery gave way not to freedom but to a kind of peonage, and though in the weird metamorphosis of race relations that followed Appomattox, the Negroes did have some voice in their own destiny, for the most part they merely obeyed new masters. Not for another hundred years were most Negroes to enjoy even in part those rights which the war and the new constitutional amendments had attempted to assure them.

What shall we say of the third objective — government of, by, and for the people? Democracy, indeed, had not 'perished from the earth,' yet for a brief interval Americans witnessed what they had never known before: military government in time of peace. The Civil War had destroyed slavery and the slaveholding class; but within a few years corporate industry would wield excessive power. Twenty years after the attack on Fort Sumter the railroads alone represented a greater investment and concentration of power than had ever the slave interest, and their influence in politics and in the economic activities of free men was far-reaching, though not so pernicious. As early as 1873 Walt Whitman, apostle of democracy, looked out upon *Democratic Vistas* and was moved to solemn warning:

> Shift and turn the combinations of the statement as we may, the problem of the future of America is in certain respects as dark as it is vast. Pride, competition, segregation, vicious wilfulness, and license beyond example brood already upon us. Unwieldy and immense, who shall hold in behemoth? who bridle leviathan? Flaunt it as we choose, athwart and over the roads of our progress loom huge uncertainty, and dreadful threatening gloom. It is useless to deny it: Democracy grows rankly up the thickest, noxious, deadliest plants and fruits of all — brings worse and worse invaders — needs newer, larger, stronger, keener compensations and compellers.

There was poetic exaggeration here, and a failure to realize that the evils complained of were common to mankind, not unique to America. Yet years later Justice John M. Harlan of the Supreme Court, looking back upon this period, remembered that 'there was everywhere among the people generally a deep feeling of unrest. The nation had been rid of human slavery . . . but the conviction was universal that the country was in real danger from another kind of slavery, namely the slavery that would result from aggregations of capital in the hands of a few.'

The cost of the war had been colossal. 'Fondly do we hope,' Lincoln had said, 'fervently do we pray, that this mighty scourge of war may speedily pass away. Yet if God wills that it continue until all the wealth piled by the bondsman's two hundred and fifty years of unrequited toil shall be sunk, and until every drop of blood drawn with the lash shall be paid by another drawn by the sword, as was said three thousand years ago, so still it must be said, "The judgments of the Lord are true and righteous altogether." ' Lincoln's tragic fears were fulfilled. Deaths from all causes in the Union army totaled some 360,000, and in the Confederate army some 260,000, and thousands more were wounded. How many lives were lost because of malnutrition, disease, and the chaotic conditions of 1865 and 1866, it is impossible to say, nor can we count the lives shattered by destruction and demoralized by defeat.

The money cost of the war was staggering; proportionally higher, indeed, than that of World War I. Loans and taxes raised by the Federal Government came to a little less than $3 billion, and the interest on the Civil War debt an additional $2.8 billion. The Confederacy floated loans of over $2 billion, but the total financial loss of the South, in property confiscated, depreciated, and destroyed, in the losses of banks and insurance companies and businesses, and in the expense of reconstruction, was incalculable. Many states, North and South, went heavily into debt for the prosecution of the war. And the country continued to pay for the war well into the twentieth century: United States government pensions amounted to almost $8 billion, and Southern states doled out additional sums to Confederate veterans. The total cost of the war to North and South may be estimated at well over $20 billion — five times all the expenditures of the federal government from 1789 to 1865!

The war left a heritage not only of death, desolation, and debt, but of practical problems of enormous complexity. The Union and Confederate armies had to be demobilized and upwards of 1.5 million men returned to the pursuits of peace. The administrative activities of the War Department and the Provost General's office had to be curbed and the supremacy of civil government restored. Currency and industry needed to adjust to a peace basis. There were staggering financial burdens of the war to be liquidated. Four million freedmen had to adapt to their new condition. Equally serious were the problems presented by the new industrial revolution in the North and the agricultural revolution in the South and the West. And foreign affairs called for immediate action.

The material problems of the war could be met; the moral devastation was never wholly repaired. During the war violence and destruction and hatred had been called virtues; it was a long time before they were again recognized as vices. The war had brutalized combatants and non-combatants alike. Ruthlessness and wastefulness, extravagance and corruption, speculation and exploitation, had accompanied the conflict, and they lingered on to trouble the postwar years. Above all, the war left a heritage of misunderstanding and even of bitterness that affected men, Northern and Southern, for over a generation. In the fiery cauldron of the Civil War not only the Old South was melted down but the old America — the federal republic of Thomas Jefferson and Andrew Jackson — was volatilized.

But the revolution wrought by the war also offered the nation an opportunity to right the grievous wrongs done to the Negro and to make this country one truly dedicated to the principles of equality. In the years after the war, for the first time, the power of the national government was employed to extend the civil rights of the Negro. One may well doubt whether, if it had not been for Reconstruction, even a century later there would be Constitutional guarantees of these rights. Only at this unique juncture in history, when the South was subjugated and the North felt some of the equalitarian spirit of the war, was it possible to write provisions into the Constitution designed to achieve these ends. If Reconstruction ultimately failed, it at least left a legal foundation for subsequent struggles against inequality. The Reconstruction period was indeed a 'tragic era,' but the tragedy lies in the blighted hopes of so many men of good will, and in the betrayal of the Negro; it lies not in the fact that the government intervened forcibly to secure equality, but in the failure of the nation to carry through this effort. That failure left a legacy of bitterness that continues to trouble us today.

2. THE REVOLUTION

The fall of the Confederacy dealt an extremely heavy blow to the planter and political aristocracy that had guided the destinies of the South since the days of Thomas Jefferson. Some of this class was excluded, for some years, from participation in the government, and for some of the abler leaders such as Davis and Lee the disability was never removed. Slave property valued in 1860 at over $2 billion evaporated, and the savings and sacrifices represented by Confederate securities were lost. A labor system which was the very basis of the Southern economy was overthrown, the agricultural regime which it served was disarranged, and a new system, no less wasteful and scarcely less oppressive, was established in its stead.

The old planter aristocracy had suffered severely in the war; for if the war had been 'a poor man's fight,' the poor white had nothing to lose, and his condition was no worse in 1870 than it had been in 1850. But the planters lost not only their youth but often their means of recuperation. Well they learned what the Knights of Aristophanes declared twenty-four centuries ago:

There are things, then, hotter than fire, there are speeches more shameless
    still
Than the shameless speeches of those who rule the City at will.

Many gave up the struggle to maintain themselves on the land. A few fled to England, Mexico, or Brazil; others migrated to the Northern cities or started life anew in the West; many moved to the towns and adapted themselves to business or professional life. At the same time the small farmers and poor whites took advantage of the prevailing disorder to enlarge their farms and elect men of their own kind, who shared instead of scorning their prejudices, to high office. A little while and the Tillmans, Watsons, and Longs would sit in the seats of the Calhouns, the Cobbs, and the Clays.

The most clean-cut stroke of the revolution in the South was the emancipation of 4 million Negro slaves. Begun during the war, this process was consummated by three amendments to the Constitution. The Thirteenth, ratified in 1865, abolished slavery in places not reached by the Emancipation Proclamation. The Fourteenth Amendment extended federal protection to the freedmen for their personal and property rights, and the Fifteenth Amendment attempted to assure them the franchise. 'The bottom rail was on top,' in the salty phrase of the time, but the whites did not let it stay there long.

While the old pattern of Southern society and economy was being rearranged into a new one, a different kind of transformation was effected in the North. With the representatives of the planter class out of Congress, the spokesmen of industry, finance, and of free Western lands were unopposed, unless by one another. During the war they pushed through legislation to fulfill the arrested hopes of the 'fifties, and after victory they garnered the fruits thereof.

The moderate tariff of 1857 gave way to the Morrill tariff of 1861, and that to a series of war tariffs with duties scaling rapidly upward, and carefully adapted to meet the need of Northern business. By the National Banking Acts of 1863 and 1864 the Independent Treasury system of 1846 was swept away, and an act of 1865 imposed a tax of 10 per cent on all state bank notes, a fatal blow which none would regret. That there might be no shortage of labor, Congress in 1864 permitted the importation of contract labor from abroad, and though this act was repealed within a few years, the practice itself was not discontinued until the decade of the 'eighties. At the same time the policy of internal improvements at national expense found expression in subsidies to telegraph and cable lines and in generous grants of millions of acres out of the public domain to railroad promoters and financiers.

While Northern industry and finance were reaping the fruits of victory, a century-old ambition of Western farmers was met by the passage of the Homestead Law in 1862. This act, limited temporarily in its application to those who 'have never borne arms against the United States Government,' granted a quarter-section (160 acres) of public domain to anyone who would undertake to cultivate it. The Morrill Act, passed the same year, subsidized agricultural education through public lands. At the same time easier access to the West was assured through the government-subsidized railroads. This legislation carried out the promise of the Republican party platform and helped bring to that party support from the agricultural West.

The Republicans came out of the war with an aura of legitimacy, for they could claim to be the party that had saved the Union, and they could brand the Democrats with the odium of secession. With a single exception, every candidate whom the Republican party named for the presidency between 1868 and 1900 had been an officer in the Union army. For a generation Republican orators rang the changes on Fort Sumter and Andersonville prison, and 'waved the bloody shirt of the rebellion,' and no appeal was more effective than that voiced by Colonel Robert Ingersoll in the campaign of 1876:

> Every State that seceded from the United States was a Democratic State. Every ordinance of secession that was drawn was drawn by a Democrat. Every man that endeavored to tear the old flag from the heaven that it enriches was a Democrat. Every man that tried to destroy this nation was a Democrat. Every enemy this great Republic had for twenty years has been a Democrat. Every man that shot Union soldiers was a Democrat. . . . Every man that loved slavery better than liberty was a Democrat. The man that assassinated Abraham Lincoln was a Democrat. . . . Every man that wanted the privilege of whipping another man to make him work for him for nothing, was a Democrat. . . . Every man that impaired the credit of the United States, every man that swore we would never pay the bonds, every man that swore we would never redeem the greenbacks, every maligner of his country's credit, or his country's honor, was a Democrat.

3. THE TRIUMPHANT NORTH

To the North the war brought not only victory, but unprecedented prosperity, a sense of power, a spirit of buoyant confidence, and exuberance of energy that found expression in a thousand outlets. To the generation that had saved the Union everything seemed possible. Men hurled themselves upon the continent with ruthless abandon as if to ravish it of its wealth. Railroads were flung across mountain barriers, and settlers crowded into half a continent, while cattle swarmed over the grasslands of the High Plains. Forests were felled, the earth gutted of coal, copper, iron ore, and precious metals; petroleum spouted from untended wells. Telegraph wires were strung across the country and cables stretched from continent to continent; factories sprang up overnight; new industries were established and old industries took on new form; speculators thronged the floors of stock and produce exchanges, inventors flooded the patent office with applications for new devices with which to conquer nature and create wealth. Cities grew so fast that no one could keep track of them, and the mansions of the rich were as vulgar as the tenements of the poor were squalid. Year after year, from every hamlet and farm, countrymen hurried into the cities, and immigrants poured into the mines and the mills.

Despite four years of war the resources of the North seemed little impaired. Population and wealth had increased; the output of factory and farm had not declined despite the drain on manpower. The census of 1870 revealed that the per capita wealth of the North had doubled in ten years. There was a universal feeling that the resources of the continent were as yet untapped. 'The truth is,' wrote Senator Sherman to his brother, the General, 'the close of the war with our resources unimpaired gives an elevation, a scope to the ideas of leading capitalists far higher than anything ever undertaken in this country before. They talk of millions as confidently as formerly of thousands.'

The war, like all wars, made special demands on some industries and depressed others, and created new opportunities for amassing private wealth. Supplying the armies with food and clothing and munitions proved immensely profitable. More profitable still was the business of financing the war. Government bonds bore from 5 to 7 per cent interest in gold. During the war they had sold at a discount; after the war they brought a premium, and many a fortune was founded upon speculation in these bonds. The National Banking Act, too, afforded a legitimate means to wealth, and in 1870 some 1600 banks reported earnings of $60 million on a capitalization of $425 million, while banks which held government bonds received an estimated aggregate of 17 per cent interest annually upon their investment. The rewards of railroad organization, financing, and construction were even greater. In the ten years after the war, the country doubled its railroad mileage, and the profits of construction and operation went, often by devious means, to establish the fortunes of Vanderbilt and Gould, Huntington and Stanford, and other multimillionaires.

No less spectacular was the exploitation of natural resources. After oil was struck in western Pennsylvania in 1859, thousands of fortune-hunters stampeded into the oil-soaked triangle between the Allegheny river and Oil Creek, and the stock of hundreds of new oil companies was hawked from town to town. During the war years the production of oil increased from 21 million to 104 million gallons, and the capitalization of new oil companies was not far from half a billion dollars. In the year of Lincoln's election the production of silver was a paltry $150,000; by the end of Reconstruction annual output had reached $38 million, and the silver barons of the West had come to exercise an influence in politics comparable to that of the bankers and industrialists in the East. Though the production of basic minerals barely held its own during the war, the postwar years saw a great upswing: coal production trebled, and iron ore production in the Lake Superior region alone increased more than tenfold.

In the decade of the 'sixties the number of manufacturing establishments in the country increased by 80 per cent. The value of manufactured products in Maine more than doubled, in Illinois it trebled, and in Michigan it increased fourfold. Four times as much timber was cut in Michigan, four times as much pig iron was smelted in Ohio, four times as much freight was handled by the Pennsylvania Railroad, four times as many miles of railroad track were laid, in 1870 as in 1860. After the war, the woolens, cotton, iron, lumber, meat, and milling industries all showed a steady and even a spectacular development. Three times as many patents were granted in 1870 as in 1860, and the transactions in the New York clearing house multiplied fivefold. And while property values in the South were suffering a cataclysmic decline, the census reported an increase in the total property value of the North and West from $10 billion in 1860 to over $25 billion a decade later.

Accompanying this extraordinary development of business was a steady growth in the population of cities and in immigration. Older cities such as New York and Philadelphia, Boston and Baltimore, continued the growth which had begun back in the 'forties, and newer cities such as Chicago and St. Louis, Cleveland and Pittsburgh, St. Paul and San Francisco, more than doubled their population in ten years. Even during the war years some 800,000 immigrants had found their way to the United States, and in the ten years after Appomattox no less than 3.25 million immigrants flooded into the cities and the farms of the North and the West.

Industry, transportation, banking, speculation, the exploitation of natural resources and of labor, all contributed to the wealth of the country and to the wealth of individuals. Observers were already remarking upon the concentration of wealth in certain fortunate areas and certain favored groups. In 1870 the wealth of New York State alone was more than twice as great as that of all the ex-Confederate states. Every business grew its own crop of millionaires, and soon the names of Morgan and Jay Cooke, Vanderbilt and Jay Gould, Armour and Swift, McCormick and Pillsbury, came to be as familiar to the average American as the names of his statesmen. A new plutocracy emerged from the War and Reconstruction, masters of money who were no less self-conscious and no less powerful than the planter aristocracy of the Old South. The war, which had gone far to flatten out class distinctions in the South, tended to accentuate class differences in the North.

4. THE PROSTRATE SOUTH

Physical devastation without parallel until 1914–18 preceded the social and economic revolution in the South. Over large sections of the country, Union and Confederate armies had tramped and fought. Sherman had left a broad belt of blackened ruin from Atlanta to Savannah and from Savannah to Raleigh: 'where our footsteps pass,' wrote one of his aides, 'fire, ashes, and desolation follow in the path.' From Fairfax Courthouse to Petersburg the region was such a wilderness that deer ran wild in the forests. Sheridan had swept down the fertile Shenandoah valley like an avenging fury, leaving a trail of ruin. 'We had no cattle, hogs, sheep, or horses or anything else,' wrote a native of Virginia. 'The fences were all gone . . . the barns were all burned; chimneys standing without houses and houses standing without roofs, or doors, or windows . . . bridges all destroyed, roads badly cut up.' In the West, conditions were just as bad. The Governor of Arkansas wrote of his state: 'The desolations of war are beyond description. . . . Besides the utter desolation that marked the tracks of war and battle, guerilla bands and scouting parties have pillaged almost every neighbourhood. . . . It would be safe to say that two thirds of the counties in the State are in destitute circumstances.'

Some of the cities presented a picture as appalling as the rural regions. Charleston, once the proudest city of the South, had been bombarded and partially burned; a Northern visitor painted it as a city of 'vacant houses, of widowed women, of rotting wharves, of deserted warehouses, of weed-wild gardens, of miles of grass-grown streets, of acres of pitiful and voiceless barrenness.' The business portion of Richmond, the capital of the Confederacy, lay in ruins 'all up and down, as far as the eye could reach. . . . Beds of cinders, cellars half filled with bricks and rubbish, broken and blackened walls, impassable streets deluged with *débris*.' In Atlanta, masses of brick and mortar, charred timber, scraps of tin roofing, engine bolts and bars, cannonballs, and long shot filled the ruined streets. Mobile, Galveston, Vicksburg, and numerous other cities of the South were in a similar plight.

With the collapse of the Confederacy, civil government and administration all but disappeared throughout the South. There was no money for the support of government and no authority which could assess or collect taxes. The postal service was paralyzed; it was fully two years before normal service was restored. There were no courts, no judges, no sheriffs, no police officers with any authority, and vandalism went unrestrained except by public opinion or by lynch law. 'Our principal danger,' observed George Cary Eggleston, 'was from lawless bands of marauders who infested the country, and our greatest difficulty in dealing with them lay in the utter absence of constituted authority of any sort.' Fraud and peculation added to the universal distress. United States Treasury agents sized hundreds of thousands of bales of cotton, and other property as well. The Federal Government subsequently reimbursed no less than 40,000 claimants because of illegal confiscation of their property.

The economic life of the South was shattered. What manufacturing there was had been all but destroyed. Few Southern banks were solvent, and it was years before the banking system was even partially restored. Confederate securities into which the people had sunk their savings were now as worthless as Continental currency. Shops were depleted of goods and almost everything had to be imported from the North on credit. Even agriculture was slow to revive. Alabama produced 989,955 bales of cotton in 1860 and only 429,472 in 1870; Mississippi turned out 1,202,507 bales in 1860 and 564,938 in 1870. Not until 1879 did the seceding states raise a cotton crop as large as that of 1860. The rice industry of South Carolina and Georgia all but disappeared; so too the sugar cane industry of Louisiana. In 1870 the tobacco crop of Virginia was one-third that of 1860 and the corn and wheat crop one-half. Farm land that had once sold for $100 an acre went begging at $5, and in Mississippi alone almost 6 million acres of land were sold for nonpayment of taxes. In the decade between 1860 and 1870 the estimated real value of all property in the eleven Confederate states decreased from $5,202,055,000 to $2,929,350,000; during the same period the estimated value of all property in the rest of the country more than doubled.

The transportation system of the region had collapsed. Roads were all but impassable, bridges destroyed or washed away, ditches filled in, river levees broken. What steamboats had not been captured or destroyed were in disrepair. Railroad transportation was paralyzed, and most of the railroad companies bankrupt. Over a stretch of 114 miles in Alabama 'every bridge and trestle was destroyed, cross-ties rotten, buildings burned, water-tanks gone, ditches filled up, and tracks grown up in weeds and bushes.' Except in Texas, public lands were not made available for Southern railway construction, and the railroad system of the South was not properly restored for almost a generation.

Starvation was imminent in certain sections. In Richmond half the population depended upon Federal Government rations. In Columbia the army fed 10,000 people and at Atlanta the army commissary distributed food to 50,000 needy whites and blacks of the surrounding territory. The Negroes suffered most. As late as December 1865 it was estimated that in Alabama, Mississippi, and Georgia over half a million people lacked the necessities of life.

Social disorganization was scarcely less complete. Much of the educational system of the South had been deranged. Schools were closed, pupils and teachers scattered; school funds had been used up in the war, endowments for colleges and universities squandered or confiscated. Churches had been destroyed and church money dissipated. Young men of family who had interrupted their education to fight for Southern independence had to labor in the fields to keep their kinfolk from starving; and a planter's family which still had young men was deemed fortunate. Seventy-year-old Thomas Dabney, once a proud Mississippi planter, did the family wash for years after the war. General Pendleton plowed his few acres and General Anderson worked as a day laborer in the yards of the South Carolina Railroad. George Fitzhugh, the philosopher of slavery who had lectured at Harvard and Yale, lived in a poor shanty among his former slaves. William Gilmore Simms, the South's leading man of letters, lost not only his 'house, stables, barns, gin house, machine and threshing houses, mules, horses, cattle, wagons, ploughs, implements, all destroyed' but what was probably the finest private library in the South. 'Pretty much the whole of life has been merely not dying,' wrote the Southern poet, Sidney Lanier, who was himself dying.

5. THE FREEDMAN

In Reconstruction the Negro was the central figure. Upwards of a million colored people had in one way or another become free before the end of the war; victory and the Thirteenth Amendment liberated about 3 million more. Never before in the history of the world had civil and political rights been conferred at one stroke on so large a body of men. Many Negroes thought that freedom meant no more work and proceeded to celebrate an endless 'day ob jubilo'; others were led to believe that the property of their former masters would be divided among them. 'Emancipation having been announced one day,' write Tom Watson about his Georgia home, 'not a Negro remained on the place the next. The fine old homestead was deserted. Every house in "the quarter" was empty. The first impulse of freedom had carried the last of the blacks to town.' Thousands took to the woods or to the road, or clustered around the United States army posts, living on doles or dying of camp diseases. As the most famous of colored leaders, Frederick Douglass, said, the Negro 'was free from the individual master but a slave of society. He had neither money, property, nor friends. He was free from the old plantation, but he had nothing but the dusty road under his feet. He was free from the old quarter that once gave him shelter, but a slave to the rains of summer and the frosts of winter. He was turned loose, naked, hungry, and destitute to the open sky.' Deaths among the black men from starvation, disease, and violence in the first two years of freedom ran into the tens of thousands.[1] Yet despite the deprivations of a slave society, the freedmen contributed leaders who faced these harsh realities with uncommon good sense.

To the average Southerner emancipation changed the position of the Negro legally rather than socially or economically. Few whites of the South were able to realize the implications of freedom or willing to acquiesce in anything approaching race equality. The Negro was still thought of as an inferior being, incapable of real independence, impossible to teach. Some of the former slaveholders tried sincerely and with some success to assist the Negro in adjusting himself to his new status. But the small farmers and the poor whites were determined to 'keep the Negro in his place,' by laws if possible, by force if necessary. J. T. Trowbridge, writing shortly after the war, remarked that 'there is at this day more prejudice against color among the middle and poorer classes . . . who owned few or no slaves, than among the planters, who owned them by the hundred,' and emancipation sharply accentuated racial antipathies in the South.

Most planters sought to keep their former slaves as hired help or as tenant farmers, or on the sharecrop system, and the Southern states attempted to assure this by a series of laws collectively known as the 'black codes.' Tennessee had none; the codes of the other states varied widely in scope and in character. The codes of Virginia and North Carolina, where the whites were in secure control were mild; those of South Carolina, Mississippi, and Louisiana, where the Negroes outnumbered the whites, were severe.

These black codes conferred upon the freedmen fairly extensive privileges, gave them the essential rights of citizens to contract, sue and be sued, own and inherit property, and testify in court, and made some provision for education. In no instance, however, were the freedmen accorded the vote or made eligible for juries, and for the most part they were not permitted to testify against white men. Because of their alleged aversion to work they were required to have some steady occupation, and subjected to special penalties for violation of labor contracts.

1. The Negro and white populations of Charleston, S.C., were substantially the same, but in the years from 1866 to 1871 Negro mortality was twice that of white, and infant mortality among the Negroes of the city three times that of the whites. However, we should keep in mind that even in the 1960's Negro infant mortality was twice that of white babies.

The especially harsh vagrancy and apprenticeship laws lent themselves readily to the establishment of a system of peonage. The penal codes provided harsher and more arbitrary punishments for blacks than for whites, and some states permitted individual masters to administer corporal punishment to 'refractory servants.' Negroes were not allowed to bear arms, or to appear in certain public places, and there were special laws governing the domestic relations of the Negroes. In some states laws that closed to the freedmen every occupation save domestic and agricultural betrayed a poor-white jealousy of the Negro artisan, and this practice of excluding the Negro from some industries and professions grew as the South became increasingly industrialized and the Negroes more competitive.

Southern whites, who had never dreamed it possible to live side by side with free Negroes, professed to believe that these laws were liberal and generous. But the philosophy which animated them was the philosophy of the Old South, and every one of the codes confessed a determination to keep the freedmen in a permanent position of tutelage, and of social and political inferiority. The Southern point of view was succinctly expressed by a writer in the most influential of Southern journals, *De Bow's Review:*

> We of the South would not find much difficulty in managing the Negroes, if left to ourselves, for we would be guided by the lights of experience and the teachings of history. . . . We should be satisfied to compel them to engage in coarse common manual labor, and to punish them for dereliction of duty or nonfulfillment of their contracts with sufficient severity to make the great majority of them productive laborers. . . . We should treat them as mere grown-up children, entitled like children, or apprentices, to the protection of guardians and masters, and bound to obey those put above them in place of parents, just as children are so bound.[2]

It was scarcely surprising that Northerners regarded the black codes as palpable evasions of the Thirteenth Amendment, and conclusive evidence that the South was not prepared to accept the 'verdict of Appomattox.' In response to the black codes the North demanded that the Federal Government step in to protect the former slaves. This object, eventually embodied in the Fourteenth and Fifteenth Amendments and the various civil rights bills, was first pursued through the agencies of the Freedmen's Bureau and the military governments.

2. June 1866, Vol. 1 (n.s.), 578.

The Freedmen's Bureau of the War Department was created by Congress 3 March 1865, for a period of one year after the close of the war — later extended to 1869 — and was given general powers of relief and guardianship over Negroes and refugees, and the administration of abandoned lands. General O. O. Howard, the 'Christian soldier,' headed the bureau, whose agents were distributed throughout the South. The chief activities of the bureau were relief work for both races, administration of justice in cases involving freedmen, and the establishment of schools for colored people. During its brief existence the Freedmen's Bureau set up over a hundred hospitals, gave medical aid to half a million patients, distributed over 20 million rations to the destitute of both races, and maintained over 4000 schools for Negro children. Yet, as the failure of the Freedmen's Bureau Bank — wiping out the savings of thousands of former slaves — revealed, the Bureau also offered an opportunity for men of low character to enrich themselves.

The most important work of the bureau was educational. As rapidly as schools were provided the freedmen took advantage of them. 'It was a whole race trying to go to school,' wrote Booker T. Washington, the greatest of Negro educational leaders. 'Few were too young and none too old to make the attempt to learn. As fast as any kind of teachers could be secured, not only were day schools filled, but night schools as well. The great ambition of the older people was to try to learn to read the Bible before they died.' Most of these freedmen's schools were taught by Northern women who volunteered for what W. E. B. DuBois has called the Ninth Crusade:

> Behind the mists of ruin and rapine waved the calico dresses of women who dared, and after the hoarse mouthings of the field guns rang the rhythm of the alphabet. Rich and poor they were, serious and curious, bereaved, now of a father, now of a brother, now of more than these, they came seeking a life work in planting New England schoolhouses among the white and black of the South. They did their work well. In that first year they taught one hundred thousand souls and more.[3]

By the end of Reconstruction there were 600,000 Negroes in elementary schools in the South; the Federal Government had set up Howard University in the national capital, and private philanthropy had founded

3. *The Souls of Black Folk* (1961 ed.), p. 38.

industrial schools like Hampton Institute in Virginia and Fisk in Tennessee.

Progress in land-ownership, the other great ambition of the freedmen, was slow and halting. This was one of the most egregious failures of reconstruction. Northern statesmen had encouraged the Negro to look to the Federal Government to provide 'forty acres and a mule.' But in the end nothing was done to help the Negro become an independent landowner. It is difficult to understand this. The Federal Government still owned enough public land in the South to have given every Negro family a 40-acre farm, while the cotton tax of some $68 million would have provided the mule! Certainly a Congress that was able to give 40 million acres of land to a single railroad might have done something to fulfill its obligation to the freedmen. Without effective assistance from federal — or state — governments, the vast majority of Negroes were unable to purchase even small farms and were forced to lease land on such terms as the whites were prepared to grant. And when the Negro did set up as an independent landowner he was severely handicapped by his unfamiliarity with farm management and marketing, and his lack of capital for farm animals and implements. In 1888 Georgia farmlands were valued at $88 million; the Negroes, who were half the population, owned land to the value of $1.8 million. By 1890 there were 121,000 Negro landowners, and ten years later 187,000 who owned a paltry percentage of the land.

Emancipation altered the form rather than the substance of the Negro's economic status for at least a generation after Appomattox. The transition from slave to independent farmer was long and painful, made usually through the medium of tenancy, and for many it was never completely made. Without the requisite capital, without credit except such as was cautiously extended by white bankers or storekeepers on usurious terms, and without agricultural skills, the vast majority of freedmen were unable to rise above the sharecropper or tenant class. They continued to work in the cotton or tobacco fields, to live in the shacks provided by the former master or by his children, and to exist on credit provided by the same hands. Some of the more ambitious drifted westward to the fertile lands of Texas or joined that curious exodus to Kansas in the late 'seventies that proved so futile. A very few achieved something more — a business or a profession which brought them social standing as well as livelihood. After 1890 some Negroes became laborers in the coal mines or the steel mills or tobacco factories that began to spring up in parts of the South; others headed northward to work in industrial centers while their wives and daughters found work as 'domestics.' But the majority remained on land that belonged to others, plodding behind the plow in spring and picking cotton in the fall, reasonably sure of food and shelter and clothing, a Saturday afternoon in town, a Sunday at revival meetings, continuing in the ways of their fathers.

XXXIX

Reconstruction, Political and Constitutional

1. RECONSTRUCTION DURING THE CIVIL WAR

Reconstruction had been a subject of discussion in the North ever since the beginning of the war. As usual with American political issues involving sectional balance, the discussion took place on the plane of constitutional theory. It turned largely on two questions: whether the seceded states were in or out of the Union when their rebellion was crushed and whether the process of restoration was presidential or congressional. From the Northern premise that secession was illegal, strict logic reached the conclusion that former states of the Confederacy had always been and were now states of the Union, with all the rights and privileges pertaining thereto. If, on the contrary, secession was valid, the South might consistently be treated as conquered territory, without any legal rights that the Union was required to respect. Both sides adopted the proper deductions from the other's premise. Radical Republicans, the most uncompromising nationalists, managed to prove to their satisfaction that the Southern states had lost or forfeited their rights, while former secessionists insisted that their rights in the Union from which they had seceded were unimpaired!

But the question of the status of the Southern states was to be decided in accordance not with theory but with political necessities. Lincoln, with his customary clarity, saw this, and saw, too, how dangerous

735

was any theoretical approach. In his last speech, on 11 April 1865, he insisted that this question whether the Southern states were in or out of the Union was 'bad as the basis of a controversy, and good for nothing at all — a merely pernicious abstraction. . . . Finding themselves safely at home, it would be utterly immaterial whether they had ever been abroad.' Obviously, these states were 'out of their proper practical relation with the Union'; the object of all should be to 'get them into their proper practical relation' again.

Lincoln had been pursuing this eminently sensible policy since the beginning of the war. As early as 1862 he had appointed provisional military governors in Tennessee, Louisiana, and North Carolina whose duty it was to re-establish loyal governments in those states. The North Carolina experiment came to naught, but in Tennessee Governor Andrew Johnson and in Louisiana General Banks made impressive progress toward the restoration of federal authority, and after the fall of Vicksburg, Arkansas was similarly restored. Encouraged by this success, Lincoln, in a proclamation of 8 December 1863, formulated what was to be the presidential plan of reconstruction.

The object of this plan was to get the seceded states back into their normal relations with the Federal Government as quickly and as painlessly as possible; the means was the presidential power to pardon. The plan itself provided for a general amnesty and restoration of property other than slaves to most of those who would take a prescribed oath of loyalty to the Union. Furthermore whenever 10 per cent of the electorate of 1860 should take this oath they might set up a state government which Lincoln promised to recognize as the true government of the state. Whether Congress would recognize any such state government, or not, was of course a matter over which the Executive had no control.

The magnanimous plan, known as the 10 per cent plan, was promptly adopted in Louisiana and Arkansas. Thousands of voters, many of them cheerfully perjuring themselves, swore that they had not willingly borne arms against the United States; they were then duly registered. They held constitutional conventions, drew up and ratified new constitutions abolishing slavery, and their states then prepared to reassume their place in the Federal Union. But all was not to be such easy sailing. Congress, which was the judge of its own membership, refused to admit the representatives of these reconstructed states, and in the presidential election of 1864 their electoral votes were not counted.

The congressional leaders had a plan of their own which carefully retained control of the entire process of reconstruction in congressional hands. This plan was embodied in the Wade-Davis Bill of 8 July 1864, which stipulated that Congress, not the President, was to have jurisdiction over the processes of reconstruction, and that a majority of the electorate, instead of merely 10 per cent, was required for the reconstitution of legal state governments. When Lincoln averted this scheme by a pocket veto, he brought down upon himself the bitter excoriation of the Wade-Davis Manifesto. 'The President . . . must understand,' said the two Congressmen, 'that the authority of Congress is paramount and must be respected . . . and if he wishes our support he must confine himself to his executive duties — to obey and execute, not make the laws — to suppress by arms armed rebellion, and leave political reorganization to Congress.' Here was the real beginning of the rift between the President and that wing of his own party called the Radicals. The term refers to those who were determined to employ the power of the national government to ensure civil and political rights for the freedmen and establish the supremacy of the Republican party in national politics and of Congress in the federal administration. Though at first small, the Radical faction included such formidable leaders as Thaddeus Stevens of Pennsylvania, Ben Wade of Ohio, Zachariah Chandler of Michigan, and Charles Sumner of Massachusetts, and during the latter part of the Johnson administration it managed to dominate the Republican party.

With the publication of the Wade-Davis Manifesto, an issue had been raised that would not be settled until a President had been impeached, a Supreme Court intimidated, and the Constitution altered. Congressional opposition to Lincoln's plan was due in part to legislative *esprit de corps,* in part to concern for the Negro, in part to the hatreds engendered by the war, and in part to persuasive constitutional considerations, for it seemed only logical that Congress, which had the power to admit new states and was the judge of its own membership, should control reconstruction. Moreover, to the Radicals it seemed monstrous that traitors and rebels should be readmitted to full fellowship in the Union they had repudiated and tried to destroy. It would be the

Union as in Buchanan's time, administered by 'rebels' and 'Copperheads' for the benefit of the unrepentant slavocracy. Even Northerners who were quite willing to admit that Davis and Stephens were honorable men did not care to see them at their old desks in the Senate, shouting for state rights. As Thaddeus Stevens put it, the Southern states 'ought never to be recognized as capable of acting in the Union, or of being counted as valid states, until the Constitution shall have been so amended . . . as to secure perpetual ascendancy to the party of the Union.' That was the nub of the matter. If the Southern states returned a solid Democratic counterpart to Congress, as appeared inevitable, a reunited Democratic party would have a majority in both houses of Congress. The amendment which Stevens had in mind was that providing for Negro suffrage, which would fulfill the moral obligation to the freedmen, satisfy the humanitarian and liberal wing of the Republican party, and create a flourishing Republican party in the South.

If the partisan considerations seem narrow, we should ask ourselves what other nation in history has ever turned over control of the government and of the spoils of victory to the leaders of a defeated rebellion?

For about six weeks after Lincoln's assassination there was a petty reign of terror, directed by Secretary Stanton and supported by President Johnson, who had always been in favor of hanging 'traitors' when apprehended. Only the stern intervention of Grant prevented the seizure of Lee and other Confederate generals. Large rewards for the apprehension of Davis and his cabinet, as alleged promoters of the murder of Lincoln, resulted in their capture and temporary imprisonment. But the charge of complicity in the murder was quickly seen to be preposterous, and since it was obviously impossible to get a Virginia jury to convict Davis of treason, that charge was quietly directed to the circumlocution office. Thirst for vengeance appeared to be slaked by the shooting or suicide of the assassin Booth, by hanging his three accomplices and the unfortunate woman who had harbored them, after an extra-legal trial by a military tribunal, and by hanging the miserable Henry Wirz, commander of the infamous Andersonville prison, for the 'murder' of Union prisoners.

All this was cause for shame, but no other great rebellion of modern times has been suppressed with so little loss of life or formal punishment of the vanquished. Not one of the rebel leaders was executed, none was brought to trial for treason. There were no mass arrests, not even of those officers of the United States who took up arms against their government. Even the civil disabilities imposed were mild; by 1872, only some 750 ex-Confederates were still barred from office-holding. For generations Southerners have rung the changes on the theme of Northern ruthlessness and Southern wretchedness during the Reconstruction years, and many historians, looking at this chapter of our history entirely through American eyes, have concluded that the North imposed upon the South a 'Carthaginian peace.' Yet we have only to recall the suppression of the Peasants' Revolt in Germany in the sixteenth century, the ravages of Alva in the rebelling Low Countries, the punishments inflicted on the Irish by Cromwell and on the Scots after Culloden, the vengeance exacted by victors over vanquished in the French Revolution, the Napoleonic Restoration, the great Chinese Rebellion of the mid-nineteeth century, or the Russian, Nazi, and Spanish revolutions of our own time, to appreciate how moderate was the conduct of the triumphant North after 1865.

2. ANDREW JOHNSON TAKES CHARGE

Lincoln's assassination and the accession to the presidency of Andrew Johnson drastically altered the political situation.[1]

Like Tyler in 1841, Johnson was the nominal head of a party of which he was not really a member. A War Democrat from a seceded state, he had been placed on the same ticket with Lincoln to emphasize the Unionism of the Republican party in 1864. Of origin as humble as Lincoln's, in early life a tailor in a Tennessee mountain village and unable to write until taught by his wife, he possessed many of Lincoln's virtues but lacked his ability to handle men. Self-educated and self-trained, he had a powerful though not well-disciplined mind. United with these intellectual qualities were the virtues of integrity, devotion to duty, and courage. But at a time when tact and flexibility were called

1. Some of the Radicals rejoiced in the removal of Lincoln and the accession of Johnson. 'I spent most of the afternoon in a political caucus,' wrote Representative George Julian of Indiana, 'and while everybody was shocked at his murder, the feeling was nearly universal that the accession of Johnson to the Presidency would prove a godsend to the country. Aside from Mr. Lincoln's known policy of tenderness to the Rebels . . . his . . . views of the subject of Reconstruction were as distasteful as possible to radical Republicans.'

for, he was stubborn and inflexible; Johnson 'had no budge in him.' And he badly missed the significance of the revolution brought by the war. At first a qualified advocate of civil rights for the Negro, he soon came to set himself against the Radicals and to blind himself to the evidence of Southern defiance.

No President ever faced a more difficult situation. He had no personal following either in the South or in the North, none of the prestige that came to Lincoln from the successful conduct of the war, and no party organization behind him, for he had broken with the Democratic party and he had not been accepted by the Republican. Seward and Welles were loyal to Johnson, but Stanton, with his customary duplicity, used the machinery of the War Department against him and kept the Radicals posted on cabinet secrets. Yet at the outset the Radicals were a minority, and they were generally well disposed toward him. It was Johnson's own blunders that isolated him not only from the Radicals but from the party's moderates.

Immediately upon his accession to the presidency, Johnson appeared to be willing to co-operate with the Radicals. 'Treason is a crime and must be punished,' he said; 'treason must be made infamous, and traitors must be impoverished,' and bluff Ben Wade exclaimed exultantly, 'Johnson, we have faith in you. By the gods, there will be no trouble now in running this government.' But soon there was trouble enough. At a time when Congress was out of session, Johnson swung around to a sharply different course.

Beginning with North Carolina, therefore, Johnson proceeded to appoint provisional civil governors in all the Confederate states where Lincoln had not already done so. These governors were enjoined to summon state constitutional conventions, which were to be elected by the 'whitewashed rebels' — former citizens of the Confederacy who took the oath of allegiance required by the presidential proclamation. Fourteen specified classes, assumed to be inveterate rebels, were excluded from this general amnesty and required to make personal application for pardon.[2] Although many of those thus proscribed did re-

2. Including all civil and diplomatic officers of the Confederacy, state governors, general officers of the Confederate Army, former U.S. Army officers and naval officers who had resigned their commissions, Congressmen and judges who had resigned their seats, and other Confederates worth over $20,000. To these classes were eventually added all who had held federal office before 1861 — coroners, constables, notaries public, and sextons of cemeteries — and who had afterwards entered the Confederate service or given aid and comfort to the rebellion.

ceive special pardons from President Johnson, the general effect was to exclude many experienced statesmen from participation in the task of establishing the new state governments.

The constitutional conventions declared invalid the ordinances of secession, repudiated the state war debts — which they could not in any event have paid — declared slavery abolished, and wrote new state constitutions. Not a single one of these granted the vote to even the most enlightened Negroes. Elections were promptly held under these new or amended constitutions, and by the autumn of 1865 regular civil administrations were functioning in all the former Confederate states except Texas.

Almost inevitably the ease and the speed with which reconstruction was being consummated excited distrust in the North. That distrust was exacerbated by the enactment of the Black Codes, and by the understandable but impolitic alacrity with which Southern voters elected their former Confederate leaders to high offices. As James G. Blaine later wrote, 'If the Southern men had intended, as their one special and desirable aim, to inflame public opinion of the North against them, they would have proceeded precisely as they did.' Certainly many Northerners came to believe that political reconstruction had been accomplished before any genuine reconciliation had been achieved, and that the South was neither repentant for her sins nor reconciled to defeat. There were many in the North who feared that the rebellious spirit of the South had been scotched, not crushed, and the rewards of victory were being wasted. To meet this criticism Johnson, in the fall of 1865, sent a number of observers to report on conditions in the South and to advise him on policies. They returned with reports to show that Southerners had fairly 'accepted defeat,' but many continued to doubt that the South was willing to accept the Negro as a free man and a citizen.

'I am satisfied that the mass of thinking people in the South accept the situation of affairs in good faith,' wrote General Grant to the President. 'Slavery and State rights they regard as having been settled forever by the highest tribunal — arms — that man can resort to. . . .' At the same time General Sherman was writing to his brother, the Senator, 'No matter what change we may desire in the feelings and thoughts of the people South, we cannot accomplish it by force. . . . You hardly yet realize how completely this country has been devastated, and how completely humble every man of the South is.' In one sense, it is clear that Grant and Sherman were right. Without in the least confessing that her cause had been wrong the South acknowledged her defeat as final and irrevocable, and put aside all thought of reopening the issue of slavery or secession. The South accepted the advice of Lee, that her allegiance was now due to the United States, and that her duty was to create a new and better South within the Union. Lee himself set a noble example to his countrymen by his serene acquiescence in trial by battle, and by devoting the rest of his life to service as president of Washington College in Lexington, Virginia. Yet this did not mean that the South accepted the logical consequences of freedom for the Negro. 'Refusing to see that a mighty cataclysm had shaken the profoundest depths of national life,' says Professor Coulter, 'they did not expect that many things would be made anew but rather looked for them to be mended as of old, — that Humpty Dumpty might after all be put back on the wall.'

3. CONGRESS INTERVENES

The Congress which met for the first time on 4 December 1865 appointed a joint committee of both Houses with authority to investigate and report on the title of Southern members-elect to be received. This Joint Committee of Fifteen, a resurrection of the old Committee on the Conduct of the War, formulated the theory and set the pace of congressional reconstruction. Yet the Committee was not controlled by the Radicals, and many of the crucial measures came from moderates like Lyman Trumbull.

The most influential member of the committee was Thaddeus Stevens of Pennsylvania, leader of the Republicans in the House. A sincere democrat, lifelong spokesman for the poor and the oppressed, and tireless champion of public education, Stevens was now a harsh embittered old man of seventy-four nursing an implacable enmity toward the Southern slavocracy and President Johnson, who, he thought, stood between them and their just deserts. 'The punishment of traitors,' he said, in a speech in Congress in the spring of 1867, 'has been wholly ignored by a treacherous Executive and a sluggish Congress. To this issue I desire to devote the small remnant of my life.' And he did. 'Strip a proud nobility of the bloated estates,' he demanded; 'reduce them to a level with plain republicans; send them forth to labor and teach their children to enter the workshops or handle a plow, and you will thus humble the proud traitors.' Partly out of passionate devotion to the Negro,[3] partly out of conviction that the welfare of the Union was identical with the triumph of the Republican party, Stevens was determined to impose Negro suffrage on the states of the South. 'I am for Negro suffrage in every rebel State,' he said. 'If it be just it should not be denied; if it be necessary it should be adopted; if it be punishment to traitors, they deserve it.' He regarded the Southern states as nothing more than conquered provinces and insisted that Congress should treat them as such.

Charles Sumner of Massachusetts, Republican leader in the Senate, was not on the Joint Committee, but next to Stevens he was the most powerful figure in congressional reconstruction. An idealist by conviction, and a reformer by training, he was a pedantic dogmatist, but in his way quite as sincere as Stevens. Against the ex-Confederates he held no vindictive feelings, but he was committed to giving Negroes the vote. Sumner advanced the theory that the Southern states had committed political suicide, had extinguished their standing as states, and were in the position of territories subject to the exclusive jurisdiction of Congress. Vain, humorless, and irritable, Sumner nevertheless had a distinguished record as a champion of good causes: the New England intellectuals looked to him for leadership, his polished orations impressed the commonalty, he was widely admired in England and on the Continent, and he infused the Radical movement with idealism and altruism.

The Joint Committee propounded the theory of reconstruction upon which Congress ultimately acted. It announced that 'the States lately in rebellion were . . . disorganized communities, without civil government and without constitutions or other forms by virtue of which political relation could legally exist between them and the federal government,' that they had 'forfeited all civil and political rights and

---

3. In his devotion to the Negro, Stevens was consistent to the last. He arranged to be buried in a Negro cemetery, and wrote his own epitaph:
I repose in this quiet and secluded spot,
Not from any natural preference for solitude
But, finding other Cemeteries limited as to Race by Charter Rules,
I have chosen this that I might illustrate in my death
The Principles which I advocated through a long life:
EQUALITY OF MAN BEFORE HIS CREATOR.

privileges under the federal Constitution,' and that they could be restored to their political rights only by Congress. In other words, the states were intact, but the state governments were, for most but not for all purposes, in a condition of suspended animation. Under this interpretation it was possible for Congress at once to deny representation to the Southern states and to accept the ratification of the Thirteenth Amendment by the legislatures of these same states.

The Radical program can be summarized briefly.

1. To keep the ex-Confederate states out of the Union until they had set up governments that could be regarded as 'republican' in nature.

2. To require them, as a prerequisite for readmission to the Union, to repeal their Black Codes, disqualify those who had been active in rebellion from holding state office, guarantee the Negro his civil rights and give him the right to vote and to hold office. When the Southern states proved unresponsive, they advocated constitutional amendments to protect the civil rights of the Negro by federal action.

3. To ensure a larger role for Congress in the process of reconstruction. The Radicals did not, as is often said, share a common attitude on economic policy. They often held diametrically opposite views on currency and the tariff, and businessmen, who had diverse interests and attitudes, were as likely to be against them as for them. Some of the Radicals, however, wished to assure permanence to that body of tariff, agricultural, and money legislation which had been written into the statute books during the war years, and were prepared to exploit the Reconstruction crisis to achieve their ends.

The Freedmen's Bureau bill, sponsored by the moderate Lyman Trumbull, represented the ideas not merely of the Radicals but of most Republicans. Opposition to it centered in the Democrats, who exploited race prejudice against Negroes; not one Democrat in either house of Congress voted for the bill. But on 19 February 1866 Johnson opened war on the advocates of civil rights by vetoing the bill to enlarge the scope of the Freedmen's Bureau.[4] In a shocking speech three days later, he denounced the campaign for Negro rights and cried that Stevens, Sumner, and Wendell Phillips were planning to assassinate him. Many Northern Republicans read Johnson out of the party, and eight state legislatures adopted resolutions rebuking the President.

4. A second Freedmen's Bureau bill was subsequently passed over the presidential veto, 16 July 1866.

Yet most Republicans still wanted conciliation with Johnson, and they hoped to win his approval for a second measure sponsored by Trumbull, a Civil Rights bill which sought to protect the rights of the freedman in the courts rather than through such institutions as the Army. Congress enacted the bill, again without a single Democratic vote, but Johnson stunned his party by vetoing this measure too. The President announced that he opposed 'the Africanization of half the United States.' After Johnson's veto of the Civil Rights bill, most Republicans broke with him. Men like Trumbull and John Sherman felt the President had betrayed them. Trumbull told the Senate that whatever obligation the President might once have felt toward securing the rights of the freedman, 'he will approve no measure that will accomplish the object'; Congress then passed the bill over Johnson's veto. Not Sumner nor Stevens but Johnson himself had turned the men of moderation in the party against the administration.

The Republicans were still not ready to insist on a federal guarantee of Negro suffrage, as Sumner wished, but after their experience with the two Trumbull bills they were determined to write new guarantees of civil rights into the Constitution and to insist that the Southern states accept these stipulations before they were accepted back into the Union. On 30 April 1866 the Committee of Fifteen reported the Fourteenth Amendment. This amendment, the most important ever added to the Constitution, was designed to guarantee the civil rights of the Negro against unfavorable legislation by the states, reduce congressional representation in proportion to the denial of suffrage to Negroes, disqualify ex-Confederates who had formerly held state or federal office, invalidate the Confederate debt, and validate the federal debt. Section I of the amendment was particularly significant. It first defined citizenship, and then provided that 'No State shall make or enforce any law which shall abridge the privileges or immunities of citizens of the United States; nor shall any State deprive any person of life, liberty, or property, without due process of law; nor deny to any person within its jurisdiction the equal protection of the laws.' It thus for the first time clearly threw the protection of the Federal Government around the rights of life, liberty, and property which might be invaded by the states, reversing the traditional relationships between these governments which had from the beginning distinguished our federal system. Designed to protect the Negro, this provision came increasingly to be interpreted as extending the protection of the Federal Government to corporations whose property rights were threatened by state legislation. There is no evidence that the framers of the amendment anticipated any such interpretation of this article.

The issue was now joined between the President and the majority in Congress. Everything turned on the election of a new Congress in the autumn of 1866, one of the most important congressional contests in our history. A National Union Convention of moderate men from both sections pledged support of the President but it did not form a new party or create party machinery. Hence in most congressional districts in the North voters had to choose between a Radical Republican and a Copperhead Democrat. Faced with this prospect many moderate Republicans went over to the Radical camp. Johnson apparently sought a party realignment in which, with the Radicals driven from the party, he could lead a union of Republicans with War Democrats and Southern loyalists. Instead, he cut himself off from the mass of his own party.

There was ample evidence that the Negro needed national protection. In some parts of the South, as in Florida, violence appears to have been rare. No doubt, too, Radical orators deliberately exaggerated, or even invented, some episodes for political effect. But the fact of the outrages was painfully real. The conservative General Jefferson C. Davis reported that in Kentucky 19 Negroes had been killed, 233 maltreated, and none of the offenders had been prosecuted by civil authorities. In Texas, one Negro was murdered for not doffing his hat; in Louisiana, a Negro who answered a white boy 'quickly' was 'taken thro' the town and across the Levee, and there stripped and terribly beaten, with raw-hides.' In May 1866 a mob of whites, aided by some of the police, burned and pillaged the Negro quarter of Memphis and killed 46 freedmen. In New Orleans on 30 July, a mob of whites, numbering many police and former Confederate soldiers, assaulted a convention of Negroes and white Radicals, and killed and wounded scores in cold blood.

In the 1866 campaign Republicans brandished reports of such atrocities to warn voters that the South was robbing them of their hard-won victory in the war. At the same time, sensitive to the racial prejudices of Northern voters, they soft-pedalled the issue of Negro suffrage. Johnson warned of the consequences of Republican policy; Southerners, he said, 'cannot be treated as subjugated people or vassal colonies without a germ of hatred being introduced, which will some day or other, though the time may be distant, develop mischief of the most serious character.' But the President proved to be an inept campaigner. He seemed incapable of advocating a policy of tolerance in a tolerant manner, and his 'swing around the circle,' a stumping tour of the Middle West, became in many instances an undignified exercise in vituperation. 'I would ask you,' the President shouted on 3 September 1866 in Cleveland, 'Why not hang Thad Stevens and Wendell Phillips?' Johnson was, said Seward, the best stump speaker in the country, but as Secretary Welles shrewdly remarked, the President should not be a stump speaker. Probably no orator, the New York *Nation* caustically observed, ever accomplished so much by a fortnight's speaking.

In the elections, the Republicans scored a smashing victory. New York gave them twice the majority it had given Lincoln two years earlier. The Republicans picked up a margin in Congress large enough to override a presidential veto.[5]

Johnson has been criticized for not bowing to the 'will of the people' and for advising the Southern state governments to ratify the Fourteenth Amendment in order to mollify Northern sentiment and get their representatives admitted. But Johnson saw himself as the champion of the Constitution, and he was a stubborn man. He nailed his colors to the mast and defied Congress to do its work. Congress was no less determined. When ten of the former Confederate states refused to ratify the Fourteenth Amendment, they left Congress with no alternative save more drastic measures or acquiescence in denying equality to the Negro. In February 1867 Congressman James Garfield cried, 'The last of the sinful ten has, with contempt and scorn, flung back into our teeth the magnanimous offer of a generous nation. It is now our turn to act.'

4. CONGRESSIONAL RECONSTRUCTION

The Radicals took the results of the fall elections as a vindication of their 'thorough' policy, and under the implacable leadership of Thaddeus Stevens a series of measures of far-reaching importance were whipped through a complaisant Congress. These measures undid the whole of presidential reconstruction, placed the Southern states back

5. The Congress that met in March 1867 contained 143 Republicans and 49 Democrats in the House, 42 Republicans and 11 Democrats in the Senate.

where they had been in April 1865, and temporarily revolutionized our political system by substituting a quasi-parliamentary for a presidential system of government.

The most important of these measures, indeed the most important piece of legislation of the entire period, was the First Reconstruction Act of 2 March 1867. This act declared that 'no legal government' existed in any Southern state except Tennessee, and divided the territory of the South into five military districts subject to military commanders who were charged with the responsibility of protecting life and property throughout their districts. For this purpose they might use, at their discretion, the ordinary civil tribunals or military tribunals. Escape from this military regime and restitution of state rights were promised on condition that a constitutional convention, chosen by universal male suffrage, set up governments based on black and white suffrage and that the new state legislatures ratify the Fourteenth Amendment.

Johnson returned the bill with a scorching message arguing the unconstitutionality of the measure, but to no avail. In March 1867 military rule replaced in the South the civil governments that had been operating for over a year. The military governors ruled with a firm hand, sometimes with a flagrant disregard for the civil rights of the white inhabitants, at the same time that they secured rights for the Negroes that these whites had denied them. Thousands of local officials were removed to make way for Northern 'carpetbaggers' or Negroes; the governors of six states were displaced and others appointed in their place; civil courts were superseded by military tribunals; the legislatures of Georgia, Alabama, and Louisiana were purged of conservatives; state legislation was set aside or modified; and an army of occupation, some 20,000 strong and aided by a force of Negro militia, kept order.

The relatively brief rule of the major generals was harsh but had the merits of honesty and a certain rude efficiency. Particularly important were the efforts made by the military to cope with economic disorganization and to regulate the social life of their satrapies. Thus in South Carolina, General Sickles abolished imprisonment for debt, stayed foreclosures on property, made the wages of farm laborers a first lien on crops, prohibited the manufacture of whiskey, and ended discrimination against the Negroes. Similar regulations were enforced in other military districts.

The principal task incumbent upon the military commanders was the creation of new electorates and the establishment of new governments. In each of the ten states over which they had jurisdiction — Tennessee, it will be remembered, had been 'reconstructed' in 1868 — the commanders enrolled a new electorate; in South Carolina, Alabama, Florida, Mississippi, and Louisiana the black voters outnumbered the white. This electorate chose in every state a constitutional convention which, under the guidance of carpetbaggers, drafted new state constitutions enfranchising the blacks and disfranchising ex-Confederate leaders,[6] and guaranteeing civil and political equality to the freedmen.

These new state constitutions represented, in almost every instance, a definite advance upon the older constitutions. The Constitution of South Carolina, for example, set up a far more democratic, humane, and efficient system of government than that which had obtained during the ante-bellum regime. In addition to providing for universal manhood suffrage it abolished property qualifications for office-holding, reapportioned representation in the legislature, drew up a new and more elaborate Bill of Rights, abolished all 'distinctions on account of color,' reformed local government and judicial administration, outlawed dueling and imprisonment for debt, protected homesteads from foreclosure, enlarged the rights of women, and provided — on paper — a system of universal public education.

By the summer of 1868 reconstructed governments had been set up in eight of the Southern states: the other three — Mississippi, Texas, and Virginia — were reconstructed in 1870.[7] After the legislatures of the reconstructed states had duly ratified the Fourteenth and Fifteenth Amendments, Congress formally readmitted them to the Union, seated their elected Representatives and Senators, and, as soon as the supremacy of the new governments appeared reasonably secure, withdrew the army.

The Radicals aimed ultimately at establishing congressional suprem-

6. Because this provision for the disfranchisement of ex-Confederates led to the defeat of the constitutions in some states, Congress permitted Southerners to vote on — and defeat — them separately. In any event the Amnesty Act of 1872 re-enfranchised all except some 500 Southerners who had held high office in the Confederate government. Not until 1898 were all disabilities finally repealed.

7. Georgia, readmitted in 1868, was once again cast into the limbo of suspended animation when her legislature unseated some duly elected Negro members; she was not finally readmitted in good standing until 1870.

acy in the American governmental system. The majority of Congress, not the Supreme Court, was to be the final judge of the powers of Congress; the President a servant of Congress. Some even thought to model Congress on the 'omnipotent' British Parliament. This new dispensation was implicit in the Reconstruction Act of 2 March 1867 and in two other pieces of legislation pushed through Congress the same day. The first of these, the Command of the Army Act, virtually deprived the Executive of control of the army by requiring that he issue all military orders through the General of the Army, who was protected against removal or suspension from office. The second, the Tenure of Office Act, by denying the President the right to remove civil officials, including members of his cabinet, without the consent of the Senate, made it impossible for him to control his own administration. The Radicals put it through in order to prevent Johnson from continuing to wield the patronage weapon against them and to stop him from removing Secretary of War Stanton, the last Radical sympathizer left in the cabinet. The next move in the game was to dispose of Johnson by impeachment, whereupon Benjamin Wade, president *pro tem.* of the Senate, would succeed to his office and title.

Impeachment had been proposed by Benjamin Butler of Massachusetts as early as October 1866, and all through the following year a House committee had been trying to gather evidence which might support such action, but without success. Now Johnson furnished the House with the excuse for which it had so long waited. Convinced that the Tenure of Office Act was unconstitutional he requested and then ordered Secretary Stanton to resign. Stanton himself thought the act unconstitutional and had even helped write the veto message, but when General Lorenzo Thomas, the newly appointed Secretary of War, sought to take possession of his office, Stanton barricaded himself in the War Department. On 24 February 1868, the House voted to impeach the President before the Senate for 'high Crimes and Misdemeanors' as the Constitution provides, and within a week eleven articles of impeachment were agreed upon by the Radicals. Ten of the eleven articles simply rang the changes on the removal of Stanton; the other consisted of garbled newspaper reports from the President's speeches. A monstrous charge to the effect that Johnson was an accomplice in the murder of Lincoln was finally excluded.

Altogether the impeachment of Johnson was one of the most dis-

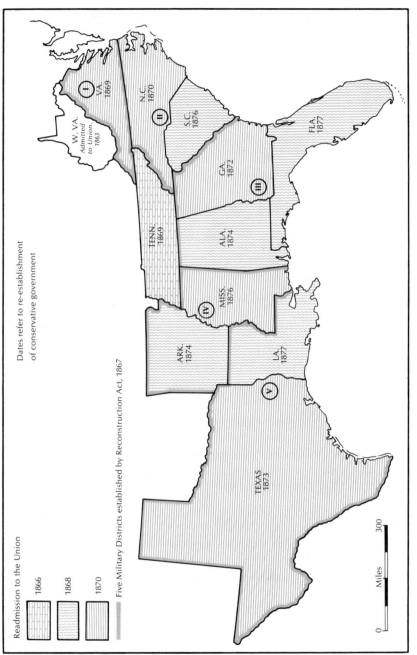

Readmission to the Union

1866

1868

1870

Five Military Districts established by Reconstruction Act, 1867

Dates refer to re-establishment of conservative government

W. VA.
Admitted
to Union,
1863

VA.
1869

N.C.
1870

S.C.
1876

FLA.
1877

GA.
1872

TENN.
1869

ALA.
1874

MISS.
1876

ARK.
1874

LA.
1877

TEXAS
1873

I

II

III

IV

V

0   Miles   300

RECONSTRUCTION IN THE SOUTH

graceful episodes in the history of the Federal Government, one that barely failed to suspend the presidential system. For had impeachment succeeded, the Radicals would have established the principle that Congress may remove a President not for 'high Crimes and Misdemeanors,' as required by the Constitution, but for purely political reasons. The managers of impeachment themselves admitted this; Johnson's crime, they asserted in their report, was 'the one great purpose of reconstructing the rebel states in accordance with his own will.' The President was defended by able counsel including William M. Evarts, leader of the American bar, and Benjamin R. Curtis, formerly a justice of the Supreme Court. These tore the case of the prosecution to shreds, and it was soon apparent to all but the most prejudiced that there were no valid grounds for impeachment. Even the Tenure of Office Act charges proved groundless, for the law restrained a President from removing a cabinet officer he had appointed, and Stanton had been named not by Johnson but by Lincoln. Yet the Radicals would have succeeded in their object but for Chief Justice Chase who insisted upon legal procedure, and for seven courageous Republican Senators who risked their political future by voting for acquittal.[8] One more affirmative vote and Ben Wade — who himself voted for conviction — would have been installed in the White House. Then, in all probability, the Court would have been battered into submission.

When the trial took place, Johnson had less than one year to serve; and the Republican nominating convention met shortly after his acquittal. There was no longer any effective opposition to the Radicals within the party ranks, and the reconstructed states gave them faithful delegates. In the ensuing election General Grant was victorious over his Democratic rival, but his popular majority was dangerously narrow. Indeed, the election revealed unmistakably that the people were growing tired of Radical reconstruction and wanted a return to representative government. To the Radicals it indicated likewise that if the Republican party was to hold its gains it was necessary to ensure Negro suffrage by Constitutional amendment. Within four months the Fifteenth Amendment to the Constitution, that 'the right of citizens of the United States to vote shall not be denied or abridged by the United

8. Fessenden, Grimes, Trumbull, Ross, Van Winkle, Fowler, and Henderson. Fessenden died in 1869; none of the others was re-elected to the Senate; yet they did not suffer as severely as the legend of their martyrdom would suggest.

States or by any State on account of race, color, or previous condition of servitude,' was passed by both Houses of Congress and sent to the states for ratification.

5. RECONSTRUCTION AND THE CONSTITUTION

At no time in American history has the Constitution been subjected to so severe or prolonged a strain as during the era of reconstruction. The theory *intra arma silent leges* had been tacitly accepted during the actual conflict without serious impairment of the laws; it remained to be seen whether reconstruction would be carried through on the same legal theory. There arose at once a number of knotty problems concerning the legal character of the war, the legal status of the seceded states after Appomattox, and the status of persons who had participated in the rebellion. There arose, too, with equal urgency, the problem of the division of powers in the Federal Government — whether Congress or the President was the proper authority to direct reconstruction, and how far the courts could go in moderating or arresting programs primarily political. Finally — and in the long run most important — there came the question of the meaning of the three constitutional amendments that were pushed through during reconstruction, particularly the Fourteenth. Some of these legal questions were settled by the courts at the time, others, especially those affecting the freedmen, lingered on into our own day, and still others remained unsettled except by rude extra-legal forces.

Throughout the war President Lincoln maintained the legal principle that the states were indestructible; that they were never out of the Union for the simple reason that they could not be. This theory, though vigorously controverted by the Radical leaders, received judicial support in the leading case of *Texas v. White,* in 1869, in which Chief Justice Chase, speaking for the majority, said:

> The Constitution, in all of its provisions, looks to an indestructible Union composed of indestructible States. . . . Considered, therefore, as transactions under the Constitution, the ordinance of secession . . . and all the acts of her legislature intended to give effect to that ordinance, were absolutely null. They were utterly without operation in law. The obligations of the State, as a member of the Union, remained perfect and unimpaired. It certainly follows that the State did not cease to be a State, nor her citizens to be citizens

of the Union. If this were otherwise, the State must have become
foreign, and her citizens foreigners. The war must have ceased to be
a war for the suppression of rebellion, and must have become a war
for conquest and subjugation. . . . Our conclusion therefore is, that
Texas continued to be a State, and a State of the Union.

Upon what theory, then, could reconstruction proceed? If the states
were still in the Union, it was only the citizens who were out of their
normal relations with the Federal Government, and these could be restored through the pardoning power of the President. This at least was
Lincoln's theory, and Johnson took it over from him; when, in a series
of proclamations, Johnson declared the insurrection at an end, the Supreme Court accepted his proclamations as legally binding.

But if the insurrection was at an end, by virtue of what authority did
Congress proceed to impose military government upon Southern states
and set up military courts? The Supreme Court had already passed
upon the question of military courts in ex parte Milligan. In this famous
case involving the validity of military courts in Indiana, the Court laid
down the doctrine that 'martial rule can never exist where the courts
are open, and in the proper and unobstructed exercise of their jurisdiction'; and to the argument of military necessity the Court said, 'No doctrine involving more pernicious consequences was ever invented by the
wit of man than that any of the [Constitution's] provisions can be suspended during any of the great exigencies of government. Such a doctrine leads directly to anarchy or despotism.' Yet within a year, in
clear violation of this decision, Congress established military tribunals
throughout the South; and when the validity of this legislation was challenged, in the McCardle case, Congress rushed through a law depriving
the Court of jurisdiction over the case, while the Supreme Court sat
idly by.

While brushing aside embarrassing legal obstacles, Radical leaders
nevertheless sought refuge in constitutional dialectics. The maintenance
of military rule in the South and the insistence upon ratification of the
Fourteenth Amendment, and later the Fifteenth Amendment, before readmission, were based theoretically upon the clause in the Constitution
that 'the United States shall guarantee to every State a Republican Form
of Government.' For three-quarters of a century this clause had been
interpreted to mean that Congress would sustain the pre-existing governments, but now the Radicals wrenched it away from this traditional

meaning and insisted that — for the Southern states at least — a 're-publican' form of government included Negro suffrage; and the Court supported them to the extent of declaring that 'the power to carry into effect the clause of guarantee is primarily a legislative power, and resides in Congress.' Yet at the beginning of the Reconstruction era only six Northern states permitted the Negro to vote, and two new states — Nebraska and Colorado — tried to come into the Union with suffrage limited to whites!

Some of the acts which Congress passed in order to carry into effect its reconstruction policy were palpably unconstitutional, but the attitude of the Radicals was well expressed by General Grant when he said of this legislation that 'much of it, no doubt, was unconstitutional; but it was hoped that the laws enacted would serve their purpose before the question of constitutionality could be submitted to the judiciary and a decision obtained.' This hope was indeed well founded, for the validity of some of the reconstruction measures never came before the courts, and others were not passed upon until long after they had 'served their purpose.' When Mississippi asked for an injunction restraining President Johnson from carrying out the Reconstruction Acts, the Supreme Court refused to accept jurisdiction. Georgia then brought suit against Secretary of War Stanton and General Grant, but once again the Court refused to intervene in what it termed a political controversy.

Individuals fared somewhat better. In *ex parte Garland* the operation of the federal test oath to exclude lawyers who had participated in the rebellion from practicing in federal courts was declared unconstitutional because *ex post facto;* and in Cummings v. Missouri similar state legislation was held invalid on the same grounds. For practical reasons it proved almost impossible to challenge the constitutionality of the confiscation of cotton or other property seized from those who were assumed to be rebels, but one notable case vindicated the right of the individual against lawless action even when committed in the name of the United States government. During the war Robert E. Lee's splendid estate at Arlington, Virginia, had been seized for nonpayment of taxes and bid in by the Federal Government, which then used it as a national cemetery. Long after the war the heirs of Lee succeeded in testing this seizure and sale in the federal courts. By a five to four vote the Supreme Court held that it would hear a suit against a sovereign — or its agents — and that the original seizure was illegal. Constitutionally, the significance of the decision lies in the assertion that no official of the government can cloak himself in the immunity of sovereignty for his illegal acts.[9] More important was the judicial emasculation of the various acts to enforce the Fourteenth and Fifteenth Amendments which made clear that the courts could not be relied upon to secure for the Negroes the rights presumably guaranteed to them.[10]

6. RADICAL RECONSTRUCTION IN THE SOUTH

From 1868 to 1877 the Radicals controlled, for varying periods, most of the reconstructed states of the South. But it was not, as it is sometimes called, 'Black Reconstruction.' In no state did the Negroes ever control the government, and only in South Carolina — where Negroes outnumbered whites four to three — did they have even a temporary majority in the legislature. There were no Negro governors, and very few Negroes in high position in the executive branch or in administration. At no time and in no state did the Negro have a representation proportional to his numbers in any branch of any government.

Radical control of Southern states was exercised by an uneasy coalition of three groups — Negroes, 'carpetbaggers,' and 'scalawags.' Both of the latter words are, of course, heavily loaded. The one conjures up the image of an impecunious Yankee adventurer descending on a prostrate South with a carpetbag to be stuffed full of loot; the other was a word commonly applied to runty cattle and, by implication, to the lowest breed of men. There were disreputable adventurers among the carpetbaggers, but most of them were Union veterans who had returned to the South to farm, businessmen looking for good investments, government agents who for one reason or another decided to stay on in the South, schoolteachers who thought of themselves as a kind of 'peace corps' to the freedmen. As for the 'scalawags' — the largest single element in the Radical coalition — these were the men who had opposed secession in the first place and were now ready to return to the old Union and to take in the Negroes as junior partners in the enterprise of restoration.

9. *United States v. Lee* 106 U.S. 196 (1882). When one of the judges asked Lee's counsel, Judge Shipman, if a claimant might eject the Government from a lighthouse, Shipman replied, 'Far better extinguish all the lighthouses in the land than put out the light of the Law.'
10. See below, Chapter XL.

The Radical governments that flourished briefly in the Southern states in these years were, in many cases, incompetent, extravagant, and corrupt. The corruption was pervasive and ostentatious. In Florida, for example, the cost of public printing in 1869 exceeded the total cost for all of the state government in 1860; in South Carolina the state maintained a restaurant and bar-room for the legislators at a cost of $125,000 for a single session, and under the head of 'legislative supplies' provided Westphalia hams, Brussels carpets, and ornamental cuspidors to the fortunate legislators; in Arkansas clerical costs of the auditor's office alone increased from $4000 to $92,000 in a single year; and in Louisiana the youthful Governor Warmoth managed to garner a fortune of half a million dollars during four years of office, while bartering away state property and dissipating school funds. But corruption did not begin with the advent of the Radicals, nor did it cease when they were forced from office. The Louisiana state convention of 1864, for example, spent $9400 on liquor and cigars for its members and $156,000 for printing the journal of the convention (in inflated currency to be sure); in 1873 the state treasurer of Virginia was indicted for looting the treasury; and as late as 1883 the treasurer of Tennessee absconded with $400,000 of state monies, while the land and railroad legislation of some of the 'Redeemer' governments was no less corrupt and considerably more expensive than anything that the Radical governments achieved. Corruption was confined to no class, no party, and no section: the corruption and extravagance of the Tweed Ring in New York City and the Gas Ring in Philadelphia made the Southern Radicals look like feckless amateurs, as most of them were.

Radical reconstruction was expensive, and taxes and indebtedness mounted throughout the South. In Alabama taxes increased fourfold, in Louisiana eightfold, and in Mississippi fourteenfold. Here, too, however, it is essential to keep a sense of perspective. Thus, in Mississippi where the new taxes were described as 'awful, monstrous, and ruinous,' the fourteenfold increase meant that taxes went up from 1 mill — or one-tenth of a cent — on the dollar, to 14 mills, or 1.4 cents on the dollar. We should keep in mind, too, a number of mitigating circumstances. With emancipation the population requiring public services had almost doubled; the task of repairing the damages of the war was herculean and made unprecedented demands on government; the Radical governments for the first time tried to set up public schools for all children;

much of the property that had customarily borne the burden of taxation — banks, railroads, and industries — had been destroyed by the war, leaving almost the whole burden of taxation to fall on real estate. And while it may be true that the Radicals added some $131 million to the indebtedness of the eleven ex-Confederate states, it must be remembered that money was depreciated and prices inflated; that most of the states were forced to float their bonds in the North at ruinous discounts; and that some two-thirds of the total new indebtedness was in the form of guarantees to railroads and other industries. In this extravagant and often corrupt policy of underwriting railroads, there was no perceptible difference between Radicals and Redeemers. Actually the conservative governments which succeeded the Radicals spent, or pledged, more money on railway subsidies than had the Radicals. In Texas, for example, a grant of $6 million in public lands to the Texas and Pacific Railroad was carried by Democratic votes over the veto of the Radical governor. Of the situation in Alabama, John Hope Franklin says, 'there was no marked difference when the Republicans came to power in 1868 or when a Democratic governor was elected in 1870, or when the Republicans were finally driven from power in 1874. Corruption was bisectional, bipartisan and biracial.'

More important than all this was the constructive side of Radical reconstruction. Much of this was directed to sheer physical rehabilitation required by the ravages of the war, but in almost every one of the Southern states a good deal of progressive legislation was written onto the statute books by the Radicals. In South Carolina, for example, the Radical legislature reformed the system of taxation, dispensed relief to the poor, distributed homesteads to Negroes, established numerous charitable and humane institutions, encouraged immigration, and, for the first time in the history of the state, provided free public schools and compelled attendance of all children from six to sixteen. It was in the realm of public education that the Radical governments made their most significant contribution. In general the Radical legislatures advanced political democracy and inaugurated social reforms, and these contributions go far to justify a favorable judgment upon them. So, too, does the consideration that the Radical legislatures enacted no vindictive or punitive legislation against the former slave-owners.

Notwithstanding these real accomplishments, the Negro was unable to make any serious dent on Southern white hostility or prejudice. Convinced that the Negro was incompetent politically, Southern whites blamed on him all the ills and burdens and humiliations of reconstruction. And because the experiment of Negro participation in politics had been associated with the Republican party, Southerners concluded that the Democratic party was the party of white supremacy and fastened upon the South a one-party system. Because some progressive laws were identified with carpetbag and Negro rule, they came to distrust such legislation and found reassurance in the return to office of an ultraconservative Democracy. Because extravagance and high taxes had accompanied Radical rule, they came to believe that economy and good government were synonymous, and renewed their ante-bellum suspicion of governmental expenditure. Even many of their quondam Northern champions came to the unhappy conclusion that Negro participation in politics had been premature.

7. THE UNDOING OF RECONSTRUCTION

Inevitably Radical reconstruction aroused vigorous and determined opposition throughout the South. This opposition took both legal and illegal form. In states such as Virginia and North Carolina, where whites greatly outnumbered blacks, the Democrats recaptured control of the state governments by regular political methods almost at once. Elsewhere it was thought necessary to resort to a much greater degree of intimidation and terror to destroy the combination that made Radical success possible. Carpetbaggers and scalawags soon felt the heavy weight of economic pressure or the sharp sting of social ostracism. Negroes were dealt with more ruthlessly, by employing terror.

Much of this violence was perpetrated by secret societies, of which the most famous, though not the largest, was the Ku Klux Klan. In 1867 a social *kuklos* (circle) of young men in Pulaski, Tennessee, organized as the 'Invisible Empire of the South,' with elaborate ritual and ceremonial. The KKK described itself as an institution of 'chivalry, humanity, mercy and patriotism,' but it was in fact quite simply an institution for the maintenance of white supremacy. During the next three or four years the KKK and other secret societies — notably the Knights of the White Camellia and the White Leagues of Louisiana and Mississippi — policed 'unruly' Negroes in the country districts, discouraged them from serving in the militia, delivered spectral warnings against using the ballot, and punished those who disregarded the warnings. The Klan and other secret societies were guilty of innumerable crimes, and their secrecy often cloaked lawlessness and outrages directed against the blacks and even against recalcitrant whites. Thus the Ku Klux Klan investigation of 1871 reported 153 Negroes murdered in a single Florida county that year; over 300 murdered in parishes outside New Orleans; bloody race riots in Mississippi and Louisiana; a reign of terror in parts of Arkansas; and in Texas, 'murders, robberies and outrages of all kinds.' It was, says the historian of reconstruction, Ellis P. Oberholtzer, 'a reign of outrage and crime which, all taken together, forms a record of wrong among the most hideous in the history of any modern state.' Not all of this could be laid at the doors of the Klan or the White Leaguers, or even of the whites, but they were responsible for most of the violence that afflicted the South during these turbulent years.

Under the impact of all this, Negro participation in politics declined sharply, and even whites began to desert the Radical cause. But the Radicals had no intention of acquiescing tamely in the undoing of reconstruction. Their answer was first a series of state laws which sought to break up the secret societies and, when these proved unavailing, an appeal to Washington for help. The Grant administration responded with renewed military occupation of evacuated districts, the unseating of Democratic administrations on the ground of fraud, and a new crop of supervisory laws of which the most important were the Force Acts of 1870 and 1871 and the drastic Ku Klux Klan Act of 1871 authorizing the President to suspend the writ of habeas corpus and suppress violence by military force. Altogether some 7000 indictments and over 1000 convictions were found under these acts, but they did not fulfill their purpose. In large areas of the South—notably in South Carolina, Louisiana, and Mississippi — violence flourished throughout the entire reconstruction period.

Public opinion in the North was no longer willing to sustain federal intervention in the affairs of the South. Much of the idealism that had gone into the anti-slavery movement had petered out, or been deflected into new channels, and the North was increasingly willing to leave the Negroes to their fate. The country was tired of the 'Southern question'; even the *Nation,* long a spokesman for ardent Radicalism, confessed that 'every Republican had become disgusted with military control of the States, and thoroughly convinced that a State government which cannot support itself should not be propped up by national soldiers.' In 1874 the Democrats captured the lower House, and the repudiation of Radicalism was all but complete. Meantime all the Southern states had been readmitted to Congress, and by the Amnesty Act of 1872 almost all Southern whites who were still disfranchised were restored to full political privileges.

In the South, too, the Radicals were in full retreat. Frightened· by the violence, Negroes were deserting their Republican allies. The merchants and businessmen who had taken over from the planters wanted peace, too — peace within the Republican party if that were necessary, but better yet peace at the expense of that party. Moreover, factional struggles between carpetbaggers and scalawags split the Republican party in almost every Southern state. As the power of the Radicals waned, demands for military intervention by Washington became more insistent, but Grant rejected these demands. 'The whole public,' he protested, 'are tired out with the annual autumnal outbreaks in the South, and the great majority are ready now to condemn any interference on the part of the government.'

So in state after state the conservative whites recaptured control of the political machinery, until by the end of 1875 only South Carolina, Louisiana, and Mississippi were still under Radical control, and even in these states that control was precarious. The process of 'redemption' was by no means confined to keeping the Negro and the carpetbagger away from the polls and restoring 'white supremacy.' Almost everywhere the struggle was also between rival economic groups, and the prizes were railroad and corporate franchises. Thus in Virginia much of the politics of reconstruction polarized about two rival groups of railroad promoters led by John W. Garrett, president of the Baltimore and Ohio Railroad, and General William Mahone, president of the Southside line — later the Norfolk and Western Railroad. The prize was control of the Virginia and Tennessee Railroad which gave a connection across the mountains to the West. The victory for Mahone was at once a triumph for the Southside Railroad and for the 'Redeemers,' though Mahone himself found no difficulty in going over to the Republicans a few years later!

Thus by one means or another conservatives triumphed. Negroes were eliminated from politics, carpetbaggers scared out, scalawags won over — and 'home rule' was restored. The Redeemer governments then proceeded to reduce expenditures and taxes — often at the expense of school children — and to wipe a good deal of progressive legislation off the statute books; it is suggestive that they did not find it necessary to draft new constitutions but mostly continued with those written by the Radicals. But acting on the assumption that the Radicals had saddled their states with fraudulent debts, and on the fact that in some instances the railroads, for whose benefit the debts had been contracted, had not carried out their part of the bargains, the Redeemers proceeded to repudiate a good part of the state obligations. By this convenient method Southern states rid themselves of perhaps $100 million of debts; efforts to collect these debts in the federal courts ran into the stone wall of the Eleventh Amendment.

When Rutherford B. Hayes was inaugurated President, 4 March 1877, the carpetbag regime had been overthrown in all the Southern states save South Carolina and Louisiana, where it was still upheld by federal bayonets. In South Carolina an army of Confederate veterans known as Red Shirts organized white voters, kept Negroes away from the polls, and elected the beloved Confederate General Wade Hampton governor and a Democratic legislature. A Republican returning board, however, sustained by federal soldiers, threw out the ballots of two counties, canceled thousands of others, and declared the carpetbag Governor D. H. Chamberlain duly re-elected to the governorship. The Democratic members then organized their own House, and with Speaker, clerks, and sergeant-at-arms forced their way into the representatives' chamber where the Radicals were sitting. During three days and nights the rival Houses sat side by side, every man armed to the teeth and ready to shoot if the rival sergeant-at-arms laid hands on one of his colleagues. At the end of that time the Democrats withdrew, leaving Governor Chamberlain in possession of the state house. For four months the two legislatures glared at each other, but the people of the state paid their taxes to Hampton's government. Chamberlain hastened to Washington to appeal for aid, but in vain. Faithful to the compromise by which he had been elected, President Hayes broke the deadlock by withdrawing the troops from Columbia, and the Democrats took possession. Two weeks later, when federal troops evacuated New Orleans, white rule was completely restored throughout the South.

Reconstruction left deep physical and moral scars upon the South. A century later, the apostles of white supremacy were able to ring the changes on the evils of Reconstruction whenever even modest changes in racial patterns were suggested. For decades after 1877, race relations were poisoned by an annual crop of outrages and lynchings. Politics were forced into an unnatural groove, and the one-party system, a hostage to white supremacy, proved inhospitable to the introduction of new issues. Southern society remained relatively static, immune to modern movements in education and social regeneration, and in the twentieth century the South was hardly more prepared to meet the industrial invasion than New England had been a century before. But Reconstruction also left another legacy: the civil rights amendments to the Constitution. In years to come, although much too tardily, Americans would begin to give to these provisions the meaning their framers intended.

Politics of the Grant
Administration

1. THE ELECTION OF 1868

Even as the Senate sat in solemn judgment on President Johnson, the triumphant Republicans met in party convention to nominate his successor. Any number of favorite sons were willing to accept the crown which sat so uneasily upon Johnson's head, but only one was considered worthy of that honor: General Grant. Before the Civil War he had seldom taken the trouble to vote, and the army was not a good school of politics. Such political principles as he professed had inclined him toward the Democratic party, but after McClellan's candidature it was inconceivable that he should have tied up with the Democrats. He had been to Lincoln a faithful subordinate but to Johnson less than faithful, and after his break with Johnson he had been captured by the Radical politicians who saw in him an unbeatable candidate.[1] On the first ballot Grant received a unanimous nomination; the selection of 'Smiling' Schuyler Colfax of Indiana as his running mate did nothing to strengthen the ticket. The Republican platform pledged the party to continue Radical reconstruction in the South, repudiated the 'Ohio

1. Gideon Welles, a Johnson partisan, observed, 'A feeling of gratitude for military services, without one thought of his capacity, intelligence, or experience in civil affairs, has enlisted popular favor for him, and the conspirators have availed themselves of it, though the knowing ones are aware of his unfitness for administrative duties. They expect to use him; he intends to use them.' Entry 21 May 1868, III *Diary*, 363.

idea' of paying the government debt in greenbacks, and preserved an eloquent silence on the tariff issue.

No such unanimity characterized the Democratic convention which met in New York City some weeks later, for the deep gash cut in that party in 1860 had not yet fully healed. The Democrats still labored under the odium of secession and were embarrassed by the leadership of the discredited President Johnson. They adopted a platform that emphasized equally the reconstruction and the money issues. That platform denounced the Republican party for 'corruption'; declared the Reconstruction Acts 'unconstitutional, revolutionary, void'; and endorsed the 'Ohio idea.' If the campaign was to be fought on the reconstruction issue, the obvious candidate was Andrew Johnson; if on the money question, 'Gentleman George' Pendleton, sponsor of the 'Ohio idea'; if on the issue of loyalty, General Winfield S. Hancock of Pennsylvania. With an evasiveness similar to that displayed in 1864, the party chose instead a man who could not dramatize the reconstruction issue, who was committed to hard money, and whose wartime record had associated him with the Copperheads — the weak and ineffectual Horatio Seymour, former governor of New York.

The campaign that followed was bitterly fought, for the stakes of victory were large. To Republicans success promised an indefinite tenure of power, during which the party might be given a national basis through the extension of Negro suffrage to the South. To the Democrats victory spelled the end of Federal backing for the Negro, and the restoration of the remaining Southern states to the Union. The Republicans waved the 'bloody shirt of the rebellion' even more effectively than in 1866. Grant carried all the states but eight, although his popular majority was only 300,000. The Negro vote of some 450,000 gave Grant his popular margin, and the exclusion of three Southern states (Mississippi, Texas, Virginia) and the control of six others through reconstruction laws assured him his large electoral college majority. Only by a willful misreading could the election be interpreted as a vote of confidence in the Radicals. But the statistics of the election strengthened the Radicals in their determination to assure the vote of the Negro and nourish a Republican party in the South, and excited Southerners to believe that restoration of home rule would mean the triumph of the Democratic party not only in the liberated states of the South but nationally as well.

2. PRESIDENT GRANT

The problems which Grant faced were varied and complex, but he brought to their solution little understanding. With less equipment for the presidency than any predecessor except Harrison and a temperament unfitted for high political office, he was unable or unwilling to overcome his deficiencies. Although a leader of men, he was not a good judge of men, and the very simplicity which had carried him safely through the intrigues of the Civil War exposed him to the wiles of politicians whose loyalty to himself he mistook for devotion to the public weal. It came as a shock that he seemed to have lost the qualities he had shown in the war — a sense of order and of command, directness, resoluteness, consistency, and intellectual honesty. The magnanimous victor of Appomattox revealed himself in office petty, vindictive, and shifty. He was naïve rather than innocent, simple rather than unsophisticated, and his simplicity, as Henry Adams remarked, 'was more disconcerting than the complexity of a Talleyrand.'

His political sense was as primitive as that of a Sioux Indian. Ignorant of the Constitution, he never came to understand properly the relations of the executive to his cabinet or to the other departments of the government, nor did he fully comprehend the character of the presidential office. To the end he regarded the presidency as a personal prerogative, a reward for services rendered rather than a responsibility, and he failed, as have so many others, to grasp the real character of the pressure groups who lobbied so successfully for favorable legislation on tariffs, finance, public lands, and even foreign affairs. He had, apparently, but one political principle — faith in his friends, a faith often mistaken and often betrayed.

Grant's only hope lay in the wisdom and integrity of his advisers, but these were chosen with bizarre irresponsibility. Grant's cabinet contained some men of ability and two or three of real talent, but these were accidents, and in time Grant came to regard them as errors. Altogether, during his eight years of office, Grant appointed no less than twenty-six men to his cabinet.[2] Six— Hoar, Cox, Creswell,

2. 'He picked his cabinet officers to suit himself, and so clumsily that the group had to be reorganized before it could function. The State Department he gave to a personal friend, Elihu B. Washburne, to gratify his pride; he allowed a military aide, John A. Rawlins, to appropriate the War Department to reward himself; he picked

Jewell, Bristow, and Fish — proved to be men of intelligence and integrity, and of these Grant managed to dismiss all but one, Secretary of State Fish.

It was fortunate that Grant was able to command, throughout the eight years of his administration, the talents of Hamilton Fish. A New York aristocrat, Grant's third choice for the State Department, and relatively unknown when he took office, Fish proved himself one of the shrewdest men who have ever directed the foreign affairs of the nation. He had what most of his colleagues in Grant's cabinet lacked, integrity of character, disciplined intelligence, learning, experience, urbanity, and a tact and patience sufficient to win and retain the confidence of his chief. To Fish must be ascribed responsibility not only for the achievements of the administration in the field of foreign affairs but also for preventing many egregious mistakes in domestic policies.

Yet for all his obvious defects, Grant wielded an immense power. The devotion which he commanded from millions of men was something stronger than integrity or political wisdom or character or intellectual pre-eminence. It was devotion to an ideal. 'The plain man,' as Allan Nevins observes, 'had not elected Grant; he had elected an indestructible legend, a folk-hero. . . . Mention that monosyllabic name, and the prosaic laborer, farmer, clerk, or business man for once in his life saw a vision. It was a vision of four years of terror and glory. Painted on the clouds above his farm or shop, he saw the torrent of muddied blue uniforms rallying on the bluffs of Shiloh . . . he saw the night ripped by shells and rockets as gunboats spouting fire raced past Vicksburg; he saw the lines at Lookout Mountain waver, reform and go on up; he saw two armies wait as Lee walked into the parlor at Appomattox.' It was well for Grant that he brought to the presidency this imperishable glamor, for he brought little else.

3. FOREIGN AFFAIRS

Thanks to Seward the Johnson administration was at its best in the realm of foreign affairs. Thanks to Hamilton Fish the Grant administra-

a great merchant with whom he had dined well, Alexander T. Stewart, to fill the treasury post, only to discover that his appointee was legally incompetent. The other places he passed around with no reference to the existence of a party that fancied it had a right to rule, or to popular sense of fitness in appointment; and he could not understand or forgive criticism of himself because of this.' F. L. Paxson in *Dictionary of American Biography* (article on Grant).

tion likewise won its most notable successes in this area. During almost the whole of Grant's two terms of office, American foreign relations were in a delicate state. The outbreak of revolution in Cuba threatened to involve the United States in war with Spain; the activities of the Fenians along the Canadian border embarrassed our relations with Canada; and the unwillingness of Lord Russell to arbitrate American claims against Great Britain for alleged failure to observe neutrality during the Civil War strained Anglo-American friendship to the breaking-point.

Many vexatious foreign questions had grown out of the Civil War. Some had been liquidated; others remained to plague the Grant administration. Seward, by his firm attitude toward the French in Mexico and the Spaniards in Santo Domingo, had sustained the Monroe Doctrine, and by strokes of diplomacy had advanced his policy of imperialism in the Pacific. Spain's attempted conquest of Santo Domingo broke down of its own accord, but the Spanish withdrawal from the ill-fated island in 1865 appeared to be a diplomatic victory for Seward. It was not until two years later that Seward persuaded Napoleon III he must abandon the Mexican venture: in June 1867 the puppet-Emperor Maximilian slumped before a firing squad and the cardboard empire collapsed. Russia had long been eager to get rid of Alaska, and in 1867 Sumner in the Senate and a well-oiled lobby in the House permitted Seward to buy that rich domain, known at the time as 'Seward's Folly,' for $7,200,000. To round out his expansionist policy Seward annexed the Midway Islands west of Hawaii, and, with a view to the construction of an isthmian canal at some future date, acquired the right of transit across Nicaragua. When he surrendered his office, a treaty for the purchase of the Danish West India islands (the present Virgin Islands) was pending in the Senate — which promptly rejected it.

President Grant, although indifferent to the Danish West Indies, was enormously interested in another of Seward's Caribbean projects — the annexation of Santo Domingo. This hare-brained proposal had originated with two Yankee fortune-hunters who planned to secure for themselves half the wealth of the island. They managed to draw into their conspiracy powerful financial and commercial interests and bought the support of such men as Ben Butler, John A. Rawlins, and Grant's personal secretary, Orville Babcock; these in turn persuaded the President to commit himself to the project. Grant sent Babcock on a tour of inspection to Santo Domingo, and Babcock returned with a treaty of annexation in his pocket. The treaty was eventually submitted to the Senate only to encounter the implacable hostility of Charles Sumner and Carl Schurz and fail of ratification. It was the most severe defeat that the administration was to suffer.

The Santo Domingo episode was not in itself of importance, but its consequences were. It revealed how easily Grant could be won over to projects of a dubious character and how naïve was his understanding of foreign affairs. It led to the deposition of Charles Sumner from his post as chairman of the Senate Committee on Foreign Affairs and caused a rift in the Republican party that widened, by 1872, into a complete breach. It distracted the attention of Grant and the Radicals from the Cuban situation and enabled Secretary Fish to sidetrack the demand for a recognition of Cuban belligerency and preserve peace with Spain.

A Cuban rebellion had broken out in 1868 and dragged on for ten dreadful years before it was finally suppressed. From the beginning the sympathy of most Americans was with the rebels, and when the Cuban junta in New York spread stories of Spanish barbarism — stories for the most part true — sympathy flamed into indignation. Early in 1869 the House passed a resolution of sympathy for the Cubans, but the movement for recognition of Cuban belligerency encountered the firm opposition of Fish. Recognition would have been a serious mistake, for it would have gravely compromised pending American claims against Great Britain for premature recognition of the belligerency of the Confederate states. As it was, the United States and Spain came to the very brink of war in 1873 over the curious *Virginius* affair. The *Virginius*, a ship flying the American flag and carrying arms for the Cuban insurgents, was captured on the high seas by a Spanish gunboat; fifty-three of her seamen, including eight Americans, were summarily executed for 'piracy.' When Spain disowned the barbarous deed and paid an indemnity, and when it was discovered that the ship had no right to her American papers or to fly the American flag, the crisis was averted and the danger of war evaporated.

To the northward as well as to the southward relations were strained. During the war Canada had furnished a base for Confederate raids on Vermont and New York. In time of peace the Fenians, or Irish Revolutionary Brother-Republics, took similar liberties in the United States. Two rival Irish republics were organized in New York City, each with its president, cabinet, and general staff in glittering uniforms of green and gold. Each planned to seize Canada with Irish veterans of the Union army, and hold it as hostage for Irish freedom. From 1866 to 1870 the Fenians harassed the Canadian border. The first invasion, in April 1866, was promptly nipped by federal authorities at Eastport, Maine. But the ensuing outcry from Irish-Americans, who carried a lot of weight at the polls, frightened President Johnson and his cabinet. Before the Attorney-General and the Secretaries of War and of the Navy could decide who should take on the onus of stopping him, 'General' John O'Neil led 1500 armed Irishmen across the Niagara river. The next day, 2 June 1866, the Canadian militia gave battle, and fled; but the Fenians fled farther — to New York State, where they were promptly arrested and as promptly released. During the following three years the Fenians collected arms and money and girded themselves for a new attack, and in the spring of 1870 tatterdemalion armies moved on Canada from St. Albans, Vermont, and Malone, New York. United States marshals arrested the Fenian leaders, and the armies disintegrated. Ridiculous as they were, the Fenian forays caused Canada much trouble and expense for which she was never reimbursed by the United States.

The greatest achievement of the Grant administration was the liquidation of all outstanding diplomatic controversies with Great Britain. The sympathy of the English ruling classes for the Confederacy and the lax enforcement of neutrality by the British government had aroused deep resentment in the United States. For some years after the war the psychological atmosphere was such that no calm adjudication of American claims was possible. The most important of these claims had to do with the alleged negligence of the British government in permitting the Confederate cruisers *Alabama, Shenandoah,* and *Florida* to be armed in, and escape from, British ports. Seward's persistent advocacy of these claims was finally rewarded in the last months of Johnson's administration by the so-called Clarendon Convention for their adjudication. In April 1869 the Senate rejected this convention as insufficient, after Sumner had charged Great Britain with responsibility for half the total cost of the war: a mere $2,125 million! Sumner's speech shocked his English friends who so faithfully had sustained the Union cause; nor were they much comforted by his explanation that the cession of Canada would be an acceptable form of payment.

After Sumner was eliminated as a result of his recalcitrance on Santo

Domingo, negotiations went forward more successfully. By this time England was ready to make amends for her support to the Confederacy. For, whatever her legal position (which was weak), she realized that her conduct had created a precedent for fitting out warships in America or other neutral waters that might be used to destroy British commerce in any future war. So the Canadian Sir John Rose staged with Hamilton Fish a diplomatic play of wooing and yielding that threw dust in the eyes of extremists on both sides. The covenant thus secretly arrived at was the famous Treaty of Washington (8 May 1871). It provided for submission to arbitration of boundary disputes, the fisheries question, and the *Alabama* claims; determined rules of neutrality that should govern the arbitral tribunal; and contained an expression of regret for the escape of the *Alabama* from British waters — a friendly gesture for which Americans had long been waiting.

In presenting its case to the arbitral tribunal at Geneva the United States claimed compensation not only for actual damage inflicted by the Confederate cruisers, but for the numerous transfers of registry occasioned by fear of capture. Hamilton Fish had no intention of pressing these 'indirect claims,' which he was anxious only to be rid of; but English opinion was deeply stirred by their presentation. Charles Francis Adams, the American member, proposed that the Geneva tribunal rule out the indirect claims in advance. This was done, and the arbitration proceeded smoothly to its conclusion: an award of $15 million for depredations committed by the *Alabama, Florida,* and *Shenandoah.* Even this sum was in excess of the actual direct damage, and part of it was never handed out to claimants.

Although the United States was thereby vindicated, the greater victory was for arbitration and peace. Never before had questions involving such touchy matters of national honor been submitted to a mere majority vote of an international tribunal. The English accepted the verdict with good grace. Charles Francis Adams never forgot that he was judge not advocate, and President Grant by his unwavering support of peaceful methods showed a quality not unusual in statesmen who know war at first hand. In a later message to the Arbitration Union of Birmingham, Grant set forth his guiding principle: 'Nothing would afford me greater happiness than to know that . . . at some future day, the nations of the earth will agree upon some sort of congress which will take cognizance of international questions of difficulty, and whose decisions will be as binding as the decisions of our Supreme Court are upon us. It is a dream of mine that some such solution may be.'

4. DOMESTIC POLITICS

No such idealism animated Grant in his handling of the more pressing problems of domestic politics. Three of these problems, reconstruction, the money question, and the tariff, were of urgent national importance; a fourth, civil service reform, was taken seriously only by a small group, but that group included many of the ablest men in American political life.

'Let us have peace,' the concluding phrase of Grant's letter accepting the presidential nomination, had led the country to believe that Grant would abandon Radical reconstruction and adopt toward the South a more conciliatory policy. In the beginning this belief seemed justified. The President suggested to his cabinet a sweeping amnesty proclamation and urged Congress to complete the reconstruction process in Virginia, Mississippi, and Texas. By 1870 representatives from these three laggard states again took their places in Congress. But despite this beginning it was soon clear that Grant, who had ardently supported the impeachment of Johnson, was still in the Radical camp. In his first annual message he recommended to Congress a drastic reconstitution of the legislature of Georgia, and Congress responded with appropriate legislation. He gave his approval to the Force Acts and the Ku Klux Act and applied them with some vigor. Faced with a revolt throughout the South against the carpetbag regime he fell back upon his military idea of restoring order, and in South Carolina, Alabama, Mississippi, Louisiana, and Arkansas supported the worst of the carpetbaggers and authorized the use of federal troops to overthrow duly elected Democratic governments and keep these states in the Radical Republican ranks.

The money question, like the Southern question, had been inherited from previous administrations. During the war the government had issued $450 million of legal tender notes, and at the close of the war some $400 million of these so-called greenbacks were still in circulation. The presence of greenbacks in the currency gave rise to two issues that divided public opinion. The first involved the medium of payment of the interest and principal of government bonds. These bonds had been purchased with depreciated greenbacks, and it was urged that they should be redeemable in greenbacks unless otherwise specified. Farmers and workingmen who would ultimately pay most of the taxes for the redemption of these bonds supported this proposal as just. Bondholders opposed it as a betrayal of national honor. The Democrats endorsed the proposal to pay government securities in greenbacks, and President Johnson went even further and urged that future interest payments be applied to the liquidation of the principal of the debt. But in his first inaugural address Grant committed himself to payment of all government obligations in gold, and the first measure passed by the new Congress (18 March 1869) pledged the faith of the United States to such payment.

The second question raised by the presence of greenbacks concerned the policy of the government toward the contraction of greenbacks and the resumption of specie payments. The inflation of the currency through greenbacks had tended to raise commodity prices, make credit easier and money cheaper. The farmer and the debtor therefore favored inflation and regarded with dismay any proposal for the contraction of the currency by calling in these greenbacks. Business interests were divided; most wanted a stable currency, and hence opposed both currency expansion and abrupt resumption. But some businessmen, such as those who had gone into debt, favored expansion, while conservative bankers and others of the creditor class demanded that the government pledge itself to redeem greenbacks with gold and thus bring this paper currency to par.

A powerful argument for stabilizing the currency was that constant fluctuation in the value of greenbacks opened a wide door to speculation. Because greenbacks were not legal tender for all purposes and because it was uncertain whether the government would ever redeem them in gold, they circulated at a discount which varied from month to month. In 1862 the gold value of a greenback dollar had been 90 cents; in 1865 it fell to 50 cents; by the time Grant assumed office it had risen to 73 cents. In September 1869 two notorious stock gamblers, Jay Gould and Jim Fisk, took advantage of this fluctuation in the value of money to organize a 'corner' in gold. With the passive connivance of persons high in the confidence of the President and the Secretary of the Treasury, the nefarious scheme almost succeeded. On 'Black Friday,' 24 September 1869, the premium on gold rose to 162, and scores of Wall Street brokers faced ruin. Then the government dumped $4 million in gold on the market, and the 'corner' collapsed. The whole country was aroused, and men everywhere blamed Grant for criminal incompetence in permitting himself to be enmeshed in the sordid affair. 'The worst scandals of the 18th century,' wrote Henry Adams, 'were relatively harmless by the side of this which smirched executive, judiciary, banks, corporate systems, professions, and people, all the great active forces of society.' Yet the episode reflected not so much upon Grant's character as upon his judgment, which vacillated. Grant favored a resumption of specie payments but he opposed contraction of the currency and was disposed to accept greenbacks as a permanent part of the currency.

In 1870 the greenback question came before the Supreme Court. When Chief Justice Chase — who as Secretary of the Treasury had originally issued them — announced that greenbacks were not legal tender for obligations entered into prior to the emission of the notes, and even made the alarming suggestion that they were completely invalid,[3] the government promptly moved for a rehearing of the case. Two vacancies on the Supreme Court afforded Grant a propitious opportunity to strengthen the government's position. In Joseph P. Bradley and William Strong, Grant found jurists upon whose faith in the constitutionality of the greenbacks he could with confidence rely.[4] He was not disappointed. In the second Legal Tender decision, *Knox v. Lee*, the Court in 1871 reversed itself and sustained the constitutionality of the Civil War greenbacks. Thirteen years later, in an even more sweeping decision, *Juilliard v. Greenman*, it proclaimed the right of the government to issue legal tender even in time of peace. When, in 1874, Congress attempted to do this, Grant interposed his veto and the threat of inflation passed. In 1875 Congress finally provided for the resumption of specie payments on 1 January 1879. This act settled, for the time being, the legal tender question, but it did not settle the money question. That remained to plague the next generation.

The tariff question also vexed the Grant administration. The Civil

3. *Hepburn v. Griswold* 8 Wallace 603 (1870).
4. It was charged at the time, and later, that Grant had 'packed' the Court. Like all Presidents he appointed to the Court men who were broadly sympathetic to his point of view; aside from this there is no evidence of any impropriety in the two appointments.

War tariffs, raising duties to unprecedented heights, were originally accepted as emergency revenue measures; protected industries soon came to regard them as permanent. After Appomattox, Western farmers and Eastern reformers joined hands in demanding tariff reduction, but the protected interests had no intention of yielding. In 1867 duties had actually been raised on a number of items, and throughout the following years Congress passed a series of 'pop' tariff bills which continued the upward course of duties. The Grant administration set itself against tariff reform. Secretary Cox was forced out of the cabinet in part because of his sympathy for it, and David A. Wells, the able economist who was a special commissioner of revenue, had to resign for the same reason. The approach of a presidential election, however, scared the administration into temporary virtue on this issue, and in 1872 Grant signed a bill providing for a horizontal slash of 10 per cent on many protected articles. At the same time, the last of the Civil War income taxes were repealed. In 1875 tariff duties were restored to their earlier status, but no effort was made to restore the income tax.

Nor did civil service reform fare better. In no department was the record of Grant's administration more discreditable. Dissatisfaction with the spoils system, voiced by such leaders as Carl Schurz, Lyman Trumbull, and Charles Sumner, appeared in the beginning to have Grant's support. The appointment of Jacob Cox to the Interior Department was a gesture toward reform, and when in 1871 a Civil Service Commission, headed by George William Curtis, submitted a list of desirable reforms, Grant promised that 'at all events the experiment shall have a fair trial.' But Cox was shoved out, and Grant soon scuttled the commission and jettisoned the reform. The recommendations of the commission were ignored, the civil service packed with party henchmen, and the system of assessments on officeholders brought to a high state of efficiency. 'There is an utter surrender of the Civil Service to the coarsest use by the coarsest men,' observed Whitelaw Reid, and reformers everywhere echoed the sentiment. Curtis, wearied of shadow-boxing with the spoilsmen, resigned in disgust, and in 1875 the commission itself was discontinued. With the appointment of the Republican boss, Zachariah Chandler, to the Department of the Interior, the administration abandoned even the pretense of interest in civil service reform and surrendered itself to the spoilsmen.

5. THE LIBERAL REPUBLICAN MOVEMENT

The Civil War had obscured the deep differences within the Republican party, and Reconstruction served as a smoke-screen behind which Radicals captured control of the party organization. Within less than a year after Grant's assumption of office, a revolt within the Republican party was in full swing. Causes for dissatisfaction were numerous. The full measure of administrative corruption was as yet unknown, but enough was suspected to outrage men who cherished standards of political decency. Grant's Southern policy was controversial, his Caribbean policy an affront, while his repudiation of civil service and tariff reform alienated even some of his own followers. Above all there was a growing distrust of Grant himself, a distrust which found dramatic expression in Sumner's speech of May 1872 wherein the President was scored for taking and giving bribes, nepotism, neglect of duty, lawless interference with the business of the other departments of the government, and for half a dozen other misdemeanors. Sumner's disapproval was something which all Presidents had had to face, and was not taken too seriously; but soon many of the most distinguished of the elder statesmen were following his lead. Grant's abuse of the civil service alienated Cox and Schurz, his Southern policy antagonized Lyman Trumbull and Gideon Welles, his tariff policy cost him the support of David A. Wells, and such men as Chief Justice Chase, Horace Greeley, Charles Francis Adams, and E. L. Godkin came to regard the President as unfit for high office.

This revolt against Grant was started by liberals and reformers, but old-line politicians and disappointed factional leaders soon flocked to it in embarrassing numbers. In the end it consisted of a group even more heterogeneous than usual in American parties. Free-traders like Wells and high protectionists like Greeley, Eastern conservatives like Adams and Western radicals like Ignatius Donnelly, civil service reformers like Carl Schurz and practical politicians like Reuben Fenton of New York, were all in the same boat. The one idea that animated them all was distrust of President Grant. It was a movement of opposition rather than of positive reform; and therein lay its chief weakness.

When the Liberal Republican convention met at Cincinnati 1 May 1872, this weakness became apparent. It was impossible for the discordant elements to agree upon a satisfactory platform or a logical candidate. The platform as finally adopted called for the withdrawal of troops from the South, civil service reform, and a resumption of specie payments; as for the tariff, the convention 'recognizing that there are in our midst honest but irreconcilable differences of opinion' remanded 'the discussion of the subject to the people in their congressional Districts.' Nor could the convention unite on a presidential candidate like Charles Francis Adams or Lyman Trumbull, the latter for almost 20 years one of the ornaments of the party. Intrigues and jealousies defeated them, and in the end the convention stampeded to Horace Greeley of New York.

No man in the country was better known than Horace Greeley, for over thirty years editor of the powerful New York *Tribune,* but he was renowned as an editor not as a statesman. A Vermont Yankee who had kept his homespun democracy and youthful idealism in the atmosphere of New York, Greeley persistently championed the cause of the underprivileged, the worker, and the farmer. He had long been a power in the councils of the Whig and Republican parties, and his advocacy of a high tariff, liberal land laws, and abolition had helped shape the course of American history. Yet for all his intellectual abilities and idealism, Greeley lacked the first qualifications for responsible political position. He was impulsive, unpredictable, intriguing, vain, and vindictive, and his eager promotion of every reform, his crotchets and caprices and carefully cultivated idiosyncrasies, laid him open to ridicule and caricature. He had championed Fourierism and vegetarianism, spiritualism and temperance, and a dozen other fads, and the average man saw in these things not the expression of a consistent social philosophy but rather the vagaries of a visionary and impractical nature. A familiar figure on the streets of New York, he wore a crumpled white coat, its pockets stuffed with newspapers, and crowning his bewhiskered face was a tall white hat. He reminded some of Mr. Pickwick, others of the Mad Hatter.

The nomination of Greeley came as a shock to the reformers who had organized the Liberal Republican movement. *The Nation* reported that 'a greater degree of incredulity and disappointment' had not been felt since the news of the first battle of Bull Run, while Lyman Trumbull said: 'If the country can stand the first outburst of mirth the nomination will call forth it may prove a strong ticket.' But the dismay of the reformers was as nothing to the dismay of Southern Democrats. For thirty years Greeley had castigated the South and the Democratic party, and much of the responsibility for anti-slavery, and later for Radical reconstruction, could justly be laid at his door. Democrats might well feel that an endorsement of Greeley would be more stultifying than an endorsement of Grant. Yet the Democrats had no alternative; bitterly they swallowed the strange pill and made Greeley their nominee. But it was hard to work up enthusiasm for a candidate who had said: 'May it be written on my grave that I was never the Democratic party's follower and lived and died in nothing its debtor.'

Greeley proved himself, surprisingly enough, an excellent campaigner, but the odds against him were insuperable. Grant could command the support of the rank and file of the Republican party, veterans of the Union armies, the Negro vote North and South, and most of the German vote alienated by Greeley's temperance views. Despite his protectionist sympathies, Greeley lost Pennsylvania by 100,000 votes. Grant won a sweeping victory. He carried all the states but six and had a popular majority of over 700,000. Greeley, with less than 44 per cent of the vote, failed to win a single state in the North or West. Three weeks later Horace Greeley died, broken-hearted. The Liberal Republican party did not long survive him, but many of the men who took part in that campaign would be active in the 'Mugwump' wing of the party for the next generation.

6. SCANDAL AND STAGNATION

'It looks at this distance,' wrote Senator Grimes to Lyman Trumbull, 'as though the Republican party were going to the dogs. . . . Like all parties that have an undisturbed power for a long time, it has become corrupt, and I believe that it is to-day the [most] corrupt and debauched political party that has ever existed.' When this was written, in July 1870, it seemed an exaggeration, but within a few years a series of sensational exposures went far to prove its accuracy. While the campaign of 1872 was still under way the country was startled by charges of wholesale corruption in connection with the construction of the Union Pacific Railroad, charges which reflected upon men high in Republican councils. The promoters of the Union Pacific, in order to divert the profits of construction to themselves, had organized a construction company, the Credit Mobilier of America. To this company the directors of the Union Pacific awarded fantastically profitable contracts. As a result of this corrupt arrangement the Union Pacific was forced to the verge of bankruptcy while the Credit Mobilier paid in a single year dividends of 348 per cent. Fearing lest Congress might interpose, the directors placed large blocks of Credit Mobilier stock 'where they would do most good.' Exposure of the scheme brought disgrace to a number of representatives, and to Vice-President Schuyler Colfax, while others such as Henry Wilson of Massachusetts and James A. Garfield of Ohio were never able to explain away their connection with the unsavory affair.

Scarcely less excusable was the so-called Salary Grab. In the closing days of Congress, February–March 1873, Ben Butler pushed through a bill doubling the salary of the President and increasing by 50 per cent the salary of Congressmen. This could be justified; what particularly affronted public opinion was that the increases granted to Congressmen were made retroactive for two years: thus each Congressman voted to himself $5000 of back salary out of public funds. The bill was an evasion if not an outright violation of the Constitution, but Grant signed it without demur. A storm of indignation against this 'steal' swept the country, and in the following session Congress hastened to restore the old salary scale.

The Credit Mobilier and the Salary Grab were merely the most sensational of the exposures which indicated the demoralization of the administration. The Navy Department sold business to contractors, and Secretary Robeson managed to accumulate a fortune of several hundred thousand dollars during his tenure of office. The Department of the Interior was working hand in glove with land speculators. The Treasury farmed out uncollected taxes to one J. D. Sanborn who promptly proceeded to highjack some $425,000 out of railroad companies and other corporations, one-half of which he took for himself. The American Minister to England, Robert Schenck, lent his name and position to the Emma Mine swindle, and the Minister to Brazil, J. W. Webb, defrauded the Brazilian government of $50,000 and fled to Europe, leaving the United States Government to refund the money, with apologies. The Custom House in New York was a sink of political corruption, and when Collector Thomas Murphy was finally forced out Grant accepted his resignation 'with regret,' while at the same time the skulduggery of

Collector Casey of the Port of New Orleans was rewarded by his reappointment to the office which he had disgraced. In the national capital 'Boss' Shepherd, head of the local ring, ran up a debt of $17 million, a large part of which was graft, and found himself appointed by a grateful President to be chairman of the Board of Public Works! It was Shepherd, too, who was largely responsible for the failure of the Freedmen's Bank, a failure which worked cruel hardship upon thousands of trusting Negroes who had deposited their savings in an institution supposedly philanthropic.

All of this was bad enough, but worse was still to come. After the Democrats carried the congressional elections of 1874, a Democratic House, the first since the Civil War, set afoot a series of investigations. In the Treasury and War departments, investigators uncovered sensational frauds. For years a 'Whiskey Ring' in St. Louis had systematically defrauded the government of millions of dollars in taxes on distilled whiskey. The Ring had operated with the collusion of Treasury officials and of the President's private secretary, Babcock. When Grant was appraised of the situation he said, 'Let no guilty man escape. Be especially vigilant against all who insinuate that they have high influence to protect or to protect them.' But most of them did escape, Babcock with the President's connivance. No sooner had the 'Whiskey Ring' been exposed than the country confronted a new scandal. In the spring of 1876 Secretary of the Treasury Benjamin H. Bristow found irrefutable proof that Secretary of War Belknap had sold Indian post-trader-ships. Faced with impeachment, Belknap hurried to resign, and his resignation was accepted 'with great regret' by the President whom he had betrayed. Impeachment proceedings were instituted, but the Secretary was finally acquitted on the technical ground that the Senate no longer had jurisdiction over his case.

Corruption was not confined to the national government. It could be found in state and municipal governments, in business and finance and transportation, and even in the professions. There was almost everywhere a breakdown of old moral standards, and to many it seemed that integrity had departed from public life. Much of the idealism of the prewar years had been burnt out in the flames of the war and reconstruction. The industrial revolution, the building of transcontinental railroads, and the exploitation of new natural resources had called into existence a class of new rich untrained to the responsibilities of their position. Never before and only once since — after World War I — have public morals fallen so low.

State legislatures, too, were guilty of gross corruption. The systematic looting in which the Southern governments indulged was matched in the Northern and Western states. In the fierce struggle between Daniel Drew and Cornelius Vanderbilt for control of the Erie Railroad the legislature of New York State was auctioned off to the highest bidder, and both the bar and the bench proved that they too were for sale. In Pennsylvania the powerful Cameron machine bought and sold legislation with bare-faced effrontery. In Illinois a corrupt legislature jammed through, in disregard of the Constitution, over 700 acts of incorporation. In Wisconsin, Minnesota, and California the legislatures were controlled by railroads; in Iowa the money for the Agricultural College realized from land-grant sales was stolen. The cities, too, presented a sorry spectacle. The brigandage of the Tweed Ring cost New York City not less than $100 million.

At a time when the Grant administration was reeling from reports of political corruption, the panic of 1873 struck an even heavier blow. Reckless speculation in railroads and wholesale stock watering in many industries played an important part in precipitating this panic. Other causes were perhaps equally important. The depression was world-wide: Germany, France, and England all felt the hard times, and European investors proceeded to call in their American loans. The unfavorable balance of trade, which had persisted all through the war and the postwar years, mounted during the early 'seventies: the total deficit for the years 1870 to 1876 was $789 million. Too rapid expansion of the agricultural West produced surplus crops which, after the Franco-Prussian War, could not be marketed abroad at satisfactory prices. The war and expansion had led to a shift of capital from productive to more speculative enterprises. Credit was overextended, currency inflated, and public finances deranged by the conflicting claims of greenbacks and of gold. With an immense self-confidence the country had mortgaged itself to the future; now it found itself unable to pay either interest or principal.

The crash came 17 September 1873 with the failure of the great banking house of Jay Cooke and Company — the house that had helped finance the war and the Northern Pacific Railroad. Soon one substantial business firm after another toppled, and the New York Stock Exchange took the unprecedented step of closing its doors for ten days. The panic lengthened into a depression. Industrial plants shut down, railway construction declined sharply, and over half the railroads defaulted on their bonds. Long bread lines began to appear in the larger cities — there was no notion of public relief — and tramps swarmed the country-side. Such a crisis was bound to have political consequences; it not only lead to the birth of a farmer-labor party, but put the chances of the Republicans in the 1876 election in serious jeopardy.

7. THE DISPUTED ELECTION OF 1876

Republican defeat seemed certain in 1876 as the bankruptcy of the Grant administration became increasingly apparent. The Republicans passed up the magnetic James G. Blaine, badly compromised by his connection with the Little Rock and Fort Smith Railroad, and chose instead the respectable but uninspiring Rutherford B. Hayes. Hayes had been thrice Governor of Ohio, and his record was good enough to command the backing of party moderates; the Old Guard had no alternative but to support the one man who might save the party from disaster. The Democrats, determined to make reform the issue of the campaign, nominated Samuel J. Tilden of New York, who had exposed and broken the notorious Tweed Ring and then, as Governor of New York, smashed the 'Canal Ring.' The newly organized Greenback party nominated Peter Cooper of New York, who received less than 82,000 votes.

When the first reports came in, Tilden appeared to have won a sweeping victory. He carried New York, New Jersey, Connecticut, Indiana, and apparently all the South. He piled up a popular plurality of over 250,000. But, scanning the returns, the Republican campaign managers became convinced that the election might yet be swung to their candidate. The votes of four states — South Carolina, Florida, Louisiana, and Oregon — were apparently in doubt. Without the vote of these states Tilden had only 184 electoral votes; 185 were necessary to win. On the morning after election Zach Chandler dispatched telegrams to each of the doubtful states, 'Can you hold your state?' — and that afternoon he announced, 'Hayes has 185 electoral votes and is elected.'

The situation was highly involved and highly precarious. In all three of the Southern states there had been intimidation and fraud on both

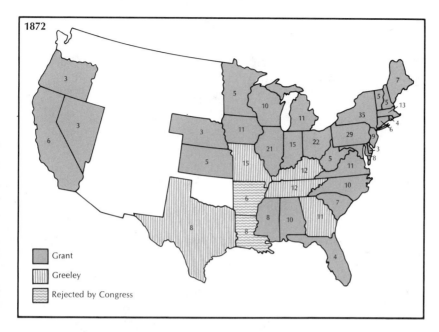

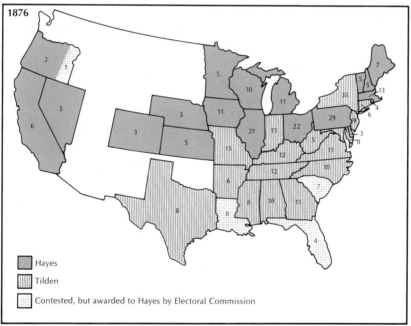

PRESIDENTIAL ELECTIONS, 1872, 1876

sides. Hayes appeared to have carried South Carolina, but, in Florida and Louisiana, Tilden seemed to have a safe majority. Republican returning boards threw out about 1000 Democratic votes in Florida and over 13,000 in Louisiana, and gave certificates to the Hayes electors. In Oregon a Democratic governor had displaced a Republican elector on a technicality and appointed a Democrat to his position. From all four states came two sets of returns.

The Constitution provides that 'The President of the Senate shall, in the presence of the Senate and the House of Representatives, open all certificates and the votes shall then be counted.' But counted by whom? If the President of the Senate did the counting, the election would go to Hayes; if the House counted the votes, Tilden would be President. And if the two houses could not agree on the procedure, there would be no President. Was the nation then to drift, distraught and confused, without a chief executive? Was the long agony of war and reconstruction to reach a new climacteric in the frustration of those constitutional mechanisms provided by the Fathers and in a new wave of violence and war?

Conservatives, North and South, hastened to head off such a crisis. By this time both sections were thoroughly tired of disorder and violence. The solution of the immediate crisis was hinted at by Representative Garfield in a letter to Hayes. Some of the extremists on both sides, he wrote, were prepared to make trouble, but 'in the meantime two forces are at work. The Democratic businessmen of the country are more anxious for quiet than for Tilden; and the old Whigs are saying that they have seen war enough, and don't care to follow the lead of their northern associates.' Garfield suggested that 'if in some discreet way, these southern men who are dissatisfied with Tilden and his violent followers, could know that the South is going to be treated with kind consideration,' they might acquiesce in Hayes's election.

Southern conservatives wanted an end to military reconstruction, the restoration of 'home rule,' some voice in the Hayes administration, and generous subsidies for internal improvements, particularly railroads. If these concessions were forthcoming, they were prepared to concede the presidency. And on his part Hayes — or those who spoke for him — were equally prepared to make the concessions.

Under these uncertain auspices, and with the reluctant support of Governor Tilden, Congress was able to act. On 29 January 1877 it set up an

Electoral Commission of fifteen members (five from the House, five from the Senate, and five from the Supreme Court) to pass on the credentials from the four states whose votes were in dispute. It was originally planned to appoint to this committee seven Democrats and seven Republicans and, as the fifteenth member, the non-partisan Judge David Davis of Illinois. At the last moment, however — and not by inadvertence — the legislature of Illinois elected Judge Davis to the Senate and, with the approval of both parties, Judge Bradley was named in his place. As it turned out it was Judge Bradley who named the next President of the United States. For on all questions submitted to it the Electoral Commission divided along strict party lines, and Judge Bradley voted invariably with the Republicans.[5] By a straight eight to seven vote the Commission awarded all four contested states to Hayes.

Would the Democrats accept a solution which seemed so partisan and so unfair? For a time it was touch and go. Indignation was intense, for Tilden had a clear majority over his rival, and the vote had constituted a sharp rebuke to the Republican administration. Northern Democrats were prepared to filibuster long enough to prevent Congress from opening and counting the votes. Such a filibuster actually flourished in the closing weeks of the Grant administration, and with a little encourage-

5. There is reason to believe that Judge Bradley's vote represented neither his original opinion nor his conviction. Abram S. Hewitt, Democratic leader of the House, wrote of Judge Bradley's vote: 'The history of this opinion forms an important feature in the final outcome of the electoral count. . . . Mr. Stevens was the intimate friend of Judge Bradley. He passed the night previous to the rendition of the judgment in the Florida case at my house. About midnight he returned from a visit to Judge Bradley and reported . . . that he had just left Judge Bradley after reading his opinion in favor of counting the vote of the Democratic electors of the state of Florida. Such a judgment insured the election of Tilden to the Presidency with three votes to spare above the necessary majority. We parted, therefore, with the assurance that all further doubt as to the Presidency was at rest. I attended the delivery of the judgment the next day without the slightest intimation from any quarter that Judge Bradley had changed his mind. In fact, the reading of the opinion, until the few concluding paragraphs were reached, was strictly in accordance with the report of Mr. Stevens. The change was made between midnight and sunrise. Mr. Stevens afterwards informed me that it was due to a visit to Judge Bradley by Senator Frelinghuysen and Secretary Robeson, made after his departure. Their appeals to Judge Bradley were said to have been reinforced by the persuasion of Mrs. Bradley. Whatever the fact may have been, Judge Bradley himself in a subsequent letter addressed to the Newark *Daily Advertiser* admitted that he had written a favorable opinion which on subsequent reflection he saw fit to modify.' 'Secret History of the Election, 1876–77,' *Selected Writings of Abram S. Hewitt*, edited by Allan Nevins, pp. 172–3.

ment from Tilden and Hewitt it might have continued to the close of Congress. But in the end wiser counsels prevailed. With renewed assurances from Hayes that he would abide by the understanding reached by his intermediaries, enough Southern Democrats deserted the Northern intransigents to permit the Congress to count the ballots, and on 2 March 1877, only two days before Inauguration Day, Hayes was declared formally elected by a majority of one vote.

This famous compromise worked well for those who contrived it, and none of those directly involved suffered as a consequence of their moderation. The real victim of the compromise was the Southern Negro, for it had been made at his expense and delayed for three generations the enforcement of those guarantees written into the Fourteenth and Fifteenth Amendments.

8. THE UNDOING OF RECONSTRUCTION

When, in 1873, the Supreme Court was called upon for the first time to interpret the phrases of the Fourteenth Amendment, Justice Samuel Miller, speaking for the Court, reviewed the history of the three Civil War Amendments and observed:

> No one can fail to be impressed with the one pervading purpose found in them all, lying at the foundation of each, and without which none of them would have been even suggested; we mean the freedom of the slave race, the security and firm establishment of that freedom, and the protection of the newly made freedman and citizen from the oppressions of those who had formerly exercised unlimited dominion over him.

At the time this seemed the common sense of the matter, and even the judges who dissented from the decision of the Court did not challenge this interpretation of the Amendments.

Each of these Amendments contained the unusual provision that 'Congress shall have power to enforce this article by appropriate legislation.' And, beginning with the ill-fated Civil Rights Act of 1866, Congress enacted a series of laws designed to do just that. The most important of these were the Enforcement Acts of 31 May 1870 and 28 February 1871 which threw the protection of the Federal Government over the Negro's right to vote; the Ku Klux Klan Act of 20 April 1871 which made it a federal offense to conspire to deprive Negroes of the equal protection of the laws; and the Civil Rights Act of 1 March 1875 which undertook to wipe out social as well as political discrimination and to secure the Negro 'full and equal enjoyment of the accommodations, advantages, facilities, and privileges of inns, public conveyances on land or water, theatres, and other places of public amusement,' as well as the right to serve on juries. During the brief period of Radical Reconstruction the Negro did enjoy both civil and political rights. He was freed from the restrictions of the black codes; he exercised the vote; he held office. He did not suffer severe economic discrimination, and that large apparatus of social indignities that came later to be called 'Jim Crow' had not yet been applied or invented.

The withdrawal of troops by President Hayes in 1877 marked the abandonment not only of reconstruction, but of the Negro. Congress, which had enacted three constitutional amendments and half a dozen Enforcement Acts all designed to protect the freedman, now threw in the sponge and turned the 'Negro problem' over to the South. That was what the South demanded as the price of reunion, and as the price would be paid by the Negro, the North did not find it exorbitant. There were three generally recognized parts to the unwritten agreement: that the North would hereafter keep hands off the 'Negro problem'; that the rules governing race relations in the South would be written by the whites; and that these rules would concede the Negro limited civil rights, but neither political nor social equality. The principle underlying this relationship was set forth succinctly by Henry Grady of the Atlanta *Constitution:* 'The supremacy of the white race of the South must be maintained forever, and the domination of the Negro race resisted at all points and at all hazards, because the white race is superior.' It was as simple as that.

Abandoned by Congress and the President, the Negro was now repudiated by the courts. If the 'one pervading purpose' of the Civil War Amendments was, indeed, the protection of the freedman from oppression, then it failed. Beginning with the Slaughterhouse case of 1873 the Supreme Court proceeded systematically to riddle the structure of Negro rights until it was, to use John Marshall's phrase, 'a magnificent structure to look at but totally unfit for use.' In the Slaughterhouse case the Court, distinguishing between the privileges and immunities derived from national and from state citizenship, asserted that all the important ones came from state citizenship and that it was not the purpose of the Fourteenth Amendment to try to extend federal protection over these. The Cruikshank case of 1875, which involved a mob attack on Negroes who were trying to vote, carefully restricted the reach of the Fourteenth Amendment to state — not private — interference with Negro rights, and to such interference as was clearly directed against Negroes on account of their race or color. 'Inasmuch' said Chief Justice Waite with sharp irony, 'as it does not appear . . . that the intent of these defendants was to prevent these parties from exercising their right to vote on account of their race, it does not appear that it was their intent to interfere with any right granted or secured by the Constitution or laws of the United States. We may suppose that "race" was the cause of the hostility, but this is not so averred.' When an election official in Kentucky — one Reese — refused to receive a Negro vote, the Court held that Congress did not have authority to protect the right to vote generally, but only where that right was denied by the *state,* and on grounds of *race* or *color.* In 1878 the Court provided the legal foundation for segregation by striking down a Louisiana statute forbidding discrimination in transportation, as an unlawful interference with congressional authority over interstate commerce! In the *United States v. Harris,* a case in which a Tennessee mob had lynched four Negro prisoners, the Court returned to the well-worn theme that the national government could protect the Negro only against acts by the *state,* and that for protection against violence by individuals or by mobs the Negro must look to the state authorities. The crucial test came with the Civil Rights Cases of 1883, where the Court, in effect, wiped off the statute book the Civil Rights Act of 1875 forbidding discrimination against Negroes in public facilities.

> It would be running the slavery argument into the ground [said Justice Bradley] to make it apply to every act of discrimination which a person may see fit to make as to the guests he will entertain, or as to the people he will take into his coach or cab or car, or admit to his concert or theatre, or deal with in other matters of intercourse or business.

And the Court added, somewhat gratuitously, that

> When a man has emerged from slavery and by the aid of beneficent legislation has shaken off the inseparable concomitants of that state, there must be some stage in the progress of his elevation when he

takes the rank of a mere citizen, and ceases to be the special favorite of the laws, and when his rights as a citizen, or a man, are to be protected in the ordinary modes by which other men's rights are protected.

This was the thesis, too, of the famous *Plessy v. Ferguson* decision of 1896 which, by accepting the doctrine of 'separate but equal accommodations,' threw the mantle of judicial approval over segregation.

> The object of the 14th Amendment [said the Court] was undoubtedly to enforce the absolute equality of the two races before the law, but in the nature of things, it could not have been intended to abolish distinctions based upon color, or to enforce social as distinguished from political equality, or a commingling of the two races upon terms unsatisfactory to either.[6]

This jettisoning of the civil rights program did not go without protest from within the Court itself. Justice Harlan of Kentucky spoke for a construction of the Constitution broad enough to embrace the rights of all citizens, Negro and white alike. His classic dissent in the Civil Rights Cases applied to the whole body of judicial construction which had by now paralyzed the wartime Amendments:

> The opinion in these cases proceeds . . . upon grounds entirely too narrow and artificial. I cannot resist the conclusion that the substance and spirit of the recent amendments of the Constitution have been sacrificed by a subtle and ingenious verbal criticism. . . . Constitutional provisions, adopted in the interest of liberty, and for the purpose of securing, through national legislation, if need be, rights inhering in a state of freedom, and belonging to American citizenship, have been so construed as to defeat the ends the people desired to accomplish, which they attempted to accomplish, and which they supposed they had accomplished by changes in their fundamental law.

And, observing that the 'separate but equal' doctrine of the Plessy case would, in time 'be quite as pernicious as the decision in the Dred Scott case,' Harlan wrote prophetically:

> The destinies of the two races in this country are indissolubly linked together, and the interests of both require that the common government of all shall not permit the seeds of race hate to be planted under the sanction of law. What can more certainly arouse race

6. This historic decision was unanimously reversed some sixty years later in the even more historic decision of *Brown v. Board of Education of Topeka*.

hate, what more certainly create and perpetuate a feeling of distrust between these races, than state enactments which in fact proceed on the ground that colored citizens are so inferior and degraded that they cannot be allowed to sit in public coaches occupied by white citizens.

What all this meant — the end of Reconstruction, the restoration of white rule, the watering down of the Enforcement Acts and their judicial nullification — was that the Southern Negro was exiled to a kind of no-man's land halfway between slavery and freedom. He was no longer a slave; he was not yet free. He was tied to the soil by the sharecrop and crop-lien systems. He was excluded from most professions and from many jobs. He was fobbed off not only with segregated schools, but with schools that were palpably inferior, and with 'separate' accommodations that were rarely 'equal.' He was expected not only to accept a position of social inferiority without protest, but to rejoice in it by playing the role of 'Uncle Tom.' At first gradually, then with dramatic speed, he was rendered politically impotent: 'grandfather' clauses, literacy tests, poll taxes, and — where these failed — naked intimidation, deprived him of the vote. In 1885 the Louisiana novelist, George Washington Cable, wrote:

> There is scarcely one public relation of life in the South where the Negro is not arbitrarily and unlawfully compelled to hold toward the white man the attitude of an alien, a menial, and a probable reprobate, by reason of his race and color. One of the marvels of future history will be that it was counted a small matter, by a majority of our nation, for six millions of people within it, made by its own decree a component part of it, to be subjected to a system of oppression so rank that nothing could make it seem small except the fact that they had already been ground under it for a century and a half. . . . It heaps upon him in every public place the most odious distinctions, without giving ear to the humblest plea concerning mental or moral character. It spurns his ambition, tramples upon his languishing self-respect, and indignantly refuses to let him either buy with money or earn by any excellence of inner life or outward behavior, the most momentary immunity from these public indignities.[7]

Thus stripped of power, of rights, and of dignity, the Negro was exposed, naked and helpless, to the mounting hostility of the white

7. G. W. Cable, 'The Freedman's Case in Equity,' *The Century Magazine*, January 1885.

tenant farmers and mill-villagers, who regarded him as a potential rival, and to the merciless enmity of popular leaders like James K. Vardaman who exploited racial hatreds for political purposes. And to add to all these injuries the Negro was abandoned by many of his quondam friends in the North. 'The fact is,' wrote the editor of *The Century Magazine*, 'that the Negroes constitute a peasantry wholly untrained in, and ignorant of, those ideas of constitutional liberty and progress which are the birthright of every white voter; that they are gregarious and emotional, and are easily led in any direction by white men of energy and determination.'

Southerners generally congratulated themselves that they had persuaded the North to concede them almost complete control of their domestic institutions. Yet the cost of the restoration of white rule on these terms was high, for white as well as for black, and for North as well as for South. By sanctioning the use of fraud and evasion to deny the Negro his legal rights, they weakened the moral standards of public life and the moral fiber of their people. By limiting Negro voting they discouraged and limited white suffrage, and thus struck a heavy blow at democracy in their section of the country. By identifying white supremacy with the Democrats they saddled a one-party system upon the South, and threw that party into the hands of the least enlightened elements of their society.

XLI

The American Mind During the Reconstruction Years

1. THE IMPACT OF WAR

Those who fight wars customarily console themselves that war is in some way creative. War, they urge, quickens the scientific spirit, inspires intellectual activity, calls forth new moral energies. This expectation was not wholly without foundation in American experience: the American Revolution, after all, loosened the floodgates of political talent, and the War of 1812 was followed by a new birth of nationalism. Would the Civil War leave the American people exhausted and embittered or would it discover new ideas and excite new energies? Would defeat produce an intellectual revival in the South or destroy initiative and hope? Would the immense organization of power and the heady sense of victory exalt the mind of the North or would habits of materialism and ruthlessness born of the war persist into the postwar era?

Defeat at the hands of Napoleon had inspired an intellectual renaissance in Prussia in the first years of the century; Denmark had emerged from the catastrophe of 1815 into a golden age of literature and philosophy; defeated France flourished far more vigorously after 1871 than did victorious Germany. But the defeated South experienced no such renaissance. The cultural life of the South did not recover for over a generation. Schools, colleges, libraries, and churches were destroyed or impoverished, and the intellectual life was paralyzed by poverty, by the preoccupation with sheer survival, and by obsession with the past and with defeat. 'You ask me to tell you the story of my last year,' wrote the poet Henry Timrod. 'I can embody it all in a few words: beggary, starvation, death, bitter grief, utter want of hope.' And the Kentucky-born scientist, Nathaniel Shaler, wrote:

> Not only did the Civil War maim the generation of Kentuckians to which I belonged, it also broke up the developing motives of intellectual culture of the commonwealth. Just before it I can see that while the ideals of culture were in a way still low and rather carnal, there was an eager reaching-out for better things; men and women were seeking, through history, literature, the fine arts, and in some measure through science, for a share in the higher life. Four years of civil war, which turned the minds of all towards what is at once the most absorbing and debasing interest of man, made an end of all this. . . .[1]

Many of the South's intellectual leaders — the novelist Simms, the poet Paul Hamilton Hayne, the sociologist George Fitzhugh — retired to live with poverty and bitterness for the rest of their lives. Others fled the South for the more prosperous or hospitable North and West: Frederick Barnard left the University of Mississippi to become president of Columbia University; the LeConte brothers gave up their scientific work in South Carolina and moved to the new University of California; the novelist George W. Cable of Louisiana took refuge in Massachusetts; the brilliant young architect Henry Hobson Richardson moved from New Orleans — via Paris — to Boston and New York; the Greek scholar Basil Gildersleeve and the poet-musician Sidney Lanier, both veterans of the Confederate army, found careers in the Johns Hopkins University in Baltimore. Such physical energies as the South was able to summon up went into material reconstruction and the building of the New South; such intellectual energies as it discovered were devoted chiefly to the elegiac celebration of the Lost Cause, or the defense of a Southern way of life.

The dream of the Old South was a phantasmagoria of the widespreading plantation and the white-pillared manor house, of families always old and distinguished, of aristocratic colonels and great ladies and girls who were lovelier and purer than girls elsewhere, of happy slaves singing in the cotton fields or dancing in the quarters on Satur-

1. Shaler, *Autobiography*, pp. 76–7.

day nights, of an independent yeomanry and picturesque mountaineers given to Elizabethan speech, of a special hospitality, a special grace, a special sense of chivalry and code of honor, a Cause forever right and forever Lost. The Old South was, in short, mankind before the Fall, but it was Southern mankind, not Yankee — a special moral and historical experience which Providence had vouchsafed to Southerners and which set them apart. As, with the passing years, the contrast between the dream of the Old South and the reality of the New — between the myth of plantation and slavery and the reality of tenant-farming and the mill villages — became ever more visible, Southerners grew more defiantly insistent upon it, for it was not only a myth but an emotional outlet and a moral value.

Meantime the North, lusty and arrogant, its power undiminished and its wealth enhanced by the war, was pushing forward to ever greater power and wealth. The decade after Appomattox was a period of relentless materialism, of tawdriness and vulgarity. It was the era of lachrymose novels like Augusta Evans's *St. Elmo* and Elizabeth Phelps's *Gates Ajar,* and the pious tales of Horatio Alger; of Rogers's plaster-cast statues and Currier and Ives lithographs and massive choruses of 10,000 voices shouting the Anvil Chorus to the accompaniment of cannon fired by electricity. It was the period of the brownstone front, the mansard roof, the stained-glass window, and the 'House Beautiful' described by Mark Twain in one of the happiest chapters of *Life on the Mississippi.*

The editor of *The Nation,* E. L. Godkin, called this a 'chromo civilization,' and Walt Whitman pronounced it:

> Cankered, crude, superstitious, and rotten. . . . Never was there, perhaps, more hollowness of heart than at present, and here in the United States. Genuine belief seems to have left us . . . I say that our New World democracy, however great a success in uplifting the masses out of their sloughs, in materialistic development, products, in a certain highly deceptive superficial popular intellectuality, is so far an almost complete failure in its social aspects, and in really grand religious, moral, literary and esthetic results.[2]

All true enough, yet we must not accept these verdicts too quickly or uncritically. In the very next year after *Democratic Vistas* came Whitman's 'Thou Mother with Thy Equal Brood' — the most exultant tribute to America that any poet has ever penned:

2. *Democratic Vistas,* 1871.

Beautiful world of new superber birth that rises to my eyes,
Like a limitless golden cloud filling the western sky,
Emblem of general maternity lifted above all,
Sacred shape of the bearer of daughters and sons, . . .
Thou wonder world yet undefined, unform'd, neither do I define thee, . . .
Land tolerating all, accepting all, not for the good alone, all good for thee,
Land in the realms of God, to be a realm unto thyself,
Under the rule of God to be a rule unto thyself.

For Whitman recognized what we are only now coming to appreciate, as we uncover the artifacts of culture beneath the debris of reconstruction, that along with so much that was tawdry and vulgar there was, in these years, an immense vitality, resourcefulness, enterprise, and imagination. For if the war had coarsened the characters of some, it had refined the spirits of others, and there was truth in the noble words of Justice Oliver Wendell Holmes, who bore the wounds of three battles:

> The generation that carried on the war has been set aside by its experience. Through our great good fortune, in our youth our hearts were touched with fire. It was given to us to learn at the outset that life is a profound and passionate thing. . . . We have seen with our own eyes, beyond and above the gold fields, the snowy heights of honor, and it is for us to bear the report to those who come after us.

2. LITERARY CURRENTS

And bear the report they did. The literary record of the war, North and South, was varied and rich. No public man of the nineteenth century wrote more eloquently than Lincoln, and a handful of his public papers can be ranked as world literature. The memoirs of the great captains like Grant and Sherman, Longstreet and Gordon, are unfailingly interesting but rarely possess the literary qualities that we find in the recollections of some of the lesser figures: Joshua Chamberlain's *The Passing of the Armies,* for example, or Thomas W. Higginson's *Army Life in a Black Regiment,* or General Taylor's brilliant *Destruction and Reconstruction.* Nor has any American war produced more memorable poetry. Henry Timrod and Paul Hayne sang the cause of the South — Lanier did not turn to poetry until after the war — and Walt Whitman was the laureate of the Union. In his poems we can read much of the history and the meaning of the war, from 'Eighteen Sixty-one':

Arm'd year—year of the struggle,
No dainty rhymes of sentimental love verses for you terrible year, . . .

to the lovely elegy for President Lincoln: 'When Lilacs Last in the Dooryard Bloom'd.'

Whitman spanned the whole period from the 'fifties to the 'eighties, linking together in his own philosophy and his poetic experiments the romanticism of the Golden Day and the naturalism of the Gilded. It was in the years after the war that he wrote many of his greatest poems — the 'Memories of President Lincoln,' 'Whispers of Heavenly Death,' 'Thou Mother with Thy Equal Brood,' and 'Passage to India.' These years, too, saw the emergence of the three great writers who were to dominate the American literary scene for almost half a century — Mark Twain, William Dean Howells, and Henry James — as well as minor writers like Bret Harte, whose sentimental stories of life in the mining camps appealed vastly to his generation, Sidney Lanier, and Emily Dickinson, whose exquisite genius awaited later recognition.

All three of the major literary figures who made their debuts during these years reached maturity only after the end of reconstruction; of the three Mark Twain alone belongs indubitably to the era which he named. Born in frontier Missouri where North meets South and East meets West, Sam Clemens spent his boyhood on the banks of the river whose epic he was to write, absorbing the rich human drama that passed before him. Before he was twenty-five he had worked as a journeyman printer and a newspaperman, and served an apprenticeship as a Mississippi pilot, learning the great river and the varied country that it traversed and the society that floated on its muddy waters. When the war came he enlisted, briefly, in a volunteer Confederate company, then — like his own Huck Finn — lit out for the Territory. It was there, in Nevada and California, that he found the material for his early stories, like 'The Celebrated Jumping Frog of Calaveras County,' and for *Roughing It*, the first full-length novel about the Far West. In 1867 he sailed to the Mediterranean and the Holy Land. *Innocents Abroad* (1869) gave him a reputation as a 'humorist' which he never quite lived down, and struck a note familiar in American literature and thought — the theme of American innocence and Old World corruption. *The Gilded Age* (1874), like *Roughing It*, drew on his acquaintance with the frontier, and with the Washington of Grant's administration. Thereafter it was the Mississippi river that provided inspiration for his greatest books. From the steamboat leadsmen's cry at two fathoms, 'by the mark, twain!' he took his literary name, and on the river were born his three immortal characters, Tom Sawyer, Huck Finn, and the Negro Jim. These early books — Roughing It, Innocents Abroad, Old Times on the Mississippi (later Life on the Mississippi), and Tom Sawyer, all written before 1877 — were, as Van Wyck Brooks observes, 'germs of a new American literature with a broader base in the national mind than the writers of New England had possessed. By his recreation of the frontier life in the great central valley, by his skill in recapturing its speech and its turns of mind, Mark Twain pre-empted for later writers a realm that was theirs by right of birth but might never have been theirs for literature if he had not cleared the way.' [3]

The second figure of the triumvirate, William Dean Howells, was, like Mark Twain, a son of the Middle Border and, like Twain too, came out of a background of printing and journalism into literature. In 1860, at the age of 23, Howells wrote an undistinguished campaign biography of Lincoln and was rewarded with the consulship at Venice. There he had time to immerse himself in European letters, and to study America from the vantage point of the Old World. Returning home at the close of the war he wrote critical essays for The Nation and travel sketches, stories, and theatricals for a wider public; in 1871 the Ohio printer's devil became editor-in-chief of the Atlantic, and made that house-organ of the Brahmins into a national periodical. Somehow he found time to carry on his editorial and critical work, while a steady stream of novels and stories flowed from his pen. As with Mark Twain's, Howells's early books anticipate his later themes: the conflict in manners, and in standards, of Boston and the hinterland (A Chance Acquaintance, 1873), the impact of the Old World on unsophisticated Americans (A Foregone Conclusion, 1875 and The Lady of the Aroostook, 1879), and the morality of the commonplace and the immorality of what passed for 'romance.' As Henry James wrote of him:

> He thinks scarcely anything too paltry to be interesting, that the small and vulgar have been terribly neglected, and would rather see an exact account of a sentiment or a character he stumbles against every day than a brilliant evocation of a passion or a type he has

3. The Times of Melville and Whitman, p. 297.

never seen. He adores the real, the natural, the colloquial, the optimistic, and the democratic.

Henry James, born eight years after Mark Twain and six after Howells, was the last of the three to make his literary bow, but he, too,
published his first important work during these reconstruction years.
Educated mostly abroad, James was never thereafter at home in America. 'It is a wretched business,' he wrote, 'this quarrel of ours with our
own society.' Although he could not come to terms with America, all his
life he remained loyal to its virtues. What fascinated him was the contrast between the simplicity and innocence of America and the rich,
dense, and often evil pattern of Europe. 'It is a complex fate being an
American,' he said, 'and one of the responsibilities it entails is fighting
against a superstitious veneration of Europe.' James's first story, 'A Passionate Pilgrim' (1871), was a variation on a theme exploited by his master, Hawthorne — the American pilgrim seeking his Old Home and suffering cruel repudiation. The theme of his first major novel, *Roderick
Hudson* (1876), was a similar one: the demoralizing effect of the Old
World — in this case the 'golden haze' of Italy — on the artistic integrity
of a young American sculptor. Here were two of the great themes with
which James was to be preoccupied for the remainder of his career
— New World innocence and Old World corruption, and the preservation of the integrity of the artist.

3. JOURNALISM

In the 'sixties and 'seventies New York City was the newspaper center
of the nation. Though such local papers as the *Springfield Republican*,
the *Boston Transcript*, the *Toledo Blade*, and the *Cincinnati Commercial* were influential, it was the great New York dailies — the *Tribune,
Sun, Evening Post*, and *Times* — that held a commanding position.

The dean of American newspapermen was the venerable William
Cullen Bryant, for half a century editor of the *Evening Post*. Few more
vigorous, discriminating and far-sighted critics have dealt with the
American scene than this poet-editor who combined respectability with
a zeal for righteousness. He lifted American journalism to a higher literary and ethical plane than it had heretofore occupied, and gave not
only his editorial column but his entire paper a dignity that assured it
the leading place in American journalism. But he lacked the talent to

appeal to a broad popular audience, and his influence was limited almost entirely to the intellectual elite.[4]

At the farthest remove from Bryant in ability to gauge and to influence popular opinion and to create a broad national paper was Horace Greeley of the *Tribune*, the greatest of American editors. Greeley was the spokesman of the plain people, not of New York alone but of the entire North. Practical, liberal, open-minded, fearless, and with boundless faith in democracy, he was a social reformer who fashioned a great paper as an instrument for social purposes. He founded the *Tribune* in 1841, drove its circulation up over the hundred thousand mark, and until the close of the Civil War exerted a greater influence over public opinion north of the Mason-Dixon Line than any other editor — and possibly than any other private citizen in the country. The weekly edition of his paper was read from Maine to Minnesota, and its fierce denunciations of the slave power did as much to inflame Northern opinion against that institution as all the agitation of the professional abolitionists. Greeley's erratic course during the war cost him some popularity, and his vindictive attacks upon President Johnson contrasted unpleasantly with the more tolerant attitude of Bryant. Yet throughout the whole of his long career Greeley found room in his paper for the liveliest literary intelligence, the most varied points of view, and the most extreme reforms. His thirty years of editorial leadership of the *Tribune* still constitutes the greatest achievement of personal journalism in our history.

A very different paper was *The Sun*, after 1868 under the control of Charles A. Dana, graduate of Harvard College and of Brook Farm. Dana had been trained to journalism under Greeley; he had seen service in the war under Grant, and was close to the center of power. By attracting to his staff some of the most skillful journalists of the day, Dana soon made *The Sun* the most popular paper in the country. With the passing of years, however, Dana grew increasingly cynical and even capricious, equally hostile to political corruption and to civil service reform, to organized capital and to organized labor; in the end he frittered away his influence and condemned his paper to sterility.

4. Says Allan Nevins, historian of the *Evening Post*, 'his journalistic vein had something of the narrowness which marked his poetic genius, and though the Post's editorials, political news, literary articles, and foreign correspondence were of the highest merit, they were for the few and not for the many.'

Less sensational than either Greeley or Dana was Henry J. Raymond of the New York *Times*. When he took over the paper he announced that he meant to 'navigate it into a position of independent thought and speech,' and that is what he did. The *Times*, under Raymond, was to its generation pretty much what the *Times* of today is to ours: intelligent, accurate, impartial, liberal, and judicious — and well-edited. In politics the *Times* tried to play a moderate and a moderating role. 'It probably came nearer the newspaper of the good time coming than any other paper in existence,' wrote Godkin of *The Nation*.

The most powerful newspaper in the country outside New York City was probably the *Springfield Republican*, edited from 1844 to 1915 by three generations of Samuel Bowleses. Like the *Tribune*, the *Republican* issued a weekly as well as a daily edition, and the weekly had a much wider circulation, spreading the liberal principles of its editors throughout New England and even west into the Ohio and Mississippi valleys. The second Samuel Bowles had charge of the paper during the critical years of the war and reconstruction; he supported Lincoln, advocated a magnanimous policy toward the defeated South, fought corruption under Grant, and held fast to principles of independence and honesty. One signal service of the *Republican* was to demonstrate the nation-wide influence that a provincial journal might wield, an example that was later to be followed by such editors as William Allen White with the Emporia (Kansas) *Gazette*.

More influential than many of the great daily papers were the weekly journals of opinion such as *The Nation, The Independent*, and *Harper's Weekly*. Of these three *The Nation*, under the Irish-born E. L. Godkin, was for the thirty years after 1865 easily the most influential journal. *The Nation*, declared James Bryce, was 'the best weekly not only in America but in the world.' A great editor, fearless, incisive, and vigorous, with high literary and intellectual standards, Godkin made his weekly the organ for enlightened liberalism and for the discussion of new ideas in every field of politics, literature, and science. Godkin enlisted the best minds in the country: Henry James and William James, Henry Adams, James Russell Lowell, William Dean Howells, C. W. Eliot and Daniel C. Gilman, Asa Gray and John Fiske — the list reads like an intellectual Who's Who of America. It was Lowell's considered opinion that 'the *Nation's* discussion of politics had done more good and influenced public opinion more than any agency, or all others combined, in the country.' Yet for all his high-mindedness, his unremitting hostility to corruption, Godkin found himself increasingly out of touch with the political and economic realities of his adopted country. His liberalism was doctrinaire; he had no understanding either of the farmer or the workingman, and was as bitter in his criticism of the Granger movement or organized labor as in his attacks on political or business corruption. 'He couldn't imagine a different kind of creature from himself in politics,' wrote William James shrewdly, and it is significant that the most fervent appreciation of Godkin came from his New England and English friends who, like him, often mistook good taste for good morals.

More securely in the American tradition was *Harper's Weekly*, long edited by the versatile and scholarly civil service reformer, George William Curtis. A family magazine, designed for entertainment rather than agitation, it was nevertheless a force for political decency, and Curtis came in time to occupy the position formerly held by Bryant. *Harper's Weekly* is chiefly remembered today for its lively coverage of the Civil War and for Winslow Homer's early drawings, as well as for being a vehicle of Thomas Nast's incomparable political cartoons. Less important than *Harper's Weekly* was *The Independent*, the leading religious paper of the postwar years, ably edited by Theodore Tilton and the famous Brooklyn preacher, Henry Ward Beecher.

The *Atlantic* and *Harper's Monthly*, high-minded but somewhat parochial, had for some time almost pre-empted the field of the monthly magazine. After the war they were joined by a number of newcomers which quickly made a place for themselves in the public affections. First in the field was *The Galaxy*, deliberately designed to compete with the *Atlantic* and ultimately absorbed by it. Mark Twain, Henry James, and many of the most popular English authors of the day wrote for the new magazine, and it gave extensive space to new developments in science. More interesting was California's bid for literary attention, the *Overland Monthly*, edited briefly by the brilliant Bret Harte whose 'Luck of Roaring Camp' and 'Outcasts of Poker Flat' first appeared in its pages. Harte abandoned the magazine at the end of a year, and though it lingered on for a long time it never lived up to its initial promise. A happier fate was reserved for that best of all children's magazines, the beloved *St. Nicholas*. Founded in 1873 by Mary Mapes Dodge — she had already written *Hans Brinker and the Silver Skates* — *St. Nicholas* managed to attract to its pages almost every distinguished author on both sides of the Atlantic, and many of the most talented artists and engravers as well. No magazine — not even *The Nation* — was better edited, and none ever gave more pleasure.

4. EDUCATION

The effect of the war on education in the South was little less than disastrous. Schoolhouses had fallen into ruin; teachers were killed or scattered; the impoverished South, less able to bear heavy taxes than at any time, now faced the additional burden of providing a public education for white and Negro alike. Higher education was all but paralyzed; many private institutions had lost part or the whole of their endowment; the very buildings of others had been destroyed; and few states were able to support their state universities. The University of North Carolina closed its doors for some years during reconstruction; the University of Louisiana was kept alive only by the heroic self-denial of a few professors who refused to abandon the stricken institution. Southern education did not fully recover from the effects of the war and reconstruction until the twentieth century.

In the North, by contrast, the temper and energy of the war and the postwar years stimulated education at almost every level. By the middle of the century the responsibility of the community to provide schooling for all its children was generally acknowledged, but that responsibility was faithfully discharged only in the realm of elementary education. In 1870, for example, there were only 200 public high schools in the entire country; a decade later the number had increased to some 800. As late as the 1870's it was still possible to challenge the propriety and even the legality of public support to high schools, and not until 1874 was this question forever laid to rest by the decision of Justice Thomas Cooley of the Michigan Supreme Court in the Kalamazoo case.

The student body of today, accustomed to a wide variety of courses, lavish equipment, well-trained teachers, and elaborate extracurricular activities, would find the schools of this postwar era shockingly primitive in almost every respect. Most children went to a 'little red schoolhouse'

— more picturesque than efficient — where some student working his way through a nearby college, or a girl too young to marry, taught all subjects and all grades. Teaching was largely by rote, discipline was capricious but severe, corporal punishment taken for granted, and extracurricular activities limited to games of marbles or of crack-the-whip on a muddy school ground. The backbone of the curriculum, a term which few of the teachers would have recognized, was the 'three R's' — reading, writing and arithmetic. Children learned spelling, and many other things, out of Noah Webster's Blue Backed Spellers, which had already done service for three generations of American boys and girls, and 'spelling-bees' were as exciting a part of school life as basketball games today. As important as Webster's *Spellers* were the McGuffey *Readers* of which over 100 million were sold in the years between 1836 and the end of the century. In an age when schools did not have libraries, and few children had any books at home, McGuffey's Readers, by introducing children to 'selections' from the best of English and American literature, set the popular literary standard for two or three generations. The novelist Hamlin Garland, who went to country schools in Iowa during these years, remembered that 'from the pages of McGuffey's Readers I learned to know and love the poems of Scott, Byron, Southey, Wordsworth, and a long line of English masters, and got my first taste of Shakespeare.' The average schoolteacher of that day was no less concerned with molding character than with molding mind, and to this purpose the McGuffey Readers, with their pious axioms of conduct and their moral tales, made a somewhat heavy-handed contribution.

The average teacher was a schoolma'am. The war had drawn men from teaching into the ranks of the army, or to industry and business, and the feminization of teaching was in full swing. By 1870 almost two-thirds of the public schoolteachers were women — a number which increased through the rest of the century. With only twelve 'normal' schools in the country at the outbreak of the Civil War, the great majority of teachers were untrained, and it was generally supposed that any girl not otherwise occupied was competent to teach school. In due course states created boards of education designed to establish minimum requirements for teaching and to maintain standards of a sort, and gradually teaching took on some of the characteristics of a profession.

During the reconstruction years nine states provided for compulsory school attendance for at least part of the year, and some even enforced these laws.

In 1867 Congress created the office of United States Commissioner of Education to 'collect statistics and facts concerning the conditions and progress of education' and 'to diffuse information regarding the organization and management of schools and methods of teaching.' Though the office was reduced to the status of a bureau, and systematically starved by a niggardly Congress, it managed nevertheless to attract to its service a number of distinguished educators: first Henry Barnard, founder and editor of the famous *American Journal of Education* and dean of educational statesmen; then the learned philosopher, William T. Harris, long-time superintendent of schools of St. Louis. It was under Harris's auspices that the first public kindergarten in the country was opened, in 1873, and it was Harris, too, whose long series of annual reports on public schools did for his generation what Horace Mann's Reports had done for an earlier generation, providing a rationalization of public education in an industrial age.

What was later known as 'progressive' education received its formulation and earliest application during these years. The doctrines of the Swiss Johann Pestalozzi, and of the German Friedrich Froebel, had been introduced to America in the years just before the war; now they triumphed in the work of Edward A. Sheldon of the famous Oswego State Normal School, whose graduates carried the new gospel from that upstate New York Zion throughout the East and the Middle West. Almost equally important was the work of Colonel Francis Parker who had studied pedagogy in Germany, returned to be superintendent of schools in Quincy, Massachusetts, and, with the support of Charles Francis Adams, quietly carried through a revolution in education whose philosophy and techniques anticipated, and deeply influenced, John Dewey two decades later.

Higher education in the North, meantime, experienced something of a renaissance. This renaissance can be traced to a number of factors: the enactment of the Morrill Land Grant Act of 1862; the demand of business and the professions for specialized knowledge and skills; the new pressures for educational facilities for those heretofore neglected; and the emergence of a remarkable group of educational statesmen, most of them deeply influenced by German educational ideas and practices.

As early as 1850 the legislature of Michigan had petitioned Congress for help in founding a college of agriculture; three years later Jonathan Turner, tireless champion of agricultural education, persuaded the legislature of his state of Illinois to second the appeal. Thereafter the idea gathered force, and in 1859 a bill looking to federal support for agricultural education passed both houses of Congress only to be vetoed by President Buchanan. Three years later President Lincoln gladly signed a similar but more generous bill sponsored by Justin Morrill of Vermont. The Morrill Land Grant Act of 1862 gave to each state 30,000 acres of public land for each Congressman, to be used as endowment or support of a college of agricultural and mechanical arts. The Morrill Act, undoubtedly the most important piece of educational legislation passed in this country in the nineteenth century, was to serve as a precedent for federal aid to education in the twentieth century. Under its generous provisions land grant colleges were founded in every state of the Union. Some states gave their lands to existing institutions; others to private universities; most established new agricultural and mechanical schools. Such varied universities as the University of Illinois, Purdue University, the Massachusetts Institute of Technology, and Cornell University — all founded during the reconstruction years — profited from the far-sighted wisdom of Jonathan Turner and Justin Morrill.

The scientific revolution and the growing complexity of American economic life gave rise to a demand for education more closely related to the needs of the day. One result was encouragement of the natural sciences at the expense of classical and humanistic studies. Another was the establishment of numerous professional and vocational schools, and soon schools of law, medicine, architecture, and engineering began to turn out graduates fitted by special training to the demands of the new economy. Some of the older states assigned their Morrill Land Grant money to schools of science or engineering at existing institutions: Massachusetts turned her money over to the new Institute of Technology, and New York's princely grant of one million acres provided a large part of the endowment of the new Cornell University. Meantime private philanthropy created a series of new engineering schools: Columbia's School of Mines in 1864, Lehigh University in 1865, Stevens Institute in 1870, and a School of Mines in Colorado as early as 1874 — two years before that Territory was admitted as a state!

In these years, too, educational leaders sought to provide in America the kind of facilities for graduate study that had long flourished abroad. Ever since George Ticknor and George Bancroft had led the way to Göttingen University in the second decade of the century, eager graduates of American colleges had poured over to Berlin, Jena, Halle, Leipzig, and Munich in ever-growing numbers, bringing back with them admiration for German scholarship, the seminar, and the Ph.D. degree. Yale awarded the first Ph.D. granted in America in 1861 and ten years later organized a graduate school; Harvard followed in 1872; and President Andrew D. White, who had studied at Berlin, made provision for graduate studies on the German model at the newly founded Cornell. With the opening of the Johns Hopkins University in 1876 the German model was firmly transplanted in the New World.

The third influence — a quickened sense of equalitarianism — required provision for higher education for women and for Negroes. Wesleyan Academy for girls had opened at Macon, Georgia, as early as 1836, and the gallant Mary Lyon had persevered against heavy odds to found Mount Holyoke College at South Hadley, Massachusetts, in 1837, while Oberlin — pioneer in this as in so many things — adopted coeducation in the late 1830's. The war and postwar years saw the founding of a number of new colleges for women: Vassar, the gift of a rich brewer of Poughkeepsie, New York, opened its doors in 1867; Wellesley College dates from 1870 and Smith College from 1871, while Hunter College in New York City, destined to be one of the largest women's colleges in the world, was likewise chartered in 1870. Meantime Iowa led the way among the state universities in adopting coeducation, and most of the state and municipal universities in the North followed its example. At a time when Englishmen were anxiously debating the propriety of establishing their first college for women — Girton, in Cambridge — the United States could boast a dozen flourishing women's colleges, and a growing acceptance of coeducation as the common sense of the matter.

Oberlin College had admitted Negroes almost from its foundation, and before the Civil War Negroes had founded a university of their own at Wilberforce, Ohio. Few Negroes in the South were prepared to take advantage of higher education in the decade after emancipation, and the institutions that were established for them were largely industrial training colleges. Thus General Clinton Fisk, who had been a colonel of a colored regiment during the war, opened a training school for Negroes in Nashville, Tennessee, in 1866 which eventually evolved into Fisk University. In 1868 General Samuel Armstrong — he too had led a Negro regiment and had worked with the Freedmen's Bureau — established Hampton Institute in Virginia; a few years later its most distinguished graduate, Booker T. Washington, was to found his famous school at Tuskegee, Alabama.

A fourth contribution to the educational renaissance was the emergence, during these postwar years, of the most remarkable group of statesmen in the history of higher education in America. As early as the 1850's Henry Tappan — the first philosopher of higher education since Jefferson — had tried to make Michigan a real university, but had been frustrated by a short-sighted board of trustees. In 1869 Harvard departed from her long tradition of clerical presidents and elected a 35-year-old chemist, Charles W. Eliot, to the presidency. Eliot summed up in himself many of the new forces that were quickening educational thought in America: he had spent some time observing universities in Germany; he was a scientist rather than a theologian, and a scientist prepared to accept the teachings of Darwinian evolution; he was peculiarly sensitive to the changes brought about by the Civil War and the industrial revolution and determined to bring Harvard abreast of those changes. He signalized his advent to the presidency by a revolution in the organization, curriculum, and academic policies of the university. Though he was not the first to advocate the elective system, his tireless championship of freedom of choice helped establish the system in public favor. Of greater ultimate significance was Eliot's rehabilitation of the schools of law and medicine, which he placed upon a sound professional basis. So significant was his achievement, and so widespread his influence — through his public statements, his famous 'five-foot shelf' of books, his service on national committees — that he came to be regarded as the first citizen of his country.

While Eliot was transforming Harvard, two other remarkable educational statesmen were making new universities. Even as Grant was hammering at the lines around Richmond, the industrialist-philanthropist, Ezra Cornell, joined hands with the statesman-scholar Andrew Dickson White, to create a university far above Cayuga's waters, at Ithaca, New York. The new Cornell University, based on income from the Morrill Land Grant and on gifts from Ezra Cornell, was to be both public and private and thus to pioneer in a new pattern of higher education. Cornell induced White to accept the presidency of the new institution. Graduate of Yale College, student at Paris and Berlin, professor at the University of Michigan, chairman of the New York State committee on education, White had long dreamed of a university that should be the equal of those of Germany and France, and now he was given a free hand to create one. He decided that Cornell would have no barriers of color, sex, or faith; it would treat students like adults, encourage mature scholarship, maintain professional standards for the study of engineering and agriculture, and be a stronghold of academic freedom. Opened in 1868, Cornell set a pattern, later followed by Hopkins and Chicago, of springing to life full-panoplied in academic armor.

The fourth important educational statesman was Daniel Coit Gilman, who created the Johns Hopkins University. A classmate of White's at Yale, Gilman had studied abroad and then returned to Yale to help found the Sheffield Scientific School, and to dream of doing for Yale what Eliot was doing for Harvard. When in 1871 the Yale Corporation elected a staunch champion of academic conservatism, Noah Porter, to the presidency, Gilman went west to take the presidency of the new University of California. In 1874 a Baltimore philanthropist, Johns Hopkins, left $7 million to found a university and a hospital; when the trustees of the university turned to President Eliot of Harvard, White of Cornell, and Angell of Michigan for advice, each one recommended that they make Gilman president and give him a free hand. They did. Gilman created a university largely on a German model, with emphasis on graduate study and scholarship. He put his money in men, not buildings, and collected not only a distinguished faculty but a distinguished group of younger 'Fellows' — among them the future President Woodrow Wilson, Josiah Royce and John Dewey, leaders of two schools of philosophy, J. Franklin Jameson and Frederick Jackson Turner, historians, Walter Hines Page and Newton D. Baker, to be prominent in the public life of the next generation. Woodrow Wilson said, later, of Gilman that he was 'the first to create and organize in America a university in which the discovery and dissemination of new truth were conceded a rank superior to mere instruction.' In all this Gilman set a standard which most great universities were to follow in the next century.

5. SCIENTIFIC INTERESTS

'Amid the din of war, the heat of party, the deviltries of politics, and the poison of hypocrisy,' wrote the Harvard mathematician, Benjamin Peirce, 'science will be inaudible, incapable, incoherent and inanimate.' The war greatly speeded up the application of science to practical problems, but retarded science itself. Out of the war came marked improvements in rifles, artillery, naval ordnance, torpedoes, and bridge building; and distinguished engineers like Washington Roebling of Brooklyn Bridge fame and James B. Eads, who spanned the Mississippi at St. Louis, learned much from their Civil War experiences. The war provided, too, a mass of experience, and of statistical data useful later for the study of medicine and especially of surgery. But, inevitably, the war drew scientists from their laboratories, interrupted the work of universities and of government bureaus and expeditions, and tended to put a premium on what was destructive in science. Yet — as with education — forces released by the war, as well as new ideas from abroad, stimulated scientific thought and achievement during the reconstruction years.

Tocqueville had observed that a democracy almost inevitably addressed itself to what was practical and immediate in science; that generalization was, for the most part, valid for this period. These years witnessed a series of large-scale geological and topographical explorations of the Far West; the organization of research at the Lawrence and Sheffield scientific schools and at government bureaus in Washington; far-reaching developments in geology, paleontology, botany, and ethnology; and the popularization of science by men like John Fiske and Edward Youmans.

The Far West had been acquired only in the 1840's, and much of it was still unexplored and unmapped; indeed the myth of the 'Great American Desert' still persisted. With settlement ready to penetrate the Last West, the need for exploring its geology and geography, its flora and fauna, was urgent, and in the decade after the war the Federal Government undertook to fill the need. The Wilkes Exploring Expedition of the 'forties, the Railroad Surveys and Boundary Surveys and Coastal Surveys of the 'fifties, provided the pattern. First in the field was the army-sponsored Geological Survey of the Fortieth Parallel under the leadership of the gifted Clarence King of the Sheffield Scientific School, whom John Hay called 'the best and brightest man of his generation.' Meanwhile the Corps of Engineers launched a large-scale expedition to explore the territory west of the 100th meridian; this was entrusted to an army engineer, George M. Wheeler, who took with him a staff of geologists, ethnologists, and zoologists and whose 40-odd volumes of reports were of immense value to American science. The Hayden Geological Survey of the Territories, sponsored by the General Land Office and directed by a distinguished professor from the University of Pennsylvania, mapped much of the *terra incognita* of the Far West and uncovered much of its mineral and botanical resources. Easily the most dramatic of the Western expeditions was that headed by the remarkable John Wesley Powell, a one-armed veteran of the Civil War who had already piloted four boats down the 900 miles of the Green and Colorado rivers of the West. In 1870 the Department of the Interior launched him upon a series of expeditions into the West, and in 1875 he directed the Survey of the Rocky Mountain Regions. Out of all this came not only a new discovery of the American West, but, in 1879, the creation of the United States Geological Survey headed first by Clarence King and then by Powell.

An important part of the discovery of America was the emergence of a new and more scientific interest in its native races. As Major Powell wrote in 1878, 'The field of research is speedily narrowing because of the rapid change in the Indian population now in progress; all habits, customs, and opinions are fading away; even languages are disappearing; and in a very few years it will be impossible to study our North American Indians in their primitive condition, except from recorded history.' Lewis Morgan had led the way with his work on the Iroquois; in the 'seventies he turned his attention to the Indians of the West and the Southwest, and in 1877 published *Ancient Society*, an argument for the common origin and evolution of all races which owed a great deal to Darwin. During these same years the historian Hubert Howe Bancroft published his five-volume *History of the Native Races of the Pacific Coast*, and the Swiss-born Adolphe Bandelier launched his pioneering explorations of the archaeology of ancient Mexico and the pueblo Indians of the Southwest which led — among other things — to his fascinating novel, *The Delight Makers*. The year 1879 saw, too, the establishment of the United States Bureau of Ethnology and the founding of the Archaeological Institute of America.

Meantime these same productive years witnessed notable contributions from the universities — particularly from Yale, Harvard, and Pennsylvania. At Harvard Asa Gray, stout champion of the Darwinian theory, brought to completion his *Flora of North America*. In the midst of the war James Dwight Dana, dean of academic geologists, published his famous *Manual of Geology*, which reflected the evolutionary findings of the great Charles Lyell in England. Dana's colleague at Yale, the paleontologist Othneil Marsh, organized a series of scientific expeditions into the West and published his famous *Vertebrate Life in America*, which placed the study of fossils on a scientific basis. At the Smithsonian Institution the veteran zoologist Spencer Baird brought to completion his *History of North American Birds*.

All this work revealed growing awareness of the urgent need to conserve resources. Everyone could see that the native races were being wiped out, or losing their identity, nor did it take much perspicacity to appreciate the disappearance of the buffalo and the wild pigeon and the beaver. More serious was the threat to soil, forest, and water, and other natural resources. Pioneer in alerting the American people to this threat was the versatile George Perkins Marsh, diplomat, historian, philologist, and scientist. From observing the waste of soil and forest in his native Vermont, and from experience in Turkey and Asia Minor, he came to appreciate the consequences of the violation of nature's laws. In 1864 he published his masterpiece, *Man and Nature* (later published as *The Earth as Modified by Human Action*), which has justly been called the most influential American geographical work of the nineteenth century. It dealt, in a broad way, with 'man as a disturbing agent,' described the destruction of animal and vegetable life by men, and argued with special emphasis the importance of conservation of forests. Once the forest is removed, he pointed out, 'the face of the earth is no longer a sponge, but a dust heap. Stripped of its vegetable glebe, the soil grows less and less productive, and less able to protect itself by weaving a new network of roots to bind its particles together, a new carpeting of turf to shield it from wind and sun and scouring rain.' Marsh's book exerted a powerful influence on contemporaries in America and Europe, and contributed to the crystallization of conservation sentiment. Ferdinand Hayden carried it with him on his expedition, and John Wesley Powell applied its central thesis to his study of the problem of land and water on the High Plains. As early as 1874 Powell had warned Congress that much of the land west of the 100th meridian, comprising some two-fifths of the entire nation, 'has a climate so arid that agriculture cannot be pursued without irrigation.' Four years later he brought out his memorable *Report on the Arid Regions of the West* which warned against the application of Eastern techniques of farming to the High Plains, argued the necessity of farm units of not less than 2500 acres, emphasized the paramount importance of water and access to water supplies, and insisted that the right to water should inhere in the land.

These fermenting years were distinguished, too, by contributions to both pure science and popular science. In 1876 Edward Pickering became director of the astronomical observatory at Harvard, and began that remarkable photographic record of the stellar universe which was to command world-wide interest. At Yale Willard Gibbs, the most gifted mathematician of his generation, made fundamental contributions to mathematical physics with his papers on the equilibrium of heterogeneous substances. William James opened the first psychological laboratory in America in the early 'seventies, and there began those studies that were to culminate in the publication of his epoch-making *Principles of Psychology*. Meantime at the other end of the scientific spectrum, John Fiske was engaged in reconciling Darwinian evolution, Spencerian sociology and liberal religion in the *Outlines of Cosmic Philosophy*, a work that sprawled through four volumes, and his friend Edward Youmans was popularizing the findings of the new science through the *Popular Science Monthly* and — more substantially — the many volumes of his International Scientific Series.

6. THE FINE ARTS

Even before the Civil War the architectural renaissance sponsored by Thomas Jefferson and Benjamin Latrobe, and its offspring the Greek Revival, had petered out, and the most promising of American architects, James Renwick and Richard Upjohn, had turned to Gothic. Renwick's Grace Church and St. Patrick's Cathedral, and Upjohn's Trinity Church and Church of the Ascension, all in New York City, gave promise of a Gothic revival like that which flourished in the England of Ruskin and Gilbert Scott. What came instead was a kind of pseudo-Gothic. Used in many large public buildings, such as the Smithsonian Institution in Washington, it had a peculiar fascination for college trustees, who littered the academic landscape from Maine to California with pseudo-Gothic structures such as Harvard's Memorial Hall or Walker Hall at Amherst College. The enraptured John Fiske of Harvard urged that 'we honestly confess our stupidity and show some grain of sense by copying the Oxford and Cambridge buildings literally.' Harvard did not accept this advice but Trinity College in Hartford, Connecticut, did, and Knox College out on the Illinois prairies, and a few years later the new University of Chicago reproduced Oxford, 'battlemented towers' and all.

By the 'sixties, says Lewis Mumford, 'architectural anarchy had reached a point at which disorder had resulted almost in physical brutality, and ugliness conducted a constant assault and battery wherever one turned one's eye. When one beholds some of the famous buildings of the period, one must charitably assume that they were built by the blind for a generation that dwelt in darkness.' Like much of the oratory of the period, this American Gothic was florid, vain, and vapid. Just as the oratory substituted rhetoric for ideas, so the architecture substituted ostentatious ornamentation for function and sincerity. Spires and battlements, gables and buttresses, stained glass windows and gargoyles, jig-saw scroll work, ornate fireplaces and mantels, elaborate hangings, endless bric-a-brac — all of this proclaimed the emptiness and insincerity of the architects of that generation and confessed the decline in American taste since the simplicity and dignity of Jefferson and Bulfinch.

Along with a yearning for the medieval went a yen for the exotic. It was a day when the *Rubáiyát* of Omar Khayyám represented the highest reaches of philosophy to many a village Socrates; when romantic ladies swooned over Bayard Taylor's *Poems of the Orient;* when P. T. Barnum erected his fantastic *Iranistan* outside Bridgeport in Indo-Persian style, and the painter Frederick Church built the dazzling *Olana* on the banks of the Hudson in the Persian manner, complete with minarets and domes and spires and a roof of green, red, and black; when Peter Wight created the National Academy of Design in New York to display a multitude of styles, and the eccentric Erastus Salisbury projected a ten-story 'Historic Monument of the American Republic' with each story in a different architectural style; and when James McNeill Whistler and Mary Cassatt were revealing the beauties of Japanese art and Henry Adams and John La Farge discovering the South Seas.

Out of all this welter of the archaeological and the exotic two distinguished architects emerged: Henry Hobson Richardson and Richard Morris Hunt. It was Richardson who ushered in the new day of American architecture. As a student in Paris, he fell under the influence of the great medievalist Viollet-le-Duc. Richardson's fame is associated with the attempt to transplant Romanesque architecture to the United States — an attempt, it would seem, foredoomed to failure. Yet by contrast with the jerry-built structures of so many of his contemporaries, Richardson's buildings have an integrity that goes far to explain their popularity. Such was Richardson's power that he enjoyed a personal success greater than any other figure in American architecture before Frank Lloyd Wright. 'To live in a house built by Richardson,' wrote one art historian, 'was a cachet of wealth and taste; to have your nest-egg in one of his banks gave you a feeling of perfect security; to worship in one of his churches made one think one had a pass key to the Golden Gates.' John Hay and Henry Adams employed Richardson to build their joint house on Lafayette Square, Washington, D.C., and while Adams took for granted that anywhere an Adams lived was better than the White House, he was happy to know that his house really was better. Richardson's greatest monuments were Trinity Church, Boston, for which John La Farge did the stained-glass windows, Austin Hall of Harvard University, and the fortresslike Marshall Field warehouse in Chicago. Although it was these public buildings that contemporaries most prized, later critics have been more impressed by Richardson's influence on domestic architecture, particularly in his use of shingles to create low, rambling houses which adapted themselves to the landscape of the New England seacoast, and which anticipated some of the innovations of Frank Lloyd Wright.

Contemporary with Richardson and, like him, trained in the École des Beaux Arts, was Richard Morris Hunt, brother of the eminent painter. Hunt was the favored architect of the new American plutocracy. He introduced to America the beauty and lavishness of the French Renaissance and built for American millionaires magnificent country houses patterned after French châteaux, or palatial town houses that resembled French hôtels-de-ville. Yet French châteaux were no more suited to the genius of America than Romanesque fortresses, and Hunt's influence remained limited.

Viollet-le-Duc had prophesied an architecture of metal and glass, and even as Richardson and Hunt wrought in their derivative styles, these materials were working a revolution in architecture. There had been anticipations abroad — London's great Crystal Palace of 1851, for example — but the first American building boldly to employ these new materials was the old Grand Central railroad station in New York, whose train-shed was modeled on those of London and Paris stations. More important architecturally was the work of the bridge-builders, notably John Roebling and his son Washington, who all through the 'sixties and 'seventies supervised the construction of that *stupor mundi*, the Brooklyn Bridge.

These years saw the beginning of the organization and professionalization of art and architecture in the United States. The American Institute of Architects had been founded in the late 'fifties, and the National Academy of Design in the early 'sixties. In that decade, too, the Massachusetts Institute of Technology, and then Cornell University, offered the first formal training for architects, and before long Pennsylvania and Columbia followed their example. In 1874 Harvard appointed the gifted but reactionary Charles Eliot Norton to the first chair of fine arts at any American university. The early 'seventies saw the beginnings of three of the greatest of American museums. Boston opened her Museum of Fine Arts; a group of New York philanthropists chartered the Metropolitan Museum of Art; and in the national capital William Corcoran — son of an Irish immigrant — built and endowed the gallery that bears his name.

Important, too, in the artistic history of the postwar generation was the development of landscape architecture and of city planning associated so largely with the work of Frederick Law Olmsted. Before the war Olmsted had won a reputation as a sociological interpreter of the South and of England. In 1858 he was appointed chief architect of the proposed Central Park in New York City, and quickly became absorbed in the three closely related problems that were to command his attention for the rest of his life: city planning, landscape architecture, and the preservation of the natural beauties of the nation. He laid out Central Park, Prospect Park in Brooklyn, the Capitol grounds in Washington, the park system of Boston and, eventually, the Chicago World's Fair of 1893. He was chiefly instrumental in preserving Yosemite valley as a national park and in protecting Niagara Falls from the worst ravages of commercialization. Through his books, editorials, and lectures he dramatized to his generation the consequences of heedless urban growth and of the reckless expropriation of the natural resources of the nation.

The most distinguished of the American landscape painters of the prewar years, George Inness, revisited Italy in the years after the war and found not only new subjects for his gifted brush, but new techniques as well. Inness's last years were in many respects like those of Whitman: the spreading canvas of 'Peace and Plenty,' painted in 1865, was the counterpart in paint of Whitman's 'Thou Mother with Thy Equal Brood.' In the next decade Inness painted a whole series of panoramic landscapes that rank among the best of their kind in American art: 'Harvest Scene in the Delaware Valley,' for example, and 'The Approaching Storm,' and Italian scenes such as 'Tivoli,' and 'Lake Albano.'

The war itself produced one of the major American artists. Trained as a lithographer, Winslow Homer had been sent to the front to do sketches for *Harper's Weekly*; his wartime drawings were the best to come out of the war — 'Prisoners at the Front' and 'The Sharpshooter,' for example, or some of his Negro sketches. In the postwar years — his middle period — Homer turned to genre painting and lifted that difficult art to the highest level it had attained in America: 'Morning Bell' (1866), 'High Tide at Long Branch' (1869), the beloved 'Snap-the-Whip' (1872), the colorful 'The Carnival' (1875). Homer's greatest period, however, was still ahead.

Meantime the most original genius among American painters was experimenting with new techniques and new subjects. Thomas Eakins had studied at the École des Beaux Arts, but that artistic finishing school left little impression on him. Back in Philadelphia in 1870 he began to turn out pictures whose unashamed realism forfeited for him the popularity that his talent merited: paintings of swimmers, fishermen, oarsmen, and professional men and women busy with their work. 'Respectability in art,' said Eakins, 'is appalling' and his own art was marked by a homespun realism and a lack of respectability reminiscent of the best seventeenth century Dutch painting. A professor of anatomy at the University of Pennsylvania, Eakins brought to his art a scientific knowledge of the human body, and portrayed it with an intimacy that shocked many of his contemporaries. His great achievement during these early years was 'The Gross Clinic' (1875); it was hung in the Centennial Exposition, not in the art collection — it was thought to be too unpleasant for that — but in the medical building. In the 'seventies Eakins turned from teaching anatomy to teaching art, and though ignored by the fashionable collectors of his own day deeply influenced the whole next generation of American painters; Sloan, Henri, Pennell, Glackens, and many others acknowledged him their master.

In art, as in literature and education, this was an era of popularization. When in the 1860's the Beecher sisters advised American women on the decoration of their homes, they recommended an expenditure of no less than $30 on chromos to be hung in the parlor: 'Miss Oakley's charming cabinet picture of The Little Scrap-book Maker; Eastman Johnson's Barefoot Boy, Newman's Blue Gentian, and Albert Bierstadt's Sunset in the Yosemite Valley.' If the frames were too expensive, the Beecher sisters added, the decorators 'could make rustic frames of twigs with the bark still on them, and glue on these a cluster of acorns or pine cones at the corners.' No wonder Godkin called this a 'chromo civilization'; certainly Currier and Ives seemed to dominate the artistic scene. Equally characteristic were the famous Rogers groups — plaster casts fashioned by John Rogers to illustrate some familiar event in history or some homely story: 'The Emancipation Proclamation,' 'The Slave Auction,' 'The Checker Game,' 'Fetching the Doctor.' Rogers himself deprecated his 'art,' but a writer in one of the popular magazines asserted confidently that 'what Hogarth is in the pencil, Canova and Michelangelo in marble, Reynolds and Landseer on canvas — all the excellences of these masters in art have their illustration in the plaster of John Rogers.' Altogether Rogers sold over 100,000 of his plaster figures in the generation after the war.

Popular art reached its climax — or its nadir — at the Centennial Exposition which opened in Fairmont Park, Philadelphia, in May 1876. America's first world exposition, it was designed to dramatize cultural independence as much as to celebrate political: Bayard Taylor wrote an ode for the occasion, the venerable Whittier composed a Hymn, Sidney Lanier provided a cantata, and Richard Wagner composed a special march. The 10 million visitors who swarmed through the fair grounds that summer could feast their eyes on a rich display of architecture: Memorial Hall — 'a noble edifice of Renaissance design' — a Turkish building 'of true Oriental type,' a Moorish Pavilion, a Tunisian Bazaar, and a Japanese pagoda. The American state buildings, most of them in Victorian Gothic, were almost as bizarre as the Oriental. Most Old World nations sent over examples of their art, and a large exhibit of American paintings included not only old masters like Stuart and Copley but younger painters like Winslow Homer, John La Farge, and Alden Weir. What made the deepest impression on the visitors, however, was the exhibit of industrial art and of machinery. As William Dean Howells wrote, 'It is still in these things of iron and steel that the national genius most freely speaks; by and by the inspired marbles, the breathing canvases, the great literature; for the present America is voluble in the strong metals and their infinite uses.' And an English reporter, contemplating the many inventions and machines on display, wrote that 'the American mechanizes as the old Greeks sculptured and as the Venetians painted.'

Two of America's major poets used the Centennial to reflect on the significance of America in history. James Russell Lowell was satirical and bitter: Columbia

> puzzled what she should display
> Of true home-make on her Centennial Day

asked Brother Jonathan, who advised her:

> Show 'em your Civil Service, and explain .
> How all men's loss is ever'body's gain. . . .
> Show your State Legislatures; show your Rings;
> And challenge Europe to produce such things. . .

Sidney Lanier's Cantata was more philosophical. When Columbia asked how long she would survive, her 'Good Angel' answered:

> Long as thine Art shall love true love,
> Long as thy Science truth shall know,
> Long as thine Eagle harms no Dove,
> Long as thy Law by law shall grow,
> Long as thy God is God above,
> Thy brother every man below,
> So long dear Land of all my love,
> Thy name shall shine, thy fame shall glow.[5]

5. Lowell's poem can be found in *The Nation*, 5 August 1875; it is not reprinted in his *Collected Works*. Lanier's Cantata is in the appendix to the *Poems of Sidney Lanier*, edited by his wife.

Bibliography

GENERAL WORKS

1. DICTIONARIES, ENCYCLOPEDIAS, AND REFERENCE BOOKS

The American Historical Review (1895–   ) reviews all new historical literature, and includes important articles and documents. The annual *Reports* of the American Historical Association (1889–   , overlapped by 5 vols. of *Papers*, 1886–91, General Index, 1884–1914) include many other articles, monographs, and source material.

The Mississippi Valley Historical Review (1915–   ), now *The Journal of American History*, also contains many general articles and documents.

Bureau of the Census, *Historical Statistics of the United States; Colonial Times to 1957*, and *Statistical Abstract of the United States* (81 annual editions through 1960).

J. R. Commons (ed.), *The Documentary History of American Industrial Society* (10 vols.).

Oscar Handlin *et al.*, *Harvard Guide to American History*. Part i, Status, Methods and Presentation; Part ii, Materials and Tools; Parts iii–vi, classified bibliographies on successive periods.

James L. Harrison, Paul C. Beach, *et al.* (eds.), *Biographical Directory of the American Congress, 1774–1949*.

Allen Johnson & Dumas Malone (eds.), *The Dictionary of American Biography* (22 vols.), and supplementary volumes.

Richard B. Morris, *Encyclopedia of American History*.

Edwin R. A. Seligman, Alvin Johnson, *et al.* (eds.), *Encyclopedia of the Social Sciences*.

2. HISTORIES OF THE UNITED STATES

Edward Channing, *History of the United States* (6 vols. and General Index, covering the period to 1865).

H. S. Commager & R. B. Morris (eds.), *The New American Nation Series.*

John B. McMaster, *History of the People of the United States from the Revolution to the Civil War* (8 vols. covering the period 1784–1861).

Arthur M. Schlesinger and Dixon R. Fox (eds.), *History of American Life* (13 vols.). Social development is stressed.

3. ECONOMIC AND SOCIAL HISTORY

GENERAL. H. U. Faulkner, *American Economic History;* E. C. Kirkland, *A History of American Economic Life;* F. J. Turner, *The Frontier in American History;* Joseph Dorfman, *The Economic Mind in American Civilization.*

LABOR. J. R. Commons *et al., History of Labour in the United States* (4 vols.); H. Harris, *American Labor;* S. Perlman, *History of Trade Unionism in the United States.*

IMMIGRATION. Louis Adamic (ed.), *The Peoples of America* (9 vols.); Maurice Davie, *World Immigration;* Oscar Handlin, *The Uprooted;* Marcus L. Hansen, *The Immigrant in American History* and *The Atlantic Migration 1607–1860;* Carl Wittke, *We Who Built America; the Saga of the Immigrant.*

OTHER PHASES. Roy M. Robbins, *Our Landed Heritage: The Public Domain, 1776–1936.* Tariff: F. W. Taussig, *Tariff History of the U.S.,* and Edward Stanwood, *American Tariff Controversies in the 19th Century* (2 vols.). Banking and Finance: D. R. Dewey, *Financial History of the U.S.;* W. J. Schultz & M. B. Caine, *Financial Development of the United States;* and Milton Friedman and Anna Jacobson Schwartz, *A Monetary History of the United States.* Agriculture: L. C. Gray, *History of Agriculture in the Southern United States to 1860;* P. W. Bidwell and J. I. Falconer, *History of Agriculture in the Northern United States, 1620–1860.*

4. FOREIGN RELATIONS

S. F. Bemis, *The Diplomatic History of the United States* and (ed.) *The American Secretaries of State and Their Diplomacy* (10 vols.); T. A. Bailey, *A Diplomatic History of the American People;* Department of State, *Papers relating to the Foreign Relations of the U.S.* (one or more annual vols.); W. M. Malloy (ed.), *Treaties . . . between the U.S. and Other Powers, 1778–1909* (2 vols.), with supplements; D. C. McKay (ed.), *The American Foreign Policy Library* (15 vols., 1948–58) is a series of popular monographs by specialists.

5. TRAVEL

H. S. Commager, *America in Perspective;* Oscar Handlin, *This Was America;* J. L. Mesick, *The English Traveler in America, 1785–1835;* Frank Monaghan, *French Travelers in the U.S., 1765–1932;* R. G. Thwaites (ed.), *Early Western Travels* (32 vols.); H. T. Tuckerman, *America and Her Commentators.*

6. GOVERNMENT AND CONSTITUTIONAL HISTORY

W. P. Binkley, *American Political Parties;* Louis Boudin, *Government by Judiciary* (2 vols.); James Bryce, *American Commonwealth* (1888); A. N. Holcombe, *State Government in the United States;* A. H. Kelly & W. A. Harbison, *The American Constitution, Its Origins and Development;* A. C. McLaughlin, *Constitutional History of the United States;* C. B. Swisher, *American Constitutional Development;* A. de Tocqueville, *Democracy in America* (translated by H. S. Commager); Charles Warren, *The Supreme Court in United States History* (2 vols.); Woodrow Wilson, *Constitutional Government in the United States.*

7. COLLECTIONS OF DOCUMENTS AND OTHER SOURCES

H. S. Commager, *Documents of American History* runs parallel to this work; R. Leopold, A. Link, and S. Coben (eds.), *Problems in American History;* Marvin Meyers *et al., Sources of the American Republic* (2 vols.); E. E. Saveth, *Understanding the American Past* (extracts from historians' writings).

8. GEOGRAPHY

Isaiah Bowman, *Forest Physiography;* Ralph H. Brown, *Historical Geography of the U.S.;* Harper's *Atlas of American History;* A. B. Hulbert (ed.), *Historic Highways of America* (16 vols.); C. O. Paullin, *Atlas of Historical Geography of the U.S.*

9. LITERATURE, PHILOSOPHY, AND RELIGION

Michael Kraus, *History of American History;* F. L. Mott, *History of American Magazines* (4 vols.) and *American Journalism, 1690–1940;* V. L. Parrington, *Main Currents of American Thought* (3 vols.); R. E. Spiller *et al.* (eds.), *Literary History of the U.S.* (3 vols.); W. P. Trent (ed.), *The Cambridge History of American Literature* (4 vols.); Joseph Blau, *Men and Movements in American Philosophy;* H. S. Commager, *The American Mind;* Merle Curti, *The Growth of American Thought;* I. Woodbridge Riley, *American Thought from Puritanism to Pragmatism;* Herbert Schneider, *History of American Philosophy;* W. W. Sweet, *The Story of Religion in America.*

10. THE FINE ARTS AND MUSIC
Wayne Andrews, *Architecture in America;* C. W. Condit, *American Building Art; the Nineteenth Century;* Royal Cortissoz, *History of American Painting;* L. H. Dodd, *The Golden Age of American Sculpture;* L. C. Elson, *The History of American Music;* A. T. Gardner, *Yankee Stonecutters, 1800– 1850;* J. T. Howard, *Our American Music;* O. W. Larkin, *Art and Life in America;* all Lewis Mumford's works; E. P. Richardson, *Painting in America, the Story of 450 Years;* Jacques Schnier, *Sculpture in Modern America.*

11. MILITARY AND NAVAL HISTORY
Robert Heinl, *A History of the U.S. Marine Corps;* Dudley W. Knox, *A History of the U.S. Navy;* Walter Millis, *Arms and Men;* E. B. Potter (ed.), *Sea Power;* Colonel O. H. Spaulding, *The U.S. Army in War and Peace.*

CHAPTER I

1. THE INDIANS AND PREHISTORIC AMERICA. W. N. Fenton, *American Indian and White Relations to 1830;* Alvin M. Josephy, Jr. (ed.), *The American Heritage Book of Indians;* Alfred V. Kidder, *Introduction to the Study of Southwestern Archaeology,* and (with C. S. Chinchilla) *The Art of Ancient Maya;* H. J. Spinden, *Ancient Civilizations of Mexico and Central America,* and *Maya Art and Civilization: The Maya and Their Neighbors;* Ruth Underhill, *Red Man's Religion;* Wilcomb Washburn (ed.), *The Indian and the White Man;* Clark Wissler, *Indians of the United States;* H. M. Wormington, *Ancient Man in North America.* For further references, *Harvard Guide to American History,* §§ 68, 69, 74.

2. NORTHMEN. Einar Haugen, *Voyages to Vinland;* H. R. Holand, *Westward from Vinland;* A. M. Reeves, *Finding of Wineland the Good;* Erik Wahlgren, *The Kensington Stone, a Mystery Solved.* For further references, *Harvard Guide,* § 70.

CHAPTER II

1. GENERAL. C. H. & Katherine George, *The Protestant Mind of the English Reformation;* J. H. Hexter, *Reappraisals in History;* H. M. Jones, *O Strange New World;* J. H. Parry, *The Age of Reconnaissance,* and *The Establishment of European Hegemony, 1415–1715;* John J. Te Paske, *Three American Empires.*

2. SPANISH AND PORTUGUESE. Herbert E. Bolton (ed.), *Spanish Borderlands,* and *Spanish Exploration in the Southwest;* E. G. Bourne, *Spain*

in America; C. R. Boxer, *Four Centuries of Portuguese Expansion, 1415–1825;* R. B. Cunninghame Graham, *The Conquest of New Granada;* C. H. Haring, *The Spanish Empire in America;* F. W. Hodge & T. H. Lewis (eds.), *Spanish Explorers in the Southern United States;* Woodbury Lowery, *Spanish Settlements in the United States;* Diego Luis Molinari, *Descubrimiento y Conquista de América;* S. E. Morison, *Admiral of the Ocean Sea* (shorter version, *Christopher Columbus, Mariner*), and *Portuguese Voyages to America before 1500;* G. T. Northup (ed.), *Vespucci Reprints;* J. E. Olson & E. G. Bourne (eds.), *The Northmen, Columbus and Cabot;* J. H. Parry, *The Spanish Seaborne Empire;* Antonio Pigafetta, *Magellan's Voyage Around the World* (James A. Robertson, ed.); William H. Prescott, *Conquest of Mexico,* and *Conquest of Peru;* Eric Wolf, *Sons of the Shaking Earth.* For further references, *Harvard Guide,* §§ 71-74.

3. ENGLISH AND FRENCH. J. B. Brebner, *The Explorers of North America;* H. S. Burrage (ed.), *Early English and French Voyages;* Sir William Foster, *England's Quest of Eastern Trade;* Richard Hakluyt (ed.), *The Principall Navigations, Voiages, Traffiques and Discoveries of the English Nation;* Wallace Notestein, *The English People on the Eve of Colonization;* Francis Parkman, *Pioneers of France in the New World* (selections in S. E. Morison, ed., *The Parkman Reader*); D. B. Quinn, *Raleigh and the British Empire;* A. L. Rowse, *The Expansion of Elizabethan England,* and *The Elizabethans and America;* H. R. Wagner, *Sir Francis Drake's Voyage around the World;* D. W. Waters, *The Art of Navigation in England in Elizabethan and Early Stuart Times;* James A. Williamson, *Voyages of John and Sebastian Cabot,* and *Age of Drake.* For further references, *Harvard Guide,* §§ 71-78.

CHAPTER III

1. VIRGINIA AND MARYLAND. Charles A. Andrews, *The Colonial Period of American History,* vols. i, ii; E. Arber (ed.), *The Travels and Works of Captain John Smith;* Philip L. Barbour, *The Three Worlds of Captain John Smith;* Philip A. Bruce, *Economic History* (2 vols.), and *Institutional History of Virginia in the Seventeenth Century* (2 vols.); W. F. Craven, *Dissolution of the Virginia Company,* and *The Southern Colonies in the 17th Century;* C. H. Firth, *An American Garland;* Ivorn Noel Hume, *Here Lies Virginia;* M. W. Jernegan, *Laboring and Dependent Classes in Colonial America, 1607–1783;* R. L. Morton, *Colonial Virginia,* vol. i; H. L. Osgood, *The American Colonies in the 17th Century* (3 vols.); H. R. Shurtleff, *The Log Cabin Myth;* Abbot Smith, *Colonists in Bondage;* James M. Smith (ed.), *Seven-*

teenth Century America: Essays in Colonial History; Louis B. Wright, *First Gentlemen of Virginia,* and *Cultural Life of the American Colonies.*

2. BERMUDA AND THE WEST INDIES. A. P. Newton, *European Nations in the West Indies;* J. H. Parry & P. M. Sherlock, *Short History of the West Indies;* Henry Wilkinson, *Adventurers of Bermuda.*

3. THE PURITAN COLONIES. Bernard Bailyn, *New England Merchants in the 17th Century;* William Bradford, *Of Plymouth Plantation* (S. E. Morison, ed.); R. S. Dunn, *Puritans and Yankees;* G. L. Haskins, *Law and Authority in Early Massachusetts;* Perry Miller, *Orthodoxy in Massachusetts, The New England Mind: The Seventeenth Century, Roger Williams* (with T. H. Johnson), *The Puritans* (an anthology), and *From Colony to Province;* E. S. Morgan, *The Puritan Family, Visible Saints,* and *The Puritan Dilemma: The Story of John Winthrop;* S. E. Morison, *The Founding of Harvard College, Harvard in the Seventeenth Century* (2 vols.), *Builders of the Bay Colony, Intellectual Life of Colonial New England,* and *Story of the "Old Colony" of New Plymouth;* Sumner Powell, *Puritan Village;* Alden Vaughan, *New England Frontier;* T. J. Wertenbaker, *The Puritan Oligarchy;* Ola Winslow, *Roger Williams;* Larzer Ziff, *The Career of John Cotton.*

4. NEW NETHERLAND. Edward Channing, *History of the United States,* vol. i, chs. 16, 17; J. F. Jameson (ed.), *Narratives of New Netherlands;* Christopher Ward, *Dutch and Swedes on the Delaware;* T. J. Wertenbaker, *The Founding of American Civilization: The Middle Colonies.*

6. NEW FRANCE. Morris Bishop, *Champlain, the Life of Fortitude;* Donald Creighton, *History of Canada,* ch. 1; W. L. Grant (ed.), *Voyages of Samuel de Champlain;* Francis Parkman, *Pioneers of France in the New World* (selections in S. E. Morison, ed., *The Parkman Reader*); J. F. Saintoyant, *Colonisation française sous l'ancien régime.*

For further references, *Harvard Guide,* §§ 88-91.

CHAPTER IV

1. GENERAL. Charles A. Andrews, E. Channing, W. F. Craven, and H. L. Osgood, as in Chaps. II, III; G. L. Beer, *The Old Colonial System* (2 vols.); D. J. Boorstin, *The Americans: The Colonial Experience;* O. M. Dickerson, *American Colonial Government, 1696–1765;* L. A. Harper, *The English Navigation Laws;* Joseph H. Smith, *Appeals to the Privy Council from the*

American Plantations; C. L. Ver Steeg, *The Formative Years;* Chilton Williamson, *From Property to Democracy.*

2. THE CAROLINAS. Louise F. Brown, *The First Earl of Shaftesbury;* V. W. Crane, *The Southern Frontier, 1670–1732;* A. S. Salley (ed.), *Narratives of Early Carolina;* D. D. Wallace, *History of South Carolina,* vol. i.

3. NEW YORK AND THE JERSEYS. A. C. Flick (ed.), *History of the State of New York,* vol. ii; John H. Kennedy, *Thomas Dongan;* T. J. Wertenbaker, *The Founding of American Civilization: The Middle Colonies.*

4. PENNSYLVANIA. H. Barbour, *Quakers in Puritan England;* W. W. Comfort, *William Penn and Our Liberties;* M. D. Learned, *Francis Daniel Pastorius;* A. C. Myers (ed.), *Narratives of Early Pennsylvania. . . ;* F. B. Tolles, *Meeting House and Counting House.* See appropriate chapters of Charles A. Andrews, E. Channing, and H. L. Osgood.

5. VIRGINIA AND NEW ENGLAND. C. M. Andrews (ed.), *Narratives of the Insurrections;* Viola F. Barnes, *The Dominion of New England;* R. E. Brown, *Middle Class Democracy and the Revolution in Massachusetts;* R. E. & B. K. Brown, *Virginia; Democracy or Aristocracy?;* G. L. Burr (ed.), *Narratives of the Witchcraft Cases;* N. H. Chamberlain, *Samuel Sewall and the World He Lived In;* D. E. Leach, *Flintlock and Tomahawk* (Philip's War); David Levin (ed.), *What Happened in Salem;* C. H. Lincoln (ed.), *Narratives of the Indian Wars;* Perry Miller, *The New England Mind: From Colony to Province;* R. L. Morton, *Colonial Virginia,* vol. i; C. S. Sydnor, *Gentlemen Freeholders;* W. E. Washburn, *The Governor and the Rebel* (Bacon); T. J. Wertenbaker, *Torch-bearer of the Revolution* (Bacon); L. B. Wright (ed.), *The Secret Diary of William Byrd of Westover, 1709–1712.*

6. CANADA AND THE WEST INDIES. V. W. Crane, *The Southern Frontier, 1670–1732;* C. H. Haring, *The Buccaneers in the West Indies in the Seventeenth Century;* L. W. Labaree, *Royal Government in America;* F. Parkman, *Frontenac and New France,* and *La Salle and the Discovery of the Great West* (extracts in S. E. Morison, ed., *Parkman Reader*).

For further references, *Harvard Guide,* §§ 92-97, 99, 100.

CHAPTER V

1. SOCIAL, ECONOMIC, AND RELIGIOUS DEVELOPMENT. Bernard Bailyn, *Education in the Forming of the American Society,* and *The New*

England Merchants in the 17th Century; Carl Bridenbaugh, Cities in the Wilderness, Rebels & Gentlemen: Philadelphia in the Age of Franklin; Cities in Revolt, The Colonial Craftsman, and Mitre and Sceptre; E. Channing, United States, vol. ii; John H. Franklin, From Slavery to Freedom, chs. 6-8; Douglas S. Freeman, George Washington, vol. i; E. S. Gaustad, The Great Awakening in New England; W. M. Gewehr, The Great Awakening in Virginia, 1740–90; L. H. Gipson, The British Empire before the American Revolution (9 vols.); Charles Grant, Democracy in the Connecticut Frontier Town of Kent; C. C. Gray, History of Agriculture in the Southern United States; Eli Heckscher, Mercantilism (2 vols.); J. B. Hedges, The Browns of Providence Plantations; Brooke Hindle, The Pursuit of Science in Revolutionary America; C. H. Maxson, The Great Awakening in the Middle Colonies; Robert Middlekauff, Ancients and Axioms; Perry Miller, Jonathan Edwards; E. S. Morgan, The Gentle Puritan: A Life of Ezra Stiles; R. B. Morris, Government and Labor in Early America; Louis Morton, Robert Carter of Nomini Hall; R. L. Morton, Colonial Virginia, vol. ii; Richard Pares, Yankees and Creoles; Alan Simpson, Puritanism in Old and New England; Abbot Smith, Colonists in Bondage; W. W. Sweet, Religion in Colonial America; F. B. Tolles, Quakers and the Atlantic Culture; Ola Winslow, Jonathan Edwards, and Meetinghouse Hill; L. B. Wright, The Cultural Life of the American Colonies.

2. GEORGIA AND NOVA SCOTIA. J. B. Brebner, New England's Outpost, and The Neutral Yankees of Nova Scotia; V. W. Crane, Promotion Literature of Georgia; A. G. Doughty, The Acadian Exiles; W. B. Kerr, The Maritime Provinces of British North America and the American Revolution; J. T. Lanning, The St. Augustine Expedition of 1740; J. R. McCain, Georgia as a Proprietary Province; Albert B. Saye, New Viewpoints in Georgia History;

3. WARS. J. S. Corbett, England in the Seven Years' War (2 vols.); Douglas S. Freeman, Washington, vol. ii; E. P. Hamilton, The French and Indian Wars; F. R. Hart, The Siege of Havana; G. S. Kimball (ed.), Correspondence of William Pitt When Secretary of State with Colonial Governors (2 vols.); J. S. McLennan, Louisbourg from Its Foundation to Its Fall; Richard Pares, War and Trade in West Indies, 1739–63; Stanley Pargellis, Lord Loudoun in North America; F. Parkman, Half-Century of Conflict, and Montcalm and Wolfe (extracts in Morison, ed., Parkman Reader); H. H. Peckham, The Colonial Wars; G. A. Wood, William Shirley; G. M. Wrong, The Fall of Canada, and The Rise and Fall of New France.

For further references, Harvard Guide, §§ 102-107.

CHAPTER VI

1. IMPERIAL PROBLEMS. C. M. Andrews, *Colonial Background of the American Revolution,* and *The Colonial Period of American History,* vol. iv; G. L. Beer, *British Colonial Policy, 1754–1765, The Old Colonial System* (2 vols.), and *The Origins of the British Colonial System;* O. M. Dickerson, *The Navigation Acts and the American Revolution;* L. H. Gipson, *British Empire before the American Revolution,* vols. ii, iii, and iv; J. P. Greene, *The Quest for Power: The Lower Houses of Assembly in the Southern Royal Colonies;* L. A. Harper, *The English Navigation Laws;* L. W. Labaree, *Royal Government in America;* E. I. McCormac, *Colonial Opposition to Imperial Authority during the French and Indian War;* C. H. McIlwain, *The American Revolution;* E. S. Morgan, *The Birth of the Republic;* Curtis Nettels, *The Money Supply of the American Colonies Before 1720;* Jack Sosin, *Agents and Merchants.*

2. THE WEST AND THE ALBANY PLAN OF UNION. L. H. Gipson, *British Empire . . .* vol. v, ch. 4; S. E. Morison, *Sources and Documents Illustrating the American Revolution;* H. M. Muhlenberg, *Notebook of a Colonial Clergyman;* Robert Newbold, *The Albany Congress and Plan of Union;* Howard Peckham, *Pontiac and the Indian Uprising;* Jack Sosin, *Whitehall and the Wilderness;* F. J. Turner, *The Frontier in American History,* chs. 1-3; Carl Van Doren, *Benjamin Franklin,* chs. 8, 13.

3. THE COLONIES, 1763–1773. John Adams, *Diary,* in *Works,* vols. ii, iii; C. M. & E. W. Andrews (eds.), *Journal of a Lady of Quality;* E. Armes (ed.), *Nancy Shippen, Her Journal Book;* William Bartram, *Travels Through North and South Carolina, Georgia, East and West;* C. L. Becker, *The History of Political Parties in the Province of New York;* Carl Bridenbaugh, *Seat of Empire* (Williamsburg); Andrew Burnaby, *Travels through the Middle Settlements in North America;* Jonathan Carver, *Travels through Interior Parts, 1766–68;* I. Bernard Cohen, *Benjamin Franklin;* Philip V. Fithian, *Journal and Letters, 1773–1774;* Anne Grant, *Memoirs of an American Lady;* Evarts B. Greene, *The Revolutionary Generation,* chs. 1-7; C. S. Sydnor, *Gentlemen Freeholders.*

4. BRITISH POLITICS. Herbert Butterfield, *George III, Lord North and the People,* and *George III and the Historians;* B. Donoghue, *British Politics and the American Revolution;* B. Knollenberg, *Origin of the American Revolution;* L. B. Namier, *England in the Age of the American Revolution;*

L. Namier & J. Brooke, *Charles Townshend;* C. R. Ritcheson, *British Politics and the American Revolution;* G. O. Trevelyan, *Early History of Charles James Fox,* and *The American Revolution,* vol. i.

For further references, *Harvard Guide,* §§ 108-111.

CHAPTER VII

1. THE WEST. T. P. Abernethy, *Western Lands and the American Revolution;* C. W. Alvord, *The Mississippi Valley in British Politics* (2 vols.); Carl Bridenbaugh, *Myths and Realities;* George Croghan, *Journal of His Trip to Detroit in 1767;* S. E. Morison, *Sources and Documents,* introd. and pp. 1-55; Theodore Roosevelt, *The Winning of the West,* vols. i, ii; Charles Wood mason, *Carolina Backcountry on the Eve of the Revolution.*

2. REVENUE AND STAMP ACTS. Bernard Bailyn (ed.), *Pamphlets of the American Revolution;* L. H. Gipson, *The Coming of the Revolution;* Bernard Knollenberg, *Origin of the American Revolution;* B. W. Labaree, *The Boston Tea Party;* John C. Miller, *Origins of the American Revolution,* and *Sam Adams;* E. S. & H. M. Morgan, *The Stamp Act Crisis;* Esmond Wright, *Fabric of Freedom.*

For further references, *Harvard Guide,* §§ 111, 112.

CHAPTER VIII

1. TOWNSHEND AND COERCIVE ACTS. E. Channing, *United States,* III, chs. iv, v; O. M. Dickerson, *Boston Under Military Rule as Revealed in the Journal of the Times;* C. H. Metzger, *The Quebec Act;* R. B. Morris, *Studies in the History of American Law,* and *The Era of the American Revolution;* A. M. Schlesinger, *The Colonial Merchants and the American Revolution,* and *Prelude to Independence: The Newspaper War in Great Britain;* Moses C. Tyler, *Literary History of the American Revolution,* i.

2. BACK-COUNTRY TURMOIL. T. P. Abernethy, *Western Lands and the American Revolution;* J. R. Alden, *John Stuart and the Southern Colonial Frontier;* J. S. Bassett, 'Regulators of North Carolina (1762–1771)' *Report* of the American Historical Ass'n. for 1894; Carl Bridenbaugh, *Myths and Realities,* ch. 3; Richard M. Brown, *The South Carolina Regulators;* Charles Woodmason, *The Carolina Backcountry.*

For further references, *Harvard Guide,* §§ 111, 113.

CHAPTER IX

1. GENERAL. R. G. Adams, *Political Ideas of the American Revolution;* C. L. Becker, *The Declaration of Independence;* Julian P. Boyd, *Anglo-American Union;* E. C. Burnett, *The Continental Congress;* Dumas Malone, *Jefferson the Viriginian;* R. L. Schuyler, *Parliament and the British Empire;* Charles Page Smith, *James Wilson.*

2. OPENING OF HOSTILITIES. J. R. Alden, *General Gage in America;* John Bakeless, *Turncoats, Traitors, and Heroes;* William B. Clark, *George Washington's Navy;* Allen French, *The First Year of the American Revolution.*

3. THE LOYALISTS. J. B. Brebner, *The Neutral Yankees of Nova Scotia;* Samuel Curwen, *Journal and Letters;* Lewis Einstein, *Divided Loyalties;* A. S. Flick, *Loyalism in New York During the American Revolution;* Thomas Hutchinson, *Diary and Letters;* Paul H. Smith, *Loyalists and Redcoats;* C. H. Van Tyne, *Loyalists in the American Revolution.*

For further references, *Harvard Guide*, §§ 113-115.

CHAPTER X

1. GENERAL. John R. Alden, *American Revolution, 1775–1783;* T. S. Anderson, *The Command of the Howe Brothers during the American Revolution;* Allen Bowman, *The Morale of the American Revolutionary Army;* H. S. Commager & R. B. Morris (eds.), *The Spirit of 'Seventy-six, the Story of the American Revolution as Told by Participants;* D. S. Freeman, *George Washington,* vols. iii–v; T. G. Frothingham, *Washington, Commander in Chief;* D. W. Knox, *The Naval Genius of Washington;* Piers Mackesy, *War for America, 1775–1783;* John C. Miller, *Triumph of Freedom, 1775–1783;* Richard B. Morris (ed.), *The Era of the American Revolution;* Howard Peckham, *War for Independence;* Eric Robson, *American Revolution in Its Political and Military Aspects, 1763–1783;* F. E. Schermerhorn, *American and French Flags of the Revolution;* Willard M. Wallace, *Appeal to Arms;* Christopher Ward, *The War of the Revolution* (2 vols.).

2. SUPPLY AND FINANCE. Anne Bezanson, *Prices and Inflation During the American Revolution;* C. J. Bullock, *Finances of the United States from 1775 to 1789;* R. A. East, *Business Enterprise in the American Revolutionary*

Era; E. James Ferguson, *Power of the Purse;* L. C. Hatch, *Administration of the American Revolutionary Army;* Curtis P. Nettels, *The Emergence of a National Economy, 1775–1815;* William G. Sumner, *The Financier and the Finances of the American Revolution* (2 vols.); C. L. Ver Steeg, *Robert Morris.*

3. MILITARY OPERATIONS, THROUGH 1777. John R. Alden, *General Charles Lee, Traitor or Patriot?;* George A. Billias, *General John Glover and His Marblehead Mariners;* Gerald S. Brown, *American Secretary: The Colonial Policy of Lord George Germain, 1775–1778;* J. F. C. Fuller, *Decisive Battles of the U.S.A.,* chs. 1, 2; Leonard Lundin, *Cockpit of the Revolution;* Hoffman Nickerson, *The Turning Point of the Revolution, Burgoyne in America;* J. M. Palmer, *General von Steuben;* Baroness Riedesel, *Letters and Journals;* Howard Swiggett, *War Out of Niagara, Butler and the Tory Rangers;* William B. Willcox, *Portrait of a General: Sir Henry Clinton in the War of Independence.*

For further references, *Harvard Guide,* § 117.

CHAPTER XI

1. FRANCE AND DIPLOMACY. T. A. Bailey, *Diplomatic History,* chs. ii–iv; S. F. Bemis, *The Diplomacy of the American Revolution;* H. Butterfield, *George III, Lord North, and the People;* E. S. Corwin, *French Policy and the American Alliance of 1778;* Verner W. Crane, *Benjamin Franklin and a Rising People;* G. H. Guttridge, *David Hartley,* for British proposals of 1778: text in S. E. Morison, *Sources and Documents;* Frank Monaghan, *John Jay;* Richard B. Morris, *The Peacemakers;* J. B. Perkins, *France in the American Revolution;* P. C. Phillips, *The West in the Diplomacy of the American Revolution;* Richard W. Van Alstyne, *Empire and Independence;* Carl Van Doren, *Benjamin Franklin,* chs. 20-24, and *Secret History of the Revolution* (Arnold, etc.); G. M. Wrong, *Canada and the American Revolution.*

2. NAVAL WAR AND MILITARY OPERATIONS, 1778–1782. J. R. Alden, *The South in the Revolution;* G. W. Allen, *Naval History of the American Revolution* (2 vols.); William B. Clark, *Lambert Wickes, Gallant John Barry,* and *Captain Dauntless* (Nicholas Biddle); W. S. Hayward, 'The Penobscot Expedition,' in *Essays in English History in Honor of Wilbur C. Abbott;* William D. James, *Sketch of the Life of Brig. Gen. Francis Marion;* William M. James, *The British Navy in Adversity;* Charles L. Lewis, *Admiral de*

Grasse and American Independence; E. S. Maclay, *History of American Privateers;* Admiral A. T. Mahan, *The Influence of Sea-Power Upon History,* and *Major Operation of the Navies in the War of Independence;* S. E. Morison, *John Paul Jones, A Sailor's Biography;* Theodore Thayer, *Nathanael Greene.*

For further references, *Harvard Guide,* §§ 117, 118.

CHAPTER XII

1. STATE CONSTITUTIONS. E. Channing, *United States,* iii, ch. 14; H. J. Eckenrode, *The Revolution in Virginia,* chs. 5-9; A. C. Flick, *History of the State of New York,* iv, ch. 5; Z. Haraszti, *John Adams and the Prophets of Progress,* chs. 2, 7, 8; Allan Nevins, *The American States during and after the Revolution;* J. P. Selsam, *The Pennsylvania Constitution of 1776.*

2. REFORM, RELIGION, SLAVERY, AND SOCIAL PROGRESS. W. E. B. Du Bois, *Suppression of the African Slave-Trade;* H. J. Eckenrode, *Separation of Church and State in Virginia;* J. H. Franklin, *From Slavery to Freedom,* ch. 10; Peter Guilday, *Life and Times of John Carroll* (2 vols.); J. F. Jameson, *The American Revolution Considered as a Social Movement;* G. A. Koch, *Republican Religion;* R. J. Purcell, *Connecticut in Transition;* Richard McCormick, *Experiment in Independence: New Jersey in the Critical Period, 1781–1789;* Max Savelle, *Seeds of Liberty.*

3. ARTS, LETTERS, EDUCATION. Abigail & John Adams, *Familiar Letters,* and *Warren-Adams Letters* (2 vols.), and (Stewart Mitchell, ed.) *New Letters of Abigail Adams;* Solon J. Buck, *The Planting of Civilization in Western Pennsylvania;* Edward Ford, *David Rittenhouse;* Nathan Goodman, *Benjamin Rush;* S. E. Morison, *Three Centuries of Harvard,* ch. 7; E. C. Shoemaker, *Noah Webster, Pioneer of Learning;* R. E. Spiller, et al., *Literary History of the U. S.,* vol. i; D. J. Struik, *Yankee Science in the Making,* part II.

4. THE WEST AND VERMONT. G. H. Alden, *New Governments west of the Alleghenies before 1780;* C. A. Hanna, *The Wilderness Trail;* Archibald Henderson, *Star of Empire;* A. B. Hulbert, *Boone's Wilderness Road;* M. B. Jones, *Vermont in the Making;* Louise P. Kellogg, *The British Regime in Wisconsin and the Northwest;* W. S. Lester, *The Transylvania Company;* John Pell, *Ethan Allen;* F. J. Turner, 'Western State Making in the Revo-

lutionary Era,' in his *Significance of Sections in American History;* S. C. Williams, *History of the Lost State of Franklin.*

For further references, *Harvard Guide,* §§ 111, 120.

CHAPTER XIII

1. GENERAL. Louise B. Dunbar, *Study of 'Monarchial' Tendencies in the United States from 1776 to 1801;* Merrill Jensen, *The Articles of Confederation,* and *The New Nation, a History of the United States during the Confederation;* Andrew C. McLaughlin, *Confederation and the Constitution;* Richard B. Morris, *The American Revolution Reconsidered.*

2. LAND POLICY AND THE ORDINANCES. T. P. Abernethy, *Western Lands and the American Revolution;* C. W. Alvord, *The Illinois Country;* K. P. Bailey, *The Ohio Company of Virginia and the Westward Movement;* R. M. Robbins, *Our Landed Heritage,* ch. 1.

3. FOREIGN AFFAIRS AND COMMERCE. S. F. Bemis, *Jay's Treaty,* chs. 1-4; E. Channing, *United States,* iii, chs. 13-15; Frank Monaghan, *John Jay;* S. E. Morison, *Maritime History of Massachusetts,* chs. 3-7; A. P. Whitaker, *The Spanish-American Frontier.*

4. DEBTORS AND SHAYS. J. Truslow Adams, *New England in the Republic;* Oscar & M. F. Handlin, *Commonwealth,* ch. 2; Marion L. Starkey, *A Little Rebellion.*

For further references, *Harvard Guide,* § 121.

CHAPTER XIV

1. GENERAL. Irving Brant, *James Madison,* vols. i-iii; Robert Brown, *Charles Beard and the Constitution;* Max Farrand (ed.), *Records of the Federal Convention* (3 vols.); Gaillard Hunt & J. B. Scott (eds.), *The Debates in the Federal Convention of 1787 . . . reported by James Madison;* Forrest McDonald, *E Pluribus Unum,* and *We the People, the Economic Origins of the Constitution;* A. C. McLaughlin, *Confederation and the Constitution;* J. T. Main, *The Antifederalists;* Saul K. Padover, *The Complete Madison;* Clinton Rossiter, *Alexander Hamilton and the Constitution;* R. L. Schuyler, *The Constitution of the United States;* C. Page Smith, *James Wilson;* Charles Warren, *The Making of the Constitution.*

2. JUDICIAL REVIEW. Charles A. Beard, *The Supreme Court and the Constitution;* E. S. Corwin, *The Doctrine of Judicial Review;* Charles Warren, *Congress, the Constitution, and the Supreme Court.*

3. RATIFICATION. F. G. Bates, *Rhode Island and the Formation of the Union;* A. J. Beveridge, *Life of John Marshall,* vol. i, chs. 9-12; S. B. Harding, *Contest over Ratification of the Federal Constitution in the State of Massachusetts;* S. E. Morison, *Sources and Documents,* pp. 233, 362 (extracts from debates in Federal and Virginia Conventions).

For further references, *Harvard Guide,* § 122.

CHAPTER XV

Stuart Bruchey, *Robert Oliver;* Bureau of the Census, *A Century of Population Growth, 1790–1900,* tabulating the Census of 1790; Luigi Castiglioni, *Viaggio negli Stati Uniti dell'America, 1785–87* (2 vols.); Marquis de Chastellux, *Travels in North America in 1780–82* (2 vols.); St. Jean de Crèvecœur, *Letters from an American Farmer;* E. B. Greene & V. D. Harrington, *American Population before the federal Census of 1790;* Joseph Hadfield, *An Englishman in America, 1785;* Thomas Jefferson, *Notes on the State of Virginia;* Francisco de Miranda, *Diary of Tour of the United States, 1783–84* (W. S. Robertson, ed.); Jedidiah Morse, *American Geography;* Richard Price, *Observations on the Importance of the American Revolution* (Turgot's letter included); Benjamin Rush, *Letters* (2 vols., L. H. Butterfield, ed.); J. D. Schöpf, *Travels in the Confederation;* R. C. Wade, *The Urban Frontier, the Rise of Western Cities, 1790–1830.*

For further references, *Harvard Guide,* § 123.

CHAPTER XVI

1. GENERAL. E. Channing, *United States,* vol. iv; D. S. Freeman, *George Washington,* vol. vi; E. S. Maclay (ed.), *Journal of William Maclay;* John C. Miller, *The Federalist Era;* Nathan Schachner, *The Founding Fathers.*

2. ORGANIZATION OF THE FEDERAL GOVERNMENT. E. C. Corwin, *The President, Office and Powers;* R. V. Harlow, *History of Legislative Methods in the Period before 1825;* Charles Warren, *The Supreme Court in United States History* (2 vols.); Leonard D. White, *The Federalists.*

3. BIOGRAPHIES. Irving Brant, *James Madison*, vol. iii; Gilbert Chinard, *Honest John Adams*, and *Thomas Jefferson: The Apostle of Americanism;* P. L. Haworth, *George Washington: Farmer;* Dumas Malone, *Jefferson and the Rights of Man;* J. C. Miller, *Alexander Hamilton, Portrait in Paradox;* Richard B. Morris (ed.), *Alexander Hamilton and the Founding of the Nation;* Nathan Schachner, *Alexander Hamilton.*

4. THE BIRTH OF PARTIES. W. N. Chambers, *Political Parties in a New Nation;* Joseph Charles, *Origins of the American Party System;* Noble Cunningham, *The Jeffersonian Republicans;* David Fischer, *Revolution of American Conservatism.*

For further references, *Harvard Guide*, §§ 124-128.

CHAPTER XVII

1. GENERAL. D. S. Freeman, *George Washington*, vol. vii; R. R. Palmer, *Age of Democratic Revolution;* Victor H. Paltsits (ed.), *Washington's Farewell Address;* see also under Chap. XVI.

2. FRENCH REVOLUTION AND FOREIGN AFFAIRS. S. F. Bemis, *Jay's Treaty and Pinckney's Treaty;* A. L. Burt, *The United States, Great Britain, and British North America,* chs. 6-8; Alexander De Conde, *Entangling Alliance;* Bernard De Voto, *The Course of Empire,* ch. 9; Felix Gilbert, *To the Farewell Address;* C. D. Hazen, *Contemporary American Opinion of the French Revolution;* H. Mumford Jones, *America and French Culture, 1750–1848;* E. P. Link, *Democratic-Republican Societies, 1790–1800;* V. L. Parrington, *Main Currents in American Thought,* vol. i; C. M. Thomas, *American Neutrality in 1793;* A. P. Whitaker, *Spanish-American Frontier.*

3. WHISKEY REBELLION, PUBLIC LAND, THE WEST. C. W. Alvord, *The Illinois Country;* Leland D. Baldwin, *Whiskey Rebels;* T. Boyd, *Mad Anthony Wayne;* B. H. Hibbard, *History of Public Land Policies;* Frederic L. Paxson, *History of the American Frontier,* chs. 8-13; M. M. Quaife, *Chicago and the Old Northwest;* R. M. Robbins, *Our Landed Heritage,* ch. 1.

CHAPTER XVIII

1. GENERAL. See Chapter XVI; Charles Francis Adams, *Life of John Adams* (vol. i of his ed. of Adams' *Works*); M. J. Dauer, *The Adams Federalists;* S. G. Kurtz, *The Presidency of John Adams.*

2. FRENCH RELATIONS AND NAVAL WAR. G. W. Allen, *Our Naval War with France;* A. J. Beveridge, *John Marshall,* vol. ii, chs. 4-9; Dudley W. Knox, *History of the U. S. Navy,* ch. 4; S. E. Morison, *Harrison Gray Otis,* vol. i, ch. 10; Moreau de Saint-Méry, *Voyage aux États-Unis, 1793–98;* Marshall Smelser, *Congress Founds the Navy;* F. J. Turner, 'Policy of France toward the Mississippi Valley,' in his *The Significance of Sections in American History;* A. P. Whitaker, *The Mississippi Question, 1795–1803.*

3. ALIEN AND SEDITION ACTS. F. M. Anderson, 'Enforcement of the Alien and Sedition Laws,' Amer. Hist. Assoc. *Report,* 1912; Irving Brant, *James Madison,* vol. iii, ch. 34; G. A. Koch, *Republican Religion,* chs. 7, 8; L. W. Levy, *Freedom of Speech and Press in Early American History,* and *Legacy of Suppression;* Dumas Malone, *The Public Life of Thomas Cooper;* James M. Smith, *Freedom's Fetters;* V. Stauffer, *New England and the Bavarian Illuminati.*

4. ELECTION OF 1800–1801. Charles A. Beard, *Economic Origins of Jeffersonian Democracy,* ch. 13; Richard Hildreth, *History of the United States,* vol. v, ch. 15; W. A. Robinson, *Jeffersonian Democracy in New England.*

CHAPTER XIX

1. GENERAL. Henry Adams, *History of the United States during the Administration of Jefferson* (4 vols., Commager ed. of 2 vols.); Sidney H. Aronson, *Status and Kinship in the Higher Civil Service;* D. J. Boorstin, *The Lost World of Thomas Jefferson;* E. S. Brown (ed.), *William Plumer's Memorandum of Proceedings in the United States Senate, 1803–1807;* N. E. Cunningham, Jr., *The Jeffersonian Republicans in Power;* W. E. Dodd, *Life of Nathaniel Macon;* Talbot Hamlin, *Benjamin H. Latrobe;* Gaillard Hunt (ed.), *First Forty Years of Washington Society in the Family Letters of Margaret Bayard Smith;* Adrienne Koch, *Jefferson and Madison: The Great Collaboration;* Alfred T. Mahan, *The Influence of Sea Power upon the French Revolution* (2 vols.); M. D. Peterson, *The Jeffersonian Image in the American Mind;* L. D. White, *The Jeffersonians;* C. M. Wiltse, *The Jeffersonian Tradition in American Democracy.*

2. TRIPOLI WAR, LOUISIANA, LEWIS AND CLARK. J. E. Bakeless, *Lewis and Clark: Partners in Discovery;* E. S. Brown, *Constitutional History of the Louisiana Purchase;* I. J. Cox, *The West Florida Controversy;* George Dangerfield, *Chancellor Robert R. Livingston of New York;* Bernard De Voto

(ed.), *The Journals of Lewis and Clark;* D. W. Knox, *History of the U. S. Navy,* chs. 6, 7; J. A. Robertson, *Louisiana under the Rule of Spain, France, and the United States* (2 vols.); Louis B. Wright & J. H. Macleod, *First Americans in North Africa.*

3. FEDERALIST AND BURR CONSPIRACIES. T. P. Abernethy, *The Burr Conspiracy;* Henry Adams (ed.), *Documents Relating to New England Federalism;* A. J. Beveridge, *John Marshall,* vol. iii, chs. 6-9; W. F. McCaleb, *The Aaron Burr Conspiracy;* S. E. Morison, *H. G. Otis,* ch. 15; Nathan Schachner, *Aaron Burr: A Biography.*

4. ASSAULT ON JUDICIARY. Beveridge, *Marshall,* vol. iii, chs. 1-4; W. C. Bruce, *John Randolph of Roanoke,* vol. i, chs. 6-7; Charles Warren, *Supreme Court in United States History,* vol. i, ch. 4.

5. EMBARGO. H. I. Chapelle, *History of the American Sailing Navy,* ch. 4; S. E. Morison, *Maritime History of Mass.,* chs. 12, 13; Bradford Perkins, *Prologue to War;* L. M. Sears, *Jefferson and the Embargo.*

For further references, *Harvard Guide,* §§ 135-137.

CHAPTER XX

1. GENERAL. Henry Adams, *History of the U. S. during the Administration of Madison* (5 vols.), and *The War of 1812* (reprint of the War chapters); F. F. Beirne, *The War of 1812;* R. A. Billington, *Westward Expansion,* ch. 13; Irving Brant, *Madison,* vol. ii., chs. 20-30; R. H. Brown, *Republic in Peril: 1812;* A. L. Burt, *The United States, Great Britain and British North America;* Albert H. Z. Carr, *The Coming of War;* E. Channing, *United States,* vol. iv, chs. 16-20; J. P. Cranwell & W. B. Crane, *Men of Marque;* Reginald Horsman,*The Causes of the War of 1812;* D. W. Knox, *History of the U. S. Navy,* chs. 8-12; C. P. Lucas, *The Canadian War of 1812;* A. T. Mahan, *Sea Power in Its Relations to the War of 1812* (2 vols.); Bernard Mayo, *Henry Clay: Spokesman of the New West;* Bradford Perkins, *Prologue to War;* J. W. Pratt, *Expansionists of 1812;* M. M. Quaife, *Chicago and the Old Northwest;* Eron Rowland, *Andrew Jackson's Campaign;* C. M. Wiltse, *John C. Calhoun: Nationalist, 1782–1828.*

2. PEACE OF GHENT AND HARTFORD CONVENTION. S. F. Bemis, *J. Q. Adams and the Foundations of American Foreign Policy;* F. L. Engelman, *The Peace of Christmas Eve;* S. E. Morison, *H. G. Otis,* vol. ii, *Mari-*

time History of Mass., chs. 12, 13, and *By Land and By Sea*, ch. 12; Bradford Perkins, *Castlereagh and Adams;* Carl Schurz, *Henry Clay*, vol. i, chs. 5, 6; F. A. Updyke, *Diplomacy of the War of 1812.*

For further references, *Harvard Guide*, §§ 138, 139.

CHAPTER XXI

1. GENERAL. Henry Adams, *United States*, vol. ix; J. Q. Adams, *Diary* (selections from 12-vol. *Memoirs*, Allan Nevins, ed.); J. Spencer Bassett, *Andrew Jackson*, vol. i, chs. 14-16; S. F. Bemis, *J. Q. Adams and the Foundations of American Foreign Policy*, chs. 11-16; W. P. Cresson, *James Monroe;* George Dangerfield, *The Era of Good Feelings*, and *The Awakening of American Nationalism;* Shaw Livermore, Jr., *The Twilight of Federalism;* Carl Schurz, *Henry Clay*, vol. i; F. J. Turner, *Rise of the New West.*

2. MARSHALL AND THE JUDICIARY. A. J. Beveridge, *John Marshall*, vol. iv; E. S. Corwin, *John Marshall and the Constitution;* Felix Frankfurter, *The Commerce Clause under Marshall, Taney, and Waite;* John T. Horton, *James Kent;* Roscoe Pound, *The Formative Era of American Law;* Joseph Story, *Commentaries on the Constitution of the United States* (2 vols.).

3. MISSOURI COMPROMISE. Timothy Flint, *Recollections of the Last Ten Years;* Glover Moore,*The Missouri Compromise;* F. C. Shoemaker, *Missouri's Struggle for Statehood, 1804–1821;* C. S. Sydnor, *Development of Southern Sectionalism.*

4. ANGLO-AMERICAN RELATIONS. T. A. Bailey, *Diplomatic History*, chs. 10-12; Dept. of State, *Naval Forces on the Great Lakes . . . the Rush-Bagot Agreement;* C. P. Lucas, *History of Canada, 1763–1812;* Frederick Merk, *Albert Gallatin and the Oregon Problem;* Richard Rush, *Memoir of a Residence at the Court of London;* C. K. Webster, *Foreign Policy of Castlereagh, 1815–22.*

For further references, *Harvard Guide*, §§ 143-145.

CHAPTER XXII

1. MONROE DOCTRINE. Alejandro Alvarez, *The Monroe Doctrine;* S. F. Bemis, *J. Q. Adams . . . Foreign Policy*, chs. 17-19, 26-27; F. A. Golder, *Russian Expansion on the Pacific;* Dexter Perkins, *Hands Off; A History of*

the Monroe Doctrine; W. S. Robertson, *Rise of the Spanish-American Republics, as told in the Lives of their Liberators;* A. P. Whitaker, *The U. S. and the Independence of Latin-America.* Also, works by W. P. Cresson, Richard Rush, and C. K. Webster, mentioned under Chapter XXI.

2. J. Q. ADAMS ADMINISTRATION. John & J. Q. Adams, *Selected Writings* (Koch & Peden, eds.), pp. 353-77; J. S. Bassett, *Andrew Jackson,* chs. 17-19; S. F. Bemis, *J. Q. Adams and the Union,* chs. 2-7; W. C. Bruce, *John Randolph,* vol. i, ch. 10; J. M. Callahan, *Cuba and International Relations;* Clement Eaton, *Henry Clay and the Art of American Politics;* W. R. Manning, *Early Diplomatic Relations between the U. S. and Mexico;* H. E. Putnam, *Joel Roberts Poinsett.*

<h2 style="text-align:center">CHAPTER XXIII</h2>

1. GENERAL. T. P. Abernethy, *From Frontier to Plantation in Tennessee;* J. S. Bassett, *Andrew Jackson;* Lee Benson, *The Concept of Jacksonian Democracy;* W. N. Chambers, *Old Bullion Benton;* Walter Hugins, *Jacksonian Democracy and the Working Class;* Marquis James, *Life of Andrew Jackson;* William MacDonald, *Jacksonian Democracy;* Marvin Meyers, *The Jacksonian Persuasion;* Robert Remini, *Andrew Jackson;* Arthur M. Schlesinger, Jr., *The Age of Jackson;* J. A. Shackford, *David Crockett, The Man and the Legend;* H. C. Syrett, *Andrew Jackson;* F. J. Turner, *Rise of the New West,* and *The United States, 1830–50;* Martin Van Buren, *Autobiography;* G. G. Van Deusen, *The Jacksonian Era;* John W. Ward, *Andrew Jackson, Symbol for an Age;* Leonard White, *The Jacksonians.*

2. POLITICAL CONDITIONS AND BACKGROUND. E. Malcolm Carroll, *Origins of the Whig Party;* Charles A. Davis, *The Letters of J. Downing;* C. R. Fish, *Civil Service and the Patronage;* D. R. Fox, *Decline of Aristocracy in the Politics of New York;* H. L. McBain, *De Witt Clinton and the Origin of the Spoils System in New York;* Richard McCormick, *The Second American Party System;* Harriet Martineau, *Society in America,* and *Retrospect of Western Travel;* Allan Nevins (ed.), *The Diary of Philip Hone;* Benjamin Perley Poore, *Perley's Reminiscences;* Josiah Quincy, *Figures of the Past;* Robert Remini, *The Election of Andrew Jackson,* and *Martin Van Buren and the Making of the Democratic Party;* Alexis de Tocqueville, *Democracy in America;* Frances Trollope, *Domestic Manners of the Americans* (Donald Smalley, ed.).

3. WEBSTER AND THE WEST. R. N. Current, *Daniel Webster and the Rise of National Conservatism;* C. M. Fuess, *Daniel Webster* (2 vols.); H. C.

Lodge, *Daniel Webster;* R. M. Robbins, *Our Landed Heritage,* chs. 3-5; Carl Schurz, *Henry Clay,* vol. ii; C. H. Van Tyne (ed.), *Letters of Daniel Webster;* R. G. Wellington, *Political and Sectional Influence of the Public Lands, 1828–42.*

4. CALHOUN AND NULLIFICATION, AND INDIAN REMOVAL. Frederic Bancroft, *Calhoun and the South Carolina Nullification Movement;* M. L. Coit, *John C. Calhoun: American Portrait;* William Freehling, *Prelude to Civil War;* D. F. Houston, *Critical Study of Nullification in South Carolina;* Dumas Malone, *Public Life of Thomas Cooper;* A. G. Smith, *Economic Readjustment of an Old Cotton State;* G. G. Van Deusen, *Economic Bases of Disunion in South Carolina;* C. M. Wiltse, *John C. Calhoun, Nullifier.*

5. FINANCE AND THE WAR ON THE BANK. R. C. H. Catterall, *The Second Bank of the U. S.;* T. P. Govan, *Nicholas Biddle;* Bray Hammond, *Banks and Politics in America from the Revolution to the Civil War;* A. B. Hepburn, *History of Currency in the U.S.;* R. C. McGrane, *Foreign Bondholders and American State Debts;* M. G. Madeleine, *Monetary and Banking Theories of Jacksonian Democracy;* W. B. Smith, *Economic Aspects of the Second Bank of the United States.*

6. INDIAN REMOVAL. Angie Debo, *The Road to Disappearance;* Grant Foreman, *Indian Removal: The Emigration of Five Civilized Tribes, The Last Trek of the Indians,* and *The Five Civilized Tribes;* G. D. Harmon, *Sixty Years of Indian Affairs, 1789–1850;* W. Lumpkin, *Removal of the Cherokee Indians from Georgia;* William MacDonald, *Jacksonian Democracy* (maps of Indian cessions); F. J. Turner, *Rise of the New West.*

7. FOREIGN RELATIONS. J. M. Callahan, *American Foreign Policy in Mexican Relations;* Julius Goebel, *The Struggle for the Falkland Islands;* D. M. Henderson, *The Hidden Coasts, a Biography of Admiral Charles Wilkes;* D. W. Knox, *History of the U. S. Navy,* ch. 14; R. A. McLemore, *Franco-American Diplomatic Relations, 1816–1836.*

For further references, *Harvard Guide,* §§ 153-158.

CHAPTER XXIV

1. GENERAL. P. W. Bidwell & J. I. Falconer, *History of Agriculture in the Northern States;* E. Channing, *United States,* vol. v; Paul W. Gates, *The*

Farmer's Age; L. M. Hacker, *The Triumph of American Capitalism,* chs. 17-20; Edward E. Hale, *A New England Boyhood;* Lucy Larcom, *A New England Girlhood;* J. B. McMaster, *History of the People of the U. S.,* vols. v-vii; Edgar W. Martin, *The Standard of Living in 1860;* Thomas L. Nichols, *Forty Years of American Life, 1821–1861;* D. C. North, *The Economic Growth of the United States;* R. H. Shryock, *Medicine and Society in America, 1660–1860;* F. J. Turner, *The United States, 1830–50;* N. J. Ware, *The Industrial Worker, 1840–1860.*

2. TRANSPORTATION AND WESTWARD MOVEMENT. C. H. Ambler, *History of Transportation in the Ohio Valley;* C. F. Carter, *When Railroads Were New;* A. D. Chandler, Jr., *Henry Varnum Poor;* A. Seymour Dunbar, *History of Travel in America* (4 vols.); R. W. Fogel, *Railroads and American Economic Growth;* Carter Goodrich, *Government Promotion of American Canals and Railroads, 1800–1890;* Carter Goodrich, et al., *Canals and American Economic Development;* A. B. Hulbert, *Paths of Inland Commerce;* Edward Hungerford, *Story of the Baltimore & Ohio Railroad;* K. W. Porter, *John Jacob Astor;* Julius Rubin, *Canal or Railroad?;* G. R. Taylor, *The Transportation Revolution;* R. L. Thompson, *Wiring a Continent;* D. B. Tyler, *Steam Conquers the Atlantic.*

3. IMMIGRATION AND PACKET SHIPS. Edith Abbott, *Historical Aspects of the Immigration Problem;* W. F. Adams, *Ireland and Irish Emigration to the New World from 1815 to the Famine;* Robert G. Albion, *Square-Riggers on Schedule,* and *The Rise of New York Port 1815–1860;* R. B. Anderson, *Norwegian Immigration to 1848;* R. T. Berthoff, *British Immigrants in Industrial America, 1825–1850;* Ray A. Billington, *The Protestant Crusade, 1800–1860;* J. R. Commons, *Races and Immigrants in America;* Robert Ernst, *Immigrant Life in New York City;* A. B. Faust, *The German Element in the United States;* Claude I. Fuess, *Carl Schurz;* Florence E. Gibson, *The Attitudes of the New York Irish toward State and National Affairs, 1848–1892;* Oscar Handlin, *The Uprooted;* Marcus L. Hansen, *The Atlantic Migration,* and *The Immigrant in American History;* Florence E. Janson, *Background of Swedish Immigration, 1840–1930;* M. A. Jones, *American Immigration.*

4. MANUFACTURING AND CITIES. Samuel Batchelder, *Introduction and Early Progress of the Cotton Manufacture in the United States;* Daniel H. Calhoun, *The American Civil Engineer;* V. S. Clark, *History of Manufacturers in the United States,* chs. 11-20; A. H. Cole, *The American Wool Manufacture* (2 vols.); Kenneth W. Porter, *The Jacksons and the Lees: Two Generations of Massachusetts Merchants;* J. M. Swank, *History of the Manu-*

facture of Iron; R. M. Tryon, *Household Manufactures in the U. S.;* Richard C. Wade, *The Urban Frontier.*

5. SCIENCE AND TECHNOLOGY. A. Hunter Dupree, *Science in the Federal Government,* and *Asa Gray;* George Daniels, *American Science in the Age of Jackson;* Bernard Jaffe, *Men of Science in America;* Edward Lurie, *Louis Agassiz, a Life of Science;* Paul H. Oehser, *Sons of Science* (the Smithsonian Institution); Carl Resek, *Lewis Henry Morgan;* R. H. Shryock, *American Medical Research Past and Present;* Mitchell Wilson, *American Science and Invention.*

6. EDUCATION. Carl Bode, *The American Lyceum;* E. Channing, *United States,* vol. v, ch. 8; Merle Curti, *Social Ideas of American Educators;* Richard Hofstadter & Walter Metzger, *The Development of Academic Freedom in the United States;* M. A. D. Howe, *Life and Letters of George Bancroft* (2 vols.), and *Classic Shades* (Williams, Mt. Holyoke, and Yale); B. A. Hinsdale, *Horace Mann and the Common School Revival in the United States;* S. E. Morison, *Three Centuries of Harvard,* chs. 10-12; F. L. Mott, *American Journalism,* and *History of American Magazines;* Frederick Rudolph, *The American College and University: A History;* Richard Storr, *The Beginnings of Graduate Education in America;* D. G. Tewkesbury, *Founding of American Colleges and Universities before the Civil War;* C. F. Thwing, *The American and the German University;* G. Ticknor, *Life, Letters, and Journals* (2 vols.); C. G. Woodson, *Education of the Negro Prior to 1861.*

For further references, *Harvard Guide,* §§ 148-151.

CHAPTER XXV

1. COTTON KINGDOM. Joseph G. Baldwin, *Flush Times in Alabama and Mississippi;* Kathleen Bruce, *Virginia Iron Manufacture in the Slave Era;* P. A. Bruce, *History of the University of Virginia* (5 vols.); Alfred Conrad & John Meyer, *The Economics of Slavery and Other Studies in Econometric History;* Avery Craven, *Edmund Ruffin, Southerner;* W. E. Dodd, *The Cotton Kingdom;* J. W. DuBose, *Life and Times of William Lowndes Yancey;* Clement Eaton, *A History of the Old South;* J. H. Franklin, *The Militant South;* F. P. Gaines, *The Southern Plantation;* Eugene D. Genovese, *The Political Economy of Slavery;* L. C. Gray, *History of Agriculture in the Southern States to 1860;* M. B. Hammond, *The Cotton Industry;* Oscar Handlin, *Race and Nationality in American Life;* Joseph H. Ingraham, *South-West, By a Yankee* (2 vols.); Frances A. Kemble, *Journal of Residence on*

a Georgian Plantation; Augustus B. Longstreet, Georgia Scenes; F. L. Olmsted, The Cotton Kingdom (A. M. Schlesinger, ed.); U. B. Phillips, Robert Toombs; Susan D. Smedes, Memorials of a Southern Planter; C. S. Sydnor, Development of Southern Sectionalism, 1819–1848; Laura White, Robert Barnwell Rhett.

2. THE NEGRO. Herbert Aptheker, American Negro Slave Revolts; Frederic Bancroft, Slave-Trading in the Old South; H. T. Catterall, Judicial Cases concerning American Slavery and the Negro; David Davis, The Problem of Slavery in Western Culture; Stanley M. Elkins, Slavery; Ralph Flanders, Plantation Slavery in Georgia; J. H. Franklin, From Slavery to Freedom; Ulrich B. Phillips, Life and Labor in the Old South, and American Negro Slavery; K. M. Stampp, The Peculiar Institution; C. S. Sydnor, Slavery in Mississippi; Frank Tannenbaum, Slave and Citizen; Richard C. Wade, Slavery in the Cities.

3. INTELLECTUAL MOVEMENT. C. H. Ambler, Thomas Ritchie; J. J. Audubon, Birds of America (William Vogt, ed.); Van Wyck Brooks, The World of Washington Irving, chs. 12-15; P. A. Bruce, History of the University of Virginia (5 vols.); W. J. Cash, The Mind of the South; Virginius Dabney, Liberalism in the South; Clement Eaton, Freedom of Thought in the Old South, and The Mind of the Old South; S. W. Geiser, Naturalists of the Frontier; W. S. Jenkins, Pro-Slavery Thought in the Old South; T. C. Johnson, Scientific Interests in the Old South; E. W. Knight, Public Education in the South; V. L. Parrington, Main Currents in American Thought, vol. ii; Linda Rhea, Hugh S. Legaré; Charles G. Sellers, Jr., The Southerner as American; William R. Taylor, Cavalier and Yankee; W. P. Trent, William Gilmore Simms.

For further references, Harvard Guide, §§ 148-151, 159.

CHAPTER XXVI

1. REFORMERS AND UTOPIAS. Edith Abbott, Women in Industry; W. Bennett, Whittier, Bard of Freedom; Gladys Brooks, Three Wise Virgins (D. L. Dix, E. P. Peabody, and C. M. Sedgwick); Charles C. Cole, Social Ideas of the Northern Evangelists, 1826–1860; W. R. Cross, The Burned-Over District; Merle Curti, The American Peace Crusade, 1815–60, and The Learned Blacksmith; R. W. Emerson, 'Life and Letters in New England,' in Lectures and Biographical Sketches; W. A. Hinds, American Communities

and Co-operative Colonies; S. M. Kingsbury (ed.), Labor Laws and Their Enforcement; J. A. Krout, The Origins of Prohibition; R. W. Leopold, Robert Dale Owen; Leon Litwack, The Negro in the Free States, 1790–1860; G. B. Lockwood, New Harmony Movement; William G. McLoughlin, Modern Revivalism; J. H. Noyes, History of American Socialisms; Pierrepont B. Noyes, My Father's House; L. E. Richards (ed.), Letters and Journals of Samuel Gridley Howe (2 vols.); Robert Riegel, American Feminists; Clara E. Sears, Days of Delusion (Millerites); T. L. Smith, Revivalism and Social Reform in Mid-Nineteenth Century America; Lindsay Swift, Brook Farm; Alice F. Tyler, Freedom's Ferment, parts ii and iii; Norman Ware, The Industrial Worker, 1840–60; W. R. Waterman, Frances Wright; Everett Webber, Escape to Utopia.

2. LITERATURE AND TRANSCENDENTALISM. G. W. Allen, The Solitary Singer: A Critical Biography of Walt Whitman; Newton Arvin, Longfellow, and Herman Melville; Van Wyck Brooks, The Flowering of New England, 1850–65, and The World of Washington Irving; H. S. Canby, Walt Whitman; William E. Channing, Collected Works; H. S. Commager, Theodore Parker; O. B. Frothingham, Transcendentalism in New England; William R. Hutchison, The Transcendentalist Ministers; J. W. Krutch, Thoreau; F. O. Matthiessen, American Renaissance; Perry Miller (ed.), The Transcendentalists, an Anthology; Lewis Mumford, The Golden Day; Bliss Perry, The American Spirit in Literature, and (ed.) The Heart of Emerson's Journals; R. L. Rusk, Life of Ralph Waldo Emerson; Odell Shepard (ed.), The Heart of Thoreau's Journals; Randall Stewart (ed.), American Notebooks, by Nathaniel Hawthorne; Mason Wade, Margaret Fuller; Stephen Whicher, Fate and Freedom: An Inner Life of Ralph Waldo Emerson.

3. ANTI-SLAVERY AND ABOLITION. G. H. Barnes, The Antislavery Impulse, 1830–44; G. H. Barnes & D. L. Dumond, Weld-Grimké Letters; Bemis, J. Q. Adams and the Union, chs. 17-19; William Birney, Sketch of the Life of James G. Birney; Henrietta Buckmaster, Let My People Go; John Jay Chapman, William Lloyd Garrison; Frederick Douglass, Life and Times; Martin Duberman (ed.), The Antislavery Vanguard; Dwight Dumond, Anti-Slavery; Louis Filler, The Crusade Against Slavery; Larry Gara, The Liberty Line; Albert Bushnell Hart, Slavery and Abolition; R. B. Nye, Fettered Freedom; W. A. Owens, Slave Mutiny (the Amistad Case); B. P. Thomas, Theodore Weld.

For further references, Harvard Guide, §§ 152, 160, 161.

CHAPTER XXVII

1. GENERAL. Lee Benson, *The Concept of Jacksonian Democracy;* O. P. Chitwood, *John Tyler;* T. C. Cochran & W. Miller, *The Age of Enterprise;* H. R. Fraser, *Democracy in the Making, the Jackson-Tyler Era;* D. B. Goebel, *William Henry Harrison;* R. G. Gunderson, *The Log-Cabin Campaign;* J. G. McMaster, *History of the People of the U. S.,* vol. vi; J. C. N. Paul, *Rift in Democracy;* Carl Schurz, *Henry Clay,* vol. ii; Robert Seager, *And Tyler Too!;* Joel Silbey, *The Transformation of American Politics, 1840–1860.*

2. PANIC AND SPLINTER PARTIES. H. D. A. Donovan, *The Barnburners;* R. C. McGrane, *The Panic of 1837;* T. C. Smith, *The Liberty and Free Soil Parties in the Northwest.*

3. TANEY AND THE SUPREME COURT. Felix Frankfurter, *Commerce Clause under Marshall, Taney and Waite;* C. B. Swisher, *Roger B. Taney;* Charles Warren, *Supreme Court,* vol. ii.

4. ANGLO-CANADIAN-AMERICAN RELATIONS. J. B. Brebner, *North Atlantic Triangle;* H. S. Burrage, *Maine in the Northeastern Boundary Controversy;* Donald Creighton, *History of Canada,* ch. 5; William Kilbourn, *The Firebrand: William Lyon Mackenzie;* T. H. Raddell, *Path of Destiny, Canada 1763–1850.*

For further references, *Harvard Guide,* §§ 162-63.

CHAPTER XXVIII

1. GENERAL. R. A. Billington, *The Far Western Frontier;* H. M. Chittenden, *The American Fur Trade of the Far West* (3 vols.); Katharine Coman, *Economic Beginnings of the Far West* (2 vols.); Bernard De Voto, *The Year of Decision, 1846,* and *Across the Wide Missouri;* N. A. Graebner, *Empire on the Pacific;* G. C. Lyman, *John Marsh, Pioneer: The Life Story of a Trail-blazer on Six Frontiers;* Frederick Merk, *Manifest Destiny and Mission in American History;* H. N. Smith, *Virgin Land;* R. G. Thwaites, *Early Western Travels;* A. K. Weinberg, *Manifest Destiny.*

2. GREAT PLAINS, OREGON, AND ROCKIES. H. C. Dale, *The Ashley-Smith Explorations and the Discovery of a Central Route to the Pacific, 1822–29;* D. O. Johansen & C. M. Gates, *Empire of the Columbia;* F. Merk

(ed.), *Fur Trade and Empire* (journal of Gov. George Simpson, 1824–25); Francis Parkman, *Oregon Trail*, and *Journals* (Mason Wade, ed.), and *Letters* (W. R. Jacobs, ed.); Joseph Schafer, *History of the Pacific Northwest;* W. P. Webb, *The Great Plains;* Dean E. Wood, *The Old Santa Fé Trail from the Missouri River.*

3. THE MORMONS. F. M. Brodie, *No Man Knows My History: The Life of Joseph Smith;* C. A. Brough, *Irrigation in Utah;* Bernard De Voto, *Year of Decision*, and *Forays and Rebuttals;* W. A. Linn, *The Story of the Mormons;* William Mulder & A. R. Mortensen, *Among the Mormons, Historic Accounts by Contemporary Observers;* T. F. O'Dea, *The Mormons;* G. Thomas, *The Development of Institutions under Irrigation;* M. R. Werner, *Brigham Young.*

For further references, *Harvard Guide*, §§ 164-66.

CHAPTER XXIX

1. GENERAL. Frances Erskine Calderon de la Barca, *Life in Mexico;* Bernard De Voto, *Year of Decision;* E. I. McCormac, *James K. Polk;* A. Nevins (ed.), *Diary of a President* (1-vol. abridgment of Polk's Diary); J. Fred Rippy, *The United States and Mexico;* C. G. Sellers, *James K. Polk: Jacksonian;* Justin H. Smith, *The War with Mexico* (2 vols.); N. W. Stephenson, *Texas and the Mexican War.*

2. TEXAS. Eugene C. Barker, *Life of Stephen F. Austin;* Jim Dan Hill, *The Texas Navy;* John H. Jenkins, *Recollections of Early Texas;* A. F. Muir (ed.), *Texas in 1837;* Stanley Siegel, *A Political History of the Texas Republic;* Justin H. Smith, *The Annexation of Texas.*

3. THE MEXICAN WAR. A. H. Bill, *Rehearsal for Conflict;* Samuel E. Chamberlain, *My Confession;* Charles W. Elliott, *Winfield Scott;* Douglas S. Freeman, *R. E. Lee*, vol. i; N. A. Graebner, *Empire on the Pacific*, ch. 10 (peace negotiations); U. S. Grant, *Personal Memoirs*, vol. i; Holman Hamilton, *Zachary Taylor;* Ethan Allen Hitchcock, *Fifty Years in Camp and Field;* D. W. Knox, *History of the U. S. Navy*, ch. 16; F. B. Rogers, *Montgomery and the Portsmouth;* Dunbar Rowland, *Jefferson Davis, Constitutionalist: His Letters*, vols. ii and iii; W. H. Samson (ed.), *Letters of Zachary Taylor from the Battlefield;* Winfield Scott, *Memoirs*, vol. i; O. A. Singletary, *The Mexican War;* W. P. Webb, *The Texas Rangers.*

For further references, *Harvard Guide*, §§ 167-168.

CHAPTER XXX

1. GENERAL. Frederic Bancroft, *Life of William H. Seward* (2 vols.); F. A. Billington, *The Protestant Crusade;* E. Channing, *United States,* vol. vi; A. C. Cole, *The Irrepressible Conflict, 1850–65;* Avery Craven, *The Growth of Southern Nationalism;* C. B. Going, *David Wilmot, Free-Soiler;* Holman Hamilton, *Zachary Taylor,* vol. ii, and *Prologue to Conflict;* G. F. Milton, *The Eve of Conflict* (life of Douglas); Allan Nevins, *Ordeal of the Union,* vol. i; James Ford Rhodes, *History of the United States from the Compromise of 1850,* vol. i; Theodore C. Smith, *Liberty and Free Soil Parties in the Northwest;* biographies of Calhoun, Clay, Rhett, Webster, and others already cited.

2. CALIFORNIA AND THE GOLD RUSH. J. W. Caughey, *Gold Is the Cornerstone;* R. G. Cleland, *From Wilderness to Empire,* and *History of California, the American Period;* Cardinal Goodwin, *Establishment of a State Government in California, 1846–1850;* L. R. Hafen, *The Overland Mail, 1849–1869;* O. T. Howe, *Argonauts of '49;* Allan Nevins, *Frémont: Pathmarker of the West;* R. W. Paul, *California Gold: The Beginning of Mining in the Far West.*

CHAPTER XXXI

1. GENERAL. Merle E. Curti, *Austria and the United States;* Roy F. Nichols, *Franklin Pierce;* works by E. Channing, Allan Nevins, and James Ford Rhodes mentioned previously.

2. OPENING OF JAPAN. Allan B. Cole, *Yankee Surveyors in the Shogun's Seas;* Tyler Dennett, *Americans in Eastern Asia;* Foster R. Dulles, *The Old China Trade;* W. E. Griffis, *Matthew C. Perry;* Townsend Harris, *Complete Journal;* Inazo Nitobe, *Intercourse between the U. S. and Japan;* P. J. Treat, *Diplomatic Relations between U. S. and Japan, 1853–95* (2 vols.); Arthur Walworth, *Black Ships off Japan.*

3. ISTHMIAN DIPLOMACY. A. A. Ettinger, *Mission to Spain to Pierre Soulé;* S. E. Morison, *Old Bruin* (Perry); Dexter Perkins, *The Monroe Doctrine, 1826–1867;* Basil Rauch, *American Interests in Cuba;* W. O. Scroggs, *Filibusters and Financiers;* I. D. Travis, *History of the Clayton-Bulwer Treaty;* William Walker, *The War in Nicaragua;* M. W. Williams, *Anglo-American Isthmian Diplomacy.* For further references, *Harvard Guide,* §§ 149-51, 170.

4. CANADIAN RELATIONS. C. D. Allin, *Annexation, Preferential Trade and Reciprocity;* Laurence Oliphant, *Episodes of a Life of Adventure;* Lester B. Shippee, *Canadian-American Relations, 1849–1874;* C. G. Tansill, *Canadian Reciprocity Treaty of 1854.*

5. THE CLIPPER SHIP AND STEAM. Arthur H. Clark, *The Clipper Ship Era;* Carl C. Cutler, *Greyhounds of the Sea;* C. L. Lewis, *Matthew Fontaine Maury;* S. E. Morison, *Maritime History of Massachusetts,* ch. 22, and *By Land and By Sea,* ch. 2; E. LeRoy Pond, *Junius Smith, a Biography of the Father of the Atlantic Liner;* D. B. Tyler, *Steam Conquers the Atlantic.*

For further references, *Harvard Guide,* § 173.

CHAPTER XXXII

1. GENERAL. A. J. Beveridge, *Life of Abraham Lincoln,* vol. ii; Avery Craven, *The Coming of the Civil War,* and *The Growth of Southern Nationalism;* Don E. Fehrenbacher, *Prelude to Greatness;* Philip S. Klein, *President James Buchanan;* George F. Milton, *The Eve of Conflict;* Allan Nevins, *Ordeal of the Union,* vol. ii, and *Emergence of Lincoln;* Roy F. Nichols, *The Democratic Machine, 1850-54, The Disruption of American Democracy,* and *Franklin Pierce;* K. M. Stampp (ed.), *The Causes of the Civil War.*

2. PRAIRIE SETTLEMENT, KANSAS, AND NEBRASKA. F. W. Blakmar, *The Life of Charles Robinson;* C. A. Dawson & E. R. Younge, *Pioneering in the Prairie Provinces;* Everett Dick, *Vanguards of the Frontier,* and *The Sod House Frontier;* David Donald, *Charles Sumner and the Coming of the Civil War;* P. W. Gates, *The Illinois Central R. R. and Its Colonization Work,* and *Fifty Million Acres;* H. C. Hubbart, *The Older Middle West, 1840–1880;* W. T. Hutchinson, *Cyrus Hall McCormick* (2 vols.); Samuel A. Johnson, *The Battle Cry of Freedom;* James C. Malin, *The Nebraska Question;* M. M. Quaife, *The Doctrine of Non-Intervention with Slavery in the Territories;* P. O. Ray, *Repeal of the Missouri Compromise;* Robert Russel, *Improvement of Communication with the Pacific Coast as an Issue in American Politics.*

3. KNOW-NOTHINGS. R. A. Billington, *The Protestant Crusade;* Oscar Handlin, *Boston's Immigrants,* ch. 7; W. D. Overdyke, *The Know-Nothing Party in the South;* L. F. Schmeckebier, *The History of the Know-Nothing Party in Maryland.*

4. DRED SCOTT. B. R. Curtis, *Memoir of Benjamin Robbins Curtis;* Vincent C. Hopkins, *Dred Scott's Case;* C. B. Swisher, *Roger B. Taney;* Charles Warren, *Supreme Court of U. S.,* vol. ii, chs. 26-27.

5. LINCOLN-DOUGLAS DEBATES. P. M. Angle (ed.), *Created Equal?,* and E. E. Sparks (ed.), *Lincoln-Douglas Debates,* for the texts; H. V. Jaffa, *Crisis of the House Divided;* Harry V. Jaffa & Robert W. Johannsen (eds.), *In the Name of the People;* Carl Sandburg, *Abraham Lincoln, the Prairie Years;* Paul Simon, *Lincoln's Preparation for Greatness.*

6. SLAVE TRADE RENEWAL. J. E. Cairns, *The Slave Power;* W. E. B. Du Bois, *Suppression of the African Slave Trade;* Peter Freuchen, *Book of the Seven Seas;* Edward A. Pollard, *Black Diamonds.*

7. FUGITIVE SLAVES AND JOHN BROWN. Daniel Aaron (ed.), *America in Crisis,* including C. Vann Woodward on the Harpers Ferry raid; H. V. Ames (ed.), *State Documents on Federal Relations, No. vi,* " 'Slavery and the Union, 1845–1861' "; Harold Schwartz, *Samuel Gridley Howe;* Oswald G. Villard, *John Brown.*

For further references, *Harvard Guide,* § 178.

CHAPTERS XXXIII–XXXVII

1. GENERAL. Bruce Catton (ed.), *American Heritage Picture History of the Civil War;* Edward Channing, *History of the United States,* vol. vi; E. M. Coulter, *The Confederate States of America;* Avery Craven, *Coming of the Civil War,* chs. 16, 17; M. B. Duberman, *Charles Francis Adams, 1807–1886,* ch. 19; Clement Eaton, *History of the Southern Confederacy;* C. R. Fish, *The American Civil War: An Interpretation;* E. D. Fite, *The Presidential Campaign of 1860;* John B. McMaster, *History of the People of the United States During Lincoln's Administration;* B. Mayo (ed.), *The American Tragedy;* Allan Nevins, *The War for the Union* (4 vols.), and *The Emergence of Lincoln,* vol. ii, chs. 1-11; Marvin Pakula, *Centennial Album of the Civil War;* Thomas J. Pressly, *Americans Interpret Their Civil War;* J. G. Randall, *Civil War and Reconstruction;* James Ford Rhodes, *History of the United States,* vols. ii-v; C. P. Roland, *The Confederacy;* Edward Stanwood, *History of the Presidency,* vol. i, ch. 21.

2. SECESSION. W. M. Caskey, *Secession and Restoration of Louisiana;* J. F. H. Claiborne, *Life and Correspondence of John A. Quitman;* A. M. B.

Coleman, *The Life of John J. Crittenden;* E. M. Coulter (ed.), *The Course of the South to Secession;* Ollinger Crenshaw, *The Slave States in the Presidential Election of 1860;* Richard Current, *Lincoln and the First Shot;* Jefferson Davis, *The Rise and Fall of the Confederate Government,* vol. i; C. P. Denman, *Secession Movement in Alabama;* D. L. Dumond, *The Secession Movement,* and (ed.), *Southern Editorials on Secession;* Norman Graebner (ed.), *The Crisis of the Union;* W. J. Grayson, *James Louis Petigru;* Robert Gunderson, *Old Gentlemen's Convention;* P. M. Hamer, *Secession Movement in South Carolina;* Joseph Hodgson, *The Cradle of the Confederacy;* George Harmon Knoles (ed.), *The Crisis of the Union;* Elizabeth Merrill, *James J. Hammond;* George F. Milton, *The Eve of Conflict;* H. C. Perkins (ed.), *Northern Editorials on Secession* (2 vols.); David M. Potter, *Lincoln and His Party in the Secession Crisis;* Percy L. Rainwater, *Mississippi: Storm Center of Secession;* R. R. Russel, *Economic Aspects of Southern Sectionalism, 1840–1861;* Henry T. Shanks, *The Secession Movement in Virginia;* Edward C. Smith, *The Borderland in the Civil War;* Kenneth Stampp, *And the War Came: The North and the Secession Crisis;* Alexander H. Stephens, *A Constitutional View of the Late War Between the States;* Arnold Whitridge, *No Compromise!;* Ralph A. Wooster, *The Secession Conventions of the South.*

3. ABRAHAM LINCOLN. C. R. Ballard, *The Military Genius of Abraham Lincoln;* Roy Basler (ed.), *Collected Works of Abraham Lincoln* (8 vols.); Robert Bruce, *Lincoln and the Tools of War;* R. N. Current, *The Lincoln Nobody Knows;* David Donald, *Lincoln Reconsidered;* B. J. Hendrick, *Lincoln's War Cabinet;* William B. Hesseltine, *Lincoln and the War Governors;* George Fort Milton, *Lincoln and the Fifth Column;* Herbert Mitgang (ed.), *Lincoln As They Saw Him;* J. G. Nicolay & John Hay, *Abraham Lincoln* (10 vols.); James G. Randall, *Constitutional Problems Under Lincoln,* and *Lincoln the President: Springfield to Gettysburg* (2 vols.); James G. Randall & Richard N. Current, *Last Full Measure* (last volume of Randall's *Lincoln);* Carl Sandburg, *Abraham Lincoln: The War Years* (4 vols.); David M. Silver, *Lincoln's Supreme Court;* Hudson Strode, *Jefferson Davis* (2 vols.); Benjamin Thomas, *Abraham Lincoln. A Biography;* T. Harry Williams, *Lincoln and His Generals;* William F. Zornow, *Lincoln and the Party Divided.*

4. BIOGRAPHIES. Rudolph von Abele, *Alexander H. Stephens;* E. P. Alexander, *Military Memoirs of a Confederate;* Gamaliel Bradford, *Union Portraits,* and *Confederate Portraits;* Fawn Brodie, *Thaddeus Stevens;* Freeman Cleaves, *The Rock of Chickamauga* (Gen. Thomas); Burke Davis, *Jeb Stuart;*

David Donald, *Charles Sumner and the Coming of the Civil War;* H. K. Douglas, *I Rode with Stonewall;* M. B. Duberman, *Charles Francis Adams, 1807–1886,* chs. 20-21; A. J. Fremantle, *Three Months in the Southern States;* Claude Fuess, *Carl Schurz;* John B. Gordon, *Reminiscences of the Civil War;* George Gorham, *Life and Public Services of Edwin M. Stanton* (2 vols.); G. E. Govan & J. W. Livingood, *A Different Valor: The Story of General Joseph E. Johnston;* U. S. Grant, *Personal Memoirs* (2 vols.); B. H. Liddell Hart, *Sherman—Soldier, Realist, American;* G. F. R. Henderson, *Stonewall Jackson and the American Civil War* (2 vols.); B. J. Hendrick, *Statesmen of the Lost Cause;* John B. Hood, *Advance and Retreat;* James Longstreet, *From Manassas to Appomattox;* Theodore Lyman, *Meade's Headquarters;* R. D. Meade, *Judah P. Benjamin;* G. B. McClellan, *McClellan's Own Story;* Robert McElroy, *Jefferson Davis* (2 vols.); Joseph Parks, *General Edmund Kirby Smith C.S.A.;* R. W. Patrick, *Jefferson Davis and His Cabinet;* Horace Porter, *Campaigning with Grant;* W. T. Sherman, *Memoirs of General William T. Sherman* (2 vols.); Robert Stiles, *Four Years Under Marse Robert;* Richard Taylor, *Destruction and Reconstruction;* John Thomason, *Jeb Stuart;* Frank Vandiver, *Mighty Stonewall* (2 vols.); R. F. Weigley, *Quarter-Master General of the Union Army* (Montgomery Meigs); Kenneth P. Williams, *Lincoln Finds a General* (U. S. Grant) (5 vols.); James H. Wilson, *Under the Old Flag;* John Wyeth, *Life of General Nathan Bedford Forrest.*

5. MILITARY. George W. Adams, *Doctors in Blue;* Richard Brownlee, *Gray Ghosts of the Confederacy: Guerrilla Warfare in the West;* Bruce Catton, *A Stillness at Appomattox, Glory Road, Grant Moves South, Mr. Lincoln's Army, Never Call Retreat, Terrible Swift Sword,* and *This Hallowed Ground;* D. T. Cornish, *The Sable Arm;* H. H. Cunningham, *Doctors in Gray;* W. F. Fox, *Regimental Losses in the American Civil War;* Douglas S. Freeman, *Lee's Lieutenants,* and *R. E. Lee;* T. R. Hay, *Hood's Tennessee Campaign;* Stanley Horn, *The Army of the Tennessee;* R. U. Johnson & C. C. Buel (eds.), *Battles and Leaders of the Civil War* (4 vols.); T. L. Livermore, *Numbers and Losses in the Civil War in America;* Frederick Maurice, *Statesmen and Soldiers of the Civil War;* E. S. Miers, *The Web of Victory: Grant at Vicksburg;* Jay Monaghan, *Civil War on the Western Border;* L. V. Naisawald, *Grape and Canister;* Frederick Phisterer, *Statistical Record of the Armies of the United States;* Benjamin Quarles, *The Negro in the Civil War;* John C. Ropes & W. R. Livermore, *The Story of the Civil War* (3 vols.); Morris Schaff, *The Sunset of the Confederacy;* Fred A. Shannon, *Organization and Administration of the Union Army* (2 vols.); Alfred Townsend,

Campaign of a Non-Combatant; Bell Wiley, *The Life of Billy Yank,* and *The Life of Johnny Reb.*

6. NAVAL. Daniel Ammen, *The Atlantic Coast;* James P. Baxter, *Introduction of the Ironclad Warship;* Florence Dorsey, *Road to the Sea: Story of James B. Eads and the Mississippi River;* H. Allen Gosnell, *Guns on the Western Waters;* Jim D. Hill, *Sea Dogs of the Sixties;* Charles L. Lewis, *David Glasgow Farragut* (2 vols.); A. T. Mahan, *Admiral Farragut,* and *The Gulf and Inland Waters;* J. M. Morgan, *Recollections of a Rebel Reefer;* J. T. Scharf, *History of the Confederate States Navy;* Gideon Welles, *Diary* (3 vols.).

7. FOREIGN RELATIONS. E. D. Adams, *Great Britain and the American Civil War* (2 vols.); Henry Adams, *The Education of Henry Adams;* Frederic Bancroft, *The Life of William H. Seward* (2 vols.); J. O. Bullock, *Secret Service of the Confederate States in Europe* (2 vols.); J. M. Callahan, *Diplomatic History of the Southern Confederacy;* Margaret Clapp, *Forgotten First Citizen: John Bigelow;* D. Jordan & E. J. Pratt, *Europe and the American Civil War;* Jay Monaghan, *Diplomat in Carpet Slippers;* Frank L. Owsley, *King Cotton Diplomacy;* S. A. Wallace & F. E. Gillespie (eds.), *The Journal of Benjamin Moran 1857–1865.*

8. BEHIND THE LINES. J. Cutler Andrew, *The North Reports the Civil War;* Robert C. Black, *The Railroads of the Confederacy;* Arthur C. Cole, *The Irrepressible Conflict;* E. M. Coulter, *The Confederate States of America;* Emmett Crozier, *Yankee Reporters 1861–65;* E. D. Fite, *Social and Industrial Conditions in the North during the Civil War;* Paul Gates, *Agriculture and the Civil War;* Wood Gray, *The Hidden Civil War;* William B. Hesseltine, *Civil War Prisons;* Harold Hyman, *Era of the Oath: Northern Loyalty Tests during the Civil War and Reconstruction;* E. C. Kirkland, *The Peacemakers of 1864;* F. L. Klement, *The Copperheads in the Middle West;* Margaret Leech, *Reveille in Washington;* Ella Lonn, *Foreigners in the Confederacy,* and *Foreigners in the Union Army and Navy;* William Q. Maxwell, *Lincoln's Fifth Wheel: The U.S. Sanitary Commission;* A. B. Moore, *Conscription and Conflict in the Confederacy;* F. L. Owsley, *States Rights in the Confederacy;* W. M. Robinson, *Justice in Grey: A History of the Judicial System of the Confederate States of America;* J. C. Schwab, *The Confederate States of America;* Louis Starr, *The Bohemian Brigade;* Richard C. Todd, *Confederate Finance;* Thomas Weber, *Northern Railroads in the Civil War;* Charles Wesley, *The Collapse of the Confederacy;* Bell Wiley, *Southern Negroes 1861–*

1865, and *The Plain People of the Confederacy;* Wilfred Yearns, *The Confederate Congress;* Edward Younger (ed.), *Inside the Confederate Government: The Diary of Robert Garlick Hill Kean.*

9. MISCELLANEOUS. H. S. Commager (ed.), *Official Atlas of the Civil War;* Edward Dicey, *Six Months in the Federal States;* Allan Nevins & M. H. Thomas (eds.), *Diary of George Templeton Strong* (4 vols.); W. H. Russell, *My Diary, North and South;* Irwin Silber, *Songs of the Civil War;* Anthony Trollope, *North America.*

10. FICTION AND POETRY. Stephen Vincent Benét, *John Brown's Body;* James Boyd, *Marching On;* Winston Churchill, *The Crisis;* John W. DeForest, *Miss Ravenel's Conversion from Secession to Loyalty;* MacKinlay Kantor, *Long Remember,* and *Andersonville;* Margaret Mitchell, *Gone with the Wind;* Evelyn Scott, *The Wave;* Walt Whitman, *Drum Taps;* Stark Young, *So Red the Rose.*

SOURCE SELECTIONS. P. M. Angle & E. S. Miers, *Tragic Years* (2 vols.); H. S. Commager, *The Blue and the Gray* (2 vols.), and (ed.), *Documents,* nos. 189-244; Frank Moore (ed.), *The Rebellion Record* (12 vols.).

CHAPTER XXXVIII

1. GENERAL. John A. Carpenter, *Sword and Olive Branch: Oliver Otis Howard;* Alan Conway, *The Reconstruction of Georgia;* Charles Crowe (ed.), *The Age of Civil War and Reconstruction;* David Donald, *The Politics of Reconstruction, 1863–1867;* Robert Franklin Durden, *James Shepherd Pike;* William A. Dunning, *Reconstruction, Political and Economic;* John Hope Franklin, *Reconstruction;* Harold M. Hyman (ed.), *New Frontiers of the American Reconstruction;* H. Wayne Morgan (ed.), *The Gilded Age: A Reappraisal;* Allan Nevins, *The Emergence of Modern America;* Ellis P. Oberholtzer, *History of the United States since the Civil War,* vol. 1; Otto H. Olsen, *Carpetbagger's Crusade: The Life of Albion Winegar Tourgee;* Rembert W. Patrick, *The Reconstruction of the Nation;* James G. Randall & David Donald, *The Civil War and Reconstruction;* James F. Rhodes, *History of the United States,* vol. v; Robert P. Sharkey, *Money, Class, and Party;* Kenneth M. Stampp, *The Era of Reconstruction, 1865–1877;* Irwin Unger, *The Greenback Era.*

2. THE PROSTRATE SOUTH. Sidney Andrews, *The South Since the War;* Myrta L. Avary, *Dixie After the War;* E. M. Coulter, *The South During*

Reconstruction; John W. DeForest, *A Union Officer in the Reconstruction;* Francis B. Leigh, *Ten Years on a Georgia Plantation since the War;* Elizabeth W. Pringle, *Chronicles of Chicora Wood;* Whitelaw Reid, *After the War;* Robert Somers, *The Southern States since the War;* Albion Tourgee, *A Fool's Errand, by One of the Fools;* J. T. Trowbridge, *The South.*

3. THE TRIUMPHANT NORTH. Paul H. Buck, *The Road to Reunion, 1865–1900;* Victor S. Clark, *History of Manufactures in the United States 1860–1914;* Charlotte Erikson, *American Industry and the European Immigrant 1860–1885;* E. D. Fite, *Social and Cultural Conditions in the North During the Civil War.*

4. THE NEGRO AS FREEDMAN. P. A. Bruce, *The Plantation Negro as Freedman;* George W. Cable, *The Negro Question* (Arlin Turner, ed.); Wilbur J. Cash, *The Mind of the South;* Henderson H. Donald, *The Negro Freedman;* W. E. B. Du Bois, *Black Reconstruction,* and *The Souls of Black Folk;* John Hope Franklin, *Reconstruction;* Frenise A. Logan, *The Negro in North Carolina, 1876–1894;* Rayford W. Logan, *The Negro in American Life and Thought, 1877–1901;* James M. McPherson, *The Struggle for Equality;* Basil Mathews, *Booker T. Washington;* August Meier, *Negro Thought in America, 1880–1915;* Gunnar Myrdal, *An American Dilemma* (2 vols.); William Peters, *The Southern Temper;* Benjamin Quarles, *Lincoln and the Negro;* Arthur Raper, *Preface to Peasantry;* Joe M. Richardson, *The Negro in the Reconstruction of Florida, 1865–1877;* Otis Singletary, *Negro Militia and Reconstruction;* S. R. Spencer, Jr., *Booker T. Washington and the Negro's Place in American Life;* Charles E. Synes, *Race Relations in Virginia, 1870–1902;* George Brown Tindall, *South Carolina Negroes, 1877–1900;* Booker T. Washington, *Up from Slavery;* Charles H. Wesley, *Negro Labor in the United States, 1850–1925;* Vernon Wharton, *The Negro in Mississippi;* Joel Williamson, *After Slavery: The Negro in South Carolina During Reconstruction, 1861–1877;* Carter G. Woodson, *A Century of Negro Migration.*

5. DOCUMENTS. Herbert Aptheker (ed.), *A Documentary History of the Negro People in the United States;* H. S. Commager, *The Blue and the Gray,* chs. 21, 26, 29, 31, and (ed.), *Documents of American History,* nos. 241, 245-247, 250, 251-253, 271-273, 291-293, 297; Walter L. Fleming, *Documentary History of Reconstruction* (2 vols.); Rayford Logan, *The Negro in the United States.*

For further references, *Harvard Guide,* §§ 195, 212.

CHAPTER XXXIX

1. PRESIDENTIAL RECONSTRUCTION. Howard Beale, *The Critical Year*, and (ed.), *The Diary of Gideon Welles* (3 vols.); LaWanda & J. H. Cox, *Politics, Principle, and Prejudice: 1865–1866;* Jonathan Dorris, *Pardon and Amnesty under Lincoln and Johnson;* W. A. Dunning, *Reconstruction, Political and Economic,* and *Essays on the Civil War and Reconstruction;* John Hope Franklin, *Reconstruction;* William B. Hesseltine, *Lincoln's Plan of Reconstruction,* and *Lincoln and the War Governors;* Charles McCarthy, *Lincoln's Plan of Reconstruction;* Eric McKitrick, *Andrew Johnson and Reconstruction;* George Fort Milton, *The Age of Hate;* James G. Randall, *Constitutional Problems under Lincoln;* Willie Lee Rose, *Rehearsal for Reconstruction: The Port Royal Experiment.*

2. CONGRESSIONAL RECONSTRUCTION. Thomas B. Alexander, *Political Reconstruction in Tennessee;* George Bentley, *A History of the Freedmen's Bureau;* W. R. Brock, *An American Crisis: Congress and Reconstruction;* Willie M. Caskey, *Secession and Restoration in Louisiana;* Walter L. Fleming, *Civil War and Reconstruction in Alabama;* J. W. Garner, *Reconstruction in Mississippi;* William Gillette, *The Right To Vote: Politics and the Passage of the Fifteenth Amendment;* Matthew Josephson, *The Politicos, 1865–1896;* Roger Shugg, *Origins of Class Struggle in Louisiana;* F. B. Simkins & R. H. Woody, *South Carolina during Reconstruction;* David Y. Thomas, *Arkansas in War and Reconstruction;* C. M. Thompson, *Reconstruction in Georgia;* H. L. Trefousse, *Benjamin Franklin Wade.*

3. RECONSTRUCTION AND THE CONSTITUTION. Harold Hyman, *The Era of the Oath;* Joseph B. James, *The Framing of the Fourteenth Amendment;* John M. Mathews, *Legislative and Judicial History of the Fifteenth Amendment;* Jacobus Ten Broek, *Antislavery Origins of the Fourteenth Amendment;* Charles Warren, *The Supreme Court in United States History,* vol. 2.

4. RADICAL RECONSTRUCTION. Fawn Brodie, *Thaddeus Stevens;* Richard N. Current, *Old Thad Stevens;* Jonathan Daniels, *Prince of Carpetbaggers: Life of M. S. Littlefield;* Mary Dearing, *Veterans in Politics: The Story of the G. A. R.;* D. M. De Witt, *Impeachment and Trial of Andrew Johnson;* David Donald, *Charles Sumner and the Coming of the Civil War* (2 vols.); W. E. B. Du Bois, *Black Reconstruction;* Harold Hyman & Benjamin P. Thomas, *The Life and Times of Lincoln's Secretary of War;*

Ralph Korngold, *Thaddeus Stevens;* George F. Milton, *The Age of Hate;* Henry White, *Life of Lyman Trumbull.*

5. UNDOING OF RECONSTRUCTION. W. G. Brown, *The Lower South in American History;* H. J. Eckenrode, *Rutherford B. Hayes, Statesman of Reunion;* Stanley Horn, *The Invisible Empire, the Story of the Ku Klux Klan;* Henry T. Thompson, *Ousting the Carpetbagger from South Carolina;* C. Vann Woodward, *Reunion and Reaction,* and *Origins of the New South.*

6. DOCUMENTS. H. S. Commager (ed.), *Documents,* nos. 245-67, 269-73, 278, 284; W. L. Fleming, *Documentary History of Reconstruction* (2 vols.); Benjamin Kendrick (ed.), *Journal of the Joint Committee of Fifteen on Reconstruction;* Samuel Klaus (ed.), *The Milligan Case.*

For further references, *Harvard Guide,* §§ 189-90.

CHAPTER XL

1. GRANT AND DOMESTIC POLITICS. Henry Adams, *The Education of Henry Adams;* D. C. Barrett, *Greenbacks and the Resumption of Specie Payments;* James G. Blaine, *Twenty Years of Congress;* Louis Boudin, *Government by Judiciary,* vol. 2, ch. 25; W. A. Cate, *L. Q. C. Lamar;* C. H. Coleman, *The Election of 1868;* D. R. Dewey, *Financial History of the United States;* Martin Duberman, *Charles Francis Adams;* C. R. Fish, *The Civil Service and the Patronage;* W. B. Hesseltine, *Ulysses S. Grant, Politician;* Matthew Josephson, *The Politicos, 1865–1896,* and *The Robber Barons;* Henrietta Larson, *Jay Cooke, Private Banker;* Hugh McCulloch, *Men and Measures of Half a Century;* Robert Stewart Mitchell, *Horatio Seymour of New York;* Wesley C. Mitchell, *A History of the Greenbacks;* A. B. Paine, *Thomas Nast, His Period and His Pictures;* E. D. Ross, *The Liberal Republican Movement;* Joseph Schafer, *Carl Schurz, Militant Liberal;* Charles Warren, *The Supreme Court in United States History,* vol. 2, ch. 31.

2. FOREIGN AFFAIRS. Frederic Bancroft, *The Life of William H. Seward;* S. F. Bemis (ed.), *The American Secretaries of State and Their Diplomacy,* vol. 7; J. M. Callahan, *The Alaska Purchase;* F. E. Chadwick, *Relations of the United States and Spain: Diplomacy;* C. L. Jones, *Caribbean Interests of the United States;* J. B. Moore, *History and Digest of International Arbitrations,* vol. 1, ch. 14; Allan Nevins, *Hamilton Fish: Inner History of the Grant Administration;* L. S. Shippee, *Canadian-American Relations 1849–1874;* Goldwin Smith, *The Treaty of Washington, 1871;* C. C. Tansill, *The United*

States and Santo Domingo 1789–1873; Sumner Welles, *Naboth's Vineyard* (2 vols.), (Santo Domingo).

3. THE ELECTION OF 1876. Harry Barnard, *Rutherford B. Hayes and His America;* H. J. Eckenrode, *Rutherford B. Hayes;* A. C. Flick, *Samuel Jones Tilden;* Paul L. Haworth, *The Hayes-Tilden Disputed Election of 1876;* Allan Nevins, *Abram S. Hewitt: With Some Account of Peter Cooper;* James Ford Rhodes, *History of the United States,* vol. 7; L. B. Richardson, *William E. Chandler, Republican;* C. R. Williams, *Life of Rutherford B. Hayes* (2 vols.); C. Vann Woodward, *Reunion and Reaction.*

4. THE NADIR OF NEGRO RIGHTS. Robert J. Harris, *The Quest for Equality;* Joseph B. James, *Framing of the Fourteenth Amendment;* Milton Konvitz, *The Constitution and Civil Rights,* and *A Century of Civil Rights;* Paul Lewinson, *Race, Class, and Party;* Samuel D. Smith, *The Negro in Congress, 1870–1901;* Gilbert T. Stephenson, *Race Distinctions in American Law;* Jacobus Ten Broek, *Antislavery Origins of the Fourteenth Amendment;* C. Vann Woodward, *The Strange Career of Jim Crow.*

5. DOCUMENTS. Ruhl J. Bartlett, *Record of American Diplomacy,* chs. 19-20; H. S. Commager (ed.), *Documents,* nos. 276-97; W. L. Fleming, *Documentary History of Reconstruction,* vol. 2.

For further references, *Harvard Guide,* §§ 192-194.

CHAPTER XLI

1. LITERATURE. Henry Adams, *The Education of Henry Adams;* Van Wyck Brooks, *New England: Indian Summer* and *The Times of Melville and Whitman;* John B. Clark, *Life and Letters of John Fiske* (2 vols.); Joseph Dorfman, *Economic Mind in American Civilization,* vol. 3; Leon Edel, *Henry James: The Untried Years;* Ralph Gabriel, *Course of American Democratic Thought;* James Hart, *The Popular Book;* William Dean Howells, *Literary Friends and Acquaintances, My Mark Twain,* and *Years of My Youth;* F. O. Matthiessen, *American Renaissance;* Vernon L. Parrington, *Main Currents of American Thought,* vol. 3; Stow Persons, *American Minds;* Aubrey H. Starke, *Sidney Lanier;* Dixon Wecter, *Sam Clemens of Hannibal.*

2. JOURNALISM. Harry Baehr, *The New York Tribune since the War;* H. S. Commager (ed.), *The St. Nicholas Anthology;* Elmer Davis, *A History of the*

New York Times; Frank L. Mott, A History of American Magazines, 1865–1885 and American Journalism; Allan Nevins, The Evening Post and American Press Opinion; F. M. O'Brien, The Story of the Sun; Rollo Ogden, E. L. Godkin (2 vols.); James Parton, Life of Horace Greeley; Gustav Pollak, Fifty Years of American Idealism (The Nation); Candace Stone, Dana and the Sun; Glyndon Van Duesen, Horace Greeley: Nineteenth-Century Crusader.

3. EDUCATION. Lawrence A. Cremin, The Transformation of the School, Progressivism in American Education, 1876–1957; Ellwood P. Cubberley, Public Education in the United States; Merle Curti, Social Ideas of American Educators; Charles W. Eliot, Educational Reform; Daniel C. Gilman, University Problems in the United States; Hugh Hawkins, Pioneer: A History of the Johns Hopkins University, 1874–1889; Paul Monroe (ed.), Cyclopaedia of Education (5 vols.); S. E. Morison, The Development of Harvard University, 1869–1929; Allan Nevins, Illinois and The Origins of Land-Grant Colleges and State Universities; George Pierson, Yale: College and University, 1871–1937; Henry Pochmann, German Culture in America; Andrew D. White, Autobiography, vol. 1.

4. SCIENCE. Edward S. Dana, et al., A Century of Science in America; W. C. Darrah, Powell of the Colorado; A. Hunter Dupree, Science in the Federal Government and Asa Gray; C. L. & M. A. Fenton, Giants of Geology; John Fiske, Excursions of an Evolutionist and Edward Livingston Youmans; Donald Fleming, John William Draper and the Religion of Science; Daniel C. Gilman, Life of James Dwight Dana; Asa Gray, Darwiniana: Essays and Reviews; David Lowenthal, George Perkins Marsh; Muriel Rukeyser, Willard Gibbs; Wallace Stegner, Beyond the 100th Meridian; Bernhard J. Stern, Lewis Henry Morgan, Social Evolutionist.

5. THE FINE ARTS. Lloyd Goodrich, Winslow Homer and Albert P. Ryder; Henry R. Hitchcock, The Architecture of H. H. Richardson and His Times; James Jackson Jarves, Art Thoughts; John Kouwenhoven, Made in America; Oliver Larkin, Art and Life in America; Russell Lynes, The Tastemakers; Elizabeth McCausland, George Inness; Roland McKinney, Thomas Eakins; Harriet Monroe, John Wellborn Root; Lewis Mumford, The Roots of Contemporary Architecture, The Brown Decades, and Sticks and Stones; Fairfield Porter, Thomas Eakins; E. P. Richardson, Painting in America; Francis Steegmuller, The Two Lives of James Jackson Jarves; M. G. Van Rensselaer, Henry Hobson Richardson.

6. DOCUMENTS. Richard Hofstadter & Wilson Smith, *American Higher Education*, vol. 2, parts 7–10; Lewis Mumford (ed.), *Roots of Contemporary American Architecture;* Allan Nevins, *American Press Opinion.*

For further references, *Harvard Guide,* §§ 217-18.

Statistical Tables

Admission of States to the Union, 859

Table of Population of the United States, 1770–1870, 860

Presidents and Their Cabinets, 862

Justices of the United States Supreme Court, 866

Speakers of the House of Representatives, 866

ADMISSION OF STATES TO THE UNION

STATE	ENTERED UNION	STATE	ENTERED UNION
Alabama	1819	Montana	1889
Alaska	1958	Nebraska	1867
Arizona	1912	Nevada	1864
Arkansas	1836	New Hampshire	1788
California	1850	New Jersey	1787
Colorado	1876	New Mexico	1912
Connecticut	1788	New York	1788
Delaware	1787	North Carolina	1789
Florida	1845	North Dakota	1889
Georgia	1788	Ohio	1803
Hawaii	1959	Oklahoma	1907
Idaho	1890	Oregon	1859
Illinois	1818	Pennsylvania	1787
Indiana	1816	Rhode Island	1790
Iowa	1846	South Carolina	1788
Kansas	1861	South Dakota	1889
Kentucky	1792	Tennessee	1796
Louisiana	1812	Texas	1845
Maine	1820	Utah	1896
Maryland	1788	Vermont	1791
Massachusetts	1788	Virginia	1788
Michigan	1837	Washington	1889
Minnesota	1858	West Virginia	1863
Mississippi	1817	Wisconsin	1848
Missouri	1821	Wyoming	1890

TABLE OF POPULATION OF THE UNITED STATES, 1770–1870

Estimates for 1770 taken from A Century of Population Growth (1909), others from the United States censuses

STATE	1770	1790	1800	1810	1820	1830	1840	1850	1860	1870
New England										
Maine	34,000	96,540	151,719	228,705	298,335	399,455	501,793	583,169	628,279	626,915
New Hampshire	60,000	141,885	183,858	214,460	244,161	269,328	284,574	317,976	326,073	318,300
Vermont	25,000	85,425	154,465	217,895	235,981	280,652	291,948	314,120	315,098	330,551
Massachusetts	265,000	378,787	422,845	472,040	523,287	610,408	737,699	994,514	1,231,066	1,457,351
Rhode Island	55,000	68,825	69,122	76,931	83,059	97,199	108,830	147,545	174,620	217,353
Connecticut	175,000	237,946	251,002	261,942	275,248	297,675	309,978	370,792	460,147	537,454
Middle Atlantic										
New York	160,000	340,120	589,051	959,049	1,372,812	1,918,608	2,428,921	3,097,394	3,880,735	4,382,759
New Jersey	110,000	184,139	211,149	245,562	277,575	320,823	373,306	489,555	672,035	906,096
Pennsylvania	250,000	434,373	602,365	810,091	1,049,458	1,348,233	1,724,033	2,311,786	2,906,215	3,521,951
South Atlantic										
Delaware	25,000	59,096	64,273	72,674	72,749	76,748	78,085	91,532	112,216	125,015
Maryland	200,000	319,728	341,548	380,546	407,350	447,040	470,019	583,034	687,049	780,894
Dist of Columbia	......	......	14,093	24,023	33,039	39,834	43,712	51,687	75,080	131,700
Virginia	450,000	747,610	880,200	974,600	1,065,366	1,211,405	1,239,797	1,421,661	1,596,318	1,225,163
West Virginia	......	......	......	......	......	......	......	......	......	442,014
North Carolina	230,000	393,751	478,103	555,500	638,829	737,987	753,419	869,039	992,622	1,071,361
South Carolina	140,000	249,073	345,591	415,115	502,741	581,185	594,398	668,507	703,708	705,606
Georgia	26,000	82,548	162,686	252,433	340,989	516,823	691,392	906,185	1,057,286	1,184,109
Florida	......	......	......	......	......	34,730	54,477	87,445	140,424	187,748
South Central										
Kentucky	......	73,677	220,955	406,511	564,317	687,917	779,828	982,405	1,155,684	1,321,011
Tennessee	......	35,691	105,602	261,727	422,823	681,904	829,210	1,002,717	1,109,801	1,258,520
Alabama	......	......	......	......	127,901	309,527	590,756	771,623	964,201	996,992
Mississippi	......	......	8,850	40,352	75,448	136,621	375,651	606,526	791,305	827,922

Arkansas				1,062	14,273	30,388	97,574	209,897	435,450	484,471
Louisiana				76,556	153,407	215,739	352,411	517,762	708,002	726,915
Oklahoma										
Texas								212,592	604,215	818,579
North Central										
Ohio			45,365	230,760	581,434	937,903	1,519,467	1,980,329	2,339,511	2,665,260
Indiana			5,641	24,520	147,178	343,031	685,866	988,416	1,350,428	1,680,637
Illinois				12,282	55,211	157,445	476,183	851,470	1,711,951	2,539,891
Michigan				4,762	8,896	31,639	212,267	397,654	749,113	1,184,059
Wisconsin							30,945	305,391	775,881	1,054,670
Minnesota								6,077	172,023	439,706
Iowa				19,783			43,112	192,214	674,913	1,194,020
Missouri					66,586	140,455	383,702	682,044	1,182,012	1,721,295
North Dakota									4,837	14,181
South Dakota										
Nebraska									28,841	122,993
Kansas									107,206	364,399
Mountain										
Montana										20,595
Idaho										14,999
Wyoming										9,118
Colorado									34,277	39,864
New Mexico								61,547	93,516	91,874
Arizona										9,658
Utah								11,380	40,273	86,786
Nevada									6,857	42,491
Pacific										
Washington									11,594	23,955
Oregon								13,294	52,465	90,923
California								92,597	379,994	560,247
	2,205,000	3,929,214	5,308,483	7,239,881	9,638,453	12,866,020	17,069,453	23,191,876	31,443,321	38,558,371

PRESIDENT AND VICE-PRESIDENT	SECRETARY OF STATE	SECRETARY OF TREASURY	SECRETARY OF WAR
George Washington-John Adams........1789	T. Jefferson ....1789 E. Randolph....1794 T. Pickering....1795	Alex. Hamilton .1789 Oliver Wolcott..1795	Henry Knox....1789 T. Pickering....1795 Jas. McHenry...1796
John Adams-Thomas Jefferson 1797	T. Pickering....1797 John Marshall..1800	Oliver Wolcott..1797 Samuel Dexter..1801	Jas. McHenry...1797 John Marshall..1800 Sam'l Dexter...1800 R. Griswold 1801
Thomas Jefferson-Aaron Burr..........1801 George Clinton 1805	James Madison..1801	Samuel Dexter..1801 Albert Gallatin..1801	H. Dearborn....1801
James Madison-George Clinton........1809 Elbridge Gerry 1813	Robert Smith ...1809 James Monroe ..1811	Albert Gallatin .1809 G. W. Campbell.1814 A. J. Dallas ....1814 W. H. Crawford 1816	Wm. Eustis ....1809 J. Armstrong ...1813 James Monroe..1814 W. H. Crawford 1815
James Monroe-D. D. Tompkins........1817	J. Q. Adams....1817	W. H. Crawford 1817	Isaac Shelby ...1817 Geo. Graham ...1817 J. C. Calhoun...1817
John Q. Adams-John C. Calhoun.......1825	Henry Clay 1825	Richard Rush...1825	Jas. Barbour....1825 Peter B. Porter..1828
Andrew Jackson-John C. Calhoun.......1829 Martin Van Buren 1833	M. Van Buren..1829 E. Livingston...1831 Louis McLane ..1833 John Forsyth ...1834	Sam. D. Ingham.1829 Louis McLane ..1831 W. J. Duane....1833 Roger B. Taney.1833 Levi Woodbury .1834	John H. Eaton ..1829 Lewis Cass.....1831 B. F. Butler 1837
Martin Van Buren-R. M. Johnson.......1837	John Forsyth ...1837	Levi Woodbury .1837	Joel R. Poinsett .1837
Wm. H. Harrison-John Tyler..........1841	Daniel Webster .1841	Thos. Ewing....1841	John Bell......1841
John Tyler.......................1841	Daniel Webster .1841 Hugh S. Legare .1843 Abel P. Upshur .1843 John C. Calhoun 1844	Thos. Ewing....1841 Walter Forward.1841 John C. Spencer.1843 Geo. M. Bibb...1844	John Bell......1841 John McLean...1841 J. C. Spencer...1841 Jas. M. Porter..1843 Wm. Wilkins...1844
James K. Polk-George M. Dallas.......1845	James Buchanan 1845	Robt. J. Walker.1845	Wm. L. Marcy..1845
Zachary Taylor-Millard Fillmore........1849	John M. Clayton 1849	W. M. Meredith .1849	G. W. Crawford.1849
Millard Fillmore...................1850	Daniel Webster .1850 Edward Everett .1852	Thomas Corwin .1850	C. M. Conrad...1850
Franklin Pierce-William R. King.......1853	W. L. Marcy ...1853	James Guthrie ..1853	Jefferson Davis .1853
James Buchanan-J. C. Breckinridge.....1857	Lewis Cass.....1857 J. S. Black.....1860	Howell Cobb ...1857 Philip F. Thomas 1860 John A. Dix....1861	John B. Floyd ..1857 Joseph Holt 1861

862

SECRETARY OF NAVY	SECRETARY OF THE INTERIOR	POSTMASTER GENERAL	ATTORNEY GENERAL
	Established March 3, 1849.	Samuel Osgood......1789 Tim. Pickering......1791 Jos. Habersham......1795	E. Randolph........1789 Wm. Bradford........1794 Charles Lee.........1795
Benj. Stoddert.......1798		Jos. Habersham......1797	Charles Lee.........1797 Theo. Parsons........1801
Benj. Stoddert.......1801 Robert Smith........1801 J. Crowninshield.....1805		Jos. Habersham......1801 Gideon Granger......1801	Levi Lincoln........1801 Robert Smith........1805 J. Breckinridge......1805 C. A. Rodney........1807
Paul Hamilton.......1809 William Jones.......1813 B. W. Crowninshield..1814		Gideon Granger......1809 R. J. Meigs, Jr.......1814	C. A. Rodney........1809 Wm. Pinkney........1811 Richard Rush........1814
B. W. Crowninshield..1817 Smith Thompson.....1818 S. L. Southard.......1823		R. J. Meigs, Jr.......1817 John McLean........1823	Richard Rush........1817 William Wirt........1817
S. L. Southard.......1825		John McLean........1825	William Wirt........1825
John Branch........1829 Levi Woodbury......1831 Mahlon Dickerson....1834		Wm. T. Barry.......1829 Amos Kendall.......1835	John M. Berrien.....1829 Roger B. Taney......1831 B. F. Butler........1833
Mahlon Dickerson....1837 Jas. K. Paulding.....1838		Amos Kendall.......1837 John M. Niles.......1840	B. F. Butler........1837 Felix Grundy........1838 H. D. Gilpin........1840
George E. Badger....1841		Francis Granger......1841	J. J. Crittenden......1841
George E. Badger....1841 Abel P. Upshur......1841 David Henshaw......1843 Thomas W. Gilmer...1844 John Y. Mason......1844		Francis Granger......1841 C. A. Wickliffe......1841	J. J. Crittenden......1841 Hugh S. Legaré......1841 John Nelson.........1843
George Bancroft.....1845 John Y. Mason.......1846		Cave Johnson........1845	John Y. Mason.......1845 Nathan Clifford......1846 Isaac Toucey........1848
Wm. B. Preston......1849	Thomas Ewing.......1849	Jacob Collamer......1849	Reverdy Johnson.....1849
Wm. A. Graham.....1850 John P. Kennedy.....1852	A. H. Stuart.........1850	Nathan K. Hall......1850 Sam D. Hubbard.....1852	J. J. Crittenden......1850
James C. Dobbin.....1853	Robert McClelland...1853	James Campbell.....1853	Caleb Cushing.......1853
Isaac Toucey........1857	Jacob Thompson.....1857	Aaron V. Brown.....1857 Joseph Holt.........1859	J. S. Black..........1857 Edw. M. Stanton.....1860

PRESIDENT AND VICE-PRESIDENT	SECRETARY OF STATE	SECRETARY OF TREASURY	SECRETARY OF WAR
Abraham Lincoln-Han'b'l Hamlin......1861 Andrew Johnson 1865	W. H. Seward . . 1861	Salmon P. Chase 1861 W. P. Fessenden 1864 Hugh McCulloch 1865	S. Cameron . . . . 1861 E. M. Stanton . . 1862
Andrew Johnson 1865	W. H. Seward . . 1865	Hugh McCulloch 1865	E. M. Stanton . . 1865 Ulysses S. Grant . 1867 Lorenzo Thomas 1868 J. M. Schofield . . 1868
Ulysses S. Grant-Schuyler Colfax . . . . . . 1869 Henry Wilson 1873	E. B. Washburn . 1869 Hamilton Fish . . 1869	Geo. S. Boutwell 1869 W. A. Richardson 1873 Ben. H. Bristow . 1874 Lot M. Morrill . . 1876	John A. Rawlins 1869 Wm. T. Sherman 1869 Wm. W. Belknap 1869 Alphonso Taft . . 1876 Jas. D. Cameron 1876
Rutherford B. Hayes-William A. Wheeler . 1877	Wm. M. Evarts . 1877	John Sherman . . 1877	G. W. McCrary . 1877 Alex. Ramsey . . . 1879

SECRETARY OF NAVY	SECRETARY OF THE INTERIOR	POSTMASTER GENERAL	ATTORNEY GENERAL
Gideon Welles......1861	Caleb B. Smith......1861 John P. Usher......1863	Horatio King......1861 M'tgomery Blair......1861 Wm. Dennison......1864	Edward Bates......1861 Titian J. Coffey......1863 James Speed......1864
Gideon Welles......1865	John P. Usher......1865 James Harlan......1865 O. H. Browning......1866	Wm. Dennison......1865 Alexander Randall....1866	James Speed......1865 Henry Stanbery......1866 William M. Evarts...1868
Adolph E. Borie.....1869 George M. Robeson...1869	Jacob D. Cox......1869 Columbus Delano....1870 Zachary Chandler....1875	John A. J. Creswell...1869 James W. Marshall...1874 Marshall Jewell......1874 James N. Tyner......1876	Ebenezer R. Hoar.....1869 Amos T. Akerman....1870 G. H. Williams......1871 Edward Pierrepont...1875 Alphonso Taft......1876
R. W. Thompson.....1877 Nathan Goff, Jr.......1881	Carl Schurz.........1877	David M. Key......1877 Horace Maynard.....1880	Charles Devens......1877

JUSTICES OF THE UNITED STATES SUPREME COURT, 1789–1877

NAME *Chief Justices in Italics*	SERVICE Term	Yrs.	NAME *Chief Justices in Italics*	SERVICE Term	Yrs.
John Jay, N.Y.	1789–1795	6	Henry Baldwin, Pa.	1830–1844	14
John Rutledge, S.C.	1789–1791	2	James M. Wayne, Ga.	1835–1867	32
William Cushing, Mass.	1789–1810	21	*Roger B. Taney,* Md.	1836–1864	28
James Wilson, Pa.	1789–1798	9	Philip P. Barbour, Va.	1836–1841	5
John Blair, Va.	1789–1796	7	John Catron, Tenn.	1837–1865	28
Robert H. Harrison, Md.	1789–1790	1	John McKinley, Ala.	1837–1852	15
James Iredell, N.C.	1790–1799	9	Peter V. Daniel, Va.	1841–1860	19
Thomas Johnson, Md.	1791–1793	2	Samuel Nelson, N.Y.	1845–1872	27
William Paterson, N.J.	1793–1806	13	Levi Woodbury, N.H.	1845–1851	6
John Rutledge, S.C.	1795–1795	..	Robert C. Grier, Pa.	1846–1870	24
Samuel Chase, Md.	1796–1811	15	Benj. R. Curtis, Mass.	1851–1857	6
Oliver Ellsworth, Conn.	1796–1799	4	John A. Campbell, Ala.	1853–1861	8
Bushrod Washington, Va.	1798–1829	31	Nathan Clifford, Me.	1858–1881	23
Alfred Moore, N.C.	1799–1804	5	Noah H. Swayne, Ohio	1862–1881	20
John Marshall, Va.	1801–1835	34	Samuel F. Miller, Iowa	1862–1890	28
William Johnson, S.C.	1804–1834	30	David Davis, Ill.	1862–1877	15
Brock Livingston, N.Y.	1806–1823	17	Stephen J. Field, Cal.	1863–1897	34
Thomas Todd, Ky.	1807–1826	19	*Salmon P. Chase,* Ohio	1864–1873	9
Joseph Story, Mass.	1811–1845	34	William Strong, Pa.	1870–1880	10
Gabriel Duval, Md.	1811–1836	25	Joseph P. Bradley, N.J.	1870–1892	22
Smith Thompson, N.Y.	1823–1843	20	Ward Hunt, N.Y.	1872 1882	10
Robert Trimble, Ky.	1826–1828	2	*Morrison R. Waite,* Ohio	1874–1888	14
John McLean, Ohio	1829–1861	32	John M. Harlan, Ky.	1877–1911	34

SPEAKERS OF THE HOUSE OF REPRESENTATIVES, 1789–1877

NAME	STATE	TIME	NAME	STATE	TIME
F. A. Muhlenburg	Pa.	1789–1791	James K. Polk	Tenn.	1835–1839
J. Trumbull	Conn.	1791–1793	R. M. T. Hunter	Va.	1839–1841
F. A. Muhlenburg	Pa.	1793–1795	John White	Ky.	1841–1843
Jonathan Dayton	N.J.	1795–1799	John W. Jones	Va.	1843–1845
Theo. Sedgwick	Mass.	1799–1801	John W. Davis	Ind.	1845–1847
Nathaniel Macon	N.C.	1801–1807	R. C. Winthrop	Mass.	1847–1849
Joseph B.Varnum	Mass.	1807–1811	Howell Cobb	Ga.	1849–1851
Henry Clay	Ky.	1811–1814	Linn Boyd	Ky.	1851–1855
Langdon Cheves	S.C.	1814–1815	N. P. Banks	Mass.	1856–1857
Henry Clay	Ky.	1815–1820	James L. Orr	S.C.	1857–1859
John W. Taylor	N.Y.	1820–1821	Wm. Pennington	N.J.	1860–1861
Philip P. Barbour	Va.	1821–1823	Galusha A. Grow	Pa.	1861–1863
Henry Clay	Ky.	1823–1825	Schuyler Colfax	Ind.	1863–1869
John W .Taylor	N.Y.	1825–1827	James G. Blaine	Me.	1869–1875
And. Stephenson	Va.	1827–1834	Michael C. Kerr	Ind.	1875–1876
John Bell	Tenn.	1834–1835	Samuel J. Randall	Pa.	1876–1881

The Constitution of
the United States of America

We the People of the United States, in order to form a more perfect union, establish Justice, insure domestic tranquility, provide for the common defence, promote the general Welfare, and secure the Blessings of Liberty to ourselves and our Posterity, do ordain and establish this Constitution for the United States of America.

ARTICLE I

SECTION 1. All legislative Powers herein granted shall be vested in a Congress of the United States, which shall consist of a Senate and a House of Representatives.

SECTION 2. The House of Representatives shall be composed of Members chosen every second Year by the People of the several States, and the Electors in each State shall have the Qualifications requisite for Electors of the most numerous Branch of the State Legislature.

No Person shall be a Representative who shall not have attained to the Age of twenty-five Years, and been seven Years a Citizen of the United States, and who shall not, when elected, be an Inhabitant of that State in which he shall be chosen.

Representatives and direct Taxes shall be apportioned among the several States which may be included within this Union, according to their respective Numbers, which shall be determined by adding to the whole Number of free Persons, including those bound to Service for a Term of Years, and excluding Indians not taxed, three fifths of all other Persons. The actual Enumeration shall be made within three Years after the first Meeting of the Congress of the United States, and within every subsequent Term of ten Years, in such Manner as they shall by Law direct. The Number of Representatives shall not exceed one for every thirty Thousand, but each State shall have at Least one Representative; and until such enumeration shall be made, the State of New Hampshire shall be entitled to chuse three, Massachusetts eight, Rhode-Island and Providence Plantations one, Connecticut five, New-York six, New Jersey four, Pennsylvania eight, Delaware one, Maryland six, Virginia ten, North Carolina five, South Carolina five, and Georgia three.

When vacancies happen in the Representation from any State, the Executive Authority thereof shall issue Writs of Election to fill such Vacancies.

The House of Representatives shall chuse their Speaker and other Officers; and shall have the sole Power of Impeachment.

SECTION 3. The Senate of the United States shall be composed of two Senators from each State, chosen by the Legislature thereof, for six Years; and each Senator shall have one Vote.

Immediately after they shall be assembled in Consequence of the first Election, they shall be divided as equally as may be into three Classes. The Seats of the Senators of the first Class shall be vacated at the Expiration of the second Year, of the second Class at the Expiration of the fourth Year, and of the third Class at the Expiration of the sixth Year, so that one-third may be chosen every second Year; and if Vacancies happen by Resignation, or otherwise, during the Recess of the Legislature of any State, the Executive thereof may make temporary Appointments until the next Meeting of the Legislature, which shall then fill such Vacancies.

No Person shall be a Senator who shall not have attained to the Age of thirty Years, and been nine Years a Citizen of the United States, and who shall not, when elected, be an Inhabitant of that State for which he shall be chosen.

The Vice President of the United States shall be President of the Senate, but shall have no Vote, unless they be equally divided.

The Senate shall chuse their other Officers, and also a President pro tempore, in the Absence of the Vice President, or when he shall exercise the Office of President of the United States.

The Senate shall have the sole Power to try all Impeachments. When sitting for that Purpose, they shall be on Oath or Affirmation. When the President of the United States is tried, the Chief Justice shall preside: And no Person shall be convicted without the Concurrence of two thirds of the Members present.

Judgment in Cases of Impeachment shall not extend further than to removal from Office, and disqualification to hold and enjoy any Office of honor, Trust or Profit under the United States: but the Party convicted shall nevertheless be liable and subject to Indictment, Trial, Judgment and Punishment, according to Law.

Section 4. The Times, Places and Manner of holding Elections for Senators and Representatives, shall be prescribed in each State by the Legislature thereof; but the Congress may at any time by Law make or alter such Regulations, except as to the Places of chusing Senators.

The Congress shall assemble at least once in every Year, and such Meeting shall be on the first Monday in December, unless they shall by Law appoint a different Day.

Section 5. Each House shall be the Judge of the Elections, Returns and Qualifications of its own Members, and a Majority of each shall constitute a Quorum to do Business; but a smaller Number may adjourn from day to day, and may be authorized to compel the Attendance of absent Members, in such Manner, and under such Penalties as each House may provide.

Each House may determine the Rules of its Proceedings, punish its Members for disorderly Behavior, and, with the Concurrence of two thirds, expel a Member.

Each House shall keep a Journal of its Proceedings, and from time to time publish the same, excepting such Parts as may in their Judgment require Secrecy; and the Yeas and Nays of the Members of either House on any question shall, at the Desire of one fifth of those present, be entered on the Journal.

Neither House, during the Session of Congress, shall, without the Consent of the other, adjourn for more than three days, nor to any other Place than that in which the two Houses shall be sitting.

SECTION 6. The Senators and Representatives shall receive a Compensation for their Services, to be ascertained by Law, and paid out of the Treasury of the United States. They shall in all Cases, except Treason, Felony and Breach of the Peace, be privileged from Arrest during their Attendance at the Session of their respective Houses, and in going to and returning from the same; and for any Speech or Debate in either House, they shall not be questioned in any other Place.

No Senator or Representative shall, during the Time for which he was elected, be appointed to any civil Office under the Authority of the United States, which shall have been created, or the Emoluments whereof shall have been encreased during such time; and no Person holding any Office under the United States, shall be a Member of either House during his Continuance in Office.

SECTION 7. All Bills for raising Revenue shall originate in the House of Representatives; but the Senate may propose or concur with Amendments as on other Bills.

Every Bill which shall have passed the House of Representatives and the Senate, shall, before it becomes a Law, be presented to the President of the United States; If he approves he shall sign it, but if not he shall return it, with his Objections to that House in which it shall have originated, who shall enter the Objections at large on their Journal, and proceed to reconsider it. If after such Reconsideration two thirds of that House shall agree to pass the Bill, it shall be sent, together with the Objections, to the other House, by which it shall likewise be reconsidered, and if approved by two thirds of that House, it shall become a Law. But in all such Cases the Votes of both Houses shall be determined by Yeas and Nays, and the Names of the Persons voting for and against the Bill shall be entered on the Journal of each House respectively. If any Bill shall not be returned by the President within ten Days (Sundays excepted) after it shall have been presented to him, the Same shall be a Law, in like Manner as if he had signed it, unless the Congress by their Adjournment prevent its Return, in which Case it shall not be a Law.

Every Order, Resolution, or Vote to which the Concurrence of the Senate and House of Representatives may be necessary (except on a question of Adjournment) shall be presented to the President of the United States; and before the Same shall take Effect, shall be approved by him, or being disapproved by him, shall be repassed by two thirds of the Senate and House of Representatives, according to the Rules and Limitations prescribed in the Case of a Bill.

SECTION 8. The Congress shall have Power To lay and collect Taxes, Duties, Imposts and Excises, to pay the Debts and provide for the common Defence and general Welfare of the United States; but all Duties, Imposts and Excises shall be uniform throughout the United States;

To borow Money on the credit of the United States;

To regulate Commerce with foreign Nations, and among the several States, and with the Indian Tribes;

To establish an uniform Rule of Naturalization, and uniform Laws on the subject of Bankruptcies throughout the United States;

To coin Money, regulate the Value thereof, and of foreign Coin, and fix the Standard of Weights and Measures;

To provide for the Punishment of counterfeiting the Securities and current Coin of the United States;

To establish Post Offices and post Roads;

To promote the Progress of Science and useful Arts, by securing for limited Times to Authors and Inventors the exclusive Right to their respective Writings and Discoveries;

To constitute Tribunals inferior to the supreme Court;

To define and punish Piracies and Felonies committed on the high Seas, and Offences against the Law of Nations;

To declare War, grant Letters of Marque and Reprisal, and make Rules concerning Captures on Land and Water;

To raise and support Armies, but no Appropriation of Money to that Use shall be for a longer Term than two Years;

To provide and maintain a Navy;

To make Rules for the Government and Regulation of the land and naval Forces;

To provide for calling forth the Militia to execute the Laws of the Union, suppress Insurrections and repel Invasions;

To provide for organizing, arming, and disciplining the Militia, and for governing such Part of them as may be employed in the Service of the United States, reserving to the States respectively, the Appointment of the Officers, and the Authority of training the Militia according to the discipline prescribed by Congress;

To exercise exclusive Legislation in all Cases whatsoever, over such District (not exceeding ten Miles square) as may, by Cession of particular States, and the Acceptance of Congress, become the Seat of the Government of the United States, and to exercise like Authority over all Places purchased by the Consent of the Legislature of the State in which the Same shall be, for the Erection of Forts, Magazines, Arsenals, dock-Yards, and other needful Buildings; — And

To make all Laws which shall be necessary and proper for carrying into Execution the foregoing Powers, and all other Powers vested by this Constitution in the Government of the United States, or in any Department or Officer thereof.

Section 9. The Migration or Importation of such Persons as any of the States now existing shall think proper to admit, shall not be prohibited by the Congress prior to the Year one thousand eight hundred and eight, but a Tax or duty may be imposed on such Importation, not exceeding ten dollars for each Person.

The Privilege of the Writ of Habeas Corpus shall not be suspended, unless when in Cases of Rebellion or Invasion the public Safety may require it.

No Bill of Attainder or ex post facto Law shall be passed.

No Capitation, or other direct, tax shall be laid, unless in Proportion to the Census or Enumeration herein before directed to be taken.

No Tax or Duty shall be laid on Articles exported from any State.

No Preference shall be given by any Regulation of Commerce or Revenue to the Ports of one State over those of another: nor shall Vessels bound to, or from, one State, be obliged to enter, clear, or pay Duties in another.

No Money shall be drawn from the Treasury, but in Consequence of

Appropriations made by Law; and a regular Statement and Account of the Receipts and Expenditures of all public Money shall be published from time to time.

No Title of Nobility shall be granted by the United States: And no Person holding any Office of Profit or Trust under them, shall, without the Consent of the Congress, accept of any present, Emolument, Office, or Title, of any kind whatever, from any King, Prince, or foreign State.

SECTION 10. No State shall enter into any Treaty, Alliance, or Confederation; grant Letters of Marque and Reprisal; coin Money; emit Bills of Credit; make any Thing but gold and silver Coin a Tender in Payment of Debts; pass any Bill of Attainder, ex post facto Law, or Law impairing the Obligation of Contracts, or grant any Title of Nobility.

No State shall, without the Consent of the Congress, lay any Imposts or Duties on Imports or Exports, except what may be absolutely necessary for executing its inspection Laws: and the net Produce of all Duties and Imposts, laid by any State on Imports or Exports, shall be for the Use of the Treasury of the United States; and all such Laws shall be subject to the Revision and Controul of the Congress.

No State shall, without the Consent of Congress, lay any Duty of Tonnage, keep Troops, or Ships of War in time of Peace, enter into any Agreement or Compact with another State, or with a foreign Power, or engage in War, unless actually invaded, or in such imminent Danger as will not admit of delay.

ARTICLE II

SECTION 1. The Executive Power shall be vested in a President of the United States of America. He shall hold his Office during the Term of four Years, and, together with the Vice President, chosen for the same Term, be elected, as follows

Each State shall appoint, in such Manner as the Legislature thereof may direct, a Number of Electors, equal to the whole Number of Senators and Representatives to which the State may be entitled in the Congress: but no Senator or Representative, or Person holding an Office of Trust or Profit under the United States, shall be appointed an Elector.   .

The electors shall meet in their respective States, and vote by ballot for two Persons, of whom one at least shall not be an Inhabitant of the same State with themselves. And they shall make a List of all the Persons voted for, and of the Number of Votes for each; which List they shall sign and certify, and transmit sealed to the Seat of the Government of the United States, directed to the President of the Senate. The President of the Senate shall, in the Presence of the Senate and House of Representatives, open all the Certificates, and the Votes shall then be counted. The Person having the greatest Number of Votes shall be the President, if such Number be a Majority of the whole Number of Electors appointed; and if there be more than one who have such Majority, and have an equal Number of Votes, then the House of Representatives shall immediately chuse by Ballot one of them for President; and if no Person have a Majority, then from the five highest on the List the said House shall in like Manner chuse the President. But in chusing the President, the Votes shall be taken by States, the Representation from each State having one Vote; A quorum for this Purpose shall consist of a Member or Members from two thirds of the States, and a Majority of all the States shall be necessary to a Choice. In every Case, after the Choice of the President, the Person having the greatest Number of Votes of the Electors shall be the Vice President. But if there should remain two or more who have equal Votes, the Senate shall chuse from them by Ballot the Vice President.

The Congress may determine the Time of chusing the Electors, and the Day on which they shall give their Votes; which Day shall be the same throughout the United States.

No Person except a natural born Citizen, or a Citizen of the United States, at the time of the Adoption of this Constitution, shall be eligible to the Office of President; neither shall any Person be eligible to that Office who shall not have attained to the Age of thirty five Years, and been fourteen Years a Resident within the United States.

In Case of the Removal of the President from Office, or of his Death, Resignation or Inability to discharge the Powers and Duties of the said Office, the same shall devolve on the Vice President, and the Congress may by Law provide for the Case of Removal, Death,

Resignation or Inability, both of the President and Vice President, declaring what Officer shall then act as President, and such Officer shall act accordingly, until the Disability be removed, or a President shall be elected.

The President shall, at stated Times, receive for his Services, a Compensation, which shall neither be encreased nor diminished during the Period for which he shall have been elected, and he shall not receive within that Period any other Emolument from the United States, or any of them.

Before he enter on the Execution of his Office, he shall take the following Oath or Affirmation: — "I do solemnly swear (or affirm) that I will faithfully execute the Office of President of the United States, and will to the best of my Ability, preserve, protect and defend the Constitution of the United States."

SECTION 2. The President shall be Commander in Chief of the Army and Navy of the United States, and of the Militia of the several States, when called into the actual Service of the United States; he may require the Opinion, in writing, of the principal Officer in each of the executive Departments, upon any Subject relating to the Duties of their respective Offices, and he shall have Power to grant Reprieves and Pardons for Offences against the United States, except in Cases of Impeachment.

He shall have Power, by and with the Advice and Consent of the Senate to make Treaties, provided two thirds of the Senators present concur and he shall nominate, and by and with the Advice and Consent of the Senate, shall appoint Ambassadors, other public Ministers and Consuls, Judges of the supreme Court, and all other Officers of the United States, whose Appointments are not herein otherwise provided for, and which shall be established by Law: but the Congress may by Law vest the Appointment of such inferior Officers, as they think proper, in the President alone, in the Courts of Law, or in the Heads of Departments.

The President shall have Power to fill up all Vacancies that may happen during the Recess of the Senate, by granting Commissions which shall expire at the End of their next Session.

SECTION 3. He shall from time to time give to the Congress Information of the State of the Union, and recommend to their Consideration such Measures as he shall judge necessary and expedient; he may, on extraordinary Occasions, convene both Houses, or either of them, and, in Case of Disagreement between them, with Respect to the Time of Adjournment, he may adjourn them to such Time as he shall think proper; he shall receive Ambassadors and other public Ministers; he shall take Care that the Laws be faithfully executed, and shall Commission all the Officers of the United States.

SECTION 4. The President, Vice President and all civil Officers of the United States, shall be removed from Office on Impeachment for, and Conviction of, Treason, Bribery, or other high Crimes and Misdemeanors.

ARTICLE III

SECTION 1. The judicial Power of the United States, shall be vested in one supreme Court, and in such inferior Courts as the Congress may from time to time ordain and establish. The Judges, both of the supreme and inferior Courts, shall hold their Offices during good Behaviour, and shall, at stated Times, receive for their Services, a Compensation, which shall not be diminished during their Continuance in Office.

SECTION 2. The judicial Power shall extend to all Cases, in Law and Equity, arising under this Constitution, the Laws of the United States, and Treaties made, or which shall be made, under their Authority; — to all Cases affecting Ambassadors, other public Ministers and Consuls; — to all Cases of admiralty and maritime Jurisdiction; — to Controversies to which the United States shall be a Party; — to Controversies between two or more States; — between a State and Citizens of another State; — between Citizens of different States, — between Citizens of the same State claiming Lands under Grants of different States, and between a State, or the Citizens thereof, and foreign States, Citizens or Subjects.
In all Cases affecting Ambassadors, other public Ministers and Consuls, and those in which a State shall be Party, the supreme Court shall have original Jurisdiction. In all other Cases before mentioned, the supreme Court shall have appellate Jurisdiction, both as to Law and

Fact, with such Exceptions, and under such Regulations as the Congress shall make.

The Trial of all Crimes, except in Cases of Impeachment, shall be by Jury; and such Trial shall be held in the State where the said Crimes shall have been committed; but when not committed within any State, the Trial shall be at such Place or Places as the Congress may by Law have directed.

SECTION 3. Treason against the United States, shall consist only in levying War against them, or in adhering to their Enemies, giving them Aid and Comfort. No Person shall be convicted of Treason unless on the Testimony of two Witnesses to the same overt Act, or on Confession in open Court.

The Congress shall have Power to declare the Punishment of Treason, but no Attainder of Treason shall work Corruption of Blood, or Forfeiture except during the Life of the Person attainted.

ARTICLE IV

SECTION 1. Full Faith and Credit shall be given in each State to the public Acts, Records, and judicial Proceedings of every other State. And the Congress may by general Laws prescribe the Manner in which such Acts, Records and Proceedings shall be proved, and the Effect thereof.

SECTION 2. The Citizens of each State shall be entitled to all Privileges and Immunities of Citizens in the several States.

A person charged in any State with Treason, Felony, or other Crime, who shall flee from Justice, and be found in another State, shall on Demand of the executive Authority of the State from which he fled, be delivered up, to be removed to the State having Jurisdiction of the Crime.

No Person held to Service or Labour in one State, under the Laws thereof, escaping into another, shall, in Consequence of any Law or Regulation therein, be discharged from such Service or Labour, but shall be delivered up on Claim of the Party to whom such Service or Labour may be due.

SECTION 3. New States may be admitted by the Congress into this Union; but no new State shall be formed or erected within the Jurisdiction of any other State; nor any State be formed by the Junction of two or more States, or Parts of States, without the Consent of the Legislatures of the States concerned as well as of the Congress.

The Congress shall have Power to dispose of and make all needful Rules and Regulations respecting the Territory or other Property belonging to the United States; and nothing in this Constitution shall be so construed as to Prejudice any Claims of the United States, or of any particular State.

SECTION 4. The United States shall guarantee to every State in this Union a Republican Form of Government, and shall protect each of them against Invasion; and on Application of the Legislature, or of the Executive (when the Legislature cannot be convened) against domestic Violence.

ARTICLE V

The Congress, whenever two thirds of both houses shall deem it necessary, shall propose Amendments to this Constitution, or, on the Application of the Legislatures of two thirds of the several States, shall call a Convention for proposing Amendments, which, in either Case, shall be valid to all Intents and Purposes, as Part of this Constitution, when ratified by the Legislatures of three fourths of the several States, or by Conventions in three fourths thereof, as the one or the other Mode of Ratification may be proposed by the Congress; Provided that no Amendment which may be made prior to the Year One thousand eight hundred and eight shall in any Manner affect the first and fourth Clauses in the Ninth Section of the first Article; and that no State, without its Consent, shall be deprived of its equal Suffrage in the Senate.

ARTICLE VI

All Debts contracted and Engagements entered into, before the Adoption of this Constitution, shall be as valid against the United States under this Constitution, as under the Confederation.

This Constitution, and the Laws of the United States which shall be made in Pursuance thereof; and all Treaties made, or which shall be made, under the Authority of the United States, shall be the supreme Law of the Land; and the Judges in every State shall be bound thereby, any Thing in the Constitution or Laws of any State to the Contrary notwithstanding.

The Senators and Representatives before mentioned, and the Members of the several State Legislatures, and all executive and judicial Officers, both of the United States and of the several States, shall be bound by Oath or Affirmation, to support this Constitution; but no religious Test shall ever be required as a Qualification to any Office or public Trust under the United States.

ARTICLE VII

The Ratification of the Conventions of nine States, shall be sufficient for the Establishment of this Constitution between the States so ratifying the Same.

DONE in Convention by the Unanimous Consent of the States present the Seventeenth Day of September in the Year of our Lord one thousand seven hundred and Eighty seven and of the Independence of the United States of America the Twelth. IN WITNESS whereof We have hereunto subscribed our Names.

G° WASHINGTON
Presid^t and deputy from Virginia

AMENDMENTS
ARTICLE I

[THE FIRST TEN ARTICLES PROPOSED 25 SEPTEMBER 1789; DECLARED IN FORCE 15 DECEMBER 1791]

ARTICLE II

Congress shall make no law respecting an establishment of religion, or prohibiting the free exercise thereof; or abridging the freedom of speech, or of the press; or the right of the people peaceably to assemble, and to petition the Government for a redress of grievances.

A well regulated Militia, being necessary to the security of a free State, the right of the people to keep and bear Arms, shall not be infringed.

ARTICLE III

No Soldier shall, in time of peace, be quartered in any house, without the consent of the Owner, nor in time of war, but in a manner to be prescribed by law.

ARTICLE IV

The right of the people to be secure in their persons, houses, papers, and effects, against unreasonable searches and seizures, shall not be violated, and no Warrants shall issue, but upon probable cause, supported by Oath or affirmation, and particularly describing the place to be searched, and the persons or things to be seized.

ARTICLE V

No person shall be held to answer for a capital, or otherwise infamous crime, unless on a presentment or indictment of a Grand Jury, except in cases arising in the land or naval forces, or in the Militia, when in actual service in time of War or public danger; nor shall any person be subject for the same offence to be twice put in jeopardy of life or limb; nor shall be compelled in any Criminal Case to be a witness against himself, nor be deprived of life, liberty, or property, without due process of law; nor shall private property be taken for public use, without just compensation.

ARTICLE VI

In all criminal prosecutions, the accused shall enjoy the right to a speedy and public trial, by an impartial jury of the State and district wherein the crime shall have been committed, which district shall have been previously ascertained by law, and to be informed of the nature and cause of the accusation; to be confronted with the witnesses against him; to have compulsory process for obtaining Witnesses in his favor, and to have the Assistance of Counsel for his defence.

ARTICLE VII

In suits at common law, where the value in controversy shall exceed twenty dollars, the right of trial by jury shall be preserved, and no fact tried by a jury shall be otherwise re-examined in any Court of the United States, than according to the rules of the common law.

ARTICLE VIII

Excessive bail shall not be required, nor excessive fines imposed, nor cruel and unusual punishments inflicted.

ARTICLE IX

The enumeration in the Constitution, of certain rights, shall not be construed to deny or disparage others retained by the people.

ARTICLE X

The powers not delegated to the United States by the Constitution, nor prohibited by it to the States, are reserved to the States respectively, or to the people.

ARTICLE XI

[PROPOSED 4 MARCH 1794; DECLARED RATIFIED 8 JANUARY 1798]

The Judicial power of the United States shall not be construed to extend to any suit in law or equity, commenced or prosecuted against one of the United States by Citizens of another State, or by Citizens or Subjects of any Foreign State.

ARTICLE XII

[PROPOSED 9 DECEMBER 1803; DECLARED RATIFIED 25 SEPTEMBER 1804]

The Electors shall meet in their respective states, and vote by ballot for President and Vice-President, one of whom, at least, shall not be an inhabitant of the same state with themselves; they shall name in their ballots the person voted for as President, and in distinct ballots the person voted for as Vice-President, and they shall make distinct lists of all persons voted for as President, and of all persons voted for as Vice-President, and of the number of votes for each, which lists they shall sign and certify, and transmit sealed to the seat of the Government of the United States, directed to the President of the Senate; — The President of the Senate shall, in the presence of the Senate and House of Representatives, open all the certificates and the votes shall then be counted; — The person having the greatest number of votes for President, shall be the President, if such number be a majority of the whole number of Electors appointed; and if no person have such majority, then from the persons having the highest numbers not exceeding three on the list of those voted for as President, the House of Representatives shall choose immediately, by ballot, the President. But in choosing the President, the votes shall be taken by states, the representation from each state having one vote; a quorum for this purpose shall consist of a member or members from two-thirds of the states, and a majority of all the states shall be necessary to a choice. And if the House of Representatives shall not choose a President whenever the right of choice shall devolve upon them, before the fourth day of March next following, then the Vice-President shall act as President, as in the case of the death or other constitutional disability of the President. The person having the greatest number of votes as Vice-President, shall be the Vice-President, if such number be a majority of the whole number of Electors appointed, and if no person have a majority, then from the two highest numbers on the list, the Senate shall choose the Vice-President; a quorum for the purpose shall consist of two-thirds of the whole number of Senators, and a majority of the whole number shall be necessary to a choice. But no person constitutionally ineligible to the office of President shall be eligible to that of Vice-President of the United States.

ARTICLE XIII

[PROPOSED 31 JANUARY 1865; DECLARED RATIFIED 18 DECEMBER 1865]

SECTION 1. Neither slavery nor involuntary servitude, except as a punishment for crime whereof the party shall have been duly convicted, shall exist within the United States, or any place subject to their jurisdiction.

SECTION 2. Congress shall have power to enforce this article by appropriate legislation.

ARTICLE XIV

[PROPOSED 13 JUNE 1866; DECLARED RATIFIED 28 JULY 1868]

SECTION 1. All persons born or naturalized in the United States, and subject to the jurisdiction thereof, are citizens of the United States and of the State wherein they reside. No State shall make or enforce any law which shall abridge the privileges or immunities of citizens of the United States; nor shall any State deprive any person of life, liberty, or property, without due process of law; nor deny to any person within its jurisdiction the equal protection of the laws.

SECTION 2. Representatives shall be apportioned among the several States according to their respective numbers, counting the whole number of persons in each State, excluding Indians not taxed. But when the right to vote at any election for the choice of electors for President and Vice President of the United States, Representatives in Congress, the Executive and Judicial officers of a State, or the members of the Legislature thereof, is denied to any of the male inhabitants of such State, being twenty-one years of age, and citizens of the United States, or in any way abridged, except for participation in rebellion, or other crime, the basis of representation therein shall be reduced in the proportion which the number of such male citizens shall bear to the whole number of male citizens twenty-one years of age in such State.

SECTION 3. No person shall be a Senator or Representative in Congress, or elector of President and Vice President, or hold any office, civil, or military, under the United States, or under any State, who, having previously taken an oath, as a member of Congress, or as an officer of the United States, or as a member of any State legislature, or as an executive or judicial officer of any State, to support the Constitution of the United States, shall have engaged in insurrection or rebellion against the same, or given aid or comfort to the enemies thereof. But Congress may by a vote of two-thirds of each House, remove such disability.

SECTION 4. The validity of the public debt of the United States, authorized by law, including debts incurred for payment of pensions and bounties for services in suppressing insurrection or rebellion, shall not be questioned. But neither the United States nor any State shall assume or pay any debt or obligation incurred in aid of insurrection or rebellion against the United States, or any claim for the loss or emancipation of any slave; but all such debts, obligations and claims shall be held illegal and void.

SECTION 5. The Congress shall have power to enforce, by appropriate legislation, the provisions of this article.

ARTICLE XV

[PROPOSED 26 FEBRUARY 1869; DECLARED RATIFIED 30 MARCH 1870]

SECTION 1. The right of citizens of the United States to vote shall not be denied or abridged by the United States or by any State on account of race, color, or previous condition of servitude.

SECTION 2. The Congress shall have power to enforce this article by appropriate legislation.

ARTICLE XVI

[PROPOSED 12 JULY 1909; DECLARED RATIFIED 25 FEBRUARY 1913]

The Congress shall have power to lay and collect taxes on incomes, from whatever source derived, without apportionment among the several States, and without regard to any census or enumeration.

ARTICLE XVII

[PROPOSED 13 MAY 1912; DECLARED RATIFIED 31 MAY 1913]

The Senate of the United States shall be composed of two senators from each State, elected by the people thereof, for six years; and each Senator shall have one vote. The electors in each State shall have the qualifications requisite for electors of the most numerous branch of the State legislature.

When vacancies happen in the representation of any State in the Senate, the executive authority of such State shall issue writs of election to fill such vacancies: PROVIDED, That the legislature of any State may empower the executive thereof to make temporary appointments until the people fill the vacancies by election as the legislature may direct.

This amendment shall not be so construed as to affect the election or term of any senator chosen before it becomes valid as part of the Constitution.

ARTICLE XVIII

[PROPOSED 18 DECEMBER 1917; DECLARED RATIFIED 29 JANUARY 1919]

After one year from the ratification of this article, the manufacture, sale, or transportation of intoxicating liquors within, the importation thereof into, or the exportation thereof from the United States and all territory subject to the jurisdiction thereof for beverage purposes is hereby prohibited.

The Congress and the several States shall have concurrent power to enforce this article by appropriate legislation.

This article shall be inoperative unless it shall have been ratified as an amendment to the Constitution by the legislatures of the several States, as provided in the Constitution, within seven years from the date of the submission hereof to the States by the Congress.

ARTICLE XIX

[PROPOSED 4 JUNE 1919; DECLARED RATIFIED 26 AUGUST 1920]

The right of citizens of the United States to vote shall not be denied or abridged by the United States or by any States on account of sex.

The Congress shall have power, by appropriate legislation, to enforce the provisions of this article.

ARTICLE XX

[PROPOSED 2 MARCH 1932; DECLARED RATIFIED 6 FEBRUARY 1933]

SECTION 1. The terms of the President and Vice-President shall end at noon on the twentieth day of January, and the terms of Senators and Representatives at noon on the third day of January, of the years in which such terms would have ended if this article had not been ratified; and the terms of their successors shall then begin.

SECTION 2. The Congress shall assemble at least once in every year, and such meeting shall begin at noon on the third day of January, unless they shall by law appoint a different day.

SECTION 3. If, at the time fixed for the beginning of the term of the President, the President-elect shall have died, the Vice-President-elect shall become President. If a President shall not have been chosen before the time fixed for the beginning of his term, or if the President-elect shall have failed to qualify, then the Vice-President-elect shall act as President until a President shall have qualified; and the Congress may by law provide for the case wherein neither a President-elect nor a Vice-President-elect shall have qualified, declaring who shall then act as President, or the manner in which one who is to act shall be selected, and such person shall act accordingly until a President or Vice-President shall have qualified.

SECTION 4. The Congress may by law provide for the case of the death of any of the persons from whom the House of Representatives may choose a President whenever the right of choice shall have devolved upon them, and for the case of the death of any of the persons from whom the Senate may choose a Vice-President whenever the right of choice shall have devolved upon them.

SECTION 5. Sections 1 and 2 shall take effect on the 15th day of October following the ratification of this article.

SECTION 6. This article shall be inoperative unless it shall have been ratified as an amendment to the Constitution by the legislatures of three-fourths of the several States within seven years from the date of its submission.

ARTICLE XXI

[PROPOSED 20 FEBRUARY 1933; ADOPTED 5 DECEMBER 1933]

SECTION 1. The eighteenth article of amendment to the Constitution of the United States is hereby repealed.

SECTION 2. The transportation or importation into any State, Territory or possession of the United States for delivery or use therein of intoxicating liquors, in violation of the laws thereof, is hereby prohibited.

SECTION 3. This article shall be inoperative unless it shall have been ratified as an amendment to the Constitution by convention in the several States, as provided in the Constitution, within seven years from the date of the submission hereof to the States by the Congress.

ARTICLE XXII

[PROPOSED 21 MARCH 1947; DECLARED RATIFIED 3 MARCH 1951]

SECTION 1. No person shall be elected to the office of the President more than twice, and no person who has held the office of President, or acted as President, for more than two years of a term to which some other person was elected President shall be elected to the office of the President more than once. But this Article shall not apply to any person holding the office of President when this Article was proposed by the Congress, and shall not prevent any person who may be holding the office of President, or acting as President, during the term within which this Article becomes operative from holding the office of President or acting as President during the remainder of such term.

ARTICLE XXIII

[PROPOSED 17 JUNE 1960; DECLARED RATIFIED 3 APRIL 1961]

SECTION 1. The District constituting the seat of Government of the United States shall appoint in such manner as the Congress may direct:

A number of electors of President and Vice President equal to the whole number of Senators and Representatives in Congress to which the District would be entitled if it were a State, but in no event more than the least populous State; they shall be in addition to those appointed by the States, but they shall be considered, for the purposes of the election of President and Vice President, to be electors appointed by a State; and they shall meet in the District and perform such duties as provided by the twelfth article of amendment.

SECTION 2. The Congress shall have power to enforce this article by appropriate legislation.

ARTICLE XXIV

[PROPOSED 27 AUGUST 1962; DECLARED RATIFIED 4 FEBRUARY 1964]

SECTION 1. The right of citizens of the United States to vote in any primary or other election for President or Vice President, for electors for President or Vice President, or for Senator or Representative in Congress, shall not be denied or abridged by the United States or any State by reason of failure to pay any poll tax or other tax.

SECTION 2. The Congress shall have power to enforce this article by appropriate legislation.

ARTICLE XXV

[PROPOSED 6 JULY 1965; DECLARED RATIFIED 23 FEBRUARY 1967]

SECTION 1. In case of the removal of the President from office or of his death or resignation, the Vice President shall become President.

SECTION 2. Whenever there is a vacancy in the office of the Vice President, the President shall nominate a Vice President who shall take office upon confirmation by a majority vote of both Houses of Congress.

SECTION 3. Whenever the President transmits to the President pro tempore of the Senate and the Speaker of the House of Representatives his written declaration that he is unable to discharge the powers and duties of his office, and until he transmits to them a written declaration to the contrary, such powers and duties shall be discharged by the Vice President as Acting President.

SECTION 4. Whenever the Vice President and a majority of either the principal officers of the executive department or of such other body as Congress may by law provide, transmit to the President pro tempore of the Senate and the Speaker of the House of Representatives their written declaration that the President is unable to discharge the powers and duties of his office, the Vice President shall immediately assume the powers and duties of the office as Acting President.

Thereafter, when the President transmits to the President pro tempore of the Senate and the Speaker of the House of Representatives his written declaration that no inability exists, he shall resume the powers and duties of his office unless the Vice President and a majority of either the principal officers of the executive department or of such other body as Congress may by law provide, transmit within four days to the President pro tempore of the Senate and the Speaker of the House of Representatives their written declaration that the President is unable to discharge the powers and duties of his office. Thereupon Congress shall decide the issue, assembling within forty-eight hours for that purpose if not in session. If the Congress, within twenty-one days after receipt of the latter written declaration, or, if Congress is not in session, within twenty-one days after Congress is required to assemble, determines by two-thirds vote of both Houses that the President is unable to discharge the powers and duties of his office, the Vice President shall continue to discharge the same as Acting President; otherwise, the President shall resume the powers and duties of his office.

ARTICLE XXVI
[PROPOSED 23 MARCH 1971; DECLARED RATIFIED 30 JUNE 1971]

SECTION 1. The right of citizens of the United States, who are 18 years of age or older, to vote shall not be denied or abridged by the United States or any state on account of age.

SECTION 2. The Congress shall have the power to enforce this article by appropriate legislation.

Index

McClellan, George B., (cont.)
at Richmond, 655, 657–62, 664, 665; and defense of Washington, 666; at Antietam, 667–68; and Democratic nomination in 1864, 708
McCormick, Cyrus H., 583
McCulloch v. Maryland, 391–93, 395–96
Macdonough, Thomas, 376, 377, 384
McDowell, Irvin, 639, 657, 658
McGuffey, William H., 461, 803
McKay, Donald, 580
Maclay, William, 294
McLoughlin, John, 526–27, 532
McLoughlin, William, 488–89
Macon, Nathaniel, 361, 385
Macon's Bill No. 2, 358–59
Madison, James, 132, 207, 213, 215, 229, 293, 312, 335, 355; and Constitution, 244, 245, 249, 253, 254, 259, 260, 282, 287, 433; on judicial review, 256; on national bank, 295; and Jeffersonian Republicans, 297–98, 302, 318; and Virginia Resolves, 326; foreign policies of, 356–61; domestic policies of, 387–88; and Anglo-American friendship, 399–402, 409
Magazines, *see* Literature.
Magellan, Ferdinand, 22, 25, 27
Mahone, William, 761
Maine, 58, 80, 88, 95, 398, 522–23, 570
Mallory, Stephen R., 628
Manassas Junction, *see* Bull Run.
Manifest destiny, 546–47, 573–79, 768
Mann, Horace, 460, 804
Mant, Thomas, 142
Manufactures, 98, 100–101, 268, 381, 472, 476, 570, 722, 818; Hamilton on protection of, 290, 294; and protective tariffs, 389–90, 426; and industrial revolution, 454–56, 583; Union superiority of, 624; growth during Civil War, 676–77; growth after Civil War, 724–26
Marbury v. Madison, 345–46, 594
Marco Polo, 17, 19
Marcos, Fray, 28
Marcy, William L., 547n., 549, 574, 579
Marion, Francis, 179, 197
Maritime commerce, 314, 318, 385, 476; New England and, 50, 134, 267, 291, 342; and Acts of Trade and Navigation, 67–69; under Constitution, 246; prospering of, 98–101, 282; and English Order in Council of 1783, 236–37; and English capture of

American ships, 303, 304–5; and Embargo Act, 352–56; and War of 1812, 358–60; and clipper ships, 579–81
Mark Twain, 470, 794, 796
Marquette, Jacques, 81
Marsh, George Perkins, 811
Marshall, John, 132, 318, 320, 322, 345, 367, 499, 514; on federal judiciary, 260; and doctrine of implied powers, 295, 392–93, 515, 516; on national sovereignty, 389, 392–95, 433, 440, 611
Martin v. Hunter's Lessee, 393, 395
Martin v. Mott, 393, 394, 395
Martineau, Harriet, 444, 445, 491
Marx, Karl, 690
Maryland, 38, 39, 46, 107, 170, 171, 215, 218, 272, 273–74, 589, 606, 618, 620; establishment of, 47–50, 83; Assembly, 48; adoption of state constitution, 208n.; and state university, 221; and Constitution, 249, 260; and War of 1812, 360, 378; *McCulloch v. Maryland,* 391–93; Civil War campaigns in, 666–68, 670
Mason, George, 210, 213, 235; and Constitution, 245, 249, 254, 258, 260
Mason, James Murray, 565, 622, 649, 691
Mason-Dixon line, 77, 219, 273, 397, 478
Massachusetts, 89, 143, 153, 218, 343, 493, 551, 588; establishment of Bay Colony, 54–59; difficulties with England, 63, 80–82; and New England Confederacy, 64; issuance of paper money, 102, 103; state constitution, 208–9, 512; Shays's Rebellion, 240–42; and Constitution, 259–60; and policies of Hamilton, 291–92; and War of 1812, 366, 381; public school system, 460–62; *Charles River Bridge v. Warren Bridge,* 515
Massachusetts Institute of Technology, 678, 805, 815
Massasoit, Chief, 9, 53
Mather, Cotton, 82, 104–5
Mather, Increase, 83
Maury, Matthew Fontaine, 484n., 580
Mayflower, 52, 53
Mayflower Compact of 1620, 52, 174
Meade, George Gordon, 680, 695–99
Medical schools, 109, 221, 466, 467
Melville, Herman, 488, 497, 498, 571
Memminger, Christopher, 628, 686